2016 EDITION

Best COLLEGES

HOW TO ORDER: Additional copies of U.S.News & World Report's Best Colleges 2016 guidebook are available for purchase at www.usnews.com/collegeguide or by calling (800) 836-6397.
To order custom reprints, please call (877) 652-5295 or email usnews@wrightsmedia.com.
For permission to republish articles, data or other content from this book, email permissions@usnews.com.

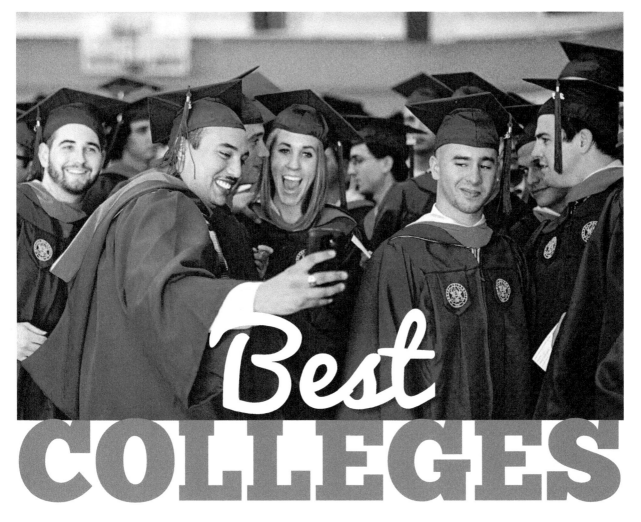

Graduation day at Drexel University

WILL FIGG FOR USN&WR

Contents

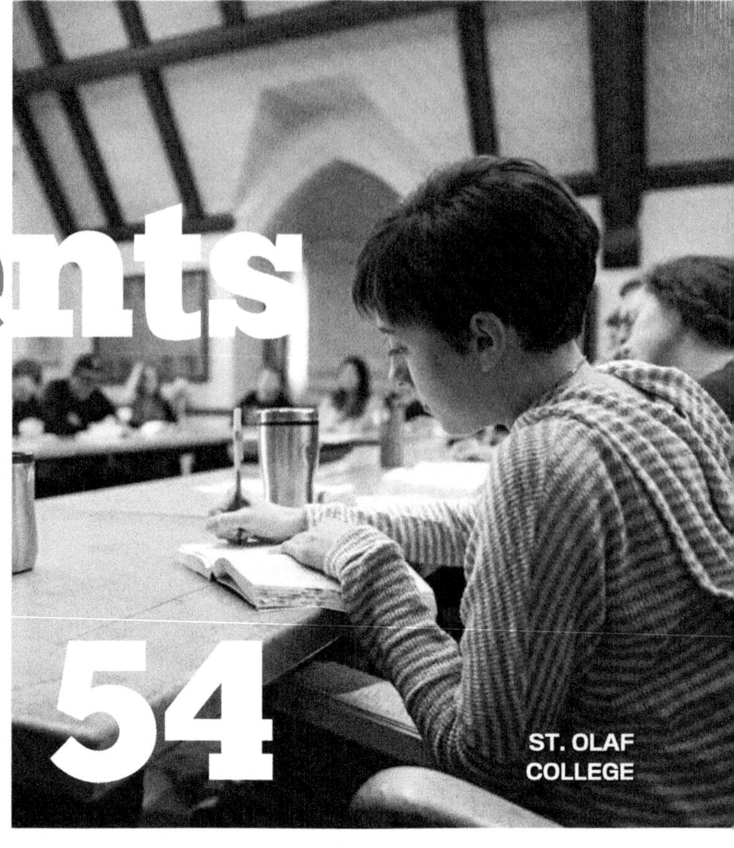

54 ST. OLAF COLLEGE

WHY I PICKED...

BRETT ZIEGLER FOR USN&WR

UC–BERKELEY

74

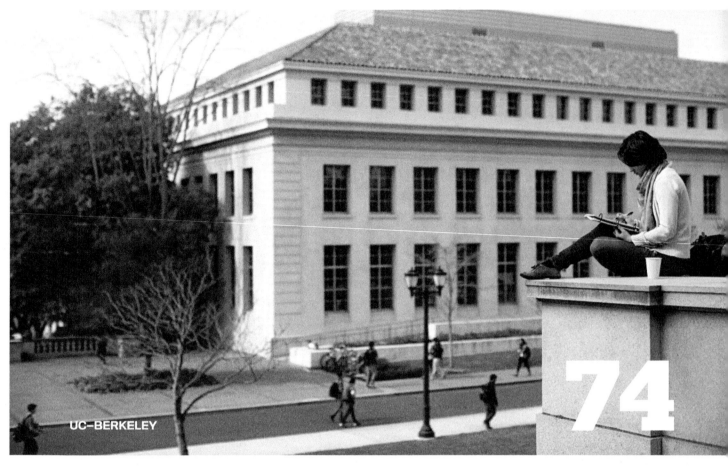

Chapter Three

The U.S. News Rankings

BRETT ZIEGLER FOR USN&WR

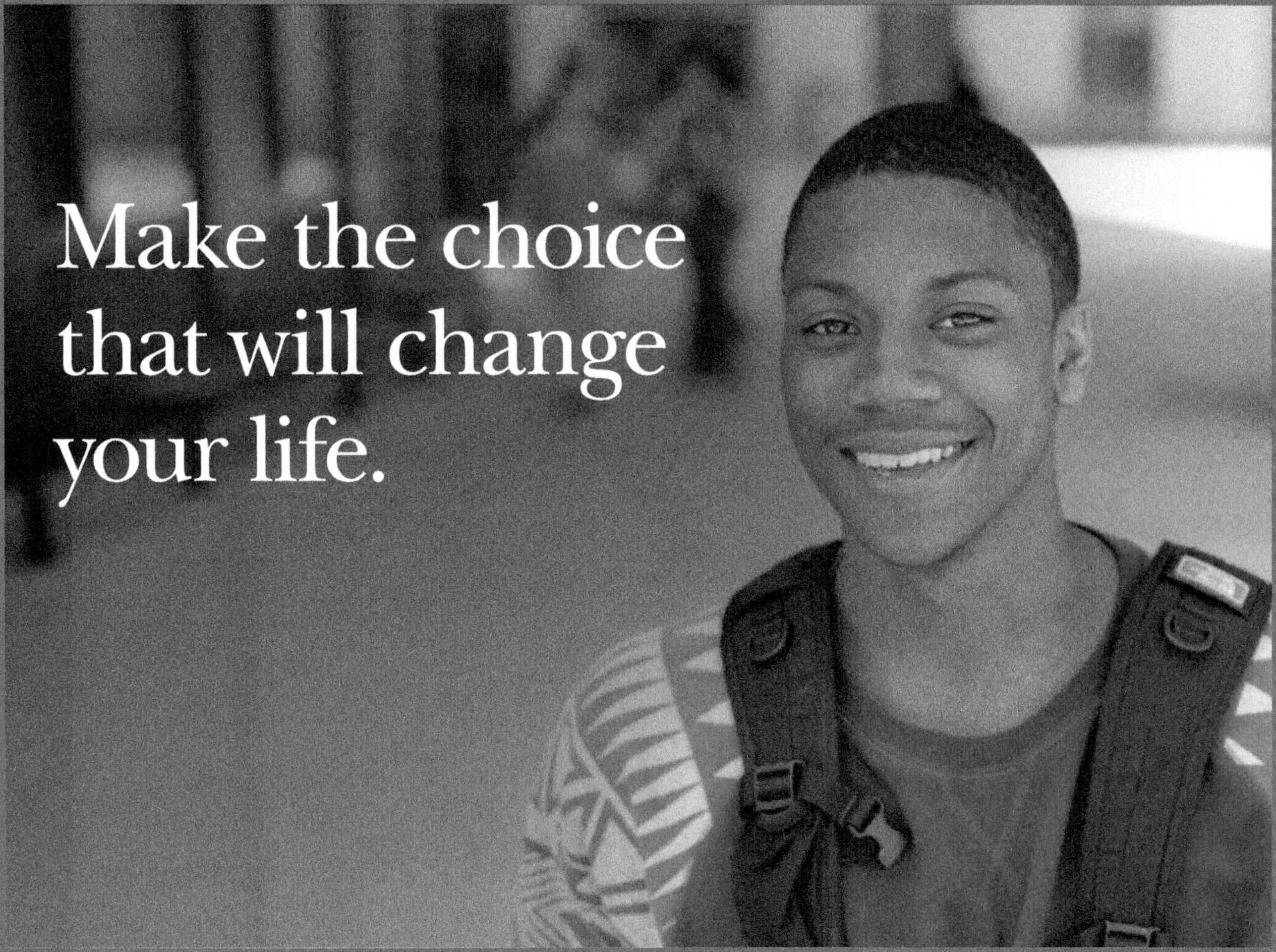

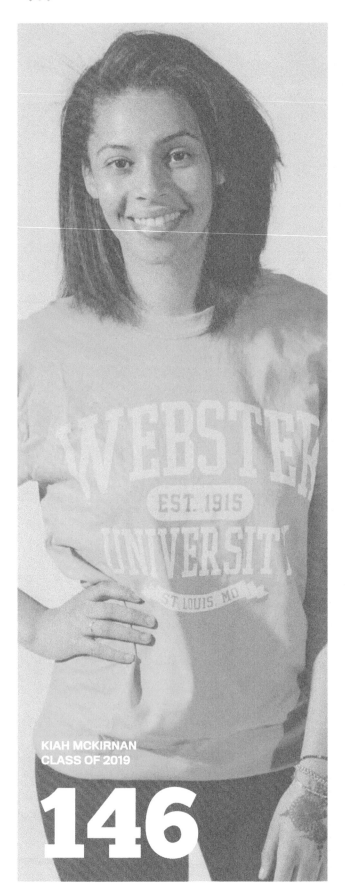

KIAH MCKIRNAN
CLASS OF 2019

146

Chapter Four
Getting In

Chapter Five
Finding the Money

FROM LEFT: BRETT ZIEGLER FOR USN&WR; GETTY IMAGES

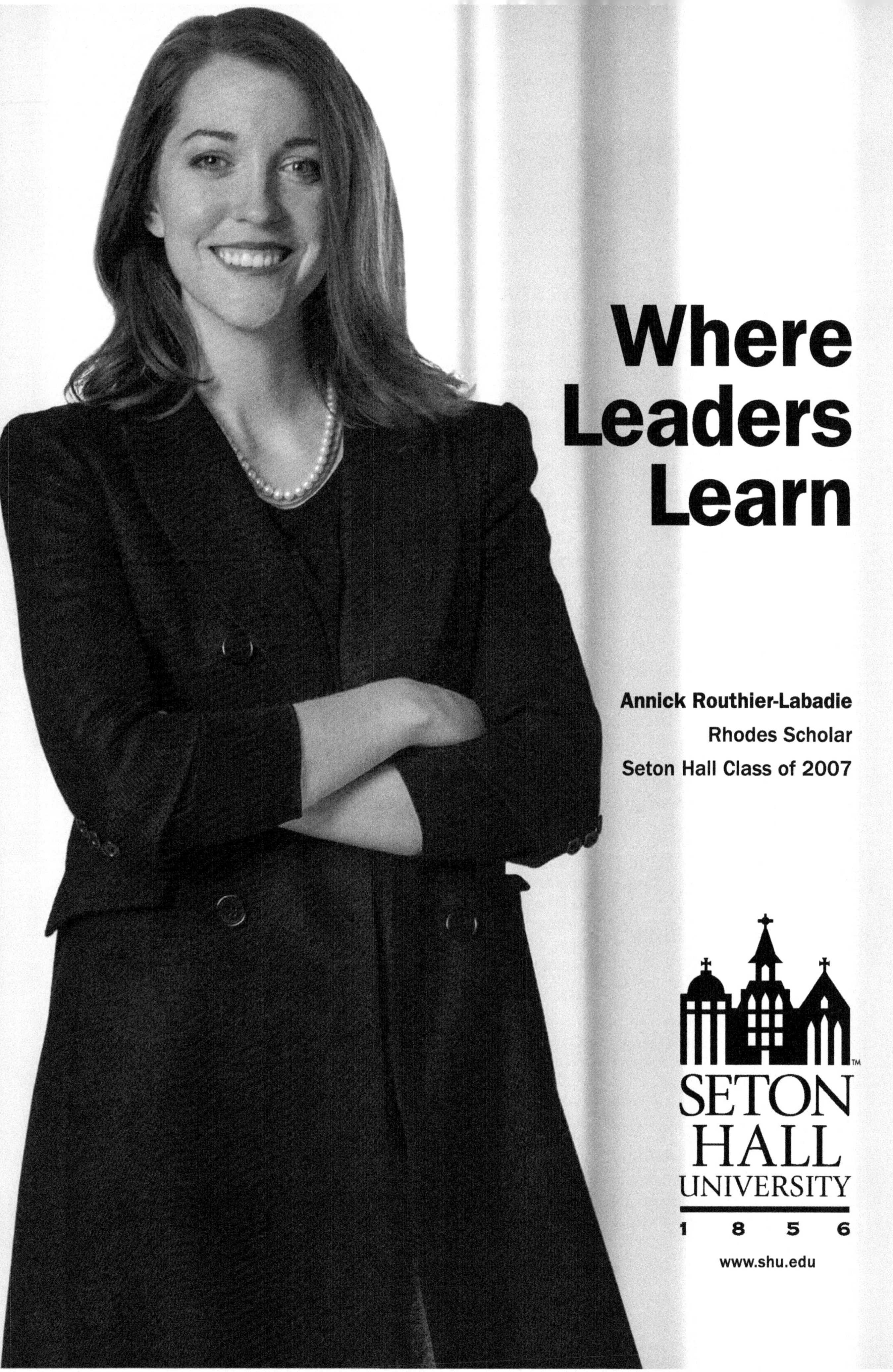
Where Leaders Learn
Annick Routhier-Labadie
Rhodes Scholar
Seton Hall Class of 2007
SETON HALL UNIVERSITY
1856
www.shu.edu

@usnews.com

GETTING IN

COLLEGE ADMISSIONS PLAYBOOK

Get tips from Varsity Tutors, an academic tutoring and test-prep provider. This blog offers advice on mastering the SAT and ACT as well as the college application process.
usnews.com/collegeplaybook

STUDENTS ON HOW THEY MADE IT IN

Seniors from high schools across the country talk about their admissions experiences and offer advice to students getting ready to apply to college.
usnews.com/studentprofiles

COLLEGE VISITS

TAKE A ROAD TRIP

We've gone on numerous trips to visit campuses in case you can't. Check out our compendium of more than 20 different trips to 100-plus schools.
usnews.com/roadtrips

RANKINGS INSIGHT

MORSE CODE BLOG

Get the inside scoop on the rankings – and the commentary and controversy surrounding them – from U.S. News' Bob Morse, the mastermind behind our education rankings projects.
usnews.com/morsecode

PAYING FOR COLLEGE

RESEARCHING AID

Visit our guide to all your possible sources of college funds. Learn about your savings options and which schools meet students' full need.
usnews.com/payforcollege

THE STUDENT LOAN RANGER

Don't fall into the trap of taking on too much debt. Bloggers from American Student Assistance provide guidance if you must turn to loans to pay for college.
usnews.com/studentloanranger

IN-DEPTH DATA

COLLEGE COMPASS

Gain access to the U.S. News College Compass, which offers comprehensive searchable data and tools for high school students starting down the path to campus. To get a 25 percent discount, subscribe at
usnews.com/compassoffer

DISTANCE LEARNING

ONLINE EDUCATION

Do you need to balance school with work or other obligations? Consult our rankings of the best online degree programs for leads on how to get your diploma without leaving home.
usnews.com/online

FOR SCHOOLS ONLY

ACADEMIC INSIGHTS

U.S. News Academic Insights is an analytics dashboard intended for use by institutions that comprises all of the undergraduate and graduate historical rankings data we've collected. The dashboard allows for peer group comparisons and includes easy-to-understand visualizations.
ai.usnews.com

BEST COLLEGES
2016 EDITION

Executive Committee Chairman and Editor-in-Chief Mortimer B. Zuckerman
Editor and Chief Content Officer Brian Kelly
Executive Editor Margaret Mannix
Managing Editor Anne McGrath
Chief Data Strategist Robert J. Morse
Senior Data Analyst Eric Brooks
Data Collection Manager Matthew Mason
Art Director Kristine L. Mehuron
Senior Designer Rebecca Pajak
Director of Photography Avijit Gupta
Photography Editor Brett Ziegler
News Editor Elizabeth Whitehead
Production Assistant Courtney Walker
Contributors Lindsay Cates, Cathie Gandel, Christopher J. Gearon, Katherine Hobson, Maura Hohman, Beth Howard, Ned Johnson, Darcy Lewis, Margaret Loftus, Michael Morella, Courtney Rubin, Arlene Weintraub
Research Manager Myke Freeman
Directory Janie S. Price

USNEWS.COM/EDUCATION
Vice President, Education Chris DiCosmo
Managing Editor, Education Anita Narayan
Assistant Education Editor Allison Gualtieri
Reporters/Writers Devon Haynie, Alexandra Pannoni, Kelly Mae Ross, Delece Smith-Barrow, Susannah Snider
Web Producers Briana Boyington, Travis Mitchell
Editorial Project Manager Erica Ryan

ACADEMIC INSIGHTS
General Manager Evan Jones
Account Manager Cale Gosnell
Sales Manager Megan Trudeau
Product Marketing Specialist Taylor Suggs

INFORMATION SERVICES
Vice President, Data and Information Strategy Stephanie Salmon
Data Analysts Kenneth Hines, Alexis Krivian, Anjelica Pitts
Data Collection Geneva Dampare, Alexandra Harris

TECHNOLOGY
Vice President, Technology Yingjie Shu
Director of Web Technology Patrick Peak
Director of Engineering Matt Kupferman
Senior Systems Manager Cathy Cacho
Software Team Lead David Jessup, Bethany Morin
Primary Developers William Garcia, Erik Gartz, Brian Stewart, Paul Pechin, Josh Brown, Dan Brown, Chris Malerich, Byron Peebles, Alan Weinstein
Digital Production Michael A. Brooks, Manager; Michael Fingerhuth

President and Chief Executive Officer William D. Holiber

ADVERTISING
Publisher and Chief Advertising Officer Kerry Dyer
National Advertising Director Ed Hannigan
Director of Sales Strategy and Planning Alexandra Kalaf
Managing Editor, BrandFuse Jada Graves
Director, Integrated Media Solutions Peter Bowes
Health Care Manager Colin Hamilton
Finance Manager Heather Levine
Senior Account Executives Steve Hiel, Michelle Rosen, Brian Roy, Shannon Tkach
Account Executives Taylor Kiefer, Ivy Zenati
Account Executive, Integrated Media Solutions Dustin Hill
Senior Manager, Programmatic and Revenue Platforms Joe Hayden
Senior Manager, Sales Strategy Freddie Zamora
Manager, Sales Strategy Tina Lopez, Riki Smolen
Sales Planners Liam Kristinnsson, Michael Machado
Senior Manager, Client Services Rachel Wulfow
Account Managers Rachel Halasz, Katie Harper, Dana Jelen
Senior Manager Advertising Operations Cory Nesser
Advertising Operations Manager Samit Khatri
Director of Advertising Services Phyllis Panza
Business Operations Karolee Jarnecki
Executive Assistant to the President Judy David
Executive Assistant to the Publisher Anny Lasso
Sales Administration Coordinator Carmen Caraballo

Vice President, Manufacturing and Specialty Marketing Mark W. White
Director of Specialty Marketing Abbe Weintraub

Senior Vice President, Operations Karen S. Chevalier
Senior Vice President, Strategic Development and General Counsel Peter M. Dwoskin
Senior Vice President, Planning Thomas H. Peck
Chief Financial Officer Neil Maheshwari
Senior Vice President, Human Resources Jeff Zomper

Additional copies of the 2016 edition of **U.S.News & World Report's Best Colleges** guidebook are available for purchase at (800) 836-6397 or online at **usnews.com/collegeguide.** To order custom reprints, please call (877) 652-5295 or email **usnews@wrightsmedia.com.** For all other permissions, email **permissions@usnews.com.**

LOYOLA
LOYOLA

LOYOLA
UNIVERSITY
NEW ORLEANS
©2015 Loyola University New Orleans

FROM THE EDITOR'S DESK

BY BRIAN KELLY

This college search thing can be a little intimidating, especially if you're going through it for the first time. This is our 31st go-round at U.S. News, so we feel like we've got some experience worth sharing.

Over the years, we've improved our information and sharpened our focus, with our primary objective being to help students and their parents make one of life's most important – and costliest – decisions. Prospective students and their parents need objective measures that allow them to evaluate and compare schools; the U.S. News rankings are one tool to help them make choices, along with all the other insights and guidance contained in these pages. This sort of assistance is more relevant than ever, with some private colleges now costing around $250,000 for a bachelor's degree. At the same time, many public high schools have greatly reduced their college counseling resources, leaving students and parents to educate themselves about the search and admission process.

Of course, we have adjusted our ranking methodology over the years to reflect changes in the world of higher education, and we make it clear that we are not doing peer-reviewed social science research, although we do maintain very high survey and data standards. We have always been open and transparent. We have always said that the rankings are not perfect. The first were based solely on schools' academic reputation among leaders at peer institutions; we later developed a formula in which reputation accounted for 25 percent of a school's score and important quantitative measures such as graduation and retention rates, average class size and student-faculty ratios, for 75 percent. Over time, we have shifted weight from inputs (indicators of the quality of students and resources) to outputs (success in graduating students). We operate under this guiding principle: The methodology is altered only if a change will better help our readers and web audience compare schools as they're deciding where to apply and enroll.

It has helped us a great deal to have these principles to focus on as we have faced the inevitable criticisms from academia about our rankings' growing influence. One main critique remains: that it is impossible to reduce the complexities of a college's offerings and attributes to one number. It's important to keep in mind that our information is a starting point. The next steps in a college search should include detailed research on a smaller list of choices, campus visits and conversations with students, faculty and alumni wherever you can find them. Feedback from academia has helped improve the rankings over time. We meet with our critics, listen to their points of view, debate them on the merits of what we do and make appropriate changes.

U.S. News is keenly aware that the higher education community is also a major audience for our rankings. We understand how seriously academics, college presidents, trustees and governing boards take our data. They study, analyze and use them in various ways, including benchmarking against peers, alumni fundraising and advertising to attract students.

BEST COLLEGES
U.S. News & WORLD REPORT
2016

What does all of this mean in today's global information marketplace? U.S. News has become a respected unbiased source that higher education administrators and policymakers and the college-bound public worldwide turn to for reliable guidance. In fact, the Best Colleges rankings have become a key part of the evolving higher education accountability movement. Universities are increasingly being held responsible for their policies, how their funds are spent, the level of student engagement, and how much graduates have learned. The U.S. News rankings have become the annual public benchmark to measure the academic performance of the country's colleges and universities.

We know our role has limits. The rankings should only be used as one factor in the college search – we've long said that there is no single "best college." There is only the best college for you or, more likely, a handful of good options, one of which will turn out to be a great fit. Besides the rankings, we can help college-bound high school students and their parents by providing a wealth of information on all aspects of the application process, from getting in to getting financial aid. Our website, usnews.com, features thousands of pages of rankings, research, sortable data, photos, videos and a personalized tool called College Compass.

We've been doing this for over three decades, so we know the process is not simple. But our experience tells us the hard work is worth it in the end. ●

Study the Schoo

IN A CHEMISTRY LAB AT MACALESTER COLLEGE

BRETT ZIEGLER FOR USN&WR

ls

1

Headed for SUCCESS

As you research schools, look for programs that aim to help students thrive. BY CHRISTOPHER J. GEARON

GEORGIA TECH, A DYNAMO AT INTERNSHIPS

Want to boost your chances of having a great college experience, finishing on time and landing a job after graduation? You can dramatically raise the odds by picking the right school – and that doesn't mean the most elite one that will take you. Doing your research now can have a huge payoff, considering that one-third of college freshmen don't return for sophomore year, and only 61 percent of students graduate in six years.

Sometimes the reasons are financial, of course. But often the problem is one of dissatisfaction, of feeling disconnected from the college community. So you'll want to zero in on places that not only feel like a good fit, but also that work at getting students engaged in campus life. A growing number of schools are implementing certain "high-impact" practices that have been shown to make a big difference to happiness and success. For example: "first-year experiences" that bond freshmen quickly to professors and a small group of other students, internships and research opportunities.

Participating in such practices, examined in the following pages, enhances students' "connection to an institution and makes their experience more meaningful," says Alexander McCormick, associate professor of educational leadership and policy studies at Indiana University–Bloomington and director of the National Survey of Student Engagement, which tracks the ways students get involved in their education. These experiences also cultivate abilities employers seek most, including critical thinking, problem-solving, and teamwork skills. "I'd be looking for [colleges] that make some of these mandatory," says George Kuh, director of the National Institute for Learning Outcomes Assessment.

Each year, U.S. News asks college presidents, chief academic officers and admissions deans to nominate up to 10 institutions with outstanding examples of high-impact programs. As you read about each program, you'll see a list of standout colleges (presented alphabetically) that got the most mentions this year; additional schools are recognized at usnews.com.

FIRST-YEAR EXPERIENCE

A FABULOUS BEGINNING

With so many students bailing after freshman year, colleges have stepped up their efforts to become "stickier." One way is to bring students together before class begins in a meaningful orientation. Another: immediately putting small groups of students into frequent contact with each other and a faculty member in a seminar or other intensive experience focused on critical inquiry, writing and team learning – the toolbox needed for success in college and a career.

"I was not totally comfortable with my decision to go to such a large school," recalls Alexandra Mooney of Highland Heights, Ohio, who just graduated from Ohio State University with a double major in economics and international studies. But then she went to a four-day leadership development conference two weeks before freshman year started that "connected me to OSU." That was followed by a required small-group course, specific to a student's intended major, in which classmates get their sea legs on everything from resources on campus to potential pathways in their field. Undecided about her major, Mooney took University Exploration, which introduced her and two dozen peers to the whole panoply of possibilities. Their professor also acted as their adviser, which further cemented the bond. "He was so invested in helping me," she notes.

"We look to get students connected early and often to the right people and right resources," says Bernie Savarese, director of University Orientation and First Year Experience at Ohio State. New students also take a series of classes designed to help them settle in and succeed, with topics ranging from personal finance, time management and study skills to healthy eating and coping with anxiety.

Peer leaders keep an eye on newbies, helping them to establish relationships on campus and supporting anyone who is having trouble transitioning to independent college life. Since initiating the program in 2001, Ohio State has watched its retention rate climb to 94 percent from the low 80s.

No matter where you choose to go, get involved in activities that will help you form ties right away, urges Savarese. "The things you do in the first six weeks of school can pay dividends 10 times going forward."

THE STANDOUTS

Alverno College (WI)
Appalachian State University (NC)*
Butler University (IN)
Elon University (NC)
Evergreen State College (WA)*
Franklin and Marshall College (PA)
Indiana Univ.-Purdue Univ.-Indianapolis*
Kennesaw State University (GA)*
Ohio State University-Columbus*
Purdue University-West Lafayette (IN)*
Skidmore College (NY)
Stanford University (CA)
University of Michigan-Ann Arbor*
Univ. of North Carolina-Chapel Hill*
University of South Carolina*
University of Texas-Austin*
University of Wisconsin-Madison*
Wagner College (NY)

(*Public)

BRETT ZIEGLER FOR USN&WR

LIVING AND WORKING AS A GROUP AT ELON

LEARNING COMMUNITIES

CLASSES THAT BUILD A BOND

Learning communities aren't just for freshmen, but they are another tool many colleges are using to provide the best possible first-year experience. A well-designed community typically puts a group of students into at least two courses together and gets them working collaboratively.

The classes often are paired to examine topics through the perspectives of different disciplines – tackling climate change through the lenses of science and economics, say. They are often intentionally demanding. Students in learning communities "spend 20 percent more time a week preparing for class," says George Kuh, director of the National Institute for Learning Outcomes Assessment.

At Elon University in North Carolina, where groups of freshmen take several core First-Year Foundations courses together, T. Giles Roll, a sophomore from Bloomington, Illinois, recalls that his Global Experience course, in particular, "challenged me like no other class." Roll, a finance major in the Leadership Fellows program, was grouped with 20 other fellows for the class, which asks students to consider such questions as individual responsibility in a global context and the relationship of humans to the natural world. Taught by a biology professor, Roll's course entailed intensive reading and monitoring of current events, as well as lots of discussion and writing. Roll framed a research paper on a local oil spill as a letter to the head of an environmental organization, for example.

Elon also has implemented a number of themed "living-learning" communities that turbocharge the experience by adding a residential component. The goal is to keep the intellectual debate and social interactions continuing outside of class, notes Jon Dooley, assistant vice president for student life. Members live on the same floor or in the same wing of a dorm based on their interest in topics such as the creative arts, gender and sexuality, and sustainable living. Roll opted this year for Innovation House, a just-launched community for budding entrepreneurs.

THE STANDOUTS

Elon University (NC)
Evergreen State College (WA)*
Franklin and Marshall College (PA)
Indiana Univ.-Purdue Univ.-Indianapolis*
Michigan State University*
Ohio State University-Columbus*
Purdue University-West Lafayette (IN)*
University of Maryland-College Park*
University of Michigan-Ann Arbor*
University of Missouri*
University of South Carolina*
University of Washington*
University of Wisconsin-Madison*
Wagner College (NY)
Yale University (CT)

(*Public)

ANDY MCMILLAN FOR USN&WR

CHRISTOPHER NEWPORT
UNIVERSITY

EDUCATING TOMORROW'S LEADERS

When former U.S. Senator Paul Trible became president of Christopher Newport University in 1996, he challenged his new colleagues to build a great university for America. "We are not interested in incremental progress. We are in the business of dramatic transformation. Everything we do will be done at the highest levels of excellence, and with the help of a lot of wonderful people, CNU will become one of America's pre-eminent public liberal arts and sciences universities."

Few schools have come so far so quickly. Since President Trible's arrival, the number of admission applications and the academic profile of the incoming freshman class have soared. This year CNU received nearly 8,000 applications for a freshman class of 1,200.

CNU offers great teaching and small classes. Hundreds of full-time faculty, drawn from the most respected graduate programs in the country, have been added, and there are no large sections or teaching assistants.

More than $1 billion in capital construction has been completed, and CNU has built a spectacularly beautiful campus with world-class facilities. "Our job is to instruct and inspire, and nothing does that more powerfully than great architecture," Trible says. "We want our students to have great dreams for their lives and for this country."

The reach and reputation of CNU is spreading. *Kiplinger's* and The Princeton Review include the University among the best values in higher education. *U.S.News & World Report* ranks CNU among the top public regional universities in the South and as a school to watch for making "the most promising and innovative changes in the areas of academics, faculty, student life, campus and facilities." Christopher Newport is also the only public institution in the nation to earn a perfect "A" from the American Council of Trustees and Alumni for the strength of its curriculum.

Christopher Newport is not a place for spectators. The academics are demanding, and students are expected to actively engage, both in class and outside of the classroom. There are more than 200 officially recognized clubs, organizations and activities from which to choose. That's a remarkable number for a school of 5,000 students.

In all things, the University emphasizes the importance of leadership, honor and civic engagement. The study of leadership is available to all students, and nearly 25 percent of CNU's students participate in the President's Leadership Program. This program combines rigorous academic courses that lead to a minor in leadership studies with community service, foreign study, outdoor adventure, and speakers who have led lives of success and significance.

"We want our students to become good citizens and leaders who possess a passion for engagement, a commitment to excellence and a powerful sense of their responsibility for making the world a better place. We want our students to lead, serve, love and set the world on fire."

INTERNSHIPS

LEARNING ON THE JOB

Employers want to hire people who can write and speak clearly, work in teams, think critically and solve real-world problems. Will you be able to do that when you graduate?

A great way to get some creds while in college is by taking on an internship – or several. That's what Hannah Sedgwick of Tewksbury, Massachusetts, was looking to do when she zeroed in on American University in Washington, D.C. "AU was my No. 1 choice because of the opportunities of interning," says the 2015 graduate in communications studies. Sedgwick, who wants to go into public relations for a large entertainment company, incorporated six gigs all-told into her schedule, including one at Washington's Newseum and two at nearby Discovery Communications. At the Newseum, Sedgwick did research related to the Berlin Wall, the assassination of Abraham Lincoln and for a potential documentary about Georgia Congressman John Lewis. But it was working as a public relations assistant at Discovery that helped her find her calling. She's now enrolled in a one-year master's in strategic communications at American.

MATT MCLOONE FOR USN&WR

HANNAH SEDGWICK AT DISCOVERY

Internships are an integral part of the learning experience for almost everyone at American, with 90 percent of undergrads doing at least one, says Gihan Fernando, executive director of the university's career center. "We're in front of [students] Day One," he says. Faculty act as interns' academic supervisors, helping them make connections between what they are learning on the job and their classwork.

All of that hands-on experience and workplace networking, plus the chance to hone your sense of what you like and don't on the job, can open up "terrific pathways to future opportunities," Fernando says. Indeed, studies have shown that having one or more internships while in college is associated with greater career satisfaction later in life.

Experiential learning is so central at many colleges that some, such as Mount Holyoke in Massachusetts, fund on-the-job experiences. If your school isn't an internship powerhouse, consider snagging one on your own.

THE STANDOUTS

Berea College (KY)
Butler University (IN)
Claremont McKenna College (CA)
Connecticut College
Drexel University (PA)
Elon University (NC)
Georgia Institute of Technology*
Harvey Mudd College (CA)
Northeastern University (MA)
Purdue University-West Lafayette (IN)*
Rochester Inst. of Technology (NY)
University of Cincinnati*
Worcester Polytechnic Institute (MA))

(*Public)

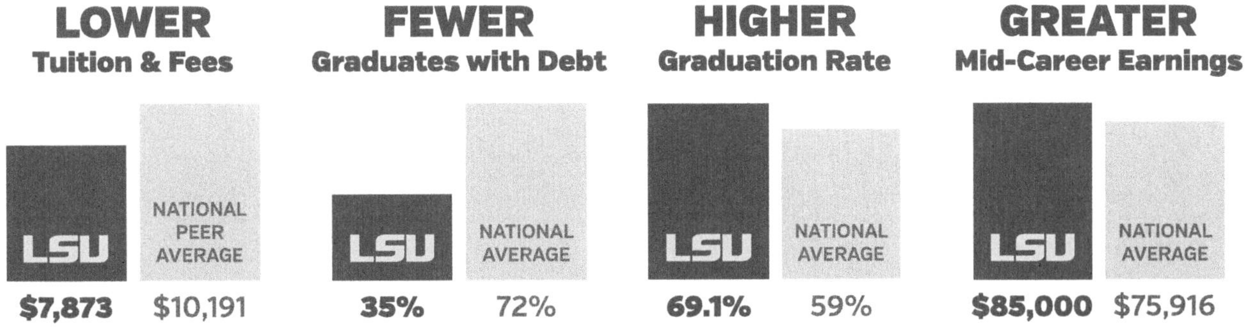

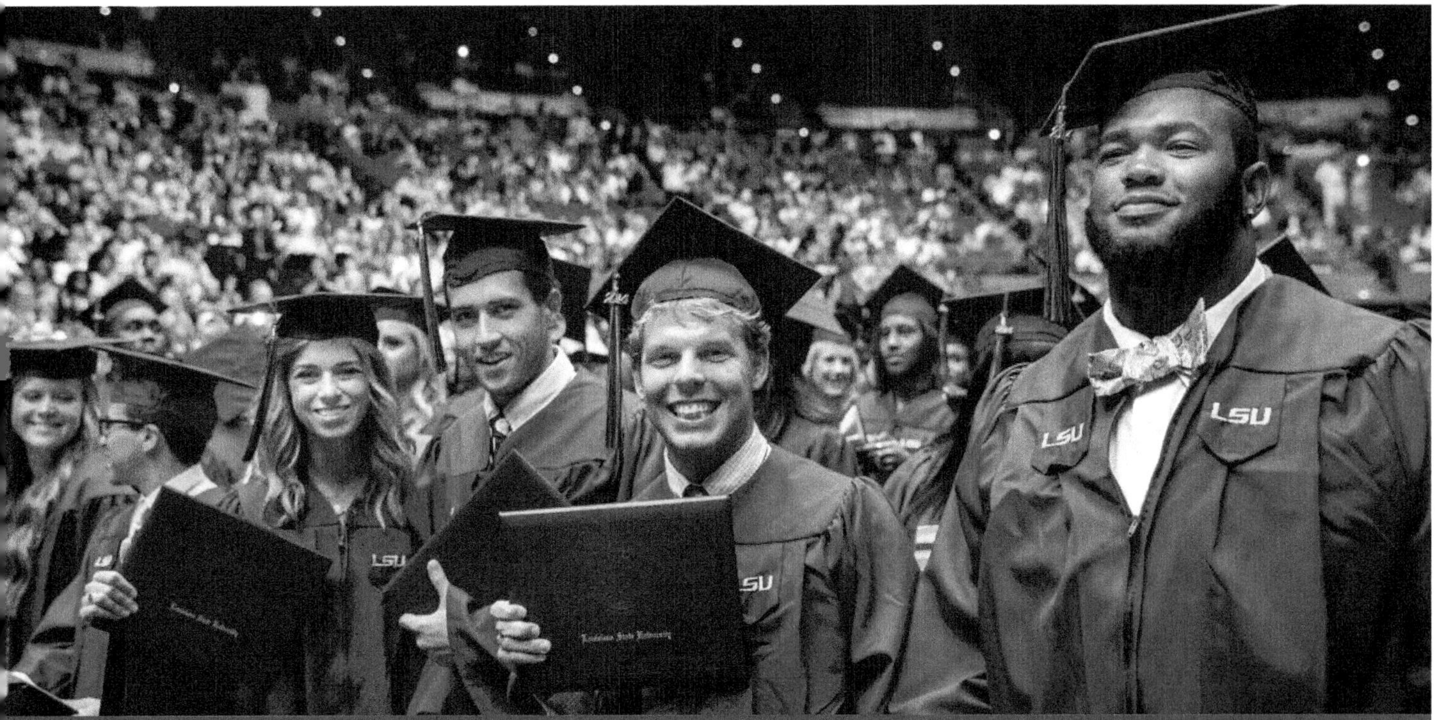

UNDERGRADUATE RESEARCH

LOOKING FOR ANSWERS

One quarter of the class of 2014 worked closely with a professor on research while in college, according to the National Survey of Student Engagement. The Association of American Colleges & Universities thinks that fraction is too low and is "really pushing" member schools to do better, says

Debra Humphreys, vice president for policy and public engagement. Collaborating on original research gets students working closely with a faculty member, posing questions, making empirical observations, and using technology in ways they can't in class.

"The stuff I'm doing is making an impact," says Anthony Recidoro, a 2015 University of Washington graduate in biology from Murrieta, California. His research on how zebrafish regenerate lost bone, skin and tails has implications for medicine, he says, and "probably ranks No. 1" among all his college experiences. Before landing his research slot sophomore year in the Musculoskeletal Systems Biology Lab, Recidoro says he felt "lost in a big old system." With research, his world "got really small, really fast."

Recidoro spent about 10 hours a week involved in the work, plus two summers, and has been published in a scientific journal. He also got to attend an international science conference in Baltimore, where he hobnobbed with Harvard University and University of Tokyo faculty.

New students at UW get a briefing on the research possibilities as early as their orientation, and some 84 percent of undergrads undertake a project. Each spring, over 1,000 students present their work at a campuswide symposium, and an impressive 87 percent of patent applications filed by the university in 2014 had student input.

When considering colleges, advises Humphreys, be sure to look for places where research opportunities are available to all students, not just honors or other subsets of students.

THE STANDOUTS

- Amherst College (MA)
- Butler University (IN)
- California Institute of Technology
- Carleton College (MN)
- Carnegie Mellon University (PA)
- College of New Jersey*
- College of Wooster (OH)
- Creighton University (NE)
- Dartmouth College (NH)
- Davidson College (NC)
- Duke University (NC)
- Elon University (NC)
- Furman University (SC)
- Harvard University (MA)
- Harvey Mudd College (CA)
- Hope College (MI)
- Johns Hopkins University (MD)
- Massachusetts Institute of Technology
- Ohio State University-Columbus*
- Pomona College (CA)
- Princeton University (NJ)
- Rice University (TX)
- Stanford University (CA)
- Trinity University (TX)
- Truman State University (MO)*
- University of California-Berkeley*
- University of California-Los Angeles*
- University of Michigan-Ann Arbor*
- University of North Carolina-Chapel Hill*
- University of Texas-Austin*
- University of Washington*
- University of Wisconsin-La Crosse*
- University of Wisconsin-Madison*
- Vanderbilt University (TN)
- Williams College (MA)
- Yale University (CT)

(*Public)

MIKE KANE FOR USN&WR

UW UNDERGRADS PRESENT THEIR RESEARCH FINDINGS.

THE STANDOUTS

Arcadia University (PA)
Boston University
Butler University (IN)
Dartmouth College (NH)
Dickinson College (PA)
Elon University (NC)
Georgetown University (DC)
Goucher College (MD)
Kalamazoo College (MI)
Macalester College (MN)
Michigan State University*
Middlebury College (VT)
New York University
Stanford University (CA)
St. John's University (MN)
St. Olaf College (MN)
Syracuse University (NY)
University of Michigan-Ann Arbor*
University of Minnesota-Twin Cities*
University of Richmond (VA)
University of Texas-Austin*
Villanova University (PA)
Wake Forest University (NC)

(*Public)

STUDY ABROAD

GETTING A GLOBAL EXPERIENCE

Colleges have been sending students abroad for a century, but the experience is no longer mainly about gaining exposure to a different culture and practicing the language. More often now "it's about making use of locations" to provide students across majors with an international perspective to take into their field, says Jim Lucas, assistant dean for global education and curriculum at Michigan State University. MSU annually sends 2,500 undergrads on nearly 300 trips to 60 countries, from Antarctica to Zambia.

The experience is "not peripheral at MSU, it's integral," says Brett Berquist, until recently the executive director of the school's Office of Study Abroad (now director of the international office at the University of Auckland in New Zealand). MSU Spartans have numerous ways to gain a global experience, from spring-break travel and study trips that run four to six weeks to the traditional semester abroad.

Recent chemical engineering grad Mario Gutierrez spent one month in Sweden and Germany exploring renewable energies. He visited a Swedish paper mill that harnesses the heat produced making paper to co-generate electricity, for example, and learned about how biogas, a gaseous fuel created by the breakdown of organic matter that isn't common in the U.S., is used in Germany. "It gave me a different perspective on engineering," says Gutierrez, a first-generation college student from Powell, Wyoming, who also took four spring break trips to volunteer at orphanages in Mexico.

An MSU study of the impact of these programs showed that students who go abroad take less time to graduate and do so with a higher GPA. Other research shows that the experiences increase participants' self-confidence and expand the diversity of their social network.

VOLUNTEERING AS PART OF THE COURSE

In "service learning" courses, students alternate time in the classroom with related community service required as part of the course. The issues students tackle out in the field are the same as or related to the ones they study in class, so they apply theory gleaned from their lessons in real settings and then reflect on the fieldwork back on campus. An accounting class might help a local charity keep the books, an architecture class might help renovate a senior center, and a sociology class might study the causes and ramifications of "food insecurity" and at the same time help operate a food pantry.

Not all service learning is equal in value. The difference is huge, for instance, between Tulane University, where students choose among 100 courses built around service and are required to take two in order to graduate, and a school that simply corrals whoever is willing for a campuswide day of volunteerism each year.

"My service learning classes were usually my favorite," says Mariana Altman, a 2015 Tulane grad with a double major in studio art and political economy. Her experiences included working with students at a local school on a mural about the scientific process, creating public health signage messages for six area clinics, and designing a brochure for a local museum. She particularly enjoyed "producing art for a cause," she says, but beyond the art, she gained invaluable exposure to the permitting process, budgeting and project management.

Another more intangible benefit is that students quickly get "embedded" in the community, observes Tulane Provost Michael Bernstein. Freshman retention and graduation rates have both risen at Tulane since university leaders challenged students to help repair the city after Hurricane Katrina.

THE STANDOUTS

Bates College (ME)
Berea College (KY)
Brown University (RI)
Butler University (IN)
Canisius College (NY)
Duke University (NC)
Elon University (NC)
Indiana U.-Purdue U.-Indianapolis*
Loyola University Maryland
Northeastern University (MA)
Portland State University (OR)*
Stanford University (CA)
Tufts University (MA)
Tulane University (LA)
University of Michigan-Ann Arbor*
Univ. of North Carolina-Chapel Hill*
University of Pennsylvania
Wagner College (NY)
Warren Wilson College (NC)

(*Public)

WILLIAM WIDMER FOR USN&WR

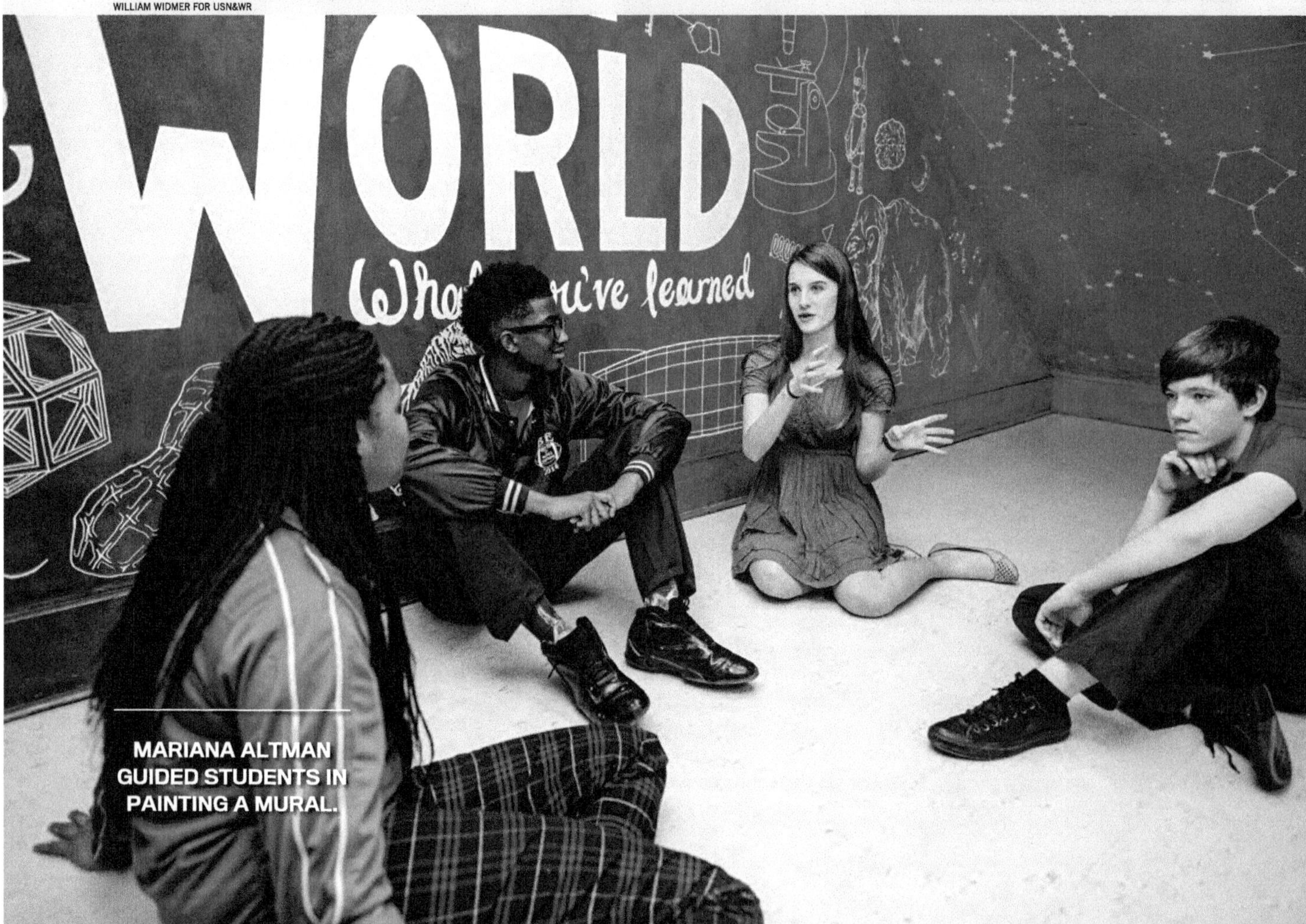

MARIANA ALTMAN GUIDED STUDENTS IN PAINTING A MURAL.

WRITING IN THE DISCIPLINES

MAKING SURE EVERYONE'S A WRITER

'There is a clear connection between writing and students' critical thinking skills," says Michelle LaFrance, director of the Writing Across the Curriculum program at George Mason University in Virginia. Students who spend time perfecting the type of writing required by their disciplines "make better connections with one another and faculty, and they learn more deeply."

Those conclusions have inspired a growing number of colleges and universities to make writing a priority at all levels of instruction and across majors. Students are producing and refining everything from traditional research papers to opinion pieces, journal articles and blog posts for a wide range of audiences. Taking one or more intensive writing courses and perhaps working for the student newspaper or literary magazine as well "will confer substantial benefits, for sure," says George Kuh, director of the National Institute for Learning Outcomes Assessment.

At George Mason, freshmen take an introductory class in which they gain an understanding of audience as they focus on writing and then revising. They later take a course on what it means to write effectively in their discipline.

"My class focused on what it looks like to write as a scientist," says Joel Mota, a 2015 graduate in biology who concentrated on analyzing scientific research, case studies and journal commentaries, then writing in those styles.

GMU students also take one of 82 writing-intensive courses within their major. As a senior, Mota chose one on animal communication and social behavior that had him stretching in various ways related to science. Among his assignments: Write a funding proposal for a health-related campus project. Besides the three required courses, instruction on communicating well in writing is woven through the curriculum.

As is true with eating vegetables, notes LaFrance, "the payoff is extensive, but not always immediately apparent."

THE STANDOUTS

Brown University (RI)
Carleton College (MN)
Clemson University (SC)*
Cornell University (NY)
Duke University (NC)
Elon University (NC)
George Mason University (VA)*
Hamilton College (NY)
Kenyon College (OH)
University of California-Davis*

(*Public)

SENIOR CAPSTONE

WRAPPING IT ALL UP WITH A PROJECT

One of the chief benefits of ending your college career with a "capstone" project is that it gives you a strong taste of the way problem-solving in the real world works. The exercise, intended to get students to integrate all that they've learned and apply it, could be a research project, a portfolio, a performance or a work experience.

As they delve into their chosen topics, says Arthur Heinricher, dean of undergraduate studies at Worcester Polytechnic Institute in Massachusetts, students often realize that success is going to require dealing with "gaps in their knowledge." WPI requires a "major qualifying project" of all seniors. Each project is guided by a faculty adviser, but many students – about one-third of the group this past year – elect an experience that involves working for an outside employer. "The goals of the project often change in the middle" when it turns out that desired data are unavailable, for instance, or when a student's initial analysis changes a company's priorities, says Heinricher. Having to "adapt on the fly" is often cited by graduates as being one of their most valuable takeaways.

"You really have to learn on the job," says Peter Shorrock, a 2014 grad in biomedical engineering whose yearlong project entailed designing a method to test a cardiac monitoring sensor developed by FLEXcon, a nearby company. Shorrock was part of a WPI team that ultimately provided recommendations on how the firm could improve the design. Today Shorrock works as a FLEXcon technical service engineer. "They knew I could do really good work, complete a project and hand it off," he says.

Capstone projects are so valuable, says Debra Humphreys, vice president for policy and public engagement at the Association of American Colleges & Universities, that the group is "doubling down" to get more members to require them. ●

THE STANDOUTS

Brown University (RI)
Carleton College (MN)
College of Wooster (OH)
Elon University (NC)
Princeton University (NJ)
Stanford University (CA)
Swarthmore College (PA)
Yale University (CT)

CONSIDER AN HONORS COLLEGE

You get VIP treatment at public prices BY MARGARET LOFTUS

Annie Brackemyre never envisioned herself going to Indiana University. Back when she was a high school senior in Fishers, Indiana, with a 4.2 GPA and an ACT score of 31, she had her sights set on a constellation of private East Coast schools, including George Washington University in Washington, D.C., and Tufts in Massachusetts. Though she applied to IU as her safety, "it was hard for me to wrap my mind around going to a state school," she admits. "I sacrificed so much for academics. And it was important that my college choice reflect that." But clarity came in the form of a full academic scholarship to IU's Hutton Honors College. As Brackemyre, now an IU senior, puts it, "Indiana made me an offer that I couldn't say no to."

With tuition at top-tier schools pushing $50,000 a year, competitive applicants (and their parents) are taking a long

PETER HOFFMAN FOR USN&WR

ANNIE BRACKEMYRE TAKES IN A HUTTON "FIRESIDE CHAT."

second look at honors colleges at public universities. Most of these schools-within-schools offer students small, seminar-style courses and a built-in community with all sorts of perks, like dinners with visiting luminaries. They encourage interdisciplinary work and study abroad, and often require capstone projects or undergraduate research – all with a state-school price tag. It's the best of both worlds, says Hutton Dean Andrea Ciccarelli. "Students receive the elite education of a smaller private university with much broader class offerings."

Swarthmore was the first university in the U.S. to institute an honors program back in the 1920s, but the movement really took off in the mid-1990s, when 60 percent of today's estimated 2,400 programs were introduced. Maryland and Florida even designated stand-alone liberal arts honors colleges within their state systems: St. Mary's College of Maryland, with just under 1,900 students, and the New College of Florida, with about 800. Never have these programs been as popular as in the aftermath of the Great Recession. "There's been an uptick in interest and applications since 2009, and it hasn't abated," says Craig Meister, president of AdmissionsIntel.com based in Baltimore, which offers guidance to college applicants and their families. Applications have gone up 43 percent over the last five years at the University of South Carolina Honors College. And the Sally McDonnell Barksdale Honors College at the University of Mississippi now sees roughly 1,300 applications a year, up from 500 in 2008. The school has tried to keep pace by expanding enrollment from 175 freshman spots a decade ago to 390 today.

"The privates have outpriced themselves," argues Douglass Sullivan-González, dean of the Ole Miss program. Even out-of-state tuition at state schools is more affordable than the tab at many private colleges. Ole Miss, for instance, charges residents $7,000 a year; out-of-state students pay $19,000. And honors colleges frequently sweeten the pot with merit-based scholarships on top of any need-based financial aid, as well as funding for studying abroad.

It didn't take Andrew Kovtun long to do the math. Intent on a career in international trade, the national merit finalist at suburban Cleveland's Solon High School had considered Georgetown University, among other top-tier schools. But a full-ride scholarship offer from South Carolina Honors College caught his eye. "I realized that in my field, a master's is becoming more and more necessary," he says. "So it wouldn't be very smart of me to get into $200,000 worth of debt for undergrad." Today, Kovtun is working toward his master's at the Johns Hopkins School of Advanced International Studies in Washington, having graduated in August with a B.S. in business administration and a B.A. in economics. "I emerged not having paid a dollar of my own," he says.

Money isn't the only factor driving interest.

Honors students typically benefit from the same sort of special attention and rigorous academics as their counterparts at elite schools, but with such large-university attractions at hand as competitive sports teams, hundreds of student organizations, and a greater range of course offerings and majors. That alone can be a game-changer for applicants who haven't decided what to major in.

Lower-division honors courses at Middle Tennessee State University, for example, are limited to 20 students, and upper-level classes max out at 15. Three advisers help the honors college's 750 students arrange internships. Honors students at the University of Pittsburgh read and discuss more material and do more writing than students in standard courses. Mississippi emphasizes discussion in small seminars taught by the most experienced professors. Sullivan-González teaches an honors course called Self and Society, for example, in which readings from Thucydides on the Peloponnesian Wars are intended to spark a debate on the question "Does might make right?" Juniors and seniors work on a thesis and are strongly encouraged to study abroad, for which grants are available.

The VIP treatment typically extends beyond academics. USC plans group outings to the opera, theater and zoo. Barrett, the honors college at Arizona State University, offers an exclusive dining program that features local organic and sustainable foods. Hutton organizes special meet-and-greets with speakers coming through campus. Brackemyre, who is majoring in political science, religious studies and journalism, was recently invited with her Hutton fellows to a breakfast with filmmaker Peter Weir. "There are so many things that you'd have no access to otherwise," she says.

Last year, during a campuswide centennial for World War I, the IU honors students sat in on a roundtable discussion about the legacy of the war by scholars and diplomats from the countries involved in it. Mississippi students have dined with Oliver Sacks, Salman Rushdie and Colin Powell.

"STUDENTS RECEIVE THE ELITE EDUCATION OF A SMALLER PRIVATE UNIVERSITY WITH MUCH BROADER CLASS OFFERINGS."

Some programs, including Mississippi's, require a separate application for admission. (Ole Miss students who maintain a 3.5 GPA for three semesters are also eligible to join the honors college.) Others, such as those at IU and the University of Maryland, automatically consider the eligibility of all applicants to the university. At Middle Tennessee State, any student who graduates from high school with a 3.5 GPA and ACT score of 25 or higher is welcome to take honors classes.

The extent to which students are required to participate in honors coursework and other activities, curricular and otherwise, ranges widely. At Hutton, students who wish to graduate with a general honors notation are required to take at least 21 credits of honors courses, in which they must maintain a 3.4 GPA, and they must have an overall 3.4 at graduation. South Carolina expects all freshmen to live in an honors residence hall. "Living together on campus is important, for one thing, because it helps to shrink the size of a large research university," says Dean Steven Lynn. "It encourages students to develop study groups, lasting friendships, and a richer college experience." Students earn at least 45 honors credits, complete two "beyond the classroom" requirements such as undergraduate research or study abroad, and wrap up with a senior thesis project. Many honors programs encourage community service, and some, including Florida International University, require it.

Some educators argue that the exclusivity of honors colleges is unfair. "The idea of giving special opportunities to some preselected group of students is not the way we do things," says Edward Stricker, dean of the University Honors College at the University of Pittsburgh. Pitt invites all undergraduate students to participate in honors classes, assuming they've taken any prerequisites and have a 3.25 GPA, as well as its intensive Brackenridge undergraduate research program, in which fellows conduct an independent research project under the guidance of a faculty mentor and present their findings at weekly seminars. "We want students to identify themselves as talented and motivated once they're in college, rather than selecting them on the basis of their high school credentials," Stricker says.

Other than students who wish to live in honors residence halls, who are asked to write two brief essays explaining why, students need not formally apply for admission, nor are they awarded special status when they take honors courses. The classes are noted on transcripts, says Stricker, "but there's no gold star or anything on their diplomas."

The honors experience isn't for everyone. While one of the best predictors of success is high school GPA, the kind of students who succeed in these programs are looking for an extra challenge and have a "fire-in-the-belly excitement" about knowledge, says Hallie Savage, executive director of the National Collegiate Honors Council, an association of honors programs and colleges. "These are people who think, 'What can I do to enrich not just my career, but learning?'" Brackemyre, who recently took a course called Where Have We Been? Where Are We? Where Are We Going?, says she found it "motivating" to be part of a community "of 15 people who wanted to hotly discuss the theories of who we are and what it means to exist."

That's the sort of enthusiasm Ole Miss looks for in the three essays applicants to the honors program are asked to complete. Admission is based on GPA and ACT scores as well, but kids with ACTs as low as 21 and as high as 36 have been admitted – "whoever's motivated to get the job done," says Sullivan-González. Retention rates are typically on par with the most elite private schools. At USC, for instance, the honors college freshman retention rate is 98 percent – Ivy League territory.

Brackemyre, for one, says she now feels she will graduate with opportunities every bit as impressive as students who graduate from elite schools. She has her sights set on getting into a top law school next year, following in the footsteps of her brother, a Hutton alumnus who is now at Harvard Law. "If you told me when I was 16 that I would end up at IU and wind up incredibly happy, I would have said 'You're crazy,'" she says. She now knows "that a state education is what you make of it, and if you put in the hard work here, it's going to get you just as far as an elite school." ●

THIS IS
A SMART
CHOICE.
THIS IS AUBURN.
Whether you've known about Auburn all your life or are just learning about this university, we invite you to discover the real Auburn.
This is a university whose alumni include the CEO of Apple, the founders of Habitat for Humanity and Wikipedia, an Oscar-winning actress, sports legends, and astronauts. Graduates are recruited by top companies around the globe.
This is a university where you will make friends for a lifetime with a 300,000-strong, worldwide network of alumni who will think of you as family.
This is a university that will surprise you, impress you, and propel you to success as it has for generations before you. auburn.edu
AUBURN
UNIVERSITY

IS GREEK LIFE FOR YOU?

BY MAURA HOHMAN

College-bound seniors might feel relieved after settling on where they'll be going come fall, but the big decisions are far from over. Is it better to pick a roommate or be randomly assigned one? What majors bear considering? Will joining a frat or sorority be the right move?

"Going Greek" entails more than an intense social life – including responsibilities to the chapter and often to the community, and money out of pocket. Yes, the occasional party is an integral part of the fraternal experience. But being active in the Greek system is supposed to be "about developing yourself as a total person," says Peter Smithhisler, president and CEO of the North-American Interfraternity Conference. The governing structure and activities are aimed at honing leadership skills, he says, and often involve managing people and a budget.

Meantime, the hard-partying lifestyle has been under attack for some time. "There have been systemic changes to the entire Greek system within the last 20 to 30 years," says Alan DeSantis, a professor of communication at University of Kentucky and author of "Inside Greek U.: Fraternities, Sororities, and the Pursuit of Pleasure, Power, and Prestige."

Especially at big state institutions, for example, "zero-tolerance policies on hazing have eliminated public humiliation in places like the quad and cafeteria," he says. And many colleges have implemented stricter alcohol policies. In January, Dartmouth College announced an aggressive plan aimed at all students, not just at the 51 percent affiliated with a Greek organization, that strengthens community life and emphasizes sexual violence prevention (story, Page 38). Here are some thoughts to contemplate as you make your own moves:

Why join?

Many students join a house to make a large community feel smaller, to establish a social safety net in one fell swoop. "Coming into your own is a hard process," says Aubrey Frazier, assistant director of fraternity and sorority life at Rollins College in Winter Park, Florida. "Connecting to a fraternity or sorority can help."

Others are attracted to the shot at leadership positions, philanthropic opportunities and strong alumni support. Students interested exclusively in parties might be surprised to find out that statistics show Greek students tend to graduate at a higher rate than average, and that the organizations pride themselves on instilling community values in members. "We enjoy our weekends, but the entire experience and process has provided me with the opportunity for self-development and self-reflection," says Frank Baptista, a 2015 grad of American University in Washington, D.C., whose experience in Sigma Chi was a lot more substantive than he expected. Baptista served as president of his fraternity and on AU's fraternity and sorority life programming board.

What % of students participate?

Smaller schools tend to have a higher percentage of Greek students, Frazier says. "On some campuses, there's the sense that you have to join fraternity and sorority life to be somebody." Similarly, on rural campuses without access to a vibrant off-campus community, notes Matthew Hughey, an associate professor of sociology at the University of Connecticut who's researched the Greek system, it's often the case that "fraternity and sorority houses are where people go." They are often social hubs on urban campuses, too, he adds, but a city setting affords non-Greeks more outlets.

A fulfilling experience without Greek life relies on finding other ways to meet like-minded people, and big schools typically have hundreds of options, as well as the chance to rally around athletics. At Washington and Lee University, a small Virginia school, 77 percent of students join, compared to about 10 percent at the University of Texas–Austin.

What's the time commitment?

As is true with most pursuits, faculty advisers say you get out what you put in. Becoming an officer or taking an active role in social and philanthropic events, for example, is apt to offer rewards in the form of experiences that just doing the bare minimum won't.

What is the bare minimum? Frazier says to expect a weekly chapter meeting at the very least; skipping often leads to fines. Most organizations also plan and host one or two social events a month, from cocktail parties to crawfish boils, and at least one community service event per semester. The size of the chapter can dictate how much time each member must commit. Baptista dedicated about 15 hours a week to Sigma Chi activities, which included chairing the chapter's Derby Days competition for cancer research. He estimates that members without leadership roles devote four to five hours a week to meetings and helping with chapter events.

What will the cost be?

Ask about the financial burden. Dues can range from $20 to $200 or more a month. (Members living in chapter housing will also pay for room and board, which may or may not compare favorably with dorm rates.)

Generally, dues follow a monthly schedule and cover social events, insurance, dues to the national (or international) chapter and operational costs, such as recruitment and upkeep of community spaces. Frazier says Greek students at Rollins pay between $300 and $900 a semester. Scholarships are often available through schools and the Greek national organizations, and some chapters have payment plans that allow members to spread the cost over an entire semester or year.

Once you decide to go through recruitment, do some research to find the place that best aligns with your interests. **"Look into each organization's events and how they convey themselves,"** advises Frazier. Other factors to think about: chapter size and housing.

How many members are in the chapter?

Big chapters tend to have money and can easily support campuswide events, and they boast big alumni networks. But the sense of brotherhood or sisterhood can suffer when members can't know everyone, and it can be tough to gain a leadership role. On the other hand, a tiny chapter is apt to lack resources and programming. DeSantis believes chapters should max out at 70 people. In addition to considering the personality of a chapter, Myrna Hernandez, assistant dean of students for campus living and community development at DePauw University in Indiana, suggests that students think about whether they're looking for the greatest number of connections or the deepest connections.

What's chapter policy on other activities?

Greek students tend to be hyperinvolved in campus life, since a big part of the system's focus is on giving back to the community. Greek-affiliated students occupy most student leadership positions at Rollins, for example, Frazier says.

Often, in fact, joining other groups is not only recommended but required by the national organization. Some frats and sororities expect to see their members prominently active in campus organizations such as student government or new student orientation; others are OK with simply attending a weekly club meeting. "It's important for students not to be one-dimensional," Smithhisler says. "The balancing act is part of the collegiate experience." The result may be a crammed schedule.

Does the chapter have a house? Will you be expected to live there?

Students at some universities hold chapter meetings in classrooms, whereas members at other schools eat, sleep, study and socialize in their fraternity or sorority house. Whenever she wanted "to crash there between classes or hang out or eat lunch," the Alpha Xi Delta house was accessible and welcoming even though she wasn't one of the 10 sisters who chose to live there, says Stephanie Riley, a 2015 grad of California State University–Northridge. Some Greek organizations do require students to live in the house for a time, regardless of whether it's more economical than dorms or off-campus apartments.

Sorority houses typically don't host parties with alcohol, so living there isn't unlike the dorm experience, says Julie Johnson, Panhellenics Committee chair of the National Panhellenic Conference of sororities. Anyone choosing a frat will want to know both whether he'll have to live in the house and what the lifestyle would entail.

Is hazing an issue?

Most campuses now ban the hazing of new pledges, as do all members of the North-American Interfraternity Conference and the National Panhellenic Conference. Forty-four states even have anti-hazing laws. "There's definitely been a concerted effort on behalf of fraternities to root out hazing," says Moe Stephens, director of Greek life and leadership at the University of Puget Sound in Washington. But it's still "a touchy subject that everyone needs to keep talking about."

For many students these days, the rituals that go along with becoming a member offer a positive and risk-free experience – "overwhelming in a good way," recalls Riley. A favorite memory: finally meeting the "big sister" assigned to mentor her, who had anonymously pampered her for a week with such treats as iced coffee delivered to class and a decorated car.

Like college campuses and the students who populate them, Greek organizations have distinct personalities. The goal is to find a great match. ●

Do You Plan to Major in BUSINESS?

If so, you might want to shop around extra carefully for a college

BY CATHIE GANDEL

It used to be that the typical undergraduate B-school program stuck pretty closely to a narrow curriculum heavily weighted in management, sales and finance, or "learning how to do business," says Jim Otteson, executive director of the BB&T Center for the Study of Capitalism at Wake Forest University in North Carolina. Many schools still do stick to that script. But beyond making sure future moguls leave with all the necessary nuts and bolts, there's a movement gaining ground to equip them with a much broader skill set and the bigger picture. These days, along with accounting and operations, business students may well find themselves analyzing Victorian literature, discussing Cicero, and debating the role of business in the world.

The goal? To turn out grads who are well-rounded, can explain complex concepts as handily as statistics, and who are good at connecting dots (beyond those on a graph) to solve problems. In ways long ingrained in the study of liberal arts, business students need to consider "who they are, what they want and where they fit" in the wider world, argues William Sullivan, a senior scholar at New American Colleges and Universities, a consortium dedicated to integrating liberal and professional education.

"You can't solve all difficult decisions by making a great Excel sheet," says Claire Preisser, associate director of the Aspen Institute Business and Society Program, an organization now working with nearly 70 colleges and universities to rethink undergraduate business education. "It's not always about plugging in the right numbers to get the right answer."

Employers seem to agree. Students who have been exposed to liberal arts and other nonbusiness courses come in "with better focus, commitment

WESTERN NEW ENGLAND STUDENTS SERVING ON THE CHILDREN'S STUDY HOME BOARD CONSULT WITH EXECUTIVE DIRECTOR ELIZA CRESCENTINI (LEFT).

ELLEN WEBBER FOR USN&WR

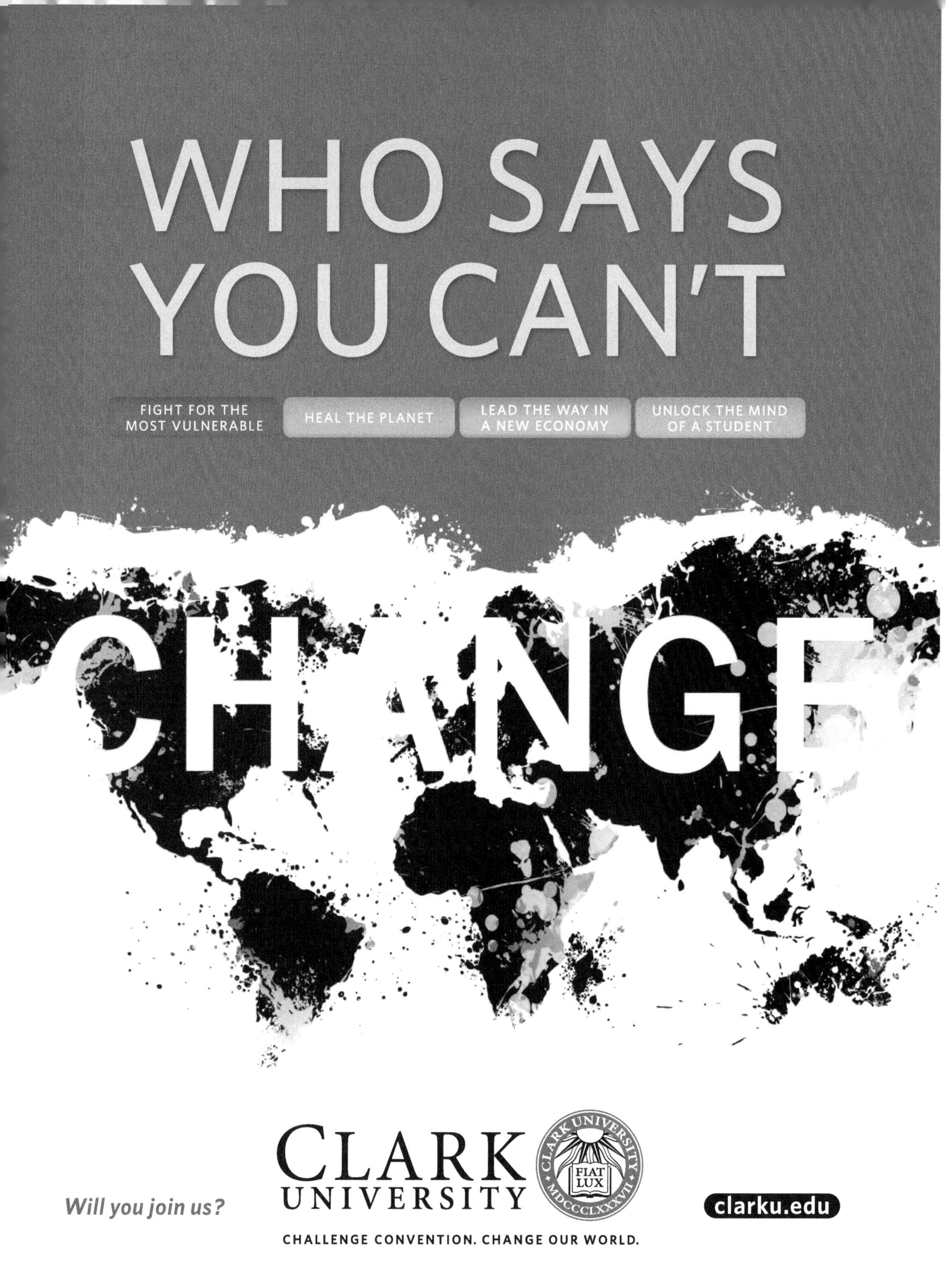
WHO SAYS
YOU CAN'T
FIGHT FOR THE MOST VULNERABLE
HEAL THE PLANET
LEAD THE WAY IN A NEW ECONOMY
UNLOCK THE MIND OF A STUDENT
CHANGE
Will you join us?
CLARK UNIVERSITY
CLARK UNIVERSITY FIAT LUX MDCCCLXXXVII
clarku.edu
CHALLENGE CONVENTION. CHANGE OUR WORLD.

and an understanding that extends beyond the individual or company," says David Mounts, chairman and CEO of Inmar, a technology and data analytics firm in Winston-Salem, North Carolina. "They are problem solvers, and their perspectives are broader and more based in reality."

The approaches colleges and universities are taking range from redesigning the curriculum or adding a brand new major to reimagining individual courses. In 2014, for instance, the University of Michigan's Stephen M. Ross School of Business unveiled its new MERGE program (for Multidisciplinary Exploration and Rigorous Guided Education). Rather than begin with the typical survey course covering the basics of economics, finance, operations and marketing, business majors now take a new introductory course called Business and Leaders: The Positive Differences. The point, through discussion, research projects and the insights of guest speakers, is for students to explore business's proper place in society as well as what role they might want to play, says Alison Davis-Blake, Ross' dean.

One issue considered by his class, recalls Joe Kuderer, a junior from Eden Prairie, Minnesota, who hopes to go into corporate finance or wealth management, was whether business should "just be focused on profits" or also on giving back to the community. The perspective he gained from the discussions "put me in the right frame of mind for the rest of my classes," he says.

THE GOAL? GRADS WHO ARE WELL-ROUNDED, CAN EXPLAIN COMPLEX CONCEPTS AS WELL AS STATISTICS AND CAN CONNECT DOTS (BEYOND THOSE ON A GRAPH) TO SOLVE PROBLEMS.

Juniors spend "an integrative learning semester" exploring business cases from different points of view, including those of operations and organizational management, business law and ethics and business communication. They also have a study-abroad experience. Senior year culminates in a capstone project that pulls all the wisdom gained over the years together.

At the Stern School of Business at New York University, students can take up to half of their courses in the College of Arts & Sciences. This builds on a set of required bigger-picture courses called the Social Impact Core. Freshmen, for example, take Business and Its Publics, which looks at the interconnections between business, government and society. As seniors, students take a capstone seminar in which they read classical texts such as Cicero's "On Duties" and reflect "on the alignment of their personal values with their professional trajectories," says Matt Statler, director of Business Ethics and Social Impact Programming.

A more values-oriented exploration is also underway at Western New England University in Massachusetts, where the aim is to send graduates into the world "with a much broader understanding of their role as business leaders," says Jeanie Forray, chair of the management department in the College of Business. Students take approximately half of their courses from outside the business program and get a big dose of "the issues of ethics, social responsibility and environmental concerns," she says.

One feature of the program: internships with local nonprofits. "Traditionally, business schools focus on for-profits," says Forray. "We wanted students to understand how nonprofits are run, but also to be better prepared to be socially responsible citizens." Some students might help a company research and analyze the distribution of services in an underserved community. Others may spend a year on the board of directors of Habitat for Humanity, say, or Children's Study Home, which provides educational and other services to families and kids with special needs. They do more than sit quietly by; they are engaged in issues that range from planning a social media campaign to creating a market analysis for a new initiative.

The approach taken by St. Lawrence University in New York, which introduced a Business in the Liberal Arts major in 2014, is to require all participants to complete a second major. They take a set of seven core courses – including economics, accounting, statistics and a philosophy course called Reasoning – designed to ground them in how markets and corporations work and to foster "the ability to make decisions under uncertainty," and to evaluate "the quality and relevance of evidence." As they work on the requirements for their biology or history or English major, they must also complete at least one internship or other off-campus experience plus electives aimed at exploring social responsibility and global citizenship, for example.

Sarah Pyc, one of the first students to sign up for the new major and now a senior, expects competition for jobs to be fierce when she graduates, especially for high-paying positions. But she's convinced that "social skills, analytical thinking and the ability to present yourself in a positive light" will be important factors setting the winners apart. "I think students with a liberal arts background are going to be a little bit better at that compared to someone who has been singularly focused on just business," says Pyc, whose second major was economics. She recalls that a class on public speaking was particularly valuable during a summer internship with GE Capital Bank in Stamford, Connecticut. "It's important in the business world to be able to communicate," Pyc says. "I gave three presenta-

tions to the president of GE Capital Bank."

Students at business-focused Bentley University in Waltham, Massachusetts, have a couple of ways to broaden their horizons. Business majors can double up, as St. Lawrence students do, by pursuing a second major in liberal studies. It's possible as well to choose a bachelor of arts degree and add a major or minor in business studies. Also, in 2014 the school introduced several six-credit "fusion" courses that combine a business course with an arts and science course to shift perspectives. A film studies professor teaches about women in film alongside a management prof focused on women in business, say. Both are "in attendance all six hours per week, discussing, debating," says Dorothy Feldmann, associate dean of the business programs.

Such innovative single courses may be a school's preferred way to give business majors that broader context. Wake Forest's Otteson teaches a course called Why Business? in which students consider the moral implications of business activities. Robins School of Business at the University of Richmond in Virginia is now experimenting with adding paired classes, one in the humanities and one on a business topic, based on a successful linkage a couple years ago of Victorian literature with government accounting.

"When you talk with a recruiter and ask them what they need, they rarely say 'someone with more accounting skills,'" says Joe Hoyle, the professor who taught the government accounting class. "Instead they say two things: employees who can write and who can think outside of the box." The goal of requiring the accounting students to also take the lit class as a group was to get them reading and enjoying such books as "Great Expectations" and "The Mill on the Floss" and discussing their ideas without being intimidated by English majors.

"Professionally you have to adapt to all kinds of situations," says Alexandria Barth, a 2013 grad now working at an accounting firm in Arlington, Virginia. "Taking that class made me step out of my comfort zone and helped me gain confidence in adapting to new situations, like talking to clients and giving presentations."

The trend toward offering a more liberal studies-oriented business degree is turning out to be quite attractive to parents, says Michigan's Davis-Blake. "Parents are often caught between wanting their children to have a broad-based education that will expand their minds and vision, and having a narrow technical education that will help them get a job," she says. The goal, she says, is to do a much better job of providing both. ●

EARN A BACHELOR'S & MBA IN ONLY FOUR YEARS!

Emily Bean always knew she wanted to work in business. So when she was offered a chance to earn both her bachelor's and MBA in just four years, she jumped. "There's some serious cost savings to earning an MBA in four years," says Bean, who will graduate from the program at Quinnipiac University in Connecticut in the spring of 2016. As part of the program, she got a spot in a dorm living alongside other B.S./MBA students and spent a semester in Rome learning about international business trends.

Quinnipiac is one of a growing group of universities offering promising business students access to rigorous accelerated programs that result in an MBA. Some consolidate traditional two-year graduate programs into a single year, then cherry-pick top juniors or seniors and persuade them to stay on past graduation. But a number, including the University of Alabama and the University of Nevada at Reno as well as Quinnipiac, are now recruiting dual-degree candidates straight out of high school.

For Bean, the benefits far outweigh the stress of the extra course load required. "I enjoy being surrounded by people who are just as motivated as I am," she says. For students arriving this fall, Quinnipiac will charge tuition, fixed for four years, of $42,270. That's 20 to 30 percent less than what it would cost to take the traditional route to its MBA, the school estimates.

While Quinnipiac, whose program launched in 2012, takes undergrads with a range of majors, many accelerated MBA programs are focused on science, technology, engineering and math; Alabama's five-year "STEM Path to the MBA," for instance, cross-trains students in engineering and business. Iowa State's five-year B.S./MBA program for STEM majors includes internships at companies like farm equipment maker John Deere and biofuels producer Renewable Energy Group. The MBA adds about 15 percent to starting salaries offered to those with an engineering degree alone, estimates Ronald Ackerman, director of MBA admissions and student services.

Most programs require students to take 16 to 20 credits per semester, forcing many to take courses over their breaks. Despite the intensity, Quinnipiac saw a 50 percent jump in applications in 2014.

By Arlene Weintraub

DEGREES *for*
DREAMERS
DOERS *and*
LEADERS

Raising the SAFETY Bar

How colleges are battling sexual violence. BY BETH HOWARD

The young man watched his fraternity brother at a large university lead a woman up the stairs at a house party. Something didn't feel right. The woman was clearly intoxicated and needed help climbing. "Hey, dude, your car is getting towed!" he yelled – with the predictable result. His quick thinking, which created an opportunity for the woman's friends to whisk her away, was inspired by training he had received a few weeks earlier.

Encouraging students to act when they see a risky situation unfolding is one of a number of ways that colleges are grappling with the sudden imperative to improve campus safety. A string of highly publicized reports of sexual violence on campus, many involving intoxication to the point of blackout, has alarmed the White House and prompted a Department of Education investigation of more than 100 colleges and universities for possible violations of Title IX, the civil rights law that prohibits discrimination based on gender. Earlier this year, a bipartisan group of senators introduced the Campus Accountability and Safety Act, which would require better coordination with local police departments when accusations are made. Says Scott Berkowitz, president of the Rape, Abuse, and Incest National Network, a nonprofit dedicated to fighting sexual violence: "There's been more movement on this front in the last year than in the entire last decade."

In January, Dartmouth College announced one of the boldest blueprints for culture change, mandating education on preventing sexual violence all four years of college and placing everybody, including fraternity members, in one of six new residential communities beginning in 2016. A community will have its own cluster of dorms and will put on social and academic programs; students living in Greek or off-campus housing will be included in community events. The school has also banned hard alcohol and will require outside security guards and bartenders at parties. "You can't address just one aspect of the problem," says Heather Lindkvist, Dartmouth's Title IX coordinator. "You need a comprehensive, integrated approach."

What kinds of initiatives can families look for when checking out schools? The most responsive institutions are now teaching classes on everything from what a healthy relationship looks like to ways both women and men can steer clear of harm, changing the way they investigate reports of sexual misconduct, and cracking down on all of the excesses associated with fraternity life. Getting a read on the scope of the problem can be tricky: Although the Department of Education compiles statistics on campus crime (ope.ed.gov/security), sexual violence is notoriously underreported. Your best bet is to ask the school and find out what is being done to improve prevention. Here's how colleges are trying to turn the tide:

Tackling the new sex education

Traditional programs aimed at prevention "are brief – one hour or less – and focused on improving knowledge about the problem," says Sarah DeGue, a behavioral scientist for the Centers for Disease Control and Prevention who has studied prevention efforts and whose findings informed a recent White House report. "Knowledge is important, but it's clear these programs don't prevent people from perpetuating sexual violence."

So a growing number of schools are mandating a deeper dive into the topic. Incoming students at Elon University in North Carolina, for example, must take a course online before they even reach campus that marches them through the ethics of relationships and alcohol's effect on behavior. Orientation at Indiana University includes a musical that covers everything from negative gender stereotypes to what constitutes sexual assault. At the University of California–Berkeley, incoming students have to participate in an educational program by Oct. 1 or have their registration for spring semester blocked until they do. The UC system has been rolling out a comprehensive new prevention and intervention plan across its 10 campuses over the past year.

But "you can't do a one-time program and expect it to make a difference," says Ruth Anne Koenick, director of the Office for Violence Prevention and Victim Assistance at Rutgers, the State University of New Jersey–New Brunswick. UC–Santa Cruz dedicated one week in April – Consent Week – to discussions on topics from violence

DARTMOUTH HAS UNVEILED A BOLD BLUEPRINT FOR CULTURE CHANGE.

in the gay community to cultural attitudes about sex and rape that need to be changed. Dartmouth students will get a refresher course every year about healthy relationships and how to prevent and respond to misconduct. Many schools are beefing up their online resources – explaining stalking, the dangers of date rape drugs, how to support a friend who's been victimized, for instance – and hosting programs for both women and men "focused on knowing what your sexual comfort zone is and feeling empowered to say that out loud," says Laurel Kennedy, vice president for student development at Denison University in Granville, Ohio. Student groups, including fraternities, are helping get the word out. When the Women's Resource Center at the University of Wisconsin–Stevens Point approached the school's frats last fall, members collected and then donned high heels for a "Walk a Mile in Her Shoes" event. Says Justin Wieseler, 20, a junior there and member of the Phi Sigma Phi fraternity: "We pride ourselves on educating ourselves about sexual assault and how to prevent it."

Because so often the unwanted advances come from "your friend or someone who you had a crush on," when both parties are drunk, the new campaigns are focused on illuminating what it means to consent, says Sara Colombo, 20, a junior and a member of the Student Organization for Sexual Safety at Colorado College. That definition is changing to make the concept of consensual sex less ambiguous – which puts a new level of responsibility on the person making advances. In California, for example, consenting no longer means simply not saying no. A student who is initiating sex must re-

ELLEN WEBBER FOR USN&WR

ceive an unambiguous yes, and that's not possible if the student being approached is incapacitated. New York enacted its own affirmative consent, or "yes means yes," law this summer, and New Jersey and Connecticut are considering similar bills. Some worry that this trend could spell trouble for students who mean no harm but mistake alcohol-facilitated flirtation as consent. There's certainly room for misunderstanding: A Washington Post-Kaiser Family Foundation survey conducted earlier this year found that 54 percent of those asked think nodding in agreement counts; 47 percent say consent is gained if the person takes off his or her clothes, and 40 percent say getting a condom means "yes."

Many campuses are pinning their hopes for prevention on educating bystanders. Traditionally, "we told men 'don't be rapists' and women 'don't get raped.' But the vast majority of men aren't rapists. The breakthrough was identifying them as allies," says Dorothy Edwards, head of the nonprofit Green Dot Violence Prevention Strategy, which teaches students to set norms that don't tolerate violence and how to intervene when they see a risk looming. "Everyone has that sixth sense of behavior they feel is over the line," says Berkowitz.

Bystander education programs like Green Dot help people pay attention to that sixth sense. Green Dot has been implemented by a slew of schools, among them the University of Virginia and the University of Dayton in Ohio. Participants brainstorm and role-play strategies, such as the use of distraction for defusing risky situations.

One bystander can "accidentally" spill a drink on a potential perpetrator or enlist him to go on a pizza run, for example, while another alerts the friends of a possible victim to what's happening. "Our goal is to make intervening the norm," says Nicole Eramo, an associate dean of students at UVA, which rolled out the program last year, before the school came under fire in a quickly discredited Rolling Stone article alleging it had mishandled assault complaints. (Eramo has sued Rolling Stone for its portrayal of her.) A 2014 study by University of Kentucky researchers showed that the Green Dot program resulted in a 50 percent drop in sexual violence over five years in the Kentucky high schools where it was implemented. At Rutgers, similar lessons are conveyed through theater productions in which students act out common scenarios that can lead to trouble, followed by discussions and training about bystander responsibilities.

Talking Points

Here are several issues families might want to discuss well before they say goodbye at the dorm:

The dangers of intoxication

A large proportion of sexual assaults involve alcohol, which, even after a few drinks, impairs judgment and memory and the ability to perceive risk, cautions George Koob, director of the National Institute on Alcohol Abuse and Alcoholism. Even when there's no ill intent, fuzzy judgment raises the risk of misreading a partner's level of impairment – and willingness.

What consent means

An enthusiastic "yes" is what you want. Short of that, it's vital to be very cautious about interpreting cues. Kissing – even disrobing – might not hold up as consent when someone has been drinking. Bottom line: If there's any doubt that your date knows what he or she is doing, you may be committing sexual assault. When there is ambiguity, that's your signal to call a halt.

The wisdom of buddying up

When drinking, women and men both benefit from being with people who will look out for each other. As a further precaution, smartphone apps such as Circle of 6 and Kitestring send prewritten texts to specified contacts letting them know where you are and that you might be in trouble.

–Maura Hohman

Putting frats on notice

Fraternities have long been hotbeds of extreme behavior, but there's a rapidly growing consensus that serious transgressions can no longer be dismissed as collegiate antics. "We're approaching zero tolerance," says Kevin Kruger, president of NASPA–Student Affairs Administrators in Higher Education. Within the past year, fraternity chapters have been suspended or put on probation for various reasons at Yale, North Carolina State University, Penn State, the University of Houston in Texas, Washington and Lee in Virginia, Furman University in South Carolina, and the University of Arizona, among others. Several colleges, including Williams and Amherst in Massachusetts and Colby and Bowdoin in Maine, have done away with fraternities altogether in recent years. Wesleyan University's tack: requiring frats to go co-ed by 2017.

Many new restrictions center around alcohol. Dartmouth's ban on hard alcohol at fraternity parties follows that of other elite schools, including Swarthmore and Brown. At Denison, parties with more than 15 students where alcohol will be served must be registered with the university. "Campus security personnel stop by the party to look at what's being served," says Kennedy.

New rules at the University of Virginia require at least three fraternity brothers to stay sober to monitor behavior at parties with wine or beer. Hard alcohol must be served from a central location by a sober brother; at larger parties it can only be served by a bartender licensed by the state. A security guard must be present at the larger parties.

Changing the college's response to accusations

Women often assume they will get more careful and sympathetic treatment if they take their case to the administration than to the police, but, in the absence of clear policies, they frequently don't get satisfaction. Complaints range from being blamed themselves

RUTGERS STUDENTS REHEARSE A SKIT DEMONSTRATING THE CONCEPT OF CONSENT, TO BE PRESENTED AT ORIENTATION.

for the behavior to allowing students found responsible to remain on campus and continue to play on teams.

When Annie E. Clark, 26, a graduate of the University of North Carolina-Chapel Hill, sought help from the school after a 2007 assault, she says she was asked, "What could you have done differently in that situation?" Clark, who didn't know who her assailant was and didn't pursue adjudication, doesn't think the comment was ill-intentioned. "It goes to a lack of training," she says. Clark has garnered national attention by filing a Title IX complaint against the university with several other women in 2013 and by assisting students on other campuses through the organization she co-founded, End Rape on Campus.

UNC has since overhauled its practices on prevention of and response to assault, says Hilary Delbridge, a spokesperson for the university's Equal Opportunity and Compliance Office. That has meant improving resources for victims and requiring students to receive online training in what behaviors are unacceptable and what support and reporting options are available.

Many colleges are revisiting the traditional disciplinary process, too, which often involves investigations and hearings by inexperienced panels of faculty and students. There's a move to outsource sexual assault cases or hire experienced investigators.

The University of Michigan and Michigan State have created a Special Victims Unit within the campus police department. This should result in better evidence gathering and more sensitive treatment of victims of sexual assault and other violent acts, predicts Holly Rider-Milkovich, director of the Sexual Assault Prevention and Awareness Center at the University of Michigan. A former sex-crimes investigator from the Philadelphia district attorney's office was recruited to preside over cases at the University of Pennsylvania. Harvard has created a central office to investigate and prosecute allegations and has hired professional investigators. Stanford relies on student and faculty reviewers but has implemented a process built on separate interviews of accuser and accused.

Last year, Princeton and Harvard lowered the required standard of proof in these cases to the widely used "preponderance of the evidence" standard that is recommended by the Department of Education. A growing number of schools are also stiffening penalties for offenders. At Duke, for example, expulsion is now the favored sanction.

Even as schools do a better job of preventing and dealing with the real problem, some experts fear that certain changes make students more vulnerable to problematic accusations. In fact, lawsuits by male students who feel they were unfairly treated are on the rise. Last fall, a large group of current and former members of Harvard's law faculty published a statement in The Boston Globe expressing concern that the university's new procedures make it difficult for a student to mount a defense – that they are "overwhelmingly stacked against the accused."

To make colleges accountable for finding solutions, the White House has called on them to conduct anonymous "climate surveys" to determine how many students have been victimized; Congress is considering making the surveys mandatory and the results public. Rutgers is working with the administration to pilot such a survey. And Koenick is guardedly optimistic that all the new efforts will pay off. "For the first time in 45 years" of doing this work, she says, it seems that real change is possible. ●

KRISANNE JOHNSON FOR USN&WR

Massachusetts Institute of Technology

Yiping Xing, CLASS OF 2015

When I first visited MIT, I fell in love with the innovative spirit that permeates the campus, which is beautifully situated along the Charles River across from downtown Boston. I saw people working to develop new treatments for diseases, computer science students coding the next great smartphone app, and engineering students building prototypes for consumer products. MIT doesn't simply teach you science or knowledge; it trains you to be a scientist and problem-solver, giving you many opportunities to apply what you learn. As a biology student interested in health care, I was able to work in a drug delivery lab tasked with developing more effective cancer therapies. I interned in the Office of the Surgeon General and traveled to Ghana to help devise natural systems to convert organic waste into animal feed for developing communities. At every step of this journey, I have enjoyed overwhelming support from my professors and my peers, who are some of the most incredible people I have ever met. As I head to medical school, I am confident that MIT has equipped me with the skills I need to thrive. ●

I FELL IN LOVE WITH THE INNOVATIVE SPIRIT THAT PERMEATES THE CAMPUS.

WHY I P

The Cooper Union

Nick Pacula, CLASS OF 2015

I chose to attend The Cooper Union because of its reputation for having one of the most innovative architecture programs in the country, its ability to take advantage of New York City's world-class cultural and professional offerings, and its strong support of student-led research projects.

The school's location in lower Manhattan allows for classes to meet at places like the Metropolitan Museum of Art and the Guggenheim. Through a school fellowship, I was able to fund a trip to Beirut, where

The Cooper Union

MARIO MORGADO – THE COOPER UNION

HEADSHOTS CLOCKWISE FROM TOP LEFT: ALLEGRA BOVERMAN – MIT NEWS OFFICE; JOYCE SEAY-KNOBLAUCH – UNIVERSITY OF ILLINOIS NEWS BUREAU; JOÃO ENXUTO – THE COOPER UNION

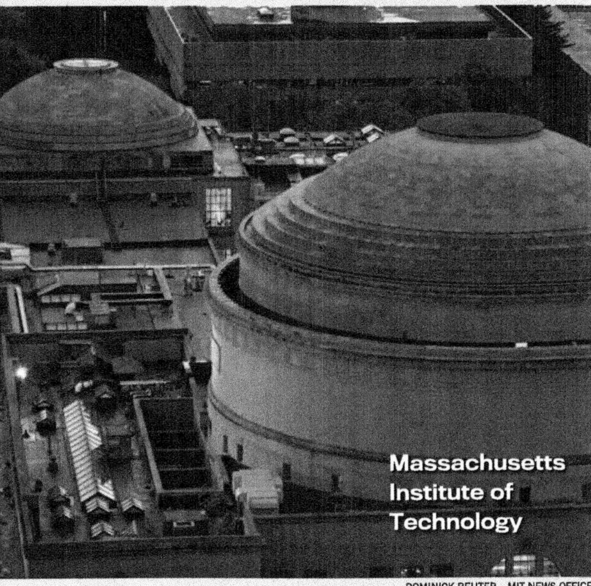
Massachusetts Institute of Technology

DOMINICK REUTER – MIT NEWS OFFICE

University of Illinois-Urbana-Champaign

Matthew Hill, CLASS OF 2015

My high school prided itself on enrolling the highest number of students at the University of Illinois, and I didn't want to get lost in that number. However, during my campus visit, I was impressed by how engaged everyone was. All the people I talked to not only had a story about where they came from, but also about where they wanted to go and how they wanted to impact the world. I was a political science major and was interested in student government. Initially I thought the school was too big for me to become a leader, but I embraced the challenge and became student body vice president. My role let me cultivate my own passion: using communication strategies to catalyze change. I helped bring the "It's On Us" campaign to campus, the national effort to stop college sexual assaults.

The best part was how administrators, faculty and other students joined us to create public service announcements and a Twitter town hall praised by Vice President Joe Biden. To me, this is what Illinois excels at: inspiring thousands of Illini to work to transform their lives and communities. ●

DURING MY CAMPUS VISIT, I WAS IMPRESSED BY HOW ENGAGED EVERYONE WAS.

ICKED...

I spent two weeks living and working in a Palestinian refugee camp. My colleagues and I imagined new infrastructures that could be developed to more easily circulate clean drinking water throughout the camp. This project was just one of the ways the school helped me better understand the critical role architects can play in improving the lives of others.

The range of opportunities available at The Cooper Union, from travel fellowships to collaborative projects with fellow students, has allowed me to find my own architectural vision that I can take forward into my career. ●

THROUGH A SCHOOL FELLOWSHIP, I WAS ABLE TO FUND A TRIP TO BEIRUT.

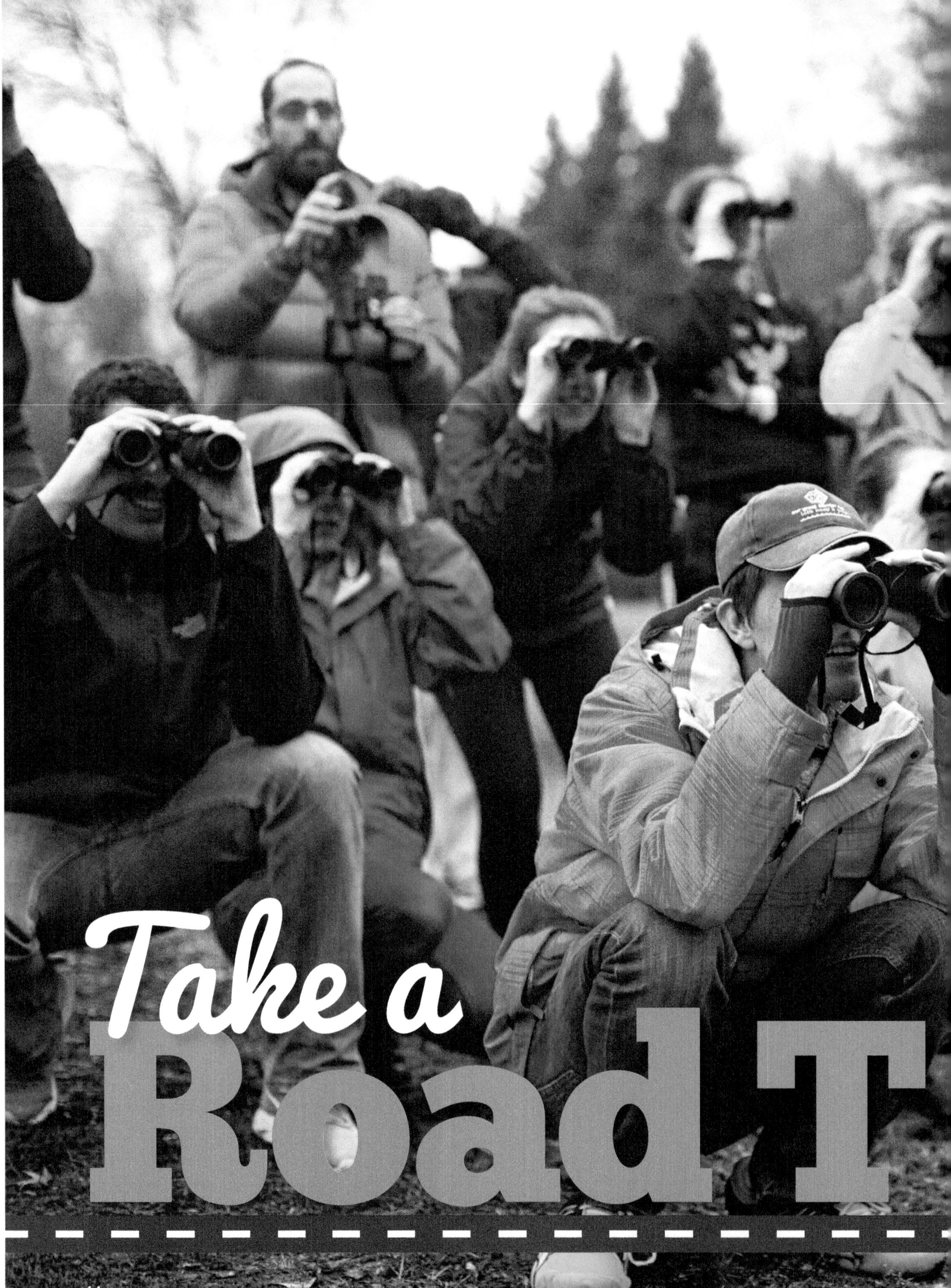

Take a Road T

A BIRD-WATCHING CLASS AT ST. OLAF COLLEGE

BRETT ZIEGLER FOR USN&WR

2

TAKE A ROAD TRIP

Massachusetts

Sit back and enjoy the ride as U.S. News hits the road for you to several college campuses in central Massachusetts. The trip begins in Amherst, at the state's flagship university. Next stop: Worcester, home to Clark University, Worcester Polytechnic Institute and College of the Holy Cross. BY CHRISTOPHER J. GEARON

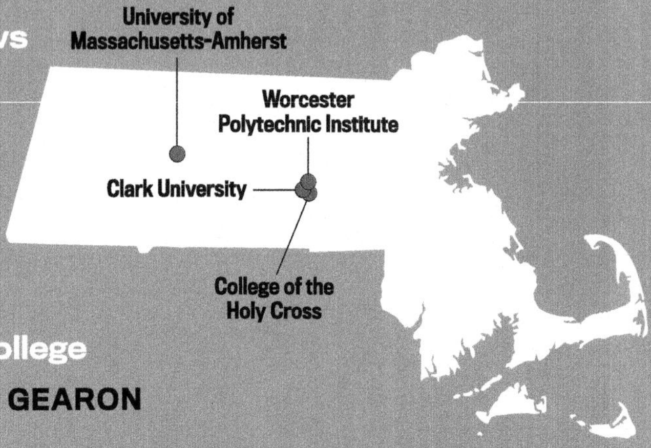

University of Massachusetts-Amherst
Worcester Polytechnic Institute
Clark University
College of the Holy Cross

University of Massachusetts

The largest public university in New England gets overshadowed in this college-rich commonwealth. But UMass-Amherst has been coming on strong. In the last decade, the university's six-year graduation rate has jumped from 68 percent to a historic high of 75 percent along with the caliber of the student body, while first-year retention rates have jumped from 83 percent to 89 percent in the last eight years. And the biggest building boom in four decades is now slotting modern sleek new entrants into the mix of unremarkable concrete and early Colonial-style architecture that dates back to the land-grant university's founding in 1863.

"I thought my dream school was Boston College," says Joanna Imbert, a 2015 grad from Everett, Massachusetts, who visited UMass after a high school teacher talked it up. The visit "clinched it for me," she says.

A psychology major, Imbert participated in undergraduate research exploring how people interpret events in conflict situations and served as a resident adviser. She really liked the fact that "UMass students are very independent, busy and focused," she says. Undergraduates have 111 majors to choose from; noted programs include linguistics, resource economics, food science, geosciences and, in the well-regarded Stockbridge School of Agriculture, such new majors as sustainable food and farming, sustainable horticulture, and turfgrass science and management.

UNDERGRADUATES
Full-time: 20,684

TOTAL COST*
In-State: $24,715
Out-of-State: $40,270

U.S. NEWS RANKING
National Universities: #75

*Tuition, fees and room & board for 2014-15

The school's improving retention record can be traced in part to a strengthened focus on academic support and advising and on faculty-student and peer interaction in first-year seminars and living-learning programs. The 51-year-old Residential Academic Programs plan, or RAP, offers a package deal: an opportunity to live on a floor or in a wing with a group of students sharing an interest plus classes with the group, often taught in the dorm.

"Our intro to psychology class was just 30 students in the RAP rather

THE OLD CHAPEL AT UMASS-AMHERST

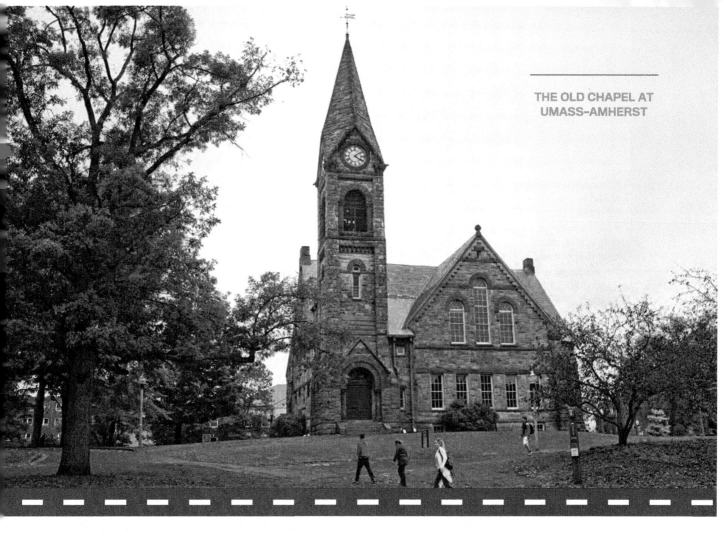

than 300," recalls Imbert. "I'm best friends with my first-year roommates." Forty percent of freshmen choose to join one of the 50 RAPs offered, which range in theme from social justice and activism to politics today to options focused around majors.

The sprawling 1,400-acre campus is located in picturesque Amherst, a town of 38,000 that also is home to Amherst and Hampshire colleges. All three schools belong to the Five College Consortium, along with Mount Holyoke and Smith, and UMass students can take classes at no extra charge at the other schools. Adam Whitcomb, a recent grad from Lunenburg, Massachusetts, double-majoring in psychology and Middle Eastern Studies, says the three Islam and Arabic classes he took at Smith and Amherst offered "an awesome opportunity to get a different perspective." Whitcomb, who plays trumpet, applied early decision to UMass, attracted by the nationally recognized Minuteman Marching Band, one of the more than 200 organizations students can join. Undergrads also can pick from 36 intramural and a dozen club sports.

Students rave about the dining halls. "Let me tell you about the breakfast burrito I had this morning," volunteers Whitcomb. Frequent surveys have found that students want "healthy, sustainable and local foods," notes Garett DiStefano, director of residential dining. The goal is that eventually half of all dining-hall food will come from New England. DiStefano even pulls from the university's five gardens, part of a student-led permaculture initiative. It won first place in 2012 among 1,500 colleges in the White House Campus Champions of Change competition recognizing student innovators. "It's a wonderful place," says Sammi Gay, a senior from the Bronx who is studying environmental design and has helped lead campus efforts in sustainability. ●

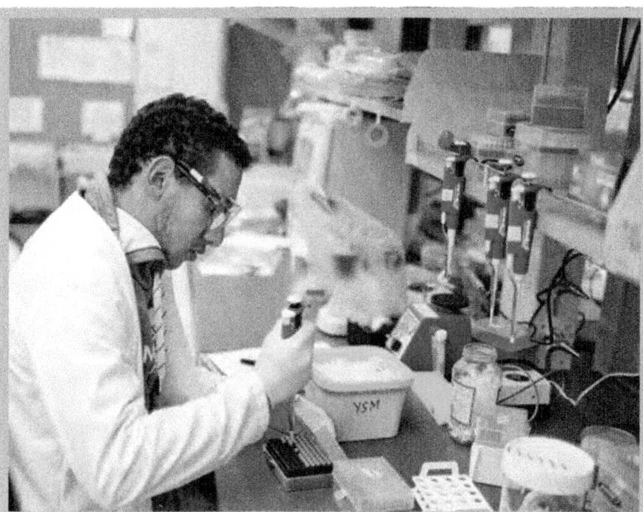

A MICROBIOLOGY STUDENT AT WORK IN THE LAB

PHOTOGRAPHY BY **MATT SLABY** – LUCEO FOR USN&WR

Worcester Polytechnic Institute

The nation's third-oldest technological school sits on a 95-acre campus atop one of seven hills that comprise Worcester, a rugged industrial city about 40 miles west of Boston. In a state known for its higher education, the school (which competes with the likes of Rochester Institute of Technology in New York, Carnegie Mellon in Pittsburgh, and Massachusetts Institute of Technology) stands out for its "WPI Plan." The plan is a project-based curriculum that is infused with the humanities and takes a collaborative, hands-on approach to learning. Some 90 percent of students major in engineering, computer science or the sciences.

UNDERGRADUATES
Full-time: 4,096

TOTAL COST*
$59,000

U.S. NEWS RANKING
National Universities: #57

*Tuition, fees and room & board for 2015-16

The school is a pioneer in problem-based learning, having dropped its conventional engineering curriculum more than 40 years ago. Today, most freshmen select a two-course "Great Problems Seminar," or GPS, which introduces them to college-level research focusing on 21st century issues such as energy and water and culminates in a project. "GPS prepared me for what was to come," says Andrew Santos, a junior from the Philippines studying electrical and computer engineering, who took a seminar in food sustainability. "Time management skills were really instilled," says Anna Civitarese, a 2015 grad in biology and biotechnology from Foxborough, Massachusetts, of her Heal the World course. The seminars and a robust system of advising by faculty and RAs result in a 97 percent first-year retention rate.

Students are required to take eight courses outside the science and technology fields, using six of those to drill deeply into one arts and humanities area. "My high school music teacher turned me onto WPI," says Luke Perreault, a recent grad from Blackstone, Massachusetts, who is studying biomedical engineering and took several music classes. Students typically take three courses during each seven-week term; classes focus on helping them identify, investigate and report on open-ended problems. "You'll know what you need to in order to be an electrical engineer or other professional, and you'll also get to solve real problems and learn how to ask the right questions," says Arthur Heinricher, dean of undergraduate studies and a mathematical sciences professor.

Two-thirds of students study or work away from campus for a term, with

STUDENTS OF INDUSTRIAL ENGINEERING WORKING TOGETHER

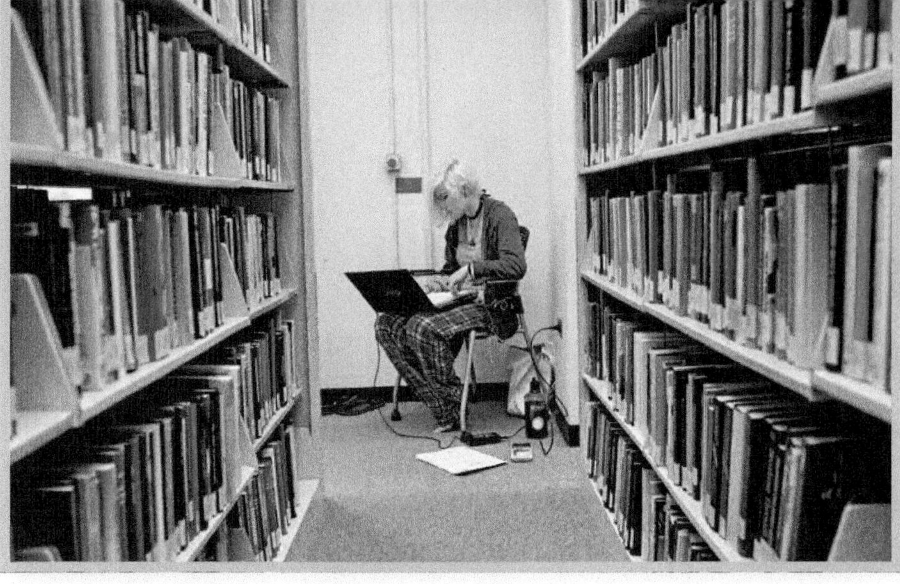

TUCKED AWAY IN A QUIET CORNER OF THE WPI LIBRARY

nearly half going abroad. Chris Long of Burlington, Connecticut, a 2015 grad, spent part of his junior year in New Zealand working on a project to improve the technology in Maori schools, for example.

The WPI Plan culminates senior year with a capstone experience, often with an outside company or nonprofit, aimed at getting students to grapple with actual problems found in the workplace and elsewhere. Civitarese, for example, researched bloodstream infection rates in intensive care units at the University of Massachusetts Medical School. Often these projects "lead to direct job offers," notes Rick Vaz, dean of the interdisciplinary and global studies division and associate professor of electrical and computer engineering.

When it comes to extracurriculars, there's everything from "LARPing" (Live Action Role Playing, which entails dressing up in medieval garb for mock battles) to athletics to musical ensembles and Greek life. WPI claims to have the nation's longest-operating student-run theater program and counts 20 NCAA Division III men's and women's teams (the Engineers) plus 31 club sports and seven intramural activities; most students participate in sports at some level. "Like all WPI students, I'm involved in many things," says Katie Picchione, a senior from Albany, New York, double majoring in mechanical engineering and security, technology and policy. She cites being president of the WPI Engineers Without Borders chapter and visiting high schools as an engineering ambassador as examples. ●

Clark University

Founded in 1887 as a graduate school, Clark today is known for combining a liberal arts undergraduate education with hands-on, real-world learning. Clark recently has packaged that approach as LEEP, for Liberal Education and Effective Practices, which focuses on getting students to put their knowledge into action and gain the capabilities employers seek through research, internships, service projects and study abroad.

The 50-acre campus along Main Street in Worcester is a mix of traditional, concrete and glass facilities, as well as nearby renovated Victorian homes purchased to accommodate growth. Clarkies quickly get acclimated to campus as they settle into a first-year "intensive" limited to just 16 students. They pick from a list of 30 seminars, from 9/11: Fact or Fiction to The Educated Robot, designed to foster the core academic skills of analytical reading, writing, speaking, thinking and debating. The professors serve as advisers to the students in their classes. Each freshman gets a LEEP adviser, too, and a peer adviser who helps with everything from transitioning to college life to finding undergrad research opportunities.

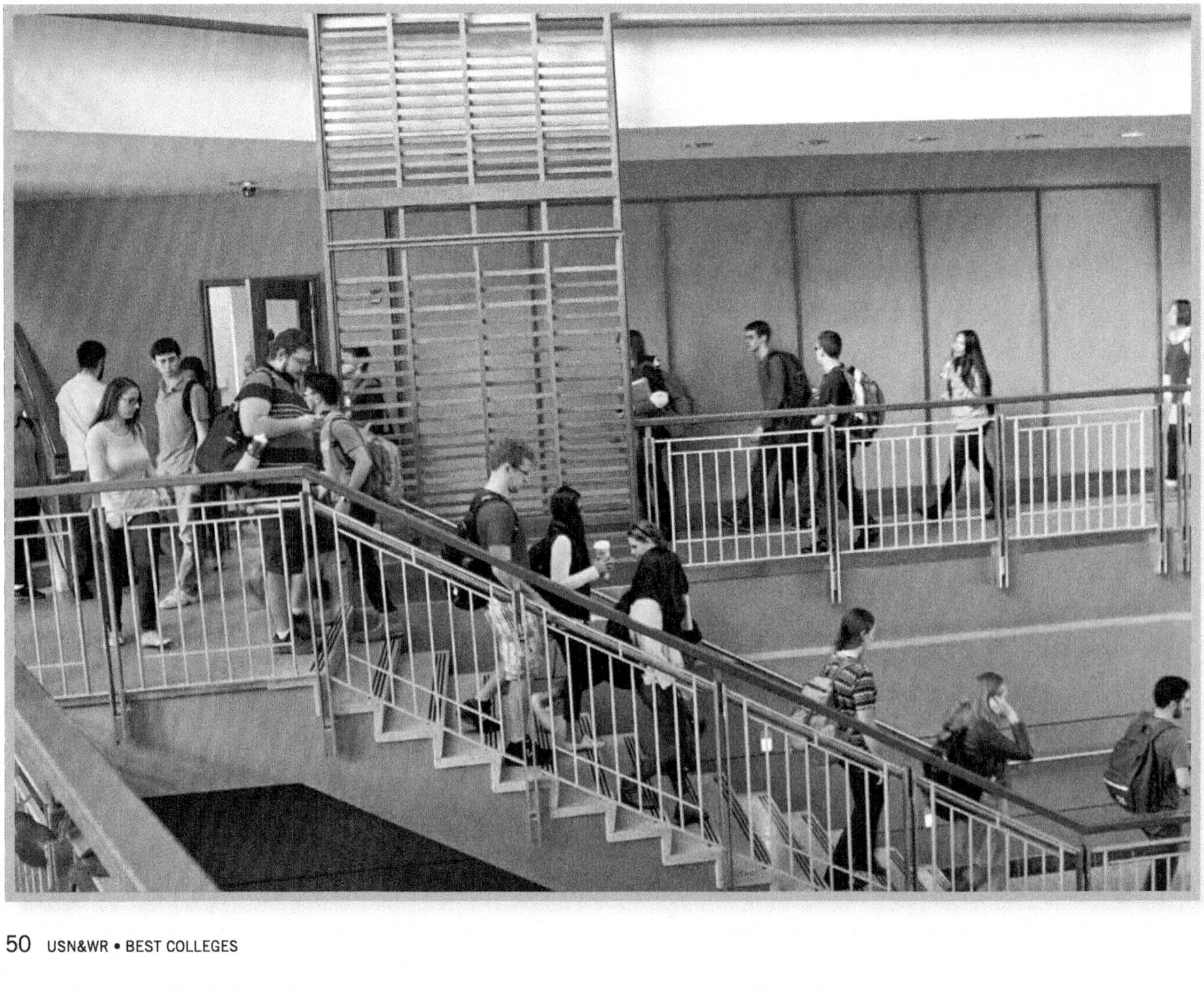

CLARK STUDENTS HEADING FROM CLASS TO CLASS

"Clarkies are just nice people," observes Nick Gerber, a recent graduate in political science from Santa Fe, New Mexico, who was attracted to the school because it is a research university but "still small" with only about 2,200 undergrads. More than a quarter of graduating seniors like it here well enough to stick around for the Accelerated B.A./Master's Degree Program, a way to earn a master's in one of 14 areas during a fifth (tuition-free) year.

Clark is noted for its psychology, geography and entrepreneurship programs. This is the

UNDERGRADUATES
Full-time: 2,213

TOTAL COST*
$50,140

U.S. NEWS RANKING
National Universities: #75

*Tuition, fees and room & board for 2015-16

birthplace of the American Psychological Association, and it takes pride in the fact that Sigmund Freud gave five lectures here in 1909. It was the university's first president who advanced the notion that adolescence is a developmental stage separate from childhood.

Eight in 10 students are engaged in community service off campus. "I'm involved in Big Brothers and Big Sisters," says Rezwana Hoque, a 2014 graduate in biology who is staying on to get a fifth-year master's.

Most undergrads also do research. And many upperclassmen take advantage of LEEP project funding to apply their classroom learning by working with an external organization – creating a product for a local business, say – for a summer or more. They receive a $2,500 stipend and attend workshops on collaboration, project management, professionalism and presentation skills, and wrap up with a presentation on their projects.

"I've never seen a student body as unafraid to take risks," says Michelle Bata, an associate dean. It's common for Clarkies from all disciplines to minor in the respected Innovation and Entrepreneurship program, and then propose an idea to improve the campus or the community through the Ureka! Big Idea Challenge, which financially supports the winning concepts.

Division III Clark participates in 17 sports; both men's and women's basketball teams traditionally have been competitive, and in recent years, men's tennis and lacrosse have had success, too. "It's not your traditional athletics department," says Alex Turgeon, a senior studying management from Holden, Massachusetts, who is captain of the lacrosse team. "You have student athletes who really are students."

Clark students tend to socialize more off campus than on, eating "a lot of good food" on trendy Shrewsbury Street, says Turgeon, as well as at the neighborhood diners, eateries and bars that are closer to campus. They also can take in Broadway-quality shows at the local Hanover Theatre for the Performing Arts and go for a hike through the nearby Broad Meadow Brook Sanctuary.

"The city has a lot of opportunities," notes Turgeon. He should know. Between hosting fundraising flag football tournaments for local nonprofits, playing lacrosse and working for Clark's IT services department, he has created a smartphone app highlighting some of the best of Worcester. It covers local nightlife and other activities, plus job and internship possibilities. ●

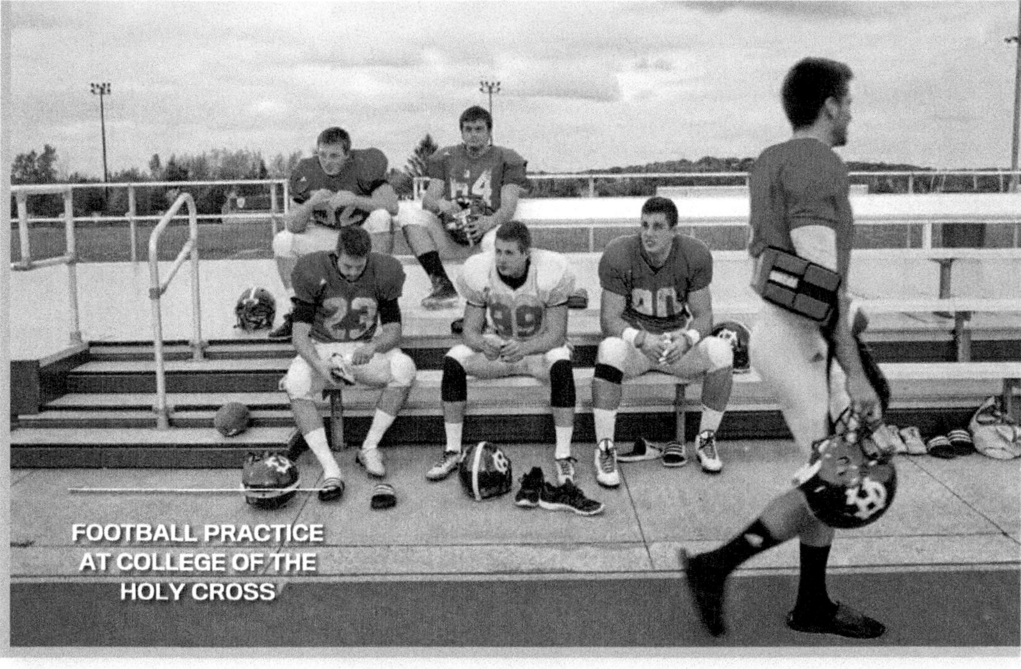
FOOTBALL PRACTICE AT COLLEGE OF THE HOLY CROSS

College of the Holy Cross

Strolling through the meticulously landscaped 174-acre campus, a registered arboretum, one might forget that this small Catholic college is located in the one-time industrial heart of New England. College of the Holy Cross, steeped in the Jesuit tradition, prides itself on intimate, contemplative classes, a close-knit community and opportunities for students to study abroad and engage in community service both near and far.

Freshmen quickly ground themselves through Montserrat, the first-year living-learning community program that involves choosing a small seminar based around one of six themes – including the natural world and core human questions – and living in a dorm with other students concentrating on the same theme. Seminars explore issues such as assimilation and rebellion, women and social change, and the gay rights movement. "We see that as an introduction to liberal arts education," says Denise Schaeffer, a professor of political science. The program plays a part in the college's 95 percent first-year retention rate. The 10-to-1 student-faculty ratio adds to the tight relationships between students and professors. Classes are small, typically with fewer than 20 students and rarely over 30.

A quarter of students play for one of the Division I college's 27 varsity sports teams, and it's common among undergrads to count a parent or sibling as a Crusader. The alumni network is extensive and engaged. "All of my professional development has been through the wonderful network here," says Jeffrey Reppucci, a 2014 graduate in Russian studies from Newburyport, Massachusetts, who thanks alumni connections for his internships with the U.S. ambassador to the Philip-

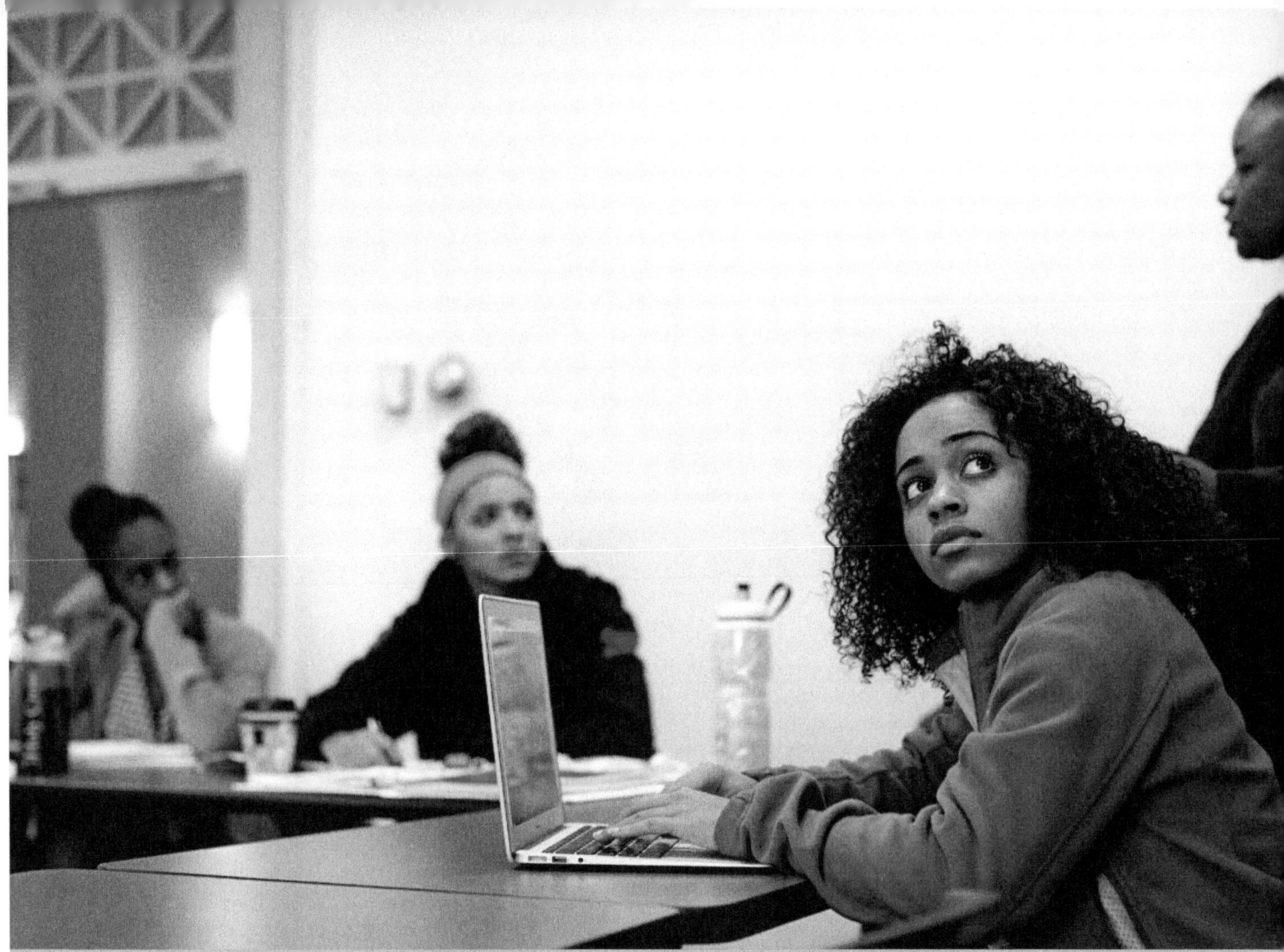

A HOLY CROSS CLASS IN TRAVEL WRITING AND AFRICAN HISTORY

pines and with a nonprofit in Washington, D.C.

The Jesuit character of the school does not imply any mandatory religious activities; one academic religion requirement can be satisfied through a wide range of classes, including introductions to Judaism or Islam. "They don't force religious activities on you, but they are available," notes Reppucci.

Students are offered 29 majors; psychology, economics and political science are the most popular. Holy Cross says it is among a small group of colleges that accept students regardless of their ability to pay and then meet 100 percent of their demonstrated financial need. About half of the 2014 freshmen class received an aid package averaging about $30,000.

"Study abroad is really popular," says Katherine Resker, a junior double-majoring in political science and Italian from North Grafton, Massachusetts. According to the Institute of International Education, Holy Cross ranks No. 1 among baccalaureate institutions for the number of students who go on long-term study abroad programs (defined as an academic or calendar year). One-third of students head out for at least a summer.

Also popular: Student Programs for Urban Development, the largest student organization on campus. "We go to local high schools to do tutoring for SATs," says Payton Shubrick, a recent grad from Springfield, Massachusetts, who studied political science. The tutoring program is one of SPUD's 46 public service programs.

"The opportunities here are endless," says Chris Campbell, a 2015 grad from Jamaica who majored in religious studies.

UNDERGRADUATES
Full-time: 2,904

TOTAL COST*
$59,924

U.S. NEWS RANKING
National Liberal Arts: #32

*Tuition, fees and room & board for 2015-16

He traveled to El Salvador, Paris and California, respectively, for a social justice immersion program, study abroad and a leadership conference. About 90 percent of students live on campus, and the social scene revolves around dorm life; there are no Greek organizations.

Holy Cross prides itself on the solid academic performance of students, including athletes. More than 90 percent of grads who apply to medical school or law school are accepted, for instance. "I was looking everywhere," says Marco Burgarello, a sophomore from Phoenix who plays baseball. "Holy Cross had the best combination of academics and athletics, and I fell in love with the campus." The graduation rate among athletes is 98 percent. ●

BRETT ZIEGLER FOR USN&WR

Minnesota

Welcome to Minnesota, the Land of 10,000 Lakes and frigid winters. (Sledding on dining hall trays, anyone?) The tour begins in Minneapolis and St. Paul at the two campuses of the University of Minnesota-Twin Cities, and then stops in at Macalester College in St. Paul. Next, we head just south to the tiny city of Northfield and visit close neighbors St. Olaf College and Carleton College. BY KELLY MAE ROSS

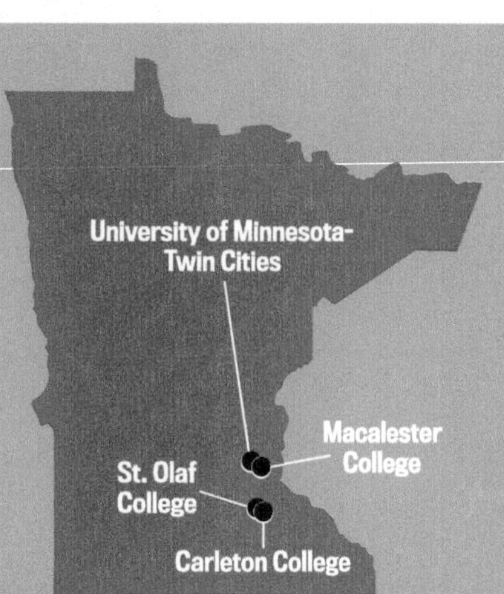

University of Minnesota

A stroll through the covered pedestrian walkway atop the Washington Avenue Bridge, which spans the Mississippi River to connect the two parts of the University of Minnesota's Minneapolis campus, offers a quick tour of the opportunities open to students at the state's flagship university. Hundreds of colorful hand-painted panels decorate the walls – a representation of some of the 900 or so student organizations, everything from the Marine Biology Club to the Minnesota Quidditch league.

All told, the land-grant university covers nearly 1,200 acres at its Twin Cities campuses in Minneapolis and St. Paul, separated by about four miles. The Minneapolis campus has the more distinctly urban feel, with its dozens of buildings, the 50,000-plus-seat TCF Bank Stadium, and a light rail line that runs through its heart. The St. Paul location houses just a few hundred students and is home to the

TACKLING A PROJECT IN TOY PRODUCTION DESIGN CLASS

PHOTOGRAPHY BY **BRETT ZIEGLER** FOR USN&WR

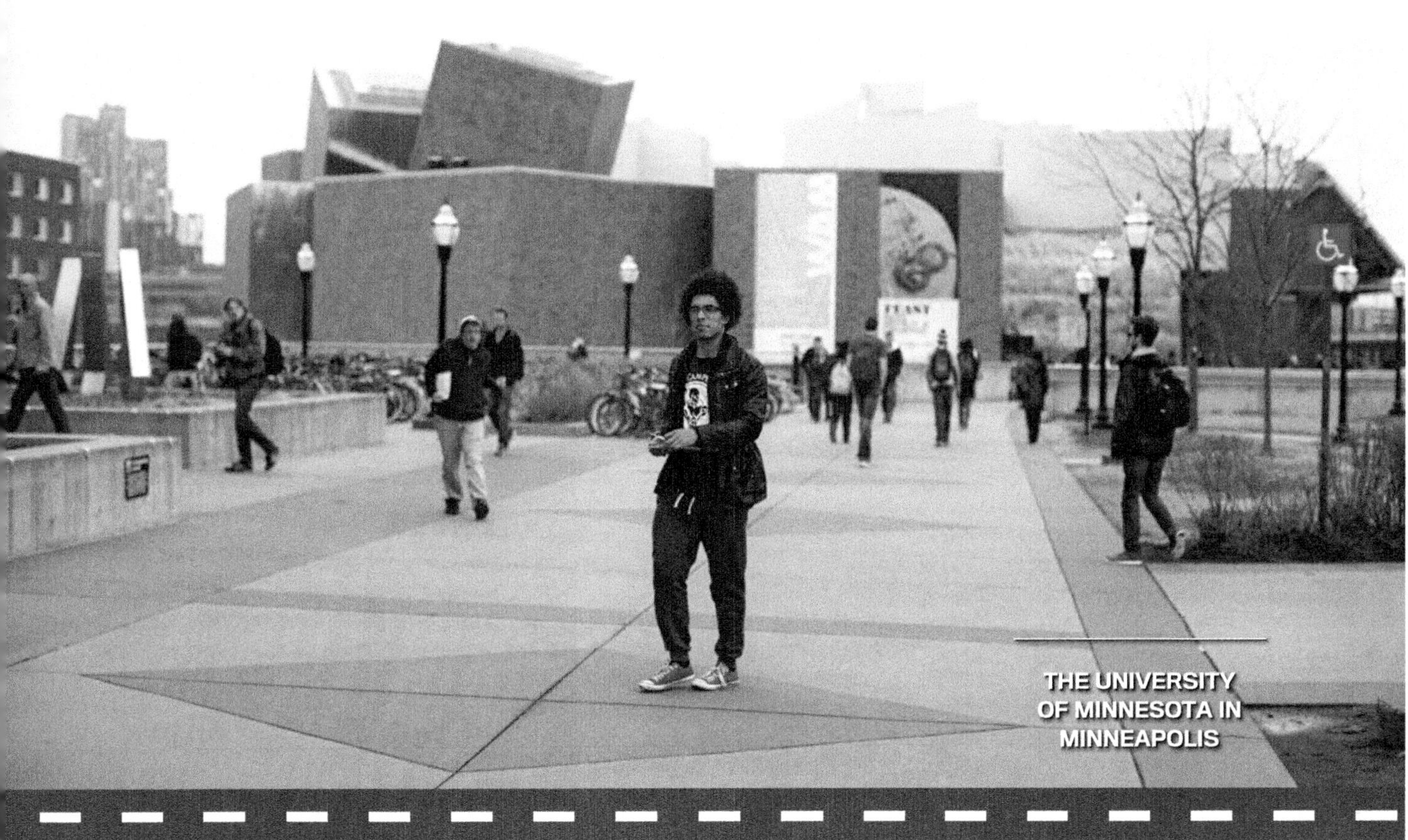
THE UNIVERSITY OF MINNESOTA IN MINNEAPOLIS

College of Food, Agricultural and Natural Resource Sciences and the College of Veterinary Medicine.

The school's size can be daunting at first, but "once you know your routes, it starts to feel a lot smaller than it is – in a good way," says Elizabeth Guzik, a sophomore from Orland Park, Illinois, majoring in vocal performance. One helpful route, particularly in the winter months, is a system of tunnels and enclosed skyways known as the "Gopher Way" in honor of the university's smiling, bucktoothed mascot.

With 51,000 undergrads and grad students (two-thirds of whom hail from Minnesota), some point out that you have to be motivated to get involved. "If you're not a self-starter it would be super easy to get lost here," says Cody Nelson, a 2015 in-state journalism grad from New Ulm.

That said, the university helps first-year students get to know a small group of classmates by offering discussion-oriented freshman seminars capped at 15 to 20 students. Examples of past seminar topics include Alpha Wives and Tiger Moms, Understanding the Evolution-Creationism Controversy, and Antioxidants: How Do They Protect Your Food and Your Body?

First-year students don't have to live on campus, but some 80 percent do. Students can apply to live in one of more than 30 living-learning communities of people who share an interest and are grouped together in residence halls, such as the American Sign Language House, STEM Diversity House or the West Bank Arts House. Some Greek housing is available for the roughly 8 percent of students who belong to a fraternity or sorority.

Undergrads have a choice of over 140 majors, more than a third of which are offered through the College of Liberal Arts, one of seven colleges that admit freshmen. Others include the College of Biological Sciences, the College of Science and Engineering, and the Carlson School of Management.

The Golden Gophers participate in 25 NCAA Division I varsity sports, including men's and women's ice hockey; those two teams have won a combined 11 national titles. Fans chant "Ski-U-Mah" (pronounced sky-you-mah), a rallying cry two rugby players coined more than 130 years ago.

The Dinkytown neighborhood north of the Minneapolis grounds, with its coffee shops and bars, is a popular place to socialize and is home to many who live off campus. The Twin Cities area has a thriving performing arts scene and several professional sports teams. The nation's largest shopping center, the Mall of America, is 13 miles away. ●

UNDERGRADUATES

Full-time: **28,904**

TOTAL COST*

In-State: **$22,480**
Out-of-State: **$29,730**

U.S. NEWS RANKING

National Universities: **#69**

*Tuition, fees and room & board for 2014-15

Macalester College

Colorful flags from 100 countries and Native American tribal nations hang above the Café Mac dining hall, representing the nationalities of members of the student body. Some 14 percent of students come to Macalester from abroad. On the Great Lawn outside Weyerhaeuser Memorial Chapel, the blue and white banner of the United Nations has been flying for more than six decades as a reminder to students, faculty and visitors that internationalism and multiculturalism are core components of the college's mission. Mac students must complete one course with an international focus and another reflecting U.S. multiculturalism, and some 60 percent of the student body "studies away" elsewhere in the U.S. or abroad.

UNDERGRADUATES
Full-time: 2,045

TOTAL COST*
$59,761

U.S. NEWS RANKING
National Liberal Arts: #23

*Tuition, fees and room & board for 2015-16

Macalester's location in St. Paul and proximity to Minneapolis – the downtown areas of both are only 10 minutes or so from campus – set it apart from many other liberal arts colleges. The setting doesn't feel urban, though, with its green lawns (when they're not covered with snow) and surrounding residential streets.

The Twin Cities area provides students ample opportunity to gain real-world experience and to enjoy a wide range of cultural offerings. Undergrads intern at places like the Minnesota House of Representatives, publisher Graywolf Press, and other businesses and nonprofits. "Macalester is centered in a really great area," says Julia Gay, a senior from Cleveland Heights, Ohio, pursuing an American studies major and a minor in theater. Her junior year work-study job involved about 10 hours a week in the St. Paul Public Schools doing theater workshops and performances with students. "It's crazy," she says, not to "take advantage of all these opportunities."

Civic engagement is another core value, and more than 90 percent of Mac's roughly 2,000 students get involved in the community

TAKING A YOGA CLASS AT MACALESTER

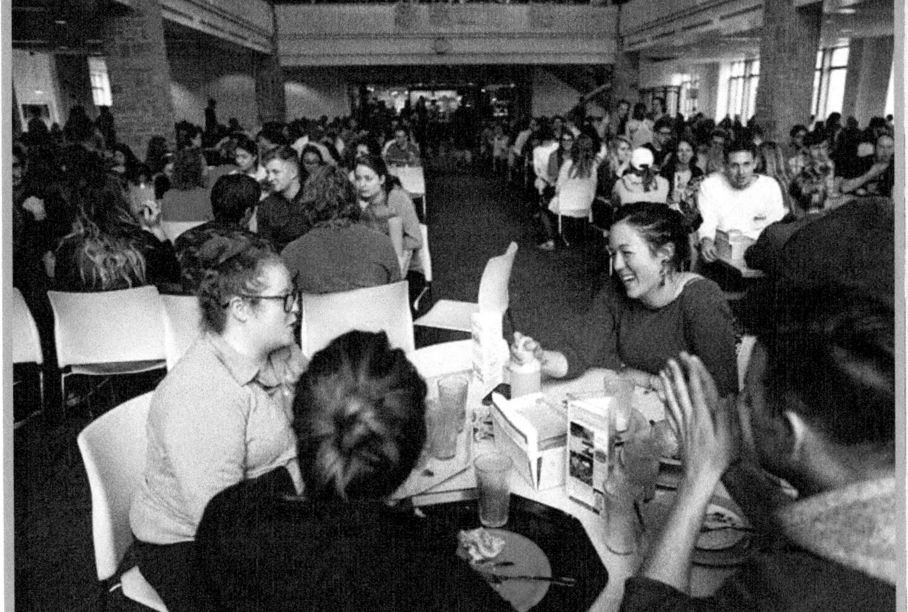

HANGING OUT IN THE ST. OLAF DINING HALL

through service, applied research or in other ways. "We educate people to think about their civic responsibility, whether it's in their local community or national community or global community," says Macalester President Brian Rosenberg. The college offers around 60 courses with a civic engagement component, such as Economics of Poverty in the U.S., in which students must work three hours a week with a nonprofit that provides aid to people who are struggling.

To enhance the transition to college life, all first-year students take a seminar capped at 16 students from an instructor who becomes their initial academic adviser, such as Ethics and the Internet or Tenors in Togas: Greek and Roman Myth in Opera. With a 10-to-1 student-faculty ratio, Macalester is the kind of place where professors quickly notice if a student misses class and will reach out, and where faculty members host dinners for students from time to time. (An endowed fund supports these gatherings.) Professors "care about you in a way that's shocking," says junior political science major Farah AlHaddad, who is from Syria.

First- and second-year students are required to live on campus, and in all, about two-thirds of the student body resides in university dorms, apartments and language or theme houses like the Veggie Co-op, which is located under the bleachers of the football stadium. The college fields 21 Division III varsity teams known as the Scots.

In a further nod to the college's heritage, which stems from its founding by a Presbyterian minister as well as the Scottish Presbyterian ancestry of early college presidents and Macalester's benefactor and namesake, Mac offers free bagpipe lessons to interested students. These instruments regularly sound during special occasions.

"When professors get tenure, they play the bagpipes into their office or whatever class they're in to announce it," says Ian Lock of Fond du Lac, Wisconsin, a junior biology major. Another fun tradition: Founders Day pushball, in which students, faculty and staff brave the March elements in a contest that involves maneuvering a giant inflatable ball across the snowy Great Lawn. ●

St. Olaf College

It's not unusual to see backpacks and coats left unsupervised in the Buntrock Commons fireside lounge or in the cubbies outside the dining hall. Oles appreciate the strong sense of trust and community that characterizes this 3,000-student liberal arts college in the rural city of Northfield. (Motto: "Cows, Colleges and Contentment.") St. Olaf's century-old honor code, which requires students to sign pledges when they take a quiz or exam stating they haven't seen any dishonest work, fosters a certain faith in each other in the classroom. Student mailboxes are not locked, and colorful flowers poke out of many of them on Fridays, purchased by undergrads for friends from local florists who come to campus each week.

The many light-colored limestone buildings give the campus, which spans 300 acres upon a hill overlooking town, a unified look. St. Olaf owns about an equal amount of restored natural lands next door where biology professors might hold a field class, say, and students can go for a jog. One landmark, the college's wind turbine, Big Ole, provides up to one-third of the power used on campus. St. Olaf is just over a mile from friendly rival Carleton College; the schools compete in athletics, but share library resources and have offered a joint class called Political Psychology of Presidential Foreign Policy Decision Making. The colleges are exploring further collaborative teaching opportunities.

St. Olaf is affiliated with the Evangelical Lutheran Church in America, though less than a third of students identify as Lutheran. (Roughly 70 percent identify as Christian.) Optional chapel services are offered six days a week, and all students are required to take a course in biblical studies and a course on Christian theology. But students say you don't have to be religious to appreciate all that St. Olaf has to offer.

About half of Oles hail from the North Star State, and nearly all live on campus, which helps build a strong feeling of closeness. There are "so many moments of just running into people," says Ashley Belisle, a 2015 grad in English and Spanish from Mahtomedi, Minnesota. Upperclassmen can apply to live in one of 19 themed houses, including several focused on a language, and others with themes

A "SOCIAL WORKER AS PROFESSIONAL" CLASS AT ST. OLAF

proposed by students that recently included sustainable food practices and mental and spiritual health awareness. Classes average 22 students.

Oles enjoy an academic calendar that includes a four-week January term between semesters, when they can study abroad or take a class like Zen and the Art of Judo, for example, or the Psychology of Hearing.

The school offers several "conversations" programs, some of which involve classmates living in the same residence hall. In the Great Conversation program, students read and discuss classic works of Western literature in a sequence of five classes over two years. (Other programs offered include American Conversations, Asian Conversations and Environmental Conversations.) Students can choose from upward of 40 majors, including computer science, nursing and Norwegian.

About one-third of Oles get involved with the musical groups on campus: eight choirs, two bands, two orchestras, several jazz ensembles, handbell groups and more. The college's music department has a faculty of more than 60 and offers several specialized degrees in such areas as performance and church music. Several ensembles perform during the annual St. Olaf Christmas Festival, which has been broadcast on public radio and TV. In addition to the concert, there's a feast of traditional Norwegian fare in the dining hall, celebrating the school's 1874 founding by Scandinavian immigrants.

"It's a lot of good feelings, I guess, is the best way I can put it," says Nick Stumo-Langer, a recent history and political science grad from White Bear Lake, Minnesota. Beyond music, the school's 200-plus student organizations range in interest from rowing to holistic medicine to fighting poverty. The college also has about a dozen sports teams each for men and women, including both Alpine and Nordic skiing.

"Everyone is just really, really involved," says Rachel Palermo, a recent grad from New Brighton, Minnesota, who studied political science and economics. "You'll never have a dull conversation." ●

UNDERGRADUATES
Full-time: **2,989**

TOTAL COST*
$52,730

U.S. NEWS RANKING
National Liberal Arts: **#51**

*Tuition, fees and room & board 2015-16

Carleton College

Carleton students expect to be busy on the eve of final exams, of course, but not just in the predictable way. At 10 p.m., Carls all over campus open their windows and scream at the top of their lungs. Soon after that, they'll be noiselessly dancing on tables (wearing headphones) in Gould Library and enjoying a late-night breakfast served up by the college's deans in one of the dining halls. These are just a few of the traditions that provide students at the private liberal arts college with a break from the books. Carleton students are "extremely high achievers" but for the most part "we don't take ourselves too seriously," says Becca Giles, a recent history grad from Eau Claire, Wisconsin.

Carleton is situated on 1,040 acres in rural Northfield, less than an hour from the Twin Cities and just a mile or so from athletic rival St. Olaf College. The annual football game between the Carleton Knights and the St. Olaf Oles is known as the Cereal Bowl, a nod to the nearby cereal factory. Bounded to the west by the Cannon River, Carleton's cozy campus contains a good deal of brick and a mix of architectural styles. Adjacent to the academic core of the campus is an 880-acre arboretum, often just called the Arb, which serves as an outdoor classroom of sorts for biology, environmental studies and even drawing courses. About 90 percent of Carleton's 2,000-some students live in college housing. First-years are mixed with upperclassmen in the residence halls, though older students can also live in shared-interest houses or highly sought-after townhomes. The residential nature of the place makes it easy to keep meeting people, and even the library "is a social hub," says recent biology grad Jorde Ranum of Spring Lake Park, Minnesota. Those craving "monastery quiet," as posters in the library call it, are directed to study on the lowest level of Gould; the main floor maintains "Blue Monday quiet," a reference to the Goodbye Blue Monday coffee shop downtown, a popular hangout.

When it comes to academics, Carls benefit from a student-faculty ratio of 9-to-1 and an average class size of 18. The college has recently been atop the U.S. News list of liberal arts institutions with a strong commitment to undergraduate teaching, posted at usnews.com (with St. Olaf close behind). Among a range of general education requirements, freshmen must complete a discussion-based Argument and Inquiry seminar during their first term; senior year, every Carl completes a capstone in his or her major that could take the form of a research paper or project. Classes are arranged in three 10-week trimesters, and the faster pace "definitely forces you to learn how to manage your time," says Matthew Pruyne, a junior from Amherst, Massachusetts, studying theater and computer science. "By the time midterms are actually done, you're getting ready for finals."

Each Friday morning, members of the campus community gather in Gothic-inspired Skinner Memorial Chapel for the weekly installment of the college's speaker series. Past speakers have included poet Javon Johnson, journalist Marco Werman and Kimberly Bryant, founder of the education organization Black Girls Code. On an open area known as the "Bald Spot" just outside the chapel, students ice skate in winter and, in warmer weather, play Ultimate Frisbee – a club sport in which both the Carleton men's and women's teams are nationally competitive.

In all, there are more than 200 organizations for undergrads to choose from, such as an anime society and CANOE, the Carleton Association of Nature and Outdoor Enthusiasts. Says Giles: "It feels sometimes like we're constantly moving."

But if undergrads need to slow down and take a break, they can head to the Dacie Moses House to bake cookies or just to relax. The house, the former residence of a longtime Carleton employee who used to host students in her home for meals and games, is stocked with the necessary baking supplies. "Dacie's occupies a pretty unique place in the community," says Pruyne. Campus a cappella groups rehearse there, and on Sundays, any member of the Carleton or Northfield community can stop by the house for a student-hosted brunch. ●

UNDERGRADUATES

Full-time: 2,044

TOTAL COST*

$62,046

U.S. NEWS RANKING

National Liberal Arts: #8

*Tuition, fees and room & board for 2015-16

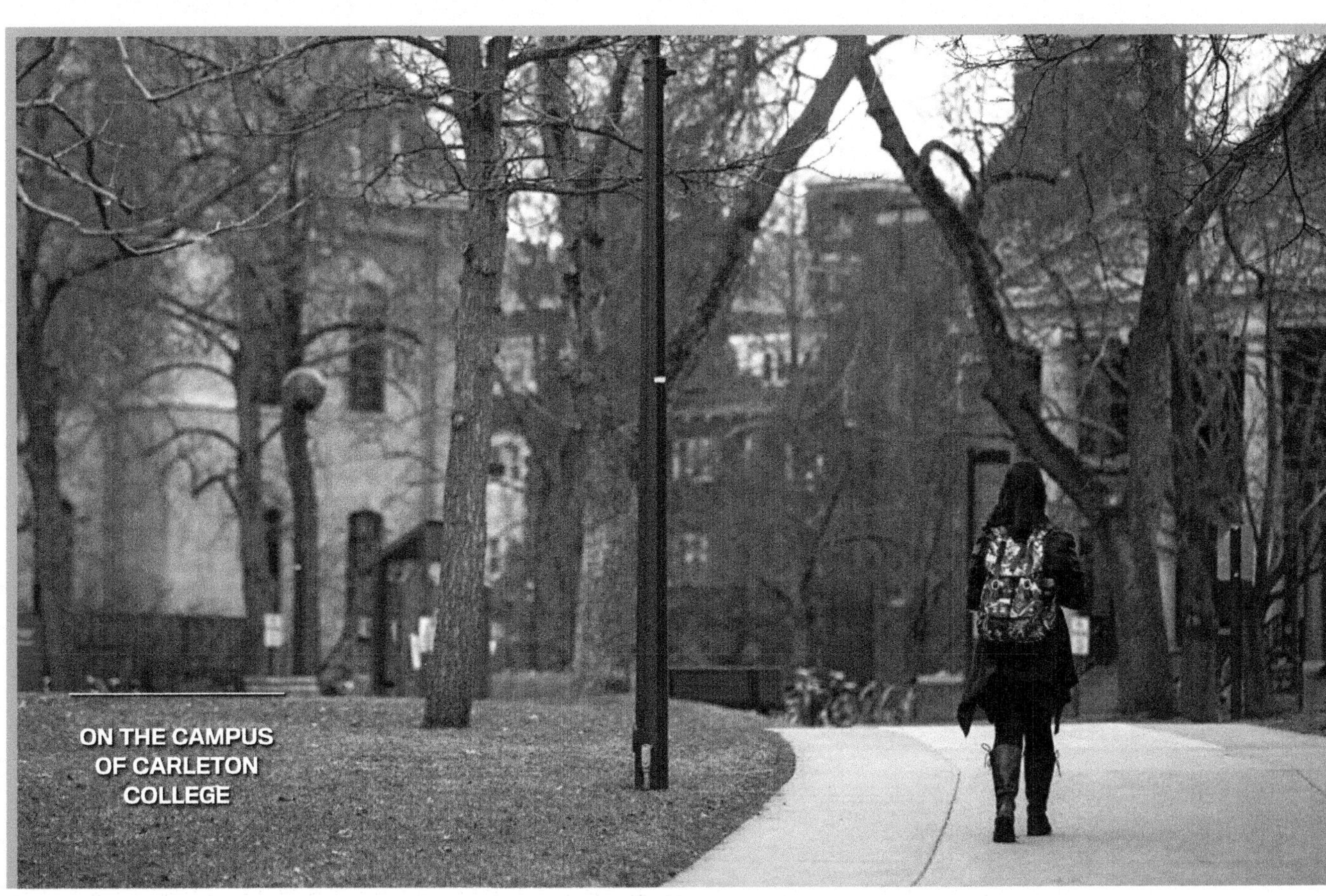

ON THE CAMPUS OF CARLETON COLLEGE

San Francisco

Home to both the storied Silicon Valley tech scene and an abundance of natural wonders, the San Francisco Bay Area is also the setting of an array of colleges, each with its own personality. Join us at the University of California-Berkeley and the University of San Francisco along the bay before we head south to Stanford and UC-Santa Cruz. BY MICHAEL MORELLA

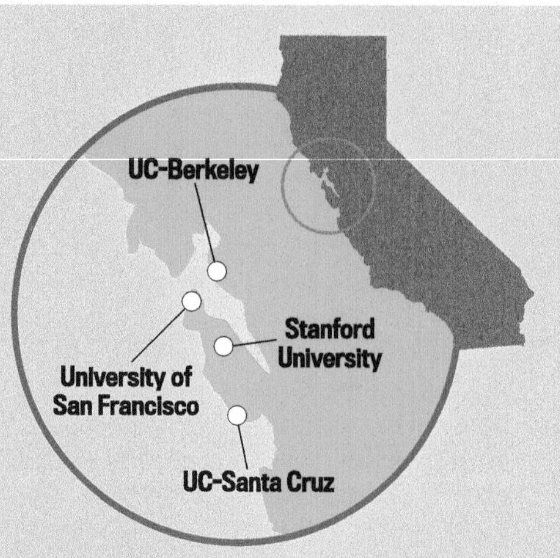

UC-Berkeley

Some 50 years ago, hundreds of students gathered at Sproul Hall on the University of California-Berkeley campus demanding that administrators not stifle their right to political free speech. That protest established Berkeley as a national hotbed of student activism. These days, the spirit of protest remains alive and well at Berkeley, the flagship campus of the University of California system and the top-ranked public university in the country. Students take issues like racial injustice and income inequality very seriously here, while also exuding a certain quirky irreverence in their daily lives. (Consider the Berkeley undergrad walking around this winter day in a pajama onesie blowing bubbles.) Besides regular demonstrations, they frequently flood Sproul Plaza for cultural performances, to socialize and to advertise clubs or events.

Undergrads attend six of the university's 14 colleges and schools, which also enroll about 10,500 graduate students. Set on 1,232 acres in downtown Berkeley, east of San Francisco Bay, the campus has an urban feel with a healthy dose of nature in the scenic Strawberry Creek and several open glades. Restaurants, theaters, record shops and other stores are just a short walk away, particularly along Telegraph Avenue to the south. Take Telegraph about five miles farther south to reach Oakland, another popular destination for food, museums, sporting events and other activities.

Commonly known as both Berkeley and Cal, the university is equal parts academic and athletic powerhouse. Students have access to about 120 majors, and faculty members include Nobel laureates, Pulitzer Prize winners and other esteemed scholars. This is a campus that has its own museum of paleontology (complete with a 40-foot T. rex skeleton) and where more than a dozen chemical elements, including plutonium, were discovered. Recent political science grad Elizabeth Kirk from Seattle says she was "inspired every day academically." The Division I Golden Bears compete in about 30 varsity sports, and students can participate in a range of intramural and club teams, martial arts, and dance and fitness classes.

More than two-thirds of students are native Californians, and roughly 14 per-

UNDERGRADUATES
Full-time: 26,320

TOTAL COST*
In-State: $28,854
Out-of-State: $53,562

U.S. NEWS RANKING
National Universities: #20

*Tuition, fees and room & board for 2015-16

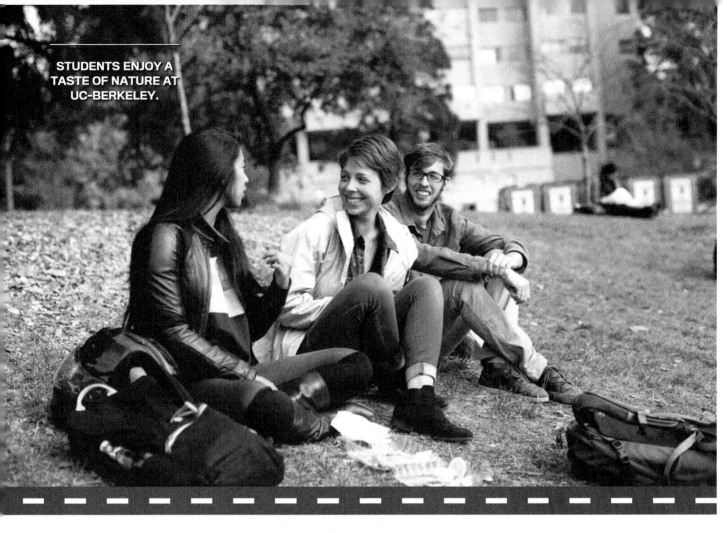

STUDENTS ENJOY A TASTE OF NATURE AT UC-BERKELEY.

cent come from outside the U.S. About 17 percent of the 78,000-plus first-year applicants for fall 2015 were offered admission, putting Berkeley among the most selective public universities in the country. Academics can be quite rigorous, students say, though they note that many Cal undergrads tend to be more competitive with themselves than with each other. But "even when stress does build up," says senior Humair Burney, a chemistry major from Pakistan, "you have a lot of outlets." The choices include taking advantage of more formal advising, counseling and tutoring plus the university's cultural resource centers, and just enjoying concerts or performances at Zellerbach Hall.

With over 1,200 student organizations, some 8,000 courses, and more than a dozen dining halls and cafes, Berkeley can feel overwhelming. "No one's going to hold your hand," says senior psychology major Andjelija Janicijevic from Serbia. But in many ways, "it's surprising how small it feels," says junior Kim Lee, a mechanical engineering major from San Rafael, California.

To make tight connections with other students and professors, first- and second-year students can choose from a range of intimate faculty-taught seminars like High Culture, Low Culture: Modernism and the Films of the Coen Brothers or Art and Science on Wheels. About three-quarters of all classes have fewer than 30 students and larger lectures typically break down into smaller discussion sections. Nearly all freshmen live in Berkeley-affiliated housing, and 10 percent of men and women belong to fraternities and sororities.

Thousands of students participate in public service each year, and Berkeley is the top producer of Peace Corps volunteers in the program's history. At Berkeley, says senior Melissa Hsu, a business major from San Marino, California, "we actually think that we can change things." ●

PASSING THROUGH SATHER GATE ON THE BERKELEY CAMPUS

PHOTOGRAPHY BY **BRETT ZIEGLER** FOR USN&WR

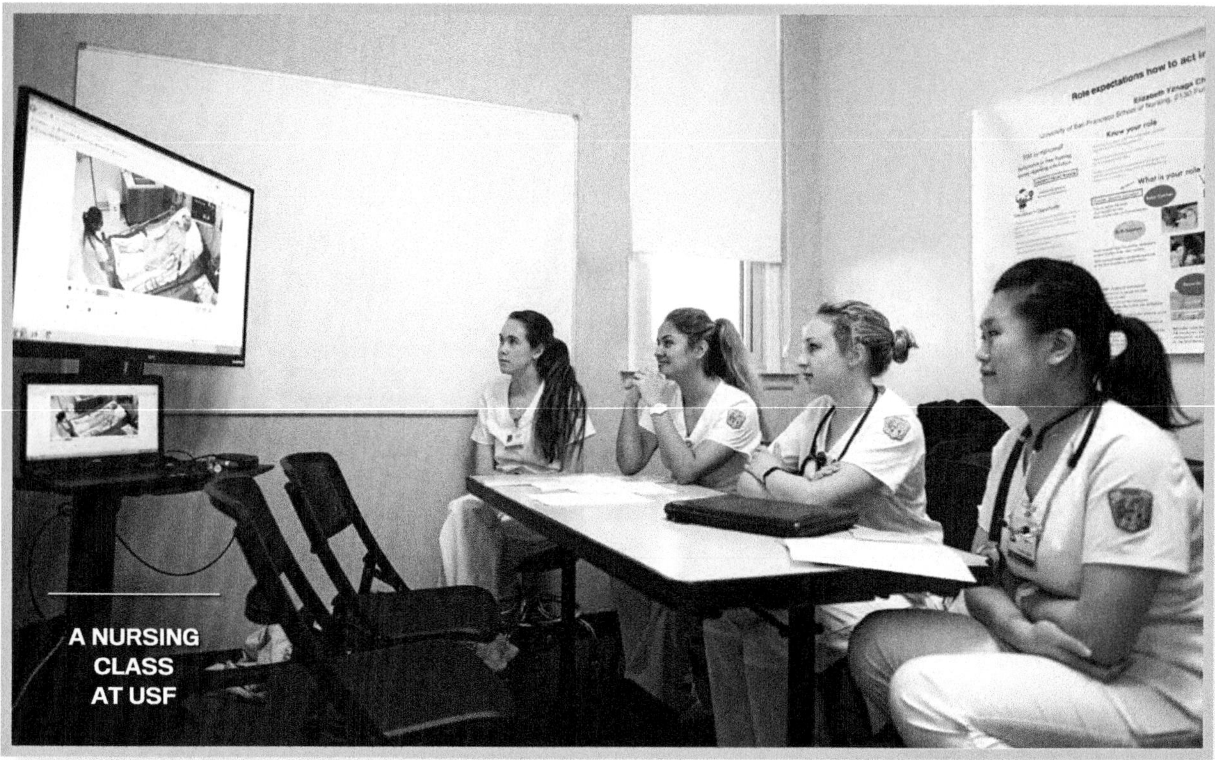

A NURSING CLASS AT USF

University of San Francisco

Like the city that it calls home, the University of San Francisco is a melting pot. About half of undergraduates are students of color, and close to 20 percent hail from outside the United States (representing 87 different countries).

Even the buildings on campus display a mix of styles, from the elegant Baroque-inspired architecture of the 100-year-old St. Ignatius Church to the modern John Lo Schiavo S.J. Center for Science and Innovation, opened in 2013, with its sleek glass-walled exterior, high-tech labs, and grass-covered "living roof."

Located near Golden Gate Park and the hip, historic Haight-Ashbury district, the private university's 55-acre campus is divided by a couple of city streets. USF students embrace their urban environs, enjoying sporting events, cultural excursions, arts and music performances and engaging energetically in community service, particularly in the underserved Western Addition neighborhood next door.

UNDERGRADUATES
Full-time: **6,529**

TOTAL COST*
$56,284

U.S. NEWS RANKING
National Universities: **#108**

*Tuition, fees and room & board for 2015-16

One of 28 Jesuit colleges and universities in the country, the university makes an effort to make people of all faiths – or none – feel welcome. In fact, just about a third of students identify as Christian. All undergrads who want to can participate in a weekly mass, interfaith retreats and other faith-based programming.

Founded in 1855, the school still stays true to the spirit of its Catholic roots. "USF is really focused on social justice, diversity and inclusion," says senior Jacqline Murillo, a philosophy major originally from the Netherlands. Undergrads can choose from 46 majors and 68 minors in the colleges of arts and sciences, management and nursing. Students must complete a core curriculum that includes courses in communication, math, arts, religion and other subjects. At least one course must have a service-learning component, such as a business class that offers a firsthand look at management and organizational dynamics issues through volunteer work with Meals on Wheels.

About 20 student organizations focus on giving back, and undergrads truly come to feel like "part of the greater San Francisco community," says recent graduate Mia Orantia, a media studies major from

San Jose, California. The Leo T. McCarthy Center for Public Service and the Common Good helps coordinate volunteer opportunities between students, faculty members and more than 200 local partners.

"It's not just about talking about it," says recent sociology grad Alexis Stanley. "There are so many opportunities that you can take advantage of." Stanley, a Phoenix native, spent a summer in Bolivia on a USF-sponsored trip working for a solar energy development organization, helping to train women in indigenous communities to use ecologically friendly cooking devices.

Enrolling about 6,500 undergrads, plus 3,800 grad students, USF "has a very familial environment," says senior nursing student Kevin Bachar of Chino Hills, California. That feeling also extends to the faculty, who are "not just professors," Bachar says, but "mentors." Core courses average about 29 students – major classes and electives are typically smaller – and about a third of undergrads live on campus, in one of several dorms, apartments or themed housing communities. Many upperclassmen live a short ride or walk from campus.

About 60 percent of those who apply to USF are granted admission, and 4 in 5 U.S. students who enroll come from California.

While the Golden Gate City is a big draw for many students, it can be expensive. At the same time, the abundance of off-campus activities makes the school occasionally feel a little empty. "It's our biggest asset, but at the same time our big challenge," notes sociology professor Jennifer Turpin, former provost and vice president for academic affairs.

On campus, the student community does come together for the Hui O Hawaii Club's annual Luau, the Spring Carnival, or to cheer on the Dons, whose Division I teams compete in the NCAA's West Coast Conference. ●

Stanford University

An estimated 13,000 bikes can be seen on Stanford's campus each day, helping students stay active and manage their usually packed schedules at the private university near Palo Alto, one of the most selective undergraduate institutions in the country. (Just over 5 percent of applicants earned a spot in the class of 2019.) But even though it's an elite university, students seem to generally agree that Stanford is not a "four-year competition," says recent grad Shelby Sinclair, a Milwaukee native who majored in Comparative Studies in Race and Ethnicity. Students work hard but preserve a healthy balance of fun and togetherness, she says.

Stanford's 8,180-acre campus includes a number of sand- and rust-colored California Mission-inspired buildings, several dozen dining options and a Rodin Sculpture Garden. Up in the southern foothills, past the Main Quad, visitors can spot "the dish," a 150-foot radio telescope.

Originally built on a horse farm, Stanford is a breeding ground for top tech talent for nearby Silicon Valley; alumni include the founders of Google, Netflix, Yahoo, Hewlett-Packard and LinkedIn, among others. Even though many students buy into the entrepreneurial mind-set, that doesn't define everyone. "There isn't one Stanford experience," says recent grad Elodie Nierenberg, a Vancouver, Washington, native who majored in Science, Technology, and Society.

While undergraduate majors in computer science, engineering and biology are among the most popular, you're hardly "being shorted" in the arts, humanities and other disciplines, says senior Cassidy Elwood, an English and economics major from Arroyo Grande, California. Stanford undergraduates can earn degrees from three of the university's seven schools, where they can choose from more than 80 majors.

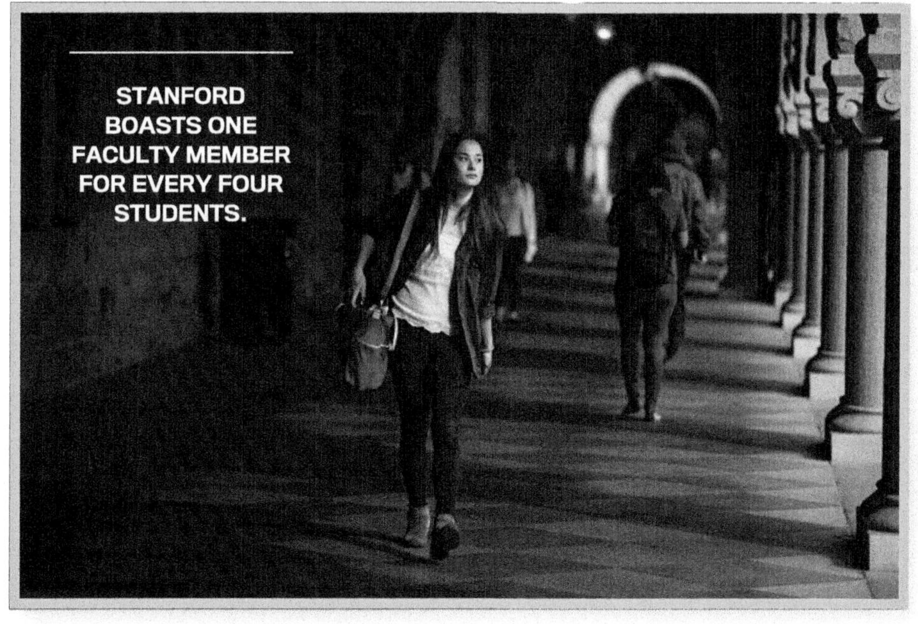
STANFORD BOASTS ONE FACULTY MEMBER FOR EVERY FOUR STUDENTS.

Thanks to a 4-to-1 student-faculty ratio, students can develop close relationships with professors, who don't "just care about me going through the motions" of learning,

WORKING INSIDE A STANFORD DRAWING STUDIO

says junior Alexa Haushalter, a mathematical and computational science major from Bellefontaine, Ohio. Undergrads regularly host their instructors for dinners, and freshmen and sophomores can take 16-student introductory seminars taught by faculty. Overall, about 70 percent of classes have fewer than 20 undergrads.

The workload is tough, but students also keep busy participating in 650-plus groups and organizations and following Stanford's varsity sports teams, which have won the second most NCAA Division I championships in history, behind UCLA. To prevent them from being lost or overextended among so many options, undergrads have access to a wide range of resources, including academic directors assigned to all first-year residences and a number of community centers for academic help or social and cultural programming, such as the Native American Cultural Center and the Diversity and First-Gen Office. "You'd almost have to actively try to not get help," says Eric Mattson, a recent human biology grad originally from Lincoln, Nebraska.

Ninety-six percent of undergrads live on "the farm," as campus is affectionately known, along with a good number of faculty members and the university's 9,100 grad students. Students have a host of housing options, from more traditional residence halls and apartments to co-ops (where students cook and clean) and themed houses like La Casa Italiana and the environmentally conscious Enchanted Broccoli Forest. About a quarter of undergraduates join fraternities and sororities.

Students talk about a "Stanford bubble," which some say can be stifling at times, but the region offers plenty of ways to branch out. Groups like Stanford Outdoor Education coordinate regular backpacking and camping trips to Big Sur and Lake Tahoe, for instance, while San Francisco and San Jose are an easy ride away by commuter rail. ●

UNDERGRADUATES
Full-time: 7,019

TOTAL COST*
$60,427

U.S. NEWS RANKING
National Universities: #4

*Tuition, fees and room & board for 2015-16

UC-Santa Cruz

Tucked in a redwood forest a couple of miles from the Pacific coast, the University of California–Santa Cruz is a nature-lover's dream, complete with some 25 miles of walking trails and a 33-acre farm, part of the Center for Agroecology and Sustainable Food Systems. Walking to class can quite literally be a hike, leading to what students wryly refer to as the "freshman minus-15," says senior Sami Chen, a Santa Cruz native studying ocean sciences.

Yet the sprawling 2,000-acre campus is made much smaller through UCSC's residential colleges. As incoming freshmen, each of the 15,800 undergraduates becomes affiliated with one of 10 of these communities, where he or she lives for at least a year and where all take a core class in small groups. Each place has its own identity and vibe, and with between 1,400 and 1,700 students per community, "you kind of get that small college feel," says Kaede Hamilton of Cupertino, California, a 2014 grad who majored in psychology and legal studies.

Every college has its own common areas, cafe or coffee house, student government, and theme – Cultural Identities and Global Consciousness at Merrill, for instance, and Science, Technology, and Society for Crown. Together, they form a ring around the central academic and administrative buildings, and each is intended to be a sort of "intellectual neighborhood," says psychology professor Faye Crosby, provost of Cowell College and one of nine faculty members who live alongside undergrads there.

With fewer than half the number of students of UC–Berkeley or UCLA,

UCSC is one of the smallest of the 10 University of California system schools, and about 93 percent of students who attend come from the Golden State. About a third of students are members of traditionally underrepresented minority groups, among the highest percentages at the UC schools. The university offers more than 60 majors, including programs in marine biology, computer game design and Jewish studies.

About two-thirds of classes enroll fewer than 30 students, though there are a fair number with 100-plus. Students say professors are highly approachable, but sometimes you have to take the initiative to get to know them personally. "I haven't come across a professor who I feel didn't really care about my progress," says senior Guillermo Rogel from Riverside, California, who is majoring in politics. (Until 2001, undergrads received narrative evaluations instead of letter grades, if they so chose.) UCSC has a modest graduate student population of about 1,600, which means there's room for more than 3 in 5 undergrads to participate in research with faculty.

While most speak highly of the residential colleges, students do admit that they can feel a little insular. "You really have to work on identifying with the larger university," Rogel says. Still, many gather for events at one of several theaters across campus, Quarry Plaza or to support the Banana Slugs, who compete in the NCAA's Division III. And "there are lots of different ways to build a community outside of your college" in the 150-plus student clubs and organizations, says recent grad Gabby Areas, a sociology major from Fairfield, California. There are about two dozen fraternities and sororities that count some 6 percent of students as members.

UNDERGRADUATES

Full-time: **15,825**

TOTAL COST*

In-State: **$28,604**
Out-of-State: **$53,312**

U.S. NEWS RANKING

National Universities: **#82**

*Tuition, fees and room & board for 2015-16

Downtown Santa Cruz, with its scenic beaches, boardwalk, shops and restaurants, is only a couple of miles up the road, and UCSC is only a short drive from several state parks, beaches, the Monterey Bay National Marine Sanctuary, and San Jose, in the heart of Silicon Valley. San Francisco is about 75 miles away.

Students say it's a myth that everyone at UCSC is a hippie, though the place is not without its offbeat touches, like the official archive of Grateful Dead artifacts in the library and the camper park, where students can live in an RV (assuming they bring one). And the university, founded in 1965, proudly bills itself as "the original authority on questioning authority." ●

A COMMUNITY GARDEN ON SANTA CRUZ'S 2,000-ACRE CAMPUS

The U.S. NEWS Ranki

3

ngs

COLLEGE OF THE HOLY CROSS

MATT SLABY – LUCEO FOR USN&WR

3

THE U.S. NEWS RANKINGS

A Close Look at the Methodology

How college-bound students can make the most of our statistics

BY ROBERT J. MORSE AND ERIC BROOKS

The host of intangibles that make up the college experience can't be measured by a series of data points. But for families concerned with finding the best academic value for their money, the U.S. News Best Colleges rankings, now in their 31st year, provide an excellent starting point for the search. They allow you to compare at a glance the relative quality of institutions based on such widely accepted indicators of excellence as freshman retention and graduation rates and the strength of the faculty. And as you check out the data for colleges already on your short list, you may discover unfamiliar schools with similar metrics, and thus broaden your options.

Yes, many factors other than those spotlighted here will figure in your decision, including location and the feel of campus life; the range of academic offerings, activities and

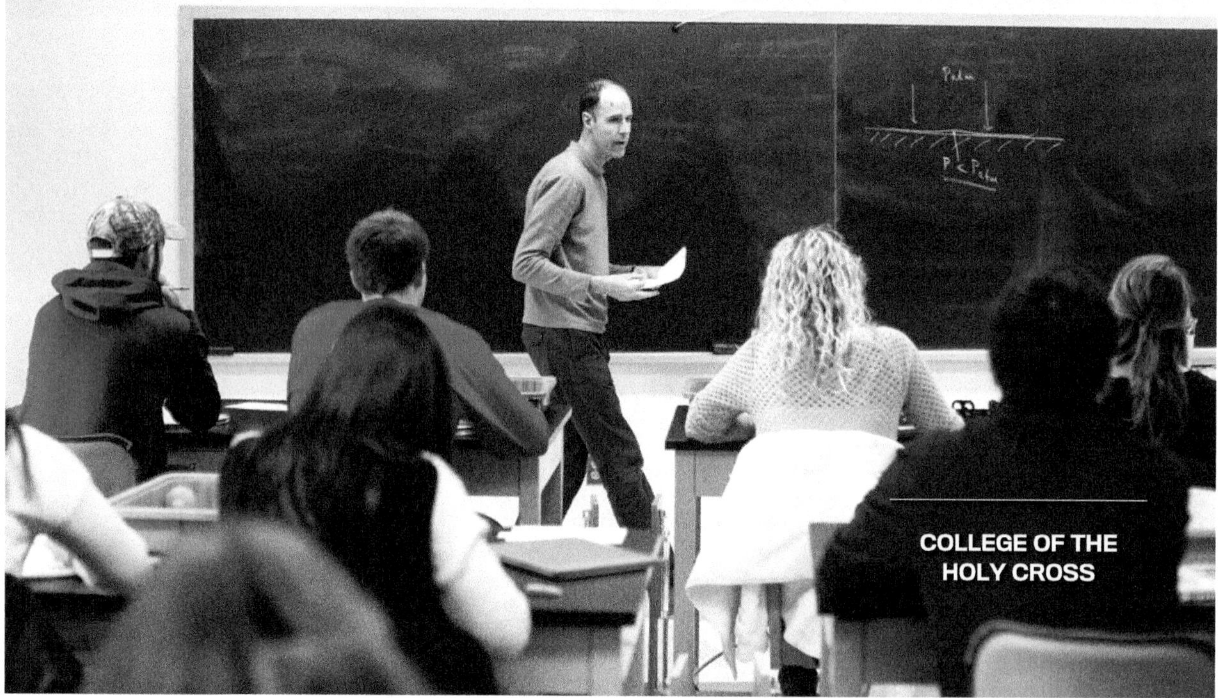

COLLEGE OF THE HOLY CROSS

BRETT ZIEGLER FOR USN&WR

sports; and the cost and availability of financial aid. But if you combine the information in this book with campus visits, interviews and your own intuition, our rankings can be a powerful tool in your quest for the right college.

How does the methodology work? The U.S. News ranking system rests on two pillars. The formula uses quantitative measures that education experts have proposed as reliable indicators of academic quality, and it's based on our researched view of what matters in education. First, schools are categorized by their mission, which is derived from the breakdown of types of higher education institutions developed by the Carnegie Foundation for the Advancement of Teaching. The Carnegie classification has been the basis of the Best Colleges ranking categories since our first ranking was published over three decades ago, given that it is used extensively by higher education researchers. The U.S. Department of Education and many higher education associations use the system to organize their data and to determine colleges' eligibility for grant money, for example.

In short, the Carnegie categories are the accepted standard. The category names we use are our own – National Universities, National Liberal Arts Colleges, Regional Universities and Regional Colleges – but the definitions of each rely on the Carnegie principles.

The national universities (Page 74) offer a full range of undergraduate majors plus master's and Ph.D. programs and emphasize faculty research. The national liberal arts colleges (Page 82) focus almost exclusively on undergraduate education. They award at least 50 percent of their degrees in the arts and sciences.

The regional universities (Page 92) offer a broad scope of undergraduate degrees and some master's degree programs but few, if any, doctoral programs. The regional colleges (Page 108) focus on undergraduate education but grant fewer than 50 percent of their degrees in liberal arts disciplines; this category also includes schools that have small bachelor's degree programs but primarily grant two-year associate degrees. The regional universities and regional colleges are further divided and ranked in four geographical groups: North, South, Midwest and West.

Next, we gather data from each college on up to 16 indicators of academic excellence. Each factor is assigned a weight that reflects our judgment about how much a measure matters. Finally, the colleges and universities in each category are ranked against their peers, based on their composite weighted score.

Some schools are not ranked and thus do not appear in the tables. The main reason a school falls into this group is that SAT or ACT test scores are not used in admissions decisions for first-time, first-year, degree-seeking applicants. In a few cases, colleges were ineligible because they received too few ratings in the peer assessment survey to be reliably ranked or had a total enrollment of fewer than 200 students, a large proportion of nontraditional students, or no first-year students (as is the situation at so-called upper-division schools). Schools that have test-optional admission policies are included in the rankings since they do use SAT or ACT scores when provided. As a result of these eligibility standards, many of the for-profit institutions are not ranked; their bachelor's degree candidates are largely nontraditional students in degree-completion programs, for example, or they don't use test scores in making admissions decisions. We also did not rank a number of highly specialized schools in the arts, business and engineering.

Most of the data come from the colleges themselves, via the U.S. News statistical survey. This year, 92.7 percent of the 1,376 ranked colleges and universities returned their statistical information during our spring and summer data collection period.

For colleges that were eligible to be ranked but declined to fill out our survey, we made extensive use of the data those institutions reported to the U.S. Department of Education's National Center for Education Statistics and other organizations. We obtained missing data on graduation rates from the National Collegiate Athletic Association and data on alumni giving from the Council for Aid to Education, for example. The National Center for Education Statistics provided data on SAT and ACT scores, acceptance rates, retention and graduation rates, faculty, student-faculty ratios, and information on financial resources.

Data that did not come from this year's survey are footnoted, and schools are identified as nonresponders. Estimates may be used in the calculations when schools fail to report data points that are not available from other sources, but estimates are not displayed in the tables. Missing data are reported as N/A.

The indicators we use to capture academic quality fall

Weighing What's Important

The U.S. News rankings are based on several key measures of quality, listed below. Scores for each measure are weighted as shown to arrive at a final overall score. In the case of the national universities and national liberal arts colleges, the assessment figure represents input from both academic peers (15 percent) and high school guidance counselors (7.5 percent); for regional universities and colleges, it reflects peer opinion only.

The Scoring Breakdown

Assessment of excellence......................22.5%
Graduation and retention rates 22.5%
Faculty resources 20%
Student selectivity 12.5%
Financial resources.................................. 10%
Graduation rate performance* 7.5%
Alumni giving 5%

*The difference between actual and predicted graduation rates.

into a number of categories: assessment by administrators at peer institutions (and, for national universities and liberal arts colleges, by high school guidance counselors as well), how well schools perform at retaining and graduating students, the quality of and investment in the faculty, student selectivity, financial resources, and the state of alumni giving. The indicators include input measures that reflect a school's student body, its faculty and its resources, along with outcome measures that signal how well the institution does its job of educating students.

An explanation of the measures and their weightings in the ranking formula follows; more detail on the methodology can be found at usnews.com/collegemeth.

Assessment by peers and counselors (22.5 percent). The ranking formula gives significant weight to the opinions of those in a position to judge a school's undergraduate academic excellence. The academic peer assessment survey allows presidents, provosts and deans of admission to account for intangibles at peer institutions such as faculty dedication to teaching. This year the academic peer scores are based on the two most recent sets of survey results, collected in spring 2014 and spring 2015. Using two years of data reduces year-to-year volatility in the results.

THE U.S. NEWS RANKINGS PROVIDE AN EXCELLENT STARTING POINT FOR A COLLEGE SEARCH.

For their views on the national universities and the national liberal arts colleges, we also surveyed 2,200 counselors at public high schools that appeared in a recent U.S. News ranking of Best High Schools and 400 college counselors at the largest independent schools.

Each person surveyed was asked to rate schools' academic programs on a 5-point scale from 1 (marginal) to 5 (distinguished). Those who didn't know enough about a school to evaluate it fairly were asked to mark "don't know." The score used in the rankings is the average of these scores; "don't knows" are not counted.

In the case of the national universities and national liberal arts colleges, the academic peer assessment accounts for 15 percentage points of the weighting, and 7.5 percentage points go to the counselors' ratings. The three most recent years' results were averaged to compute the high school counselor score (up from two). For the full results of the high school counselors' ratings of the colleges, visit usnews.com/counselors. The regional universities and the regional colleges are judged by peers only.

In order to reduce the impact of strategic voting by respondents, we eliminated the two highest and two lowest scores each school received before calculating the average score. Ipsos Public Affairs collected the most recent year's data in the spring of 2015; of the 4,530 academics who were sent questionnaires, 40 percent responded. The counselors' response rate for just this past spring was 7 percent.

Retention (22.5 percent). The higher the proportion of freshmen who return to campus for sophomore year and eventually graduate, the better a school most likely is at offering the classes and services that students need to succeed. This measure has two components: six-year graduation rate (80 percent of the retention score) and freshman retention rate (20 percent).

The graduation rate indicates the average proportion of a graduating class earning a degree in six years or less. We consider freshman classes that started from fall 2005 through fall 2008. Freshman retention indicates the average proportion of freshmen who entered the school in the fall of 2010 through fall 2013 and returned the following fall.

Faculty resources (20 percent). Research shows that the more satisfied students are about their contact with professors, the more they will learn and the more likely they are to graduate. We use six factors from the 2014-2015 academic year to assess a school's commitment to instruction.

Class size has two components, the proportion of classes with fewer than 20 students (30 percent of the faculty resources score) and the proportion with 50 or more students (10 percent of the score). Faculty salary (35 percent) is the average faculty pay, plus benefits, during the 2013-14 and 2014-2015 academic years, adjusted for regional differences in the cost of living using indexes from the consulting firm Runzheimer International.

We also weigh the proportion of professors with the highest degree in their field (15 percent), the student-faculty ratio (5 percent) and the proportion of faculty who are full time (5 percent).

Student selectivity (12.5 percent). A school's academic atmosphere is determined in part by the abilities and ambitions of the students. We factor in the admissions test scores for all enrollees who took the critical reading and math portions of the SAT and the composite ACT score (65 percent of the selectivity

score); the proportion of enrolled freshmen at national universities and national liberal arts colleges who graduated in the top 10 percent of their high school classes or in the top quarter at regional universities and regional colleges (25 percent); and the acceptance rate, or the ratio of students admitted to applicants (10 percent). The data are all for the fall 2014 entering class. While the ranking calculation takes account of both the SAT and ACT scores of all entering students, the table displays the score range for whichever test was taken by most students. Footnotes clearly indicate the schools that did not report fall 2014 SAT and ACT test scores for all new students for whom they had scores (including athletes, international students, minority students, legacies, those admitted by special arrangement, and those who started in the summer of 2014) or schools that declined to tell us whether all students with scores were represented. We discount the value of these schools' reported scores in the ranking model since the effect of leaving students out could be that lower scores are omitted.

Financial resources (10 percent). Generous per-student spending indicates that a college can offer a wide variety of programs and services. U.S. News measures financial resources by using the average spending per student on instruction, research, student services and related educational expenditures in the 2013 and 2014 fiscal years. Spending on sports, dorms and hospitals doesn't count.

Graduation rate performance (7.5 percent). This indicator shows the effect of programs and policies on the graduation rate after controlling for spending and student characteristics such as test scores and the proportion receiving Pell grants.

We measure the difference between a school's six-year graduation rate for the class that entered in 2008 and the rate we predicted for the class. If the actual graduation rate is higher than the predicted rate, then the college is enhancing achievement.

Alumni giving rate (5 percent). This reflects the average percentage of living alumni with bachelor's degrees who gave to their school during 2012-13 and 2013-2014, an indirect measure of student satisfaction.

To arrive at a school's rank, we calculated the weighted sum of its scores. The final scores were rescaled so that the top college or university in each category received a value of 100, and the other schools' weighted scores were calculated as a proportion of that top score. Final scores were rounded to the nearest whole number and ranked in descending order. Schools that are tied appear in alphabetical order.

Be sure to check out usnews.com regularly over the coming year, since we may add content to the Best Colleges pages as we obtain additional information. And as you mine the tables that follow for insights (a sense of which schools might be impressed enough by your SAT or ACT scores to offer some merit aid, for example, or where you will be apt to get the most attention from professors), keep in mind that the rankings provide a launching pad for more research – not an easy answer. ●

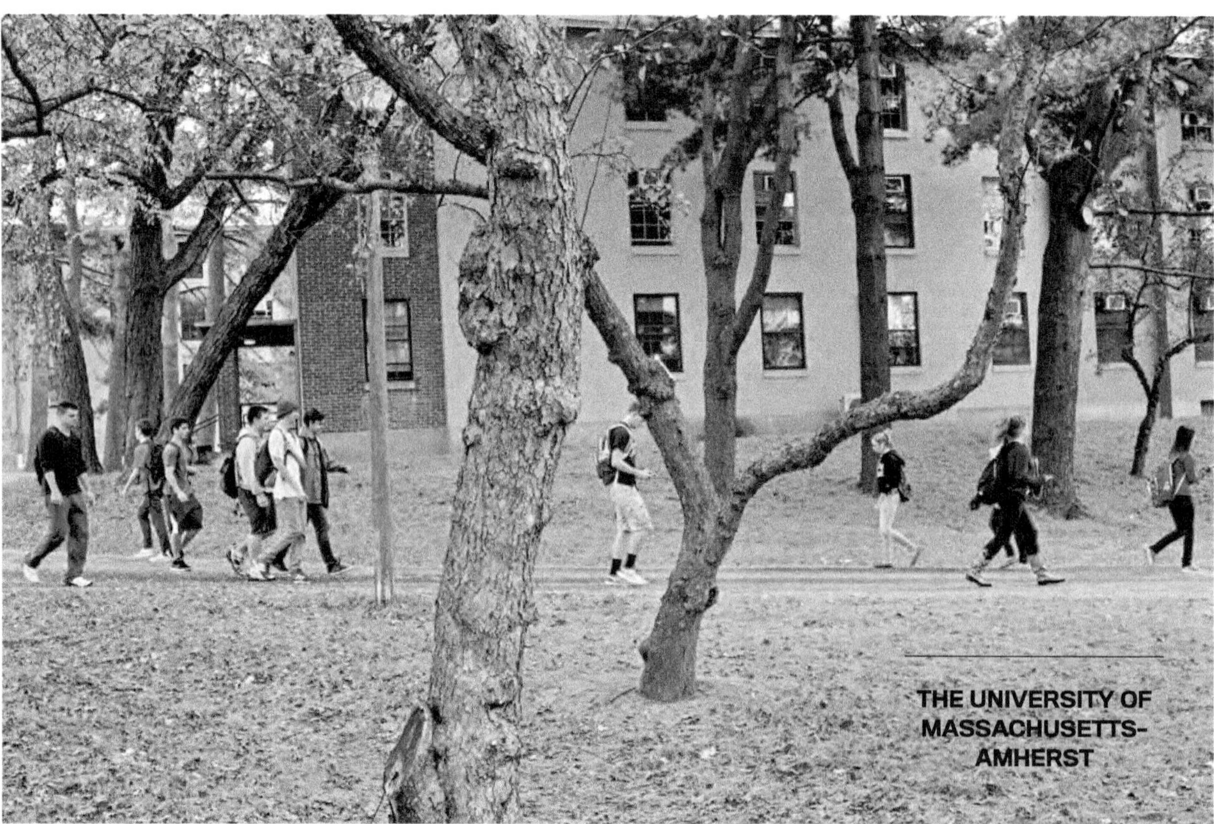

THE UNIVERSITY OF MASSACHUSETTS-AMHERST

MATT SLABY – LUCEO FOR USN&WR

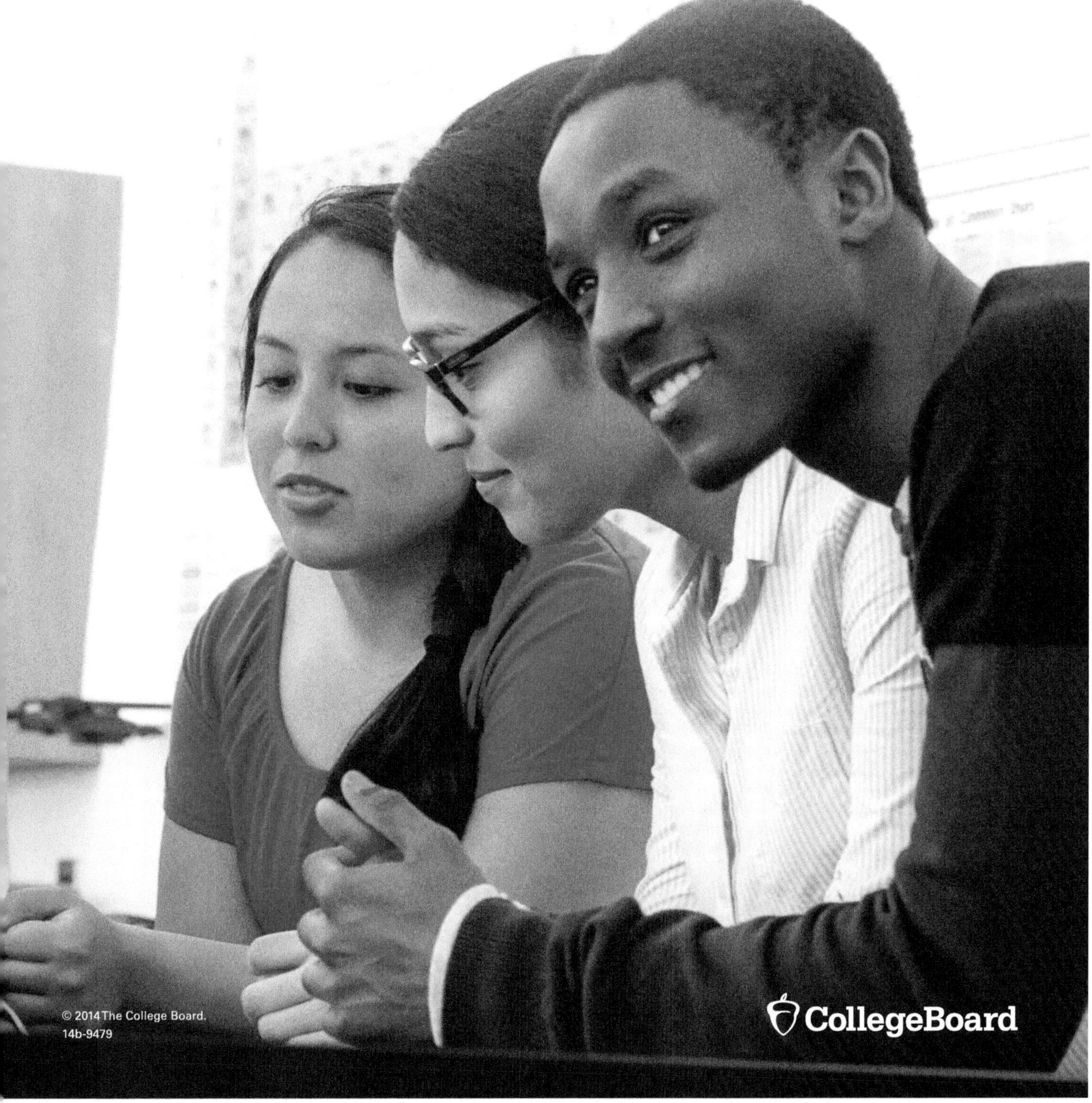

Best National Univer

Rank	School (State) (*Public)	Overall score	Peer assessment score (5.0=highest)	High school counselor assessment score	Graduation and retention rank	Average freshman retention rate	2014 graduation rate: Predicted	2014 graduation rate: Actual	2014 graduation rate: Over-performance(+) Under-performance(-)	Faculty resources rank
1.	**Princeton University** (NJ)	100	4.8	4.9	3	98%	96%	97%	+1	5
2.	**Harvard University** (MA)	99	4.9	5.0	1	97%	95%	98%	+3	4
3.	**Yale University** (CT)	97	4.8	4.9	1	99%	96%	96%	None	9
4.	**Columbia University** (NY)	95	4.6	4.9	5	99%	94%	96%	+2	3
4.	**Stanford University** (CA)	95	4.9	4.9	5	98%	95%	95%	None	10
4.	**University of Chicago**	95	4.5	4.7	11	99%	94%	93%	-1	1
7.	**Massachusetts Inst. of Technology**	93	4.9	5.0	16	98%	96%	91%	-5	15
8.	**Duke University** (NC)	92	4.4	4.8	10	97%	95%	95%	None	1
9.	**University of Pennsylvania**	91	4.4	4.8	3	98%	97%	96%	-1	7
10.	**California Institute of Technology**	90	4.6	4.7	20	97%	96%	92%	-4	11
10.	**Johns Hopkins University** (MD)	90	4.6	4.9	16	97%	93%	94%	+1	18
12.	**Dartmouth College** (NH)	89	4.2	4.8	5	98%	95%	95%	None	13
12.	**Northwestern University** (IL)	89	4.3	4.7	11	97%	94%	94%	None	5
14.	**Brown University** (RI)	85	4.4	4.8	5	98%	95%	96%	+1	17
15.	**Cornell University** (NY)	84	4.5	4.8	16	97%	94%	93%	-1	20
15.	**Vanderbilt University** (TN)	84	4.1	4.7	16	97%	93%	93%	None	12
15.	**Washington University in St. Louis**	84	4.0	4.6	11	97%	97%	95%	-2	13
18.	**Rice University** (TX)	82	4.0	4.5	20	97%	93%	93%	None	8
18.	**University of Notre Dame** (IN)	82	3.9	4.7	5	98%	94%	96%	+2	16
20.	**University of California–Berkeley***	77	4.7	4.7	23	97%	92%	91%	-1	33
21.	**Emory University** (GA)	76	4.0	4.4	28	95%	93%	91%	-2	20
21.	**Georgetown University** (DC)	76	4.0	4.8	11	96%	95%	95%	None	38
23.	**Carnegie Mellon University** (PA)	74	4.2	4.7	32	95%	90%	88%	-2	24
23.	**Univ. of California–Los Angeles***	74	4.2	4.4	23	97%	90%	91%	+1	30
23.	**Univ. of Southern California**	74	3.9	4.4	23	97%	92%	91%	-1	43
26.	**University of Virginia***	73	4.2	4.5	11	97%	92%	94%	+2	35
27.	**Tufts University** (MA)	72	3.6	4.5	20	96%	93%	92%	-1	30
27.	**Wake Forest University** (NC)	72	3.5	4.4	34	94%	87%	88%	+1	35
29.	**University of Michigan–Ann Arbor***	71	4.4	4.4	23	97%	92%	91%	-1	67
30.	**Boston College**	68	3.6	4.4	23	95%	90%	91%	+1	51
30.	**U. of North Carolina–Chapel Hill***	68	4.0	4.5	28	97%	88%	90%	+2	86
32.	**New York University**	67	3.8	4.5	40	92%	87%	82%	-5	19
33.	**University of Rochester** (NY)	66	3.4	4.0	38	96%	88%	84%	-4	20
34.	**Brandeis University** (MA)	65	3.5	4.1	31	94%	91%	91%	None	48
34.	**College of William and Mary** (VA)*	65	3.7	4.4	28	96%	90%	90%	None	54
36.	**Georgia Institute of Technology***	64	4.1	4.4	49	96%	86%	82%	-4	116
37.	**Case Western Reserve Univ.** (OH)	63	3.5	4.3	65	93%	85%	81%	-4	46
37.	**Univ. of California–Santa Barbara***	63	3.5	3.9	54	92%	84%	87%	+3	20
39.	**University of California–Irvine***	62	3.6	4.1	36	93%	85%	87%	+2	28
39.	**Univ. of California–San Diego***	62	3.8	4.1	36	95%	89%	86%	-3	111
41.	**Boston University**	61	3.4	4.2	40	93%	82%	85%	+3	39
41.	**Rensselaer Polytechnic Inst.** (NY)	61	3.4	4.2	40	93%	86%	82%	-4	39
41.	**Tulane University** (LA)	61	3.4	4.2	74	90%	85%	83%	-2	25
41.	**University of California–Davis***	61	3.8	4.2	47	93%	84%	87%	+3	82
41.	**U. of Illinois–Urbana-Champaign***	61	3.9	4.0	40	94%	82%	84%	+2	58
41.	**Univ. of Wisconsin–Madison***	61	4.1	4.1	40	95%	83%	85%	+2	86
47.	**Lehigh University** (PA)	60	3.2	4.1	32	95%	93%	87%	-6	39
47.	**Northeastern University** (MA)	60	3.2	4.2	54	96%	80%	82%	+2	28
47.	**Pennsylvania State U.–Univ. Park***	60	3.6	4.1	38	92%	71%	86%	+15	102
47.	**University of Florida***	60	3.6	3.8	34	96%	84%	88%	+4	82

Note: Key to footnotes, Page 80.

sities

% of classes under 20 ('14)	% of classes of 50 or more ('14)	Student/ faculty ratio ('14)	Selectivity rank	SAT/ACT 25th-75th percentile ('14)	Freshmen in top 10% of HS class ('14)	Acceptance rate ('14)	Financial resources rank	Alumni giving rank	Average alumni giving rate
72%	11%	6/1	4	1400-1600	96%[5]	7%	10	1	63%
74%	10%	7/1	4	1410-1600	95%[5]	6%	4	11	35%
75%	9%	6/1	4	1410-1600	96%[5]	6%	1	13	34%
82%	9%	6/1	8	1390-1570	93%[5]	7%	12	13	34%
70%	11%	4/1	4	1380-1570	95%[5]	5%	7	9	36%
77%	6%	6/1	2	1430-1590	98%	9%	6	4	41%
67%	14%	8/1	2	1420-1570	97%[5]	8%	7	5	37%
73%	6%	7/1	13	1370-1550	91%[5]	11%	15	11	35%
67%	10%	6/1	8	1360-1550	93%[5]	10%	12	13	33%
65%	9%	3/1	1	1500-1600	100%[5]	9%	2	33	22%
72%	10%	10/1	16	1360-1530	88%[5]	15%	3	9	35%
64%	8%	7/1	8	1360-1550	93%[5]	12%	15	2	46%
76%	7%	7/1	13	1390-1560	90%[5]	13%	9	20	26%
68%	10%	9/1	13	1330-1550	92%[5]	9%	24	6	36%
55%	18%	9/1	20	1330-1510	87%[5]	14%	17	17	30%
66%	9%	8/1	8	32-34	91%[5]	13%	14	18	27%
66%	11%	8/1	8	32-34	92%[5]	17%	4	26	24%
68%	8%	6/1	16	1390-1550	88%[5]	15%	22	16	30%
58%	10%	10/1	16	32-34	90%[5]	21%	27	3	42%
59%	15%	17/1	20	1290-1490	98%	16%	39	84	13%
61%	9%	8/1	26	1280-1460	81%[5]	27%	17	26	24%
61%	7%	11/1	20	1320-1520	92%[5]	17%	32	18	27%
65%	11%	13/1	24	1340-1540	79%[5]	25%	32	54	17%
51%	22%	17/1	25	1190-1460	97%	19%	20	106	11%
57%	13%	9/1	23	1280-1480	88%[4]	18%	25	6	36%
55%	15%	15/1	26	1250-1460	89%[5]	29%	67	35	21%
69%	7%	9/1	16	1360-1520	90%[5]	17%	27	37	20%
55%	1%	11/1	36	1210-1420[2]	77%[5]	34%	11	24	25%
48%	18%	15/1	31	29-33	73%[5]	32%	41	43	19%
52%	7%	12/1	26	1270-1460	81%[5]	34%	69	20	26%
39%	15%	13/1	36	1210-1400	78%	29%	32	50	18%
61%	8%	10/1	49	1240-1450	54%[5]	35%	32	139	9%
69%	12%	10/1	34	1240-1450[2]	72%[4]	36%	22	46	18%
62%	10%	10/1[4]	36	1250-1480	71%[5]	35%	51	20	26%
48%	9%	12/1	31	1270-1470	81%[5]	33%	113	26	24%
39%	25%	19/1	26	1310-1490	79%[5]	33%	44	20	26%
62%	13%	11/1	34	1270-1470	68%[5]	38%	27	35	21%
49%	18%	17/1	40	1120-1380	100%	36%	67	62	16%
58%	20%	19/1	63	1040-1310	96%	37%	51	182	6%
38%	36%	19/1	30	1180-1420	100%	33%	21	167	7%
60%	12%	13/1	55	1190-1410	59%[5]	35%	47	127	9%
52%	12%	15/1	36	1300-1490	69%[5]	38%	47	93	13%
65%	6%	9/1	45	29-32	56%[5]	28%	61	50	17%
35%	27%	18/1	55	1080-1350	100%	41%	32	156	8%
42%	20%	18/1	49	26-32	59%[5]	59%	56	119	10%
46%	20%	17/1	58	26-31	52%	50%	62	106	11%
49%	11%	10/1	46	1230-1410	62%[5]	34%	56	37	21%
64%	8%	14/1	31	1340-1500	66%[5]	32%	78	98	12%
38%	15%	16/1	93	1090-1290	40%[5]	50%	56	74	15%
49%	16%	21/1	49	1170-1360	75%	47%	45	56	16%

What Is a National University?

To assess nearly 1,600 of the country's four-year colleges and universities, U.S. News first assigns each to a group of its peers, based on the categories of higher education institutions developed in 2010 by the Carnegie Foundation for the Advancement of Teaching. The National Universities category consists of the 280 institutions (173 public, 100 private and seven for-profit) that offer a wide range of undergraduate majors as well as master's and doctoral degrees; some emphasize research. A list of the top 30 public national universities appears on Page 80.

Data on up to 16 indicators of academic quality are gathered from each institution and tabulated. Schools are ranked by their total weighted score; those receiving the same rank are tied and listed in alphabetical order. For a description of the methodology, see Page 68, and for more on a college, turn to the directory at the back of the book.

BEST NATIONAL UNIVERSITIES

Rank	School (State) (*Public)	Overall score	Peer assessment score (5.0=highest)	High school counselor assessment score	Average freshman retention rate	2014 graduation rate: Predicted	2014 graduation rate: Actual	% of classes under 20 ('14)	% of classes of 50 or more ('14)	SAT/ACT 25th-75th percentile ('14)	Freshmen in top 10% of HS class ('14)	Acceptance rate ('14)	Average alumni giving rate
51.	University of Miami (FL)	59	3.2	3.9	92%	85%	81%	52%	8%	1220-1420	66%[5]	38%	16%
52.	Ohio State University–Columbus*	58	3.7	4.1	93%	77%	83%	30%	22%	27-31	61%	53%	15%
52.	Pepperdine University (CA)	58	3.2	4.3	92%	77%	84%	69%	2%	1120-1330	46%[5]	35%	8%
52.	University of Texas–Austin*	58	4.0	4.2	94%	83%	81%	37%	25%	1170-1390	69%	40%	11%
52.	University of Washington*	58	3.8	4.0	93%	84%	84%	35%	22%	1110-1350	92%[5]	55%	13%
52.	Yeshiva University (NY)	58	2.7	3.4	91%	78%	89%	62%	1%	1120-1360	39%	82%	16%
57.	George Washington University (DC)	56	3.4	4.3	93%	86%	79%	57%	10%	1200-1390	52%[5]	44%	8%
57.	University of Connecticut*	56	3.1	4.0	93%	74%	81%	52%	15%	1150-1350	50%[5]	50%	16%
57.	Univ. of Maryland–College Park*	56	3.6	4.1	95%	86%	85%	45%	16%	1210-1420	73%	48%	7%
57.	Worcester Polytechnic Inst. (MA)	56	2.9	4.0	96%	81%	85%	66%	10%	1210-1410[2]	68%	44%	13%
61.	Clemson University (SC)*	55	3.1	4.0	91%	78%	82%	52%	14%	1160-1350	53%	53%	23%
61.	Purdue Univ.–West Lafayette (IN)*	55	3.6	4.2	92%	69%	74%	39%	18%	1080-1330	42%[5]	59%	19%
61.	Southern Methodist University (TX)	55	3.0	3.9	90%	78%	77%	59%	7%	28-31	46%[5]	52%	22%
61.	Syracuse University (NY)	55	3.3	4.0	92%	72%	80%	63%	9%	1070-1280	37%[5]	53%	16%
61.	University of Georgia*	55	3.4	4.0	94%	78%	85%	39%	12%	1140-1330	52%	56%	11%
66.	Brigham Young Univ.–Provo (UT)	54	3.0	3.9	88%	77%	79%	57%	14%	27-31	55%	47%	13%
66.	Fordham University (NY)	54	3.2	4.1	89%	76%	80%	48%	2%	1150-1350	47%[5]	48%	17%
66.	University of Pittsburgh*	54	3.4	3.8	92%	78%	82%	40%	20%	1180-1360	54%	53%	11%
69.	Univ. of Minnesota–Twin Cities*	53	3.7	3.9	91%	75%	78%	38%	20%	26-30	47%	45%	10%
70.	Texas A&M Univ.–College Station*	52	3.6	4.1	91%	77%	79%	22%	26%	1060-1310	65%	71%	22%
70.	Virginia Tech*	52	3.4	4.1	92%	75%	83%	28%	20%	1110-1320	41%	73%	12%
72.	American University (DC)	51	3.0	4.0	89%	80%	82%	50%	1%	1150-1340[2]	69%	46%	8%
72.	Baylor University (TX)	51	3.2	4.1	87%	73%	72%	49%	9%	24-30	39%	55%	18%
72.	Rutgers, St. U. of N.J.–New Brunswick*	51	3.4	4.0	92%	73%	80%	38%	20%	1090-1340[3]	39%[5]	61%	8%
75.	Clark University (MA)	49	2.8	3.8	89%	73%	78%	56%	5%	1108-1333[2]	37%[5]	54%	19%
75.	Colorado School of Mines*	49	3.3	4.2	91%	80%	76%	27%	19%	28-32	58%[5]	36%	16%
75.	Indiana University–Bloomington*	49	3.6	4.0	89%	69%	78%	36%	18%	1060-1290	33%[5]	76%	13%
75.	Michigan State University*	49	3.5	3.9	91%	68%	79%	24%	24%	23-28	31%[5]	66%	10%
75.	Stevens Institute of Technology (NJ)	49	2.7	3.8	95%	79%	82%	34%	10%	1255-1425	70%[5]	44%	15%
75.	University of Delaware*	49	3.1	3.8	92%	76%	81%	32%	15%	1100-1300	37%[5]	66%	9%
75.	Univ. of Massachusetts–Amherst*	49	3.2	3.9	89%	67%	76%	45%	19%	1120-1310	33%[5]	61%	10%
82.	Miami University–Oxford (OH)*	48	3.1	3.9	90%	70%	79%	33%	10%	25-30	34%[5]	66%	20%
82.	Texas Christian University	48	2.8	3.8	89%	71%	76%	40%	6%	24-30	42%[5]	49%	20%
82.	Univ. of California–Santa Cruz*	48	3.0	3.8	90%	81%	80%	50%	22%	1010-1280	96%	57%	6%
82.	University of Iowa*	48	3.5	3.8	86%	70%	70%	51%	13%	23-28	29%	81%	9%
86.	Marquette University (WI)	47	3.0	3.9	90%	73%	79%	36%	14%	25-29	32%[5]	67%	15%
86.	University of Denver	47	2.8	3.6	87%	75%	76%	56%	7%	25-30	42%[5]	76%	9%
86.	University of Tulsa (OK)	47	2.6	3.6	88%	83%	70%	62%	3%	26-32	75%[5]	40%	20%
89.	Binghamton University–SUNY*	46	2.9	3.8	91%	79%	81%	44%	15%	1210-1370	48%[5]	44%	7%
89.	North Carolina State U.–Raleigh*	46	3.1	3.7	92%	72%	76%	28%	17%	1160-1330	52%	51%	13%
89.	Stony Brook–SUNY*	46	3.2	3.6	90%	71%	69%	45%	20%	1150-1350	48%[5]	41%	10%
89.	SUNY Col. of Envir. Sci. and Forestry*	46	2.8	3.7	85%	67%	68%	67%	10%	1090-1280	28%	51%	22%
89.	University of Colorado–Boulder*	46	3.5	3.8	84%	70%	70%	48%	15%	24-30	27%[5]	84%	8%
89.	University of San Diego	46	2.8	3.8	89%	74%	77%	41%	0.1%	1130-1320	45%[5]	46%	12%
89.	University of Vermont*	46	2.9	3.7	86%	71%	76%	52%	13%	1080-1290	29%[5]	73%	10%
96.	Florida State University*	45	3.0	3.5	92%	70%	79%	33%	16%	26-29	40%	55%	18%
96.	Saint Louis University	45	2.9	3.8	88%	72%	72%	50%	9%	25-30	43%[5]	60%	13%
96.	University of Alabama*	45	3.1	3.7	87%	67%	66%	41%	19%	22-31	41%	51%	36%
99.	Drexel University (PA)	44	3.0	3.9	85%	72%	67%	57%	9%	1090-1300	29%[5]	76%	8%
99.	Loyola University Chicago	44	2.9	4.0	86%	71%	73%	39%	7%	25-29	34%[5]	63%	9%
99.	University at Buffalo–SUNY*	44	3.0	3.7	88%	67%	72%	36%	20%	1050-1250	29%[5]	58%	8%
102.	Auburn University (AL)*	43	3.2	3.9	90%	73%	71%	32%	16%	24-30	29%	83%	12%
103.	Univ. of Missouri*	42	3.2	3.7	85%	69%	69%	40%	17%	23-28	27%	78%	15%
103.	Univ. of Nebraska–Lincoln*	42	3.2	3.7	84%	67%	67%	39%	17%	22-28	24%	70%	20%
103.	University of New Hampshire*	42	2.8	3.6	86%	64%	77%	43%	17%	1000-1200	17%	80%	7%
103.	University of Oregon*	42	3.3	3.8	86%	63%	69%	41%	20%	990-1230	23%[5]	75%	9%
103.	University of Tennessee*	42	3.1	3.8	86%	74%	69%	28%	14%	24-29	50%[5]	75%	10%
108.	Illinois Institute of Technology	41	2.7	3.7	93%	75%	65%	56%	8%	25-31	45%[5]	51%	9%
108.	Iowa State University*	41	3.2	3.8	87%	67%	69%	31%	24%	21-29	26%	87%	13%
108.	University of Dayton (OH)	41	2.6	3.4	89%	69%	76%	34%	4%	24-29	24%[5]	59%	15%
108.	University of Oklahoma*	41	3.0	3.7	85%	72%	67%	42%	11%	23-29	35%	81%	18%
108.	University of San Francisco	41	2.8	3.8	87%	66%	70%	49%	2%	1040-1250	22%[4]	60%	7%
108.	Univ. of South Carolina*	41	2.9	3.7	88%	70%	73%	39%	16%	1110-1300	29%	65%	16%
108.	University of the Pacific (CA)	41	2.5	3.6	85%	69%	67%	53%	5%	1038-1313	37%[5]	55%	10%

Note: Key to footnotes, Page 80.

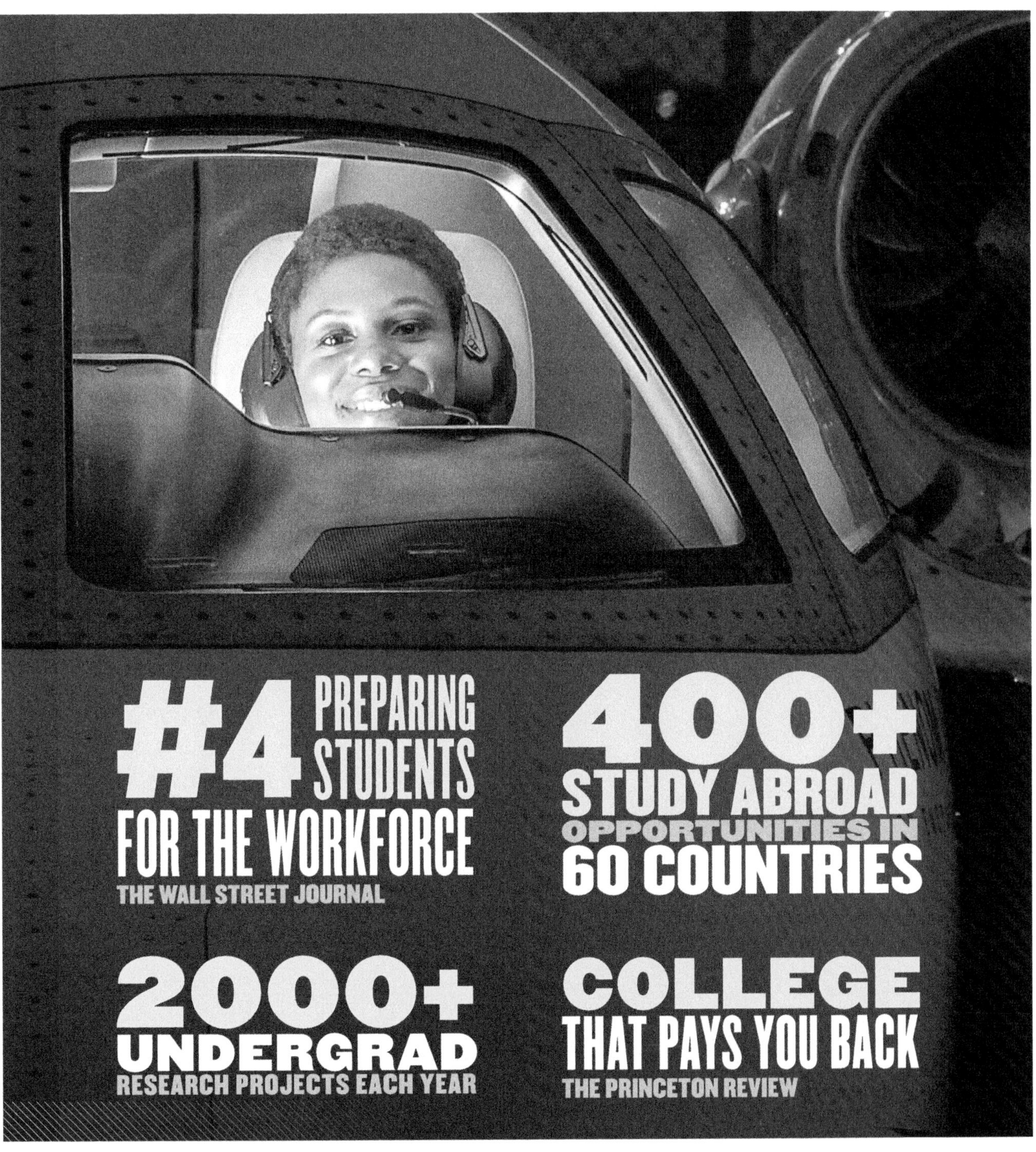
#4 PREPARING STUDENTS
FOR THE WORKFORCE
THE WALL STREET JOURNAL
400+
STUDY ABROAD
OPPORTUNITIES IN
60 COUNTRIES
2000+
UNDERGRAD
RESEARCH PROJECTS EACH YEAR
COLLEGE
THAT PAYS YOU BACK
THE PRINCETON REVIEW

Rank	School (State) (*Public)	Overall score	Peer assessment score (5.0=highest)	High school counselor assessment score	Average freshman retention rate	2014 graduation rate: Predicted	2014 graduation rate: Actual	% of classes under 20 ('14)	% of classes of 50 or more ('14)	SAT/ACT 25th-75th percentile ('14)	Freshmen in top 10% of HS class ('14)	Acceptance rate ('14)	Average alumni giving rate
115.	**Clarkson University** (NY)	40	2.6	3.6	88%	71%	73%	42%	23%	1090-1290	41%	62%	14%
115.	**Duquesne University** (PA)	40	2.6	3.6	89%	64%	76%	41%	9%	1040-1230[2]	30%	73%	7%
115.	**Temple University** (PA)*	40	2.9	3.8	88%	60%	69%	38%	8%	1010-1230[2]	21%[5]	62%	6%
115.	**University of Kansas***	40	3.3	3.7	80%	68%	60%	45%	11%	22-28	26%	91%	15%
115.	**University of St. Thomas** (MN)	40	2.5	3.5	87%	66%	72%	39%	2%	24-29	29%[5]	87%	18%
115.	**University of Utah***	40	3.0	3.5	88%	64%	62%	50%	15%	21-28	22%[5]	81%	10%
121.	**University of Arizona***	39	3.5	3.7	80%	64%	60%	39%	15%	970-1220[2]	31%[5]	75%	6%
121.	**Univ. of California–Riverside***	39	3.1	3.7	89%	69%	69%	20%	36%	1010-1250	94%	58%	4%
123.	**Catholic University of America** (DC)	38	2.7	3.6	82%	64%	67%	59%	5%	1020-1230	N/A	75%	8%
123.	**DePaul University** (IL)	38	2.8	3.7	86%	64%	71%	40%	1%	23-28[2]	21%[5]	70%	7%
123.	**Michigan Technological University***	38	2.6	3.9	83%	70%	64%	46%	14%	25-30	31%	76%	11%
123.	**Seton Hall University** (NJ)	38	2.7	3.8	84%	62%	66%	47%	2%	1040-1220	38%[5]	76%	8%
127.	**Colorado State University***	37	2.9	3.5	85%	63%	65%	38%	18%	22-27	21%	80%	10%
127.	**New School** (NY)	37	2.7	3.9	83%	61%	66%	90%	1%	990-1240[2]	15%[5]	66%	2%
129.	**Arizona State University–Tempe***	36	3.2	3.5	84%	61%	63%	41%	18%	1020-1270[2]	30%	84%	9%
129.	**Louisiana State Univ.–Baton Rouge***	36	2.8	3.5	84%	68%	67%	37%	21%	23-28	25%	77%	10%
129.	**University at Albany–SUNY***	36	2.8	3.6	83%	60%	66%	23%	17%	1010-1180	18%[5]	56%	7%
129.	**University of Arkansas***	36	2.8	3.4	82%	70%	62%	46%	17%	23-28	26%	62%	26%
129.	**University of Illinois–Chicago***	36	3.0	3.6	79%	55%	60%	39%	19%	22-27[3]	24%	73%	4%
129.	**University of Kentucky***	36	2.9	3.7	82%	64%	60%	30%	16%	22-28	30%	72%	16%
135.	**George Mason University** (VA)*	35	2.9	3.9	87%	62%	67%	31%	14%	1050-1250[2]	26%[5]	67%	4%
135.	**Hofstra University** (NY)	35	2.7	3.7	79%	69%	60%	51%	3%	1050-1230[2]	28%[5]	62%	11%
135.	**Howard University** (DC)	35	2.8	4.0	82%	60%	60%	52%	6%	990-1220	26%[5]	48%	6%
135.	**Ohio University***	35	2.9	3.6	80%	56%	67%	33%	18%	22-26	15%	74%	7%
135.	**Oregon State University***	35	2.9	3.6	83%	57%	63%	29%	21%	980-1230	27%	78%	10%
140.	**New Jersey Inst. of Technology***	34	2.6	3.5	84%	65%	59%	34%	6%	1080-1300	26%[5]	63%	8%
140.	**Rutgers, The State U. of N.J.–Newark***	34	2.7	3.8	85%	59%	66%	28%	18%	940-1130[3]	20%	63%	4%
140.	**University of Cincinnati***	34	2.7	3.4	86%	63%	65%	44%	13%	23-28	20%	76%	13%
140.	**University of Mississippi***	34	2.7	3.5	83%	56%	61%	44%	16%	21-27[2]	22%	81%	15%
140.	**University of Texas–Dallas***	34	2.6	3.7	86%	74%	71%	24%	25%	1140-1370	38%	62%	2%
140.	**Washington State University***	34	3.0	3.5	82%	67%	67%	36%	21%	910-1130	35%[5]	80%	13%
146.	**Kansas State University***	33	2.9	3.6	82%	64%	59%	40%	13%	22-28[2]	22%	95%	24%
146.	**Missouri Univ. of Science & Tech.***	33	2.6	3.6	84%	74%	63%	27%	22%	26-31	40%	86%	15%[4]
146.	**St. John Fisher College** (NY)	33	2.2	3.2	85%	59%	70%	48%	1%	970-1160	18%	68%	14%
149.	**Illinois State University***	32	2.4	3.4	83%	62%	72%	34%	11%	22-26	N/A	74%	7%
149.	**Oklahoma State University***	32	2.7	3.5	80%	65%	61%	34%	16%	22-28	26%	75%	13%
149.	**San Diego State University***	32	2.8	3.6	89%	52%	67%	29%	25%	1000-1220	29%[5]	34%	5%
149.	**University of Alabama–Birmingham***	32	2.7	3.4	81%	64%	55%	40%	17%	21-27	28%	86%	12%
153.	**Adelphi University** (NY)	31	2.2	3.3	82%	59%	64%	55%	2%	1010-1220[9]	29%[5]	72%	8%
153.	**Southern Illinois U.–Carbondale***	31	2.4	3.2	64%	32%	44%	62%	5%	19-26	14%	82%	5%
153.	**St. John's University** (NY)	31	2.7	3.7	79%	58%	59%	38%	6%	990-1210	19%[5]	63%	5%
156.	**Univ. of Maryland–Baltimore County***	30	2.8	3.6	87%	69%	61%	38%	12%	1110-1310	25%[5]	60%	4%
156.	**Univ. of Massachusetts–Lowell***	30	2.4	3.5	82%	56%	54%	50%	6%	1050-1240	23%[5]	62%	11%
156.	**University of South Florida***	30	2.6	3.3	89%	63%	67%	32%	14%	1070-1250	30%	47%	9%
156.	**Virginia Commonwealth University***	30	2.8	3.7	86%	58%	59%	34%	16%	1000-1210[2]	19%	69%	5%
160.	**University of La Verne** (CA)	29	1.9	3.3	86%	48%	59%	66%	0.3%	930-1100	20%[5]	47%	5%
161.	**Biola University** (CA)	28	1.8	3.5	86%	65%	71%	49%	7%	980-1240	30%[5]	75%	11%
161.	**Florida Institute of Technology**	28	2.3	3.3	79%	61%	55%	51%	6%	1020-1260	31%[5]	62%	12%
161.	**Immaculata University** (PA)	28	1.9	3.0	81%	45%	61%	83%	0.4%	870-1060	N/A	76%	11%
161.	**Maryville Univ. of St. Louis**	28	1.8	3.3	86%	62%	66%	71%	0.2%	23-27	28%	72%	6%
161.	**Mississippi State University***	28	2.5	3.3	81%	63%	60%[6]	38%	14%	21-28	28%	71%	16%
161.	**University of Hawaii–Manoa***	28	2.7	3.2	79%	61%	56%	49%	13%	980-1190[3]	27%	78%	6%
161.	**University of Rhode Island***	28	2.7	3.5	82%	59%	59%	33%	11%	1010-1200[3]	19%	76%	6%
168.	**Ball State University** (IN)*	27	2.5	3.3	79%	52%	60%	41%	8%	1000-1190[2]	19%	60%	12%
168.	**Texas Tech University***	27	2.7	3.6	82%	61%	59%	25%	20%	1000-1200	20%	66%	14%
168.	**University of Central Florida***	27	2.6	3.1	88%	67%	70%	29%	24%	1090-1280	31%	50%	7%
168.	**University of Idaho***	27	2.6	3.4	78%	57%	58%	49%	10%	910-1170	20%	67%	9%
168.	**University of Louisville** (KY)*	27	2.7	3.5	79%	64%	54%	32%	9%	22-28[3]	26%[5]	72%	14%
168.	**University of Maine***	27	2.5	3.4	78%	58%	60%	41%	16%	960-1190	20%	83%	7%[7]
168.	**University of Wyoming***	27	2.6	3.4	75%	63%	54%	40%	12%	22-27	19%	98%	9%
175.	**Andrews University** (MI)	26	1.7	3.3	79%	58%	60%	69%	4%	20-27	21%[5]	37%	6%
175.	**Azusa Pacific University** (CA)	26	1.9	3.4	85%	62%	67%	63%	2%	980-1080	25%	82%	N/A
175.	**Edgewood College** (WI)	26	1.7	3.1	81%	51%	62%	79%	0.4%	20-25	17%	76%	10%
175.	**Kent State University** (OH)*	26	2.5	3.3	78%	45%	55%	54%	8%	20-25	15%	84%	4%

Note: Key to footnotes, Page 80.

Rank	School (State) (*Public)	Overall score	Peer assessment score (5.0=highest)	High school counselor assessment score	Average freshman retention rate	2014 graduation rate: Predicted	2014 graduation rate: Actual	% of classes under 20 ('14)	% of classes of 50 or more ('14)	SAT/ACT 25th-75th percentile ('14)	Freshmen in top 10% of HS class ('14)	Acceptance rate ('14)	Average alumni giving rate
175.	**West Virginia University***	26	2.7	3.2	77%	58%	57%	36%	18%	21-26	19%[5]	86%	11%
180.	**Pace University** (NY)	25	2.3	3.5	77%	58%	55%	50%	2%	950-1150[2]	14%[5]	85%	5%
180.	**St. Mary's Univ. of Minnesota**	25	2.0	3.5	78%	56%	65%	57%	0%	20-26	16%[5]	74%	12%
180.	**University of New Mexico***	25	2.7	3.6	77%	52%	48%	33%	15%	20-25	N/A	46%	4%
180.	**University of North Dakota***	25	2.5	3.6	77%	58%	54%	41%	8%	21-26[3]	17%	86%	10%
180.	**University of South Dakota***	25	2.4	3.5	76%	55%	57%	52%	6%	20-25	15%	89%	7%
185.	**Bowling Green State University** (OH)*	24	2.5	3.4	72%	49%	54%	43%	8%	20-25	13%	53%	7%
185.	**North Dakota State University***	24	2.4	3.6	79%	57%	56%	32%	21%	21-26[3]	17%	83%	10%
187.	**South Dakota State University***	23	2.3	3.5	75%	56%	58%[8]	30%	16%	20-26	13%	92%	15%[4]
187.	**University of Alabama–Huntsville***	23	2.4	3.4	79%	62%	46%	38%	13%	24-30	29%[5]	82%	2%
187.	**University of Houston***	23	2.5	3.3	84%	55%	48%	30%	23%	1040-1250	32%	63%	12%
187.	**University of Nevada–Reno***	23	2.3	3.1	80%	58%	55%	36%	17%	960-1190	23%	84%	9%
187.	**U. of North Carolina–Greensboro***	23	2.5	3.5	76%	51%	56%	41%	17%	940-1100	16%	60%	5%[7]
187.	**Western Michigan University***	23	2.3	3.2	75%	50%	54%	37%	11%	19-25	12%	84%	4%
187.	**Widener University** (PA)	23	2.0	3.2	74%	51%	53%	63%	2%	920-1130	12%	65%	3%
194.	**Central Michigan University***	22	2.2	3.2	76%	50%	56%	33%	9%	20-25	15%	69%	5%
194.	**East Carolina University** (NC)*	22	2.2	3.2	80%	50%	59%	30%	16%	950-1110	13%	77%	4%
194.	**South Carolina State University***	22	2.1	3.3	63%	22%	38%	52%	2%	15-18	6%	85%	N/A
194.	**Univ. of Missouri–Kansas City***	22	2.5	3.3	73%	64%	51%	53%	11%	21-27	29%	64%	7%
194.	**U. of North Carolina–Charlotte***	22	2.6	3.6	79%	52%	55%	25%	25%	1000-1170	23%	64%	4%
199.	**Ashland University** (OH)	21	1.7	3.1	74%	52%	57%	60%	0%	20-25	18%	72%	5%
199.	**Indiana U.-Purdue U.–Indianapolis***	21	2.8	3.7	72%	50%	44%	36%	11%	880-1120	15%	70%	8%
199.	**Louisiana Tech University***	21	2.2	3.2	78%	57%	54%	51%	8%	21-27	24%	65%	13%
199.	**New Mexico State University***	21	2.4	3.4	73%	43%	46%	47%	11%	18-24	19%	70%	6%
199.	**University of Colorado–Denver***	21	2.7	3.5	74%	56%	40%	35%	8%	20-25	18%[5]	73%	3%

School (State) (*Public)	Peer assessment score (5.0=highest)	High school counselor assessment score	Average freshman retention rate	2014 graduation rate: Predicted	2014 graduation rate: Actual	% of classes under 20 ('14)	% of classes of 50 or more ('14)	SAT/ACT 25th-75th percentile ('14)	Freshmen in top 10% of HS class ('14)	Acceptance rate ('14)	Average alumni giving rate
SECOND TIER (SCHOOLS RANKED 204 THROUGH 268 ARE LISTED HERE ALPHABETICALLY)											
Barry University (FL)	1.9	3.1	58%[8]	42%	36%	68%[4]	1%[4]	840-1023	N/A	46%	4%
Benedictine University (IL)	1.9	3.4	75%	56%	51%	72%	0.3%	19-25[3]	12%[5]	77%	5%
Bowie State University (MD)*	1.9	3.2	73%	31%	37%[6]	45%	1%	881-960[3]	N/A	54%	5%
Cardinal Stritch University (WI)	1.7	3.2	69%[8]	52%	49%	83%	0.2%	19-24[2]	10%	83%	4%
Clark Atlanta University	2.1	3.3	63%	36%	41%	44%	4%	770-930	7%[5]	85%	N/A
Cleveland State University*	2.1	2.9	67%	45%	39%	36%[4]	11%[4]	19-25[4]	12%	67%	4%
East Tennessee State University*	2.0	3.1	68%	51%	43%	46%	8%	19-25	19%	92%	3%
Florida A&M University*	2.0	3.3	81%	38%	40%	33%	14%	18-22	13%[5]	49%	5%
Florida Atlantic University*	2.2	3.1	77%	50%	46%	22%	19%	960-1140	12%	66%	3%
Florida International University*	2.2	3.3	83%	65%	54%	22%	22%	1030-1200	21%[5]	48%	7%
Georgia Southern University*	2.2	3.1	80%	57%	51%	27%	10%	1030-1180[3]	19%[5]	63%	7%
Georgia State University*	2.6	3.5	83%	58%	54%	17%	15%	950-1180[3]	18%	57%	5%
Indiana State University*	2.4	3.4	62%	39%	40%	29%	12%	810-1020	9%	83%	6%
Indiana Univ. of Pennsylvania*	2.0	3.0	75%	44%	53%	33%	14%	860-1060[3]	8%	95%	6%
Jackson State University (MS)*	1.8	2.8	78%[8]	37%	43%	53%	7%	17-21[3]	N/A	26%	4%
Lamar University (TX)*	2.0	2.9	59%	37%	33%	33%	9%	870-1080	15%	78%	2%
Lynn University (FL)	1.7	2.8	67%	37%	39%	39%	0.2%	870-1075[2]	10%[5]	75%	7%
Middle Tennessee State Univ.*	2.1	3.1	70%	49%	46%	42%	7%	19-25[3]	19%[5]	72%	5%[4]
Montana State University*	2.5	3.4	75%	61%	50%	41%	14%	21-28	19%	84%	8%
Morgan State University (MD)*	1.9	3.1	74%	34%	33%	34%	2%	800-960[9]	4%	65%	14%
National Louis University[1] (IL)	1.7	2.8	72%[8]	28%	38%[6]	N/A	N/A	N/A[2]	N/A	N/A	N/A
North Carolina A&T State Univ.*	2.0	3.1	77%	33%	47%	33%	7%	830-990	11%	58%	6%
Northern Arizona University*	2.4	3.3	74%	56%	52%	34%	11%	930-1150[2]	21%	91%	4%
Northern Illinois University*	2.3	3.2	70%	50%	50%	49%	10%	19-25[3]	11%	51%	5%
Nova Southeastern University (FL)	1.7	2.7	72%	48%	46%	78%	0.1%	1010-1240	31%	49%	2%
Oakland University (MI)*	2.1	3.1	75%	51%	46%	36%	15%	20-26	16%	67%	4%
Old Dominion University (VA)*	2.6	3.5	80%	52%	52%	33%	10%	920-1120	10%	82%	6%
Our Lady of the Lake University (TX)	1.6	3.4	63%	39%	38%	60%	0%	840-1030	13%	50%	14%
Portland State University (OR)*	2.5	3.5	73%[8]	52%	39%	32%	16%	910-1160[2]	13%	85%	3%[7]
Regent University (VA)	1.8	3.4	77%	53%	53%	62%	0%	910-1130	8%[5]	80%	4%
Sam Houston State University (TX)*	2.0	3.2	76%	45%	53%	29%	13%	880-1070[3]	14%	74%	9%
Spalding University[1] (KY)	1.7	3.3	73%[8]	34%	41%[6]	N/A	N/A	880-1045[4]	N/A	81%[4]	N/A

School (State) (*Public)	Peer assessment score (5.0=highest)	High school counselor assessment score	Average freshman retention rate	2014 graduation rate Predicted	2014 graduation rate Actual	% of classes under 20 ('14)	% of classes of 50 or more ('14)	SAT/ACT 25th-75th percentile ('14)	Freshmen in top 10% of HS class ('14)	Acceptance rate ('14)	Average alumni giving rate
SECOND TIER CONTINUED (SCHOOLS RANKED 204 THROUGH 268 ARE LISTED HERE ALPHABETICALLY)											
Tennessee State University*	1.9	3.2	62%[8]	30%	33%[8]	50%	2%	15-20	N/A	53%	N/A
Texas A&M University–Commerce*	2.1	3.7	69%	42%	52%	40%	4%	870-1080[3]	11%	48%	4%
Texas A&M Univ.–Corpus Christi*	2.0	3.7	58%	42%	38%	22%	18%	870-1070[3]	10%	61%	N/A
Texas A&M Univ.–Kingsville*	2.0	3.6	62%	35%	36%	41%	5%	17-21	11%	84%	18%
Texas Southern University*	1.9	3.2	58%	12%	16%	37%	14%	730-900[3]	6%	51%	2%
Texas Woman's University*	2.2	3.4	69%	47%	47%	46%	10%	840-1060[9]	14%	85%	1%[4]
Trevecca Nazarene University (TN)	1.5	3.3	74%	51%	51%	68%	3%	20-26[3]	N/A	73%	7%
Trinity International Univ. (IL)	1.7	3.2	73%[8]	56%	46%	73%	0.4%	20-26	12%[5]	97%	7%[4]
University of Akron (OH)*	2.2	3.1	70%	45%	41%	41%	8%	19-26	16%	96%	14%
University of Alaska–Fairbanks*	2.4	3.2	76%	52%	43%	66%	4%	19-26	18%	74%	5%
Univ. of Arkansas–Little Rock*	2.2	3.1	78%[8]	52%	24%	73%	3%	22	N/A	62%	2%
University of Louisiana–Lafayette*	2.1	3.1	75%	44%	48%	37%	8%	21-25	19%	56%	7%
Univ. of Massachusetts–Boston*	2.5	3.6	78%	56%	42%	35%	6%	950-1150	N/A	71%	5%
University of Memphis*	2.3	3.3	77%	50%	42%	45%	10%	20-26	16%	49%	5%
Univ. of Missouri–St. Louis*	2.4	3.3	78%	57%	42%	47%	8%	21-27	29%	76%	5%
University of Montana*	2.6	3.4	73%	55%	50%	47%	11%	20-26[3]	18%	94%	6%
University of Nebraska–Omaha*	2.5	3.4	74%	55%	45%	36%	11%	19-26	14%	79%	5%
University of Nevada–Las Vegas*	2.4	3.2	77%	52%	39%	21%	19%	880-1110	21%	87%	5%
University of New Orleans*	2.0	3.2	67%	53%	34%	33%	14%	21-25	16%	44%	2%
University of Northern Colorado*	2.2	3.3	68%[8]	51%	46%	28%	13%	19-25[2]	12%	71%	4%
University of North Texas*	2.4	3.2	77%	58%	50%	26%	23%	990-1210[3]	20%	62%	5%
University of South Alabama*	2.0	2.8	68%	53%	37%	43%	8%	20-25[2]	N/A	84%	N/A
Univ. of Southern Mississippi*	2.2	3.1	73%	51%	48%	45%	9%	19-25	19%[5]	67%	9%
University of Texas–Arlington*	2.5	3.5	74%	54%	42%	31%	23%	910-1178	27%	61%	2%
University of Texas–El Paso*	2.2	3.3	74%[8]	38%	38%[6]	34%	16%	17-23[3]	18%	100%	N/A
University of Texas–San Antonio*	2.4	3.5	63%	48%	31%	17%	31%	930-1150	19%	76%	5%
University of Toledo (OH)*	2.3	3.1	66%	50%	44%	35%	13%	19-25	17%	95%	4%
University of West Florida*	2.0	3.0	72%	55%	51%	32%	8%	21-26[3]	17%	42%	4%
Univ. of Wisconsin–Milwaukee*	2.7	3.5	70%	50%	44%	43%	10%	19-24	9%	75%	4%
Utah State University*	2.5	3.3	70%	59%	49%	47%	13%	20-26	19%	98%	6%
Wayne State University (MI)*	2.5	3.3	76%	44%	34%	53%	8%	20-26	21%	77%	5%
Wichita State University (KS)*	2.4	3.2	72%	57%	44%	45%	11%	21-26[2]	21%	96%	7%
Wright State University (OH)*	2.2	3.2	62%	46%	39%	44%	13%	18-25	15%	97%	4%

▶ The Top 30 Public National Universities

Rank School (State)

1. **University of California–Berkeley**
2. **Univ. of California–Los Angeles**
3. **University of Virginia**
4. **University of Michigan–Ann Arbor**
5. **University of North Carolina–Chapel Hill**
6. **College of William and Mary** (VA)
7. **Georgia Institute of Technology**
8. **Univ. of California–Santa Barbara**
9. **University of California–Irvine**
9. **Univ. of California–San Diego**
11. **University of California–Davis**
11. **University of Illinois–Urbana-Champaign**
11. **Univ. of Wisconsin–Madison**
14. **Pennsylvania State U.–Univ. Park**
14. **University of Florida**
16. **Ohio State University–Columbus**
16. **University of Texas–Austin**
16. **University of Washington**
19. **University of Connecticut**
19. **Univ. of Maryland–College Park**
21. **Clemson University** (SC)
21. **Purdue Univ.–West Lafayette** (IN)
21. **University of Georgia**
24. **University of Pittsburgh**
25. **Univ. of Minnesota–Twin Cities**
26. **Texas A&M Univ.–College Station**
26. **Virginia Tech**
28. **Rutgers, State University of New Jersey–New Brunswick**
29. **Colorado School of Mines**
29. **Indiana University–Bloomington**
29. **Michigan State University**
29. **University of Delaware**
29. **Univ. of Massachusetts–Amherst**

Footnotes:
1. School refused to fill out U.S. News statistical survey. Data that appear are from school in previous years or from another source such as the National Center for Education Statistics.
2. SAT and/or ACT not required by school for some or all applicants.
3. In reporting SAT/ACT scores, the school did not include all students for whom it had scores or refused to tell U.S. News whether all students with scores had been included.
4. Data reported to U.S. News in previous years.
5. Data based on fewer than 51 percent of enrolled freshmen.
6. Some or all data reported to the NCAA and/or the National Center for Education Statistics.
7. Data reported to the Council for Aid to Education.
8. This rate, normally based on four years of data, is given here for less than four years because school didn't report rate for the most recent year or years to U.S. News.
9. SAT and/or ACT may not be required by school for some or all applicants, and in reporting SAT/ACT scores, the school did not include all students for whom it had scores or refused to tell U.S. News whether all students with scores had been included.

N/A means not available.

Best National Liberal

Rank	School (State) (*Public)	Overall score	Peer assessment score (5.0=highest)	High school counselor assessment score	Graduation and retention rank	Average freshman retention rate	2014 graduation rate: Predicted	2014 graduation rate: Actual	2014 graduation rate: Over-performance(+) Under-performance(-)	Faculty resources rank
1.	**Williams College** (MA)	100	4.7	4.7	3	97%	94%	95%	+1	2
2.	**Amherst College** (MA)	96	4.6	4.5	1	98%	90%	94%	+4	14
3.	**Swarthmore College** (PA)	94	4.6	4.5	4	96%	95%	94%	-1	12
4.	**Bowdoin College** (ME)	92	4.4	4.5	4	97%	93%	93%	None	15
4.	**Middlebury College** (VT)	92	4.3	4.3	4	96%	97%	94%	-3	18
4.	**Pomona College** (CA)	92	4.4	4.4	1	98%	93%	93%	None	23
4.	**Wellesley College** (MA)	92	4.4	4.6	10	96%	90%	91%	+1	20
8.	**Carleton College** (MN)	91	4.3	4.4	4	97%	90%	93%	+3	12
9.	**Claremont McKenna College** (CA)	89	4.1	4.5	10	96%	94%	90%	-4	6
9.	**Davidson College** (NC)	89	4.1	4.3	9	96%	93%	93%	None	4
9.	**United States Naval Academy** (MD)*	89	4.1	4.8	20	97%	69%	89%	+20	58
12.	**Haverford College** (PA)	88	4.0	4.3	4	97%	95%	94%	-1	20
12.	**Vassar College** (NY)	88	4.2	4.6	10	96%	87%	92%	+5	23
14.	**Hamilton College** (NY)	86	3.9	4.3	15	95%	91%	91%	None	8
14.	**Harvey Mudd College** (CA)	86	4.3	4.6	15	98%	95%	94%	-1	67
14.	**Smith College** (MA)	86	4.3	4.6	36	94%	84%	87%	+3	23
14.	**Washington and Lee University** (VA)	86	3.8	4.1	20	96%	96%	88%	-8	2
14.	**Wesleyan University** (CT)	86	4.1	4.4	10	95%	85%	93%	+8	20
19.	**Colby College** (ME)	85	4.0	4.3	15	94%	87%	90%	+3	17
19.	**Colgate University** (NY)	85	4.0	4.4	15	95%	88%	92%	+4	8
19.	**Grinnell College** (IA)	85	4.2	4.2	28	94%	85%	89%	+4	23
22.	**United States Military Academy** (NY)*	83	4.1	4.8	45	95%	81%	80%	-1	52
23.	**Macalester College** (MN)	82	4.0	4.3	24	94%	86%	90%	+4	37
23.	**Oberlin College** (OH)	82	4.1	4.3	30	93%	88%	87%	-1	23
25.	**Bates College** (ME)	81	4.0	4.3	20	94%	84%	88%	+4	52
25.	**Bryn Mawr College** (PA)	81	4.0	4.3	51	91%	86%	82%	-4	28
25.	**Colorado College**	81	3.8	4.1	28	95%	89%	86%	-3	6
25.	**Kenyon College** (OH)	81	3.8	4.2	24	96%	87%	89%	+2	33
29.	**Barnard College** (NY)	80	3.9	4.4	15	96%	87%	89%	+2	58
29.	**Scripps College** (CA)	80	3.7	4.3	30	93%	90%	87%	-3	18
29.	**United States Air Force Acad.** (CO)*	80	4.0	4.7	45	92%	85%	84%	-1	104
32.	**Bucknell University** (PA)	79	3.8	4.3	20	94%	89%	89%	None	75
32.	**College of the Holy Cross** (MA)	79	3.6	4.1	10	95%	84%	92%	+8	40
32.	**University of Richmond** (VA)	79	3.8	4.0	41	94%	85%	84%	-1	8
35.	**Mount Holyoke College** (MA)	78	4.0	4.2	51	91%	83%	80%	-3	37
36.	**Pitzer College** (CA)	77	3.6	4.3	41	92%	81%	84%	+3	33
37.	**Lafayette College** (PA)	76	3.4	4.0	24	94%	89%	90%	+1	47
38.	**Skidmore College** (NY)	75	3.5	4.2	30	94%	77%	87%	+10	43
38.	**Union College** (NY)	75	3.3	4.0	36	93%	83%	86%	+3	28
40.	**Dickinson College** (PA)	74	3.6	4.1	45	90%	82%	84%	+2	33
40.	**Franklin and Marshall College** (PA)	74	3.6	4.0	38	92%	84%	87%	+3	52
40.	**Whitman College** (WA)	74	3.4	4.0	30	94%	88%	87%	-1	40
43.	**Occidental College** (CA)	73	3.7	4.0	38	93%	83%	85%	+2	87
43.	**Trinity College** (CT)	73	3.6	4.1	41	90%	82%	84%	+2	82
45.	**Bard College** (NY)	72	3.4	4.0	82	87%	87%	75%	-12	15
45.	**Centre College** (KY)	72	3.5	4.1	45	91%	81%	82%	+1	94
45.	**Soka University of America** (CA)	72	2.3	3.1	30	96%	78%	79%	+1	1
48.	**Connecticut College**	71	3.5	4.1	45	90%	87%	83%	-4	58
48.	**Gettysburg College** (PA)	71	3.4	3.9	41	90%	87%	84%	-3	47
48.	**Sewanee–University of the South** (TN)	71	3.5	4.1	61	89%	82%	79%	-3	47

Note: Key to footnotes, Page 89.

Arts Colleges

% of classes under 20 ('14)	% of classes of 50 or more ('14)	Student/ faculty ratio ('14)	Selectivity rank	SAT/ACT 25th-75th percentile ('14)	Freshmen in top 10% of HS class ('14)	Acceptance rate ('14)	Financial resources rank	Alumni giving rank	Average alumni giving rate
77%	3%	7/1	1	1350-1560	95%[5]	19%	5	3	57%
71%	2%	8/1	4	1350-1550	84%[5]	14%	10	9	49%
75%	2%	8/1	4	1360-1540	88%[5]	17%	7	16	43%
70%	2%	9/1	19	1370-1520[2]	86%[5]	15%	11	4	54%
67%	2%	9/1	9	1260-1470	76%[5]	17%	3	5	53%
69%	2%	8/1	1	1380-1540	91%[5]	12%	6	41	33%
67%	1%	7/1	9	1290-1480	78%[5]	30%	7	7	51%
71%	1%	9/1	12	1320-1510	70%[5]	23%	27	7	51%
82%	1%	8/1	7	1350-1520	78%[4]	11%	13	17	41%
74%	0.2%	10/1	15	1230-1440	74%[5]	22%	27	5	53%
70%	0.1%	8/1	21	1180-1390	59%	8%	2	121	19%
77%	3%	9/1	4	1330-1490	94%[5]	25%	11	15	45%
65%	1%	8/1	12	1320-1490	70%	24%	16	46	31%
74%	1%	9/1	12	1310-1470	75%[5]	26%	20	19	40%
58%	5%	9/1	3	1418-1570	88%[5]	14%	17	54	29%
68%	6%	9/1	28	1240-1470[2]	62%[5]	42%	17	38	34%
72%	0%	8/1	7	1320-1460	81%[5]	20%	23	12	48%
72%	3%	8/1	18	1290-1480[2]	64%[5]	24%	46	17	41%
72%	2%	10/1	24	1230-1430[2]	61%[5]	28%	27	22	40%
74%	2%	9/1	37	1280-1470[3]	72%[5]	26%	32	19	40%
65%	0%	9/1	15	30-33	69%[5]	28%	22	41	33%
95%	0%	7/1	32	1160-1390	52%	9%	7	54	29%
71%	1%	10/1	19	1270-1465	65%[5]	36%	48	32	36%
74%	2%	9/1	24	1260-1450	61%[5]	33%	35	46	31%
65%	4%	10/1	41	1280-1430[2]	69%[5]	25%	43	14	47%
74%	3%	8/1	28	1200-1440[2]	65%[5]	40%	17	27	37%
69%	0.2%	10/1	15	28-32[2]	69%[5]	18%	32	108	21%
70%	1%	10/1	21	1230-1420	65%[5]	25%	35	25	38%
72%	9%	10/1	9	1250-1440	82%[5]	24%	54	71	26%
83%	1%	10/1	33	1260-1460[3]	83%[5]	27%	23	27	37%
68%	0%	8/1	24	28-32	56%	17%	4	168	13%
57%	2%	9/1	21	1210-1400	68%[5]	31%	40	46	31%
68%	1%	10/1	57	1230-1380[2]	56%[5]	43%	50	9	49%
67%	0%	8/1	28	1220-1430	59%[5]	32%	23	82	24%
71%	2%	10/1	35	1220-1450[2]	56%[5]	55%	40	51	30%
71%	0%	10/1	46	1240-1420[2]	60%[5]	13%	27	32	36%
57%	1%	10/1	28	1200-1400	63%[5]	30%	32	41	33%
73%	1%	8/1	47	1130-1350	43%[5]	37%	46	71	25%
66%	1%	10/1	24	1210-1400[2]	70%[5]	41%	50	44	32%
75%	0%	9/1	43	1190-1370[2]	46%[5]	48%	54	64	26%
63%	1%	9/1	53	1220-1390[2]	62%[4]	39%	40	64	27%
69%	0%	9/1	37	1200-1430	53%[5]	41%	60	34	35%
59%	0.2%	10/1	35	1210-1390	55%[5]	42%	60	97	22%
62%	2%	10/1	50	1150-1340	43%[5]	33%	23	57	28%
78%	1%	10/1	64	1170-1390[2]	60%[5]	45%	13	27	37%
60%	0%	10/1	43	26-31	53%[5]	72%	73	12	48%
95%	0%	8/1	70	1090-1370	28%[5]	43%	1	113	20%
68%	1%	9/1	57	1250-1410[2]	48%[5]	38%	43	57	28%
68%	1%	10/1	33	1210-1360	70%[5]	45%	54	89	23%
56%	1%	10/1	57	26-30[2]	35%[5]	65%	63	34	35%

What Is a National Liberal Arts College?

The country's 245 liberal arts colleges emphasize undergraduate education and award at least half of their degrees in the arts and sciences, which include such disciplines as English, the biological and physical sciences, history, foreign languages and the visual and performing arts but exclude professional disciplines such as business, education and nursing. There are 217 private and 27 public liberal arts colleges; one is for-profit. The top public colleges appear below.

The Top Public Colleges

Rank School (State)

1. **United States Naval Academy** (MD)
2. **United States Military Academy** (NY)
3. **United States Air Force Acad.** (CO)
4. **New College of Florida**
4. **Virginia Military Institute**
6. **St. Mary's College of Maryland**
7. **University of Minnesota–Morris**
8. **U. of North Carolina–Asheville**
9. **Purchase College–SUNY**

BEST NATIONAL LIBERAL ARTS COLLEGES

Rank	School (State) (*Public)	Overall score	Peer assessment score (5.0=highest)	High school counselor assessment score	Average freshman retention rate	2014 graduation rate: Predicted	2014 graduation rate: Actual	% of classes under 20 ('14)	% of classes of 50 or more ('14)	SAT/ACT 25th-75th percentile ('14)	Freshmen in top 10% of HS class ('14)	Acceptance rate ('14)	Average alumni giving rate
51.	**DePauw University** (IN)	69	3.3	3.9	92%	80%	80%	69%	0%	25-29	48%	57%	27%
51.	**Furman University** (SC)	69	3.4	3.9	89%	84%	84%	58%	0%	1130-1340[2]	38%	69%	25%
51.	**Rhodes College** (TN)	69	3.5	4.1	91%	81%	80%	68%	1%	27-31	48%[5]	60%	38%
51.	**St. Olaf College** (MN)	69	3.6	4.0	94%	82%	89%	58%	4%	26-32	52%[5]	51%	21%
55.	**Denison University** (OH)	68	3.3	3.9	90%	80%	82%	73%	0%	26-31[9]	45%[5]	51%	23%
55.	**St. John's College** (MD)	68	3.4	4.0	86%	75%	70%	99%	1%	1200-1440[2]	33%[5]	87%	21%
57.	**Lawrence University** (WI)	67	3.1	3.9	89%	75%	80%	76%	2%	25-31[2]	42%[5]	73%	32%
57.	**Sarah Lawrence College** (NY)	67	3.4	4.2	87%	72%	77%	93%	1%	1160-1380[2]	41%[5]	53%	18%
57.	**Wheaton College** (IL)	67	3.2	4.0	95%	81%	89%	59%	5%	27-32	52%[5]	69%	24%
60.	**St. Lawrence University** (NY)	66	3.2	3.7	91%	77%	85%	64%	1%	1110-1290[2]	37%[5]	48%	26%
61.	**Beloit College** (WI)	65	3.2	3.8	89%	74%	80%	72%	0%	24-30[2]	42%[5]	69%	23%
61.	**College of Wooster** (OH)	65	3.2	3.8	89%	71%	76%	70%	1%	25-30	41%[5]	59%	25%
61.	**Earlham College** (IN)	65	3.3	3.9	85%	71%	72%	80%	2%	1150-1370[2]	40%[5]	65%	25%
61.	**Hobart & William Smith Colleges** (NY)	65	3.2	3.9	86%	72%	79%	66%	0%	1140-1320[2]	30%[5]	50%	28%
61.	**Wabash College** (IN)	65	3.3	3.8	86%	72%	73%	74%	2%	1020-1240	29%	70%	40%
66.	**Kalamazoo College** (MI)	64	3.3	3.9	92%	77%	82%	61%	1%	25-30	35%[5]	70%	27%
67.	**Agnes Scott College** (GA)	63	3.1	3.7	83%	68%	74%	73%	0%	1060-1260[2]	37%[5]	68%	39%
67.	**Berea College** (KY)	63	3.3	3.5	82%	48%	62%	76%	0%	22-27	24%	34%	16%
67.	**Hillsdale College** (MI)	63	2.5	3.5	96%	78%	82%	71%	0.2%	27-31	50%[5]	53%	13%

BRETT ZIEGLER FOR USN&WR

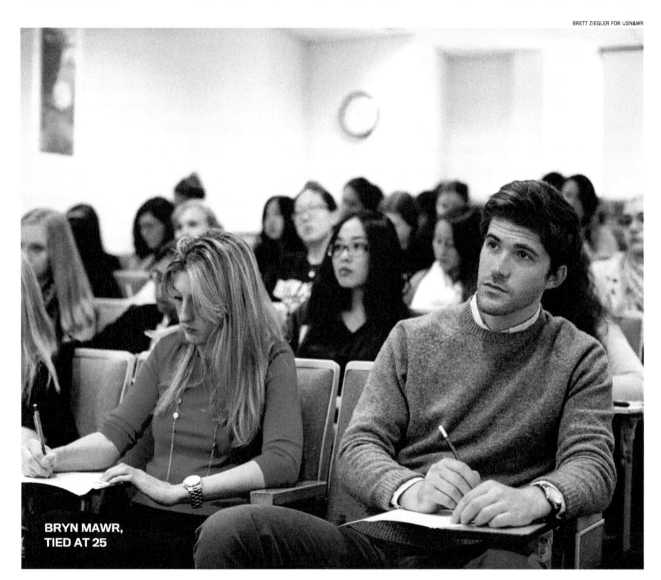

BRYN MAWR, TIED AT 25

Note: Key to footnotes, Page 89.

BEST NATIONAL LIBERAL ARTS COLLEGES

Rank	School (State) (*Public)	Overall score	Peer assessment score (5.0=highest)	High school counselor assessment score	Average freshman retention rate	2014 graduation rate: Predicted	2014 graduation rate: Actual	% of classes under 20 ('14)	% of classes of 50 or more ('14)	SAT/ACT 25th-75th percentile ('14)	Freshmen in top 10% of HS class ('14)	Acceptance rate ('14)	Average alumni giving rate
67.	**Wheaton College** (MA)	63	3.4	4.0	85%	80%	77%	71%	1%	1120-1350[2]	34%[5]	70%	25%
67.	**Willamette University** (OR)	63	3.2	3.8	86%	75%	77%	61%	0%	1080-1320	40%	81%	14%
72.	**Allegheny College** (PA)	62	3.0	3.6	86%	74%	78%	71%	1%	1050-1270	43%	72%	23%
72.	**Illinois Wesleyan University**	62	3.0	3.6	90%	76%	81%	65%	1%	25-30	38%[5]	60%	23%
72.	**Knox College** (IL)	62	3.0	3.5	88%	73%	80%	76%	0%	23-30[2]	31%[5]	68%	31%
72.	**Lewis & Clark College** (OR)	62	3.3	3.8	87%	76%	79%	68%	1%	1190-1380[2]	38%[5]	67%	19%
72.	**Muhlenberg College** (PA)	62	2.8	3.5	91%	81%	85%	68%	1%	1120-1330[2]	43%[5]	53%	19%
72.	**Spelman College** (GA)	62	3.4	3.8	89%	61%	74%	65%	2%	900-1100	25%	54%	37%
72.	**University of Puget Sound** (WA)	62	3.2	3.7	87%	74%	76%	60%	1%	1110-1330	35%[5]	79%	16%
79.	**Austin College** (TX)	61	3.1	3.7	83%	70%	77%	72%	1%	22-27	24%	54%	13%[7]
79.	**Gustavus Adolphus College** (MN)	61	3.1	3.7	91%	71%	82%	56%	2%	24-30[2]	31%	61%	23%
79.	**St. John's University** (MN)	61	3.2	3.7	89%	69%	80%	56%	1%	23-28	16%	79%	26%
82.	**College of the Atlantic** (ME)	60	2.6	3.3	83%	66%	71%	93%	0%	1100-1340[2]	55%[5]	71%	39%
82.	**Hendrix College** (AR)	60	3.3	3.8	85%	75%	71%	56%	0%	25-31	42%	83%	26%
82.	**New College of Florida***	60	3.0	3.9	83%	71%	69%	75%	1%	1180-1380	45%	60%	19%
82.	**St. Mary's College** (IN)	60	2.9	3.9	88%	72%	81%	56%	1%	23-28	35%[5]	83%	30%
82.	**Thomas Aquinas College** (CA)	60	2.7	3.1	90%	76%	72%	100%	0%	1180-1350	36%[5]	83%	58%
82.	**Transylvania University** (KY)	60	2.8	3.4	86%	73%	70%	76%	0%	25-30	51%	83%	35%
82.	**Virginia Military Institute***	60	3.1	3.8	86%	65%	71%	61%	0.2%	1070-1250[3]	21%	44%	31%
82.	**Wofford College** (SC)	60	3.0	3.6	89%	80%	78%	57%	1%	24-30	46%	77%	26%
90.	**College of St. Benedict** (MN)	59	3.0	3.3	89%	71%	81%	56%	1%	23-29	40%	82%	19%
90.	**Luther College** (IA)	59	3.1	3.5	87%	72%	82%	61%	2%	23-28	29%	71%	25%
90.	**Southwestern University** (TX)	59	3.0	3.6	85%	78%	73%	77%	1%	1050-1260	36%	49%	21%
93.	**Bennington College** (VT)	58	2.8	3.7	84%	71%	67%	86%	1%	1170-1400[9]	44%[4]	67%	22%
93.	**Cornell College** (IA)	58	2.9	3.8	82%	63%	67%	80%	0%	23-30	17%	74%	24%
93.	**Millsaps College** (MS)	58	2.9	3.6	80%	74%	64%	85%	0%	23-29	36%	57%	20%
93.	**Reed College**[1] (OR)	58	3.7	4.3	94%[8]	84%	79%[6]	N/A	N/A	1280-1470[4]	N/A	49%[4]	N/A
93.	**St. Mary's College of Maryland***	58	2.9	3.6	88%	79%	81%	70%	1%	1104-1283	28%[4]	79%	12%
93.	**Ursinus College** (PA)	58	2.9	3.4	90%	77%	80%	75%	0.3%	1050-1260[2]	24%[5]	83%	17%
93.	**Westmont College** (CA)	58	2.8	3.3	87%	75%	78%	64%	2%	1050-1290	29%[5]	79%	22%
100.	**Albion College** (MI)	57	2.8	3.5	81%	68%	72%	70%	0.3%	22-27	21%[4]	61%	22%
100.	**Hope College** (MI)	57	3.1	3.6	90%	70%	80%	54%	2%	23-29	30%	82%	23%
100.	**St. John's College** (NM)	57	3.1	4.0	76%	68%	50%	95%	0%	1210-1450[2]	32%[5]	93%	16%
100.	**Washington and Jefferson Col.** (PA)	57	2.8	3.5	N/A	73%	76%	67%	0%	1040-1230[2]	31%	42%	16%
100.	**Washington College** (MD)	57	2.8	3.6	83%	73%	74%	71%	1%	1040-1270[2]	34%[5]	56%	18%
105.	**Augustana College** (IL)	56	2.9	3.4	85%	69%	74%	62%	0.2%	23-29[2]	29%	54%	25%
105.	**Juniata College** (PA)	56	2.7	3.5	88%	73%	78%	75%	1%	1040-1250[9]	33%	74%	28%
105.	**St. Michael's College** (VT)	56	2.8	3.5	89%	69%	79%	59%	2%	1050-1250[2]	22%	80%	17%
108.	**Hampden-Sydney College** (VA)	55	2.8	3.3	80%	67%	67%	70%	0%	995-1210	8%	47%	34%
108.	**Hollins University** (VA)	55	2.7	3.5	71%	65%	62%	91%	0%	960-1200	15%	57%	30%
108.	**Lake Forest College** (IL)	55	2.9	3.7	84%	65%	73%	59%	1%	23-28[2]	27%[5]	55%	23%
108.	**Ohio Wesleyan University**	55	2.9	3.7	81%	69%	65%	68%	0%	22-28[2]	24%[5]	74%	22%
112.	**Drew University** (NJ)	54	2.8	3.4	79%	72%	62%	73%	0.3%	1000-1220[2]	28%[5]	70%	24%
112.	**Goucher College** (MD)	54	3.0	3.7	82%	70%	63%	78%	0%	1020-1280[2]	27%[5]	76%	16%
112.	**Siena College** (NY)	54	2.7	3.4	87%	62%	80%	43%	0%	1020-1220[2]	23%	58%	17%
112.	**St. Anselm College** (NH)	54	2.6	3.2	87%	68%	75%	68%	3%	1050-1230[2]	27%[5]	76%	20%
116.	**Coe College** (IA)	53	2.8	3.3	80%	66%	71%	76%	1%	22-28	34%	55%	20%
116.	**Hanover College** (IN)	53	2.7	3.4	82%	65%	69%	77%	0%	940-1170	29%	64%	18%
116.	**Ripon College** (WI)	53	2.5	3.2	85%	62%	68%	76%	1%	21-27	25%	67%	29%
116.	**Stonehill College** (MA)	53	2.7	3.5	88%	82%	82%	53%	1%	1010-1220[2]	29%	77%	15%
120.	**Birmingham-Southern Col.** (AL)	52	2.8	3.3	81%	71%	64%	72%	0.3%	23-29	25%	53%	24%
120.	**Calvin College** (MI)	52	2.8	3.4	87%	68%	74%	32%	2%	23-29[2]	32%	73%	24%
120.	**Concordia College–Moorhead** (MN)	52	2.8	3.5	83%	67%	72%	57%	1%	23-28	30%	64%	19%
120.	**Linfield College** (OR)	52	2.6	3.4	85%	63%	71%	70%	1%	960-1200	27%	94%	15%
120.	**Susquehanna University** (PA)	52	2.8	3.1	84%	67%	76%	57%	0%	1020-1210[2]	28%	78%	13%
125.	**Randolph-Macon College** (VA)	51	2.8	3.4	79%	58%	62%	62%	0%	980-1190	22%	60%	35%
125.	**Westminster College** (PA)	51	2.6	3.3	85%	63%	76%	69%	0%	940-1160	22%	94%	19%
127.	**Berry College** (GA)	50	2.8	3.4	78%	70%	62%	55%	0.2%	24-29	34%	61%	18%
127.	**Eckerd College** (FL)	50	2.9	3.6	82%	61%	65%	54%	0.3%	1010-1240[3]	N/A	76%	N/A
127.	**Goshen College** (IN)	50	2.6	3.3	79%	65%	72%	70%	1%	975-1255	38%	95%	24%
127.	**Presbyterian College** (SC)	50	2.7	3.4	82%	70%	65%	66%	0%	970-1210[2]	29%	54%	15%
127.	**Principia College** (IL)	50	2.2	3.0	82%	77%	87%	N/A	N/A	920-1230	23%[4]	79%	25%
127.	**St. Norbert College** (WI)	50	2.7	3.4	83%	65%	70%	44%	1%	22-27	31%	82%	18%
127.	**Whittier College** (CA)	50	3.0	3.3	84%	61%	65%	58%	2%	960-1170	25%	62%	20%

Note: Key to footnotes, Page 89.

Rank	School (State) (*Public)	Overall score	Peer assessment score (5.0=highest)	High school counselor assessment score	Average freshman retention rate	2014 graduation rate Predicted	2014 graduation rate Actual	% of classes under 20 ('14)	% of classes of 50 or more ('14)	SAT/ACT 25th-75th percentile ('14)	Freshmen in top 10% of HS class ('14)	Acceptance rate ('14)	Average alumni giving rate
134.	**Grove City College** (PA)	49	2.4	3.2	90%	73%	83%	43%	5%	1070-1334	45%	88%	21%
134.	**McDaniel College** (MD)	49	2.7	3.4	82%	65%	68%	67%	0%	980-1200	26%	76%	15%
136.	**Central College** (IA)	48	2.6	3.3	81%	64%	68%	61%	1%	21-27	22%	66%	16%
136.	**Houghton College** (NY)	48	2.4	3.1	87%	65%	76%	71%	1%	980-1260	23%	94%	18%[4]
136.	**Illinois College**	48	2.5	2.9	78%	64%	75%	75%	0%	18-26[2]	22%	54%	25%
136.	**Marlboro College** (VT)	48	2.2	3.2	74%	78%	59%	98%	0%	1080-1370[2]	8%[5]	82%	26%
136.	**Salem College** (NC)	48	2.2	3.2	78%	52%	65%	91%	0%	21-27	40%	60%	22%[4]
136.	**University of Minnesota–Morris***	48	2.8	3.6	82%	61%	67%	64%	3%	22-28	27%	64%	11%
136.	**Wells College** (NY)	48	2.6	3.7	71%[8]	63%	58%	89%[4]	0%[4]	930-1070[4]	32%[4]	58%	22%
143.	**Alma College** (MI)	47	2.5	3.2	80%	63%	60%	70%	1%	21-27	23%	72%	21%
143.	**Nebraska Wesleyan University**	47	2.5	3.4	80%	63%	69%	71%	0%	22-27	21%	78%	16%
143.	**Roanoke College** (VA)	47	2.8	3.3	80%	65%	64%	54%	0.4%	980-1210	18%	69%	20%
143.	**Simpson College** (IA)	47	2.5	3.2	80%	63%	73%	65%	1%	22-27	24%	85%	15%
143.	**Wartburg College** (IA)	47	2.6	3.3	78%	66%	71%	49%	2%	21-27	29%	79%	22%
148.	**Centenary College of Louisiana**	46	2.3	3.3	73%	65%	52%	78%	0%	21-28	25%	66%	12%
148.	**Moravian College** (PA)	46	2.4	3.1	78%	65%	69%	66%	1%	910-1130	17%	86%	17%
148.	**Morehouse College** (GA)	46	3.2	3.7	83%	53%	53%	51%	1%	880-1120	19%	84%	16%
148.	**U. of North Carolina–Asheville***	46	2.9	3.5	79%	59%	64%	50%	1%	1100-1290	21%	73%	9%
148.	**Westminster College** (MO)	46	2.5	3.3	79%	61%	67%	66%	0%	22-27	27%	67%	13%
148.	**Wittenberg University** (OH)	46	2.5	3.6	78%	70%	69%	50%	1%	22-28[2]	22%	91%	13%
154.	**Carthage College** (WI)	45	2.5	3.4	77%	58%	61%	60%	0.3%	21-27	29%	72%	13%
154.	**Georgetown College** (KY)	45	2.5	3.5	72%	62%	55%	83%	0%	21-27	26%	89%	14%
154.	**Hiram College** (OH)	45	2.4	3.4	74%	55%	63%	80%	0%	18-25	15%	62%	13%
154.	**Saint Vincent College** (PA)	45	2.3	3.0	83%	63%	74%	45%	0%	910-1160	25%	72%	20%
158.	**Doane College** (NE)	44	2.1	3.1	75%	44%	59%	75%	0.2%	21-25[3]	17%	79%	19%
158.	**Gordon College** (MA)	44	2.4	3.2	82%	69%	71%	62%	4%	1030-1280[3]	36%[5]	88%	8%

BEST NATIONAL LIBERAL ARTS COLLEGES

Rank	School (State) (*Public)	Overall score	Peer assessment score (5.0=highest)	High school counselor assessment score	Average freshman retention rate	2014 graduation rate: Predicted	2014 graduation rate: Actual	% of classes under 20 ('14)	% of classes of 50 or more ('14)	SAT/ACT 25th-75th percentile ('14)	Freshmen in top 10% of HS class ('14)	Acceptance rate ('14)	Average alumni giving rate
158.	**Guilford College** (NC)	44	2.9	3.3	73%	52%	61%	63%	0%	910-1170[2]	12%	62%	12%
158.	**Randolph College** (VA)	44	2.5	3.2	76%	66%	41%	88%	0%	950-1200	7%	81%	22%
158.	**Wesleyan College** (GA)	44	2.7	3.6	78%	61%	48%	83%	1%	870-1110	N/A	45%	27%
158.	**William Jewell College** (MO)	44	2.4	3.4	76%	67%	60%	72%	1%	22-28[2]	37%	63%	10%
164.	**Hartwick College** (NY)	43	2.7	3.4	75%	60%	57%	66%	0.2%	1010-1200[2]	15%	90%	16%
164.	**Lycoming College** (PA)	43	2.5	3.2	82%	57%	62%	58%	2%	930-1153[2]	20%	72%	19%
164.	**Warren Wilson College** (NC)	43	2.5	3.3	67%	62%	51%	84%	0%	1010-1220[2]	28%[5]	72%	13%
167.	**Monmouth College** (IL)	42	2.5	3.1	76%	53%	56%	68%	0%	19-25	13%	69%	19%
167.	**Oglethorpe University** (GA)	42	2.6	3.4	76%	59%	51%	73%	0%	1040-1230	29%	78%	12%
169.	**College of Idaho**	41	2.6	3.1	84%	63%	59%	59%	1%	920-1190	18%	69%	35%
170.	**Ouachita Baptist University** (AR)	40	2.3	3.2	78%	67%	58%	59%	1%	21-28	27%	71%	19%
171.	**Eastern Mennonite University** (VA)	39	2.4	3.0	78%	59%	61%	66%	3%	860-1130	16%[4]	60%	21%
171.	**Fisk University** (TN)	39	2.7	3.4	82%[8]	59%	50%[6]	71%	3%	17-23[3]	N/A	83%	24%
171.	**Purchase College–SUNY***	39	2.4	3.3	82%	58%	68%	65%	3%	990-1210	13%[4]	41%	5%
174.	**Claflin University** (SC)	38	2.2	2.7	73%	33%	49%	62%	1%	700-880	10%	44%	49%
174.	**Emory and Henry College** (VA)	38	2.5	3.2	73%	54%	47%	74%	0%	860-1115	N/A	72%	25%
174.	**Wisconsin Lutheran College**	38	2.1	2.8	76%	58%	61%	72%	0.3%	21-26	13%	64%	18%

School (State) (*Public)	Peer assessment score (5.0=highest)	High school counselor assessment score	Average freshman retention rate	2014 graduation rate: Predicted	2014 graduation rate: Actual	% of classes under 20 ('14)	% of classes of 50 or more ('14)	SAT/ACT 25th-75th percentile ('14)	Freshmen in top 10% of HS class ('14)	Acceptance rate ('14)	Average alumni giving rate
SECOND TIER (SCHOOLS RANKED 177 THROUGH 235 ARE LISTED HERE ALPHABETICALLY)											
Albright College (PA)	2.5	3.1	74%	55%	52%	60%	1%	960-1150[2]	23%	50%	9%
Allen University (SC)	1.8	2.4	54%	36%	28%	N/A	N/A	16[4]	N/A	43%	100%
American Jewish University (CA)	2.3	2.8	68%[8]	72%	62%[6]	N/A	N/A	16-27[9]	N/A	58%	N/A
Amridge University (AL)	1.5	2.1	N/A	N/A	N/A	N/A	N/A	N/A[2]	N/A	N/A	N/A
Ave Maria University[1] (FL)	2.1	2.6	71%[8]	59%	54%[6]	N/A	N/A	930-1210[4]	N/A	60%[4]	N/A
Bay Path University (MA)	2.1	2.6	75%	44%	60%	79%	0%	840-1063	10%	63%	5%
Bennett College (NC)	2.1	2.4	61%	36%	45%	75%	0%	680-845	4%	92%	38%
Bethany College (WV)	2.4	3.0	61%	49%	47%	71%	1%	17-23	6%	62%	17%
Bethany Lutheran College (MN)	2.1	2.7	72%	57%	54%	76%	1%	20-26	15%	78%	15%
Bloomfield College (NJ)	2.0	2.5	67%	33%	33%	73%	0%	730-910	6%	63%	5%
Brevard College (NC)	2.2	3.1	58%	48%	43%	68%	0%	840-1050[2]	6%	43%	5%
Bridgewater College (VA)	2.3	3.0	76%	57%	61%	49%	0%	950-1140	21%	48%	16%
Bryn Athyn Col. of New Church[1] (PA)	1.9	2.9	64%[8]	74%	40%[6]	N/A	N/A	920-1130[4]	N/A	52%[4]	N/A
Burlington College[1] (VT)	2.2	3.2	44%[8]	49%	25%[6]	N/A	N/A	17-23[4]	5%[4]	83%[4]	9%[4]
Castleton State College (VT)*	2.0	2.6	71%	52%	50%	70%	2%	850-1070	6%	78%	8%
Colorado Mesa University*	2.1	3.0	65%	38%	32%	51%	7%	18-23	10%	82%	1%
Dillard University (LA)	2.2	3.1	66%[8]	38%	38%	57%	1%	17-20	9%	41%	7%
Eastern Nazarene College (MA)	2.1	2.6	70%	47%	51%	79%	4%	800-1050	7%	49%	N/A
East-West University[1] (IL)	1.6	2.2	31%[8]	25%	9%[6]	N/A	N/A	N/A	N/A	N/A	N/A
Erskine College (SC)	2.3	3.3	71%	65%	48%	82%	0%	900-1140	15%	61%	16%
Fort Lewis College (CO)*	2.4	3.0	63%	48%	38%	45%	2%	19-24[3]	11%	91%	2%
Green Mountain College (VT)	2.1	2.8	70%[8]	54%	48%	56%	0%	920-1200[4]	N/A	68%	7%[4]
Harrisburg Univ. of Science and Tech. (PA)	2.0	2.9	59%[8]	72%	18%	76%[4]	0%[4]	830-1050[4]	N/A	N/A	N/A
Holy Cross College[1] (IN)	2.6	3.6	61%[8]	48%	26%[6]	N/A	N/A	870-1080[4]	N/A	72%[4]	N/A
Huston-Tillotson University (TX)	2.1	2.9	57%[8]	26%	31%	67%	0%	720-920[3]	N/A	N/A	N/A
Johnson C. Smith University (NC)	2.1	2.7	67%	32%	44%	80%	0%	720-900	4%	42%	16%
Judson College[1] (AL)	2.2	2.8	60%[8]	54%	39%[6]	N/A	N/A	1050-1240[4]	N/A	74%[4]	N/A
Kentucky State University*	2.0	3.3	48%	39%	20%	74%	1%	16-21[3]	9%	48%	4%
The King's College (NY)	2.2	2.8	65%[8]	68%	53%	41%	0%	1000-1220	15%[4]	70%	14%[4]
Lane College (TN)	2.0	2.4	50%	27%	32%	69%	0.2%	14-17	N/A	43%	N/A
Life University (GA)	1.7	2.6	66%	42%	28%	86%	0%	918[3]	N/A	57%	1%
Louisiana State University–Alexandria*	2.1	3.1	56%	41%	25%	42%	4%	19-23	14%	55%	3%
Lyon College (AR)	2.5	3.0	69%	60%	48%	57%	0%	22-27	24%	61%	14%
Marymount Manhattan College (NY)	2.3	3.2	69%	62%	44%	67%	0%	940-1170	N/A	74%	9%
Maryville College (TN)	2.4	2.9	72%	58%	55%	55%	0%	20-26	15%[5]	71%	25%
Massachusetts Col. of Liberal Arts*	2.4	3.3	76%	52%	52%	63%	0.2%	860-1090[3]	8%[5]	72%	11%
Northland College (WI)	2.2	3.0	69%	59%	46%	65%	0%	21-26	13%	63%	13%
Pacific Union College (CA)	2.5	3.2	78%	52%	45%	61%	6%	860-1130	N/A	47%	7%
Pine Manor College (MA)	1.9	2.5	60%	36%	35%	84%	0%	680-880	N/A	68%	6%[4]
Rust College (MS)	2.1	2.8	61%[8]	21%	18%	N/A	N/A	14-17	N/A	18%	N/A
San Diego Christian College[1]	2.0	3.0	66%[8]	43%	38%[6]	N/A	N/A	870-1120[4]	N/A	49%[4]	N/A

School (State) (*Public)	Peer assessment score (5.0=highest)	High school counselor assessment score	Average freshman retention rate	2014 graduation rate: Predicted	2014 graduation rate: Actual	% of classes under 20 ('14)	% of classes of 50 or more ('14)	SAT/ACT 25th-75th percentile ('14)	Freshmen in top 10% of HS class ('14)	Accept-ance rate ('14)	Average alumni giving rate
SECOND TIER (SCHOOLS RANKED 177 THROUGH 235 ARE LISTED HERE ALPHABETICALLY)											
Savannah State University (GA)*	2.1	2.9	70%[8]	20%	28%	22%	22%	770-920[3]	N/A	34%	5%
Shawnee State University (OH)*	2.0	2.6	53%	38%	27%	50%	4%	18-24	12%	74%	1%
Shorter University[1] (GA)	2.0	2.6	71%[8]	52%	47%[6]	N/A	N/A	820-1060[4]	N/A	68%[4]	N/A
Simpson University (CA)	2.4	3.2	73%	34%	52%	69%	2%	940-1120	16%[5]	57%	4%
Stillman College[1] (AL)	2.4	3.2	61%[8]	32%	24%[6]	N/A	N/A	733-888[4]	N/A	43%[4]	N/A
SUNY College–Old Westbury*	2.4	3.1	79%	45%	38%	30%	1%	910-1080[3]	N/A	62%	1%[4]
Tougaloo College (MS)	2.1	2.2	77%	45%	49%	77%	1%	15-21	19%	42%	16%
University of Hawaii–Hilo*	2.5	3.1	69%[8]	52%	38%	48%	4%	830-1050[3]	23%	71%	N/A
University of Maine–Machias*	2.2	2.8	69%	49%	31%	79%	0%	780-1030[3]	N/A	87%	0.2%
University of Pikeville (KY)	1.8	3.3	52%	39%	38%	54%	2%	18-23	14%	100%	5%
Univ. of Science and Arts of Okla.*	2.5	3.2	69%	48%	46%	74%	1%	20-25	27%	68%	5%[4]
University of Virginia–Wise*	2.4	3.4	68%	47%	42%	74%	1%	840-1050	23%	69%	9%
Univ. of Wisconsin–Parkside*	2.1	2.9	67%	46%	31%	47%	7%	19-23[2]	8%	71%	1%
Virginia Wesleyan College	2.5	3.1	66%	56%	48%	78%	0.2%	870-1100[2]	13%	89%	6%
Western State Colorado University*	2.2	3.1	66%	51%	37%	54%	0.2%	19-24	6%[4]	97%	N/A
West Virginia State University*	2.1	3.1	55%	43%	22%	51%	1%	18-22	N/A	41%	2%
William Peace University[1] (NC)	1.9	2.9	67%[8]	46%	40%[6]	N/A	N/A	810-1030[4]	N/A	91%[4]	N/A
Xavier University of Louisiana	2.8	3.4	69%	48%	43%	41%	3%	20-25	36%	66%	13%

Footnotes:

1. School refused to fill out U.S. News statistical survey. Data that appear are from school in previous years or from another source such as the National Center for Education Statistics.
2. SAT and/or ACT not required by school for some or all applicants.
3. In reporting SAT/ACT scores, the school did not include all students for whom it had scores or refused to tell U.S. News whether all students with scores had been included.
4. Data reported to U.S. News in previous years.
5. Data based on fewer than 51 percent of enrolled freshmen.
6. Some or all data reported to the NCAA and/or the National Center for Education Statistics.
7. Data reported to the Council for Aid to Education.
8. This rate, normally based on four years of data, is given here for less than four years because school didn't report rate for the most recent year or years to U.S. News.
9. SAT and/or ACT may not be required by school for some or all applicants, and in reporting SAT/ACT scores, the school did not include all students for whom it had scores or refused to tell U.S. News whether all students with scores had been included.

N/A means not available.

Wake Forest University

Harsh Patolia, CLASS OF 2016

It took only one visit for me to fall in love with Wake Forest. I walked through the beautiful campus, sat in on some amazing classes (including an energetic philosophy class discussion on free will) and saw a community engaged and supportive of each other.

The university offers stellar research opportunities for undergraduates. As a researcher at the school's Institute for Regenerative Medicine, I have worked in a lab to process 3-D images of organs, which allowed me to see some of the cutting-edge advances that technology is bringing to medicine. I am a biophysics major but have thrived by taking advantage of the diverse experiences Wake offers. Two of my favorite classes have included one on Latin American literature and a survey of Slavic literature.

> ON ONE UNIVERSITY-SPONSORED TRIP, I SPENT TWO WEEKS IN RWANDA SERVING STUDENTS IN KIGALI.

Wake Forest also encourages students to take advantage of study abroad opportunities. On one university-sponsored trip, I spent two weeks in Rwanda serving students in Kigali through lesson planning and team-building activities. On another, I spent my spring break working on an organic farm. It is this combination of classroom, research and service experience – Wake's motto is "Pro Humanitate" ("For Humanity") – that has prepared me well for a medical career and developed my interest in public policy. •

WHY I P

University of Notre Dame

Lesley Stevenson, CLASS OF 2016

For college, I wanted more than great academics; I wanted a community. Notre Dame gave me both. The residential hall system, academic advisers and alumni network offered me not only unparalleled individualized attention but also a push to serve a purpose greater than myself. I discovered my passion for media studies with the help of my first-year adviser and my advisers in Film, Television and Theatre and American Studies, who got me into small classes with in-demand professors. My FTT adviser agreed to direct

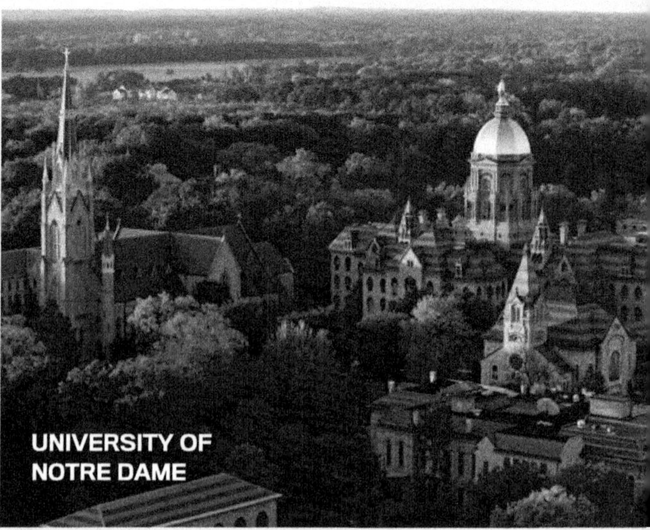

UNIVERSITY OF NOTRE DAME

UNIVERSITY OF NOTRE DAME

HEADSHOTS CLOCKWISE FROM TOP LEFT: KEN BENNETT – WAKE FOREST UNIVERSITY; SPENCER BRUTTIG; BRIAN LACH

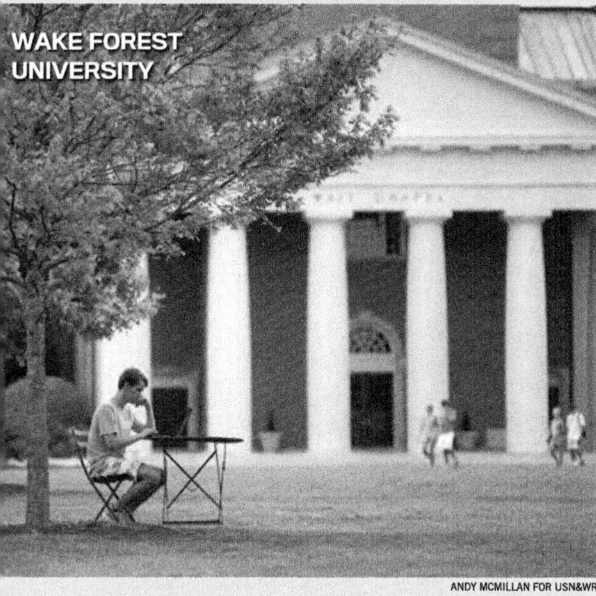

ANDY MCMILLAN FOR USN&WR

UC-Santa Barbara

Amy Levitt, CLASS OF 2015

I chose the University of California-Santa Barbara because of its beautiful surroundings overlooking the Pacific, its supportive community, and its reputation as a top academic institution. As a freshman, I knew I wanted to study political science, but I didn't realize how hugely supportive the faculty would be, as when they encouraged me to intern with my local congresswoman and to seize the opportunity to spend six months in Ireland studying international relations and law at Trinity College Dublin.

The professors at UCSB are extremely friendly and accessible. They have always answered my questions and given me great advice so that I now find myself headed to law school and a career in international law.

Of course, studying at a university set in such an idyllic location has been an incredible experience. Over the past four years, I have found it easy to forget the stress of finals by taking a break to run on the beach or to hike in the nearby mountains. The fantastic weather makes studying outside possible almost every day of the year. I can't think of a better place to live and learn. ●

THE FANTASTIC WEATHER MAKES STUDYING OUT-SIDE POSSIBLE ALMOST EVERY DAY OF THE YEAR.

ICKED...

my senior thesis on the "Harry Potter" films, for which I received funding to do research in London.

This student body that lives and learns together continually challenges me to think beyond my homework, too. I spent two months in rural Peru teaching English through a Notre Dame-sponsored service-learning program that changed my understanding of global communications. The school's religious identity encourages the belief that knowledge can be used as a force for good. Notre Dame truly cares for its students, and for that reason I call it my home. ●

THIS STUDENT BODY THAT LIVES AND LEARNS TOGETHER CONTINUALLY CHALLENGES ME.

Best Regional Universities

What Is a Regional University?

Like the national universities, the institutions that appear here provide a full range of undergraduate majors and master's programs; the difference is that they offer few, if any, doctoral programs. The 618 universities in this category are not ranked nationally but rather against their peer group in one of four regions – North, South, Midwest and West – because, in general, they tend to draw students most heavily from surrounding states.

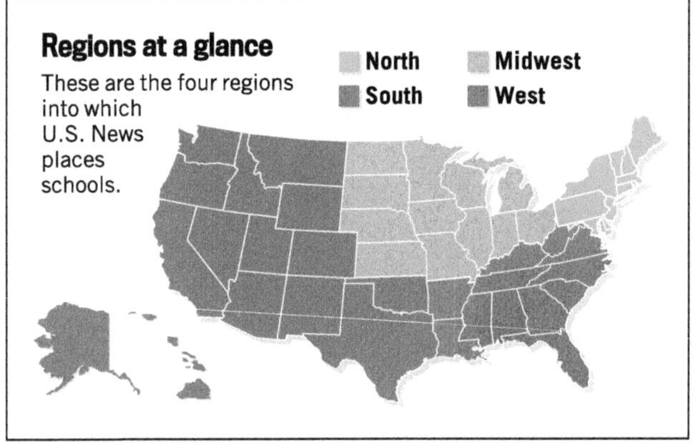
Regions at a glance
These are the four regions into which U.S. News places schools.
North
South
Midwest
West

NORTH ▶

Rank	School (State) (*Public)	Overall score	Peer assessment score (5.0=highest)	Average freshman retention rate	2014 graduation rate: Predicted	2014 graduation rate: Actual	% of classes under 20 ('14)	% of classes of 50 or more ('14)	Student/ faculty ratio ('14)	SAT/ACT 25th-75th percentile ('14)	Freshmen in top 25% of HS class ('14)	Acceptance rate ('14)	Average alumni giving rate
1.	Villanova University (PA)	100	4.3	94%	88%	89%	44%	2%	12/1	1220-1400	87%[5]	49%	24%
2.	Providence College (RI)	83	3.7	91%	79%	86%	53%	3%	12/1	1040-1250[2]	65%[5]	63%	18%
3.	Bentley University (MA)	80	3.4	94%	83%	88%	25%	0.1%	12/1	1150-1330	75%[5]	46%	7%
3.	College of New Jersey*	80	3.5	94%	83%	87%	40%	0.2%	13/1	1120-1310	85%	49%	7%
3.	Loyola University Maryland	80	3.6	88%	79%	83%	40%	1%	12/1	1100-1270[2]	65%[4]	60%	13%
6.	Fairfield University (CT)	78	3.5	88%	78%	80%	46%	1%	11/1	1090-1260[2]	N/A	72%	15%
7.	Rochester Inst. of Technology (NY)	75	4.0	87%	71%	65%	47%	5%	12/1	1110-1320	67%	57%	6%
8.	University of Scranton (PA)	74	3.3	89%	70%	80%	49%	0.2%	11/1	1040-1210	57%[5]	77%	13%
9.	Ithaca College (NY)	72	3.5	85%	76%	78%	62%	4%	11/1	1100-1300[2]	68%[5]	59%	9%
10.	Emerson College (MA)	71	3.3	88%	80%	80%	66%	1%	13/1	1140-1330	73%[5]	49%	7%
11.	Bryant University (RI)	69	3.0	88%	74%	78%	26%	0%	14/1	1065-1240[2]	52%[5]	75%	8%
11.	Quinnipiac University (CT)	69	3.3	87%	76%	76%	47%	3%	11/1	1010-1210	66%	66%	9%
13.	Marist College (NY)	68	3.3	91%	74%	78%	49%	0.1%	16/1	1090-1270[9]	58%[5]	39%	13%
14.	SUNY–Geneseo*	67	3.5	90%	79%	78%	30%	9%	20/1	1120-1320	76%	59%	12%
15.	St. Joseph's University (PA)	66	3.2	89%	70%	73%	27%	1%	13/1	1030-1220[2]	44%[5]	85%	11%
16.	Simmons College (MA)	65	3.0	86%	69%	65%	66%	4%	10/1	1070-1260	64%[5]	52%	18%
17.	Manhattan College (NY)	62	3.0	86%	67%	74%	46%	0.1%	12/1	990-1190[3]	52%[5]	67%	16%
18.	Pratt Institute (NY)	61	3.2	84%	71%	64%	72%	1%	10/1	1060-1290	N/A	63%	6%
19.	Gallaudet University (DC)	60	3.1	71%	50%	46%	96%	0%	6/1	15-20	N/A	65%	N/A
19.	Le Moyne College (NY)	60	2.9	86%	61%	72%	47%	1%	13/1	950-1160	50%	65%	16%
19.	Rowan University (NJ)*	60	3.0	86%	61%	66%	43%	1%	17/1	1010-1220	63%[4]	65%	3%
22.	Mount St. Mary's University (MD)	58	3.0	80%	63%	64%	46%	0%	13/1	950-1150	39%	67%	22%
22.	Rider University (NJ)	58	2.9	80%	61%	63%	50%	1%	12/1	930-1120	47%[5]	71%	10%
24.	St. Bonaventure University (NY)	57	2.9	82%	58%	68%	60%	0%	11/1	940-1160	43%	70%	20%
24.	SUNY–New Paltz*	57	3.0	88%	63%	74%	36%	3%	15/1	1030-1200	80%[5]	42%	5%
26.	La Salle University (PA)	56	3.1	81%	59%	67%	49%	1%	12/1	900-1100	35%	78%	11%
26.	Ramapo College of New Jersey*	56	2.8	88%	67%	72%	33%	0%	18/1	980-1200	26%[5]	53%	14%
26.	Wagner College (NY)	56	2.9	84%	74%	64%	64%	2%	15/1	1060-1270[2]	73%	72%	11%
29.	Hood College (MD)	55	2.9	77%	61%	71%	73%	0%	11/1	920-1140[2]	32%[5]	81%	18%
29.	Nazareth College (NY)	55	2.5	82%	61%	76%	58%	0%	9/1	980-1190[2]	56%	70%	11%
29.	Springfield College (MA)	55	2.8	84%	50%	69%	53%	3%	13/1	910-1170	39%	71%	11%
32.	Assumption College (MA)	54	2.8	83%	62%	70%	41%	0.2%	12/1	1020-1200[2]	43%	81%	13%
32.	CUNY–Baruch College*	54	3.2	90%	61%	66%	21%	15%	16/1	1120-1330[3]	78%	28%	4%
34.	Canisius College (NY)	53	2.8	79%	66%	68%	46%	1%	12/1	970-1180	52%	80%	11%
34.	Montclair State University (NJ)*	53	3.0	83%	48%	64%	39%	2%	17/1	880-1070[2]	37%	67%	3%
36.	Molloy College (NY)	52	2.3	89%	57%	70%	68%	1%	10/1	980-1140	54%	75%	10%
36.	Monmouth University (NJ)	52	2.8	81%	64%	67%	46%	0%	14/1	960-1140	49%[5]	74%	5%
36.	Roger Williams University (RI)	52	2.9	80%	67%	62%	48%	0.1%	15/1	1030-1200[2]	44%[5]	78%	6%

Note: Key to footnotes, Page 106.

BEST REGIONAL UNIVERSITIES

NORTH ▶

Rank	School (State) (*Public)	Overall score	Peer assessment score (5.0=highest)	Average freshman retention rate	2014 graduation rate: Predicted	2014 graduation rate: Actual	% of classes under 20 ('14)	% of classes of 50 or more ('14)	Student/faculty ratio ('14)	SAT/ACT 25th-75th percentile ('14)	Freshmen in top 25% of HS class ('14)	Acceptance rate ('14)	Average alumni giving rate
36.	**Rutgers, The State U. of N.J.–Camden***	52	3.1	82%	63%	52%	40%	8%	10/1	920-1130	45%	60%	3%
36.	**Salve Regina University** (RI)	52	2.7	81%	66%	67%	46%	0.2%	13/1	1010-1180[2]	45%	71%	16%
41.	**Arcadia University** (PA)	51	2.7	81%	62%	60%	70%	4%	13/1	1000-1200	60%	59%	13%
41.	**Marywood University** (PA)	51	2.5	82%	57%	69%	63%	1%	11/1	930-1130	45%	74%	14%
41.	**Mercyhurst University** (PA)	51	2.6	80%	47%	67%	57%	0.3%	13/1	880-1210[2]	16%	80%	14%
41.	**New York Inst. of Technology**	51	2.9	74%	69%	45%	62%	1%	14/1	1040-1270	52%[5]	64%	14%
41.	**Sacred Heart University** (CT)	51	2.9	80%	66%	67%	41%	2%	15/1	955-1229[2]	39%[4]	57%	6%
41.	**St. Francis University** (PA)	51	2.5	81%[8]	62%	72%	62%	2%	14/1[4]	920-1130	54%	69%	16%
47.	**Alfred University** (NY)	50	2.9	74%	64%	56%	59%	3%	13/1	950-1170	41%	69%	13%
47.	**CUNY–Hunter College***	50	3.2	86%	59%	52%	43%	7%	11/1	1060-1270	57%	35%	11%
47.	**CUNY–Queens College***	50	2.9	86%	54%	57%	32%	8%	15/1	1020-1180	65%[5]	40%	20%
47.	**Misericordia University** (PA)	50	2.5	83%	59%	71%	49%	0%	13/1	970-1170[3]	60%	71%	19%
47.	**Niagara University** (NY)	50	2.8	82%	57%	64%	46%	2%	13/1	940-1130	44%	66%	10%
47.	**SUNY College–Oneonta***	50	2.9	86%	63%	73%	30%	6%	19/1	1000-1170[3]	54%[5]	50%	7%
53.	**Chatham University** (PA)	49	2.5	75%	59%	56%	86%	0%	9/1	915-1160[2]	54%	53%	18%
53.	**College of St. Rose** (NY)	49	2.5	78%	58%	66%	59%	1%	14/1	940-1150[9]	34%	76%	18%
53.	**King's College** (PA)	49	2.6	77%	57%	62%	64%	0%	12/1	920-1140[2]	39%	67%	14%
53.	**Stockton University** (NJ)*	49	2.7	86%	60%	67%	23%	3%	17/1	980-1200	54%	65%	3%
53.	**Towson University** (MD)*	49	3.1	85%	59%	68%	31%	2%	17/1	1000-1170	49%[5]	59%	4%
58.	**College at Brockport–SUNY***	48	2.7	82%	58%	68%	33%	6%	17/1	950-1150	44%	49%	5%
58.	**Gannon University** (PA)	48	2.7	80%	56%	65%	53%	0%	14/1	930-1130	45%	78%	10%
58.	**Johnson & Wales University** (RI)	48	2.9	77%	35%	54%	47%	0%	24/1	N/A[2]	N/A	81%	N/A
58.	**Notre Dame of Maryland University**	48	2.7	75%	61%	57%	90%	0%	11/1	930-1140	49%	49%	9%
58.	**Philadelphia University**	48	2.7	76%	61%	66%	63%	0.1%	13/1	970-1180	46%[5]	64%	7%
58.	**Suffolk University** (MA)	48	2.9	76%	58%	55%	38%	1%	11/1	890-1130	41%[5]	84%	5%
58.	**SUNY–Oswego***	48	2.9	79%	58%	63%	55%	6%	18/1	1020-1190[3]	53%	48%	8%
58.	**Western New England Univ.** (MA)	48	2.7	74%	61%	60%	49%	0.1%	13/1	970-1170	44%[5]	80%	6%
66.	**CUNY–City College***	47	3.0	85%	50%	44%	44%	0.4%	14/1	980-1220[3]	44%[4]	35%	21%
66.	**Emmanuel College** (MA)	47	2.6	81%	61%	64%	38%	0%	14/1	990-1190[2]	54%[4]	69%	13%
66.	**Endicott College** (MA)	47	2.5	84%	61%	73%	53%	0%	14/1	980-1170[2]	40%[5]	73%	16%
66.	**Robert Morris University** (PA)	47	2.7	80%	53%	62%	54%	4%	15/1	950-1160	48%	76%	6%
66.	**SUNY–Fredonia***	47	2.7	80%	59%	67%	54%	5%	16/1	940-1140	39%	53%	6%
71.	**DeSales University** (PA)	46	2.5	83%	64%	70%	53%	2%	14/1	890-1150	44%[5]	80%	9%
71.	**Salisbury University** (MD)*	46	2.9	83%	61%	66%	33%	4%	16/1	1070-1230[9]	55%[5]	55%	9%
71.	**West Chester Univ. of Pennsylvania***	46	2.8	87%	56%	67%	24%	7%	19/1	990-1160	39%	53%	6%
74.	**St. Joseph's College New York**	45	2.4	85%	57%	68%	75%	0.1%	12/1	920-1130	N/A	71%	5%
74.	**SUNY College–Cortland***	45	2.7	82%	58%	67%	29%	6%	17/1	970-1130[2]	52%[5]	49%	7%
76.	**Keene State College** (NH)*	44	2.7	77%	52%	63%	52%	2%	16/1	870-1060	18%	79%	6%
76.	**Norwich University** (VT)	44	2.7	78%	58%	57%	53%	1%	16/1	930-1160[2]	39%[5]	66%	13%
76.	**SUNY–Plattsburgh***	44	2.7	82%	56%	61%	46%	4%	15/1	970-1160[3]	40%	48%	7%
79.	**Iona College** (NY)	43	2.8	83%	65%	58%	39%	0.1%	15/1	920-1110[3]	29%[5]	87%	9%
79.	**Slippery Rock U. of Pennsylvania***	43	2.8	82%	53%	67%	15%	10%	22/1	910-1080	36%	66%	8%
79.	**Stevenson University** (MD)	43	2.7	75%	58%	63%	64%	0.1%	15/1	900-1090	42%	62%	4%
79.	**University of St. Joseph** (CT)	43	2.5	77%	53%	51%	74%	0%	11/1	870-1060	41%[4]	80%	14%
83.	**CUNY–Brooklyn College***	42	2.9	84%	52%	50%	30%	4%	16/1	970-1160	49%[5]	35%	6%
83.	**Eastern University** (PA)	42	2.3	80%	55%	62%	86%	0.1%	11/1	910-1150	51%	68%	12%
83.	**Fairleigh Dickinson Univ.** (NJ)	42	3.0	74%	58%	53%	68%	1%	15/1	890-1090	36%	63%	4%
83.	**Millersville U. of Pennsylvania***	42	2.7	80%	57%	64%	27%	7%	21/1	920-1110	37%	69%	5%
83.	**Roberts Wesleyan College** (NY)	42	2.5	80%	55%	61%	66%	3%	11/1	950-1160	42%	69%	11%
83.	**Univ. of Massachusetts–Dartmouth***	42	3.1	76%	57%	47%	39%	12%	19/1	920-1130	37%	77%	5%
83.	**University of New England** (ME)	42	2.7	76%	62%	61%	48%	7%	13/1	970-1170	N/A	86%	8%
83.	**Wilkes University** (PA)	42	2.5	80%	59%	56%	48%	6%	15/1	930-1160	53%	79%	14%
83.	**York College of Pennsylvania**	42	2.5	76%	64%	61%	50%	0.1%	16/1	950-1150	42%	45%	8%
92.	**Eastern Connecticut State Univ.***	41	2.6	77%	55%	56%	32%	1%	16/1	920-1120[2]	28%	63%	8%
92.	**Manhattanville College** (NY)	41	2.6	74%	63%	61%	59%	0.2%	12/1	970-1160[2]	N/A	74%	13%
92.	**Shippensburg U. of Pennsylvania***	41	2.8	71%	50%	55%	27%	2%	20/1	890-1080	25%	83%	12%
92.	**St. Peter's University** (NJ)	41	2.5	77%	46%	53%	60%	0%	13/1	810-990	39%	57%	13%
92.	**SUNY College–Potsdam***	41	2.6	77%	52%	54%	68%	2%	13/1	900-1140[2]	32%[5]	68%	8%
92.	**University of Hartford** (CT)	41	2.7	73%	61%	55%	71%	1%	10/1	880-1110	N/A	72%	4%
92.	**University of New Haven** (CT)	41	2.6	77%	53%	49%	42%	4%	15/1	950-1160	50%[5]	81%	9%
92.	**Wheelock College** (MA)	41	2.5	71%	53%	55%	62%	0.4%	11/1	850-1080	35%[5]	88%	13%

Note: Key to footnotes, Page 106.

NORTH ►

Rank	School (State) (*Public)	Overall score	Peer assessment score (5.0=highest)	Average freshman retention rate	2014 graduation rate Predicted	2014 graduation rate Actual	% of classes under 20 ('14)	% of classes of 50 or more ('14)	Student/ faculty ratio ('14)	SAT/ACT 25th-75th percentile ('14)	Freshmen in top 25% of HS class ('14)	Acceptance rate ('14)	Average alumni giving rate
100.	**Plymouth State University** (NH)*	40	2.6	74%	45%	58%	57%	1%	16/1	890-1060[2]	20%	75%	7%
100.	**The Sage Colleges** (NY)	40	2.4	77%	55%	59%	53%	0%	12/1	830-1090[2]	48%	55%	11%
100.	**Waynesburg University** (PA)	40	2.4	81%	55%	59%	72%	0.4%	13/1	900-1090	46%	84%	7%
103.	**Caldwell University** (NJ)	39	2.2	78%	50%	62%	71%	0%	9/1	830-1070[3]	37%[5]	64%	14%
104.	**Bloomsburg U. of Pennsylvania***	38	2.6	80%	53%	65%	20%	7%	21/1	880-1070	27%	88%	6%
104.	**William Paterson Univ. of N.J.***	38	2.5	77%	49%	51%	54%	0.4%	14/1	890-1070	N/A	75%	5%
106.	**Cairn University**	37	2.2	76%[8]	53%	64%	73%	2%	14/1	870-1110	31%	98%	10%
106.	**Central Connecticut State Univ.***	37	2.6	77%	53%	52%	45%	2%	15/1	920-1110	19%	60%	5%
106.	**Mount St. Mary College** (NY)	37	2.3	71%	53%	59%	51%	1%	14/1	910-1100	37%	89%	11%
109.	**Albertus Magnus College** (CT)	36	2.3	84%[8]	40%	44%	84%	0%	14/1	19-29[3]	24%[5]	67%	18%
109.	**Alvernia University** (PA)	36	2.4	74%	46%	53%	70%	1%	12/1	870-1070	32%	75%	8%
109.	**St. Thomas Aquinas College** (NY)	36	2.4	77%	53%	57%	57%	0.3%	14/1	837-1082	29%[4]	81%	15%
112.	**College of Mount St. Vincent** (NY)	35	2.3	71%	46%	57%	51%	0.3%	13/1	840-1010	9%[5]	87%	16%
112.	**College of St. Elizabeth** (NJ)	35	2.2	68%	48%	50%	90%	0%	12/1	750-905	10%[4]	58%	12%
112.	**Lesley University** (MA)	35	2.5	77%[8]	57%	58%	78%	0%	10/1	980-1190	43%[5]	71%	N/A
112.	**Point Park University** (PA)	35	2.3	76%	51%	58%	73%	0.4%	13/1	880-1100	31%[5]	71%	3%
116.	**College of New Rochelle** (NY)	34	2.3	71%	33%	40%	78%	1%	8/1	880-1030	N/A	28%	18%
116.	**CUNY–Lehman College***	34	2.8	82%	37%	37%	39%	1%	14/1	870-1020[3]	N/A	29%	16%
116.	**Rosemont College** (PA)	34	2.2	72%	42%	43%	79%	0%	10/1	800-1063	49%[5]	58%	13%
116.	**Utica College** (NY)	34	2.5	69%	47%	44%	70%	0%	11/1	870-1070[2]	30%	82%	8%
116.	**Westfield State University** (MA)*	34	2.4	79%	51%	63%	37%	1%	16/1	910-1090	27%	75%	4%
116.	**Worcester State University** (MA)*	34	2.6	80%	52%	53%	74%	0.2%	16/1	890-1100	N/A	61%	7%
122.	**SUNY Buffalo State***	33	2.7	75%	46%	45%	45%	6%	16/1	820-1010	30%[5]	62%	3%
122.	**SUNY Polytechnic Institute***	33	2.5	75%	58%	43%	43%	3%	18/1	920-1260[3]	43%	57%	5%
122.	**University of Baltimore***	33	2.7	78%[8]	46%	43%	20%	4%	15/1	810-1030	N/A	62%	7%
125.	**Bridgewater State University** (MA)*	32	2.5	81%	50%	59%	42%	1%	19/1	890-1090	N/A	79%	6%
125.	**CUNY–John Jay Col. of Crim. Justice***	32	3.0	78%	41%	44%	31%[4]	1%[4]	N/A	860-1040[3]	N/A	51%	2%
125.	**Delaware State University***	32	2.5	66%	40%	43%	48%	3%	15/1	820-970	27%	44%	7%
125.	**Frostburg State University** (MD)*	32	2.6	74%	48%	49%	49%	2%	16/1	870-1080	30%	59%	5%
125.	**Holy Family University** (PA)	32	2.1	76%	52%	56%	72%	0%	13/1	830-1020	28%	73%	3%
125.	**Southern Connecticut State Univ.***	32	2.6	75%	49%	53%	45%	1%	14/1	830-1030	8%	72%	3%
131.	**Chestnut Hill College** (PA)	31	2.2	75%	45%	47%	85%	0%	9/1	850-1080	28%	62%	15%
131.	**East Stroudsburg Univ. of Pa.**[1]*	31	2.6	71%[8]	49%	57%[8]	28%[4]	11%[4]	22/1[4]	880-1010[4]	10%[4]	78%[4]	N/A
131.	**Georgian Court University** (NJ)	31	2.1	69%	54%	48%	77%	0%	12/1	840-1050	29%	68%	11%
131.	**Gwynedd Mercy University** (PA)	31	2.3	80%[8]	47%	56%	61%	4%	13/1	860-1060	25%	76%	5%
131.	**Kutztown Univ. of Pennsylvania***	31	2.6	74%	49%	56%	22%	10%	20/1	870-1060	17%	79%	5%
131.	**Mansfield Univ. of Pennsylvania***	31	2.3	73%	47%	54%	36%	9%	18/1	850-1050[2]	30%	91%	8%
131.	**Rhode Island College***	31	2.8	77%	48%	43%	49%	1%	15/1	810-1030[3]	34%	65%	5%
131.	**Southern New Hampshire University**	31	2.7	74%	41%	49%	62%	0%	16/1	870-1060[9]	20%	84%	3%

School (State) (*Public)	Peer assessment score (5.0=highest)	Average freshman retention rate	2014 graduation rate Predicted	2014 graduation rate Actual	% of classes under 20 ('14)	% of classes of 50 or more ('14)	Student/ faculty ratio ('14)	SAT/ACT 25th-75th percentile ('14)	Freshmen in top 25% of HS class ('14)	Acceptance rate ('14)	Average alumni giving rate
SECOND TIER (SCHOOLS RANKED 139 THROUGH 183 ARE LISTED HERE ALPHABETICALLY)											
American International College (MA)	2.0	65%	43%	38%	58%	4%	13/1	780-980	N/A	68%	8%[4]
Anna Maria College (MA)	1.9	65%[8]	38%	40%	77%	0%	11/1	N/A[2]	N/A	78%	8%
Cabrini College (PA)	2.2	74%	51%	50%	77%	0.2%	11/1	790-990[9]	17%	75%	8%
California U. of Pennsylvania*	2.3	77%[8]	50%	57%	24%	13%	19/1	840-1030[3]	24%	74%	5%
Carlow University[1] (PA)	2.3	72%[8]	48%	56%[6]	N/A	N/A	11/1[4]	855-1035[4]	N/A	95%[4]	N/A
Centenary College (NJ)	2.1	76%	49%	61%	82%	0%	17/1	820-1040	31%[5]	82%	7%
Cheyney U. of Pennsylvania[1]*	1.8	55%[8]	33%	24%[6]	47%[4]	10%[4]	16/1[4]	13-16[4]	9%[4]	88%[4]	3%[4]
Clarion U. of Pennsylvania*	2.3	72%[8]	45%	49%	26%	9%	19/1	830-1030	27%	93%	6%
College of St. Joseph[1] (VT)	2.3	56%[8]	35%	39%[6]	97%[4]	0%[4]	7/1[4]	16-18[4]	N/A	73%[4]	3%[4]
Coppin State University (MD)*	2.2	69%[8]	37%	21%	61%	1%	14/1	810-960	N/A	42%	11%
CUNY–College of Staten Island*	2.7	83%	48%	47%	18%	9%	18/1	910-1100	N/A	100%	2%
Curry College (MA)	2.2	69%	46%	45%	60%	0%	11/1	850-1040[2]	18%[5]	87%	6%
Daemen College (NY)	2.2	79%	52%	48%	61%	2%	13/1	920-1130[2]	54%	55%	5%
Dominican College (NY)	2.1	68%	42%	39%	58%	0%	15/1	780-960	N/A	63%	N/A
Dowling College (NY)	1.8	66%	44%	34%	81%	0%	13/1	N/A[2]	N/A	78%	N/A
D'Youville College (NY)	2.0	75%	53%	44%	61%	7%	9/1	910-1120	51%	85%	16%

BEST REGIONAL UNIVERSITIES

NORTH ▶

School (State) (*Public)	Peer assessment score (5.0=highest)	Average freshman retention rate	2014 graduation rate: Predicted	2014 graduation rate: Actual	% of classes under 20 ('14)	% of classes of 50 or more ('14)	Student/faculty ratio ('14)	SAT/ACT 25th-75th percentile ('14)	Freshmen in top 25% of HS class ('14)	Acceptance rate ('14)	Average alumni giving rate
SECOND TIER CONTINUED (SCHOOLS RANKED 139 THROUGH 183 ARE LISTED HERE ALPHABETICALLY)											
Edinboro Univ. of Pennsylvania*	2.5	71%	41%	49%	27%	10%	20/1	820-1050	24%	99%	4%
Felician College (NJ)	2.0	74%	40%	35%	75%	0%	14/1	790-960	23%	84%	3%
Fitchburg State University (MA)*	2.4	76%	51%	57%	42%	0.2%	16/1	900-1110	N/A	72%	4%
Framingham State University (MA)*	2.5	74%	54%	51%	43%	1%	16/1	920-1100	26%[5]	62%	4%
Franklin Pierce University (NH)	2.4	65%	52%	45%	62%	2%	12/1	850-1050	28%	84%	5%[4]
Husson University (ME)	2.2	73%	41%	40%	56%	0%	16/1	860-1050	45%	72%	4%
Johnson State College (VT)*	2.2	N/A	42%	34%[6]	N/A	N/A	N/A	N/A[2]	N/A	N/A	N/A
Kean University (NJ)*	2.4	75%	43%	48%	35%	0%	17/1	820-1000	26%[5]	70%	2%
Keuka College (NY)	2.3	73%	45%	47%	62%	0.4%	14/1	875-1050[9]	26%	83%	12%
Lincoln University (PA)*	2.1	71%	35%	43%	43%	0%	14/1	772-940	23%[5]	27%	9%
LIU Post (NY)	2.3	71%	55%	40%	64%	3%	13/1	840-1053	N/A	83%	2%
Lock Haven U. of Pennsylvania*	2.4	69%[8]	44%	47%	29%	12%	21/1	850-1050	30%	93%	5%
Medaille College[1] (NY)	1.9	65%[8]	42%	49%[6]	52%[4]	1%[4]	18/1[4]	760-970[4]	N/A	54%[4]	N/A
Metropolitan College of New York	1.9	42%[8]	53%	36%	87%	0%	11/1	N/A[2]	N/A	43%	N/A
Monroe College (NY)	2.0	75%	52%	71%	43%	0.1%	15/1	710-960[2]	N/A	40%	2%
Neumann University (PA)	2.3	72%	49%	54%	57%	1%	14/1	760-950	N/A	94%	9%
New England College (NH)	2.4	60%	36%	35%	73%	0%	19/1	770-1000[2]	14%	96%	6%
New Jersey City University*	2.3	70%	35%	32%	55%	0%	14/1	800-980	33%[5]	77%	3%
Nyack College (NY)	2.1	67%	38%	42%	77%	2%	12/1	760-1010[2]	27%[5]	99%	7%
Rivier University[1] (NH)	2.1	77%[8]	49%	49%[6]	N/A	N/A	17/1[4]	860-1020[4]	N/A	89%[4]	N/A
Salem State University (MA)*	2.5	77%	49%	46%	43%	1%	15/1	883-1080	N/A	71%	5%
St. Joseph's College[1] (ME)	2.5	72%[8]	55%	56%[6]	N/A	N/A	12/1[4]	870-1050[4]	N/A	78%[4]	N/A
Touro College (NY)	1.8	73%	56%	55%	87%	1%	16/1	830-1180[9]	N/A	37%	2%
Trinity Washington University[1] (DC)	2.7	55%[8]	31%	36%[6]	N/A	N/A	11/1[4]	N/A[2]	N/A	52%[4]	N/A
University of Bridgeport (CT)	2.1	62%	42%	28%	60%	0.4%	17/1	820-980	30%[5]	61%	2%
Univ. of Maryland–Eastern Shore*	2.5	70%	36%	37%	54%	3%	14/1	760-930	N/A	61%	3%
University of Southern Maine*	2.6	66%	52%	31%	45%	4%	15/1	880-1110	30%	84%	1%
Univ. of the District of Columbia*	1.9	54%[8]	51%	16%[6]	57%	0%	8/1	700-910[9]	22%[5]	93%	N/A
Western Connecticut State Univ.*	2.5	74%	52%	42%	34%	1%	14/1	890-1080	24%	57%	2%

SOUTH ▶

Rank	School (State) (*Public)	Overall score	Peer assessment score (5.0=highest)	Average freshman retention rate	2014 graduation rate: Predicted	2014 graduation rate: Actual	% of classes under 20 ('14)	% of classes of 50 or more ('14)	Student/faculty ratio ('14)	SAT/ACT 25th-75th percentile ('14)	Freshmen in top 25% of HS class ('14)	Acceptance rate ('14)	Average alumni giving rate
1.	**Elon University** (NC)	100	4.0	90%	80%	81%	49%	0%	12/1	1130-1320	62%[5]	54%	21%
1.	**Rollins College** (FL)	100	3.9	83%	72%	71%	73%	0.2%	10/1	1100-1280[2]	64%[5]	57%	14%
3.	**The Citadel** (SC)*	90	3.9	84%	61%	69%	39%	2%	13/1	990-1190	33%	76%	26%
4.	**Samford University** (AL)	87	3.8	87%	72%	66%	63%	1%	13/1	23-29	56%[5]	82%	10%
5.	**Belmont University** (TN)	86	3.8	81%[8]	73%	70%	41%	0.3%	13/1	23-29	60%	83%	22%
5.	**Stetson University** (FL)	86	3.6	78%	68%	61%	61%	0.2%	12/1	1070-1275[2]	58%	61%	11%
7.	**James Madison University** (VA)*	84	3.9	88%	71%	82%	34%	11%	16/1	1050-1230	43%	66%	7%
8.	**Mercer University** (GA)	83	3.7	82%	69%	63%	62%	3%	13/1	1090-1290	70%	67%	10%
9.	**Embry-Riddle Aeronautical U.** (FL)	79	3.6	77%	54%	52%	24%	2%	14/1	980-1240[2]	49%[5]	73%	2%
10.	**Appalachian State University** (NC)*	78	3.6	88%	64%	70%	36%	8%	16/1	1060-1240	56%	63%	8%
11.	**College of Charleston** (SC)*	77	3.7	82%	69%	67%	36%	4%	15/1	1030-1230	55%	78%	8%
11.	**Loyola University New Orleans**	77	3.5	78%	71%	62%	50%	1%	11/1	22-28	39%[5]	90%	8%
13.	**Bellarmine University** (KY)	76	3.3	80%	65%	67%	55%	1%	12/1	22-27	53%[5]	83%	17%
14.	**Christopher Newport Univ.** (VA)*	74	3.2	85%	68%	68%	57%	3%	15/1	1060-1250[2]	54%	56%	14%
14.	**Union University** (TN)	74	3.1	92%	65%	66%	72%	0.3%	10/1	22-29	57%	69%	8%
16.	**Univ. of Mary Washington** (VA)*	72	3.3	82%	70%	70%	57%	3%	15/1	1020-1200	45%	77%	14%
16.	**Univ. of North Carolina–Wilmington***	72	3.3	86%	65%	70%	30%	9%	17/1	1110-1270	69%	59%	6%
18.	**Hampton University** (VA)	70	3.0	77%	58%	67%	62%	3%	9/1	910-1100[2]	52%	29%	13%
18.	**Lipscomb University** (TN)	70	3.0	76%	64%	62%	55%	6%	12/1	23-29	51%[5]	56%	13%
20.	**Queens University of Charlotte** (NC)	69	3.0	71%	60%	62%	68%	0%	10/1	920-1160	46%	78%	25%
21.	**Spring Hill College** (AL)	66	2.9	75%	63%	58%	57%	0%	13/1	22-27	55%	52%	17%
22.	**Harding University** (AR)	65	3.0	82%	63%	63%	54%	7%	16/1	22-28	55%	99%	11%
22.	**University of Tampa** (FL)	65	3.1	74%	60%	62%	39%	3%	17/1	990-1160	48%[5]	52%	19%
24.	**Campbell University** (NC)	64	3.1	75%	56%	51%	61%	7%	16/1	802-1248	53%	68%	10%
25.	**Converse College** (SC)	63	2.7	69%[8]	60%	60%	81%	0%	12/1	930-1150	48%	54%	9%
26.	**Winthrop University** (SC)*	62	3.2	74%	57%	52%	45%	2%	14/1	940-1170	55%	71%	7%

Note: Key to footnotes, Page 106.

SOUTH ▶

Rank	School (State) (*Public)	Overall score	Peer assessment score (5.0=highest)	Average freshman retention rate	2014 graduation rate: Predicted	2014 graduation rate: Actual	% of classes under 20 ('14)	% of classes of 50 or more ('14)	Student/ faculty ratio ('14)	SAT/ACT 25th-75th percentile ('14)	Freshmen in top 25% of HS class ('14)	Acceptance rate ('14)	Average alumni giving rate
27.	**Christian Brothers University** (TN)	61	2.8	78%	60%	55%	63%	0.3%	10/1	21-27	68%	50%	14%
28.	**Georgia College & State Univ.***	60	3.1	85%	63%	61%	38%	6%	18/1	23-26	N/A	76%	4%
28.	**Longwood University** (VA)*	60	2.8	79%	57%	66%	49%	2%	17/1	930-1090	36%	73%	10%
28.	**Murray State University** (KY)*	60	3.1	72%	59%	52%	56%	4%	16/1	20-26	43%	80%	14%
31.	**Western Kentucky University***	58	3.0	72%	48%	50%	48%	6%	18/1	19-26	48%[5]	93%	10%
32.	**Lynchburg College** (VA)	57	2.7	74%	55%	56%	63%	0.1%	11/1	900-1090	N/A	67%	13%
32.	**Mississippi College**	57	3.0	73%	55%	54%	56%	2%	16/1	21-28[3]	47%	63%	5%
32.	**Western Carolina University** (NC)*	57	3.0	76%	51%	58%	28%	6%	16/1	930-1120	39%	43%	5%
35.	**Columbia International Univ.** (SC)	56	2.4	79%	53%	66%	61%	11%	14/1	980-1190	34%	33%	8%
35.	**Tennessee Technological Univ.***	56	3.0	73%	54%	49%	40%	12%	20/1	21-27	54%	94%	9%
37.	**Columbia College** (SC)	55	2.7	66%	47%	47%	78%	0%	11/1	900-1140	52%	79%	11%
37.	**Radford University** (VA)*	55	3.0	76%	49%	59%	31%	9%	18/1	890-1060[2]	20%	79%	5%
37.	**University of Montevallo** (AL)*	55	3.0	77%	55%	44%	48%	1%	16/1	20-26	N/A	74%	15%
37.	**Wingate University** (NC)	55	2.9	73%	55%	51%	44%	1%	15/1	907-1110	45%	75%	13%
41.	**Gardner-Webb University** (NC)	54	2.7	71%	50%	53%	67%	0%	13/1	900-1130	53%	67%	7%
41.	**Mary Baldwin College** (VA)	54	3.0	63%	47%	43%	59%	0%	11/1	850-1090	42%	51%	17%[4]
41.	**Shenandoah University** (VA)	54	2.8	77%	58%	55%	63%	1%	10/1	880-1110	36%[4]	83%	6%
41.	**William Carey University** (MS)	54	2.7	76%	54%	58%	71%	1%	14/1	20-27[3]	60%	52%	5%
45.	**Marshall University** (WV)*	53	3.3	71%	51%	45%	44%	4%	19/1	19-24	N/A	87%	5%
46.	**Freed-Hardeman University** (TN)	51	2.5	74%	58%	51%	47%	2%	14/1	22-27	54%	93%	12%
46.	**Lee University** (TN)	51	2.8	75%	51%	54%	55%	5%	17/1	21-27[3]	49%	89%	8%
46.	**Mississippi Univ. for Women***	51	3.0	74%	46%	41%	66%	3%	14/1	18-23	63%	94%	5%
46.	**Palm Beach Atlantic University** (FL)	51	2.7	72%	58%	55%	61%	2%	13/1	930-1158	N/A	95%	4%
50.	**Lincoln Memorial University** (TN)	50	2.4	70%	46%	40%	82%	1%	13/1	19-27	N/A	74%	7%
50.	**University of North Florida***	50	2.8	83%	56%	55%	28%	10%	20/1	22-26	41%	61%	7%
50.	**University of Tennessee–Martin***	50	2.7	73%	50%	47%	58%	5%	17/1	20-25	62%[5]	73%	6%
53.	**Arkansas State University***	49	2.9	72%	39%	37%	50%	5%	17/1	21-26	49%	72%	10%
53.	**Marymount University** (VA)	49	2.8	74%	58%	51%	51%	0.2%	13/1	910-1100	15%[5]	84%	4%
53.	**Piedmont College** (GA)	49	2.4	74%	42%	50%	78%	0.2%	14/1	860-1050	37%	58%	4%
53.	**Thomas More College** (KY)	49	2.6	67%	53%	46%	74%	1%	15/1	19-23	27%	93%	15%
53.	**University of North Georgia***	49	2.8	80%	53%	52%	33%	3%	21/1	1010-1200	66%[5]	65%	7%
58.	**Belhaven University** (MS)	48	2.7	65%	43%	49%	79%	2%	10/1	18-23	37%[5]	72%	6%
58.	**U. of South Florida–St. Petersburg***	48	2.8	66%	42%	32%	37%	10%	19/1	1050-1230	58%	35%	20%
58.	**Univ. of Tennessee–Chattanooga***	48	3.1	69%	51%	40%	37%	9%	18/1	21-26	47%	77%	5%
61.	**Brenau University** (GA)	47	2.7	67%	49%	47%	84%	1%	11/1	890-1080	N/A	76%	4%
61.	**Morehead State University** (KY)*	47	2.7	69%	51%	46%	53%	4%	18/1	19-25	42%	84%	8%
63.	**Coastal Carolina University** (SC)*	46	2.8	63%	50%	45%	32%	3%	17/1	910-1090	29%	64%	5%
63.	**St. Thomas University** (FL)	46	2.6	68%	40%	33%	73%	0%	11/1	810-1040	27%[4]	85%	1%
65.	**Jacksonville University** (FL)	45	2.6	67%	54%	39%	76%	0.1%	11/1	910-1110[2]	N/A	56%	6%
65.	**North Carolina Central Univ.***	45	2.3	73%	34%	47%	41%	3%	15/1	810-950	24%	43%	10%
65.	**Troy University** (AL)*	45	2.7	71%	36%	34%[6]	48%	4%	18/1	19-26[3]	54%[5]	44%	8%
68.	**Alcorn State University** (MS)*	44	2.4	70%	27%	40%	55%	5%	17/1	16-20	N/A	78%	N/A
68.	**Austin Peay State University** (TN)*	44	2.9	69%	44%	39%	53%	4%	19/1	19-24[2]	36%	89%	4%[4]
68.	**University of Central Arkansas***	44	2.8	70%	52%	45%	46%	3%	17/1	20-26	43%	94%	5%
71.	**Georgia Regents University***	43	2.9	69%[8]	55%	32%	N/A	N/A	N/A	N/A[2]	N/A	N/A	2%
71.	**Kennesaw State University** (GA)*	43	3.1	77%	53%	43%	24%	16%	21/1	990-1170	35%	54%	5%
71.	**King University** (TN)	43	2.3	72%	47%	55%	81%	0.2%	11/1	20-26[3]	53%	57%	9%
71.	**Saint Leo University** (FL)	43	2.7	69%	46%	42%	49%	0%	15/1	900-1090[2]	26%	72%	5%
71.	**University of North Alabama***	43	2.9	71%	48%	39%	55%	2%	17/1	19-25	N/A	68%	6%
76.	**Eastern Kentucky University***	42	2.8	66%	49%	42%	52%	5%	16/1	19-24	34%	74%	5%
76.	**Francis Marion University** (SC)*	42	2.6	67%	41%	41%	44%	6%	15/1	17-21[3]	46%	59%	4%
76.	**Pfeiffer University** (NC)	42	2.4	68%	43%	35%	75%	0%	12/1	17-21	31%	47%	11%
76.	**Valdosta State University** (GA)*	42	2.8	69%	45%	39%	49%	4%	19/1	930-1100	N/A	54%	3%
80.	**Florida Gulf Coast University***	41	2.7	76%	51%	49%	20%	16%	23/1	970-1120	41%[4]	59%	7%
80.	**Liberty University** (VA)	41	2.5	77%	37%	52%	33%	6%	18/1	910-1160[3]	42%	20%	2%
80.	**Northern Kentucky University***	41	2.7	67%	49%	36%	39%	3%	17/1	20-25	32%	93%	7%
83.	**Union College**[1] (KY)	39	2.4	55%[8]	35%	34%[6]	78%[4]	0%[4]	13/1[4]	19-24[4]	N/A	75%[4]	16%[4]
84.	**Campbellsville University**[1] (KY)	37	2.5	69%[8]	47%	42%[6]	59%[4]	0.2%[4]	13/1[4]	18-24[4]	N/A	68%[4]	10%[4]
84.	**Fayetteville State University** (NC)*	37	2.3	73%	29%	35%	41%	1%	18/1	810-960	26%	50%	2%
84.	**Winston-Salem State Univ.**[1] (NC)*	37	2.5	79%[8]	36%	43%[6]	N/A	N/A	N/A	N/A	N/A	N/A	N/A
87.	**Arkansas Tech University***	36	2.6	68%	43%	45%	43%	6%	20/1	18-25	34%	86%	4%

Note: Key to footnotes, Page 106.

FLORIDA
SOUTHERN
COLLEGE

SOUTH ▶

Rank	School (State) (*Public)	Overall score	Peer assessment score (5.0=highest)	Average freshman retention rate	2014 graduation rate Predicted	Actual	% of classes under 20 ('14)	% of classes of 50 or more ('14)	Student/faculty ratio ('14)	SAT/ACT 25th-75th percentile ('14)	Freshmen in top 25% of HS class ('14)	Acceptance rate ('14)	Average alumni giving rate
87.	Henderson State University (AR)*	36	2.7	59%	45%	34%	54%	2%	17/1	18-24	36%	63%	3%
87.	McNeese State University (LA)*	36	2.6	69%	44%	41%	40%	7%	21/1	20-24	44%	75%	7%
87.	Nicholls State University (LA)*	36	2.5	70%[8]	48%	37%	39%	10%	20/1	20-24	42%	88%	5%
87.	University of the Cumberlands (KY)	36	2.4	60%	43%	36%	62%	1%	14/1	20-25	39%	66%	18%
87.	University of West Georgia*	36	2.8	72%	42%	41%	30%	12%	24/1	870-1030	N/A	49%	4%
93.	Albany State University (GA)*	35	2.3	68%	29%	40%	52%	2%	16/1	820-940[3]	24%[5]	47%	4%
93.	Charleston Southern University (SC)	35	2.6	65%[8]	44%	34%	53%	3%	15/1	890-1080	51%	59%	4%
93.	Montreat College (NC)	35	2.1	61%[8]	49%	39%[6]	87%	0%	12/1	820-1080	40%	46%	5%
93.	University of Louisiana–Monroe*	35	2.6	69%	51%	40%	36%	14%	21/1	19-25	56%	77%	4%
93.	U. of North Carolina–Pembroke*	35	2.6	66%	38%	34%	39%	3%	15/1	850-1000	34%	73%	4%

School (State) (*Public)	Peer assessment score (5.0=highest)	Average freshman retention rate	2014 graduation rate Predicted	Actual	% of classes under 20 ('14)	% of classes of 50 or more ('14)	Student/faculty ratio ('14)	SAT/ACT 25th-75th percentile ('14)	Freshmen in top 25% of HS class ('14)	Acceptance rate ('14)	Average alumni giving rate
SECOND TIER (SCHOOLS RANKED 98 THROUGH 127 ARE LISTED HERE ALPHABETICALLY)											
Alabama A&M University*	2.3	67%	36%	35%	48%[4]	4%[4]	21/1	15-19[3]	N/A	53%	8%
Alabama State University*	2.4	59%	27%	26%	43%	0.3%	15/1	16-19	7%	53%	3%
Armstrong State University (GA)*	2.4	68%	44%	30%	36%	3%	18/1	920-1090	N/A	67%	5%
Auburn University–Montgomery (AL)*	2.9	60%	45%	25%	40%	1%	15/1	19-24	46%	80%	3%
Bethel University (TN)	2.2	62%[8]	36%	36%	78%	1%	13/1[4]	17-23[2]	N/A	63%	3%[4]
Columbus State University (GA)*	2.6	69%	44%	34%	45%	4%	17/1	860-1100	37%	56%	3%
Cumberland University (TN)	2.5	66%	47%	37%	65%	2%	14/1	20-25	34%	46%	4%
Delta State University (MS)*	2.5	65%	43%	34%	64%	1%	14/1	18-22[4]	40%[4]	92%	N/A
Fairmont State University (WV)*	2.3	64%	41%	32%	50%	5%	15/1	18-23	35%	59%	2%
Florida Memorial University	2.0	70%[8]	26%	38%	N/A	N/A	N/A	N/A[2]	N/A	21%	N/A
Georgia Southwestern State University*	2.4	66%	43%	32%	52%	2%	17/1	880-1060	42%	70%	1%
Grambling State University (LA)*	2.4	69%	32%	31%	46%	9%	18/1	16-20[3]	28%	44%	N/A
Jacksonville State University (AL)*	2.7	70%	40%	30%	37%	6%	19/1	19-26[3]	42%	83%	8%
Lindsey Wilson College (KY)	2.5	57%	36%	34%	63%	0%	14/1	19-24[9]	34%	73%	12%
Louisiana State U.–Shreveport*	2.6	66%	49%	30%	50%	5%	19/1	20-25[3]	N/A	77%	N/A
Mississippi Valley State Univ.*	2.2	65%[8]	25%	29%	62%	2%	16/1	15-19[3]	N/A	16%	N/A
Norfolk State University (VA)*	2.4	N/A	33%	34%	N/A	N/A	18/1[4]	790-950[3]	N/A	65%[4]	N/A
Northwestern State U. of La.[1]*	2.4	70%[8]	45%	37%[6]	45%[4]	10%[4]	19/1[4]	19-24[4]	44%[4]	58%[4]	5%[4]
Our Lady of Holy Cross College[1] (LA)	2.5	71%[8]	36%	26%[6]	N/A	N/A	11/1[4]	N/A[2]	N/A	48%[4]	N/A
Shepherd University (WV)*	2.5	67%	47%	40%	55%	1%	16/1	890-1090	N/A	98%	6%
Southeastern Louisiana University*	2.4	65%	44%	37%	34%	7%	20/1	20-24	31%	87%	5%
Southern Arkansas University*	2.3	62%	41%	36%	48%	4%	16/1	18-24	41%	71%	5%
Southern Univ. and A&M College (LA)*	2.2	69%	30%	32%	N/A	N/A	17/1	17-20	11%	N/A	N/A
Southern University–New Orleans[1]*	2.2	52%[8]	23%	14%[6]	N/A	N/A	18/1[4]	N/A[2]	N/A	N/A	N/A
Southern Wesleyan University[1] (SC)	2.4	66%[8]	39%	47%[6]	N/A	N/A	18/1[4]	810-1050[4]	N/A	94%[4]	N/A
South University[1] (GA)	1.9	45%[8]	51%	16%[6]	N/A	N/A	15/1[4]	N/A[2]	N/A	52%[4]	N/A
Tusculum College (TN)	2.4	57%	40%	36%	79%	0%	15/1	18-23	N/A	72%	5%
University of West Alabama*	2.4	58%	32%	32%	55%	2%	14/1	19-23	N/A	72%	4%
Virginia State University[1]*	2.4	65%[8]	31%	43%[6]	N/A	N/A	16/1[4]	730-910[4]	17%[4]	54%[4]	N/A
Warner University (FL)	2.3	66%[8]	39%	35%	60%	1%	17/1	17-19[3]	22%	26%	1%

MIDWEST ▶

Rank	School (State) (*Public)	Overall score	Peer assessment score (5.0=highest)	Average freshman retention rate	2014 graduation rate Predicted	Actual	% of classes under 20 ('14)	% of classes of 50 or more ('14)	Student/faculty ratio ('14)	SAT/ACT 25th-75th percentile ('14)	Freshmen in top 25% of HS class ('14)	Acceptance rate ('14)	Average alumni giving rate
1.	Creighton University (NE)	100	4.1	90%	79%	78%	48%	6%	11/1	24-29	72%	73%	15%
2.	Butler University (IN)	95	4.0	90%	79%	78%	57%	3%	11/1	25-30[3]	79%	68%	22%
3.	Drake University (IA)	91	3.9	88%	76%	78%	49%	6%	12/1	25-30	71%	69%	12%
4.	Bradley University (IL)	86	3.6	87%	70%	74%	58%	3%	12/1	23-28	63%	64%	12%
5.	Valparaiso University (IN)	85	3.8	85%	69%	67%	55%	5%	13/1	23-29	64%	82%	16%
6.	Xavier University (OH)	82	3.7	83%	71%	71%	37%	1%	12/1	22-27[3]	48%[5]	73%	15%
7.	John Carroll University (OH)	79	3.4	88%	61%	71%	44%	0.1%	13/1	22-27	44%[5]	83%	15%
8.	Truman State University (MO)*	74	3.6	88%	73%	71%	42%	2%	17/1	24-30	80%	74%	9%
8.	University of Evansville (IN)	74	3.3	85%	68%	64%	67%	1%	14/1	1020-1230	62%	83%	14%
10.	Elmhurst College (IL)	72	3.2	80%	63%	74%	64%	0.3%	13/1	21-26	45%	68%	8%

Note: Key to footnotes, Page 106.

MIDWEST ▶

Rank	School (State) (*Public)	Overall score	Peer assessment score (5.0=highest)	Average freshman retention rate	2014 graduation rate Predicted	Actual	% of classes under 20 ('14)	% of classes of 50 or more ('14)	Student/ faculty ratio ('14)	SAT/ACT 25th-75th percentile ('14)	Freshmen in top 25% of HS class ('14)	Accept-ance rate ('14)	Average alumni giving rate
11.	**Drury University** (MO)	69	2.9	83%	70%	71%	69%	1%	10/1	23-29	62%	81%	14%
12.	**Hamline University** (MN)	67	3.2	81%	61%	65%	54%	4%	13/1	21-27	41%	70%	15%
13.	**Baldwin Wallace University** (OH)	66	3.0	81%	61%	68%	62%	1%	13/1	20-25[2]	46%	64%	11%
13.	**Otterbein University** (OH)	66	3.1	76%	61%	59%	73%	1%	10/1	21-26	55%	75%	15%
15.	**Milwaukee School of Engineering**	65	3.4	81%	73%	56%	44%	0%	15/1	25-30	N/A	69%	8%
15.	**North Central College** (IL)	65	3.0	79%	64%	63%	38%	0%	15/1	22-27	52%	60%	20%
15.	**St. Catherine University** (MN)	65	3.1	81%	57%	60%	66%	2%	10/1	21-26	60%	67%	14%
18.	**Rockhurst University** (MO)	64	3.0	86%	68%	69%	38%	3%	12/1	23-28	58%[5]	77%	14%
18.	**University of Northern Iowa***	64	3.2	83%	60%	64%	39%	7%	16/1	20-25	47%	77%	9%
20.	**Augsburg College** (MN)	63	3.0	79%	53%	63%	62%	0%	12/1	20-26[3]	43%[4]	68%	11%
20.	**Dominican University** (IL)	63	2.8	82%	54%	63%	59%	0.2%	10/1	20-24	48%	61%	17%
20.	**Franciscan Univ. of Steubenville** (OH)	63	2.4	86%	64%	75%	58%	1%	14/1	23-29	60%[5]	78%	13%
23.	**Bethel University** (MN)	61	2.7	84%	65%	73%	49%	3%	12/1	22-28	57%	95%	10%
23.	**Kettering University** (MI)	61	2.7	91%	75%	57%	55%	1%	13/1	25-29	71%	72%	4%
23.	**University of Detroit Mercy**	61	2.7	81%	64%	54%	60%	2%	11/1	22-26	55%	66%	10%
26.	**Grand Valley State University** (MI)*	60	3.1	82%	59%	65%	23%	7%	17/1	21-26	48%	80%	5%
26.	**Webster University** (MO)	60	2.7	79%	63%	64%	85%	0%	9/1	21-27	42%	56%	5%
28.	**Lewis University** (IL)	59	2.7	81%	55%	62%	66%	0.2%	13/1	21-25	44%	62%	7%
29.	**Univ. of Wisconsin–La Crosse***	58	3.1	86%	68%	70%	29%	11%	19/1	23-27	65%	76%	4%
30.	**Eastern Illinois University***	56	2.7	78%	51%	59%	47%	3%	14/1	19-24	33%	50%	5%
30.	**Indiana Wesleyan University**	56	2.6	77%	61%	64%	64%	2%	14/1	21-27	58%	96%	8%
30.	**University of Indianapolis**	56	3.1	74%	55%	51%	55%	1%	11/1	900-1120	54%	66%	11%
33.	**College of St. Scholastica** (MN)	55	2.7	82%	58%	61%	55%	2%	14/1	21-27	50%	66%	10%

MIDWEST ▶

Rank	School (State) (*Public)	Overall score	Peer assessment score (5.0=highest)	Average freshman retention rate	2014 graduation rate: Predicted	2014 graduation rate: Actual	% of classes under 20 ('14)	% of classes of 50 or more ('14)	Student/faculty ratio ('14)	SAT/ACT 25th-75th percentile ('14)	Freshmen in top 25% of HS class ('14)	Acceptance rate ('14)	Average alumni giving rate
33.	**Univ. of Wisconsin–Eau Claire***	55	3.0	83%	63%	69%	26%	11%	21/1	22-26	47%	84%	9%
35.	**Anderson University** (IN)	54	2.7	76%	57%	63%	68%	2%	12/1	920-1140	52%	55%	7%
36.	**Baker University** (KS)	53	2.4	77%	43%	58%	71%	1%	11/1	20-26	42%	76%	15%
36.	**Capital University** (OH)	53	2.6	75%	63%	59%	60%	2%	12/1	21-27[3]	44%	73%	8%
36.	**St. Ambrose University** (IA)	53	2.8	78%	56%	57%	70%	0.2%	10/1	20-25	34%	96%	8%
36.	**University of Michigan–Dearborn***	53	2.9	82%	59%	51%	35%	7%	15/1	21-27	58%	64%	9%
36.	**University of Minnesota–Duluth***	53	3.0	76%	59%	59%	40%	14%	19/1	22-26	45%	77%	9%[4]
36.	**University of St. Francis** (IL)	53	2.6	80%	55%	56%	63%	0%	11/1	21-25	44%	51%	6%
42.	**Carroll University** (WI)	52	2.8	78%	58%	61%	52%	4%	14/1	21-26	58%[4]	81%	11%
42.	**Univ. of Illinois–Springfield***	52	2.8	75%	59%	49%	54%	1%	14/1	20-27	43%	62%	5%
44.	**Concordia University** (NE)	50	2.4	79%	58%	66%	59%	1%	13/1	20-27	43%	77%	22%
44.	**Southern Illinois U.–Edwardsville***	50	2.9	71%	58%	50%	40%	12%	19/1	20-26	45%	87%	5%
46.	**St. Xavier University** (IL)	48	2.8	73%	53%	54%	46%	1%	13/1	19-24[3]	54%	75%	7%
46.	**Univ. of Nebraska–Kearney***	48	2.9	78%	49%	56%	46%	4%	15/1	20-25	42%	84%	8%
46.	**Western Illinois University***	48	2.7	69%	48%	54%	48%	3%	15/1	18-23	28%	70%	5%
49.	**Heidelberg University** (OH)	47	2.7	65%	54%	47%	62%	0.3%	14/1	19-25	N/A	75%	19%
50.	**Muskingum University** (OH)	46	2.5	70%	54%	53%	70%	0.4%	13/1	19-24[3]	37%	78%	17%
50.	**Univ. of Wisconsin–Stevens Point***	46	2.8	80%	55%	61%	32%	4%	20/1	20-25[9]	40%	81%	5%
50.	**Univ. of Wisconsin–Whitewater***	46	2.9	79%	50%	57%	33%	7%	21/1	20-25[2]	28%	70%	10%
50.	**Ursuline College** (OH)	46	2.3	70%	52%	49%	93%	0%	6/1	18-25[3]	31%	66%	17%
54.	**Aquinas College** (MI)	45	2.5	77%	55%	52%	62%	0.4%	12/1	21-26[3]	45%[4]	65%	13%
54.	**Concordia University Wisconsin**	45	2.6	74%	49%	61%	52%	2%	13/1	21-26[3]	48%	75%	4%
54.	**Lawrence Technological Univ.** (MI)	45	2.6	79%	64%	45%	74%	1%	11/1	21-28	50%	57%	4%
54.	**North Park University** (IL)	45	2.7	76%	54%	53%	56%	2%	13/1	19-25	N/A	55%	8%
54.	**Olivet Nazarene University** (IL)	45	2.6	75%	61%	56%	45%	7%	16/1	21-27	47%	74%	14%
54.	**University of Findlay** (OH)	45	2.6	79%	63%	55%	52%	2%	16/1	20-25	45%	72%	9%
54.	**Walsh University** (OH)	45	2.3	75%	51%	55%	70%	0.3%	13/1	20-25	45%	81%	11%
61.	**Ferris State University** (MI)*	44	2.8	73%	47%	51%	41%	4%	16/1	19-24[3]	N/A	78%	3%
61.	**Malone University** (OH)	44	2.3	69%	53%	51%	60%	1%	12/1	20-25	44%	72%	10%
61.	**Mount Vernon Nazarene U.** (OH)	44	2.3	76%	53%	59%	82%	1%	14/1	20-25	44%	76%	7%
64.	**Alverno College** (WI)	43	2.9	72%	41%	36%	72%	0%	10/1	17-22	40%	65%	12%
64.	**Missouri State Univ.***	43	2.8	76%	55%	55%	27%	13%	20/1	21-26	54%	85%	7%
64.	**Spring Arbor University** (MI)	43	2.4	76%	51%	54%	71%	1%	15/1	19-25	44%	67%	10%
64.	**University of Wisconsin–Stout***	43	2.8	73%	48%	53%	36%	2%	17/1	20-24	29%	82%	5%
68.	**McKendree University** (IL)	42	2.4	77%	55%	56%	72%	0%	14/1	20-25	37%	61%	8%
68.	**Mount St. Joseph University** (OH)	42	2.3	71%	52%	54%	70%	0%	11/1	19-24	34%	88%	10%
68.	**Quincy University** (IL)	42	2.5	71%	48%	49%	71%	0%	13/1	19-25	32%	89%	13%
68.	**Tiffin University** (OH)	42	2.4	66%	22%	48%	58%	0%	15/1	17-22[3]	N/A	54%	11%
72.	**Univ. of Wisconsin–River Falls***	41	2.7	72%	52%	54%	41%	5%	20/1	20-25	33%	78%	7%
72.	**Winona State University** (MN)*	41	2.9	78%	53%	57%	26%	10%	20/1	20-25	30%	63%	8%
74.	**Northwest Missouri State Univ.***	40	2.8	68%	47%	49%	44%	7%	22/1	20-25	41%	74%	5%
75.	**College of St. Mary** (NE)	39	2.3	72%	45%	49%	74%	0%	10/1	20-25	52%	54%[4]	21%
75.	**Concordia University Chicago**	39	2.5	65%	52%	59%	58%	6%	17/1	20-25	10%[5]	54%	9%
75.	**Minnesota State Univ.–Mankato***	39	2.8	74%	49%	50%	32%	10%	23/1	19-24	24%	67%	6%
75.	**Mount Mary University** (WI)	39	2.3	71%	46%	49%	87%	0%	10/1	17-22	45%	55%	14%
75.	**University of Central Missouri***	39	2.7	69%[8]	47%	52%	45%	4%	20/1	19-24[2]	32%	78%	2%[7]
75.	**Univ. of Wisconsin–Green Bay***	39	2.8	74%	55%	51%	36%	10%	21/1	20-25	N/A	84%	5%
75.	**Univ. of Wisconsin–Oshkosh***	39	2.8	76%	52%	54%	37%	9%	22/1	20-24[3]	35%	68%	5%
75.	**Wayne State College** (NE)*	39	2.5	67%	43%	49%	48%	1%	19/1	18-24[2]	29%	100%	13%
83.	**Marian University** (WI)	38	2.2	69%	45%	56%	76%	0.4%	11/1	17-23	28%	77%	8%
83.	**Univ. of Wisconsin–Platteville***	38	2.8	77%	51%	52%	29%	6%	21/1	21-25[3]	36%	79%	N/A
85.	**Eastern Michigan University***	37	2.8	74%	48%	37%	40%	4%	18/1	19-25	39%	69%	3%
85.	**Fontbonne University** (MO)	37	2.4	73%	50%	48%	83%	0%	11/1	20-25	N/A	93%	4%
85.	**Northern Michigan University***	37	2.8	73%[8]	53%	49%	37%	8%	21/1	19-24[3]	N/A	72%	6%
85.	**Ohio Dominican University**	37	2.6	67%[8]	44%	43%	57%	0%	15/1	19-24	42%	47%	8%
85.	**Pittsburg State University** (KS)*	37	2.6	72%	48%	53%	38%	9%	19/1	19-24	35%	79%	8%
90.	**Rockford University** (IL)	36	2.3	63%	43%	45%	81%	0.3%	10/1	19-24	N/A	55%	8%
90.	**William Woods University** (MO)	36	2.3	74%	50%	52%	78%	0%	10/1	19-26	39%	76%	10%
92.	**Dakota State University** (SD)*	35	2.5	65%	50%	41%	61%	1%	16/1	19-25	20%	84%	10%
92.	**Siena Heights University** (MI)	35	2.3	64%	44%	51%	82%	0%	11/1	19-24	38%	74%	6%
92.	**Southeast Missouri State Univ.***	35	2.6	73%	52%	51%	42%	4%	22/1	20-25[3]	41%	85%	6%

Note: Key to footnotes, Page 106.

MIDWEST ▶

Rank	School (State) (*Public)	Overall score	Peer assessment score (5.0=highest)	Average freshman retention rate	2014 graduation rate Predicted	2014 graduation rate Actual	% of classes under 20 ('14)	% of classes of 50 or more ('14)	Student/ faculty ratio ('14)	SAT/ACT 25th-75th percentile ('14)	Freshmen in top 25% of HS class ('14)	Acceptance rate ('14)	Average alumni giving rate
92.	**University of Saint Francis** (IN)	35	2.6	71%	48%	50%	59%	2%	12/1	870-1060	24%	97%	6%
92.	**Univ. of Wisconsin–Superior***	35	2.5	70%	48%	43%	59%	2%	14/1	19-24	17%	68%	4%
92.	**Washburn University** (KS)*	35	2.7	65%	49%	35%	47%	2%	14/1	19-25	35%	98%	9%
98.	**Madonna University** (MI)	34	2.3	83%[8]	50%	50%	69%	2%	11/1	19-26	35%	59%	2%
99.	**Bemidji State University** (MN)*	33	2.6	68%	48%	46%	45%	7%	21/1	19-24	20%	94%	5%
99.	**Concordia University–St. Paul** (MN)	33	2.6	70%	48%	46%	69%	0%	19/1	18-24[3]	31%	53%	4%
99.	**Southwestern College** (KS)	33	2.0	64%	56%	54%	77%	1%	10/1	19-25	36%	88%	6%
99.	**St. Cloud State University** (MN)*	33	2.7	70%	47%	44%	41%	4%	17/1	19-24	27%	82%	3%
99.	**University of Michigan–Flint***	33	2.7	74%	47%	34%	52%	3%	15/1	18-24	41%	79%	N/A
104.	**Emporia State University** (KS)*	32	2.6	71%	50%	39%	44%	6%	17/1	19-24[3]	35%	77%	10%
104.	**Graceland University** (IA)	32	2.1	66%	55%	54%	64%	5%	13/1	18-23	25%	50%	18%
104.	**Robert Morris University** (IL)	32	2.3	48%	31%	47%	51%	0.3%	21/1	16-21[3]	15%	24%	1%
104.	**Viterbo University**[1] (WI)	32	2.5	81%[8]	50%	50%[6]	N/A	N/A	12/1[4]	21-26[4]	N/A	71%[4]	N/A
108.	**Cornerstone University** (MI)	31	2.0	74%[8]	49%	47%	59%	2%	24/1[4]	20-25	45%	69%	21%
108.	**Lindenwood University** (MO)	31	2.0	71%	43%	50%	70%	0%	14/1	20-25	33%	53%	12%
108.	**Minnesota State Univ.–Moorhead***	31	2.7	68%	47%	42%	36%	7%	17/1	20-25	31%	84%	N/A
108.	**University of Dubuque** (IA)	31	2.5	67%[8]	45%	48%	N/A	N/A	13/1	17-23[3]	22%	78%	12%
112.	**Minot State University** (ND)*	30	2.4	66%	54%	40%	65%[4]	1%[4]	13/1	20-25	31%[5]	58%	4%
112.	**Roosevelt University** (IL)	30	2.4	62%	47%	30%	53%	1%	11/1	20-25	9%	76%	N/A

School (State) (*Public)	Peer assessment score (5.0=highest)	Average freshman retention rate	2014 graduation rate Predicted	2014 graduation rate Actual	% of classes under 20 ('14)	% of classes of 50 or more ('14)	Student/ faculty ratio ('14)	SAT/ACT 25th-75th percentile ('14)	Freshmen in top 25% of HS class ('14)	Acceptance rate ('14)	Average alumni giving rate
SECOND TIER (SCHOOLS RANKED 114 THROUGH 149 ARE LISTED HERE ALPHABETICALLY)											
Aurora University[1] (IL)	2.3	72%[8]	50%	51%[6]	N/A	N/A	15/1[4]	920-1120[4]	N/A	76%[4]	4%[7]
Avila University[1] (MO)	2.2	70%[8]	48%	45%[6]	N/A	N/A	14/1[4]	850-1140[4]	N/A	61%[4]	N/A
Black Hills State University[1] (SD)*	2.5	60%[8]	44%	33%[6]	N/A	N/A	20/1[4]	853-1229[4]	N/A	89%[4]	N/A
Calumet College of St. Joseph (IN)	2.1	58%	43%	25%	77%	1%	12/1	15-19[9]	15%	30%	3%
Chicago State University*	1.9	53%	36%	19%	54%	0%	12/1[4]	16-20	N/A	30%	N/A
Columbia College Chicago[1]	2.6	67%[8]	53%	41%[6]	N/A	N/A	12/1[4]	N/A[2]	N/A	91%[4]	N/A
Davenport University (MI)	2.0	69%	27%	37%	64%	0%	12/1	21[2]	N/A	93%	1%
DeVry University (IL)	1.6	N/A	32%	32%	N/A	N/A	13/1	N/A[2]	N/A	N/A	N/A
Fort Hays State University (KS)*	2.4	68%[8]	33%	41%	43%	3%	17/1	N/A[2]	30%	88%	N/A
Friends University (KS)	2.2	N/A	47%	38%	N/A	N/A	N/A	N/A[2]	33%	84%	N/A
Governors State University (IL)*	2.1	N/A	N/A	N/A	60%	1%	10/1	17-21	N/A	94%	N/A
Indiana University Northwest*	2.2	66%	34%	29%	35%	9%	15/1	790-1020	28%	77%	6%
Indiana U.-Purdue U.–Fort Wayne*	2.7	63%	43%	25%	49%	4%	17/1	880-1100	38%	91%	4%[4]
Indiana University–South Bend*	2.5	64%	40%	26%	45%	2%	13/1	840-1040	28%	73%	7%
Indiana University Southeast*	2.3	62%	39%	32%	43%	1%	14/1	850-1050	31%	80%	8%
Lake Erie College (OH)	1.9	66%	47%	47%	70%	0%	14/1	18-23[3]	28%[4]	69%	8%
Lakeland College[1] (WI)	2.0	70%[8]	47%	46%[6]	N/A	N/A	15/1[4]	830-960[4]	N/A	55%[4]	N/A
Lincoln University (MO)*	2.0	50%	55%	25%	49%	2%	17/1	15-21	17%	54%	8%
Lourdes University (OH)	2.1	60%	37%	25%	70%	0%	9/1	18-22	33%	65%	7%[4]
Marygrove College[1] (MI)	2.1	67%[8]	24%	22%[6]	N/A	N/A	11/1[4]	14-18[4]	N/A	94%[4]	N/A
Metropolitan State University[1] (MN)*	2.3	61%[8]	47%	33%[6]	N/A	N/A	17/1[4]	N/A[2]	N/A	100%[4]	2%[7]
MidAmerica Nazarene University (KS)	2.2	N/A	51%	50%	65%	2%	23/1	19-21	N/A	69%	N/A
Missouri Baptist University[1]	2.0	62%[8]	50%	36%[6]	N/A	N/A	20/1[4]	810-1040[4]	N/A	61%[4]	N/A
Newman University (KS)	2.2	71%	54%	48%	68%	1%	14/1	20-27[9]	50%	53%	6%
Northeastern Illinois University*	2.4	62%	42%	22%	42%	1%	16/1	16-21	23%	57%	2%
Oakland City University (IN)	1.9	75%	51%	52%	N/A	N/A	12/1	18-23[9]	N/A	55%	N/A
Park University (MO)	2.2	64%[8]	43%	42%	N/A	0%	12/1	22[3]	34%[5]	66%	1%
Purdue University–Calumet (IN)*	2.5	70%	31%	31%	27%	8%	19/1	860-1070	37%	60%	5%[4]
Saginaw Valley State Univ. (MI)*	2.4	70%	46%	40%	33%	4%	18/1	19-25	43%	79%	N/A
Southwest Baptist University[1] (MO)	2.2	64%[8]	48%	43%[6]	N/A	N/A	15/1[4]	830-1110[4]	N/A	90%[4]	N/A
Southwest Minnesota State University*	2.4	68%[8]	50%	43%	37%	4%	16/1	19-23[3]	24%	67%	10%
University of Mary (ND)	2.4	77%[8]	47%	46%	73%	2%	11/1	20-25[3]	N/A	79%	24%
University of Southern Indiana*	2.5	68%	44%	39%	42%	5%	17/1	890-1100	37%	71%	5%
University of St. Mary (KS)	2.2	63%	49%	35%	72%[4]	0%[4]	10/1[4]	19-24[4]	3%[4]	47%	N/A
Upper Iowa University	2.2	66%	38%	38%	78%	0.1%	18/1	17-23	44%	70%	4%
Youngstown State University (OH)*	2.3	68%	37%	33%	39%	6%	17/1	18-24	30%	83%	4%

WEST ▶

Rank	School (State) (*Public)	Overall score	Peer assessment score (5.0=highest)	Average freshman retention rate	2014 graduation rate		% of classes under 20 ('14)	% of classes of 50 or more ('14)	Student/ faculty ratio ('14)	SAT/ACT 25th-75th percentile ('14)	Freshmen in top 25% of HS class ('14)	Accept-ance rate ('14)	Average alumni giving rate
					Predicted	Actual							
1.	**Trinity University** (TX)	100	4.1	89%	88%	81%	61%	2%	9/1	1170-1360	70%	48%	14%
2.	**Santa Clara University** (CA)	98	3.9	95%	82%	85%	42%	2%	12/1	1210-1390	86%[4]	49%	22%
3.	**Loyola Marymount University** (CA)	95	3.8	91%	77%	78%	51%	1%	11/1	1100-1300	74%[4]	53%	19%
4.	**Gonzaga University** (WA)	89	3.9	93%	75%	83%	48%	2%	11/1	1100-1290	71%	68%	18%
5.	**Mills College** (CA)	85	3.4	77%	68%	69%	74%	0%	11/1	1020-1250	64%	76%	23%
6.	**Seattle University**	79	3.5	87%	72%	78%	58%	1%	12/1	1060-1280	62%[5]	73%	10%
7.	**Chapman University** (CA)	78	3.5	91%	82%	74%	43%	2%	14/1	1110-1290	80%[5]	47%	10%
7.	**University of Portland** (OR)	78	3.7	90%	74%	80%	32%	2%	14/1	1080-1310	73%[5]	63%	13%
9.	**St. Mary's College of California**	74	3.4	88%	62%	65%	52%	0.2%	12/1	980-1200	64%[4]	75%	15%
10.	**Cal. Poly. State U.–San Luis Obispo***	72	3.8	93%	75%	78%	15%	13%	20/1	1130-1320[3]	85%[5]	31%	5%
10.	**Whitworth University** (WA)	72	3.5	86%	74%	75%	56%	3%	11/1	1050-1280[9]	N/A	82%	17%
12.	**University of Redlands** (CA)	69	3.1	88%	68%	69%	61%	0.2%	14/1	1000-1200	62%	73%	12%
13.	**St. Edward's University** (TX)	67	3.3	82%	63%	67%	61%	0.1%	13/1	1010-1210	58%	78%	6%
14.	**Pacific Lutheran University** (WA)	66	3.2	82%	69%	68%	50%	2%	12/1	980-1210	63%[5]	75%	11%
15.	**University of Dallas**	65	3.2	79%	73%	70%	62%	3%	10/1	1080-1320[3]	58%[5]	85%	18%
16.	**California Lutheran University**	64	3.2	84%	66%	66%	59%	1%	16/1	1000-1200	63%	61%	14%
17.	**Abilene Christian University** (TX)	63	3.3	76%	65%	62%	46%	8%	14/1	21-27	64%	50%	10%
17.	**Point Loma Nazarene University** (CA)	63	3.0	85%	69%	73%	43%	4%	14/1	1010-1220	67%	70%	8%
17.	**Seattle Pacific University**	63	3.1	85%	68%	75%	48%	3%	15/1	1030-1250[3]	57%[4]	83%	8%[7]
20.	**Westminster College** (UT)	62	3.1	76%	65%	61%	68%	0%	9/1	22-27	55%	97%	15%
21.	**Western Washington University***	61	3.3	84%	62%	72%	35%	17%	19/1	1000-1210	51%	85%	5%
22.	**St. Mary's Univ. of San Antonio**	56	3.0	73%	58%	63%	23%	0.4%	12/1	940-1130[3]	57%[4]	59%	9%
23.	**Mount Saint Mary's University** (CA)	54	3.0	80%	47%	66%	62%	0.2%	12/1	810-1020	42%	78%	13%
23.	**Oklahoma City University**	54	3.0	79%	71%	59%	76%	1%	11/1	23-28[3]	64%	68%	5%
25.	**Dominican University of California**	53	2.8	83%	61%	62%	68%	0%	9/1	940-1150	57%	81%	9%
25.	**N.M. Inst. of Mining and Tech.***	53	3.2	76%	78%	45%	60%	6%	12/1	23-29	64%	36%	N/A
25.	**Pacific University** (OR)	53	3.0	79%	67%	59%	54%	4%	11/1	980-1200[3]	N/A	80%	9%
28.	**George Fox University** (OR)	52	3.0	82%	61%	69%	55%	4%	14/1	960-1210	57%[5]	76%	4%
28.	**Regis University** (CO)	52	3.1	83%	62%	60%	67%	1%	14/1	22-27[3]	50%	96%	5%
30.	**University of St. Thomas** (TX)	51	3.0	82%	65%	52%	66%	0.2%	9/1	990-1220	49%	79%	6%
31.	**Calif. State Poly. Univ.–Pomona***	50	3.5	90%	45%	57%	15%	13%	25/1	930-1210[3]	N/A	52%	3%
32.	**California State U.–Long Beach***	49	3.2	89%	55%	65%	22%	10%	24/1	940-1170	N/A	36%	4%
32.	**LeTourneau University** (TX)	49	2.7	78%	62%	51%	60%	3%	14/1	1030-1310[2]	56%	49%	7%
34.	**Hardin-Simmons University** (TX)	48	2.8	65%	53%	53%	68%	1%	12/1	20-25[3]	46%	57%	8%
35.	**Dallas Baptist University**	47	2.8	72%	58%	55%	67%	2%	13/1	18-27	46%	46%	1%
35.	**Evergreen State College** (WA)*	47	3.2	72%	52%	56%	35%	13%	22/1	880-1200	18%[5]	99%	5%
37.	**California State U.–Fullerton***	46	3.1	88%	48%	56%	25%	9%	25/1	920-1130	66%	44%	2%
37.	**Fresno Pacific University** (CA)	46	2.7	78%	51%	64%	64%	2%	12/1	900-1110	63%	67%	N/A
39.	**California Baptist University**	45	2.8	79%	49%	55%	56%	5%	18/1	840-1100	40%	80%	2%
39.	**Notre Dame de Namur University** (CA)	45	2.8	78%[8]	46%	53%	67%	0%	11/1	850-1040	35%[5]	78%	9%
39.	**San Jose State University** (CA)*	45	3.1	86%	48%	51%	18%	17%	28/1	900-1200	N/A	60%	2%
42.	**Alaska Pacific University**	43	2.5	73%[8]	62%	60%	96%[4]	0%[4]	8/1[4]	950-1165[3]	N/A	42%	N/A
42.	**California State Univ.–Chico***	43	2.8	87%	57%	59%	28%	14%	24/1	993-1100[3]	76%[5]	75%	5%[4]
42.	**Oklahoma Christian U.**	43	2.9	76%	60%	46%	60%	5%	14/1	22-28[3]	52%	64%	16%
42.	**Walla Walla University** (WA)	43	2.7	79%	56%	56%	62%	7%	13/1	930-1230	33%	58%	9%
46.	**St. Martin's University** (WA)	42	2.7	78%	53%	48%	63%	6%	12/1	935-1155	58%	89%	6%
46.	**Univ. of Colo.–Colorado Springs***	42	3.2	69%	52%	47%	45%	7%	15/1	21-26	35%	92%	2%
48.	**Sonoma State University** (CA)*	41	2.9	81%	52%	55%	32%	10%	25/1	880-1100	N/A	92%	1%
48.	**Texas Wesleyan University**	41	2.7	62%	46%	39%	76%	0%	15/1	900-1060	39%	38%	7%
50.	**Holy Names University** (CA)	40	2.5	73%	48%	50%	72%	0%	9/1	785-980	31%[5]	57%	8%
50.	**Oral Roberts University** (OK)	40	2.5	80%	54%	53%	54%	5%	15/1	19-25	44%	45%	8%
52.	**California State Univ.–Fresno***	39	2.9	84%	47%	52%	17%	11%	22/1	790-1010	80%	59%	3%
52.	**Central Washington University***	39	2.8	77%	48%	53%	46%	6%	19/1	870-1080[3]	N/A	87%	2%
52.	**Texas State University***	39	2.8	77%	54%	55%	28%	16%	20/1	930-1130	43%	73%	4%
55.	**Concordia University** (CA)	38	2.6	76%	55%	56%	53%	0.2%	18/1	910-1150	42%[5]	63%	5%
55.	**Univ. of Mary Hardin-Baylor** (TX)	38	2.8	67%	55%	48%	49%	3%	17/1	950-1140[3]	48%	80%	6%
57.	**California State U.–Stanislaus***	37	2.6	86%	39%	54%	20%	9%	22/1	810-1010[2]	N/A	73%	1%
57.	**Humboldt State University** (CA)*	37	2.8	75%	51%	44%	29%	14%	24/1	870-1100[2]	46%	77%	7%
57.	**La Sierra University** (CA)	37	2.4	77%	52%	50%	70%	3%	15/1	800-1070	24%	41%	4%
57.	**Woodbury University** (CA)	37	2.4	78%	35%	43%	80%	0%	11/1	830-1058	N/A	71%	3%
61.	**Boise State University** (ID)*	36	3.2	72%	47%	37%	35%	10%	19/1	920-1140[3]	36%	77%	7%

Note: Key to footnotes, Page 106.

WEST ▸

Rank	School (State) (*Public)	Overall score	Peer assessment score (5.0=highest)	Average freshman retention rate	2014 graduation rate: Predicted	2014 graduation rate: Actual	% of classes under 20 ('14)	% of classes of 50 or more ('14)	Student/ faculty ratio ('14)	SAT/ACT 25th-75th percentile ('14)	Freshmen in top 25% of HS class ('14)	Accept-ance rate ('14)	Average alumni giving rate
61.	**Northwest Nazarene University** (ID)	36	2.6	76%[8]	53%	52%	63%	4%	17/1	900-1180[3]	46%	65%	N/A
63.	**California State U.–Los Angeles***	35	2.9	82%	25%	41%	28%	8%	26/1	780-980[2]	3%[4]	61%	2%
63.	**California State U.–Monterey Bay***	35	2.8	81%	47%	45%	19%	6%	29/1	860-1080	43%	45%[4]	2%
63.	**California State U.–Sacramento***	35	3.0	82%	39%	44%	21%	17%	26/1	830-1050[2]	N/A	73%	2%[7]
63.	**Eastern Washington University***	35	2.7	76%	44%	45%	37%	11%	22/1	850-1070	N/A	74%	3%
63.	**San Francisco State University***	35	3.0	82%	49%	50%	25%[4]	20%[4]	24/1	870-1110	N/A	66%	2%
63.	**Univ. of the Incarnate Word** (TX)	35	2.7	74%	47%	42%	54%	1%	14/1	850-1070	37%	93%	6%
69.	**Calif. State U.–San Bernardino***	34	2.7	89%	34%	47%	26%	19%	30/1	790-990[2]	N/A	65%	2%
70.	**California State U.–Northridge***	33	3.1	76%	39%	47%	10%	16%	28/1	800-1030	N/A	53%	2%[7]
70.	**Southern Utah University***	33	2.6	66%	52%	38%	42%	7%	18/1	20-26	43%	63%	3%
70.	**Texas A&M International University***	33	2.6	78%	38%	41%	33%	14%	20/1	820-1010	51%	48%	8%
73.	**Chaminade Univ. of Honolulu**	32	2.6	73%	40%	48%	59%	1%	12/1	860-1040	5%	85%	4%
73.	**Houston Baptist University**	32	2.6	66%	54%	44%	49%	1%	16/1	960-1160	57%	36%	4%[4]
73.	**Southern Oregon University***	32	2.8	70%	49%	41%	44%	4%	21/1	910-1150	N/A	93%	2%
73.	**University of Texas–Tyler***	32	2.7	64%	55%	45%	35%	11%	16/1	953-1150	37%[5]	84%	N/A
77.	**Hawaii Pacific University**	31	2.8	69%	58%	42%	51%	1%	13/1	890-1120	61%	83%	1%
77.	**University of Alaska–Anchorage***	31	2.9	72%	49%	28%	56%	4%	12/1	880-1120[2]	33%	80%	5%
77.	**Weber State University** (UT)*	31	2.9	71%	38%	35%	47%	6%	20/1	18-24[2]	18%	100%	1%
77.	**Western Oregon University***	31	2.7	70%[8]	46%	46%	56%	3%	15/1	860-1180	35%	89%	N/A
81.	**University of Central Oklahoma***	30	3.0	58%	46%	37%	35%	3%	20/1	18-24	21%	90%	1%
81.	**University of Houston–Clear Lake***	30	2.7	N/A	N/A	N/A	29%	6%	16/1	960-1150	55%	34%	2%
83.	**California State Univ.–Bakersfield***	29	2.7	73%[8]	33%	40%[6]	N/A	N/A	N/A	N/A[2]	N/A	N/A	0.4%[7]
83.	**Lubbock Christian University** (TX)	29	2.5	67%	50%	43%	65%	2%	12/1	19-24[3]	42%	94%	5%
83.	**Prescott College** (AZ)	29	2.5	69%[8]	52%	35%	99%	1%	9/1	890-1205[3]	N/A	68%	N/A
83.	**Southern Nazarene University** (OK)	29	2.5	53%[8]	47%	47%[6]	70%[4]	2%[4]	15/1[4]	N/A	49%[4]	37%	N/A
87.	**California State U.–Channel Islands**[1]*	28	2.6	78%[8]	56%	52%[6]	N/A	N/A	20/1[4]	N/A[2]	N/A	N/A	N/A
87.	**California State Univ.–San Marcos***	28	2.6	81%	46%	47%	14%	8%	27/1	860-1050[2]	N/A	85%	1%[7]
87.	**Stephen F. Austin State Univ.** (TX)*	28	2.7	66%	46%	43%	26%	11%	20/1	900-1080	40%	59%	4%

COURTESY OF TRINITY UNIVERSITY

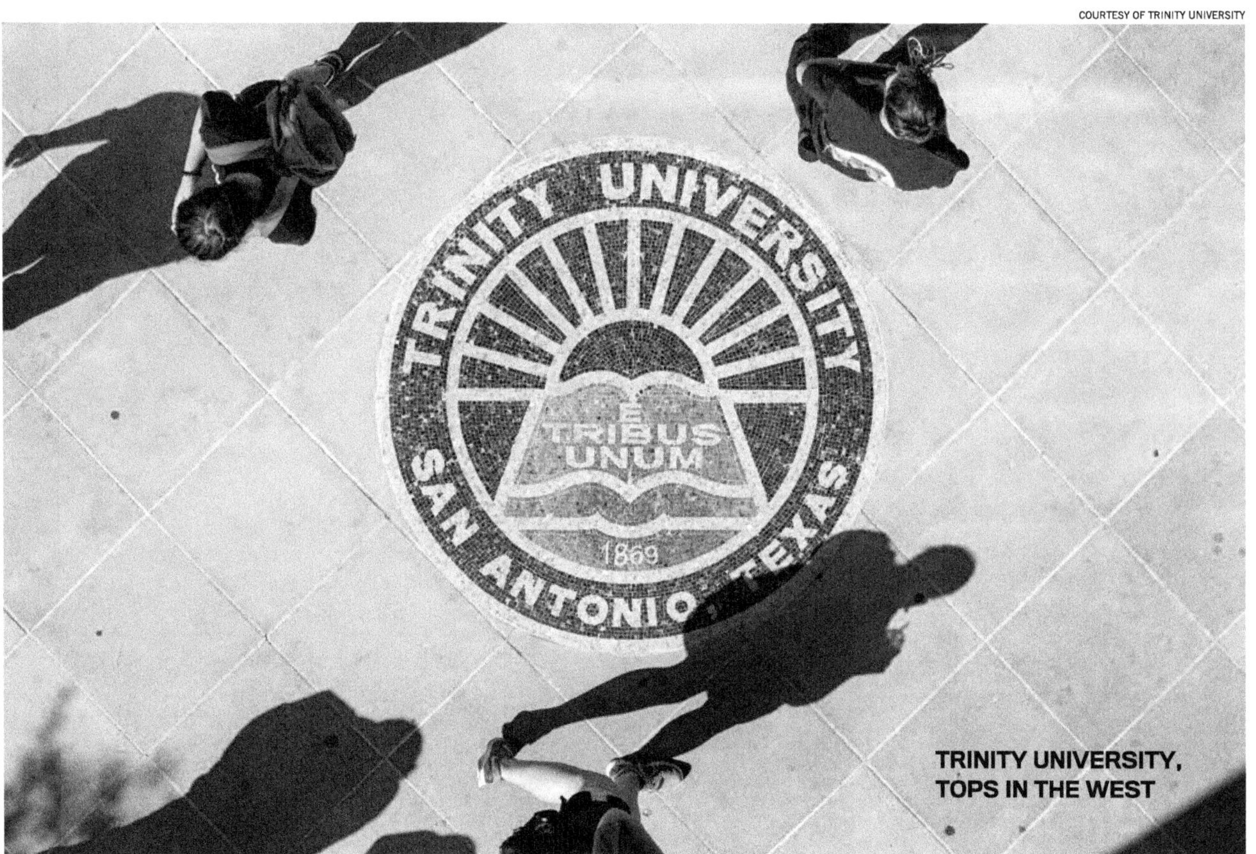

TRINITY UNIVERSITY, TOPS IN THE WEST

WEST ▶

School (State) (*Public)	Peer assessment score (5.0=highest)	Average freshman retention rate	2014 graduation rate: Predicted	2014 graduation rate: Actual	% of classes under 20 ('14)	% of classes of 50 or more ('14)	Student/faculty ratio ('14)	SAT/ACT 25th-75th percentile ('14)	Freshmen in top 25% of HS class ('14)	Acceptance rate ('14)	Average alumni giving rate
SECOND TIER (SCHOOLS RANKED 90 THROUGH 118 ARE LISTED HERE ALPHABETICALLY)											
Adams State University[1] (CO)*	2.5	56%[8]	37%	24%[6]	N/A	N/A	15/1[4]	890-1083[4]	N/A	53%[4]	N/A
Angelo State University (TX)*	2.4	59%	42%	31%	25%	9%	19/1	18-24	34%	89%	2%
California State U.–Dominguez Hills*	2.4	79%	30%	32%	22%	11%	26/1	760-940[2]	N/A	81%	2%
California State Univ.–East Bay*	2.5	77%	41%	37%	18%	16%	28/1	790-1010[9]	N/A	70%	N/A
Cameron University (OK)*	2.3	59%	37%	23%	46%	1%	19/1	17-23[2]	13%	100%	3%
Colorado Christian University[1]	2.5	69%[8]	51%	40%[6]	N/A	N/A	14/1[4]	N/A[2]	N/A	N/A	N/A
Colorado State University–Pueblo*	2.5	63%	33%	32%	48%	6%	16/1	18-23[3]	31%	93%	2%
Concordia University[1] (OR)	2.5	71%[8]	46%	50%[6]	N/A	N/A	23/1[4]	890-1100[4]	N/A	56%[4]	N/A
Concordia University Texas[1]	2.5	53%[8]	50%	36%[6]	N/A	N/A	11/1[4]	930-1120[4]	N/A	47%[4]	N/A
East Central University[1] (OK)*	2.4	63%[8]	38%	34%[6]	N/A	N/A	19/1[4]	800-1090[4]	N/A	98%[4]	N/A
Eastern New Mexico University[1]*	2.4	61%[8]	39%	27%[6]	N/A	N/A	18/1[4]	820-1080[4]	N/A	63%[4]	N/A
Eastern Oregon University*	2.4	65%[8]	36%	29%[6]	74%	3%	22/1	820-1050	36%	64%	1%
Grand Canyon University[1] (AZ)	1.9	59%[8]	47%	31%[6]	N/A	N/A	21/1[4]	N/A[2]	N/A	55%[4]	N/A
Midwestern State University (TX)*	2.4	69%[8]	49%	45%	37%	12%	17/1	900-1100	38%	62%	5%
Montana State Univ.–Billings*	2.9	57%	43%	24%	51%	6%	17/1	18-23[2]	27%	100%	6%
Northeastern State University (OK)*	2.5	64%	43%	31%	53%	3%	18/1	19-24[3]	46%	75%	2%
Northwestern Oklahoma State U.*	2.3	62%	37%	39%	53%	2%	15/1	18-22	26%	65%	3%
Prairie View A&M University (TX)*	2.2	66%	31%	36%	22%	10%	18/1	770-940	16%	86%	N/A
Sierra Nevada College[1] (NV)	2.1	71%[8]	52%	47%[6]	81%[4]	0%[4]	11/1[4]	870-1070[4]	20%[4]	87%[4]	4%[4]
Southeastern Oklahoma State U.*	2.4	58%	40%	28%	53%	3%	17/1	18-22[3]	34%	79%	4%
Southwestern Assemblies of God University (TX)	2.2	66%[8]	40%	36%[6]	N/A	N/A	18/1[4]	18-24[3]	N/A	34%	1%
Southwestern Oklahoma State U.*	2.4	65%	44%	33%	47%	6%	18/1	19-24	46%	85%	1%[4]
Sul Ross State University (TX)*	2.2	51%[8]	36%	26%	65%	3%	15/1	15-21	12%	93%	N/A
Tarleton State University (TX)*	2.4	68%	45%	45%	33%	9%	19/1	860-1050	23%	77%[4]	2%[7]
Texas A&M University–Texarkana[1]*	2.4	42%[8]	N/A	N/A	N/A	N/A	16/1[4]	830-1030[4]	39%[4]	36%[4]	N/A
University of Houston–Victoria[1]*	2.5	N/A	N/A	N/A	30%[4]	2%[4]	19/1[4]	810-1005[4]	23%[4]	52%[4]	N/A
U. of Texas of the Permian Basin*	2.4	65%	52%	34%	37%	12%	21/1	880-1068	55%	87%	7%
Wayland Baptist University (TX)	2.1	48%	41%	32%	86%	0.1%	8/1	17-23	29%	97%	1%
West Texas A&M University*	2.6	65%	48%	43%	29%	11%	20/1	18-23	39%	67%	3%

The Top Public Regional Universities ▶

NORTH

Rank School (State)

1. **College of New Jersey**
2. **SUNY–Geneseo**
3. **Rowan University** (NJ)
4. **SUNY–New Paltz**
5. **Ramapo College of New Jersey**
6. **CUNY–Baruch College**
7. **Montclair State University** (NJ)
8. **Rutgers, The State University of New Jersey–Camden**
9. **CUNY–Hunter College**
9. **CUNY–Queens College**
9. **SUNY College–Oneonta**
12. **Stockton University** (NJ)
12. **Towson University** (MD)
14. **College at Brockport–SUNY**
14. **SUNY–Oswego**

SOUTH

Rank School (State)

1. **The Citadel** (SC)
2. **James Madison University** (VA)
3. **Appalachian State University** (NC)
4. **College of Charleston** (SC)
5. **Christopher Newport Univ.** (VA)
6. **Univ. of Mary Washington** (VA)
6. **University of North Carolina–Wilmington**
8. **Winthrop University** (SC)
9. **Georgia College & State Univ.**
9. **Longwood University** (VA)
9. **Murray State University** (KY)
12. **Western Kentucky University**
13. **Western Carolina University** (NC)
14. **Tennessee Technological Univ.**
15. **Radford University** (VA)
15. **University of Montevallo** (AL)

MIDWEST

Rank School (State)

1. **Truman State University** (MO)
2. **University of Northern Iowa**
3. **Grand Valley State University** (MI)
4. **Univ. of Wisconsin–La Crosse**
5. **Eastern Illinois University**
6. **Univ. of Wisconsin–Eau Claire**
7. **University of Michigan–Dearborn**
7. **University of Minnesota–Duluth**
9. **University of Illinois–Springfield**
10. **Southern Illinois University–Edwardsville**
11. **Univ. of Nebraska–Kearney**
11. **Western Illinois University**
13. **Univ. of Wisconsin–Stevens Point**
13. **Univ. of Wisconsin–Whitewater**
15. **Ferris State University** (MI)

WEST

Rank School (State)

1. **California Polytechnic State University–San Luis Obispo**
2. **Western Washington University**
3. **N.M. Inst. of Mining and Tech.**
4. **Calif. State Poly. Univ.–Pomona**
5. **California State U.–Long Beach**
6. **Evergreen State College** (WA)
7. **California State U.–Fullerton**
8. **San Jose State University** (CA)
9. **California State Univ.–Chico**
10. **Univ. of Colo.–Colorado Springs**
11. **Sonoma State University** (CA)
12. **California State Univ.–Fresno**
12. **Central Washington University**
12. **Texas State University**
15. **California State U.–Stanislaus**
15. **Humboldt State University** (CA)

Footnotes:

1. School refused to fill out U.S. News statistical survey. Data that appear are from school in previous years or from another source such as the National Center for Education Statistics.
2. SAT and/or ACT not required by school for some or all applicants.
3. In reporting SAT/ACT scores, the school did not include all students for whom it had scores or refused to tell U.S. News whether all students with scores had been included.
4. Data reported to U.S. News in previous years.
5. Data based on fewer than 51 percent of enrolled freshmen.
6. Some or all data reported to the NCAA and/or the National Center for Education Statistics.
7. Data reported to the Council for Aid to Education.
8. This rate, normally based on four years of data, is given here for less than four years because school didn't report rate for the most recent year or years to U.S. News.
9. SAT and/or ACT may not be required by school for some or all applicants, and in reporting SAT/ACT scores, the school did not include all students for whom it had scores or refused to tell U.S. News whether all students with scores had been included.

N/A means not available.

ANDY MCMILLAN FOR USN&WR

ELON UNIVERSITY, TIED AT NO. 1 IN THE SOUTH

Best Regional Colleges

What Is a Regional College?

According to the Carnegie Classification of Institutions of Higher Education, these schools focus almost entirely on the undergraduate experience and offer a broad range of programs in the liberal arts (which account for fewer than half of all bachelor's degrees granted) and in fields such as business, nursing and education. They grant few graduate degrees. Because most of the 363 colleges in the category draw heavily from nearby states, they are ranked by region.

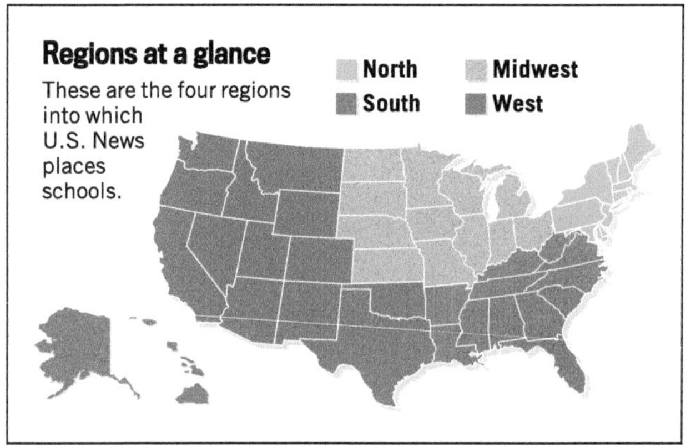

NORTH ▶

Rank	School (State) (*Public)	Overall score	Peer assessment score (5.0=highest)	Average freshman retention rate	2014 graduation rate: Predicted	2014 graduation rate: Actual	% of classes under 20 ('14)	% of classes of 50 or more ('14)	Student/faculty ratio ('14)	SAT/ACT 25th-75th percentile ('14)	Freshmen in top 25% of HS class ('14)	Acceptance rate ('14)	Average alumni giving rate
1.	**U.S. Coast Guard Acad.** (CT)*	100	4.1	92%	83%	85%	67%	0%	7/1	1170-1340	76%	18%	29%[4]
2.	**Cooper Union** (NY)	94	4.1	94%[8]	94%	83%	70%	1%	7/1[4]	1250-1500	90%[5]	15%	23%[4]
3.	**U.S. Merchant Marine Acad.** (NY)*	74	3.7	91%[8]	73%	68%	70%[4]	3%[4]	13/1	26-30	68%	22%	N/A
4.	**Elizabethtown College** (PA)	67	3.3	83%	66%	69%	64%	1%	11/1	1020-1240	64%	71%	20%
5.	**Messiah College** (PA)	65	3.4	86%	68%	80%	48%	2%	13/1	1010-1240	63%	80%	13%
6.	**Lebanon Valley College** (PA)	60	3.1	85%	64%	75%	56%	1%	11/1	970-1210[2]	66%	71%	16%
7.	**Maine Maritime Academy***	59	3.4	80%	55%	65%	54%	2%	12/1	920-1130	35%	64%	17%
8.	**Massachusetts Maritime Academy***	58	3.4	89%	57%	70%	46%	2%	16/1	1030-1190	N/A	62%	13%
9.	**Merrimack College** (MA)	52	3.3	83%	56%	68%	39%	2%	13/1	930-1120[2]	34%[4]	78%	13%
10.	**Seton Hill University** (PA)	51	3.1	77%[8]	52%	60%	61%	0%	13/1	940-1180[2]	51%	69%	17%
11.	**Bard College at Simon's Rock** (MA)	50	3.3	76%	61%	29%[8]	98%	0%	6/1	29-31[9]	81%[5]	89%	13%[4]
11.	**Elmira College** (NY)	50	3.1	76%	62%	58%	66%	1%	11/1	940-1180	58%[4]	82%	17%
13.	**Wentworth Inst. of Technology** (MA)	48	3.3	81%	56%	64%	35%	2%	16/1	1010-1220	40%[4]	83%	5%
14.	**Cedar Crest College** (PA)	46	2.8	71%	58%	69%	79%	2%	10/1	888-1120	44%	52%	12%
14.	**Champlain College** (VT)	46	3.0	79%	57%	57%	68%	0%	14/1	1030-1250[3]	44%[5]	64%	7%
16.	**Geneva College** (PA)	45	2.6	79%	51%	65%	68%	4%	13/1	920-1190	51%	71%	11%
17.	**SUNY Maritime College***	43	3.2	80%	55%	47%	29%	3%	15/1	1020-1190	44%[5]	53%	4%
18.	**Delaware Valley University** (PA)	42	3.0	72%	54%	58%	54%	3%	14/1	870-1110[3]	29%	76%	8%
19.	**SUNY College of Technology–Alfred***	40	2.8	83%	32%	55%	47%	3%	19/1	840-1090[2]	N/A	55%	3%
19.	**University of Maine–Farmington***	40	2.8	73%	47%	54%	63%	1%	13/1	870-1100[2]	37%	85%	4%
21.	**St. Francis College** (NY)	39	2.8	80%	41%	55%	56%	0.3%	17/1	830-1040	N/A	77%	9%
21.	**Wilson College** (PA)	39	2.4	69%	55%	41%	89%	0%	9/1	870-1090[2]	34%	31%	20%
23.	**College of Our Lady of the Elms** (MA)	38	2.3	82%	42%	66%	68%	1%	13/1	840-1060[3]	N/A	79%	15%
24.	**Cazenovia College** (NY)	37	2.6	68%	50%	58%	76%	0%	12/1	830-1060[2]	34%	76%	9%
24.	**Vermont Technical College***	37	2.5	74%	50%	65%	74%	0.2%	10/1	810-1050[9]	23%[5]	69%	1%
26.	**Lasell College** (MA)	36	2.7	71%	48%	57%	70%	0%	13/1	880-1070	N/A	76%	12%
26.	**Vaughn Col. of Aeron. and Tech.** (NY)	36	2.6	74%	45%	52%	70%	0%	15/1	891-1093	N/A	75%	2%
28.	**SUNY College of A&T–Cobleskill***	33	2.6	76%	41%	59%	41%	6%	20/1	740-1010[2]	19%	73%	5%
28.	**SUNY College of Technology–Delhi***	33	2.6	70%	30%	63%	45%	3%	17/1	18-22[4]	13%[5]	68%	3%
28.	**Unity College** (ME)	33	2.5	75%	45%	58%	64%	3%	11/1	900-1127[2]	33%	93%	3%
31.	**Dean College** (MA)	31	2.6	65%	34%	43%	56%	0%	16/1	760-960[2]	11%[4]	68%	8%
32.	**Farmingdale State College–SUNY***	30	2.7	82%	47%	43%	26%	1%	19/1	900-1060	24%[5]	47%	0.3%
33.	**Morrisville State College** (NY)*	28	2.4	66%	31%	48%	51%	3%	16/1	840-1000[2]	25%	56%	4%
34.	**La Roche College** (PA)	27	2.3	71%[8]	41%	44%	71%	0%	11/1	840-1010	37%	94%	4%
34.	**Thiel College** (PA)	27	2.5	64%	44%	36%	61%	2%	14/1	860-1060	35%	69%	14%
36.	**Nichols College** (MA)	26	2.5	65%	40%	48%	29%	0%	17/1	840-1030[9]	13%[4]	76%	10%
37.	**Pennsylvania College of Technology***	25	2.8	69%	48%	41%	64%	0%	18/1	N/A[2]	16%	88%	N/A
38.	**Mount Ida College** (MA)	24	2.4	62%	41%	40%	76%	1%	15/1	780-990	N/A	68%	2%

Note: Key to footnotes, Page 115.

NORTH ►

Rank	School (State) (*Public)	Overall score	Peer assessment score (5.0=highest)	Average freshman retention rate	2014 graduation rate: Predicted	2014 graduation rate: Actual	% of classes under 20 ('14)	% of classes of 50 or more ('14)	Student/ faculty ratio ('14)	SAT/ACT 25th-75th percentile ('14)	Freshmen in top 25% of HS class ('14)	Accept-ance rate ('14)	Average alumni giving rate
38.	University of Maine–Fort Kent*	24	2.4	62%	42%	52%	71%	1%	16/1	810-990[2]	18%	90%	6%
40.	Concordia College (NY)	23	2.7	72%[8]	40%	48%	N/A	N/A	N/A	N/A	N/A	74%	N/A
40.	Univ. of Maine–Presque Isle*	23	2.4	62%	47%	46%	74%	0%	13/1	793-1062[2]	19%	83%	2%
42.	Mount Aloysius College (PA)	22	2.8	64%[8]	36%	33%[6]	72%	0%	12/1	840-1010[3]	N/A	74%	N/A
43.	Washington Adventist University (MD)	21	2.2	68%	44%	40%	85%	0.3%	9/1	740-1030	N/A	45%	3%
44.	Keystone College (PA)	20	2.3	66%	35%	36%	73%	0%	11/1	810-1030	17%	92%	N/A
44.	Paul Smith's College[1] (NY)	20	2.6	69%[8]	45%	39%[6]	N/A	N/A	15/1[4]	880-1060[4]	N/A	75%[4]	N/A
44.	SUNY College of Technology–Canton*	20	2.6	76%	27%	31%	44%	3%	17/1	780-1020[2]	16%	81%	3%
44.	Thomas College (ME)	20	2.3	65%	37%	46%	59%	0%	21/1	805-1050[2]	40%	74%	5%
44.	University of Valley Forge[1] (PA)	20	2.2	74%[8]	41%	49%[6]	N/A	N/A	14/1[4]	890-1040[4]	N/A	66%[4]	N/A

School (State) (*Public)	Peer assessment score (5.0=highest)	Average freshman retention rate	2014 graduation rate: Predicted	2014 graduation rate: Actual	% of classes under 20 ('14)	% of classes of 50 or more ('14)	Student/ faculty ratio ('14)	SAT/ACT 25th-75th percentile ('14)	Freshmen in top 25% of HS class ('14)	Accept-ance rate ('14)	Average alumni giving rate
SECOND TIER (SCHOOLS RANKED 49 THROUGH 61 ARE LISTED HERE ALPHABETICALLY)											
Bay State College (MA)	2.1	N/A	32%	16%[6]	60%	0%	17/1	N/A[2]	N/A	59%[4]	N/A
Becker College[1] (MA)	2.5	64%[8]	37%	27%[6]	59%[4]	1%[4]	17/1[4]	19-24[4]	26%[4]	63%[4]	N/A
CUNY–Medgar Evers College*	2.3	N/A	22%	13%	18%	0.3%	17/1	680-870[9]	N/A	91%	N/A
CUNY–New York City Col. of Tech.*	2.7	76%	22%	20%	28%	0.1%	17/1	740-950[2]	N/A	73%	1%
CUNY–York College[1]*	2.5	76%[8]	33%	24%[6]	20%[4]	43%[4]	21/1[4]	N/A	N/A	65%[4]	N/A
Daniel Webster College[1] (NH)	2.4	66%[8]	53%	48%[6]	N/A	N/A	14/1[4]	830-1100[4]	N/A	60%[4]	N/A
Fisher College (MA)	2.3	62%	37%	33%	78%	0%	16/1	710-940[2]	N/A	66%	2%
Five Towns College (NY)	2.2	60%[8]	38%	34%	89%	0%	15/1[4]	760-1000	39%[5]	56%	N/A
Lyndon State College[1] (VT)*	2.4	64%[8]	42%	33%[6]	N/A	N/A	14/1[4]	810-1050[4]	N/A	99%[4]	N/A
Post University[1] (CT)	2.3	44%[8]	30%	32%[8]	59%[4]	0%[4]	19/1[4]	16-22[4]	20%[4]	64%[4]	N/A
Southern Vermont College	2.4	62%[8]	38%	35%	N/A	N/A	14/1	770-940[3]	N/A	94%	N/A
University of Maine–Augusta*	2.7	52%	35%	12%	76%	0.3%	17/1	770-970[2]	14%	97%	0.3%
Wesley College[1] (DE)	2.7	47%[8]	43%	30%[8]	N/A	N/A	16/1[4]	750-940[4]	23%[4]	N/A	N/A

SOUTH ►

Rank	School (State) (*Public)	Overall score	Peer assessment score (5.0=highest)	Average freshman retention rate	2014 graduation rate: Predicted	2014 graduation rate: Actual	% of classes under 20 ('14)	% of classes of 50 or more ('14)	Student/ faculty ratio ('14)	SAT/ACT 25th-75th percentile ('14)	Freshmen in top 25% of HS class ('14)	Accept-ance rate ('14)	Average alumni giving rate
1.	High Point University (NC)	100	3.5	77%	57%	63%	56%	1%	14/1	1009-1192	48%[5]	80%	9%
2.	John Brown University (AR)	97	3.2	82%	61%	61%	52%	0.3%	14/1	22-29	59%	70%	17%
3.	Asbury University (KY)	96	3.2	81%	59%	65%	64%	0.3%	12/1	22-28	54%	69%	18%
4.	Florida Southern College	95	3.2	78%	56%	65%	60%	0%	13/1	1040-1220	58%	45%	13%
5.	Meredith College (NC)	91	3.1	75%	56%	62%	63%	0.2%	12/1	920-1130	46%	61%	20%
6.	Flagler College (FL)	89	3.4	70%	52%	58%	48%	0%	19/1	960-1140	38%	48%	19%
6.	Milligan College (TN)	89	3.0	82%	55%	58%	77%	2%	12/1	22-26	65%	62%	24%
8.	University of the Ozarks (AR)	86	3.2	66%	57%	48%	73%	0%	12/1	20-26	47%	89%	14%
9.	Covenant College (GA)	85	2.9	85%	62%	57%	52%	1%	14/1	23-29	50%[5]	97%	14%
10.	Tuskegee University (AL)	83	3.0	76%	48%	43%	56%	9%	13/1	17-23	60%	48%	25%
11.	Wheeling Jesuit University (WV)	81	2.9	71%	58%	64%	69%	0.3%	12/1	20-25	38%	63%	12%
12.	LaGrange College (GA)	79	2.9	62%	57%	53%	74%	0.4%	10/1	20-24	47%	55%	15%
13.	Lenoir-Rhyne University (NC)	78	3.1	66%	49%	54%	71%	0%	12/1	870-1090	39%	66%	15%
14.	West Virginia Wesleyan College	76	3.0	67%	54%	58%	56%	1%	13/1	19-25	56%	78%	18%
15.	Catawba College (NC)	73	2.9	70%	53%	53%	65%	0%	13/1	860-1090[9]	36%	36%	18%
16.	Anderson University (SC)	71	3.2	75%	45%	49%	45%	5%	14/1	920-1170	63%	63%	7%
16.	Carson-Newman University (TN)	71	3.1	66%	52%	48%	60%	1%	11/1	21-26	N/A	62%	8%
18.	Univ. of South Carolina–Aiken*	70	3.2	67%	44%	39%	55%	1%	15/1	860-1080	43%	65%	6%
19.	Aquinas College (TN)	68	2.7	69%	48%	29%	83%	6%	8/1	20-29	60%[5]	61%	N/A
20.	Coker College (SC)	67	2.8	72%[8]	46%	49%	74%	0%	13/1	910-1108	18%	51%	10%[4]
21.	Huntingdon College (AL)	65	2.8	62%	48%	45%	59%	0.4%	15/1	20-24	32%	58%	28%
22.	Barton College (NC)	64	2.6	71%	43%	44%	66%	0.3%	11/1	860-1050	41%	38%	8%
22.	Blue Mountain College (MS)	64	2.6	72%	41%	46%	80%	0%	14/1	17-26	48%	55%	7%
24.	University of Charleston (WV)	63	3.2	65%	51%	36%	59%	2%	14/1[4]	19-23	N/A	61%	7%
25.	Southern Adventist University (TN)	61	2.7	75%	50%	46%	60%	5%	14/1	20-26	N/A	86%	11%
25.	University of Mobile (AL)	61	3.0	75%	45%	42%	61%	1%	12/1	20-24	48%	58%	1%
27.	Averett University (VA)	60	2.7	58%	32%	32%	80%	0%	11/1	830-1028	30%	60%	5%

SOUTH ▶

Rank	School (State) (*Public)	Overall score	Peer assessment score (5.0=highest)	Average freshman retention rate	2014 graduation rate: Predicted	2014 graduation rate: Actual	% of classes under 20 ('14)	% of classes of 50 or more ('14)	Student/ faculty ratio ('14)	SAT/ACT 25th-75th percentile ('14)	Freshmen in top 25% of HS class ('14)	Acceptance rate ('14)	Average alumni giving rate
27.	**Kentucky Wesleyan College**	60	2.7	62%	46%	41%	84%	0.4%	13/1	19-25	39%	67%[4]	15%
27.	**North Greenville University** (SC)	60	2.8	72%	47%	50%	69%	1%	14/1	22-30[3]	37%	59%	5%
30.	**Alice Lloyd College** (KY)	59	2.8	60%	45%	36%	49%	1%	17/1	19-24[3]	47%	7%	42%
30.	**Bryan College** (TN)	59	2.6	68%	54%	53%	68%	3%	15/1	20-26	48%	48%	10%
30.	**Elizabeth City State Univ.**[1] (NC)*	59	2.4	76%[8]	31%	38%[6]	66%[4]	1%[4]	16/1[4]	16-19[4]	5%[4]	52%[4]	9%[4]
33.	**Tennessee Wesleyan College**	57	2.6	63%	43%	45%	77%	4%	12/1	18-25	41%[5]	67%	10%
33.	**Toccoa Falls College** (GA)	57	2.6	70%	44%	52%	65%	1%	15/1	840-1080[2]	29%	37%	3%
33.	**U. of South Carolina–Upstate***	57	3.0	68%	44%	38%	50%	1%	17/1	850-1040	37%	53%	1%
36.	**Keiser University** (FL)	56	2.1	82%	45%	63%[8]	81%[4]	0%[4]	12/1[4]	N/A[2]	N/A	N/A	N/A
36.	**Mars Hill University** (NC)	56	2.9	57%	38%	37%	72%	0%	12/1	810-1030[3]	27%	62%	10%
38.	**Methodist University** (NC)	55	2.8	64%[8]	44%	38%	65%	0%	12/1	870-1080	33%	57%	8%
39.	**Belmont Abbey College** (NC)	54	2.9	64%[8]	44%	38%	63%	0%	16/1	890-1120[9]	15%	69%	8%
39.	**Bethune-Cookman University** (FL)	54	2.7	66%	30%	50%	45%	2%	17/1	15-18	33%	64%	3%
41.	**Newberry College** (SC)	53	2.6	68%	48%	41%	63%	0%	12/1	830-1050[3]	25%	57%	14%
42.	**Emmanuel College** (GA)	51	2.5	61%	36%	44%	70%	0%	12/1	790-1130	N/A	49%	7%
42.	**Southeastern University** (FL)	51	2.7	66%	45%	42%	63%	4%	19/1	18-23[3]	N/A	44%	4%
44.	**Lander University** (SC)*	50	2.6	68%[8]	38%	45%	36%	5%	22/1	840-1040	40%	58%	9%
45.	**Alderson Broaddus University** (WV)	49	2.5	62%	47%	43%	65%	5%	16/1	19-24	32%	43%	15%
45.	**Univ. of Arkansas–Pine Bluff***	49	2.7	57%	29%	27%	57%	4%	15/1	16-21	31%	39%	8%
47.	**Concord University** (WV)*	48	2.8	64%	37%	34%	64%	2%	15/1	19-24	48%	38%	4%
47.	**Philander Smith College** (AR)	48	2.2	64%	36%	37%	81%	1%	11/1	15-21	32%	52%	13%[4]
49.	**Bluefield College** (VA)	47	2.5	53%	38%	50%	71%	0%	14/1	800-1010	23%	98%	8%
50.	**Brescia University** (KY)	46	2.6	61%	41%	26%	89%	0%	13/1	20-25	N/A	49%	13%
51.	**Louisiana College**	45	2.4	61%	50%	47%	77%	1%	11/1	18-24	N/A	61%	N/A
51.	**University of Mount Olive** (NC)	45	2.4	66%	35%	43%	68%	0%	15/1	805-1020[2]	N/A	47%	3%[7]
51.	**Williams Baptist College** (AR)	45	2.6	59%[8]	44%	41%	60%	0%	14/1	20-25[4]	N/A	67%	4%

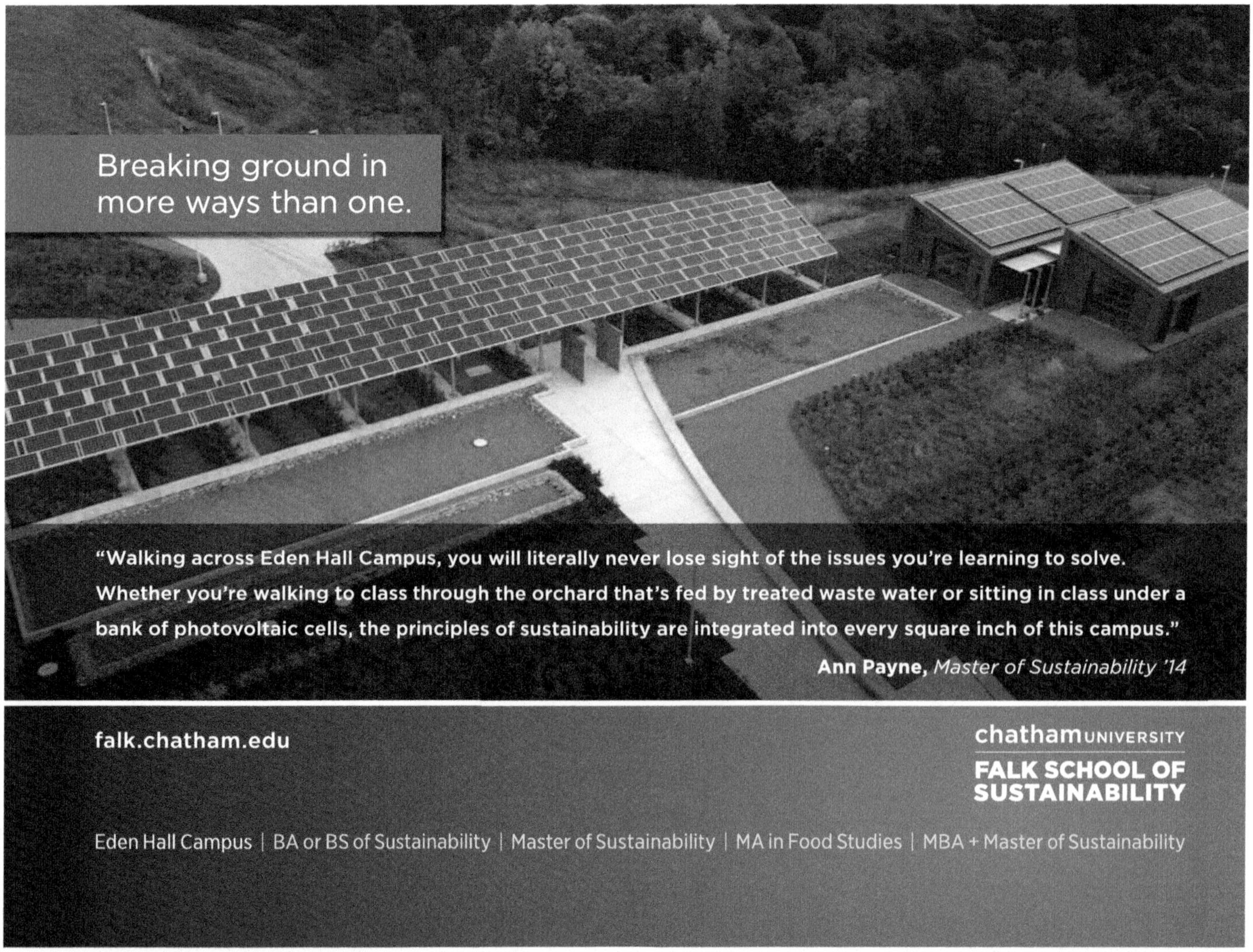

SOUTH ▶

Rank	School (State) (*Public)	Overall score	Peer assessment score (5.0=highest)	Average freshman retention rate	2014 graduation rate: Predicted	2014 graduation rate: Actual	% of classes under 20 ('14)	% of classes of 50 or more ('14)	Student/faculty ratio ('14)	SAT/ACT 25th-75th percentile ('14)	Freshmen in top 25% of HS class ('14)	Acceptance rate ('14)	Average alumni giving rate
54.	Faulkner University (AL)	44	2.6	58%[8]	38%	30%	74%	3%	18/1	18-22	19%[5]	50%	2%
54.	Florida College	44	2.5	N/A	52%	57%	N/A	0%	13/1	20-26[3]	N/A	77%	54%
54.	Midway College[1] (KY)	44	2.2	83%[8]	35%	50%[6]	N/A	N/A	13/1[4]	920-1180[4]	N/A	54%[4]	N/A
54.	Reinhardt University (GA)	44	2.6	62%	45%	36%	78%	1%	12/1	890-1095	30%	90%	4%
58.	Kentucky Christian University	43	2.5	62%	40%	34%	72%	0%	12/1	18-23[3]	33%	48%	4%
58.	Univ. of South Carolina–Beaufort*	43	2.9	53%	42%	26%	47%	2%	19/1	840-1030	25%	57%	3%
60.	Clayton State University (GA)*	42	2.7	69%	38%	33%	43%	3%	17/1	860-1000	N/A	42%	4%
60.	Lees-McRae College (NC)	42	2.6	62%	43%	36%[6]	70%	0%	15/1	840-1060[9]	22%	62%	9%
60.	West Liberty University (WV)*	42	2.5	69%[8]	37%	40%	62%	1%	14/1	18-23[3]	35%	72%	N/A
63.	Davis and Elkins College[1] (WV)	41	2.6	50%[8]	40%	44%[6]	N/A	N/A	16/1[4]	810-1060[4]	N/A	57%[4]	N/A
63.	Ferrum College (VA)	41	2.9	51%	34%	25%	50%	0%	16/1	740-940[2]	12%	73%	8%
63.	North Carolina Wesleyan College	41	2.5	53%	25%	35%	76%	0%	13/1	756-1144[2]	26%	53%	3%
63.	Welch College (TN)	41	2.2	66%	49%	38%	91%	1%	10/1	17-25	59%[5]	55%	12%
67.	Oakwood University[1] (AL)	40	2.8	77%[8]	38%	37%[6]	N/A	N/A	14/1[4]	N/A	N/A	N/A	N/A
67.	Point University[1] (GA)	40	2.2	55%[8]	22%	41%[6]	N/A	N/A	19/1[4]	18-22[4]	34%[4]	54%[4]	N/A
69.	Everglades University (FL)	39	2.2	N/A	N/A	51%	N/A	N/A	N/A	N/A[2]	N/A	86%	N/A
70.	Ohio Valley University (WV)	36	2.2	57%	46%	30%	87%	0%	9/1	17-23	17%	32%	7%
71.	Central Baptist College (AR)	35	2.2	60%	33%	37%	82%	0.4%	20/1	19-23	35%	58%	9%
72.	Fort Valley State University (GA)*	34	2.3	60%	30%	30%	36%	22%	17/1	820-930	26%[5]	24%	14%
73.	Georgia Gwinnett College*	33	2.7	65%	29%	27%	46%	0%	19/1	840-1060[2]	15%[4]	91%	3%
73.	Limestone College (SC)	33	2.2	58%	35%	29%	69%	0%	10/1	960-1100	19%	52%	5%

School (State) (*Public)	Peer assessment score (5.0=highest)	Average freshman retention rate	2014 graduation rate: Predicted	2014 graduation rate: Actual	% of classes under 20 ('14)	% of classes of 50 or more ('14)	Student/faculty ratio ('14)	SAT/ACT 25th-75th percentile ('14)	Freshmen in top 25% of HS class ('14)	Acceptance rate ('14)	Average alumni giving rate
SECOND TIER (SCHOOLS RANKED 75 THROUGH 98 ARE LISTED HERE ALPHABETICALLY)											
Abraham Baldwin Agricultural College (GA)*	2.6	55%[8]	23%	16%	26%	3%	22/1[4]	820-1030[3]	39%	79%	N/A
Benedict College (SC)	2.2	58%[8]	20%	31%	N/A	N/A	N/A	17[9]	N/A	73%	N/A
Bluefield State College (WV)*	2.3	57%	34%	33%	72%	0%	15/1	17-22	49%[5]	38%	4%
Brewton-Parker College[1] (GA)	2.1	60%[8]	37%	18%[6]	N/A	N/A	17/1[4]	810-990[4]	N/A	51%[4]	N/A
Chipola College[1] (FL)*	2.4	N/A	N/A	N/A	N/A	N/A	20/1[4]	N/A[2]	N/A	N/A	N/A
Chowan University (NC)	2.4	46%	29%	25%	48%	1%	16/1	710-880	11%	60%	10%
Edward Waters College[1] (FL)	1.9	51%[8]	47%	20%[6]	N/A	N/A	15/1[4]	710-880[4]	N/A	27%[4]	N/A
Glenville State College (WV)*	2.3	66%	38%	28%	68%	0.4%	16/1	17-21	35%	47%	5%
Gordon State College[1] (GA)*	2.5	N/A	N/A	N/A	N/A	N/A	21/1[4]	750-950[4]	N/A	45%[4]	N/A
Greensboro College[1] (NC)	2.6	60%[8]	42%	36%[6]	N/A	N/A	12/1[4]	790-1020[4]	N/A	78%[4]	N/A
Indian River State College (FL)*	2.6	N/A	N/A	N/A	34%	2%	22/1	N/A[2]	N/A	100%	N/A
LeMoyne-Owen College (TN)	2.5	50%[8]	30%	15%[6]	60%	0%	13/1[4]	13-17[3]	N/A	52%	N/A
Livingstone College (NC)	2.0	52%	24%	24%	46%	1%	17/1	645-800[3]	6%	64%	24%
Middle Georgia State University[1]*	2.5	N/A	30%	22%[6]	N/A	N/A	N/A	N/A[2]	N/A	45%[4]	N/A
Paine College[1] (GA)	2.2	59%[8]	26%	25%[6]	65%[4]	0%[4]	13/1[4]	14-18[4]	15%[4]	44%[4]	14%[4]
Shaw University[1] (NC)	2.1	46%[8]	23%	28%[6]	N/A	N/A	15/1[4]	N/A[2]	N/A	54%[4]	N/A
St. Augustine's University (NC)	2.1	49%	25%	34%	72%	0%	14/1	665-790[3]	N/A	74%	5%
St. Catharine College (KY)	2.2	57%[8]	41%	33%	85%	0%	10/1	18-22	N/A	69%	4%
Thomas University (GA)	2.1	56%	36%	16%	77%	1%	10/1	20-24[2]	N/A	60%	N/A
Truett McConnell College (GA)	2.4	66%	33%	18%	64%	6%	14/1	863-1080	26%	96%	6%
University of Arkansas–Fort Smith*	2.7	64%[8]	42%	27%	48%	4%	18/1	19-25	N/A	56%	N/A
Virginia Union University	2.4	54%[8]	25%	26%	56%	1%	14/1	690-860	20%	83%[4]	9%
Voorhees College[1] (SC)	2.1	46%[8]	29%	32%[6]	N/A	N/A	11/1[4]	N/A[2]	N/A	51%[4]	N/A
Webber International University (FL)	2.3	51%	31%	28%	70%	0%	15/1	17-23[3]	22%[4]	57%	N/A

MIDWEST ▶

Rank	School (State) (*Public)	Overall score	Peer assessment score (5.0=highest)	Average freshman retention rate	2014 graduation rate: Predicted	2014 graduation rate: Actual	% of classes under 20 ('14)	% of classes of 50 or more ('14)	Student/faculty ratio ('14)	SAT/ACT 25th-75th percentile ('14)	Freshmen in top 25% of HS class ('14)	Acceptance rate ('14)	Average alumni giving rate
1.	Taylor University (IN)	100	3.9	88%	69%	74%	61%	5%	13/1	24-30	66%[5]	88%	21%
2.	Augustana College (SD)	89	3.6	82%	65%	66%	45%	2%	12/1	23-28	65%	61%	17%
2.	Ohio Northern University	89	3.5	87%	66%	65%	58%	2%	12/1	23-29[3]	62%	69%	13%
4.	College of the Ozarks (MO)	86	3.6	86%	47%	63%	52%	1%	15/1	21-25[3]	52%	8%	20%
5.	Marietta College[1] (OH)	85	3.3	76%[8]	58%	56%[8]	78%[4]	0%[4]	11/1[4]	21-27[4]	59%[4]	64%[4]	20%[4]
5.	Northwestern College (IA)	85	3.4	77%	61%	64%	70%	0%	11/1	21-27	55%	78%	21%
7.	Dordt College (IA)	84	3.5	81%	61%	65%	61%	5%	13/1	21-27[3]	39%	72%	25%
8.	University of Mount Union (OH)	81	3.2	75%	51%	63%	53%	1%	13/1	21-25	44%	74%	20%

Note: Key to footnotes, Page 115.

MIDWEST ▶

Rank	School (State) (*Public)	Overall score	Peer assessment score (5.0=highest)	Average freshman retention rate	2014 graduation rate Predicted	2014 graduation rate Actual	% of classes under 20 ('14)	% of classes of 50 or more ('14)	Student/ faculty ratio ('14)	SAT/ACT 25th-75th percentile ('14)	Freshmen in top 25% of HS class ('14)	Accept-ance rate ('14)	Average alumni giving rate
9.	**Cedarville University** (OH)	80	3.3	86%	67%	70%	63%	6%	13/1	23-29	65%	74%	10%
10.	**Millikin University** (IL)	79	3.5	78%	56%	61%	60%	1%	11/1	19-26	40%	63%	13%
11.	**Buena Vista University** (IA)	78	3.1	73%	55%	46%	79%	0.3%	9/1	20-25	49%	68%	7%
11.	**Franklin College** (IN)	78	3.0	76%	55%	61%	77%	0%	12/1	910-1100[3]	46%	69%	24%
13.	**Loras College** (IA)	77	3.2	80%	59%	64%	44%	0.3%	12/1	21-26	40%	95%	20%
14.	**Clarke University** (IA)	76	2.8	79%[8]	52%	64%[8]	76%	1%	10/1	20-25[4]	55%	70%	17%
14.	**Hastings College** (NE)	76	3.1	72%	54%	59%	68%	0.4%	14/1	20-27	45%	70%	22%
16.	**Huntington University** (IN)	75	3.1	80%	55%	59%	65%	1%	13/1	880-1128	47%	97%	17%
16.	**Univ. of Northwestern–St. Paul** (MN)	75	3.0	78%[8]	56%	63%	56%	3%	18/1	21-27	48%	82%	16%
18.	**Benedictine College** (KS)	74	3.3	78%	48%	60%	49%	2%	14/1	22-27	44%[5]	98%	24%
19.	**Adrian College** (MI)	73	3.2	64%	53%	57%	73%	1%	13/1	19-24	57%	62%	16%
19.	**Bethel College** (IN)	73	2.9	81%	48%	68%	66%	2%	12/1	890-1170	45%	70%	9%
21.	**Saint Mary-of-the-Woods College** (IN)	70	3.0	75%	47%	47%	95%	0%	8/1	830-1050	35%	100%	24%
22.	**Manchester University** (IN)	69	3.2	70%	50%	55%	56%	0.3%	17/1	890-1100	45%	74%	17%
22.	**Mount Mercy University** (IA)	69	2.6	79%	52%	72%	66%	1%	14/1	19-25	38%	57%	13%
24.	**Marian University** (IN)	68	3.1	71%	49%	53%	63%	5%	13/1	20-26[3]	39%	75%	13%
24.	**Morningside College** (IA)	68	3.0	73%	50%	54%	48%	1%	13/1	20-25	40%	57%	21%
24.	**Trinity Christian College** (IL)	68	2.9	80%	54%	58%	58%	0.4%	11/1	20-27	42%	78%	12%
27.	**Bethel College** (KS)	67	2.8	68%	59%	58%	68%	2%	10/1	19-25	38%	49%	22%
27.	**Bluffton University** (OH)	67	2.8	67%	49%	60%	63%	1%	12/1	19-25	36%	56%	16%
29.	**Eureka College** (IL)	65	2.6	63%[8]	52%	53%	78%	0%	12/1	19-26	35%	65%	18%
29.	**Stephens College** (MO)	65	2.9	67%	53%	53%	78%	0%	8/1	20-26[3]	41%[5]	54%	12%
29.	**Trine University** (IN)	65	3.0	72%	53%	53%	49%	0.2%	11/1	945-1160	57%	76%	10%[4]
32.	**St. Joseph's College** (IN)	62	2.9	70%	48%	45%	76%	1%	11/1	18-24[3]	37%	66%	19%
33.	**Judson University** (IL)	61	2.7	71%	51%	50%	74%	2%	10/1	20-26	44%	73%	6%
33.	**University of Sioux Falls** (SD)	61	2.8	68%	52%	53%	66%	1%	14/1	19-25	40%	97%	4%
35.	**Greenville College** (IL)	60	2.8	70%[8]	50%	48%	66%	4%	14/1	20-26	39%	56%	16%[4]
36.	**Central Methodist University** (MO)	58	2.8	64%	49%	52%	54%	2%	13/1	20-25	41%	61%	9%
36.	**University of Jamestown** (ND)	58	2.9	67%	53%	49%	58%	2%	13/1	20-25[3]	45%	64%	17%
38.	**Briar Cliff University** (IA)	56	2.6	62%	48%	47%	71%	0%	12/1	19-24	37%	62%	15%
38.	**Grace College and Seminary** (IN)	56	2.5	81%	54%	66%	52%	3%	26/1	930-1170[3]	48%	80%	15%
38.	**Martin Luther College**[1] (MN)	56	2.2	85%[8]	60%	74%[6]	N/A	N/A	12/1[4]	22-27[4]	N/A	96%[4]	N/A
41.	**Defiance College** (OH)	55	2.6	58%	47%	49%	73%	0%	12/1	18-23	29%	65%	9%
41.	**Tabor College** (KS)	55	2.5	62%	47%	50%	68%	2%	12/1	20-25	23%	86%	32%
43.	**Culver-Stockton College** (MO)	54	2.9	69%	48%	41%	58%	0%	15/1	19-23	32%	58%	17%
43.	**Valley City State University** (ND)*	54	2.5	61%	46%	48%	78%	1%	11/1	19-25	25%	90%	12%
45.	**Dakota Wesleyan University** (SD)	53	2.7	67%[8]	44%	42%	66%	1%	13/1	18-27	36%	73%	17%
46.	**Blackburn College** (IL)	52	2.5	67%	48%	39%	75%	0%	12/1	18-24	31%	65%	17%
46.	**Mount Marty College** (SD)	52	2.2	68%	51%	54%	71%	1%	10/1	19-23	36%	72%	5%
48.	**Union College** (NE)	51	2.3	72%	53%	47%	69%	3%	10/1	19-25	29%[4]	52%	22%
48.	**University of Minnesota–Crookston***	51	2.5	70%	48%	48%	64%	2%	20/1	19-24[3]	31%	71%	6%
50.	**McPherson College** (KS)	50	2.3	57%	49%	48%	69%	1%	13/1	18-25	25%	88%	8%
51.	**Grand View University** (IA)	48	2.6	69%[8]	42%	46%	59%	0%	13/1	18-23	31%	99%	4%
52.	**Northern State University** (SD)*	47	2.6	69%	47%	49%	54%	4%	21/1	19-25	20%	83%	12%
52.	**Olivet College** (MI)	47	2.6	65%	35%	39%	65%	2%	16/1	18-23	N/A	61%	11%[4]
54.	**Wilmington College**[1] (OH)	46	2.7	82%[8]	43%	45%[6]	N/A	N/A	15/1[4]	850-1120[4]	N/A	46%[4]	N/A
55.	**Evangel University** (MO)	45	2.6	72%[8]	49%	47%	N/A	N/A	14/1	20-26[3]	N/A	65%	N/A
55.	**Kansas Wesleyan University**	45	2.4	58%	47%	33%	69%	0%	11/1	20-26	43%	62%	12%
57.	**Lake Superior State University** (MI)*	44	2.7	71%[8]	44%	48%	60%	6%	15/1[4]	21-25[2]	26%	91%	3%
57.	**MacMurray College** (IL)	44	2.3	64%	41%	29%	76%	0%	13/1	18-22	24%	78%	18%[4]
59.	**North Central University** (MN)	43	2.5	67%[8]	41%	43%	N/A	N/A	N/A	19-25	41%	55%	3%[4]
60.	**Midland University** (NE)	41	2.2	66%[8]	47%	47%[6]	N/A	N/A	10/1	17-26[3]	N/A	60%	10%
60.	**Sterling College** (KS)	41	2.3	67%	44%	43%	70%	0.4%	14/1	18-24	18%	43%	N/A
62.	**Hannibal-LaGrange University** (MO)	40	2.1	60%[8]	46%	50%[6]	76%[4]	1%[4]	N/A	19-25[4]	N/A	61%	5%
62.	**Mayville State University** (ND)*	40	2.1	53%	48%	42%	77%	1%	13/1	17-22	34%[4]	57%	8%
62.	**Ohio Christian University**	40	2.1	64%[8]	23%	41%[6]	N/A	N/A	9/1	17-22	N/A	65%	N/A
62.	**Ottawa University** (KS)	40	2.5	58%	56%	31%	68%	1%	14/1	19-24	32%	64%	4%
66.	**Bethany College**[1] (KS)	39	2.3	64%[8]	46%	38%[6]	75%[4]	1%[4]	12/1[4]	18-23[4]	20%[4]	59%[4]	13%[4]
66.	**Maranatha Baptist University** (WI)	39	1.6	71%	45%	49%	79%	3%	12/1	20-25	N/A	76%	N/A
66.	**Silver Lake College** (WI)	39	2.0	70%	49%	39%	95%	0%	7/1	14-20	25%	83%	5%
69.	**Iowa Wesleyan College**	38	2.0	47%	42%	32%	94%	0%	N/A	18-24	12%	41%	6%
69.	**Kuyper College**[1] (MI)	38	2.3	67%[8]	51%	47%[6]	N/A	N/A	11/1[4]	860-1130[4]	N/A	68%[4]	N/A
69.	**Rochester College** (MI)	38	2.2	60%	43%	39%	85%	0.3%	11/1	18-23[9]	N/A	41%	N/A
69.	**York College** (NE)	38	2.0	69%[8]	45%	37%	80%	0%	15/1	18-22	25%	46%	5%

Note: Key to footnotes, Page 115.

AT COLLEGE OF THE OZARKS, NO. 4 IN THE MIDWEST

MATT SLABY – LUCEO FOR USN&WR

MIDWEST ▶

School (State) (*Public)	Peer assessment score (5.0=highest)	Average freshman retention rate	2014 graduation rate: Predicted	2014 graduation rate: Actual	% of classes under 20 ('14)	% of classes of 50 or more ('14)	Student/faculty ratio ('14)	SAT/ACT 25th-75th percentile ('14)	Freshmen in top 25% of HS class ('14)	Acceptance rate ('14)	Average alumni giving rate
SECOND TIER (SCHOOLS RANKED 73 THROUGH 96 ARE LISTED HERE ALPHABETICALLY)											
Bismarck State College (ND)*	2.3	N/A	N/A	N/A	71%	0.2%	14/1	17-22[2]	N/A	100%	3%
Central Christian College (KS)	1.8	60%[8]	31%	34%	91%	1%	21/1	18-23	N/A	42%	15%
Central State University (OH)*	1.8	51%	26%	22%	60%	1%	12/1	15-18	21%	38%	13%[4]
Crown College[1] (MN)	2.4	50%[8]	46%	51%[6]	N/A	N/A	17/1[4]	765-890[4]	N/A	55%[4]	N/A
Dickinson State University (ND)*	2.2	56%[8]	52%	33%[6]	82%	1%	12/1	18-23[9]	N/A	61%	N/A
Dunwoody College of Tech. (MN)	2.0	50%[8]	N/A	N/A	87%	0%	9/1	N/A[2]	1%[4]	N/A	5%
Finlandia University[1] (MI)	2.1	57%[8]	47%	43%[6]	N/A	N/A	10/1[4]	17-22[4]	N/A	59%[4]	N/A
Grace Bible College[1] (MI)	1.8	66%[8]	33%	34%[6]	N/A	N/A	11/1[4]	N/A[2]	N/A	75%[4]	N/A
Grace University[1] (NE)	2.0	72%[8]	28%	40%[6]	N/A	N/A	13/1[4]	823-993[4]	N/A	58%[4]	N/A
Harris-Stowe State University (MO)*	1.5	46%	31%	8%	83%	0%	13/1	14-18	15%	93%	4%
Herzing University[1] (WI)	1.5	43%[8]	39%	38%[6]	N/A	N/A	15/1[4]	N/A[2]	N/A	N/A	N/A
Indiana University East*	2.3	66%	27%	27%	64%	2%	15/1	830-1030	37%	64%	7%
Indiana University–Kokomo*	2.4	63%	37%	27%	49%	1%	16/1	830-1040	31%	67%	8%
Kendall College[1] (IL)	2.2	56%[8]	47%	35%[6]	N/A	N/A	10/1[4]	N/A[2]	N/A	N/A	N/A
Lincoln College[1] (IL)	2.0	43%[8]	N/A	N/A	N/A	N/A	15/1[4]	16-19[4]	N/A	87%[4]	N/A
Missouri Southern State University*	2.3	63%	41%	36%	49%	0%	18/1	18-24	37%	96%	3%
Missouri Valley College[1]	1.9	44%[8]	31%	25%[6]	N/A	N/A	14/1[4]	790-900[4]	N/A	22%[4]	N/A
Missouri Western State University*	2.2	61%	37%	35%	52%	6%	17/1	17-23[2]	26%	99%	7%
Notre Dame College of Ohio[1]	2.6	62%[8]	43%	41%[6]	N/A	N/A	15/1[4]	816-1020[4]	N/A	90%[4]	N/A
Presentation College[1] (SD)	2.1	58%[8]	41%	42%[6]	N/A	N/A	12/1[4]	790-940[4]	N/A	66%[4]	N/A
Purdue Univ.–North Central (IN)*	2.9	58%	29%	21%	58%	2%	15/1	850-1060[9]	26%	74%	N/A
Waldorf College[1] (IA)	1.9	49%[8]	34%	43%[6]	N/A	N/A	20/1[4]	855-1000[4]	N/A	51%[4]	N/A
Wilberforce University[1] (OH)	2.1	74%[8]	34%	43%[6]	N/A	N/A	8/1[4]	N/A[2]	N/A	58%[4]	N/A
William Penn University[1] (IA)	2.0	59%[8]	32%	32%[6]	N/A	N/A	17/1[4]	760-1050[4]	N/A	58%[4]	N/A

WEST ▶

Rank	School (State) (*Public)	Overall score	Peer assessment score (5.0=highest)	Average freshman retention rate	2014 graduation rate: Predicted	2014 graduation rate: Actual	% of classes under 20 ('14)	% of classes of 50 or more ('14)	Student/faculty ratio ('14)	SAT/ACT 25th-75th percentile ('14)	Freshmen in top 25% of HS class ('14)	Acceptance rate ('14)	Average alumni giving rate
1.	**Carroll College** (MT)	100	3.7	81%	59%	63%	66%	2%	12/1	22-28	64%	58%	15%
2.	**Texas Lutheran University**	90	3.6	71%	51%	44%	66%	0.2%	13/1	920-1130	50%	56%	14%
3.	**Master's Col. and Seminary** (CA)	84	3.3	82%	60%	62%	68%	7%	10/1	960-1200	54%[5]	76%	8%
4.	**Oklahoma Baptist University**	82	3.5	76%	58%	51%	68%	3%	16/1	21-27	49%	60%	7%
5.	**Corban University** (OR)	80	3.2	75%	51%	56%	63%	2%	14/1	895-1140	58%	37%	13%[4]
5.	**Montana Tech of the Univ. of Mont.***	80	3.4	69%	53%	43%	56%	9%	15/1	22-27	57%	90%	16%
5.	**Oregon Inst. of Technology***	80	3.9	72%	49%	47%	62%	2%	13/1	19-26	54%[5]	40%	3%
8.	**California Maritime Academy**[1]*	76	3.4	82%[8]	58%	60%[6]	N/A	N/A	14/1[4]	990-1200[4]	N/A	63%[4]	N/A
9.	**Menlo College** (CA)	74	3.0	78%	50%	59%	51%	0%	15/1	898-1095	N/A	45%	6%
10.	**Warner Pacific College** (OR)	73	3.2	67%	42%	41%	72%	1%	12/1	815-1020	18%	63%	4%
11.	**Howard Payne University** (TX)	71	3.3	58%	47%	45%	73%	0.3%	10/1	860-1070	34%	82%	7%
12.	**Oklahoma Wesleyan University**	69	3.5	59%	51%	37%	74%	3%	15/1	18-25	N/A	63%	N/A
13.	**Brigham Young University–Idaho**[1]	68	3.7	68%[8]	42%	53%[6]	N/A	N/A	24/1[4]	890-1120[4]	N/A	100%[4]	N/A
13.	**Vanguard Univ. of Southern California**	68	3.0	76%	46%	55%	63%	3%	15/1	850-1090	21%	58%	5%
15.	**Rocky Mountain College** (MT)	66	2.8	69%	44%	42%	73%	1%	12/1	20-26	49%	65%	7%
16.	**Schreiner University** (TX)	65	3.1	66%[8]	45%	43%	60%	0%	14/1	890-1090	40%	93%	4%
17.	**East Texas Baptist University**	64	3.3	57%	46%	38%	60%	0%	14/1	18-22	39%	58%	5%
17.	**McMurry University** (TX)	64	3.1	58%	42%	36%	75%	0.3%	10/1	810-1010	27%	61%	8%
17.	**Northwest University** (WA)	64	3.2	79%	48%	52%	61%	3%	12/1	880-1145[3]	N/A	86%	N/A
20.	**Hope International University** (CA)	61	3.1	71%	42%	47%	73%	0%	10/1	800-990	4%	31%	7%
20.	**University of Montana–Western***	61	2.8	73%	36%	54%	69%	0%	17/1	17-22[3]	17%	71%	3%
22.	**Brigham Young University–Hawaii**[1]	60	3.5	61%[8]	58%	49%[6]	N/A	N/A	14/1[4]	950-1170[4]	N/A	36%[4]	N/A
22.	**Northwest Christian University** (OR)	60	2.8	66%[8]	46%	64%	77%	1%	15/1	888-1103	N/A	72%	N/A
22.	**Southwestern Adventist Univ.**[1] (TX)	60	2.8	63%[8]	46%	35%[6]	77%[4]	2%[4]	12/1[4]	830-1060[4]	26%[4]	32%[4]	8%[4]
25.	**Trinity Lutheran College**[1] (WA)	54	2.8	67%[8]	46%	67%[6]	N/A	N/A	14/1[4]	733-1062[4]	N/A	96%[4]	N/A
26.	**Lewis-Clark State College** (ID)*	53	3.4	57%[8]	39%	31%	70%	1%	16/1	810-1030[2]	18%	99%	N/A
27.	**St. Gregory's University** (OK)	52	2.9	60%[8]	36%	47%	87%	1%	N/A	19-23[3]	N/A	63%	N/A
28.	**Southwestern Christian Univ.**[1] (OK)	44	3.0	59%[8]	25%	35%[6]	N/A	N/A	17/1[4]	860-1180[4]	N/A	88%[4]	N/A
29.	**University of Great Falls** (MT)	43	2.9	62%[8]	27%	27%[6]	67%	0%	14/1	N/A	N/A	N/A	N/A
30.	**Oklahoma St. U. Inst. of Tech.–Okmulgee***	42	3.3	55%	33%	31%	83%	0%	17/1	16-21	14%	47%	1%
31.	**University of Houston–Downtown***	36	3.4	64%	34%	19%	27%	4%	22/1	820-980	35%	84%	2%

WEST ▸

School (State) (*Public)	Peer assessment score (5.0=highest)	Average freshman retention rate	2014 graduation rate Predicted	Actual	% of classes under 20 ('14)	% of classes of 50 or more ('14)	Student/ faculty ratio ('14)	SAT/ACT 25th-75th percentile ('14)	Freshmen in top 25% of HS class ('14)	Accept-ance rate ('14)	Average alumni giving rate
SECOND TIER (SCHOOLS RANKED 32 THROUGH 41 ARE LISTED HERE ALPHABETICALLY)											
Bacone College (OK)	2.3	N/A	31%	10%	N/A	N/A	15/1	16-19	N/A	N/A	N/A
Jarvis Christian College (TX)	2.5	55%	20%	14%	57%	4%	24/1	660-880	10%	80%	3%
Metropolitan State Univ. of Denver*	2.9	64%[8]	32%	24%	36%	1%	N/A	18-23[3]	20%	65%	N/A
Montana State Univ.–Northern[1]*	2.9	59%[8]	38%	24%[6]	N/A	N/A	16/1[4]	770-995[4]	N/A	100%[4]	N/A
Nevada State College*	2.6	N/A	44%	12%	N/A	N/A	N/A	N/A[2]	N/A	62%	N/A
Oklahoma Panhandle State Univ.*	2.3	N/A	37%	43%	N/A	N/A	N/A	17-21[2]	N/A	60%	N/A
Rogers State University (OK)*	2.8	60%	34%	22%[6]	53%	1%	19/1	16-19[3]	14%	77%	N/A
University of the Southwest[1] (NM)	3.2	45%[8]	28%	18%[6]	N/A	N/A	15/1[4]	N/A	N/A	N/A	N/A
Utah Valley University*	2.8	61%	31%	25%	44%	5%	22/1	18-24	19%	100%	N/A
Wiley College[1] (TX)	2.4	50%[8]	20%	18%[6]	58%[4]	2%[4]	17/1[4]	14-18[4]	8%[4]	94%[4]	4%[4]

The Top Public Regional Colleges ▸

NORTH

Rank	School (State)
1.	**U.S. Coast Guard Acad.** (CT)
2.	**U.S. Merchant Marine Acad.** (NY)
3.	**Maine Maritime Academy**
4.	**Massachusetts Maritime Academy**
5.	**SUNY Maritime College**

SOUTH

Rank	School (State)
1.	**Univ. of South Carolina–Aiken**
2.	**Elizabeth City State Univ.**[1] (NC)
3.	**U. of South Carolina–Upstate**
4.	**Lander University** (SC)
5.	**Univ. of Arkansas–Pine Bluff**

MIDWEST

Rank	School (State)
1.	**Valley City State University** (ND)
2.	**University of Minnesota–Crookston**
3.	**Northern State University** (SD)
4.	**Lake Superior State University** (MI)
5.	**Mayville State University** (ND)

WEST

Rank	School (State)
1.	**Montana Tech of the Univ. of Mont.**
1.	**Oregon Inst. of Technology**
3.	**California Maritime Academy**[1]
4.	**University of Montana–Western**
5.	**Lewis-Clark State College** (ID)

Footnotes:

1. School refused to fill out U.S. News statistical survey. Data that appear are from school in previous years or from another source such as the National Center for Education Statistics.
2. SAT and/or ACT not required by school for some or all applicants.
3. In reporting SAT/ACT scores, the school did not include all students for whom it had scores or refused to tell U.S. News whether all students with scores had been included.
4. Data reported to U.S. News in previous years.
5. Data based on fewer than 51 percent of enrolled freshmen.
6. Some or all data reported to the NCAA and/or the National Center for Education Statistics.
7. Data reported to the Council for Aid to Education.
8. This rate, normally based on four years of data, is given here for less than four years because school didn't report rate for the most recent year or years to U.S. News.
9. SAT and/or ACT may not be required by school for some or all applicants, and in reporting SAT/ACT scores, the school did not include all students for whom it had scores, or refused to tell U.S. News whether all students with scores had been included.

N/A means not available.

THE U.S. COAST GUARD ACADEMY

PABLO MARTINEZ MONSIVAIS – AP

Best Historically Black Colleges

Increasingly, the nation's top historically black colleges and universities are an appealing option for applicants of all races; many HBCUs, in fact, now actively recruit Hispanic, international and white students in addition to the African-American high school grads heading to college in record numbers. Which schools offer the best undergraduate education? U.S. News each year surveys administrators at the HBCUs, asking the president, provost and admissions dean at each to rate the academic quality of all other HBCUs with which they are familiar. In addition to the two most recent years of survey results, reflected in the peer assessment score, the rankings below are based on nearly all the same ranking indicators (although weighted slightly differently) as those used in ranking the regional universities. These include retention and graduation rates, high school class standing, admission test scores and the strength of the faculty, among others.

To be part of the universe, a school must be designated by the Department of Education as an HBCU, be a baccalaureate-granting institution that enrolls primarily first-year, first-time students, and have been part of this year's Best Colleges survey and ranking process. If an HBCU is unranked in the 2016 Best Colleges rankings, it is also unranked here; reasons that schools are not ranked vary, but include a school's policy not to use test scores in admissions decisions. There are 80 HBCUs; 72 were ranked. HBCUs in the top three-quarters are numerically ranked, and those in the bottom quarter are listed alphabetically. For more detail, visit usnews.com/hbcu.

Key Measures

Graduation and retention rates	27.5%
Peer assessment	25%
Faculty resources	20%
Student selectivity	12.5%
Financial resources	10%
Alumni giving	5%

Rank	School (State) (*Public)	Overall score	Peer assessment score (5.0=highest)	Average freshman retention rate	Average graduation rate	% of classes under 20 ('14)	% of classes of 50 or more ('14)	Student/faculty ratio ('14)	% of faculty who are full time ('14)	SAT/ACT 25th-75th percentile ('14)	Freshmen in top 25% of HS class ('14)	Acceptance rate ('14)	Average alumni giving rate
1.	**Spelman College** (GA)	100	4.7	89%	73%	65%	2%	10/1	89%	900-1100	57%	54%	37%
2.	**Howard University** (DC)	86	4.4	82%	62%[6]	52%	6%	10/1	90%	990-1220	55%[5]	48%	6%
3.	**Hampton University** (VA)	85	4.5	77%	61%[6]	62%	3%	9/1	92%	910-1100[2]	52%	29%	13%
4.	**Morehouse College** (GA)	77	4.5	83%	55%[6]	51%	1%	12/1	91%	880-1120	41%	84%	16%
5.	**Tuskegee University** (AL)	71	4.1	76%	44%[6]	56%	9%	13/1	96%	17-23	60%	48%	25%
6.	**Xavier University of Louisiana**	67	4.2	69%	48%[6]	41%	3%	14/1	96%	20-25	58%	66%	13%
7.	**Fisk University** (TN)	64	3.6	82%[8]	50%[6]	71%	3%	13/1	80%	17-23[3]	2%	83%	24%
8.	**Claflin University** (SC)	57	3.6	73%	44%	62%	1%	13/1	88%	700-880	26%	44%	49%
9.	**North Carolina A&T State Univ.***	56	4.1	77%	43%[6]	33%	7%	18/1	86%	830-990	34%	58%	6%
10.	**Florida A&M University***	55	4.0	81%	40%	33%	14%	15/1	87%	18-22	36%[5]	49%	5%
11.	**Tougaloo College** (MS)	54	3.2	77%	50%[6]	77%	1%	13/1	89%	15-21	25%	42%	16%
12.	**North Carolina Central Univ.***	53	3.7	73%	42%	41%	3%	15/1	89%	810-950	24%	43%	10%
13.	**Jackson State University** (MS)*	51	3.7	78%[8]	44%[6]	53%	7%	17/1	87%	17-21[3]	N/A	26%	4%
14.	**Dillard University** (LA)	49	3.6	66%[8]	35%[6]	57%	1%	14/1	76%	17-20	23%	41%	7%
15.	**Bennett College** (NC)	47	3.2	61%	41%[6]	75%	0%	9/1	92%	680-845	14%	92%	38%
16.	**Johnson C. Smith University** (NC)	46	3.2	67%	42%	80%	0%	11/1	84%	720-900	17%	42%	16%
17.	**Lincoln University** (PA)*	43	3.0	71%	40%[6]	43%	0%	14/1	81%	772-940	23%[5]	27%	9%
18.	**Elizabeth City State Univ.**[1] (NC)*	41	2.9	76%[8]	38%[6]	66%[4]	1%[4]	16/1[4]	86%[4]	16-19[4]	5%[4]	52%[4]	9%[4]
19.	**Clark Atlanta University**	40	3.6	63%	40%[6]	44%	4%	17/1	82%	770-930	26%[5]	85%	N/A
19.	**Morgan State University** (MD)*	40	3.6	74%	32%	34%	2%	14/1	93%	800-960[9]	9%	65%	14%
21.	**Delaware State University***	38	3.4	66%	37%	48%	3%	15/1	82%	820-970	27%	44%	7%
21.	**Tennessee State University***	38	3.5	62%[8]	33%[8]	50%	2%	17/1	88%	15-20	N/A	53%	N/A
23.	**Bethune-Cookman University** (FL)	37	3.4	66%	46%[6]	45%	2%	17/1	88%	15-18	33%	64%	3%
24.	**Bowie State University** (MD)*	36	3.3	73%	37%[6]	45%	1%	16/1	77%	881-960[3]	N/A	54%	5%
25.	**Alabama A&M University***	35	3.5	67%	32%[6]	48%[4]	4%[4]	21/1	98%	15-19[3]	N/A	53%	8%
25.	**Fayetteville State University** (NC)*	35	3.2	73%	32%	41%	1%	18/1	90%	810-960	26%	50%	2%
27.	**Albany State University** (GA)*	34	3.1	68%	41%[6]	52%	2%	16/1	96%	820-940[3]	24%[5]	47%	4%
27.	**Alcorn State University** (MS)*	34	3.1	70%	35%[6]	55%	5%	17/1	90%	16-20	N/A	78%	N/A
29.	**Univ. of Arkansas–Pine Bluff***	33	3.0	57%	26%	57%	4%	15/1	92%	16-21	31%	39%	8%

Note: Key to footnotes, Page 106.

Rank	School (State) (*Public)	Overall score	Peer assessment score (5.0=highest)	Average freshman retention rate	Average graduation rate	% of classes under 20 ('14)	% of classes of 50 or more ('14)	Student/ faculty ratio ('14)	% of faculty who are full time ('14)	SAT/ACT 25th-75th percentile ('14)	Freshmen in top 25% of HS class ('14)	Accept-ance rate ('14)	Average alumni giving rate
30.	**Univ. of Maryland–Eastern Shore***	32	3.4	70%	35%[6]	54%	3%	14/1	82%	760-930	N/A	61%	3%
30.	**Winston-Salem State Univ.**[1] (NC)*	32	3.3	79%[8]	43%[6]	N/A	N/A	N/A	N/A	N/A	N/A	N/A	N/A
32.	**Alabama State University***	31	3.2	59%	26%[6]	43%	0.3%	15/1	84%	16-19	7%	53%	3%
32.	**Prairie View A&M University** (TX)*	31	3.3	66%	36%[6]	22%	10%	18/1	93%	770-940	16%	86%	N/A
34.	**Kentucky State University***	30	3.1	48%	18%[6]	74%	1%	12/1	93%	16-21[3]	24%	48%	4%
34.	**Philander Smith College** (AR)	30	2.7	64%	36%	81%	1%	11/1	96%	15-21	32%	52%	13%[4]
36.	**Norfolk State University** (VA)*	28	3.3	N/A	36%[6]	N/A	N/A	18/1[4]	N/A	790-950[3]	N/A	65%[4]	N/A
36.	**Virginia State University**[1]*	28	3.2	65%[8]	43%[6]	N/A	N/A	16/1[4]	86%[4]	730-910[4]	17%[4]	54%[4]	N/A
38.	**South Carolina State University***	26	2.5	63%	38%[6]	52%	2%	15/1	90%	15-18	35%	85%	N/A
39.	**Fort Valley State University** (GA)*	25	2.9	60%	31%	36%	22%	17/1	97%	820-930	26%[5]	24%	14%
39.	**Grambling State University** (LA)*	25	3.0	69%	30%[6]	46%	9%	18/1	98%	16-20[3]	28%	44%	N/A
39.	**Mississippi Valley State Univ.***	25	2.8	65%[8]	25%[6]	62%	2%	16/1	92%	15-19[3]	N/A	16%	N/A
42.	**Southern U. and A&M College** (LA)*	23	3.1	69%	30%[6]	N/A	N/A	17/1	88%	17-20	11%	N/A	N/A
43.	**Bluefield State College** (WV)*	22	2.7	57%	28%[6]	72%	0%	15/1	80%	17-22	49%[5]	38%	4%
43.	**Central State University** (OH)*	22	2.8	51%	25%	60%	1%	12/1	70%	15-18	21%	38%	13%[4]
43.	**Virginia Union University**	22	3.0	54%[8]	30%	56%	1%	14/1	87%	690-860	20%	83%[4]	9%
46.	**Cheyney U. of Pennsylvania**[1]*	21	2.7	55%[8]	24%[6]	47%[4]	10%[4]	16/1[4]	90%[4]	13-16[4]	9%[4]	88%[4]	3%[4]
46.	**West Virginia State University***	21	2.8	55%	21%[6]	51%	1%	16/1	81%	18-22	N/A	41%	2%
48.	**Lincoln University** (MO)*	20	3.0	50%	23%	49%	2%	17/1	81%	15-21	17%	54%	8%
48.	**Oakwood University**[1] (AL)	20	3.0	77%[8]	37%[6]	N/A	N/A	14/1[4]	91%[4]	N/A	N/A	N/A	N/A
48.	**St. Augustine's University** (NC)	20	2.6	49%	23%[6]	72%	0%	14/1	87%	665-790[3]	N/A	74%	5%
48.	**Texas Southern University***	20	3.2	58%	14%	37%	14%	18/1	80%	730-900[3]	19%	51%	2%
52.	**Huston-Tillotson University** (TX)	19	2.9	57%[8]	26%[6]	67%	0%	16/1	80%	720-920[3]	N/A	N/A	N/A
52.	**Paine College**[1] (GA)	19	2.7	59%[8]	25%[6]	65%[4]	0%[4]	13/1[4]	86%[4]	14-18[4]	15%[4]	44%[4]	14%[4]
54.	**Univ. of the District of Columbia***	18	2.6	54%[8]	16%[6]	57%	0%	8/1	71%	700-910[9]	22%[5]	93%	N/A
54.	**Wilberforce University**[1] (OH)	18	2.6	74%[8]	43%[6]	N/A	N/A	8/1[4]	66%[4]	N/A[2]	N/A	58%[4]	N/A

School (State) (*Public)	Peer assessment score (5.0=highest)	Average freshman retention rate	Average graduation rate	% of classes under 20 ('14)	% of classes of 50 or more ('14)	Student/ faculty ratio ('14)	% of faculty who are full time ('14)	SAT/ACT 25th-75th percentile ('14)	Freshmen in top 25% of HS class ('14)	Accept-ance rate ('14)	Average alumni giving rate
SECOND TIER (SCHOOLS RANKED 56 THROUGH 72 ARE LISTED HERE ALPHABETICALLY)											
Allen University (SC)	2.4	54%	20%	N/A	N/A	14/1	100%	16[4]	N/A	43%	N/A
Benedict College (SC)	2.8	58%[8]	28%[6]	N/A	N/A	N/A	N/A	17[9]	N/A	73%	N/A
Coppin State University (MD)*	2.8	69%[8]	17%[6]	61%	1%	14/1	76%	810-960	N/A	42%	11%
Edward Waters College[1] (FL)	2.3	51%[8]	20%[6]	N/A	N/A	15/1[4]	80%[4]	710-880[4]	N/A	27%[4]	N/A
Florida Memorial University	2.7	70%[8]	40%[6]	N/A	N/A	N/A	N/A	N/A[2]	N/A	21%	N/A
Harris-Stowe State University (MO)*	2.6	46%	9%[6]	83%	0%	13/1	48%	14-18	15%	93%	4%
Jarvis Christian College (TX)	2.5	55%	13%[6]	57%	4%	24/1	100%	660-880	10%	80%	3%
Lane College (TN)	2.6	50%	33%[6]	69%	0.2%	15/1	98%	14-17	N/A	43%	N/A
LeMoyne-Owen College (TN)	2.4	50%[8]	15%[6]	60%	0%	13/1[4]	N/A	13-17[3]	N/A	52%	N/A
Livingstone College (NC)	2.5	52%	31%[6]	46%	1%	17/1	98%	645-800[3]	6%	64%	24%
Rust College (MS)	2.7	61%[8]	25%[6]	N/A	N/A	19/1	99%	14-17	N/A	18%	N/A
Savannah State University (GA)*	3.2	70%[8]	30%[6]	22%	22%	21/1	94%	770-920[3]	N/A	34%	5%
Shaw University[1] (NC)	2.7	46%[8]	28%[6]	N/A	N/A	15/1[4]	75%[4]	N/A[2]	N/A	54%[4]	N/A
Southern University–New Orleans[1]*	2.8	52%[8]	14%[6]	N/A	N/A	18/1[4]	87%[4]	N/A[2]	N/A	N/A	N/A
Stillman College[1] (AL)	2.7	61%[8]	24%[6]	N/A	N/A	14/1[4]	96%[4]	733-888[4]	N/A	43%[4]	N/A
Voorhees College[1] (SC)	2.5	46%[8]	32%[6]	N/A	N/A	11/1[4]	94%[4]	N/A[2]	N/A	51%[4]	N/A
Wiley College[1] (TX)	2.8	50%[8]	18%[6]	58%[4]	2%[4]	17/1[4]	83%[4]	14-18[4]	8%[4]	94%[4]	4%[4]

Sources: Statistical data from the schools. Peer assessment data collected by Ipsos Public Affairs.

Best Business Programs

Each year, U.S. News ranks undergraduate business programs accredited by the Association to Advance Collegiate Schools of Business; the results are based solely on surveys of B-school deans and senior faculty. Participants were asked to rate the quality of business programs with which they're familiar on a scale of 1 (marginal) to 5 (distinguished); 37 percent of those surveyed responded to the most recent survey conducted in the spring of 2015. Two years of data were used to calculate the peer assessment score. Deans and faculty members also were asked to nominate the 10 best programs in a number of specialty areas; the five schools receiving the most mentions in the 2015 survey appear here.

Top Programs

Rank	School (State) (*Public)	Peer assessment score (5.0=highest)
1.	University of Pennsylvania (Wharton)	4.8
2.	Massachusetts Inst. of Technology (Sloan)	4.6
2.	University of California–Berkeley (Haas)*	4.6
4.	University of Michigan–Ann Arbor (Ross)*	4.5
5.	New York University (Stern)	4.4
6.	University of Virginia (McIntire)*	4.3
7.	Carnegie Mellon University (Tepper) (PA)	4.2
7.	U. of N. Carolina–Chapel Hill (Kenan-Flagler)*	4.2
7.	University of Texas–Austin (McCombs)*	4.2
10.	Cornell University (Dyson) (NY)	4.1
10.	Indiana University–Bloomington (Kelley)*	4.1
10.	University of Notre Dame (Mendoza) (IN)	4.1
10.	Univ. of Southern California (Marshall)	4.1
14.	Washington University in St. Louis (Olin)	4.0
15.	Emory University (Goizueta) (GA)	3.9
15.	Georgetown University (McDonough) (DC)	3.9
15.	Georgia Institute of Technology (Scheller)*	3.9
15.	U. of Illinois–Urbana-Champaign*	3.9
15.	Univ. of Minnesota–Twin Cities (Carlson)*	3.9
15.	Univ. of Wisconsin–Madison*	3.9
21.	Ohio State University–Columbus (Fisher)*	3.8
22.	Boston College (Carroll)	3.7
22.	Michigan State University (Broad)*	3.7
22.	Pennsylvania State U.–Univ. Park (Smeal)*	3.7
22.	Purdue Univ.–West Lafayette (Krannert) (IN)*	3.7
22.	University of Arizona (Eller)*	3.7
22.	Univ. of Maryland–College Park (Smith)*	3.7
22.	University of Washington (Foster)*	3.7
29.	Arizona State University–Tempe (Carey)*	3.6
29.	Babson College (MA)	3.6
29.	Texas A&M Univ.–College Station (Mays)*	3.6
29.	University of Florida (Warrington)*	3.6
29.	University of Georgia (Terry)*	3.6
34.	Brigham Young Univ.–Provo (Marriott) (UT)	3.5
34.	University of California–Irvine (Merage)*	3.5
34.	University of Colorado–Boulder (Leeds)*	3.5
34.	University of Iowa (Tippie)*	3.5
34.	Wake Forest University (NC)	3.5
39.	Boston University	3.4
39.	Case Western Reserve U. (Weatherhead) (OH)	3.4
39.	College of William and Mary (Mason) (VA)*	3.4
39.	University of Pittsburgh*	3.4
43.	George Washington University (DC)	3.3
43.	Southern Methodist University (Cox) (TX)	3.3
43.	Syracuse University (Whitman) (NY)	3.3
43.	Tulane University (Freeman) (LA)	3.3
43.	University of Arkansas (Walton)*	3.3
43.	Univ. of South Carolina (Moore)*	3.3
43.	Virginia Tech (Pamplin)*	3.3
50.	Auburn University (Harbert) (AL)*	3.2
50.	Bentley University (MA)	3.2
50.	Georgia State University (Robinson)*	3.2
50.	Pepperdine University (Graziadio) (CA)	3.2
50.	Univ. of California–San Diego (Rady)*	3.2
50.	University of Connecticut*	3.2
50.	Univ. of Massachusetts–Amherst (Isenberg)*	3.2
50.	Univ. of Missouri (Trulaske)*	3.2
50.	University of Oregon (Lundquist)*	3.2
50.	University of Tennessee (Haslam)*	3.2
50.	University of Utah (Eccles)*	3.2
61.	Baylor University (Hankamer) (TX)	3.1
61.	Clemson University (SC)*	3.1
61.	CUNY–Baruch College (Zicklin)*	3.1
61.	Florida State University*	3.1
61.	Miami University–Oxford (Farmer) (OH)*	3.1
61.	Northeastern Univ. (D'Amore-McKim) (MA)	3.1
61.	Rensselaer Polytechnic Inst. (Lally) (NY)	3.1
61.	Santa Clara University (Leavey) (CA)	3.1
61.	Temple University (Fox) (PA)*	3.1
61.	Texas Christian University (Neeley)	3.1
61.	United States Air Force Acad. (CO)*	3.1
61.	University of Alabama (Culverhouse)*	3.1
61.	University of Kansas*	3.1
61.	University of Kentucky (Gatton)*	3.1
61.	University of Miami (FL)	3.1
61.	Univ. of Nebraska–Lincoln*	3.1
61.	University of Oklahoma (Price)*	3.1
61.	University of Richmond (Robins) (VA)	3.1
61.	Villanova University (PA)	3.1
80.	American University (Kogod) (DC)	3.0
80.	DePaul University (Driehaus) (IL)	3.0
80.	Fordham University (Gabelli) (NY)	3.0
80.	George Mason University (VA)*	3.0
80.	Iowa State University*	3.0
80.	Louisiana State Univ.–Baton Rouge (Ourso)*	3.0
80.	Loyola University Chicago (Quinlan)	3.0
80.	University at Buffalo–SUNY*	3.0
80.	Univ. of California–Riverside*	3.0
80.	University of Delaware (Lerner)*	3.0
80.	University of Denver (Daniels)	3.0
80.	University of Illinois–Chicago*	3.0
80.	University of Louisville (KY)*	3.0
93.	Brandeis University (MA)	2.9
93.	Colorado State University*	2.9
93.	Drexel University (LeBow) (PA)	2.9
93.	Gonzaga University (WA)	2.9
93.	Lehigh University (PA)	2.9
93.	Loyola Marymount University (CA)	2.9
93.	Marquette University (WI)	2.9
93.	North Carolina State U.–Raleigh (Poole)*	2.9
93.	Oklahoma State University (Spears)*	2.9
93.	Rochester Inst. of Technology (Saunders) (NY)	2.9
93.	Rutgers, St. U. of N.J.–New Brunswick*	2.9
93.	San Diego State University*	2.9
93.	Seattle University (Albers)	2.9
93.	St. Joseph's University (Haub) (PA)	2.9
93.	Saint Louis University (Cook)	2.9
93.	Texas Tech University (Rawls)*	2.9
93.	University of Colorado–Denver*	2.9
93.	University of Houston (Bauer)*	2.9
93.	University of Mississippi*	2.9
93.	University of Texas–Dallas (Jindal)*	2.9
93.	Washington State University (Carson)*	2.9
114.	Creighton University (NE)	2.8
114.	James Madison University (VA)*	2.8
114.	Kansas State University*	2.8
114.	Ohio University*	2.8
114.	Oregon State University*	2.8
114.	Rutgers, The State U. of N.J.–Newark*	2.8
114.	University at Albany–SUNY*	2.8
114.	University of Alabama–Birmingham (Collat)*	2.8
114.	University of Cincinnati (Lindner)*	2.8
114.	University of Memphis (Fogelman)*	2.8
114.	University of New Mexico (Anderson)*	2.8
114.	U. of North Carolina–Charlotte (Belk)*	2.8
114.	University of San Diego	2.8
114.	University of San Francisco	2.8
114.	Univ. of Wisconsin–Milwaukee (Lubar)*	2.8
114.	Virginia Commonwealth University*	2.8

Top Programs

Rank	School (State) (*Public)	Peer assessment score (5.0=highest)
114.	**Washington and Lee Univ.** (Williams) (VA)	2.8
131.	**Ball State University** (Miller) (IN)*	2.7
131.	**Binghamton University–SUNY***	2.7
131.	**Bucknell University** (PA)	2.7
131.	**Butler University** (IN)	2.7
131.	**Cal. Poly. State U.–San Luis Obispo** (Orfalea)*	2.7
131.	**Hofstra University** (Zarb) (NY)	2.7
131.	**Kennesaw State University** (Coles) (GA)*	2.7
131.	**Loyola University Maryland** (Sellinger)	2.7
131.	**Northern Illinois University***	2.7
131.	**Rollins College** (FL)	2.7
131.	**Rutgers, The State U. of N.J.–Camden***	2.7
131.	**San Jose State University** (Lucas) (CA)*	2.7
131.	**Seton Hall University** (Stillman) (NJ)	2.7
131.	**U. S. Coast Guard Acad.** (CT)*	2.7
131.	**University of Central Florida***	2.7
131.	**Univ. of Colo.–Colorado Springs***	2.7
131.	**University of Hawaii–Manoa** (Shidler)*	2.7
131.	**University of Idaho***	2.7
131.	**Univ. of Missouri–St. Louis***	2.7
131.	**University of Montana***	2.7
131.	**University of Nebraska–Omaha***	2.7
131.	**University of Rhode Island***	2.7
131.	**University of Texas–Arlington***	2.7
131.	**University of Vermont***	2.7
131.	**Xavier University** (Williams) (OH)	2.7
156.	**Boise State University** (ID)*	2.6
156.	**Bowling Green State University** (OH)*	2.6
156.	**Bradley University** (Foster) (IL)	2.6
156.	**Calif. State Poly. Univ.–Pomona***	2.6
156.	**California State U.–Fullerton** (Mihaylo)*	2.6
156.	**California State U.–Los Angeles***	2.6
156.	**Chapman University** (Argyros) (CA)	2.6
156.	**Clark University** (MA)	2.6
156.	**Drake University** (IA)	2.6
156.	**Elon University** (Love) (NC)	2.6
156.	**Fairfield University** (Dolan) (CT)	2.6
156.	**Howard University** (DC)	2.6
156.	**Kent State University** (OH)*	2.6
156.	**Mississippi State University***	2.6
156.	**Portland State University** (OR)*	2.6
156.	**Quinnipiac University** (CT)	2.6
156.	**Southern Illinois U.–Carbondale***	2.6
156.	**St. John's University** (Tobin) (NY)	2.6
156.	**University of Alabama–Huntsville***	2.6
156.	**Univ. of Arkansas–Little Rock***	2.6
156.	**University of Baltimore** (Merrick)*	2.6
156.	**University of Dayton** (OH)	2.6
156.	**University of Maine***	2.6
156.	**Univ. of Massachusetts–Boston***	2.6
156.	**University of Minnesota–Duluth** (Labovitz)*	2.6
156.	**Univ. of Missouri–Kansas City** (Bloch)*	2.6
156.	**University of Nevada–Las Vegas** (Lee)*	2.6
156.	**U. of North Carolina–Greensboro** (Bryan)*	2.6
156.	**University of Portland** (Pamplin) (OR)	2.6
156.	**University of St. Thomas** (Opus) (MN)	2.6
156.	**University of Tulsa** (Collins) (OK)	2.6
156.	**University of Wyoming***	2.6
156.	**Utah State University** (Huntsman)*	2.6
156.	**West Virginia University***	2.6
156.	**Worcester Polytechnic Inst.** (MA)	2.6

Note: Peer assessment survey conducted by Ipsos Public Affairs. To be ranked in a specialty, an undergraduate business school may have either a program or course offerings in that subject area. Extended undergraduate business rankings can be found at usnews.com/bestcolleges.

Best in the Specialties

(*Public)

ACCOUNTING
1. **University of Texas–Austin** (McCombs)*
2. **U. of Illinois–Urbana-Champaign***
3. **Brigham Young Univ.–Provo** (Marriott) (UT)
4. **University of Notre Dame** (Mendoza) (IN)
4. **University of Pennsylvania** (Wharton)

ENTREPRENEURSHIP
1. **Babson College** (MA)
2. **Massachusetts Inst. of Technology** (Sloan)
3. **Univ. of Southern California** (Marshall)
4. **University of California–Berkeley** (Haas)*
4. **University of Pennsylvania** (Wharton)

FINANCE
1. **University of Pennsylvania** (Wharton)
2. **New York University** (Stern)
3. **University of Michigan–Ann Arbor** (Ross)*
4. **Massachusetts Inst. of Technology** (Sloan)
5. **University of California–Berkeley** (Haas)*

INSURANCE/RISK MANAGEMENT
1. **University of Pennsylvania** (Wharton)
2. **University of Georgia** (Terry)*
3. **St. Joseph's University** (Haub) (PA)
4. **Univ. of Wisconsin–Madison***
5. **Temple University** (Fox) (PA)*

INTERNATIONAL BUSINESS
1. **Univ. of South Carolina** (Moore)*
2. **New York University** (Stern)
3. **Univ. of Southern California** (Marshall)
4. **University of Pennsylvania** (Wharton)
5. **University of California–Berkeley** (Haas)*

MANAGEMENT
1. **University of Michigan–Ann Arbor** (Ross)*
2. **University of Pennsylvania** (Wharton)
3. **University of California–Berkeley** (Haas)*
4. **University of Virginia** (McIntire)*
5. **U. of North Carolina–Chapel Hill** (Kenan-Flagler)*

MANAGEMENT INFORMATION SYSTEMS
1. **Massachusetts Inst. of Technology** (Sloan)
2. **Carnegie Mellon University** (Tepper) (PA)
3. **Univ. of Minnesota–Twin Cities** (Carlson)*
4. **University of Arizona** (Eller)*
5. **University of Texas–Austin** (McCombs)*

MARKETING
1. **University of Pennsylvania** (Wharton)
2. **University of Michigan–Ann Arbor** (Ross)*
3. **New York University** (Stern)
4. **University of California–Berkeley** (Haas)*
5. **University of Texas–Austin** (McCombs)*

PRODUCTION/OPERATIONS MANAGEMENT
1. **Massachusetts Inst. of Technology** (Sloan)
2. **Carnegie Mellon University** (Tepper) (PA)
3. **Purdue Univ.–West Lafayette** (Krannert) (IN)*
4. **University of Michigan–Ann Arbor** (Ross)*
5. **University of California–Berkeley** (Haas)*

QUANTITATIVE ANALYSIS/METHODS
1. **Massachusetts Inst. of Technology** (Sloan)
2. **Carnegie Mellon University** (Tepper) (PA)
3. **University of Pennsylvania** (Wharton)
4. **University of California–Berkeley** (Haas)*
5. **Georgia Institute of Technology** (Scheller)*

REAL ESTATE
1. **University of Pennsylvania** (Wharton)
2. **Univ. of Wisconsin–Madison***
3. **University of Georgia** (Terry)*
4. **University of California–Berkeley** (Haas)*
5. **Univ. of Southern California** (Marshall)

SUPPLY CHAIN MANAGEMENT/LOGISTICS
1. **Michigan State University** (Broad)*
2. **Massachusetts Inst. of Technology** (Sloan)
3. **Ohio State University–Columbus** (Fisher)*
3. **Pennsylvania State U.–Univ. Park** (Smeal)*
5. **Arizona State University–Tempe** (Carey)*
5. **University of Tennessee** (Haslam)*

Best Engineering Programs

On these pages, U.S. News ranks undergraduate engineering programs accredited by ABET. The rankings are based solely on surveys of engineering deans and senior faculty at accredited programs. Participants were asked to rate programs with which they're familiar on a scale from 1 (marginal) to 5 (distinguished); the two most recent years' survey results were used to calculate the peer assessment score. Students who prefer a program that focuses on its undergrads can use the list below of top institutions whose terminal engineering degree is a bachelor's or master's; universities that grant doctorates in engineering, whose programs are ranked separately, may boast a wider range of offerings at the undergraduate level. For the spring 2015 surveys, 30 percent of those surveyed returned ratings of the group below; 51 percent did so for the doctorate group. Respondents were also asked to name 10 top programs in specialty areas; those mentioned most often in the 2015 survey alone appear here.

Top Programs ▸ AT ENGINEERING SCHOOLS WHOSE HIGHEST DEGREE IS A BACHELOR'S OR MASTER'S

Rank	School (State) (*Public)	Peer assessment score (5.0=highest)
1.	**Harvey Mudd College** (CA)	4.4
1.	**Rose-Hulman Inst. of Tech.** (IN)	4.4
3.	**Franklin W. Olin College of Engineering** (MA)	4.1
3.	**United States Military Academy** (NY)*	4.1
5.	**United States Air Force Acad.** (CO)*	3.9
5.	**United States Naval Academy** (MD)*	3.9
7.	**Cal. Poly. State U.–San Luis Obispo***	3.8
8.	**Bucknell University** (PA)	3.7
8.	**Cooper Union** (NY)	3.7
8.	**Embry-Riddle Aeronautical U.** (FL)	3.7
11.	**Villanova University** (PA)	3.5
12.	**Baylor University** (TX)	3.4
12.	**Milwaukee School of Engineering**	3.4
12.	**Santa Clara University** (CA)	3.4
15.	**Calif. State Poly. Univ.–Pomona***	3.3
15.	**Embry-Riddle Aeronautical U.–Prescott** (AZ)	3.3
15.	**Kettering University** (MI)	3.3
15.	**Lafayette College** (PA)	3.3
15.	**Swarthmore College** (PA)	3.3
15.	**U. S. Coast Guard Acad.** (CT)*	3.3
15.	**University of San Diego**	3.3
22.	**The Citadel** (SC)*	3.2
22.	**Lawrence Technological Univ.** (MI)	3.2
22.	**Smith College** (MA)	3.2
22.	**Univ. of Colo.–Colorado Springs***	3.2
22.	**Valparaiso University** (IN)	3.2
22.	**Virginia Military Institute***	3.2
28.	**Gonzaga University** (WA)	3.1
28.	**Loyola Marymount University** (CA)	3.1
28.	**Rowan University** (NJ)*	3.1
28.	**San Jose State University** (CA)*	3.1
28.	**U.S. Merchant Marine Acad.** (NY)*	3.1
33.	**Boise State University** (ID)*	3.0
33.	**Bradley University** (IL)	3.0
33.	**Miami University–Oxford** (OH)*	3.0
33.	**Seattle University**	3.0
33.	**Trinity University** (TX)	3.0
33.	**Union College** (NY)	3.0
39.	**Brigham Young University–Idaho**	2.9
39.	**California State U.–Los Angeles***	2.9
39.	**LeTourneau University** (TX)	2.9
39.	**Mercer University** (GA)	2.9
39.	**Ohio Northern University**	2.9
39.	**Univ. of Massachusetts–Dartmouth***	2.9
39.	**University of Michigan–Dearborn***	2.9
46.	**California State U.–Long Beach***	2.8
46.	**California State U.–Northridge***	2.8
46.	**Grand Valley State University** (MI)*	2.8
46.	**Loyola University Maryland**	2.8
46.	**Northern Illinois University***	2.8
46.	**Oregon Inst. of Technology***	2.8
46.	**Trinity College** (CT)	2.8
46.	**University of Alaska–Anchorage***	2.8
46.	**University of Minnesota–Duluth***	2.8
46.	**University of Portland** (OR)	2.8
46.	**University of St. Thomas** (MN)	2.8
46.	**Univ. of Wisconsin–Platteville***	2.8

Best in the Specialties ▸

(*Public)

AEROSPACE/AERONAUTICAL/ASTRONAUTICAL

1. **Embry-Riddle Aeronautical U.** (FL)
2. **United States Air Force Acad.** (CO)*
3. **Embry-Riddle Aeronautical U.–Prescott** (AZ)

BIOMEDICAL/BIOMEDICAL ENGINEERING

1. **Rose-Hulman Inst. of Technology** (IN)

CHEMICAL

1. **Rose-Hulman Institute of Technology** (IN)

CIVIL

1. **Rose-Hulman Institute of Technology** (IN)
2. **United States Military Academy** (NY)*
3. **California Polytechnic State University–San Luis Obispo***
4. **Bucknell University** (PA)
5. **Lawrence Technological University** (MI)

COMPUTER ENGINEERING

1. **Rose-Hulman Institute of Technology** (IN)
2. **Harvey Mudd College** (CA)
3. **Bucknell University** (PA)
4. **Cooper Union** (NY)
5. **Franklin W. Olin College of Engineering** (MA)

ELECTRICAL/ELECTRONIC/COMMUNICATIONS

1. **Rose-Hulman Institute of Technology** (IN)
2. **Bucknell University** (PA)
2. **Franklin W. Olin College of Engineering** (MA)
4. **Harvey Mudd College** (CA)
4. **United States Air Force Acad.** (CO)*

MECHANICAL

1. **Rose-Hulman Institute of Technology** (IN)
2. **Franklin W. Olin College of Engineering** (MA)
3. **California Polytechnic State University–San Luis Obispo***
4. **United States Military Academy** (NY)*
5. **Harvey Mudd College** (CA)
5. **United States Air Force Acad.** (CO)*

Note: Peer assessment survey conducted by Ipsos Public Affairs. To be ranked in a specialty, a school may have either a program or course offerings in that subject area; ABET accreditation of that program is not needed. Based on a recommendation by the American Society for Engineering Education, a few schools with small doctoral programs are part of the bachelor's and master's category. Extended rankings can be found at usnews.com/bestcolleges.

Top Programs ▸ AT ENGINEERING SCHOOLS WHOSE HIGHEST DEGREE IS A DOCTORATE

Rank	School (State) (*Public)	Peer assessment score (5.0=highest)
1.	Massachusetts Inst. of Technology	4.8
1.	Stanford University (CA)	4.8
3.	University of California–Berkeley*	4.7
4.	California Institute of Technology	4.6
5.	U. of Illinois–Urbana-Champaign*	4.4
6.	Carnegie Mellon University (PA)	4.3
6.	Georgia Institute of Technology*	4.3
6.	University of Michigan–Ann Arbor*	4.3
9.	Cornell University (NY)	4.2
9.	Purdue Univ.–West Lafayette (IN)*	4.2
11.	Princeton University (NJ)	4.1
11.	University of Texas–Austin*	4.1
13.	Northwestern University (IL)	4.0
14.	Univ. of Wisconsin–Madison*	3.9
15.	Johns Hopkins University (MD)	3.8
15.	Texas A&M Univ.–College Station*	3.8
15.	Virginia Tech*	3.8
18.	Columbia University (NY)	3.7
18.	Duke University (NC)	3.7
18.	Pennsylvania State U.–Univ. Park*	3.7
18.	Rice University (TX)	3.7
18.	Univ. of California–Los Angeles*	3.7
23.	Univ. of California–San Diego*	3.6
23.	Univ. of Maryland–College Park*	3.6
23.	Univ. of Minnesota–Twin Cities*	3.6
23.	University of Washington*	3.6
27.	Harvard University (MA)	3.5
27.	Ohio State University–Columbus*	3.5
27.	University of Pennsylvania	3.5
27.	Univ. of Southern California	3.5
31.	North Carolina State U.–Raleigh*	3.4
31.	Rensselaer Polytechnic Inst. (NY)	3.4
31.	University of California–Davis*	3.4
31.	Univ. of California–Santa Barbara*	3.4
31.	University of Virginia*	3.4
36.	Iowa State University*	3.3
36.	University of Colorado–Boulder*	3.3
36.	University of Florida*	3.3
36.	Vanderbilt University (TN)	3.3
36.	Yale University (CT)	3.3
41.	Arizona State University–Tempe*	3.2
41.	Brown University (RI)	3.2
41.	Case Western Reserve Univ. (OH)	3.2
41.	Colorado School of Mines*	3.2
41.	Lehigh University (PA)	3.2
41.	University of Notre Dame (IN)	3.2
41.	Washington University in St. Louis	3.2
48.	Dartmouth College (NH)	3.1
48.	Michigan State University*	3.1
48.	University of California–Irvine*	3.1
51.	Boston University	3.0
51.	Northeastern University (MA)	3.0
51.	Rutgers, St. U. of N.J.–New Brunswick*	3.0
51.	University of Arizona*	3.0
51.	University of Pittsburgh*	3.0
56.	Auburn University (AL)*	2.9
56.	Clemson University (SC)*	2.9
56.	Drexel University (PA)	2.9
56.	Tufts University (MA)	2.9
56.	University of Delaware*	2.9
56.	Univ. of Massachusetts–Amherst*	2.9
56.	University of Utah*	2.9
63.	Illinois Institute of Technology	2.8
63.	Rochester Inst. of Technology (NY)	2.8
63.	Stony Brook–SUNY*	2.8
63.	University at Buffalo–SUNY*	2.8
63.	University of Iowa*	2.8
63.	University of Tennessee*	2.8
63.	Worcester Polytechnic Inst. (MA)	2.8

Best in the Specialties ▸

(*Public)

AEROSPACE/AERONAUTICAL/ASTRONAUTICAL
1. Massachusetts Institute of Technology
2. Georgia Institute of Technology*
3. University of Michigan–Ann Arbor*
4. Purdue University–West Lafayette (IN)*
5. California Institute of Technology

BIOLOGICAL/AGRICULTURAL
1. Purdue University–West Lafayette (IN)*
2. Iowa State University*
2. Texas A&M Univ.–College Station*
2. University of Illinois–Urbana-Champaign*
5. University of California–Davis*

BIOMEDICAL/BIOMEDICAL ENGINEERING
1. Johns Hopkins University (MD)
2. Duke University (NC)
3. Georgia Institute of Technology*
4. Massachusetts Institute of Technology
4. Rice University (TX)
4. Stanford University (CA)

CHEMICAL
1. Massachusetts Institute of Technology
2. University of California–Berkeley*
3. Stanford University (CA)
4. University of Texas–Austin*
5. University of Minnesota–Twin Cities*

CIVIL
1. University of California–Berkeley*
2. University of Illinois–Urbana-Champaign*
3. Georgia Institute of Technology*
4. Stanford University (CA)
5. Purdue University–West Lafayette (IN)*

COMPUTER ENGINEERING
1. Massachusetts Institute of Technology
2. Stanford University (CA)
3. Carnegie Mellon University (PA)
4. University of California–Berkeley*
5. University of Illinois–Urbana-Champaign*

ELECTRICAL/ELECTRONIC/COMMUNICATIONS
1. Massachusetts Institute of Technology
2. Stanford University (CA)
3. University of California–Berkeley*
4. Georgia Institute of Technology*
5. University of Illinois–Urbana-Champaign*

ENGINEERING SCIENCE/ENGINEERING PHYSICS
1. Massachusetts Institute of Technology
2. University of Illinois–Urbana-Champaign*
3. University of California–Berkeley*
4. Virginia Tech*
5. Cornell University (NY)
5. Stanford University (CA)

ENVIRONMENTAL/ENVIRONMENTAL HEALTH
1. Stanford University (CA)
1. University of California–Berkeley*
3. University of Michigan–Ann Arbor*
4. University of Illinois–Urbana-Champaign*
5. University of Texas–Austin*

INDUSTRIAL/MANUFACTURING
1. Georgia Institute of Technology*
2. University of Michigan–Ann Arbor*
3. Purdue University–West Lafayette (IN)*
3. University of California–Berkeley*
5. Northwestern University (IL)
5. Stanford University (CA)
5. Virginia Tech*

MATERIALS
1. Massachusetts Institute of Technology
2. University of Illinois–Urbana-Champaign*
3. University of California–Berkeley*
4. Northwestern University (IL)
5. University of Michigan–Ann Arbor*

MECHANICAL
1. Massachusetts Institute of Technology
2. Georgia Institute of Technology*
3. University of California–Berkeley*
4. Stanford University (CA)
5. University of Michigan–Ann Arbor*

Best Online Degree Programs

When we surveyed colleges in 2014 about their online options, 296 schools reported having bachelor's programs that can be completed without showing up in person for class (though attendance may be required for testing, orientations or support services). These offerings, typically degree-completion programs aimed at working adults and community college grads, were evaluated on their success at engaging students, the credentials of their faculty and the services and technologies made available remotely. The table below features some of the most significant ranking factors, such as the prevalence of faculty holding a Ph.D. or other terminal degree, class size, the percentages of new entrants who stayed enrolled and later graduated, and the debt load of recent graduates. The top half of programs are listed here. Ranks are determined by the institutions' rounded overall program score, displayed below. To see the rest of the ranked online bachelor's programs and to read the full methodology, visit usnews.com/online. You'll also find detail-rich profile pages for each of the schools and (in case you want to plan ahead) rankings of online MBA programs and graduate programs in engineering, nursing, education and more.

(*Public, **For profit)

Rank	School	Overall program score	Average peer assessment score (5.0=highest)	'14 total program enrollment	'14 - '15 tuition[1]	'14 full-time faculty with Ph.D.	'14 average class size	'14 retention rate	'14 graduation rate[2]	% graduates with debt ('14)	Average debt of graduates ('14)
1.	**Pennsylvania State University–World Campus***	100	4.2	4,361	$535	59%	27	72%	52%	74%	$39,977
2.	**Daytona State College*** (FL)	97	3.5	1,656	$560	65%	24	81%	60%	18%	$24,097
2.	**University of Illinois–Chicago***	97	3.4	171	$575	38%	17	96%	N/A	39%	$15,638
2.	**Western Kentucky University***	97	3.2	2,401	$463	69%	18	81%	N/A	66%	$17,269
5.	**Embry-Riddle Aeronautical U.–Worldwide** (FL)	95	3.6	13,826	$335	39%	19	75%	2%	18%	$3,718
5.	**Oregon State University***	95	3.5	3,040	$191	62%	26	73%	52%	75%	$25,654
7.	**Colorado State University–Global Campus***	94	3.4	7,411	$350	N/A	13	71%	N/A	62%	$23,342
8.	**Arizona State University***	93	3.7	10,339	$480	70%	46	80%	N/A	75%	$27,108
8.	**Ohio State University–Columbus***	93	3.5	301	$1,070	40%	152	70%	N/A	42%	$11,518
10.	**Pace University** (NY)	92	3.1	343	$570	92%	14	69%	55%	26%	$32,721
11.	**Regent University** (VA)	91	3.1	2,380	$395	90%	18	72%	42%	77%	$32,646
11.	**Savannah College of Art and Design** (GA)	91	3.3	606	$751	29%	18	84%	46%	79%	$36,656
13.	**Central Michigan University***	90	3.2	1,485	$387	79%	19	53%	22%	39%	$7,543
13.	**University of Florida***	90	3.5	1,122	$500	79%	59	90%	60%	62%	$18,839
13.	**Utah State University***	90	3.7	1,813	$290	55%	55	70%	60%	67%	$25,422
16.	**Creighton University** (NE)	89	3.4	62	$412	79%	12	63%	N/A	100%	$19,855
16.	**Fort Hays State University*** (KS)	89	3.1	6,965	$187	60%	21	86%	73%	18%	$23,118
18.	**SUNY College of Technology–Delhi*** (NY)	88	3.3	828	$257	50%	17	57%	N/A	N/A	N/A
18.	**University of La Verne** (CA)	88	2.9	295	$565	89%	17	77%	58%	75%	$28,822
20.	**George Washington University** (DC)	87	3.6	182	$552	73%	14	77%	67%	19%	$25,495
20.	**University of Illinois–Springfield***	87	3.5	1,022	$359	79%	N/A	74%	48%	59%	$23,667
20.	**Washington State University***	87	3.4	2,197	$569	80%	38	61%	53%	72%	$25,806
23.	**California Baptist University**	86	3.4	1,765	$511	68%	15	88%	N/A	91%	$30,620
23.	**University of Wisconsin–Superior***	86	3.6	684	$305	33%	11	92%	15%	N/A	N/A
25.	**Palm Beach Atlantic University** (FL)	85	2.9	87	$445	72%	10	55%	50%	100%	$26,845
25.	**Siena Heights University** (MI)	85	N/A	526	$455	70%	16	37%	91%	64%	$21,704
27.	**American Public University System**** (WV)	84	3.0	61,874	$250	49%	15	51%	39%	32%	$21,695
27.	**City University of Seattle** (WA)	84	N/A	2,540	$388	27%	9	67%	52%	32%	$9,916
27.	**CUNY School of Professional Studies*** (NY)	84	N/A	1,271	$260	90%	16	59%	33%	60%	$3,729
27.	**University of Denver** (CO)	84	3.2	142	$539	75%	9	79%	45%	76%	N/A
31.	**Brandman University** (CA)	83	2.5	1,184	$500	97%	25	76%	N/A	77%	$28,446
31.	**Old Dominion University*** (VA)	83	3.1	4,060	$314	60%	42	78%	51%	N/A	N/A
31.	**Temple University*** (PA)	83	N/A	96	$726	83%	30	69%	N/A	80%	$29,083
34.	**Ball State University*** (IN)	82	3.5	472	$499	68%	22	68%	59%	68%	$30,542
34.	**Charleston Southern University** (SC)	82	N/A	312	$490	60%	12	78%	N/A	94%	$31,308
34.	**Indiana University-Purdue Univ.–Fort Wayne***	82	3.7	397	$355	71%	N/A	75%	N/A	50%	$5,160
34.	**St. John's University** (NY)	82	3.2	41	$1,262	85%	19	100%	N/A	80%	$29,818
34.	**University of Minnesota–Crookston***	82	3.5	1,115	$385	34%	25	67%	31%	54%	$27,207
34.	**University of Missouri–Kansas City***	82	2.9	N/A	$705	78%	21	89%	N/A	N/A	N/A
40.	**Colorado State University***	81	3.3	1,542	$397	71%	21	78%	69%	N/A	N/A
40.	**Concordia University–St. Paul** (MN)	81	2.7	897	$420	53%	11	79%	71%	72%	$33,726
40.	**Eastern Kentucky University***	81	N/A	1,484	$398	64%	17	51%	60%	81%	$23,692

Note: Key to footnotes, Page 126.

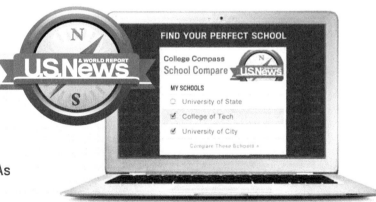

BEST ONLINE DEGREE PROGRAMS

(*Public, **For profit)

Rank	School	Overall program score	Average peer assessment score (5.0=highest)	'14 total program enrollment	'14 - '15 tuition[1]	'14 full-time faculty with Ph.D.	'14 average class size	'14 retention rate	'14 graduation rate[2]	% graduates with debt ('14)	Average debt of graduates ('14)
40.	**Florida Institute of Technology**	81	3.2	3,051	$510	60%	20	71%	N/A	82%	$44,500
40.	**Malone University** (OH)	81	N/A	86	$485	40%	13	94%	84%	76%	$23,395
40.	**University of Maine–Augusta***	81	N/A	3,338	$271	68%	27	77%	23%	77%	$23,246
40.	**University of Nebraska–Lincoln***	81	3.5	25	$501	95%	40	100%	N/A	100%	$21,567
47.	**Lamar University*** (TX)	80	2.3	972	$208	71%	N/A	72%	N/A	32%	$22,868
47.	**Loyola University Chicago** (IL)	80	3.2	327	$630	60%	19	58%	N/A	66%	$25,688
47.	**Marist College** (NY)	80	3.3	256	$600	67%	24	77%	48%	82%	$23,548
50.	**Saint Leo University** (FL)	79	N/A	5,985	$470	74%	18	73%	N/A	70%	N/A
50.	**University of Central Florida***	79	N/A	8,425	$749	67%	79	87%	80%	55%	$16,924
50.	**University of Missouri–St. Louis***	79	3.2	86	$452	20%	19	61%	93%	51%	$17,506
50.	**University of the Incarnate Word** (TX)	79	N/A	2,594	$495	100%	21	72%	63%	70%	$22,583
50.	**University of Wisconsin–Platteville***	79	3.7	731	$370	71%	18	20%	N/A	N/A	N/A
55.	**University of Massachusetts–Dartmouth***	78	3.7	166	$304	67%	13	47%	N/A	N/A	N/A
55.	**University of North Florida***	78	N/A	N/A	$285	78%	40	N/A	N/A	39%	$11,525
55.	**Wayne State University*** (MI)	78	3.3	45	$397	67%	23	95%	N/A	83%	$27,088
58.	**Regis University** (CO)	77	2.8	2,207	$460	48%	11	80%	42%	66%	$31,702
58.	**SUNY College of Technology–Canton*** (NY)	77	3.2	797	$659	56%	23	82%	34%	N/A	N/A
58.	**University of Nebraska–Omaha***	77	3.4	N/A	$464	81%	25	78%	N/A	80%	$24,371
58.	**Westfield State University*** (MA)	77	N/A	212	$260	88%	18	79%	N/A	67%	$19,244
62.	**Drexel University** (PA)	76	3.4	2,329	$502	58%	22	77%	53%	N/A	N/A
63.	**Bellevue University** (NE)	75	2.3	7,341	$385	42%	16	95%	N/A	73%	N/A
63.	**Granite State College*** (NH)	75	N/A	1,929	$315	50%	16	73%	52%	72%	$21,771
63.	**Linfield College** (OR)	75	N/A	766	$450	62%	16	87%	66%	47%	$11,571
63.	**University of Alabama–Huntsville***	75	3.0	34	$440	0%	43	85%	N/A	N/A	N/A
63.	**Western Illinois University***	75	3.0	734	$288	74%	35	79%	63%	N/A	N/A
68.	**Sam Houston State University*** (TX)	74	3.0	1,026	$204	80%	44	78%	N/A	64%	$23,899
68.	**Southeast Missouri State University***	74	3.2	658	$381	76%	25	72%	35%	39%	$23,416
68.	**University of Bridgeport** (CT)	74	N/A	157	$500	40%	15	85%	N/A	N/A	N/A
68.	**University of Oklahoma***	74	N/A	1,391	$563	100%	17	79%	41%	53%	$21,562
72.	**Boise State University*** (ID)	73	N/A	709	$317	21%	20	86%	72%	76%	$19,930
72.	**California State University–Chico***	73	3.2	274	$619	75%	24	78%	51%	N/A	N/A
72.	**Franklin University** (OH)	73	N/A	5,981	$464	88%	15	70%	38%	67%	$28,113
72.	**Indiana University–Online***	73	N/A	1,693	$298	59%	26	78%	N/A	N/A	N/A
72.	**Peirce College** (PA)	73	N/A	1,280	$550	71%	17	68%	48%	82%	$22,714
72.	**University of Alabama–Birmingham***	73	3.2	106	$573	83%	24	100%	N/A	N/A	N/A
72.	**University of Wisconsin–Green Bay***	73	3.5	1,493	$578	88%	25	N/A	59%	65%	$19,424
79.	**Kaplan University**** (IA)	72	1.9	39,440	$371	23%	22	55%	16%	86%	$31,363
79.	**Liberty University** (VA)	72	2.7	40,444	$360	43%	20	70%	40%	73%	$28,869
79.	**University of West Georgia***	72	N/A	N/A	$260	83%	47	N/A	N/A	N/A	N/A
82.	**California University of Pennsylvania***	71	N/A	1,199	$347	0%	40	80%	90%	N/A	$18,970
82.	**Lynn University** (FL)	71	N/A	1,009	$355	70%	12	54%	N/A	37%	$29,139
82.	**North Carolina State University–Raleigh***	71	3.6	81	$408	100%	40	N/A	N/A	N/A	N/A
82.	**University of Illinois–Urbana-Champaign***	71	N/A	N/A	$397	100%	24	92%	N/A	N/A	N/A
82.	**University of Phoenix**** (AZ)	71	1.9	213,944	$469	35%	14	72%	39%	84%	$28,621
87.	**Berkeley College**** (NY)	70	2.6	1,496	$525	70%	21	84%	32%	95%	$34,689
87.	**Sacred Heart University** (CT)	70	N/A	392	$530	82%	14	22%	N/A	42%	$38,120
87.	**Upper Iowa University**	70	2.6	2,200	$405	71%	13	98%	N/A	N/A	N/A
90.	**Charter Oak State College*** (CT)	69	2.3	1,898	$346	N/A	13	82%	63%	N/A	N/A
90.	**Duquesne University** (PA)	69	3.3	273	$687	100%	15	N/A	N/A	N/A	N/A
90.	**Herzing University** (WI)	69	N/A	758	$525	22%	19	23%	28%	85%	$30,574
90.	**Northwestern State University of Louisiana***	69	N/A	3,369	$206	45%	28	80%	42%	61%	$15,752
90.	**Oklahoma Panhandle State University***	69	N/A	N/A	N/A	67%	19	N/A	77%	N/A	N/A
90.	**University of Georgia***	69	N/A	24	$893	50%	16	N/A	100%	N/A	$19,411
90.	**University of Texas of the Permian Basin***	69	N/A	506	$530	69%	32	52%	N/A	100%	N/A
90.	**Western Carolina University*** (NC)	69	N/A	1,115	$475	80%	N/A	73%	N/A	33%	$11,819
98.	**Columbia College** (MO)	68	2.7	14,350	$260	89%	18	81%	20%	61%	$28,480
98.	**Cornerstone University** (MI)	68	N/A	N/A	$385	20%	12	N/A	N/A	N/A	N/A
98.	**Everglades University** (FL)	68	N/A	595	$600	84%	12	N/A	24%	N/A	N/A
98.	**Florida International University***	68	3.1	1,059	$279	89%	N/A	N/A	N/A	N/A	N/A
98.	**Lindenwood University** (MO)	68	N/A	71	$484	69%	14	50%	N/A	N/A	N/A
98.	**McKendree University** (IL)	68	N/A	223	$350	87%	15	98%	N/A	N/A	N/A
98.	**Norwich University** (VT)	68	3.5	443	$375	100%	9	52%	N/A	10%	$7,103

Note: Key to footnotes, Page 126.

(*Public, **For profit)

Rank	School	Overall program score	Average peer assessment score (5.0=highest)	'14 total program enrollment	'14 - '15 tuition[1]	'14 full-time faculty with Ph.D.	'14 average class size	'14 retention rate	'14 graduation rate[2]	% graduates with debt ('14)	Average debt of graduates ('14)
98.	**University of Missouri***	68	3.3	897	$350	70%	25	N/A	N/A	N/A	N/A
98.	**University of Tennessee–Martin***	68	3.3	612	$308	83%	16	N/A	N/A	N/A	N/A
107.	**Concordia University** (OR)	67	N/A	N/A	$425	33%	10	N/A	N/A	N/A	N/A
107.	**Georgia Southern University***	67	N/A	707	$199	89%	40	78%	N/A	80%	$22,853
107.	**John Brown University** (AR)	67	1.9	162	$410	71%	12	82%	N/A	78%	$18,514
107.	**University of St. Francis** (IL)	67	N/A	424	$599	55%	11	67%	54%	67%	$29,401
111.	**DeVry University**** (IL)	66	2.1	24,644	$609	40%	25	81%	16%	79%	$42,643
111.	**Ferris State University*** (MI)	66	3.0	842	$381	50%	19	N/A	N/A	N/A	N/A
111.	**Lawrence Technological University** (MI)	66	N/A	124	$986	50%	18	69%	N/A	N/A	N/A
111.	**Northwood University** (MI)	66	N/A	301	$420	42%	20	N/A	49%	66%	$26,483
111.	**Robert Morris University** (PA)	66	2.4	423	$695	80%	13	80%	N/A	66%	$20,137
111.	**Toccoa Falls College** (GA)	66	N/A	44	$295	72%	15	50%	N/A	46%	$4,967
111.	**University of Houston–Victoria*** (TX)	66	N/A	N/A	$535	87%	25	48%	N/A	N/A	N/A
111.	**Valley City State University*** (ND)	66	N/A	N/A	$168	61%	11	N/A	N/A	N/A	N/A
119.	**Chatham University** (PA)	65	N/A	109	$782	100%	N/A	76%	63%	88%	$16,153
119.	**Davenport University** (MI)	65	N/A	4,099	$613	27%	20	54%	N/A	N/A	N/A
119.	**North Carolina A&T State University***	65	N/A	429	$544	87%	N/A	74%	47%	N/A	N/A

PHOTO ILLUSTRATION BY WILLIAM DUKE FOR USN&WR

(*Public, **For profit)

Rank	School	Overall program score	Average peer assessment score (5.0=highest)	'14 total program enrollment	'14-'15 tuition[1]	'14 full-time faculty with Ph.D.	'14 average class size	'14 retention rate	'14 graduation rate[2]	% graduates with debt ('14)	Average debt of graduates ('14)
119.	**Post University**** (CT)	65	N/A	10,684	$570	34%	12	84%	2%	54%	$30,095
119.	**University of South Carolina–Aiken***	65	N/A	107	$777	76%	21	100%	N/A	70%	$10,922
119.	**West Texas A&M University***	65	N/A	N/A	$277	69%	N/A	82%	N/A	N/A	N/A
125.	**Colorado Technical University****	64	N/A	22,967	$325	88%	24	N/A	N/A	85%	$38,220
125.	**Dominican College** (NY)	64	N/A	N/A	$753	48%	10	N/A	N/A	N/A	N/A
125.	**Fitchburg State University*** (MA)	64	N/A	159	$294	58%	18	91%	N/A	66%	N/A
125.	**Georgia College & State University***	64	3.2	36	$232	80%	25	94%	N/A	N/A	N/A
125.	**Limestone College** (SC)	64	N/A	1,063	$390	58%	16	68%	44%	98%	$34,556
125.	**Wheeling Jesuit University** (WV)	64	N/A	89	$365	78%	20	N/A	55%	68%	$31,257
131.	**Gallaudet University** (DC)	63	2.8	23	$725	73%	N/A	25%	N/A	80%	$14,189
131.	**Lee University** (TN)	63	N/A	788	$182	93%	11	85%	N/A	64%	$30,298
131.	**New England College** (NH)	63	N/A	1,035	$395	57%	18	76%	N/A	68%	$12,026
131.	**Northern Arizona University***	63	3.5	3,487	$771	N/A	13	59%	66%	N/A	N/A
131.	**United States Sports Academy** (AL)	63	2.3	318	$360	100%	N/A	N/A	N/A	69%	$22,917
136.	**Concordia University Chicago** (IL)	62	N/A	122	$475	35%	9	76%	N/A	N/A	N/A
136.	**Madonna University** (MI)	62	N/A	123	N/A	67%	N/A	94%	78%	N/A	N/A
136.	**Southwestern College** (KS)	62	N/A	1,805	$427	100%	13	82%	57%	39%	$23,285
136.	**University at Buffalo–SUNY*** (NY)	62	N/A	33	$816	83%	17	N/A	N/A	N/A	N/A
140.	**California State University–Dominguez Hills***	61	2.9	785	N/A	93%	N/A	79%	20%	41%	$16,667
140.	**New England Institute of Technology** (RI)	61	N/A	34	$350	64%	14	91%	N/A	N/A	N/A
142.	**Minot State University*** (ND)	60	3.2	N/A	$206	57%	17	N/A	N/A	N/A	N/A
142.	**Monroe College**** (NY)	60	N/A	583	$535	7%	19	56%	61%	82%	$21,227
142.	**Oral Roberts University** (OK)	60	N/A	274	$349	N/A	10	60%	14%	75%	$41,433
142.	**Southern Arkansas University***	60	N/A	N/A	$325	57%	16	N/A	N/A	N/A	N/A
142.	**University of Toledo*** (OH)	60	N/A	3,328	$385	68%	N/A	77%	53%	74%	$28,736
142.	**University of Wisconsin–Stout***	60	N/A	874	$334	56%	25	N/A	N/A	87%	$22,141

Best Online Bachelor's Programs For Veterans

Which programs offer military veterans and active-duty service members the best distance education? To ensure academic quality, all schools included in this ranking had to first qualify for a spot by being in the top three-quarters of the Best Online Degree Programs ranking, above. They had to be housed in a regionally accredited institution and were judged on a multitude of factors, including program reputation, faculty credentials, student graduation rate and graduate debt load. Secondly, because veterans and active-duty members often wish to take full advantage of federal benefits designed to make their coursework less expensive, programs also had to be certified for the GI Bill and participate in the Yellow Ribbon Program or charge in-state tuition – that can be fully covered by the GI Bill – to veterans from out of state. Programs that met all criteria were ranked in descending order based on their position in the overall ranking.

Rank	School (State)
1.	**Pennsylvania State University–World Campus***
2.	**Daytona State College** (FL)*
2.	**Western Kentucky University***
4.	**Embry-Riddle Aeronautical University–Worldwide** (FL)
4.	**Oregon State University***
6.	**Colorado State University–Global Campus***
7.	**Arizona State University***
7.	**Ohio State University–Columbus***
9.	**Pace University** (NY)
10.	**Regent University** (VA)
10.	**Savannah College of Art and Design** (GA)
12.	**Central Michigan University***
12.	**University of Florida***
12.	**Utah State University***
15.	**Creighton University** (NE)
15.	**Fort Hays State University** (KS)*
17.	**University of La Verne** (CA)
18.	**George Washington University** (DC)
18.	**Washington State University***
20.	**California Baptist University**
21.	**Palm Beach Atlantic University** (FL)
21.	**Siena Heights University** (MI)
23.	**City University of Seattle** (WA)
23.	**CUNY School of Professional Studies** (NY)*
23.	**University of Denver** (CO)
26.	**Brandman University** (CA)
26.	**Old Dominion University** (VA)*
26.	**Temple University** (PA)*
29.	**Ball State University** (IN)*
29.	**Charleston Southern University** (SC)
29.	**Indiana University-Purdue University–Fort Wayne***
29.	**St. John's University** (NY)
29.	**University of Minnesota–Crookston***
29.	**University of Missouri–Kansas City***
35.	**Colorado State University***
35.	**Concordia University–St. Paul** (MN)
35.	**Eastern Kentucky University***
35.	**Florida Institute of Technology**
35.	**Malone University** (OH)
35.	**University of Maine–Augusta***
35.	**University of Nebraska–Lincoln***
42.	**Lamar University** (TX)*
42.	**Loyola University Chicago** (IL)
42.	**Marist College** (NY)
45.	**Saint Leo University** (FL)
45.	**University of Central Florida***
45.	**University of Missouri–St. Louis***
45.	**University of the Incarnate Word** (TX)
45.	**University of Wisconsin–Platteville***
50.	**University of Massachusetts–Dartmouth***
50.	**Wayne State University** (MI)*

N/A=Data were not provided by the school.
1. Tuition is reported on a per-credit-hour basis. Out-of-state tuition is listed for public institutions. **2.** Displayed here for standardization are six-year graduation rates.

Getting In

4

BASKETBALL PRACTICE AT CLARK UNIVERSITY

MATT SLABY – LUCEO FOR USN&WR

GETTING IN

9 Ways to WOW Admissions

The experts share their tips on how to make yourself stand out in the college application contest

BY KATHERINE HOBSON

Clara Perez knew she wanted to study architecture by freshman year of high school, when she spent hours building virtual houses for the characters in the computer game The Sims. Her college search was equally focused; she worked with her family and an independent counselor to come up with a short list of schools with strong architecture programs. When she decided after a campus visit that Syracuse University was the place, she made frequent contact with the recruiter for SU's architecture school as she worked on a portfolio. She scheduled an interview to show off her ability to speak on her feet. "I wasn't the girl with the strongest grades in high school, but I put myself out there," she says. This fall she'll be a junior at Syracuse.

An academic passion, initiative and a proven interest in a school are key to getting your foot in the door – and they're only some of the attributes admissions officers are looking for in their ever more competitive applicant pools. Sixty-five percent of colleges and universities surveyed by the National Association for College Admission Counseling saw a jump in the number of applications for entry in the fall of 2013, the most recent stats available, as students continued to apply to a greater number of schools and interest increased from abroad. There are roughly 55 percent more international students in the U.S. now than a decade ago, according to the Institute of International Education.

The same forces are persisting this year, particularly at the top of the heap. Stanford University accepted just over 5 percent of the 42,487 applications it received for the class of 2019; Columbia's acceptance rate was 6.1 percent.

Scary as those statistics may be, it's important to remember that, on average, colleges are accepting almost two-thirds of their applicants, according to NACAC. "For most kids, it's not that hard to get into college as long as you're doing the right thing," says Mark Montgomery, an educational consultant in Denver. U.S. News talked with admissions officers, independent college counselors and high school guidance counselors to find out what the right thing is. Read on:

DARREN HAUCK FOR USN&WR

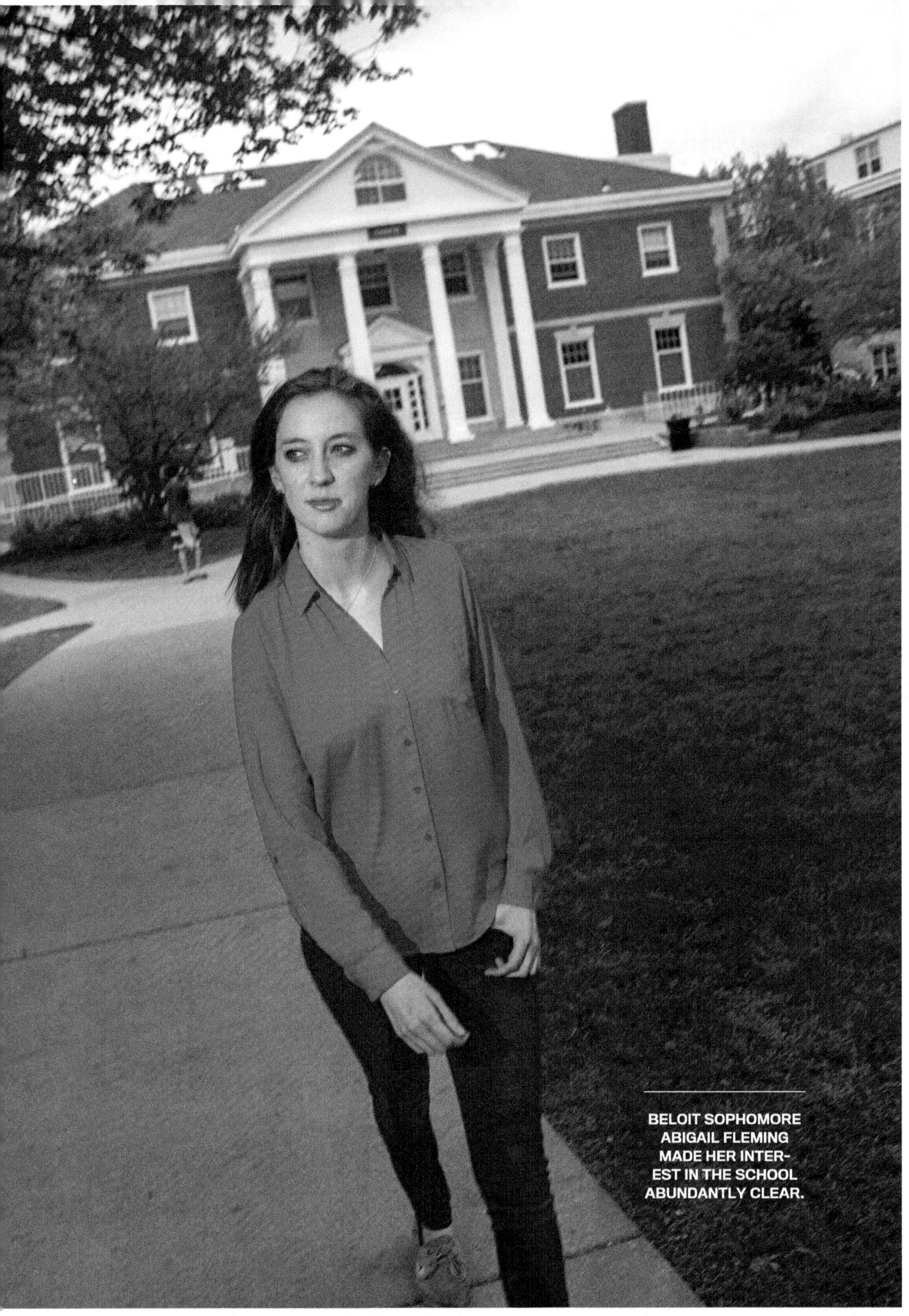

BELOIT SOPHOMORE ABIGAIL FLEMING MADE HER INTEREST IN THE SCHOOL ABUNDANTLY CLEAR.

GET A HEAD START

Plenty of kids enter high school figuring they've got lots of time to perfect their act. But freshman year is not a dress rehearsal. "We do start really paying attention to students' grades in the ninth grade year," says Rick Clark, director of undergraduate admission at Georgia Institute of Technology. "Selective schools will take the whole high school career into account."

Beyond attending to your grades, that means making sure you're on track from the outset to fit in all the courses you might need for admission, advises Thyra Briggs, vice president for admission and financial aid at Harvey Mudd College in Claremont, California. That might mean making sure you have advanced algebra under your belt by the end of sophomore year if a college wants to see a year of calculus, or that you're taking Spanish as a freshman if schools strongly prefer four years of a foreign language.

CONSIDER YOUR CURRICULUM

Some things haven't changed. Grades in college prep courses still carry the most weight in admissions decisions. People who can show they've successfully challenged themselves in high school are "better prepared to handle college work," says Paul Marthers, associate vice chancellor for enrollment management and student success at The State University of New York. At the same time, no one expects students to take every AP class offered. Better to do the best you can in the highest level classes that make sense given your interests and aptitudes, while getting eight to nine hours of sleep a night, advises Katy Murphy, director of college counseling at Bellarmine College Preparatory in San Jose, California, and immediate past president of NACAC. "We see too many kids taking advanced courses across the curriculum who crash and burn because they've taken on too much."

To repeat: It's most important to take AP classes in your areas of strength. And because your guidance counselor will send colleges a detailed profile of your school and its curriculum, the people vetting applications will know if you've taken wise advantage or gone after easy A's. "We don't need to see the student who intends to pursue magazine journalism in AP biology, chemistry, physics and calculus," says Laura Linn, director of admission at Drake University in Des Moines, Iowa. That person is probably better off with two advanced English courses; someone planning on majoring in engineering, on the other hand, can prioritize AP math and science.

HONE YOUR EXTRACURRICULARS

Have you been joining a laundry list of clubs in order to look impressive? Stop, says Murphy. "Colleges are looking for two or three things done in depth," she says. The goal is to select a well-rounded class of freshmen who are passionate about their particular interests, and admissions wants to get a sense from your application of who you really are. It's even better if your activities show off your different facets – that you're an athlete also doing community service, or an actor performing research.

Even if you need to focus on making money during the summer, those months can often be used strategically to develop your story. Far from expecting you to treat July and August as vacation, "we want to see you doing something generally meaningful," says Georgia Tech's Clark. That doesn't imply an expensive enrichment or study abroad program, he says. Those are no more impressive than a summer job or volunteer activity close to home, and time spent sharpening your skills in a sport or artistic pursuit.

The key is to follow up on academic or extracurricular interests rather than just fill time between trips to the beach. But best not to repeat the same experience over and over again, cautions Judy Muir, an independent college consultant in Houston. A dedicated baseball player who spends much of one summer practic-

The Pros' Pet Peeves

Here are a few moves it's best not to make. Don't:

Use inappropriate email addresses. "Like hotlady@gmail.com," says Laura Linn, director of admission at Drake University.

Ignore directions. "Give us what we ask for," says Thyra Briggs, vice president for admission and financial aid at Harvey Mudd College. "We require one recommendation from a math or science teacher and one from a humanities or social science teacher." Students who bother only to ask for the math or science letter seem to be suggesting that "they're not going to embrace that [other] important part of the curriculum."

Neglect email. "You may prefer texting and Twitter, but check your email," says Mike Sexton, vice president for enrollment management at Santa Clara University. "That's how we send out information about incomplete files and admissions decisions."

Get sloppy. "Don't use the wrong school name in your statement!" says Kasey Urquidez, dean of undergraduate admissions at the University of Arizona. Adds Ted Spencer, Michigan's senior adviser on admissions outreach: "We had a student who wrote how much time he'd spent after school torturing – not tutoring – students. Give it to an outside reader. And proofread." *–K.H.*

ing and playing, for example, might the next summer volunteer to help coach Little League.

DEVELOP A SMART SHORT LIST

Picking colleges requires a long look inward as well as study of all those websites. "Pause and assess who you are, what you're good at," advises Muir. Then consider how your learning style and other preferences (large lectures? discussion-intensive seminars? a tight college community? Big Ten sports?) fit with each college's strengths.

Ted Spencer, senior adviser on admissions outreach at the University of Michigan in Ann Arbor, says you should be able to come up with five reasons for applying to every school on your list. Then run the list by your guidance counselor to be sure you're being realistic about the chances for admission. Some high schools have software that can tell you where you'd stack up against past applicants to a college. Make sure to include a few safe bets, suggests Caroline Brokaw Tucker, an independent college consultant at New Canaan, Connecticut-based Dunbar Educational Consultants, and that they are places where you'll be happy. Just in case.

CONSIDER EARLY OPTIONS

Some 49 percent of colleges reported an increase in the number of applicants accepted through binding early decision for the fall of 2013 (meaning the students promised to attend if accepted), and 68 percent saw a jump in nonbinding early-action acceptances (students get word early, without an obligation), according to NACAC. Montgomery always advises students to apply early decision if they absolutely know where they want to go and won't need to weigh financial aid offers, since colleges like to admit students who are a sure thing, and the odds of clearing the bar are often better. "We have students whose applications we're reading in the regular decision round who go on the waitlist, when they would have been admitted early decision or early action," says Mike Sexton, vice president for enrollment management at Santa Clara University in California.

But early decision has its disadvantages. You have to know your first choice very early senior year. And you have less bargaining power when it comes to financial aid, says Teresa Lloyd, founder of Grosse Pointe College Consulting in Grosse Pointe Park, Michigan.

SHOW SINCERE INTEREST

As it becomes easier for students to apply to multiple schools electronically and by using the Common Application, admissions officers are alert for "stealth candidates" who do nothing but fill out the forms. If you want to be taken seriously, "you've got to show them some love," says Tucker.

Visiting, the best way to get a feel for schools, is also the best way to show you're interested. Take the tour, but also meet with admissions officers. Ask questions. With a little notice, you can arrange to attend classes and meet with a professor whose area of research intrigues you. If you can't visit, take advantage of local college fairs and every other option for contact. "Write to the admissions office, sign up on their Facebook page – anything to let them know you think they're the bee's knees," says Montgomery.

"I made sure I stood out," says Abigail Fleming of Evansville, Indiana, who applied to 10 small liberal arts colleges and, after visiting a few, zeroed in on Beloit College in Wisconsin. She stayed in touch with the admissions office when she had questions, and even drove three hours to a college fair to connect with the school again. She's now a sophomore at Beloit.

MAX FARBMAN WROTE ABOUT BEING PART OF AN ORCHESTRA.

CHRISTOPHER CUNNINGHAM FOR USN&WR

ACE THE ESSAY

The goal in choosing an essay topic is to give a sense of your personality to go with the grades and test scores, not to deliver a Big Think piece on world affairs, a common mistake. Often the best inspiration is a routine experience that can be mined for a larger theme saying something about how you tick. That's the approach taken by Max Farbman, an avid percussionist from Arlington Heights, Illinois. After several revisions, he sent off an essay about how he's happiest when he's part of the bigger picture of the orchestra, enjoying the moment as he waits for his parts. One college liked the essay so much it planned to include it in a packet for applicants. Farbman is now at Yale.

The essay (or an optional personal statement) also provides a great opportunity to address apparent flaws in your application – poor grades during that long bout with mono sophomore year, for example. "Don't let us interpret that blindly," says Linn. If you simply screwed up, tell us the specifics of how you bounced back, suggests Kasey Urquidez, dean of undergraduate admissions at the University of Arizona.

PAY ATTENTION TO DETAILS

Optional essays? Write them. A chance to elaborate on your extracurricular activities? Take it. For students on the bubble, that bit of extra effort can make the difference in whether or not you're admitted. Briggs of Harvey Mudd College advises putting serious thought into the teachers you ask for recommendations. "Don't always choose teachers who gave you a straight A," she says. A recommendation from a teacher who watched you struggle can "show how you respond to challenge." Finally, keep careful track of deadlines. And meet them.

TAKE THE LEAD

Throughout the process, it's really crucial to remember that you, not your parents, are running the show. Take charge of creating your list, of arranging visits and interviews (and then do the talking), and of reaching out to the admissions office with questions on your own, rather than having your mom do it on her lunch hour. "It's refreshing when a student does that," says Clark, "because it's so rare." ●

HOW A MOOC CAN BUFF YOUR CREDS

BY ARLENE WEINTRAUB

Rachael McIver wanted to explore a career in marketing, but there were no courses in the topic at her high school, the Woodward School for Girls in Quincy, Massachusetts. So she signed on for a college-level "massive open online course" (MOOC) in introductory marketing taught by faculty members at the University of Pennsylvania's Wharton School. She loved it. "This definitely helped me determine that business is something I'd like to pursue in college," she says.

And, like many of the rapidly growing ranks of high school students enrolling in MOOCs, McIver also hopes the course will bolster her college résumé. Daphne Koller, president of the large MOOC platform Coursera, estimates that nearly 400,000 students in Coursera offerings are in high school. Even though these online offerings don't typically award college credit, Koller says, "students think of MOOCs like AP credits or chess club" or other activities that boost their admissions chances.

Admissions officers are starting to pay attention, says Suzanne McCray, vice provost for enrollment management and dean of admissions at the University of Arkansas. "We look for anything that shows engagement, especially for scholarships, and I think most schools do," McCray says. "MOOCs would certainly fit into that." She adds that it's important to show that you completed the MOOC. Coursera and other major MOOC platforms generally offer certificates of completion, though there may be a fee involved.

Some colleges are reaching out directly to high school students with MOOCs designed to prepare them for college level work or to introduce them to potential majors. The University of Wisconsin, for example, offers College Readiness Math, which has proven so popular that more than 2,500 students have signed up since it was tested in the summer of 2012. And in 2013, Brown University launched a MOOC called Exploring Engineering that has already attracted 4,000 high school students. During the two-week course, students build prototypes responding to a design challenge and get feedback on the designs from fellow students and lecturer Karen Haberstroh, Brown's associate director of engineering programs.

Haberstroh notes that many of the students who complete the MOOC go on to take more intensive online courses in engineering at Brown – further grist for their applications. ●

Getting IN

A+ Schools for B Students

So you're a scholar with lots to offer and the GPA of a B student, and your heart is set on going to a great college. No problem. U.S. News has screened the universe of colleges and universities to identify those where nonsuperstars have a decent shot at being accepted and thriving – where spirit and hard work could make all the difference to the admissions office. To make this list, which is presented alphabetically, schools had to admit a meaningful proportion of applicants whose test scores and class standing put them in non-A territory (methodology, Page 141). Since many truly seek a broad and engaged student body, be sure to display your individuality and seriousness of purpose as you apply.

National Universities

School (State) (*Public)	SAT/ACT 25th-75th percentile ('14)	Average high school GPA ('14)	Freshmen in top 25% of class ('14)
Adelphi University (NY)	1010-1220[9]	3.4	62%[5]
Andrews University (MI)	20-27	N/A	44%[5]
Arizona State University–Tempe*	1020-1270[2]	3.5	60%
Auburn University (AL)*	24-30	3.8	61%
Azusa Pacific University (CA)	980-1080	3.6	55%
Ball State University (IN)*	1000-1190[2]	3.4	52%
Baylor University (TX)	24-30	N/A	74%
Biola University (CA)	980-1240	3.5	58%[5]
Clarkson University (NY)	1090-1290	3.7	76%
Clark University (MA)	1108-1333[2]	3.6	73%[5]
Colorado State University*	22-27	3.6	50%
DePaul University (IL)	23-28[2]	3.3	53%[5]
Drexel University (PA)	1090-1300	3.5	61%[5]
Duquesne University (PA)	1040-1230[2]	3.7	58%
Edgewood College (WI)	20-25	3.4	44%
Florida Institute of Technology	1020-1260	3.6	63%[5]
Florida State University*	26-29	3.9	76%
Fordham University (NY)	1150-1350	3.6	80%[5]
George Mason University (VA)*	1050-1250[2]	3.7	65%[5]
Hofstra University (NY)	1050-1230[2]	3.6	57%[5]
Howard University (DC)	990-1220	3.3	55%[5]
Indiana University–Bloomington*	1060-1290	3.6	69%[5]
Iowa State University*	21-29	3.6	58%
Kansas State University*	22-28[2]	3.5	47%
Kent State University (OH)*	20-25	3.3	40%
Louisiana State Univ.–Baton Rouge*	23-28	3.5	54%
Louisiana Tech University*	21-27	3.5	51%
Loyola University Chicago	25-29	3.8	72%[5]
Marquette University (WI)	25-29	N/A	67%[5]
Maryville University of St. Louis	23-27	3.7	61%
Miami University–Oxford (OH)*	25-30	3.7	68%[5]
Michigan State University*	23-28	3.7	68%[5]
Michigan Technological University*	25-30	3.7	65%
Mississippi State University*	21-28	3.4	54%
New Jersey Institute of Technology*	1080-1300	3.4	54%[5]
New School (NY)	990-1240[2]	N/A	42%[5]
North Dakota State University*	21-26[3]	3.4	42%
Ohio University*	22-26	3.4	43%
Oklahoma State University*	22-28	3.5	54%
Oregon State University*	980-1230	3.6	57%
Pepperdine University (CA)	1120-1330	3.6	80%[5]
Purdue University–West Lafayette (IN)*	1080-1330	3.7	77%[5]
Rutgers, The St. U. of N.J.–New Brunswick*	1090-1340[3]	N/A	74%[5]
San Diego State University*	1000-1220	3.7	77%[5]
Seton Hall University (NJ)	1040-1220	3.5	69%[5]
St. John's University (NY)	990-1210	3.4	43%[5]
Saint Louis University	25-30	3.8	72%[5]
SUNY Col. of Envir. Sci. and Forestry*	1090-1280	3.8	68%
Syracuse University (NY)	1070-1280	3.6	71%[5]
Temple University (PA)*	1010-1230[2]	3.5	51%[5]
Texas Christian University	24-30	N/A	73%[5]
Texas Tech University*	1000-1200	N/A	54%
University at Albany–SUNY*	1010-1180	3.5	49%[5]
University at Buffalo–SUNY*	1050-1250	3.2	63%[5]
University of Alabama–Birmingham*	21-27	3.6	55%
University of Alabama–Huntsville*	24-30	3.7	54%[5]
University of Arkansas*	23-28	3.6	55%
University of Central Florida*	1090-1280	3.9	71%
University of Cincinnati*	23-28	3.5	48%
University of Colorado–Boulder*	24-30	3.6	54%[5]
University of Dayton (OH)	24-29	3.6	54%[5]
University of Delaware*	1100-1300	3.7	72%[5]
University of Denver	25-30	3.7	74%[5]
University of Hawaii–Manoa*	980-1190[3]	3.5	60%
University of Houston*	1040-1250	N/A	63%
University of Illinois–Chicago*	22-27[3]	3.3	62%
University of Iowa*	23-28	3.6	56%
University of Kansas*	22-28	3.5	56%
University of Kentucky*	22-28	3.6	57%
University of Louisville (KY)*	22-28[3]	3.5	55%[5]
Univ. of Maryland–Baltimore County*	1110-1310	3.8	54%[5]
University of Massachusetts–Amherst*	1120-1310	3.8	72%[5]
University of Massachusetts–Lowell*	1050-1240	3.4	52%[5]
University of Mississippi*	21-27[2]	3.5	47%
University of Missouri*	23-28	N/A	57%
University of Nebraska–Lincoln*	22-28	3.5	51%
University of New Hampshire*	1000-1200	N/A	48%
University of North Carolina–Charlotte*	1000-1170	3.3	56%
University of Oklahoma*	23-29	3.6	65%
University of Oregon*	990-1230	3.6	66%[5]
University of Rhode Island*	1010-1200[3]	3.4	49%
University of San Diego	1130-1320	3.9	78%[5]
University of San Francisco	1040-1250	3.6	60%[4]
University of South Carolina*	1110-1300	4.0	64%
University of South Florida*	1070-1250	3.9	56%
University of St. Thomas (MN)	24-29	3.6	58%[5]
University of the Pacific (CA)	1038-1313	3.5	62%[5]
University of Utah*	21-28	3.6	49%[5]
University of Vermont*	1080-1290	3.4	68%[5]
University of Wyoming*	22-27	3.5	48%
Virginia Commonwealth University*	1000-1210[2]	3.6	47%
West Virginia University*	21-26	3.4	44%[5]

Note: Key to footnotes, Page 80.

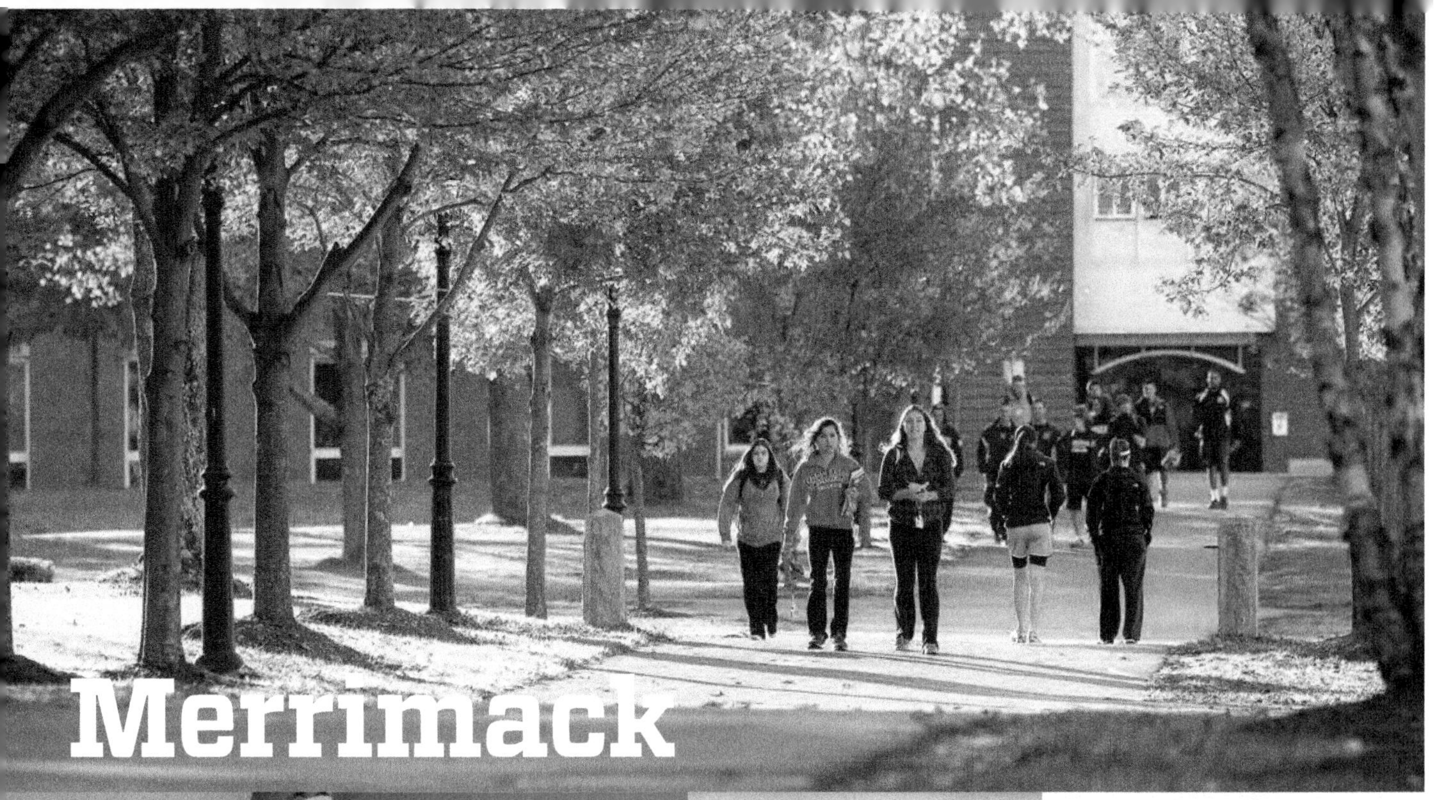

PEPPERDINE UNIVERSITY IN CALIFORNIA

BRETT ZIEGLER FOR USN&WR

National Liberal Arts Colleges

School (State) (*Public)	SAT/ACT 25th-75th percentile ('14)	Average high school GPA ('14)	Freshmen in top 25% of class ('14)
Agnes Scott College (GA)	1060-1260[2]	3.7	70%[5]
Allegheny College (PA)	1050-1270	3.8	73%
Alma College (MI)	21-27	3.5	53%
Augustana College (IL)	23-29[2]	3.3	66%
Austin College (TX)	22-27	3.5	72%
Beloit College (WI)	24-30[2]	3.3	75%[5]
Berea College (KY)	22-27	3.4	69%
Berry College (GA)	24-29	3.7	66%
Birmingham-Southern College (AL)	23-29	3.5	53%
Calvin College (MI)	23-29[2]	3.7	58%
Carthage College (WI)	21-27	N/A	50%
Central College (IA)	21-27	3.6	48%
Coe College (IA)	22-28	3.7	67%
College of St. Benedict (MN)	23-29	3.7	70%
College of Wooster (OH)	25-30	3.6	71%[5]
Concordia College–Moorhead (MN)	23-28	3.6	61%
Cornell College (IA)	23-30	3.4	45%
Doane College (NE)	21-25[3]	3.5	42%
Drew University (NJ)	1000-1220[2]	3.5	54%[5]
Furman University (SC)	1130-1340[2]	N/A	72%
Gordon College (MA)	1030-1280[3]	3.6	67%[5]
Goucher College (MD)	1020-1280[2]	3.2	53%[5]
Grove City College (PA)	1070-1334	3.7	79%
Gustavus Adolphus College (MN)	24-30[2]	3.6	64%
Hartwick College (NY)	1010-1200[2]	3.2	45%
Hobart and William Smith Colleges (NY)	1140-1320[2]	3.4	70%[5]
Hope College (MI)	23-29	3.8	62%
Houghton College (NY)	980-1260	3.5	55%
Illinois Wesleyan University	25-30	N/A	76%[5]
Juniata College (PA)	1040-1250[9]	3.7	64%
Kalamazoo College (MI)	25-30	3.8	75%[5]
Knox College (IL)	23-30[2]	N/A	58%[5]
Lake Forest College (IL)	23-28[2]	3.7	56%[5]
Luther College (IA)	23-28	3.7	63%
McDaniel College (MD)	980-1200	3.5	50%
Millsaps College (MS)	23-29	3.6	61%
Muhlenberg College (PA)	1120-1330[2]	3.3	74%[5]
Nebraska Wesleyan University	22-27	3.7	54%
Oglethorpe University (GA)	1040-1230	3.5	58%
Ohio Wesleyan University	22-28[2]	3.5	56%[5]
Ouachita Baptist University (AR)	21-28	3.6	55%
Randolph-Macon College (VA)	980-1190	3.6	52%
Ripon College (WI)	21-27	3.4	46%
Roanoke College (VA)	980-1210	3.5	43%
Salem College (NC)	21-27	N/A	76%
Sewanee–University of the South (TN)	26-30[2]	3.7	68%[5]
Siena College (NY)	1020-1220[2]	3.5	53%
Simpson College (IA)	22-27	N/A	57%
Skidmore College (NY)	1130-1350	N/A	78%[5]
Southwestern University (TX)	1050-1260	N/A	66%
St. Anselm College (NH)	1050-1230[2]	3.2	58%[5]
St. John's University (MN)	23-28	3.4	50%
St. Lawrence University (NY)	1110-1290[2]	3.5	78%[5]
St. Mary's College (IN)	23-28	3.8	62%[5]
St. Michael's College (VT)	1050-1250[2]	3.4	49%
St. Norbert College (WI)	22-27	3.5	61%
Stonehill College (MA)	1010-1220[2]	3.3	62%
Susquehanna University (PA)	1020-1210[2]	3.4	54%
Thomas Aquinas College (CA)	1180-1350	3.8	71%[5]
Trinity College (CT)	1150-1340	N/A	80%[5]
University of Minnesota–Morris*	22-28	3.6	55%
University of North Carolina–Asheville*	1100-1290	3.4	54%
University of Puget Sound (WA)	1110-1330	3.5	64%[5]
Ursinus College (PA)	1050-1260[2]	N/A	54%[5]
Virginia Military Institute*	1070-1250[3]	3.6	58%
Wabash College (IN)	1020-1240	3.6	66%
Wartburg College (IA)	21-27	3.5	57%
Washington College (MD)	1040-1270[2]	3.6	62%[5]
Westminster College (MO)	22-27	3.4	48%
Westmont College (CA)	1050-1290	3.5	60%[5]
Wheaton College (MA)	1120-1350[2]	3.3	69%[5]
Willamette University (OR)	1080-1320	3.8	72%
William Jewell College (MO)	22-28[2]	3.8	60%
Wisconsin Lutheran College	21-26	3.4	41%
Wittenberg University (OH)	22-28[2]	3.4	46%
Wofford College (SC)	24-30	3.5	77%

Regional Universities

School (State) (*Public)	SAT/ACT 25th-75th percentile ('14)	Average high school GPA ('14)	Freshmen in top 25% of class ('14)
NORTH			
Arcadia University (PA)	1000-1200	3.6	60%
Assumption College (MA)	1020-1200[2]	3.4	43%
Bentley University (MA)	1150-1330	N/A	75%[5]
Bryant University (RI)	1065-1240[2]	3.4	52%[5]
CUNY–Baruch College*	1120-1330[3]	3.3	78%
CUNY–Hunter College*	1060-1270	3.4	57%
CUNY–Queens College*	1020-1180	N/A	65%[5]
Emerson College (MA)	1140-1330	3.6	73%[5]
Endicott College (MA)	980-1170[2]	N/A	40%[5]
Ithaca College (NY)	1100-1300[2]	N/A	68%[5]
Lesley University (MA)	980-1190	3.0	43%[5]
Loyola University Maryland	1100-1270[2]	3.4	65%[4]
Manhattan College (NY)	990-1190[3]	N/A	52%[5]
Marist College (NY)	1090-1270[9]	3.3	58%[5]
Molloy College (NY)	980-1140	3.0	54%
Nazareth College (NY)	980-1190[2]	3.4	56%
Providence College (RI)	1040-1250[2]	3.4	65%[5]
Quinnipiac University (CT)	1010-1210	3.4	66%
Rochester Institute of Technology (NY)	1110-1320	3.7	67%
Roger Williams University (RI)	1030-1200[2]	3.3	44%[5]
Salisbury University (MD)*	1070-1230[9]	3.8	55%[5]
Salve Regina University (RI)	1010-1180[2]	3.2	45%
Simmons College (MA)	1070-1260	3.3	64%[5]
St. Joseph's University (PA)	1030-1220[2]	3.5	44%[5]
Stockton University (NJ)*	980-1200	N/A	54%
SUNY College–Oneonta*	1000-1170[3]	3.7	54%[5]
SUNY–Geneseo*	1120-1320	3.7	76%
SUNY–New Paltz*	1030-1200	3.6	80%[5]
SUNY–Oswego*	1020-1190[3]	3.5	53%

Note: Key to footnotes, Page 80.

Regional Universities (continued)

School (State) (*Public)	SAT/ACT 25th-75th percentile ('14)	Average high school GPA ('14)	Freshmen in top 25% of class ('14)
Towson University (MD)*	1000-1170	3.6	49%[5]
University of Scranton (PA)	1040-1210	3.4	57%[5]
Wagner College (NY)	1060-1270[2]	3.6	73%
SOUTH			
Appalachian State University (NC)*	1060-1240	4.0	56%
Bellarmine University (KY)	22-27	3.5	53%[5]
Belmont University (TN)	23-29	3.5	60%
Christian Brothers University (TN)	21-27	3.7	68%
Christopher Newport University (VA)*	1060-1250[2]	3.8	54%
College of Charleston (SC)*	1030-1230	3.9	55%
Elon University (NC)	1130-1320	4.0	62%[5]
Embry-Riddle Aeronautical Univ. (FL)	980-1240[2]	3.6	49%[5]
Harding University (AR)	22-28	3.6	55%
James Madison University (VA)*	1050-1230	N/A	43%
Lee University (TN)	21-27[3]	3.6	49%
Lipscomb University (TN)	23-29	3.6	51%[5]
Mercer University (GA)	1090-1290	3.8	70%
Rollins College (FL)	1100-1280[2]	3.3	64%[5]
Samford University (AL)	23-29	3.6	56%[5]
Spring Hill College (AL)	22-27	3.5	55%
Stetson University (FL)	1070-1275[2]	3.7	58%
Union University (TN)	22-29	3.7	57%
University of Mary Washington (VA)*	1020-1200	3.5	45%
Univ. of North Carolina–Wilmington*	1110-1270	4.0	69%
University of North Florida*	22-26	3.7	41%
University of North Georgia*	1010-1200	3.2	66%[5]
William Carey University (MS)	20-27[3]	3.5	60%
MIDWEST			
Baker University (KS)	20-26	3.4	42%
Baldwin Wallace University (OH)	20-25[2]	3.4	46%
Bethel University (MN)	22-28	3.5	57%
Bradley University (IL)	23-28	3.6	63%
Butler University (IN)	25-30[3]	3.8	79%
Capital University (OH)	21-27[3]	3.5	44%
College of St. Scholastica (MN)	21-27	3.5	50%
Concordia University (NE)	20-27	3.5	43%
Creighton University (NE)	24-29	3.8	72%
Dominican University (IL)	20-24	3.6	48%

School (State) (*Public)	SAT/ACT 25th-75th percentile ('14)	Average high school GPA ('14)	Freshmen in top 25% of class ('14)
Drake University (IA)	25-30	3.7	71%
Drury University (MO)	23-29	3.8	62%
Elmhurst College (IL)	21-26	3.4	45%
Franciscan Univ. of Steubenville (OH)	23-29	3.8	60%[5]
Grand Valley State University (MI)*	21-26	3.3	48%
Hamline University (MN)	21-27	3.4	41%
Indiana Wesleyan University	21-27	3.6	58%
John Carroll University (OH)	22-27	3.5	44%[5]
Kettering University (MI)	25-29	3.7	71%
Lawrence Technological Univ. (MI)	21-28	3.4	50%
Lewis University (IL)	21-25	3.4	44%
Missouri State University*	21-26	3.6	54%
Mount Vernon Nazarene Univ. (OH)	20-25	3.4	44%
North Central College (IL)	22-27	3.6	52%
Olivet Nazarene University (IL)	21-27	3.5	47%
Otterbein University (OH)	21-26	3.5	55%
Rockhurst University (MO)	23-28	3.6	58%[5]
St. Catherine University (MN)	21-26	3.6	60%
Truman State University (MO)*	24-30	3.8	80%
University of Detroit Mercy	22-26	3.5	55%
University of Evansville (IN)	1020-1230	3.6	62%
University of Findlay (OH)	20-25	3.6	45%
University of Illinois–Springfield*	20-27	3.4	43%
University of Michigan–Dearborn*	21-27	3.6	58%
University of Minnesota–Duluth*	22-26	3.4	45%
University of Nebraska–Kearney*	20-25	3.4	42%
University of Northern Iowa*	20-25	3.5	47%
University of St. Francis (IL)	21-25	3.4	44%
University of Wisconsin–Eau Claire*	22-26	N/A	47%
University of Wisconsin–La Crosse*	23-27	N/A	65%
Univ. of Wisconsin–Stevens Point*	20-25[9]	3.3	40%
Valparaiso University (IN)	23-29	3.7	64%
Walsh University (OH)	20-25	3.4	45%
Webster University (MO)	21-27	3.5	42%
Xavier University (OH)	22-27[3]	3.5	48%[5]
WEST			
Abilene Christian University (TX)	21-27	3.7	64%
California Lutheran University	1000-1200	3.7	63%
California State University–Chico*	993-1100[3]	3.2	76%[5]
Chapman University (CA)	1110-1290	3.7	80%[5]
Gonzaga University (WA)	1100-1290	3.7	71%
LeTourneau University (TX)	1030-1310[2]	3.6	56%
Loyola Marymount University (CA)	1100-1300	3.8	74%[4]
Mills College (CA)	1020-1250	3.6	64%
New Mexico Inst. of Mining and Tech.*	23-29	3.6	64%
Oklahoma Christian University	22-28[3]	3.5	52%
Oklahoma City University	23-28[3]	3.6	64%
Pacific Lutheran University (WA)	980-1210	3.7	63%[5]
Point Loma Nazarene University (CA)	1010-1220	3.8	67%
Regis University (CO)	22-27[3]	3.5	50%
Seattle University	1060-1280	3.6	62%[5]
St. Edward's University (TX)	1010-1210	N/A	58%
University of Dallas	1080-1320[3]	3.7	58%[5]
University of Portland (OR)	1080-1310	3.6	73%[5]
University of Redlands (CA)	1000-1200	N/A	62%
University of St. Thomas (TX)	990-1220	3.5	49%
Western Washington University*	1000-1210	3.4	51%
Westminster College (UT)	22-27	3.6	55%

Regional Colleges

School (State) (*Public)	SAT/ACT 25th-75th percentile ('14)	Average high school GPA ('14)	Freshmen in top 25% of class ('14)
NORTH			
Champlain College (VT)	1030-1250[3]	3.2	44%[5]
Elizabethtown College (PA)	1020-1240	N/A	64%
Messiah College (PA)	1010-1240	3.7	63%
SUNY Maritime College*	1020-1190	3.2	44%[5]
United States Coast Guard Acad. (CT)*	1170-1340	3.8	76%
U.S. Merchant Marine Acad. (NY)*	26-30	N/A	68%
SOUTH			
Asbury University (KY)	22-28	N/A	54%
Covenant College (GA)	23-29	3.6	50%[5]
Florida Southern College	1040-1220	3.7	58%
High Point University (NC)	1009-1192	3.3	48%[5]
John Brown University (AR)	22-29	3.7	59%
Milligan College (TN)	22-26	3.7	65%
University of Mobile (AL)	20-24	3.3	48%
MIDWEST			
Augustana College (SD)	23-28	3.7	65%
Benedictine College (KS)	22-27	3.5	44%[5]
Cedarville University (OH)	23-29	3.7	65%
College of the Ozarks (MO)	21-25[3]	3.6	52%
Loras College (IA)	21-26	3.4	40%
Northwestern College (IA)	21-27	3.6	55%
Ohio Northern University	23-29[3]	3.7	62%
Taylor University (IN)	24-30	3.7	66%[5]
Trinity Christian College (IL)	20-27	3.5	42%
University of Mount Union (OH)	21-25	3.4	44%
Univ. of Northwestern–St. Paul (MN)	21-27	3.5	48%
WEST			
Carroll College (MT)	22-28	3.6	64%
Oklahoma Baptist University	21-27	3.6	49%

Methodology: To be eligible, national universities, liberal arts colleges, regional universities and regional colleges all had to be ranked among the top three-quarters of their peer groups in the 2016 Best Colleges rankings. They had to admit a meaningful proportion of non-A students, as indicated by fall 2014 admissions data on SAT Critical Reading and Math or Composite ACT scores and high school class standing. The cutoffs were: The 75th percentile for the SAT had to be less than or equal to 1,350; the 25th percentile, greater than or equal to 980. The ACT composite range: less than or equal to 30 and greater than or equal to 20. The proportion of freshmen from the top 10 percent of their high school class had to be less than or equal to 50 percent (for national universities and liberal arts colleges only); for all schools, the proportion of freshmen from the top 25 percent of their high school class had to be less than or equal to 80 percent, and greater than or equal to 40 percent. Average freshman retention rates for all schools had to be greater than or equal to 75 percent. Average high school GPA itself was not used in the calculations identifying the A-plus schools. N/A means not available.

Note: Key to footnotes, Page 80.

Meet the New SAT

Here's what to expect from both the current version and the overhaul, coming in 2016

BY DARCY LEWIS

If you're reading this book as a senior, you're preparing to sit – or have already sat – for the familiar 2400-point SAT, complete with its fancy vocabulary words and mandatory essay. But members of the class of 2017 will soon begin prepping for a completely overhauled test. Last year, College Board President David Coleman announced major revisions to the fall 2015 PSAT and the spring 2016 SAT, saying the SAT had "become disconnected from the work of high schools."

The changes, which include going back to the old 1600-point composite score based on 800-point math and "evidence-based" reading and writing sections and making the essay optional, are intended to better reflect the material students are, or should be, learning in high school. They also are aimed at improving the SAT's reliability as an indicator of how prepared applicants are to tackle college work. The current test is designed more to get at innate abilities; hence the "scholastic aptitude" of the SAT's original name.

The new test "aligns with the Common Core curriculum standards," says Kasey Urquidez, dean of undergraduate admissions at the University of Arizona, who believes that the changes will be beneficial. Defenders of the current test think the change could weaken what they see as an effective tool to identify smart, capable students at academically weaker schools.

One big innovation is the way vocabulary will be handled; rather than test students' knowledge of obscure words out of context (like "cruciverbalist," "mellifluous" or "prestidigitation"), the focus will be on so-called high-utility words that appear in many disciplines, and they'll be used in a passage.

For example, after reading a selection about population density that uses the word "intense," test-takers might be asked which word has the closest meaning: "emotional," "concentrated," "brilliant" or "determined." Many college officials think this shift will let students from all backgrounds show what they really know, not just what they've memorized in prepping. But others remain a fan of the way the current test gets students to tap their critical thinking skills and knowledge of Greek and Latin roots.

The new SAT will also require students to draw conclusions by taking account of evidence, to revise and edit text, to analyze data and interpret graphs, and to solve the types of math problems most commonly seen in college courses and the workplace. It's no coincidence, observers say, that the new test will more closely resemble the ACT, which has been growing ever more popular. (The format of the ACT isn't changing, but the company is making the optional essay a more analytical exercise and is breaking out new scores measuring job skills and proficiency in science, technology, engineering and math.) The redesigned SAT will last three hours, with an extra 50 minutes allotted for an optional essay in which students will analyze a passage and how the author builds an argument. Another popular change is the elimination of the guessing penalty, the practice of subtracting points for wrong answers.

Everyone can take advantage of one much-heralded development already in effect: the College Board's partnership with the nonprofit Khan Academy to provide free online test prep materials. The idea is to start by taking a practice SAT, then master the material by watching in-depth explanatory videos and answering as many practice questions as you want. Starting with the 2015 PSAT, a personalized dashboard will allow students to track their progress.

Whichever test you take, devoting time to practice should increase your comfort level. But some experts advise against sitting for the real thing several times in an attempt to raise your score; some colleges may ask to see all your results – and they certainly want to see you engaged in more activities than test prep. Try to keep the testing in perspective, urges Stuart Schmill, dean of admissions at Massachusetts Institute of Technology. "There is some predictive value in SAT scores, but they are not determinative," he says. "And factors like persistence, resilience and organizational skills, which aren't measured on tests, also predict future academic success."

In fact, many fine colleges have concluded that they don't need test scores to make admissions decisions (story, Page 145). The National Center for Fair & Open Testing (fairtest.org) maintains a database of those that de-emphasize the tests or are "test-optional," meaning applicants choose whether to submit scores or not. ●

GETTY IMAGES

Taming TEST Anxiety

Calming tips from a test-prep pro

Test day is on the horizon, and the mere thought is making you sweat. How to get a grip? First, take a deep breath and tell yourself it's normal to be anxious – in fact, some anxiety is good, since it will provide focus and an incentive to prepare. The problem is that being really anxious may actually hurt your performance. The good news: You can do quite a bit to stop test anxiety before it stops you!

First, a lesson on how brains work. Two parts of the brain play a big role in anxiety, the amygdala and the prefrontal cortex. The amygdala is basically a really good built-in threat detector. Imagine strolling through the forest thousands of years ago, when suddenly a hungry tiger rushes up to grab you for lunch. You would not want to pause and think – you would want to either run or fight immediately. Your amygdala would send out chemical signals (cortisol and adrenaline) that would rapidly increase your heart rate and breathing, elevate your blood pressure, put sugar into your bloodstream for fuel and focus your attention on running away or fighting.

Unfortunately, neither of those responses will help you take a high-stakes test like the ACT or SAT.

The prefrontal cortex, on the other hand, handles planning and goal-setting, and allows you to work toward what you want and resist temptations that might throw you off course. The trouble starts when the amygdala fires up and seizes control in the absence of any real danger: Your ability to solve problems using the calm and thoughtful approach goes straight out the window. So the key is to lower the level of threat your amygdala detects and give your thinking center the advantage. One scientist researching how brains react to stress, the University of Montreal's Sonia Lupien, has a clever model summarizing what causes anxiety, or what, she observes, makes people "nuts":

- **Novelty.** New situations, while they may be fun, are also generally stressful.
- **Unpredictability.** Not knowing how things will turn out is unnerving.
- **Threat to the ego.** Feeling that your abilities are in doubt is nerve-wracking.
- **Sense of low control.** Feeling a lack of control or a sense of helplessness is about as bad as it gets. Being aware of these factors should help you gain perspective and reduce their impact, Lupien says.

Here are some ways to minimize your anxiety and maximize your test performance:

#1

Prep for the test by learning how it works.

However you feel about the ACT and SAT, you have to give them this: They are consistent. (Thus the name standardized tests.) So your test will be a heck of a lot like the previous ones. You already may have a feel for what to expect if you sat for the PSAT last year, or the similar preview of the ACT, known as ACT Aspire.

Now you want to work through lots of practice tests, on your own and under conditions that mimic as much as possible the conditions and

GETTY IMAGES

the stresses of the real thing. Be strict about time. Do the whole darned test to develop stamina. Take it in a library to add the distractions of other people. As they say in sports, "practice like you'll play, so you can play like you've practiced."

Research shows that one of the best antidotes for students who suffer from excessive test anxiety is more practice tests. In light of this research, The College Board recently launched a collaboration with Khan Academy to offer a wealth of practice opportunities for the SAT online. Free! Many students approach these tests as if they're school exams. They are not. Your job is to figure out (and get used to) the ways they differ.

#2

Learn how YOU react to the test.

If you did not do as well as you would have liked on a practice test, ask: Why not? Did you run out of time? If so, where and why? Identify questions that were difficult for you. Did you make silly errors that you can avoid making next time? When you take the test the first time, notice if something about the testing situation affected your concentration. Not getting enough sleep, showing up late or forgetting to bring snacks, for example, can throw you off balance. Recognizing your own patterns as well as those of the tests can help you avoid subpar performance.

#3

Keep the tests in perspective.

Remember: You are not your test score. Knowing the meaning of "laconic" and "lugubrious" does not prove you are smart. Nor does memorizing the rules of logarithms, apostrophes or parallel structure. The ACT and SAT are tests of acquired skills, and you may have some work to do to acquire them. But a low score does not mean you lack intelligence or are a poor learner. Understanding that distinction should help make the test less stressful.

In her book "Mindset," psychologist Carol Dweck makes the case for thinking of learning as a way to grow your abilities rather than show how smart you are. Low scores are not a measurement of you, but rather of the material you have not mastered yet.

#4

Get more sleep.

Ever notice how, when you are tired, your mom/friend/teacher/little brother is even more annoying than usual? It's not your mom/friend/teacher/little brother who's the problem – it's you. Your highly sensitive amygdala is getting the upper hand, which makes you much more likely to feel and act stressed. Being well rested when you deal with a challenging situation increases the chances that your prefrontal cortex will stay firmly in charge.

Getting enough sleep also strengthens the brain pathways that help you retrieve information. When you are exhausted, the little guy who goes to pull the answer from the filing cabinet in the back of your head waves you off, yawning, "Sorry! I am on a break. Come back later." You may be aware that you have learned the material, but your ability to access it becomes compromised, slowing you down or foiling you altogether. In the days leading up to the test, do essential homework, be antisocial, and go to sleep.

#5

Focus on the test process, not the score.

Obsessing about what your score will be is bound to jangle your nerves. As you practice and on the big day, try to laser in on the process of taking the test, the part that you can control. Better technique – not worry – leads to better outcomes. Psychologist Mihaly Csikszentmihalyi found that two requirements of a top performance are "concentration on the task at hand and loss of self-consciousness." In other words, to find your groove while prepping and on test day, focus on the job itself and not on your results.

#6

Get the logistics sorted out ahead of time.

Make sure you consult your test registration form or admission ticket for what to bring (photo ID, an acceptable calculator, say) and pack your "test kit" in advance so you can grab it and go. Be clear about where you need to be, and allow plenty of time to arrive early. The stress of running late can take a toll on your sense of control.

#7

Have a Plan B.

First of all, remember that you can take the ACT or SAT (or both) again if you don't like your score – and again. Knowing you have several chances at success should help lower that threat level. And if you still don't like your score when all is said and done, there are hundreds of "test-optional" colleges that have concluded that they don't need the tests to make admissions decisions. Seriously! Go to fairtest.org to learn more.

Finally, I like to tell students to get up on test day and locate their swagger. Listen to your favorite music. Wear the clothes that make you feel like all that. Think about the places in your life where you are at your best. Throw your shoulders back and think "Oh, yeah!"

We all have strengths that tests do not capture – think about yours. Psychologists have found that when students take a few minutes before a big test to write about the strengths and values that make them who they are, they perform better. Good luck! •

By Ned Johnson, founder of PrepMatters (prepmatters.com) and co-author of "Conquering the SAT: How Parents Can Help Teens Overcome the Pressure and Succeed."

TEST SCORES:

You May Not Need Them!

A growing number of colleges are choosing not to require SAT or ACT results. BY DARCY LEWIS

Olivia Rossetti was hoping to apply to colleges with strong English and social science programs, flexible curricula and admissions policies that considered her as a whole person. When the Brookfield, Massachusetts, student visited Smith College, she was glad to find campuswide support for a test-optional admissions policy and the belief that standardized exams do not necessarily reflect a student's abilities. "I felt validated," the Smith junior says.

Welcome to the world of test-optional admissions, where applicants – not colleges – decide whether to supply schools with their SAT or ACT scores. Bowdoin College went test-optional in 1969, which at first created only a trickle of interest among other institutions. But now the floodgates have opened. "Hundreds of top-notch colleges are willing to view applicants as more than a test score," says Bob Schaeffer, public education director at the National Center for Fair and Open Testing, better known as FairTest.

Research has confirmed what many schools have long suspected: Test scores do not always predict which students will excel after reaching campus. A 2014 report from two former Bates admissions officials, William Hiss and Valerie Franks, analyzed student performance data from 33 test-optional schools and showed a difference of just five-hundredths of a point in GPA and six-tenths of one percent in graduation rates between nonsubmitters and submitters.

In the past year, more than 30 schools have dropped their testing requirements, more than in any previous year, FairTest has noted. Among them: George Washington University in D.C., Drake University in Iowa and the University of Puget Sound in Washington. Another reason schools cited for ditching the test requirements: They can help boost racial and socioeconomic diversity on campus, a point also noted in the Hiss and Franks study. DePaul University in Chicago went test-optional in 2012 with the aim of drawing in more applications from bright Chicago Public Schools students and others whose test scores don't necessarily reflect their potential. It worked. And when associate vice president for enrollment management Jon Boeckenstedt crunched the numbers, he found "CPS graduates with lower test scores did just as well here as CPS graduates with higher test scores."

> THE SAT OR ACT WON'T ALWAYS PREDICT WHICH STUDENTS WILL EXCEL ONCE THEY REACH CAMPUS.

What to consider

Applicants mulling over this route can begin by checking the FairTest database, fairtest.org, for its list of some 840 accredited bachelor degree-granting schools that are test-optional. (Some only allow this choice to students who meet certain GPA or related requirements.) The list includes a handful of "test-flexible" schools that allow applicants to submit other results like Advanced Placement or International Baccalaureate subject test scores in place of the SAT and ACT.

How can you decide whether to send in scores? Generally, you may want to go ahead if you feel they will improve how admissions will rank your application in their mix. If you do some research and find that your results fall below those of the top third of accepted students at more selective schools or below the median at more inclusive institutions, you may want to hold them back, experts suggest. Jane H. Dané, associate vice president for enrollment management at Old Dominion University in Virginia, whose first test-optional class arrives on campus this fall, notes that applicants to ODU (and elsewhere) who don't submit scores will be particularly scrutinized for other evidence of potential for success, like challenging coursework and leadership skills. The more well-rounded you are, the better your chances of impressing without scores.

Keep in mind that even test-optional schools may require scores to dole out their merit aid awards and decide class placement. So if a good financial aid package is important, check school policies to be sure you won't lose out by holding back.

At the very least, knowing the choice exists may ease your stress. "We want to remove fear and frenzy from the application equation," says Martha Allman, dean of admissions at test-optional Wake Forest University in North Carolina. "We're more interested in who you really are." ●

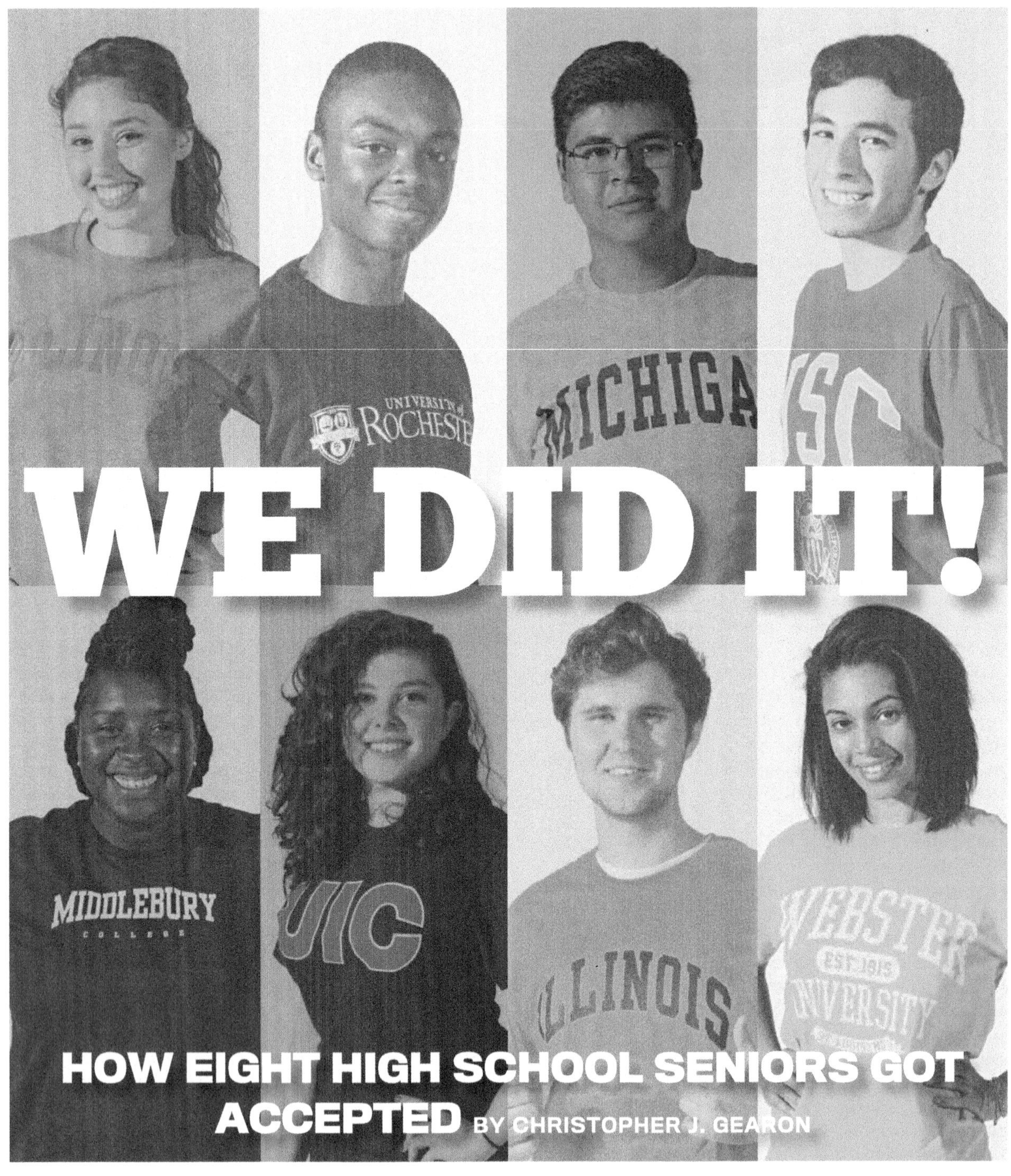

WE DID IT!

HOW EIGHT HIGH SCHOOL SENIORS GOT ACCEPTED

BY CHRISTOPHER J. GEARON

Is college in your near future? Get the scoop on what the path to campus is really like from recent high school grads who have just taken it. As the May 1 decision day approached, U.S. News visited Lincoln Park High School in Chicago to ask a number of seniors about their college application experience and for tips for students now getting started. Built more than a century ago on Chicago's north side, Lincoln Park High is both a neighborhood school and home to three magnet programs open to students from across the city – in performing arts, college prep and the International Baccalaureate diploma option. The school offers robust college readiness programs; College Ambassadors, for example, has seniors assisting their peers with all facets of the application process. The 2,200 students come from a wide range of backgrounds; Lincoln Park describes itself as "a slice of the real world." More than one-third are Hispanic, 28 percent are white, 22 percent are black, and 10 percent are Asian. About 80 percent of graduates go on to college. Check out how eight members of the Class of 2015 found the right fit – and what it took for each to get in:

PHOTOGRAPHY BY **BRETT ZIEGLER** FOR USN&WR

Paulina Rodriguez

Even as she applied to 10 colleges last fall, Rodriguez figured she would end up at a local community college for financial reasons. The road to medical school and a career as a neurosurgeon seemed particularly daunting for the budding first-generation college student. But Rodriguez was used to doing what needs to be done, having started helping her mom (who speaks mostly Spanish) at age 7 with her tasks as a housekeeper.

Alongside her college applications, Rodriguez applied for the Gates Millennium Scholars Program, which covers tuition and expenses for underrepresented students with financial need. After getting into seven schools, including Loyola University, St. Xavier University and the University of Illinois in Chicago, as well as UI–Urbana-Champaign, she got word in April that she was selected as a Gates scholar. Besides providing undergrads a free ride, the program extends recipients free graduate schooling in certain fields.

Although Loyola had been her top choice, a visit to the campus along Lake Michigan on a "really cold" day dampened her enthusiasm. When she visited Urbana-Champaign, she was sold. "It was sunny and pretty, and the people were so nice," she says. She also liked that the university was farther from home and has a good psychology program. Schools that denied her: the University of Chicago, Northwestern University in nearby Evanston, and Boston University.

GPA: 3.7 unweighted
ACT Score: 22
Extracurrics: LPHS College Ambassador, Ecology Club, National Honor Society; co-president of the Fuego Dance Crew, New Era Dance Company member, worked as a hostess and waitress, youth group volunteer
Essay: Her early transition from childhood to adulthood as she helped her mom support the two of them.
Regret: That she didn't start the process earlier than October. "There were a lot of essays."
Big help: "I had people proofread. There wasn't an application I didn't redo."
Oops: "I sent Northwestern essays to BU."

DON'T MAKE YOURSELF SOUND LIKE EVERYONE ELSE.

Paulina Rodriguez

Notable essay prompt: For the University of Chicago: "What's so odd about odd numbers?"
Beware: In contacting schools to make sure they had received everything, she discovered Loyola was missing her transcript.
Advice: "Don't make yourself sound like everyone else" in your application. To help show who she is, Rodriguez gave a personal reason for her interest in the brain: her chronic migraines.

Elijah Mitchell

After applying to 20 colleges, Mitchell is attending the University of Rochester in New York, where he plans to study engineering and business. He also got into seven other schools: Case Western Reserve and Denison universities in Ohio, Northeastern in Boston, Purdue in Indiana, the University of Wisconsin, the University of Illinois–Urbana-Champaign, and the University of Southern California. Besides being a great fit, he says, Rochester will cover all but $10,000 of his annual costs.

Mitchell got a lot of support, including waived application fees and inside tracks to college admissions officers, from two programs that help disadvantaged or underrepresented students navigate the college-application process: QuestBridge and Kappa Leadership Institute–Chicago. While many of the highly selective schools he applied to through the programs denied him (including the University of Pennsylvania, Massachusetts Institute of Technology, Vanderbilt University in Tennessee, and Stanford in California), Mitchell "highly recommends" the programs to students with limited resources. However, he wouldn't advise applying to so many schools.

GPA: 3.33 unweighted
ACT Score: 28
Extracurrics: Tinikling (a popular traditional Filipino dance) team, intern at Roseland Community Hospital, science archivist at Museum of Science and Industry, volunteer at Brookfield Zoo, plays cello.
Essay: How he wants to parlay his "entrepreneurial adventures" (which have included making and selling Yugioh cards in 6th grade and, as a junior, selling candy he bought at a store in school for higher

prices) into running his own engineering firm.
Biggest surprise: "I didn't know how much there was to it," says Mitchell of the application process. He also applied for 30 scholarships.
Upside: "I improved my time management" skills.
Biggest mistake: Thinks he could have gotten more financial aid if he had been more organized about filling out colleges' forms.
Advice: Have some idea of what you want to study, and get internships and volunteer positions and do other activities to show schools your interest and that you've got exposure to these areas.

Christian Rios

Rios, too, applied to a lot of colleges – and he got into all 16. They include DePaul, the University of Illinois and Loyola in Chicago, as well as Carleton College in Minnesota, the University of Iowa, the University of Missouri, DePauw University in Indiana, and Marquette University in Wisconsin. The prospective chemical engineering major, who wants to eventually get into salt water desalination, picked the University of Michigan in Ann Arbor for its highly regarded program. He also likes the way Michigan "does a good job of keeping a big school small" by putting interested students in living-learning communities and that it's big on service learning ("that's my passion"). It didn't hurt that he'll enjoy a full ride. (Rios also was offered full rides by Iowa, Carleton and DePauw.) His visit to Michigan sealed the deal: "Ann Arbor was great," he says. "Everyone wanted to change the world."
GPA: 3.87 unweighted
ACT Score: 27
Extracurrics: Orchestra (violin), vice president of the Key Club, tutor, National Honor Society; violinist for his church
Essay: His interest in service learning and his experience tutoring kids at his former elementary school during the summer.
Hardest step: Starting the essay.

I DIDN'T KNOW HOW MUCH THERE WAS TO IT!

Elijah Mitchell
Christian Rios

START YOUR ESSAY EARLY SO A TOPIC WILL TAKE HOLD.

Biggest mistake: Provided the wrong Social Security number on the FAFSA. He overnighted a corrected version.
Notable essay prompt: One university asked applicants to name a song that describes them. Rios discussed Beethoven's Fifth Symphony.
Advice: Start writing your essay early so you have lots of time to noodle around for a topic. "Something will take hold at some point."

Martin Torres

After applying to 25 schools, Torres settled on the University of Southern California based on the strength of its biology program and its medium-sized campus nestled in a big city. Several other schools he got into also fit that bill, including New York University, Boston University, Boston College and the University of California–San Diego (along with some that rejected him, such as Harvard, Columbia and the

University of California–Berkeley). He was also denied by Northwestern and Vanderbilt and wait-listed by the University of Pennsylvania. All told, it "was a win," says Torres. "I did not want to live my whole life knowing I did not try but rather try, and if rejected, know I tried."

INTERVIEWS LET SCHOOLS KNOW YOU AREN'T JUST A NUMBER.

Fighting the odds is something he knows, and Torres highlighted that in his application. For example, the Spanish-speaking immigrant worked hard to excel in Lincoln Park's IB program and managed a perfect score on the English section of his ACT. "The colleges noticed that," he says. He also wrote about how he had been bullied when he was younger.

With USC paying half his way, he has been applying for private scholarships to help with the other half. His long-range goal is to become a genetic research engineer.

GPA: 3.80 unweighted
ACT Score: 30
Extracurrics: LPHS varsity debate team, which advanced to the city finals, freshman mentor, National Honor Society
Essay: The experience of having to transfer to a different middle school after being bullied. "Writing it helped me let go of the past," he says.
Notable: Torres flagged his independent IB research on the effect of pH on intestinal pathogenic bacteria. In their acceptances, USC, UC–San Diego and the University of Rochester all "said they really liked my research paper."
Smart move: The Common Application opened Aug. 1 and Torres got started right away. He took advantage of evenings when homework was light to work on an essay or his application.
Worthwhile: He visited five schools, including NYU and Miami University Ohio's "gorgeous" campus, where he did a two-week summer scholars program. "I thought NYU was the place until I visited," he says; that's when it dawned on him that studying at NYU's Polytechnic School in Brooklyn just wouldn't be the same as being at the Manhattan campus.
Advice: Do interviews. "They let schools know you are not a number," he says. "And you get a feel of the school."

Martin Torres

Briana Garrett

Briana Garrett

Garrett is off to Middlebury College in Vermont, where she plans to pursue either international studies or film and media culture. Garrett applied to 17 schools after her counselor suggested she better have some backups to top picks Connecticut College and Middlebury. She got into 10, including Ithaca College in New York, Boston University, Illinois Wesleyan University, Bradley University in Illinois, and Butler University and DePauw in Indiana. The schools that turned her down included Connecticut College, Harvard University, Syracuse University in New York, and Carleton

TEST SCORES AND GPA ALONE DO NOT DEFINE YOU.

College in Minnesota.

"I love languages," says Garrett, an IB student who speaks French and Spanish and cites Middlebury's renowned language programs as one of the chief reasons she chose the school. Another reason: The college will cover her full tuition.

To deal with the stress of applying to so many colleges, Garrett says, she made a habit of logging on to the Common App every day and tackling it in small doses. She also took up kickboxing and made a practice of calming down by listening to music.

GPA: 3.2 unweighted
ACT Score: 26
Extracurrics: LPHS College Ambassador, French movie club, member of school's "She's the First" chapter supporting education for girls around the world; member of her church's youth and speech clubs.
Essay: On diversity and how preconceived notions can be eliminated. Wanting to make sure her quirkiness came through, she started off with an attention grabber: "School sucks: That's a statement that spreads like butter on toast."
Smart Move: To write letters of recommendation, Garrett chose her French, Spanish and English teachers, all of whom she felt knew her well. Wanting to get into "THE language school," she says, "I needed people to attest to my language abilities" who also could speak to other personal qualities.
Regret: "Not believing in myself enough," she says. "That added more stress to the process."
Remember: Test scores and GPA alone "do not define you." She gave a fuller picture when she "showcased my language abilities."
Visits: Do them, but make sure you don't let your schoolwork slip.
Advice: Stay in touch with your colleges' reps, and follow up with schools to make sure they've received all your materials.

Sandra Dib

Sandra Dib

Dib and her family traveled from Syria to Chicago to visit relatives in July 2013. With the war in Syria worsening, it was decided that she and her mother would stay on, with Dib enrolling at Lincoln Park for her junior and senior years despite being unable to speak much English at the time. Late in 11th grade, a teacher alerted her to the ins and outs of the American college application process. "I had no idea of what I was doing," says Dib, noting that in Syria only senior-year performance counts.

GET TIPS FROM STUDENTS WHO HAVE JUST BEEN THROUGH IT.

Dib worked hard to become proficient in English and adapted easily to life at LPHS, even as she continued to worry about her father and friends back home. She navigated her college search by turning for advice to recent high school graduates who had just gone through the process themselves. "I plan to go to pharmacy school," says Dib, who got into six schools, including Butler in Indiana, Drake University in Iowa, and the University of Illinois–Chicago and DePaul University.

Because it took some time to get her legal status established, Dib was able to get an extension past the May 1 decision day to apply for financial aid and see where she would get a better deal – Butler, her top choice, or UIC, which offered her in-state tuition. UIC won out.

GPA: 3.74 unweighted
ACT Score: 21
Extracurrics: College Ambassador, Model United Nations, school choir; plays guitar and piano and enjoys ping pong
Essay: The moment her life changed, when a building she was in was bombed. "I became a different person," more focused and having a better understanding of the importance of family and friends.
Stressor: Living in the U.S. with her father still in Syria.
Best part: "I value the opportunities here," she says. "In Syria, I would not have that many options."
Advice: "Students who have just been through this know the details" of how to apply to college better than the adults, who give more generic advice.

Sergej Radovanovic

Interested in bioengineering and agriculture, Radovanovic started with a list of 20 colleges and put each to the test. The German-born student of Bosnian parents considered school rankings, talked to teachers and checked out College Confidential for reviews of professors. "What matters to me is the teacher/student interaction," he says.

Eventually he narrowed the list to seven schools and got into Arizona State University, Ohio State University and both the Chicago and Urbana-Champaign campuses of the University of Illinois;

the latter is where he is going. He was rejected by the University of Florida and San Diego State University and waitlisted by Michigan. While at first Radovanovic favored ASU, a visit to the Fighting Illini's campus impressed him, plus he realized that he didn't really want to go so far away from home. The in-state tuition also was attractive.
GPA: 3.4 unweighted
ACT Score: 29
Extracurrics: Varsity lacrosse, co-captain of the varsity rowing team, orchestra (cello); worked at a local hot dog restaurant as a cook and cashier.
Essay: How he broke away from his Baptist religious beliefs.
Presentation: The aspiring engineer "presented myself as a well-rounded person" who works well with other people, highlighting his athletic and musical endeavors.
Do-over: If he'd known then what he knows now, "I definitely would have listened to my parents when they got on me about doing my applications," says Radovanovic, who didn't start until October. He thinks "a couple more days" of work "would have been the difference between getting accepted to Michigan and being waitlisted."
Advice: Students are told how to structure their college essays to hit key points, which can be formulaic, he thinks. Toss the template aside and "write more emotionally." Also, be active mentally and physically. How you feel will affect how you present yourself.

TOSS THE TEMPLATE AND WRITE MORE EMOTIONALLY.

Kiah McKirnan

As a drama student in the performing arts magnet program, McKirnan considered bypassing more education in favor of starting an acting career. But she decided that college would be "a time to train myself as an artist." Since she wants to continue in drama, she applied to seven schools with theater programs (plus one business program for good measure).

She got into top choice Emerson College in Boston, UIC, Cornell College in Iowa, Ball State University in Indiana and Webster University in St. Louis and was rejected by the New School in New York City, DePaul University and Michigan State University's business program. All of the theater programs required an audition, so she had to prepare to give two monologues and then sit for a follow-up interview. In the end, Webster's program won out, partly because a scholarship will reduce her annual cost to a little more than $30,000 vs. almost double that at Emerson.
GPA: 2.87 unweighted
ACT Score: 26
Extracurrics: Senior class vice president, yearbook, concert choir; member of American Theater Company Youth Ensemble and another youth theater, as well as president of a youth arts council.
Essay: Focused on "my cultural ambiguity" (she's multiracial and was raised by white adoptive parents) as well as her artistic and personal conflicts.
On fit: Besides its lower cost, Webster's program is "more structured." She expects that will be helpful with her attention-deficit disorder.
Turn-on: When visiting Webster, "my name was on the parking spot." Better yet, she got her financial award during her visit.
Do-over: Having "no idea the college process would take so much out of me, mentally and academically," she overcommitted by taking two APs and one IB class as a senior. "If I could redo it, I would limit myself to one AP or IB and take honors level courses."
Biggest misconception: That most schools will give you money. "I was so sure that Emerson would give me money."
Advice: "Have someone you can talk to, and preferably not a teacher or a parent. Find someone that has gone through this recently or even someone that is going through it right now." ●

HAVE SOMEONE YOU CAN TALK TO BESIDES A TEACHER OR PARENT.

Kiah McKirnan

Sergej Radovanovic

TO-DO LIST

FOR YOUR COLLEGE SEARCH BY NED JOHNSON

✔ FRESHMAN YEAR

Get set for a great high school career. It's important to remember that what lies ahead is more than just a four-year audition for college. Still, it will help later to think now about what admissions staffers will look for three (short) years from now.

☐ **Seek advice and teacher feedback.**
Ask someone you trust to help you map out your classes. Grades are important in ninth grade. But rigor is key, too, so don't just go for easy A's. If you get a bad grade, accept it as constructive criticism, really read (or listen) to your teacher's comments and figure out how to do better. Check in with older students or, if you have one, your peer mentor to get advice from upperclassmen.

☐ **Read voraciously.**
Books, newspapers, magazines, blogs - choose what engages you and remember to look up unfamiliar words.

☐ **Get involved.**
Not only will you develop talents and interests that will catch a college's eye, but also you'll find school is more fun when you have activities to look forward to.

☐ **Use social media wisely.**
Be responsible. What you post will follow you - which could be a good or bad thing. Use social media productively (e.g., build a website, tweet about current events). The technological profile you build is a part of your narrative.

✔ SOPHOMORE YEAR

Now that you're no longer a rookie, you'll want to focus on evolving as a learner. Besides studying the material, take note of what your teachers value and consider how you can learn more efficiently - and better.

☐ **Refine your route.**
Look ahead to which 11th and 12th grade courses you might be interested in taking and plan to work in any prerequisites.

☐ **Challenge yourself (wisely).**
Create a balanced schedule. You want to strive for the best possible grades, but overtaxing yourself is bound to be counterproductive.

☐ **Get some practice.**
Will you take the PSAT this year? You'll get a better sense of where you stand if you know what is on the test before you take it. Also, consider whether an SAT subject test makes sense in the spring. If you're enrolled in an AP or honors course now, the timing may be good. The College Board makes practice versions. Take at least one.

☐ **Put together a résumé.**
Start jotting down your hobbies, jobs and extracurricular activities. The résumé is a living document and should evolve as your experience does.

☐ **Make the most of your summer(s).**
Don't just hang out at the beach or pool. Work, volunteer, play sports or take a class. Find an activity that builds on a favorite subject or extracurricular interest. And keep in contact with your mentors, advisers, counselors, etc. They are all a part of your support system.

✔ JUNIOR YEAR

Essays and testing and APs, oh my! Your grades, test scores and activities junior year constitute a big chunk of what colleges consider for admissions. Do your best in class and truly prepare for the tests you take. This can also be the time to step forward as a

leader. Explore pursuits that interest you, not just because they'll look good on an application, but also because they'll help you grow as a person.

☐ Ask for help.

As Einstein allegedly put it, insanity is "doing the same thing over and over again and expecting different results." So if you feel stuck in your studies and in need of a breakthrough, ask teachers, parents or friends for help in finding a new approach.

☐ Speak up in class.

You will need to ask two junior-year teachers to write recommendations. They can't know you without hearing your thoughts, so make sure to contribute in class. In addition, your counselor will write a letter of recommendation, so visit the counseling office and make him or her a part of your growing network.

☐ Sleep.

The average 16-year-old brain needs over nine hours of sleep to function at 100 percent, and that's exactly where you want to be.

☐ Plan your testing calendar.

Test scores matter (along with grades), so talk with your parents and guidance counselor about which ones to take and when, and how to prepare for them. First up, the PSAT. If your 10th-grade scores put you in reach of a national merit scholarship, it might be wise to spend concentrated time prepping. Then take the SAT or ACT in winter or early spring. Don't worry if you don't get your ideal score; you can try again. The SAT subject tests are also an option for May or June in areas where you shine or in subjects you covered junior year.

☐ Get involved.

It's great to show you've worked hard, are dedicated to an activity, play well with others - and can lead them. Start an arts discussion group that goes to museum openings, say, or be voted team captain.

☐ Begin building your college list.

Once you have gotten your test scores, talk to a counselor and start putting together a list of target schools, reaches and safeties. Make use of new technology and apps to aid your research. Explore college websites and resources like ed.gov/finaid and usnews.com/bestcolleges. (Again, be mindful of your online presence and be sure to clean up your Facebook and Twitter accounts. They might get a look.)

☐ Make some campus visits.

Spring break and summer vacation are ideal times to check out a few campuses. Attend college fairs and talk with the folks behind the tables. They can give you a feel for their school and some good future contacts.

☐ Write.

Procrastination doesn't make for a good college essay. Aim to have first drafts done by Labor Day. Share them with an English teacher or counselor.

✔ Senior Year

You made it. Let's party! Well, not quite yet. This will also be a year of hard work and continued preparation. Colleges do consider senior-year transcripts. They can and will rescind offers to students who slack off, so stay focused.

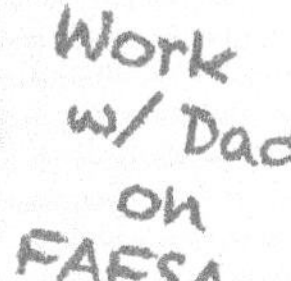

☐ Finish testing and check the boxes.

You're in the final stretch. If necessary, retake the SAT, ACT or subject tests. The early fall test dates will give you time to apply early. Also, make sure you're completing all graduation requirements as well as course requirements for your target colleges.

☐ Ask for recommendations.

Engage the network you've created for yourself. Early in the school year, ask two teachers if they are willing to write a letter of recommendation for you. Choose teachers with whom you have a good relationship and who will effectively communicate your academic and personal qualities. You will want people who can offer different perspectives on your performance. Be sure to update and polish your résumé, too; it will come in handy when you're filling out applications and preparing for admissions interviews.

☐ Apply.

Select a core group of schools to which you will apply and consider which deadlines (e.g., early decision, early action) are most appropriate. Fill out each application carefully and ask someone to look over your essays critically. Check that your colleges have received records and recs from your high school, and have your SAT or ACT scores officially sent in. A month from the date you submit your application, call the college and confirm that it is complete.

☐ Follow the money.

Many colleges require that all of your financial aid application forms be turned in by February. But the earlier the better.

☐ Make a choice.

Try to visit the colleges where you've been accepted again. Talk with alumni, attend an accepted-student reception. Then confidently make your college choice official by sending in your deposit. Done!

Ned Johnson is founder of and tutor-geek at PrepMatters (prepmatters.com) where, along with colleagues, he torments teens with test prep, educational counseling and general attempts to help them thrive. He also is co-author of "Conquering the SAT: How Parents Can Help Teens Overcome the Pressure and Succeed."

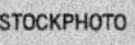
ISTOCKPHOTO

New Mexico Institute of Mining and Technology

Austin Dehart, CLASS OF 2015

New Mexico Tech is a comfortably small state technical school set an hour outside Albuquerque that focuses almost exclusively on science and engineering. I decided to go to NMT because it was easy to get into (a one-page application form!), affordable, and offers a specialization in astrophysics – my focus. (The faculty works with the Expanded Very Large Array, the iconic radio telescope featured in the film "Contact.")

Once you are in, the school demands a lot of you. The math and science courses are extremely tough, but professors are always eager to help, even out of the classroom. NMT encourages students to do as much hands-on research as possible; it even has its own explosives facility, where students frequently detonate experiments. This past year, I did a research project on rotational periods of asteroids and presented my finding at NMT's annual student research symposium.

NMT ENCOURAGES STUDENTS TO DO AS MUCH HANDS-ON RESEARCH AS POSSIBLE.

The school has given me a rigorous, quality education that has enabled me to head debt-free to grad school, where I will now be pursuing my doctorate in astrophysics. •

WHY I P

Villanova University

Margaret Lamb, CLASS OF 2016

Villanova was the first place I visited because my parents met and married at the university and loved it. I was eager to embrace their experience, but wanted to follow my own path. Villanova reflects the spirit of St. Augustine, who once said, "The world is a book and those who do not travel read only one page."

Located just a half hour outside of Philadelphia, this 175-year-old Catholic university emphasizes academic growth and exploration. I found a home in the Villanova Honors program, where I took part in the two-year

VILLANOVA UNIVERSITY

HEADSHOTS CLOCKWISE FROM TOP LEFT: ALEX BURD; KELLEY COX; DIAN LAMB

COURTESY OF NEW MEXICO TECH

University of Denver

Anna Gaulding, CLASS OF 2015

As soon as I visited the campus, I knew DU would be a great fit for me. Not only is it beautiful – a mix of historic buildings and modern architecture just 15 minutes from downtown Denver – but it also boasts one of the top study abroad programs in the country. Through the Cherrington Global Scholars program, nearly three-quarters of undergraduates study at more than 150 partner programs around the world. My junior year, I spent four months living in Cork, Ireland, while my peers traversed the globe, landing everywhere from Peru to Australia.

DU HAS SIX LIVING-AND-LEARNING COMMUNITIES THAT BRING LIKE-MINDED STUDENTS TOGETHER.

DU also has six living-and-learning communities that bring like-minded students together. As a member of the Pioneer Leadership Program, I spent two years living among a tightknit group of undergrads passionate about leading change, and I earned a minor in leadership studies to boot. Beyond academics, DU is ideally situated for outdoor adventurers with its proximity to ski resorts and 14,000-foot mountain peaks for hiking enthusiasts. On campus, there are countless ways to get involved, from club sports to the grilling society. I know I will leave the university a well-rounded student, prepared for a career in education. ●

ICKED...

Global Scholars: Politics, Philosophy, and Economics program that culminated in a semester abroad in London. I found another home in Campus Ministry, which I joined on three service trips including a civil rights pilgrimage to Selma, Alabama, and a Habitat for Humanity trip to Hickory, North Carolina. I found a home in my majors, especially Global Interdisciplinary Studies, where I had the chance to craft my own understanding of Augustine's quote – to become a global citizen aware of the world's complexities. It was an experience that's leading me toward a career in international development and human rights. ●

THIS 175-YEAR-OLD CATHOLIC UNIVERSITY EMPHASIZES ACADEMIC GROWTH AND EXPLORATION.

Finding the Mone

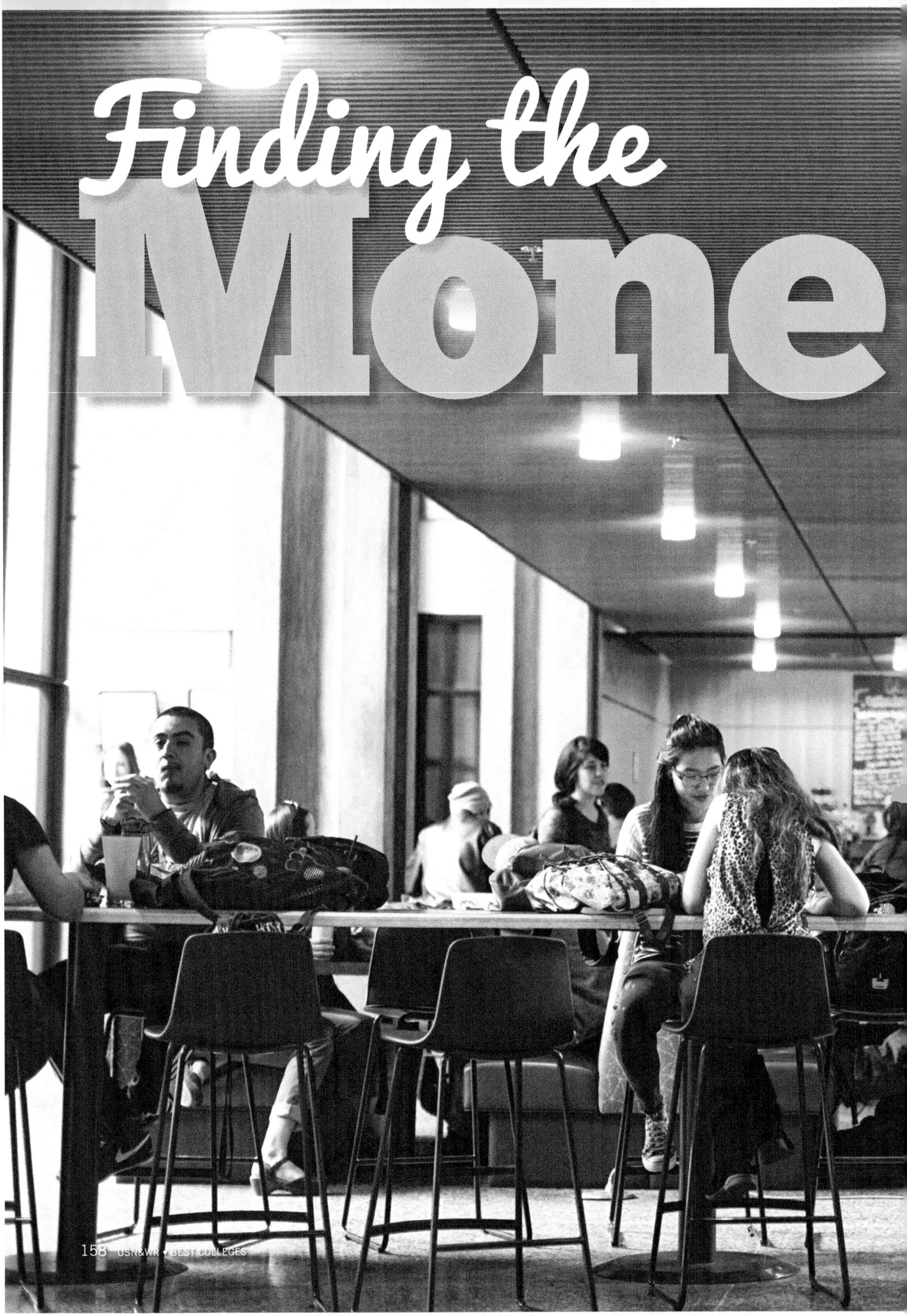

5

THE UNIVERSITY OF CALIFORNIA-SANTA CRUZ

BRETT ZIEGLER FOR USN&WR

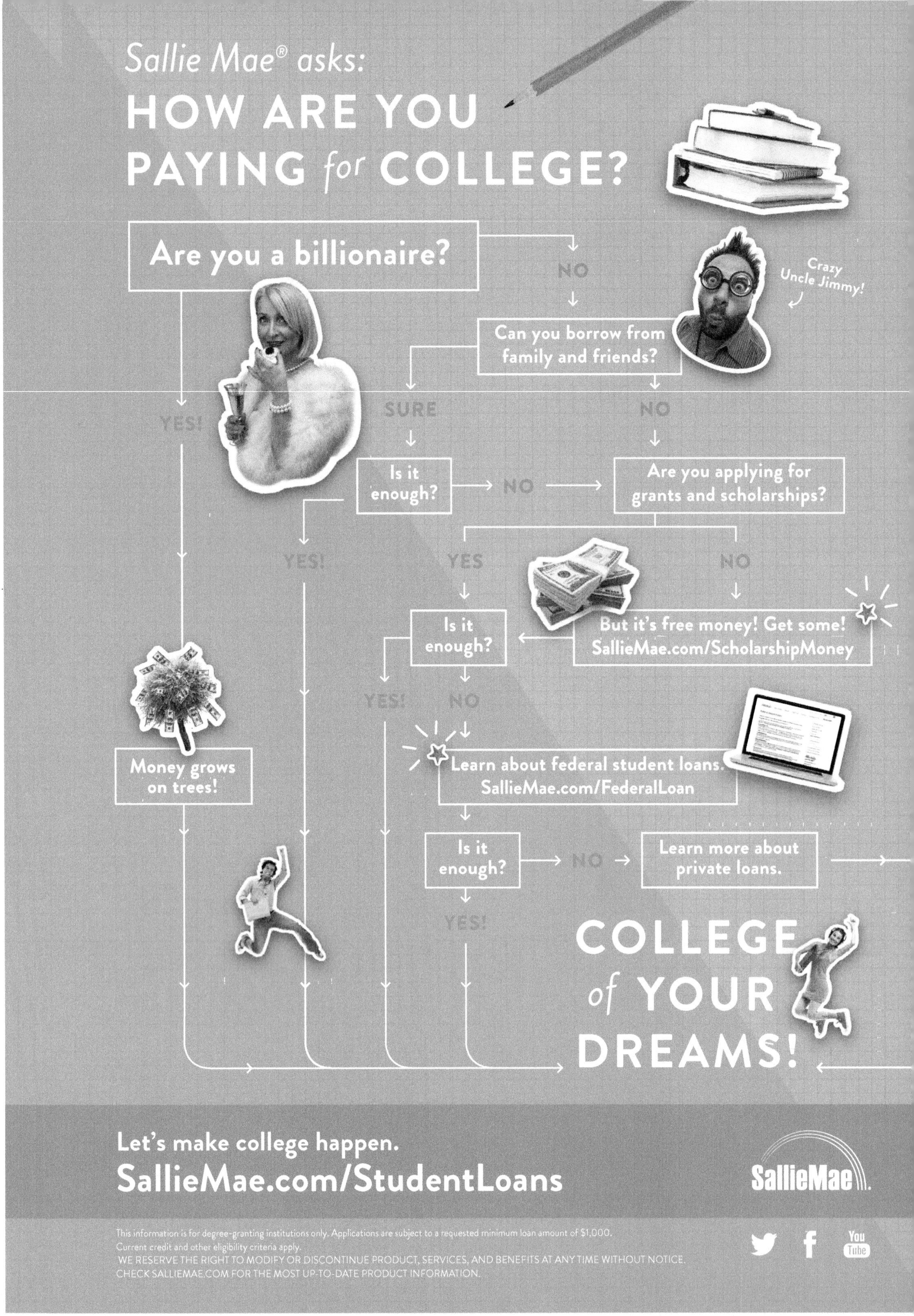
Sallie Mae® asks:
HOW ARE YOU PAYING for COLLEGE?
Are you a billionaire?
NO
Crazy Uncle Jimmy!
Can you borrow from family and friends?
YES!
SURE
NO
Is it enough?
NO
Are you applying for grants and scholarships?
YES!
YES
NO
Is it enough?
But it's free money! Get some! SallieMae.com/ScholarshipMoney
YES!
NO
Money grows on trees!
Learn about federal student loans. SallieMae.com/FederalLoan
Is it enough?
NO
Learn more about private loans.
YES!
COLLEGE of YOUR DREAMS!
Let's make college happen.
SallieMae.com/StudentLoans
SallieMae
This information is for degree-granting institutions only. Applications are subject to a requested minimum loan amount of $1,000.
Current credit and other eligibility criteria apply.
WE RESERVE THE RIGHT TO MODIFY OR DISCONTINUE PRODUCT, SERVICES, AND BENEFITS AT ANY TIME WITHOUT NOTICE.
CHECK SALLIEMAE.COM FOR THE MOST UP-TO-DATE PRODUCT INFORMATION.
You Tube

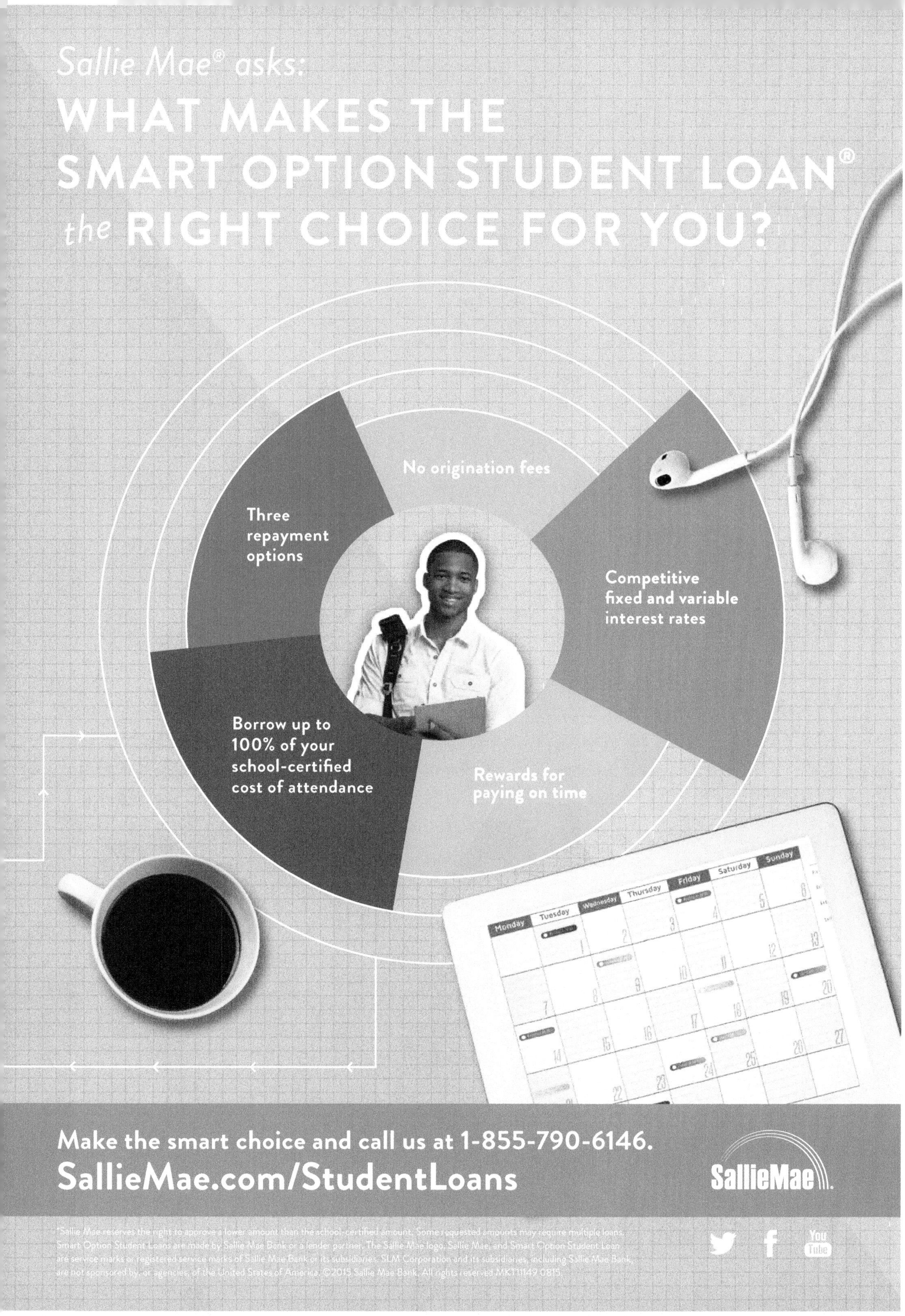

6 Things You Need to Know to Get a GREAT DEAL

Each year the federal government hands out billions in grants and loans to young people headed to college – some $138 billion during the latest fiscal year alone. States, colleges and other organizations award big handouts, too. Here are six things families need to know to be sure of getting their share:

You don't have to automatically rule out high-priced colleges

New York students enjoy a relative bargain in The State University of New York and The City University of New York systems; room and board aside, tuition at the four-year colleges now runs just over $6,300 a year for state residents. For the 2015-16 school year, in-state students at the University of California–Berkeley are paying a little more than a third of the $38,000 or so that out-of-staters owe for tuition and fees.

Still, many colleges with large endowments want to enroll smart, capable students regardless of their ability to pay, and they have the deep pockets to make that happen. A number of schools, such as Princeton, the University of Pennsylvania and the University of Chicago, have

GETTY IMAGES

adopted no-loan or minimal-loan policies for many or all students with need. So a college with a high sticker price can sometimes actually be the cheapest choice.

You do have to fill out the FAFSA

The Free Application for Federal Student Aid determines how much a family is expected to contribute to college costs and must be completed for a student to receive any money from federal government coffers. Parents provide information about their income and assets (assuming the student is still a dependent) and their child's at fafsa.gov; the result is an "expected family contribution," or EFC, that colleges use to put together an aid package. The value of the family home and retirement savings aren't held against you in the federal aid formula. Many colleges require an additional form, the CSS/Financial Aid Profile, to calculate whether a student is eligible for nonfederal awards.

Your child's "need" may not be what you think

The federal aid a college offers you is keyed not to how smart a student is but to need – the difference between that expected family contribution and the cost of college. Families are sometimes shocked to discover that, based on their income, their EFC runs to thousands of dollars that they haven't socked away. Colleges that say they "meet full need" are talking about bridging the gap between expected family contribution and the cost. They aren't volunteering to help out with the family contribution, too.

There are several parts to a financial aid package

Uncle Sam's contributions are: outright grants such as the Pell Grant for lower-income students (the maximum award for 2015-16 is $5,775); student loans that don't have to be repaid until college is over, the most common of which is the Stafford; and a work-study job on campus. Parents who qualify can borrow up to the full cost of college (minus any aid received) under the PLUS loan program. State funds might be given out, too, and colleges often add "merit" aid that is based not on need but on grades, leadership or musical talent, for example.

Students with need get "subsidized" Stafford loans, meaning the government covers the interest for them until after graduation. Any student, regardless of need, can take out an unsubsidized Stafford. They still won't have to make payments on the loans while in school, but the interest they owe will accumulate. Currently, the cap on Staffords for a typical dependent freshman is $5,500, of which up to $3,500 can be subsidized. (Freshmen who are not dependent on their parents can borrow $9,500.) The caps rise in later years.

It's critical to compare financial aid award letters carefully

Colleges have leeway in how they put their packages together and often are more generous to students they really want. So it's vital to look beyond the bottom line. For example, a $20,000 award from one school might include $3,000 in federal grants, $2,000 in scholarships, $2,500 in work-study and $12,500 in loans, while a $20,000 offer elsewhere might include $3,000 in federal grants, $4,000 in scholarships, $2,500 in work-study, and $10,500 in loans. Borrowing less is generally better. Tip: Students may improve their chances of getting generous merit aid by applying to schools where their grades and SAT or ACT scores put them near the top of the applicant pool.

It's OK to ask for more

Colleges often say they don't negotiate, but many will take a second look if a family gets a better offer elsewhere. And they do want to know if your situation has suddenly changed – Mom lost her job, say, or Dad incurred big medical bills. Financial aid staffers might not be receptive to an angry phone call, but a polite request for a hearing could get results.

Learn & EARN

Taking a work-study job can pay off in more ways than one. BY MICHAEL MORELLA

Like all first-year work-study students at Dickinson College, Angeline Apostolou started with a stint in the cafeteria, cleaning tables and washing dishes. By senior year, the international studies major from Livingston, New Jersey, had transitioned to a job as a student supervisor at the Clarke Forum for Contemporary Issues, which coordinates visits with scholars, authors and other guest speakers who come to the Carlisle, Pennsylvania, college each semester. "It was great meeting people you see on the news or in books," says the 2015 grad, noting that the job was her favorite part about Dickinson.

Apostolou started at the forum as a sophomore project manager, earning $8.25 an hour and working 10 hours per week. When she was promoted to supervisor as a junior, she was logging a couple more hours each week with a small bump in pay. In addition to sharpening her communications and research skills, Apostolou hired and led a staff of her peers and ran events. She now hopes to put those experiences to use in a foreign affairs job in Washington, D.C.

Hundreds of thousands of college students participate in the federal government's work-study program, part of its financial-aid superstructure for those who demonstrate need. The first step: Opt in when you're asked if you'd like to be considered for the program in question 31 of the Free Application for Federal Student Aid, or FAFSA. If you're eligible, and if you follow through by actually finding a position once you get to college, then you can expect to earn at least federal minimum wage - currently $7.25 an hour - or the state or local baseline, if higher.

Most jobs are on campus in the dining hall, bookstore or athletic department, say, though some might be with local employers. The government awarded a yearly average of nearly $1,400 per student at about 3,300 colleges in 2013-14, according to the latest data.

Schools are required to kick in 25 percent of every student's funding, which means that annual awards often run around $2,000 or $2,500. You'll coordinate your own work schedule and may work as much as you like up to the ceiling imposed by the size of your award. (An award of slightly more than $1,000 per 14-week semester would work out to 10 hours a week at $7.25 per hour, for example.)

There are "a lot of different models out there" for actually securing a job, says Joe Weglarz, executive director of student financial services at Marist College in Poughkeepsie, New York. Marist holds a work-study job fair to introduce new students to prospective employers, and the student financial services office helps facilitate the job search. At Iowa State University, for example, students have access to a jobs portal of available positions, which they apply for on their own. Other schools place students in positions based on their skills and academic interests.

Besides providing some tuition or spending money, work-study jobs can help you build a résumé, establish a network of mentors and potential references and learn useful skills. "My public speaking ability skyrocketed from having to be on the balls of my feet at all times to answer fairly abstract questions about specific pieces of art," notes Jeremiah O'Leary, a 2015 graduate in service design from Savannah College of Art and Design in Georgia, who spent four years in a work-study gig as a docent at the SCAD Museum of Art.

And research shows that students who work about 10 to 15 hours a week tend to perform better academically, adds Desiree Noah, who coordinates student employment at La Sierra University in Riverside, California, and is president of the National Student Employment Association. One great perk of a work-study job is that your employer will probably give you a break when you're swamped at exam time and pulling all-nighters. ●

With Lindsay Cates

GETTY IMAGES

Scholarship Focus: Science, Technology, Engineering, Math

Scholarships to reel students into STEM fields are multiplying, and an online search will turn up hundreds of sources. Below is a sampling of what students with the right qualifications can compete for; some are open to all STEM students, while many target members of underrepresented groups. Requirements vary. College-bound seniors can apply for many; some are only for students already in college.

For all STEM students

- **Intertek Scholarship:** Five scholarships of up to $10,000 and an internship go to engineering students (intertek.com).
- **Buick Achievers Scholarship Program:** Fifty incoming or current college students get up to $25,000 (buickachievers.com).
- **Great Lakes Higher Education Corporation awards:** The student loan servicer offers up to 750 STEM scholarships of $2,500 (community.mygreatlakes.org).
- **The SMART Scholarship:** This Department of Defense program provides full tuition and a stipend to students in STEM willing to work for the DOD upon graduation (smart.asee.org).
- **Scholarship America Dream Award:** This renewable STEM award goes to students entering at least their second year of college (scholarshipamerica.org).
- **American Society of Civil Engineers scholarships:** Awards of $2,500 to $5,000 go to ASCE student members (asce.org).
- **American Society of Mechanical Engineers awards:** ASME offers scholarships for current undergrads and graduating high schoolers studying mechanical engineering or mechanical engineering technology (asme.org).
- **American Institute of Aeronautics and Astronautics awards:** For undergrads in aerospace-related or engineering programs (aiaa-awards.org).

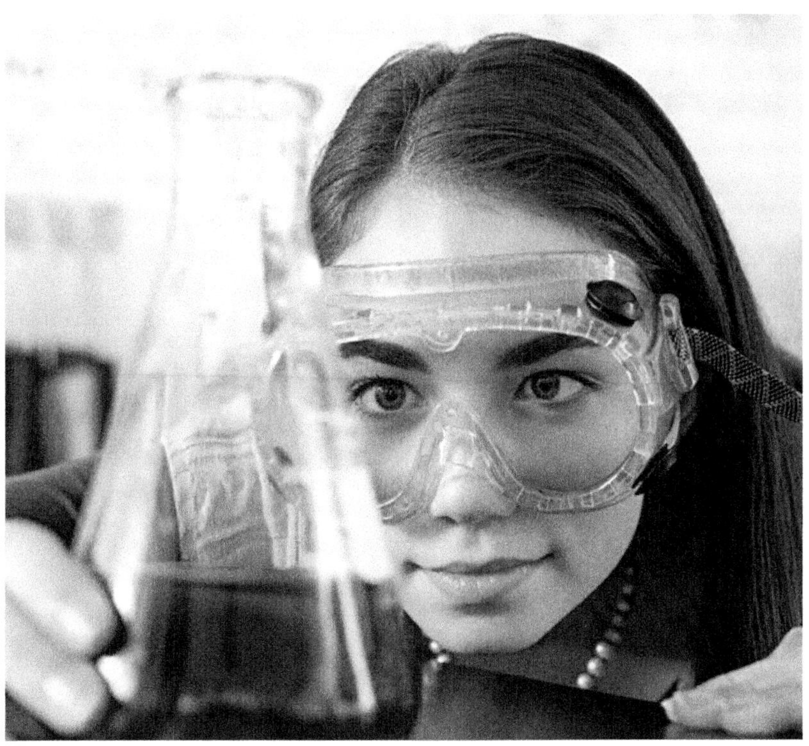

GETTY IMAGES

- **Siemens Competition in Math, Science & Technology:** Winners and finalists get from $1,000 to $100,000 (siemenscompetition.discoveryeducation.com).
- **The Intel Science Talent Search:** Hundreds of semifinalists win $1,000 each. Finalists compete for additional awards (student.societyforscience.org).

For women

- **Google Anita Borg Memorial Scholarship:** In honor of the founder of the Institute for Women and Technology, Google awards $10,000 to students of computer science or computer engineering (google.com/edu/students).
- **HP Helion OpenStack Scholarship:** Four scholarships of $10,000 are presented to students pursuing a career in technology (go.hpcloud.com).
- **Palantir Scholarship for Women in Engineering:** The global software technology company offers grants ranging from $1,500 to $10,000 to women studying computer science or STEM fields (palantir.com/college/scholarship).
- **Society of Women Engineers:** Offers scholarships and fellowships from $1,000 to $20,000 for women pursuing undergraduate and graduate degrees in engineering, engineering technology and computer science (swe.org).
- **Women in Technology Scholarship program:** Offers multiple scholarships of up to $2,500 each for women who are attending or are planning to attend a two- or four-year college (trustvip.com).
- **Association for Women Geoscientists:** AWG awards scholarships (and in some cases offers mentoring) to undergraduate women pursuing degrees and careers in the geosciences (awg.org).

For underrepresented minorities

- **Gates Millennium Scholars Program:** Tuition and expenses for undergraduate minority students with need in any field (gmsp.org).
- **Xerox Technical Minority Scholarship:** Up to $10,000 for minority students in a technical or engineering field (xerox.com/jobs/).
- **National Action Council for Minorities in Engineering STEM Scholarships:** For African-American, Latino or American Indian seniors in a precollege program or current college students pursuing degrees in STEM (nacme.org).
- **National Society of Black Engineers awards:** NSBE and corporate partners such as Northrop Grumman and Chevron award engineering scholarships (nsbe.org).
- **United Negro College Fund awards:** Numerous scholarship programs for students in various fields (uncf.org).
- **Society of Hispanic Professional Engineers Foundation awards:** For students of Hispanic descent (shpefoundation.org).
- **Hispanic Scholarship Fund awards:** A host of scholarships for students studying the broad spectrum of disciplines (hsf.net).
- **Great Minds in STEM scholarships:** The organization offers college students of Hispanic descent scholarships ranging from $500 to $10,000 (greatmindsinstem.org).
- **The Google Lime Scholarship:** Google offers $10,000 scholarships for computer science or computer engineering students with disabilities (google.com/edu/students).
- **The Generation Google Scholarship:** High school and college students in underrepresented groups are eligible for a $10,000 scholarship (google.com/edu/students).
- **The National Institutes of Health Undergraduate Scholarship:** Up to $20,000, renewable for four years, for disadvantaged students pursuing biomedical, behavioral and social science health-related research (training.nih.gov/programs).
- **Microsoft Scholarships:** Priority given to minority students, women and people with disabilities (careers.microsoft.com). ●

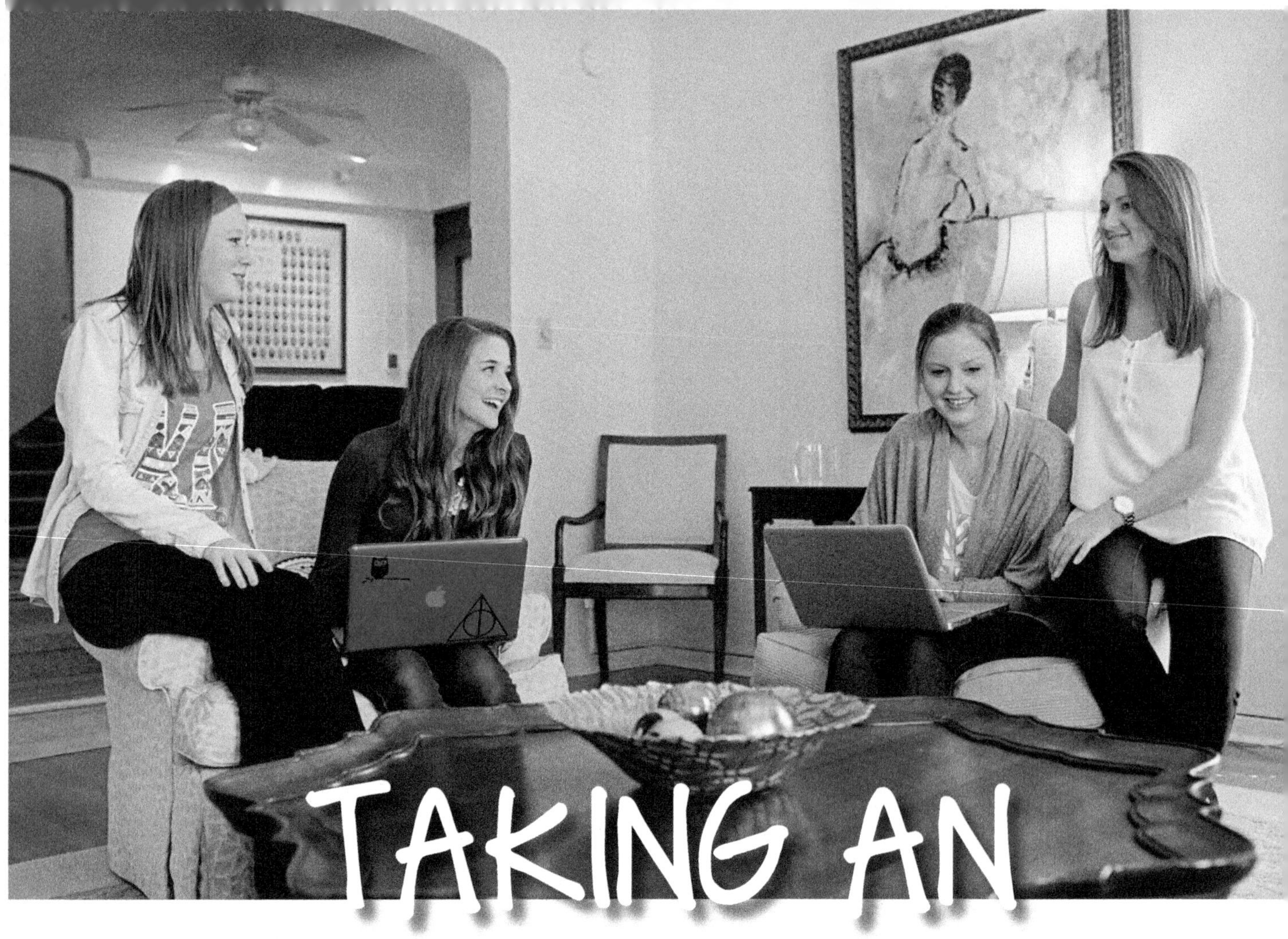

TAKING AN EARLY OUT

Will shaving off a year be a wise move for you?

BY COURTNEY RUBIN

While most of Alyssa Lowery's classmates at the University of Illinois–Urbana-Champaign were enjoying their month of winter break this year, Lowery was at her computer, spending hours watching lectures and doing homework for an online science course. This summer, she took two classes at a community college. All of this extra effort is so Lowery, who is double majoring in Spanish and linguistics, can graduate in three years and, she estimates, save $25,000.

ALYSSA LOWERY (SECOND FROM LEFT) HAS SQUEEZED FOUR YEARS INTO THREE.

With college costs climbing and outstanding student loan debt at a record $1.2 trillion, little wonder that many students try to pare a semester or a full year of expenses off the tally, especially if they're planning to go on to graduate school. But is the time (and money) saved as smart a financial move as you might think? "I definitely sacrifice on sleep and some of the typical college experience," Lowery admits, noting that although she's found a community as a member of Kappa Delta sorority, she has managed to squeeze in only a handful of social functions because of her heavy courseload. Still, she says, "I've talked to people who've graduated early and most of them don't have regrets." Here are some factors to weigh before making the decision:

PETER HOFFMAN FOR USN&WR

What do you want to get out of college?

If you view school purely as a means to a job or entrée to professional school, then getting to that goal as fast as possible may be the right move. But many educators point out that the college experience is also about putting time and effort into developing a network, as well as critical thinking and writing skills and key professional capabilities like teamwork and communication. "You don't get those skills because you pushed the right buttons on a Scantron to pass a test," says David Laude, the University of Texas–Austin's senior vice provost of enrollment and curriculum services.

Just how much are you saving?

Be sure to factor in the cost of summer school and winter break classes, plus extra charges you may rack up during the regular semester above a certain number of credits.

Will you suffer from missing classes and internships?

Marissa Johnson, who graduated from Anderson University in Indiana in three years in 2013, hoped to put her public relations major to use in communications or admissions at a university. But the crunched timeline meant she hadn't managed to take any business courses, which she thinks would have made her a more attractive candidate, and she had time for only one internship. "My one regret," she says, "is that maybe I wasn't able to make as many connections." Johnson, who lives in Indianapolis, is currently working as an administrative assistant at an elementary school and is glad that she can at least use her PR skills to work on the school's website and yearbook.

Indeed, largely in response to employers' interest in hiring young people with real-world perspective, there's greater emphasis these days on participating in experiential learning through internships, study abroad and service activities, for example. Michael Sciola, associate vice president for institutional advancement and director of career services at Colgate University in New York, suggests that anyone intent on a shortened stay visit the career services office "the second day you're on campus." And often.

Keep in mind that many companies hire almost exclusively out of internship programs, among them Wall Street banks, insurance firms and entertainment companies.

Are you willing to sacrifice the chance to explore widely?

Johnson notes that she had to take some courses that "weren't my first choice" just because they fulfilled a requirement at the right moment, and she's sure that she missed out on "fun" classes. And according to some estimates, about 85 percent of students change their majors at least once. Lack of time to look into possible options during college may mean you'll end up paying for more education later. On the other hand, you may be better able to afford graduate school. Christen Robinson, 32, finished her degree in economics at UNC–Greensboro in just 2.5 years, graduated in 2014 and works for an attorney; she now has her sights set on a master's degree in digital forensics and cyber investigation at University of Maryland University College.

Do you think the fast track will make you seem a whiz kid?

"I wish I knew how that folklore got started," says Margaret Bruzelius, senior class dean at Smith College in Massachusetts, who encounters it frequently. "Actually, employers will just think you're really young." (Not yet 21? You won't be able to rent a car or take a client for a drink, Sciola points out.) As for grad schools, they want to see the best possible academic record. "It doesn't do you much good to graduate quickly with a really mediocre record," Bruzelius says.

If you're set on graduating early, it's never too soon to start planning, since one way to earn (cheap) credits is to pick them up during high school. Advanced Placement exams cost $91, compared to the hundreds or thousands you might pay for the same credits on campus. If your school offers the International Baccalaureate program, you could potentially enter college as a sophomore. And many high schools partner with community colleges in dual-enrollment arrangements that grant both high school and college credit. Caveat: Elite schools may accept few or none of these credits (Brown University, for example, does not accept AP credit), and those that do often won't count them toward your major.

Once you get to college, you'll need to map out your strategy as soon as possible to make sure you don't end up having to hang around to get a required course. One cost-cutting option is to take summer classes at a community college or public university. Another is to earn credit by passing exams. The College Board's College Level Examination Program (clep.collegeboard.org) features 33 tests, in subjects ranging from foreign language to math, that cover material typically taught during the first two years of college. The 90- to 120-minute computerized CLEP exams are $80 apiece; some 2,900 colleges nationwide accept these credits. One way to prepare is to take the free self-paced courses available from the nonprofit Saylor Foundation (saylor.org).

Finally, the American Council on Education (acenet.edu), an association of college presidents and other institutions, offers a service that, for a one-time fee of $40, evaluates military experience, workplace training, and online courses from nonaccredited providers to determine what sort of course credit they might be worth. More than 2,000 schools say they will consider ACE recommendations. ●

How to Save Money on Your TEXTBOOKS

Buy or rent? Hard copy or e-book? A whole array of smartphone apps can help you figure out the cheapest way to go. BY LINDSAY CATES

Smart book buying is one college skill you might want to master quickly. Incoming freshmen may assume the campus bookstore and Amazon.com amount to the list of choices, but upperclassmen know better. These days, there's an entire arsenal of apps that streamline the process of buying and selling books. Or renting them. Pick your favorites and start searching for the best deals from your phone.

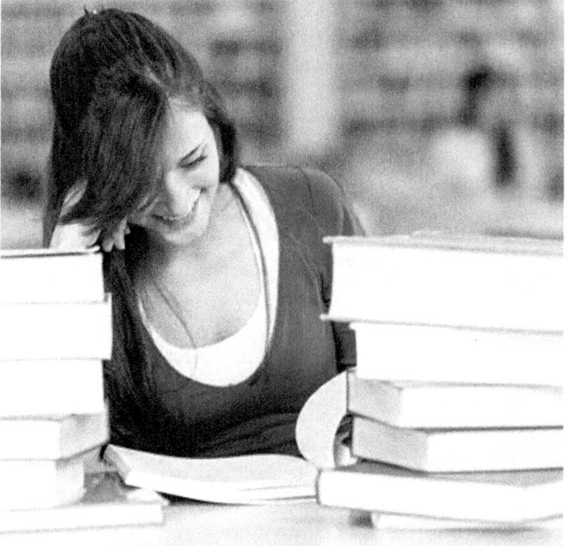

The higher-tech book acquisition methods appear to be saving students serious money. The National Association of College Stores published a report in July revealing that students bought the same quantity of course materials in 2014 as they did in 2007 but spent 20 percent less on average – $563 versus $701. Because of the many options now available, which include buying new or used books, renting, choosing e-textbooks and using custom-created course packs, "we do see students doing their research," says Elizabeth Riddle, director of NACS OnCampus Research.

The report found that for the spring 2015 semester, 38 percent of students shopped around using their smartphone, and 23 percent used a tablet. The number of students who chose to rent, whether via app, online or in the store, has doubled since 2011. Although campus stores were still the top source of textbooks, online retailers like Amazon are gaining ground.

Apps for Amazon, Chegg and the many other textbook retailers can turn the book-buying chore into a bargain-hunting adventure. A Chemistry 100 textbook available in one campus bookstore this fall for $205.75 new or $154.50 used was recently available through the Chegg app for $30.99 as a rental, $103.50 as an e-textbook rental, $122.99 as a used textbook, and $164.49 as a new book – still 20 percent less than the same version at the campus store.

Some apps, such as CampusBooks and BIGWORDS, do the comparison legwork for you, examining prices available through the most popular textbook apps and at other retailers to find the best deal. You can complete the entire transaction from your phone and email titles and prices to your friends.

Lightening your load. If you'd rather not lug any books around at all, renting or buying e-textbooks can be an appealing way to bring your costs down. Apps such as Intel Education Study and CourseSmart allow students to rent e-textbooks and read them on any device. Intel Education Study, formerly known as Kno, lets users highlight, take notes and master flashcards, for instance. Using the CourseSmart app, students can buy textbooks, search for topics in the book, add notes and print pages. Rather than buy a politics book at the campus store new for $89.95 or used for $67.50, say, students can rent the e-textbook for a semester from CourseSmart for $44.98.

Although renting or buying an e-textbook is usually cheaper than getting a physical copy, one potential downside to consider is that you won't be able to sell it back.

When your textbooks are novels or other trade books, the apps available for reading via Kindle, NOOK and iBooks might be a good bet. If a textbook you purchased is republished with new content, iBooks lets you download the updated version for free.

When the time comes to get rid of your books, there are apps that can help with that chore, too. Using Textbook Buyback, CampusBooks or BIGWORDS, you can scan the barcode on your book and see what different retailers would be willing to pay you; you then send the retailer the book, often with free shipping. (The three outfits also have websites where you can get a quote by entering your book's ISBN number.) Cash4Books lets users scan all their barcodes at once and get an instant quote for the grand total. ●

GETTY IMAGES

Finding THE MONEY

Great Schools, Great Prices

Which colleges and universities offer students the best value? The calculation used here takes into account a school's academic quality, based on its U.S. News Best Colleges ranking, and the 2014-2015 net cost of attendance for a student who received the average level of need-based financial aid. The higher the quality of the program and the lower the cost, the better the deal. Only schools in or near the top half of their U.S. News ranking categories are included because U.S. News considers the most significant values to be among colleges that perform well academically.

National Universities

Rank	School (State) (*Public)	% receiving grants based on need ('14)	Average cost after receiving grants based on need ('14)	Average discount from total cost ('14)
1.	**Princeton University** (NJ)	59%	$16,868	71%
2.	**Harvard University** (MA)	59%	$17,820	71%
3.	**Yale University** (CT)	50%	$18,260	71%
4.	**Stanford University** (CA)	47%	$19,713	69%
5.	**Massachusetts Inst. of Technology**	57%	$21,454	65%
6.	**Columbia University** (NY)	48%	$21,717	67%
7.	**Duke University** (NC)	43%	$22,305	65%
8.	**California Institute of Technology**	50%	$23,433	62%
9.	**Dartmouth College** (NH)	49%	$23,522	64%
10.	**Brown University** (RI)	45%	$22,256	65%
11.	**University of Pennsylvania**	47%	$24,156	62%
12.	**Vanderbilt University** (TN)	45%	$22,367	64%
13.	**U. of North Carolina–Chapel Hill***	41%	$18,069	63%
14.	**Rice University** (TX)	39%	$21,612	62%
15.	**University of Chicago**	45%	$26,651	60%
16.	**Brigham Young Univ.–Provo** (UT)	39%	$13,097	27%
17.	**Cornell University** (NY)	46%	$26,045	59%
18.	**Emory University** (GA)	40%	$23,687	61%
19.	**Northwestern University** (IL)	43%	$28,245	57%
20.	**Johns Hopkins University** (MD)	43%	$29,717	54%
21.	**Texas A&M Univ.–College Station***	62%	$21,248	46%
22.	**University of Notre Dame** (IN)	43%	$29,436	53%
23.	**Washington University in St. Louis**	39%	$29,587	55%
24.	**Tufts University** (MA)	37%	$26,453	58%
25.	**Pepperdine University** (CA)	54%	$26,189	59%
26.	**University of Rochester** (NY)	51%	$28,192	55%
27.	**Brandeis University** (MA)	50%	$27,746	56%
28.	**Georgetown University** (DC)	35%	$27,982	57%
29.	**Univ. of California–Santa Cruz***	52%	$22,152	61%
30.	**Wake Forest University** (NC)	33%	$26,987	57%
31.	**University of California–Irvine***	21%	$21,368	61%
32.	**Clark University** (MA)	59%	$24,454	51%
33.	**University of Virginia***	28%	$26,380	53%
34.	**Clarkson University** (NY)	84%	$31,023	48%
35.	**Boston College**	36%	$27,740	56%
36.	**Lehigh University** (PA)	40%	$25,840	56%
37.	**Carnegie Mellon University** (PA)	44%	$33,208	48%
38.	**Rensselaer Polytechnic Inst.** (NY)	63%	$35,671	44%
39.	**Univ. of Southern California**	36%	$32,380	50%
40.	**Univ. of California–Santa Barbara***	20%	$24,004	56%
41.	**SUNY Col. of Envir. Sci. and Forestry***	70%	$26,661	21%
42.	**Case Western Reserve Univ.** (OH)	48%	$33,101	45%
43.	**Duquesne University** (PA)	65%	$27,145	41%
44.	**Yeshiva University** (NY)	48%	$31,576	45%
45.	**Syracuse University** (NY)	52%	$32,548	45%
46.	**Worcester Polytechnic Inst.** (MA)	64%	$37,703	37%
47.	**Illinois Institute of Technology**	54%	$27,202	52%
48.	**Univ. of California–San Diego***	17%	$25,511	53%
49.	**University of California–Davis***	26%	$27,699	51%
50.	**North Carolina State U.–Raleigh***	42%	$23,559	38%

National Liberal Arts Colleges

Rank	School (State) (*Public)	% receiving grants based on need ('14)	Average cost after receiving grants based on need ('14)	Average discount from total cost ('14)
1.	**Amherst College** (MA)	58%	$17,413	73%
2.	**Pomona College** (CA)	56%	$18,637	71%
3.	**Williams College** (MA)	50%	$20,331	68%
4.	**Soka University of America** (CA)	88%	$17,754	60%
5.	**Vassar College** (NY)	58%	$20,836	67%
6.	**Washington and Lee University** (VA)	41%	$18,612	69%
7.	**Grinnell College** (IA)	70%	$22,164	63%
8.	**Swarthmore College** (PA)	51%	$22,136	65%
9.	**Haverford College** (PA)	49%	$21,810	66%
10.	**Middlebury College** (VT)	42%	$22,122	64%
11.	**College of the Atlantic** (ME)	86%	$19,730	62%
12.	**Bowdoin College** (ME)	45%	$22,672	63%
13.	**Colby College** (ME)	38%	$20,665	67%
14.	**Smith College** (MA)	59%	$23,924	62%
15.	**Colgate University** (NY)	34%	$20,977	66%
16.	**Davidson College** (NC)	48%	$23,751	61%
17.	**Wesleyan University** (CT)	44%	$22,731	65%
18.	**Hamilton College** (NY)	47%	$23,508	62%
19.	**Macalester College** (MN)	69%	$25,716	57%
20.	**Agnes Scott College** (GA)	78%	$21,587	56%
21.	**Claremont McKenna College** (CA)	38%	$23,777	63%
22.	**Colorado College**	35%	$21,944	64%
23.	**University of Richmond** (VA)	40%	$22,371	62%
24.	**Hollins University** (VA)	80%	$21,115	57%
25.	**Bates College** (ME)	44%	$23,849	62%
26.	**Earlham College** (IN)	81%	$25,040	54%
27.	**Mount Holyoke College** (MA)	67%	$26,339	54%
28.	**Knox College** (IL)	79%	$23,684	54%
29.	**Carleton College** (MN)	55%	$28,390	55%
30.	**Thomas Aquinas College** (CA)	70%	$19,951	44%
31.	**Franklin and Marshall College** (PA)	50%	$23,805	62%
32.	**Bryn Mawr College** (PA)	52%	$25,938	58%
33.	**Kenyon College** (OH)	39%	$24,111	61%
34.	**Ripon College** (WI)	84%	$22,187	51%
35.	**Trinity College** (CT)	39%	$22,572	65%
36.	**Barnard College** (NY)	40%	$24,378	61%
37.	**St. Olaf College** (MN)	66%	$24,906	53%
38.	**Lake Forest College** (IL)	78%	$23,275	57%
39.	**Lawrence University** (WI)	66%	$24,679	54%
40.	**Gustavus Adolphus College** (MN)	71%	$23,689	54%

Methodology: The rankings were based on the following three variables: **1.** Ratio of quality to price: a school's overall score in the latest Best Colleges rankings divided by the net cost to a student receiving the average need-based scholarship or grant. The higher the ratio of rank to the discounted cost (tuition, fees, room and board, and other expenses less average scholarship or grant), the better the value. **2.** Percentage of all undergrads receiving need-based scholarships or grants during the 2014-2015 year. **3.** Average discount: percentage of a school's 2014-2015 total costs covered by the average need-based scholarship or grant to undergrads. For public institutions, 2014-2015 out-of-state tuition and percentage of out-of-state students receiving need-based scholarships or grants were used. Only those schools ranked in or near the top half of their U.S. News ranking categories were considered. Ranks were determined by standardizing scores achieved by every school in each of the three variables and weighting those scores. Ratio of quality to price accounted for 60 percent of the overall score; percentage of undergrads receiving need-based grants, for 25 percent; and average discount, for 15 percent. The school with the most total weighted points became No. 1 in its category.

More @ usnews.com/bestcolleges

Regional Universities

Rank	School (State) (*Public)	% receiving grants based on need ('14)	Average cost after receiving grants based on need ('14)	Average discount from total cost ('14)
NORTH				
1.	**Gallaudet University** (DC)	86%	$16,433	53%
2.	**Villanova University** (PA)	45%	$31,039	49%
3.	**Bentley University** (MA)	43%	$29,152	50%
4.	**Rochester Inst. of Technology** (NY)	71%	$30,361	38%
5.	**St. Bonaventure University** (NY)	74%	$23,839	45%
6.	**Alfred University** (NY)	87%	$22,873	49%
7.	**Le Moyne College** (NY)	83%	$26,617	42%
8.	**Simmons College** (MA)	78%	$30,246	44%
9.	**Gannon University** (PA)	78%	$23,429	45%
10.	**Providence College** (RI)	52%	$36,343	39%
11.	**Niagara University** (NY)	75%	$24,265	44%
12.	**Ithaca College** (NY)	66%	$33,611	41%
13.	**Canisius College** (NY)	74%	$26,400	46%
14.	**Hood College** (MD)	83%	$27,996	44%
15.	**University of Scranton** (PA)	69%	$35,509	38%
SOUTH				
1.	**William Carey University** (MS)	91%	$14,950	38%
2.	**Mercer University** (GA)	73%	$24,983	49%
3.	**Converse College** (SC)	79%	$18,947	37%
4.	**Harding University** (AR)	58%	$18,283	34%
5.	**The Citadel** (SC)*	40%	$25,665	44%
6.	**Coastal Carolina University** (SC)*	22%	$13,734	63%
7.	**Stetson University** (FL)	73%	$29,659	47%
8.	**Wingate University** (NC)	78%	$19,645	50%
9.	**Christian Brothers University** (TN)	75%	$21,621	46%
10.	**Columbia College** (SC)	84%	$21,027	48%
11.	**Mississippi College**	52%	$18,803	35%
12.	**Loyola University New Orleans**	68%	$28,176	47%
13.	**Appalachian State University** (NC)*	23%	$23,400	28%
14.	**Lee University** (TN)	64%	$17,736	32%
15.	**Samford University** (AL)	39%	$28,234	33%
MIDWEST				
1.	**Valparaiso University** (IN)	73%	$22,328	53%
2.	**Creighton University** (NE)	53%	$26,691	46%
3.	**Drury University** (MO)	61%	$20,692	42%
4.	**University of Evansville** (IN)	64%	$23,192	50%
5.	**Truman State University** (MO)*	38%	$19,734	25%
6.	**Dominican University** (IL)	87%	$22,154	46%
7.	**John Carroll University** (OH)	72%	$26,840	46%
8.	**Univ. of Wisconsin–Oshkosh***	14%	$11,502	56%
9.	**Elmhurst College** (IL)	72%	$25,498	46%
10.	**Drake University** (IA)	58%	$29,647	36%
11.	**Bradley University** (IL)	61%	$28,361	35%
12.	**Indiana Wesleyan University**	79%	$20,429	42%
13.	**Butler University** (IN)	62%	$32,368	37%
14.	**Grand Valley State University** (MI)*	3%	$16,978	36%
15.	**Hamline University** (MN)	83%	$26,136	46%
WEST				
1.	**Trinity University** (TX)	44%	$24,741	51%
2.	**Seattle Pacific University**	71%	$23,592	52%
3.	**Whitworth University** (WA)	69%	$27,181	46%
4.	**Gonzaga University** (WA)	56%	$30,318	40%
5.	**Abilene Christian University** (TX)	66%	$25,034	42%
6.	**Westminster College** (UT)	58%	$24,409	44%
7.	**Pacific Lutheran University** (WA)	75%	$28,809	43%
8.	**University of Dallas**	60%	$27,208	46%
9.	**Mills College** (CA)	81%	$38,814	35%
10.	**LeTourneau University** (TX)	85%	$25,166	38%
11.	**St. Martin's University** (WA)	89%	$24,707	46%
12.	**University of Portland** (OR)	50%	$33,116	40%
13.	**Seattle University**	53%	$34,016	38%
14.	**St. Mary's College of California**	68%	$36,144	39%
15.	**Loyola Marymount University** (CA)	53%	$40,896	33%

Regional Colleges

Rank	School (State) (*Public)	% receiving grants based on need ('14)	Average cost after receiving grants based on need ('14)	Average discount from total cost ('14)
NORTH				
1.	**Cooper Union** (NY)	32%	$10,380	82%
2.	**Lebanon Valley College** (PA)	84%	$27,255	47%
3.	**Cedar Crest College** (PA)	92%	$23,917	48%
4.	**Elmira College** (NY)	82%	$24,476	52%
5.	**Wilson College** (PA)	89%	$19,952	47%
6.	**Elizabethtown College** (PA)	75%	$28,871	44%
7.	**Geneva College** (PA)	83%	$21,681	41%
8.	**Messiah College** (PA)	71%	$27,538	38%
9.	**Unity College** (ME)	87%	$22,545	38%
10.	**College of Our Lady of the Elms** (MA)	87%	$27,871	39%
SOUTH				
1.	**University of the Ozarks** (AR)	73%	$15,957	57%
2.	**Alice Lloyd College** (KY)	90%	$13,650	41%
3.	**Milligan College** (TN)	79%	$20,648	47%
4.	**John Brown University** (AR)	65%	$21,409	40%
5.	**West Virginia Wesleyan College**	73%	$20,561	51%
6.	**Meredith College** (NC)	75%	$24,233	45%
7.	**Flagler College** (FL)	61%	$21,217	29%
8.	**Florida Southern College**	69%	$24,951	42%
9.	**Carson-Newman University** (TN)	79%	$20,164	46%
10.	**Lenoir-Rhyne University** (NC)	87%	$24,277	47%
MIDWEST				
1.	**College of the Ozarks** (MO)	94%	$12,058	57%
2.	**Augustana College** (SD)	62%	$18,988	51%
3.	**Buena Vista University** (IA)	83%	$20,868	51%
4.	**Manchester University** (IN)	89%	$19,978	51%
5.	**Blackburn College** (IL)	85%	$14,983	46%
6.	**Huntington University** (IN)	84%	$21,476	41%
7.	**Hastings College** (NE)	75%	$20,668	46%
8.	**St. Joseph's College** (IN)	85%	$19,168	51%
9.	**Franklin College** (IN)	83%	$22,954	44%
10.	**Clarke University** (IA)	86%	$23,310	45%
WEST				
1.	**Carroll College** (MT)	65%	$25,770	39%
2.	**Howard Payne University** (TX)	70%	$19,790	44%
3.	**Corban University** (OR)	79%	$24,010	42%
4.	**Schreiner University** (TX)	88%	$20,315	42%
5.	**Northwest University** (WA)	80%	$20,749	45%
6.	**Master's Col. and Seminary** (CA)	76%	$26,940	39%
7.	**McMurry University** (TX)	90%	$21,807	41%
8.	**Oklahoma Wesleyan University**	74%	$23,108	35%
9.	**Oklahoma Baptist University**	62%	$26,851	22%
10.	**Warner Pacific College** (OR)	64%	$26,370	20%

Finding THE MONEY

The Payback Picture

With tuition rising and financial aid budgets shrinking, many undergrads have to borrow their way to a degree. U.S. News has compiled a list of the schools whose class of 2014 graduated with the heaviest and lightest debt loads. The data include loans taken out by students from their colleges, from private financial institutions, and from federal, state and local governments. Loans directly to parents are not included. The first data column indicates what percentage of the class graduated owing money and, by extrapolation, what percentage graduated debt free. "Average amount of debt" refers to the cumulative amount borrowed by students who incurred debt; it's not an average for all students.

MOST DEBT

National Universities

School (State) (*Public)	% of grads with debt	Average amount of debt
Rensselaer Polytechnic Institute (NY)	66%	$41,814
Florida Institute of Technology	60%	$40,383
Texas Christian University	43%	$39,584
Boston University	57%	$39,166
Barry University (FL)	71%	$38,342
University of St. Thomas (MN)	65%	$37,131
University of New Hampshire*	79%	$36,965
Pennsylvania State University–University Park*	63%	$36,955
Regent University (VA)	82%	$36,564
Andrews University (MI)	62%	$36,536
University of Pittsburgh*	67%	$36,466
Clarkson University (NY)	85%	$36,304
Michigan Technological University*	73%	$36,041
Temple University (PA)*	77%	$35,752
Tennessee State University*	86%	$35,645

National Liberal Arts Colleges

School (State) (*Public)	% of grads with debt	Average amount of debt
Pacific Union College (CA)	77%	$45,390
Life University (GA)	77%	$40,000
College of St. Benedict (MN)	75%	$39,437
Wartburg College (IA)	80%	$39,414
Gordon College (MA)	84%	$38,456
St. John's University (MN)	70%	$38,089
Whittier College (CA)	75%	$37,379
Hollins University (VA)	77%	$37,332
Albion College (MI)	65%	$37,151
Harrisburg Univ. of Science and Technology (PA)	75%	$37,078
St. Michael's College (VT)	75%	$36,967
Luther College (IA)	74%	$36,918
Gustavus Adolphus College (MN)	76%	$36,636
Wells College (NY)	88%	$36,498
Washington College (MD)	73%	$35,833

Regional Universities

School (State) (*Public)	% of grads with debt	Average amount of debt
NORTH		
Wheelock College (MA)	85%	$46,690
Quinnipiac University (CT)	71%	$45,711
University of New Haven (CT)	84%	$43,472
Curry College (MA)	81%	$43,388
Utica College (NY)	93%	$42,083
SOUTH		
Albany State University (GA)*	93%	$39,014
Alabama A&M University*	77%	$38,819
Coastal Carolina University (SC)*	80%	$34,654
University of Tampa (FL)	61%	$34,212
Lynchburg College (VA)	83%	$33,592
MIDWEST		
College of St. Scholastica (MN)	77%	$42,792
St. Catherine University (MN)	87%	$39,748
Rockford University (IL)	86%	$39,619
Lawrence Technological University (MI)	72%	$39,033
Alverno College (WI)	93%	$38,642
WEST		
Abilene Christian University (TX)	67%	$43,841
Texas Wesleyan University	78%	$42,565
Woodbury University (CA)	92%	$40,699
Walla Walla University (WA)	67%	$38,778
Western Oregon University*	68%	$38,331

Regional Colleges

School (State) (*Public)	% of grads with debt	Average amount of debt
NORTH		
Wentworth Institute of Technology (MA)	82%	$48,980
Mount Ida College (MA)	91%	$46,430
Dean College (MA)	73%	$44,063
Cedar Crest College (PA)	92%	$41,939
Maine Maritime Academy*	88%	$40,909
SOUTH		
Fort Valley State University (GA)*	63%	$40,700
Livingstone College (NC)	95%	$40,574
Tuskegee University (AL)	63%	$39,000
Chowan University (NC)	96%	$36,006
Southern Adventist University (TN)	70%	$34,790
MIDWEST		
MacMurray College (IL)	86%	$50,039
Grand View University (IA)	89%	$38,160
Clarke University (IA)	90%	$37,200
Iowa Wesleyan College	91%	$36,797
Bluffton University (OH)	82%	$35,883
WEST		
Howard Payne University (TX)	67%	$33,329
Warner Pacific College (OR)	89%	$31,338
East Texas Baptist University	88%	$30,718
McMurry University (TX)	92%	$30,694
Oregon Institute of Technology*	73%	$30,060

Note: Student debt data are as of July 29, 2015.

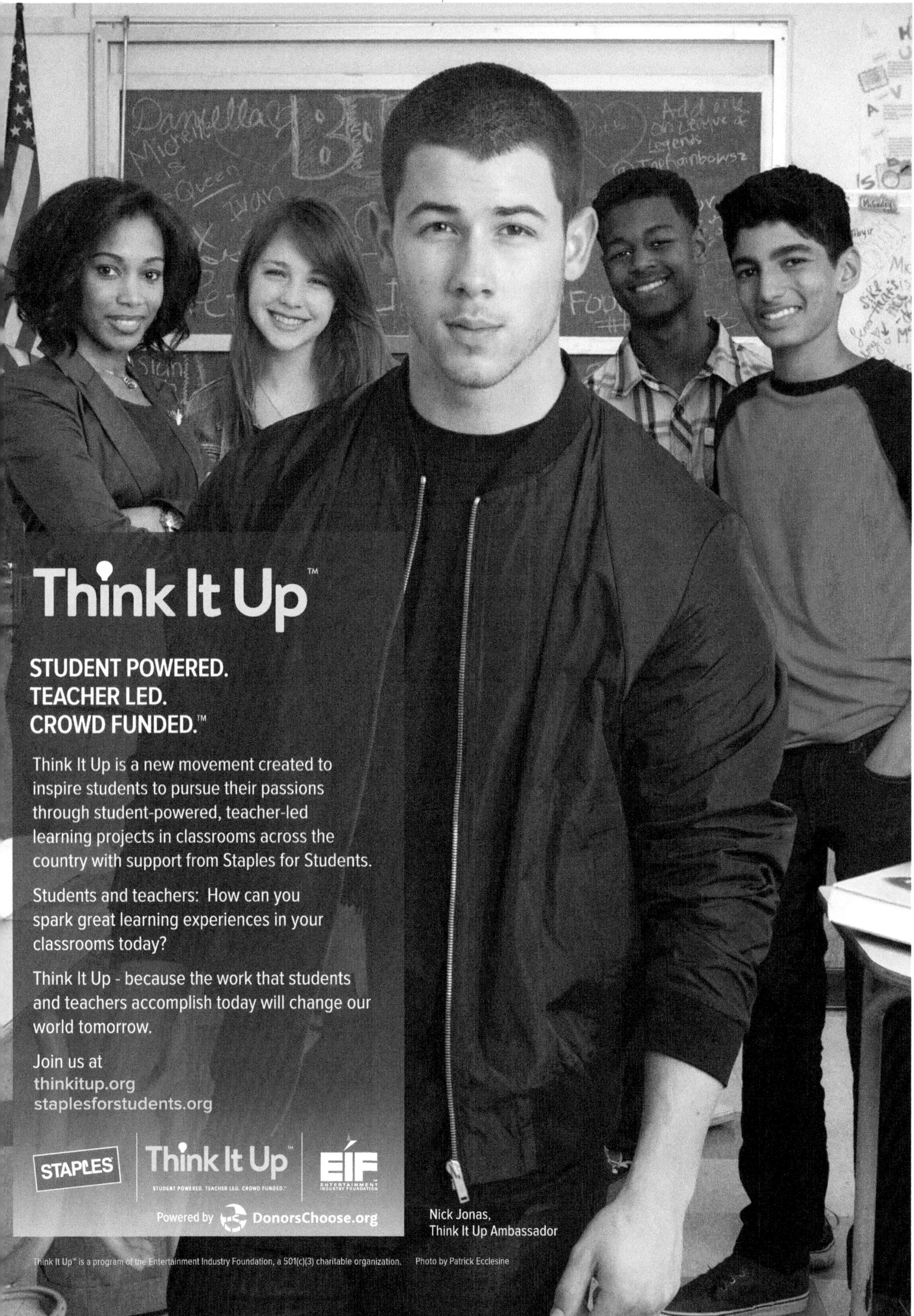

Think It Up™
STUDENT POWERED.
TEACHER LED.
CROWD FUNDED.™
Think It Up is a new movement created to inspire students to pursue their passions through student-powered, teacher-led learning projects in classrooms across the country with support from Staples for Students.
Students and teachers: How can you spark great learning experiences in your classrooms today?
Think It Up - because the work that students and teachers accomplish today will change our world tomorrow.
Join us at
thinkitup.org
staplesforstudents.org
STAPLES
Think It Up™
STUDENT POWERED. TEACHER LED. CROWD FUNDED.™
EIF
ENTERTAINMENT INDUSTRY FOUNDATION
Powered by DonorsChoose.org
Nick Jonas,
Think It Up Ambassador
Think It Up™ is a program of the Entertainment Industry Foundation, a 501(c)(3) charitable organization.
Photo by Patrick Ecclesine

LEAST DEBT

National Universities

School (State) (*Public)	% of grads with debt	Average amount of debt
Princeton University (NJ)	17%	$6,600
California Institute of Technology	32%	$12,104
Brigham Young University–Provo (UT)	26%	$14,021
Yale University (CT)	16%	$14,853
Harvard University (MA)	26%	$15,117
Louisiana Tech University*	51%	$16,855
Dartmouth College (NH)	46%	$17,171
University of California–Berkeley*	39%	$17,584
University of Southern Mississippi*	67%	$17,806
San Diego State University*	49%	$18,400
University of Houston*	48%	$18,453
Florida International University*	48%	$18,519
University of Nevada–Las Vegas*	46%	$18,542
University of New Orleans*	53%	$18,850
University of North Carolina–Chapel Hill*	41%	$18,945
Massachusetts Institute of Technology	40%	$19,064
Stanford University (CA)	23%	$19,230
University of Pennsylvania	36%	$19,442
University of California–Davis*	56%	$19,705
Northwestern University (IL)	46%	$19,864
University of Texas–Dallas*	48%	$19,884
University of Utah*	39%	$20,019
Wichita State University (KS)*	62%	$20,044
University of California–Irvine*	55%	$20,319
North Carolina State University–Raleigh*	57%	$20,482

National Liberal Arts Colleges

School (State) (*Public)	% of grads with debt	Average amount of debt
Berea College (KY)	64%	$6,186
Louisiana State University–Alexandria*	61%	$10,114
Sarah Lawrence College (NY)	59%	$12,483
University of Virginia–Wise*	65%	$12,496
Wellesley College (MA)	52%	$12,956
Williams College (MA)	35%	$14,103
Amherst College (MA)	31%	$14,490
Thomas Aquinas College (CA)	85%	$16,263
Pomona College (CA)	34%	$16,273
Grinnell College (IA)	56%	$16,315
Rust College (MS)	78%	$17,035
Vassar College (NY)	57%	$17,476
New College of Florida*	38%	$17,553
Barnard College (NY)	49%	$17,660
Middlebury College (VT)	44%	$17,975
Carleton College (MN)	39%	$18,302
Hamilton College (NY)	44%	$18,491
Bates College (ME)	40%	$18,929
Whitman College (WA)	49%	$19,147
Pitzer College (CA)	44%	$19,422
Fort Lewis College (CO)*	62%	$19,491
Soka University of America (CA)	61%	$19,563
Colorado College	34%	$19,756
Scripps College (CA)	50%	$20,060
University of Science and Arts of Okla.*	61%	$20,074

Regional Universities

School (State) (*Public)	% of grads with debt	Average amount of debt
NORTH		
CUNY–Baruch College*	29%	$7,737
CUNY–John Jay College of Crim. Justice*	20%	$11,246
CUNY–Hunter College*	71%	$12,400
CUNY–Queens College*	19%	$14,000
CUNY–Lehman College*	25%	$15,000
SOUTH		
University of North Georgia*	51%	$12,892
William Carey University (MS)	85%	$16,000
University of Mary Washington (VA)*	48%	$17,460
Southeastern Louisiana University*	57%	$18,433
Tennessee Technological University*	53%	$18,477
MIDWEST		
Northeastern Illinois University*	18%	$13,366
University of Wisconsin–Platteville*	79%	$18,822
William Woods University (MO)	71%	$21,260
McKendree University (IL)	83%	$21,731
North Central College (IL)	76%	$22,064
WEST		
New Mexico Institute of Mining and Technology*	38%	$9,567
California State University–Bakersfield*	90%	$11,735
California State University–Los Angeles*	54%	$14,788
California State University–Fullerton*	44%	$14,965
Southern Utah University*	53%	$14,978

Regional Colleges

School (State) (*Public)	% of grads with debt	Average amount of debt
NORTH		
U.S. Merchant Marine Academy (NY)*	35%	$5,500
SUNY College of Technology–Delhi*	75%	$14,670
Farmingdale State College–SUNY*	42%	$17,238
Cooper Union (NY)	26%	$19,072
Vermont Technical College*	80%	$23,530
SOUTH		
Alice Lloyd College (KY)	52%	$9,949
Bryan College (TN)	60%	$11,643
Truett McConnell College (GA)	62%	$13,508
North Greenville University (SC)	70%	$15,000
Georgia Gwinnett College*	45%	$19,487
MIDWEST		
College of the Ozarks (MO)	8%	$7,808
Dunwoody College of Tech. (MN)	89%	$18,014
Maranatha Baptist University (WI)	66%	$18,475
University of Minnesota–Crookston*	77%	$23,621
Dickinson State University (ND)*	67%	$23,838
WEST		
Oklahoma State Univ. Inst. of Technology–Okmulgee*	75%	$8,785
Rogers State University (OK)*	51%	$13,403
Utah Valley University*	87%	$16,784
Lewis-Clark State College (ID)*	68%	$18,065
Master's Col. and Seminary (CA)	73%	$18,750

Note: Student debt data are as of July 29, 2015.

2016 EDITION

DIRECTORY OF COLLEGES AND UNIVERSITIES

INSIDE

The latest facts and figures on nearly 1,600 American colleges and universities, including schools' U.S. News rankings

New data on tuition, admissions, the makeup of the undergraduate student body, popular majors and financial aid

Statistical profiles of freshman classes, including entrance exam scores and high school class standing

Using the Directory

How to interpret the statistics in the following entries on nearly 1,600 American colleges and universities - and how to get the most out of them

The snapshots of colleges and universities presented here, alphabetized by state, contain a wealth of helpful information on everything from the most popular majors offered to the stats on the freshman class that arrived in the fall of 2014. The statistics were collected in the spring and summer of 2015 and are as of Aug. 14, 2015; they are explained in detail below. A school whose name has been footnoted did not return the U.S. News statistical questionnaire, so limited data appear. If a college did not reply to a particular question, you'll see N/A, for "not available." By tapping our online directory at usnews.com/collegesearch, you can experiment with a customized search of our database that allows you to pick schools based on major, location and other criteria. To find a school of interest in the rankings tables, consult the index at the back of the book.

EXAMPLE

Fairfield University

Fairfield CT

1 — (203) 254-4100

2 — **U.S. News ranking:** Reg. U. (N), No. 6

3 — **Website:** www.fairfield.edu

4 — **Admissions email:** admis@fairfield.edu

5 — **Private;** founded 1942 **Affiliation:** Roman Catholic (Jesuit)

6 — **Freshman admissions:** selective; 2014-2015: 9,978 applied, 7,137 accepted. Neither SAT nor ACT required. SAT 25/75 percentile: 1090-1260. High school rank: N/A

7 — **Early decision deadline:** 11/15, notification date: 12/15 **Early action deadline:** 11/1, notification date: 12/20

8 — **Application deadline (fall):** 1/15

9 — **Undergraduate student body:** 3,688 full time, 294 part time; 41% male, 59% female; 0% American Indian, 2% Asian, 2% black, 7% Hispanic, 1% multiracial, 0% Pacific Islander, 75% white, 2% international; 29% from in state; 76% live on campus; N/A of students in fraternities, N/A in sororities

10 — **Most popular majors:** 28% Business, Management, Marketing, and Related Support Services, 11% Communication, Journalism, and Related Programs, 7% English Language and Literature/Letters, 12% Health Professions and Related Programs, 14% Social Sciences

11 — **Expenses:** 2015-2016: $44,875; room/board: $13,520

12 — **Financial aid:** (203) 254-4125; 49% of undergrads determined to have financial need; average aid package $30,054

1. TELEPHONE NUMBER

This number reaches the admissions office.

2. U.S. NEWS RANKING

The abbreviation indicates which category of institution the school falls into: National Universities (Nat. U.), National Liberal Arts Colleges (Nat. Lib. Arts), Regional Universities (Reg. U.), or Regional Colleges (Reg. Coll.). The regional universities and regional colleges are further divided by region: North (N), South (S), Midwest (MidW), and West (W). "Business" refers to business specialty schools, and "Engineering" refers to engineering specialty schools. "Arts" refers to schools devoted to the fine and performing arts.

Next, you'll find the school's 2016 rank within its category. Colleges and universities falling in the top three-fourths of their categories are ranked numerically. Those ranked in the bottom 25 percent of their respective category are placed in the second tier, listed alphabetically. But remember: You cannot compare school ranks in different categories; U.S. News ranks schools only against their peers. Specialty schools that focus on business, engineering and the arts aren't ranked and are listed as unranked. Also unranked are schools with fewer than 200 students, a high percentage of older or part-time students, that don't use SAT or ACT test scores for admission decisions or that have received a very small number of peer assessment votes in a survey conducted in spring 2015.

3. WEBSITE

Visit the school's website to research programs, take a virtual tour or submit an application. You can also find a link to each site at usnews.com.

4. ADMISSIONS EMAIL

You can use this email address to request information or to submit an application.

5. TYPE/AFFILIATION

Is the school public, private or for-profit? Affiliated with a religious denomination?

6. FRESHMAN ADMISSIONS

How competitive is the admissions process at this institution? Schools are designated "most selective," "more selective," "selective," "less selective" or "least selective." The more selective a school, the harder it will probably be to get in. All of the admissions statistics reported are for the class that entered in the fall of 2014. The 25/75 percentiles for the SAT Math and Critical Reading or ACT Composite show the range in which half the students scored: 25 percent of students scored at or below the lower end, and 75 percent scored at or below the upper end. If a school reported the averages and not the 25/75 percentiles, the average score is listed. The test score that is published represents the test that the greatest percentage of the entering students took.

7. EARLY DECISION/ EARLY ACTION DEADLINES

Applicants who plan to take the early decision route to fall 2016 enrollment will have to meet the deadline listed for the school. If the school offers an early action option, the application deadline and notification date are also shown.

8. APPLICATION DEADLINE

The date shown is the regular admission deadline for the academic year starting in the fall of 2016. "Rolling" means the school makes admissions decisions as applications come in until the class is filled.

9. UNDERGRADUATE STUDENT BODY

This section gives you the breakdown of full-time vs. part-time students, male and female enrollment, the ethnic makeup of the student body, in-state and out-of-state populations, the percentage of students living on campus, and the percentage in fraternities and sororities. All figures are for the 2014-15 academic year.

10. MOST POPULAR MAJORS

The five most popular majors appear, along with the percentage majoring in each among 2014 graduates with a bachelor's degree.

11. EXPENSES

The first figure represents tuition (including required fees); next is total room and board. Figures are for the 2015-16 academic year; if data are not available, we use figures for the 2014-15 academic year. For public schools, we list both in-state and out-of-state tuition.

12. FINANCIAL AID

The percentage of undergrads determined to have financial need and the amount of the average package (grants, loans and jobs) in 2014-15. We also provide the phone number of the financial aid office.

ALABAMA

Alabama Agricultural and Mechanical University
Normal AL
(256) 372-5245
U.S. News ranking: Reg. U. (S), second tier
Website: www.aamu.edu
Admissions email: admissions@aamu.edu
Public; founded 1875
Freshman admissions: less selective; 2014-2015: 9,790 applied, 5,204 accepted. ACT required. ACT 25/75 percentile: 15-19. High school rank: N/A
Early decision deadline: N/A, notification date: N/A
Early action deadline: N/A, notification date: N/A
Application deadline (fall): 7/15
Undergraduate student body: 3,930 full time, 280 part time; 48% male, 52% female; 0% American Indian, 0% Asian, 94% black, 1% Hispanic, N/A multiracial, 0% Pacific Islander, 2% white, 1% international; 79% from in state; 45% live on campus; N/A of students in fraternities, N/A in sororities
Most popular majors: 6% Biology/Biological Sciences, General, 6% Business/Commerce, General, 6% Food Science, 5% Physical Education Teaching and Coaching, 10% Social Work
Expenses: 2015-2016: $9,096 in state, $16,596 out of state; room/board: $5,440
Financial aid: (256) 372-5400; 92% of undergrads determined to have financial need; average aid package $10,708

Alabama State University
Montgomery AL
(334) 229-4291
U.S. News ranking: Reg. U. (S), second tier
Website: www.alasu.edu
Admissions email: mpettway@alasu.edu
Public; founded 1887
Freshman admissions: less selective; 2014-2015: 7,673 applied, 4,087 accepted. Either SAT or ACT required. ACT 25/75 percentile: 16-19. High school rank: 3% in top tenth, 7% in top quarter, 22% in top half
Early decision deadline: N/A, notification date: N/A
Early action deadline: N/A, notification date: N/A
Application deadline (fall): 7/30
Undergraduate student body: 4,374 full time, 429 part time; 39% male, 61% female; 0% American Indian, 0% Asian, 92% black, 1% Hispanic, 1% multiracial, 0% Pacific Islander, 2% white, 2% international; 67% from in state; 34% live on campus; 3% of students in fraternities, 5% in sororities
Most popular majors: 10% Biology/Biological Sciences, General, 10% Computer Science, 20% Criminal Justice/Safety Studies, 20% Rehabilitation and Therapeutic Professions, Other, 40% Secondary Education and Teaching
Expenses: 2015-2016: $8,720 in state, $15,656 out of state; room/board: $5,422
Financial aid: (334) 229-4323; 96% of undergrads determined to have financial need; average aid package $18,358

Amridge University
Montgomery AL
(800) 351-4040
U.S. News ranking: Nat. Lib. Arts, second tier
Website: www.amridgeuniversity.edu/
Admissions email: admissions@amridgeuniversity.edu
Private; founded 1967
Affiliation: Church of Christ
Freshman admissions: selective; 2014-2015: N/A applied, N/A accepted. Neither SAT nor ACT required. ACT 25/75 percentile: N/A. High school rank: N/A
Early decision deadline: N/A, notification date: N/A
Early action deadline: N/A, notification date: N/A
Application deadline (fall): rolling
Undergraduate student body: 159 full time, 132 part time; 40% male, 60% female; 0% American Indian, 0% Asian, 42% black, 1% Hispanic, 0% multiracial, 0% Pacific Islander, 30% white, 0% international
Most popular majors: 7% Business, Management, Marketing, and Related Support Services, 4% Computer and Information Sciences and Support Services, 61% Liberal Arts and Sciences, General Studies and Humanities, 28% Theology and Religious Vocations
Expenses: 2015-2016: $13,800; room/board: N/A
Financial aid: (800) 351-4040; 94% of undergrads determined to have financial need; average aid package $7,870

Athens State University
Athens AL
(256) 233-8217
U.S. News ranking: Reg. Coll. (S), unranked
Website: www.athens.edu/
Admissions email: N/A
Public; founded 1822
Freshman admissions: N/A; 2014-2015: N/A applied, N/A accepted. Neither SAT nor ACT required. ACT 25/75 percentile: N/A. High school rank: N/A
Early decision deadline: N/A, notification date: N/A
Early action deadline: N/A, notification date: N/A
Application deadline (fall): N/A
Undergraduate student body: 1,342 full time, 1,787 part time; 35% male, 65% female; 2% American Indian, 1% Asian, 12% black, 2% Hispanic, 2% multiracial, 0% Pacific Islander, 78% white, 1% international
Most popular majors: 10% Accounting, 18% Business Administration and Management, General, 5% Business, Management, Marketing, and Related Support Services, Other, 16% Elementary Education and Teaching, 4% Liberal Arts and Sciences/Liberal Studies
Expenses: 2015-2016: $6,270 in state, $11,790 out of state; room/board: N/A
Financial aid: (256) 233-8122; 71% of undergrads determined to have financial need; average aid package $9,462

Auburn University
Auburn AL
(334) 844-6425
U.S. News ranking: Nat. U., No. 102
Website: www.auburn.edu
Admissions email: admissions@auburn.edu
Public; founded 1856
Freshman admissions: more selective; 2014-2015: 16,958 applied, 14,154 accepted. Either SAT or ACT required. ACT 25/75 percentile: 24-30. High school rank: 29% in top tenth, 61% in top quarter, 88% in top half
Early decision deadline: N/A, notification date: N/A
Early action deadline: 2/1, notification date: 10/15
Application deadline (fall): 6/1
Undergraduate student body: 18,853 full time, 1,776 part time; 51% male, 49% female; 1% American Indian, 2% Asian, 7% black, 2% Hispanic, N/A multiracial, N/A Pacific Islander, 85% white, 1% international; 62% from in state; 22% live on campus; 24% of students in fraternities, 38% in sororities
Most popular majors: 9% Biological and Biomedical Sciences, 19% Business, Management, Marketing, and Related Support Services, 6% Communication, Journalism, and Related Programs, 9% Education, 16% Engineering
Expenses: 2015-2016: $10,424 in state, $28,040 out of state; room/board: $12,584
Financial aid: (334) 844-4634; 38% of undergrads determined to have financial need; average aid package $10,531

Auburn University–Montgomery
Montgomery AL
(334) 244-3611
U.S. News ranking: Reg. U. (S), second tier
Website: www.aum.edu
Admissions email: vsamuel@aum.edu
Public; founded 1967
Freshman admissions: selective; 2014-2015: 2,123 applied, 1,702 accepted. Either SAT or ACT required. ACT 25/75 percentile: 19-24. High school rank: 18% in top tenth, 46% in top quarter, 79% in top half
Early decision deadline: N/A, notification date: N/A
Early action deadline: N/A, notification date: N/A
Application deadline (fall): 8/15
Undergraduate student body: 3,081 full time, 1,296 part time; 37% male, 63% female; 0% American Indian, 2% Asian, 34% black, 1% Hispanic, 3% multiracial, 0% Pacific Islander, 54% white, 4% international; 96% from in state; 20% live on campus; 1% of students in fraternities, 3% in sororities
Most popular majors: 9% Biological and Biomedical Sciences, 31% Business, Management, Marketing, and Related Support Services, 11% Education, 18% Health Professions and Related Programs, 6% Psychology
Expenses: 2015-2016: $9,350 in state, $20,210 out of state; room/board: $5,520
Financial aid: (334) 244-3571; 66% of undergrads determined to have financial need; average aid package $7,236

Birmingham-Southern College
Birmingham AL
(205) 226-4696
U.S. News ranking: Nat. Lib. Arts, No. 120
Website: www.bsc.edu
Admissions email: admission@bsc.edu
Private; founded 1856
Affiliation: United Methodist
Freshman admissions: more selective; 2014-2015: 2,770 applied, 1,479 accepted. Either SAT or ACT required. ACT 25/75 percentile: 23-29. High school rank: 25% in top tenth, 53% in top quarter, 81% in top half
Early decision deadline: N/A, notification date: N/A
Early action deadline: 11/15, notification date: 12/15
Application deadline (fall): 7/15
Undergraduate student body: 1,178 full time, 7 part time; 54% male, 46% female; 1% American Indian, 3% Asian, 11% black, 2% Hispanic, 1% multiracial, 0% Pacific Islander, 78% white, 4% international; 57% from in state; 62% live on campus; 34% of students in fraternities, 53% in sororities
Most popular majors: 13% Biology/Biological Sciences, General, 18% Business Administration and Management, General, 6% History, General, 10% Psychology, General, 7% Teacher Education, Multiple Levels
Expenses: 2015-2016: $33,128; room/board: $11,350
Financial aid: (205) 226-4688; 55% of undergrads determined to have financial need; average aid package $30,038

Concordia College[1]
Selma AL
(334) 874-5700
U.S. News ranking: Reg. Coll. (S), unranked
Website: www.ccal.edu/
Admissions email: admission@ccal.edu
Private; founded 1922
Affiliation: Lutheran
Application deadline (fall): rolling
Undergraduate student body: N/A full time, N/A part time
Expenses: 2014-2015: $10,320; room/board: $5,600
Financial aid: (334) 874-5700

Faulkner University
Montgomery AL
(334) 386-7200
U.S. News ranking: Reg. Coll. (S), No. 54
Website: www.faulkner.edu
Admissions email: admissions@faulkner.edu
Private; founded 1942
Affiliation: Church of Christ
Freshman admissions: selective; 2014-2015: 2,319 applied, 1,153 accepted. Either SAT or ACT required. ACT 25/75 percentile: 18-22. High school rank: 6% in top tenth, 19% in top quarter, 58% in top half
Early decision deadline: N/A, notification date: N/A
Early action deadline: N/A, notification date: N/A
Application deadline (fall): rolling
Undergraduate student body: 1,821 full time, 847 part time; 40% male, 60% female; 1% American Indian, 0% Asian, 51% black, 3% Hispanic, 2% multiracial, 0% Pacific Islander, 39% white, 2% international; 86% from in state; 26% live on campus; 17% of students in fraternities, 12% in sororities
Most popular majors: 46% Business Administration and Management, General, 17% Criminal Justice/Safety Studies, 2% Elementary Education and Teaching, 19% Human Resources Management/Personnel Administration, General, 2% Sport and Fitness Administration/Management
Expenses: 2015-2016: $19,250; room/board: $7,130
Financial aid: (334) 386-7195; 63% of undergrads determined to have financial need; average aid package $6,100

Huntingdon College
Montgomery AL
(334) 833-4497
U.S. News ranking: Reg. Coll. (S), No. 21
Website: www.huntingdon.edu
Admissions email: admiss@huntingdon.edu
Private; founded 1854
Affiliation: Methodist
Freshman admissions: selective; 2014-2015: 1,437 applied, 839 accepted. Either SAT or ACT required. ACT 25/75 percentile: 20-24. High school rank: 14% in top tenth, 32% in top quarter, 78% in top half
Early decision deadline: N/A, notification date: N/A
Early action deadline: N/A, notification date: N/A
Application deadline (fall): rolling
Undergraduate student body: 912 full time, 248 part time; 51% male, 49% female; 1% American Indian, 1% Asian, 20% black, 2% Hispanic, 3% multiracial, 0% Pacific Islander, 64% white, 1% international; 82% from in state; 62% live on campus; 26% of students in fraternities, 42% in sororities
Most popular majors: 12% Biological and Biomedical Sciences, 46% Business, Management, Marketing, and Related Support Services, 5% Communication, Journalism, and Related Programs, 5% Education, 10% Parks, Recreation, Leisure, and Fitness Studies
Expenses: 2015-2016: $25,050; room/board: $8,850
Financial aid: (334) 833-4519; 74% of undergrads determined to have financial need; average aid package $17,249

Jacksonville State University
Jacksonville AL
(256) 782-5268
U.S. News ranking: Reg. U. (S), second tier
Website: www.jsu.edu
Admissions email: info@jsu.edu
Public; founded 1883
Freshman admissions: selective; 2014-2015: 2,969 applied, 2,472 accepted. Either SAT or ACT required. ACT 25/75 percentile: 19-26. High school rank: 20% in top tenth, 42% in top quarter, 73% in top half
Early decision deadline: N/A, notification date: N/A
Early action deadline: N/A, notification date: N/A
Application deadline (fall): rolling
Undergraduate student body: 5,733 full time, 1,914 part time; 43% male, 57% female; 1% American Indian, 1% Asian, 24% black, 1% Hispanic, 0% multiracial, 0% Pacific Islander, 68% white, 2% international; 82% from in state; 25% live on campus; 13% of students in fraternities, 15% in sororities
Most popular majors: 5% Business Administration and Management, General, 6% Criminal Justice/Safety Studies, 5% Educational Leadership and Administration, General, 8% Elementary Education and Teaching, 17% Registered Nursing/Registered Nurse
Expenses: 2014-2015: $8,790 in state, $17,280 out of state; room/board: $6,985
Financial aid: (256) 782-5006; 86% of undergrads determined to have financial need; average aid package $9,251

Judson College[1]
Marion AL
(800) 447-9472
U.S. News ranking: Nat. Lib. Arts, second tier
Website: www.judson.edu/
Admissions email: admissions@judson.edu
Private
Application deadline (fall): N/A
Undergraduate student body: N/A full time, N/A part time
Expenses: 2014-2015: $16,258; room/board: $9,334
Financial aid: (334) 683-5170

Miles College[1]
Birmingham AL
(800) 445-0708
U.S. News ranking: Reg. Coll. (S), unranked
Website: www.miles.edu
Admissions email: admissions@mail.miles.edu
Private
Application deadline (fall): N/A
Undergraduate student body: N/A full time, N/A part time
Expenses: 2014-2015: $11,604; room/board: $7,042
Financial aid: (205) 929-1665

Oakwood University[1]
Huntsville AL
(256) 726-7356
U.S. News ranking: Reg. Coll. (S), No. 67
Website: www.oakwood.edu
Admissions email: admissions@oakwood.edu
Private; founded 1896
Affiliation: Seventh-day Adventist
Application deadline (fall): rolling
Undergraduate student body: N/A full time, N/A part time
Expenses: 2014-2015: $16,720; room/board: $9,700
Financial aid: (256) 726-7210

Samford University
Birmingham AL
(800) 888-7218
U.S. News ranking: Reg. U. (S), No. 4
Website: www.samford.edu
Admissions email: admission@samford.edu
Private; founded 1841
Affiliation: Baptist
Freshman admissions: more selective; 2014-2015: 3,327 applied, 2,725 accepted. Either SAT or ACT required. ACT 25/75 percentile: 23-29. High school rank: 30% in top tenth, 56% in top quarter, 82% in top half
Early decision deadline: N/A, notification date: N/A
Early action deadline: N/A, notification date: N/A
Application deadline (fall): 7/31
Undergraduate student body: 2,915 full time, 136 part time; 35% male, 65% female; 0% American Indian, 1% Asian, 7% black, 6% Hispanic, 1% multiracial, 0% Pacific Islander, 82% white, 3% international; 35% from in state; 72% live on campus; 36% of students in fraternities, 49% in sororities
Most popular majors: 19% Business, Management, Marketing, and Related Support Services, 6% Communication, Journalism, and Related Programs, 17% Health Professions and Related Programs, 7% Parks, Recreation, Leisure, and Fitness Studies, 8% Visual and Performing Arts
Expenses: 2015-2016: $28,370; room/board: $10,234
Financial aid: (205) 726-2905; 41% of undergrads determined to have financial need; average aid package $18,141

Spring Hill College
Mobile AL
(251) 380-3030
U.S. News ranking: Reg. U. (S), No. 21
Website: www.shc.edu
Admissions email: admit@shc.edu
Private; founded 1830
Affiliation: Catholic
Freshman admissions: more selective; 2014-2015: 6,245 applied, 3,233 accepted. Either SAT or ACT required. ACT 25/75 percentile: 22-27. High school rank: 32% in top tenth, 55% in top quarter, 85% in top half
Early decision deadline: N/A, notification date: N/A
Early action deadline: N/A, notification date: N/A
Application deadline (fall): 7/15
Undergraduate student body: 1,215 full time, 59 part time; 40% male, 60% female; 1% American Indian, 1% Asian, 15% black, 6% Hispanic, 3% multiracial, 0% Pacific Islander, 67% white, 2% international; 40% from in state; 80% live on campus; 24% of students in fraternities, 31% in sororities
Most popular majors: 9% Biological and Biomedical Sciences, 22% Business, Management, Marketing, and Related Support Services, 10% Communication, Journalism, and Related Programs, 15% Psychology, 8% Social Sciences
Expenses: 2015-2016: $34,091; room/board: $12,090
Financial aid: (251) 380-3460; 69% of undergrads determined to have financial need; average aid package $26,574

Stillman College[1]
Tuscaloosa AL
(205) 366-8837
U.S. News ranking: Nat. Lib. Arts, second tier
Website: www.stillman.edu
Admissions email: admissions@stillman.edu
Private; founded 1876
Affiliation: Presbyterian Church (USA)
Application deadline (fall): rolling
Undergraduate student body: N/A full time, N/A part time
Expenses: 2014-2015: $15,865; room/board: $7,056
Financial aid: (205) 366-8817

Talladega College[1]
Talladega AL
(256) 761-6235
U.S. News ranking: Nat. Lib. Arts, unranked
Website: www.talladega.edu
Admissions email: admissions@talladega.edu
Private
Application deadline (fall): N/A
Undergraduate student body: N/A full time, N/A part time
Expenses: 2014-2015: $12,509; room/board: $6,504
Financial aid: (256) 761-6341

Troy University
Troy AL
(334) 670-3179
U.S. News ranking: Reg. U. (S), No. 65
Website: www.troy.edu/
Admissions email: admit@troy.edu
Public; founded 1887
Freshman admissions: selective; 2014-2015: 6,336 applied, 2,797 accepted. Either SAT or ACT required. ACT 25/75 percentile: 19-26. High school rank: N/A in top tenth, 54% in top quarter, 85% in top half
Early decision deadline: N/A, notification date: N/A
Early action deadline: N/A, notification date: N/A
Application deadline (fall): rolling
Undergraduate student body: 9,018 full time, 6,097 part time; 39% male, 61% female; 1% American Indian, 1% Asian, 34% black, 3% Hispanic, 2% multiracial, 0% Pacific Islander, 51% white, 3% international; 68% from in state; 29% live on campus; 13% of students in fraternities, 15% in sororities
Most popular majors: 31% Business, Management, Marketing, and Related Support Services, 6% Education, 13% Homeland Security, Law Enforcement, Firefighting and Related Protective Services, 15% Psychology, 6% Social Sciences
Expenses: 2015-2016: $9,646 in state, $18,256 out of state; room/board: $6,525
Financial aid: (334) 670-3186; 70% of undergrads determined to have financial need; average aid package $2,297

Tuskegee University
Tuskegee AL
(334) 727-8500
U.S. News ranking: Reg. Coll. (S), No. 10
Website: www.tuskegee.edu
Admissions email: admiweb@tusk.edu
Private; founded 1881
Freshman admissions: selective; 2014-2015: 7,151 applied, 3,428 accepted. Either SAT or ACT required. ACT 25/75 percentile: 17-23. High school rank: 21% in top tenth, 60% in top quarter, 100% in top half
Early decision deadline: N/A, notification date: N/A
Early action deadline: N/A, notification date: N/A
Application deadline (fall): 3/15
Undergraduate student body: 2,489 full time, 99 part time; 43% male, 57% female; 0% American Indian, 0% Asian, 77% black, 0% Hispanic, 0% multiracial, 0% Pacific Islander, 0% white, 0% international; 37% from in state; 0% live on campus; 4% of students in fraternities, 6% in sororities
Most popular majors: 11% Agriculture, Agriculture Operations, and Related Sciences, 7% Biology/Biological Sciences, General, 20% Engineering, 10% Psychology, General, 5% Registered Nursing, Nursing Administration, Nursing Research and Clinical Nursing
Expenses: 2015-2016: $21,535; room/board: $9,104
Financial aid: (334) 727-8201; 73% of undergrads determined to have financial need; average aid package $18,000

University of Alabama
Tuscaloosa AL
(205) 348-5666
U.S. News ranking: Nat. U., No. 96
Website: www.ua.edu
Admissions email: admissions@ua.edu
Public; founded 1831
Freshman admissions: more selective; 2014-2015: 33,736 applied, 17,221 accepted. Either SAT or ACT required. ACT 25/75 percentile: 22-31. High school rank: 41% in top tenth, 61% in top quarter, 83% in top half
Early decision deadline: N/A, notification date: N/A
Early action deadline: N/A, notification date: N/A
Application deadline (fall): rolling
Undergraduate student body: 27,737 full time, 3,015 part time; 46% male, 54% female; 0% American Indian, 1% Asian, 11% black, 3% Hispanic, 3% multiracial, 0% Pacific Islander, 78% white, 3% international; 50% from in state; 27% live on campus; 26% of students in fraternities, 40% in sororities
Most popular majors: 29% Business, Management, Marketing, and Related Support Services, 11% Communication, Journalism, and Related Programs, 7% Education, 7% Engineering, 8% Health Professions and Related Programs
Expenses: 2015-2016: $10,170 in state, $25,950 out of state; room/board: $9,030
Financial aid: (205) 348-2976; 43% of undergrads determined to have financial need; average aid package $12,431

University of Alabama–Birmingham
Birmingham AL
(205) 934-8221
U.S. News ranking: Nat. U., No. 149
Website: www.uab.edu
Admissions email: chooseuab@uab.edu
Public; founded 1969
Freshman admissions: more selective; 2014-2015: 5,710 applied, 4,893 accepted. Either SAT or ACT required. ACT 25/75 percentile: 21-27. High school rank: 28% in top tenth, 55% in top quarter, 83% in top half
Early decision deadline: N/A, notification date: N/A
Early action deadline: N/A, notification date: N/A
Application deadline (fall): rolling
Undergraduate student body: 8,472 full time, 3,207 part time; 42% male, 58% female; 0% American Indian, 5% Asian, 26% black, 3% Hispanic, 4% multiracial, 0% Pacific Islander, 59% white, 2% international; 91% from in state; 21% live on campus; 4% of students in fraternities, 4% in sororities
Most popular majors: 8% Biological and Biomedical Sciences, 19% Business, Management, Marketing, and Related Support Services, 9% Education, 20% Health Professions and Related Programs, 8% Psychology
Expenses: 2014-2015: $9,280 in state, $21,220 out of state; room/board: $10,112
Financial aid: (205) 934-8223; 62% of undergrads determined to have financial need; average aid package $9,148

University of Alabama–Huntsville
Huntsville AL
(256) 824-6070
U.S. News ranking: Nat. U., No. 187
Website: www.uah.edu
Admissions email: uahadmissions@uah.edu
Public; founded 1950
Freshman admissions: more selective; 2014-2015: 2,104 applied, 1,726 accepted. Either SAT or ACT required. ACT 25/75 percentile: 24-30. High school rank: 29% in top tenth, 54% in top quarter, 84% in top half
Early decision deadline: N/A, notification date: N/A
Early action deadline: N/A, notification date: N/A
Application deadline (fall): 8/19
Undergraduate student body: 4,304 full time, 1,314 part time; 57% male, 43% female; 1% American Indian, 4% Asian, 13% black, 4% Hispanic, 2% multiracial, 0% Pacific Islander, 70% white, 3% international; 90% from in

More at usnews.com/college

state; 21% live on campus; 8% of students in fraternities, 8% in sororities
Most popular majors: 9% Biological and Biomedical Sciences, 20% Business, Management, Marketing, and Related Support Services, 26% Engineering, 21% Health Professions and Related Programs, 3% Visual and Performing Arts
Expenses: 2015-2016: $9,128 in state, $20,622 out of state; room/board: $8,433
Financial aid: (256) 824-6241; 54% of undergrads determined to have financial need; average aid package $9,868

University of Mobile

Mobile AL
(251) 442-2273
U.S. News ranking: Reg. Coll. (S), No. 25
Website: www.umobile.edu
Admissions email: umadminfo@umobile.edu
Private; founded 1961
Affiliation: Southern Baptist
Freshman admissions: selective; 2014-2015: 1,009 applied, 590 accepted. Either SAT or ACT required. ACT 25/75 percentile: 20-24. High school rank: 18% in top tenth, 48% in top quarter, 76% in top half
Early decision deadline: N/A, notification date: N/A
Early action deadline: N/A, notification date: N/A
Application deadline (fall): 8/1
Undergraduate student body: 1,282 full time, 184 part time; 35% male, 65% female; 2% American Indian, 0% Asian, 21% black, 2% Hispanic, 2% multiracial, 0% Pacific Islander, 65% white, 4% international; 74% from in state; 49% live on campus; 0% of students in fraternities, 0% in sororities
Most popular majors: 15% Business, Management, Marketing, and Related Support Services, 22% Education, 21% Health Professions and Related Programs, 10% Liberal Arts and Sciences, General Studies and Humanities, 5% Theology and Religious Vocations
Expenses: 2015-2016: $19,970; room/board: $9,670
Financial aid: (251) 442-2385; 74% of undergrads determined to have financial need; average aid package $17,569

University of Montevallo

Montevallo AL
(205) 665-6030
U.S. News ranking: Reg. U. (S), No. 37
Website: www.montevallo.edu
Admissions email: admissions@montevallo.edu
Public; founded 1896
Freshman admissions: selective; 2014-2015: 1,821 applied, 1,353 accepted. Either SAT or ACT required. ACT 25/75 percentile: 20-26. High school rank: N/A
Early decision deadline: N/A, notification date: N/A
Early action deadline: N/A, notification date: N/A
Application deadline (fall): 8/1
Undergraduate student body: 2,361 full time, 304 part time; 34% male, 66% female; 1% American Indian, 1% Asian, 14% black, 3% Hispanic, 2% multiracial, 0% Pacific Islander, 73% white, 1% international; 95% from in state; 47% live on campus; 12% of students in fraternities, 17% in sororities
Most popular majors: Information not available
Expenses: 2015-2016: $11,410 in state, $22,780 out of state; room/board: $6,900
Financial aid: (205) 665-6050; 65% of undergrads determined to have financial need; average aid package $10,076

University of North Alabama

Florence AL
(256) 765-4608
U.S. News ranking: Reg. U. (S), No. 71
Website: www.una.edu
Admissions email: admissions@una.edu
Public; founded 1830
Freshman admissions: selective; 2014-2015: 2,765 applied, 1,877 accepted. Either SAT or ACT required. ACT 25/75 percentile: 19-25. High school rank: N/A
Early decision deadline: N/A, notification date: N/A
Early action deadline: N/A, notification date: N/A
Application deadline (fall): rolling
Undergraduate student body: 4,648 full time, 1,237 part time; 43% male, 57% female; 1% American Indian, 0% Asian, 14% black, 3% Hispanic, 2% multiracial, 0% Pacific Islander, 71% white, 4% international; 84% from in state; 22% live on campus; 11% of students in fraternities, 12% in sororities
Most popular majors: 17% Business, Management, Marketing, and Related Support Services, 7% Communication, Journalism, and Related Programs, 12% Education, 16% Health Professions and Related Programs, 6% Social Sciences
Expenses: 2014-2015: $9,073 in state, $16,393 out of state; room/board: $6,327
Financial aid: (256) 765-4278; 69% of undergrads determined to have financial need; average aid package $7,752

University of South Alabama

Mobile AL
(251) 460-6141
U.S. News ranking: Nat. U., second tier
Website: www.southalabama.edu/departments/admissions/index.html
Admissions email: recruitment@southalabama.edu
Public; founded 1963
Freshman admissions: selective; 2014-2015: 5,614 applied, 4,688 accepted. Neither SAT nor ACT required. ACT 25/75 percentile: 20-25. High school rank: N/A
Early decision deadline: N/A, notification date: N/A
Early action deadline: N/A, notification date: N/A
Application deadline (fall): 7/15
Undergraduate student body: 9,090 full time, 2,389 part time; 44% male, 56% female; 1% American Indian, 3% Asian, 24% black, 3% Hispanic, 2% multiracial, 0% Pacific Islander, 61% white, 4% international; 82% from in state; 29% live on campus; N/A of students in fraternities, N/A in sororities
Most popular majors: 4% Biology/Biological Sciences, General, 4% Elementary Education and Teaching, 4% Multi/Interdisciplinary Studies, General, 19% Registered Nursing/Registered Nurse, 4% Speech Communication and Rhetoric
Expenses: 2015-2016: $9,026 in state, $17,628 out of state; room/board: $8,266
Financial aid: (251) 460-6231

University of West Alabama

Livingston AL
(205) 652-3578
U.S. News ranking: Reg. U. (S), second tier
Website: www.uwa.edu
Admissions email: admissions@uwa.edu
Public; founded 1835
Freshman admissions: selective; 2014-2015: 1,014 applied, 730 accepted. Either SAT or ACT required. ACT 25/75 percentile: 19-23. High school rank: N/A
Early decision deadline: N/A, notification date: N/A
Early action deadline: N/A, notification date: N/A
Application deadline (fall): rolling
Undergraduate student body: 1,694 full time, 228 part time; 44% male, 56% female; 0% American Indian, 0% Asian, 41% black, 2% Hispanic, 1% multiracial, 0% Pacific Islander, 44% white, 6% international; 79% from in state; 47% live on campus; 11% of students in fraternities, 11% in sororities
Most popular majors: 8% Accounting, 13% Finance, General, 7% Kinesiology and Exercise Science, 10% Physical Education Teaching and Coaching, 9% Teacher Education, Multiple Levels
Expenses: 2014-2015: $8,018 in state, $14,886 out of state; room/board: $6,256
Financial aid: (205) 652-3576; 79% of undergrads determined to have financial need; average aid package $10,803

ALASKA

Alaska Pacific University

Anchorage AK
(800) 252-7528
U.S. News ranking: Reg. U. (W), No. 42
Website: www.alaskapacific.edu
Admissions email: admissions@alaskapacific.edu
Private; founded 1957
Affiliation: United Methodist
Freshman admissions: selective; 2014-2015: 328 applied, 138 accepted. Either SAT or ACT required. SAT 25/75 percentile: 950-1165. High school rank: N/A
Early decision deadline: N/A, notification date: N/A
Early action deadline: N/A, notification date: N/A
Application deadline (fall): rolling
Undergraduate student body: 215 full time, 111 part time; 37% male, 63% female; 18% American Indian, 3% Asian, 3% black, 4% Hispanic, 9% multiracial, 1% Pacific Islander, 53% white, 0% international
Most popular majors: 23% Business Administration and Management, General, 12% Liberal Arts and Sciences/Liberal Studies, 17% Parks, Recreation and Leisure Studies
Expenses: 2015-2016: $19,680; room/board: $7,000
Financial aid: (907) 564-8341; 61% of undergrads determined to have financial need; average aid package $9,714

University of Alaska–Anchorage

Anchorage AK
(907) 786-1480
U.S. News ranking: Reg. U. (W), No. 77
Website: www.uaa.alaska.edu
Admissions email: enroll@uaa.alaska.edu
Public; founded 1954
Freshman admissions: selective; 2014-2015: 3,533 applied, 2,838 accepted. Neither SAT nor ACT required. SAT 25/75 percentile: 880-1120. High school rank: 13% in top tenth, 33% in top quarter, 62% in top half
Early decision deadline: N/A, notification date: N/A
Early action deadline: N/A, notification date: N/A
Application deadline (fall): 7/1
Undergraduate student body: 7,485 full time, 8,978 part time; 42% male, 58% female; 7% American Indian, 8% Asian, 4% black, 7% Hispanic, 10% multiracial, 1% Pacific Islander, 57% white, 2% international; 91% from in state; N/A live on campus; N/A of students in fraternities, N/A in sororities
Most popular majors: 19% Business, Management, Marketing, and Related Support Services, 8% Engineering, 15% Health Professions and Related Programs, 8% Psychology, 6% Social Sciences
Expenses: 2015-2016: $5,490 in state, $19,470 out of state; room/board: $11,362
Financial aid: (907) 786-1586; 54% of undergrads determined to have financial need; average aid package $8,793

University of Alaska–Fairbanks

Fairbanks AK
(800) 478-1823
U.S. News ranking: Nat. U., second tier
Website: www.uaf.edu
Admissions email: admissions@uaf.edu
Public; founded 1917
Freshman admissions: selective; 2014-2015: 1,575 applied, 1,164 accepted. Either SAT or ACT required. ACT 25/75 percentile: 19-26. High school rank: 18% in top tenth, 40% in top quarter, 68% in top half
Early decision deadline: N/A, notification date: N/A
Early action deadline: N/A, notification date: N/A
Application deadline (fall): 6/15
Undergraduate student body: 3,491 full time, 4,072 part time; 42% male, 58% female; 13% American Indian, 1% Asian, 2% black, 5% Hispanic, 4% multiracial, 0% Pacific Islander, 43% white, 1% international; 86% from in state; 29% live on campus; N/A of students in fraternities, N/A in sororities
Most popular majors: 8% Biological and Biomedical Sciences, 14% Business, Management, Marketing, and Related Support Services, 18% Engineering, 6% Psychology, 6% Public Administration and Social Service Professions
Expenses: 2015-2016: $7,370 in state, $21,350 out of state; room/board: $8,242
Financial aid: (907) 474-7256; 55% of undergrads determined to have financial need; average aid package $7,745

University of Alaska–Southeast[1]

Juneau AK
(907) 465-6350
U.S. News ranking: Reg. U. (W), unranked
Website: www.uas.alaska.edu
Admissions email: admissions@uas.alaska.edu
Public
Application deadline (fall): N/A
Undergraduate student body: N/A full time, N/A part time
Expenses: 2014-2015: $5,901 in state, $16,705 out of state; room/board: $10,310
Financial aid: (907) 796-6255

ARIZONA

American Indian College[1]

Phoenix AZ
(800) 933-3828
U.S. News ranking: Reg. Coll. (W), unranked
Website: www.aicag.edu
Admissions email: aicadm@aicag.edu
Private
Application deadline (fall): N/A
Undergraduate student body: N/A full time, N/A part time
Expenses: 2014-2015: $11,700; room/board: $6,202
Financial aid: (800) 933-3828

Arizona State University–Tempe

Tempe AZ
(480) 965-7788
U.S. News ranking: Nat. U., No. 129
Website: www.asu.edu
Admissions email: admissions@asu.edu
Public; founded 1885
Freshman admissions: selective; 2014-2015: 22,581 applied, 19,042 accepted. Neither SAT nor ACT required. SAT 25/75 percentile: 1020-1270. High school rank: 30% in top tenth, 60% in top quarter, 89% in top half

Early decision deadline: N/A, notification date: N/A
Early action deadline: N/A, notification date: N/A
Undergraduate student body: 36,265 full time, 3,703 part time; 56% male, 44% female; 1% American Indian, 7% Asian, 4% black, 19% Hispanic, 4% multiracial, 0% Pacific Islander, 55% white, 9% international; 76% from in state; 23% live on campus; 9% of students in fraternities, 15% in sororities
Most popular majors: 9% Biological and Biomedical Sciences, 22% Business, Management, Marketing, and Related Support Services, 8% Engineering, 10% Social Sciences, 8% Visual and Performing Arts
Expenses: 2014-2015: $10,127 in state, $24,503 out of state; room/board: $10,010
Financial aid: (480) 965-3355; 56% of undergrads determined to have financial need; average aid package $14,002

Everest College–Phoenix[1]

Phoenix AZ
(888) 523-3117
U.S. News ranking: Reg. Coll. (W), unranked
Website: www.everestcollegephoenix.edu
Admissions email: N/A
For-profit
Application deadline (fall): N/A
Undergraduate student body: N/A full time, N/A part time
Expenses: 2014-2015: $12,204; room/board: $7,839
Financial aid: N/A

Frank Lloyd Wright School of Architecture[1]

Scottsdale AZ
(608) 588-4770
U.S. News ranking: Arts, unranked
Website: www.taliesin.edu/
Admissions email: N/A
Private
Application deadline (fall): 4/1
Undergraduate student body: N/A full time, N/A part time
Expenses: N/A
Financial aid: N/A

Grand Canyon University[1]

Phoenix AZ
(800) 800-9776
U.S. News ranking: Reg. U. (W), second tier
Website: https://apply.gcu.edu
Admissions email: golopes@gcu.edu
For-profit; founded 1949
Application deadline (fall): rolling
Undergraduate student body: N/A full time, N/A part time
Expenses: 2014-2015: $17,050; room/board: $8,550
Financial aid: (602) 639-6600

Northcentral University[1]

Prescott Valley AZ
(888) 327-2877
U.S. News ranking: Nat. U., unranked
Website: www.ncu.edu
Admissions email: admissions@ncu.edu
For-profit; founded 1996
Application deadline (fall): rolling
Undergraduate student body: N/A full time, N/A part time
Expenses: N/A
Financial aid: (928) 541-7777

Northern Arizona University

Flagstaff AZ
(928) 523-5511
U.S. News ranking: Nat. U., second tier
Website: www.nau.edu
Admissions email: undergraduate.admissions@nau.edu
Public; founded 1899
Freshman admissions: selective; 2014-2015: 27,780 applied, 25,153 accepted. Neither SAT nor ACT required. SAT 25/75 percentile: 930-1150. High school rank: 21% in top tenth, 50% in top quarter, 83% in top half
Early decision deadline: N/A, notification date: N/A
Early action deadline: N/A, notification date: N/A
Application deadline (fall): rolling
Undergraduate student body: 19,361 full time, 4,484 part time; 42% male, 58% female; 3% American Indian, 2% Asian, 3% black, 20% Hispanic, 5% multiracial, 0% Pacific Islander, 61% white, 5% international; 72% from in state; 29% live on campus; N/A of students in fraternities, N/A in sororities
Most popular majors: 18% Business, Management, Marketing, and Related Support Services, 13% Education, 11% Health Professions and Related Programs, 12% Liberal Arts and Sciences, General Studies and Humanities, 8% Social Sciences
Expenses: 2015-2016: $10,358 in state, $23,348 out of state; room/board: N/A
Financial aid: (928) 523-4951

Prescott College

Prescott AZ
(877) 350-2100
U.S. News ranking: Reg. U. (W), No. 83
Website: www.prescott.edu/
Admissions email: admissions@prescott.edu
Private; founded 1966
Freshman admissions: selective; 2014-2015: 573 applied, 388 accepted. Either SAT or ACT required. SAT 25/75 percentile: 890-1205. High school rank: N/A
Early decision deadline: 12/1, notification date: 12/15
Early action deadline: N/A, notification date: N/A
Application deadline (fall): 8/15
Undergraduate student body: 371 full time, 93 part time; 41% male, 59% female; 4% American Indian, 2% Asian, 2% black, 6% Hispanic, 4% multiracial, 0% Pacific Islander, 70% white, 1% international; 11% from in state; 16% live on campus; N/A of students in fraternities, N/A in sororities
Most popular majors: 26% Education, 6% Multi/Interdisciplinary Studies, 14% Natural Resources and Conservation, 9% Parks, Recreation, Leisure, and Fitness Studies, 15% Psychology
Expenses: 2015-2016: $27,505; room/board: $8,374
Financial aid: (928) 350-1111; 67% of undergrads determined to have financial need; average aid package $19,456

Southwest University of Visual Arts[1]

Tucson AZ
(800) 825-8753
U.S. News ranking: Arts, unranked
Website: suva.edu/
Admissions email: N/A
For-profit
Application deadline (fall): N/A
Undergraduate student body: N/A full time, N/A part time
Expenses: 2014-2015: $23,069; room/board: $12,660
Financial aid: N/A

University of Advancing Technology[1]

Tempe AZ
(602) 383-8228
U.S. News ranking: Reg. Coll. (W), unranked
Website: www.uat.edu
Admissions email: admissions@uat.edu
For-profit
Application deadline (fall): N/A
Undergraduate student body: N/A full time, N/A part time
Expenses: 2014-2015: $21,150; room/board: $8,480
Financial aid: (800) 658-5744

University of Arizona

Tucson AZ
(520) 621-3237
U.S. News ranking: Nat. U., No. 121
Website: www.arizona.edu
Admissions email: admissions@arizona.edu
Public; founded 1885
Freshman admissions: selective; 2014-2015: 32,723 applied, 24,417 accepted. Neither SAT nor ACT required. SAT 25/75 percentile: 970-1220. High school rank: 31% in top tenth, 57% in top quarter, 85% in top half
Early decision deadline: N/A, notification date: N/A
Early action deadline: N/A, notification date: N/A
Application deadline (fall): 5/1
Undergraduate student body: 29,529 full time, 3,458 part time; 48% male, 52% female; 1% American Indian, 6% Asian, 4% black, 25% Hispanic, 4% multiracial, 0% Pacific Islander, 53% white, 6% international; 72% from in state; 20% live on campus; 10% of students in fraternities, 19% in sororities
Most popular majors: 10% Biological and Biomedical Sciences, 16% Business, Management, Marketing, and Related Support Services, 6% Multi/Interdisciplinary Studies, 8% Psychology, 9% Social Sciences
Expenses: 2015-2016: $10,872 in state, $30,025 out of state; room/board: N/A
Financial aid: (520) 621-5200; 54% of undergrads determined to have financial need; average aid package $11,507

University of Phoenix[1]

Phoenix AZ
(866) 766-0766
U.S. News ranking: Nat. U., unranked
Website: www.phoenix.edu
Admissions email: N/A
For-profit
Application deadline (fall): N/A
Undergraduate student body: N/A full time, N/A part time
Expenses: N/A
Financial aid: N/A

Western International University

Tempe AZ
(602) 943-2311
U.S. News ranking: Reg. U. (W), unranked
Website: www.west.edu/
Admissions email: N/A
For-profit; founded 1978
Freshman admissions: N/A; 2014-2015: 8 applied, 8 accepted. Neither SAT nor ACT required. ACT 25/75 percentile: N/A. High school rank: N/A
Early decision deadline: N/A, notification date: N/A
Early action deadline: N/A, notification date: N/A
Application deadline (fall): rolling
Undergraduate student body: 1,036 full time, N/A part time; 37% male, 63% female; 2% American Indian, 1% Asian, 15% black, 17% Hispanic, 5% multiracial, 1% Pacific Islander, 48% white, 1% international
Most popular majors: 15% Accounting, 15% Behavioral Sciences, 45% Business/Commerce, General, 8% Information Technology, 12% Organizational Behavior Studies
Expenses: 2015-2016: $7,500; room/board: N/A
Financial aid: (602) 943-2311

ARKANSAS

Arkansas Baptist College[1]

Little Rock AR
(501) 244-5104
U.S. News ranking: Reg. Coll. (S), unranked
Website: www.arkansasbaptist.edu
Admissions email: jocelyn.spriggs@arkansasbaptist.edu
Private
Application deadline (fall): N/A
Undergraduate student body: N/A full time, N/A part time
Expenses: 2014-2015: $8,040; room/board: $7,256
Financial aid: (501) 374-0804

Arkansas State University

State University AR
(870) 972-3024
U.S. News ranking: Reg. U. (S), No. 53
Website: www.astate.edu
Admissions email: admissions@astate.edu
Public; founded 1909
Freshman admissions: selective; 2014-2015: 5,086 applied, 3,682 accepted. Either SAT or ACT required. ACT 25/75 percentile: 21-26. High school rank: 27% in top tenth, 49% in top quarter, 74% in top half
Early decision deadline: N/A, notification date: N/A
Early action deadline: N/A, notification date: N/A
Application deadline (fall): 8/24
Undergraduate student body: 7,465 full time, 2,392 part time; 43% male, 57% female; 0% American Indian, 1% Asian, 14% black, 2% Hispanic, 2% multiracial, 0% Pacific Islander, 74% white, 6% international; 90% from in state; 30% live on campus; 5% of students in fraternities, 5% in sororities
Most popular majors: 15% Business, Management, Marketing, and Related Support Services, 18% Education, 15% Health Professions and Related Programs, 10% Liberal Arts and Sciences, General Studies and Humanities, 7% Social Sciences
Expenses: 2014-2015: $7,720 in state, $13,480 out of state; room/board: $7,750
Financial aid: (870) 972-2310; 85% of undergrads determined to have financial need; average aid package $10,500

Arkansas Tech University

Russellville AR
(479) 968-0343
U.S. News ranking: Reg. U. (S), No. 87
Website: www.atu.edu
Admissions email: tech.enroll@atu.edu
Public; founded 1909
Freshman admissions: selective; 2014-2015: 4,162 applied, 3,590 accepted. Either SAT or ACT required. ACT 25/75 percentile: 18-25. High school rank: 13% in top tenth, 34% in top quarter, 64% in top half
Early decision deadline: N/A, notification date: N/A
Early action deadline: N/A, notification date: N/A
Application deadline (fall): rolling
Undergraduate student body: 7,028 full time, 4,071 part time; 45% male, 55% female; 1% American Indian, 1% Asian, 9% black, 5% Hispanic, 2% multiracial, 0% Pacific Islander, 78% white, 4% international; 95% from in state; 31% live on campus; 4% of students in fraternities, 7% in sororities
Most popular majors: 5% Business Administration and Management, General, 5% Crisis/Emergency/Disaster Management, 7% Early Childhood Education and Teaching, 21% Multi/Interdisciplinary Studies, Other, 9% Registered Nursing/Registered Nurse
Expenses: 2014-2015: $7,248 in state, $13,518 out of state; room/board: $6,734
Financial aid: (479) 968-0399; 68% of undergrads determined to have financial need; average aid package $8,760

Central Baptist College

Conway AR
(501) 329-6873
U.S. News ranking: Reg. Coll. (S), No. 71
Website: www.cbc.edu
Admissions email: admissions@cbc.edu

Private; founded 1952
Affiliation: Baptist Missionary Association of America
Freshman admissions: selective; 2014-2015: 492 applied, 283 accepted. Either SAT or ACT required. ACT 25/75 percentile: 19-23. High school rank: 12% in top tenth, 35% in top quarter, 63% in top half
Early decision deadline: N/A, notification date: N/A
Early action deadline: N/A, notification date: N/A
Application deadline (fall): rolling
Undergraduate student body: 664 full time, 194 part time; 53% male, 47% female; 3% American Indian, 0% Asian, 22% black, 3% Hispanic, 2% multiracial, 0% Pacific Islander, 67% white, 3% international; 84% from in state; 20% live on campus; 0% of students in fraternities, 0% in sororities
Most popular majors: 29% Bible/ Biblical Studies, 10% Business, Management, Marketing, and Related Support Services, Other, 9% General Studies, 13% Organizational Behavior Studies, 11% Psychology, General
Expenses: 2015-2016: $14,400; room/board: $7,500
Financial aid: (501) 329-6872; 79% of undergrads determined to have financial need; average aid package $11,431

Harding University

Searcy AR
(800) 477-4407
U.S. News ranking: Reg. U. (S), No. 22
Website: www.harding.edu
Admissions email: admissions@harding.edu
Private; founded 1924
Affiliation: Church of Christ
Freshman admissions: more selective; 2014-2015: 2,269 applied, 2,249 accepted. Either SAT or ACT required. ACT 25/75 percentile: 22-28. High school rank: 27% in top tenth, 55% in top quarter, 82% in top half
Early decision deadline: N/A, notification date: N/A
Early action deadline: 11/15, notification date: N/A
Application deadline (fall): rolling
Undergraduate student body: 4,158 full time, 334 part time; 45% male, 55% female; 1% American Indian, 1% Asian, 4% black, 3% Hispanic, 2% multiracial, 0% Pacific Islander, 83% white, 6% international; 31% from in state; 74% live on campus; 45% of students in fraternities, 49% in sororities
Most popular majors: 16% Business, Management, Marketing, and Related Support Services, 14% Education, 14% Health Professions and Related Programs, 8% Liberal Arts and Sciences, General Studies and Humanities, 9% Parks, Recreation, Leisure, and Fitness Studies
Expenses: 2015-2016: $17,670; room/board: $6,668
Financial aid: (501) 279-5278; 62% of undergrads determined to have financial need; average aid package $15,896

Henderson State University

Arkadelphia AR
(870) 230-5028
U.S. News ranking: Reg. U. (S), No. 87
Website: www.hsu.edu/admissions
Admissions email: admissions@hsu.edu
Public; founded 1890
Freshman admissions: selective; 2014-2015: 3,571 applied, 2,242 accepted. Either SAT or ACT required. ACT 25/75 percentile: 18-24. High school rank: 14% in top tenth, 36% in top quarter, 68% in top half
Early decision deadline: N/A, notification date: N/A
Early action deadline: N/A, notification date: N/A
Application deadline (fall): rolling
Undergraduate student body: 2,923 full time, 307 part time; 45% male, 55% female; 0% American Indian, 1% Asian, 24% black, 4% Hispanic, 5% multiracial, 0% Pacific Islander, 66% white, 1% international; 86% from in state; 46% live on campus; N/A of students in fraternities, N/A in sororities
Most popular majors: 16% Business, Management, Marketing, and Related Support Services, 19% Education, 11% Liberal Arts and Sciences, General Studies and Humanities, 8% Psychology, 7% Visual and Performing Arts
Expenses: 2014-2015: $7,561 in state, $13,921 out of state; room/ board: $6,500
Financial aid: (870) 230-5148; 83% of undergrads determined to have financial need; average aid package $11,778

Hendrix College

Conway AR
(800) 277-9017
U.S. News ranking: Nat. Lib. Arts, No. 82
Website: www.hendrix.edu
Admissions email: adm@hendrix.edu
Private; founded 1876
Affiliation: United Methodist
Freshman admissions: more selective; 2014-2015: 1,665 applied, 1,379 accepted. Either SAT or ACT required. ACT 25/75 percentile: 25-31. High school rank: 42% in top tenth, 76% in top quarter, 92% in top half
Early decision deadline: N/A, notification date: N/A
Early action deadline: 11/15, notification date: 12/15
Application deadline (fall): 6/1
Undergraduate student body: 1,339 full time, 9 part time; 45% male, 55% female; 2% American Indian, 6% Asian, 5% black, 5% Hispanic, 1% multiracial, 0% Pacific Islander, 78% white, 4% international; 50% from in state; 88% live on campus; 0% of students in fraternities, 0% in sororities
Most popular majors: 19% Biology/ Biological Sciences, General, 8% Foreign Languages, Literatures, and Linguistics, 7% Physical Sciences, 11% Psychology, General, 17% Sociology
Expenses: 2015-2016: $40,870; room/board: $11,244
Financial aid: (501) 450-1368; 61% of undergrads determined to have financial need; average aid package $30,702

John Brown University

Siloam Springs AR
(877) 528-4636
U.S. News ranking: Reg. Coll. (S), No. 2
Website: www.jbu.edu
Admissions email: jbuinfo@jbu.edu
Private; founded 1919
Affiliation: Interdenominational
Freshman admissions: more selective; 2014-2015: 1,201 applied, 837 accepted. Either SAT or ACT required. ACT 25/75 percentile: 22-29. High school rank: 30% in top tenth, 59% in top quarter, 85% in top half
Early decision deadline: N/A, notification date: N/A
Early action deadline: N/A, notification date: N/A
Application deadline (fall): rolling
Undergraduate student body: 1,565 full time, 666 part time; 44% male, 56% female; 2% American Indian, 1% Asian, 3% black, 6% Hispanic, 3% multiracial, 0% Pacific Islander, 76% white, 6% international; 43% from in state; 77% live on campus; 0% of students in fraternities, 0% in sororities
Most popular majors: 49% Business, Management, Marketing, and Related Support Services, 6% Education, 6% Engineering, 7% Family and Consumer Sciences/Human Sciences, 8% Visual and Performing Arts
Expenses: 2015-2016: $24,468; room/board: $8,664
Financial aid: (479) 524-7115; 70% of undergrads determined to have financial need; average aid package $18,043

Lyon College

Batesville AR
(800) 423-2542
U.S. News ranking: Nat. Lib. Arts, second tier
Website: www.lyon.edu
Admissions email: admissions@lyon.edu
Private; founded 1872
Affiliation: Presbyterian
Freshman admissions: more selective; 2014-2015: 1,952 applied, 1,199 accepted. Either SAT or ACT required. ACT 25/75 percentile: 22-27. High school rank: 24% in top tenth, 53% in top quarter, 85% in top half
Early decision deadline: N/A, notification date: N/A
Early action deadline: 10/31, notification date: 11/15
Application deadline (fall): rolling
Undergraduate student body: 689 full time, 22 part time; 54% male, 46% female; 1% American Indian, 2% Asian, 7% black, 6% Hispanic, 0% multiracial, 0% Pacific Islander, 74% white, 3% international; 73% from in state; 73% live on campus; 21% of students in fraternities, 32% in sororities
Most popular majors: 22% Biology/ Biological Sciences, General, 11% Business Administration and Management, General, 10% English Language and Literature, General, 7% Fine/Studio Arts, General, 14% Social Sciences, General
Expenses: 2015-2016: $25,280; room/board: $8,110
Financial aid: (870) 698-4257; 78% of undergrads determined to have financial need; average aid package $20,898

Ouachita Baptist University

Arkadelphia AR
(870) 245-5110
U.S. News ranking: Nat. Lib. Arts, No. 170
Website: www.obu.edu
Admissions email: admissions@obu.edu
Private; founded 1886
Affiliation: Arkansas Baptist State Convention
Freshman admissions: more selective; 2014-2015: 1,732 applied, 1,223 accepted. Either SAT or ACT required. ACT 25/75 percentile: 21-28. High school rank: 27% in top tenth, 55% in top quarter, 81% in top half
Early decision deadline: N/A, notification date: N/A
Early action deadline: N/A, notification date: N/A
Application deadline (fall): rolling
Undergraduate student body: 1,452 full time, 49 part time; 49% male, 51% female; 1% American Indian, 1% Asian, 8% black, 4% Hispanic, 0% multiracial, 0% Pacific Islander, 84% white, 2% international; 64% from in state; 94% live on campus; 20% of students in fraternities, 30% in sororities
Most popular majors: 13% Biological and Biomedical Sciences, 18% Business, Management, Marketing, and Related Support Services, 8% Education, 10% Theology and Religious Vocations, 11% Visual and Performing Arts
Expenses: 2015-2016: $24,120; room/board: $7,140
Financial aid: (870) 245-5570; 62% of undergrads determined to have financial need; average aid package $21,016

Philander Smith College

Little Rock AR
(501) 370-5221
U.S. News ranking: Reg. Coll. (S), No. 47
Website: www.philander.edu
Admissions email: admissions@philander.edu
Private; founded 1877
Affiliation: United Methodist
Freshman admissions: less selective; 2014-2015: 3,330 applied, 1,730 accepted. Either SAT or ACT required. ACT 25/75 percentile: 15-21. High school rank: 15% in top tenth, 32% in top quarter, 59% in top half
Early decision deadline: N/A, notification date: N/A
Early action deadline: N/A, notification date: N/A
Application deadline (fall): 7/1
Undergraduate student body: 521 full time, 46 part time; 36% male, 64% female; 0% American Indian, 1% Asian, 90% black, 0% Hispanic, 2% multiracial, 0% Pacific Islander, 1% white, 6% international; 53% from in state; 40% live on campus; N/A of students in fraternities, N/A in sororities
Most popular majors: 13% Biological and Biomedical Sciences, 22% Business, Management, Marketing, and Related Support Services, 8% Education, 13% Public Administration and Social Service Professions, 14% Social Sciences
Expenses: 2015-2016: $12,414; room/board: $9,064
Financial aid: (501) 370-5350; 87% of undergrads determined to have financial need; average aid package $13,452

Southern Arkansas University

Magnolia AR
(870) 235-4040
U.S. News ranking: Reg. U. (S), second tier
Website: www.saumag.edu
Admissions email: muleriders@saumag.edu
Public; founded 1909
Freshman admissions: selective; 2014-2015: 2,502 applied, 1,787 accepted. Either SAT or ACT required. ACT 25/75 percentile: 18-24. High school rank: 18% in top tenth, 41% in top quarter, 71% in top half
Early decision deadline: N/A, notification date: N/A
Early action deadline: N/A, notification date: N/A
Application deadline (fall): 8/27
Undergraduate student body: 2,531 full time, 505 part time; 43% male, 57% female; 0% American Indian, 1% Asian, 29% black, 3% Hispanic, 0% multiracial, 0% Pacific Islander, 63% white, 3% international; 78% from in state; 53% live on campus; 1% of students in fraternities, 2% in sororities
Most popular majors: 20% Business, Management, Marketing, and Related Support Services, 17% Education, 13% Health Professions and Related Programs, 6% Homeland Security, Law Enforcement, Firefighting and Related Protective Services, 7% Psychology
Expenses: 2014-2015: $7,736 in state, $11,186 out of state; room/ board: $6,140
Financial aid: (870) 235-4023

University of Arkansas

Fayetteville AR
(800) 377-8632
U.S. News ranking: Nat. U., No. 129
Website: www.uark.edu
Admissions email: uofa@uark.edu
Public; founded 1871
Freshman admissions: more selective; 2014-2015: 18,984 applied, 11,777 accepted. Either SAT or ACT required. ACT 25/75 percentile: 23-28. High school rank: 26% in top tenth, 55% in top quarter, 86% in top half
Early decision deadline: N/A, notification date: N/A
Early action deadline: 11/1, notification date: 12/15
Application deadline (fall): 8/1

Undergraduate student body: 19,243 full time, 2,593 part time; 48% male, 52% female; 1% American Indian, 3% Asian, 5% black, 7% Hispanic, 3% multiracial, 0% Pacific Islander, 78% white, 3% international; 61% from in state; 25% live on campus; 21% of students in fraternities, 36% in sororities
Most popular majors: 20% Business, Management, Marketing, and Related Support Services, 7% Communication, Journalism, and Related Programs, 9% Engineering, 8% Health Professions and Related Programs, 9% Social Sciences
Expenses: 2015-2016: $8,522 in state, $23,320 out of state; room/board: $9,880
Financial aid: (479) 575-3806; 45% of undergrads determined to have financial need; average aid package $9,264

University of Arkansas–Fort Smith

Fort Smith AR
(479) 788-7120
U.S. News ranking: Reg. Coll. (S), second tier
Website: www.uafortsmith.edu/Home/Index
Admissions email: N/A
Public; founded 1928
Freshman admissions: selective; 2014-2015: 4,001 applied, 2,252 accepted. Either SAT or ACT required. ACT 25/75 percentile: 19-25. High school rank: N/A
Early decision deadline: N/A, notification date: N/A
Early action deadline: N/A, notification date: N/A
Application deadline (fall): rolling
Undergraduate student body: 4,581 full time, 2,242 part time; 44% male, 56% female; 3% American Indian, 5% Asian, 5% black, 9% Hispanic, 5% multiracial, 0% Pacific Islander, 72% white, 2% international; 86% from in state; 13% live on campus; N/A of students in fraternities, N/A in sororities
Most popular majors: 8% Business Administration and Management, General, 7% Criminal Justice/Law Enforcement Administration, 9% Early Childhood Education and Teaching, 12% Multi/Interdisciplinary Studies, Other, 8% Registered Nursing/Registered Nurse
Expenses: 2014-2015: $4,727 in state, $10,511 out of state; room/board: $8,077
Financial aid: (479) 788-7090

University of Arkansas–Little Rock

Little Rock AR
(501) 569-3127
U.S. News ranking: Nat. U., second tier
Website: www.ualr.edu/
Admissions email: admissions@ualr.edu
Public; founded 1927
Freshman admissions: selective; 2014-2015: 1,204 applied, 747 accepted. Either SAT or ACT required. Average composite ACT score: 22. High school rank: N/A
Early decision deadline: N/A, notification date: N/A
Early action deadline: N/A, notification date: N/A
Application deadline (fall): 8/1
Undergraduate student body: 4,921 full time, 4,463 part time; 41% male, 59% female; 0% American Indian, 2% Asian, 27% black, 7% Hispanic, 8% multiracial, 0% Pacific Islander, 53% white, 3% international; 98% from in state; 2% live on campus; 3% of students in fraternities, 2% in sororities
Most popular majors: 16% Business, Management, Marketing, and Related Support Services, 16% Health Professions and Related Programs, 6% Homeland Security, Law Enforcement, Firefighting and Related Protective Services, 5% Liberal Arts and Sciences, General Studies and Humanities, 6% Psychology
Expenses: 2015-2016: $8,165 in state, $19,235 out of state; room/board: $8,780
Financial aid: (501) 569-3035; 76% of undergrads determined to have financial need; average aid package $11,848

University of Arkansas–Monticello[1]

Monticello AR
(870) 460-1026
U.S. News ranking: Reg. U. (S), unranked
Website: www.uamont.edu
Admissions email: admissions@uamont.edu
Public
Application deadline (fall): N/A
Undergraduate student body: N/A full time, N/A part time
Expenses: 2014-2015: $6,082 in state, $12,052 out of state; room/board: $5,994
Financial aid: (870) 460-1050

University of Arkansas–Pine Bluff

Pine Bluff AR
(870) 575-8492
U.S. News ranking: Reg. Coll. (S), No. 45
Website: www.uapb.edu/
Admissions email: jonesm@uapb.edu
Public; founded 1873
Freshman admissions: less selective; 2014-2015: 3,508 applied, 1,357 accepted. Either SAT or ACT required. ACT 25/75 percentile: 16-21. High school rank: 15% in top tenth, 31% in top quarter, 64% in top half
Early decision deadline: N/A, notification date: N/A
Early action deadline: N/A, notification date: N/A
Application deadline (fall): rolling
Undergraduate student body: 2,188 full time, 213 part time; 46% male, 54% female; 0% American Indian, 0% Asian, 93% black, 1% Hispanic, 0% multiracial, 0% Pacific Islander, 4% white, 1% international; 38% from in state; 43% live on campus; 25% of students in fraternities, 25% in sororities
Most popular majors: 11% Biology/Biological Sciences, General, 11% Business Administration and Management, General, 11% Criminal Justice/Safety Studies, 12% General Studies, 9% Industrial Technology/Technician
Expenses: 2014-2015: $5,956 in state, $11,626 out of state; room/board: $7,200
Financial aid: (870) 575-8302; 93% of undergrads determined to have financial need; average aid package $11,508

University of Central Arkansas

Conway AR
(501) 450-3128
U.S. News ranking: Reg. U. (S), No. 68
Website: www.uca.edu
Admissions email: admissions@uca.edu
Public; founded 1907
Freshman admissions: selective; 2014-2015: 5,160 applied, 4,864 accepted. Either SAT or ACT required. ACT 25/75 percentile: 20-26. High school rank: 17% in top tenth, 43% in top quarter, 75% in top half
Early decision deadline: N/A, notification date: N/A
Early action deadline: N/A, notification date: N/A
Application deadline (fall): rolling
Undergraduate student body: 8,172 full time, 1,670 part time; 42% male, 58% female; 0% American Indian, 2% Asian, 20% black, 4% Hispanic, 3% multiracial, 0% Pacific Islander, 65% white, 4% international; 91% from in state; 51% live on campus; 23% of students in fraternities, 23% in sororities
Most popular majors: 5% Biology/Biological Sciences, General, 4% Community Health Services/Liaison/Counseling, 7% Health Professions and Related Clinical Sciences, Other, 6% Kindergarten/Preschool Education and Teaching, 4% Registered Nursing/Registered Nurse
Expenses: 2015-2016: $7,889 in state, $13,806 out of state; room/board: $5,778
Financial aid: (501) 450-3140

University of the Ozarks

Clarksville AR
(479) 979-1227
U.S. News ranking: Reg. Coll. (S), No. 8
Website: www.ozarks.edu
Admissions email: admiss@ozarks.edu
Private; founded 1834
Affiliation: Presbyterian
Freshman admissions: selective; 2014-2015: 668 applied, 594 accepted. Either SAT or ACT required. ACT 25/75 percentile: 20-26. High school rank: 23% in top tenth, 47% in top quarter, 82% in top half
Early decision deadline: N/A, notification date: N/A
Early action deadline: N/A, notification date: N/A
Application deadline (fall): rolling
Undergraduate student body: 570 full time, 17 part time; 48% male, 52% female; 1% American Indian, 0% Asian, 6% black, 15% Hispanic, 4% multiracial, 0% Pacific Islander, 67% white, 6% international; 72% from in state; 75% live on campus; 0% of students in fraternities, 0% in sororities
Most popular majors: 8% Biology/Biological Sciences, General, 15% Business Administration and Management, General, 13% Early Childhood Education and Teaching, 10% Marketing/Marketing Management, General, 10% Physical Education Teaching and Coaching
Expenses: 2015-2016: $24,440; room/board: $7,100
Financial aid: (479) 979-1221; 73% of undergrads determined to have financial need; average aid package $24,452

Williams Baptist College

Walnut Ridge AR
(800) 722-4434
U.S. News ranking: Reg. Coll. (S), No. 51
Website: www.williamsbaptistcollege.com
Admissions email: admissions@wbcoll.edu
Private; founded 1941
Affiliation: Southern Baptist Convention
Freshman admissions: selective; 2014-2015: 619 applied, 412 accepted. Either SAT or ACT required. ACT 25/75 percentile: 20-25. High school rank: N/A
Early decision deadline: N/A, notification date: N/A
Early action deadline: N/A, notification date: N/A
Application deadline (fall): rolling
Undergraduate student body: 495 full time, 65 part time; 46% male, 54% female; 1% American Indian, 0% Asian, 9% black, 2% Hispanic, 0% multiracial, 0% Pacific Islander, 86% white, 2% international
Most popular majors: 9% Bible/Biblical Studies, 13% Business Administration and Management, General, 14% Elementary Education and Teaching, 15% Liberal Arts and Sciences/Liberal Studies, 20% Psychology, General
Expenses: 2015-2016: $16,430; room/board: $7,000
Financial aid: (870) 759-4112; 70% of undergrads determined to have financial need; average aid package $17,732

CALIFORNIA

Academy of Art University

San Francisco CA
(800) 544-2787
U.S. News ranking: Arts, unranked
Website: www.academyart.edu/
Admissions email: admissions@academyart.edu
For-profit; founded 1929
Freshman admissions: N/A; 2014-2015: 2,852 applied, 2,852 accepted. Neither SAT nor ACT required. ACT 25/75 percentile: N/A. High school rank: N/A
Early decision deadline: N/A, notification date: N/A
Early action deadline: N/A, notification date: N/A
Application deadline (fall): rolling
Undergraduate student body: 5,622 full time, 4,422 part time; 43% male, 57% female; 1% American Indian, 8% Asian, 7% black, 11% Hispanic, 2% multiracial, 1% Pacific Islander, 24% white, 25% international; 60% from in state; 14% live on campus; N/A of students in fraternities, N/A in sororities
Most popular majors: 15% Animation, Interactive Technology, Video Graphics and Special Effects, 9% Cinematography and Film/Video Production, 17% Fashion/Apparel Design, 8% Illustration, 7% Photography
Expenses: 2015-2016: $25,350; room/board: $14,160
Financial aid: (415) 274-2223; 43% of undergrads determined to have financial need; average aid package $10,819

Alliant International University

San Diego CA
(858) 635-4772
U.S. News ranking: Nat. U., unranked
Website: www.alliant.edu
Admissions email: admissions@alliant.edu
Private; founded 1969
Freshman admissions: N/A; 2014-2015: N/A applied, N/A accepted. Neither SAT nor ACT required. ACT 25/75 percentile: N/A. High school rank: N/A
Early decision deadline: N/A, notification date: N/A
Early action deadline: N/A, notification date: N/A
Application deadline (fall): rolling
Undergraduate student body: 189 full time, 1,261 part time; 48% male, 52% female; 1% American Indian, 2% Asian, 11% black, 34% Hispanic, 2% multiracial, 0% Pacific Islander, 22% white, 25% international; 100% from in state; 30% live on campus; 0% of students in fraternities, 0% in sororities
Most popular majors: Information not available
Expenses: 2014-2015: $19,930; room/board: $7,790
Financial aid: (858) 635-4700

American Jewish University

Bel-Air CA
(310) 440-1247
U.S. News ranking: Nat. Lib. Arts, second tier
Website: www.aju.edu
Admissions email: admissions@aju.edu
Private; founded 1947
Affiliation: Jewish
Freshman admissions: selective; 2014-2015: 92 applied, 53 accepted. Neither SAT nor ACT required. ACT 25/75 percentile: 16-27. High school rank: N/A
Early decision deadline: N/A, notification date: N/A
Early action deadline: 11/15, notification date: 12/15
Application deadline (fall): rolling
Undergraduate student body: N/A full time, N/A part time; N/A male, N/A female; N/A American Indian, N/A Asian, N/A black, N/A Hispanic, N/A multiracial, N/A Pacific Islander, N/A white, N/A international
Most popular majors: Information not available
Expenses: 2015-2016: $29,606; room/board: $15,706
Financial aid: (310) 476-9777; 63% of undergrads determined to have financial need; average aid package $29,132

More at usnews.com/college

Argosy University[1]
Orange CA
(800) 377-0617
U.S. News ranking: Nat. U., unranked
Website: www.argosy.edu/
Admissions email: N/A
For-profit
Application deadline (fall): N/A
Undergraduate student body: N/A full time, N/A part time
Expenses: 2014-2015: $13,663; room/board: $10,016
Financial aid: (714) 620-3687

Art Center College of Design
Pasadena CA
(626) 396-2373
U.S. News ranking: Arts, unranked
Website: www.artcenter.edu
Admissions email: admissions@artcenter.edu
Private; founded 1930
Freshman admissions: N/A; 2014-2015: 534 applied, 432 accepted. Neither SAT nor ACT required. ACT 25/75 percentile: N/A. High school rank: N/A
Early decision deadline: N/A, notification date: N/A
Early action deadline: N/A, notification date: N/A
Application deadline (fall): rolling
Undergraduate student body: 1,578 full time, 246 part time; 50% male, 50% female; 0% American Indian, 35% Asian, 1% black, 11% Hispanic, 4% multiracial, 0% Pacific Islander, 20% white, 27% international; 100% from in state; 0% live on campus; 0% of students in fraternities, 0% in sororities
Most popular majors: 100% Visual and Performing Arts
Expenses: 2014-2015: $37,830; room/board: N/A
Financial aid: (626) 396-2215

Ashford University[1]
San Diego CA
(563) 242-4153
U.S. News ranking: Reg. U. (W), unranked
Website: www.ashford.edu
Admissions email: admissions@ashford.edu
For-profit
Application deadline (fall): N/A
Undergraduate student body: N/A full time, N/A part time
Expenses: 2014-2015: $10,480; room/board: $6,300
Financial aid: (563) 242-4023

Azusa Pacific University
Azusa CA
(800) 825-5278
U.S. News ranking: Nat. U., No. 175
Website: www.apu.edu
Admissions email: admissions@apu.edu
Private; founded 1899
Affiliation: Christian interdenominational
Freshman admissions: selective; 2014-2015: 5,202 applied, 4,257 accepted. Either SAT or ACT required. SAT 25/75 percentile: 980-1080. High school rank: 25% in top tenth, 55% in top quarter, 86% in top half
Early decision deadline: N/A, notification date: N/A
Early action deadline: 11/15, notification date: 1/15
Application deadline (fall): 6/1
Undergraduate student body: 5,400 full time, 518 part time; 35% male, 65% female; 0% American Indian, 9% Asian, 4% black, 26% Hispanic, 7% multiracial, 1% Pacific Islander, 47% white, 2% international; 82% from in state; 57% live on campus; 0% of students in fraternities, 0% in sororities
Most popular majors: 23% Business, Management, Marketing, and Related Support Services, 20% Health Professions and Related Programs, 8% Liberal Arts and Sciences, General Studies and Humanities, 8% Psychology, 9% Visual and Performing Arts
Expenses: 2015-2016: $34,754; room/board: $9,218
Financial aid: (626) 815-6000

Biola University
La Mirada CA
(562) 903-4752
U.S. News ranking: Nat. U., No. 161
Website: www.biola.edu
Admissions email: admissions@biola.edu
Private; founded 1908
Affiliation: Christian, Interdenominational
Freshman admissions: selective; 2014-2015: 3,874 applied, 2,921 accepted. Either SAT or ACT required. SAT 25/75 percentile: 980-1240. High school rank: 30% in top tenth, 58% in top quarter, 88% in top half
Early decision deadline: N/A, notification date: N/A
Early action deadline: 11/15, notification date: 1/15
Application deadline (fall): rolling
Undergraduate student body: 4,268 full time, 105 part time; 37% male, 63% female; 0% American Indian, 16% Asian, 2% black, 18% Hispanic, 6% multiracial, 0% Pacific Islander, 52% white, 3% international; 78% from in state; 61% live on campus; 0% of students in fraternities, 0% in sororities
Most popular majors: 12% Business, Management, Marketing, and Related Support Services, 11% Communication, Journalism, and Related Programs, 9% Psychology, 11% Theology and Religious Vocations, 12% Visual and Performing Arts
Expenses: 2015-2016: $34,498; room/board: $10,224
Financial aid: (562) 903-4742; 68% of undergrads determined to have financial need; average aid package $18,900

Brandman University
Irvine CA
(877) 516-4501
U.S. News ranking: Reg. U. (W), unranked
Website: www.brandman.edu
Admissions email: apply@brandman.edu
Private; founded 1958
Freshman admissions: N/A; 2014-2015: 82 applied, 60 accepted. Neither SAT nor ACT required. ACT 25/75 percentile: N/A. High school rank: N/A
Early decision deadline: N/A, notification date: N/A
Early action deadline: N/A, notification date: N/A
Application deadline (fall): rolling
Undergraduate student body: 1,478 full time, 2,512 part time; 39% male, 61% female; 1% American Indian, 3% Asian, 10% black, 29% Hispanic, 4% multiracial, 1% Pacific Islander, 45% white, 0% international
Most popular majors: 10% Business Administration and Management, General, 8% Early Childhood Education and Teaching, 9% Liberal Arts and Sciences/Liberal Studies, 15% Organizational Behavior Studies, 18% Psychology, General
Expenses: 2015-2016: $12,240; room/board: N/A
Financial aid: (415) 575-6122; 73% of undergrads determined to have financial need; average aid package $27,168

California Baptist University
Riverside CA
(877) 228-8866
U.S. News ranking: Reg. U. (W), No. 39
Website: www.calbaptist.edu
Admissions email: admissions@calbaptist.edu
Private; founded 1950
Affiliation: California Southern Baptist Convention
Freshman admissions: less selective; 2014-2015: 4,211 applied, 3,355 accepted. Either SAT or ACT required. SAT 25/75 percentile: 840-1100. High school rank: 13% in top tenth, 40% in top quarter, 77% in top half
Early decision deadline: N/A, notification date: N/A
Early action deadline: 12/15, notification date: 1/31
Application deadline (fall): rolling
Undergraduate student body: 5,571 full time, 864 part time; 37% male, 63% female; 1% American Indian, 5% Asian, 8% black, 32% Hispanic, 5% multiracial, 1% Pacific Islander, 41% white, 2% international; 94% from in state; 39% live on campus; 0% of students in fraternities, 0% in sororities
Most popular majors: 8% Business/Commerce, General, 6% Kinesiology and Exercise Science, 7% Liberal Arts and Sciences/Liberal Studies, 10% Psychology, General, 10% Registered Nursing/Registered Nurse
Expenses: 2015-2016: $30,384; room/board: $8,060
Financial aid: (951) 343-4236; 85% of undergrads determined to have financial need; average aid package $16,344

California College of the Arts
San Francisco CA
(800) 447-1278
U.S. News ranking: Arts, unranked
Website: www.cca.edu
Admissions email: enroll@cca.edu
Private; founded 1907
Freshman admissions: N/A; 2014-2015: 1,547 applied, 1,277 accepted. Neither SAT nor ACT required. SAT 25/75 percentile: 950-1230. High school rank: N/A
Early decision deadline: N/A, notification date: N/A
Early action deadline: N/A, notification date: N/A
Application deadline (fall): rolling
Undergraduate student body: 1,479 full time, 63 part time; 38% male, 62% female; 0% American Indian, 16% Asian, 4% black, 13% Hispanic, N/A multiracial, 1% Pacific Islander, 29% white, 27% international; 66% from in state; 22% live on campus; 1% of students in fraternities, 0% in sororities
Most popular majors: 8% Architecture, 10% Graphic Design, 13% Illustration, 11% Industrial and Product Design, 10% Painting
Expenses: 2015-2016: $43,708; room/board: $9,050
Financial aid: (415) 703-9573; 60% of undergrads determined to have financial need; average aid package $27,460

California Institute of Integral Studies[1]
San Francisco CA
(415) 575-6100
U.S. News ranking: Nat. U., unranked
Website: www.ciis.edu
Admissions email: N/A
Private
Application deadline (fall): N/A
Undergraduate student body: N/A full time, N/A part time
Expenses: N/A
Financial aid: N/A

California Institute of Technology
Pasadena CA
(626) 395-6341
U.S. News ranking: Nat. U., No. 10
Website: www.caltech.edu
Admissions email: ugadmissions@caltech.edu
Private; founded 1891
Freshman admissions: most selective; 2014-2015: 6,525 applied, 576 accepted. Either SAT or ACT required. SAT 25/75 percentile: 1500-1600. High school rank: 100% in top tenth, 100% in top quarter, 100% in top half
Early decision deadline: N/A, notification date: N/A
Early action deadline: 11/1, notification date: 12/15
Application deadline (fall): 1/3
Undergraduate student body: 983 full time, N/A part time; 64% male, 36% female; 0% American Indian, 44% Asian, 2% black, 12% Hispanic, 6% multiracial, 0% Pacific Islander, 28% white, 9% international; 37% from in state; 85% live on campus; N/A of students in fraternities, N/A in sororities
Most popular majors: 13% Biological and Biomedical Sciences, 18% Computer and Information Sciences and Support Services, 36% Engineering, 11% Mathematics and Statistics, 22% Physical Sciences
Expenses: 2015-2016: $45,390; room/board: $13,371
Financial aid: (626) 395-6280; 50% of undergrads determined to have financial need; average aid package $41,669

California Institute of the Arts
Valencia CA
(661) 255-1050
U.S. News ranking: Arts, unranked
Website: www.calarts.edu
Admissions email: admiss@calarts.edu
Private; founded 1961
Freshman admissions: N/A; 2014-2015: 1,914 applied, 531 accepted. Neither SAT nor ACT required. ACT 25/75 percentile: N/A. High school rank: N/A
Early decision deadline: N/A, notification date: N/A
Early action deadline: N/A, notification date: N/A
Application deadline (fall): 1/5
Undergraduate student body: 961 full time, 9 part time; 42% male, 58% female; 0% American Indian, 13% Asian, 7% black, 13% Hispanic, 1% multiracial, 1% Pacific Islander, 39% white, 9% international
Most popular majors: Information not available
Expenses: 2014-2015: $42,276; room/board: $13,000
Financial aid: (661) 253-7869

California Lutheran University
Thousand Oaks CA
(877) 258-3678
U.S. News ranking: Reg. U. (W), No. 16
Website: www.callutheran.edu
Admissions email: admissions@callutheran.edu
Private; founded 1959
Affiliation: Lutheran
Freshman admissions: selective; 2014-2015: 6,490 applied, 3,958 accepted. Either SAT or ACT required. SAT 25/75 percentile: 1000-1200. High school rank: 23% in top tenth, 63% in top quarter, 92% in top half
Early decision deadline: N/A, notification date: N/A
Early action deadline: 11/1, notification date: 1/15
Application deadline (fall): 6/30
Undergraduate student body: 2,649 full time, 159 part time; 44% male, 56% female; 1% American Indian, 7% Asian, 4% black, 25% Hispanic, 3% multiracial, 1% Pacific Islander, 51% white, 4% international; 81% from in state; 51% live on campus; 0% of students in fraternities, 0% in sororities
Most popular majors: 8% Biological and Biomedical Sciences, 22% Business, Management, Marketing, and Related Support Services, 18% Communication, Journalism, and Related Programs, 11% Psychology, 8% Social Sciences
Expenses: 2015-2016: $38,430; room/board: $12,740
Financial aid: (805) 493-3115; 65% of undergrads determined to have financial need; average aid package $25,729

California Maritime Academy[1]
Vallejo CA
(707) 654-1330
U.S. News ranking: Reg. Coll. (W), No. 8
Website: www.csum.edu

Admissions email: admission@csum.edu
Public; founded 1929
Application deadline (fall): rolling
Undergraduate student body: N/A full time, N/A part time
Expenses: 2014-2015: $6,598 in state, $17,758 out of state; room/board: $11,610
Financial aid: (707) 654-1275

California Polytechnic State University–San Luis Obispo

San Luis Obispo CA
(805) 756-2311
U.S. News ranking: Reg. U. (W), No. 10
Website: www.calpoly.edu
Admissions email: admissions@calpoly.edu
Public; founded 1901
Freshman admissions: more selective; 2014-2015: 43,812 applied, 13,533 accepted. Either SAT or ACT required. SAT 25/75 percentile: 1130-1320. High school rank: 52% in top tenth, 85% in top quarter, 98% in top half
Early decision deadline: 10/31, notification date: 12/15
Early action deadline: N/A, notification date: N/A
Application deadline (fall): 11/30
Undergraduate student body: 18,578 full time, 668 part time; 54% male, 46% female; 0% American Indian, 12% Asian, 1% black, 15% Hispanic, 7% multiracial, 0% Pacific Islander, 59% white, 1% international; 88% from in state; 37% live on campus; N/A of students in fraternities, N/A in sororities
Most popular majors: 13% Agriculture, Agriculture Operations, and Related Sciences, 6% Biological and Biomedical Sciences, 13% Business, Management, Marketing, and Related Support Services, 26% Engineering, 6% Parks, Recreation, Leisure, and Fitness Studies
Expenses: 2015-2016: $9,000 in state, $20,160 out of state; room/board: $12,009
Financial aid: (805) 756-2927; 43% of undergrads determined to have financial need; average aid package $10,279

California State Polytechnic University–Pomona

Pomona CA
(909) 869-5299
U.S. News ranking: Reg. U. (W), No. 31
Website: www.cpp.edu
Admissions email: admissions@cpp.edu
Public; founded 1938
Freshman admissions: selective; 2014-2015: 32,801 applied, 17,014 accepted. Either SAT or ACT required. SAT 25/75 percentile: 930-1210. High school rank: N/A
Early decision deadline: N/A, notification date: N/A
Early action deadline: N/A, notification date: N/A
Application deadline (fall): 11/30
Undergraduate student body: 19,717 full time, 2,678 part time; 56% male, 44% female; 0% American Indian, 25% Asian, 3% black, 39% Hispanic, 4% multiracial, 0% Pacific Islander, 20% white, 5% international; 99% from in state; 11% live on campus; 2% of students in fraternities, 1% in sororities
Most popular majors: 23% Business Administration and Management, General, 4% Civil Engineering, General, 6% Hospitality Administration/Management, General, 4% Mechanical Engineering, 4% Psychology, General
Expenses: 2015-2016: $6,976 in state, $18,136 out of state; room/board: $15,238
Financial aid: (909) 869-3700; 68% of undergrads determined to have financial need; average aid package $10,714

California State University–Bakersfield

Bakersfield CA
(661) 654-3036
U.S. News ranking: Reg. U. (W), No. 83
Website: www.csub.edu
Admissions email: admissions@csub.edu
Public
Freshman admissions: less selective; 2014-2015: N/A applied, N/A accepted. Neither SAT nor ACT required. ACT 25/75 percentile: N/A. High school rank: N/A
Early decision deadline: N/A, notification date: N/A
Early action deadline: N/A, notification date: N/A
Undergraduate student body: 6,605 full time, 939 part time; 39% male, 61% female; 1% American Indian, 7% Asian, 6% black, 52% Hispanic, 3% multiracial, 0% Pacific Islander, 18% white, 3% international; 99% from in state; N/A live on campus; N/A of students in fraternities, N/A in sororities
Most popular majors: Information not available
Expenses: 2015-2016: $5,472 in state, $16,632 out of state; room/board: $10,926
Financial aid: (661) 654-3016; 70% of undergrads determined to have financial need; average aid package $4,245

California State University–Channel Islands[1]

Camarillo CA
(805) 437-8500
U.S. News ranking: Reg. U. (W), No. 87
Website: www.csuci.edu
Admissions email: N/A
Public
Application deadline (fall): N/A
Undergraduate student body: N/A full time, N/A part time
Expenses: 2014-2015: $6,521 in state, $17,681 out of state; room/board: $14,170
Financial aid: (805) 437-8530

California State University–Chico

Chico CA
(800) 542-4426
U.S. News ranking: Reg. U. (W), No. 42
Website: www.csuchico.edu
Admissions email: info@csuchico.edu
Public; founded 1887
Freshman admissions: selective; 2014-2015: 20,360 applied, 15,250 accepted. Either SAT or ACT required. SAT 25/75 percentile: 993-1100. High school rank: 35% in top tenth, 76% in top quarter, 100% in top half
Early decision deadline: N/A, notification date: N/A
Early action deadline: N/A, notification date: N/A
Application deadline (fall): 11/30
Undergraduate student body: 14,605 full time, 1,650 part time; 48% male, 52% female; 1% American Indian, 6% Asian, 2% black, 26% Hispanic, 5% multiracial, 0% Pacific Islander, 49% white, 4% international; 99% from in state; 1% live on campus; 1% of students in fraternities, 1% in sororities
Most popular majors: 16% Business, Management, Marketing, and Related Support Services, 10% Health Professions and Related Programs, 9% Parks, Recreation, Leisure, and Fitness Studies, 9% Social Sciences, 7% Visual and Performing Arts
Expenses: 2015-2016: $8,532 in state, $19,692 out of state; room/board: $11,626
Financial aid: (530) 898-6451; 64% of undergrads determined to have financial need; average aid package $16,090

California State University–Dominguez Hills

Carson CA
(310) 243-3300
U.S. News ranking: Reg. U. (W), second tier
Website: www.csudh.edu
Admissions email: info@csudh.edu
Public; founded 1960
Freshman admissions: least selective; 2014-2015: 8,257 applied, 6,691 accepted. Neither SAT nor ACT required. SAT 25/75 percentile: 760-940. High school rank: N/A
Early decision deadline: N/A, notification date: N/A
Early action deadline: N/A, notification date: N/A
Application deadline (fall): rolling
Undergraduate student body: 8,790 full time, 3,827 part time; 37% male, 63% female; 0% American Indian, 9% Asian, 15% black, 58% Hispanic, 3% multiracial, 0% Pacific Islander, 8% white, 3% international; 100% from in state; 5% live on campus; 1% of students in fraternities, 1% in sororities
Most popular majors: 20% Business, Management, Marketing, and Related Support Services, 13% Health Professions and Related Programs, 8% Liberal Arts and Sciences, General Studies and Humanities, 10% Psychology, 10% Social Sciences
Expenses: 2015-2016: $6,274 in state, $15,202 out of state; room/board: $12,790
Financial aid: (310) 243-3691; 76% of undergrads determined to have financial need; average aid package $6,278

California State University–East Bay

Hayward CA
(510) 885-2784
U.S. News ranking: Reg. U. (W), second tier
Website: www.csueastbay.edu
Admissions email: admissions@csueastbay.edu
Public; founded 1957
Freshman admissions: less selective; 2014-2015: 14,179 applied, 9,967 accepted. Neither SAT nor ACT required. SAT 25/75 percentile: 790-1010. High school rank: N/A
Early decision deadline: N/A, notification date: N/A
Early action deadline: N/A, notification date: N/A
Application deadline (fall): 11/30
Undergraduate student body: 10,663 full time, 1,579 part time; 38% male, 62% female; 0% American Indian, 24% Asian, 11% black, 29% Hispanic, 6% multiracial, 1% Pacific Islander, 19% white, 6% international; 99% from in state; N/A live on campus; N/A of students in fraternities, N/A in sororities
Most popular majors: 26% Business Administration and Management, General, 16% Health Services/Allied Health/Health Sciences, General, 6% Psychology, General, 10% Social Sciences, General, 5% Visual and Performing Arts, General
Expenses: 2015-2016: $6,564 in state, $17,724 out of state; room/board: $12,849
Financial aid: (510) 885-2784; average aid package $11,016

California State University–Fresno

Fresno CA
(559) 278-2191
U.S. News ranking: Reg. U. (W), No. 52
Website: www.csufresno.edu
Admissions email: tinab@csufresno.edu
Public; founded 1911
Freshman admissions: less selective; 2014-2015: 18,953 applied, 11,256 accepted. Either SAT or ACT required. SAT 25/75 percentile: 790-1010. High school rank: 15% in top tenth, 80% in top quarter, 100% in top half
Early decision deadline: N/A, notification date: N/A
Early action deadline: N/A, notification date: N/A
Application deadline (fall): 11/30
Undergraduate student body: 17,752 full time, 2,758 part time; 43% male, 57% female; 0% American Indian, 15% Asian, 4% black, 45% Hispanic, 3% multiracial, 0% Pacific Islander, 23% white, 4% international; 99% from in state; 5% live on campus; 6% of students in fraternities, 6% in sororities
Most popular majors: 13% Business, Management, Marketing, and Related Support Services, 13% Health Professions and Related Programs, 7% Homeland Security, Law Enforcement, Firefighting and Related Protective Services, 8% Liberal Arts and Sciences, General Studies and Humanities, 7% Psychology
Expenses: 2015-2016: $6,298 in state, $17,458 out of state; room/board: $10,604
Financial aid: (559) 278-2182; 76% of undergrads determined to have financial need; average aid package $12,478

California State University–Fullerton

Fullerton CA
(657) 278-7788
U.S. News ranking: Reg. U. (W), No. 37
Website: www.fullerton.edu
Admissions email: admissions@fullerton.edu
Public; founded 1957
Freshman admissions: selective; 2014-2015: 40,955 applied, 18,212 accepted. SAT required. SAT 25/75 percentile: 920-1130. High school rank: 24% in top tenth, 66% in top quarter, 96% in top half
Early decision deadline: N/A, notification date: N/A
Early action deadline: N/A, notification date: N/A
Application deadline (fall): 11/30
Undergraduate student body: 26,762 full time, 5,964 part time; 45% male, 55% female; 0% American Indian, 22% Asian, 2% black, 39% Hispanic, 4% multiracial, 0% Pacific Islander, 24% white, 5% international; 99% from in state; 6% live on campus; 2% of students in fraternities, 2% in sororities
Most popular majors: 24% Business, Management, Marketing, and Related Support Services, 9% Communication, Journalism, and Related Programs, 5% Family and Consumer Sciences/Human Sciences, 6% Parks, Recreation, Leisure, and Fitness Studies, 7% Psychology
Expenses: 2015-2016: $6,436 in state, $17,596 out of state; room/board: $13,510
Financial aid: (714) 278-3128; 81% of undergrads determined to have financial need; average aid package $13,500

California State University–Long Beach

Long Beach CA
(562) 985-5471
U.S. News ranking: Reg. U. (W), No. 32
Website: www.csulb.edu
Admissions email: N/A
Public; founded 1949
Freshman admissions: selective; 2014-2015: 56,357 applied, 20,326 accepted. Either SAT or ACT required. SAT 25/75 percentile: 940-1170. High school rank: N/A
Early decision deadline: N/A, notification date: N/A
Early action deadline: N/A, notification date: N/A
Application deadline (fall): 11/30
Undergraduate student body: 27,174 full time, 4,349 part time; 44% male, 56% female; 0% American Indian, 23% Asian, 4% black, 38% Hispanic, 5% multiracial, 0% Pacific Islander, 20% white, 6% international;

99% from in state; 9% live on campus; 3% of students in fraternities, 3% in sororities
Most popular majors: Information not available
Expenses: 2015-2016: $6,452 in state, $12,140 out of state; room/board: $11,880
Financial aid: (562) 985-8403; 77% of undergrads determined to have financial need; average aid package $13,662

California State University–Los Angeles

Los Angeles CA
(323) 343-3901
U.S. News ranking: Reg. U. (W), No. 63
Website: www.calstatela.edu
Admissions email: admission@calstatela.edu
Public; founded 1947
Freshman admissions: least selective; 2014-2015: 31,011 applied, 18,939 accepted. Neither SAT nor ACT required. SAT 25/75 percentile: 780-980. High school rank: N/A
Early decision deadline: N/A, notification date: N/A
Early action deadline: N/A, notification date: N/A
Application deadline (fall): 11/30
Undergraduate student body: 17,741 full time, 2,927 part time; 42% male, 58% female; 0% American Indian, 16% Asian, 4% black, 61% Hispanic, 2% multiracial, 0% Pacific Islander, 8% white, 6% international; 100% from in state; 5% live on campus; 2% of students in fraternities, 2% in sororities
Most popular majors: 20% Business, Management, Marketing, and Related Support Services, 10% Health Professions and Related Programs, 7% Homeland Security, Law Enforcement, Firefighting and Related Protective Services, 6% Psychology, 10% Social Sciences
Expenses: 2015-2016: $6,345 in state, $17,505 out of state; room/board: $12,833
Financial aid: (323) 343-1784; 84% of undergrads determined to have financial need; average aid package $11,764

California State University–Monterey Bay

Seaside CA
(831) 582-3738
U.S. News ranking: Reg. U. (W), No. 63
Website: www.csumb.edu
Admissions email: admissions@csumb.edu
Public; founded 1994
Freshman admissions: selective; 2014-2015: N/A applied, N/A accepted. Either SAT or ACT required. SAT 25/75 percentile: 860-1080. High school rank: 12% in top tenth, 43% in top quarter, 83% in top half
Early decision deadline: N/A, notification date: N/A
Early action deadline: N/A, notification date: N/A
Application deadline (fall): 11/30
Undergraduate student body: 5,783 full time, 451 part time; 38% male, 62% female; 1% American Indian, 6% Asian, 7% black, 35% Hispanic, 7% multiracial, 1% Pacific Islander, 35% white, 5% international; 98% from in state; 43% live on campus; 4% of students in fraternities, 3% in sororities
Most popular majors: Information not available
Expenses: 2014-2015: $5,963 in state, $17,123 out of state; room/board: $10,112
Financial aid: (831) 582-5100; 67% of undergrads determined to have financial need; average aid package $11,055

California State University–Northridge

Northridge CA
(818) 677-3700
U.S. News ranking: Reg. U. (W), No. 70
Website: www.csun.edu
Admissions email: admissions.records@csun.edu
Public; founded 1958
Freshman admissions: less selective; 2014-2015: 33,386 applied, 17,647 accepted. Either SAT or ACT required. SAT 25/75 percentile: 800-1030. High school rank: N/A
Early decision deadline: N/A, notification date: N/A
Early action deadline: N/A, notification date: N/A
Application deadline (fall): 11/30
Undergraduate student body: 29,341 full time, 6,275 part time; 46% male, 54% female; 0% American Indian, 11% Asian, 6% black, 42% Hispanic, 3% multiracial, 0% Pacific Islander, 24% white, 8% international; 97% from in state; N/A live on campus; N/A of students in fraternities, N/A in sororities
Most popular majors: Information not available
Expenses: 2015-2016: $6,525 in state, $17,685 out of state; room/board: $10,628
Financial aid: (818) 677-4085; 74% of undergrads determined to have financial need; average aid package $18,276

California State University–Sacramento

Sacramento CA
(916) 278-3901
U.S. News ranking: Reg. U. (W), No. 63
Website: www.csus.edu
Admissions email: outreach@csus.edu
Public; founded 1947
Freshman admissions: less selective; 2014-2015: 21,550 applied, 15,657 accepted. Neither SAT nor ACT required. SAT 25/75 percentile: 830-1050. High school rank: N/A in top tenth, N/A in top quarter, 100% in top half
Early decision deadline: N/A, notification date: N/A
Early action deadline: 11/30, notification date: N/A
Application deadline (fall): 11/30
Undergraduate student body: 21,276 full time, 5,372 part time; 44% male, 56% female; 1% American Indian, 21% Asian, 6% black, 23% Hispanic, 6% multiracial, 1% Pacific Islander, 34% white, 2% international; 99% from in state; 4% live on campus; 7% of students in fraternities, 5% in sororities
Most popular majors: 13% Business, Management, Marketing, and Related Support Services, 9% Communication, Journalism, and Related Programs, 8% Homeland Security, Law Enforcement, Firefighting and Related Protective Services, 8% Parks, Recreation, Leisure, and Fitness Studies, 10% Social Sciences
Expenses: 2015-2016: $6,648 in state, $17,808 out of state; room/board: N/A
Financial aid: (916) 278-6554; 75% of undergrads determined to have financial need; average aid package $10,808

California State University–San Bernardino

San Bernardino CA
(909) 537-5188
U.S. News ranking: Reg. U. (W), No. 69
Website: www.csusb.edu
Admissions email: moreinfo@csusb.edu
Public; founded 1962
Freshman admissions: less selective; 2014-2015: 12,951 applied, 8,372 accepted. Neither SAT nor ACT required. SAT 25/75 percentile: 790-990. High school rank: N/A
Early decision deadline: N/A, notification date: N/A
Early action deadline: N/A, notification date: 5/1
Application deadline (fall): rolling
Undergraduate student body: 14,769 full time, 1,907 part time; 39% male, 61% female; 0% American Indian, 6% Asian, 6% black, 58% Hispanic, 3% multiracial, 0% Pacific Islander, 16% white, 7% international; 99% from in state; 8% live on campus; 4% of students in fraternities, 5% in sororities
Most popular majors: 21% Business Administration and Management, General, 8% Health Professions and Related Programs, 7% Homeland Security, Law Enforcement, Firefighting and Related Protective Services, 13% Psychology, General, 10% Social Sciences
Expenses: 2015-2016: $6,577 in state, $17,737 out of state; room/board: $9,372
Financial aid: (909) 537-7800; 83% of undergrads determined to have financial need; average aid package $8,781

California State University–San Marcos

San Marcos CA
(760) 750-4848
U.S. News ranking: Reg. U. (W), No. 87
Website: www.csusm.edu
Admissions email: apply@csusm.edu
Public; founded 1989
Freshman admissions: less selective; 2014-2015: 10,728 applied, 9,102 accepted. Neither SAT nor ACT required. SAT 25/75 percentile: 860-1050. High school rank: N/A
Early decision deadline: N/A, notification date: N/A
Early action deadline: N/A, notification date: N/A
Undergraduate student body: 9,099 full time, 2,456 part time; 40% male, 60% female; 0% American Indian, 10% Asian, 3% black, 40% Hispanic, 5% multiracial, 0% Pacific Islander, 32% white, 2% international; 98% from in state; 99% live on campus; N/A of students in fraternities, N/A in sororities
Most popular majors: Information not available
Expenses: 2014-2015: $7,704 in state, $24,336 out of state; room/board: N/A
Financial aid: (760) 750-4850

California State University–Stanislaus

Turlock CA
(209) 667-3152
U.S. News ranking: Reg. U. (W), No. 57
Website: www.csustan.edu
Admissions email: Outreach_Help_Desk@csustan.edu
Public; founded 1957
Freshman admissions: less selective; 2014-2015: 6,265 applied, 4,555 accepted. Neither SAT nor ACT required. SAT 25/75 percentile: 810-1010. High school rank: N/A
Early decision deadline: N/A, notification date: N/A
Early action deadline: N/A, notification date: N/A
Application deadline (fall): 11/30
Undergraduate student body: 6,698 full time, 1,149 part time; 36% male, 64% female; 0% American Indian, 11% Asian, 2% black, 48% Hispanic, 4% multiracial, 1% Pacific Islander, 26% white, 3% international; 99% from in state; 8% live on campus; 6% of students in fraternities, 6% in sororities
Most popular majors: 20% Business Administration and Management, General, 9% Liberal Arts and Sciences/Liberal Studies, 13% Psychology, General, 12% Social Sciences, General
Expenses: 2015-2016: $6,700 in state, $17,860 out of state; room/board: $8,612
Financial aid: (209) 667-3336; 82% of undergrads determined to have financial need; average aid package $8,006

Chapman University

Orange CA
(888) 282-7759
U.S. News ranking: Reg. U. (W), No. 7
Website: www.chapman.edu
Admissions email: admit@chapman.edu
Private; founded 1861
Affiliation: Christian Church (Disciples of Christ)
Freshman admissions: more selective; 2014-2015: 12,507 applied, 5,883 accepted. Either SAT or ACT required. SAT 25/75 percentile: 1110-1290. High school rank: 42% in top tenth, 80% in top quarter, 95% in top half
Early decision deadline: N/A, notification date: N/A
Early action deadline: 11/1, notification date: 1/10
Application deadline (fall): 1/15
Undergraduate student body: 6,004 full time, 277 part time; 40% male, 60% female; 0% American Indian, 10% Asian, 1% black, 14% Hispanic, 6% multiracial, 0% Pacific Islander, 60% white, 4% international; 74% from in state; 32% live on campus; 28% of students in fraternities, 38% in sororities
Most popular majors: 17% Business Administration and Management, General, 10% Cinematography and Film/Video Production, 7% Psychology, General, 5% Public Relations/Image Management, 10% Speech Communication and Rhetoric
Expenses: 2015-2016: $47,234; room/board: $14,580
Financial aid: (714) 997-6741; 59% of undergrads determined to have financial need; average aid package $32,340

Claremont McKenna College

Claremont CA
(909) 621-8088
U.S. News ranking: Nat. Lib. Arts, No. 9
Website: www.claremontmckenna.edu
Admissions email: admission@cmc.edu
Private; founded 1946
Freshman admissions: most selective; 2014-2015: 6,043 applied, 651 accepted. Either SAT or ACT required. SAT 25/75 percentile: 1350-1520. High school rank: 78% in top tenth, 97% in top quarter, 100% in top half
Early decision deadline: 11/1, notification date: 12/15
Early action deadline: N/A, notification date: N/A
Application deadline (fall): 1/1
Undergraduate student body: 1,298 full time, 3 part time; 52% male, 48% female; 0% American Indian, 10% Asian, 4% black, 12% Hispanic, 8% multiracial, 0% Pacific Islander, 43% white, 17% international; 44% from in state; 97% live on campus; N/A of students in fraternities, N/A in sororities
Most popular majors: 13% Accounting, 27% Economics, General, 12% International Relations and Affairs, 14% Political Science and Government, General, 14% Psychology, General
Expenses: 2015-2016: $49,045; room/board: $15,280
Financial aid: (909) 621-8356; 39% of undergrads determined to have financial need; average aid package $42,538

Cogswell Polytechnical College[1]

Sunnyvale CA
(408) 541-0100
U.S. News ranking: Reg. Coll. (W), unranked
Website: www.cogswell.edu
Admissions email: info@cogswell.edu
Private; founded 1887
Application deadline (fall): rolling
Undergraduate student body: N/A full time, N/A part time

Expenses: 2014-2015: $16,160; room/board: $7,200
Financial aid: (408) 541-0100

Concordia University
Irvine CA
(949) 214-3010
U.S. News ranking: Reg. U. (W), No. 55
Website: www.cui.edu
Admissions email: admission@cui.edu
Private; founded 1972
Affiliation: Lutheran Church-Missouri Synod
Freshman admissions: selective; 2014-2015: 3,050 applied, 1,911 accepted. Either SAT or ACT required. SAT 25/75 percentile: 910-1150. High school rank: 15% in top tenth, 42% in top quarter, 80% in top half
Early decision deadline: N/A, notification date: N/A
Early action deadline: 12/1, notification date: 12/15
Application deadline (fall): rolling
Undergraduate student body: 1,760 full time, 158 part time; 36% male, 64% female; 0% American Indian, 6% Asian, 3% black, 18% Hispanic, 4% multiracial, 0% Pacific Islander, 46% white, 4% international; 89% from in state; 46% live on campus; N/A of students in fraternities, N/A in sororities
Most popular majors: 25% Business Administration and Management, General, 8% Communication, General, 6% Health and Physical Education/Fitness, General, 9% Psychology, General, 19% Registered Nursing/Registered Nurse
Expenses: 2015-2016: $31,690; room/board: $9,890
Financial aid: (949) 854-8002; 69% of undergrads determined to have financial need; average aid package $18,883

Dominican University of California
San Rafael CA
(415) 485-3204
U.S. News ranking: Reg. U. (W), No. 25
Website: www.dominican.edu
Admissions email: enroll@dominican.edu
Private; founded 1890
Freshman admissions: selective; 2014-2015: 2,076 applied, 1,680 accepted. Either SAT or ACT required. SAT 25/75 percentile: 940-1150. High school rank: 25% in top tenth, 57% in top quarter, 86% in top half
Early decision deadline: N/A, notification date: N/A
Early action deadline: N/A, notification date: N/A
Application deadline (fall): rolling
Undergraduate student body: 1,213 full time, 265 part time; 26% male, 74% female; 0% American Indian, 20% Asian, 4% black, 21% Hispanic, 4% multiracial, 1% Pacific Islander, 33% white, 1% international; 92% from in state; 32% live on campus; N/A of students in fraternities, N/A in sororities
Most popular majors: 12% Biological and Biomedical Sciences, 17% Business, Management, Marketing, and Related Support Services, 31% Health Professions and Related Programs, 7% Liberal Arts and Sciences, General Studies and Humanities, 11% Psychology
Expenses: 2014-2015: $41,730; room/board: $13,940
Financial aid: (415) 257-1321

Fashion Institute of Design & Merchandising
Los Angeles CA
(800) 624-1200
U.S. News ranking: Arts, unranked
Website: fidm.edu/
Admissions email: admissions@fidm.edu
For-profit; founded 1969
Freshman admissions: N/A; 2014-2015: 2,021 applied, 1,100 accepted. Neither SAT nor ACT required. SAT 25/75 percentile: N/A. High school rank: N/A
Early decision deadline: N/A, notification date: N/A
Early action deadline: N/A, notification date: N/A
Application deadline (fall): rolling
Undergraduate student body: 3,519 full time, 448 part time; 10% male, 90% female; 0% American Indian, 13% Asian, 5% black, 23% Hispanic, 3% multiracial, 1% Pacific Islander, 36% white, 12% international; 73% from in state; N/A live on campus; N/A of students in fraternities, N/A in sororities
Most popular majors: 86% Business, Management, Marketing, and Related Support Services, Other
Expenses: N/A
Financial aid: N/A

Fresno Pacific University
Fresno CA
(559) 453-2039
U.S. News ranking: Reg. U. (W), No. 37
Website: www.fresno.edu
Admissions email: ugadmis@fresno.edu
Private; founded 1944
Affiliation: Mennonite Brethren
Freshman admissions: selective; 2014-2015: 765 applied, 509 accepted. Either SAT or ACT required. SAT 25/75 percentile: 900-1110. High school rank: 31% in top tenth, 63% in top quarter, 93% in top half
Early decision deadline: N/A, notification date: N/A
Early action deadline: N/A, notification date: N/A
Application deadline (fall): 7/31
Undergraduate student body: 2,229 full time, 489 part time; 32% male, 68% female; 1% American Indian, 4% Asian, 5% black, 42% Hispanic, 2% multiracial, 1% Pacific Islander, 37% white, 2% international; 99% from in state; 17% live on campus; 0% of students in fraternities, 0% in sororities
Most popular majors: 22% Business, Management, Marketing, and Related Support Services, 25% Education, 16% Family and Consumer Sciences/Human Sciences, 8% Homeland Security, Law Enforcement, Firefighting and Related Protective Services, 9% Psychology
Expenses: 2015-2016: $27,854; room/board: $7,690
Financial aid: (559) 453-2027; 84% of undergrads determined to have financial need; average aid package $15,829

Golden Gate University[1]
San Francisco CA
(415) 442-7800
U.S. News ranking: Reg. U. (W), unranked
Website: www.ggu.edu
Admissions email: info@ggu.edu
Private; founded 1901
Application deadline (fall): rolling
Undergraduate student body: N/A full time, N/A part time
Expenses: 2014-2015: $14,640; room/board: $13,200
Financial aid: (415) 442-7270

Harvey Mudd College
Claremont CA
(909) 621-8011
U.S. News ranking: Nat. Lib. Arts, No. 14
Website: www.hmc.edu
Admissions email: admission@hmc.edu
Private; founded 1955
Freshman admissions: most selective; 2014-2015: 3,678 applied, 524 accepted. Either SAT or ACT required. SAT 25/75 percentile: 1418-1570. High school rank: 88% in top tenth, 99% in top quarter, 100% in top half
Early decision deadline: 11/15, notification date: 12/15
Early action deadline: N/A, notification date: N/A
Application deadline (fall): 1/1
Undergraduate student body: 802 full time, 2 part time; 54% male, 46% female; 0% American Indian, 21% Asian, 2% black, 10% Hispanic, 6% multiracial, 0% Pacific Islander, 44% white, 12% international; 42% from in state; 98% live on campus; 0% of students in fraternities, 0% in sororities
Most popular majors: 1% Biological and Biomedical Sciences, 27% Computer and Information Sciences and Support Services, 38% Engineering, 15% Mathematics and Statistics, 17% Physical Sciences
Expenses: 2014-2015: $48,594; room/board: $15,833
Financial aid: (909) 621-8055

Holy Names University
Oakland CA
(510) 436-1351
U.S. News ranking: Reg. U. (W), No. 50
Website: www.hnu.edu
Admissions email: admissions@hnu.edu
Private; founded 1868
Affiliation: Roman Catholic
Freshman admissions: less selective; 2014-2015: 489 applied, 279 accepted. Either SAT or ACT required. SAT 25/75 percentile: 785-980. High school rank: 6% in top tenth, 31% in top quarter, 76% in top half
Early decision deadline: N/A, notification date: N/A
Early action deadline: N/A, notification date: N/A
Application deadline (fall): rolling
Undergraduate student body: 615 full time, 138 part time; 35% male, 65% female; 1% American Indian, 15% Asian, 20% black, 31% Hispanic, 3% multiracial, 4% Pacific Islander, 21% white, 3% international; 92% from in state; 51% live on campus; N/A of students in fraternities, N/A in sororities
Most popular majors: 16% Business, Management, Marketing, and Related Support Services, 5% Communication, Journalism, and Related Programs, 36% Health Professions and Related Programs, 14% Psychology, 10% Social Sciences
Expenses: 2015-2016: $35,666; room/board: $12,072
Financial aid: (510) 436-1327; 87% of undergrads determined to have financial need; average aid package $29,708

Hope International University
Fullerton CA
(714) 879-3901
U.S. News ranking: Reg. Coll. (W), No. 20
Website: www.hiu.edu
Admissions email: admissions@hiu.edu
Private; founded 1928
Affiliation: Christian Churches/Churches of Christ
Freshman admissions: less selective; 2014-2015: 635 applied, 196 accepted. Either SAT or ACT required. SAT 25/75 percentile: 800-990. High school rank: 0% in top tenth, 4% in top quarter, 76% in top half
Early decision deadline: N/A, notification date: N/A
Early action deadline: N/A, notification date: N/A
Application deadline (fall): rolling
Undergraduate student body: 648 full time, 171 part time; 45% male, 55% female; 1% American Indian, 3% Asian, 6% black, 19% Hispanic, 12% multiracial, 1% Pacific Islander, 40% white, 0% international; 92% from in state; 46% live on campus; N/A of students in fraternities, N/A in sororities
Most popular majors: 19% Business Administration and Management, General, 16% Human Development and Family Studies, General, 17% Psychology, General, 9% Social Sciences, General, 27% Theological and Ministerial Studies, Other
Expenses: 2015-2016: $28,550; room/board: $9,050
Financial aid: (714) 879-3901; 87% of undergrads determined to have financial need; average aid package $15,340

Humboldt State University
Arcata CA
(707) 826-4402
U.S. News ranking: Reg. U. (W), No. 57
Website: www.humboldt.edu
Admissions email: hsuinfo@humboldt.edu
Public; founded 1913
Freshman admissions: selective; 2014-2015: 11,912 applied, 9,119 accepted. Neither SAT nor ACT required. SAT 25/75 percentile: 870-1100. High school rank: 13% in top tenth, 46% in top quarter, 80% in top half
Early decision deadline: N/A, notification date: N/A
Early action deadline: N/A, notification date: N/A
Application deadline (fall): 11/30
Undergraduate student body: 7,446 full time, 516 part time; 46% male, 54% female; 1% American Indian, 3% Asian, 4% black, 30% Hispanic, 6% multiracial, 0% Pacific Islander, 47% white, 1% international; 94% from in state; 25% live on campus; 2% of students in fraternities, 2% in sororities
Most popular majors: 11% Biological and Biomedical Sciences, 9% Liberal Arts and Sciences, General Studies and Humanities, 15% Natural Resources and Conservation, 9% Social Sciences, 8% Visual and Performing Arts
Expenses: 2015-2016: $7,164 in state, $18,324 out of state; room/board: $12,114
Financial aid: (707) 826-4321; 77% of undergrads determined to have financial need; average aid package $13,494

Humphreys College[1]
Stockton CA
(209) 478-0800
U.S. News ranking: Reg. Coll. (W), unranked
Website: www.humphreys.edu
Admissions email: ugadmission@humphreys.edu
Private
Application deadline (fall): N/A
Undergraduate student body: N/A full time, N/A part time
Expenses: 2014-2015: $12,456; room/board: $11,493
Financial aid: (209) 478-0800

John F. Kennedy University
Pleasant Hill CA
(925) 969-3330
U.S. News ranking: Reg. U. (W), unranked
Website: www.jfku.edu
Admissions email: proginfo@jfku.edu
Private; founded 1964
Freshman admissions: N/A; 2014-2015: N/A applied, N/A accepted. Neither SAT nor ACT required. ACT 25/75 percentile: N/A. High school rank: N/A
Early decision deadline: N/A, notification date: N/A
Early action deadline: N/A, notification date: N/A
Application deadline (fall): rolling
Undergraduate student body: 85 full time, 166 part time; 31% male, 69% female; 2% American Indian, 8% Asian, 16% black, 26% Hispanic, 4% multiracial, 1% Pacific Islander, 37% white, 3% international
Most popular majors: Information not available
Expenses: N/A
Financial aid: (925) 969-3385

More at usnews.com/college

Laguna College of Art and Design[1]
Laguna Beach CA
(949) 376-6000
U.S. News ranking: Arts, unranked
Website: www.lcad.edu/
Admissions email: admissions@lcad.edu
Private
Application deadline (fall): 8/1
Undergraduate student body: N/A full time, N/A part time
Expenses: 2015-2016: $28,100; room/board: N/A
Financial aid: (949) 376-6000

La Sierra University
Riverside CA
(951) 785-2176
U.S. News ranking: Reg. U. (W), No. 57
Website: www.lasierra.edu
Admissions email: admissions@lasierra.edu
Private; founded 1922
Affiliation: Seventh-day Adventist
Freshman admissions: less selective; 2014-2015: 4,707 applied, 1,913 accepted. Either SAT or ACT required. SAT 25/75 percentile: 800-1070. High school rank: 10% in top tenth, 24% in top quarter, 78% in top half
Early decision deadline: N/A, notification date: N/A
Early action deadline: N/A, notification date: N/A
Application deadline (fall): 7/1
Undergraduate student body: 1,899 full time, 220 part time; 42% male, 58% female; 0% American Indian, 15% Asian, 7% black, 43% Hispanic, 4% multiracial, 2% Pacific Islander, 15% white, 13% international; 93% from in state; 32% live on campus; 0% of students in fraternities, 0% in sororities
Most popular majors: 13% Biology/Biological Sciences, General, 7% Kinesiology and Exercise Science, 5% Liberal Arts and Sciences/Liberal Studies, 13% Marketing/Marketing Management, General, 6% Social Work
Expenses: 2015-2016: $30,471; room/board: $7,800
Financial aid: (909) 785-2175; 81% of undergrads determined to have financial need; average aid package $22,616

Loyola Marymount University
Los Angeles CA
(310) 338-2750
U.S. News ranking: Reg. U. (W), No. 3
Website: www.lmu.edu
Admissions email: admissions@lmu.edu
Private; founded 1911
Affiliation: Roman Catholic
Freshman admissions: more selective; 2014-2015: 12,117 applied, 6,387 accepted. Either SAT or ACT required. SAT 25/75 percentile: 1100-1300. High school rank: 36% in top tenth, 74% in top quarter, 96% in top half
Early decision deadline: N/A, notification date: N/A
Early action deadline: 11/1, notification date: 12/20
Application deadline (fall): 1/15
Undergraduate student body: 5,925 full time, 259 part time; 43% male, 57% female; 0% American Indian, 11% Asian, 6% black, 22% Hispanic, 8% multiracial, 0% Pacific Islander, 47% white, 7% international; 78% from in state; 53% live on campus; 22% of students in fraternities, 33% in sororities
Most popular majors: 7% Biology/Biological Sciences, General, 21% Business/Commerce, General, 14% Social Sciences, General, 8% Speech Communication and Rhetoric, 16% Visual and Performing Arts, General
Expenses: 2015-2016: $42,569; room/board: $14,470
Financial aid: (310) 338-2753; 57% of undergrads determined to have financial need; average aid package $28,400

Master's College and Seminary
Santa Clarita CA
(800) 568-6248
U.S. News ranking: Reg. Coll. (W), No. 3
Website: www.masters.edu
Admissions email: admissions@masters.edu
Private; founded 1927
Affiliation: Evangelical
Freshman admissions: selective; 2014-2015: 485 applied, 368 accepted. Either SAT or ACT required. SAT 25/75 percentile: 960-1200. High school rank: 29% in top tenth, 54% in top quarter, 79% in top half
Early decision deadline: N/A, notification date: N/A
Early action deadline: 11/15, notification date: 12/22
Application deadline (fall): rolling
Undergraduate student body: 992 full time, 145 part time; 52% male, 48% female; 0% American Indian, 7% Asian, 4% black, 10% Hispanic, 7% multiracial, 1% Pacific Islander, 61% white, 5% international; 73% from in state; 82% live on campus; N/A of students in fraternities, N/A in sororities
Most popular majors: 25% Bible/Biblical Studies, 21% Business, Management, Marketing, and Related Support Services, 13% Communication, Journalism, and Related Programs, 7% Liberal Arts and Sciences, General Studies and Humanities, 8% Visual and Performing Arts
Expenses: 2015-2016: $30,920; room/board: $10,060
Financial aid: (661) 259-3540; 78% of undergrads determined to have financial need; average aid package $21,665

Menlo College
Atherton CA
(800) 556-3656
U.S. News ranking: Reg. Coll. (W), No. 9
Website: www.menlo.edu
Admissions email: admissions@menlo.edu
Private; founded 1927
Freshman admissions: selective; 2014-2015: 3,935 applied, 1,773 accepted. Either SAT or ACT required. SAT 25/75 percentile: 898-1095. High school rank: N/A
Early decision deadline: N/A, notification date: N/A
Early action deadline: 11/15, notification date: 1/15
Application deadline (fall): 4/1
Undergraduate student body: 760 full time, 12 part time; 60% male, 40% female; 1% American Indian, 7% Asian, 7% black, 21% Hispanic, 8% multiracial, 2% Pacific Islander, 34% white, 13% international; 83% from in state; 60% live on campus; N/A of students in fraternities, N/A in sororities
Most popular majors: Information not available
Expenses: 2014-2015: $37,520; room/board: $12,260
Financial aid: (650) 543-3880

Mills College
Oakland CA
(510) 430-2135
U.S. News ranking: Reg. U. (W), No. 5
Website: www.mills.edu
Admissions email: admission@mills.edu
Private; founded 1852
Freshman admissions: selective; 2014-2015: 1,869 applied, 1,423 accepted. Either SAT or ACT required. SAT 25/75 percentile: 1020-1250. High school rank: 29% in top tenth, 64% in top quarter, 97% in top half
Early decision deadline: N/A, notification date: N/A
Early action deadline: 11/15, notification date: 12/15
Application deadline (fall): 3/1
Undergraduate student body: 875 full time, 42 part time; 0% male, 100% female; 1% American Indian, 11% Asian, 7% black, 23% Hispanic, 10% multiracial, 1% Pacific Islander, 45% white, 1% international; 76% from in state; 58% live on campus; 0% of students in fraternities, 0% in sororities
Most popular majors: 11% Area, Ethnic, Cultural, Gender, and Group Studies, 16% English Language and Literature/Letters, 9% Psychology, 20% Social Sciences, 10% Visual and Performing Arts
Expenses: 2015-2016: $44,002; room/board: $13,200
Financial aid: (510) 430-2000; 84% of undergrads determined to have financial need; average aid package $38,470

Minerva Schools at Keck Graduate Institute[1]
San Francisco CA
U.S. News ranking: Reg. Coll. (W), unranked
Website: www.minerva.kgi.edu
Admissions email: admissions@minerva.kgi.edu
Private
Application deadline (fall): N/A
Undergraduate student body: N/A full time, N/A part time
Expenses: N/A
Financial aid: N/A

Mount Saint Mary's University
Los Angeles CA
(310) 954-4250
U.S. News ranking: Reg. U. (W), No. 23
Website: www.msmu.edu
Admissions email: admissions@msmu.edu
Private; founded 1925
Affiliation: Roman Catholic
Freshman admissions: less selective; 2014-2015: 2,161 applied, 1,692 accepted. Either SAT or ACT required. SAT 25/75 percentile: 810-1020. High school rank: 14% in top tenth, 42% in top quarter, 83% in top half
Early decision deadline: N/A, notification date: N/A
Early action deadline: 12/1, notification date: 1/30
Application deadline (fall): 8/1
Undergraduate student body: 2,047 full time, 620 part time; 7% male, 93% female; 0% American Indian, 17% Asian, 7% black, 60% Hispanic, 2% multiracial, 1% Pacific Islander, 10% white, 0% international; 99% from in state; 22% live on campus; N/A of students in fraternities, 1% in sororities
Most popular majors: 10% Business, Management, Marketing, and Related Support Services, 33% Health Professions and Related Programs, 11% Psychology, 7% Public Administration and Social Service Professions, 18% Social Sciences
Expenses: 2015-2016: $35,944; room/board: $11,117
Financial aid: (310) 954-4191; 92% of undergrads determined to have financial need; average aid package $25,295

National Hispanic University[1]
San Jose CA
(408) 254-2772
U.S. News ranking: Nat. Lib. Arts, unranked
Website: www.nhu.edu
Admissions email: university@nhu.edu
For-profit
Application deadline (fall): N/A
Undergraduate student body: N/A full time, N/A part time
Expenses: 2014-2015: $8,196; room/board: $10,050
Financial aid: (408) 254-2708

National University
La Jolla CA
(800) 628-8648
U.S. News ranking: Reg. U. (W), unranked
Website: www.nu.edu
Admissions email: advisor@nu.edu
Private; founded 1971
Freshman admissions: N/A; 2014-2015: N/A applied, N/A accepted. Neither SAT nor ACT required. ACT 25/75 percentile: N/A. High school rank: N/A
Early decision deadline: N/A, notification date: N/A
Early action deadline: N/A, notification date: N/A
Application deadline (fall): rolling
Undergraduate student body: 3,798 full time, 5,923 part time; 43% male, 57% female; N/A American Indian, N/A Asian, N/A black, N/A Hispanic, N/A multiracial, N/A Pacific Islander, N/A white, N/A international
Most popular majors: 5% Accounting, 18% Business Administration and Management, General, 9% Early Childhood Education and Teaching, 12% Psychology, General, 13% Registered Nursing/Registered Nurse
Expenses: 2014-2015: $12,384; room/board: $10,216
Financial aid: (858) 642-8500

NewSchool of Architecture and Design[1]
San Diego CA
(619) 684-7081
U.S. News ranking: Arts, unranked
Website: newschoolarch.edu/
Admissions email: N/A
For-profit
Application deadline (fall): N/A
Undergraduate student body: N/A full time, N/A part time
Expenses: 2015-2016: $35,284; room/board: $18,276
Financial aid: N/A; 83% of undergrads determined to have financial need; average aid package $13,832

Notre Dame de Namur University
Belmont CA
(650) 508-3600
U.S. News ranking: Reg. U. (W), No. 39
Website: www.ndnu.edu
Admissions email: admissions@ndnu.edu
Private; founded 1851
Affiliation: Catholic
Freshman admissions: less selective; 2014-2015: 2,167 applied, 1,684 accepted. Either SAT or ACT required. SAT 25/75 percentile: 850-1040. High school rank: 13% in top tenth, 35% in top quarter, 76% in top half
Early decision deadline: N/A, notification date: N/A
Early action deadline: 12/1, notification date: 12/15
Application deadline (fall): rolling
Undergraduate student body: 806 full time, 372 part time; 33% male, 67% female; 1% American Indian, 12% Asian, 6% black, 37% Hispanic, 4% multiracial, 3% Pacific Islander, 25% white, 3% international; 94% from in state; 40% live on campus; N/A of students in fraternities, N/A in sororities
Most popular majors: 14% Biological and Biomedical Sciences, 20% Business, Management, Marketing, and Related Support Services, 16% Psychology, 12% Public Administration and Social Service Professions, 10% Social Sciences
Expenses: 2015-2016: $32,608; room/board: N/A
Financial aid: (650) 508-3600; 90% of undergrads determined to have financial need; average aid package $24,678

Occidental College
Los Angeles CA
(800) 825-5262
U.S. News ranking: Nat. Lib. Arts, No. 43
Website: www.oxy.edu
Admissions email: admission@oxy.edu
Private; founded 1887
Freshman admissions: more selective; 2014-2015: 6,071 applied, 2,552 accepted. Either SAT or ACT required. SAT 25/75 percentile: 1210-1390. High school rank: 55% in top tenth, 85% in top quarter, 99% in top half

Early decision deadline: 11/15, notification date: 12/15
Early action deadline: N/A, notification date: N/A
Application deadline (fall): 1/10
Undergraduate student body: 2,024 full time, 16 part time; 44% male, 56% female; 0% American Indian, 13% Asian, 4% black, 15% Hispanic, 9% multiracial, 0% Pacific Islander, 51% white, 6% international; 52% from in state; 81% live on campus; 13% of students in fraternities, 19% in sororities
Most popular majors: 8% Biology/ Biological Sciences, General, 16% Economics, General, 7% International Relations and Affairs, 7% Political Science and Government, General, 7% Psychology, General
Expenses: 2015-2016: $49,278; room/board: $13,946
Financial aid: (323) 259-2548; 57% of undergrads determined to have financial need; average aid package $43,221

Otis College of Art and Design

Los Angeles CA
(310) 665-6820
U.S. News ranking: Arts, unranked
Website: www.otis.edu
Admissions email: admissions@ otis.edu
Private; founded 1918
Freshman admissions: N/A; 2014-2015: 1,160 applied, 1,053 accepted. Either SAT or ACT required. ACT 25/75 percentile: 18-25. High school rank: N/A
Early decision deadline: N/A, notification date: N/A
Early action deadline: N/A, notification date: N/A
Application deadline (fall): rolling
Undergraduate student body: 1,080 full time, 13 part time; 33% male, 67% female; 1% American Indian, 29% Asian, 4% black, 10% Hispanic, 6% multiracial, 0% Pacific Islander, 24% white, 22% international
Most popular majors: Information not available
Expenses: 2015-2016: $41,854; room/board: $11,800
Financial aid: (310) 665-6880; 65% of undergrads determined to have financial need; average aid package $26,104

Pacific Union College

Angwin CA
(707) 965-6336
U.S. News ranking: Nat. Lib. Arts, second tier
Website: www.puc.edu
Admissions email: enroll@puc.edu
Private; founded 1882
Affiliation: Seventh-day Adventist
Freshman admissions: selective; 2014-2015: 2,051 applied, 973 accepted. Either SAT or ACT required. SAT 25/75 percentile: 860-1130. High school rank: N/A
Early decision deadline: N/A, notification date: N/A
Early action deadline: N/A, notification date: N/A
Application deadline (fall): rolling
Undergraduate student body: 1,459 full time, 181 part time; 44% male, 56% female; 0% American Indian, 18% Asian, 9% black, 27% Hispanic, 8% multiracial, 2% Pacific Islander, 28% white, 3% international; 86% from in state; 76% live on campus; N/A of students in fraternities, N/A in sororities
Most popular majors: 15% Biology/ Biological Sciences, General, 14% Business/Commerce, General, 7% Communication, General, 9% Early Childhood Education and Teaching, 19% Registered Nursing/Registered Nurse
Expenses: 2015-2016: $29,064; room/board: $7,695
Financial aid: (707) 965-7200; 80% of undergrads determined to have financial need; average aid package $24,107

Patten University[1]

Oakland CA
(877) 472-8836
U.S. News ranking: Reg. Coll. (W), unranked
Website: www.patten.edu/
Admissions email: Admissions@ patten.edu
Private
Application deadline (fall): N/A
Undergraduate student body: N/A full time, N/A part time
Expenses: N/A
Financial aid: (510) 261-8500

Pepperdine University

Malibu CA
(310) 506-4392
U.S. News ranking: Nat. U., No. 52
Website: www.pepperdine.edu
Admissions email: admission-seaver@pepperdine.edu
Private; founded 1937
Affiliation: Church of Christ
Freshman admissions: more selective; 2014-2015: 8,914 applied, 3,161 accepted. Either SAT or ACT required. SAT 25/75 percentile: 1120-1330. High school rank: 46% in top tenth, 80% in top quarter, 96% in top half
Early decision deadline: N/A, notification date: N/A
Early action deadline: N/A, notification date: N/A
Application deadline (fall): 1/5
Undergraduate student body: 3,129 full time, 322 part time; 41% male, 59% female; 0% American Indian, 13% Asian, 6% black, 13% Hispanic, 9% multiracial, 0% Pacific Islander, 45% white, 9% international; 59% from in state; 54% live on campus; 18% of students in fraternities, 31% in sororities
Most popular majors: 30% Business, Management, Marketing, and Related Support Services, 16% Communication, Journalism, and Related Programs, 6% Multi/Interdisciplinary Studies, 8% Psychology, 11% Social Sciences
Expenses: 2015-2016: $48,342; room/board: $13,810
Financial aid: (310) 506-4301; 56% of undergrads determined to have financial need; average aid package $40,757

Pitzer College

Claremont CA
(909) 621-8129
U.S. News ranking: Nat. Lib. Arts, No. 36
Website: www.pitzer.edu
Admissions email: admission@ pitzer.edu
Private; founded 1963
Freshman admissions: most selective; 2014-2015: 4,324 applied, 563 accepted. Neither SAT nor ACT required. SAT 25/75 percentile: 1240-1420. High school rank: 60% in top tenth, 99% in top quarter, 100% in top half
Early decision deadline: 11/15, notification date: 12/22
Early action deadline: N/A, notification date: N/A
Application deadline (fall): 1/1
Undergraduate student body: 1,038 full time, 38 part time; 42% male, 58% female; 0% American Indian, 6% Asian, 4% black, 15% Hispanic, 9% multiracial, 0% Pacific Islander, 50% white, 7% international; 45% from in state; 75% live on campus; 0% of students in fraternities, 0% in sororities
Most popular majors: 8% Economics, General, 10% Environmental Studies, 12% Multi/Interdisciplinary Studies, Other, 13% Psychology, General, 6% Sociology
Expenses: 2015-2016: $48,660; room/board: $15,210
Financial aid: (909) 621-8208; 34% of undergrads determined to have financial need; average aid package $40,250

Point Loma Nazarene University

San Diego CA
(619) 849-2273
U.S. News ranking: Reg. U. (W), No. 17
Website: www.pointloma.edu
Admissions email: admissions@ pointloma.edu
Private; founded 1902
Affiliation: Church of the Nazarene
Freshman admissions: selective; 2014-2015: 3,036 applied, 2,111 accepted. Either SAT or ACT required. SAT 25/75 percentile: 1010-1220. High school rank: 34% in top tenth, 67% in top quarter, 91% in top half
Early decision deadline: N/A, notification date: N/A
Early action deadline: 11/15, notification date: 12/21
Application deadline (fall): 2/15
Undergraduate student body: 2,493 full time, 75 part time; 36% male, 64% female; 1% American Indian, 5% Asian, 2% black, 22% Hispanic, 6% multiracial, 1% Pacific Islander, 62% white, 1% international; 83% from in state; 67% live on campus; N/A of students in fraternities, N/A in sororities
Most popular majors: 9% Biological and Biomedical Sciences, 21% Business, Management, Marketing, and Related Support Services, 17% Health Professions and Related Programs, 6% Parks, Recreation, Leisure, and Fitness Studies, 8% Psychology
Expenses: 2015-2016: $32,400; room/board: $9,800
Financial aid: (619) 849-2538; 69% of undergrads determined to have financial need; average aid package $21,589

Pomona College

Claremont CA
(909) 621-8134
U.S. News ranking: Nat. Lib. Arts, No. 4
Website: www.pomona.edu
Admissions email: admissions@ pomona.edu
Private; founded 1887
Freshman admissions: most selective; 2014-2015: 7,727 applied, 942 accepted. Either SAT or ACT required. SAT 25/75 percentile: 1380-1540. High school rank: 91% in top tenth, 99% in top quarter, 100% in top half
Early decision deadline: 11/1, notification date: 12/15
Early action deadline: N/A, notification date: N/A
Application deadline (fall): 1/1
Undergraduate student body: 1,634 full time, 16 part time; 49% male, 51% female; 0% American Indian, 13% Asian, 7% black, 14% Hispanic, 7% multiracial, 0% Pacific Islander, 43% white, 9% international; 31% from in state; 98% live on campus; 5% of students in fraternities, 0% in sororities
Most popular majors: 6% Biology/ Biological Sciences, General, 9% Economics, General, 6% Environmental Science, 10% Mathematics, General, 5% Neuroscience
Expenses: 2015-2016: $47,620; room/board: $15,150
Financial aid: (909) 621-8205; 56% of undergrads determined to have financial need; average aid package $47,119

San Diego Christian College[1]

El Cajon CA
(619) 588-7747
U.S. News ranking: Nat. Lib. Arts, second tier
Website: www.sdcc.edu/
Admissions email: admissions@ sdcc.edu
Private; founded 1970
Application deadline (fall): rolling
Undergraduate student body: N/A full time, N/A part time
Expenses: 2014-2015: $27,090; room/board: $10,100
Financial aid: (619) 590-1786

San Diego State University

San Diego CA
(619) 594-6336
U.S. News ranking: Nat. U., No. 149
Website: www.sdsu.edu
Admissions email: admissions@ sdsu.edu
Public; founded 1897
Freshman admissions: more selective; 2014-2015: 56,921 applied, 19,625 accepted. Either SAT or ACT required. SAT 25/75 percentile: 1000-1220. High school rank: 29% in top tenth, 77% in top quarter, 98% in top half
Early decision deadline: N/A, notification date: N/A
Early action deadline: N/A, notification date: N/A
Application deadline (fall): 11/30
Undergraduate student body: 25,088 full time, 3,274 part time; 45% male, 55% female; 0% American Indian, 13% Asian, 4% black, 31% Hispanic, 6% multiracial, 0% Pacific Islander, 35% white, 6% international; 93% from in state; 14% live on campus; 9% of students in fraternities, 10% in sororities
Most popular majors: 18% Business, Management, Marketing, and Related Support Services, 7% English Language and Literature/Letters, 7% Health Professions and Related Programs, 8% Psychology, 12% Social Sciences
Expenses: 2015-2016: $6,976 in state, $18,136 out of state; room/ board: $15,826
Financial aid: (619) 594-6323; 58% of undergrads determined to have financial need; average aid package $10,800

San Francisco Art Institute

San Francisco CA
(800) 345-7324
U.S. News ranking: Arts, unranked
Website: www.sfai.edu
Admissions email: admissions@ sfai.edu
Private; founded 1871
Freshman admissions: N/A; 2014-2015: 427 applied, 406 accepted. Neither SAT nor ACT required. SAT 25/75 percentile: 930-1110. High school rank: N/A
Early decision deadline: N/A, notification date: N/A
Early action deadline: N/A, notification date: N/A
Application deadline (fall): rolling
Undergraduate student body: 430 full time, 37 part time; 43% male, 57% female; 0% American Indian, 4% Asian, 2% black, 17% Hispanic, 8% multiracial, 0% Pacific Islander, 48% white, 18% international; 63% from in state; 27% live on campus; 0% of students in fraternities, 0% in sororities
Most popular majors: 8% Design and Visual Communications, General, 32% Painting, 36% Photography, 7% Sculpture, 5% Visual and Performing Arts, Other
Expenses: 2015-2016: $41,272; room/board: $11,500
Financial aid: (415) 749-4520

San Francisco Conservatory of Music

San Francisco CA
(800) 899-7326
U.S. News ranking: Arts, unranked
Website: www.sfcm.edu
Admissions email: admit@sfcm.edu
Private; founded 1917
Freshman admissions: N/A; 2014-2015: 330 applied, 123 accepted. Neither SAT nor ACT required. ACT 25/75 percentile: N/A. High school rank: N/A
Early decision deadline: N/A, notification date: N/A
Early action deadline: N/A, notification date: N/A
Application deadline (fall): 12/1
Undergraduate student body: 170 full time, 1 part time; 56% male, 44% female; 0% American Indian, 10% Asian, 2% black, 8% Hispanic, 9% multiracial, 1% Pacific Islander, 34% white, 28% international; 65% from in state; 46% live on campus; 0% of students in fraternities, 0% in sororities

More at usnews.com/college

Most popular majors: 8% Keyboard Instruments, 10% Music Theory and Composition, 41% Stringed Instruments, 31% Voice and Opera, 8% Woodwind Instruments
Expenses: 2015-2016: $42,210; room/board: $15,500
Financial aid: (415) 759-3414; 92% of undergrads determined to have financial need; average aid package $30,600

San Francisco State University

San Francisco CA
(415) 338-6486
U.S. News ranking: Reg. U. (W), No. 63
Website: www.sfsu.edu
Admissions email: ugadmit@sfsu.edu
Public; founded 1899
Freshman admissions: selective; 2014-2015: 31,963 applied, 21,087 accepted. Either SAT or ACT required. SAT 25/75 percentile: 870-1110. High school rank: N/A
Early decision deadline: N/A, notification date: N/A
Early action deadline: N/A, notification date: N/A
Application deadline (fall): 11/30
Undergraduate student body: 21,713 full time, 4,225 part time; 43% male, 57% female; 0% American Indian, 28% Asian, 5% black, 22% Hispanic, 6% multiracial, 1% Pacific Islander, 23% white, 6% international; 99% from in state; 13% live on campus; N/A of students in fraternities, N/A in sororities
Most popular majors: 24% Business, Management, Marketing, and Related Support Services, 9% Communication, Journalism, and Related Programs, 7% Health Professions and Related Programs, 10% Social Sciences, 9% Visual and Performing Arts
Expenses: 2015-2016: $6,476 in state, $17,636 out of state; room/board: N/A
Financial aid: (415) 338-7000; 70% of undergrads determined to have financial need; average aid package $11,297

San Jose State University

San Jose CA
(408) 283-7500
U.S. News ranking: Reg. U. (W), No. 39
Website: www.sjsu.edu
Admissions email: admissions@sjsu.edu
Public; founded 1857
Freshman admissions: selective; 2014-2015: 29,734 applied, 17,793 accepted. Either SAT or ACT required. SAT 25/75 percentile: 900-1200. High school rank: N/A
Early decision deadline: N/A, notification date: N/A
Early action deadline: N/A, notification date: N/A
Application deadline (fall): 11/30
Undergraduate student body: 21,341 full time, 5,323 part time; 52% male, 48% female; 0% American Indian, 35% Asian, 3% black, 25% Hispanic, 5% multiracial, 1% Pacific Islander, 21% white, 5% international; 99% from in state; 14% live on campus; N/A of students in fraternities, N/A in sororities
Most popular majors: 25% Business, Management, Marketing, and Related Support Services, 8% Communication, Journalism, and Related Programs, 9% Engineering, 9% Health Professions and Related Programs, 8% Visual and Performing Arts
Expenses: 2015-2016: $9,174 in state, $13,011 out of state; room/board: $14,217
Financial aid: (408) 283-7500; 67% of undergrads determined to have financial need; average aid package $13,269

Santa Clara University

Santa Clara CA
(408) 554-4700
U.S. News ranking: Reg. U. (W), No. 2
Website: www.scu.edu
Admissions email: Admission@scu.edu
Private; founded 1851
Affiliation: Catholic
Freshman admissions: more selective; 2014-2015: 14,985 applied, 7,395 accepted. Either SAT or ACT required. SAT 25/75 percentile: 1210-1390. High school rank: 54% in top tenth, 86% in top quarter, 97% in top half
Early decision deadline: 11/1, notification date: 12/23
Early action deadline: 11/1, notification date: 12/23
Application deadline (fall): 1/7
Undergraduate student body: 5,389 full time, 97 part time; 50% male, 50% female; 0% American Indian, 15% Asian, 3% black, 17% Hispanic, 7% multiracial, 0% Pacific Islander, 48% white, 3% international; 74% from in state; 52% live on campus; 0% of students in fraternities, 0% in sororities
Most popular majors: 22% Business, Management, Marketing, and Related Support Services, 7% Communication, Journalism, and Related Programs, 16% Engineering, 7% Psychology, 17% Social Sciences
Expenses: 2015-2016: $45,300; room/board: $13,425
Financial aid: (408) 554-4505; 48% of undergrads determined to have financial need; average aid package $30,016

Scripps College

Claremont CA
(909) 621-8149
U.S. News ranking: Nat. Lib. Arts, No. 29
Website: www.scrippscollege.edu/
Admissions email: admission@scrippscollege.edu
Private; founded 1926
Freshman admissions: more selective; 2014-2015: 2,782 applied, 758 accepted. Either SAT or ACT required. SAT 25/75 percentile: 1260-1460. High school rank: 83% in top tenth, 97% in top quarter, 100% in top half
Early decision deadline: 11/15, notification date: 12/15
Early action deadline: N/A, notification date: N/A
Application deadline (fall): 1/1
Undergraduate student body: 968 full time, 4 part time; 0% male, 100% female; 0% American Indian, 19% Asian, 3% black, 9% Hispanic, 6% multiracial, 0% Pacific Islander, 49% white, 4% international; 50% from in state; 97% live on campus; N/A of students in fraternities, N/A in sororities
Most popular majors: 8% Area, Ethnic, Cultural, Gender, and Group Studies, 15% Biological and Biomedical Sciences, 7% Psychology, General, 17% Social Sciences, 9% Visual and Performing Arts
Expenses: 2015-2016: $49,152; room/board: $15,108
Financial aid: (909) 621-8275; 37% of undergrads determined to have financial need; average aid package $42,638

Simpson University

Redding CA
(530) 226-4606
U.S. News ranking: Nat. Lib. Arts, second tier
Website: www.simpsonu.edu
Admissions email: admissions@simpsonu.edu
Private; founded 1921
Affiliation: Christian and Missionary Alliance
Freshman admissions: selective; 2014-2015: 598 applied, 343 accepted. Either SAT or ACT required. SAT 25/75 percentile: 940-1120. High school rank: 16% in top tenth, 28% in top quarter, 79% in top half
Early decision deadline: N/A, notification date: N/A
Early action deadline: 8/31, notification date: 12/1
Application deadline (fall): rolling
Undergraduate student body: 1,019 full time, 49 part time; 34% male, 66% female; 3% American Indian, 3% Asian, 3% black, 12% Hispanic, 3% multiracial, 0% Pacific Islander, 62% white, 2% international; 89% from in state; 40% live on campus; 0% of students in fraternities, 0% in sororities
Most popular majors: 30% Business, Management, Marketing, and Related Support Services, 4% Communication, Journalism, and Related Programs, 14% Health Professions and Related Programs, 22% Psychology, 10% Theology and Religious Vocations
Expenses: 2015-2016: $25,200; room/board: $7,700
Financial aid: (530) 226-4111; 89% of undergrads determined to have financial need; average aid package $19,571

Soka University of America

Aliso Viejo CA
(888) 600-Soka
U.S. News ranking: Nat. Lib. Arts, No. 45
Website: www.soka.edu
Admissions email: admission@soka.edu
Private; founded 1987
Freshman admissions: more selective; 2014-2015: 405 applied, 176 accepted. Either SAT or ACT required. SAT 25/75 percentile: 1090-1370. High school rank: 28% in top tenth, 64% in top quarter, 100% in top half
Early decision deadline: N/A, notification date: N/A
Early action deadline: 11/1, notification date: 12/1
Application deadline (fall): 1/15
Undergraduate student body: 411 full time, 1 part time; 40% male, 60% female; 1% American Indian, 19% Asian, 5% black, 10% Hispanic, 2% multiracial, 0% Pacific Islander, 19% white, 38% international; 57% from in state; 99% live on campus; 0% of students in fraternities, 0% in sororities
Most popular majors: 100% Liberal Arts and Sciences/Liberal Studies
Expenses: 2015-2016: $30,642; room/board: $11,468
Financial aid: N/A; 90% of undergrads determined to have financial need; average aid package $34,356

Sonoma State University

Rohnert Park CA
(707) 664-2778
U.S. News ranking: Reg. U. (W), No. 48
Website: www.sonoma.edu
Admissions email: student.outreach@sonoma.edu
Public; founded 1960
Freshman admissions: less selective; 2014-2015: 14,438 applied, 13,351 accepted. Either SAT or ACT required. SAT 25/75 percentile: 880-1100. High school rank: N/A
Early decision deadline: N/A, notification date: N/A
Early action deadline: N/A, notification date: N/A
Application deadline (fall): 11/30
Undergraduate student body: 7,315 full time, 1,162 part time; 38% male, 62% female; 1% American Indian, 5% Asian, 3% black, 21% Hispanic, 8% multiracial, 1% Pacific Islander, 57% white, 2% international; N/A from in state; 36% live on campus; N/A of students in fraternities, N/A in sororities
Most popular majors: 19% Business Administration and Management, General, 4% Criminology, 8% Liberal Arts and Sciences/Liberal Studies, 9% Psychology, General, 8% Sociology
Expenses: 2015-2016: $7,324 in state, $18,484 out of state; room/board: $12,814
Financial aid: (707) 664-2287; 59% of undergrads determined to have financial need; average aid package $10,092

Southern California Institute of Architecture[1]

Los Angeles CA
(800) 774-7242
U.S. News ranking: Arts, unranked
Website: www.sciarc.edu
Admissions email: admissions@sciarc.edu
Private
Application deadline (fall): 1/15
Undergraduate student body: N/A full time, N/A part time
Expenses: 2014-2015: $40,262; room/board: $13,846
Financial aid: (213) 613-2200

Stanford University

Stanford CA
(650) 723-2091
U.S. News ranking: Nat. U., No. 4
Website: www.stanford.edu
Admissions email: admission@stanford.edu
Private; founded 1885
Freshman admissions: most selective; 2014-2015: 42,167 applied, 2,145 accepted. Either SAT or ACT required. SAT 25/75 percentile: 1380-1570. High school rank: 95% in top tenth, 99% in top quarter, 100% in top half
Early decision deadline: N/A, notification date: N/A
Early action deadline: 11/1, notification date: 12/15
Application deadline (fall): 1/3
Undergraduate student body: 7,019 full time, 0 part time; 53% male, 47% female; 1% American Indian, 20% Asian, 6% black, 16% Hispanic, 11% multiracial, 0% Pacific Islander, 38% white, 8% international; 41% from in state; 92% live on campus; 24% of students in fraternities, 28% in sororities
Most popular majors: 12% Computer and Information Sciences and Support Services, 16% Engineering, 18% Multi/Interdisciplinary Studies, 5% Physical Sciences, 15% Social Sciences
Expenses: 2015-2016: $46,320; room/board: $14,107
Financial aid: (650) 723-3058; 48% of undergrads determined to have financial need; average aid package $47,000

St. Mary's College of California

Moraga CA
(925) 631-4224
U.S. News ranking: Reg. U. (W), No. 9
Website: www.stmarys-ca.edu
Admissions email: smcadmit@stmarys-ca.edu
Private; founded 1863
Affiliation: Roman Catholic
Freshman admissions: selective; 2014-2015: 4,863 applied, 3,656 accepted. Either SAT or ACT required. SAT 25/75 percentile: 980-1200. High school rank: N/A
Early decision deadline: N/A, notification date: N/A
Early action deadline: 11/15, notification date: 12/15
Application deadline (fall): 2/1
Undergraduate student body: 2,701 full time, 257 part time; 41% male, 59% female; 0% American Indian, 10% Asian, 4% black, 25% Hispanic, 7% multiracial, 1% Pacific Islander, 46% white, 2% international; 90% from in state; 56% live on campus; 0% of students in fraternities, 0% in sororities
Most popular majors: 24% Business, Management, Marketing, and Related Support Services, 11% Communication, Journalism, and Related Programs, 7% Liberal Arts and Sciences, General Studies and Humanities, 12% Psychology, 12% Social Sciences
Expenses: 2015-2016: $42,930; room/board: $14,490

Financial aid: (925) 631-4370; 71% of undergrads determined to have financial need; average aid package $29,383

Thomas Aquinas College

Santa Paula CA
(800) 634-9797
U.S. News ranking: Nat. Lib. Arts, No. 82
Website: www.thomasaquinas.edu
Admissions email: admissions@thomasaquinas.edu
Private; founded 1971
Affiliation: Catholic
Freshman admissions: more selective; 2014-2015: 185 applied, 153 accepted. Either SAT or ACT required. SAT 25/75 percentile: 1180-1350. High school rank: 36% in top tenth, 71% in top quarter, 93% in top half
Early decision deadline: N/A, notification date: N/A
Early action deadline: N/A, notification date: N/A
Application deadline (fall): rolling
Undergraduate student body: 378 full time, 0 part time; 51% male, 49% female; 1% American Indian, 1% Asian, 0% black, 15% Hispanic, 6% multiracial, 0% Pacific Islander, 71% white, 4% international; 41% from in state; 99% live on campus; 0% of students in fraternities, 0% in sororities
Most popular majors: 100% Liberal Arts and Sciences, General Studies and Humanities
Expenses: 2015-2016: $24,500; room/board: $7,950
Financial aid: (805) 525-4417; 76% of undergrads determined to have financial need; average aid package $22,171

Trident University International[1]

Cypress CA
(800) 579-3170
U.S. News ranking: Nat. U., unranked
Website: www.trident.edu
Admissions email: N/A
For-profit
Application deadline (fall): rolling
Undergraduate student body: N/A full time, N/A part time
Expenses: 2014-2015: $8,400; room/board: $6,880
Financial aid: (877) 835-9818

University of California–Berkeley

Berkeley CA
(510) 642-3175
U.S. News ranking: Nat. U., No. 20
Website: students.berkeley.edu/admissions/
Admissions email: N/A
Public; founded 1868
Freshman admissions: most selective; 2014-2015: 73,779 applied, 11,816 accepted. Either SAT or ACT required. SAT 25/75 percentile: 1290-1490. High school rank: 98% in top tenth, 100% in top quarter, 100% in top half
Early decision deadline: N/A, notification date: N/A
Early action deadline: N/A, notification date: N/A
Application deadline (fall): 11/30
Undergraduate student body: 26,320 full time, 806 part time; 48% male, 52% female; 0% American Indian, 35% Asian, 2% black, 14% Hispanic, 5% multiracial, 0% Pacific Islander, 28% white, 14% international; 85% from in state; 26% live on campus; 10% of students in fraternities, 10% in sororities
Most popular majors: 13% Biological and Biomedical Sciences, 13% Engineering, 5% English Language and Literature/Letters, 5% Natural Resources and Conservation, 20% Social Sciences
Expenses: 2015-2016: $13,432 in state, $38,140 out of state; room/board: $15,422
Financial aid: (510) 642-6442; 51% of undergrads determined to have financial need; average aid package $23,345

University of California–Davis

Davis CA
(530) 752-2971
U.S. News ranking: Nat. U., No. 41
Website: www.ucdavis.edu
Admissions email: undergraduateadmissions@ucdavis.edu
Public; founded 1905
Freshman admissions: more selective; 2014-2015: 60,506 applied, 24,541 accepted. Either SAT or ACT required. SAT 25/75 percentile: 1080-1350. High school rank: 100% in top tenth, 100% in top quarter, 100% in top half
Early decision deadline: N/A, notification date: N/A
Early action deadline: N/A, notification date: N/A
Application deadline (fall): 11/30
Undergraduate student body: 27,314 full time, 414 part time; 42% male, 58% female; 0% American Indian, 34% Asian, 2% black, 18% Hispanic, 5% multiracial, 0% Pacific Islander, 29% white, 8% international; 96% from in state; 25% live on campus; N/A of students in fraternities, N/A in sororities
Most popular majors: 5% Biology/Biological Sciences, General, 5% Business/Managerial Economics, 7% Economics, General, 4% Neurobiology and Anatomy, 11% Research and Experimental Psychology, Other
Expenses: 2015-2016: $13,951 in state, $38,659 out of state; room/board: $14,517
Financial aid: (530) 752-2396; 65% of undergrads determined to have financial need; average aid package $20,093

University of California–Irvine

Irvine CA
(949) 824-6703
U.S. News ranking: Nat. U., No. 39
Website: www.uci.edu
Admissions email: admissions@uci.edu
Public; founded 1965
Freshman admissions: more selective; 2014-2015: 66,505 applied, 24,890 accepted. Either SAT or ACT required. SAT 25/75 percentile: 1040-1310. High school rank: 96% in top tenth, 100% in top quarter, 100% in top half
Early decision deadline: N/A, notification date: N/A
Early action deadline: N/A, notification date: N/A
Application deadline (fall): 11/30
Undergraduate student body: 24,139 full time, 350 part time; 46% male, 54% female; 0% American Indian, 41% Asian, 2% black, 24% Hispanic, 4% multiracial, 0% Pacific Islander, 14% white, 12% international; 98% from in state; 41% live on campus; 10% of students in fraternities, 10% in sororities
Most popular majors: 13% Biology/Biological Sciences, General, 5% Business/Managerial Economics, 6% Political Science and Government, General, 17% Public Health, Other, 10% Social Psychology
Expenses: 2014-2015: $14,577 in state, $37,455 out of state; room/board: $12,638
Financial aid: (949) 824-5337; 69% of undergrads determined to have financial need; average aid package $21,475

University of California–Los Angeles

Los Angeles CA
(310) 825-3101
U.S. News ranking: Nat. U., No. 23
Website: www.ucla.edu/
Admissions email: ugadm@saonet.ucla.edu
Public; founded 1919
Freshman admissions: most selective; 2014-2015: 86,548 applied, 16,059 accepted. Either SAT or ACT required. SAT 25/75 percentile: 1190-1460. High school rank: 97% in top tenth, 100% in top quarter, 100% in top half
Early decision deadline: N/A, notification date: N/A
Early action deadline: N/A, notification date: N/A
Application deadline (fall): 11/30
Undergraduate student body: 29,033 full time, 600 part time; 44% male, 56% female; 0% American Indian, 30% Asian, 3% black, 20% Hispanic, 5% multiracial, 0% Pacific Islander, 28% white, 13% international; 91% from in state; 43% live on campus; 15% of students in fraternities, 15% in sororities
Most popular majors: 5% English Language and Literature/Letters, 5% History, 6% Psychology, 5% Social Sciences, 7% Social Sciences
Expenses: 2015-2016: $12,753 in state, $35,631 out of state; room/board: $14,903
Financial aid: (310) 206-0400; 55% of undergrads determined to have financial need; average aid package $22,405

University of California–Riverside

Riverside CA
(951) 827-3411
U.S. News ranking: Nat. U., No. 121
Website: www.ucr.edu
Admissions email: admit@ucr.edu
Public; founded 1954
Freshman admissions: more selective; 2014-2015: 36,101 applied, 21,044 accepted. Either SAT or ACT required. SAT 25/75 percentile: 1010-1250. High school rank: 94% in top tenth, 100% in top quarter, 100% in top half
Early decision deadline: N/A, notification date: N/A
Early action deadline: N/A, notification date: N/A
Application deadline (fall): 11/30
Undergraduate student body: 18,445 full time, 337 part time; 48% male, 52% female; 0% American Indian, 36% Asian, 5% black, 37% Hispanic, 4% multiracial, 0% Pacific Islander, 14% white, 3% international; 99% from in state; 34% live on campus; 7% of students in fraternities, 8% in sororities
Most popular majors: 14% Biological and Biomedical Sciences, 16% Business, Management, Marketing, and Related Support Services, 7% Engineering, 9% Psychology, 21% Social Sciences
Expenses: 2015-2016: $14,050 in state, $40,973 out of state; room/board: $13,950
Financial aid: (951) 827-3878; 78% of undergrads determined to have financial need; average aid package $20,928

University of California–San Diego

La Jolla CA
(858) 534-4831
U.S. News ranking: Nat. U., No. 39
Website: www.ucsd.edu/
Admissions email: admissionsinfo@ucsd.edu
Public; founded 1960
Freshman admissions: most selective; 2014-2015: 73,440 applied, 24,595 accepted. Either SAT or ACT required. SAT 25/75 percentile: 1180-1420. High school rank: 100% in top tenth, 100% in top quarter, 100% in top half
Early decision deadline: N/A, notification date: N/A
Early action deadline: N/A, notification date: N/A
Application deadline (fall): 11/30
Undergraduate student body: 24,428 full time, 382 part time; 52% male, 48% female; 0% American Indian, 35% Asian, 2% black, 15% Hispanic, 0% multiracial, 0% Pacific Islander, 20% white, 20% international; 94% from in state; 44% live on campus; 12% of students in fraternities, 12% in sororities
Most popular majors: 22% Biology, General, 9% Computer Engineering, 11% Economics, 5% Electrical and Electronics Engineering, 5% Psychology, General
Expenses: 2015-2016: $14,042 in state, $38,066 out of state; room/board: $12,243
Financial aid: (858) 534-4480; 61% of undergrads determined to have financial need; average aid package $22,196

University of California–Santa Barbara

Santa Barbara CA
(805) 893-2485
U.S. News ranking: Nat. U., No. 37
Website: www.ucsb.edu
Admissions email: admissions@sa.ucsb.edu
Public; founded 1909
Freshman admissions: most selective; 2014-2015: 66,813 applied, 24,283 accepted. Either SAT or ACT required. SAT 25/75 percentile: 1120-1380. High school rank: 100% in top tenth, 100% in top quarter, 100% in top half
Early decision deadline: N/A, notification date: N/A
Early action deadline: N/A, notification date: N/A
Application deadline (fall): 11/30
Undergraduate student body: 19,913 full time, 325 part time; 47% male, 53% female; 0% American Indian, 21% Asian, 2% black, 25% Hispanic, 6% multiracial, 0% Pacific Islander, 38% white, 6% international; 96% from in state; 38% live on campus; 8% of students in fraternities, 13% in sororities
Most popular majors: 8% Biological and Biomedical Sciences, 7% Communication, Journalism, and Related Programs, 10% Psychology, 26% Social Sciences, 7% Visual and Performing Arts
Expenses: 2015-2016: $13,865 in state, $38,573 out of state; room/board: $14,192
Financial aid: (805) 893-2432; 62% of undergrads determined to have financial need; average aid package $22,572

University of California–Santa Cruz

Santa Cruz CA
(831) 459-4008
U.S. News ranking: Nat. U., No. 82
Website: www.ucsc.edu
Admissions email: admissions@ucsc.edu
Public; founded 1965
Freshman admissions: more selective; 2014-2015: 40,193 applied, 22,914 accepted. Either SAT or ACT required. SAT 25/75 percentile: 1010-1280. High school rank: 96% in top tenth, 100% in top quarter, 100% in top half
Early decision deadline: N/A, notification date: N/A
Early action deadline: N/A, notification date: N/A
Application deadline (fall): 11/30
Undergraduate student body: 15,825 full time, 452 part time; 47% male, 53% female; 0% American Indian, 20% Asian, 2% black, 32% Hispanic, 7% multiracial, 0% Pacific Islander, 35% white, 2% international; 97% from in state; 51% live on campus; 0% of students in fraternities, 4% in sororities
Most popular majors: 7% Business/Managerial Economics, 6% Cell/Cellular and Molecular Biology, 5% Environmental Studies, 13% Psychology, General, 5% Sociology
Expenses: 2015-2016: $13,481 in state, $38,189 out of state; room/board: $15,123

More at usnews.com/college

Financial aid: (831) 459-2963; 70% of undergrads determined to have financial need; average aid package $23,134

University of La Verne

La Verne CA
(800) 876-4858
U.S. News ranking: Nat. U., No. 160
Website: www.laverne.edu
Admissions email: admission@laverne.edu
Private; founded 1891
Freshman admissions: selective; 2014-2015: 8,233 applied, 3,833 accepted. Either SAT or ACT required. SAT 25/75 percentile: 930-1100. High school rank: 20% in top tenth, 52% in top quarter, 86% in top half
Early decision deadline: N/A, notification date: N/A
Early action deadline: N/A, notification date: N/A
Application deadline (fall): rolling
Undergraduate student body: 2,626 full time, 87 part time; 41% male, 59% female; 0% American Indian, 6% Asian, 5% black, 52% Hispanic, 5% multiracial, 1% Pacific Islander, 25% white, 5% international; 96% from in state; 31% live on campus; 8% of students in fraternities, 16% in sororities
Most popular majors: 23% Business, Management, Marketing, and Related Support Services, 11% Communication, Journalism, and Related Programs, 7% Education, 14% Psychology, 16% Social Sciences
Expenses: 2015-2016: $38,560; room/board: $12,510
Financial aid: (800) 649-0160; 82% of undergrads determined to have financial need; average aid package $29,286

University of Redlands

Redlands CA
(800) 455-5064
U.S. News ranking: Reg. U. (W), No. 12
Website: www.redlands.edu
Admissions email: admissions@redlands.edu
Private; founded 1907
Freshman admissions: selective; 2014-2015: 4,533 applied, 3,313 accepted. Either SAT or ACT required. SAT 25/75 percentile: 1000-1200. High school rank: 32% in top tenth, 62% in top quarter, 90% in top half
Early decision deadline: N/A, notification date: N/A
Early action deadline: 11/15, notification date: 12/31
Application deadline (fall): 1/15
Undergraduate student body: 2,911 full time, 868 part time; 43% male, 57% female; 1% American Indian, 5% Asian, 4% black, 27% Hispanic, 4% multiracial, 0% Pacific Islander, 47% white, 1% international
Most popular majors: 9% Biology/Biological Sciences, General, 9% Business/Commerce, General, 16% Health Services/Allied Health/Health Sciences, General, 22% Multi/Interdisciplinary Studies, General, 22% Psychology, General
Expenses: 2014-2015: $43,186; room/board: $12,710
Financial aid: (909) 335-4047

University of San Diego

San Diego CA
(619) 260-4506
U.S. News ranking: Nat. U., No. 89
Website: www.SanDiego.edu
Admissions email: admissions@SanDiego.edu
Private; founded 1949
Affiliation: Roman Catholic
Freshman admissions: more selective; 2014-2015: 14,247 applied, 6,589 accepted. Either SAT or ACT required. SAT 25/75 percentile: 1130-1320. High school rank: 45% in top tenth, 78% in top quarter, 94% in top half
Early decision deadline: N/A, notification date: N/A
Early action deadline: N/A, notification date: N/A
Application deadline (fall): 12/15
Undergraduate student body: 5,541 full time, 200 part time; 45% male, 55% female; 0% American Indian, 6% Asian, 3% black, 19% Hispanic, 6% multiracial, 0% Pacific Islander, 54% white, 7% international; 63% from in state; 40% live on campus; 24% of students in fraternities, 37% in sororities
Most popular majors: 8% Biological and Biomedical Sciences, 41% Business, Management, Marketing, and Related Support Services, 9% Communication, Journalism, and Related Programs, 7% Psychology, 14% Social Sciences
Expenses: 2015-2016: $44,586; room/board: $12,042
Financial aid: (619) 260-4514; 54% of undergrads determined to have financial need; average aid package $31,971

University of San Francisco

San Francisco CA
(415) 422-6563
U.S. News ranking: Nat. U., No. 108
Website: www.usfca.edu
Admissions email: admission@usfca.edu
Private; founded 1855
Affiliation: Jesuit Catholic
Freshman admissions: more selective; 2014-2015: 17,448 applied, 10,478 accepted. Either SAT or ACT required. SAT 25/75 percentile: 1040-1250. High school rank: 22% in top tenth, 60% in top quarter, 90% in top half
Early decision deadline: 11/15, notification date: 1/1
Early action deadline: 11/15, notification date: 1/1
Application deadline (fall): rolling
Undergraduate student body: 6,529 full time, 316 part time; 38% male, 62% female; 0% American Indian, 20% Asian, 3% black, 20% Hispanic, 7% multiracial, 1% Pacific Islander, 29% white, 19% international; 79% from in state; 35% live on campus; 4% of students in fraternities, 6% in sororities
Most popular majors: 33% Business, Management, Marketing, and Related Support Services, 10% Communication, Journalism, and Related Programs, 11% Health Professions and Related Programs, 7% Psychology, 11% Social Sciences
Expenses: 2015-2016: $42,634; room/board: $13,650
Financial aid: (415) 422-2620; 54% of undergrads determined to have financial need; average aid package $27,879

University of Southern California

Los Angeles CA
(213) 740-1111
U.S. News ranking: Nat. U., No. 23
Website: www.usc.edu/
Admissions email: admitusc@usc.edu
Private; founded 1880
Freshman admissions: most selective; 2014-2015: 51,920 applied, 9,358 accepted. Either SAT or ACT required. SAT 25/75 percentile: 1280-1480. High school rank: 88% in top tenth, 97% in top quarter, 100% in top half
Early decision deadline: N/A, notification date: N/A
Early action deadline: N/A, notification date: N/A
Application deadline (fall): 1/15
Undergraduate student body: 18,058 full time, 682 part time; 50% male, 50% female; 0% American Indian, 22% Asian, 4% black, 14% Hispanic, 5% multiracial, 0% Pacific Islander, 36% white, 13% international; 68% from in state; 33% live on campus; 25% of students in fraternities, 20% in sororities
Most popular majors: 24% Business, Management, Marketing, and Related Support Services, 9% Communication, Journalism, and Related Programs, 10% Engineering, 13% Social Sciences, 13% Visual and Performing Arts
Expenses: 2015-2016: $50,210; room/board: $13,855
Financial aid: (213) 740-1111; 39% of undergrads determined to have financial need; average aid package $45,308

University of the Pacific

Stockton CA
(209) 946-2285
U.S. News ranking: Nat. U., No. 108
Website: www.pacific.edu
Admissions email: admissions@pacific.edu
Private; founded 1851
Freshman admissions: more selective; 2014-2015: 15,183 applied, 8,335 accepted. Either SAT or ACT required. SAT 25/75 percentile: 1038-1313. High school rank: 37% in top tenth, 62% in top quarter, 89% in top half
Early decision deadline: N/A, notification date: N/A
Early action deadline: 11/15, notification date: 1/15
Application deadline (fall): 1/15
Undergraduate student body: 3,713 full time, 97 part time; 48% male, 52% female; 1% American Indian, 33% Asian, 2% black, 18% Hispanic, 5% multiracial, 1% Pacific Islander, 30% white, 7% international; 93% from in state; 46% live on campus; 17% of students in fraternities, 20% in sororities
Most popular majors: 10% Biology/Biological Sciences, General, 16% Business Administration and Management, General, 6% Curriculum and Instruction, 11% Engineering, General, 9% Social Sciences
Expenses: 2015-2016: $42,934; room/board: $12,858
Financial aid: (209) 946-2421; 71% of undergrads determined to have financial need; average aid package $31,221

University of the West[1]

Rosemead CA
(855) 469-3378
U.S. News ranking: Reg. Coll. (W), unranked
Website: www.uwest.edu
Admissions email: N/A
Private; founded 1991
Application deadline (fall): N/A
Undergraduate student body: N/A full time, N/A part time
Expenses: 2014-2015: $9,968; room/board: $6,820
Financial aid: (626) 571-8811

Vanguard University of Southern California

Costa Mesa CA
(800) 722-6279
U.S. News ranking: Reg. Coll. (W), No. 13
Website: www.vanguard.edu
Admissions email: admissions@vanguard.edu
Private; founded 1920
Affiliation: Assemblies of God
Freshman admissions: less selective; 2014-2015: 1,352 applied, 787 accepted. Either SAT or ACT required. SAT 25/75 percentile: 850-1090. High school rank: 13% in top tenth, 21% in top quarter, 68% in top half
Early decision deadline: N/A, notification date: N/A
Early action deadline: 12/1, notification date: 1/15
Application deadline (fall): 8/1
Undergraduate student body: 1,504 full time, 483 part time; 33% male, 67% female; 0% American Indian, 4% Asian, 4% black, 36% Hispanic, 5% multiracial, 1% Pacific Islander, 46% white, 1% international; 90% from in state; 47% live on campus; 0% of students in fraternities, 0% in sororities
Most popular majors: 21% Business, Management, Marketing, and Related Support Services, 11% Communication, Journalism, and Related Programs, 8% Education, 14% Health Professions and Related Programs, 17% Psychology
Expenses: 2015-2016: $30,050; room/board: $9,010
Financial aid: (714) 556-3610; 85% of undergrads determined to have financial need; average aid package $13,017

Westmont College

Santa Barbara CA
(800) 777-9011
U.S. News ranking: Nat. Lib. Arts, No. 93
Website: www.westmont.edu
Admissions email: admissions@westmont.edu
Private; founded 1937
Affiliation: Christian nondenominational
Freshman admissions: more selective; 2014-2015: 2,103 applied, 1,669 accepted. Either SAT or ACT required. SAT 25/75 percentile: 1050-1290. High school rank: 29% in top tenth, 60% in top quarter, 93% in top half
Early decision deadline: N/A, notification date: N/A
Early action deadline: 11/15, notification date: 1/5
Application deadline (fall): rolling
Undergraduate student body: 1,303 full time, 10 part time; 40% male, 60% female; 0% American Indian, 7% Asian, 1% black, 14% Hispanic, 8% multiracial, 0% Pacific Islander, 65% white, 2% international; 75% from in state; 84% live on campus; 0% of students in fraternities, 0% in sororities
Most popular majors: 12% Biology/Biological Sciences, General, 14% Business/Managerial Economics, 9% English Language and Literature, General, 15% Kinesiology and Exercise Science, 11% Speech Communication and Rhetoric
Expenses: 2015-2016: $41,360; room/board: $13,040
Financial aid: (805) 565-6063; 66% of undergrads determined to have financial need; average aid package $30,373

Whittier College

Whittier CA
(562) 907-4238
U.S. News ranking: Nat. Lib. Arts, No. 127
Website: www.whittier.edu
Admissions email: admission@whittier.edu
Private; founded 1887
Freshman admissions: selective; 2014-2015: 4,850 applied, 3,001 accepted. Either SAT or ACT required. SAT 25/75 percentile: 960-1170. High school rank: 25% in top tenth, 38% in top quarter, 91% in top half
Early decision deadline: N/A, notification date: N/A
Early action deadline: 11/15, notification date: 12/30
Application deadline (fall): rolling
Undergraduate student body: 1,640 full time, 25 part time; 45% male, 55% female; 1% American Indian, 10% Asian, 5% black, 44% Hispanic, 4% multiracial, 0% Pacific Islander, 31% white, 4% international; 84% from in state; 50% live on campus; 9% of students in fraternities, 14% in sororities
Most popular majors: 7% Biological and Biomedical Sciences, 18% Business, Management, Marketing, and Related Support Services, 12% Parks, Recreation, Leisure, and Fitness Studies, 11% Psychology, 15% Social Sciences
Expenses: 2015-2016: $43,080; room/board: $12,672

Financial aid: (562) 907-4285; 77% of undergrads determined to have financial need; average aid package $33,071

Woodbury University

Burbank CA
(818) 767-0888
U.S. News ranking: Reg. U. (W), No. 57
Website: www.woodbury.edu
Admissions email: info@woodbury.edu
Private; founded 1884
Freshman admissions: less selective; 2014-2015: 1,068 applied, 763 accepted. Either SAT or ACT required. SAT 25/75 percentile: 830-1058. High school rank: N/A
Early decision deadline: N/A, notification date: N/A
Early action deadline: N/A, notification date: N/A
Application deadline (fall): rolling
Undergraduate student body: 1,161 full time, 177 part time; 50% male, 50% female; 0% American Indian, 10% Asian, 5% black, 27% Hispanic, 0% multiracial, 0% Pacific Islander, 36% white, 22% international; 96% from in state; N/A live on campus; N/A of students in fraternities, N/A in sororities
Most popular majors: 8% Accounting, 30% Architecture, 11% Business Administration and Management, General, 8% Communications Technologies/ Technicians and Support Services, Other, 7% Fashion/Apparel Design
Expenses: 2014-2015: $35,048; room/board: $10,522
Financial aid: (818) 767-0888; 87% of undergrads determined to have financial need; average aid package $23,356

COLORADO

Adams State University[1]

Alamosa CO
(800) 824-6494
U.S. News ranking: Reg. U. (W), second tier
Website: www.adams.edu
Admissions email: ascadmit@adams.edu
Public
Application deadline (fall): N/A
Undergraduate student body: N/A full time, N/A part time
Expenses: 2014-2015: $8,014 in state, $18,814 out of state; room/ board: $8,572
Financial aid: (719) 587-7306

Art Institute of Colorado[1]

Denver CO
(800) 275-2420
U.S. News ranking: Arts, unranked
Website: www.artinstitutes.edu/ denver/
Admissions email: N/A
For-profit
Application deadline (fall): N/A
Undergraduate student body: N/A full time, N/A part time
Expenses: 2014-2015: $17,632; room/board: $11,550
Financial aid: (800) 275-2420

Colorado Christian University[1]

Lakewood CO
(303) 963-3200
U.S. News ranking: Reg. U. (W), second tier
Website: www.ccu.edu
Admissions email: admission@ccu.edu
Private
Application deadline (fall): N/A
Undergraduate student body: N/A full time, N/A part time
Expenses: 2014-2015: $26,430; room/board: $10,917
Financial aid: (303) 963-3230

Colorado College

Colorado Springs CO
(719) 389-6344
U.S. News ranking: Nat. Lib. Arts, No. 25
Website: www.ColoradoCollege.edu
Admissions email: admission@ColoradoCollege.edu
Private; founded 1874
Freshman admissions: most selective; 2014-2015: 7,602 applied, 1,361 accepted. Neither SAT nor ACT required. ACT 25/75 percentile: 28-32. High school rank: 69% in top tenth, 90% in top quarter, 99% in top half
Early decision deadline: 11/10, notification date: 12/15
Early action deadline: 11/10, notification date: 12/18
Application deadline (fall): 1/15
Undergraduate student body: 2,036 full time, 14 part time; 47% male, 53% female; 0% American Indian, 5% Asian, 2% black, 9% Hispanic, 8% multiracial, 0% Pacific Islander, 66% white, 6% international; 18% from in state; 76% live on campus; 10% of students in fraternities, 11% in sororities
Most popular majors: 8% Ecology and Evolutionary Biology, 9% Economics, General, 5% Fine/ Studio Arts, General, 4% Neuroscience, 4% Sociology
Expenses: 2015-2016: $48,996; room/board: $11,215
Financial aid: (719) 389-6651; 37% of undergrads determined to have financial need; average aid package $45,111

Colorado Mesa University

Grand Junction CO
(800) 982-6372
U.S. News ranking: Nat. Lib. Arts, second tier
Website: www.coloradomesa.edu/
Admissions email: admissions@coloradomesa.edu
Public; founded 1925
Freshman admissions: selective; 2014-2015: 5,881 applied, 4,842 accepted. Either SAT or ACT required. ACT 25/75 percentile: 18-23. High school rank: 10% in top tenth, 26% in top quarter, 54% in top half
Early decision deadline: N/A, notification date: N/A
Early action deadline: N/A, notification date: N/A
Application deadline (fall): rolling
Undergraduate student body: 6,969 full time, 2,034 part time; 46% male, 54% female; 1% American Indian, 1% Asian, 3% black, 16% Hispanic, 4% multiracial, 1% Pacific Islander, 72% white, 1% international; 87% from in state; 23% live on campus; N/A of students in fraternities, N/A in sororities
Most popular majors: 6% Biology/ Biological Sciences, General, 13% Business/Commerce, General, 8% Criminal Justice/Safety Studies, 6% Psychology, General, 10% Registered Nursing/Registered Nurse
Expenses: 2015-2016: $8,008 in state, $19,363 out of state; room/ board: $10,526
Financial aid: (970) 248-1396; 68% of undergrads determined to have financial need; average aid package $8,317

Colorado School of Mines

Golden CO
(303) 273-3220
U.S. News ranking: Nat. U., No. 75
Website: www.mines.edu
Admissions email: admit@mines.edu
Public; founded 1874
Freshman admissions: most selective; 2014-2015: 12,340 applied, 4,501 accepted. Either SAT or ACT required. ACT 25/75 percentile: 28-32. High school rank: 58% in top tenth, 91% in top quarter, 100% in top half
Early decision deadline: N/A, notification date: N/A
Early action deadline: N/A, notification date: N/A
Application deadline (fall): 4/1
Undergraduate student body: 4,241 full time, 215 part time; 74% male, 26% female; 0% American Indian, 5% Asian, 1% black, 8% Hispanic, 5% multiracial, 0% Pacific Islander, 75% white, 5% international; 67% from in state; 35% live on campus; 14% of students in fraternities, 18% in sororities
Most popular majors: 4% Computer and Information Sciences and Support Services, 87% Engineering, 5% Mathematics and Statistics, 3% Physical Sciences, 1% Social Sciences
Expenses: 2015-2016: $17,383 in state, $34,828 out of state; room/board: $11,008
Financial aid: (303) 273-3220; 52% of undergrads determined to have financial need; average aid package $12,191

Colorado State University

Fort Collins CO
(970) 491-6909
U.S. News ranking: Nat. U., No. 127
Website: www.colostate.edu
Admissions email: admissions@colostate.edu
Public; founded 1870
Freshman admissions: more selective; 2014-2015: 16,655 applied, 13,404 accepted. Either SAT or ACT required. ACT 25/75 percentile: 22-27. High school rank: 21% in top tenth, 50% in top quarter, 85% in top half
Early decision deadline: N/A, notification date: N/A
Early action deadline: 12/1, notification date: 2/1
Application deadline (fall): 2/1
Undergraduate student body: 21,253 full time, 2,605 part time; 49% male, 51% female; 1% American Indian, 2% Asian, 2% black, 10% Hispanic, 3% multiracial, 0% Pacific Islander, 74% white, 4% international; 80% from in state; 25% live on campus; 8% of students in fraternities, 12% in sororities
Most popular majors: 10% Biological and Biomedical Sciences, 14% Business, Management, Marketing, and Related Support Services, 9% Family and Consumer Sciences/ Human Sciences, 8% Parks, Recreation, Leisure, and Fitness Studies, 9% Social Sciences
Expenses: 2015-2016: $10,590 in state, $27,258 out of state; room/board: $11,526
Financial aid: (970) 491-6321; 52% of undergrads determined to have financial need; average aid package $10,498

Colorado State University–Pueblo

Pueblo CO
(719) 549-2461
U.S. News ranking: Reg. U. (W), second tier
Website: www.csupueblo.edu
Admissions email: info@colostate-pueblo.edu
Public; founded 1933
Freshman admissions: less selective; 2014-2015: 4,236 applied, 3,930 accepted. Either SAT or ACT required. ACT 25/75 percentile: 18-23. High school rank: 10% in top tenth, 31% in top quarter, 64% in top half
Early decision deadline: N/A, notification date: N/A
Early action deadline: N/A, notification date: N/A
Application deadline (fall): 8/1
Undergraduate student body: 3,644 full time, 1,548 part time; 46% male, 54% female; 1% American Indian, 1% Asian, 8% black, 32% Hispanic, 4% multiracial, 0% Pacific Islander, 50% white, 2% international; 93% from in state; 19% live on campus; 2% of students in fraternities, 2% in sororities
Most popular majors: 10% Business/Commerce, General, 10% Kinesiology and Exercise Science, 8% Psychology, General, 9% Registered Nursing/Registered Nurse, 12% Sociology
Expenses: 2014-2015: $7,833 in state, $18,774 out of state; room/ board: $8,962
Financial aid: (719) 549-2753; 74% of undergrads determined to have financial need; average aid package $9,669

Colorado Technical University[1]

Colorado Springs CO
(888) 897-6555
U.S. News ranking: Nat. U., unranked
Website: www.coloradotech.edu
Admissions email: info@ctuonline.edu
For-profit
Application deadline (fall): N/A
Undergraduate student body: N/A full time, N/A part time
Expenses: 2014-2015: $11,327; room/board: $9,072
Financial aid: (719) 598-2900

Fort Lewis College

Durango CO
(970) 247-7184
U.S. News ranking: Nat. Lib. Arts, second tier
Website: www.fortlewis.edu
Admissions email: admission@fortlewis.edu
Public; founded 1911
Freshman admissions: selective; 2014-2015: 2,439 applied, 2,215 accepted. Either SAT or ACT required. ACT 25/75 percentile: 19-24. High school rank: 11% in top tenth, 31% in top quarter, 69% in top half
Early decision deadline: N/A, notification date: N/A
Early action deadline: 1/15, notification date: 3/15
Application deadline (fall): 8/1
Undergraduate student body: 3,479 full time, 272 part time; 52% male, 48% female; 24% American Indian, 1% Asian, 1% black, 10% Hispanic, 6% multiracial, 0% Pacific Islander, 55% white, 1% international; 53% from in state; 38% live on campus; 0% of students in fraternities, 0% in sororities
Most popular majors: 7% Biological and Biomedical Sciences, 20% Business, Management, Marketing, and Related Support Services, 9% Psychology, 13% Social Sciences, 9% Visual and Performing Arts
Expenses: 2015-2016: $7,600 in state, $17,816 out of state; room/ board: $10,680
Financial aid: (970) 247-7142; 65% of undergrads determined to have financial need; average aid package $14,668

Jones International University[1]

Centennial CO
(800) 811-5663
U.S. News ranking: Reg. U. (W), unranked
Website: www.jonesinternational.edu/
Admissions email: info@jonesinternational.edu
For-profit; founded 1995
Application deadline (fall): rolling
Undergraduate student body: N/A full time, N/A part time
Expenses: 2014-2015: $12,720; room/board: $6,144
Financial aid: (800) 811-5663

Metropolitan State University of Denver

Denver CO
(303) 556-3058
U.S. News ranking: Reg. Coll. (W), second tier
Website: www.mscd.edu
Admissions email: askmetro@mscd.edu
Public; founded 1963
Freshman admissions: less selective; 2014-2015: 6,172 applied, 4,024 accepted. Either SAT or ACT required. ACT 25/75 percentile: 18-23. High school rank: 7% in top tenth, 20% in top quarter, 53% in top half
Early decision deadline: N/A, notification date: N/A
Early action deadline: N/A, notification date: N/A
Application deadline (fall): 4/30

Undergraduate student body: 12,718 full time, 8,478 part time; 46% male, 54% female; 1% American Indian, 4% Asian, 6% black, 22% Hispanic, 4% multiracial, 0% Pacific Islander, 60% white, 1% international; 97% from in state; N/A live on campus; N/A of students in fraternities, N/A in sororities
Most popular majors: 18% Business, Management, Marketing, and Related Support Services, 6% Health Professions and Related Programs, 7% Homeland Security, Law Enforcement, Firefighting and Related Protective Services, 9% Multi/Interdisciplinary Studies, 8% Psychology
Expenses: 2014-2015: $6,070 in state, $18,888 out of state; room/board: $9,072
Financial aid: (303) 556-4741

Naropa University

Boulder CO
(303) 546-3572
U.S. News ranking: Reg. U. (W), unranked
Website: www.naropa.edu
Admissions email: admissions@naropa.edu
Private; founded 1974
Freshman admissions: N/A; 2014-2015: 157 applied, 110 accepted. Neither SAT nor ACT required. ACT 25/75 percentile: N/A. High school rank: N/A
Early decision deadline: N/A, notification date: N/A
Early action deadline: N/A, notification date: N/A
Application deadline (fall): rolling
Undergraduate student body: 366 full time, 20 part time; 33% male, 67% female; 0% American Indian, 1% Asian, 2% black, 11% Hispanic, 11% multiracial, 0% Pacific Islander, 62% white, 3% international; 37% from in state; 19% live on campus; 0% of students in fraternities, 0% in sororities
Most popular majors: 8% English Language and Literature, General, 13% Health and Physical Education/Fitness, Other, 13% Multi/Interdisciplinary Studies, Other, 34% Psychology, General, 12% Visual and Performing Arts, General
Expenses: 2015-2016: $30,760; room/board: $9,604
Financial aid: (303) 546-3565; 75% of undergrads determined to have financial need; average aid package $35,101

Regis University

Denver CO
(303) 458-4900
U.S. News ranking: Reg. U. (W), No. 28
Website: www.regis.edu
Admissions email: regisadm@regis.edu
Private; founded 1877
Affiliation: Roman Catholic (Jesuit)
Freshman admissions: selective; 2014-2015: 2,422 applied, 2,326 accepted. Either SAT or ACT required. ACT 25/75 percentile: 22-27. High school rank: 22% in top tenth, 50% in top quarter, 79% in top half
Early decision deadline: N/A, notification date: N/A
Early action deadline: N/A, notification date: N/A
Application deadline (fall): 8/1
Undergraduate student body: 2,501 full time, 2,508 part time; 39% male, 61% female; 1% American Indian, 4% Asian, 5% black, 19% Hispanic, 3% multiracial, 0% Pacific Islander, 61% white, 1% international; 67% from in state; 48% live on campus; N/A of students in fraternities, N/A in sororities
Most popular majors: 28% Business, Management, Marketing, and Related Support Services, 5% Computer and Information Sciences and Support Services, 36% Health Professions and Related Programs, 5% Liberal Arts and Sciences, General Studies and Humanities, 5% Psychology
Expenses: 2015-2016: $33,710; room/board: $9,830
Financial aid: (303) 458-4066; 69% of undergrads determined to have financial need; average aid package $26,920

Rocky Mountain College of Art and Design[1]

Lakewood CO
(303) 225-8576
U.S. News ranking: Arts, unranked
Website: www.rmcad.edu/
Admissions email: admissions@rmcad.edu
For-profit; founded 1963
Application deadline (fall): rolling
Undergraduate student body: N/A full time, N/A part time
Expenses: 2014-2015: $22,470; room/board: N/A
Financial aid: (303) 753-6046

United States Air Force Academy

USAF Academy CO
(800) 443-9266
U.S. News ranking: Nat. Lib. Arts, No. 29
Website: academyadmissions.com
Admissions email: rr_webmail@usafa.edu
Public; founded 1954
Freshman admissions: most selective; 2014-2015: 9,050 applied, 1,498 accepted. Either SAT or ACT required. ACT 25/75 percentile: 28-32. High school rank: 56% in top tenth, 85% in top quarter, 98% in top half
Early decision deadline: N/A, notification date: N/A
Early action deadline: N/A, notification date: N/A
Application deadline (fall): 12/31
Undergraduate student body: 3,952 full time, 0 part time; 78% male, 22% female; 0% American Indian, 4% Asian, 6% black, 10% Hispanic, 6% multiracial, 1% Pacific Islander, 65% white, 1% international; 13% from in state; 100% live on campus; 0% of students in fraternities, 0% in sororities
Most popular majors: 7% Biological and Biomedical Sciences, 17% Business, Management, Marketing, and Related Support Services, 34% Engineering, 9% Multi/Interdisciplinary Studies, 15% Social Sciences
Expenses: N/A
Financial aid: (719) 333-3160; 0% of undergrads determined to have financial need; average aid package $0

University of Colorado–Boulder

Boulder CO
(303) 492-6301
U.S. News ranking: Nat. U., No. 89
Website: www.colorado.edu
Admissions email: apply@colorado.edu
Public; founded 1876
Freshman admissions: more selective; 2014-2015: 28,768 applied, 24,230 accepted. Either SAT or ACT required. ACT 25/75 percentile: 24-30. High school rank: 27% in top tenth, 54% in top quarter, 87% in top half
Early decision deadline: N/A, notification date: N/A
Early action deadline: 11/15, notification date: 2/1
Application deadline (fall): 1/15
Undergraduate student body: 24,245 full time, 2,181 part time; 56% male, 44% female; 0% American Indian, 5% Asian, 2% black, 10% Hispanic, 4% multiracial, 0% Pacific Islander, 72% white, 5% international; 62% from in state; 29% live on campus; 11% of students in fraternities, 19% in sororities
Most popular majors: 12% Biological and Biomedical Sciences, 11% Business, Management, Marketing, and Related Support Services, 10% Engineering, 10% Psychology, 15% Social Sciences
Expenses: 2015-2016: $11,091 in state, $34,125 out of state; room/board: $13,194
Financial aid: (303) 492-5091; 38% of undergrads determined to have financial need; average aid package $16,269

University of Colorado–Colorado Springs

Colorado Springs CO
(719) 255-3383
U.S. News ranking: Reg. U. (W), No. 46
Website: www.uccs.edu
Admissions email: admrecor@uccs.edu
Public; founded 1965
Freshman admissions: selective; 2014-2015: 7,619 applied, 7,036 accepted. Either SAT or ACT required. ACT 25/75 percentile: 21-26. High school rank: 13% in top tenth, 35% in top quarter, 71% in top half
Early decision deadline: N/A, notification date: N/A
Early action deadline: N/A, notification date: N/A
Application deadline (fall): rolling
Undergraduate student body: 7,365 full time, 2,124 part time; 48% male, 52% female; 0% American Indian, 3% Asian, 4% black, 15% Hispanic, 7% multiracial, 0% Pacific Islander, 67% white, 1% international; 88% from in state; 13% live on campus; 1% of students in fraternities, 2% in sororities
Most popular majors: 17% Business Administration, Management and Operations, 9% Communication, Journalism, and Related Programs, 14% Health Professions and Related Programs, 9% Psychology, 13% Social Sciences
Expenses: 2014-2015: $8,982 in state, $21,522 out of state; room/board: N/A
Financial aid: (719) 262-3460

University of Colorado–Denver

Denver CO
(303) 556-2704
U.S. News ranking: Nat. U., No. 199
Website: www.ucdenver.edu
Admissions email: admissions@ucdenver.edu
Public; founded 1912
Freshman admissions: selective; 2014-2015: 7,220 applied, 5,270 accepted. Either SAT or ACT required. ACT 25/75 percentile: 20-25. High school rank: 18% in top tenth, 47% in top quarter, 78% in top half
Early decision deadline: N/A, notification date: N/A
Early action deadline: N/A, notification date: N/A
Application deadline (fall): rolling
Undergraduate student body: 7,996 full time, 5,513 part time; 46% male, 54% female; 0% American Indian, 10% Asian, 5% black, 17% Hispanic, 4% multiracial, 0% Pacific Islander, 50% white, 10% international; 92% from in state; 5% live on campus; N/A of students in fraternities, N/A in sororities
Most popular majors: 10% Biology/Biological Sciences, General, 15% Business Administration and Management, General, 6% Psychology, General, 12% Registered Nursing/Registered Nurse, 5% Speech Communication and Rhetoric
Expenses: 2015-2016: $10,404 in state, $29,334 out of state; room/board: N/A
Financial aid: (303) 556-2886; 60% of undergrads determined to have financial need; average aid package $9,059

University of Denver

Denver CO
(303) 871-2036
U.S. News ranking: Nat. U., No. 86
Website: www.du.edu
Admissions email: admission@du.edu
Private; founded 1864
Freshman admissions: more selective; 2014-2015: 13,670 applied, 10,456 accepted. Either SAT or ACT required. ACT 25/75 percentile: 25-30. High school rank: 42% in top tenth, 74% in top quarter, 95% in top half
Early decision deadline: 11/1, notification date: 12/15
Early action deadline: 11/1, notification date: 1/15
Application deadline (fall): 1/15
Undergraduate student body: 5,304 full time, 339 part time; 46% male, 54% female; 0% American Indian, 4% Asian, 3% black, 9% Hispanic, 3% multiracial, 0% Pacific Islander, 68% white, 10% international; 43% from in state; 47% live on campus; 24% of students in fraternities, 32% in sororities
Most popular majors: 28% Business, Management, Marketing, and Related Support Services, 8% Communication, Journalism, and Related Programs, 7% Psychology, 18% Social Sciences, 10% Visual and Performing Arts
Expenses: 2015-2016: $44,178; room/board: $11,498
Financial aid: (303) 871-4020; 42% of undergrads determined to have financial need; average aid package $34,455

University of Northern Colorado

Greeley CO
(970) 351-2881
U.S. News ranking: Nat. U., second tier
Website: www.unco.edu
Admissions email: admissions.help@unco.edu
Public; founded 1890
Freshman admissions: selective; 2014-2015: 7,831 applied, 5,551 accepted. Neither SAT nor ACT required. ACT 25/75 percentile: 19-25. High school rank: 12% in top tenth, 35% in top quarter, 73% in top half
Early decision deadline: N/A, notification date: N/A
Early action deadline: N/A, notification date: N/A
Application deadline (fall): 8/1
Undergraduate student body: 8,324 full time, 1,100 part time; 37% male, 63% female; 0% American Indian, 2% Asian, 4% black, 17% Hispanic, 3% multiracial, 0% Pacific Islander, 56% white, 1% international; 87% from in state; 37% live on campus; 6% of students in fraternities, 6% in sororities
Most popular majors: 8% Business, Management, Marketing, and Related Support Services, 7% Communication, Journalism, and Related Programs, 16% Health Professions and Related Programs, 16% Multi/Interdisciplinary Studies, 8% Parks, Recreation, Leisure, and Fitness Studies
Expenses: 2015-2016: $7,733 in state, $19,277 out of state; room/board: $10,360
Financial aid: (970) 351-2502; 71% of undergrads determined to have financial need; average aid package $7,298

Western State Colorado University

Gunnison CO
(800) 876-5309
U.S. News ranking: Nat. Lib. Arts, second tier
Website: www.western.edu
Admissions email: discover@western.edu
Public; founded 1901
Freshman admissions: selective; 2014-2015: 1,199 applied, 1,168 accepted. Either SAT or ACT required. ACT 25/75 percentile: 19-24. High school rank: N/A
Early decision deadline: N/A, notification date: N/A
Early action deadline: N/A, notification date: N/A
Application deadline (fall): rolling
Undergraduate student body: 1,855 full time, 483 part time; 58% male, 42% female; 0% American Indian, 1% Asian, 3% black, 9% Hispanic, 4% multiracial, 1% Pacific Islander, 75% white, 1% international; 73% from in state; 45% live on campus; N/A of students in fraternities, N/A in sororities

Most popular majors: 11% Biological and Biomedical Sciences, 21% Business, Management, Marketing, and Related Support Services, 15% Parks, Recreation, Leisure, and Fitness Studies, 8% Psychology, 10% Social Sciences
Expenses: 2015-2016: $8,451 in state, $19,455 out of state; room/board: $9,307
Financial aid: (970) 943-3085; 58% of undergrads determined to have financial need; average aid package $12,202

CONNECTICUT

Albertus Magnus College

New Haven CT
(800) 578-9160
U.S. News ranking: Reg. U. (N), No. 109
Website: www.albertus.edu
Admissions email: admissions@albertus.edu
Private; founded 1925
Affiliation: Roman Catholic
Freshman admissions: less selective; 2014-2015: 780 applied, 519 accepted. Either SAT or ACT required. ACT 25/75 percentile: 19-29. High school rank: 7% in top tenth, 24% in top quarter, 68% in top half
Early decision deadline: N/A, notification date: N/A
Early action deadline: N/A, notification date: N/A
Application deadline (fall): rolling
Undergraduate student body: 1,146 full time, 110 part time; 35% male, 65% female; 0% American Indian, 0% Asian, 34% black, 15% Hispanic, 1% multiracial, 0% Pacific Islander, 41% white, 1% international
Most popular majors: 53% Business, Management, Marketing, and Related Support Services, 5% English Language and Literature/Letters, 10% Homeland Security, Law Enforcement, Firefighting and Related Protective Services, 10% Psychology, 10% Social Sciences
Expenses: 2015-2016: $29,650; room/board: $13,608
Financial aid: (203) 773-8508; 88% of undergrads determined to have financial need; average aid package $15,663

Central Connecticut State University

New Britain CT
(860) 832-2278
U.S. News ranking: Reg. U. (N), No. 106
Website: www.ccsu.edu
Admissions email: admissions@ccsu.edu
Public; founded 1849
Freshman admissions: selective; 2014-2015: 8,173 applied, 4,940 accepted. Either SAT or ACT required. SAT 25/75 percentile: 920-1110. High school rank: 9% in top tenth, 19% in top quarter, 68% in top half
Early decision deadline: N/A, notification date: N/A
Early action deadline: N/A, notification date: N/A
Application deadline (fall): 6/1
Undergraduate student body: 7,702 full time, 2,169 part time; 53% male, 47% female; 0% American Indian, 4% Asian, 11% black, 13% Hispanic, 3% multiracial, 0% Pacific Islander, 66% white, 1% international; 97% from in state; 22% live on campus; N/A of students in fraternities, N/A in sororities
Most popular majors: 24% Business, Management, Marketing, and Related Support Services, 11% Education, 6% Engineering Technologies and Engineering-Related Fields, 7% Psychology, 15% Social Sciences
Expenses: 2015-2016: $9,300 in state, $20,410 out of state; room/board: $11,134
Financial aid: (860) 832-2200; 78% of undergrads determined to have financial need; average aid package $8,672

Charter Oak State College

New Britain CT
(860) 832-3855
U.S. News ranking: Nat. Lib. Arts, unranked
Website: www.charteroak.edu
Admissions email: info@charteroak.edu
Public
Freshman admissions: N/A; 2014-2015: N/A applied, N/A accepted. Neither SAT nor ACT required. ACT 25/75 percentile: N/A. High school rank: N/A
Early decision deadline: N/A, notification date: N/A
Early action deadline: N/A, notification date: N/A
Application deadline (fall): rolling
Undergraduate student body: 386 full time, 1,543 part time; 33% male, 67% female; 0% American Indian, 1% Asian, 18% black, 13% Hispanic, 3% multiracial, 0% Pacific Islander, 61% white, 1% international; 78% from in state; N/A live on campus; N/A of students in fraternities, N/A in sororities
Most popular majors: Information not available
Expenses: 2015-2016: $9,015 in state, $11,625 out of state; room/board: N/A
Financial aid: N/A

Connecticut College

New London CT
(860) 439-2200
U.S. News ranking: Nat. Lib. Arts, No. 48
Website: www.conncoll.edu
Admissions email: admission@conncoll.edu
Private; founded 1911
Freshman admissions: more selective; 2014-2015: 5,394 applied, 2,028 accepted. Neither SAT nor ACT required. SAT 25/75 percentile: 1250-1410. High school rank: 48% in top tenth, 92% in top quarter, 98% in top half
Early decision deadline: 11/15, notification date: 12/15
Early action deadline: N/A, notification date: N/A
Application deadline (fall): 1/1
Undergraduate student body: 1,873 full time, 20 part time; 38% male, 62% female; 0% American Indian, 3% Asian, 3% black, 9% Hispanic, 3% multiracial, 0% Pacific Islander, 72% white, 5% international; 17% from in state; 99% live on campus; 0% of students in fraternities, 0% in sororities
Most popular majors: 15% Economics, 6% English Language and Literature, General, 8% International Relations and National Security Studies, 8% Political Science and Government, 10% Psychology, General
Expenses: 2015-2016: $49,350; room/board: $13,615
Financial aid: (860) 439-2058; 52% of undergrads determined to have financial need; average aid package $39,458

Eastern Connecticut State University

Willimantic CT
(860) 465-5286
U.S. News ranking: Reg. U. (N), No. 92
Website: www.easternct.edu
Admissions email: admissions@easternct.edu
Public; founded 1889
Freshman admissions: selective; 2014-2015: 4,756 applied, 3,001 accepted. Neither SAT nor ACT required. SAT 25/75 percentile: 920-1120. High school rank: 6% in top tenth, 28% in top quarter, 71% in top half
Early decision deadline: N/A, notification date: N/A
Early action deadline: N/A, notification date: N/A
Application deadline (fall): rolling
Undergraduate student body: 4,288 full time, 851 part time; 47% male, 53% female; 0% American Indian, 2% Asian, 7% black, 9% Hispanic, 3% multiracial, 0% Pacific Islander, 69% white, 1% international; 96% from in state; 53% live on campus; N/A of students in fraternities, N/A in sororities
Most popular majors: 15% Business, Management, Marketing, and Related Support Services, 9% Communication, Journalism, and Related Programs, 14% Liberal Arts and Sciences, General Studies and Humanities, 10% Psychology, 12% Social Sciences
Expenses: 2015-2016: $10,016 in state, $21,126 out of state; room/board: $12,108
Financial aid: (860) 465-5205; 70% of undergrads determined to have financial need; average aid package $8,843

Fairfield University

Fairfield CT
(203) 254-4100
U.S. News ranking: Reg. U. (N), No. 6
Website: www.fairfield.edu
Admissions email: admis@fairfield.edu
Private; founded 1942
Affiliation: Roman Catholic (Jesuit)
Freshman admissions: selective; 2014-2015: 9,978 applied, 7,137 accepted. Neither SAT nor ACT required. SAT 25/75 percentile: 1090-1260. High school rank: N/A
Early decision deadline: 11/15, notification date: 12/15
Early action deadline: 11/1, notification date: 12/20
Application deadline (fall): 1/15
Undergraduate student body: 3,688 full time, 294 part time; 41% male, 59% female; 0% American Indian, 2% Asian, 2% black, 7% Hispanic, 1% multiracial, 0% Pacific Islander, 75% white, 2% international; 29% from in state; 76% live on campus; N/A of students in fraternities, N/A in sororities
Most popular majors: 28% Business, Management, Marketing, and Related Support Services, 11% Communication, Journalism, and Related Programs, 7% English Language and Literature/Letters, 12% Health Professions and Related Programs, 14% Social Sciences
Expenses: 2015-2016: $44,875; room/board: $13,520
Financial aid: (203) 254-4125; 49% of undergrads determined to have financial need; average aid package $30,054

Lyme Academy College of Fine Arts[1]

Old Lyme CT
(860) 434-5232
U.S. News ranking: Arts, unranked
Website: www.lymeacademy.edu
Admissions email: admissions@lymeacademy.edu
Private
Application deadline (fall): N/A
Undergraduate student body: N/A full time, N/A part time
Expenses: 2014-2015: $30,456; room/board: $10,463
Financial aid: (860) 434-5232

Mitchell College[1]

New London CT
(800) 443-2811
U.S. News ranking: Reg. Coll. (N), unranked
Website: www.mitchell.edu
Admissions email: admissions@mitchell.edu
Private
Application deadline (fall): N/A
Undergraduate student body: N/A full time, N/A part time
Expenses: 2014-2015: $30,012; room/board: $12,492
Financial aid: (860) 701-5061

Post University[1]

Waterbury CT
(203) 596-4520
U.S. News ranking: Reg. Coll. (N), second tier
Website: www.post.edu
Admissions email: admissions@post.edu
For-profit; founded 1890
Application deadline (fall): rolling
Undergraduate student body: N/A full time, N/A part time
Expenses: 2014-2015: $16,510; room/board: $10,500
Financial aid: (203) 596-4526

Quinnipiac University

Hamden CT
(800) 462-1944
U.S. News ranking: Reg. U. (N), No. 11
Website: www.quinnipiac.edu
Admissions email: admissions@quinnipiac.edu
Private; founded 1929
Freshman admissions: selective; 2014-2015: 23,240 applied, 15,318 accepted. Either SAT or ACT required. SAT 25/75 percentile: 1010-1210. High school rank: 27% in top tenth, 66% in top quarter, 93% in top half
Early decision deadline: 11/1, notification date: 12/1
Early action deadline: N/A, notification date: N/A
Application deadline (fall): 2/1
Undergraduate student body: 6,335 full time, 218 part time; 40% male, 60% female; 0% American Indian, 3% Asian, 5% black, 9% Hispanic, 2% multiracial, 0% Pacific Islander, 77% white, 2% international; 25% from in state; 77% live on campus; 19% of students in fraternities, 30% in sororities
Most popular majors: 4% Biological and Biomedical Sciences, 20% Business, Management, Marketing, and Related Support Services, 18% Communication, Journalism, and Related Programs, 33% Health Professions and Related Programs, 7% Psychology
Expenses: 2015-2016: $42,270; room/board: $14,820
Financial aid: (203) 582-8750; 62% of undergrads determined to have financial need; average aid package $25,571

Sacred Heart University

Fairfield CT
(203) 371-7880
U.S. News ranking: Reg. U. (N), No. 41
Website: www.sacredheart.edu
Admissions email: enroll@sacredheart.edu
Private; founded 1963
Affiliation: Roman Catholic
Freshman admissions: selective; 2014-2015: 9,114 applied, 5,209 accepted. Neither SAT nor ACT required. SAT 25/75 percentile: 955-1229. High school rank: N/A
Early decision deadline: 12/1, notification date: 12/15
Early action deadline: 12/15, notification date: 1/31
Application deadline (fall): rolling
Undergraduate student body: 4,232 full time, 765 part time; 36% male, 64% female; 0% American Indian, 2% Asian, 4% black, 7% Hispanic, 1% multiracial, 0% Pacific Islander, 69% white, 1% international; 40% from in state; 53% live on campus; 16% of students in fraternities, 30% in sororities
Most popular majors: 5% Biological and Biomedical Sciences, 26% Business, Management, Marketing, and Related Support Services, 30% Business, Management, Marketing, and Related Support Services, 5% Homeland Security, Law Enforcement, Firefighting and Related Protective Services, 12% Psychology
Expenses: 2015-2016: $37,170; room/board: $14,142
Financial aid: (203) 371-7980; 70% of undergrads determined to have financial need; average aid package $19,572

Southern Connecticut State University
New Haven CT
(203) 392-5656
U.S. News ranking: Reg. U. (N), No. 125
Website: www.southernct.edu/
Admissions email: information@southernct.edu
Public; founded 1893
Freshman admissions: less selective; 2014-2015: 4,568 applied, 3,268 accepted. Either SAT or ACT required. SAT 25/75 percentile: 830-1030. High school rank: 1% in top tenth, 8% in top quarter, 41% in top half
Early decision deadline: N/A, notification date: N/A
Early action deadline: N/A, notification date: N/A
Application deadline (fall): rolling
Undergraduate student body: 6,802 full time, 1,331 part time; 40% male, 60% female; 0% American Indian, 3% Asian, 16% black, 12% Hispanic, 2% multiracial, 0% Pacific Islander, 58% white, 0% international; 96% from in state; 31% live on campus; 1% of students in fraternities, 1% in sororities
Most popular majors: 13% Business/Commerce, General, 8% Education, General, 15% Health and Wellness, General, 13% Liberal Arts and Sciences/Liberal Studies, 11% Psychology, General
Expenses: 2015-2016: $9,600 in state, $20,710 out of state; room/board: $11,614
Financial aid: (203) 392-5222; 68% of undergrads determined to have financial need; average aid package $13,602

Trinity College
Hartford CT
(860) 297-2180
U.S. News ranking: Nat. Lib. Arts, No. 43
Website: www.trincoll.edu
Admissions email: admissions.office@trincoll.edu
Private; founded 1823
Freshman admissions: more selective; 2014-2015: 7,507 applied, 2,480 accepted. Either SAT or ACT required. SAT 25/75 percentile: 1150-1340. High school rank: 43% in top tenth, 80% in top quarter, 97% in top half
Early decision deadline: 11/15, notification date: 12/15
Early action deadline: N/A, notification date: N/A
Application deadline (fall): 1/1
Undergraduate student body: 2,146 full time, 109 part time; 53% male, 47% female; 0% American Indian, 4% Asian, 6% black, 7% Hispanic, 3% multiracial, 0% Pacific Islander, 65% white, 10% international; 17% from in state; 91% live on campus; 21% of students in fraternities, 12% in sororities
Most popular majors: 5% African Studies, 12% Economics, General, 7% English Language and Literature, General, 11% Political Science and Government, General, 8% Psychology, General
Expenses: 2015-2016: $50,776; room/board: $13,144
Financial aid: (860) 297-2046; 41% of undergrads determined to have financial need; average aid package $44,424

United States Coast Guard Academy
New London CT
(800) 883-8724
U.S. News ranking: Reg. Coll. (N), No. 1
Website: www.uscga.edu
Admissions email: admissions@uscga.edu
Public; founded 1931
Freshman admissions: more selective; 2014-2015: 2,096 applied, 379 accepted. Either SAT or ACT required. SAT 25/75 percentile: 1170-1340. High school rank: 40% in top tenth, 76% in top quarter, 97% in top half
Early decision deadline: N/A, notification date: N/A
Early action deadline: 11/15, notification date: 2/1
Application deadline (fall): 2/1
Undergraduate student body: 896 full time, N/A part time; 65% male, 35% female; 1% American Indian, 6% Asian, 4% black, 12% Hispanic, 7% multiracial, 0% Pacific Islander, 65% white, 3% international; 6% from in state; 100% live on campus; 0% of students in fraternities, 0% in sororities
Most popular majors: Information not available
Expenses: 2015-2016: $942 in state, $942 out of state; room/board: $0
Financial aid: N/A; 0% of undergrads determined to have financial need; average aid package $0

University of Bridgeport
Bridgeport CT
(203) 576-4552
U.S. News ranking: Reg. U. (N), second tier
Website: www.bridgeport.edu
Admissions email: admit@bridgeport.edu
Private; founded 1927
Freshman admissions: less selective; 2014-2015: 5,990 applied, 3,637 accepted. Either SAT or ACT required. SAT 25/75 percentile: 820-980. High school rank: 7% in top tenth, 30% in top quarter, 62% in top half
Early decision deadline: N/A, notification date: N/A
Early action deadline: N/A, notification date: N/A
Application deadline (fall): rolling
Undergraduate student body: 2,254 full time, 767 part time; 35% male, 65% female; 1% American Indian, 3% Asian, 38% black, 17% Hispanic, 2% multiracial, 0% Pacific Islander, 25% white, 15% international; 64% from in state; 30% live on campus; 5% of students in fraternities, 5% in sororities
Most popular majors: 18% Business/Commerce, General, 13% Dental Hygiene/Hygienist, 18% General Studies, 11% Human Services, General, 15% Psychology, General
Expenses: 2015-2016: $30,850; room/board: $12,990
Financial aid: (203) 576-4568; 81% of undergrads determined to have financial need; average aid package $25,487

University of Connecticut
Storrs CT
(860) 486-3137
U.S. News ranking: Nat. U., No. 57
Website: www.uconn.edu
Admissions email: beahusky@uconn.edu
Public; founded 1881
Freshman admissions: more selective; 2014-2015: 31,280 applied, 15,629 accepted. Either SAT or ACT required. SAT 25/75 percentile: 1150-1350. High school rank: 50% in top tenth, 85% in top quarter, 98% in top half
Early decision deadline: N/A, notification date: N/A
Early action deadline: N/A, notification date: N/A
Application deadline (fall): 1/15
Undergraduate student body: 17,677 full time, 718 part time; 50% male, 50% female; 0% American Indian, 10% Asian, 5% black, 8% Hispanic, 3% multiracial, 0% Pacific Islander, 62% white, 4% international; 78% from in state; 71% live on campus; 8% of students in fraternities, 12% in sororities
Most popular majors: 8% Biological and Biomedical Sciences, 11% Business, Management, Marketing, and Related Support Services, 8% Engineering, 12% Health Professions and Related Programs, 12% Social Sciences
Expenses: 2015-2016: $13,364 in state, $34,908 out of state; room/board: $12,174
Financial aid: (860) 486-2819; 57% of undergrads determined to have financial need; average aid package $13,545

University of Hartford
West Hartford CT
(860) 768-4296
U.S. News ranking: Reg. U. (N), No. 92
Website: www.hartford.edu
Admissions email: admission@hartford.edu
Private; founded 1877
Freshman admissions: selective; 2014-2015: 14,444 applied, 10,419 accepted. Either SAT or ACT required. SAT 25/75 percentile: 880-1110. High school rank: N/A
Early decision deadline: N/A, notification date: N/A
Early action deadline: 11/15, notification date: 12/1
Application deadline (fall): rolling
Undergraduate student body: 4,446 full time, 734 part time; 50% male, 50% female; 0% American Indian, 3% Asian, 15% black, 10% Hispanic, 3% multiracial, 0% Pacific Islander, 58% white, 6% international; 51% from in state; 61% live on campus; N/A of students in fraternities, N/A in sororities
Most popular majors: 13% Business, Management, Marketing, and Related Support Services, Other, 6% Education, Other, 8% Engineering, Other, 12% Health Professions and Related Clinical Sciences, Other, 19% Visual and Performing Arts, Other
Expenses: 2015-2016: $36,460; room/board: $11,638
Financial aid: (860) 768-4296

University of New Haven
West Haven CT
(203) 932-7319
U.S. News ranking: Reg. U. (N), No. 92
Website: www.newhaven.edu
Admissions email: adminfo@newhaven.edu
Private; founded 1920
Freshman admissions: selective; 2014-2015: 9,006 applied, 7,282 accepted. Either SAT or ACT required. SAT 25/75 percentile: 950-1160. High school rank: 17% in top tenth, 50% in top quarter, 82% in top half
Early decision deadline: 12/1, notification date: 12/15
Early action deadline: 12/15, notification date: 1/15
Application deadline (fall): rolling
Undergraduate student body: 4,674 full time, 374 part time; 50% male, 50% female; 0% American Indian, 2% Asian, 9% black, 10% Hispanic, 2% multiracial, 0% Pacific Islander, 59% white, 8% international; 42% from in state; 54% live on campus; N/A of students in fraternities, N/A in sororities
Most popular majors: 8% Biological and Biomedical Sciences, 14% Business, Management, Marketing, and Related Support Services, 7% Health Professions and Related Programs, 39% Homeland Security, Law Enforcement, Firefighting and Related Protective Services, 9% Visual and Performing Arts
Expenses: 2015-2016: $35,650; room/board: $14,720
Financial aid: (203) 932-7315; 73% of undergrads determined to have financial need; average aid package $21,989

University of St. Joseph
West Hartford CT
(860) 231-5216
U.S. News ranking: Reg. U. (N), No. 79
Website: www.usj.edu
Admissions email: admissions@usj.edu
Private; founded 1932
Affiliation: Roman Catholic
Freshman admissions: less selective; 2014-2015: 724 applied, 579 accepted. Either SAT or ACT required. SAT 25/75 percentile: 870-1060. High school rank: N/A
Early decision deadline: N/A, notification date: N/A
Early action deadline: N/A, notification date: N/A
Application deadline (fall): rolling
Undergraduate student body: 761 full time, 226 part time; 2% male, 98% female; 0% American Indian, 2% Asian, 16% black, 15% Hispanic, 1% multiracial, 0% Pacific Islander, 54% white, 0% international; 95% from in state; 32% live on campus; N/A of students in fraternities, N/A in sororities
Most popular majors: 8% Biological and Biomedical Sciences, 15% Family and Consumer Sciences/Human Sciences, 22% Health Professions and Related Programs, 11% Psychology, 19% Public Administration and Social Service Professions
Expenses: 2015-2016: $36,170; room/board: $14,850
Financial aid: (860) 231-5223; 90% of undergrads determined to have financial need; average aid package $24,930

Wesleyan University
Middletown CT
(860) 685-3000
U.S. News ranking: Nat. Lib. Arts, No. 14
Website: www.wesleyan.edu
Admissions email: admissions@wesleyan.edu
Private; founded 1831
Freshman admissions: most selective; 2014-2015: 9,390 applied, 2,245 accepted. Neither SAT nor ACT required. SAT 25/75 percentile: 1290-1480. High school rank: 64% in top tenth, N/A in top quarter, 97% in top half
Early decision deadline: 11/15, notification date: 12/15
Early action deadline: N/A, notification date: N/A
Application deadline (fall): 1/1
Undergraduate student body: 2,914 full time, 14 part time; 48% male, 52% female; 0% American Indian, 9% Asian, 7% black, 10% Hispanic, 6% multiracial, 0% Pacific Islander, 53% white, 9% international; 8% from in state; 99% live on campus; 1% of students in fraternities, 1% in sororities
Most popular majors: 9% Economics, General, 7% English Language and Literature, General, 6% Physiological Psychology/Psychobiology, 6% Political Science and Government, General, 9% Psychology, General
Expenses: 2015-2016: $48,974; room/board: $13,504
Financial aid: (860) 685-2800; 46% of undergrads determined to have financial need; average aid package $45,507

Western Connecticut State University
Danbury CT
(203) 837-9000
U.S. News ranking: Reg. U. (N), second tier
Website: www.wcsu.edu
Admissions email: admissions@wcsu.edu
Public; founded 1903
Freshman admissions: selective; 2014-2015: 3,825 applied, 2,191 accepted. Either SAT or ACT required. SAT 25/75 percentile: 890-1080. High school rank: 7% in top tenth, 24% in top quarter, 63% in top half
Early decision deadline: N/A, notification date: N/A
Early action deadline: N/A, notification date: N/A
Application deadline (fall): rolling
Undergraduate student body: 4,365 full time, 1,077 part time; 47% male, 53% female; 0% American Indian, 3% Asian, 12% black, 16% Hispanic, 1% multiracial, 0% Pacific Islander, 65% white, 0% international; 94% from in state; 38% live on campus; 4% of students in fraternities, 5% in sororities
Most popular majors: 21% Business, Management, Marketing, and Related Support Services, 9% Communication,

Journalism, and Related Programs, 12% Health Professions and Related Programs, 14% Homeland Security, Law Enforcement, Firefighting and Related Protective Services, 9% Psychology
Expenses: 2015-2016: $9,516 in state, $20,626 out of state; room/board: $11,738
Financial aid: (203) 837-8580; 68% of undergrads determined to have financial need; average aid package $7,153

Yale University
New Haven CT
(203) 432-9300
U.S. News ranking: Nat. U., No. 3
Website: www.yale.edu/
Admissions email: student.questions@yale.edu
Private; founded 1701
Freshman admissions: most selective; 2014-2015: 30,932 applied, 1,950 accepted. Either SAT or ACT required. SAT 25/75 percentile: 1410-1600. High school rank: 96% in top tenth, 99% in top quarter, 100% in top half
Early decision deadline: N/A, notification date: N/A
Early action deadline: 11/1, notification date: 12/15
Application deadline (fall): 1/1
Undergraduate student body: 5,470 full time, 7 part time; 51% male, 49% female; 1% American Indian, 17% Asian, 7% black, 11% Hispanic, 6% multiracial, 0% Pacific Islander, 47% white, 10% international; 6% from in state; 86% live on campus; N/A of students in fraternities, N/A in sororities
Most popular majors: 7% Biology/Biological Sciences, General, 12% Economics, General, 7% History, General, 10% Political Science and Government, General, 6% Psychology, General
Expenses: 2015-2016: $47,600; room/board: $14,600
Financial aid: (203) 432-2700; 50% of undergrads determined to have financial need; average aid package $48,261

DELAWARE

Delaware State University
Dover DE
(302) 857-6353
U.S. News ranking: Reg. U. (N), No. 125
Website: www.desu.edu
Admissions email: admissions@desu.edu
Public; founded 1891
Freshman admissions: less selective; 2014-2015: 7,191 applied, 3,145 accepted. Either SAT or ACT required. SAT 25/75 percentile: 820-970. High school rank: 9% in top tenth, 27% in top quarter, 65% in top half
Early decision deadline: N/A, notification date: N/A
Early action deadline: N/A, notification date: N/A
Application deadline (fall): rolling
Undergraduate student body: 3,479 full time, 533 part time; 37% male, 63% female; 0% American Indian, 1% Asian, 75% black, 6% Hispanic, 4% multiracial, 0% Pacific Islander, 11% white, 2% international; 56% from in state; 55% live on campus; 4% of students in fraternities, 7% in sororities
Most popular majors: 13% Business, Management, Marketing, and Related Support Services, 8% Communication, Journalism, and Related Programs, 11% Parks, Recreation, Leisure, and Fitness Studies, 10% Psychology, 12% Social Sciences
Expenses: 2015-2016: $7,532 in state, $16,138 out of state; room/board: $10,820
Financial aid: (302) 857-6250; 83% of undergrads determined to have financial need; average aid package $11,631

Goldey-Beacom College
Wilmington DE
(302) 225-6248
U.S. News ranking: Business, unranked
Website: gbc.edu
Admissions email: admissions@gbc.edu
Private; founded 1886
Freshman admissions: less selective; 2014-2015: 710 applied, 371 accepted. SAT required. SAT 25/75 percentile: N/A. High school rank: N/A
Early decision deadline: N/A, notification date: N/A
Early action deadline: N/A, notification date: N/A
Application deadline (fall): rolling
Undergraduate student body: 492 full time, 147 part time; 46% male, 54% female; 1% American Indian, 1% Asian, 26% black, 4% Hispanic, 2% multiracial, 0% Pacific Islander, 43% white, 22% international
Most popular majors: Information not available
Expenses: 2014-2015: $22,500; room/board: $6,740
Financial aid: (302) 225-6265

University of Delaware
Newark DE
(302) 831-8123
U.S. News ranking: Nat. U., No. 75
Website: www.udel.edu/
Admissions email: admissions@udel.edu
Public; founded 1743
Freshman admissions: more selective; 2014-2015: 25,032 applied, 16,491 accepted. Either SAT or ACT required. SAT 25/75 percentile: 1100-1300. High school rank: 37% in top tenth, 72% in top quarter, 95% in top half
Early decision deadline: N/A, notification date: N/A
Early action deadline: N/A, notification date: N/A
Application deadline (fall): 1/15
Undergraduate student body: 16,703 full time, 1,438 part time; 42% male, 58% female; 0% American Indian, 4% Asian, 5% black, 7% Hispanic, 3% multiracial, 0% Pacific Islander, 76% white, 4% international; 39% from in state; 45% live on campus; 17% of students in fraternities, 21% in sororities
Most popular majors: 21% Business, Management, Marketing, and Related Support Services, 8% Education, 10% Engineering, 9% Health Professions and Related Programs, 11% Social Sciences
Expenses: 2015-2016: $12,342 in state, $30,692 out of state; room/board: $11,868
Financial aid: (302) 831-8761; 50% of undergrads determined to have financial need; average aid package $15,854

Wesley College[1]
Dover DE
(302) 736-2400
U.S. News ranking: Reg. Coll. (N), second tier
Website: www.wesley.edu
Admissions email: admissions@wesley.edu
Private; founded 1873
Affiliation: United Methodist
Application deadline (fall): 4/30
Undergraduate student body: N/A full time, N/A part time
Expenses: 2014-2015: $24,100; room/board: $10,890
Financial aid: (302) 736-2321

Wilmington University
New Castle DE
(302) 328-9407
U.S. News ranking: Nat. U., unranked
Website: www.wilmu.edu
Admissions email: undergradadmissions@wilmu.edu
Private; founded 1967
Freshman admissions: N/A; 2014-2015: 1,660 applied, 1,658 accepted. Neither SAT nor ACT required. ACT 25/75 percentile: N/A. High school rank: N/A
Early decision deadline: N/A, notification date: N/A
Early action deadline: N/A, notification date: N/A
Application deadline (fall): rolling
Undergraduate student body: 3,760 full time, 5,468 part time; 36% male, 64% female; 1% American Indian, 2% Asian, 25% black, 3% Hispanic, 0% multiracial, 0% Pacific Islander, 52% white, 2% international; 71% from in state; 0% live on campus; 0% of students in fraternities, 0% in sororities
Most popular majors: Information not available
Expenses: 2015-2016: $10,430; room/board: N/A
Financial aid: (302) 328-9437

DISTRICT OF COLUMBIA

American University
Washington DC
(202) 885-6000
U.S. News ranking: Nat. U., No. 72
Website: www.american.edu
Admissions email: admissions@american.edu
Private; founded 1893
Affiliation: United Methodist
Freshman admissions: more selective; 2014-2015: 15,119 applied, 6,931 accepted. Neither SAT nor ACT required. SAT 25/75 percentile: 1150-1340. High school rank: 69% in top tenth, 88% in top quarter, 98% in top half
Early decision deadline: 11/15, notification date: 12/31
Early action deadline: N/A, notification date: N/A
Application deadline (fall): 1/15
Undergraduate student body: 7,386 full time, 320 part time; 38% male, 62% female; 0% American Indian, 7% Asian, 6% black, 11% Hispanic, 5% multiracial, 0% Pacific Islander, 58% white, 7% international; 19% from in state; N/A live on campus; N/A of students in fraternities, N/A in sororities
Most popular majors: 13% Business Administration and Management, General, 4% Economics, General, 26% International Relations and Affairs, 5% Mass Communication/Media Studies, 9% Political Science and Government, General
Expenses: 2015-2016: $43,103; room/board: $14,354
Financial aid: (202) 885-6100; 55% of undergrads determined to have financial need; average aid package $29,054

The Catholic University of America
Washington DC
(800) 673-2772
U.S. News ranking: Nat. U., No. 123
Website: www.cua.edu
Admissions email: cua-admissions@cua.edu
Private; founded 1887
Affiliation: Roman Catholic
Freshman admissions: selective; 2014-2015: 6,363 applied, 4,753 accepted. Either SAT or ACT required. SAT 25/75 percentile: 1020-1230. High school rank: N/A
Early decision deadline: N/A, notification date: N/A
Early action deadline: 11/15, notification date: 12/15
Application deadline (fall): 2/15
Undergraduate student body: 3,355 full time, 217 part time; 47% male, 53% female; 0% American Indian, 3% Asian, 6% black, 12% Hispanic, 4% multiracial, 0% Pacific Islander, 63% white, 5% international; 4% from in state; 58% live on campus; 1% of students in fraternities, 1% in sororities
Most popular majors: 7% Architecture, 5% History, General, 10% Political Science and Government, General, 10% Psychology, General, 9% Registered Nursing/Registered Nurse
Expenses: 2015-2016: $40,932; room/board: $13,356
Financial aid: (202) 319-5307; 59% of undergrads determined to have financial need; average aid package $25,560

Corcoran College of Art and Design[1]
Washington DC
(202) 639-1814
U.S. News ranking: Arts, unranked
Website: www.corcoran.edu
Admissions email: admissions@corcoran.org
Private; founded 1890
Application deadline (fall): rolling
Undergraduate student body: N/A full time, N/A part time
Expenses: N/A
Financial aid: (202) 639-1818

Gallaudet University
Washington DC
(202) 651-5750
U.S. News ranking: Reg. U. (N), No. 19
Website: www.gallaudet.edu
Admissions email: admissions.office@gallaudet.edu
Private; founded 1864
Freshman admissions: less selective; 2014-2015: 496 applied, 324 accepted. Either SAT or ACT required. ACT 25/75 percentile: 15-20. High school rank: N/A
Early decision deadline: N/A, notification date: N/A
Early action deadline: N/A, notification date: N/A
Application deadline (fall): rolling
Undergraduate student body: 951 full time, 80 part time; 45% male, 55% female; 0% American Indian, 4% Asian, 12% black, 15% Hispanic, 3% multiracial, 0% Pacific Islander, 56% white, 8% international; 3% from in state; 72% live on campus; 17% of students in fraternities, 9% in sororities
Most popular majors: 11% Business, Management, Marketing, and Related Support Services, 10% Foreign Languages, Literatures, and Linguistics, 9% Parks, Recreation, Leisure, and Fitness Studies, 12% Psychology, 9% Visual and Performing Arts
Expenses: 2015-2016: $15,604; room/board: $12,630
Financial aid: (202) 651-5290; 88% of undergrads determined to have financial need; average aid package $20,376

Georgetown University
Washington DC
(202) 687-3600
U.S. News ranking: Nat. U., No. 21
Website: www.georgetown.edu
Admissions email: guadmiss@georgetown.edu
Private; founded 1789
Affiliation: Roman Catholic (Jesuit)
Freshman admissions: most selective; 2014-2015: 19,505 applied, 3,384 accepted. Either SAT or ACT required. SAT 25/75 percentile: 1320-1520. High school rank: 92% in top tenth, 99% in top quarter, 100% in top half
Early decision deadline: N/A, notification date: N/A
Early action deadline: 11/1, notification date: 12/15
Application deadline (fall): 1/10
Undergraduate student body: 7,226 full time, 369 part time; 45% male, 55% female; 0% American Indian, 10% Asian, 6% black, 8% Hispanic, 4% multiracial, 0% Pacific Islander, 58% white, 12% international; 3% from in state; 63% live on campus; N/A of students in fraternities, N/A in sororities
Most popular majors: 23% Business, Management, Marketing, and Related Support Services, 6% English Language and Literature/Letters, 5% Foreign Languages, Literatures, and Linguistics, 7% Health Professions and Related Programs, 33% Social Sciences
Expenses: 2015-2016: $48,611; room/board: $14,902

More at usnews.com/college

Financial aid: (202) 687-4547; 38% of undergrads determined to have financial need; average aid package $39,693

George Washington University

Washington DC
(202) 994-6040
U.S. News ranking: Nat. U., No. 57
Website: www.gwu.edu
Admissions email: gwadm@gwu.edu
Private; founded 1821
Freshman admissions: more selective; 2014-2015: 19,069 applied, 8,351 accepted. Either SAT or ACT required. SAT 25/75 percentile: 1200-1390. High school rank: 52% in top tenth, 86% in top quarter, 99% in top half
Early decision deadline: 11/1, notification date: 12/15
Early action deadline: N/A, notification date: N/A
Application deadline (fall): 1/15
Undergraduate student body: 9,830 full time, 910 part time; 44% male, 56% female; 0% American Indian, 10% Asian, 6% black, 8% Hispanic, 4% multiracial, 0% Pacific Islander, 58% white, 9% international; 2% from in state; 63% live on campus; 26% of students in fraternities, 31% in sororities
Most popular majors: 17% Business, Management, Marketing, and Related Support Services, 5% Engineering, 7% Health Professions and Related Programs, 6% Psychology, 36% Social Sciences
Expenses: 2015-2016: $50,435; room/board: $12,050
Financial aid: (202) 994-6620; 47% of undergrads determined to have financial need; average aid package $42,872

Howard University

Washington DC
(202) 806-2755
U.S. News ranking: Nat. U., No. 135
Website: www.howard.edu
Admissions email: admission@howard.edu
Private; founded 1867
Freshman admissions: selective; 2014-2015: 13,760 applied, 6,661 accepted. Either SAT or ACT required. SAT 25/75 percentile: 990-1220. High school rank: 26% in top tenth, 55% in top quarter, 86% in top half
Early decision deadline: N/A, notification date: N/A
Early action deadline: 11/1, notification date: 12/20
Application deadline (fall): 2/15
Undergraduate student body: 6,513 full time, 500 part time; 33% male, 67% female; 1% American Indian, 2% Asian, 91% black, 0% Hispanic, 0% multiracial, 0% Pacific Islander, 1% white, 4% international; 5% from in state; 59% live on campus; 4% of students in fraternities, 6% in sororities
Most popular majors: 10% Biological and Biomedical Sciences, 13% Business, Management, Marketing, and Related Support Services, 18% Communication, Journalism, and Related Programs, 12% Health Professions and Related Programs, 15% Social Sciences
Expenses: 2015-2016: $23,970; room/board: $13,814
Financial aid: (202) 806-2762; 84% of undergrads determined to have financial need; average aid package $14,864

Strayer University[1]

Washington DC
(202) 408-2400
U.S. News ranking: Reg. U. (N), unranked
Website: www.strayer.edu
Admissions email: mzm@strayer.edu
For-profit
Application deadline (fall): N/A
Undergraduate student body: N/A full time, N/A part time
Expenses: 2014-2015: $12,975; room/board: $10,917
Financial aid: (888) 311-0355

Trinity Washington University[1]

Washington DC
(202) 884-9400
U.S. News ranking: Reg. U. (N), second tier
Website: www.trinitydc.edu
Admissions email: admissions@trinitydc.edu
Private
Application deadline (fall): N/A
Undergraduate student body: N/A full time, N/A part time
Expenses: 2014-2015: $22,316; room/board: $9,840
Financial aid: (202) 884-9530

University of the District of Columbia

Washington DC
(202) 274-5010
U.S. News ranking: Reg. U. (N), second tier
Website: www.udc.edu/
Admissions email: N/A
Public; founded 1976
Freshman admissions: least selective; 2014-2015: 1,954 applied, 1,821 accepted. Neither SAT nor ACT required. SAT 25/75 percentile: 700-910. High school rank: 11% in top tenth, 22% in top quarter, 37% in top half
Early decision deadline: N/A, notification date: N/A
Early action deadline: N/A, notification date: N/A
Application deadline (fall): rolling
Undergraduate student body: 1,902 full time, 2,589 part time; 37% male, 63% female; 0% American Indian, 3% Asian, 63% black, 9% Hispanic, 2% multiracial, 0% Pacific Islander, 4% white, 3% international
Most popular majors: 8% Accounting, 7% Human Development and Family Studies, General, 10% Legal Studies, General, 5% Mass Communication/Media Studies, 5% Social Work
Expenses: 2014-2015: $7,255 in state, $14,535 out of state; room/board: N/A
Financial aid: (202) 274-5060; 70% of undergrads determined to have financial need; average aid package $8,200

University of the Potomac[1]

Washington DC
(202) 686-0876
U.S. News ranking: Business, unranked
Website: www.potomac.edu
Admissions email: admissions@potomac.edu
For-profit; founded 1989
Application deadline (fall): rolling
Undergraduate student body: N/A full time, N/A part time
Expenses: 2014-2015: $13,434; room/board: $6,240
Financial aid: (888) 635-1121

FLORIDA

Ave Maria University[1]

Ave Maria FL
(877) 283-8648
U.S. News ranking: Nat. Lib. Arts, second tier
Website: www.avemaria.edu
Admissions email: N/A
Private; founded 2003
Affiliation: Catholic
Application deadline (fall): rolling
Undergraduate student body: N/A full time, N/A part time
Expenses: 2014-2015: $17,940; room/board: $9,746
Financial aid: N/A

Barry University

Miami Shores FL
(305) 899-3100
U.S. News ranking: Nat. U., second tier
Website: www.barry.edu
Admissions email: admissions@mail.barry.edu
Private; founded 1940
Affiliation: Roman Catholic
Freshman admissions: less selective; 2014-2015: 7,587 applied, 3,497 accepted. Either SAT or ACT required. SAT 25/75 percentile: 840-1023. High school rank: N/A
Early decision deadline: N/A, notification date: N/A
Early action deadline: N/A, notification date: N/A
Application deadline (fall): rolling
Undergraduate student body: 3,365 full time, 631 part time; 39% male, 61% female; 0% American Indian, 2% Asian, 32% black, 29% Hispanic, 2% multiracial, 0% Pacific Islander, 20% white, 7% international
Most popular majors: Information not available
Expenses: 2015-2016: $28,160; room/board: $10,200
Financial aid: (800) 899-3673; 80% of undergrads determined to have financial need; average aid package $20,058

Beacon College[1]

Leesburg FL
(706) 323-5364
U.S. News ranking: Nat. Lib. Arts, unranked
Website: www.beaconcollege.edu/
Admissions email: admissions@beaconcollege.edu
Private; founded 1989
Application deadline (fall): rolling
Undergraduate student body: N/A full time, N/A part time
Expenses: 2014-2015: $33,016; room/board: $9,304
Financial aid: (352) 787-7660

Bethune-Cookman University

Daytona Beach FL
(800) 448-0228
U.S. News ranking: Reg. Coll. (S), No. 39
Website: www.bethune.cookman.edu
Admissions email: admissions@cookman.edu
Private; founded 1904
Affiliation: Methodist
Freshman admissions: less selective; 2014-2015: 7,936 applied, 5,056 accepted. Either SAT or ACT required. ACT 25/75 percentile: 15-18. High school rank: 13% in top tenth, 33% in top quarter, 67% in top half
Early decision deadline: N/A, notification date: N/A
Early action deadline: N/A, notification date: N/A
Application deadline (fall): rolling
Undergraduate student body: 3,696 full time, 204 part time; 41% male, 59% female; 0% American Indian, 0% Asian, 89% black, 3% Hispanic, 2% multiracial, 0% Pacific Islander, 2% white, 2% international; 70% from in state; 51% live on campus; 2% of students in fraternities, 75% in sororities
Most popular majors: 13% Business Administration and Management, General, 15% Corrections and Criminal Justice, Other, 11% Liberal Arts and Sciences/Liberal Studies, 9% Mass Communication/Media Studies, 12% Psychology, General
Expenses: 2014-2015: $14,410; room/board: $8,560
Financial aid: (386) 481-2620; 97% of undergrads determined to have financial need; average aid package $13,672

Chipola College[1]

Marianna FL
(850) 718-2211
U.S. News ranking: Reg. Coll. (S), second tier
Website: www.chipola.edu
Admissions email: N/A
Public
Application deadline (fall): N/A
Undergraduate student body: N/A full time, N/A part time
Expenses: 2014-2015: $3,120 in state, $8,950 out of state; room/board: $4,560
Financial aid: (800) 433-3243

Daytona State College[1]

Daytona Beach FL
(386) 506-3059
U.S. News ranking: Reg. Coll. (S), unranked
Website: www.daytonastate.edu
Admissions email: N/A
Public; founded 1957
Application deadline (fall): rolling
Undergraduate student body: N/A full time, N/A part time
Expenses: 2014-2015: $3,306 in state, $12,376 out of state; room/board: $6,000
Financial aid: (386) 506-3015

Eckerd College

St. Petersburg FL
(727) 864-8331
U.S. News ranking: Nat. Lib. Arts, No. 127
Website: www.eckerd.edu
Admissions email: admissions@eckerd.edu
Private; founded 1958
Affiliation: Presbyterian
Freshman admissions: selective; 2014-2015: 3,963 applied, 3,028 accepted. Either SAT or ACT required. SAT 25/75 percentile: 1010-1240. High school rank: N/A
Early decision deadline: N/A, notification date: N/A
Early action deadline: 11/15, notification date: 12/15
Application deadline (fall): rolling
Undergraduate student body: 1,776 full time, 39 part time; 39% male, 61% female; 0% American Indian, 2% Asian, 2% black, 8% Hispanic, 3% multiracial, 0% Pacific Islander, 80% white, 4% international
Most popular majors: 6% Biology, General, 10% Environmental Studies, 5% International Relations and Affairs, 12% Marine Sciences, 8% Psychology, General
Expenses: 2015-2016: $40,020; room/board: $10,920
Financial aid: (727) 864-8334; 60% of undergrads determined to have financial need; average aid package $31,297

Edward Waters College[1]

Jacksonville FL
(904) 470-8200
U.S. News ranking: Reg. Coll. (S), second tier
Website: www.ewc.edu
Admissions email: admissions@ewc.edu
Private
Application deadline (fall): N/A
Undergraduate student body: N/A full time, N/A part time
Expenses: 2014-2015: $12,525; room/board: $7,282
Financial aid: (904) 470-8192

Embry-Riddle Aeronautical University

Daytona Beach FL
(800) 862-2416
U.S. News ranking: Reg. U. (S), No. 9
Website: www.embryriddle.edu
Admissions email: dbadmit@erau.edu
Private; founded 1926
Freshman admissions: selective; 2014-2015: 4,087 applied, 2,986 accepted. Neither SAT nor ACT required. SAT 25/75 percentile: 980-1240. High school rank: 21% in top tenth, 49% in top quarter, 81% in top half
Early decision deadline: N/A, notification date: N/A
Early action deadline: N/A, notification date: N/A
Application deadline (fall): rolling
Undergraduate student body: 4,647 full time, 320 part time; 81% male, 19% female; 0% American Indian, 4% Asian, 6% black, 6% Hispanic, 6% multiracial, 0% Pacific Islander, 53% white, 15% international; 36% from in state; 41% live on campus; 10% of

students in fraternities, 14% in sororities
Most popular majors: 15% Aeronautics/Aviation/Aerospace Science and Technology, General, 24% Aerospace, Aeronautical and Astronautical/Space Engineering, 7% Air Traffic Controller, 16% Airline/Commercial/Professional Pilot and Flight Crew, 6% Homeland Security
Expenses: 2015-2016: $33,218; room/board: $10,382
Financial aid: (800) 943-6279; 68% of undergrads determined to have financial need; average aid package $15,986

Everglades University
Boca Raton FL
(888) 772-6077
U.S. News ranking: Reg. Coll. (S), No. 69
Website: www.evergladesuniversity.edu
Admissions email: N/A
Private
Freshman admissions: least selective; 2014-2015: 177 applied, 152 accepted. Neither SAT nor ACT required. ACT 25/75 percentile: N/A. High school rank: N/A
Early decision deadline: N/A, notification date: N/A
Early action deadline: N/A, notification date: N/A
Application deadline (fall): rolling
Undergraduate student body: 1,284 full time, 29 part time; 47% male, 53% female; 1% American Indian, 2% Asian, 17% black, 15% Hispanic, 5% multiracial, 0% Pacific Islander, 59% white, 0% international
Most popular majors: 45% Alternative and Complementary Medicine and Medical Systems, General, 30% Construction Management
Expenses: 2014-2015: $16,000; room/board: $23,448
Financial aid: (888) 772-6077

Flagler College
St. Augustine FL
(800) 304-4208
U.S. News ranking: Reg. Coll. (S), No. 6
Website: www.flagler.edu
Admissions email: admiss@flagler.edu
Private; founded 1968
Freshman admissions: selective; 2014-2015: 6,585 applied, 3,153 accepted. Either SAT or ACT required. SAT 25/75 percentile: 960-1140. High school rank: 10% in top tenth, 38% in top quarter, 71% in top half
Early decision deadline: 11/1, notification date: 12/15
Early action deadline: N/A, notification date: N/A
Application deadline (fall): 3/1
Undergraduate student body: 2,682 full time, 92 part time; 40% male, 60% female; 0% American Indian, 1% Asian, 3% black, 10% Hispanic, 3% multiracial, 0% Pacific Islander, 74% white, 4% international; 61% from in state; 37% live on campus; 0% of students in fraternities, 0% in sororities
Most popular majors: 14% Business, Management, Marketing, and Related Support Services, 13% Communication, Journalism, and Related Programs, 12% Psychology, 13% Public Administration and Social Service Professions, 15% Visual and Performing Arts
Expenses: 2015-2016: $16,830; room/board: $9,630
Financial aid: (904) 819-6225; 63% of undergrads determined to have financial need; average aid package $12,194

Florida A&M University
Tallahassee FL
(850) 599-3796
U.S. News ranking: Nat. U., second tier
Website: www.famu.edu
Admissions email: ugradmissions@famu.edu
Public; founded 1887
Freshman admissions: selective; 2014-2015: 5,017 applied, 2,456 accepted. Either SAT or ACT required. ACT 25/75 percentile: 18-22. High school rank: 13% in top tenth, 36% in top quarter, 78% in top half
Early decision deadline: N/A, notification date: N/A
Early action deadline: N/A, notification date: N/A
Application deadline (fall): 5/15
Undergraduate student body: 7,230 full time, 1,265 part time; 38% male, 62% female; 0% American Indian, 1% Asian, 94% black, 1% Hispanic, 0% multiracial, 0% Pacific Islander, 3% white, 1% international; 85% from in state; 28% live on campus; 2% of students in fraternities, 3% in sororities
Most popular majors: 11% Business, Management, Marketing, and Related Support Services, 20% Health Professions and Related Programs, 12% Homeland Security, Law Enforcement, Firefighting and Related Protective Services, 7% Psychology, 7% Social Sciences
Expenses: 2015-2016: $5,784 in state, $17,726 out of state; room/board: $10,100
Financial aid: (850) 412-7927; 82% of undergrads determined to have financial need; average aid package $13,259

Florida Atlantic University
Boca Raton FL
(561) 297-3040
U.S. News ranking: Nat. U., second tier
Website: www.fau.edu
Admissions email: Admissions@fau.edu
Public; founded 1961
Freshman admissions: selective; 2014-2015: 14,944 applied, 9,867 accepted. Either SAT or ACT required. SAT 25/75 percentile: 960-1140. High school rank: 12% in top tenth, 37% in top quarter, 78% in top half
Early decision deadline: N/A, notification date: N/A
Early action deadline: N/A, notification date: N/A
Application deadline (fall): 5/1
Undergraduate student body: 15,524 full time, 9,685 part time; 44% male, 56% female; 0% American Indian, 4% Asian, 20% black, 25% Hispanic, 3% multiracial, 0% Pacific Islander, 45% white, 2% international; 96% from in state; 15% live on campus; 2% of students in fraternities, 4% in sororities
Most popular majors: 7% Biological and Biomedical Sciences, 24% Business, Management, Marketing, and Related Support Services, 7% Education, 7% Health Professions and Related Programs, 9% Social Sciences
Expenses: 2014-2015: $6,039 in state, $21,595 out of state; room/board: $11,924
Financial aid: (561) 297-3530; 63% of undergrads determined to have financial need; average aid package $10,199

Florida College
Temple Terrace FL
(800) 326-7655
U.S. News ranking: Reg. Coll. (S), No. 54
Website: www.floridacollege.edu/
Admissions email: N/A
Private
Freshman admissions: selective; 2014-2015: 346 applied, 265 accepted. Either SAT or ACT required. ACT 25/75 percentile: 20-26. High school rank: N/A
Early decision deadline: N/A, notification date: N/A
Early action deadline: N/A, notification date: N/A
Application deadline (fall): 8/1
Undergraduate student body: 528 full time, 27 part time; 50% male, 50% female; 1% American Indian, 1% Asian, 5% black, 4% Hispanic, 5% multiracial, 1% Pacific Islander, 81% white, 2% international; 33% from in state; 82% live on campus; N/A of students in fraternities, N/A in sororities
Most popular majors: Information not available
Expenses: 2015-2016: $16,074; room/board: $8,090
Financial aid: N/A; 71% of undergrads determined to have financial need; average aid package $10,841

Florida Gulf Coast University
Fort Myers FL
(239) 590-7878
U.S. News ranking: Reg. U. (S), No. 80
Website: www.fgcu.edu
Admissions email: admissions@fgcu.edu
Public; founded 1991
Freshman admissions: selective; 2014-2015: 13,773 applied, 8,110 accepted. Either SAT or ACT required. SAT 25/75 percentile: 970-1120. High school rank: 15% in top tenth, 41% in top quarter, 82% in top half
Early decision deadline: N/A, notification date: N/A
Early action deadline: N/A, notification date: N/A
Application deadline (fall): 5/1
Undergraduate student body: 10,564 full time, 2,736 part time; 44% male, 56% female; 0% American Indian, 2% Asian, 8% black, 19% Hispanic, 3% multiracial, 0% Pacific Islander, 66% white, 2% international; 92% from in state; 36% live on campus; 8% of students in fraternities, 14% in sororities
Most popular majors: 33% Business, Management, Marketing, and Related Support Services, 10% Communication, Journalism, and Related Programs, 8% Education, 8% Health Professions and Related Programs, 6% Psychology
Expenses: 2014-2015: $6,118 in state, $24,255 out of state; room/board: $9,820
Financial aid: (239) 590-7920; 49% of undergrads determined to have financial need; average aid package $9,313

Florida Institute of Technology
Melbourne FL
(800) 888-4348
U.S. News ranking: Nat. U., No. 161
Website: www.fit.edu
Admissions email: admission@fit.edu
Private; founded 1958
Freshman admissions: more selective; 2014-2015: 8,573 applied, 5,278 accepted. Either SAT or ACT required. SAT 25/75 percentile: 1020-1260. High school rank: 31% in top tenth, 63% in top quarter, 87% in top half
Early decision deadline: N/A, notification date: N/A
Early action deadline: N/A, notification date: N/A
Application deadline (fall): rolling
Undergraduate student body: 3,352 full time, 284 part time; 71% male, 29% female; 0% American Indian, 3% Asian, 6% black, 7% Hispanic, 2% multiracial, 0% Pacific Islander, 40% white, 33% international; 55% from in state; 45% live on campus; 13% of students in fraternities, 12% in sororities
Most popular majors: 9% Aerospace, Aeronautical and Astronautical/Space Engineering, 9% Aviation/Airway Management and Operations, 7% Electrical and Electronics Engineering, 4% Marine Biology and Biological Oceanography, 12% Mechanical Engineering
Expenses: 2015-2016: $39,290; room/board: $13,500
Financial aid: (321) 674-8070; 52% of undergrads determined to have financial need; average aid package $34,092

Florida International University
Miami FL
(305) 348-2363
U.S. News ranking: Nat. U., second tier
Website: www.fiu.edu
Admissions email: admiss@fiu.edu
Public; founded 1972
Freshman admissions: selective; 2014-2015: 17,617 applied, 8,380 accepted. Either SAT or ACT required. SAT 25/75 percentile: 1030-1200. High school rank: 21% in top tenth, 49% in top quarter, 86% in top half
Early decision deadline: N/A, notification date: N/A
Early action deadline: N/A, notification date: N/A
Undergraduate student body: 25,645 full time, 15,329 part time; 44% male, 56% female; 0% American Indian, 3% Asian, 12% black, 67% Hispanic, 2% multiracial, 0% Pacific Islander, 10% white, 5% international; 97% from in state; 8% live on campus; N/A of students in fraternities, N/A in sororities
Most popular majors: 6% Biological and Biomedical Sciences, 32% Business, Management, Marketing, and Related Support Services, 6% Health Professions and Related Programs, 11% Psychology, 9% Social Sciences
Expenses: 2014-2015: $6,496 in state, $18,895 out of state; room/board: $10,702
Financial aid: (305) 348-2431; 75% of undergrads determined to have financial need; average aid package $7,529

Florida Memorial University
Miami FL
(305) 626-3750
U.S. News ranking: Reg. U. (S), second tier
Website: www.fmuniv.edu/
Admissions email: admit@fmuniv.edu
Private; founded 1879
Affiliation: Baptist
Freshman admissions: selective; 2014-2015: 5,195 applied, 1,067 accepted. Neither SAT nor ACT required. ACT 25/75 percentile: N/A. High school rank: N/A
Early decision deadline: 4/1, notification date: 4/1
Early action deadline: N/A, notification date: N/A
Application deadline (fall): rolling
Undergraduate student body: 1,413 full time, 65 part time; 39% male, 61% female; 0% American Indian, 0% Asian, 72% black, 4% Hispanic, 1% multiracial, 0% Pacific Islander, 0% white, 13% international
Most popular majors: Information not available
Expenses: 2014-2015: $14,776; room/board: $6,112
Financial aid: (305) 626-3745

Florida Southern College
Lakeland FL
(863) 680-4131
U.S. News ranking: Reg. Coll. (S), No. 4
Website: www.flsouthern.edu
Admissions email: fscadm@flsouthern.edu
Private; founded 1883
Affiliation: United Methodist
Freshman admissions: selective; 2014-2015: 5,590 applied, 2,505 accepted. Either SAT or ACT required. SAT 25/75 percentile: 1040-1220. High school rank: 29% in top tenth, 58% in top quarter, 85% in top half
Early decision deadline: 12/1, notification date: 12/15
Early action deadline: N/A, notification date: N/A
Application deadline (fall): rolling
Undergraduate student body: 2,115 full time, 57 part time; 39% male, 61% female; 1% American Indian, 1% Asian, 6% black, 10% Hispanic, 4% multiracial,

0% Pacific Islander, 73% white, 5% international; 64% from in state; 80% live on campus; 34% of students in fraternities, 35% in sororities
Most popular majors: 23% Business, Management, Marketing, and Related Support Services, 8% Communication, Journalism, and Related Programs, 11% Health Professions and Related Programs, 11% Social Sciences, 9% Visual and Performing Arts
Expenses: 2015-2016: $31,460; room/board: $10,210
Financial aid: (863) 680-4140; 70% of undergrads determined to have financial need; average aid package $24,441

Florida SouthWestern State College

Fort Myers FL
(800) 749-2322
U.S. News ranking: Reg. Coll. (S), unranked
Website: www.fsw.edu/
Admissions email: N/A
Public; founded 1962
Freshman admissions: N/A; 2014-2015: 4,972 applied, 3,994 accepted. Neither SAT nor ACT required. ACT 25/75 percentile: N/A. High school rank: N/A
Early decision deadline: N/A, notification date: N/A
Early action deadline: N/A, notification date: N/A
Application deadline (fall): 8/14
Undergraduate student body: 5,387 full time, 10,318 part time; 39% male, 61% female; 0% American Indian, 2% Asian, 11% black, 26% Hispanic, 2% multiracial, 0% Pacific Islander, 52% white, 2% international; 98% from in state; 3% live on campus; N/A of students in fraternities, N/A in sororities
Most popular majors: 40% Business, Management, Marketing, and Related Support Services, 32% Education, 28% Health Professions and Related Programs
Expenses: 2014-2015: $3,340 in state, $10,654 out of state; room/board: N/A
Financial aid: (239) 489-9127; 63% of undergrads determined to have financial need; average aid package $5,880

Florida State College–Jacksonville[1]

Jacksonville FL
(877) 633-5950
U.S. News ranking: Reg. Coll. (S), unranked
Website: www.fscj.edu
Admissions email: N/A
Public
Application deadline (fall): N/A
Undergraduate student body: N/A full time, N/A part time
Expenses: 2014-2015: $2,830 in state, $9,944 out of state; room/board: $8,260
Financial aid: (904) 359-5433

Florida State University

Tallahassee FL
(850) 644-6200
U.S. News ranking: Nat. U., No. 96
Website: www.fsu.edu
Admissions email: admissions@admin.fsu.edu
Public; founded 1851
Freshman admissions: more selective; 2014-2015: 30,266 applied, 16,763 accepted. Either SAT or ACT required. ACT 25/75 percentile: 26-29. High school rank: 40% in top tenth, 76% in top quarter, 97% in top half
Early decision deadline: N/A, notification date: N/A
Early action deadline: N/A, notification date: N/A
Application deadline (fall): 1/15
Undergraduate student body: 29,211 full time, 3,737 part time; 45% male, 55% female; 0% American Indian, 2% Asian, 8% black, 18% Hispanic, 3% multiracial, 0% Pacific Islander, 66% white, 1% international; 90% from in state; 20% live on campus; 17% of students in fraternities, 24% in sororities
Most popular majors: 4% Biology/Biological Sciences, General, 6% Criminal Justice/Safety Studies, 5% English Language and Literature, General, 5% Finance, General, 6% Psychology, General
Expenses: 2014-2015: $6,507 in state, $21,673 out of state; room/board: $10,208
Financial aid: (850) 644-1993; 53% of undergrads determined to have financial need; average aid package $8,370

Hodges University

Naples FL
(239) 513-1122
U.S. News ranking: Reg. U. (S), unranked
Website: www.hodges.edu
Admissions email: admit@hodges.edu
Private; founded 1990
Freshman admissions: N/A; 2014-2015: N/A applied, N/A accepted. Neither SAT nor ACT required. ACT 25/75 percentile: N/A. High school rank: N/A
Early decision deadline: N/A, notification date: N/A
Early action deadline: N/A, notification date: N/A
Application deadline (fall): rolling
Undergraduate student body: 1,137 full time, 541 part time; 37% male, 63% female; 1% American Indian, 2% Asian, 13% black, 35% Hispanic, 1% multiracial, 0% Pacific Islander, 45% white, 0% international; 96% from in state; N/A live on campus; N/A of students in fraternities, N/A in sororities
Most popular majors: Information not available
Expenses: 2015-2016: $500; room/board: N/A
Financial aid: (239) 513-1122; 95% of undergrads determined to have financial need; average aid package $10,050

Indian River State College

Fort Pierce FL
(772) 462-7460
U.S. News ranking: Reg. Coll. (S), second tier
Website: www.irsc.edu
Admissions email: N/A
Public
Freshman admissions: least selective; 2014-2015: 1,877 applied, 1,877 accepted. Neither SAT nor ACT required. ACT 25/75 percentile: N/A. High school rank: N/A
Early decision deadline: N/A, notification date: N/A
Early action deadline: N/A, notification date: N/A
Application deadline (fall): rolling
Undergraduate student body: 5,950 full time, 11,715 part time; 40% male, 60% female; 0% American Indian, 2% Asian, 18% black, 18% Hispanic, 2% multiracial, 0% Pacific Islander, 56% white, 1% international
Most popular majors: Information not available
Expenses: 2014-2015: $8,460 in state, $15,912 out of state; room/board: $5,700
Financial aid: (772) 462-7450; average aid package $4,705

Jacksonville University

Jacksonville FL
(800) 225-2027
U.S. News ranking: Reg. U. (S), No. 65
Website: www.jacksonville.edu
Admissions email: admissions@ju.edu
Private; founded 1934
Freshman admissions: selective; 2014-2015: 2,939 applied, 1,648 accepted. Neither SAT nor ACT required. SAT 25/75 percentile: 910-1110. High school rank: N/A
Early decision deadline: N/A, notification date: N/A
Early action deadline: N/A, notification date: N/A
Application deadline (fall): rolling
Undergraduate student body: 2,111 full time, 1,112 part time; 36% male, 64% female; 1% American Indian, 3% Asian, 16% black, 7% Hispanic, 0% multiracial, 0% Pacific Islander, 51% white, 3% international; 61% from in state; 28% live on campus; 43% of students in fraternities, 56% in sororities
Most popular majors: 4% Biological and Biomedical Sciences, 8% Business, Management, Marketing, and Related Support Services, 55% Health Professions and Related Programs, 5% Social Sciences, 5% Visual and Performing Arts
Expenses: 2015-2016: $32,620; room/board: $13,320
Financial aid: (904) 256-7060; 71% of undergrads determined to have financial need; average aid package $23,040

Keiser University

Ft. Lauderdale FL
(954) 776-4456
U.S. News ranking: Reg. Coll. (S), No. 36
Website: www.keiseruniversity.edu
Admissions email: N/A
Private; founded 1977
Freshman admissions: least selective; 2014-2015: N/A applied, N/A accepted. Neither SAT nor ACT required. ACT 25/75 percentile: N/A. High school rank: N/A
Early decision deadline: N/A, notification date: N/A
Early action deadline: N/A, notification date: N/A
Application deadline (fall): rolling
Undergraduate student body: 13,386 full time, 4,715 part time; 30% male, 70% female; 0% American Indian, 2% Asian, 20% black, 34% Hispanic, 3% multiracial, 0% Pacific Islander, 38% white, 0% international
Most popular majors: 21% Business Administration and Management, General, 20% Criminal Justice/Safety Studies, 13% Health Services Administration, 25% Health Services/Allied Health/Health Sciences, General, 15% Multi/Interdisciplinary Studies, General
Expenses: 2014-2015: $16,936; room/board: $8,488
Financial aid: (954) 351-4456

Lynn University

Boca Raton FL
(800) 888-5966
U.S. News ranking: Nat. U., second tier
Website: www.lynn.edu
Admissions email: admission@lynn.edu
Private; founded 1962
Freshman admissions: less selective; 2014-2015: 3,557 applied, 2,663 accepted. Neither SAT nor ACT required. SAT 25/75 percentile: 870-1075. High school rank: 10% in top tenth, 19% in top quarter, 45% in top half
Early decision deadline: N/A, notification date: N/A
Early action deadline: 11/15, notification date: 12/15
Application deadline (fall): rolling
Undergraduate student body: 1,815 full time, 161 part time; 53% male, 47% female; 1% American Indian, 1% Asian, 9% black, 14% Hispanic, 1% multiracial, 0% Pacific Islander, 43% white, 23% international; 47% from in state; 51% live on campus; 5% of students in fraternities, 6% in sororities
Most popular majors: 42% Business, Management, Marketing, and Related Support Services, 12% Communication, Journalism, and Related Programs, 7% Homeland Security, Law Enforcement, Firefighting and Related Protective Services, 9% Psychology, 8% Visual and Performing Arts
Expenses: 2015-2016: $35,200; room/board: $11,300
Financial aid: (561) 237-7186; 43% of undergrads determined to have financial need; average aid package $20,349

Miami Dade College[1]

Miami FL
(305) 237-8888
U.S. News ranking: Reg. Coll. (S), unranked
Website: www.mdc.edu/
Admissions email: mdcinfo@mdc.edu
Public
Application deadline (fall): N/A
Undergraduate student body: N/A full time, N/A part time
Expenses: 2014-2015: $3,486 in state, $12,015 out of state; room/board: $21,768
Financial aid: (305) 237-6040

Miami International University of Art & Design[1]

Miami FL
(305) 428-5700
U.S. News ranking: Arts, unranked
Website: www.aimiu.aii.edu/
Admissions email: N/A
For-profit
Application deadline (fall): N/A
Undergraduate student body: N/A full time, N/A part time
Expenses: N/A
Financial aid: N/A

New College of Florida

Sarasota FL
(941) 487-5000
U.S. News ranking: Nat. Lib. Arts, No. 82
Website: www.ncf.edu
Admissions email: admissions@ncf.edu
Public; founded 2001
Freshman admissions: more selective; 2014-2015: 1,570 applied, 940 accepted. Either SAT or ACT required. SAT 25/75 percentile: 1180-1380. High school rank: 45% in top tenth, 78% in top quarter, 99% in top half
Early decision deadline: N/A, notification date: N/A
Early action deadline: N/A, notification date: N/A
Application deadline (fall): 4/15
Undergraduate student body: 834 full time, 0 part time; 41% male, 59% female; 0% American Indian, 2% Asian, 3% black, 15% Hispanic, 5% multiracial, 0% Pacific Islander, 71% white, 2% international; 81% from in state; 77% live on campus; 0% of students in fraternities, 0% in sororities
Most popular majors: 100% Liberal Arts and Sciences, General Studies and Humanities, Other
Expenses: 2015-2016: $7,040 in state, $30,069 out of state; room/board: $9,009
Financial aid: (941) 359-4255; 56% of undergrads determined to have financial need; average aid package $12,940

Northwest Florida State College[1]

Niceville FL
(850) 729-6922
U.S. News ranking: Reg. Coll. (S), unranked
Website: www.owcc.cc.fl.us/
Admissions email: N/A
Public
Application deadline (fall): N/A
Undergraduate student body: N/A full time, N/A part time
Expenses: 2014-2015: $3,124 in state, $11,434 out of state; room/board: $8,930
Financial aid: (850) 729-5370

Nova Southeastern University

Ft. Lauderdale FL
(954) 262-8000
U.S. News ranking: Nat. U., second tier
Website: www.nova.edu
Admissions email: admissions@nova.edu
Private; founded 1964
Freshman admissions: more selective; 2014-2015: 4,364 applied, 2,130 accepted. Either SAT or ACT required. SAT 25/75 percentile: 1010-1240. High school rank: 31% in top tenth, 62% in top quarter, 88% in top half
Early decision deadline: N/A, notification date: N/A
Early action deadline: N/A, notification date: N/A
Application deadline (fall): rolling
Undergraduate student body: 3,162 full time, 1,537 part time; 30% male, 70% female; 0% American Indian, 8% Asian, 18% black, 31% Hispanic, 2% multiracial, 0% Pacific Islander, 32% white, 5% international; 84% from in state; 20% live on campus; 8% of students in fraternities, 7% in sororities
Most popular majors: 17% Biological and Biomedical Sciences, 18% Business, Management, Marketing, and Related Support Services, 5% Education, 36% Health Professions and Related Programs, 7% Psychology
Expenses: 2015-2016: $27,660; room/board: $10,874
Financial aid: (954) 262-3380; 76% of undergrads determined to have financial need; average aid package $25,774

Palm Beach Atlantic University

West Palm Beach FL
(888) 468-6722
U.S. News ranking: Reg. U. (S), No. 46
Website: www.pba.edu
Admissions email: admit@pba.edu
Private; founded 1968
Affiliation: Christian Interdenominational
Freshman admissions: selective; 2014-2015: 1,564 applied, 1,490 accepted. Either SAT or ACT required. SAT 25/75 percentile: 930-1158. High school rank: N/A
Early decision deadline: N/A, notification date: N/A
Early action deadline: 3/31, notification date: 4/15
Application deadline (fall): rolling
Undergraduate student body: 2,424 full time, 597 part time; 35% male, 65% female; 0% American Indian, 1% Asian, 13% black, 17% Hispanic, 3% multiracial, 0% Pacific Islander, 61% white, 4% international; 64% from in state; 46% live on campus; N/A of students in fraternities, N/A in sororities
Most popular majors: 31% Business, Management, Marketing, and Related Support Services, 11% Health Professions and Related Programs, 10% Psychology, 11% Theology and Religious Vocations, 10% Visual and Performing Arts
Expenses: 2015-2016: $27,150; room/board: $8,932
Financial aid: (561) 803-2000; 75% of undergrads determined to have financial need; average aid package $17,688

Ringling College of Art and Design

Sarasota FL
(800) 255-7695
U.S. News ranking: Arts, unranked
Website: www.ringling.edu
Admissions email: admissions@ringling.edu
Private; founded 1931
Freshman admissions: N/A; 2014-2015: 1,409 applied, 980 accepted. Neither SAT nor ACT required. ACT 25/75 percentile: N/A. High school rank: N/A
Early decision deadline: N/A, notification date: N/A
Early action deadline: N/A, notification date: N/A
Application deadline (fall): rolling
Undergraduate student body: 1,170 full time, 49 part time; 40% male, 60% female; 1% American Indian, 8% Asian, 3% black, 15% Hispanic, 2% multiracial, 0% Pacific Islander, 55% white, 16% international; 54% from in state; 65% live on campus; 0% of students in fraternities, 0% in sororities
Most popular majors: 23% Animation, Interactive Technology, Video Graphics and Special Effects, 6% Fine/Studio Arts, General, 5% Game and Interactive Media Design, 11% Graphic Design, 36% Illustration
Expenses: 2015-2016: $41,480; room/board: $13,850
Financial aid: (941) 351-5100; 61% of undergrads determined to have financial need; average aid package $20,276

Rollins College

Winter Park FL
(407) 646-2161
U.S. News ranking: Reg. U. (S), No. 1
Website: www.rollins.edu
Admissions email: admission@rollins.edu
Private; founded 1885
Freshman admissions: more selective; 2014-2015: 4,858 applied, 2,783 accepted. Neither SAT nor ACT required. SAT 25/75 percentile: 1100-1280. High school rank: 33% in top tenth, 64% in top quarter, 91% in top half
Early decision deadline: 11/15, notification date: 12/15
Early action deadline: N/A, notification date: N/A
Application deadline (fall): 2/15
Undergraduate student body: 1,932 full time, N/A part time; 41% male, 59% female; 0% American Indian, 3% Asian, 3% black, 13% Hispanic, 3% multiracial, 0% Pacific Islander, 67% white, 8% international; 53% from in state; 60% live on campus; 42% of students in fraternities, 45% in sororities
Most popular majors: 13% Business, Management, Marketing, and Related Support Services, 15% Communication, Journalism, and Related Programs, 10% Psychology, 24% Social Sciences, 10% Visual and Performing Arts
Expenses: 2015-2016: $44,760; room/board: $13,910
Financial aid: (407) 646-2395; 51% of undergrads determined to have financial need; average aid package $31,352

Saint Leo University

Saint Leo FL
(800) 334-5532
U.S. News ranking: Reg. U. (S), No. 71
Website: www.saintleo.edu
Admissions email: admission@saintleo.edu
Private; founded 1889
Affiliation: Roman Catholic
Freshman admissions: selective; 2014-2015: 3,490 applied, 2,511 accepted. Neither SAT nor ACT required. SAT 25/75 percentile: 900-1090. High school rank: 10% in top tenth, 26% in top quarter, 63% in top half
Early decision deadline: N/A, notification date: N/A
Early action deadline: N/A, notification date: N/A
Application deadline (fall): rolling
Undergraduate student body: 2,193 full time, 97 part time; 48% male, 52% female; 0% American Indian, 1% Asian, 13% black, 17% Hispanic, 2% multiracial, 0% Pacific Islander, 46% white, 13% international; 72% from in state; 63% live on campus; 13% of students in fraternities, 21% in sororities
Most popular majors: 26% Business, Management, Marketing, and Related Support Services, 9% Education, 14% Homeland Security, Law Enforcement, Firefighting and Related Protective Services, 10% Parks, Recreation, Leisure, and Fitness Studies, 8% Psychology
Expenses: 2015-2016: $20,880; room/board: N/A
Financial aid: (352) 588-8270; 71% of undergrads determined to have financial need; average aid package $19,034

Southeastern University

Lakeland FL
(800) 500-8760
U.S. News ranking: Reg. Coll. (S), No. 42
Website: www.seu.edu
Admissions email: admission@seu.edu
Private; founded 1935
Affiliation: Assemblies of God
Freshman admissions: selective; 2014-2015: 3,402 applied, 1,495 accepted. Either SAT or ACT required. ACT 25/75 percentile: 18-23. High school rank: N/A
Early decision deadline: N/A, notification date: N/A
Early action deadline: N/A, notification date: N/A
Application deadline (fall): 5/1
Undergraduate student body: 2,715 full time, 721 part time; 45% male, 55% female; 0% American Indian, 1% Asian, 15% black, 17% Hispanic, 1% multiracial, 0% Pacific Islander, 61% white, 2% international; 68% from in state; 52% live on campus; 0% of students in fraternities, 0% in sororities
Most popular majors: 18% Business, Management, Marketing, and Related Support Services, 10% Communication, Journalism, and Related Programs, 12% Education, 11% Public Administration and Social Service Professions, 23% Theology and Religious Vocations
Expenses: 2015-2016: $22,840; room/board: $9,148
Financial aid: (863) 667-5026; 83% of undergrads determined to have financial need; average aid package $15,094

Stetson University

DeLand FL
(800) 688-0101
U.S. News ranking: Reg. U. (S), No. 5
Website: www.stetson.edu
Admissions email: admissions@stetson.edu
Private; founded 1883
Freshman admissions: more selective; 2014-2015: 10,986 applied, 6,728 accepted. Neither SAT nor ACT required. SAT 25/75 percentile: 1070-1275. High school rank: 26% in top tenth, 58% in top quarter, 90% in top half
Early decision deadline: N/A, notification date: N/A
Early action deadline: N/A, notification date: N/A
Application deadline (fall): rolling
Undergraduate student body: 2,804 full time, 37 part time; 42% male, 58% female; 0% American Indian, 2% Asian, 8% black, 14% Hispanic, 3% multiracial, 0% Pacific Islander, 65% white, 5% international; 72% from in state; 64% live on campus; 28% of students in fraternities, 27% in sororities
Most popular majors: 29% Business, Management, Marketing, and Related Support Services, 6% Education, 7% Psychology, 10% Social Sciences, 10% Visual and Performing Arts
Expenses: 2015-2016: $41,590; room/board: $11,944
Financial aid: (386) 822-7120; 74% of undergrads determined to have financial need; average aid package $33,033

St. Petersburg College[1]

St. Petersburg FL
(727) 341-4772
U.S. News ranking: Reg. Coll. (S), unranked
Website: www.spcollege.edu/
Admissions email: information@spcollege.edu
Public
Application deadline (fall): N/A
Undergraduate student body: N/A full time, N/A part time
Expenses: 2014-2015: $3,292 in state, $11,524 out of state; room/board: $9,431
Financial aid: (727) 791-2442

St. Thomas University

Miami Gardens FL
(305) 628-6546
U.S. News ranking: Reg. U. (S), No. 63
Website: www.stu.edu
Admissions email: signup@stu.edu
Private; founded 1961
Affiliation: Roman Catholic
Freshman admissions: less selective; 2014-2015: 874 applied, 742 accepted. Either SAT or ACT required. SAT 25/75 percentile: 810-1040. High school rank: 13% in top tenth, 27% in top quarter, 54% in top half
Early decision deadline: N/A, notification date: N/A
Early action deadline: N/A, notification date: N/A
Application deadline (fall): rolling
Undergraduate student body: 878 full time, 53 part time; 49% male, 51% female; 0% American Indian, 0% Asian, 22% black, 46% Hispanic, 1% multiracial, 0% Pacific Islander, 9% white, 18% international; N/A from in state; 27% live on campus; N/A of students in fraternities, N/A in sororities
Most popular majors: 7% Biological and Biomedical Sciences, 42% Business, Management, Marketing, and Related Support Services, 6% Communication, Journalism, and Related Programs, 15% Homeland Security, Law Enforcement, Firefighting and Related Protective Services, 10% Psychology
Expenses: 2015-2016: $28,710; room/board: $7,820
Financial aid: (305) 474-6960; 70% of undergrads determined to have financial need

University of Central Florida

Orlando FL
(407) 823-3000
U.S. News ranking: Nat. U., No. 168
Website: www.ucf.edu
Admissions email: admission@ucf.edu
Public; founded 1963
Freshman admissions: more selective; 2014-2015: 33,226 applied, 16,483 accepted. Either SAT or ACT required. SAT 25/75 percentile: 1090-1280. High school rank: 31% in top tenth, 71% in top quarter, 96% in top half
Early decision deadline: N/A, notification date: N/A
Early action deadline: N/A, notification date: N/A
Application deadline (fall): 5/1
Undergraduate student body: 36,428 full time, 16,104 part time; 45% male, 55% female; 0% American Indian, 6% Asian, 11% black, 23% Hispanic, 3% multiracial, 0% Pacific Islander, 55% white, 1% international; 95% from in state; 18% live on campus; 7% of students in fraternities, 7% in sororities
Most popular majors: 22% Business, Management, Marketing, and Related Support Services, 9% Education, 6% Engineering, 15% Health Professions and Related Programs, 9% Psychology
Expenses: 2014-2015: $6,368 in state, $22,467 out of state; room/board: $9,300
Financial aid: (407) 823-2827; 66% of undergrads determined to have financial need; average aid package $8,295

More at usnews.com/college

University of Florida

Gainesville FL
(352) 392-1365
U.S. News ranking: Nat. U., No. 47
Website: www.ufl.edu
Admissions email: N/A
Public; founded 1853
Freshman admissions: more selective; 2014-2015: 27,852 applied, 13,111 accepted. Either SAT or ACT required. SAT 25/75 percentile: 1170-1360. High school rank: 75% in top tenth, 97% in top quarter, 100% in top half
Early decision deadline: N/A, notification date: N/A
Early action deadline: N/A, notification date: N/A
Application deadline (fall): 11/1
Undergraduate student body: 30,248 full time, 3,472 part time; 45% male, 55% female; 0% American Indian, 8% Asian, 7% black, 20% Hispanic, 3% multiracial, 1% Pacific Islander, 58% white, 1% international; 96% from in state; 23% live on campus; 21% of students in fraternities, 23% in sororities
Most popular majors: 10% Biological and Biomedical Sciences, 11% Business, Management, Marketing, and Related Support Services, 8% Communication, Journalism, and Related Programs, 12% Engineering, 13% Social Sciences
Expenses: 2014-2015: $6,313 in state, $28,591 out of state; room/board: $9,630
Financial aid: (352) 392-1271; 52% of undergrads determined to have financial need; average aid package $12,517

University of Miami

Coral Gables FL
(305) 284-4323
U.S. News ranking: Nat. U., No. 51
Website: www.miami.edu
Admissions email: admission@miami.edu
Private; founded 1925
Freshman admissions: more selective; 2014-2015: 31,607 applied, 12,064 accepted. Either SAT or ACT required. SAT 25/75 percentile: 1220-1420. High school rank: 66% in top tenth, 87% in top quarter, 95% in top half
Early decision deadline: 11/1, notification date: 12/20
Early action deadline: 11/1, notification date: 2/1
Application deadline (fall): 1/1
Undergraduate student body: 10,619 full time, 654 part time; 49% male, 51% female; 0% American Indian, 6% Asian, 7% black, 21% Hispanic, 3% multiracial, 0% Pacific Islander, 43% white, 14% international; 45% from in state; 37% live on campus; 16% of students in fraternities, 19% in sororities
Most popular majors: 15% Biological and Biomedical Sciences, 19% Business, Management, Marketing, and Related Support Services, 10% Communication, Journalism, and Related Programs, 10% Health Professions and Related Programs, 10% Social Sciences
Expenses: 2015-2016: $45,724; room/board: $13,066
Financial aid: (305) 284-5212; 44% of undergrads determined to have financial need; average aid package $33,539

University of North Florida

Jacksonville FL
(904) 620-2624
U.S. News ranking: Reg. U. (S), No. 50
Website: www.unf.edu
Admissions email: admissions@unf.edu
Public; founded 1965
Freshman admissions: selective; 2014-2015: 11,154 applied, 6,756 accepted. Either SAT or ACT required. ACT 25/75 percentile: 22-26. High school rank: 13% in top tenth, 41% in top quarter, 79% in top half
Early decision deadline: N/A, notification date: N/A
Early action deadline: N/A, notification date: N/A
Application deadline (fall): rolling
Undergraduate student body: 9,901 full time, 4,220 part time; 45% male, 55% female; 0% American Indian, 4% Asian, 10% black, 10% Hispanic, 5% multiracial, 0% Pacific Islander, 69% white, 1% international; 97% from in state; 22% live on campus; N/A of students in fraternities, N/A in sororities
Most popular majors: 20% Business, Management, Marketing, and Related Support Services, 9% Communication, Journalism, and Related Programs, 8% Education, 15% Health Professions and Related Programs, 10% Psychology
Expenses: 2015-2016: $6,394 in state, $20,112 out of state; room/board: $9,487
Financial aid: (904) 620-2604; 58% of undergrads determined to have financial need; average aid package $8,668

University of South Florida

Tampa FL
(813) 974-3350
U.S. News ranking: Nat. U., No. 156
Website: www.usf.edu
Admissions email: admission@admin.usf.edu
Public; founded 1956
Freshman admissions: more selective; 2014-2015: 27,987 applied, 13,285 accepted. Either SAT or ACT required. SAT 25/75 percentile: 1070-1250. High school rank: 30% in top tenth, 56% in top quarter, 70% in top half
Early decision deadline: N/A, notification date: N/A
Early action deadline: N/A, notification date: N/A
Application deadline (fall): 3/1
Undergraduate student body: 23,783 full time, 7,284 part time; 45% male, 55% female; 0% American Indian, 6% Asian, 11% black, 20% Hispanic, 4% multiracial, 0% Pacific Islander, 53% white, 4% international; 94% from in state; 18% live on campus; 7% of students in fraternities, 8% in sororities
Most popular majors: 9% Biomedical Sciences, General, 15% Criminology, 17% Finance, General, 8% Psychology, General, 13% Registered Nursing/Registered Nurse
Expenses: 2014-2015: $6,410 in state, $17,325 out of state; room/board: $9,400
Financial aid: (813) 974-4700; 72% of undergrads determined to have financial need; average aid package $9,506

University of South Florida–St. Petersburg

St. Petersburg FL
(727) 873-4142
U.S. News ranking: Reg. U. (S), No. 58
Website: www.usfsp.edu
Admissions email: admissions@usfsp.edu
Public; founded 1965
Freshman admissions: more selective; 2014-2015: 2,997 applied, 1,059 accepted. Either SAT or ACT required. SAT 25/75 percentile: 1050-1230. High school rank: 47% in top tenth, 58% in top quarter, 88% in top half
Early decision deadline: N/A, notification date: N/A
Early action deadline: 11/15, notification date: 12/1
Application deadline (fall): 4/15
Undergraduate student body: 2,543 full time, 1,452 part time; 40% male, 60% female; 0% American Indian, 4% Asian, 7% black, 15% Hispanic, 3% multiracial, 0% Pacific Islander, 68% white, 0% international
Most popular majors: 33% Business, Management, Marketing, and Related Support Services, 10% Education, 6% English Language and Literature/Letters, 14% Psychology, 18% Social Sciences
Expenses: 2015-2016: $5,830 in state, $16,746 out of state; room/board: $9,250
Financial aid: (727) 873-4128; 73% of undergrads determined to have financial need; average aid package $8,562

University of Tampa

Tampa FL
(888) 646-2738
U.S. News ranking: Reg. U. (S), No. 22
Website: www.ut.edu
Admissions email: admissions@ut.edu
Private; founded 1931
Freshman admissions: selective; 2014-2015: 17,208 applied, 8,927 accepted. Either SAT or ACT required. SAT 25/75 percentile: 990-1160. High school rank: 20% in top tenth, 48% in top quarter, 83% in top half
Early decision deadline: N/A, notification date: N/A
Early action deadline: 11/15, notification date: 12/15
Application deadline (fall): rolling
Undergraduate student body: 6,545 full time, 278 part time; 44% male, 56% female; 0% American Indian, 1% Asian, 5% black, 12% Hispanic, 3% multiracial, 0% Pacific Islander, 59% white, 10% international; 33% from in state; 61% live on campus; 4% of students in fraternities, 13% in sororities
Most popular majors: 30% Business, Management, Marketing, and Related Support Services, 12% Communication, Journalism, and Related Programs, 9% Parks, Recreation, Leisure, and Fitness Studies, 11% Social Sciences, 7% Visual and Performing Arts
Expenses: 2015-2016: $27,044; room/board: $9,900
Financial aid: (813) 253-6219; 60% of undergrads determined to have financial need; average aid package $16,219

University of West Florida

Pensacola FL
(850) 474-2230
U.S. News ranking: Nat. U., second tier
Website: uwf.edu
Admissions email: admissions@uwf.edu
Public; founded 1963
Freshman admissions: selective; 2014-2015: 10,138 applied, 4,229 accepted. Either SAT or ACT required. ACT 25/75 percentile: 21-26. High school rank: 17% in top tenth, 42% in top quarter, 71% in top half
Early decision deadline: N/A, notification date: N/A
Early action deadline: N/A, notification date: N/A
Application deadline (fall): 6/30
Undergraduate student body: 7,394 full time, 2,678 part time; 43% male, 57% female; 1% American Indian, 3% Asian, 12% black, 9% Hispanic, 5% multiracial, 0% Pacific Islander, 66% white, 2% international; 92% from in state; 59% live on campus; N/A of students in fraternities, N/A in sororities
Most popular majors: 10% Health Services/Allied Health/Health Sciences, General, 9% Health and Physical Education/Fitness, General, 10% Mass Communication/Media Studies, 9% Psychology, General, 14% Registered Nursing/Registered Nurse
Expenses: 2014-2015: $8,956 in state, $21,838 out of state; room/board: $9,580
Financial aid: (850) 474-3127; 67% of undergrads determined to have financial need; average aid package $8,868

Warner University

Lake Wales FL
(800) 309-9563
U.S. News ranking: Reg. U. (S), second tier
Website: www.warner.edu
Admissions email: admissions@warner.edu
Private
Affiliation: Church of God, Anderson IN
Freshman admissions: less selective; 2014-2015: 1,139 applied, 298 accepted. Either SAT or ACT required. ACT 25/75 percentile: 17-19. High school rank: 5% in top tenth, 22% in top quarter, 53% in top half
Early decision deadline: N/A, notification date: N/A
Early action deadline: N/A, notification date: N/A
Application deadline (fall): rolling
Undergraduate student body: 882 full time, 155 part time; 52% male, 48% female; 0% American Indian, 1% Asian, 41% black, 13% Hispanic, 2% multiracial, 0% Pacific Islander, 39% white, 2% international; 94% from in state; 35% live on campus; N/A of students in fraternities, N/A in sororities
Most popular majors: 5% Biology/Biological Sciences, General, 10% Business Administration and Management, General, 29% Business Administration, Management and Operations, Other, 20% Elementary Education and Teaching, 6% Psychology, General
Expenses: 2014-2015: $18,966; room/board: $7,879
Financial aid: (863) 638-7202

Webber International University

Babson Park FL
(800) 741-1844
U.S. News ranking: Reg. Coll. (S), second tier
Website: www.webber.edu
Admissions email: admissions@webber.edu
Private; founded 1927
Freshman admissions: less selective; 2014-2015: 926 applied, 529 accepted. Either SAT or ACT required. ACT 25/75 percentile: 17-23. High school rank: N/A
Early decision deadline: N/A, notification date: N/A
Early action deadline: N/A, notification date: N/A
Application deadline (fall): 8/1
Undergraduate student body: 568 full time, 49 part time; 46% male, 54% female; N/A American Indian, 1% Asian, 11% black, 1% Hispanic, 2% multiracial, N/A Pacific Islander, 58% white, 11% international; 41% from in state; 85% live on campus; N/A of students in fraternities, N/A in sororities
Most popular majors: Information not available
Expenses: 2015-2016: $24,772; room/board: $8,712
Financial aid: (863) 638-2930; 63% of undergrads determined to have financial need; average aid package $19,410

GEORGIA

Abraham Baldwin Agricultural College

Tifton GA
(800) 733-3653
U.S. News ranking: Reg. Coll. (S), second tier
Website: www.abac.edu/
Admissions email: N/A
Public; founded 1908
Freshman admissions: less selective; 2014-2015: 2,714 applied, 2,138 accepted. Either SAT or ACT required. SAT 25/75 percentile: 820-1030. High school rank: 15% in top tenth, 39% in top quarter, 71% in top half
Early decision deadline: N/A, notification date: N/A
Early action deadline: N/A, notification date: N/A
Application deadline (fall): 8/1

Undergraduate student body: 2,469 full time, 989 part time; 47% male, 53% female; 0% American Indian, 1% Asian, 12% black, 6% Hispanic, 1% multiracial, 0% Pacific Islander, 79% white, 1% international
Most popular majors: Information not available
Expenses: 2014-2015: $3,394 in state, $9,839 out of state; room/board: $11,040
Financial aid: (229) 391-4910

Agnes Scott College
Decatur GA
(800) 868-8602
U.S. News ranking: Nat. Lib. Arts, No. 67
Website: www.agnesscott.edu
Admissions email: admission@agnesscott.edu
Private; founded 1889
Affiliation: Presbyterian Church (USA)
Freshman admissions: more selective; 2014-2015: 1,394 applied, 944 accepted. Neither SAT nor ACT required. SAT 25/75 percentile: 1060-1260. High school rank: 37% in top tenth, 70% in top quarter, 94% in top half
Early decision deadline: 11/1, notification date: 12/1
Early action deadline: 11/15, notification date: 12/15
Undergraduate student body: 847 full time, 26 part time; 1% male, 99% female; 0% American Indian, 5% Asian, 35% black, 9% Hispanic, 6% multiracial, 0% Pacific Islander, 32% white, 9% international; 58% from in state; 84% live on campus; N/A of students in fraternities, N/A in sororities
Most popular majors: 14% Biological and Biomedical Sciences, 11% English Language and Literature/Letters, 8% Mathematics and Statistics, 14% Psychology, 22% Social Sciences
Expenses: 2015-2016: $37,236; room/board: $11,150
Financial aid: (404) 471-6395; 78% of undergrads determined to have financial need; average aid package $33,244

Albany State University
Albany GA
(229) 430-4646
U.S. News ranking: Reg. U. (S), No. 93
Website: www.asurams.edu/
Admissions email: admissions@asurams.edu
Public; founded 1903
Freshman admissions: less selective; 2014-2015: 2,381 applied, 1,126 accepted. Either SAT or ACT required. SAT 25/75 percentile: 820-940. High school rank: 10% in top tenth, 24% in top quarter, 66% in top half
Early decision deadline: N/A, notification date: N/A
Early action deadline: N/A, notification date: N/A
Application deadline (fall): 7/1
Undergraduate student body: 2,780 full time, 536 part time; 33% male, 67% female; 0% American Indian, 0% Asian, 89% black, 1% Hispanic, 1% multiracial, 0% Pacific Islander, 5% white, 0% international; 98% from in state; 47% live on campus; 7% of students in fraternities, 10% in sororities
Most popular majors: 6% Biology/Biological Sciences, General, 10% Business Administration and Management, General, 10% Criminal Justice/Safety Studies, 15% Early Childhood Education and Teaching, 6% Psychology, General
Expenses: 2015-2016: $6,258 in state, $19,078 out of state; room/board: $9,704
Financial aid: (229) 430-4650; 94% of undergrads determined to have financial need; average aid package $5,164

Armstrong State University
Savannah GA
(912) 344-2503
U.S. News ranking: Reg. U. (S), second tier
Website: www.armstrong.edu
Admissions email: adm-info@mail.armstrong.edu
Public; founded 1935
Freshman admissions: selective; 2014-2015: 2,405 applied, 1,622 accepted. Either SAT or ACT required. SAT 25/75 percentile: 920-1090. High school rank: N/A
Early decision deadline: N/A, notification date: N/A
Early action deadline: N/A, notification date: N/A
Application deadline (fall): 7/1
Undergraduate student body: 4,702 full time, 1,644 part time; 33% male, 67% female; 0% American Indian, 3% Asian, 25% black, 7% Hispanic, 4% multiracial, 0% Pacific Islander, 58% white, 2% international; 94% from in state; 19% live on campus; 4% of students in fraternities, 3% in sororities
Most popular majors: 7% Biological and Biomedical Sciences, 11% Education, 39% Health Professions and Related Programs, 9% Liberal Arts and Sciences, General Studies and Humanities, 5% Psychology
Expenses: 2015-2016: $6,214 in state, $18,720 out of state; room/board: $10,266
Financial aid: (912) 921-5990; 32% of undergrads determined to have financial need; average aid package $8,499

Art Institute of Atlanta[1]
Atlanta GA
(770) 394-8300
U.S. News ranking: Arts, unranked
Website: www.artinstitutes.edu/atlanta/
Admissions email: aiaadm@aii.edu
For-profit
Application deadline (fall): N/A
Undergraduate student body: N/A full time, N/A part time
Expenses: 2014-2015: $17,596; room/board: $11,268
Financial aid: (770) 394-8300

Bauder College[1]
Atlanta GA
(800) 241-3797
U.S. News ranking: Reg. Coll. (S), unranked
Website: www.bauder.edu
Admissions email: N/A
For-profit
Application deadline (fall): N/A
Undergraduate student body: N/A full time, N/A part time
Expenses: 2014-2015: $13,356; room/board: $5,648
Financial aid: N/A

Berry College
Mount Berry GA
(706) 236-2215
U.S. News ranking: Nat. Lib. Arts, No. 127
Website: www.berry.edu
Admissions email: admissions@berry.edu
Private; founded 1902
Freshman admissions: more selective; 2014-2015: 3,801 applied, 2,312 accepted. Either SAT or ACT required. ACT 25/75 percentile: 24-29. High school rank: 34% in top tenth, 66% in top quarter, 93% in top half
Early decision deadline: N/A, notification date: N/A
Early action deadline: N/A, notification date: N/A
Application deadline (fall): 7/24
Undergraduate student body: 2,060 full time, 25 part time; 39% male, 61% female; 0% American Indian, 1% Asian, 4% black, 6% Hispanic, 3% multiracial, 0% Pacific Islander, 83% white, 1% international; 71% from in state; 87% live on campus; 0% of students in fraternities, 0% in sororities
Most popular majors: 12% Agriculture, Agriculture Operations, and Related Sciences, 10% Biological and Biomedical Sciences, 16% Business, Management, Marketing, and Related Support Services, 7% Education, 10% Psychology
Expenses: 2015-2016: $31,996; room/board: $11,190
Financial aid: (706) 236-1714; 73% of undergrads determined to have financial need; average aid package $25,079

Brenau University
Gainesville GA
(770) 534-6100
U.S. News ranking: Reg. U. (S), No. 61
Website: www.brenau.edu
Admissions email: admissions@brenau.edu
Private; founded 1878
Freshman admissions: less selective; 2014-2015: 2,563 applied, 1,943 accepted. Either SAT or ACT required. SAT 25/75 percentile: 890-1080. High school rank: N/A
Early decision deadline: N/A, notification date: N/A
Early action deadline: N/A, notification date: N/A
Application deadline (fall): rolling
Undergraduate student body: 1,000 full time, 596 part time; 10% male, 90% female; 0% American Indian, 2% Asian, 32% black, 8% Hispanic, 3% multiracial, 0% Pacific Islander, 50% white, 3% international; 95% from in state; 24% live on campus; 0% of students in fraternities, 12% in sororities
Most popular majors: 4% Biological and Biomedical Sciences, 29% Business, Management, Marketing, and Related Support Services, 9% Education, 34% Health Professions and Related Programs, 12% Visual and Performing Arts
Expenses: 2015-2016: $25,878; room/board: $11,998
Financial aid: (770) 534-6176; 85% of undergrads determined to have financial need; average aid package $16,472

Brewton-Parker College[1]
Mount Vernon GA
(912) 583-3265
U.S. News ranking: Reg. Coll. (S), second tier
Website: www.bpc.edu
Admissions email: admissions@bpc.edu
Private; founded 1904
Affiliation: Baptist
Application deadline (fall): rolling
Undergraduate student body: N/A full time, N/A part time
Expenses: 2014-2015: $14,200; room/board: $7,615
Financial aid: (912) 583-3215

Clark Atlanta University
Atlanta GA
(800) 688-3228
U.S. News ranking: Nat. U., second tier
Website: www.cau.edu
Admissions email: cauadmissions@cau.edu
Private; founded 1988
Affiliation: Methodist
Freshman admissions: least selective; 2014-2015: 5,140 applied, 4,352 accepted. Either SAT or ACT required. SAT 25/75 percentile: 770-930. High school rank: 7% in top tenth, 26% in top quarter, 68% in top half
Early decision deadline: N/A, notification date: N/A
Early action deadline: N/A, notification date: N/A
Application deadline (fall): 6/1
Undergraduate student body: 2,441 full time, 126 part time; 25% male, 75% female; 0% American Indian, 0% Asian, 87% black, 0% Hispanic, N/A multiracial, N/A Pacific Islander, 0% white, 1% international; 37% from in state; 61% live on campus; 2% of students in fraternities, 3% in sororities
Most popular majors: 8% Biological and Biomedical Sciences, 17% Business, Management, Marketing, and Related Support Services, 20% Communication, Journalism, and Related Programs, 16% Psychology, 10% Visual and Performing Arts
Expenses: 2015-2016: $20,886; room/board: $10,478
Financial aid: (404) 880-8111; 93% of undergrads determined to have financial need; average aid package $7,553

Clayton State University
Morrow GA
(678) 466-4115
U.S. News ranking: Reg. Coll. (S), No. 60
Website: www.clayton.edu
Admissions email: ccsu-info@mail.clayton.edu
Public; founded 1969
Freshman admissions: less selective; 2014-2015: 2,199 applied, 927 accepted. Either SAT or ACT required. SAT 25/75 percentile: 860-1000. High school rank: N/A
Early decision deadline: N/A, notification date: N/A
Early action deadline: N/A, notification date: N/A
Application deadline (fall): 7/1
Undergraduate student body: 3,711 full time, 2,921 part time; 31% male, 69% female; 0% American Indian, 5% Asian, 65% black, 3% Hispanic, 3% multiracial, 0% Pacific Islander, 19% white, 1% international; 98% from in state; 14% live on campus; 2% of students in fraternities, 1% in sororities
Most popular majors: 4% Business Administration and Management, General, 11% Community Psychology, 13% Hospital and Health Care Facilities Administration/Management, 12% Liberal Arts and Sciences/Liberal Studies, 14% Registered Nursing/Registered Nurse
Expenses: 2015-2016: $6,312 in state, $19,132 out of state; room/board: $9,926
Financial aid: (678) 466-4185; 88% of undergrads determined to have financial need; average aid package $9,007

Columbus State University
Columbus GA
(706) 507-8800
U.S. News ranking: Reg. U. (S), second tier
Website: www.columbusstate.edu
Admissions email: admissions@columbusstate.edu
Public; founded 1958
Freshman admissions: selective; 2014-2015: 2,828 applied, 1,583 accepted. Either SAT or ACT required. SAT 25/75 percentile: 860-1100. High school rank: 11% in top tenth, 37% in top quarter, 68% in top half
Early decision deadline: N/A, notification date: N/A
Early action deadline: N/A, notification date: N/A
Application deadline (fall): 6/30
Undergraduate student body: 4,844 full time, 2,035 part time; 40% male, 60% female; 0% American Indian, 2% Asian, 36% black, 6% Hispanic, 2% multiracial, 0% Pacific Islander, 52% white, 1% international; 84% from in state; 18% live on campus; 4% of students in fraternities, 4% in sororities
Most popular majors: 17% Business, Management, Marketing, and Related Support Services, 12% Education, 21% Health Professions and Related Programs, 9% Homeland Security, Law Enforcement, Firefighting and Related Protective Services, 8% Visual and Performing Arts
Expenses: 2015-2016: $7,056 in state, $20,274 out of state; room/board: $9,920
Financial aid: (706) 568-2036; 74% of undergrads determined to have financial need; average aid package $9,057

Covenant College

Lookout Mountain GA
(706) 820-2398
U.S. News ranking: Reg. Coll. (S), No. 9
Website: www.covenant.edu
Admissions email: admissions@covenant.edu
Private; founded 1955
Affiliation: Presbyterian Church in America
Freshman admissions: more selective; 2014-2015: 655 applied, 633 accepted. Either SAT or ACT required. ACT 25/75 percentile: 23-29. High school rank: 26% in top tenth, 50% in top quarter, 76% in top half
Early decision deadline: N/A, notification date: N/A
Early action deadline: N/A, notification date: N/A
Application deadline (fall): rolling
Undergraduate student body: 1,049 full time, 56 part time; 42% male, 58% female; 0% American Indian, 2% Asian, 3% black, 3% Hispanic, 2% multiracial, 0% Pacific Islander, 87% white, 2% international; 22% from in state; 85% live on campus; 0% of students in fraternities, 0% in sororities
Most popular majors: 10% Education, 13% English Language and Literature/Letters, 8% Multi/Interdisciplinary Studies, 14% Social Sciences, 9% Visual and Performing Arts
Expenses: 2015-2016: $31,320; room/board: $9,170
Financial aid: (706) 419-1126; 63% of undergrads determined to have financial need; average aid package $24,114

Dalton State College[1]

Dalton GA
(706) 272-4436
U.S. News ranking: Reg. Coll. (S), unranked
Website: www.daltonstate.edu/
Admissions email: N/A
Public
Application deadline (fall): N/A
Undergraduate student body: N/A full time, N/A part time
Expenses: 2014-2015: $3,982 in state, $12,038 out of state; room/board: $6,720
Financial aid: (706) 272-4545

Emmanuel College

Franklin Springs GA
(800) 860-8800
U.S. News ranking: Reg. Coll. (S), No. 42
Website: www.ec.edu
Admissions email: admissions@ec.edu
Private; founded 1919
Affiliation: International Pentecostal Holiness
Freshman admissions: less selective; 2014-2015: 1,480 applied, 727 accepted. Either SAT or ACT required. SAT 25/75 percentile: 790-1130. High school rank: N/A
Early decision deadline: N/A, notification date: N/A
Early action deadline: N/A, notification date: N/A
Application deadline (fall): 8/1
Undergraduate student body: 723 full time, 93 part time; 50% male, 50% female; N/A American Indian, 1% Asian, 18% black, 5% Hispanic, 1% multiracial, 0% Pacific Islander, 71% white, 4% international; 75% from in state; 58% live on campus; N/A of students in fraternities, N/A in sororities
Most popular majors: 9% Biological and Biomedical Sciences, 15% Education, 23% Parks, Recreation, Leisure, and Fitness Studies, 14% Theology and Religious Vocations
Expenses: 2015-2016: $18,870; room/board: $7,200
Financial aid: (706) 245-2843; 81% of undergrads determined to have financial need; average aid package $15,519

Emory University

Atlanta GA
(404) 727-6036
U.S. News ranking: Nat. U., No. 21
Website: www.emory.edu
Admissions email: admission@emory.edu
Private; founded 1836
Affiliation: Methodist
Freshman admissions: most selective; 2014-2015: 17,796 applied, 4,773 accepted. Either SAT or ACT required. SAT 25/75 percentile: 1280-1460. High school rank: 81% in top tenth, 95% in top quarter, 100% in top half
Early decision deadline: 11/1, notification date: 12/15
Early action deadline: N/A, notification date: N/A
Application deadline (fall): 1/1
Undergraduate student body: 7,732 full time, 97 part time; 44% male, 56% female; 0% American Indian, 21% Asian, 9% black, 7% Hispanic, 3% multiracial, 0% Pacific Islander, 41% white, 15% international; 22% from in state; 73% live on campus; 28% of students in fraternities, 30% in sororities
Most popular majors: 9% Biology/Biological Sciences, General, 14% Business Administration and Management, General, 10% Economics, General, 7% Neuroscience, 7% Psychology, General
Expenses: 2015-2016: $46,314; room/board: $13,130
Financial aid: (404) 727-6039; 44% of undergrads determined to have financial need; average aid package $40,309

Fort Valley State University

Fort Valley GA
(478) 825-6307
U.S. News ranking: Reg. Coll. (S), No. 72
Website: www.fvsu.edu
Admissions email: admissap@mail.fvsu.edu
Public; founded 1895
Freshman admissions: less selective; 2014-2015: 2,228 applied, 539 accepted. Either SAT or ACT required. SAT 25/75 percentile: 820-930. High school rank: 4% in top tenth, 26% in top quarter, 65% in top half
Early decision deadline: N/A, notification date: N/A
Early action deadline: N/A, notification date: N/A
Application deadline (fall): 7/19
Undergraduate student body: 1,947 full time, 282 part time; 41% male, 59% female; 0% American Indian, 0% Asian, 96% black, 0% Hispanic, 0% multiracial, 0% Pacific Islander, 3% white, 0% international; 96% from in state; 40% live on campus; N/A of students in fraternities, N/A in sororities
Most popular majors: 10% Biology, General, 12% Business Administration, Management and Operations, 12% Criminal Justice and Corrections, 11% Education, General, 11% Psychology, General
Expenses: 2014-2015: $6,448 in state, $18,954 out of state; room/board: $8,508
Financial aid: (478) 825-6351; 98% of undergrads determined to have financial need; average aid package $9,076

Georgia College & State University

Milledgeville GA
(478) 445-1283
U.S. News ranking: Reg. U. (S), No. 28
Website: www.gcsu.edu
Admissions email: info@gcsu.edu
Public; founded 1889
Freshman admissions: selective; 2014-2015: 3,978 applied, 3,033 accepted. Either SAT or ACT required. ACT 25/75 percentile: 23-26. High school rank: N/A
Early decision deadline: N/A, notification date: N/A
Early action deadline: 11/1, notification date: 12/15
Application deadline (fall): 4/1
Undergraduate student body: 5,521 full time, 406 part time; 39% male, 61% female; 0% American Indian, 1% Asian, 5% black, 5% Hispanic, 2% multiracial, 0% Pacific Islander, 84% white, 1% international; 99% from in state; 36% live on campus; 6% of students in fraternities, 12% in sororities
Most popular majors: 9% Business Administration and Management, General, 9% Health Teacher Education, 7% Journalism, 10% Registered Nursing/Registered Nurse, 9% Research and Experimental Psychology, Other
Expenses: 2015-2016: $9,170 in state, $27,518 out of state; room/board: $11,612
Financial aid: (478) 445-5149; 51% of undergrads determined to have financial need; average aid package $9,465

Georgia Gwinnett College

Lawrenceville GA
(877) 704-4422
U.S. News ranking: Reg. Coll. (S), No. 73
Website: www.ggc.edu
Admissions email: N/A
Public; founded 2005
Freshman admissions: less selective; 2014-2015: 3,817 applied, 3,472 accepted. Neither SAT nor ACT required. SAT 25/75 percentile: 840-1060. High school rank: N/A
Early decision deadline: N/A, notification date: N/A
Early action deadline: N/A, notification date: N/A
Application deadline (fall): 6/1
Undergraduate student body: 7,527 full time, 3,301 part time; 45% male, 55% female; 0% American Indian, 9% Asian, 32% black, 15% Hispanic, 4% multiracial, 0% Pacific Islander, 38% white, 2% international; 99% from in state; 7% live on campus; 0% of students in fraternities, 0% in sororities
Most popular majors: 12% Biological and Biomedical Sciences, 34% Business, Management, Marketing, and Related Support Services, 13% Education, 7% Homeland Security, Law Enforcement, Firefighting and Related Protective Services, 12% Psychology
Expenses: 2015-2016: $5,648 in state, $16,152 out of state; room/board: $12,300
Financial aid: N/A; 78% of undergrads determined to have financial need; average aid package $9,062

Georgia Institute of Technology

Atlanta GA
(404) 894-4154
U.S. News ranking: Nat. U., No. 36
Website: admission.gatech.edu/information/
Admissions email: admission@gatech.edu
Public; founded 1885
Freshman admissions: most selective; 2014-2015: 25,884 applied, 8,641 accepted. Either SAT or ACT required. SAT 25/75 percentile: 1310-1490. High school rank: 79% in top tenth, 97% in top quarter, 99% in top half
Early decision deadline: N/A, notification date: N/A
Early action deadline: 10/15, notification date: 1/10
Application deadline (fall): 1/10
Undergraduate student body: 13,253 full time, 1,429 part time; 66% male, 34% female; 0% American Indian, 18% Asian, 6% black, 7% Hispanic, 4% multiracial, 0% Pacific Islander, 53% white, 11% international; 69% from in state; 54% live on campus; 23% of students in fraternities, 30% in sororities
Most popular majors: 5% Biological and Biomedical Sciences, 13% Business, Management, Marketing, and Related Support Services, 8% Computer and Information Sciences and Support Services, 61% Engineering, 2% Physical Sciences
Expenses: 2015-2016: $12,204 in state, $32,396 out of state; room/board: $13,194
Financial aid: (404) 894-4582; 41% of undergrads determined to have financial need; average aid package $11,415

Georgia Regents University

Augusta GA
(706) 721-2725
U.S. News ranking: Reg. U. (S), No. 71
Website: www.georgiahealth.edu/
Admissions email: admissions@georgiahealth.edu
Public; founded 1828
Freshman admissions: less selective; 2014-2015: N/A applied, N/A accepted. Neither SAT nor ACT required. ACT 25/75 percentile: N/A. High school rank: N/A
Early decision deadline: N/A, notification date: N/A
Early action deadline: N/A, notification date: N/A
Application deadline (fall): N/A
Undergraduate student body: 4,077 full time, 1,147 part time; 36% male, 64% female; 0% American Indian, 1% Asian, 26% black, 5% Hispanic, 3% multiracial, 0% Pacific Islander, 56% white, 1% international; N/A from in state; 15% live on campus; N/A of students in fraternities, N/A in sororities
Most popular majors: 5% Business Administration and Management, General, 5% Early Childhood Education and Teaching, 5% Psychology, General, 17% Registered Nursing/Registered Nurse, 6% Speech Communication and Rhetoric
Expenses: N/A
Financial aid: (706) 721-4901

Georgia Southern University

Statesboro GA
(912) 478-5391
U.S. News ranking: Nat. U., second tier
Website: www.georgiasouthern.edu/
Admissions email: admissions@georgiasouthern.edu
Public; founded 1906
Freshman admissions: selective; 2014-2015: 9,679 applied, 6,107 accepted. Either SAT or ACT required. SAT 25/75 percentile: 1030-1180. High school rank: 19% in top tenth, 47% in top quarter, 77% in top half
Early decision deadline: N/A, notification date: N/A
Early action deadline: N/A, notification date: N/A
Application deadline (fall): 5/1
Undergraduate student body: 15,844 full time, 2,160 part time; 50% male, 50% female; 0% American Indian, 1% Asian, 26% black, 5% Hispanic, 2% multiracial, 0% Pacific Islander, 63% white, 1% international; 97% from in state; 28% live on campus; 13% of students in fraternities, 16% in sororities
Most popular majors: 18% Business, Management, Marketing, and Related Support Services, 7% Education, 6% Health Professions and Related Programs, 8% Liberal Arts and Sciences, General Studies and Humanities, 8% Parks, Recreation, Leisure, and Fitness Studies
Expenses: 2015-2016: $7,318 in state, $20,536 out of state; room/board: $9,800
Financial aid: (912) 681-5413; 67% of undergrads determined to have financial need; average aid package $9,474

Georgia Southwestern State University

Americus GA
(229) 928-1273
U.S. News ranking: Reg. U. (S), second tier
Website: www.gsw.edu
Admissions email: admissions@gsw.edu
Public; founded 1906

Freshman admissions: selective; 2014-2015: 1,179 applied, 821 accepted. Either SAT or ACT required. SAT 25/75 percentile: 880-1060. High school rank: 15% in top tenth, 42% in top quarter, 74% in top half
Early decision deadline: 12/15, notification date: 1/15
Early action deadline: N/A, notification date: N/A
Application deadline (fall): 7/21
Undergraduate student body: 1,752 full time, 775 part time; 37% male, 63% female; 0% American Indian, 1% Asian, 28% black, 4% Hispanic, 2% multiracial, 0% Pacific Islander, 63% white, 2% international; 97% from in state; 31% live on campus; 8% of students in fraternities, 8% in sororities
Most popular majors: 12% Accounting, 17% Business Administration and Management, General, 10% Elementary Education and Teaching, 9% Psychology, General, 17% Registered Nursing/Registered Nurse
Expenses: 2015-2016: $6,234 in state, $19,054 out of state; room/board: $7,390
Financial aid: (229) 928-1378; 76% of undergrads determined to have financial need; average aid package $9,373

Georgia State University

Atlanta GA
(404) 413-2500
U.S. News ranking: Nat. U., second tier
Website: www.gsu.edu
Admissions email: admissions@gsu.edu
Public; founded 1913
Freshman admissions: selective; 2014-2015: 12,518 applied, 7,144 accepted. Either SAT or ACT required. SAT 25/75 percentile: 950-1180. High school rank: 18% in top tenth, 47% in top quarter, 82% in top half
Early decision deadline: N/A, notification date: N/A
Early action deadline: 11/15, notification date: 1/30
Application deadline (fall): 3/1
Undergraduate student body: 18,976 full time, 6,339 part time; 41% male, 59% female; 0% American Indian, 12% Asian, 41% black, 9% Hispanic, 5% multiracial, 0% Pacific Islander, 29% white, 2% international; 96% from in state; 17% live on campus; 4% of students in fraternities, 4% in sororities
Most popular majors: 7% Biological and Biomedical Sciences, 27% Business, Management, Marketing, and Related Support Services, 7% Education, 9% Psychology, 11% Social Sciences
Expenses: 2015-2016: $10,686 in state, $28,896 out of state; room/board: $13,700
Financial aid: (404) 651-2227; 79% of undergrads determined to have financial need; average aid package $10,669

Gordon State College[1]

Barnesville GA
(678) 359-5021
U.S. News ranking: Reg. Coll. (S), second tier
Website: www.gordonstate.edu/
Admissions email: N/A
Public
Application deadline (fall): N/A
Undergraduate student body: N/A full time, N/A part time
Expenses: 2014-2015: $3,510 in state, $9,937 out of state; room/board: $6,487
Financial aid: N/A

Kennesaw State University

Kennesaw GA
(770) 423-6300
U.S. News ranking: Reg. U. (S), No. 71
Website: www.kennesaw.edu
Admissions email: ksuadmit@kennesaw.edu
Public; founded 1963
Freshman admissions: selective; 2014-2015: 11,309 applied, 6,073 accepted. Either SAT or ACT required. SAT 25/75 percentile: 990-1170. High school rank: 27% in top tenth, 35% in top quarter, 98% in top half
Early decision deadline: N/A, notification date: N/A
Early action deadline: N/A, notification date: N/A
Application deadline (fall): 5/8
Undergraduate student body: 17,732 full time, 5,860 part time; 43% male, 57% female; 0% American Indian, 3% Asian, 19% black, 7% Hispanic, 4% multiracial, 0% Pacific Islander, 61% white, 2% international; 94% from in state; 16% live on campus; 4% of students in fraternities, 5% in sororities
Most popular majors: 23% Business, Management, Marketing, and Related Support Services, 9% Communication, Journalism, and Related Programs, 12% Education, 6% Health Professions and Related Programs, 8% Social Sciences
Expenses: 2014-2015: $6,932 in state, $19,828 out of state; room/board: $6,014
Financial aid: (770) 423-6074; 68% of undergrads determined to have financial need; average aid package $4,322

LaGrange College

LaGrange GA
(706) 880-8005
U.S. News ranking: Reg. Coll. (S), No. 12
Website: www.lagrange.edu
Admissions email: admission@lagrange.edu
Private; founded 1831
Affiliation: United Methodist
Freshman admissions: selective; 2014-2015: 1,343 applied, 742 accepted. Either SAT or ACT required. ACT 25/75 percentile: 20-24. High school rank: 15% in top tenth, 47% in top quarter, 80% in top half
Early decision deadline: N/A, notification date: N/A
Early action deadline: N/A, notification date: N/A
Application deadline (fall): rolling
Undergraduate student body: 804 full time, 76 part time; 47% male, 53% female; 1% American Indian, 1% Asian, 23% black, 2% Hispanic, 4% multiracial, 0% Pacific Islander, 69% white, 1% international; 84% from in state; 60% live on campus; 20% of students in fraternities, 33% in sororities
Most popular majors: 11% Biology/Biological Sciences, General, 5% Business Administration, Management and Operations, 8% Elementary Education and Teaching, 23% Registered Nursing/Registered Nurse, 8% Visual and Performing Arts, General
Expenses: 2015-2016: $27,510; room/board: $11,240
Financial aid: (706) 880-8229; 86% of undergrads determined to have financial need; average aid package $22,667

Life University

Marietta GA
(770) 426-2884
U.S. News ranking: Nat. Lib. Arts, second tier
Website: www.life.edu
Admissions email: admissions@life.edu
Private; founded 1974
Freshman admissions: less selective; 2014-2015: 331 applied, 189 accepted. Either SAT or ACT required. Average composite SAT score: 918. High school rank: N/A
Early decision deadline: N/A, notification date: N/A
Early action deadline: N/A, notification date: N/A
Application deadline (fall): 9/1
Undergraduate student body: 534 full time, 240 part time; 50% male, 50% female; 1% American Indian, 3% Asian, 24% black, 9% Hispanic, 0% multiracial, 0% Pacific Islander, 34% white, 3% international; 42% from in state; 7% live on campus; 0% of students in fraternities, 0% in sororities
Most popular majors: 28% Biology/Biological Sciences, General, 10% Business Administration and Management, General, 9% Dietetics/Dietitian, 13% Kinesiology and Exercise Science, 13% Psychology, General
Expenses: 2014-2015: $10,500; room/board: $12,480
Financial aid: (770) 426-2901; 78% of undergrads determined to have financial need; average aid package $10,700

Mercer University

Macon GA
(478) 301-2650
U.S. News ranking: Reg. U. (S), No. 8
Website: www.mercer.edu
Admissions email: admissions@mercer.edu
Private; founded 1833
Freshman admissions: more selective; 2014-2015: 4,375 applied, 2,919 accepted. Either SAT or ACT required. SAT 25/75 percentile: 1090-1290. High school rank: 38% in top tenth, 70% in top quarter, 93% in top half
Early decision deadline: N/A, notification date: N/A
Early action deadline: 11/1, notification date: 11/15
Application deadline (fall): 7/1
Undergraduate student body: 3,833 full time, 737 part time; 39% male, 61% female; 1% American Indian, 6% Asian, 32% black, 5% Hispanic, 2% multiracial, 0% Pacific Islander, 48% white, 3% international; 81% from in state; 74% live on campus; 21% of students in fraternities, 25% in sororities
Most popular majors: 14% Biological and Biomedical Sciences, 14% Business, Management, Marketing, and Related Support Services, 13% Engineering, 8% Psychology, 10% Social Sciences
Expenses: 2015-2016: $34,450; room/board: $11,460
Financial aid: (478) 301-2670; 74% of undergrads determined to have financial need; average aid package $32,468

Middle Georgia State University[1]

Macon GA
(800) 272-7619
U.S. News ranking: Reg. Coll. (S), second tier
Website: www.mga.edu/
Admissions email: N/A
Public
Application deadline (fall): 7/16
Undergraduate student body: N/A full time, N/A part time
Expenses: N/A
Financial aid: (800) 272-7619

Morehouse College

Atlanta GA
(404) 215-2632
U.S. News ranking: Nat. Lib. Arts, No. 148
Website: www.morehouse.edu
Admissions email: admissions@morehouse.edu
Private; founded 1867
Freshman admissions: selective; 2014-2015: 1,678 applied, 1,410 accepted. Either SAT or ACT required. SAT 25/75 percentile: 880-1120. High school rank: 19% in top tenth, 41% in top quarter, 74% in top half
Early decision deadline: 11/1, notification date: 12/15
Early action deadline: 11/1, notification date: 12/15
Application deadline (fall): 2/1
Undergraduate student body: 2,003 full time, 106 part time; 100% male, 0% female; 0% American Indian, 0% Asian, 94% black, 1% Hispanic, 0% multiracial, 0% Pacific Islander, 0% white, 3% international; 27% from in state; 72% live on campus; 4% of students in fraternities, N/A in sororities
Most popular majors: 7% Biology/Biological Sciences, General, 29% Business Administration and Management, General, 8% Political Science and Government, General, 7% Psychology, General
Expenses: 2014-2015: $26,090; room/board: $13,322
Financial aid: (404) 681-2800; 78% of undergrads determined to have financial need; average aid package $21,295

Oglethorpe University

Atlanta GA
(404) 364-8307
U.S. News ranking: Nat. Lib. Arts, No. 167
Website: www.oglethorpe.edu
Admissions email: admission@oglethorpe.edu
Private; founded 1835
Freshman admissions: selective; 2014-2015: 2,768 applied, 2,172 accepted. Either SAT or ACT required. SAT 25/75 percentile: 1040-1230. High school rank: 29% in top tenth, 58% in top quarter, 87% in top half
Early decision deadline: N/A, notification date: N/A
Early action deadline: 11/15, notification date: 12/5
Application deadline (fall): rolling
Undergraduate student body: 1,035 full time, 60 part time; 42% male, 58% female; 0% American Indian, 4% Asian, 19% black, 11% Hispanic, 3% multiracial, N/A Pacific Islander, 34% white, 5% international; 72% from in state; 58% live on campus; 17% of students in fraternities, 15% in sororities
Most popular majors: 18% Business, Management, Marketing, and Related Support Services, 25% English Language and Literature/Letters, 14% Social Sciences, 10% Visual and Performing Arts
Expenses: 2015-2016: $33,800; room/board: $12,180
Financial aid: (404) 364-8356; 69% of undergrads determined to have financial need; average aid package $27,485

Paine College[1]

Augusta GA
(706) 821-8320
U.S. News ranking: Reg. Coll. (S), second tier
Website: www.paine.edu
Admissions email: admissions@paine.edu
Private; founded 1882
Affiliation: Christian Methodist Episcopal and United Methodist Churches
Application deadline (fall): 7/15
Undergraduate student body: N/A full time, N/A part time
Expenses: 2014-2015: $13,332; room/board: $6,494
Financial aid: (706) 821-8262

Piedmont College

Demorest GA
(800) 277-7020
U.S. News ranking: Reg. U. (S), No. 53
Website: www.piedmont.edu
Admissions email: ugrad@piedmont.edu
Private; founded 1897
Affiliation: Nat. Assoc. of Congreg. Christ. Churches & United Church of Christ
Freshman admissions: selective; 2014-2015: 994 applied, 572 accepted. Either SAT or ACT required. SAT 25/75 percentile: 860-1050. High school rank: 14% in top tenth, 37% in top quarter, 78% in top half
Early decision deadline: N/A, notification date: N/A
Early action deadline: N/A, notification date: N/A
Application deadline (fall): 7/1

Undergraduate student body: 1,137 full time, 149 part time; 34% male, 66% female; 1% American Indian, 1% Asian, 9% black, 4% Hispanic, 2% multiracial, 0% Pacific Islander, 73% white, 0% international; 92% from in state; 64% live on campus; N/A of students in fraternities, N/A in sororities
Most popular majors: 17% Business, Management, Marketing, and Related Support Services, 29% Education, General, 18% Health Professions and Related Programs, 14% Social Sciences, 10% Visual and Performing Arts
Expenses: 2015-2016: $21,990; room/board: $9,050
Financial aid: (706) 776-0114; 81% of undergrads determined to have financial need; average aid package $18,169

Point University[1]

West Point GA
(706) 385-1202
U.S. News ranking: Reg. Coll. (S), No. 67
Website: www.point.edu
Admissions email: admissions@point.edu
Private; founded 1937
Affiliation: Christian Churches/Churches of Christ
Application deadline (fall): 8/5
Undergraduate student body: N/A full time, N/A part time
Expenses: 2014-2015: $17,650; room/board: $6,350
Financial aid: (800) 766-1222

Reinhardt University

Waleska GA
(770) 720-5526
U.S. News ranking: Reg. Coll. (S), No. 54
Website: www.reinhardt.edu/
Admissions email: admissions@reinhardt.edu
Private
Affiliation: United Methodist
Freshman admissions: less selective; 2014-2015: 1,172 applied, 1,055 accepted. Either SAT or ACT required. SAT 25/75 percentile: 890-1095. High school rank: 8% in top tenth, 30% in top quarter, 64% in top half
Early decision deadline: N/A, notification date: N/A
Early action deadline: N/A, notification date: N/A
Application deadline (fall): 8/15
Undergraduate student body: 1,231 full time, 103 part time; 52% male, 48% female; 0% American Indian, 1% Asian, 6% black, 18% Hispanic, 0% multiracial, 0% Pacific Islander, 69% white, 0% international; 95% from in state; 53% live on campus; N/A of students in fraternities, N/A in sororities
Most popular majors: Information not available
Expenses: 2015-2016: $20,266; room/board: $7,568
Financial aid: (770) 720-5667; 77% of undergrads determined to have financial need; average aid package $14,124

Savannah College of Art and Design

Savannah GA
(912) 525-5100
U.S. News ranking: Arts, unranked
Website: www.scad.edu
Admissions email: admission@scad.edu
Private; founded 1978
Freshman admissions: N/A; 2014-2015: 9,656 applied, 6,344 accepted. Either SAT or ACT required. SAT 25/75 percentile: 940-1180. High school rank: 15% in top tenth, 41% in top quarter, 75% in top half
Early decision deadline: N/A, notification date: N/A
Early action deadline: N/A, notification date: N/A
Application deadline (fall): rolling
Undergraduate student body: 8,043 full time, 1,652 part time; 35% male, 65% female; 1% American Indian, 8% Asian, 11% black, 8% Hispanic, 0% multiracial, 0% Pacific Islander, 53% white, 14% international; 22% from in state; 41% live on campus; N/A of students in fraternities, N/A in sororities
Most popular majors: 8% Animation, Interactive Technology, Video Graphics and Special Effects, 5% Fashion/Apparel Design, 11% Graphic Design, 7% Illustration, 6% Photography
Expenses: 2015-2016: $34,970; room/board: $13,677
Financial aid: (912) 525-6104; 54% of undergrads determined to have financial need; average aid package $27,795

Savannah State University

Savannah GA
(912) 356-2181
U.S. News ranking: Nat. Lib. Arts, second tier
Website: www.savannahstate.edu
Admissions email: admissions@savannahstate.edu
Public; founded 1890
Freshman admissions: less selective; 2014-2015: 7,916 applied, 2,706 accepted. Either SAT or ACT required. SAT 25/75 percentile: 770-920. High school rank: N/A
Early decision deadline: N/A, notification date: N/A
Early action deadline: N/A, notification date: N/A
Application deadline (fall): 7/15
Undergraduate student body: 4,196 full time, 573 part time; 44% male, 56% female; 0% American Indian, 0% Asian, 88% black, 3% Hispanic, 3% multiracial, 0% Pacific Islander, 4% white, 1% international; 93% from in state; 49% live on campus; N/A of students in fraternities, N/A in sororities
Most popular majors: 7% Biology/Biological Sciences, General, 8% Business Administration and Management, General, 9% Corrections and Criminal Justice, Other, 7% Journalism, 9% Social Work
Expenses: 2015-2016: $6,617 in state, $19,435 out of state; room/board: N/A
Financial aid: (912) 356-2253

Shorter University[1]

Rome GA
(800) 868-6980
U.S. News ranking: Nat. Lib. Arts, second tier
Website: www.shorter.edu
Admissions email: admissions@shorter.edu
Private
Application deadline (fall): N/A
Undergraduate student body: N/A full time, N/A part time
Expenses: 2014-2015: $20,250; room/board: $9,400
Financial aid: (706) 233-7227

South University[1]

Savannah GA
(912) 201-8000
U.S. News ranking: Reg. U. (S), second tier
Website: www.southuniversity.edu
Admissions email: cshall@southuniversity.edu
Private
Application deadline (fall): N/A
Undergraduate student body: N/A full time, N/A part time
Expenses: 2014-2015: $16,360; room/board: $9,105
Financial aid: (912) 201-8000

Spelman College

Atlanta GA
(800) 982-2411
U.S. News ranking: Nat. Lib. Arts, No. 72
Website: www.spelman.edu
Admissions email: admiss@spelman.edu
Private; founded 1881
Freshman admissions: selective; 2014-2015: 4,324 applied, 2,335 accepted. Either SAT or ACT required. SAT 25/75 percentile: 900-1100. High school rank: 25% in top tenth, 57% in top quarter, 88% in top half
Early decision deadline: 11/1, notification date: 12/15
Early action deadline: 11/15, notification date: 12/31
Application deadline (fall): 2/1
Undergraduate student body: 2,072 full time, 63 part time; 0% male, 100% female; 0% American Indian, 0% Asian, 87% black, 0% Hispanic, 3% multiracial, N/A Pacific Islander, 0% white, 1% international; 27% from in state; 69% live on campus; 0% of students in fraternities, 1% in sororities
Most popular majors: 16% Biology/Biological Sciences, General, 8% Economics, General, 7% English Language and Literature, General, 11% Political Science and Government, General, 25% Psychology, General
Expenses: 2015-2016: $26,388; room/board: $12,363
Financial aid: (404) 270-5212; 83% of undergrads determined to have financial need; average aid package $19,489

Thomas University

Thomasville GA
(229) 227-6934
U.S. News ranking: Reg. Coll. (S), second tier
Website: www.thomasu.edu
Admissions email: rgagliano@thomasu.edu
Private; founded 1950
Freshman admissions: less selective; 2014-2015: 219 applied, 132 accepted. Neither SAT nor ACT required. ACT 25/75 percentile: 20-24. High school rank: N/A
Early decision deadline: N/A, notification date: N/A
Early action deadline: N/A, notification date: N/A
Application deadline (fall): rolling
Undergraduate student body: 508 full time, 362 part time; 43% male, 57% female; 0% American Indian, 1% Asian, 19% black, 2% Hispanic, 0% multiracial, 0% Pacific Islander, 53% white, 5% international; 70% from in state; 8% live on campus; N/A of students in fraternities, N/A in sororities
Most popular majors: 11% Clinical/Medical Laboratory Technician, 22% Criminal Justice/Law Enforcement Administration, 11% Registered Nursing, Nursing Administration, Nursing Research and Clinical Nursing, Other, 10% Social Work, 7% Vocational Rehabilitation Counseling/Counselor
Expenses: 2015-2016: $16,400; room/board: $4,650
Financial aid: (229) 227-6925; average aid package $6,893

Toccoa Falls College

Toccoa Falls GA
(888) 785-5624
U.S. News ranking: Reg. Coll. (S), No. 33
Website: www.tfc.edu
Admissions email: admissions@tfc.edu
Private; founded 1907
Affiliation: Christian and Missionary Alliance
Freshman admissions: selective; 2014-2015: 583 applied, 216 accepted. Neither SAT nor ACT required. SAT 25/75 percentile: 840-1080. High school rank: 9% in top tenth, 29% in top quarter, 62% in top half
Early decision deadline: N/A, notification date: N/A
Early action deadline: N/A, notification date: N/A
Application deadline (fall): rolling
Undergraduate student body: 780 full time, 140 part time; 47% male, 53% female; 0% American Indian, 9% Asian, 7% black, 4% Hispanic, 1% multiracial, 0% Pacific Islander, 78% white, 1% international; 59% from in state; 81% live on campus; 0% of students in fraternities, 0% in sororities
Most popular majors: 8% Business Administration and Management, General, 16% Counseling Psychology, 7% Elementary Education and Teaching, 14% Missions/Missionary Studies and Missiology, 9% Youth Ministry
Expenses: 2015-2016: $20,710; room/board: $7,260
Financial aid: (706) 886-6831; 87% of undergrads determined to have financial need; average aid package $17,611

Truett McConnell College

Cleveland GA
(706) 865-2134
U.S. News ranking: Reg. Coll. (S), second tier
Website: www.truett.edu
Admissions email: admissions@truett.edu
Private; founded 1946
Affiliation: Southern Baptist
Freshman admissions: less selective; 2014-2015: 490 applied, 472 accepted. Either SAT or ACT required. SAT 25/75 percentile: 863-1080. High school rank: 12% in top tenth, 26% in top quarter, 53% in top half
Early decision deadline: N/A, notification date: N/A
Early action deadline: N/A, notification date: N/A
Application deadline (fall): 8/1
Undergraduate student body: 752 full time, 911 part time; 47% male, 53% female; 0% American Indian, 0% Asian, 7% black, 5% Hispanic, 0% multiracial, 0% Pacific Islander, 84% white, 1% international; 96% from in state; 81% live on campus; N/A of students in fraternities, N/A in sororities
Most popular majors: 27% Business, Management, Marketing, and Related Support Services, 15% Education, 6% History, 8% Psychology, 39% Theology and Religious Vocations
Expenses: 2015-2016: $17,900; room/board: $7,220
Financial aid: (800) 226-8621; 86% of undergrads determined to have financial need; average aid package $14,314

University of Georgia

Athens GA
(706) 542-8776
U.S. News ranking: Nat. U., No. 61
Website: www.admissions.uga.edu
Admissions email: adm-info@uga.edu
Public; founded 1785
Freshman admissions: more selective; 2014-2015: 20,877 applied, 11,644 accepted. Either SAT or ACT required. SAT 25/75 percentile: 1140-1330. High school rank: 52% in top tenth, 92% in top quarter, 99% in top half
Early decision deadline: N/A, notification date: N/A
Early action deadline: 10/15, notification date: 12/1
Application deadline (fall): 1/15
Undergraduate student body: 25,371 full time, 1,511 part time; 43% male, 57% female; 0% American Indian, 9% Asian, 8% black, 5% Hispanic, 3% multiracial, 0% Pacific Islander, 72% white, 1% international; 91% from in state; 28% live on campus; 22% of students in fraternities, 29% in sororities
Most popular majors: 6% Biology/Biological Sciences, General, 5% Finance, General, 3% International Relations and Affairs, 4% Marketing/Marketing Management, General, 7% Psychology, General
Expenses: 2015-2016: $11,622 in state, $29,832 out of state; room/board: $9,450

Financial aid: (706) 542-6147; 44% of undergrads determined to have financial need; average aid package $11,479

University of North Georgia

Dahlonega GA
(706) 864-1800
U.S. News ranking: Reg. U. (S), No. 53
Website: ung.edu/
Admissions email: bacheloradmissions@ung.edu
Public; founded 1873
Freshman admissions: selective; 2014-2015: 4,904 applied, 3,180 accepted. Either SAT or ACT required. SAT 25/75 percentile: 1010-1200. High school rank: 26% in top tenth, 66% in top quarter, 95% in top half
Early decision deadline: N/A, notification date: N/A
Early action deadline: N/A, notification date: N/A
Application deadline (fall): 7/1
Undergraduate student body: 10,745 full time, 4,762 part time; 45% male, 55% female; 0% American Indian, 3% Asian, 4% black, 9% Hispanic, 3% multiracial, 0% Pacific Islander, 78% white, 1% international; 97% from in state; 14% live on campus; 4% of students in fraternities, 5% in sororities
Most popular majors: 10% Business Administration and Management, General, 7% Criminal Justice/Safety Studies, 9% Early Childhood Education and Teaching, 7% Psychology, General, 7% Special Education and Teaching, General
Expenses: 2015-2016: $7,178 in state, $20,720 out of state; room/board: $9,494
Financial aid: (706) 864-1412; 61% of undergrads determined to have financial need; average aid package $13,652

University of West Georgia

Carrollton GA
(678) 839-5600
U.S. News ranking: Reg. U. (S), No. 87
Website: www.westga.edu
Admissions email: admiss@westga.edu
Public; founded 1906
Freshman admissions: less selective; 2014-2015: 7,868 applied, 3,825 accepted. Either SAT or ACT required. SAT 25/75 percentile: 870-1030. High school rank: N/A
Early decision deadline: N/A, notification date: N/A
Early action deadline: N/A, notification date: N/A
Application deadline (fall): 6/1
Undergraduate student body: 8,531 full time, 1,718 part time; 37% male, 63% female; 0% American Indian, 1% Asian, 36% black, 4% Hispanic, 4% multiracial, 0% Pacific Islander, 51% white, 1% international; 97% from in state; 29% live on campus; 3% of students in fraternities, 4% in sororities
Most popular majors: 22% Business, Management, Marketing, and Related Support Services, 14% Education, 15% Health Professions and Related Programs, 7% Psychology, 13% Social Sciences
Expenses: 2014-2015: $6,956 in state, $19,852 out of state; room/board: $8,532
Financial aid: (678) 839-6421; 76% of undergrads determined to have financial need; average aid package $8,242

Valdosta State University

Valdosta GA
(229) 333-5791
U.S. News ranking: Reg. U. (S), No. 76
Website: www.valdosta.edu
Admissions email: admissions@valdosta.edu
Public; founded 1906
Freshman admissions: selective; 2014-2015: 5,427 applied, 2,938 accepted. Either SAT or ACT required. SAT 25/75 percentile: 930-1100. High school rank: N/A
Early decision deadline: N/A, notification date: N/A
Early action deadline: N/A, notification date: N/A
Application deadline (fall): 8/1
Undergraduate student body: 7,815 full time, 1,513 part time; 41% male, 59% female; 0% American Indian, 1% Asian, 36% black, 5% Hispanic, 3% multiracial, 0% Pacific Islander, 51% white, 2% international; 95% from in state; 27% live on campus; 2% of students in fraternities, 2% in sororities
Most popular majors: 8% Architecture and Related Services, 17% Business, Management, Marketing, and Related Support Services, 9% Communication, Journalism, and Related Programs, 13% Education, 11% Health Professions and Related Programs
Expenses: 2015-2016: $7,342 in state, $20,560 out of state; room/board: $7,912
Financial aid: (229) 333-5935; 73% of undergrads determined to have financial need; average aid package $15,045

Wesleyan College

Macon GA
(800) 447-6610
U.S. News ranking: Nat. Lib. Arts, No. 158
Website: www.wesleyancollege.edu
Admissions email: admissions@wesleyancollege.edu
Private; founded 1836
Affiliation: United Methodist
Freshman admissions: selective; 2014-2015: 829 applied, 369 accepted. Either SAT or ACT required. SAT 25/75 percentile: 870-1110. High school rank: N/A
Early decision deadline: 11/15, notification date: 12/15
Early action deadline: 2/15, notification date: 3/15
Application deadline (fall): rolling
Undergraduate student body: 489 full time, 176 part time; 0% male, 100% female; 0% American Indian, 2% Asian, 28% black, 4% Hispanic, 2% multiracial, 0% Pacific Islander, 41% white, 20% international; 92% from in state; 76% live on campus; 0% of students in fraternities, 0% in sororities
Most popular majors: 10% Biology/Biological Sciences, General, 22% Business Administration, Management and Operations, Other, 10% Psychology, General, 10% Social Sciences, General, 18% Visual and Performing Arts, General
Expenses: 2015-2016: $20,290; room/board: $9,020
Financial aid: (888) 665-5723; 63% of undergrads determined to have financial need; average aid package $19,067

HAWAII

Brigham Young University–Hawaii[1]

Laie Oahu HI
(808) 293-3738
U.S. News ranking: Reg. Coll. (W), No. 22
Website: www.byuh.edu
Admissions email: admissions@byuh.edu
Private
Application deadline (fall): N/A
Undergraduate student body: N/A full time, N/A part time
Expenses: 2014-2015: $4,940; room/board: $5,746
Financial aid: (808) 293-3530

Chaminade University of Honolulu

Honolulu HI
(808) 735-4735
U.S. News ranking: Reg. U. (W), No. 73
Website: www.chaminade.edu
Admissions email: admissions@chaminade.edu
Private; founded 1955
Affiliation: Roman Catholic
Freshman admissions: less selective; 2014-2015: 918 applied, 784 accepted. Either SAT or ACT required. SAT 25/75 percentile: 860-1040. High school rank: 3% in top tenth, 5% in top quarter, 18% in top half
Early decision deadline: N/A, notification date: N/A
Early action deadline: N/A, notification date: N/A
Application deadline (fall): rolling
Undergraduate student body: 1,270 full time, 36 part time; 32% male, 68% female; 0% American Indian, 37% Asian, 3% black, 5% Hispanic, 17% multiracial, 18% Pacific Islander, 14% white, 2% international; 68% from in state; 27% live on campus; 0% of students in fraternities, 0% in sororities
Most popular majors: 12% Business Administration and Management, General, 22% Criminal Justice/Safety Studies, 9% Elementary Education and Teaching, 13% Psychology, General, 14% Registered Nursing/Registered Nurse
Expenses: 2015-2016: $21,780; room/board: $12,290
Financial aid: (808) 735-4780; 72% of undergrads determined to have financial need; average aid package $18,271

Hawaii Pacific University

Honolulu HI
(808) 544-0238
U.S. News ranking: Reg. U. (W), No. 77
Website: www.hpu.edu
Admissions email: admissions@hpu.edu
Private; founded 1965
Freshman admissions: selective; 2014-2015: 3,481 applied, 2,884 accepted. Either SAT or ACT required. SAT 25/75 percentile: 890-1120. High school rank: 25% in top tenth, 61% in top quarter, 87% in top half
Early decision deadline: N/A, notification date: N/A
Early action deadline: 12/1, notification date: 12/31
Application deadline (fall): rolling
Undergraduate student body: 3,145 full time, 1,690 part time; 43% male, 57% female; 0% American Indian, 17% Asian, 6% black, 14% Hispanic, 18% multiracial, 2% Pacific Islander, 29% white, 12% international; 65% from in state; 2% live on campus; 0% of students in fraternities, 0% in sororities
Most popular majors: 7% Biological and Biomedical Sciences, 30% Business, Management, Marketing, and Related Support Services, 6% Communication, Journalism, and Related Programs, 23% Health Professions and Related Programs, 6% Psychology
Expenses: 2015-2016: $22,360; room/board: $13,610
Financial aid: (808) 544-0253; 51% of undergrads determined to have financial need; average aid package $19,337

University of Hawaii–Hilo

Hilo HI
(800) 897-4456
U.S. News ranking: Nat. Lib. Arts, second tier
Website: www.uhh.hawaii.edu
Admissions email: uhhadm@hawaii.edu
Public; founded 1947
Freshman admissions: less selective; 2014-2015: 1,679 applied, 1,195 accepted. Either SAT or ACT required. SAT 25/75 percentile: 830-1050. High school rank: 23% in top tenth, 53% in top quarter, 88% in top half
Early decision deadline: N/A, notification date: N/A
Early action deadline: N/A, notification date: N/A
Application deadline (fall): 7/1
Undergraduate student body: 2,726 full time, 636 part time; 40% male, 60% female; 1% American Indian, 17% Asian, 1% black, 13% Hispanic, 30% multiracial, 11% Pacific Islander, 23% white, 5% international; 72% from in state; N/A live on campus; N/A of students in fraternities, N/A in sororities
Most popular majors: 8% Biological and Biomedical Sciences, 8% Business, Management, Marketing, and Related Support Services, 18% Health Professions and Related Programs, 10% Psychology, 11% Social Sciences
Expenses: 2014-2015: $7,036 in state, $19,036 out of state; room/board: $9,382
Financial aid: (808) 974-7323

University of Hawaii–Manoa

Honolulu HI
(808) 956-8975
U.S. News ranking: Nat. U., No. 161
Website: www.manoa.hawaii.edu/
Admissions email: ar-info@hawaii.edu
Public; founded 1907
Freshman admissions: selective; 2014-2015: 7,604 applied, 5,920 accepted. Either SAT or ACT required. SAT 25/75 percentile: 980-1190. High school rank: 27% in top tenth, 60% in top quarter, 90% in top half
Early decision deadline: N/A, notification date: N/A
Early action deadline: N/A, notification date: N/A
Application deadline (fall): 3/1
Undergraduate student body: 11,741 full time, 2,385 part time; 45% male, 55% female; 0% American Indian, 41% Asian, 2% black, 2% Hispanic, 15% multiracial, 18% Pacific Islander, 20% white, 3% international; 75% from in state; 25% live on campus; 1% of students in fraternities, 1% in sororities
Most popular majors: 20% Business, Management, Marketing, and Related Support Services, 7% Education, 8% Health Professions and Related Programs, 6% Psychology, 9% Social Sciences
Expenses: 2015-2016: $11,404 in state, $31,516 out of state; room/board: $13,898
Financial aid: (808) 956-7251; 57% of undergrads determined to have financial need; average aid package $13,754

University of Hawaii–Maui College[1]

Kahului HI
(800) 479-6692
U.S. News ranking: Reg. Coll. (W), unranked
Website: maui.hawaii.edu/
Admissions email: N/A
Public
Application deadline (fall): N/A
Undergraduate student body: N/A full time, N/A part time
Expenses: 2014-2015: $2,862 in state, $7,710 out of state; room/board: $11,782
Financial aid: (808) 984-3277

University of Hawaii–West Oahu[1]

Kapolei HI
(808) 689-2900
U.S. News ranking: Reg. Coll. (W), unranked
Website: www.uhwo.hawaii.edu
Admissions email: uhwo.admissions@hawaii.edu
Public; founded 1976
Application deadline (fall): 8/1
Undergraduate student body: N/A full time, N/A part time
Expenses: 2015-2016: $7,380 in state, $19,620 out of state; room/board: N/A
Financial aid: (808) 689-2900

IDAHO

Boise State University
Boise ID
(208) 426-1156
U.S. News ranking: Reg. U. (W), No. 61
Website: www.BoiseState.edu
Admissions email: bsuinfo@boisestate.edu
Public; founded 1932
Freshman admissions: less selective; 2014-2015: 8,163 applied, 6,284 accepted. Either SAT or ACT required. SAT 25/75 percentile: 920-1140. High school rank: 14% in top tenth, 36% in top quarter, 73% in top half
Early decision deadline: N/A, notification date: N/A
Early action deadline: N/A, notification date: N/A
Application deadline (fall): 5/15
Undergraduate student body: 12,155 full time, 7,178 part time; 46% male, 54% female; 1% American Indian, 2% Asian, 2% black, 10% Hispanic, 4% multiracial, 0% Pacific Islander, 75% white, 4% international; 79% from in state; 6% live on campus; 1% of students in fraternities, 2% in sororities
Most popular majors: 5% Business/Commerce, General, 6% Health Professions and Related Clinical Sciences, Other, 5% Psychology, General, 9% Registered Nursing/Registered Nurse, 6% Speech Communication and Rhetoric
Expenses: 2015-2016: $6,876 in state, $20,926 out of state; room/board: $7,566
Financial aid: (208) 426-1540; 62% of undergrads determined to have financial need; average aid package $9,118

Brigham Young University–Idaho[1]
Rexburg ID
(208) 496-1036
U.S. News ranking: Reg. Coll. (W), No. 13
Website: www.byui.edu
Admissions email: admissions@byui.edu
Private
Application deadline (fall): N/A
Undergraduate student body: N/A full time, N/A part time
Expenses: 2014-2015: $3,950; room/board: $4,200
Financial aid: (208) 496-1600

College of Idaho
Caldwell ID
(800) 224-3246
U.S. News ranking: Nat. Lib. Arts, No. 169
Website: www.collegeofidaho.edu
Admissions email: admissions@collegeofidaho.edu
Private; founded 1891
Freshman admissions: selective; 2014-2015: 1,276 applied, 877 accepted. Either SAT or ACT required. SAT 25/75 percentile: 920-1190. High school rank: 18% in top tenth, 41% in top quarter, 70% in top half
Early decision deadline: N/A, notification date: N/A
Early action deadline: 11/15, notification date: 12/15
Application deadline (fall): 7/15
Undergraduate student body: 1,085 full time, 35 part time; 48% male, 52% female; 1% American Indian, 3% Asian, 2% black, 15% Hispanic, 2% multiracial, 0% Pacific Islander, 64% white, 7% international; 83% from in state; 65% live on campus; 18% of students in fraternities, 17% in sororities
Most popular majors: 12% Biological and Biomedical Sciences, 13% Business, Management, Marketing, and Related Support Services, 9% Education, 10% Psychology, 10% Social Sciences
Expenses: 2015-2016: $25,825; room/board: $8,894
Financial aid: (208) 459-5307; 73% of undergrads determined to have financial need; average aid package $23,635

Idaho State University[1]
Pocatello ID
(208) 282-2475
U.S. News ranking: Nat. U., unranked
Website: www.isu.edu
Admissions email: info@isu.edu
Public
Application deadline (fall): N/A
Undergraduate student body: N/A full time, N/A part time
Expenses: 2014-2015: $6,566 in state, $19,326 out of state; room/board: $8,280
Financial aid: (208) 282-2756

Lewis-Clark State College
Lewiston ID
(208) 792-2210
U.S. News ranking: Reg. Coll. (W), No. 26
Website: www.lcsc.edu
Admissions email: admissions@lcsc.edu
Public; founded 1893
Freshman admissions: least selective; 2014-2015: 852 applied, 844 accepted. Neither SAT nor ACT required. SAT 25/75 percentile: 810-1030. High school rank: 5% in top tenth, 18% in top quarter, 46% in top half
Early decision deadline: N/A, notification date: N/A
Early action deadline: N/A, notification date: N/A
Application deadline (fall): 8/8
Undergraduate student body: 2,436 full time, 1,868 part time; 39% male, 61% female; 2% American Indian, 1% Asian, 1% black, 6% Hispanic, 3% multiracial, 0% Pacific Islander, 82% white, 4% international; 80% from in state; N/A live on campus; N/A of students in fraternities, N/A in sororities
Most popular majors: 25% Business, Management, Marketing, and Related Support Services, 7% Education, 23% Health Professions and Related Programs, 5% Parks, Recreation, Leisure, and Fitness Studies, 8% Public Administration and Social Service Professions
Expenses: 2015-2016: $6,150 in state, $17,150 out of state; room/board: $6,570
Financial aid: (208) 792-2224; 53% of undergrads determined to have financial need; average aid package $8,602

Northwest Nazarene University
Nampa ID
(208) 467-8000
U.S. News ranking: Reg. U. (W), No. 61
Website: www.nnu.edu
Admissions email: Admissions@nnu.edu
Private; founded 1913
Affiliation: Church of the Nazarene
Freshman admissions: selective; 2014-2015: 1,603 applied, 1,043 accepted. Either SAT or ACT required. SAT 25/75 percentile: 900-1180. High school rank: 19% in top tenth, 46% in top quarter, 80% in top half
Early decision deadline: N/A, notification date: N/A
Early action deadline: 12/15, notification date: 1/15
Application deadline (fall): 8/15
Undergraduate student body: 1,167 full time, 357 part time; 43% male, 57% female; 1% American Indian, 1% Asian, 1% black, 9% Hispanic, 2% multiracial, 0% Pacific Islander, 76% white, 3% international; 58% from in state; 71% live on campus; N/A of students in fraternities, N/A in sororities
Most popular majors: 6% Basic Skills and Developmental/Remedial Education, 20% Business, Management, Marketing, and Related Support Services, 15% Education, 13% Health Professions and Related Programs, 8% Liberal Arts and Sciences, General Studies and Humanities
Expenses: 2015-2016: $27,950; room/board: N/A
Financial aid: (208) 467-8347; 83% of undergrads determined to have financial need; average aid package $19,993

University of Idaho
Moscow ID
(888) 884-3246
U.S. News ranking: Nat. U., No. 168
Website: www.uidaho.edu/admissions
Admissions email: admissions@uidaho.edu
Public; founded 1889
Freshman admissions: selective; 2014-2015: 8,515 applied, 5,746 accepted. Either SAT or ACT required. SAT 25/75 percentile: 910-1170. High school rank: 20% in top tenth, 45% in top quarter, 73% in top half
Early decision deadline: N/A, notification date: N/A
Early action deadline: N/A, notification date: N/A
Application deadline (fall): 8/1
Undergraduate student body: 7,824 full time, 1,564 part time; 52% male, 48% female; 1% American Indian, 1% Asian, 1% black, 9% Hispanic, 4% multiracial, 0% Pacific Islander, 77% white, 4% international; 77% from in state; 23% live on campus; 14% of students in fraternities, 14% in sororities
Most popular majors: 3% Finance, General, 4% General Studies, 3% Human Resources Management/Personnel Administration, General, 4% Mechanical Engineering, 7% Psychology, General
Expenses: 2015-2016: $7,020 in state, $21,024 out of state; room/board: $8,328
Financial aid: (208) 885-6312; 65% of undergrads determined to have financial need; average aid package $13,366

ILLINOIS

American Academy of Art[1]
Chicago IL
(312) 461-0600
U.S. News ranking: Arts, unranked
Website: www.aaart.edu
Admissions email: N/A
For-profit
Application deadline (fall): N/A
Undergraduate student body: N/A full time, N/A part time
Expenses: 2014-2015: $30,220; room/board: $6,354
Financial aid: N/A

American InterContinental University[1]
Hoffman Estates IL
(855) 377-1888
U.S. News ranking: Reg. U. (Mid.W), unranked
Website: www.aiuniv.edu
Admissions email: N/A
For-profit
Application deadline (fall): N/A
Undergraduate student body: N/A full time, N/A part time
Expenses: 2014-2015: $11,104; room/board: $6,480
Financial aid: N/A

Augustana College
Rock Island IL
(800) 798-8100
U.S. News ranking: Nat. Lib. Arts, No. 105
Website: www.augustana.edu
Admissions email: admissions@augustana.edu
Private; founded 1860
Affiliation: Evangelical Lutheran Church in America
Freshman admissions: more selective; 2014-2015: 6,053 applied, 3,245 accepted. Neither SAT nor ACT required. ACT 25/75 percentile: 23-29. High school rank: 29% in top tenth, 66% in top quarter, 91% in top half
Early decision deadline: N/A, notification date: N/A
Early action deadline: N/A, notification date: N/A
Application deadline (fall): rolling
Undergraduate student body: 2,472 full time, 25 part time; 42% male, 58% female; 0% American Indian, 2% Asian, 4% black, 10% Hispanic, 4% multiracial, 0% Pacific Islander, 76% white, 2% international; 84% from in state; 70% live on campus; 23% of students in fraternities, 36% in sororities
Most popular majors: 22% Biological and Biomedical Sciences, 16% Business, Management, Marketing, and Related Support Services, 10% Health Professions and Related Programs, 7% Psychology, 9% Social Sciences
Expenses: 2015-2016: $38,466; room/board: $9,746
Financial aid: (309) 794-7207; 77% of undergrads determined to have financial need; average aid package $27,752

Aurora University[1]
Aurora IL
(800) 742-5281
U.S. News ranking: Reg. U. (Mid.W), second tier
Website: www.aurora.edu
Admissions email: admission@aurora.edu
Private
Application deadline (fall): N/A
Undergraduate student body: N/A full time, N/A part time
Expenses: 2014-2015: $21,320; room/board: $8,710
Financial aid: (630) 844-5533

Benedictine University
Lisle IL
(630) 829-6000
U.S. News ranking: Nat. U., second tier
Website: www.ben.edu
Admissions email: admissions@ben.edu
Private; founded 1887
Affiliation: Roman Catholic
Freshman admissions: selective; 2014-2015: 2,558 applied, 1,974 accepted. Either SAT or ACT required. ACT 25/75 percentile: 19-25. High school rank: 12% in top tenth, 35% in top quarter, 67% in top half
Early decision deadline: N/A, notification date: N/A
Early action deadline: N/A, notification date: N/A
Application deadline (fall): rolling
Undergraduate student body: 3,071 full time, 747 part time; 42% male, 58% female; 0% American Indian, 15% Asian, 9% black, 11% Hispanic, N/A multiracial, 0% Pacific Islander, 46% white, 1% international; 90% from in state; 18% live on campus; 0% of students in fraternities, 0% in sororities
Most popular majors: Information not available
Expenses: 2014-2015: $26,950; room/board: $8,280
Financial aid: (630) 829-6108

Blackburn College
Carlinville IL
(800) 233-3550
U.S. News ranking: Reg. Coll. (Mid.W), No. 46
Website: www.blackburn.edu
Admissions email: admit@mail.blackburn.edu
Private; founded 1837
Affiliation: Presbyterian
Freshman admissions: selective; 2014-2015: 788 applied, 513 accepted. Either SAT or ACT required. ACT 25/75 percentile: 18-24. High school rank: 13% in top tenth, 31% in top quarter, 63% in top half
Early decision deadline: N/A, notification date: N/A
Early action deadline: N/A, notification date: N/A
Application deadline (fall): rolling
Undergraduate student body: 554 full time, 31 part time; 45% male, 55% female; 1% American Indian, 1% Asian, 11% black, 2% Hispanic, 2% multiracial,

0% Pacific Islander, 82% white, 0% international; 89% from in state; 69% live on campus; 0% of students in fraternities, 0% in sororities
Most popular majors: 12% Biology/Biological Sciences, General, 9% Business Administration, Management and Operations, Other, 9% Criminal Justice/Safety Studies, 13% Psychology, General
Expenses: 2015-2016: $20,364; room/board: $7,034
Financial aid: (800) 233-3550; 85% of undergrads determined to have financial need; average aid package $17,524

Bradley University

Peoria IL
(800) 447-6460
U.S. News ranking: Reg. U. (Mid.W), No. 4
Website: www.bradley.edu
Admissions email: admissions@bradley.edu
Private; founded 1897
Freshman admissions: more selective; 2014-2015: 9,009 applied, 5,793 accepted. Either SAT or ACT required. ACT 25/75 percentile: 23-28. High school rank: 28% in top tenth, 63% in top quarter, 90% in top half
Early decision deadline: N/A, notification date: N/A
Early action deadline: N/A, notification date: N/A
Application deadline (fall): rolling
Undergraduate student body: 4,373 full time, 215 part time; 49% male, 51% female; 0% American Indian, 3% Asian, 5% black, 6% Hispanic, 1% multiracial, 0% Pacific Islander, 70% white, 1% international; 83% from in state; 69% live on campus; 33% of students in fraternities, 33% in sororities
Most popular majors: 16% Business, Management, Marketing, and Related Support Services, 8% Communication, Journalism, and Related Programs, 8% Education, 20% Engineering, 14% Health Professions and Related Programs
Expenses: 2015-2016: $31,480; room/board: $9,700
Financial aid: (309) 677-3089; 75% of undergrads determined to have financial need; average aid package $20,117

Chicago State University

Chicago IL
(773) 995-2513
U.S. News ranking: Reg. U. (Mid.W), second tier
Website: www.csu.edu
Admissions email: ug-admissions@csu.edu
Public; founded 1867
Freshman admissions: less selective; 2014-2015: 5,517 applied, 1,653 accepted. ACT required. ACT 25/75 percentile: 16-20. High school rank: N/A
Early decision deadline: N/A, notification date: N/A
Early action deadline: N/A, notification date: N/A
Application deadline (fall): rolling
Undergraduate student body: 2,498 full time, 1,414 part time; 29% male, 71% female; 0% American Indian, 1% Asian, 74% black, 8% Hispanic, N/A multiracial, N/A Pacific Islander, 2% white, N/A international
Most popular majors: Information not available
Expenses: 2014-2015: $11,396 in state, $20,096 out of state; room/board: $8,724
Financial aid: (773) 995-2304

Columbia College Chicago[1]

Chicago IL
(312) 344-7130
U.S. News ranking: Reg. U. (Mid.W), second tier
Website: www.colum.edu
Admissions email: admissions@colum.edu
Private
Application deadline (fall): N/A
Undergraduate student body: N/A full time, N/A part time
Expenses: 2014-2015: $23,544; room/board: $12,450
Financial aid: (312) 344-7054

Concordia University Chicago

River Forest IL
(877) 282-4422
U.S. News ranking: Reg. U. (Mid.W), No. 75
Website: www.cuchicago.edu/
Admissions email: admission@cuchicago.edu
Private; founded 1864
Affiliation: Lutheran
Freshman admissions: selective; 2014-2015: 3,723 applied, 2,005 accepted. Either SAT or ACT required. ACT 25/75 percentile: 20-25. High school rank: 10% in top tenth, 10% in top quarter, 82% in top half
Early decision deadline: N/A, notification date: N/A
Early action deadline: N/A, notification date: N/A
Application deadline (fall): rolling
Undergraduate student body: 1,397 full time, 141 part time; 39% male, 61% female; 0% American Indian, 2% Asian, 13% black, 24% Hispanic, 3% multiracial, 0% Pacific Islander, 55% white, 1% international; 78% from in state; 36% live on campus; 0% of students in fraternities, 0% in sororities
Most popular majors: Information not available
Expenses: 2015-2016: $29,520; room/board: $8,992
Financial aid: (708) 209-3113; 86% of undergrads determined to have financial need; average aid package $20,479

DePaul University

Chicago IL
(312) 362-8300
U.S. News ranking: Nat. U., No. 123
Website: www.depaul.edu
Admissions email: admission@depaul.edu
Private; founded 1898
Affiliation: Roman Catholic
Freshman admissions: more selective; 2014-2015: 19,533 applied, 13,649 accepted. Neither SAT nor ACT required. ACT 25/75 percentile: 23-28. High school rank: 21% in top tenth, 53% in top quarter, 86% in top half
Early decision deadline: N/A, notification date: N/A
Early action deadline: 11/15, notification date: 1/15
Application deadline (fall): 2/1
Undergraduate student body: 13,643 full time, 2,510 part time; 47% male, 53% female; 0% American Indian, 8% Asian, 8% black, 18% Hispanic, 4% multiracial, 0% Pacific Islander, 55% white, 3% international; 79% from in state; 16% live on campus; N/A of students in fraternities, N/A in sororities
Most popular majors: 28% Business/Commerce, General, 11% Liberal Arts and Sciences/Liberal Studies, 7% Psychology, General, 9% Social Sciences, General, 14% Speech Communication and Rhetoric
Expenses: 2015-2016: $36,361; room/board: $12,873
Financial aid: (312) 362-8091; 70% of undergrads determined to have financial need; average aid package $21,173

DeVry University

Downers Grove IL
(866) 338-7940
U.S. News ranking: Reg. U. (Mid.W), second tier
Website: www.devry.edu
Admissions email: N/A
For-profit; founded 1931
Freshman admissions: less selective; 2014-2015: N/A applied, N/A accepted. Neither SAT nor ACT required. ACT 25/75 percentile: N/A. High school rank: N/A
Early decision deadline: N/A, notification date: N/A
Early action deadline: N/A, notification date: N/A
Application deadline (fall): rolling
Undergraduate student body: 16,741 full time, 25,641 part time; 54% male, 46% female; 1% American Indian, 5% Asian, 23% black, 18% Hispanic, 1% multiracial, 1% Pacific Islander, 40% white, 1% international
Most popular majors: 21% Business Administration and Management, General, 42% Business Administration, Management and Operations, Other, 11% Computer Systems Analysis/Analyst, 8% Computer Systems Networking and Telecommunications, 4% Web Page, Digital/Multimedia and Information Resources Design
Expenses: 2014-2015: $17,132; room/board: N/A
Financial aid: N/A

Dominican University

River Forest IL
(708) 524-6800
U.S. News ranking: Reg. U. (Mid.W), No. 20
Website: public.dom.edu/
Admissions email: domadmis@dom.edu
Private; founded 1901
Affiliation: Roman Catholic
Freshman admissions: selective; 2014-2015: 3,692 applied, 2,240 accepted. Either SAT or ACT required. ACT 25/75 percentile: 20-24. High school rank: 22% in top tenth, 48% in top quarter, 85% in top half
Early decision deadline: N/A, notification date: N/A
Early action deadline: N/A, notification date: N/A
Application deadline (fall): 7/1
Undergraduate student body: 1,996 full time, 184 part time; 34% male, 66% female; 0% American Indian, 3% Asian, 6% black, 44% Hispanic, 1% multiracial, 0% Pacific Islander, 41% white, 3% international; 93% from in state; 27% live on campus; 0% of students in fraternities, 0% in sororities
Most popular majors: 16% Business, Management, Marketing, and Related Support Services, 11% Health Professions and Related Programs, 9% Psychology, 21% Social Sciences, 9% Visual and Performing Arts
Expenses: 2015-2016: $30,670; room/board: $9,380
Financial aid: (708) 524-6809; 90% of undergrads determined to have financial need; average aid package $22,638

Eastern Illinois University

Charleston IL
(877) 581-2348
U.S. News ranking: Reg. U. (Mid.W), No. 30
Website: www.eiu.edu
Admissions email: admissions@eiu.edu
Public; founded 1895
Freshman admissions: selective; 2014-2015: 8,918 applied, 4,438 accepted. Either SAT or ACT required. ACT 25/75 percentile: 19-24. High school rank: 12% in top tenth, 33% in top quarter, 68% in top half
Early decision deadline: N/A, notification date: N/A
Early action deadline: N/A, notification date: N/A
Application deadline (fall): 8/15
Undergraduate student body: 6,676 full time, 964 part time; 40% male, 60% female; 0% American Indian, 1% Asian, 19% black, 5% Hispanic, 2% multiracial, 0% Pacific Islander, 70% white, 1% international; 96% from in state; 38% live on campus; 20% of students in fraternities, 18% in sororities
Most popular majors: 9% Business, Management, Marketing, and Related Support Services, 9% Communication, Journalism, and Related Programs, 21% Education, 7% Liberal Arts and Sciences, General Studies and Humanities, 10% Parks, Recreation, Leisure, and Fitness Studies
Expenses: 2015-2016: $11,312 in state, $13,442 out of state; room/board: $9,546
Financial aid: (217) 581-3713; 69% of undergrads determined to have financial need; average aid package $11,392

East-West University[1]

Chicago IL
(312) 939-0111
U.S. News ranking: Nat. Lib. Arts, second tier
Website: www.eastwest.edu
Admissions email: seeyou@eastwest.edu
Private; founded 1980
Application deadline (fall): rolling
Undergraduate student body: N/A full time, N/A part time
Expenses: 2014-2015: $19,545; room/board: $11,331
Financial aid: (312) 939-0111

Elmhurst College

Elmhurst IL
(630) 617-3400
U.S. News ranking: Reg. U. (Mid.W), No. 10
Website: www.elmhurst.edu
Admissions email: admit@elmhurst.edu
Private; founded 1871
Affiliation: United Church of Christ
Freshman admissions: selective; 2014-2015: 3,193 applied, 2,162 accepted. Either SAT or ACT required. ACT 25/75 percentile: 21-26. High school rank: 17% in top tenth, 45% in top quarter, 75% in top half
Early decision deadline: N/A, notification date: N/A
Early action deadline: N/A, notification date: N/A
Application deadline (fall): rolling
Undergraduate student body: 2,699 full time, 154 part time; 40% male, 60% female; 0% American Indian, 5% Asian, 4% black, 16% Hispanic, 3% multiracial, 0% Pacific Islander, 70% white, 0% international; 90% from in state; 35% live on campus; 10% of students in fraternities, 16% in sororities
Most popular majors: 18% Business, Management, Marketing, and Related Support Services, 10% Education, 8% English Language and Literature/Letters, 14% Health Professions and Related Programs, 11% Psychology
Expenses: 2015-2016: $34,450; room/board: $9,816
Financial aid: (630) 617-3075; 72% of undergrads determined to have financial need; average aid package $27,279

Eureka College

Eureka IL
(309) 467-6350
U.S. News ranking: Reg. Coll. (Mid.W), No. 29
Website: www.eureka.edu
Admissions email: admissions@eureka.edu
Private; founded 1855
Affiliation: Christian Church (Disciples of Christ)
Freshman admissions: selective; 2014-2015: 1,164 applied, 759 accepted. Either SAT or ACT required. ACT 25/75 percentile: 19-26. High school rank: 19% in top tenth, 35% in top quarter, 67% in top half
Early decision deadline: N/A, notification date: N/A
Early action deadline: N/A, notification date: N/A
Application deadline (fall): 8/1
Undergraduate student body: 636 full time, 18 part time; 44% male, 56% female; 0% American Indian, 1% Asian, 5% black, 2% Hispanic, 3% multiracial, 0% Pacific Islander, 84% white, 1% international; 93% from in state; 59% live on campus; 25% of students in fraternities, 12% in sororities
Most popular majors: 15% Business Administration and Management, General, 10% Corrections and Criminal Justice, Other, 9% Elementary Education and Teaching, 8% History, Other, 9% Kinesiology and Exercise Science
Expenses: 2015-2016: $20,510; room/board: $8,835

More at usnews.com/college

Financial aid: (309) 467-6311; 79% of undergrads determined to have financial need; average aid package $15,558

Governors State University

University Park IL
(708) 534-4490
U.S. News ranking: Reg. U. (Mid.W), second tier
Website: www.govst.edu/
Admissions email: GSUNOW@govst.edu
Public; founded 1969
Freshman admissions: less selective; 2014-2015: 422 applied, 398 accepted. Either SAT or ACT required. ACT 25/75 percentile: 17-21. High school rank: 17% in top tenth, N/A in top quarter, 77% in top half
Early decision deadline: 11/15, notification date: 12/15
Early action deadline: 11/15, notification date: 12/15
Application deadline (fall): 4/1
Undergraduate student body: 1,713 full time, 1,872 part time; 33% male, 67% female; 0% American Indian, 2% Asian, 37% black, 11% Hispanic, 2% multiracial, 0% Pacific Islander, 38% white, 1% international; 98% from in state; 5% live on campus; 0% of students in fraternities, 0% in sororities
Most popular majors: 16% Business, Management, Marketing, and Related Support Services, 19% Health Professions and Related Programs, 11% Homeland Security, Law Enforcement, Firefighting and Related Protective Services, 22% Liberal Arts and Sciences, General Studies and Humanities, 10% Psychology
Expenses: 2014-2015: $9,386 in state, $17,036 out of state; room/board: $9,000
Financial aid: (708) 534-4480; 50% of undergrads determined to have financial need

Greenville College

Greenville IL
(618) 664-7100
U.S. News ranking: Reg. Coll. (Mid.W), No. 35
Website: www.greenville.edu
Admissions email: admissions@greenville.edu
Private; founded 1892
Affiliation: Free Methodist
Freshman admissions: selective; 2014-2015: 2,321 applied, 1,291 accepted. Either SAT or ACT required. ACT 25/75 percentile: 20-26. High school rank: 16% in top tenth, 39% in top quarter, 75% in top half
Early decision deadline: N/A, notification date: N/A
Early action deadline: N/A, notification date: N/A
Application deadline (fall): rolling
Undergraduate student body: 1,031 full time, 72 part time; 52% male, 48% female; N/A American Indian, 1% Asian, 9% black, 5% Hispanic, 2% multiracial, 0% Pacific Islander, 76% white, 2% international; 65% from in state; 90% live on campus; 0% of students in fraternities, 0% in sororities
Most popular majors: 8% Biological and Biomedical Sciences, 22% Business, Management, Marketing, and Related Support Services, 27% Education, 5% Homeland Security, Law Enforcement, Firefighting and Related Protective Services, 7% Visual and Performing Arts
Expenses: 2015-2016: $25,088; room/board: $8,288
Financial aid: (618) 664-7110; 86% of undergrads determined to have financial need; average aid package $19,037

Harrington College of Design[1]

Chicago IL
(866) 590-4423
U.S. News ranking: Arts, unranked
Website: www.harrington.edu/
Admissions email: N/A
For-profit
Application deadline (fall): N/A
Undergraduate student body: N/A full time, N/A part time
Expenses: 2014-2015: $18,357; room/board: $6,952
Financial aid: N/A

Illinois College

Jacksonville IL
(217) 245-3030
U.S. News ranking: Nat. Lib. Arts, No. 136
Website: www.ic.edu
Admissions email: admissions@ic.edu
Private; founded 1829
Affiliation: Presbyterian Church (USA) and United Church of Christ
Freshman admissions: selective; 2014-2015: 2,749 applied, 1,488 accepted. Neither SAT nor ACT required. ACT 25/75 percentile: 18-26. High school rank: 22% in top tenth, 52% in top quarter, 88% in top half
Early decision deadline: N/A, notification date: N/A
Early action deadline: 12/15, notification date: 12/23
Application deadline (fall): rolling
Undergraduate student body: 952 full time, 5 part time; 50% male, 50% female; 0% American Indian, 1% Asian, 13% black, 9% Hispanic, 3% multiracial, 0% Pacific Islander, 71% white, 3% international; 86% from in state; 83% live on campus; 0% of students in fraternities, 0% in sororities
Most popular majors: 17% Biological and Biomedical Sciences, 11% Business, Management, Marketing, and Related Support Services, 11% English Language and Literature/Letters, 14% Multi/Interdisciplinary Studies, 9% Social Sciences
Expenses: 2015-2016: $31,660; room/board: $9,190
Financial aid: (217) 245-3035; 84% of undergrads determined to have financial need; average aid package $26,431

Illinois Institute of Art–Chicago[1]

Chicago IL
(800) 351-3450
U.S. News ranking: Arts, unranked
Website: www.artinstitutes.edu/chicago/
Admissions email: N/A
For-profit
Application deadline (fall): N/A
Undergraduate student body: N/A full time, N/A part time
Expenses: 2014-2015: $17,488; room/board: $12,897
Financial aid: N/A

Illinois Institute of Technology

Chicago IL
(800) 448-2329
U.S. News ranking: Nat. U., No. 108
Website: iit.edu/undergrad_admission/
Admissions email: admission@iit.edu
Private; founded 1890
Freshman admissions: more selective; 2014-2015: 3,559 applied, 1,801 accepted. Either SAT or ACT required. ACT 25/75 percentile: 25-31. High school rank: 45% in top tenth, 77% in top quarter, 94% in top half
Early decision deadline: N/A, notification date: N/A
Early action deadline: N/A, notification date: N/A
Application deadline (fall): 8/1
Undergraduate student body: 2,922 full time, 177 part time; 69% male, 31% female; 0% American Indian, 11% Asian, 6% black, 14% Hispanic, 1% multiracial, 0% Pacific Islander, 33% white, 30% international; 80% from in state; 62% live on campus; 12% of students in fraternities, 13% in sororities
Most popular majors: 18% Architecture and Related Services, 5% Business, Management, Marketing, and Related Support Services, 10% Computer and Information Sciences and Support Services, 49% Engineering, 4% Physical Sciences
Expenses: 2015-2016: $43,680; room/board: $11,300
Financial aid: (312) 567-7219; 55% of undergrads determined to have financial need; average aid package $35,527

Illinois State University

Normal IL
(309) 438-2181
U.S. News ranking: Nat. U., No. 149
Website: www.ilstu.edu
Admissions email: admissions@ilstu.edu
Public; founded 1857
Freshman admissions: selective; 2014-2015: 15,297 applied, 11,301 accepted. Either SAT or ACT required. ACT 25/75 percentile: 22-26. High school rank: N/A
Early decision deadline: N/A, notification date: N/A
Early action deadline: N/A, notification date: N/A
Application deadline (fall): 4/1
Undergraduate student body: 17,040 full time, 1,115 part time; 45% male, 55% female; 0% American Indian, 2% Asian, 7% black, 9% Hispanic, 2% multiracial, 0% Pacific Islander, 78% white, 0% international; 97% from in state; 34% live on campus; 3% of students in fraternities, 4% in sororities
Most popular majors: 19% Business, Management, Marketing, and Related Support Services, 7% Communication, Journalism, and Related Programs, 13% Education, 8% Health Professions and Related Programs, 6% Social Sciences
Expenses: 2014-2015: $12,830 in state, $20,420 out of state; room/board: $9,970
Financial aid: (309) 438-2231; 65% of undergrads determined to have financial need; average aid package $10,482

Illinois Wesleyan University

Bloomington IL
(800) 332-2498
U.S. News ranking: Nat. Lib. Arts, No. 72
Website: www.iwu.edu
Admissions email: iwuadmit@iwu.edu
Private; founded 1850
Affiliation: Methodist
Freshman admissions: more selective; 2014-2015: 3,427 applied, 2,071 accepted. Either SAT or ACT required. ACT 25/75 percentile: 25-30. High school rank: 38% in top tenth, 76% in top quarter, 99% in top half
Early decision deadline: N/A, notification date: N/A
Early action deadline: 11/15, notification date: 1/15
Application deadline (fall): rolling
Undergraduate student body: 1,885 full time, 8 part time; 44% male, 56% female; 0% American Indian, 4% Asian, 5% black, 7% Hispanic, 2% multiracial, 0% Pacific Islander, 71% white, 8% international; 89% from in state; 71% live on campus; 33% of students in fraternities, 33% in sororities
Most popular majors: 8% Accounting, 7% Biological and Biomedical Sciences, 15% Business/Commerce, General, 12% Psychology, General, 6% Registered Nursing/Registered Nurse
Expenses: 2015-2016: $42,490; room/board: $9,796
Financial aid: (309) 556-3096; 64% of undergrads determined to have financial need; average aid package $29,999

Judson University

Elgin IL
(800) 879-5376
U.S. News ranking: Reg. Coll. (Mid.W), No. 33
Website: www.judsonu.edu
Admissions email: admissions@judsonu.edu
Private; founded 1913
Affiliation: American Baptist
Freshman admissions: selective; 2014-2015: 703 applied, 514 accepted. Either SAT or ACT required. ACT 25/75 percentile: 20-26. High school rank: 22% in top tenth, 44% in top quarter, 82% in top half
Early decision deadline: N/A, notification date: N/A
Early action deadline: N/A, notification date: N/A
Application deadline (fall): rolling
Undergraduate student body: 781 full time, 373 part time; 40% male, 60% female; 0% American Indian, 2% Asian, 8% black, 13% Hispanic, 2% multiracial, 0% Pacific Islander, 62% white, 3% international; 73% from in state; 48% live on campus; 0% of students in fraternities, 0% in sororities
Most popular majors: 9% Architecture and Related Services, 29% Business, Management, Marketing, and Related Support Services, 9% Education, 8% Military Technologies and Applied Sciences, 7% Public Administration and Social Service Professions
Expenses: 2015-2016: $28,170; room/board: $9,450
Financial aid: (847) 628-2532; 83% of undergrads determined to have financial need; average aid package $19,023

Kendall College[1]

Chicago IL
(877) 588-8860
U.S. News ranking: Reg. Coll. (Mid.W), second tier
Website: www.kendall.edu
Admissions email: admissions@kendall.edu
For-profit; founded 1934
Application deadline (fall): rolling
Undergraduate student body: N/A full time, N/A part time
Expenses: 2014-2015: $25,173; room/board: $10,305
Financial aid: (312) 752-2028

Knox College

Galesburg IL
(800) 678-5669
U.S. News ranking: Nat. Lib. Arts, No. 72
Website: www.knox.edu
Admissions email: admission@knox.edu
Private; founded 1837
Freshman admissions: more selective; 2014-2015: 3,221 applied, 2,198 accepted. Neither SAT nor ACT required. ACT 25/75 percentile: 23-30. High school rank: 31% in top tenth, 58% in top quarter, 89% in top half
Early decision deadline: N/A, notification date: N/A
Early action deadline: 12/1, notification date: 12/31
Application deadline (fall): 1/15
Undergraduate student body: 1,367 full time, 32 part time; 42% male, 58% female; 0% American Indian, 6% Asian, 8% black, 13% Hispanic, 4% multiracial, 0% Pacific Islander, 53% white, 13% international; 57% from in state; 80% live on campus; 17% of students in fraternities, 17% in sororities
Most popular majors: 11% Creative Writing, 8% Economics, General, 9% Elementary Education and Teaching, 6% Psychology, General, 6% Social Sciences, Other
Expenses: 2015-2016: $41,847; room/board: $9,012
Financial aid: (309) 341-7130; 80% of undergrads determined to have financial need; average aid package $32,942

Lake Forest College

Lake Forest IL
(847) 735-5000
U.S. News ranking: Nat. Lib. Arts, No. 108
Website: www.lakeforest.edu

Admissions email: admissions@lakeforest.edu
Private; founded 1857
Freshman admissions: more selective; 2014-2015: 3,451 applied, 1,905 accepted. Neither SAT nor ACT required. ACT 25/75 percentile: 23-28. High school rank: 27% in top tenth, 56% in top quarter, 86% in top half
Early decision deadline: 11/15, notification date: 12/15
Early action deadline: 11/15, notification date: 12/15
Application deadline (fall): 2/15
Undergraduate student body: 1,589 full time, 18 part time; 43% male, 57% female; 0% American Indian, 5% Asian, 7% black, 15% Hispanic, 4% multiracial, 0% Pacific Islander, 58% white, 9% international; 64% from in state; 72% live on campus; 12% of students in fraternities, 16% in sororities
Most popular majors: 7% Biological and Biomedical Sciences, 11% Business, Management, Marketing, and Related Support Services, 11% Communication, Journalism, and Related Programs, 6% Psychology, 24% Social Sciences
Expenses: 2015-2016: $42,644; room/board: $9,570
Financial aid: (847) 735-5104; 78% of undergrads determined to have financial need; average aid package $34,865

Lewis University

Romeoville IL
(800) 897-9000
U.S. News ranking: Reg. U. (Mid.W), No. 28
Website: www.lewisu.edu
Admissions email: admissions@lewisu.edu
Private; founded 1932
Affiliation: Roman Catholic
Freshman admissions: selective; 2014-2015: 5,786 applied, 3,582 accepted. Either SAT or ACT required. ACT 25/75 percentile: 21-25. High school rank: 18% in top tenth, 44% in top quarter, 83% in top half
Early decision deadline: N/A, notification date: N/A
Early action deadline: N/A, notification date: N/A
Application deadline (fall): rolling
Undergraduate student body: 3,816 full time, 936 part time; 44% male, 56% female; 0% American Indian, 3% Asian, 7% black, 18% Hispanic, 2% multiracial, 0% Pacific Islander, 66% white, 1% international; 94% from in state; 28% live on campus; 4% of students in fraternities, 4% in sororities
Most popular majors: 5% Aviation/Airway Management and Operations, 7% Business Administration and Management, General, 11% Criminal Justice/Safety Studies, 6% Psychology, General, 20% Registered Nursing/Registered Nurse
Expenses: 2015-2016: $29,040; room/board: $9,930
Financial aid: (815) 836-5263; 76% of undergrads determined to have financial need; average aid package $20,334

Lincoln College[1]

Lincoln IL
(800) 569-0556
U.S. News ranking: Reg. Coll. (Mid.W), second tier
Website: www.lincolncollege.edu
Admissions email: admission@lincolncollege.edu
Private; founded 1865
Application deadline (fall): rolling
Undergraduate student body: N/A full time, N/A part time
Expenses: 2014-2015: $17,500; room/board: $7,000
Financial aid: (309) 452-0500

Loyola University Chicago

Chicago IL
(312) 915-6500
U.S. News ranking: Nat. U., No. 99
Website: www.luc.edu
Admissions email: admission@luc.edu
Private; founded 1870
Affiliation: Roman Catholic
Freshman admissions: more selective; 2014-2015: 20,414 applied, 12,931 accepted. Either SAT or ACT required. ACT 25/75 percentile: 25-29. High school rank: 34% in top tenth, 72% in top quarter, 96% in top half
Early decision deadline: N/A, notification date: N/A
Early action deadline: N/A, notification date: N/A
Application deadline (fall): rolling
Undergraduate student body: 9,331 full time, 991 part time; 36% male, 64% female; 0% American Indian, 11% Asian, 4% black, 13% Hispanic, 6% multiracial, 0% Pacific Islander, 60% white, 4% international; 65% from in state; 44% live on campus; 9% of students in fraternities, 10% in sororities
Most popular majors: 14% Biological and Biomedical Sciences, 18% Business, Management, Marketing, and Related Support Services, 11% Health Professions and Related Programs, 12% Psychology, 11% Social Sciences
Expenses: 2015-2016: $39,179; room/board: $13,310
Financial aid: (773) 508-3155; 69% of undergrads determined to have financial need; average aid package $30,916

MacMurray College

Jacksonville IL
(217) 479-7056
U.S. News ranking: Reg. Coll. (Mid.W), No. 57
Website: www.mac.edu
Admissions email: admissions@mac.edu
Private; founded 1846
Affiliation: United Methodist
Freshman admissions: selective; 2014-2015: 624 applied, 489 accepted. Either SAT or ACT required. ACT 25/75 percentile: 18-22. High school rank: 8% in top tenth, 24% in top quarter, 57% in top half
Early decision deadline: N/A, notification date: N/A
Early action deadline: N/A, notification date: N/A
Application deadline (fall): 8/25
Undergraduate student body: 525 full time, 29 part time; 45% male, 55% female; 0% American Indian, 0% Asian, 13% black, 5% Hispanic, 2% multiracial, 0% Pacific Islander, 75% white, 0% international; 86% from in state; 55% live on campus; 0% of students in fraternities, 0% in sororities
Most popular majors: 16% Business Administration and Management, General, 14% Criminal Justice/Law Enforcement Administration, 9% Psychology, General, 18% Registered Nursing/Registered Nurse, 10% Social Work
Expenses: 2015-2016: $24,172; room/board: $8,112
Financial aid: (217) 479-7041; 89% of undergrads determined to have financial need; average aid package $20,581

McKendree University

Lebanon IL
(618) 537-6831
U.S. News ranking: Reg. U. (Mid.W), No. 68
Website: www.mckendree.edu
Admissions email: inquiry@mckendree.edu
Private; founded 1828
Affiliation: Methodist
Freshman admissions: selective; 2014-2015: 1,965 applied, 1,201 accepted. Either SAT or ACT required. ACT 25/75 percentile: 20-25. High school rank: 10% in top tenth, 37% in top quarter, 76% in top half
Early decision deadline: N/A, notification date: N/A
Early action deadline: N/A, notification date: N/A
Application deadline (fall): rolling
Undergraduate student body: 1,950 full time, 571 part time; 44% male, 56% female; 1% American Indian, 1% Asian, 14% black, 4% Hispanic, 2% multiracial, 0% Pacific Islander, 69% white, 2% international; 82% from in state; 73% live on campus; 4% of students in fraternities, 20% in sororities
Most popular majors: 11% Business Administration and Management, General, 7% Management Science, 7% Psychology, General, 21% Registered Nursing/Registered Nurse, 5% Sociology
Expenses: 2015-2016: $27,930; room/board: $9,020
Financial aid: (618) 537-6828; 84% of undergrads determined to have financial need; average aid package $20,754

Midstate College[1]

Peoria IL
(309) 692-4092
U.S. News ranking: Reg. Coll. (Mid.W), unranked
Website: www.midstate.edu/
Admissions email: jauer@midstate.edu
For-profit
Application deadline (fall): rolling
Undergraduate student body: N/A full time, N/A part time
Expenses: 2014-2015: $16,230; room/board: $7,395
Financial aid: (309) 692-4092

Millikin University

Decatur IL
(217) 424-6210
U.S. News ranking: Reg. Coll. (Mid.W), No. 10
Website: www.millikin.edu
Admissions email: admis@millikin.edu
Private; founded 1901
Affiliation: Presbyterian
Freshman admissions: selective; 2014-2015: 3,255 applied, 2,042 accepted. Either SAT or ACT required. ACT 25/75 percentile: 19-26. High school rank: 14% in top tenth, 40% in top quarter, 71% in top half
Early decision deadline: N/A, notification date: N/A
Early action deadline: N/A, notification date: N/A
Application deadline (fall): rolling
Undergraduate student body: 2,018 full time, 94 part time; 41% male, 59% female; 0% American Indian, 1% Asian, 14% black, 6% Hispanic, 4% multiracial, 0% Pacific Islander, 74% white, 1% international; 87% from in state; 67% live on campus; 26% of students in fraternities, 26% in sororities
Most popular majors: 23% Business, Management, Marketing, and Related Support Services, 7% Communication, Journalism, and Related Programs, 10% Education, 12% Health Professions and Related Programs, 17% Visual and Performing Arts
Expenses: 2015-2016: $30,630; room/board: $9,916
Financial aid: (217) 424-6343; 84% of undergrads determined to have financial need; average aid package $22,679

Monmouth College

Monmouth IL
(800) 747-2687
U.S. News ranking: Nat. Lib. Arts, No. 167
Website: www.monmouthcollege.edu/admissions
Admissions email: admissions@monmouthcollege.edu
Private; founded 1853
Affiliation: Presbyterian USA
Freshman admissions: selective; 2014-2015: 2,849 applied, 1,969 accepted. Either SAT or ACT required. ACT 25/75 percentile: 19-25. High school rank: 13% in top tenth, 35% in top quarter, 75% in top half
Early decision deadline: N/A, notification date: N/A
Early action deadline: N/A, notification date: N/A
Application deadline (fall): rolling
Undergraduate student body: 1,278 full time, 22 part time; 46% male, 54% female; 1% American Indian, 1% Asian, 11% black, 13% Hispanic, 1% multiracial, 0% Pacific Islander, 64% white, 3% international; 92% from in state; 92% live on campus; 22% of students in fraternities, 18% in sororities
Most popular majors: 22% Business, Management, Marketing, and Related Support Services, 15% Communication, Journalism, and Related Programs, 9% Education, 7% Psychology, 11% Social Sciences
Expenses: 2015-2016: $34,200; room/board: $8,060
Financial aid: (309) 457-2129; 86% of undergrads determined to have financial need; average aid package $30,380

National Louis University[1]

Chicago IL
(888) 658-8632
U.S. News ranking: Nat. U., second tier
Website: www.nl.edu
Admissions email: nluinfo@nl.edu
Private
Application deadline (fall): rolling
Undergraduate student body: N/A full time, N/A part time
Expenses: 2014-2015: $12,867; room/board: $15,300
Financial aid: (847) 465-5350

North Central College

Naperville IL
(630) 637-5800
U.S. News ranking: Reg. U. (Mid.W), No. 15
Website: www.noctrl.edu
Admissions email: ncadm@noctrl.edu
Private; founded 1861
Affiliation: United Methodist
Freshman admissions: more selective; 2014-2015: 5,807 applied, 3,475 accepted. Either SAT or ACT required. ACT 25/75 percentile: 22-27. High school rank: 22% in top tenth, 52% in top quarter, 81% in top half
Early decision deadline: N/A, notification date: N/A
Early action deadline: N/A, notification date: N/A
Application deadline (fall): rolling
Undergraduate student body: 2,601 full time, 181 part time; 45% male, 55% female; 0% American Indian, 2% Asian, 4% black, 10% Hispanic, 3% multiracial, 0% Pacific Islander, 73% white, 2% international; 93% from in state; 57% live on campus; N/A of students in fraternities, N/A in sororities
Most popular majors: 8% Business Administration and Management, General, 5% Kinesiology and Exercise Science, 7% Marketing/Marketing Management, General, 11% Psychology, General, 6% Sociology
Expenses: 2015-2016: $35,421; room/board: $10,089
Financial aid: (630) 637-5600; 78% of undergrads determined to have financial need; average aid package $23,538

Northeastern Illinois University

Chicago IL
(773) 442-4000
U.S. News ranking: Reg. U. (Mid.W), second tier
Website: www.neiu.edu
Admissions email: admrec@neiu.edu
Public; founded 1867
Freshman admissions: less selective; 2014-2015: 4,986 applied, 2,825 accepted. ACT required. ACT 25/75 percentile: 16-21. High school rank: 8% in top tenth, 23% in top quarter, 55% in top half
Early decision deadline: N/A, notification date: N/A
Early action deadline: N/A, notification date: N/A
Application deadline (fall): 7/1
Undergraduate student body: 4,695 full time, 3,717 part time; 44% male, 56% female; 0% American Indian, 9% Asian, 10% black, 36% Hispanic, 2% multiracial,

0% Pacific Islander, 36% white, 4% international; 98% from in state; 0% live on campus; 1% of students in fraternities, 1% in sororities
Most popular majors: 17% Business, Management, Marketing, and Related Support Services, 8% Education, 11% Liberal Arts and Sciences, General Studies and Humanities, 8% Public Administration and Social Service Professions, 9% Social Sciences
Expenses: 2015-2016: $10,318 in state, $18,992 out of state; room/board: N/A
Financial aid: (773) 442-5000; 73% of undergrads determined to have financial need; average aid package $8,284

Northern Illinois University

DeKalb IL
(815) 753-0446
U.S. News ranking: Nat. U., second tier
Website: www.niu.edu/
Admissions email: admission@niu.edu
Public; founded 1895
Freshman admissions: selective; 2014-2015: 19,814 applied, 10,083 accepted. Either SAT or ACT required. ACT 25/75 percentile: 19-25. High school rank: 11% in top tenth, 31% in top quarter, 70% in top half
Early decision deadline: N/A, notification date: N/A
Early action deadline: N/A, notification date: N/A
Application deadline (fall): 8/1
Undergraduate student body: 13,489 full time, 1,946 part time; 51% male, 49% female; 0% American Indian, 5% Asian, 16% black, 14% Hispanic, 3% multiracial, 0% Pacific Islander, 58% white, 2% international; 98% from in state; 28% live on campus; 6% of students in fraternities, 4% in sororities
Most popular majors: 5% Accounting, 4% Health/Medical Preparatory Programs, Other, 6% Psychology, General, 6% Registered Nursing/Registered Nurse, 7% Speech Communication and Rhetoric
Expenses: 2015-2016: $14,426 in state, $23,891 out of state; room/board: $10,756
Financial aid: (815) 753-1300; 75% of undergrads determined to have financial need; average aid package $12,946

North Park University

Chicago IL
(773) 244-5500
U.S. News ranking: Reg. U. (Mid.W), No. 54
Website: www.northpark.edu
Admissions email: admissions@northpark.edu
Private; founded 1891
Affiliation: Evangelical Covenant Church
Freshman admissions: selective; 2014-2015: 2,655 applied, 1,450 accepted. Either SAT or ACT required. ACT 25/75 percentile: 19-25. High school rank: N/A
Early decision deadline: N/A, notification date: N/A
Early action deadline: N/A, notification date: N/A
Application deadline (fall): 7/1
Undergraduate student body: 1,911 full time, 289 part time; 37% male, 63% female; 0% American Indian, 6% Asian, 9% black, 20% Hispanic, 4% multiracial, 1% Pacific Islander, 50% white, 5% international; 77% from in state; 39% live on campus; 0% of students in fraternities, 0% in sororities
Most popular majors: 6% Biology/Biological Sciences, General, 18% Business Administration and Management, General, 5% Health and Physical Education/Fitness, General, 5% Psychology, General, 22% Registered Nursing/Registered Nurse
Expenses: 2014-2015: $24,540; room/board: $8,660
Financial aid: (773) 244-5526

Northwestern University

Evanston IL
(847) 491-7271
U.S. News ranking: Nat. U., No. 12
Website: www.northwestern.edu
Admissions email: ug-admission@northwestern.edu
Private; founded 1851
Freshman admissions: most selective; 2014-2015: 33,674 applied, 4,416 accepted. Either SAT or ACT required. SAT 25/75 percentile: 1390-1560. High school rank: 90% in top tenth, 100% in top quarter, 100% in top half
Early decision deadline: 11/1, notification date: 12/15
Early action deadline: N/A, notification date: N/A
Application deadline (fall): 1/1
Undergraduate student body: 8,278 full time, 127 part time; 49% male, 51% female; 0% American Indian, 17% Asian, 6% black, 11% Hispanic, 5% multiracial, 0% Pacific Islander, 52% white, 8% international; 33% from in state; 40% live on campus; 29% of students in fraternities, 32% in sororities
Most popular majors: 7% Biology/Biological Sciences, General, 4% Drama and Dramatics/Theatre Arts, General, 12% Economics, General, 8% Journalism, 7% Psychology, General
Expenses: 2015-2016: $49,047; room/board: $14,936
Financial aid: (847) 491-7400; 44% of undergrads determined to have financial need; average aid package $40,978

Olivet Nazarene University

Bourbonnais IL
(815) 939-5011
U.S. News ranking: Reg. U. (Mid.W), No. 54
Website: www.olivet.edu
Admissions email: admissions@olivet.edu
Private; founded 1907
Affiliation: Church of the Nazarene
Freshman admissions: selective; 2014-2015: 4,783 applied, 3,563 accepted. Either SAT or ACT required. ACT 25/75 percentile: 21-27. High school rank: 22% in top tenth, 47% in top quarter, 79% in top half
Early decision deadline: N/A, notification date: N/A
Early action deadline: N/A, notification date: N/A
Application deadline (fall): 8/1
Undergraduate student body: 3,082 full time, 439 part time; 38% male, 62% female; 0% American Indian, 2% Asian, 7% black, 7% Hispanic, 2% multiracial, 0% Pacific Islander, 80% white, 1% international; 65% from in state; 68% live on campus; 0% of students in fraternities, 0% in sororities
Most popular majors: 5% Business Administration and Management, General, 5% Elementary Education and Teaching, 4% Psychology, General, 30% Registered Nursing/Registered Nurse, 5% Social Work
Expenses: 2015-2016: $32,790; room/board: $7,900
Financial aid: (815) 939-5249; 83% of undergrads determined to have financial need; average aid package $24,719

Principia College

Elsah IL
(618) 374-5181
U.S. News ranking: Nat. Lib. Arts, No. 127
Website: www.principiacollege.edu
Admissions email: collegeadmissions@principia.edu
Private; founded 1910
Affiliation: Christian Science
Freshman admissions: selective; 2014-2015: 211 applied, 167 accepted. Either SAT or ACT required. SAT 25/75 percentile: 920-1230. High school rank: 23% in top tenth, 48% in top quarter, 68% in top half
Early decision deadline: N/A, notification date: N/A
Early action deadline: N/A, notification date: N/A
Application deadline (fall): 7/25
Undergraduate student body: 488 full time, 7 part time; 49% male, 51% female; 0% American Indian, 1% Asian, 1% black, 2% Hispanic, 2% multiracial, 1% Pacific Islander, 69% white, 15% international; 7% from in state; 99% live on campus; N/A of students in fraternities, N/A in sororities
Most popular majors: 8% Biology, General, 16% Business Administration and Management, General, 8% English Language and Literature, General, 9% Fine/Studio Arts, General, 8% Mass Communication/Media Studies
Expenses: 2015-2016: $27,440; room/board: $10,810
Financial aid: (618) 374-5186

Quincy University

Quincy IL
(217) 228-5210
U.S. News ranking: Reg. U. (Mid.W), No. 68
Website: www.quincy.edu
Admissions email: admissions@quincy.edu
Private; founded 1860
Affiliation: Catholic
Freshman admissions: selective; 2014-2015: 903 applied, 803 accepted. Either SAT or ACT required. ACT 25/75 percentile: 19-25. High school rank: 10% in top tenth, 32% in top quarter, 62% in top half
Early decision deadline: N/A, notification date: N/A
Early action deadline: N/A, notification date: N/A
Application deadline (fall): rolling
Undergraduate student body: 1,019 full time, 78 part time; 44% male, 56% female; 1% American Indian, 2% Asian, 11% black, 3% Hispanic, 2% multiracial, 1% Pacific Islander, 71% white, 1% international; 69% from in state; 56% live on campus; 6% of students in fraternities, 8% in sororities
Most popular majors: 10% Biological and Biomedical Sciences, 21% Business, Management, Marketing, and Related Support Services, 14% Education, 8% Health Professions and Related Programs, 7% Homeland Security, Law Enforcement, Firefighting and Related Protective Services
Expenses: 2015-2016: $26,998; room/board: $10,000
Financial aid: (217) 228-5260; 86% of undergrads determined to have financial need; average aid package $24,349

Robert Morris University

Chicago IL
(312) 935-4400
U.S. News ranking: Reg. U. (Mid.W), No. 104
Website: www.robertmorris.edu/
Admissions email: enroll@robertmorris.edu
Private; founded 1913
Freshman admissions: less selective; 2014-2015: 3,412 applied, 830 accepted. Either SAT or ACT required. ACT 25/75 percentile: 16-21. High school rank: 3% in top tenth, 15% in top quarter, 49% in top half
Early decision deadline: N/A, notification date: N/A
Early action deadline: N/A, notification date: N/A
Application deadline (fall): rolling
Undergraduate student body: 2,666 full time, 113 part time; 50% male, 50% female; 0% American Indian, 3% Asian, 27% black, 29% Hispanic, 2% multiracial, 0% Pacific Islander, 37% white, 1% international; 92% from in state; 9% live on campus; 0% of students in fraternities, 0% in sororities
Most popular majors: 75% Business, Management, Marketing, and Related Support Services, 6% Computer and Information Sciences and Support Services, 14% Multi/Interdisciplinary Studies, 5% Visual and Performing Arts
Expenses: 2015-2016: $25,650; room/board: $13,479
Financial aid: (312) 935-4408; 92% of undergrads determined to have financial need; average aid package $16,097

Rockford University

Rockford IL
(815) 226-4050
U.S. News ranking: Reg. U. (Mid.W), No. 90
Website: www.rockford.edu
Admissions email: Admissions@Rockford.edu
Private; founded 1847
Freshman admissions: selective; 2014-2015: 1,958 applied, 1,068 accepted. Either SAT or ACT required. ACT 25/75 percentile: 19-24. High school rank: N/A
Early decision deadline: N/A, notification date: N/A
Early action deadline: N/A, notification date: N/A
Application deadline (fall): rolling
Undergraduate student body: 901 full time, 131 part time; 38% male, 62% female; 0% American Indian, 2% Asian, 9% black, 5% Hispanic, 9% multiracial, 0% Pacific Islander, 67% white, 1% international; 87% from in state; 31% live on campus; 0% of students in fraternities, 0% in sororities
Most popular majors: 24% Business, Management, Marketing, and Related Support Services, 15% Education, 22% Health Professions and Related Programs, 6% Psychology, 9% Social Sciences
Expenses: 2015-2016: $28,330; room/board: $7,940
Financial aid: (815) 226-3396; 90% of undergrads determined to have financial need; average aid package $19,566

Roosevelt University

Chicago IL
(877) 277-5978
U.S. News ranking: Reg. U. (Mid.W), No. 112
Website: www.roosevelt.edu
Admissions email: admission@roosevelt.edu
Private; founded 1945
Freshman admissions: selective; 2014-2015: 5,409 applied, 4,122 accepted. Either SAT or ACT required. ACT 25/75 percentile: 20-25. High school rank: 2% in top tenth, 9% in top quarter, 31% in top half
Early decision deadline: N/A, notification date: N/A
Early action deadline: N/A, notification date: N/A
Application deadline (fall): rolling
Undergraduate student body: 2,953 full time, 840 part time; 37% male, 63% female; 0% American Indian, 5% Asian, 19% black, 22% Hispanic, 3% multiracial, 0% Pacific Islander, 45% white, 3% international; 92% from in state; 23% live on campus; 0% of students in fraternities, 2% in sororities
Most popular majors: 35% Business, Management, Marketing, and Related Support Services, 15% Psychology, 7% Social Sciences, 8% Visual and Performing Arts
Expenses: 2015-2016: $27,300; room/board: $12,532
Financial aid: (312) 341-3565; 82% of undergrads determined to have financial need; average aid package $21,900

School of the Art Institute of Chicago

Chicago IL
(312) 629-6100
U.S. News ranking: Arts, unranked
Website: www.saic.edu
Admissions email: admiss@saic.edu
Private; founded 1866

Freshman admissions: N/A; 2014-2015: 3,737 applied, 2,584 accepted. Either SAT or ACT required. SAT 25/75 percentile: 900-1330. High school rank: N/A
Early decision deadline: N/A, notification date: N/A
Early action deadline: 1/3, notification date: 9/1
Application deadline (fall): 6/1
Undergraduate student body: 2,602 full time, 181 part time; 28% male, 72% female; 0% American Indian, 13% Asian, 3% black, 7% Hispanic, 2% multiracial, 0% Pacific Islander, 40% white, 31% international
Most popular majors: Information not available
Expenses: 2015-2016: $43,960; room/board: $12,850
Financial aid: (312) 629-6600

Shimer College[1]

Chicago IL
(312) 235-3500
U.S. News ranking: Nat. Lib. Arts, unranked
Website: www.shimer.edu
Admissions email: admission@shimer.edu
Private
Application deadline (fall): N/A
Undergraduate student body: N/A full time, N/A part time
Expenses: 2014-2015: $32,499; room/board: $10,000
Financial aid: (847) 249-7180

Southern Illinois University–Carbondale

Carbondale IL
(618) 536-4405
U.S. News ranking: Nat. U., No. 153
Website: www.siu.edu
Admissions email: admissions@siu.edu
Public; founded 1869
Freshman admissions: selective; 2014-2015: 10,877 applied, 8,883 accepted. Either SAT or ACT required. ACT 25/75 percentile: 19-26. High school rank: 14% in top tenth, 34% in top quarter, 64% in top half
Early decision deadline: N/A, notification date: N/A
Early action deadline: N/A, notification date: N/A
Application deadline (fall): 5/1
Undergraduate student body: 11,873 full time, 1,588 part time; 54% male, 46% female; 0% American Indian, 2% Asian, 20% black, 8% Hispanic, 3% multiracial, 0% Pacific Islander, 63% white, 3% international; 85% from in state; 33% live on campus; 7% of students in fraternities, 6% in sororities
Most popular majors: 8% Business, Management, Marketing, and Related Support Services, 16% Education, 7% Engineering Technologies and Engineering-Related Fields, 8% Health Professions and Related Programs, 7% Social Sciences
Expenses: 2015-2016: $13,137 in state, $26,390 out of state; room/board: $9,996
Financial aid: (618) 453-4334; 72% of undergrads determined to have financial need; average aid package $14,366

Southern Illinois University–Edwardsville

Edwardsville IL
(618) 650-3705
U.S. News ranking: Reg. U. (Mid.W), No. 44
Website: www.siue.edu
Admissions email: admissions@siue.edu
Public; founded 1957
Freshman admissions: selective; 2014-2015: 7,594 applied, 6,604 accepted. Either SAT or ACT required. ACT 25/75 percentile: 20-26. High school rank: 19% in top tenth, 45% in top quarter, 78% in top half
Early decision deadline: N/A, notification date: N/A
Early action deadline: N/A, notification date: N/A
Application deadline (fall): 5/1
Undergraduate student body: 9,714 full time, 1,707 part time; 47% male, 53% female; 0% American Indian, 2% Asian, 15% black, 4% Hispanic, 3% multiracial, 0% Pacific Islander, 74% white, 1% international; 93% from in state; 30% live on campus; 8% of students in fraternities, 10% in sororities
Most popular majors: 5% Accounting, 7% Biology/Biological Sciences, General, 10% Business Administration and Management, General, 8% Psychology, General, 11% Registered Nursing/Registered Nurse
Expenses: 2015-2016: $10,247 in state, $21,740 out of state; room/board: $9,570
Financial aid: (618) 650-3839; 66% of undergrads determined to have financial need; average aid package $11,570

St. Augustine College[1]

Chicago IL
(773) 878-3656
U.S. News ranking: Reg. Coll. (Mid.W), unranked
Website: www.staugustinecollege.edu/index.asp
Admissions email: info@staugustine.edu
Private
Application deadline (fall): N/A
Undergraduate student body: N/A full time, N/A part time
Expenses: 2014-2015: $9,576; room/board: $8,500
Financial aid: (773) 878-3813

St. Xavier University

Chicago IL
(773) 298-3050
U.S. News ranking: Reg. U. (Mid.W), No. 46
Website: www.sxu.edu
Admissions email: admission@sxu.edu
Private; founded 1846
Affiliation: Roman Catholic
Freshman admissions: selective; 2014-2015: 8,140 applied, 6,083 accepted. Either SAT or ACT required. ACT 25/75 percentile: 19-24. High school rank: 21% in top tenth, 54% in top quarter, 86% in top half
Early decision deadline: N/A, notification date: N/A
Early action deadline: N/A, notification date: N/A
Application deadline (fall): rolling
Undergraduate student body: 2,557 full time, 417 part time; 33% male, 67% female; 0% American Indian, 3% Asian, 14% black, 28% Hispanic, 2% multiracial, 0% Pacific Islander, 48% white, 0% international; 95% from in state; 21% live on campus; 0% of students in fraternities, 0% in sororities
Most popular majors: 20% Business, Management, Marketing, and Related Support Services, 8% Education, 22% Health Professions and Related Programs, 9% Liberal Arts and Sciences, General Studies and Humanities, 12% Psychology
Expenses: 2015-2016: $30,920; room/board: $10,620
Financial aid: (773) 298-3070; 88% of undergrads determined to have financial need; average aid package $23,760

Trinity Christian College

Palos Heights IL
(800) 748-0085
U.S. News ranking: Reg. Coll. (Mid.W), No. 24
Website: www.trnty.edu
Admissions email: admissions@trnty.edu
Private; founded 1959
Affiliation: Reformed
Freshman admissions: selective; 2014-2015: 805 applied, 627 accepted. Either SAT or ACT required. ACT 25/75 percentile: 20-27. High school rank: 20% in top tenth, 42% in top quarter, 70% in top half
Early decision deadline: N/A, notification date: N/A
Early action deadline: N/A, notification date: N/A
Application deadline (fall): rolling
Undergraduate student body: 1,114 full time, 223 part time; 35% male, 65% female; 0% American Indian, 2% Asian, 10% black, 11% Hispanic, 2% multiracial, 0% Pacific Islander, 69% white, 4% international; 65% from in state; 49% live on campus; N/A of students in fraternities, N/A in sororities
Most popular majors: 19% Business, Management, Marketing, and Related Support Services, 31% Education, 13% Health Professions and Related Programs, 5% Homeland Security, Law Enforcement, Firefighting and Related Protective Services, 7% Psychology
Expenses: 2015-2016: $26,440; room/board: $9,390
Financial aid: (708) 239-4706; 70% of undergrads determined to have financial need; average aid package $17,489

Trinity International University

Deerfield IL
(800) 822-3225
U.S. News ranking: Nat. U., second tier
Website: www.tiu.edu
Admissions email: tcadmissions@tiu.edu
Private; founded 1897
Affiliation: Evangelical Free Church of America
Freshman admissions: selective; 2014-2015: 393 applied, 381 accepted. Either SAT or ACT required. ACT 25/75 percentile: 20-26. High school rank: 12% in top tenth, 35% in top quarter, 58% in top half
Early decision deadline: N/A, notification date: N/A
Early action deadline: N/A, notification date: N/A
Application deadline (fall): rolling
Undergraduate student body: 812 full time, 287 part time; 48% male, 52% female; 0% American Indian, 3% Asian, 19% black, 18% Hispanic, 2% multiracial, 0% Pacific Islander, 48% white, 1% international; 67% from in state; N/A live on campus; 0% of students in fraternities, 0% in sororities
Most popular majors: 11% Business/Commerce, General, 7% Elementary Education and Teaching, 18% Psychology, General, 22% Religious Education
Expenses: 2015-2016: $28,700; room/board: $8,830
Financial aid: (847) 317-8060; 81% of undergrads determined to have financial need; average aid package $23,171

University of Chicago

Chicago IL
(773) 702-8650
U.S. News ranking: Nat. U., No. 4
Website: www.uchicago.edu
Admissions email: collegeadmissions@uchicago.edu
Private; founded 1890
Freshman admissions: most selective; 2014-2015: 27,500 applied, 2,409 accepted. Either SAT or ACT required. SAT 25/75 percentile: 1430-1590. High school rank: 98% in top tenth, 99% in top quarter, 100% in top half
Early decision deadline: N/A, notification date: N/A
Early action deadline: 11/1, notification date: 12/20
Application deadline (fall): 1/4
Undergraduate student body: 5,616 full time, 65 part time; 53% male, 47% female; 0% American Indian, 17% Asian, 5% black, 9% Hispanic, 4% multiracial, 0% Pacific Islander, 45% white, 10% international; 17% from in state; 54% live on campus; 8% of students in fraternities, 12% in sororities
Most popular majors: 12% Biological and Biomedical Sciences, 18% Economics, 5% English Language and Literature/Letters, 8% Mathematics and Statistics, 8% Political Science and Government
Expenses: 2015-2016: $50,193; room/board: $14,772
Financial aid: (773) 702-8666; 46% of undergrads determined to have financial need; average aid package $43,220

University of Illinois–Chicago

Chicago IL
(312) 996-4350
U.S. News ranking: Nat. U., No. 129
Website: www.uic.edu
Admissions email: uicadmit@uic.edu
Public; founded 1982
Freshman admissions: selective; 2014-2015: 15,949 applied, 11,598 accepted. Either SAT or ACT required. ACT 25/75 percentile: 22-27. High school rank: 24% in top tenth, 62% in top quarter, 92% in top half
Early decision deadline: N/A, notification date: N/A
Early action deadline: N/A, notification date: N/A
Application deadline (fall): 1/15
Undergraduate student body: 15,459 full time, 1,248 part time; 50% male, 50% female; 0% American Indian, 23% Asian, 8% black, 26% Hispanic, 2% multiracial, 0% Pacific Islander, 36% white, 2% international; 98% from in state; 17% live on campus; 1% of students in fraternities, 1% in sororities
Most popular majors: 5% Accounting, 11% Biology/Biological Sciences, General, 5% Finance, General, 14% Psychology, General, 6% Registered Nursing/Registered Nurse
Expenses: 2015-2016: $13,670 in state, $26,526 out of state; room/board: $10,882
Financial aid: (312) 996-3126; 76% of undergrads determined to have financial need; average aid package $14,401

University of Illinois–Springfield

Springfield IL
(217) 206-4847
U.S. News ranking: Reg. U. (Mid.W), No. 42
Website: www.uis.edu
Admissions email: admissions@uis.edu
Public; founded 1969
Freshman admissions: selective; 2014-2015: 1,460 applied, 899 accepted. Either SAT or ACT required. ACT 25/75 percentile: 20-27. High school rank: 21% in top tenth, 43% in top quarter, 77% in top half
Early decision deadline: N/A, notification date: N/A
Early action deadline: N/A, notification date: N/A
Application deadline (fall): rolling
Undergraduate student body: 1,935 full time, 1,103 part time; 49% male, 51% female; 0% American Indian, 4% Asian, 15% black, 6% Hispanic, 3% multiracial, 0% Pacific Islander, 66% white, 4% international; 86% from in state; 30% live on campus; 0% of students in fraternities, 0% in sororities
Most popular majors: 15% Business Administration and Management, General, 8% Communication, General, 10% Computer Science, 7% English Language and Literature, General, 11% Psychology, General
Expenses: 2015-2016: $11,413 in state, $20,938 out of state; room/board: $9,650
Financial aid: (217) 206-6724; 70% of undergrads determined to have financial need; average aid package $12,948

University of Illinois–Urbana-Champaign

Champaign IL
(217) 333-0302
U.S. News ranking: Nat. U., No. 41
Website: www.illinois.edu
Admissions email: ugradadmissions@illinois.edu

Public; founded 1867
Freshman admissions: more selective; 2014-2015: 35,822 applied, 21,150 accepted. Either SAT or ACT required. ACT 25/75 percentile: 26-32. High school rank: 59% in top tenth, 90% in top quarter, 99% in top half
Early decision deadline: N/A, notification date: N/A
Early action deadline: N/A, notification date: N/A
Application deadline (fall): 12/1
Undergraduate student body: 31,742 full time, 1,217 part time; 56% male, 44% female; 0% American Indian, 16% Asian, 5% black, 9% Hispanic, 3% multiracial, 0% Pacific Islander, 51% white, 15% international; 89% from in state; 50% live on campus; 23% of students in fraternities, 23% in sororities
Most popular majors: 7% Biological and Biomedical Sciences, 13% Business, Management, Marketing, and Related Support Services, 8% Communication, Journalism, and Related Programs, 18% Engineering, 8% Social Sciences
Expenses: 2015-2016: $15,626 in state, $30,786 out of state; room/board: $11,010
Financial aid: (217) 333-0100; 45% of undergrads determined to have financial need; average aid package $15,793

University of St. Francis

Joliet IL
(800) 735-7500
U.S. News ranking: Reg. U. (Mid.W), No. 36
Website: www.stfrancis.edu
Admissions email: admissions@stfrancis.edu
Private; founded 1920
Affiliation: Roman Catholic
Freshman admissions: selective; 2014-2015: 1,509 applied, 763 accepted. Either SAT or ACT required. ACT 25/75 percentile: 21-25. High school rank: 10% in top tenth, 44% in top quarter, 77% in top half
Early decision deadline: N/A, notification date: N/A
Early action deadline: N/A, notification date: N/A
Application deadline (fall): 8/1
Undergraduate student body: 1,316 full time, 65 part time; 36% male, 64% female; 0% American Indian, 2% Asian, 8% black, 17% Hispanic, 3% multiracial, 0% Pacific Islander, 68% white, 2% international; 95% from in state; 26% live on campus; 0% of students in fraternities, 2% in sororities
Most popular majors: 8% Biology/Biological Sciences, General, 15% Business, Management, Marketing, and Related Support Services, 12% Education, 8% Homeland Security, Law Enforcement, Firefighting and Related Protective Services, 21% Registered Nursing/Registered Nurse
Expenses: 2015-2016: $29,950; room/board: $9,084
Financial aid: (815) 740-3403; 86% of undergrads determined to have financial need; average aid package $22,972

VanderCook College of Music

Chicago IL
(800) 448-2655
U.S. News ranking: Arts, unranked
Website: www.vandercook.edu
Admissions email: admissions@vandercook.edu
Private; founded 1909
Freshman admissions: N/A; 2014-2015: 46 applied, 35 accepted. Neither SAT nor ACT required. ACT 25/75 percentile: 20-28. High school rank: 10% in top tenth, 60% in top quarter, 85% in top half
Early decision deadline: N/A, notification date: N/A
Early action deadline: N/A, notification date: N/A
Application deadline (fall): rolling
Undergraduate student body: 105 full time, 43 part time; 53% male, 47% female; 0% American Indian, 1% Asian, 6% black, 21% Hispanic, 4% multiracial, 0% Pacific Islander, 66% white, 2% international; 76% from in state; 6% live on campus; N/A of students in fraternities, N/A in sororities
Most popular majors: Information not available
Expenses: 2014-2015: $25,690; room/board: $10,888
Financial aid: (312) 225-6288

Western Illinois University

Macomb IL
(309) 298-3157
U.S. News ranking: Reg. U. (Mid.W), No. 46
Website: www.wiu.edu
Admissions email: admissions@wiu.edu
Public; founded 1899
Freshman admissions: selective; 2014-2015: 10,671 applied, 7,431 accepted. Either SAT or ACT required. ACT 25/75 percentile: 18-23. High school rank: 9% in top tenth, 28% in top quarter, 63% in top half
Early decision deadline: N/A, notification date: N/A
Early action deadline: N/A, notification date: N/A
Application deadline (fall): 5/15
Undergraduate student body: 8,607 full time, 1,038 part time; 51% male, 49% female; 0% American Indian, 1% Asian, 19% black, 9% Hispanic, 2% multiracial, 0% Pacific Islander, 63% white, 2% international; 88% from in state; 44% live on campus; 6% of students in fraternities, 6% in sororities
Most popular majors: 12% Business Administration and Management, General, 18% Criminal Justice/Law Enforcement Administration, 14% Liberal Arts and Sciences, General Studies and Humanities, Other, 7% Parks, Recreation and Leisure Facilities Management, General, 7% Speech Communication and Rhetoric
Expenses: 2015-2016: $11,509 in state, $15,912 out of state; room/board: $9,760
Financial aid: (309) 298-2446; 75% of undergrads determined to have financial need; average aid package $11,221

Wheaton College

Wheaton IL
(630) 752-5005
U.S. News ranking: Nat. Lib. Arts, No. 57
Website: www.wheaton.edu
Admissions email: admissions@wheaton.edu
Private; founded 1860
Affiliation: Christian nondenominational
Freshman admissions: more selective; 2014-2015: 2,010 applied, 1,390 accepted. Either SAT or ACT required. ACT 25/75 percentile: 27-32. High school rank: 52% in top tenth, 75% in top quarter, 93% in top half
Early decision deadline: N/A, notification date: N/A
Early action deadline: 11/1, notification date: 12/31
Application deadline (fall): 1/10
Undergraduate student body: 2,368 full time, 64 part time; 48% male, 52% female; 0% American Indian, 9% Asian, 2% black, 5% Hispanic, 5% multiracial, 0% Pacific Islander, 76% white, 3% international; 26% from in state; 90% live on campus; N/A of students in fraternities, N/A in sororities
Most popular majors: 11% Business, Management, Marketing, and Related Support Services, 7% Education, 8% English Language and Literature/Letters, 14% Social Sciences, 10% Visual and Performing Arts
Expenses: 2015-2016: $32,950; room/board: $9,200
Financial aid: (630) 752-5021; 52% of undergrads determined to have financial need; average aid package $24,003

INDIANA

Anderson University

Anderson IN
(765) 641-4080
U.S. News ranking: Reg. U. (Mid.W), No. 35
Website: www.anderson.edu
Admissions email: info@anderson.edu
Private; founded 1917
Affiliation: Church of God
Freshman admissions: selective; 2014-2015: 2,659 applied, 1,460 accepted. Either SAT or ACT required. SAT 25/75 percentile: 920-1140. High school rank: 23% in top tenth, 52% in top quarter, 82% in top half
Early decision deadline: N/A, notification date: N/A
Early action deadline: N/A, notification date: N/A
Application deadline (fall): rolling
Undergraduate student body: 1,674 full time, 302 part time; 40% male, 60% female; 0% American Indian, 1% Asian, 6% black, 3% Hispanic, 1% multiracial, 0% Pacific Islander, 80% white, 3% international; 74% from in state; 60% live on campus; N/A of students in fraternities, N/A in sororities
Most popular majors: 21% Business, Management, Marketing, and Related Support Services, 12% Education, 8% Health Professions and Related Programs, 8% Psychology, 7% Visual and Performing Arts
Expenses: 2014-2015: $26,850; room/board: $9,250
Financial aid: (765) 641-4180

Ball State University

Muncie IN
(765) 285-8300
U.S. News ranking: Nat. U., No. 168
Website: www.bsu.edu
Admissions email: askus@bsu.edu
Public; founded 1918
Freshman admissions: selective; 2014-2015: 18,107 applied, 10,842 accepted. Neither SAT nor ACT required. SAT 25/75 percentile: 1000-1190. High school rank: 19% in top tenth, 52% in top quarter, 90% in top half
Early decision deadline: N/A, notification date: N/A
Early action deadline: N/A, notification date: N/A
Application deadline (fall): 8/10
Undergraduate student body: 15,018 full time, 1,397 part time; 42% male, 58% female; 0% American Indian, 1% Asian, 7% black, 4% Hispanic, 2% multiracial, 0% Pacific Islander, 81% white, 3% international; 88% from in state; 41% live on campus; 12% of students in fraternities, 14% in sororities
Most popular majors: 16% Business, Management, Marketing, and Related Support Services, 13% Communication, Journalism, and Related Programs, 11% Education, 8% Health Professions and Related Programs, 8% Liberal Arts and Sciences, General Studies and Humanities
Expenses: 2015-2016: $9,624 in state, $25,348 out of state; room/board: $9,656
Financial aid: (765) 285-5600; 68% of undergrads determined to have financial need; average aid package $11,822

Bethel College

Mishawaka IN
(800) 422-4101
U.S. News ranking: Reg. Coll. (Mid.W), No. 19
Website: www.bethelcollege.edu
Admissions email: admissions@bethelcollege.edu
Private; founded 1947
Affiliation: Missionary Church
Freshman admissions: selective; 2014-2015: 1,211 applied, 853 accepted. Either SAT or ACT required. SAT 25/75 percentile: 890-1170. High school rank: 23% in top tenth, 45% in top quarter, 75% in top half
Early decision deadline: N/A, notification date: N/A
Early action deadline: N/A, notification date: N/A
Application deadline (fall): rolling
Undergraduate student body: 1,227 full time, 373 part time; 35% male, 65% female; 0% American Indian, 1% Asian, 11% black, 6% Hispanic, 3% multiracial, 1% Pacific Islander, 77% white, 2% international; 73% from in state; 48% live on campus; 0% of students in fraternities, 0% in sororities
Most popular majors: 29% Business, Management, Marketing, and Related Support Services, 8% Education, 15% Health Professions and Related Programs, 10% Liberal Arts and Sciences, General Studies and Humanities, 5% Theology and Religious Vocations
Expenses: 2015-2016: $26,590; room/board: $8,340
Financial aid: (574) 257-3316

Butler University

Indianapolis IN
(888) 940-8100
U.S. News ranking: Reg. U. (Mid.W), No. 2
Website: www.butler.edu
Admissions email: admission@butler.edu
Private; founded 1855
Freshman admissions: more selective; 2014-2015: 10,103 applied, 6,917 accepted. Either SAT or ACT required. ACT 25/75 percentile: 25-30. High school rank: 49% in top tenth, 79% in top quarter, 97% in top half
Early decision deadline: N/A, notification date: N/A
Early action deadline: 11/1, notification date: 12/20
Application deadline (fall): 2/1
Undergraduate student body: 3,980 full time, 82 part time; 40% male, 60% female; 0% American Indian, 3% Asian, 4% black, 3% Hispanic, 2% multiracial, 0% Pacific Islander, 83% white, 2% international; 49% from in state; 66% live on campus; 29% of students in fraternities, 37% in sororities
Most popular majors: 21% Business, Management, Marketing, and Related Support Services, 8% Communication, Journalism, and Related Programs, 13% Education, 13% Health Professions and Related Programs, 8% Social Sciences
Expenses: 2015-2016: $37,010; room/board: $12,055
Financial aid: (317) 940-8200; 63% of undergrads determined to have financial need; average aid package $23,034

Calumet College of St. Joseph

Whiting IN
(219) 473-4295
U.S. News ranking: Reg. U. (Mid.W), second tier
Website: www.ccsj.edu
Admissions email: admissions@ccsj.edu
Private; founded 1951
Affiliation: Roman Catholic
Freshman admissions: less selective; 2014-2015: 519 applied, 157 accepted. Neither SAT nor ACT required. ACT 25/75 percentile: 15-19. High school rank: 2% in top tenth, 15% in top quarter, 47% in top half
Early decision deadline: N/A, notification date: N/A
Early action deadline: N/A, notification date: N/A
Application deadline (fall): rolling
Undergraduate student body: 532 full time, 375 part time; 53% male, 47% female; 0% American Indian, 1% Asian, 29% black, 29% Hispanic, 1% multiracial, 0% Pacific Islander, 40% white, 0% international; 59% from in state; 0% live on campus; N/A of students in fraternities, N/A in sororities
Most popular majors: 4% Accounting, 11% Business Administration and Management,

General, 21% Business Administration, Management and Operations, Other, 42% Criminal Justice/Safety Studies, 4% Elementary Education and Teaching
Expenses: 2015-2016: $17,000; room/board: N/A
Financial aid: (219) 473-4213; 81% of undergrads determined to have financial need; average aid package $13,290

DePauw University

Greencastle IN
(765) 658-4006
U.S. News ranking: Nat. Lib. Arts, No. 51
Website: www.depauw.edu
Admissions email: admission@depauw.edu
Private; founded 1837
Freshman admissions: more selective; 2014-2015: 5,282 applied, 3,002 accepted. Either SAT or ACT required. ACT 25/75 percentile: 25-29. High school rank: 48% in top tenth, 83% in top quarter, 97% in top half
Early decision deadline: 11/1, notification date: 1/1
Early action deadline: 12/1, notification date: 1/31
Application deadline (fall): 2/1
Undergraduate student body: 2,186 full time, 30 part time; 46% male, 54% female; 0% American Indian, 3% Asian, 6% black, 3% Hispanic, 7% multiracial, 0% Pacific Islander, 69% white, 9% international; 37% from in state; 96% live on campus; 77% of students in fraternities, 63% in sororities
Most popular majors: 10% Biological and Biomedical Sciences, 14% Communication, Journalism, and Related Programs, 11% English Language and Literature/Letters, 22% Social Sciences, 8% Visual and Performing Arts
Expenses: 2015-2016: $44,678; room/board: $11,700
Financial aid: (765) 658-4030; 55% of undergrads determined to have financial need; average aid package $35,694

Earlham College

Richmond IN
(765) 983-1600
U.S. News ranking: Nat. Lib. Arts, No. 61
Website: www.earlham.edu/admissions
Admissions email: admission@earlham.edu
Private; founded 1847
Affiliation: Quaker
Freshman admissions: more selective; 2014-2015: 2,001 applied, 1,291 accepted. Neither SAT nor ACT required. SAT 25/75 percentile: 1150-1370. High school rank: 40% in top tenth, 74% in top quarter, 92% in top half
Early decision deadline: 11/1, notification date: 12/1
Early action deadline: 12/1, notification date: 2/1
Application deadline (fall): 2/15
Undergraduate student body: 981 full time, 12 part time; 45% male, 55% female; 1% American Indian, 6% Asian, 13% black, 6% Hispanic, 0% multiracial, 0% Pacific Islander, 53% white, 18% international; 35% from in state; 92% live on campus; 0% of students in fraternities, 0% in sororities
Most popular majors: 16% Biology, General, 16% Multi/Interdisciplinary Studies, Other, 7% Psychology, General, 14% Social Sciences, General, 8% Visual and Performing Arts, General
Expenses: 2015-2016: $44,390; room/board: $9,120
Financial aid: (765) 983-1217; 82% of undergrads determined to have financial need; average aid package $38,220

Franklin College

Franklin IN
(317) 738-8062
U.S. News ranking: Reg. Coll. (Mid.W), No. 11
Website: www.franklincollege.edu
Admissions email: admissions@franklincollege.edu
Private; founded 1834
Affiliation: American Baptist
Freshman admissions: selective; 2014-2015: 2,050 applied, 1,419 accepted. Either SAT or ACT required. SAT 25/75 percentile: 910-1100. High school rank: 18% in top tenth, 46% in top quarter, 85% in top half
Early decision deadline: N/A, notification date: N/A
Early action deadline: N/A, notification date: N/A
Application deadline (fall): rolling
Undergraduate student body: 1,008 full time, 67 part time; 46% male, 54% female; 0% American Indian, 1% Asian, 4% black, 2% Hispanic, 4% multiracial, 0% Pacific Islander, 84% white, 2% international; 89% from in state; 80% live on campus; 43% of students in fraternities, 50% in sororities
Most popular majors: 12% Biology/Biological Sciences, General, 16% Business Administration and Management, General, 12% Health Services/Allied Health/Health Sciences, General, 15% Journalism, 17% Sociology
Expenses: 2015-2016: $29,025; room/board: $9,040
Financial aid: (317) 738-8075; 83% of undergrads determined to have financial need; average aid package $22,635

Goshen College

Goshen IN
(574) 535-7535
U.S. News ranking: Nat. Lib. Arts, No. 127
Website: www.goshen.edu
Admissions email: admissions@goshen.edu
Private; founded 1894
Affiliation: Mennonite Church USA
Freshman admissions: selective; 2014-2015: 655 applied, 621 accepted. Either SAT or ACT required. SAT 25/75 percentile: 975-1255. High school rank: 38% in top tenth, 63% in top quarter, 85% in top half
Early decision deadline: N/A, notification date: N/A
Early action deadline: N/A, notification date: N/A
Application deadline (fall): 8/15
Undergraduate student body: 702 full time, 72 part time; 42% male, 58% female; 0% American Indian, 2% Asian, 4% black, 13% Hispanic, 3% multiracial, 0% Pacific Islander, 68% white, 9% international; 52% from in state; N/A live on campus; N/A of students in fraternities, N/A in sororities
Most popular majors: 9% Biological and Biomedical Sciences, 16% Business, Management, Marketing, and Related Support Services, 6% Communication, Journalism, and Related Programs, 10% Education, 22% Health Professions and Related Programs
Expenses: 2015-2016: $30,590; room/board: $9,985
Financial aid: (574) 535-7583; 72% of undergrads determined to have financial need; average aid package $24,844

Grace College and Seminary

Winona Lake IN
(574) 372-5100
U.S. News ranking: Reg. Coll. (Mid.W), No. 38
Website: www.grace.edu
Admissions email: enroll@grace.edu
Private; founded 1948
Affiliation: Fellowship of Grace Brethren Churches
Freshman admissions: selective; 2014-2015: 3,519 applied, 2,808 accepted. Either SAT or ACT required. SAT 25/75 percentile: 930-1170. High school rank: 21% in top tenth, 48% in top quarter, 81% in top half
Early decision deadline: N/A, notification date: N/A
Early action deadline: 12/1, notification date: 12/20
Application deadline (fall): 3/1
Undergraduate student body: 1,347 full time, 510 part time; 45% male, 55% female; 0% American Indian, 1% Asian, 5% black, 4% Hispanic, 2% multiracial, 0% Pacific Islander, 76% white, 1% international; 72% from in state; 53% live on campus; 0% of students in fraternities, 0% in sororities
Most popular majors: 14% Business Administration and Management, General, 8% Business Administration, Management and Operations, Other, 10% Counseling Psychology, 8% Psychology, General, 5% Special Education and Teaching, General
Expenses: 2015-2016: $22,450; room/board: $8,160
Financial aid: (574) 372-5100; 53% of undergrads determined to have financial need; average aid package $16,475

Hanover College

Hanover IN
(812) 866-7021
U.S. News ranking: Nat. Lib. Arts, No. 116
Website: www.hanover.edu
Admissions email: admission@hanover.edu
Private; founded 1827
Affiliation: Presbyterian
Freshman admissions: selective; 2014-2015: 2,888 applied, 1,862 accepted. Either SAT or ACT required. SAT 25/75 percentile: 940-1170. High school rank: 29% in top tenth, 62% in top quarter, 93% in top half
Early decision deadline: N/A, notification date: N/A
Early action deadline: 12/1, notification date: 12/20
Application deadline (fall): 3/1
Undergraduate student body: 1,134 full time, 11 part time; 42% male, 58% female; 1% American Indian, 1% Asian, 5% black, 2% Hispanic, 2% multiracial, N/A Pacific Islander, 82% white, 5% international; 71% from in state; 92% live on campus; 44% of students in fraternities, 32% in sororities
Most popular majors: 8% Biology/Biological Sciences, General, 6% Kinesiology and Exercise Science, 7% Political Science and Government, General, 9% Psychology, General, 9% Speech Communication and Rhetoric
Expenses: 2015-2016: $34,514; room/board: $10,452
Financial aid: (800) 213-2178; 77% of undergrads determined to have financial need; average aid package $27,762

Holy Cross College[1]

Notre Dame IN
(574) 239-8400
U.S. News ranking: Nat. Lib. Arts, second tier
Website: www.hcc-nd.edu/home
Admissions email: admissions@hcc-nd.edu
Private; founded 1966
Affiliation: Roman Catholic
Application deadline (fall): rolling
Undergraduate student body: N/A full time, N/A part time
Expenses: 2014-2015: $27,150; room/board: $9,500
Financial aid: (574) 239-8408

Huntington University

Huntington IN
(800) 642-6493
U.S. News ranking: Reg. Coll. (Mid.W), No. 16
Website: www.huntington.edu
Admissions email: admissions@huntington.edu
Private; founded 1897
Affiliation: United Brethren in Christ
Freshman admissions: selective; 2014-2015: 760 applied, 738 accepted. Either SAT or ACT required. SAT 25/75 percentile: 880-1128. High school rank: 22% in top tenth, 47% in top quarter, 77% in top half
Early decision deadline: N/A, notification date: N/A
Early action deadline: N/A, notification date: N/A
Application deadline (fall): 8/1
Undergraduate student body: 955 full time, 119 part time; 43% male, 57% female; 1% American Indian, 1% Asian, 2% black, 3% Hispanic, 2% multiracial, 0% Pacific Islander, 87% white, 4% international; 69% from in state; 74% live on campus; 0% of students in fraternities, 0% in sororities
Most popular majors: 28% Business, Management, Marketing, and Related Support Services, 13% Education, 7% Psychology, 11% Theology and Religious Vocations, 8% Visual and Performing Arts
Expenses: 2015-2016: $24,822; room/board: $8,456
Financial aid: (260) 359-4015; 80% of undergrads determined to have financial need; average aid package $17,228

Indiana Institute of Technology[1]

Fort Wayne IN
(800) 937-2448
U.S. News ranking: Business, unranked
Website: www.indianatech.edu
Admissions email: admissions@indianatech.edu
Private; founded 1930
Application deadline (fall): rolling
Undergraduate student body: N/A full time, N/A part time
Expenses: 2015-2016: $25,600; room/board: $11,240
Financial aid: (260) 422-5561; 87% of undergrads determined to have financial need; average aid package $18,563

Indiana State University

Terre Haute IN
(812) 237-2121
U.S. News ranking: Nat. U., second tier
Website: web.indstate.edu/
Admissions email: admissions@indstate.edu
Public; founded 1865
Freshman admissions: less selective; 2014-2015: 11,258 applied, 9,292 accepted. Either SAT or ACT required. SAT 25/75 percentile: 810-1020. High school rank: 9% in top tenth, 27% in top quarter, 64% in top half
Early decision deadline: N/A, notification date: N/A
Early action deadline: N/A, notification date: N/A
Application deadline (fall): 8/15
Undergraduate student body: 9,459 full time, 1,422 part time; 46% male, 54% female; 0% American Indian, 1% Asian, 19% black, 3% Hispanic, 3% multiracial, 0% Pacific Islander, 66% white, 6% international; 85% from in state; 33% live on campus; 6% of students in fraternities, 6% in sororities
Most popular majors: 17% Business, Management, Marketing, and Related Support Services, 9% Education, 6% Engineering Technologies and Engineering-Related Fields, 17% Health Professions and Related Programs, 11% Social Sciences
Expenses: 2014-2015: $8,416 in state, $18,346 out of state; room/board: $9,182
Financial aid: (812) 237-2215; 72% of undergrads determined to have financial need; average aid package $10,935

Indiana University–Bloomington

Bloomington IN
(812) 855-0661
U.S. News ranking: Nat. U., No. 75
Website: www.iub.edu
Admissions email: iuadmit@indiana.edu
Public; founded 1820
Freshman admissions: more selective; 2014-2015: 36,362 applied, 27,668 accepted. Either SAT or ACT required. SAT 25/75 percentile: 1060-1290. High school rank: 33% in top tenth, 69% in top quarter, 95% in top half
Early decision deadline: N/A, notification date: N/A

Early action deadline: N/A, notification date: N/A
Application deadline (fall): rolling
Undergraduate student body: 31,370 full time, 5,049 part time; 49% male, 51% female; 0% American Indian, 4% Asian, 4% black, 5% Hispanic, 3% multiracial, 0% Pacific Islander, 72% white, 11% international; 69% from in state; 37% live on campus; 22% of students in fraternities, 18% in sororities
Most popular majors: 8% Biological and Biomedical Sciences, 17% Business, Management, Marketing, and Related Support Services, 9% Communication, Journalism, and Related Programs, 7% Parks, Recreation, Leisure, and Fitness Studies, 9% Social Sciences
Expenses: 2015-2016: $10,388 in state, $33,741 out of state; room/board: $9,795
Financial aid: (812) 855-0321; 43% of undergrads determined to have financial need; average aid package $12,352

Indiana University East

Richmond IN
(765) 973-8208
U.S. News ranking: Reg. Coll. (Mid.W), second tier
Website: www.iue.edu
Admissions email: eaadmit@indiana.edu
Public; founded 1971
Freshman admissions: less selective; 2014-2015: 1,388 applied, 885 accepted. Either SAT or ACT required. SAT 25/75 percentile: 830-1030. High school rank: 11% in top tenth, 37% in top quarter, 73% in top half
Early decision deadline: N/A, notification date: N/A
Early action deadline: N/A, notification date: N/A
Application deadline (fall): rolling
Undergraduate student body: 2,015 full time, 2,415 part time; 37% male, 63% female; 0% American Indian, 1% Asian, 4% black, 3% Hispanic, 2% multiracial, 0% Pacific Islander, 88% white, 1% international; 77% from in state; 0% live on campus; N/A of students in fraternities, N/A in sororities
Most popular majors: 27% Business, Management, Marketing, and Related Support Services, 7% Education, 17% Health Professions and Related Programs, 18% Liberal Arts and Sciences, General Studies and Humanities, 6% Psychology
Expenses: 2015-2016: $6,930 in state, $18,379 out of state; room/board: N/A
Financial aid: (765) 973-8206; 82% of undergrads determined to have financial need; average aid package $8,757

Indiana University–Kokomo

Kokomo IN
(765) 455-9217
U.S. News ranking: Reg. Coll. (Mid.W), second tier
Website: www.iuk.edu
Admissions email: Iuadmiss@iuk.edu
Public; founded 1945
Freshman admissions: less selective; 2014-2015: 1,408 applied, 947 accepted. Either SAT or ACT required. SAT 25/75 percentile: 830-1040. High school rank: 8% in top tenth, 31% in top quarter, 70% in top half
Early decision deadline: N/A, notification date: N/A
Early action deadline: N/A, notification date: N/A
Application deadline (fall): rolling
Undergraduate student body: 2,077 full time, 1,927 part time; 34% male, 66% female; 0% American Indian, 1% Asian, 4% black, 5% Hispanic, 2% multiracial, 0% Pacific Islander, 84% white, 0% international; 100% from in state; 0% live on campus; 3% of students in fraternities, 1% in sororities
Most popular majors: 6% Business, Management, Marketing, and Related Support Services, 9% Education, 36% Health Professions and Related Programs, 16% Liberal Arts and Sciences, General Studies and Humanities, 6% Psychology
Expenses: 2015-2016: $6,941 in state, $18,379 out of state; room/board: N/A
Financial aid: (765) 455-9216; 77% of undergrads determined to have financial need; average aid package $8,437

Indiana University Northwest

Gary IN
(219) 980-6991
U.S. News ranking: Reg. U. (Mid.W), second tier
Website: www.iun.edu
Admissions email: admit@iun.edu
Public; founded 1948
Freshman admissions: less selective; 2014-2015: 1,658 applied, 1,273 accepted. Either SAT or ACT required. SAT 25/75 percentile: 790-1020. High school rank: 8% in top tenth, 28% in top quarter, 63% in top half
Early decision deadline: N/A, notification date: N/A
Early action deadline: N/A, notification date: N/A
Application deadline (fall): rolling
Undergraduate student body: 3,114 full time, 2,547 part time; 33% male, 67% female; 0% American Indian, 2% Asian, 18% black, 19% Hispanic, 2% multiracial, 0% Pacific Islander, 56% white, 0% international; 98% from in state; 0% live on campus; N/A of students in fraternities, N/A in sororities
Most popular majors: 11% Business, Management, Marketing, and Related Support Services, 8% Education, 20% Health Professions and Related Programs, 10% Homeland Security, Law Enforcement, Firefighting and Related Protective Services, 17% Liberal Arts and Sciences, General Studies and Humanities
Expenses: 2015-2016: $6,963 in state, $18,379 out of state; room/board: N/A
Financial aid: (877) 280-4593; 72% of undergrads determined to have financial need; average aid package $8,250

Indiana University-Purdue University–Fort Wayne

Fort Wayne IN
(260) 481-6812
U.S. News ranking: Reg. U. (Mid.W), second tier
Website: www.ipfw.edu
Admissions email: ask@ipfw.edu
Public; founded 1964
Freshman admissions: selective; 2014-2015: 3,386 applied, 3,077 accepted. Either SAT or ACT required. SAT 25/75 percentile: 880-1100. High school rank: 14% in top tenth, 38% in top quarter, 75% in top half
Early decision deadline: N/A, notification date: N/A
Early action deadline: N/A, notification date: N/A
Application deadline (fall): 8/1
Undergraduate student body: 6,971 full time, 5,703 part time; 45% male, 55% female; 0% American Indian, 2% Asian, 5% black, 5% Hispanic, 3% multiracial, 0% Pacific Islander, 83% white, 2% international; 95% from in state; 8% live on campus; 1% of students in fraternities, 0% in sororities
Most popular majors: 16% Business Administration and Management, General, 15% General Studies, 13% Health Services/Allied Health/Health Sciences, General, 7% Human Services, General, 6% Visual and Performing Arts, General
Expenses: 2015-2016: $8,199 in state, $19,565 out of state; room/board: $9,270
Financial aid: (260) 481-6820; 74% of undergrads determined to have financial need; average aid package $9,525

Indiana University-Purdue University–Indianapolis

Indianapolis IN
(317) 274-4591
U.S. News ranking: Nat. U., No. 199
Website: www.iupui.edu
Admissions email: apply@iupui.edu
Public; founded 1969
Freshman admissions: selective; 2014-2015: 12,920 applied, 9,107 accepted. Either SAT or ACT required. SAT 25/75 percentile: 880-1120. High school rank: 15% in top tenth, 42% in top quarter, 86% in top half
Early decision deadline: N/A, notification date: N/A
Early action deadline: N/A, notification date: N/A
Application deadline (fall): 5/1
Undergraduate student body: 17,262 full time, 5,263 part time; 44% male, 56% female; 0% American Indian, 4% Asian, 10% black, 6% Hispanic, 4% multiracial, 0% Pacific Islander, 72% white, 4% international; 98% from in state; 9% live on campus; 3% of students in fraternities, 4% in sororities
Most popular majors: 17% Business, Management, Marketing, and Related Support Services, 5% Communication, Journalism, and Related Programs, 5% Education, 16% Health Professions and Related Programs, 11% Liberal Arts and Sciences, General Studies and Humanities
Expenses: 2015-2016: $9,056 in state, $29,774 out of state; room/board: $8,154
Financial aid: (317) 274-4162; 71% of undergrads determined to have financial need; average aid package $9,974

Indiana University–South Bend

South Bend IN
(574) 520-4839
U.S. News ranking: Reg. U. (Mid.W), second tier
Website: www.iusb.edu
Admissions email: admissions@iusb.edu
Public; founded 1922
Freshman admissions: less selective; 2014-2015: 2,430 applied, 1,782 accepted. Either SAT or ACT required. SAT 25/75 percentile: 840-1040. High school rank: 7% in top tenth, 28% in top quarter, 68% in top half
Early decision deadline: N/A, notification date: N/A
Early action deadline: N/A, notification date: N/A
Application deadline (fall): rolling
Undergraduate student body: 3,857 full time, 3,436 part time; 39% male, 61% female; 0% American Indian, 1% Asian, 8% black, 8% Hispanic, 3% multiracial, 0% Pacific Islander, 75% white, 3% international; 97% from in state; 9% live on campus; N/A of students in fraternities, N/A in sororities
Most popular majors: 17% Business, Management, Marketing, and Related Support Services, 8% Education, 17% Health Professions and Related Programs, 14% Liberal Arts and Sciences, General Studies and Humanities, 7% Social Sciences
Expenses: 2015-2016: $6,986 in state, $18,379 out of state; room/board: N/A
Financial aid: (574) 237-4357; 78% of undergrads determined to have financial need; average aid package $8,669

Indiana University Southeast

New Albany IN
(812) 941-2212
U.S. News ranking: Reg. U. (Mid.W), second tier
Website: www.ius.edu
Admissions email: admissions@ius.edu
Public; founded 1941
Freshman admissions: less selective; 2014-2015: 2,038 applied, 1,637 accepted. Either SAT or ACT required. SAT 25/75 percentile: 850-1050. High school rank: 10% in top tenth, 31% in top quarter, 69% in top half
Early decision deadline: N/A, notification date: N/A
Early action deadline: N/A, notification date: N/A
Application deadline (fall): rolling
Undergraduate student body: 3,587 full time, 2,402 part time; 41% male, 59% female; 0% American Indian, 1% Asian, 6% black, 3% Hispanic, 2% multiracial, 0% Pacific Islander, 86% white, 0% international; 70% from in state; 11% live on campus; N/A of students in fraternities, N/A in sororities
Most popular majors: 19% Business, Management, Marketing, and Related Support Services, 14% Education, 11% Health Professions and Related Programs, 12% Liberal Arts and Sciences, General Studies and Humanities, 9% Psychology
Expenses: 2015-2016: $6,949 in state, $18,379 out of state; room/board: N/A
Financial aid: (812) 941-2246; 72% of undergrads determined to have financial need; average aid package $7,881

Indiana Wesleyan University

Marion IN
(866) 468-6498
U.S. News ranking: Reg. U. (Mid.W), No. 30
Website: www.indwes.edu
Admissions email: admissions@indwes.edu
Private; founded 1920
Affiliation: Wesleyan Church
Freshman admissions: selective; 2014-2015: 2,444 applied, 2,340 accepted. Either SAT or ACT required. ACT 25/75 percentile: 21-27. High school rank: 30% in top tenth, 58% in top quarter, 86% in top half
Early decision deadline: N/A, notification date: N/A
Early action deadline: N/A, notification date: N/A
Application deadline (fall): rolling
Undergraduate student body: 2,699 full time, 211 part time; 34% male, 66% female; 0% American Indian, 1% Asian, 2% black, 3% Hispanic, 3% multiracial, 0% Pacific Islander, 90% white, 1% international; 52% from in state; 82% live on campus; 0% of students in fraternities, 0% in sororities
Most popular majors: 3% Business Administration and Management, General, 7% Elementary Education and Teaching, 6% Psychology, General, 22% Registered Nursing/Registered Nurse, 3% Social Work
Expenses: 2015-2016: $24,728; room/board: $7,988
Financial aid: (765) 677-2116; 80% of undergrads determined to have financial need; average aid package $22,840

Manchester University

North Manchester IN
(800) 852-3648
U.S. News ranking: Reg. Coll. (Mid.W), No. 22
Website: www.manchester.edu
Admissions email: admitinfo@manchester.edu
Private; founded 1889
Affiliation: Church of the Brethren
Freshman admissions: selective; 2014-2015: 2,551 applied, 1,895 accepted. Either SAT or ACT required. SAT 25/75 percentile: 890-1100. High school rank: 16% in top tenth, 45% in top quarter, 84% in top half
Early decision deadline: N/A, notification date: N/A
Early action deadline: N/A, notification date: N/A
Application deadline (fall): rolling
Undergraduate student body: 1,233 full time, 24 part time; 48% male, 52% female; 0% American

Indian, 1% Asian, 4% black, 5% Hispanic, 3% multiracial, 0% Pacific Islander, 84% white, 2% international; 88% from in state; 73% live on campus; N/A of students in fraternities, N/A in sororities
Most popular majors: 24% Business, Management, Marketing, and Related Support Services, 11% Education, 9% Health Professions and Related Programs, 8% Parks, Recreation, Leisure, and Fitness Studies, 6% Social Sciences
Expenses: 2015-2016: $29,910; room/board: $9,510
Financial aid: (260) 982-5066; 89% of undergrads determined to have financial need; average aid package $25,265

Marian University

Indianapolis IN
(317) 955-6300
U.S. News ranking: Reg. Coll. (Mid.W), No. 24
Website: www.marian.edu
Admissions email: admissions@marian.edu
Private; founded 1851
Affiliation: Roman Catholic
Freshman admissions: selective; 2014-2015: 1,825 applied, 1,377 accepted. Either SAT or ACT required. ACT 25/75 percentile: 20-26. High school rank: 17% in top tenth, 39% in top quarter, 75% in top half
Early decision deadline: N/A, notification date: N/A
Early action deadline: N/A, notification date: N/A
Application deadline (fall): 8/1
Undergraduate student body: 1,712 full time, 425 part time; 36% male, 64% female; 0% American Indian, 1% Asian, 13% black, 5% Hispanic, 3% multiracial, 0% Pacific Islander, 73% white, 1% international; 86% from in state; 34% live on campus; 0% of students in fraternities, 0% in sororities
Most popular majors: 10% Business Administration and Management, General, 5% Management Science, 4% Marketing/Marketing Management, General, 3% Psychology, General, 46% Registered Nursing/Registered Nurse
Expenses: 2015-2016: $30,500; room/board: $9,436
Financial aid: (317) 955-6040; 82% of undergrads determined to have financial need; average aid package $24,361

Martin University[1]

Indianapolis IN
(317) 543-3243
U.S. News ranking: Nat. Lib. Arts, unranked
Website: www.martin.edu
Admissions email: bshaheed@martin.edu
Private
Application deadline (fall): N/A
Undergraduate student body: N/A full time, N/A part time
Expenses: 2014-2015: $11,960; room/board: $7,728
Financial aid: (317) 543-3258

Oakland City University

Oakland City IN
(800) 737-5125
U.S. News ranking: Reg. U. (Mid.W), second tier
Website: www.oak.edu
Admissions email: admission@oak.edu
Private; founded 1885
Affiliation: General Association of General Baptist
Freshman admissions: selective; 2014-2015: 675 applied, 371 accepted. Neither SAT nor ACT required. ACT 25/75 percentile: 18-23. High school rank: N/A
Early decision deadline: N/A, notification date: N/A
Early action deadline: N/A, notification date: N/A
Application deadline (fall): 9/8
Undergraduate student body: 576 full time, 1,435 part time; 43% male, 57% female; 0% American Indian, 0% Asian, 2% black, 2% Hispanic, 1% multiracial, 0% Pacific Islander, 88% white, 1% international; 85% from in state; 50% live on campus; N/A of students in fraternities, N/A in sororities
Most popular majors: 40% Business, Management, Marketing, and Related Support Services, 22% Education, 8% Homeland Security, Law Enforcement, Firefighting and Related Protective Services, 9% Liberal Arts and Sciences, General Studies and Humanities, 4% Psychology
Expenses: 2014-2015: $19,800; room/board: $8,700
Financial aid: (812) 749-1224

Purdue University–Calumet

Hammond IN
(219) 989-2213
U.S. News ranking: Reg. U. (Mid.W), second tier
Website: www.purduecal.edu/
Admissions email: adms@purduecal.edu
Public; founded 1946
Freshman admissions: selective; 2014-2015: 2,351 applied, 1,403 accepted. Either SAT or ACT required. SAT 25/75 percentile: 860-1070. High school rank: 14% in top tenth, 37% in top quarter, 76% in top half
Early decision deadline: N/A, notification date: N/A
Early action deadline: N/A, notification date: N/A
Application deadline (fall): 8/1
Undergraduate student body: 4,905 full time, 3,586 part time; 44% male, 56% female; 0% American Indian, 2% Asian, 13% black, 18% Hispanic, 2% multiracial, 0% Pacific Islander, 55% white, 7% international; 78% from in state; 7% live on campus; 1% of students in fraternities, 1% in sororities
Most popular majors: 13% Business, Management, Marketing, and Related Support Services, 5% Communication, Journalism, and Related Programs, 4% Engineering, 7% Engineering Technologies and Engineering-Related Fields, 47% Health Professions and Related Programs
Expenses: 2014-2015: $7,241 in state, $16,356 out of state; room/board: $8,075
Financial aid: (219) 989-2301; 67% of undergrads determined to have financial need; average aid package $9,047

Purdue University–North Central

Westville IN
(219) 785-5505
U.S. News ranking: Reg. Coll. (Mid.W), second tier
Website: www.pnc.edu/admissions
Admissions email: admissions@pnc.edu
Public; founded 1946
Freshman admissions: less selective; 2014-2015: 1,416 applied, 1,044 accepted. Neither SAT nor ACT required. SAT 25/75 percentile: 850-1060. High school rank: 7% in top tenth, 26% in top quarter, 65% in top half
Early decision deadline: N/A, notification date: N/A
Early action deadline: N/A, notification date: N/A
Application deadline (fall): rolling
Undergraduate student body: 2,566 full time, 3,576 part time; 40% male, 60% female; 0% American Indian, 1% Asian, 5% black, 9% Hispanic, 2% multiracial, 0% Pacific Islander, 82% white, 1% international
Most popular majors: 5% Behavioral Sciences, 19% Business, Management, Marketing, and Related Support Services, Other, 8% Elementary Education and Teaching, 12% Liberal Arts and Sciences/Liberal Studies, 18% Registered Nursing/Registered Nurse
Expenses: 2014-2015: $7,329 in state, $17,445 out of state; room/board: N/A
Financial aid: (219) 785-5653

Purdue University–West Lafayette

West Lafayette IN
(765) 494-1776
U.S. News ranking: Nat. U., No. 61
Website: www.purdue.edu
Admissions email: admissions@purdue.edu
Public; founded 1869
Freshman admissions: more selective; 2014-2015: 39,706 applied, 23,506 accepted. Either SAT or ACT required. SAT 25/75 percentile: 1080-1330. High school rank: 42% in top tenth, 77% in top quarter, 97% in top half
Early decision deadline: N/A, notification date: N/A
Early action deadline: 11/1, notification date: 12/12
Application deadline (fall): rolling
Undergraduate student body: 27,881 full time, 1,374 part time; 57% male, 43% female; 0% American Indian, 6% Asian, 3% black, 4% Hispanic, 2% multiracial, 0% Pacific Islander, 65% white, 18% international; 67% from in state; 37% live on campus; 17% of students in fraternities, 20% in sororities
Most popular majors: 9% Agriculture, Agriculture Operations, and Related Sciences, 18% Business, Management, Marketing, and Related Support Services, 5% Education, 22% Engineering, 13% Liberal Arts and Sciences, General Studies and Humanities
Expenses: 2015-2016: $10,002 in state, $28,804 out of state; room/board: $10,030
Financial aid: (765) 494-5090; 43% of undergrads determined to have financial need; average aid package $13,076

Rose-Hulman Institute of Technology

Terre Haute IN
(812) 877-8213
U.S. News ranking: Engineering, unranked
Website: www.rose-hulman.edu
Admissions email: admissions@rose-hulman.edu
Private; founded 1874
Freshman admissions: more selective; 2014-2015: 4,404 applied, 2,589 accepted. Either SAT or ACT required. ACT 25/75 percentile: 27-32. High school rank: 63% in top tenth, 94% in top quarter, 100% in top half
Early decision deadline: N/A, notification date: N/A
Early action deadline: 11/1, notification date: 12/15
Application deadline (fall): 3/1
Undergraduate student body: 2,258 full time, 22 part time; 78% male, 22% female; 0% American Indian, 4% Asian, 2% black, 3% Hispanic, 4% multiracial, 0% Pacific Islander, 76% white, 11% international; 36% from in state; 59% live on campus; 35% of students in fraternities, 36% in sororities
Most popular majors: 8% Bioengineering and Biomedical Engineering, 14% Chemical Engineering, 7% Civil Engineering, General, 10% Electrical and Electronics Engineering, 35% Mechanical Engineering
Expenses: 2015-2016: $42,741; room/board: $12,660
Financial aid: (812) 877-8259; 63% of undergrads determined to have financial need; average aid package $28,720

Saint Mary-of-the-Woods College

St. Mary-of-the-Woods IN
(800) 926-7692
U.S. News ranking: Reg. Coll. (Mid.W), No. 21
Website: www.smwc.edu
Admissions email: smwcadms@smwc.edu
Private; founded 1840
Affiliation: Roman Catholic
Freshman admissions: less selective; 2014-2015: 284 applied, 284 accepted. Either SAT or ACT required. SAT 25/75 percentile: 830-1050. High school rank: 11% in top tenth, 35% in top quarter, 76% in top half
Early decision deadline: N/A, notification date: N/A
Early action deadline: N/A, notification date: N/A
Application deadline (fall): rolling
Undergraduate student body: 407 full time, 339 part time; 7% male, 93% female; 1% American Indian, 0% Asian, 4% black, 1% Hispanic, 0% multiracial, 0% Pacific Islander, 72% white, 1% international; 20% from in state; 60% live on campus; N/A of students in fraternities, N/A in sororities
Most popular majors: 7% Accounting, 29% Education, 6% Horse Husbandry/Equine Science and Management, 9% Human Resources Management and Services, 12% Psychology
Expenses: 2015-2016: $28,932; room/board: $10,500
Financial aid: (812) 535-5109

St. Joseph's College

Rensselaer IN
(219) 866-6170
U.S. News ranking: Reg. Coll. (Mid.W), No. 32
Website: www.saintjoe.edu
Admissions email: admissions@saintjoe.edu
Private; founded 1889
Affiliation: Roman Catholic
Freshman admissions: selective; 2014-2015: 1,572 applied, 1,044 accepted. Either SAT or ACT required. ACT 25/75 percentile: 18-24. High school rank: 15% in top tenth, 37% in top quarter, 68% in top half
Early decision deadline: N/A, notification date: N/A
Early action deadline: N/A, notification date: N/A
Application deadline (fall): rolling
Undergraduate student body: 1,012 full time, 130 part time; 40% male, 60% female; 1% American Indian, 0% Asian, 9% black, 4% Hispanic, 3% multiracial, 0% Pacific Islander, 81% white, 1% international; 76% from in state; 64% live on campus; 0% of students in fraternities, 0% in sororities
Most popular majors: 12% Biology/Biological Sciences, General, 16% Business/Commerce, General, 8% Criminal Justice/Safety Studies, 6% Political Science and Government, General, 23% Registered Nursing/Registered Nurse
Expenses: 2015-2016: $28,690; room/board: $8,900
Financial aid: (219) 866-6163; 87% of undergrads determined to have financial need; average aid package $28,055

St. Mary's College

Notre Dame IN
(574) 284-4587
U.S. News ranking: Nat. Lib. Arts, No. 82
Website: www.saintmarys.edu
Admissions email: admission@saintmarys.edu
Private; founded 1844
Affiliation: Roman Catholic
Freshman admissions: more selective; 2014-2015: 1,687 applied, 1,406 accepted. Either SAT or ACT required. ACT 25/75 percentile: 23-28. High school rank: 35% in top tenth, 62% in top quarter, 94% in top half
Early decision deadline: 11/15, notification date: 12/15
Early action deadline: N/A, notification date: N/A
Application deadline (fall): rolling
Undergraduate student body: 1,501 full time, 18 part time; 0% male, 100% female; 0% American Indian, 2% Asian, 1% black, 11% Hispanic, 3% multiracial, 0% Pacific Islander, 78% white, 2% international; 26% from in state; 87% live on campus; 0% of students in fraternities, 0% in sororities

Most popular majors: 8% Business Administration and Management, General, 7% Communication Disorders Sciences and Services, Other, 11% Psychology, General, 20% Registered Nursing/ Registered Nurse, 13% Speech Communication and Rhetoric
Expenses: 2015-2016: $37,400; room/board: $11,320
Financial aid: (574) 284-4557; 58% of undergrads determined to have financial need; average aid package $29,773

Taylor University

Upland IN
(765) 998-5134
U.S. News ranking: Reg. Coll. (Mid.W), No. 1
Website: www.taylor.edu
Admissions email: admissions_u@taylor.edu
Private; founded 1846
Affiliation: Christian interdenominational
Freshman admissions: more selective; 2014-2015: 1,496 applied, 1,317 accepted. Either SAT or ACT required. ACT 25/75 percentile: 24-30. High school rank: 34% in top tenth, 66% in top quarter, 90% in top half
Early decision deadline: N/A, notification date: N/A
Early action deadline: N/A, notification date: N/A
Application deadline (fall): rolling
Undergraduate student body: 1,824 full time, 279 part time; 44% male, 56% female; 0% American Indian, 2% Asian, 3% black, 3% Hispanic, 1% multiracial, 0% Pacific Islander, 87% white, 5% international; 39% from in state; 85% live on campus; N/A of students in fraternities, N/A in sororities
Most popular majors: 17% Business, Management, Marketing, and Related Support Services, 15% Education, 8% Parks, Recreation, Leisure, and Fitness Studies, 7% Psychology, 9% Visual and Performing Arts
Expenses: 2015-2016: $30,270; room/board: $8,497
Financial aid: (765) 998-5358; 60% of undergrads determined to have financial need; average aid package $19,626

Trine University

Angola IN
(260) 665-4100
U.S. News ranking: Reg. Coll. (Mid.W), No. 29
Website: www.trine.edu
Admissions email: admit@trine.edu
Private; founded 1884
Freshman admissions: selective; 2014-2015: 2,890 applied, 2,196 accepted. Either SAT or ACT required. SAT 25/75 percentile: 945-1160. High school rank: 31% in top tenth, 57% in top quarter, 84% in top half
Early decision deadline: N/A, notification date: N/A
Early action deadline: N/A, notification date: N/A
Application deadline (fall): 8/1
Undergraduate student body: 1,622 full time, 1,169 part time; 58% male, 42% female; 0% American Indian, 0% Asian, 2% black, 4% Hispanic, 3% multiracial, 0% Pacific Islander, 78% white, 8% international; 61% from in state; 69% live on campus; 26% of students in fraternities, 19% in sororities
Most popular majors: 10% CAD/ CADD Drafting and/or Design Technology/Technician, 9% Criminal Justice/Law Enforcement Administration, 9% Education, General, 33% Engineering, General, 11% Kinesiology and Exercise Science
Expenses: 2015-2016: $30,350; room/board: $10,200
Financial aid: (260) 665-4175; 79% of undergrads determined to have financial need; average aid package $25,519

University of Evansville

Evansville IN
(812) 488-2468
U.S. News ranking: Reg. U. (Mid.W), No. 8
Website: www.evansville.edu
Admissions email: admission@evansville.edu
Private; founded 1854
Affiliation: Methodist
Freshman admissions: selective; 2014-2015: 2,762 applied, 2,291 accepted. Either SAT or ACT required. SAT 25/75 percentile: 1020-1230. High school rank: 30% in top tenth, 62% in top quarter, 93% in top half
Early decision deadline: N/A, notification date: N/A
Early action deadline: 12/1, notification date: 12/15
Application deadline (fall): rolling
Undergraduate student body: 2,265 full time, 155 part time; 45% male, 55% female; 0% American Indian, 1% Asian, 3% black, 3% Hispanic, 2% multiracial, 0% Pacific Islander, 74% white, 14% international; 59% from in state; 64% live on campus; 29% of students in fraternities, 27% in sororities
Most popular majors: 12% Business, Management, Marketing, and Related Support Services, 9% Engineering, 13% Health Professions and Related Programs, 8% Parks, Recreation, Leisure, and Fitness Studies, 10% Visual and Performing Arts
Expenses: 2015-2016: $32,946; room/board: $11,240
Financial aid: (812) 488-2364; 65% of undergrads determined to have financial need; average aid package $26,090

University of Indianapolis

Indianapolis IN
(317) 788-3216
U.S. News ranking: Reg. U. (Mid.W), No. 30
Website: www.uindy.edu
Admissions email: admissions@uindy.edu
Private; founded 1902
Affiliation: United Methodist
Freshman admissions: selective; 2014-2015: 6,796 applied, 4,518 accepted. Either SAT or ACT required. SAT 25/75 percentile: 900-1120. High school rank: 21% in top tenth, 54% in top quarter, 86% in top half
Early decision deadline: N/A, notification date: N/A
Early action deadline: N/A, notification date: N/A
Application deadline (fall): rolling
Undergraduate student body: 3,364 full time, 805 part time; 35% male, 65% female; 0% American Indian, 1% Asian, 6% black, 4% Hispanic, 3% multiracial, 0% Pacific Islander, 69% white, 10% international; 93% from in state; 79% live on campus; 0% of students in fraternities, 0% in sororities
Most popular majors: 22% Business Administration and Management, General, 5% Kinesiology and Exercise Science, 5% Liberal Arts and Sciences/ Liberal Studies, 9% Psychology, General, 26% Registered Nursing/ Registered Nurse
Expenses: 2015-2016: $26,290; room/board: $9,930
Financial aid: (317) 788-3217; 72% of undergrads determined to have financial need; average aid package $17,983

University of Notre Dame

Notre Dame IN
(574) 631-7505
U.S. News ranking: Nat. U., No. 18
Website: www.nd.edu
Admissions email: admissions@nd.edu
Private; founded 1842
Affiliation: Roman Catholic
Freshman admissions: most selective; 2014-2015: 17,901 applied, 3,785 accepted. Either SAT or ACT required. ACT 25/75 percentile: 32-34. High school rank: 90% in top tenth, 97% in top quarter, 100% in top half
Early decision deadline: N/A, notification date: N/A
Early action deadline: 11/1, notification date: 12/21
Application deadline (fall): 1/1
Undergraduate student body: 8,430 full time, 18 part time; 52% male, 48% female; 0% American Indian, 6% Asian, 4% black, 10% Hispanic, 4% multiracial, 0% Pacific Islander, 71% white, 5% international; 8% from in state; 76% live on campus; N/A of students in fraternities, N/A in sororities
Most popular majors: 5% Accounting, 5% Economics, General, 9% Finance, General, 6% Political Science and Government, General, 5% Psychology, General
Expenses: 2015-2016: $47,929; room/board: $13,846
Financial aid: (574) 631-6436; 45% of undergrads determined to have financial need; average aid package $41,932

University of Saint Francis

Fort Wayne IN
(260) 399-8000
U.S. News ranking: Reg. U. (Mid.W), No. 92
Website: www.sf.edu
Admissions email: admis@sf.edu
Private; founded 1890
Affiliation: Roman Catholic
Freshman admissions: less selective; 2014-2015: 954 applied, 924 accepted. Either SAT or ACT required. SAT 25/75 percentile: 870-1060. High school rank: 14% in top tenth, 24% in top quarter, 72% in top half
Early decision deadline: N/A, notification date: N/A
Early action deadline: N/A, notification date: N/A
Application deadline (fall): rolling
Undergraduate student body: 1,558 full time, 303 part time; 30% male, 70% female; 0% American Indian, 1% Asian, 7% black, 6% Hispanic, 2% multiracial, 0% Pacific Islander, 79% white, 1% international; 90% from in state; 20% live on campus; 0% of students in fraternities, 0% in sororities
Most popular majors: 7% Biological and Biomedical Sciences, 9% Business, Management, Marketing, and Related Support Services, 32% Health Professions and Related Programs, 7% Psychology, 16% Visual and Performing Arts
Expenses: 2015-2016: $27,220; room/board: $9,276
Financial aid: (260) 434-3283; 89% of undergrads determined to have financial need; average aid package $18,569

University of Southern Indiana

Evansville IN
(812) 464-1765
U.S. News ranking: Reg. U. (Mid.W), second tier
Website: www.usi.edu
Admissions email: enroll@usi.edu
Public; founded 1965
Freshman admissions: selective; 2014-2015: 5,831 applied, 4,160 accepted. Either SAT or ACT required. SAT 25/75 percentile: 890-1100. High school rank: 12% in top tenth, 37% in top quarter, 74% in top half
Early decision deadline: N/A, notification date: N/A
Early action deadline: N/A, notification date: N/A
Application deadline (fall): 8/15
Undergraduate student body: 6,980 full time, 1,434 part time; 40% male, 60% female; 0% American Indian, 1% Asian, 4% black, 2% Hispanic, 2% multiracial, 0% Pacific Islander, 86% white, 2% international; 89% from in state; 30% live on campus; 8% of students in fraternities, 11% in sororities
Most popular majors: 17% Business, Management, Marketing, and Related Support Services, 6% Communication, Journalism, and Related Programs, 6% Education, 26% Health Professions and Related Programs, 5% Psychology
Expenses: 2015-2016: $6,957 in state, $16,297 out of state; room/ board: $7,928
Financial aid: (812) 464-1767; 64% of undergrads determined to have financial need; average aid package $9,015

Valparaiso University

Valparaiso IN
(888) 468-2576
U.S. News ranking: Reg. U. (Mid.W), No. 5
Website: www.valpo.edu
Admissions email: undergrad.admission@valpo.edu
Private; founded 1859
Affiliation: Lutheran
Freshman admissions: more selective; 2014-2015: 6,491 applied, 5,346 accepted. Either SAT or ACT required. ACT 25/75 percentile: 23-29. High school rank: 35% in top tenth, 64% in top quarter, 94% in top half
Early decision deadline: N/A, notification date: N/A
Early action deadline: N/A, notification date: N/A
Application deadline (fall): rolling
Undergraduate student body: 3,159 full time, 101 part time; 48% male, 52% female; 0% American Indian, 2% Asian, 5% black, 8% Hispanic, 2% multiracial, 0% Pacific Islander, 73% white, 8% international; 41% from in state; 65% live on campus; 18% of students in fraternities, 17% in sororities
Most popular majors: 4% Atmospheric Sciences and Meteorology, General, 4% Biology/ Biological Sciences, General, 5% Mechanical Engineering, 5% Psychology, General, 22% Registered Nursing/Registered Nurse
Expenses: 2015-2016: $36,160; room/board: $10,520
Financial aid: (219) 464-5015; 73% of undergrads determined to have financial need; average aid package $29,780

Vincennes University

Vincennes IN
(800) 742-9198
U.S. News ranking: Reg. Coll. (Mid.W), unranked
Website: www.vinu.edu
Admissions email: N/A
Public; founded 1801
Freshman admissions: N/A; 2014-2015: N/A applied, N/A accepted. Neither SAT nor ACT required. ACT 25/75 percentile: N/A. High school rank: N/A
Early decision deadline: N/A, notification date: N/A
Early action deadline: N/A, notification date: N/A
Application deadline (fall): rolling
Undergraduate student body: 6,175 full time, 13,030 part time; 55% male, 45% female; 0% American Indian, 1% Asian, 13% black, 3% Hispanic, 2% multiracial, 0% Pacific Islander, 72% white, 0% international
Most popular majors: Information not available
Expenses: 2014-2015: $5,174 in state, $12,234 out of state; room/ board: $8,732
Financial aid: (812) 888-4361

Wabash College

Crawfordsville IN
(800) 345-5385
U.S. News ranking: Nat. Lib. Arts, No. 61
Website: www.wabash.edu
Admissions email: admissions@wabash.edu
Private; founded 1832
Freshman admissions: selective; 2014-2015: 1,259 applied, 881 accepted. Either SAT or ACT required. SAT 25/75 percentile: 1020-1240. High school rank: 29% in top tenth, 66% in top quarter, 90% in top half
Early decision deadline: 11/15, notification date: 12/1
Early action deadline: 12/1, notification date: 12/19
Application deadline (fall): rolling
Undergraduate student body: 924 full time, 2 part time; 100% male, 0% female; 1% American Indian, 1% Asian, 6% black,

6% Hispanic, 3% multiracial, 0% Pacific Islander, 75% white, 7% international; 75% from in state; 86% live on campus; 53% of students in fraternities, N/A in sororities
Most popular majors: 11% Biology/Biological Sciences, General, 11% Economics, General, 12% History, General, 8% Political Science and Government, General, 14% Psychology, General
Expenses: 2015-2016: $39,980; room/board: $9,360
Financial aid: (765) 361-6370; 80% of undergrads determined to have financial need; average aid package $32,812

IOWA

AIB College of Business[1]

Des Moines IA
(515) 246-5358
U.S. News ranking: Business, unranked
Website: www.aib.edu
Admissions email: admissions@aib.edu
Private; founded 1921
Application deadline (fall): rolling
Undergraduate student body: N/A full time, N/A part time
Expenses: 2014-2015: $15,600; room/board: N/A
Financial aid: N/A

Briar Cliff University

Sioux City IA
(712) 279-5200
U.S. News ranking: Reg. Coll. (Mid.W), No. 38
Website: www.briarcliff.edu
Admissions email: admissions@briarcliff.edu
Private; founded 1930
Affiliation: Roman Catholic
Freshman admissions: selective; 2014-2015: 1,775 applied, 1,095 accepted. Either SAT or ACT required. ACT 25/75 percentile: 19-24. High school rank: 13% in top tenth, 37% in top quarter, 66% in top half
Early decision deadline: N/A, notification date: N/A
Early action deadline: N/A, notification date: N/A
Application deadline (fall): rolling
Undergraduate student body: 774 full time, 267 part time; 41% male, 59% female; 1% American Indian, 2% Asian, 5% black, 9% Hispanic, 2% multiracial, 0% Pacific Islander, 78% white, 3% international; 55% from in state; 44% live on campus; 0% of students in fraternities, 0% in sororities
Most popular majors: 7% Biological and Biomedical Sciences, 27% Business, Management, Marketing, and Related Support Services, 8% Education, 27% Health Professions and Related Programs, 9% Social Sciences
Expenses: 2015-2016: $27,910; room/board: $8,124
Financial aid: (712) 279-5239; 85% of undergrads determined to have financial need; average aid package $29,213

Buena Vista University

Storm Lake IA
(800) 383-9600
U.S. News ranking: Reg. Coll. (Mid.W), No. 11
Website: www.bvu.edu
Admissions email: admissions@bvu.edu
Private; founded 1891
Affiliation: Presbyterian
Freshman admissions: selective; 2014-2015: 1,227 applied, 833 accepted. Either SAT or ACT required. ACT 25/75 percentile: 20-25. High school rank: 20% in top tenth, 49% in top quarter, 82% in top half
Early decision deadline: N/A, notification date: N/A
Early action deadline: N/A, notification date: N/A
Application deadline (fall): rolling
Undergraduate student body: 844 full time, 17 part time; 49% male, 51% female; 0% American Indian, 3% Asian, 2% black, 8% Hispanic, 2% multiracial, 0% Pacific Islander, 76% white, 6% international; 77% from in state; 88% live on campus; 0% of students in fraternities, 0% in sororities
Most popular majors: 9% Biological and Biomedical Sciences, 26% Business, Management, Marketing, and Related Support Services, 7% Communication, Journalism, and Related Programs, 12% Education, 10% Visual and Performing Arts
Expenses: 2015-2016: $31,318; room/board: $9,046
Financial aid: (712) 749-2164; 83% of undergrads determined to have financial need; average aid package $27,355

Central College

Pella IA
(641) 628-5286
U.S. News ranking: Nat. Lib. Arts, No. 136
Website: www.central.edu
Admissions email: admission@central.edu
Private; founded 1853
Affiliation: Reformed Church in America
Freshman admissions: selective; 2014-2015: 3,068 applied, 2,024 accepted. Either SAT or ACT required. ACT 25/75 percentile: 21-27. High school rank: 22% in top tenth, 48% in top quarter, 84% in top half
Early decision deadline: N/A, notification date: N/A
Early action deadline: N/A, notification date: N/A
Application deadline (fall): 8/15
Undergraduate student body: 1,365 full time, 46 part time; 48% male, 52% female; 0% American Indian, 1% Asian, 2% black, 3% Hispanic, 1% multiracial, 0% Pacific Islander, 90% white, 0% international; 80% from in state; 94% live on campus; 4% of students in fraternities, 3% in sororities
Most popular majors: 11% Biological and Biomedical Sciences, 15% Business, Management, Marketing, and Related Support Services, 9% Education, 14% Parks, Recreation, Leisure, and Fitness Studies, 13% Social Sciences
Expenses: 2015-2016: $33,345; room/board: $9,980
Financial aid: (641) 628-5187; 81% of undergrads determined to have financial need; average aid package $24,872

Clarke University

Dubuque IA
(563) 588-6316
U.S. News ranking: Reg. Coll. (Mid.W), No. 14
Website: www.clarke.edu
Admissions email: admissions@clarke.edu
Private; founded 1843
Affiliation: Roman Catholic
Freshman admissions: selective; 2014-2015: 1,359 applied, 958 accepted. Either SAT or ACT required. ACT 25/75 percentile: 20-25. High school rank: 13% in top tenth, 55% in top quarter, 84% in top half
Early decision deadline: N/A, notification date: N/A
Early action deadline: N/A, notification date: N/A
Application deadline (fall): rolling
Undergraduate student body: 835 full time, 114 part time; 32% male, 68% female; 0% American Indian, 1% Asian, 4% black, 5% Hispanic, 0% multiracial, 0% Pacific Islander, 89% white, 1% international; 62% from in state; 56% live on campus; N/A of students in fraternities, N/A in sororities
Most popular majors: 10% Business Administration and Management, General, 13% Education, General, 13% Psychology, General, 35% Registered Nursing/Registered Nurse
Expenses: 2015-2016: $29,940; room/board: $9,000
Financial aid: (563) 588-6327; 86% of undergrads determined to have financial need; average aid package $23,657

Coe College

Cedar Rapids IA
(319) 399-8500
U.S. News ranking: Nat. Lib. Arts, No. 116
Website: www.coe.edu
Admissions email: admission@coe.edu
Private; founded 1851
Affiliation: Presbyterian
Freshman admissions: more selective; 2014-2015: 3,403 applied, 1,882 accepted. Either SAT or ACT required. ACT 25/75 percentile: 22-28. High school rank: 34% in top tenth, 67% in top quarter, 91% in top half
Early decision deadline: N/A, notification date: N/A
Early action deadline: 12/10, notification date: 1/20
Application deadline (fall): 3/1
Undergraduate student body: 1,360 full time, 75 part time; 44% male, 56% female; 0% American Indian, 2% Asian, 5% black, 8% Hispanic, 3% multiracial, 0% Pacific Islander, 76% white, 2% international; 49% from in state; 89% live on campus; 30% of students in fraternities, 26% in sororities
Most popular majors: 9% Biological and Biomedical Sciences, 19% Business, Management, Marketing, and Related Support Services, 8% Psychology, 8% Social Sciences, 9% Visual and Performing Arts
Expenses: 2015-2016: $39,080; room/board: $8,510
Financial aid: (319) 399-8540; 84% of undergrads determined to have financial need; average aid package $30,351

Cornell College

Mount Vernon IA
(800) 747-1112
U.S. News ranking: Nat. Lib. Arts, No. 93
Website: www.cornellcollege.edu
Admissions email: admissions@cornellcollege.edu
Private; founded 1853
Affiliation: United Methodist
Freshman admissions: more selective; 2014-2015: 1,915 applied, 1,410 accepted. Either SAT or ACT required. ACT 25/75 percentile: 23-30. High school rank: 17% in top tenth, 45% in top quarter, 76% in top half
Early decision deadline: 11/1, notification date: 12/15
Early action deadline: 12/1, notification date: 2/1
Application deadline (fall): 2/1
Undergraduate student body: 1,072 full time, 5 part time; 47% male, 53% female; 0% American Indian, 2% Asian, 5% black, 13% Hispanic, 4% multiracial, 0% Pacific Islander, 66% white, 4% international; 18% from in state; 92% live on campus; 16% of students in fraternities, 22% in sororities
Most popular majors: 10% Biological and Biomedical Sciences, 8% English Language and Literature/Letters, 9% Psychology, 18% Social Sciences, 7% Visual and Performing Arts
Expenses: 2015-2016: $38,700; room/board: $8,700
Financial aid: (319) 895-4216; 76% of undergrads determined to have financial need; average aid package $32,245

Dordt College

Sioux Center IA
(800) 343-6738
U.S. News ranking: Reg. Coll. (Mid.W), No. 7
Website: www.dordt.edu
Admissions email: admissions@dordt.edu
Private; founded 1955
Affiliation: Christian Reformed
Freshman admissions: selective; 2014-2015: 1,275 applied, 924 accepted. Either SAT or ACT required. ACT 25/75 percentile: 21-27. High school rank: 15% in top tenth, 39% in top quarter, 70% in top half
Early decision deadline: N/A, notification date: N/A
Early action deadline: N/A, notification date: N/A
Application deadline (fall): 8/1
Undergraduate student body: 1,344 full time, 55 part time; 54% male, 46% female; 0% American Indian, 1% Asian, 1% black, 1% Hispanic, 9% multiracial, 0% Pacific Islander, 73% white, 9% international; 31% from in state; 89% live on campus; 0% of students in fraternities, 0% in sororities
Most popular majors: 7% Agricultural Business and Management, General, 19% Business/Commerce, General, 19% Elementary Education and Teaching, 5% Health and Wellness, General, 7% Parks, Recreation and Leisure Studies
Expenses: 2015-2016: $28,280; room/board: $8,350
Financial aid: (712) 722-6087; 70% of undergrads determined to have financial need; average aid package $21,965

Drake University

Des Moines IA
(800) 443-7253
U.S. News ranking: Reg. U. (Mid.W), No. 3
Website: www.drake.edu
Admissions email: admission@drake.edu
Private; founded 1881
Freshman admissions: more selective; 2014-2015: 6,476 applied, 4,485 accepted. Either SAT or ACT required. ACT 25/75 percentile: 25-30. High school rank: 41% in top tenth, 71% in top quarter, 94% in top half
Early decision deadline: N/A, notification date: N/A
Early action deadline: N/A, notification date: N/A
Application deadline (fall): rolling
Undergraduate student body: 3,177 full time, 187 part time; 44% male, 56% female; 0% American Indian, 4% Asian, 3% black, 4% Hispanic, 2% multiracial, 0% Pacific Islander, 79% white, 7% international; 32% from in state; 72% live on campus; 9% of students in fraternities, 8% in sororities
Most popular majors: Information not available
Expenses: 2015-2016: $33,696; room/board: $9,596
Financial aid: (515) 271-2905; 59% of undergrads determined to have financial need; average aid package $25,015

Graceland University

Lamoni IA
(866) 472-2352
U.S. News ranking: Reg. U. (Mid.W), No. 104
Website: www.graceland.edu
Admissions email: admissions@graceland.edu
Private; founded 1895
Affiliation: Community of Christ
Freshman admissions: selective; 2014-2015: 2,169 applied, 1,081 accepted. Either SAT or ACT required. ACT 25/75 percentile: 18-23. High school rank: 9% in top tenth, 25% in top quarter, 55% in top half
Early decision deadline: N/A, notification date: N/A
Early action deadline: N/A, notification date: N/A
Application deadline (fall): rolling
Undergraduate student body: 1,255 full time, 339 part time; 44% male, 56% female; 0% American Indian, 1% Asian, 10% black, 9% Hispanic, 3% multiracial, 1% Pacific Islander, 64% white, 6% international; 25% from in state; 71% live on campus; 0% of students in fraternities, 0% in sororities
Most popular majors: 12% Business, Management, Marketing, and Related Support Services, 32% Education, 27% Health Professions and Related Programs, 8% Liberal Arts and Sciences, General Studies

More at usnews.com/college

and Humanities, 7% Parks, Recreation, Leisure, and Fitness Studies
Expenses: 2015-2016: $25,890; room/board: $8,100
Financial aid: (641) 784-5136; 81% of undergrads determined to have financial need; average aid package $22,106

Grand View University

Des Moines IA
(515) 263-2810
U.S. News ranking: Reg. Coll. (Mid.W), No. 51
Website: admissions.grandview.edu/
Admissions email: admissions@grandview.edu
Private; founded 1896
Affiliation: Evangelical Lutheran Church in America
Freshman admissions: selective; 2014-2015: 772 applied, 762 accepted. Either SAT or ACT required. ACT 25/75 percentile: 18-23. High school rank: 11% in top tenth, 31% in top quarter, 69% in top half
Early decision deadline: N/A, notification date: N/A
Early action deadline: N/A, notification date: N/A
Application deadline (fall): 8/15
Undergraduate student body: 1,679 full time, 326 part time; 44% male, 56% female; 0% American Indian, 3% Asian, 8% black, 4% Hispanic, 3% multiracial, 0% Pacific Islander, 73% white, 2% international; 85% from in state; 39% live on campus; 0% of students in fraternities, 0% in sororities
Most popular majors: Information not available
Expenses: 2015-2016: $24,544; room/board: $7,866
Financial aid: (515) 263-2820; 81% of undergrads determined to have financial need; average aid package $17,223

Grinnell College

Grinnell IA
(800) 247-0113
U.S. News ranking: Nat. Lib. Arts, No. 19
Website: www.grinnell.edu
Admissions email: askgrin@grinnell.edu
Private; founded 1846
Freshman admissions: most selective; 2014-2015: 6,058 applied, 1,697 accepted. Either SAT or ACT required. ACT 25/75 percentile: 30-33. High school rank: 69% in top tenth, 89% in top quarter, 99% in top half
Early decision deadline: 11/15, notification date: 12/15
Early action deadline: N/A, notification date: N/A
Application deadline (fall): 1/15
Undergraduate student body: 1,672 full time, 62 part time; 45% male, 55% female; 0% American Indian, 7% Asian, 6% black, 8% Hispanic, 4% multiracial, 0% Pacific Islander, 58% white, 14% international; 8% from in state; 88% live on campus; 0% of students in fraternities, 0% in sororities
Most popular majors: 13% Biology/Biological Sciences, General, 7% Foreign Languages and Literatures, General, 6% History, General, 9% Psychology, General, 31% Social Sciences, General
Expenses: 2015-2016: $46,990; room/board: $11,408
Financial aid: (641) 269-3250; 70% of undergrads determined to have financial need; average aid package $43,287

Iowa State University

Ames IA
(800) 262-3810
U.S. News ranking: Nat. U., No. 108
Website: www.iastate.edu
Admissions email: admissions@iastate.edu
Public; founded 1858
Freshman admissions: more selective; 2014-2015: 18,399 applied, 15,990 accepted. Either SAT or ACT required. ACT 25/75 percentile: 21-29. High school rank: 26% in top tenth, 58% in top quarter, 91% in top half
Early decision deadline: N/A, notification date: N/A
Early action deadline: N/A, notification date: N/A
Application deadline (fall): rolling
Undergraduate student body: 27,436 full time, 1,457 part time; 57% male, 43% female; 0% American Indian, 3% Asian, 3% black, 4% Hispanic, 2% multiracial, 0% Pacific Islander, 76% white, 7% international; 69% from in state; 35% live on campus; 12% of students in fraternities, 18% in sororities
Most popular majors: 11% Agriculture, Agriculture Operations, and Related Sciences, 5% Biological and Biomedical Sciences, 19% Business, Management, Marketing, and Related Support Services, 4% Communication, Journalism, and Related Programs, 19% Engineering
Expenses: 2015-2016: $7,736 in state, $20,856 out of state; room/board: $8,070
Financial aid: (515) 294-2223; 53% of undergrads determined to have financial need; average aid package $11,793

Iowa Wesleyan College

Mount Pleasant IA
(319) 385-6231
U.S. News ranking: Reg. Coll. (Mid.W), No. 69
Website: www.iwc.edu
Admissions email: admit@iwc.edu
Private; founded 1842
Affiliation: United Methodist
Freshman admissions: selective; 2014-2015: 1,696 applied, 700 accepted. Either SAT or ACT required. ACT 25/75 percentile: 18-24. High school rank: 10% in top tenth, 12% in top quarter, 40% in top half
Early decision deadline: N/A, notification date: N/A
Early action deadline: N/A, notification date: N/A
Application deadline (fall): rolling
Undergraduate student body: 386 full time, 87 part time; 40% male, 60% female; 1% American Indian, 1% Asian, 6% black, 4% Hispanic, 2% multiracial, 0% Pacific Islander, 60% white, 5% international
Most popular majors: Information not available
Expenses: 2015-2016: $27,286; room/board: $9,576
Financial aid: (319) 385-6242; 86% of undergrads determined to have financial need; average aid package $22,216

Kaplan University[1]

Davenport IA
(800) 987-7734
U.S. News ranking: Reg. U. (Mid.W), unranked
Website: www.kaplan.edu
Admissions email: N/A
For-profit
Application deadline (fall): N/A
Undergraduate student body: N/A full time, N/A part time
Expenses: 2014-2015: $13,956; room/board: $4,624
Financial aid: (866) 428-2008

Loras College

Dubuque IA
(800) 245-6727
U.S. News ranking: Reg. Coll. (Mid.W), No. 13
Website: www.loras.edu
Admissions email: admissions@loras.edu
Private; founded 1839
Affiliation: Roman Catholic
Freshman admissions: selective; 2014-2015: 1,293 applied, 1,230 accepted. Either SAT or ACT required. ACT 25/75 percentile: 21-26. High school rank: 16% in top tenth, 40% in top quarter, 73% in top half
Early decision deadline: N/A, notification date: N/A
Early action deadline: N/A, notification date: N/A
Application deadline (fall): rolling
Undergraduate student body: 1,446 full time, 44 part time; 52% male, 48% female; 0% American Indian, 1% Asian, 3% black, 6% Hispanic, 1% multiracial, 0% Pacific Islander, 84% white, 2% international; 37% from in state; 68% live on campus; 4% of students in fraternities, 4% in sororities
Most popular majors: 7% Biology/Biological Sciences, General, 5% Elementary Education and Teaching, 5% Marketing/Marketing Management, General, 7% Psychology, General, 6% Sport and Fitness Administration/Management
Expenses: 2015-2016: $30,628; room/board: $7,489
Financial aid: (563) 588-7136; 76% of undergrads determined to have financial need; average aid package $20,971

Luther College

Decorah IA
(563) 387-1287
U.S. News ranking: Nat. Lib. Arts, No. 90
Website: www.luther.edu
Admissions email: admissions@luther.edu
Private; founded 1861
Affiliation: Lutheran
Freshman admissions: more selective; 2014-2015: 3,440 applied, 2,448 accepted. Either SAT or ACT required. ACT 25/75 percentile: 23-28. High school rank: 29% in top tenth, 63% in top quarter, 91% in top half
Early decision deadline: N/A, notification date: N/A
Early action deadline: N/A, notification date: N/A
Application deadline (fall): rolling
Undergraduate student body: 2,339 full time, 46 part time; 44% male, 56% female; 0% American Indian, 2% Asian, 1% black, 3% Hispanic, 2% multiracial, 0% Pacific Islander, 85% white, 6% international; 33% from in state; 85% live on campus; 1% of students in fraternities, 2% in sororities
Most popular majors: 10% Biology/Biological Sciences, General, 9% Business Administration and Management, General, 6% Elementary Education and Teaching, 10% Music, General, 8% Psychology, General
Expenses: 2015-2016: $39,190; room/board: $7,920
Financial aid: (563) 387-1018; 69% of undergrads determined to have financial need; average aid package $30,365

Maharishi University of Management[1]

Fairfield IA
(641) 472-1110
U.S. News ranking: Reg. U. (Mid.W), unranked
Website: www.mum.edu
Admissions email: admissions@mum.edu
Private
Application deadline (fall): N/A
Undergraduate student body: N/A full time, N/A part time
Expenses: 2014-2015: $26,430; room/board: $7,400
Financial aid: (641) 472-1156

Morningside College

Sioux City IA
(712) 274-5111
U.S. News ranking: Reg. Coll. (Mid.W), No. 24
Website: www.morningside.edu
Admissions email: mscadm@morningside.edu
Private; founded 1894
Affiliation: United Methodist
Freshman admissions: selective; 2014-2015: 4,150 applied, 2,358 accepted. Either SAT or ACT required. ACT 25/75 percentile: 20-25. High school rank: 12% in top tenth, 40% in top quarter, 73% in top half
Early decision deadline: N/A, notification date: N/A
Early action deadline: N/A, notification date: N/A
Application deadline (fall): rolling
Undergraduate student body: 1,279 full time, 42 part time; 48% male, 52% female; 1% American Indian, 1% Asian, 2% black, 6% Hispanic, 2% multiracial, 0% Pacific Islander, 83% white, 2% international; 65% from in state; 62% live on campus; 5% of students in fraternities, 2% in sororities
Most popular majors: 9% Biological and Biomedical Sciences, 25% Business, Management, Marketing, and Related Support Services, 21% Education, 9% Health Professions and Related Programs, 7% Psychology
Expenses: 2015-2016: $28,155; room/board: $8,710
Financial aid: (712) 274-5159; 86% of undergrads determined to have financial need; average aid package $21,392

Mount Mercy University

Cedar Rapids IA
(319) 368-6460
U.S. News ranking: Reg. Coll. (Mid.W), No. 22
Website: www.mtmercy.edu
Admissions email: admission@mtmercy.edu
Private; founded 1928
Affiliation: Roman Catholic
Freshman admissions: selective; 2014-2015: 695 applied, 395 accepted. Either SAT or ACT required. ACT 25/75 percentile: 19-25. High school rank: 10% in top tenth, 38% in top quarter, 72% in top half
Early decision deadline: N/A, notification date: N/A
Early action deadline: N/A, notification date: N/A
Application deadline (fall): rolling
Undergraduate student body: 858 full time, 586 part time; 30% male, 70% female; 0% American Indian, 1% Asian, 4% black, 1% Hispanic, 1% multiracial, 0% Pacific Islander, 84% white, 3% international; 93% from in state; N/A live on campus; N/A of students in fraternities, N/A in sororities
Most popular majors: 8% Accounting, 5% Business Administration and Management, General, 10% Business/Commerce, General, 7% Marketing/Marketing Management, General, 25% Registered Nursing/Registered Nurse
Expenses: 2015-2016: $28,226; room/board: $8,600
Financial aid: (319) 368-6467; 73% of undergrads determined to have financial need; average aid package $19,750

Northwestern College

Orange City IA
(712) 707-7130
U.S. News ranking: Reg. Coll. (Mid.W), No. 5
Website: www.nwciowa.edu
Admissions email: admissions@nwciowa.edu
Private; founded 1882
Affiliation: Reformed Church in America
Freshman admissions: selective; 2014-2015: 1,254 applied, 976 accepted. Either SAT or ACT required. ACT 25/75 percentile: 21-27. High school rank: 23% in top tenth, 55% in top quarter, 87% in top half
Early decision deadline: N/A, notification date: N/A
Early action deadline: N/A, notification date: N/A
Application deadline (fall): rolling
Undergraduate student body: 1,100 full time, 105 part time; 41% male, 59% female; 0% American Indian, 1% Asian, 1% black, 5% Hispanic, 2% multiracial, 0% Pacific Islander, 84% white, 3% international; 53% from in state; 89% live on campus; 0% of students in fraternities, 0% in sororities
Most popular majors: 7% Biology/Biological Sciences, General, 17% Business Administration and Management, General, 16% Elementary Education and Teaching, 10% Registered Nursing/Registered Nurse, 7% Spanish Language and Literature

Expenses: 2015-2016: $28,950; room/board: $8,750
Financial aid: (712) 707-7131; 78% of undergrads determined to have financial need; average aid package $25,135

Simpson College
Indianola IA
(515) 961-1624
U.S. News ranking: Nat. Lib. Arts, No. 143
Website: www.simpson.edu
Admissions email: admiss@simpson.edu
Private; founded 1860
Affiliation: United Methodist
Freshman admissions: more selective; 2014-2015: 1,312 applied, 1,121 accepted. Either SAT or ACT required. ACT 25/75 percentile: 22-27. High school rank: 24% in top tenth, 57% in top quarter, 88% in top half
Early decision deadline: N/A, notification date: N/A
Early action deadline: N/A, notification date: N/A
Application deadline (fall): rolling
Undergraduate student body: 1,466 full time, 194 part time; 44% male, 56% female; 1% American Indian, 1% Asian, 2% black, 2% Hispanic, 2% multiracial, 0% Pacific Islander, 79% white, 1% international; 86% from in state; 86% live on campus; 23% of students in fraternities, 22% in sororities
Most popular majors: 12% Accounting, 25% Business/Commerce, General, 7% Computer and Information Sciences, General, 7% Criminal Justice/Safety Studies, 9% Elementary Education and Teaching
Expenses: 2015-2016: $34,175; room/board: $7,963
Financial aid: (515) 961-1630; 82% of undergrads determined to have financial need; average aid package $29,037

St. Ambrose University
Davenport IA
(563) 333-6300
U.S. News ranking: Reg. U. (Mid.W), No. 36
Website: www.sau.edu
Admissions email: admit@sau.edu
Private; founded 1882
Affiliation: Roman Catholic
Freshman admissions: selective; 2014-2015: 2,954 applied, 2,838 accepted. Either SAT or ACT required. ACT 25/75 percentile: 20-25. High school rank: 15% in top tenth, 34% in top quarter, 72% in top half
Early decision deadline: N/A, notification date: N/A
Early action deadline: N/A, notification date: N/A
Application deadline (fall): rolling
Undergraduate student body: 2,401 full time, 313 part time; 43% male, 57% female; 0% American Indian, 1% Asian, 3% black, 6% Hispanic, 2% multiracial, 0% Pacific Islander, 81% white, 3% international; 44% from in state; 61% live on campus; 0% of students in fraternities, 0% in sororities
Most popular majors: 25% Business, Management, Marketing, and Related Support Services, 11% Education, 11% Health Professions and Related Programs, 11% Parks, Recreation, Leisure, and Fitness Studies, 11% Psychology
Expenses: 2015-2016: $28,380; room/board: $9,582
Financial aid: (563) 333-6314; 72% of undergrads determined to have financial need; average aid package $20,016

University of Dubuque
Dubuque IA
(800) 722-5583
U.S. News ranking: Reg. U. (Mid.W), No. 108
Website: www.dbq.edu
Admissions email: admssns@univ.dbq.edu
Private; founded 1852
Affiliation: Presbyterian
Freshman admissions: less selective; 2014-2015: 1,451 applied, 1,130 accepted. Either SAT or ACT required. ACT 25/75 percentile: 17-23. High school rank: 7% in top tenth, 22% in top quarter, 53% in top half
Early decision deadline: N/A, notification date: N/A
Early action deadline: N/A, notification date: N/A
Application deadline (fall): rolling
Undergraduate student body: 1,589 full time, 186 part time; 58% male, 42% female; 1% American Indian, 2% Asian, 12% black, 8% Hispanic, 3% multiracial, 0% Pacific Islander, 67% white, 1% international
Most popular majors: 11% Aviation/Airway Management and Operations, 7% Biology/Biological Sciences, General, 25% Business Administration and Management, General, 9% Criminal Justice/Safety Studies, 8% Parks, Recreation, Leisure, and Fitness Studies, Other
Expenses: 2015-2016: $27,896; room/board: $9,070
Financial aid: (563) 589-3396; 88% of undergrads determined to have financial need; average aid package $22,760

University of Iowa
Iowa City IA
(319) 335-3847
U.S. News ranking: Nat. U., No. 82
Website: www.uiowa.edu
Admissions email: admissions@uiowa.edu
Public; founded 1847
Freshman admissions: more selective; 2014-2015: 24,097 applied, 19,506 accepted. Either SAT or ACT required. ACT 25/75 percentile: 23-28. High school rank: 29% in top tenth, 56% in top quarter, 90% in top half
Early decision deadline: N/A, notification date: N/A
Early action deadline: N/A, notification date: N/A
Application deadline (fall): 4/1
Undergraduate student body: 19,546 full time, 2,808 part time; 48% male, 52% female; 0% American Indian, 3% Asian, 3% black, 6% Hispanic, 2% multiracial, 0% Pacific Islander, 68% white, 11% international; 66% from in state; 26% live on campus; 14% of students in fraternities, 19% in sororities
Most popular majors: 18% Business, Management, Marketing, and Related Support Services, 7% Communication, Journalism, and Related Programs, 6% Engineering, 11% Parks, Recreation, Leisure, and Fitness Studies, 9% Social Sciences
Expenses: 2015-2016: $8,104 in state, $27,890 out of state; room/board: $9,728
Financial aid: (319) 335-1450; 46% of undergrads determined to have financial need; average aid package $13,515

University of Northern Iowa
Cedar Falls IA
(800) 772-2037
U.S. News ranking: Reg. U. (Mid.W), No. 18
Website: www.uni.edu/
Admissions email: admissions@uni.edu
Public; founded 1876
Freshman admissions: selective; 2014-2015: 5,509 applied, 4,222 accepted. Either SAT or ACT required. ACT 25/75 percentile: 20-25. High school rank: 17% in top tenth, 47% in top quarter, 83% in top half
Early decision deadline: N/A, notification date: N/A
Early action deadline: N/A, notification date: N/A
Application deadline (fall): 8/15
Undergraduate student body: 9,122 full time, 1,020 part time; 44% male, 56% female; 0% American Indian, 1% Asian, 3% black, 3% Hispanic, 2% multiracial, 0% Pacific Islander, 85% white, 4% international; 94% from in state; 37% live on campus; 4% of students in fraternities, 6% in sororities
Most popular majors: 7% Biological and Biomedical Sciences, 19% Business, Management, Marketing, and Related Support Services, 7% Communication, Journalism, and Related Programs, 18% Education, 8% Social Sciences
Expenses: 2015-2016: $7,817 in state, $18,005 out of state; room/board: $8,320
Financial aid: (319) 273-2700; 63% of undergrads determined to have financial need; average aid package $7,352

Upper Iowa University
Fayette IA
(563) 425-5281
U.S. News ranking: Reg. U. (Mid.W), second tier
Website: www.uiu.edu
Admissions email: admission@uiu.edu
Private; founded 1857
Freshman admissions: selective; 2014-2015: 1,397 applied, 977 accepted. SAT required. ACT 25/75 percentile: 17-23. High school rank: 8% in top tenth, 44% in top quarter, 67% in top half
Early decision deadline: N/A, notification date: N/A
Early action deadline: N/A, notification date: N/A
Application deadline (fall): rolling
Undergraduate student body: 2,684 full time, 1,755 part time; 42% male, 58% female; 0% American Indian, 1% Asian, 18% black, 4% Hispanic, 2% multiracial, 0% Pacific Islander, 66% white, 5% international; 40% from in state; 65% live on campus; 10% of students in fraternities, 10% in sororities
Most popular majors: 39% Business, Management, Marketing, and Related Support Services, 8% Health Professions and Related Programs, 13% Psychology, 11% Public Administration and Social Service Professions, 13% Social Sciences
Expenses: 2015-2016: $28,073; room/board: $8,057
Financial aid: (563) 425-5274; 92% of undergrads determined to have financial need; average aid package $12,097

Waldorf College[1]
Forest City IA
(641) 585-8112
U.S. News ranking: Reg. Coll. (Mid.W), second tier
Website: www.waldorf.edu
Admissions email: admissions@waldorf.edu
For-profit
Application deadline (fall): N/A
Undergraduate student body: N/A full time, N/A part time
Expenses: 2014-2015: $20,316; room/board: $6,856
Financial aid: (641) 585-8120

Wartburg College
Waverly IA
(319) 352-8264
U.S. News ranking: Nat. Lib. Arts, No. 143
Website: www.wartburg.edu
Admissions email: admissions@wartburg.edu
Private; founded 1852
Affiliation: Lutheran
Freshman admissions: more selective; 2014-2015: 2,310 applied, 1,821 accepted. Either SAT or ACT required. ACT 25/75 percentile: 21-27. High school rank: 29% in top tenth, 57% in top quarter, 82% in top half
Early decision deadline: N/A, notification date: N/A
Early action deadline: 12/1, notification date: N/A
Application deadline (fall): rolling
Undergraduate student body: 1,596 full time, 65 part time; 48% male, 52% female; 0% American Indian, 1% Asian, 5% black, 3% Hispanic, 2% multiracial, 0% Pacific Islander, 78% white, 10% international; 73% from in state; 78% live on campus; 0% of students in fraternities, 0% in sororities
Most popular majors: 17% Biology/Biological Sciences, General, 16% Business/Commerce, General, 14% Elementary Education and Teaching, 8% Social Sciences, General, 7% Speech Communication and Rhetoric
Expenses: 2015-2016: $37,190; room/board: $9,010
Financial aid: (319) 352-8262; 72% of undergrads determined to have financial need; average aid package $27,267

William Penn University[1]
Oskaloosa IA
(641) 673-1012
U.S. News ranking: Reg. Coll. (Mid.W), second tier
Website: www.wmpenn.edu
Admissions email: admissions@wmpenn.edu
Private
Application deadline (fall): N/A
Undergraduate student body: N/A full time, N/A part time
Expenses: 2014-2015: $23,480; room/board: $6,298
Financial aid: (641) 673-1040

KANSAS

Baker University
Baldwin City KS
(800) 873-4282
U.S. News ranking: Reg. U. (Mid.W), No. 36
Website: www.bakeru.edu
Admissions email: admission@bakeru.edu
Private; founded 1858
Affiliation: United Methodist
Freshman admissions: selective; 2014-2015: 971 applied, 737 accepted. Either SAT or ACT required. ACT 25/75 percentile: 20-26. High school rank: 15% in top tenth, 42% in top quarter, 78% in top half
Early decision deadline: N/A, notification date: N/A
Early action deadline: N/A, notification date: N/A
Application deadline (fall): rolling
Undergraduate student body: 818 full time, 192 part time; 50% male, 50% female; 3% American Indian, 0% Asian, 9% black, 6% Hispanic, 1% multiracial, 0% Pacific Islander, 73% white, 3% international; 68% from in state; 80% live on campus; 32% of students in fraternities, 43% in sororities
Most popular majors: 7% Biological and Biomedical Sciences, 19% Business, Management, Marketing, and Related Support Services, 14% Education, 20% Parks, Recreation, Leisure, and Fitness Studies, 12% Social Sciences
Expenses: 2015-2016: $30,080; room/board: $8,270
Financial aid: (785) 594-4595; 81% of undergrads determined to have financial need; average aid package $20,203

Benedictine College
Atchison KS
(800) 467-5340
U.S. News ranking: Reg. Coll. (Mid.W), No. 18
Website: www.benedictine.edu
Admissions email: bcadmiss@benedictine.edu
Private; founded 1859
Affiliation: Roman Catholic
Freshman admissions: selective; 2014-2015: 2,249 applied, 2,199 accepted. Either SAT or ACT required. ACT 25/75 percentile: 22-27. High school rank: 22% in top tenth, 44% in top quarter, 72% in top half
Early decision deadline: N/A, notification date: N/A
Early action deadline: N/A, notification date: N/A
Application deadline (fall): rolling
Undergraduate student body: 1,838 full time, 262 part time; 48% male, 52% female; 0% American Indian, 1% Asian, 4% black, 6% Hispanic, 4% multiracial, 0% Pacific Islander, 79% white, 3% international; 26% from in state; 84% live on campus; 0%

More at usnews.com/college

of students in fraternities, 0% in sororities
Most popular majors: 12% Business, Management, Marketing, and Related Support Services, 20% Education, 7% Health Professions and Related Programs, 10% Social Sciences, 9% Theology and Religious Vocations
Expenses: 2015-2016: $26,200; room/board: $9,165
Financial aid: (913) 360-7484; 67% of undergrads determined to have financial need; average aid package $19,687

Bethany College[1]

Lindsborg KS
(800) 826-2281
U.S. News ranking: Reg. Coll. (Mid.W), No. 66
Website: www.bethanylb.edu
Admissions email: admissions@bethanylb.edu
Private
Affiliation: Evangelical Luteran Chuch in America (ELCA)
Application deadline (fall): rolling
Undergraduate student body: N/A full time, N/A part time
Expenses: 2014-2015: $24,390; room/board: $7,610
Financial aid: (785) 227-3311

Bethel College

North Newton KS
(800) 522-1887
U.S. News ranking: Reg. Coll. (Mid.W), No. 27
Website: www.bethelks.edu
Admissions email: admissions@bethelks.edu
Private; founded 1887
Affiliation: Mennonite Church USA
Freshman admissions: selective; 2014-2015: 833 applied, 409 accepted. Either SAT or ACT required. ACT 25/75 percentile: 19-25. High school rank: 17% in top tenth, 38% in top quarter, 73% in top half
Early decision deadline: N/A, notification date: N/A
Early action deadline: N/A, notification date: N/A
Application deadline (fall): rolling
Undergraduate student body: 468 full time, 15 part time; 49% male, 51% female; 0% American Indian, 0% Asian, 15% black, 10% Hispanic, 2% multiracial, 0% Pacific Islander, 71% white, 2% international; 62% from in state; 71% live on campus; 0% of students in fraternities, 0% in sororities
Most popular majors: 13% Business, Management, Marketing, and Related Support Services, 9% Communication, Journalism, and Related Programs, 8% Education, 19% Health Professions and Related Programs, 13% Visual and Performing Arts
Expenses: 2015-2016: $25,410; room/board: $8,610
Financial aid: (316) 284-5232; 86% of undergrads determined to have financial need; average aid package $24,404

Central Christian College

McPherson KS
(800) 835-0078
U.S. News ranking: Reg. Coll. (Mid.W), second tier
Website: www.centralchristian.edu/
Admissions email: rick.wyatt@centralchristian.edu
Private; founded 1184
Affiliation: Free Metodist Church of North America
Freshman admissions: selective; 2014-2015: 588 applied, 248 accepted. Either SAT or ACT required. ACT 25/75 percentile: 18-23. High school rank: N/A
Early decision deadline: N/A, notification date: N/A
Early action deadline: 11/30, notification date: 12/1
Application deadline (fall): rolling
Undergraduate student body: 962 full time, 23 part time; 51% male, 49% female; 2% American Indian, 1% Asian, 21% black, 11% Hispanic, 2% multiracial, 0% Pacific Islander, 43% white, 1% international; 26% from in state; 27% live on campus; 0% of students in fraternities, 0% in sororities
Most popular majors: Information not available
Expenses: 2014-2015: $16,204; room/board: $7,600
Financial aid: (620) 241-0723

Donnelly College

Kansas City KS
(913) 621-8700
U.S. News ranking: Reg. Coll. (Mid.W), unranked
Website: donnelly.edu
Admissions email: N/A
Private; founded 1949
Affiliation: Catholic
Freshman admissions: N/A; 2014-2015: N/A applied, N/A accepted. Neither SAT nor ACT required. ACT 25/75 percentile: N/A. High school rank: N/A
Early decision deadline: N/A, notification date: N/A
Early action deadline: N/A, notification date: N/A
Application deadline (fall): rolling
Undergraduate student body: 310 full time, 153 part time; 29% male, 71% female; 0% American Indian, 10% Asian, 29% black, 40% Hispanic, 5% multiracial, 0% Pacific Islander, 10% white, 6% international; 75% from in state; N/A live on campus; N/A of students in fraternities, N/A in sororities
Most popular majors: 24% Liberal Arts and Sciences/Liberal Studies, 19% Non-Profit/Public/Organizational Management
Expenses: 2014-2015: $7,111; room/board: $7,270
Financial aid: (913) 621-8700

Emporia State University

Emporia KS
(620) 341-5465
U.S. News ranking: Reg. U. (Mid.W), No. 104
Website: www.emporia.edu
Admissions email: go2esu@emporia.edu
Public; founded 1863
Freshman admissions: selective; 2014-2015: 1,979 applied, 1,515 accepted. Either SAT or ACT required. ACT 25/75 percentile: 19-24. High school rank: 14% in top tenth, 35% in top quarter, 70% in top half
Early decision deadline: N/A, notification date: N/A
Early action deadline: N/A, notification date: N/A
Application deadline (fall): rolling
Undergraduate student body: 3,527 full time, 397 part time; 40% male, 60% female; 1% American Indian, 1% Asian, 6% black, 6% Hispanic, 6% multiracial, 0% Pacific Islander, 71% white, 8% international; 91% from in state; 28% live on campus; 12% of students in fraternities, 9% in sororities
Most popular majors: 14% Business, Management, Marketing, and Related Support Services, 23% Education, 12% Health Professions and Related Programs, 6% Liberal Arts and Sciences, General Studies and Humanities, 9% Social Sciences
Expenses: 2014-2015: $5,746 in state, $17,896 out of state; room/board: $7,582
Financial aid: (620) 341-5457; 66% of undergrads determined to have financial need; average aid package $8,805

Fort Hays State University

Hays KS
(800) 628-3478
U.S. News ranking: Reg. U. (Mid.W), second tier
Website: www.fhsu.edu
Admissions email: tigers@fhsu.edu
Public; founded 1902
Freshman admissions: less selective; 2014-2015: 2,427 applied, 2,142 accepted. Neither SAT nor ACT required. ACT 25/75 percentile: N/A. High school rank: 11% in top tenth, 30% in top quarter, 62% in top half
Early decision deadline: N/A, notification date: N/A
Early action deadline: N/A, notification date: N/A
Application deadline (fall): rolling
Undergraduate student body: 5,644 full time, 5,999 part time; 40% male, 60% female; 0% American Indian, 1% Asian, 4% black, 7% Hispanic, 2% multiracial, 0% Pacific Islander, 56% white, 29% international; 71% from in state; 12% live on campus; 2% of students in fraternities, 1% in sororities
Most popular majors: Information not available
Expenses: 2014-2015: $4,469 in state, $13,159 out of state; room/board: $7,280
Financial aid: (785) 628-4408; 69% of undergrads determined to have financial need; average aid package $7,199

Friends University

Wichita KS
(316) 295-5100
U.S. News ranking: Reg. U. (Mid.W), second tier
Website: www.friends.edu
Admissions email: learn@friends.edu
Private; founded 1898
Affiliation: Quaker
Freshman admissions: selective; 2014-2015: 487 applied, 410 accepted. Neither SAT nor ACT required. ACT 25/75 percentile: N/A. High school rank: 12% in top tenth, 33% in top quarter, 67% in top half
Early decision deadline: N/A, notification date: N/A
Early action deadline: N/A, notification date: N/A
Application deadline (fall): N/A
Undergraduate student body: 1,025 full time, 392 part time; 46% male, 54% female; 1% American Indian, 2% Asian, 9% black, 4% Hispanic, 6% multiracial, 0% Pacific Islander, 69% white, 0% international
Most popular majors: Information not available
Expenses: 2014-2015: $24,630; room/board: $7,320
Financial aid: (316) 295-5200; 80% of undergrads determined to have financial need; average aid package $14,589

Kansas State University

Manhattan KS
(785) 532-6250
U.S. News ranking: Nat. U., No. 146
Website: www.k-state.edu
Admissions email: k-state@k-state.edu
Public; founded 1863
Freshman admissions: selective; 2014-2015: 9,614 applied, 9,127 accepted. Neither SAT nor ACT required. ACT 25/75 percentile: 22-28. High school rank: 22% in top tenth, 47% in top quarter, 75% in top half
Early decision deadline: N/A, notification date: N/A
Early action deadline: N/A, notification date: N/A
Application deadline (fall): rolling
Undergraduate student body: 18,258 full time, 2,069 part time; 52% male, 48% female; 0% American Indian, 1% Asian, 4% black, 6% Hispanic, 3% multiracial, 0% Pacific Islander, 78% white, 6% international; 83% from in state; 22% live on campus; 15% of students in fraternities, 18% in sororities
Most popular majors: 12% Agriculture, Agriculture Operations, and Related Sciences, 18% Business, Management, Marketing, and Related Support Services, 11% Engineering, 8% Family and Consumer Sciences/Human Sciences, 10% Social Sciences
Expenses: 2014-2015: $9,034 in state, $22,624 out of state; room/board: $8,060
Financial aid: (785) 532-6420; 52% of undergrads determined to have financial need; average aid package $11,423

Kansas Wesleyan University

Salina KS
(785) 827-5541
U.S. News ranking: Reg. Coll. (Mid.W), No. 55
Website: www.kwu.edu
Admissions email: admissions@kwu.edu
Private; founded 1886
Affiliation: United Methodist
Freshman admissions: selective; 2014-2015: 605 applied, 373 accepted. Either SAT or ACT required. ACT 25/75 percentile: 20-26. High school rank: 21% in top tenth, 43% in top quarter, 81% in top half
Early decision deadline: N/A, notification date: N/A
Early action deadline: N/A, notification date: N/A
Application deadline (fall): rolling
Undergraduate student body: 593 full time, 74 part time; 45% male, 55% female; 1% American Indian, 1% Asian, 6% black, 13% Hispanic, 2% multiracial, 0% Pacific Islander, 74% white, 3% international; 60% from in state; 61% live on campus; N/A of students in fraternities, N/A in sororities
Most popular majors: 10% Business Administration and Management, General, 11% Criminal Justice/Law Enforcement Administration, 10% Kinesiology and Exercise Science, 25% Registered Nursing/Registered Nurse, 5% Secondary Education and Teaching
Expenses: 2014-2015: $25,200; room/board: $8,000
Financial aid: (785) 827-5541

McPherson College

McPherson KS
(800) 365-7402
U.S. News ranking: Reg. Coll. (Mid.W), No. 50
Website: www.mcpherson.edu
Admissions email: admissions@mcpherson.edu
Private; founded 1887
Affiliation: Church of the Brethren
Freshman admissions: selective; 2014-2015: 623 applied, 551 accepted. Either SAT or ACT required. ACT 25/75 percentile: 18-25. High school rank: 10% in top tenth, 25% in top quarter, 49% in top half
Early decision deadline: N/A, notification date: N/A
Early action deadline: N/A, notification date: N/A
Application deadline (fall): 8/1
Undergraduate student body: 580 full time, 39 part time; 61% male, 39% female; 0% American Indian, 1% Asian, 14% black, 11% Hispanic, 3% multiracial, 1% Pacific Islander, 68% white, 2% international; 50% from in state; 72% live on campus; 0% of students in fraternities, 0% in sororities
Most popular majors: 26% Business, Management, Marketing, and Related Support Services, 20% Engineering Technologies and Engineering-Related Fields, 15% Parks, Recreation, Leisure, and Fitness Studies, 6% Public Administration and Social Service Professions, 11% Visual and Performing Arts
Expenses: 2015-2016: $25,236; room/board: $8,441
Financial aid: (620) 241-0731; 80% of undergrads determined to have financial need; average aid package $24,734

MidAmerica Nazarene University

Olathe KS
(913) 971-3380
U.S. News ranking: Reg. U. (Mid.W), second tier
Website: www.mnu.edu
Admissions email: admissions@mnu.edu
Private; founded 1966

Affiliation: International Church of the Nazarene
Freshman admissions: selective; 2014-2015: 841 applied, 580 accepted. Either SAT or ACT required. ACT 25/75 percentile: 19-21. High school rank: N/A
Early decision deadline: N/A, notification date: N/A
Early action deadline: N/A, notification date: N/A
Application deadline (fall): 8/1
Undergraduate student body: 1,026 full time, 342 part time; 42% male, 58% female; 1% American Indian, 1% Asian, 8% black, 6% Hispanic, 0% multiracial, 0% Pacific Islander, 57% white, 0% international
Most popular majors: 2% Bible/ Biblical Studies, 30% Business Administration and Management, General, 3% Elementary Education and Teaching, 3% Kinesiology and Exercise Science, 39% Registered Nursing/ Registered Nurse
Expenses: 2014-2015: $24,250; room/board: $7,550
Financial aid: (913) 791-3298

Newman University

Wichita KS
(877) 639-6268
U.S. News ranking: Reg. U. (Mid.W), second tier
Website: www.newmanu.edu
Admissions email: admissions@newmanu.edu
Private; founded 1933
Affiliation: Roman Catholic
Freshman admissions: selective; 2014-2015: 2,473 applied, 1,306 accepted. Neither SAT nor ACT required. ACT 25/75 percentile: 20-27. High school rank: 19% in top tenth, 50% in top quarter, 78% in top half
Early decision deadline: N/A, notification date: N/A
Early action deadline: N/A, notification date: N/A
Application deadline (fall): rolling
Undergraduate student body: 1,045 full time, 1,687 part time; 38% male, 62% female; 1% American Indian, 4% Asian, 5% black, 14% Hispanic, 3% multiracial, 0% Pacific Islander, 66% white, 6% international; 90% from in state; 11% live on campus; 0% of students in fraternities, 0% in sororities
Most popular majors: 11% Biology/ Biological Sciences, General, 11% Business Administration and Management, General, 11% Elementary Education and Teaching, 6% Multi/ Interdisciplinary Studies, 16% Registered Nursing/Registered Nurse
Expenses: 2014-2015: $24,800; room/board: $7,060
Financial aid: (316) 942-4291

Ottawa University

Ottawa KS
(785) 242-5200
U.S. News ranking: Reg. Coll. (Mid.W), No. 62
Website: www.ottawa.edu
Admissions email: admiss@ottawa.edu
Private; founded 1865
Affiliation: American Baptist
Freshman admissions: selective; 2014-2015: 585 applied, 375 accepted. Either SAT or ACT required. ACT 25/75 percentile: 19-24. High school rank: 10% in top tenth, 32% in top quarter, 63% in top half
Early decision deadline: N/A, notification date: N/A
Early action deadline: N/A, notification date: N/A
Application deadline (fall): rolling
Undergraduate student body: 572 full time, 20 part time; 60% male, 40% female; 6% American Indian, 0% Asian, 11% black, 7% Hispanic, 0% multiracial, 0% Pacific Islander, 65% white, 0% international; 56% from in state; 71% live on campus; 0% of students in fraternities, 0% in sororities
Most popular majors: 6% Biology/ Biological Sciences, General, 15% Business Administration and Management, General, 12% Human Services, General, 17% Kinesiology and Exercise Science, 11% Speech Communication and Rhetoric
Expenses: 2015-2016: $26,204; room/board: $8,910
Financial aid: (785) 242-5200; 87% of undergrads determined to have financial need; average aid package $12,518

Pittsburg State University

Pittsburg KS
(800) 854-7488
U.S. News ranking: Reg. U. (Mid.W), No. 85
Website: www.pittstate.edu
Admissions email: psuadmit@pittstate.edu
Public; founded 1903
Freshman admissions: selective; 2014-2015: 2,758 applied, 2,184 accepted. Either SAT or ACT required. ACT 25/75 percentile: 19-24. High school rank: 13% in top tenth, 35% in top quarter, 67% in top half
Early decision deadline: N/A, notification date: N/A
Early action deadline: N/A, notification date: N/A
Application deadline (fall): rolling
Undergraduate student body: 5,586 full time, 684 part time; 52% male, 48% female; 1% American Indian, 1% Asian, 4% black, 5% Hispanic, 5% multiracial, 0% Pacific Islander, 81% white, 3% international; 73% from in state; 19% live on campus; N/A of students in fraternities, N/A in sororities
Most popular majors: 5% Accounting and Related Services, 6% Business/Commerce, General, 5% Psychology, General, 9% Registered Nursing, Nursing Administration, Nursing Research and Clinical Nursing, 7% Teacher Education and Professional Development, Specific Levels and Methods
Expenses: 2014-2015: $6,230 in state, $16,336 out of state; room/ board: $6,936
Financial aid: (620) 235-4240; 63% of undergrads determined to have financial need; average aid package $6,505

Southwestern College

Winfield KS
(620) 229-6236
U.S. News ranking: Reg. U. (Mid.W), No. 99
Website: www.sckans.edu
Admissions email: scadmit@sckans.edu
Private; founded 1885
Affiliation: United Methodist
Freshman admissions: selective; 2014-2015: 439 applied, 386 accepted. Either SAT or ACT required. ACT 25/75 percentile: 19-25. High school rank: 13% in top tenth, 36% in top quarter, 73% in top half
Early decision deadline: N/A, notification date: N/A
Early action deadline: N/A, notification date: N/A
Application deadline (fall): 8/25
Undergraduate student body: 557 full time, 766 part time; 58% male, 42% female; 2% American Indian, 1% Asian, 10% black, 8% Hispanic, 4% multiracial, 0% Pacific Islander, 62% white, 5% international; 55% from in state; 69% live on campus; N/A of students in fraternities, N/A in sororities
Most popular majors: 16% Biological and Biomedical Sciences, 23% Business, Management, Marketing, and Related Support Services, 8% Education, 18% Parks, Recreation, Leisure, and Fitness Studies, 10% Visual and Performing Arts
Expenses: 2015-2016: $25,946; room/board: $7,080
Financial aid: (620) 229-6215; 76% of undergrads determined to have financial need; average aid package $21,161

Sterling College

Sterling KS
(800) 346-1017
U.S. News ranking: Reg. Coll. (Mid.W), No. 60
Website: www.sterling.edu
Admissions email: admissions@sterling.edu
Private; founded 1887
Affiliation: Presbyterian
Freshman admissions: selective; 2014-2015: 1,497 applied, 644 accepted. Either SAT or ACT required. ACT 25/75 percentile: 18-24. High school rank: 16% in top tenth, 18% in top quarter, 68% in top half
Early decision deadline: N/A, notification date: N/A
Early action deadline: N/A, notification date: N/A
Application deadline (fall): rolling
Undergraduate student body: 595 full time, 76 part time; 54% male, 46% female; 3% American Indian, N/A Asian, 11% black, 11% Hispanic, N/A multiracial, 2% Pacific Islander, 67% white, 0% international; 48% from in state; 77% live on campus; 0% of students in fraternities, 0% in sororities
Most popular majors: 8% Health Professions and Related Programs, 20% Kinesiology and Exercise Science, 18% Marketing/ Marketing Management, General, 8% Philosophy and Religious Studies, 17% Teacher Education and Professional Development, Specific Levels and Methods
Expenses: 2015-2016: $23,350; room/board: $7,060
Financial aid: (620) 278-4207; 88% of undergrads determined to have financial need; average aid package $21,618

Tabor College

Hillsboro KS
(620) 947-3121
U.S. News ranking: Reg. Coll. (Mid.W), No. 41
Website: www.tabor.edu
Admissions email: admissions@tabor.edu
Private; founded 1908
Affiliation: Mennonite Brethren
Freshman admissions: selective; 2014-2015: 482 applied, 413 accepted. Either SAT or ACT required. ACT 25/75 percentile: 20-25. High school rank: 20% in top tenth, 23% in top quarter, 69% in top half
Early decision deadline: N/A, notification date: N/A
Early action deadline: N/A, notification date: N/A
Application deadline (fall): rolling
Undergraduate student body: 736 full time, 0 part time; 50% male, 50% female; 0% American Indian, 1% Asian, 9% black, 12% Hispanic, 3% multiracial, 0% Pacific Islander, 68% white, 2% international; 51% from in state; 86% live on campus; N/A of students in fraternities, N/A in sororities
Most popular majors: 5% Business Administration and Management, General, 7% Elementary Education and Teaching, 8% Psychology, General, 21% Registered Nursing, Nursing Administration, Nursing Research and Clinical Nursing, Other, 6% Social Work, Other
Expenses: 2015-2016: $25,280; room/board: $8,880
Financial aid: (620) 947-3121; 82% of undergrads determined to have financial need; average aid package $20,198

University of Kansas

Lawrence KS
(785) 864-3911
U.S. News ranking: Nat. U., No. 115
Website: www.ku.edu/
Admissions email: adm@ku.edu
Public; founded 1865
Freshman admissions: more selective; 2014-2015: 15,767 applied, 14,414 accepted. Either SAT or ACT required. ACT 25/75 percentile: 22-28. High school rank: 26% in top tenth, 56% in top quarter, 87% in top half
Early decision deadline: N/A, notification date: N/A
Early action deadline: N/A, notification date: N/A
Application deadline (fall): rolling
Undergraduate student body: 17,335 full time, 2,008 part time; 50% male, 50% female; 0% American Indian, 4% Asian, 5% black, 7% Hispanic, 5% multiracial, 0% Pacific Islander, 73% white, 5% international; 76% from in state; 25% live on campus; 18% of students in fraternities, 21% in sororities
Most popular majors: 15% Business, Management, Marketing, and Related Support Services, 10% Communication, Journalism, and Related Programs, 8% Engineering, 12% Health Professions and Related Programs, 7% Social Sciences
Expenses: 2014-2015: $10,448 in state, $25,731 out of state; room/board: $7,896
Financial aid: (785) 864-4700; 48% of undergrads determined to have financial need; average aid package $9,267

University of St. Mary

Leavenworth KS
(913) 758-6118
U.S. News ranking: Reg. U. (Mid.W), second tier
Website: www.stmary.edu
Admissions email: admiss@stmary.edu
Private; founded 1923
Affiliation: Roman Catholic
Freshman admissions: selective; 2014-2015: 737 applied, 350 accepted. Either SAT or ACT required. ACT 25/75 percentile: 19-24. High school rank: N/A
Early decision deadline: N/A, notification date: N/A
Early action deadline: N/A, notification date: N/A
Application deadline (fall): rolling
Undergraduate student body: 593 full time, 324 part time; 36% male, 64% female; 1% American Indian, 1% Asian, 10% black, 11% Hispanic, 3% multiracial, 1% Pacific Islander, 60% white, 1% international
Most popular majors: Information not available
Expenses: 2015-2016: $25,620; room/board: $7,750
Financial aid: (800) 752-7043; 71% of undergrads determined to have financial need; average aid package $24,485

Washburn University

Topeka KS
(785) 670-1030
U.S. News ranking: Reg. U. (Mid.W), No. 92
Website: www.washburn.edu
Admissions email: admissions@washburn.edu
Public; founded 1865
Freshman admissions: selective; 2014-2015: 1,416 applied, 1,390 accepted. ACT required. ACT 25/75 percentile: 19-25. High school rank: 13% in top tenth, 35% in top quarter, 67% in top half
Early decision deadline: N/A, notification date: N/A
Early action deadline: N/A, notification date: N/A
Application deadline (fall): 8/1
Undergraduate student body: 3,903 full time, 1,998 part time; 41% male, 59% female; N/A American Indian, N/A Asian, N/A black, N/A Hispanic, N/A multiracial, N/A Pacific Islander, N/A white, N/A international; 91% from in state; 16% live on campus; 6% of students in fraternities, 8% in sororities
Most popular majors: 14% Business, Management, Marketing, and Related Support Services, 5% Communication, Journalism, and Related Programs, 7% Education, 30% Health Professions and Related Programs, 8% Homeland Security, Law Enforcement, Firefighting and Related Protective Services
Expenses: 2014-2015: $6,038 in state, $13,526 out of state; room/ board: $6,541
Financial aid: (785) 670-1151; 64% of undergrads determined to have financial need; average aid package $9,613

Wichita State University

Wichita KS
(316) 978-3085
U.S. News ranking: Nat. U., second tier
Website: www.wichita.edu
Admissions email: admissions@wichita.edu
Public; founded 1895
Freshman admissions: selective; 2014-2015: 4,517 applied, 4,315 accepted. Neither SAT nor ACT required. ACT 25/75 percentile: 21-26. High school rank: 21% in top tenth, 48% in top quarter, 80% in top half
Early decision deadline: N/A, notification date: N/A
Early action deadline: N/A, notification date: N/A
Application deadline (fall): rolling
Undergraduate student body: 8,909 full time, 3,070 part time; 48% male, 52% female; 1% American Indian, 7% Asian, 6% black, 10% Hispanic, 3% multiracial, 0% Pacific Islander, 63% white, 6% international; 94% from in state; 9% live on campus; 3% of students in fraternities, 4% in sororities
Most popular majors: 17% Business, Management, Marketing, and Related Support Services, 9% Education, 11% Engineering, 17% Health Professions and Related Programs, 6% Homeland Security, Law Enforcement, Firefighting and Related Protective Services
Expenses: 2014-2015: $7,267 in state, $16,697 out of state; room/board: $8,373
Financial aid: (316) 978-3430; 54% of undergrads determined to have financial need; average aid package $7,582

KENTUCKY

Alice Lloyd College

Pippa Passes KY
(888) 280-4252
U.S. News ranking: Reg. Coll. (S), No. 30
Website: www.alc.edu
Admissions email: admissions@alc.edu
Private; founded 1923
Freshman admissions: selective; 2014-2015: 4,120 applied, 293 accepted. Either SAT or ACT required. ACT 25/75 percentile: 19-24. High school rank: 19% in top tenth, 47% in top quarter, 83% in top half
Early decision deadline: N/A, notification date: N/A
Early action deadline: N/A, notification date: N/A
Application deadline (fall): 7/1
Undergraduate student body: 589 full time, 30 part time; 46% male, 54% female; 0% American Indian, 0% Asian, 0% black, 0% Hispanic, 0% multiracial, 0% Pacific Islander, 97% white, 0% international; 80% from in state; 85% live on campus; 0% of students in fraternities, 0% in sororities
Most popular majors: 32% Biological and Biomedical Sciences, 16% Business, Management, Marketing, and Related Support Services, 20% Education, 9% Parks, Recreation, Leisure, and Fitness Studies, 9% Social Sciences
Expenses: 2015-2016: $11,460; room/board: $5,940
Financial aid: (606) 368-6059; 91% of undergrads determined to have financial need; average aid package $12,998

Asbury University

Wilmore KY
(800) 888-1818
U.S. News ranking: Reg. Coll. (S), No. 3
Website: www.asbury.edu
Admissions email: admissions@asbury.edu
Private; founded 1890
Affiliation: non-denominational
Freshman admissions: more selective; 2014-2015: 1,328 applied, 913 accepted. Either SAT or ACT required. ACT 25/75 percentile: 22-28. High school rank: 24% in top tenth, 54% in top quarter, 80% in top half
Early decision deadline: N/A, notification date: N/A
Early action deadline: N/A, notification date: N/A
Application deadline (fall): rolling
Undergraduate student body: 1,326 full time, 296 part time; 41% male, 59% female; 0% American Indian, 1% Asian, 4% black, 2% Hispanic, 6% multiracial, 0% Pacific Islander, 80% white, 2% international; 52% from in state; 85% live on campus; N/A of students in fraternities, N/A in sororities
Most popular majors: 6% Business/Commerce, General, 12% Elementary Education and Teaching, 5% Equestrian/Equine Studies, 5% Psychology, General, 13% Radio, Television, and Digital Communication, Other
Expenses: 2014-2015: $26,868; room/board: $6,132
Financial aid: (800) 888-1818

Bellarmine University

Louisville KY
(502) 272-8131
U.S. News ranking: Reg. U. (S), No. 13
Website: www.bellarmine.edu
Admissions email: admissions@bellarmine.edu
Private; founded 1950
Affiliation: Roman Catholic
Freshman admissions: more selective; 2014-2015: 5,631 applied, 4,696 accepted. Either SAT or ACT required. ACT 25/75 percentile: 22-27. High school rank: 21% in top tenth, 53% in top quarter, 87% in top half
Early decision deadline: N/A, notification date: N/A
Early action deadline: 11/1, notification date: 11/15
Application deadline (fall): 8/15
Undergraduate student body: 2,383 full time, 202 part time; 36% male, 64% female; 0% American Indian, 2% Asian, 4% black, 3% Hispanic, 3% multiracial, 0% Pacific Islander, 84% white, 1% international; 68% from in state; 43% live on campus; 1% of students in fraternities, 1% in sororities
Most popular majors: 5% Biological and Biomedical Sciences, 12% Business, Management, Marketing, and Related Support Services, 35% Health Professions and Related Programs, 6% Parks, Recreation, Leisure, and Fitness Studies, 9% Psychology
Expenses: 2015-2016: $37,650; room/board: $10,990
Financial aid: (502) 452-8124; 77% of undergrads determined to have financial need; average aid package $28,838

Berea College

Berea KY
(859) 985-3500
U.S. News ranking: Nat. Lib. Arts, No. 67
Website: www.berea.edu
Admissions email: admissions@berea.edu
Private; founded 1855
Freshman admissions: more selective; 2014-2015: 1,648 applied, 555 accepted. Either SAT or ACT required. ACT 25/75 percentile: 22-27. High school rank: 24% in top tenth, 69% in top quarter, 95% in top half
Early decision deadline: N/A, notification date: N/A
Early action deadline: N/A, notification date: N/A
Application deadline (fall): 4/30
Undergraduate student body: 1,578 full time, 43 part time; 44% male, 56% female; 0% American Indian, 2% Asian, 15% black, 6% Hispanic, 6% multiracial, 0% Pacific Islander, 63% white, 8% international; 47% from in state; 82% live on campus; N/A of students in fraternities, N/A in sororities
Most popular majors: 9% Biological and Biomedical Sciences, 8% Education, 8% Family and Consumer Sciences/Human Sciences, 7% Social Sciences, 9% Visual and Performing Arts
Expenses: 2015-2016: $870; room/board: $6,410
Financial aid: (859) 985-3310; 100% of undergrads determined to have financial need; average aid package $30,448

Brescia University

Owensboro KY
(270) 686-4241
U.S. News ranking: Reg. Coll. (S), No. 50
Website: www.brescia.edu
Admissions email: admissions@brescia.edu
Private; founded 1950
Affiliation: Roman Catholic
Freshman admissions: selective; 2014-2015: 3,748 applied, 1,851 accepted. Either SAT or ACT required. ACT 25/75 percentile: 20-25. High school rank: N/A
Early decision deadline: N/A, notification date: N/A
Early action deadline: N/A, notification date: N/A
Application deadline (fall): rolling
Undergraduate student body: 762 full time, 272 part time; 26% male, 74% female; 1% American Indian, 0% Asian, 12% black, 5% Hispanic, 0% multiracial, 0% Pacific Islander, 71% white, 1% international; 47% from in state; 40% live on campus; 0% of students in fraternities, 0% in sororities
Most popular majors: 13% Audiology/Audiologist and Speech-Language Pathology/Pathologist, 11% Business/Commerce, General, 4% Liberal Arts and Sciences/Liberal Studies, 13% Psychology, General, 34% Social Work
Expenses: 2014-2015: $19,990; room/board: $9,500
Financial aid: (270) 686-4253

Campbellsville University[1]

Campbellsville KY
(270) 789-5220
U.S. News ranking: Reg. U. (S), No. 84
Website: www.campbellsville.edu
Admissions email: admissions@campbellsville.edu
Private; founded 1906
Affiliation: Baptist
Application deadline (fall): 8/1
Undergraduate student body: N/A full time, N/A part time
Expenses: 2014-2015: $22,842; room/board: $7,550
Financial aid: (270) 789-5013; 86% of undergrads determined to have financial need; average aid package $18,904

Centre College

Danville KY
(859) 238-5350
U.S. News ranking: Nat. Lib. Arts, No. 45
Website: www.centre.edu
Admissions email: admission@centre.edu
Private; founded 1819
Freshman admissions: more selective; 2014-2015: 2,494 applied, 1,785 accepted. Either SAT or ACT required. ACT 25/75 percentile: 26-31. High school rank: 53% in top tenth, 79% in top quarter, 96% in top half
Early decision deadline: 12/1, notification date: 12/31
Early action deadline: 12/1, notification date: 1/15
Application deadline (fall): 1/15
Undergraduate student body: 1,386 full time, 1 part time; 48% male, 52% female; 0% American Indian, 3% Asian, 5% black, 2% Hispanic, 3% multiracial, 0% Pacific Islander, 80% white, 6% international; 56% from in state; 98% live on campus; 40% of students in fraternities, 41% in sororities
Most popular majors: 14% Economics, Other, 9% English Language and Literature, General, 7% History, General, 7% International/Global Studies, 8% Political Science and Government, General
Expenses: 2015-2016: $38,200; room/board: $9,620
Financial aid: (859) 238-5365; 58% of undergrads determined to have financial need; average aid package $28,761

Eastern Kentucky University

Richmond KY
(800) 465-9191
U.S. News ranking: Reg. U. (S), No. 76
Website: www.eku.edu
Admissions email: admissions@eku.edu
Public; founded 1906
Freshman admissions: selective; 2014-2015: 9,776 applied, 7,222 accepted. Either SAT or ACT required. ACT 25/75 percentile: 19-24. High school rank: 13% in top tenth, 34% in top quarter, 66% in top half
Early decision deadline: N/A, notification date: N/A
Early action deadline: N/A, notification date: N/A
Application deadline (fall): 8/1
Undergraduate student body: 11,178 full time, 2,800 part time; 44% male, 56% female; 0% American Indian, 1% Asian, 6% black, 2% Hispanic, 2% multiracial, 0% Pacific Islander, 85% white, 2% international; 87% from in state; 25% live on campus; 18% of students in fraternities, 27% in sororities
Most popular majors: 15% Aeronautics/Aviation/Aerospace Science and Technology, General, 24% Aerospace, Aeronautical and Astronautical/Space Engineering, 7% Air Traffic Controller, 16% Airline/Commercial/Professional Pilot and Flight Crew, 6% Homeland Security
Expenses: 2015-2016: $8,150 in state, $17,640 out of state; room/board: $8,158
Financial aid: (859) 622-2361; 73% of undergrads determined to have financial need; average aid package $10,970

Georgetown College

Georgetown KY
(502) 863-8009
U.S. News ranking: Nat. Lib. Arts, No. 154
Website: www.georgetowncollege.edu
Admissions email: admissions@georgetowncollege.edu
Private; founded 1829
Affiliation: Baptist
Freshman admissions: selective; 2014-2015: 2,089 applied, 1,854 accepted. Either SAT or ACT required. ACT 25/75 percentile: 21-27. High school rank: 26% in top tenth, 49% in top quarter, 82% in top half
Early decision deadline: N/A, notification date: N/A
Early action deadline: N/A, notification date: N/A
Application deadline (fall): 8/15
Undergraduate student body: 952 full time, 27 part time; 46% male, 54% female; 0% American Indian, 1% Asian, 9% black, 4% Hispanic, 3% multiracial, 0% Pacific Islander, 79% white, 2% international; 74% from in state; 91% live on campus; 25% of students in fraternities, 28% in sororities
Most popular majors: 10% Biology/Biological Sciences, General, 9% Business/Commerce, General, 13% Communication and Media Studies, Other, 9% Elementary Education and Teaching, 15% Psychology, General
Expenses: 2015-2016: $34,280; room/board: $8,710
Financial aid: (502) 863-8027; 85% of undergrads determined to have financial need; average aid package $36,430

Kentucky Christian University

Grayson KY
(800) 522-3181
U.S. News ranking: Reg. Coll. (S), No. 58
Website: www.kcu.edu
Admissions email: knights@kcu.edu
Private; founded 1919

Affiliation: Christian Church/Church of Christ
Freshman admissions: selective; 2014-2015: 886 applied, 423 accepted. Either SAT or ACT required. ACT 25/75 percentile: 18-23. High school rank: 15% in top tenth, 33% in top quarter, 64% in top half
Early decision deadline: N/A, notification date: N/A
Early action deadline: N/A, notification date: N/A
Application deadline (fall): 8/1
Undergraduate student body: 497 full time, 105 part time; 51% male, 49% female; 0% American Indian, 1% Asian, 10% black, 1% Hispanic, 1% multiracial, 0% Pacific Islander, 68% white, 2% international; 49% from in state; 68% live on campus; 0% of students in fraternities, 0% in sororities
Most popular majors: 10% Elementary Education and Teaching, 18% Multi/Interdisciplinary Studies, Other, 21% Registered Nursing/Registered Nurse, 21% Social Work, 9% Theological and Ministerial Studies, Other
Expenses: 2015-2016: $17,810; room/board: $7,800
Financial aid: (606) 474-3226; 89% of undergrads determined to have financial need; average aid package $15,407

Kentucky State University

Frankfort KY
(800) 325-1716
U.S. News ranking: Nat. Lib. Arts, second tier
Website: www.kysu.edu
Admissions email: admissions@kysu.edu
Public; founded 1886
Freshman admissions: less selective; 2014-2015: 6,540 applied, 3,119 accepted. Either SAT or ACT required. ACT 25/75 percentile: 16-21. High school rank: 9% in top tenth, 24% in top quarter, 55% in top half
Early decision deadline: N/A, notification date: N/A
Early action deadline: N/A, notification date: N/A
Application deadline (fall): 4/1
Undergraduate student body: 1,397 full time, 357 part time; 39% male, 61% female; 0% American Indian, 0% Asian, 58% black, 2% Hispanic, 2% multiracial, 0% Pacific Islander, 25% white, 0% international; 58% from in state; 34% live on campus; 2% of students in fraternities, 4% in sororities
Most popular majors: 6% Business/Commerce, General, 8% Criminal Justice/Safety Studies, 10% Liberal Arts and Sciences/Liberal Studies, 11% Psychology, General, 20% Registered Nursing/Registered Nurse
Expenses: 2014-2015: $7,404 in state, $17,214 out of state; room/board: $6,690
Financial aid: (502) 597-5960; 89% of undergrads determined to have financial need; average aid package $12,182

Kentucky Wesleyan College

Owensboro KY
(800) 999-0592
U.S. News ranking: Reg. Coll. (S), No. 27
Website: www.kwc.edu/page.php?page=354
Admissions email: rsmith@kwc.edu
Private; founded 1858
Affiliation: United Methodist
Freshman admissions: selective; 2014-2015: N/A applied, N/A accepted. Either SAT or ACT required. ACT 25/75 percentile: 19-25. High school rank: 13% in top tenth, 39% in top quarter, 69% in top half
Early decision deadline: N/A, notification date: N/A
Early action deadline: N/A, notification date: N/A
Application deadline (fall): rolling
Undergraduate student body: 662 full time, 47 part time; 54% male, 46% female; N/A American Indian, N/A Asian, N/A black, N/A Hispanic, N/A multiracial, N/A Pacific Islander, N/A white, N/A international
Most popular majors: Information not available
Expenses: 2015-2016: $23,120; room/board: $8,150
Financial aid: (270) 926-3111; 86% of undergrads determined to have financial need; average aid package $20,508

Lindsey Wilson College

Columbia KY
(270) 384-8100
U.S. News ranking: Reg. U. (S), second tier
Website: www.lindsey.edu
Admissions email: admissions@lindsey.edu
Private; founded 1903
Affiliation: United Methodist
Freshman admissions: selective; 2014-2015: 2,997 applied, 2,183 accepted. Neither SAT nor ACT required. ACT 25/75 percentile: 19-24. High school rank: 12% in top tenth, 34% in top quarter, 68% in top half
Early decision deadline: N/A, notification date: N/A
Early action deadline: N/A, notification date: N/A
Application deadline (fall): rolling
Undergraduate student body: 2,079 full time, 126 part time; 42% male, 58% female; 0% American Indian, 1% Asian, 10% black, 1% Hispanic, 1% multiracial, 0% Pacific Islander, 68% white, N/A international; 80% from in state; 50% live on campus; N/A of students in fraternities, N/A in sororities
Most popular majors: 9% Business Administration and Management, General, 6% Criminal Justice/Safety Studies, 52% Human Services, General, 4% Registered Nursing/Registered Nurse, 5% Speech Communication and Rhetoric
Expenses: 2015-2016: $23,162; room/board: $8,900
Financial aid: (270) 384-8022; 94% of undergrads determined to have financial need; average aid package $18,865

Midway College[1]

Midway KY
(800) 755-0031
U.S. News ranking: Reg. Coll. (S), No. 54
Website: www.midway.edu
Admissions email: admissions@midway.edu
Private
Application deadline (fall): N/A
Undergraduate student body: N/A full time, N/A part time
Expenses: 2014-2015: $22,300; room/board: $8,000
Financial aid: (859) 846-5745

Morehead State University

Morehead KY
(606) 783-2000
U.S. News ranking: Reg. U. (S), No. 61
Website: www.moreheadstate.edu
Admissions email: admissions@moreheadstate.edu
Public; founded 1887
Freshman admissions: selective; 2014-2015: 5,236 applied, 4,421 accepted. Either SAT or ACT required. ACT 25/75 percentile: 19-25. High school rank: 17% in top tenth, 42% in top quarter, 76% in top half
Early decision deadline: N/A, notification date: N/A
Early action deadline: N/A, notification date: N/A
Application deadline (fall): rolling
Undergraduate student body: 6,258 full time, 3,694 part time; 40% male, 60% female; 0% American Indian, 0% Asian, 4% black, 1% Hispanic, 1% multiracial, 0% Pacific Islander, 90% white, 1% international; 87% from in state; 48% live on campus; 13% of students in fraternities, 10% in sororities
Most popular majors: 6% Elementary Education and Teaching, 13% General Studies, 7% Registered Nursing/Registered Nurse, 6% Social Work, 4% Special Education and Teaching, General
Expenses: 2015-2016: $8,098 in state, $20,246 out of state; room/board: $8,420
Financial aid: (606) 783-2011; 78% of undergrads determined to have financial need; average aid package $10,961

Murray State University

Murray KY
(270) 809-3741
U.S. News ranking: Reg. U. (S), No. 28
Website: www.murraystate.edu
Admissions email: msu.admissions@murraystate.edu
Public; founded 1922
Freshman admissions: selective; 2014-2015: 4,760 applied, 3,806 accepted. Either SAT or ACT required. ACT 25/75 percentile: 20-26. High school rank: 18% in top tenth, 43% in top quarter, 77% in top half
Early decision deadline: N/A, notification date: N/A
Early action deadline: N/A, notification date: N/A
Application deadline (fall): 8/15
Undergraduate student body: 7,370 full time, 2,074 part time; 44% male, 56% female; 0% American Indian, 1% Asian, 8% black, 2% Hispanic, 2% multiracial, 0% Pacific Islander, 82% white, 4% international; 69% from in state; 33% live on campus; 14% of students in fraternities, 16% in sororities
Most popular majors: 6% Business/Commerce, General, 5% Elementary Education and Teaching, 9% General Studies, 7% Registered Nursing/Registered Nurse, 7% Veterinary/Animal Health Technology/Technician and Veterinary Assistant
Expenses: 2015-2016: $7,608 in state, $20,712 out of state; room/board: $8,206
Financial aid: (270) 809-2546; 61% of undergrads determined to have financial need; average aid package $10,461

Northern Kentucky University

Highland Heights KY
(800) 637-9948
U.S. News ranking: Reg. U. (S), No. 80
Website: www.nku.edu
Admissions email: admitnku@nku.edu
Public; founded 1968
Freshman admissions: selective; 2014-2015: 6,957 applied, 6,489 accepted. Either SAT or ACT required. ACT 25/75 percentile: 20-25. High school rank: 11% in top tenth, 32% in top quarter, 66% in top half
Early decision deadline: N/A, notification date: N/A
Early action deadline: N/A, notification date: N/A
Application deadline (fall): 8/18
Undergraduate student body: 9,433 full time, 3,376 part time; 45% male, 55% female; 0% American Indian, 1% Asian, 7% black, 3% Hispanic, 2% multiracial, 0% Pacific Islander, 82% white, 3% international; 69% from in state; 16% live on campus; 7% of students in fraternities, 10% in sororities
Most popular majors: 4% Accounting, 5% Elementary Education and Teaching, 3% Health Services/Allied Health/Health Sciences, General, 8% Organizational Behavior Studies, 4% Speech Communication and Rhetoric
Expenses: 2015-2016: $9,120 in state, $17,856 out of state; room/board: $8,768
Financial aid: (859) 572-5143; 65% of undergrads determined to have financial need; average aid package $10,528

Spalding University[1]

Louisville KY
(502) 585-7111
U.S. News ranking: Nat. U., second tier
Website: www.spalding.edu
Admissions email: admissions@spalding.edu
Private; founded 1814
Affiliation: Roman Catholic
Application deadline (fall): rolling
Undergraduate student body: N/A full time, N/A part time
Expenses: 2014-2015: $22,950; room/board: $8,400
Financial aid: (502) 585-9911

St. Catharine College

St. Catharine KY
(800) 599-2000
U.S. News ranking: Reg. Coll. (S), second tier
Website: www.sccky.edu
Admissions email: admissions@sccky.edu
Private; founded 1931
Affiliation: Roman Catholic
Freshman admissions: selective; 2014-2015: 614 applied, 421 accepted. Either SAT or ACT required. ACT 25/75 percentile: 18-22. High school rank: N/A
Early decision deadline: N/A, notification date: N/A
Early action deadline: N/A, notification date: N/A
Application deadline (fall): rolling
Undergraduate student body: 571 full time, 368 part time; 40% male, 60% female; 0% American Indian, 0% Asian, 11% black, 6% Hispanic, 3% multiracial, 0% Pacific Islander, 78% white, 2% international; 87% from in state; 53% live on campus; 0% of students in fraternities, 0% in sororities
Most popular majors: 4% Biology/Biological Sciences, General, 8% Business Administration and Management, General, 6% Criminal Justice/Law Enforcement Administration, 6% Psychology, General, 8% Registered Nursing/Registered Nurse
Expenses: 2014-2015: $18,926; room/board: $9,392
Financial aid: (859) 336-5082

Sullivan University[1]

Louisville KY
(502) 456-6504
U.S. News ranking: Reg. U. (S), unranked
Website: www.sullivan.edu
Admissions email: admissions@sullivan.edu
Private
Application deadline (fall): N/A
Undergraduate student body: N/A full time, N/A part time
Expenses: 2014-2015: $19,740; room/board: $9,810
Financial aid: (800) 844-1354

Thomas More College

Crestview Hills KY
(800) 825-4557
U.S. News ranking: Reg. U. (S), No. 53
Website: www.thomasmore.edu
Admissions email: admissions@thomasmore.edu
Private; founded 1921
Affiliation: Roman Catholic
Freshman admissions: selective; 2014-2015: 1,190 applied, 1,109 accepted. Either SAT or ACT required. ACT 25/75 percentile: 19-23. High school rank: 3% in top tenth, 27% in top quarter, 64% in top half
Early decision deadline: N/A, notification date: N/A
Early action deadline: N/A, notification date: N/A
Application deadline (fall): 8/1
Undergraduate student body: 1,214 full time, 283 part time; 49% male, 51% female; 0% American Indian, 1% Asian, 8% black, 2% Hispanic, 2% multiracial, 0% Pacific Islander, 74% white, 1% international; 48% from in

state; 31% live on campus; 2% of students in fraternities, 2% in sororities
Most popular majors: 8% Biological and Biomedical Sciences, 42% Business, Management, Marketing, and Related Support Services, 7% Education, 7% Health Professions and Related Programs
Expenses: 2015-2016: $28,668; room/board: $7,770
Financial aid: (859) 344-3319; 68% of undergrads determined to have financial need; average aid package $20,495

Transylvania University

Lexington KY
(859) 233-8242
U.S. News ranking: Nat. Lib. Arts, No. 82
Website: www.transy.edu
Admissions email: admissions@transy.edu
Private; founded 1780
Affiliation: Christian Church (Disciples of Christ)
Freshman admissions: more selective; 2014-2015: 1,444 applied, 1,193 accepted. Either SAT or ACT required. ACT 25/75 percentile: 25-30. High school rank: 51% in top tenth, 76% in top quarter, 94% in top half
Early decision deadline: N/A, notification date: N/A
Early action deadline: 12/1, notification date: 1/15
Application deadline (fall): 2/1
Undergraduate student body: 1,010 full time, 4 part time; 42% male, 58% female; 0% American Indian, 2% Asian, 3% black, 5% Hispanic, 3% multiracial, 0% Pacific Islander, 80% white, 4% international; 77% from in state; 75% live on campus; 44% of students in fraternities, 60% in sororities
Most popular majors: 10% Biology/Biological Sciences, General, 13% Business/Commerce, General, 10% Parks, Recreation and Leisure Studies, 10% Psychology, General, 12% Social Sciences, General
Expenses: 2015-2016: $34,370; room/board: $9,560
Financial aid: (859) 233-8239; 67% of undergrads determined to have financial need; average aid package $27,365

Union College[1]

Barbourville KY
(800) 489-8646
U.S. News ranking: Reg. U. (S), No. 83
Website: www.unionky.edu
Admissions email: enroll@unionky.edu
Private; founded 1879
Affiliation: United Methodist
Application deadline (fall): rolling
Undergraduate student body: N/A full time, N/A part time
Expenses: 2015-2016: $24,000; room/board: $7,075
Financial aid: (606) 546-1229; 89% of undergrads determined to have financial need; average aid package $21,434

University of Kentucky

Lexington KY
(859) 257-2000
U.S. News ranking: Nat. U., No. 129
Website: www.uky.edu
Admissions email: admissions@uky.edu
Public; founded 1865
Freshman admissions: more selective; 2014-2015: 20,677 applied, 14,930 accepted. Either SAT or ACT required. ACT 25/75 percentile: 22-28. High school rank: 30% in top tenth, 57% in top quarter, 85% in top half
Early decision deadline: N/A, notification date: N/A
Early action deadline: 12/1, notification date: N/A
Application deadline (fall): rolling
Undergraduate student body: 20,690 full time, 1,533 part time; 48% male, 52% female; 0% American Indian, 3% Asian, 8% black, 4% Hispanic, 3% multiracial, 0% Pacific Islander, 77% white, 3% international; 73% from in state; 29% live on campus; 18% of students in fraternities, 30% in sororities
Most popular majors: 4% Biology/Biological Sciences, General, 4% Business/Commerce, General, 4% Marketing/Marketing Management, General, 6% Psychology, General, 5% Registered Nursing/Registered Nurse
Expenses: 2015-2016: $10,936 in state, $24,268 out of state; room/board: $11,434
Financial aid: (859) 257-3172; 52% of undergrads determined to have financial need; average aid package $11,740

University of Louisville

Louisville KY
(502) 852-6531
U.S. News ranking: Nat. U., No. 168
Website: www.louisville.edu
Admissions email: admitme@louisville.edu
Public; founded 1798
Freshman admissions: selective; 2014-2015: 9,711 applied, 6,979 accepted. Either SAT or ACT required. ACT 25/75 percentile: 22-28. High school rank: 26% in top tenth, 55% in top quarter, 81% in top half
Early decision deadline: N/A, notification date: N/A
Early action deadline: N/A, notification date: N/A
Application deadline (fall): 8/25
Undergraduate student body: 12,494 full time, 3,468 part time; 49% male, 51% female; 0% American Indian, 3% Asian, 11% black, 4% Hispanic, 4% multiracial, 0% Pacific Islander, 76% white, 1% international; 85% from in state; 17% live on campus; 20% of students in fraternities, 17% in sororities
Most popular majors: 14% Business, Management, Marketing, and Related Support Services, 8% Education, 9% Engineering, 9% Health Professions and Related Programs, 11% Parks, Recreation, Leisure, and Fitness Studies
Expenses: 2015-2016: $10,738 in state, $24,626 out of state; room/board: $8,120
Financial aid: (502) 852-5511; 62% of undergrads determined to have financial need; average aid package $11,342

University of Pikeville

Pikeville KY
(606) 218-5251
U.S. News ranking: Nat. Lib. Arts, second tier
Website: www.pc.edu/
Admissions email: wewantyou@pc.edu
Private; founded 1889
Affiliation: Presbyterian Church (USA)
Freshman admissions: selective; 2014-2015: 2,278 applied, 2,278 accepted. Either SAT or ACT required. ACT 25/75 percentile: 18-23. High school rank: 14% in top tenth, 32% in top quarter, 61% in top half
Early decision deadline: N/A, notification date: N/A
Early action deadline: N/A, notification date: N/A
Application deadline (fall): 8/16
Undergraduate student body: 1,295 full time, 634 part time; 46% male, 54% female; 0% American Indian, 0% Asian, 12% black, 2% Hispanic, 0% multiracial, 0% Pacific Islander, 82% white, 3% international; 80% from in state; 60% live on campus; N/A of students in fraternities, N/A in sororities
Most popular majors: 17% Biological and Biomedical Sciences, 26% Business, Management, Marketing, and Related Support Services, 9% Homeland Security, Law Enforcement, Firefighting and Related Protective Services, 12% Psychology, 5% Social Sciences
Expenses: 2015-2016: $18,840; room/board: $7,600
Financial aid: (606) 218-5253; 99% of undergrads determined to have financial need; average aid package $20,661

University of the Cumberlands

Williamsburg KY
(800) 343-1609
U.S. News ranking: Reg. U. (S), No. 87
Website: www.ucumberlands.edu
Admissions email: admiss@ucumberlands.edu
Private; founded 1888
Affiliation: Baptist
Freshman admissions: selective; 2014-2015: 2,322 applied, 1,539 accepted. Either SAT or ACT required. ACT 25/75 percentile: 20-25. High school rank: 18% in top tenth, 39% in top quarter, 74% in top half
Early decision deadline: N/A, notification date: N/A
Early action deadline: N/A, notification date: N/A
Application deadline (fall): 8/15
Undergraduate student body: 1,697 full time, 958 part time; 45% male, 55% female; 0% American Indian, 0% Asian, 7% black, 2% Hispanic, 1% multiracial, 0% Pacific Islander, 77% white, 6% international; 68% from in state; 80% live on campus; N/A of students in fraternities, N/A in sororities
Most popular majors: 19% Business, Management, Marketing, and Related Support Services, 10% Homeland Security, Law Enforcement, Firefighting and Related Protective Services, 12% Parks, Recreation, Leisure, and Fitness Studies, 11% Psychology, 9% Public Administration and Social Service Professions
Expenses: 2015-2016: $22,000; room/board: $8,500
Financial aid: (800) 532-0828

Western Kentucky University

Bowling Green KY
(270) 745-2551
U.S. News ranking: Reg. U. (S), No. 31
Website: www.wku.edu
Admissions email: admission@wku.edu
Public; founded 1906
Freshman admissions: selective; 2014-2015: 8,462 applied, 7,897 accepted. Either SAT or ACT required. ACT 25/75 percentile: 19-26. High school rank: 25% in top tenth, 48% in top quarter, 75% in top half
Early decision deadline: N/A, notification date: N/A
Early action deadline: N/A, notification date: N/A
Application deadline (fall): 8/1
Undergraduate student body: 13,297 full time, 4,155 part time; 43% male, 57% female; 0% American Indian, 1% Asian, 10% black, 3% Hispanic, 2% multiracial, 0% Pacific Islander, 76% white, 6% international; 82% from in state; 32% live on campus; 12% of students in fraternities, 15% in sororities
Most popular majors: 14% Business, Management, Marketing, and Related Support Services, 11% Education, 11% Health Professions and Related Programs, 9% Liberal Arts and Sciences, General Studies and Humanities, 8% Social Sciences
Expenses: 2015-2016: $9,482 in state, $24,132 out of state; room/board: $7,368
Financial aid: (270) 745-2755; 64% of undergrads determined to have financial need; average aid package $13,785

LOUISIANA

Centenary College of Louisiana

Shreveport LA
(800) 234-4448
U.S. News ranking: Nat. Lib. Arts, No. 148
Website: www.centenary.edu
Admissions email: admission@centenary.edu
Private; founded 1825
Affiliation: United Methodist
Freshman admissions: more selective; 2014-2015: 769 applied, 505 accepted. Either SAT or ACT required. ACT 25/75 percentile: 21-28. High school rank: 25% in top tenth, 57% in top quarter, 87% in top half
Early decision deadline: N/A, notification date: N/A
Early action deadline: 12/15, notification date: N/A
Application deadline (fall): rolling
Undergraduate student body: 544 full time, 9 part time; 43% male, 57% female; 1% American Indian, 4% Asian, 15% black, 6% Hispanic, 4% multiracial, 0% Pacific Islander, 68% white, 2% international; 63% from in state; 66% live on campus; 29% of students in fraternities, 43% in sororities
Most popular majors: 24% Biology/Biological Sciences, General, 8% Business Administration and Management, General, 8% Mass Communication/Media Studies, 4% Music Performance, General, 14% Psychology, General
Expenses: 2015-2016: $32,960; room/board: $10,540
Financial aid: (318) 869-5137; 75% of undergrads determined to have financial need; average aid package $26,598

Dillard University

New Orleans LA
(800) 216-6637
U.S. News ranking: Nat. Lib. Arts, second tier
Website: www.dillard.edu
Admissions email: admissions@dillard.edu
Private; founded 1869
Affiliation: United Methodist
Freshman admissions: selective; 2014-2015: 6,142 applied, 2,493 accepted. Either SAT or ACT required. ACT 25/75 percentile: 17-20. High school rank: 9% in top tenth, 23% in top quarter, 55% in top half
Early decision deadline: N/A, notification date: N/A
Early action deadline: N/A, notification date: N/A
Application deadline (fall): 8/1
Undergraduate student body: 1,138 full time, 62 part time; 27% male, 73% female; N/A American Indian, N/A Asian, N/A black, N/A Hispanic, N/A multiracial, N/A Pacific Islander, N/A white, N/A international
Most popular majors: 8% Biology/Biological Sciences, General, 12% Mass Communication/Media Studies, 9% Public Health, General, 14% Registered Nursing/Registered Nurse, 12% Sociology
Expenses: 2015-2016: $16,252; room/board: $9,920
Financial aid: (504) 816-4677; 90% of undergrads determined to have financial need; average aid package $15,756

Grambling State University

Grambling LA
(318) 274-6183
U.S. News ranking: Reg. U. (S), second tier
Website: www.gram.edu/
Admissions email: admissions@gram.edu
Public
Freshman admissions: less selective; 2014-2015: 2,894 applied, 1,272 accepted. Either SAT or ACT required. ACT 25/75 percentile: 16-20. High school rank: 8% in top tenth, 28% in top quarter, 59% in top half
Early decision deadline: N/A, notification date: N/A
Early action deadline: N/A, notification date: N/A
Application deadline (fall): 8/15

Undergraduate student body: 3,264 full time, 260 part time; 40% male, 60% female; 0% American Indian, 0% Asian, 91% black, 1% Hispanic, 2% multiracial, 0% Pacific Islander, 1% white, 4% international; 73% from in state; 75% live on campus; 2% of students in fraternities, 2% in sororities
Most popular majors: 18% Business Administration and Management, General, 19% Criminal Justice/Safety Studies, 6% Education, General, 7% Psychology, General, 9% Registered Nursing/Registered Nurse
Expenses: 2015-2016: $7,063 in state, $16,282 out of state; room/board: $8,638
Financial aid: (318) 274-6056; 94% of undergrads determined to have financial need; average aid package $3,935

Louisiana College

Pineville LA
(318) 487-7259
U.S. News ranking: Reg. Coll. (S), No. 51
Website: www.lacollege.edu
Admissions email: admissions@lacollege.edu
Private; founded 1906
Affiliation: Southern Baptist
Freshman admissions: selective; 2014-2015: 809 applied, 494 accepted. Either SAT or ACT required. ACT 25/75 percentile: 18-24. High school rank: N/A
Early decision deadline: N/A, notification date: N/A
Early action deadline: 12/1, notification date: N/A
Application deadline (fall): rolling
Undergraduate student body: 931 full time, 54 part time; 52% male, 48% female; 1% American Indian, 1% Asian, 21% black, 3% Hispanic, 1% multiracial, 0% Pacific Islander, 65% white, 7% international; 90% from in state; 55% live on campus; 0% of students in fraternities, 0% in sororities
Most popular majors: 8% Biological and Biomedical Sciences, 12% Business, Management, Marketing, and Related Support Services, 23% Health Professions and Related Programs, 9% Parks, Recreation, Leisure, and Fitness Studies, 9% Visual and Performing Arts
Expenses: 2014-2015: $14,570; room/board: $5,074
Financial aid: (318) 487-7386

Louisiana State University–Alexandria

Alexandria LA
(318) 473-6417
U.S. News ranking: Nat. Lib. Arts, second tier
Website: www.lsua.edu
Admissions email: admissions@lsua.edu
Public; founded 1960
Freshman admissions: selective; 2014-2015: 1,056 applied, 576 accepted. Either SAT or ACT required. ACT 25/75 percentile: 19-23. High school rank: 14% in top tenth, 35% in top quarter, 68% in top half
Early decision deadline: N/A, notification date: N/A
Early action deadline: N/A, notification date: N/A
Application deadline (fall): 8/1
Undergraduate student body: 1,549 full time, 1,153 part time; 31% male, 69% female; 2% American Indian, 1% Asian, 17% black, 5% Hispanic, 3% multiracial, 0% Pacific Islander, 72% white, 1% international; 95% from in state; N/A live on campus; 0% of students in fraternities, 0% in sororities
Most popular majors: 16% Business Administration and Management, General, 10% Criminal Justice/Safety Studies, 10% Elementary Education and Teaching, 17% General Studies, 13% Psychology, General
Expenses: 2014-2015: $6,010 in state, $12,868 out of state; room/board: N/A
Financial aid: (318) 473-6423; 72% of undergrads determined to have financial need; average aid package $7,566

Louisiana State University–Baton Rouge

Baton Rouge LA
(225) 578-1175
U.S. News ranking: Nat. U., No. 129
Website: www.lsu.edu
Admissions email: admissions@lsu.edu
Public; founded 1860
Freshman admissions: more selective; 2014-2015: 16,580 applied, 12,706 accepted. Either SAT or ACT required. ACT 25/75 percentile: 23-28. High school rank: 25% in top tenth, 54% in top quarter, 82% in top half
Early decision deadline: N/A, notification date: N/A
Early action deadline: N/A, notification date: N/A
Application deadline (fall): 4/15
Undergraduate student body: 23,195 full time, 2,377 part time; 49% male, 51% female; 0% American Indian, 4% Asian, 11% black, 6% Hispanic, 2% multiracial, 0% Pacific Islander, 74% white, 2% international; 82% from in state; 25% live on campus; 17% of students in fraternities, 28% in sororities
Most popular majors: 8% Biological and Biomedical Sciences, 20% Business, Management, Marketing, and Related Support Services, 7% Communication, Journalism, and Related Programs, 10% Education, 12% Engineering
Expenses: 2014-2015: $8,750 in state, $26,467 out of state; room/board: $10,804
Financial aid: (225) 578-3103; 50% of undergrads determined to have financial need; average aid package $14,780

Louisiana State University–Shreveport

Shreveport LA
(318) 797-5061
U.S. News ranking: Reg. U. (S), second tier
Website: www.lsus.edu
Admissions email: admissions@pilot.lsus.edu
Public; founded 1967
Freshman admissions: selective; 2014-2015: 690 applied, 529 accepted. Either SAT or ACT required. ACT 25/75 percentile: 20-25. High school rank: N/A
Early decision deadline: N/A, notification date: N/A
Early action deadline: N/A, notification date: N/A
Application deadline (fall): rolling
Undergraduate student body: 1,967 full time, 1,253 part time; 40% male, 60% female; 1% American Indian, 2% Asian, 22% black, 4% Hispanic, 3% multiracial, 0% Pacific Islander, 59% white, 2% international; 91% from in state; 0% live on campus; 1% of students in fraternities, 1% in sororities
Most popular majors: 11% Biological and Biomedical Sciences, 25% Business, Management, Marketing, and Related Support Services, 10% Education, 11% Liberal Arts and Sciences, General Studies and Humanities, 12% Psychology
Expenses: 2014-2015: $6,168 in state, N/A out of state; room/board: $8,921
Financial aid: (318) 797-5363

Louisiana Tech University

Ruston LA
(318) 257-3036
U.S. News ranking: Nat. U., No. 199
Website: www.latech.edu
Admissions email: bulldog@latech.edu
Public; founded 1894
Freshman admissions: more selective; 2014-2015: 5,863 applied, 3,813 accepted. Either SAT or ACT required. ACT 25/75 percentile: 21-27. High school rank: 24% in top tenth, 51% in top quarter, 82% in top half
Early decision deadline: N/A, notification date: N/A
Early action deadline: N/A, notification date: N/A
Application deadline (fall): rolling
Undergraduate student body: 6,891 full time, 2,641 part time; 53% male, 47% female; 0% American Indian, 1% Asian, 14% black, 1% Hispanic, 2% multiracial, 0% Pacific Islander, 71% white, 4% international; 89% from in state; 15% live on campus; N/A of students in fraternities, N/A in sororities
Most popular majors: 5% Biological and Biomedical Sciences, 17% Business, Management, Marketing, and Related Support Services, 6% Education, 14% Engineering, 6% Health Professions and Related Programs
Expenses: 2015-2016: $8,853 in state, $25,851 out of state; room/board: $6,702
Financial aid: (318) 257-2643; 57% of undergrads determined to have financial need; average aid package $10,878

Loyola University New Orleans

New Orleans LA
(800) 456-9652
U.S. News ranking: Reg. U. (S), No. 11
Website: www.loyno.edu
Admissions email: admit@loyno.edu
Private; founded 1912
Affiliation: Roman Catholic (Jesuit)
Freshman admissions: selective; 2014-2015: 4,491 applied, 4,053 accepted. Either SAT or ACT required. ACT 25/75 percentile: 22-28. High school rank: 19% in top tenth, 39% in top quarter, 74% in top half
Early decision deadline: N/A, notification date: N/A
Early action deadline: N/A, notification date: N/A
Application deadline (fall): rolling
Undergraduate student body: 2,618 full time, 178 part time; 41% male, 59% female; 1% American Indian, 4% Asian, 16% black, 16% Hispanic, 4% multiracial, 0% Pacific Islander, 51% white, 3% international; 43% from in state; 46% live on campus; 3% of students in fraternities, 7% in sororities
Most popular majors: 5% Biology/Biological Sciences, General, 6% Marketing/Marketing Management, General, 9% Music Management, 13% Psychology, General, 10% Speech Communication and Rhetoric
Expenses: 2015-2016: $37,580; room/board: $12,808
Financial aid: (504) 865-3231; 69% of undergrads determined to have financial need; average aid package $29,614

McNeese State University

Lake Charles LA
(337) 475-5356
U.S. News ranking: Reg. U. (S), No. 87
Website: www.mcneese.edu
Admissions email: admissions@mcneese.edu
Public; founded 1939
Freshman admissions: selective; 2014-2015: 2,734 applied, 2,058 accepted. Either SAT or ACT required. ACT 25/75 percentile: 20-24. High school rank: 21% in top tenth, 44% in top quarter, 76% in top half
Early decision deadline: N/A, notification date: N/A
Early action deadline: N/A, notification date: N/A
Application deadline (fall): 8/17
Undergraduate student body: 5,831 full time, 1,600 part time; 39% male, 61% female; 1% American Indian, 2% Asian, 19% black, 3% Hispanic, 2% multiracial, 0% Pacific Islander, 70% white, 4% international; 92% from in state; 10% live on campus; N/A of students in fraternities, N/A in sororities
Most popular majors: 6% Criminal Justice/Safety Studies, 5% Engineering, General, 14% General Studies, 5% Kinesiology and Exercise Science, 14% Registered Nursing/Registered Nurse
Expenses: 2014-2015: $6,334 in state, $17,404 out of state; room/board: $7,464
Financial aid: (337) 475-5065

Nicholls State University

Thibodaux LA
(985) 448-4507
U.S. News ranking: Reg. U. (S), No. 87
Website: www.nicholls.edu
Admissions email: nicholls@nicholls.edu
Public; founded 1948
Freshman admissions: selective; 2014-2015: 2,424 applied, 2,142 accepted. Either SAT or ACT required. ACT 25/75 percentile: 20-24. High school rank: 16% in top tenth, 42% in top quarter, 74% in top half
Early decision deadline: N/A, notification date: N/A
Early action deadline: N/A, notification date: N/A
Application deadline (fall): rolling
Undergraduate student body: 4,769 full time, 926 part time; 38% male, 62% female; 2% American Indian, 1% Asian, 20% black, 3% Hispanic, 3% multiracial, 0% Pacific Islander, 67% white, 2% international; 95% from in state; 18% live on campus; 8% of students in fraternities, 8% in sororities
Most popular majors: 24% Business, Management, Marketing, and Related Support Services, 11% Education, 17% Health Professions and Related Programs, 14% Liberal Arts and Sciences, General Studies and Humanities, 5% Personal and Culinary Services
Expenses: 2014-2015: $7,234 in state, $17,481 out of state; room/board: $8,580
Financial aid: (985) 448-4048; 64% of undergrads determined to have financial need; average aid package $8,948

Northwestern State University of Louisiana[1]

Natchitoches LA
(800) 426-3754
U.S. News ranking: Reg. U. (S), second tier
Website: www.nsula.edu
Admissions email: admissions@nsula.edu
Public; founded 1884
Application deadline (fall): 7/6
Undergraduate student body: N/A full time, N/A part time
Expenses: 2014-2015: $6,807 in state, $17,595 out of state; room/board: $6,846
Financial aid: (318) 357-5961

Our Lady of Holy Cross College[1]

New Orleans LA
(504) 398-2175
U.S. News ranking: Reg. U. (S), second tier
Website: www.olhcc.edu
Admissions email: admissions@olhcc.edu
Private
Application deadline (fall): N/A
Undergraduate student body: N/A full time, N/A part time
Expenses: 2014-2015: $12,620; room/board: N/A
Financial aid: (504) 398-2165

Southeastern Louisiana University

Hammond LA
(985) 549-5637
U.S. News ranking: Reg. U. (S), second tier
Website: www.selu.edu
Admissions email: admissions@selu.edu
Public; founded 1925

More at usnews.com/college

Freshman admissions: selective; 2014-2015: 3,725 applied, 3,229 accepted. Either SAT or ACT required. ACT 25/75 percentile: 20-24. High school rank: 11% in top tenth, 31% in top quarter, 66% in top half
Early decision deadline: N/A, notification date: N/A
Early action deadline: N/A, notification date: N/A
Application deadline (fall): 8/1
Undergraduate student body: 9,732 full time, 3,644 part time; 39% male, 61% female; 0% American Indian, 1% Asian, 16% black, 7% Hispanic, 6% multiracial, 0% Pacific Islander, 67% white, 2% international; 96% from in state; 21% live on campus; 9% of students in fraternities, 8% in sororities
Most popular majors: 23% Business, Management, Marketing, and Related Support Services, 11% Education, 13% Health Professions and Related Programs, 5% Homeland Security, Law Enforcement, Firefighting and Related Protective Services, 12% Liberal Arts and Sciences, General Studies and Humanities
Expenses: 2014-2015: $6,547 in state, $19,111 out of state; room/board: N/A
Financial aid: (985) 549-2244

Southern University and A&M College

Baton Rouge LA
(225) 771-2430
U.S. News ranking: Reg. U. (S), second tier
Website: www.subr.edu/
Admissions email: admit@subr.edu
Public; founded 1880
Freshman admissions: less selective; 2014-2015: N/A applied, N/A accepted. Either SAT or ACT required. ACT 25/75 percentile: 17-20. High school rank: 3% in top tenth, 11% in top quarter, 34% in top half
Early decision deadline: N/A, notification date: N/A
Early action deadline: N/A, notification date: N/A
Application deadline (fall): 7/1
Undergraduate student body: 4,446 full time, 768 part time; 36% male, 64% female; 0% American Indian, 0% Asian, 93% black, 1% Hispanic, 1% multiracial, 0% Pacific Islander, 3% white, 0% international; 88% from in state; N/A live on campus; N/A of students in fraternities, N/A in sororities
Most popular majors: 13% Business, Management, Marketing, and Related Support Services, 7% Engineering, 21% Health Professions and Related Programs, 8% Homeland Security, Law Enforcement, Firefighting and Related Protective Services, 6% Psychology
Expenses: 2014-2015: $6,630 in state, $8,274 out of state; room/board: $8,003
Financial aid: (225) 771-2790

Southern University–New Orleans[1]

New Orleans LA
(504) 286-5314
U.S. News ranking: Reg. U. (S), second tier
Website: www.suno.edu
Admissions email: N/A
Public
Application deadline (fall): N/A
Undergraduate student body: N/A full time, N/A part time
Expenses: 2014-2015: $5,218 in state, $6,517 out of state; room/board: $7,080
Financial aid: (504) 286-5263

Tulane University

New Orleans LA
(504) 865-5731
U.S. News ranking: Nat. U., No. 41
Website: www.tulane.edu
Admissions email: undergrad.admission@tulane.edu
Private; founded 1834
Freshman admissions: most selective; 2014-2015: 28,901 applied, 8,078 accepted. Either SAT or ACT required. ACT 25/75 percentile: 29-32. High school rank: 56% in top tenth, 84% in top quarter, 97% in top half
Early decision deadline: N/A, notification date: N/A
Early action deadline: 11/15, notification date: 12/15
Application deadline (fall): 1/15
Undergraduate student body: 6,606 full time, 1,747 part time; 42% male, 58% female; 0% American Indian, 3% Asian, 9% black, 6% Hispanic, 3% multiracial, 0% Pacific Islander, 72% white, 3% international; 26% from in state; 44% live on campus; 30% of students in fraternities, 50% in sororities
Most popular majors: 10% Biological and Biomedical Sciences, 23% Business, Management, Marketing, and Related Support Services, 7% Health Professions and Related Programs, 6% Psychology, 16% Social Sciences
Expenses: 2015-2016: $49,638; room/board: $13,758
Financial aid: (504) 865-5723; 36% of undergrads determined to have financial need; average aid package $40,884

University of Louisiana–Lafayette

Lafayette LA
(337) 482-6553
U.S. News ranking: Nat. U., second tier
Website: www.louisiana.edu
Admissions email: enroll@louisiana.edu
Public; founded 1898
Freshman admissions: selective; 2014-2015: 9,386 applied, 5,237 accepted. Either SAT or ACT required. ACT 25/75 percentile: 21-25. High school rank: 19% in top tenth, 43% in top quarter, 74% in top half
Early decision deadline: N/A, notification date: N/A
Early action deadline: N/A, notification date: N/A
Application deadline (fall): rolling
Undergraduate student body: 12,498 full time, 3,076 part time; 44% male, 56% female; 0% American Indian, 2% Asian, 21% black, 3% Hispanic, 2% multiracial, 0% Pacific Islander, 68% white, 2% international; 92% from in state; 18% live on campus; 10% of students in fraternities, 10% in sororities
Most popular majors: 17% Business, Management, Marketing, and Related Support Services, 14% Education, 7% Engineering, 12% Health Professions and Related Programs, 13% Liberal Arts and Sciences, General Studies and Humanities
Expenses: 2014-2015: $6,948 in state, $19,348 out of state; room/board: $8,566
Financial aid: (337) 482-6506; 57% of undergrads determined to have financial need; average aid package $8,757

University of Louisiana–Monroe

Monroe LA
(318) 342-5430
U.S. News ranking: Reg. U. (S), No. 93
Website: www.ulm.edu
Admissions email: admissions@ulm.edu
Public; founded 1931
Freshman admissions: selective; 2014-2015: 3,863 applied, 2,983 accepted. Either SAT or ACT required. ACT 25/75 percentile: 19-25. High school rank: 28% in top tenth, 56% in top quarter, 84% in top half
Early decision deadline: N/A, notification date: N/A
Early action deadline: N/A, notification date: N/A
Application deadline (fall): rolling
Undergraduate student body: 4,916 full time, 2,299 part time; 36% male, 64% female; 0% American Indian, 2% Asian, 26% black, 2% Hispanic, 2% multiracial, 0% Pacific Islander, 63% white, 3% international; 91% from in state; 28% live on campus; 11% of students in fraternities, 8% in sororities
Most popular majors: 7% Business Administration and Management, General, 9% General Studies, 7% Kinesiology and Exercise Science, 8% Psychology, General, 9% Registered Nursing/Registered Nurse
Expenses: 2014-2015: $6,963 in state, $19,121 out of state; room/board: $6,830
Financial aid: (318) 342-5320

University of New Orleans

New Orleans LA
(504) 280-6595
U.S. News ranking: Nat. U., second tier
Website: www.uno.edu
Admissions email: unopec@uno.edu
Public; founded 1956
Freshman admissions: selective; 2014-2015: 3,828 applied, 1,674 accepted. Either SAT or ACT required. ACT 25/75 percentile: 21-25. High school rank: 16% in top tenth, 39% in top quarter, 67% in top half
Early decision deadline: N/A, notification date: N/A
Early action deadline: N/A, notification date: N/A
Application deadline (fall): 7/25
Undergraduate student body: 5,280 full time, 1,872 part time; 49% male, 51% female; 0% American Indian, 8% Asian, 16% black, 10% Hispanic, 4% multiracial, 0% Pacific Islander, 55% white, 4% international; 95% from in state; 10% live on campus; 2% of students in fraternities, 2% in sororities
Most popular majors: 8% Biological and Biomedical Sciences, 31% Business, Management, Marketing, and Related Support Services, 10% Engineering, 11% Multi/Interdisciplinary Studies, 9% Visual and Performing Arts
Expenses: 2014-2015: $7,482 in state, $21,092 out of state; room/board: $9,274
Financial aid: (504) 280-6603; 74% of undergrads determined to have financial need; average aid package $9,389

Xavier University of Louisiana

New Orleans LA
(504) 520-7388
U.S. News ranking: Nat. Lib. Arts, second tier
Website: www.xula.edu
Admissions email: apply@xula.edu
Private; founded 1915
Affiliation: Roman Catholic
Freshman admissions: selective; 2014-2015: 3,963 applied, 2,615 accepted. Either SAT or ACT required. ACT 25/75 percentile: 20-25. High school rank: 36% in top tenth, 58% in top quarter, 83% in top half
Early decision deadline: N/A, notification date: N/A
Early action deadline: N/A, notification date: N/A
Application deadline (fall): 7/1
Undergraduate student body: 2,238 full time, 121 part time; 27% male, 73% female; 0% American Indian, 10% Asian, 77% black, 3% Hispanic, 3% multiracial, 0% Pacific Islander, 4% white, 2% international; 51% from in state; 47% live on campus; 1% of students in fraternities, 3% in sororities
Most popular majors: 29% Biological and Biomedical Sciences, 11% Business, Management, Marketing, and Related Support Services, 24% Physical Sciences, 12% Psychology, 5% Social Sciences
Expenses: 2015-2016: $22,349; room/board: $8,200
Financial aid: (504) 520-7517; 84% of undergrads determined to have financial need; average aid package $22,224

MAINE

Bates College

Lewiston ME
(855) 228-3755
U.S. News ranking: Nat. Lib. Arts, No. 25
Website: www.bates.edu
Admissions email: admission@bates.edu
Private; founded 1855
Freshman admissions: most selective; 2014-2015: 5,044 applied, 1,282 accepted. Neither SAT nor ACT required. SAT 25/75 percentile: 1280-1430. High school rank: 69% in top tenth, 95% in top quarter, 100% in top half
Early decision deadline: 11/15, notification date: 12/20
Early action deadline: N/A, notification date: N/A
Application deadline (fall): 1/1
Undergraduate student body: 1,773 full time, 0 part time; 50% male, 50% female; 0% American Indian, 5% Asian, 5% black, 7% Hispanic, 4% multiracial, 0% Pacific Islander, 72% white, 7% international; 11% from in state; 91% live on campus; N/A of students in fraternities, N/A in sororities
Most popular majors: 12% Biological and Biomedical Sciences, 7% English Language and Literature/Letters, 7% Natural Resources and Conservation, 10% Psychology, 26% Social Sciences
Expenses: 2015-2016: $48,435; room/board: $14,105
Financial aid: (207) 786-6096; 44% of undergrads determined to have financial need; average aid package $42,718

Bowdoin College

Brunswick ME
(207) 725-3100
U.S. News ranking: Nat. Lib. Arts, No. 4
Website: www.bowdoin.edu
Admissions email: admissions@bowdoin.edu
Private; founded 1794
Freshman admissions: most selective; 2014-2015: 6,935 applied, 1,034 accepted. Neither SAT nor ACT required. SAT 25/75 percentile: 1370-1520. High school rank: 86% in top tenth, 97% in top quarter, 100% in top half
Early decision deadline: 11/15, notification date: 12/15
Early action deadline: N/A, notification date: N/A
Application deadline (fall): 1/1
Undergraduate student body: 1,802 full time, 3 part time; 50% male, 50% female; 0% American Indian, 6% Asian, 5% black, 13% Hispanic, 7% multiracial, 0% Pacific Islander, 64% white, 5% international; 11% from in state; 92% live on campus; N/A of students in fraternities, N/A in sororities
Most popular majors: 8% Biology/Biological Sciences, General, 12% Economics, General, 7% History, General, 9% Mathematics, General, 16% Political Science and Government, General
Expenses: 2015-2016: $48,212; room/board: $13,142
Financial aid: (207) 725-3273; 45% of undergrads determined to have financial need; average aid package $40,549

Colby College

Waterville ME
(800) 723-3032
U.S. News ranking: Nat. Lib. Arts, No. 19
Website: www.colby.edu
Admissions email: admissions@colby.edu
Private; founded 1813
Freshman admissions: more selective; 2014-2015: 5,148 applied, 1,444 accepted. Neither SAT nor ACT required. SAT 25/75 percentile: 1230-1430. High school rank: 61% in top tenth, 86% in top quarter, 96% in top half
Early decision deadline: 11/15, notification date: 12/15
Early action deadline: N/A, notification date: N/A
Application deadline (fall): 1/1

Undergraduate student body: 1,847 full time, 0 part time; 47% male, 53% female; 0% American Indian, 6% Asian, 3% black, 6% Hispanic, 5% multiracial, 0% Pacific Islander, 60% white, 11% international; 14% from in state; 95% live on campus; 0% of students in fraternities, 0% in sororities
Most popular majors: 11% Biological and Biomedical Sciences, 7% English Language and Literature/Letters, 11% Multi/ Interdisciplinary Studies, 7% Physical Sciences, 23% Social Sciences
Expenses: 2015-2016: $49,120; room/board: $12,610
Financial aid: (800) 723-3032; 39% of undergrads determined to have financial need; average aid package $42,858

College of the Atlantic
Bar Harbor ME
(800) 528-0025
U.S. News ranking: Nat. Lib. Arts, No. 82
Website: www.coa.edu/
Admissions email: inquiry@coa.edu
Private; founded 1969
Freshman admissions: more selective; 2014-2015: 429 applied, 305 accepted. Neither SAT nor ACT required. SAT 25/75 percentile: 1100-1340. High school rank: 55% in top tenth, 79% in top quarter, 100% in top half
Early decision deadline: 12/1, notification date: 12/15
Early action deadline: N/A, notification date: N/A
Application deadline (fall): 2/15
Undergraduate student body: 364 full time, 14 part time; 30% male, 70% female; 1% American Indian, 2% Asian, 1% black, 6% Hispanic, 1% multiracial, 0% Pacific Islander, 70% white, 16% international; 21% from in state; 37% live on campus; 0% of students in fraternities, 0% in sororities
Most popular majors: Information not available
Expenses: 2015-2016: $42,084; room/board: $9,432
Financial aid: (800) 528-0025; 89% of undergrads determined to have financial need; average aid package $35,649

Husson University
Bangor ME
(207) 941-7100
U.S. News ranking: Reg. U. (N), second tier
Website: www.husson.edu
Admissions email: admit@husson.edu
Private; founded 1898
Freshman admissions: less selective; 2014-2015: 2,130 applied, 1,527 accepted. Either SAT or ACT required. SAT 25/75 percentile: 860-1050. High school rank: 15% in top tenth, 45% in top quarter, 73% in top half
Early decision deadline: N/A, notification date: N/A
Early action deadline: N/A, notification date: N/A
Application deadline (fall): 8/15
Undergraduate student body: 2,230 full time, 474 part time; 46% male, 54% female; 0% American Indian, 1% Asian, 3% black, 1% Hispanic, 1% multiracial, 0% Pacific Islander, 90% white, 2% international; 82% from in state; 39% live on campus; 3% of students in fraternities, 6% in sororities
Most popular majors: 35% Business, Management, Marketing, and Related Support Services, 4% Education, 24% Health Professions and Related Programs, 13% Homeland Security, Law Enforcement, Firefighting and Related Protective Services, 15% Psychology
Expenses: 2015-2016: $16,060; room/board: $8,922
Financial aid: (207) 941-7156; 81% of undergrads determined to have financial need; average aid package $12,711

Maine College of Art
Portland ME
(800) 699-1509
U.S. News ranking: Arts, unranked
Website: www.meca.edu
Admissions email: admissions@meca.edu
Private; founded 1882
Freshman admissions: N/A; 2014-2015: 484 applied, 407 accepted. Neither SAT nor ACT required. SAT 25/75 percentile: 920-1210. High school rank: N/A
Early decision deadline: N/A, notification date: N/A
Early action deadline: 12/1, notification date: 12/24
Application deadline (fall): rolling
Undergraduate student body: 410 full time, 17 part time; 27% male, 73% female; 0% American Indian, 2% Asian, 1% black, 6% Hispanic, 5% multiracial, 0% Pacific Islander, 82% white, 1% international
Most popular majors: 11% Crafts/ Craft Design, Folk Art and Artisanry, 19% Graphic Design, 10% Illustration, 12% Painting, 10% Photography
Expenses: 2015-2016: $32,240; room/board: $10,872
Financial aid: (207) 775-3052; 81% of undergrads determined to have financial need; average aid package $20,089

Maine Maritime Academy
Castine ME
(207) 326-2206
U.S. News ranking: Reg. Coll. (N), No. 7
Website: www.mainemaritime.edu
Admissions email: admissions@mma.edu
Public; founded 1941
Freshman admissions: selective; 2014-2015: 796 applied, 512 accepted. Either SAT or ACT required. SAT 25/75 percentile: 920-1130. High school rank: 9% in top tenth, 35% in top quarter, 70% in top half
Early decision deadline: N/A, notification date: N/A
Early action deadline: 12/31, notification date: 2/15
Application deadline (fall): 3/31
Undergraduate student body: 1,018 full time, 13 part time; 87% male, 13% female; 0% American Indian, 1% Asian, 1% black, 1% Hispanic, 0% multiracial, 0% Pacific Islander, 95% white, N/A international
Most popular majors: 8% Biological and Biomedical Sciences, Other, 34% Engineering Technologies and Engineering-Related Fields, Other, 7% International Business/ Trade/Commerce, 29% Marine Science/Merchant Marine Officer, 21% Naval Architecture and Marine Engineering
Expenses: 2015-2016: $17,668 in state, $25,372 out of state; room/board: $9,830
Financial aid: (207) 326-2339; 76% of undergrads determined to have financial need; average aid package $4,342

St. Joseph's College[1]
Standish ME
(207) 893-7746
U.S. News ranking: Reg. U. (N), second tier
Website: www.sjcme.edu
Admissions email: admission@sjcme.edu
Private
Application deadline (fall): N/A
Undergraduate student body: N/A full time, N/A part time
Expenses: 2014-2015: $31,920; room/board: $11,900
Financial aid: (800) 752-1266

Thomas College
Waterville ME
(800) 339-7001
U.S. News ranking: Reg. Coll. (N), No. 44
Website: www.thomas.edu
Admissions email: admiss@thomas.edu
Private; founded 1894
Freshman admissions: less selective; 2014-2015: 1,134 applied, 840 accepted. Neither SAT nor ACT required. SAT 25/75 percentile: 805-1050. High school rank: 23% in top tenth, 40% in top quarter, 66% in top half
Early decision deadline: N/A, notification date: N/A
Early action deadline: N/A, notification date: N/A
Application deadline (fall): rolling
Undergraduate student body: 779 full time, 441 part time; 47% male, 53% female; 0% American Indian, 0% Asian, 3% black, 2% Hispanic, 10% multiracial, 0% Pacific Islander, 75% white, 3% international; 79% from in state; 64% live on campus; 1% of students in fraternities, 0% in sororities
Most popular majors: 13% Accounting, 14% Business Administration and Management, General, 17% Criminal Justice/ Safety Studies, 10% Psychology, General, 13% Sport and Fitness Administration/Management
Expenses: 2015-2016: $24,300; room/board: $10,430
Financial aid: (207) 859-1112; 86% of undergrads determined to have financial need; average aid package $20,385

Unity College
Unity ME
(207) 948-3131
U.S. News ranking: Reg. Coll. (N), No. 28
Website: www.unity.edu
Admissions email: admissions@unity.edu
Private; founded 1965
Freshman admissions: selective; 2014-2015: 638 applied, 594 accepted. Neither SAT nor ACT required. SAT 25/75 percentile: 900-1127. High school rank: 14% in top tenth, 33% in top quarter, 67% in top half
Early decision deadline: N/A, notification date: N/A
Early action deadline: 12/15, notification date: 12/31
Application deadline (fall): 6/15
Undergraduate student body: 583 full time, 18 part time; 48% male, 52% female; 2% American Indian, 0% Asian, 1% black, 2% Hispanic, 4% multiracial, 0% Pacific Islander, 90% white, 0% international; 27% from in state; 72% live on campus; 0% of students in fraternities, 0% in sororities
Most popular majors: 20% Natural Resources Law Enforcement and Protective Services, 8% Wildlife Biology, 33% Wildlife, Fish and Wildlands Science and Management
Expenses: 2015-2016: $26,300; room/board: $9,800
Financial aid: (207) 948-3131; 87% of undergrads determined to have financial need; average aid package $19,914

University of Maine
Orono ME
(877) 486-2364
U.S. News ranking: Nat. U., No. 168
Website: www.umaine.edu
Admissions email: um-admit@maine.edu
Public; founded 1865
Freshman admissions: selective; 2014-2015: 11,552 applied, 9,539 accepted. Either SAT or ACT required. SAT 25/75 percentile: 960-1190. High school rank: 20% in top tenth, 46% in top quarter, 81% in top half
Early decision deadline: N/A, notification date: N/A
Early action deadline: 12/15, notification date: 1/31
Application deadline (fall): rolling
Undergraduate student body: 8,129 full time, 1,210 part time; 52% male, 48% female; 1% American Indian, 1% Asian, 2% black, 2% Hispanic, 3% multiracial, 0% Pacific Islander, 82% white, 2% international; 76% from in state; 38% live on campus; N/A of students in fraternities, N/A in sororities
Most popular majors: 13% Business, Management, Marketing, and Related Support Services, 10% Education, 11% Engineering, 7% Psychology, 9% Social Sciences
Expenses: 2015-2016: $10,610 in state, $28,880 out of state; room/board: $9,576
Financial aid: (207) 581-1324; 72% of undergrads determined to have financial need; average aid package $16,083

University of Maine–Augusta
Augusta ME
(207) 621-3465
U.S. News ranking: Reg. Coll. (N), second tier
Website: www.uma.edu
Admissions email: umaadm@maine.edu
Public; founded 1965
Freshman admissions: least selective; 2014-2015: 856 applied, 830 accepted. Neither SAT nor ACT required. SAT 25/75 percentile: 770-970. High school rank: 3% in top tenth, 14% in top quarter, 35% in top half
Early decision deadline: N/A, notification date: N/A
Early action deadline: N/A, notification date: N/A
Application deadline (fall): 9/1
Undergraduate student body: 1,641 full time, 3,023 part time; 28% male, 72% female; 2% American Indian, 0% Asian, 1% black, 2% Hispanic, 2% multiracial, 0% Pacific Islander, 86% white, 0% international; 97% from in state; 0% live on campus; 0% of students in fraternities, 0% in sororities
Most popular majors: 10% Business, Management, Marketing, and Related Support Services, 31% Health Professions and Related Programs, 5% Homeland Security, Law Enforcement, Firefighting and Related Protective Services, 26% Liberal Arts and Sciences, General Studies and Humanities, 8% Library Science
Expenses: 2015-2016: $7,448 in state, $16,688 out of state; room/ board: N/A
Financial aid: (207) 621-3163; 87% of undergrads determined to have financial need; average aid package $9,172

University of Maine–Farmington
Farmington ME
(207) 778-7050
U.S. News ranking: Reg. Coll. (N), No. 19
Website: www.farmington.edu
Admissions email: umfadmit@maine.edu
Public; founded 1864
Freshman admissions: less selective; 2014-2015: 1,463 applied, 1,237 accepted. Neither SAT nor ACT required. SAT 25/75 percentile: 870-1100. High school rank: 10% in top tenth, 37% in top quarter, 75% in top half
Early decision deadline: N/A, notification date: N/A
Early action deadline: 11/15, notification date: 12/15
Application deadline (fall): rolling
Undergraduate student body: 1,658 full time, 115 part time; 35% male, 65% female; 1% American Indian, 1% Asian, 2% black, 1% Hispanic, 2% multiracial, 0% Pacific Islander, 86% white, 0% international; 84% from in state; 50% live on campus; N/A of students in fraternities, N/A in sororities
Most popular majors: 7% Business, Management, Marketing, and Related Support Services, 35% Education, 9% English Language and Literature/Letters, 12% Health Professions and Related Programs, 9% Psychology
Expenses: 2015-2016: $9,217 in state, $18,305 out of state; room/ board: $8,970
Financial aid: (207) 778-7100; 81% of undergrads determined to have financial need; average aid package $13,999

More at usnews.com/college

University of Maine–Fort Kent

Fort Kent ME
(207) 834-7600
U.S. News ranking: Reg. Coll. (N), No. 38
Website: www.umfk.maine.edu
Admissions email: umfkadm@maine.edu
Public; founded 1878
Freshman admissions: least selective; 2014-2015: 231 applied, 207 accepted. Neither SAT nor ACT required. SAT 25/75 percentile: 810-990. High school rank: 5% in top tenth, 18% in top quarter, 60% in top half
Early decision deadline: N/A, notification date: N/A
Early action deadline: N/A, notification date: N/A
Application deadline (fall): rolling
Undergraduate student body: 578 full time, 749 part time; 32% male, 68% female; 1% American Indian, 1% Asian, 3% black, 2% Hispanic, 2% multiracial, 0% Pacific Islander, 74% white, 12% international; 90% from in state; 23% live on campus; 1% of students in fraternities, 2% in sororities
Most popular majors: 9% Business, Management, Marketing, and Related Support Services, 5% Education, 62% Health Professions and Related Programs, 9% Public Administration and Social Service Professions, 8% Social Sciences
Expenses: 2015-2016: $7,575 in state, $10,875 out of state; room/board: $7,910
Financial aid: (888) 879-8635; 77% of undergrads determined to have financial need; average aid package $11,455

University of Maine–Machias

Machias ME
(888) 468-6866
U.S. News ranking: Nat. Lib. Arts, second tier
Website: www.umm.maine.edu
Admissions email: ummadmissions@maine.edu
Public; founded 1909
Freshman admissions: less selective; 2014-2015: 363 applied, 317 accepted. Either SAT or ACT required. SAT 25/75 percentile: 780-1030. High school rank: N/A
Early decision deadline: N/A, notification date: N/A
Early action deadline: 12/15, notification date: N/A
Application deadline (fall): 8/15
Undergraduate student body: 434 full time, 376 part time; 32% male, 68% female; 3% American Indian, 1% Asian, 4% black, 4% Hispanic, 2% multiracial, 0% Pacific Islander, 78% white, 2% international; 81% from in state; 37% live on campus; 14% of students in fraternities, 8% in sororities
Most popular majors: 16% Biology/Biological Sciences, General, 25% Community Psychology, 16% Entrepreneurial and Small Business Operations, 12% General Studies, 11% Parks, Recreation and Leisure Studies
Expenses: 2014-2015: $7,490 in state, $19,370 out of state; room/board: $8,178
Financial aid: (207) 255-1203

University of Maine–Presque Isle

Presque Isle ME
(207) 768-9532
U.S. News ranking: Reg. Coll. (N), No. 40
Website: www.umpi.edu
Admissions email: admissions@umpi.edu
Public; founded 1903
Freshman admissions: less selective; 2014-2015: 580 applied, 480 accepted. Neither SAT nor ACT required. SAT 25/75 percentile: 793-1062. High school rank: 7% in top tenth, 19% in top quarter, 46% in top half
Early decision deadline: N/A, notification date: N/A
Early action deadline: N/A, notification date: N/A
Application deadline (fall): rolling
Undergraduate student body: 659 full time, 479 part time; 36% male, 64% female; 3% American Indian, 0% Asian, 1% black, 1% Hispanic, 3% multiracial, 0% Pacific Islander, 80% white, 8% international; 96% from in state; 22% live on campus; 1% of students in fraternities, 1% in sororities
Most popular majors: 17% Business, Management, Marketing, and Related Support Services, 10% Education, 17% Liberal Arts and Sciences, General Studies and Humanities, 8% Psychology, 6% Public Administration and Social Service Professions
Expenses: 2015-2016: $7,436 in state, $10,736 out of state; room/board: $8,044
Financial aid: (207) 768-9511; 77% of undergrads determined to have financial need; average aid package $11,575

University of New England

Biddeford ME
(207) 283-0171
U.S. News ranking: Reg. U. (N), No. 83
Website: www.une.edu
Admissions email: admissions@une.edu
Private; founded 1831
Freshman admissions: selective; 2014-2015: 4,317 applied, 3,699 accepted. Either SAT or ACT required. SAT 25/75 percentile: 970-1170. High school rank: N/A
Early decision deadline: N/A, notification date: N/A
Early action deadline: 12/1, notification date: 12/31
Application deadline (fall): 2/15
Undergraduate student body: 2,202 full time, 547 part time; 29% male, 71% female; 0% American Indian, 3% Asian, 1% black, 0% Hispanic, 1% multiracial, 0% Pacific Islander, 74% white, 1% international; 33% from in state; 63% live on campus; N/A of students in fraternities, N/A in sororities
Most popular majors: 30% Biological and Biomedical Sciences, 3% Business, Management, Marketing, and Related Support Services, 35% Health Professions and Related Programs, 12% Parks, Recreation, Leisure, and Fitness Studies, 6% Psychology
Expenses: 2015-2016: $34,760; room/board: $12,920
Financial aid: (207) 602-2342

University of Southern Maine

Portland ME
(207) 780-5670
U.S. News ranking: Reg. U. (N), second tier
Website: www.usm.maine.edu
Admissions email: usmadm@usm.maine.edu
Public; founded 1878
Freshman admissions: less selective; 2014-2015: 3,781 applied, 3,174 accepted. Either SAT or ACT required. SAT 25/75 percentile: 880-1110. High school rank: 7% in top tenth, 30% in top quarter, 67% in top half
Early decision deadline: N/A, notification date: N/A
Early action deadline: N/A, notification date: N/A
Application deadline (fall): rolling
Undergraduate student body: 3,985 full time, 2,643 part time; 43% male, 57% female; 1% American Indian, 2% Asian, 3% black, 2% Hispanic, 3% multiracial, 0% Pacific Islander, 81% white, 1% international; 92% from in state; 18% live on campus; N/A of students in fraternities, N/A in sororities
Most popular majors: 18% Business, Management, Marketing, and Related Support Services, 8% Communication, Journalism, and Related Programs, 18% Health Professions and Related Programs, 5% Liberal Arts and Sciences, General Studies and Humanities, 13% Social Sciences
Expenses: 2015-2016: $8,920 in state, $21,280 out of state; room/board: $9,150
Financial aid: (207) 780-5250; 76% of undergrads determined to have financial need; average aid package $13,146

MARYLAND

Bowie State University

Bowie MD
(301) 860-3415
U.S. News ranking: Nat. U., second tier
Website: www.bowiestate.edu
Admissions email: ugradadmissions@bowiestate.edu
Public; founded 1865
Freshman admissions: less selective; 2014-2015: 3,033 applied, 1,626 accepted. Either SAT or ACT required. SAT 25/75 percentile: 881-960. High school rank: N/A
Early decision deadline: N/A, notification date: N/A
Early action deadline: N/A, notification date: N/A
Application deadline (fall): rolling
Undergraduate student body: 3,675 full time, 781 part time; 38% male, 62% female; 0% American Indian, 1% Asian, 87% black, 3% Hispanic, 3% multiracial, 0% Pacific Islander, 3% white, 1% international; 91% from in state; 45% live on campus; 25% of students in fraternities, 20% in sororities
Most popular majors: Information not available
Expenses: 2015-2016: $7,657 in state, $18,140 out of state; room/board: $10,850
Financial aid: (301) 860-3540

Capitol Technology University[1]

Laurel MD
(800) 950-1992
U.S. News ranking: Engineering, unranked
Website: captechu.edu/
Admissions email: N/A
Private
Application deadline (fall): N/A
Undergraduate student body: N/A full time, N/A part time
Expenses: 2014-2015: $22,896; room/board: $6,964
Financial aid: (301) 369-2800

Coppin State University

Baltimore MD
(410) 951-3600
U.S. News ranking: Reg. U. (N), second tier
Website: www.coppin.edu
Admissions email: admissions@coppin.edu
Public
Freshman admissions: less selective; 2014-2015: 4,388 applied, 1,842 accepted. Either SAT or ACT required. SAT 25/75 percentile: 810-960. High school rank: N/A
Early decision deadline: N/A, notification date: N/A
Early action deadline: N/A, notification date: N/A
Application deadline (fall): rolling
Undergraduate student body: 2,046 full time, 638 part time; 28% male, 72% female; 0% American Indian, 0% Asian, 85% black, 1% Hispanic, 2% multiracial, 0% Pacific Islander, 2% white, 6% international; 93% from in state; 22% live on campus; 1% of students in fraternities, 1% in sororities
Most popular majors: 10% Criminal Justice/Safety Studies, 8% Health Information/Medical Records Administration/Administrator, 12% Psychology, General, 28% Registered Nursing/Registered Nurse, 9% Social Work
Expenses: 2014-2015: $6,624 in state, $11,885 out of state; room/board: $9,336
Financial aid: (410) 951-3636

Frostburg State University

Frostburg MD
(301) 687-4201
U.S. News ranking: Reg. U. (N), No. 125
Website: www.frostburg.edu
Admissions email: fsuadmissions@frostburg.edu
Public; founded 1898
Freshman admissions: selective; 2014-2015: 4,252 applied, 2,488 accepted. Either SAT or ACT required. SAT 25/75 percentile: 870-1080. High school rank: 11% in top tenth, 30% in top quarter, 64% in top half
Early decision deadline: 12/15, notification date: N/A
Early action deadline: N/A, notification date: N/A
Application deadline (fall): rolling
Undergraduate student body: 4,228 full time, 687 part time; 49% male, 51% female; 0% American Indian, 2% Asian, 30% black, 5% Hispanic, 4% multiracial, 0% Pacific Islander, 57% white, 1% international; 93% from in state; 33% live on campus; N/A of students in fraternities, N/A in sororities
Most popular majors: 11% Business Administration and Management, General, 6% Criminal Justice/Safety Studies, 5% Early Childhood Education and Teaching, 9% Liberal Arts and Sciences/Liberal Studies, 9% Psychology, General
Expenses: 2015-2016: $8,488 in state, $20,588 out of state; room/board: $9,878
Financial aid: (301) 687-4301; 57% of undergrads determined to have financial need; average aid package $9,335

Goucher College

Baltimore MD
(410) 337-6100
U.S. News ranking: Nat. Lib. Arts, No. 112
Website: www.goucher.edu
Admissions email: admissions@goucher.edu
Private; founded 1885
Freshman admissions: selective; 2014-2015: 3,340 applied, 2,528 accepted. Neither SAT nor ACT required. SAT 25/75 percentile: 1020-1280. High school rank: 27% in top tenth, 53% in top quarter, 81% in top half
Early decision deadline: 11/15, notification date: 12/15
Early action deadline: 12/1, notification date: 2/1
Application deadline (fall): rolling
Undergraduate student body: 1,447 full time, 24 part time; 33% male, 67% female; 0% American Indian, 3% Asian, 10% black, 8% Hispanic, 4% multiracial, 0% Pacific Islander, 67% white, 2% international; 27% from in state; 81% live on campus; 0% of students in fraternities, 0% in sororities
Most popular majors: 8% Business, Management, Marketing, and Related Support Services, 9% Communication, Journalism, and Related Programs, 12% Psychology, 17% Social Sciences, 14% Visual and Performing Arts
Expenses: 2015-2016: $42,180; room/board: $11,942
Financial aid: (410) 337-6141; 66% of undergrads determined to have financial need; average aid package $31,019

Hood College

Frederick MD
(800) 922-1599
U.S. News ranking: Reg. U. (N), No. 29
Website: www.hood.edu
Admissions email: admission@hood.edu
Private; founded 1893
Affiliation: United Church of Christ
Freshman admissions: selective; 2014-2015: 1,590 applied, 1,283 accepted. Neither SAT nor ACT required. SAT 25/75 percentile: 920-1140. High school rank: 14% in top tenth, 32% in top quarter, 70% in top half

Early decision deadline: N/A, notification date: N/A
Early action deadline: N/A, notification date: N/A
Application deadline (fall): rolling
Undergraduate student body: 1,264 full time, 95 part time; 37% male, 63% female; 0% American Indian, 4% Asian, 13% black, 8% Hispanic, 4% multiracial, 0% Pacific Islander, 65% white, 2% international; 76% from in state; 56% live on campus; 0% of students in fraternities, 0% in sororities
Most popular majors: 10% Biological and Biomedical Sciences, 13% Business, Management, Marketing, and Related Support Services, 10% Education, 7% Psychology, 8% Social Sciences
Expenses: 2015-2016: $35,150; room/board: $11,840
Financial aid: (301) 696-3411; 83% of undergrads determined to have financial need; average aid package $26,070

Johns Hopkins University

Baltimore MD
(410) 516-8171
U.S. News ranking: Nat. U., No. 10
Website: www.jhu.edu
Admissions email: gotojhu@jhu.edu
Private; founded 1876
Freshman admissions: most selective; 2014-2015: 23,877 applied, 3,587 accepted. Either SAT or ACT required. SAT 25/75 percentile: 1360-1530. High school rank: 88% in top tenth, 98% in top quarter, 100% in top half
Early decision deadline: 11/1, notification date: 12/15
Early action deadline: N/A, notification date: N/A
Application deadline (fall): 1/1
Undergraduate student body: 6,161 full time, 308 part time; 47% male, 53% female; 0% American Indian, 20% Asian, 5% black, 12% Hispanic, 5% multiracial, 0% Pacific Islander, 46% white, 10% international; 12% from in state; 52% live on campus; 23% of students in fraternities, 25% in sororities
Most popular majors: 7% Bioengineering and Biomedical Engineering, 4% Cell/Cellular and Molecular Biology, 6% International Relations and Affairs, 6% Neuroscience, 6% Public Health, General
Expenses: 2015-2016: $48,710; room/board: $14,540
Financial aid: (410) 516-8028; 47% of undergrads determined to have financial need; average aid package $37,632

Loyola University Maryland

Baltimore MD
(410) 617-5012
U.S. News ranking: Reg. U. (N), No. 3
Website: www.loyola.edu
Admissions email: admissions@loyola.edu
Private; founded 1852
Affiliation: Roman Catholic
Freshman admissions: more selective; 2014-2015: 13,863 applied, 8,266 accepted. Neither SAT nor ACT required. SAT 25/75 percentile: 1100-1270. High school rank: 27% in top tenth, 65% in top quarter, 87% in top half
Early decision deadline: N/A, notification date: N/A
Early action deadline: 11/1, notification date: 1/15
Application deadline (fall): 1/15
Undergraduate student body: 4,035 full time, 49 part time; 42% male, 58% female; 0% American Indian, 3% Asian, 5% black, 9% Hispanic, 2% multiracial, 0% Pacific Islander, 79% white, 0% international; 17% from in state; 82% live on campus; 0% of students in fraternities, 0% in sororities
Most popular majors: 33% Business/Commerce, General, 9% Psychology, General, 9% Social Sciences, General, 11% Speech Communication and Rhetoric, 7% Speech-Language Pathology/Pathologist
Expenses: 2015-2016: $45,365; room/board: $13,310
Financial aid: (410) 617-2576; 59% of undergrads determined to have financial need; average aid package $28,440

Maryland Institute College of Art

Baltimore MD
(410) 225-2222
U.S. News ranking: Arts, unranked
Website: www.mica.edu
Admissions email: admissions@mica.edu
Private; founded 1826
Freshman admissions: N/A; 2014-2015: 3,067 applied, 1,661 accepted. Either SAT or ACT required. SAT 25/75 percentile: 1030-1300. High school rank: N/A
Early decision deadline: 11/15, notification date: 12/15
Early action deadline: N/A, notification date: N/A
Application deadline (fall): 2/1
Undergraduate student body: 1,817 full time, 29 part time; 28% male, 72% female; 0% American Indian, 13% Asian, 6% black, 4% Hispanic, 8% multiracial, 0% Pacific Islander, 52% white, 12% international
Most popular majors: 17% Graphic Design, 17% Illustration, 12% Intermedia/Multimedia, 14% Painting, 8% Sculpture
Expenses: 2015-2016: $43,870; room/board: $12,030
Financial aid: (410) 225-2285

McDaniel College

Westminster MD
(800) 638-5005
U.S. News ranking: Nat. Lib. Arts, No. 134
Website: www.mcdaniel.edu
Admissions email: admissions@mcdaniel.edu
Private; founded 1867
Freshman admissions: selective; 2014-2015: 2,966 applied, 2,258 accepted. Either SAT or ACT required. SAT 25/75 percentile: 980-1200. High school rank: 26% in top tenth, 50% in top quarter, 85% in top half
Early decision deadline: N/A, notification date: N/A
Early action deadline: 12/1, notification date: 12/21
Application deadline (fall): 6/1
Undergraduate student body: 1,665 full time, 41 part time; 47% male, 53% female; 0% American Indian, 3% Asian, 12% black, 6% Hispanic, 3% multiracial, 0% Pacific Islander, 73% white, 1% international; 36% from in state; 78% live on campus; 19% of students in fraternities, 21% in sororities
Most popular majors: 11% Business, Management, Marketing, and Related Support Services, 8% Parks, Recreation, Leisure, and Fitness Studies, 12% Psychology, 14% Social Sciences, 9% Visual and Performing Arts
Expenses: 2015-2016: $39,900; room/board: $10,300
Financial aid: (410) 857-2233; 75% of undergrads determined to have financial need; average aid package $33,346

Morgan State University

Baltimore MD
(800) 332-6674
U.S. News ranking: Nat. U., second tier
Website: www.morgan.edu
Admissions email: admissions@morgan.edu
Public; founded 1867
Freshman admissions: least selective; 2014-2015: 4,808 applied, 3,137 accepted. Neither SAT nor ACT required. SAT 25/75 percentile: 800-960. High school rank: 4% in top tenth, 9% in top quarter, 41% in top half
Early decision deadline: N/A, notification date: N/A
Early action deadline: 11/15, notification date: 2/15
Application deadline (fall): rolling
Undergraduate student body: 5,544 full time, 758 part time; 45% male, 55% female; 0% American Indian, 1% Asian, 81% black, 3% Hispanic, 3% multiracial, 0% Pacific Islander, 2% white, 9% international; 78% from in state; 44% live on campus; N/A of students in fraternities, N/A in sororities
Most popular majors: 22% Business, Management, Marketing, and Related Support Services, 8% Computer and Information Sciences and Support Services, 8% Engineering, 10% Health Professions and Related Programs, 8% Public Administration and Social Service Professions
Expenses: 2014-2015: $7,378 in state, $16,862 out of state; room/board: $9,492
Financial aid: (443) 885-3170; 82% of undergrads determined to have financial need; average aid package $21,418

Mount St. Mary's University

Emmitsburg MD
(800) 448-4347
U.S. News ranking: Reg. U. (N), No. 22
Website: www.msmary.edu
Admissions email: admissions@msmary.edu
Private; founded 1808
Affiliation: Roman Catholic
Freshman admissions: selective; 2014-2015: 6,142 applied, 4,107 accepted. Either SAT or ACT required. SAT 25/75 percentile: 950-1150. High school rank: 13% in top tenth, 39% in top quarter, 71% in top half
Early decision deadline: N/A, notification date: N/A
Early action deadline: 12/1, notification date: 12/25
Application deadline (fall): 3/1
Undergraduate student body: 1,723 full time, 87 part time; 44% male, 56% female; 0% American Indian, 2% Asian, 11% black, 9% Hispanic, 4% multiracial, 0% Pacific Islander, 71% white, 1% international; 51% from in state; 83% live on campus; N/A of students in fraternities, N/A in sororities
Most popular majors: 8% Accounting, 8% Biology/Biological Sciences, General, 21% Business/Commerce, General, 8% Criminology, 10% Elementary Education and Teaching
Expenses: 2015-2016: $37,500; room/board: $12,400
Financial aid: (301) 447-5207; 69% of undergrads determined to have financial need; average aid package $24,665

Notre Dame of Maryland University

Baltimore MD
(410) 532-5330
U.S. News ranking: Reg. U. (N), No. 58
Website: www.ndm.edu
Admissions email: admiss@ndm.edu
Private; founded 1873
Affiliation: Roman Catholic
Freshman admissions: selective; 2014-2015: 827 applied, 409 accepted. Either SAT or ACT required. SAT 25/75 percentile: 930-1140. High school rank: 24% in top tenth, 49% in top quarter, 85% in top half
Early decision deadline: N/A, notification date: N/A
Early action deadline: 12/1, notification date: 12/15
Application deadline (fall): rolling
Undergraduate student body: 538 full time, 631 part time; 5% male, 95% female; 3% American Indian, 5% Asian, 27% black, 6% Hispanic, 0% multiracial, 0% Pacific Islander, 57% white, 1% international; 93% from in state; 29% live on campus; 0% of students in fraternities, 0% in sororities
Most popular majors: 3% Biology, General, 9% Business/Commerce, General, 11% Liberal Arts and Sciences, General Studies and Humanities, 11% Multi/Interdisciplinary Studies, Other, 47% Registered Nursing, Nursing Administration, Nursing Research and Clinical Nursing, Other
Expenses: 2014-2015: $33,010; room/board: $10,716
Financial aid: (410) 532-5369

Salisbury University

Salisbury MD
(410) 543-6161
U.S. News ranking: Reg. U. (N), No. 71
Website: www.salisbury.edu/
Admissions email: admissions@salisbury.edu
Public; founded 1925
Freshman admissions: selective; 2014-2015: 8,723 applied, 4,771 accepted. Neither SAT nor ACT required. SAT 25/75 percentile: 1070-1230. High school rank: 23% in top tenth, 55% in top quarter, 91% in top half
Early decision deadline: 11/15, notification date: 12/15
Early action deadline: 12/1, notification date: 1/15
Application deadline (fall): 1/15
Undergraduate student body: 7,350 full time, 647 part time; 43% male, 57% female; 0% American Indian, 3% Asian, 12% black, 4% Hispanic, 4% multiracial, 0% Pacific Islander, 73% white, 1% international; 86% from in state; 28% live on campus; 10% of students in fraternities, 10% in sororities
Most popular majors: 6% Biology/Biological Sciences, General, 7% Elementary Education and Teaching, 8% Kinesiology and Exercise Science, 7% Psychology, General, 10% Speech Communication and Rhetoric
Expenses: 2014-2015: $8,560 in state, $16,906 out of state; room/board: $10,620
Financial aid: (410) 543-6165; 53% of undergrads determined to have financial need; average aid package $8,174

Sojourner-Douglass College[1]

Baltimore MD
(800) 732-2630
U.S. News ranking: Reg. Coll. (N), unranked
Website: www.sdc.edu/
Admissions email: N/A
Private
Application deadline (fall): N/A
Undergraduate student body: N/A full time, N/A part time
Expenses: 2014-2015: $9,830; room/board: $7,100
Financial aid: (410) 276-0306

Stevenson University

Stevenson MD
(410) 486-7001
U.S. News ranking: Reg. U. (N), No. 79
Website: www.stevenson.edu/
Admissions email: admissions@stevenson.edu
Private; founded 1947
Freshman admissions: selective; 2014-2015: 5,086 applied, 3,169 accepted. Either SAT or ACT required. SAT 25/75 percentile: 900-1090. High school rank: 14% in top tenth, 42% in top quarter, 77% in top half
Early decision deadline: N/A, notification date: N/A
Early action deadline: N/A, notification date: N/A
Application deadline (fall): rolling
Undergraduate student body: 3,203 full time, 605 part time; 35% male, 65% female; 0% American Indian, 3% Asian, 29% black, 5% Hispanic, 3% multiracial, 0% Pacific Islander, 56% white, 0% international; 82% from in state; 48% live on campus; 0% of students in fraternities, 2% in sororities
Most popular majors: 16% Business, Management, Marketing, and Related Support Services, 11% Computer and Information Sciences and Support Services, 24% Health Professions and Related Programs,

7% Homeland Security, Law Enforcement, Firefighting and Related Protective Services, 10% Legal Professions and Studies
Expenses: 2015-2016: $30,998; room/board: $12,490
Financial aid: (443) 334-2559; 77% of undergrads determined to have financial need; average aid package $19,286

St. John's College
Annapolis MD
(410) 626-2522
U.S. News ranking: Nat. Lib. Arts, No. 55
Website: sjc.edu
Admissions email: annapolis.admissions@sjc.edu
Private; founded 1696
Freshman admissions: more selective; 2014-2015: 345 applied, 299 accepted. Neither SAT nor ACT required. SAT 25/75 percentile: 1200-1440. High school rank: 33% in top tenth, 56% in top quarter, 79% in top half
Early decision deadline: N/A, notification date: N/A
Early action deadline: 1/15, notification date: 2/15
Application deadline (fall): rolling
Undergraduate student body: 426 full time, 0 part time; 55% male, 45% female; 0% American Indian, 3% Asian, 1% black, 5% Hispanic, 3% multiracial, 0% Pacific Islander, 76% white, 10% international; 19% from in state; 80% live on campus; 0% of students in fraternities, 0% in sororities
Most popular majors: 100% Liberal Arts and Sciences, General Studies and Humanities
Expenses: 2015-2016: $49,119; room/board: $11,598
Financial aid: (410) 626-2502; 73% of undergrads determined to have financial need; average aid package $35,892

St. Mary's College of Maryland
St. Mary's City MD
(800) 492-7181
U.S. News ranking: Nat. Lib. Arts, No. 93
Website: www.smcm.edu
Admissions email: admissions@smcm.edu
Public; founded 1840
Freshman admissions: more selective; 2014-2015: 1,874 applied, 1,478 accepted. Either SAT or ACT required. SAT 25/75 percentile: 1104-1283. High school rank: N/A
Early decision deadline: 11/1, notification date: 11/20
Early action deadline: N/A, notification date: N/A
Application deadline (fall): 2/15
Undergraduate student body: 1,626 full time, 62 part time; 43% male, 57% female; 0% American Indian, 3% Asian, 8% black, 7% Hispanic, 4% multiracial, 0% Pacific Islander, 73% white, 1% international; 91% from in state; 82% live on campus; 0% of students in fraternities, 0% in sororities
Most popular majors: 9% Biology/Biological Sciences, General, 9% Economics, General, 9% English Language and Literature, General, 16% Psychology, General, 7% Social Sciences, General
Expenses: 2015-2016: $13,895 in state, $28,745 out of state; room/board: $12,290
Financial aid: (240) 895-3000; 50% of undergrads determined to have financial need; average aid package $15,468

Towson University
Towson MD
(410) 704-2113
U.S. News ranking: Reg. U. (N), No. 53
Website: www.towson.edu
Admissions email: admissions@towson.edu
Public; founded 1866
Freshman admissions: selective; 2014-2015: 18,134 applied, 10,738 accepted. Either SAT or ACT required. SAT 25/75 percentile: 1000-1170. High school rank: 19% in top tenth, 49% in top quarter, 86% in top half
Early decision deadline: N/A, notification date: N/A
Early action deadline: N/A, notification date: N/A
Application deadline (fall): 1/15
Undergraduate student body: 16,575 full time, 2,232 part time; 40% male, 60% female; 0% American Indian, 5% Asian, 16% black, 6% Hispanic, 4% multiracial, 0% Pacific Islander, 63% white, 2% international; 85% from in state; 26% live on campus; 10% of students in fraternities, 9% in sororities
Most popular majors: 14% Business, Management, Marketing, and Related Support Services, 12% Education, 11% Health Professions and Related Programs, 8% Psychology, 10% Social Sciences
Expenses: 2015-2016: $9,182 in state, $20,788 out of state; room/board: $11,638
Financial aid: (410) 704-4236; 55% of undergrads determined to have financial need; average aid package $9,675

United States Naval Academy
Annapolis MD
(410) 293-4361
U.S. News ranking: Nat. Lib. Arts, No. 9
Website: www.usna.edu
Admissions email: webmail@usna.edu
Public; founded 1845
Freshman admissions: most selective; 2014-2015: 17,618 applied, 1,398 accepted. Either SAT or ACT required. SAT 25/75 percentile: 1180-1390. High school rank: 59% in top tenth, 81% in top quarter, 95% in top half
Early decision deadline: N/A, notification date: N/A
Early action deadline: N/A, notification date: N/A
Application deadline (fall): 1/31
Undergraduate student body: 4,511 full time, 0 part time; 77% male, 23% female; 0% American Indian, 7% Asian, 7% black, 11% Hispanic, 8% multiracial, 0% Pacific Islander, 65% white, 1% international; 6% from in state; 100% live on campus; 0% of students in fraternities, 0% in sororities
Most popular majors: 9% Economics, General, 8% History, General, 8% Mechanical Engineering, 10% Oceanography, Chemical and Physical, 10% Political Science and Government, General
Expenses: N/A
Financial aid: N/A

University of Baltimore
Baltimore MD
(410) 837-4777
U.S. News ranking: Reg. U. (N), No. 122
Website: www.ubalt.edu
Admissions email: admissions@ubalt.edu
Public; founded 1925
Freshman admissions: less selective; 2014-2015: 540 applied, 335 accepted. Either SAT or ACT required. SAT 25/75 percentile: 810-1030. High school rank: N/A
Early decision deadline: N/A, notification date: N/A
Early action deadline: N/A, notification date: N/A
Application deadline (fall): rolling
Undergraduate student body: 2,089 full time, 1,396 part time; 43% male, 57% female; 0% American Indian, 4% Asian, 47% black, 5% Hispanic, 4% multiracial, 0% Pacific Islander, 34% white, 2% international; 97% from in state; N/A live on campus; N/A of students in fraternities, N/A in sororities
Most popular majors: 6% Animation, Interactive Technology, Video Graphics and Special Effects, 36% Business/Commerce, General, 9% Criminal Justice/Police Science, 8% Health Services Administration, 5% Human Services, General
Expenses: 2015-2016: $4,163 in state, $9,872 out of state; room/board: $14,200
Financial aid: (410) 837-4763; 73% of undergrads determined to have financial need; average aid package $11,631

University of Maryland–Baltimore County
Baltimore MD
(410) 455-2291
U.S. News ranking: Nat. U., No. 156
Website: www.umbc.edu
Admissions email: admissions@umbc.edu
Public; founded 1963
Freshman admissions: more selective; 2014-2015: 10,217 applied, 6,090 accepted. SAT required. SAT 25/75 percentile: 1110-1310. High school rank: 25% in top tenth, 54% in top quarter, 84% in top half
Early decision deadline: N/A, notification date: N/A
Early action deadline: 11/1, notification date: 12/15
Application deadline (fall): 2/1
Undergraduate student body: 9,653 full time, 1,726 part time; 55% male, 45% female; 0% American Indian, 20% Asian, 16% black, 6% Hispanic, 4% multiracial, 0% Pacific Islander, 44% white, 5% international; 94% from in state; 34% live on campus; 4% of students in fraternities, 5% in sororities
Most popular majors: 16% Biological and Biomedical Sciences, 15% Computer and Information Sciences and Support Services, 13% Psychology, 12% Social Sciences, 8% Visual and Performing Arts
Expenses: 2015-2016: $11,006 in state, $23,770 out of state; room/board: $11,454
Financial aid: (410) 455-2387; 53% of undergrads determined to have financial need; average aid package $10,333

University of Maryland–College Park
College Park MD
(301) 314-8385
U.S. News ranking: Nat. U., No. 57
Website: www.maryland.edu
Admissions email: um-admit@umd.edu
Public; founded 1856
Freshman admissions: more selective; 2014-2015: 26,268 applied, 12,556 accepted. Either SAT or ACT required. SAT 25/75 percentile: 1210-1420. High school rank: 73% in top tenth, 90% in top quarter, 98% in top half
Early decision deadline: N/A, notification date: N/A
Early action deadline: 11/1, notification date: 1/31
Application deadline (fall): 1/20
Undergraduate student body: 25,027 full time, 2,029 part time; 54% male, 46% female; 0% American Indian, 16% Asian, 13% black, 9% Hispanic, 4% multiracial, 0% Pacific Islander, 53% white, 3% international; 80% from in state; 44% live on campus; 13% of students in fraternities, 14% in sororities
Most popular majors: 4% Accounting, 7% Biology/Biological Sciences, General, 5% Criminology, 5% Economics, General, 5% Psychology, General
Expenses: 2015-2016: $9,996 in state, $31,144 out of state; room/board: $10,972
Financial aid: (301) 314-9000; 43% of undergrads determined to have financial need; average aid package $13,667

University of Maryland–Eastern Shore
Princess Anne MD
(410) 651-6410
U.S. News ranking: Reg. U. (N), second tier
Website: www.umes.edu
Admissions email: umesadmissions@umes.edu
Public; founded 1886
Freshman admissions: least selective; 2014-2015: 4,141 applied, 2,537 accepted. Either SAT or ACT required. SAT 25/75 percentile: 760-930. High school rank: N/A
Early decision deadline: N/A, notification date: N/A
Early action deadline: N/A, notification date: N/A
Application deadline (fall): 6/30
Undergraduate student body: 3,192 full time, 379 part time; 45% male, 55% female; 0% American Indian, 1% Asian, 74% black, 2% Hispanic, 9% multiracial, 0% Pacific Islander, 10% white, 2% international; 83% from in state; 63% live on campus; N/A of students in fraternities, N/A in sororities
Most popular majors: 9% Biology/Biological Sciences, General, 16% Criminal Justice/Police Science, 7% English Language and Literature, General, 6% Family and Consumer Sciences/Human Sciences, General, 9% Hotel/Motel Administration/Management
Expenses: 2015-2016: $7,625 in state, $16,687 out of state; room/board: $9,114
Financial aid: (410) 651-6172; 84% of undergrads determined to have financial need; average aid package $12,559

University of Maryland University College
Adelphi MD
(800) 888-8682
U.S. News ranking: Reg. U. (N), unranked
Website: www.umuc.edu/
Admissions email: enroll@umuc.edu
Public; founded 1947
Freshman admissions: N/A; 2014-2015: 1,789 applied, 1,789 accepted. Neither SAT nor ACT required. ACT 25/75 percentile: N/A. High school rank: N/A
Early decision deadline: N/A, notification date: N/A
Early action deadline: N/A, notification date: N/A
Application deadline (fall): rolling
Undergraduate student body: 8,261 full time, 26,893 part time; 53% male, 47% female; 0% American Indian, 4% Asian, 27% black, 11% Hispanic, 4% multiracial, 1% Pacific Islander, 42% white, 1% international; 46% from in state; N/A live on campus; N/A of students in fraternities, N/A in sororities
Most popular majors: 39% Business, Management, Marketing, and Related Support Services, 26% Computer and Information Sciences and Support Services, 7% Homeland Security, Law Enforcement, Firefighting and Related Protective Services, 7% Psychology
Expenses: 2014-2015: $6,744 in state, $12,336 out of state; room/board: N/A
Financial aid: (301) 985-7510; 61% of undergrads determined to have financial need; average aid package $7,752

Washington Adventist University
Takoma Park MD
(301) 891-4080
U.S. News ranking: Reg. Coll. (N), No. 43
Website: www.wau.edu
Admissions email: enroll@wau.edu
Private; founded 1904
Affiliation: Seventh-day Adventist
Freshman admissions: least selective; 2014-2015: 1,179 applied, 530 accepted. Either SAT or ACT required. SAT 25/75 percentile: 740-1030. High school rank: N/A

Early decision deadline: N/A, notification date: N/A
Early action deadline: N/A, notification date: N/A
Application deadline (fall): 8/1
Undergraduate student body: 705 full time, 171 part time; 35% male, 65% female; 1% American Indian, 8% Asian, 53% black, 14% Hispanic, 1% multiracial, 0% Pacific Islander, 13% white, N/A international
Most popular majors: Information not available
Expenses: 2015-2016: $22,790; room/board: $8,650
Financial aid: (301) 891-4005; 95% of undergrads determined to have financial need; average aid package $10,442

Washington College

Chestertown MD
(410) 778-7700
U.S. News ranking: Nat. Lib. Arts, No. 100
Website: www.washcoll.edu
Admissions email: adm.off@washcoll.edu
Private; founded 1782
Freshman admissions: more selective; 2014-2015: 5,318 applied, 2,960 accepted. Neither SAT nor ACT required. SAT 25/75 percentile: 1040-1270. High school rank: 34% in top tenth, 62% in top quarter, 88% in top half
Early decision deadline: 11/15, notification date: 12/15
Early action deadline: 12/1, notification date: 1/15
Application deadline (fall): 2/15
Undergraduate student body: 1,417 full time, 50 part time; 43% male, 57% female; 0% American Indian, 2% Asian, 4% black, 4% Hispanic, 2% multiracial, 0% Pacific Islander, 76% white, 8% international; 45% from in state; 85% live on campus; 8% of students in fraternities, 11% in sororities
Most popular majors: 10% Biological and Biomedical Sciences, 12% Business, Management, Marketing, and Related Support Services, 7% English Language and Literature/Letters, 12% Psychology, 24% Social Sciences
Expenses: 2015-2016: $43,850; room/board: $10,612
Financial aid: (410) 778-7214; 59% of undergrads determined to have financial need; average aid package $29,263

MASSACHUSETTS

American International College

Springfield MA
(413) 205-3201
U.S. News ranking: Reg. U. (N), second tier
Website: www.aic.edu
Admissions email: inquiry@aic.edu
Private; founded 1885
Freshman admissions: less selective; 2014-2015: 2,026 applied, 1,369 accepted. Either SAT or ACT required. SAT 25/75 percentile: 780-980. High school rank: N/A
Early decision deadline: N/A, notification date: N/A
Early action deadline: N/A, notification date: N/A
Application deadline (fall): rolling
Undergraduate student body: 1,376 full time, 97 part time; 41% male, 59% female; 0% American Indian, 2% Asian, 25% black, 10% Hispanic, 4% multiracial, 1% Pacific Islander, 42% white, 0% international; 63% from in state; 47% live on campus; 1% of students in fraternities, 1% in sororities
Most popular majors: 17% Business, Management, Marketing, and Related Support Services, 38% Health Professions and Related Programs, 12% Homeland Security, Law Enforcement, Firefighting and Related Protective Services, 6% Liberal Arts and Sciences, General Studies and Humanities, 8% Social Sciences
Expenses: 2015-2016: $31,868; room/board: $12,892
Financial aid: (413) 205-3259; 83% of undergrads determined to have financial need; average aid package $25,587

Amherst College

Amherst MA
(413) 542-2328
U.S. News ranking: Nat. Lib. Arts, No. 2
Website: www.amherst.edu
Admissions email: admission@amherst.edu
Private; founded 1821
Freshman admissions: most selective; 2014-2015: 8,478 applied, 1,173 accepted. Either SAT or ACT required. SAT 25/75 percentile: 1350-1550. High school rank: 84% in top tenth, 97% in top quarter, 99% in top half
Early decision deadline: 11/15, notification date: 12/15
Early action deadline: N/A, notification date: N/A
Application deadline (fall): 1/1
Undergraduate student body: 1,792 full time, N/A part time; 52% male, 48% female; 0% American Indian, 13% Asian, 12% black, 13% Hispanic, 5% multiracial, 0% Pacific Islander, 42% white, 10% international; 12% from in state; 98% live on campus; 0% of students in fraternities, 0% in sororities
Most popular majors: 16% Economics, General, 11% English Language and Literature, General, 8% History, General, 9% Political Science and Government, General, 11% Psychology, General
Expenses: 2015-2016: $50,562; room/board: $13,210
Financial aid: (413) 542-2296; 58% of undergrads determined to have financial need; average aid package $48,535

Anna Maria College

Paxton MA
(508) 849-3360
U.S. News ranking: Reg. U. (N), second tier
Website: www.annamaria.edu
Admissions email: admissions@annamaria.edu
Private; founded 1946
Affiliation: Roman Catholic
Freshman admissions: less selective; 2014-2015: 1,944 applied, 1,508 accepted. Neither SAT nor ACT required. ACT 25/75 percentile: N/A. High school rank: N/A
Early decision deadline: N/A, notification date: N/A
Early action deadline: N/A, notification date: N/A
Application deadline (fall): rolling
Undergraduate student body: 769 full time, 347 part time; 40% male, 60% female; 0% American Indian, 2% Asian, 8% black, 6% Hispanic, 2% multiracial, 0% Pacific Islander, 72% white, 1% international; 75% from in state; 60% live on campus; N/A of students in fraternities, N/A in sororities
Most popular majors: Information not available
Expenses: 2014-2015: $34,330; room/board: $12,730
Financial aid: (508) 849-3366; 88% of undergrads determined to have financial need; average aid package $25,752

Assumption College

Worcester MA
(866) 477-7776
U.S. News ranking: Reg. U. (N), No. 32
Website: www.assumption.edu
Admissions email: admiss@assumption.edu
Private; founded 1904
Affiliation: Roman Catholic
Freshman admissions: selective; 2014-2015: 4,402 applied, 3,579 accepted. Neither SAT nor ACT required. SAT 25/75 percentile: 1020-1200. High school rank: 15% in top tenth, 43% in top quarter, 79% in top half
Early decision deadline: N/A, notification date: N/A
Early action deadline: 11/1, notification date: 12/15
Application deadline (fall): 2/15
Undergraduate student body: 1,997 full time, 11 part time; 42% male, 58% female; 0% American Indian, 2% Asian, 5% black, 7% Hispanic, 2% multiracial, 0% Pacific Islander, 74% white, 2% international; 66% from in state; 89% live on campus; N/A of students in fraternities, N/A in sororities
Most popular majors: 10% Accounting, 6% Chemistry, General, 6% Marketing/Marketing Management, General, 11% Psychology, General, 12% Rehabilitation and Therapeutic Professions, Other
Expenses: 2015-2016: $36,160; room/board: $11,264
Financial aid: (508) 767-7158; 78% of undergrads determined to have financial need; average aid package $26,459

Babson College

Babson Park MA
(781) 239-5522
U.S. News ranking: Business, unranked
Website: www.babson.edu
Admissions email: ugradadmission@babson.edu
Private; founded 1919
Freshman admissions: more selective; 2014-2015: 6,199 applied, 1,631 accepted. Either SAT or ACT required. SAT 25/75 percentile: 1180-1370. High school rank: N/A
Early decision deadline: 11/1, notification date: 12/15
Early action deadline: 11/1, notification date: 1/1
Application deadline (fall): 1/4
Undergraduate student body: 2,107 full time, N/A part time; 53% male, 47% female; 0% American Indian, 11% Asian, 5% black, 10% Hispanic, 2% multiracial, 0% Pacific Islander, 39% white, 27% international; 28% from in state; 76% live on campus; 15% of students in fraternities, 25% in sororities
Most popular majors: 100% Business Administration, Management and Operations
Expenses: 2015-2016: $46,784; room/board: $14,928
Financial aid: (781) 239-4219; 43% of undergrads determined to have financial need; average aid package $38,749

Bard College at Simon's Rock

Great Barrington MA
(800) 234-7186
U.S. News ranking: Reg. Coll. (N), No. 11
Website: www.simons-rock.edu
Admissions email: admit@simons-rock.edu
Private; founded 1966
Freshman admissions: more selective; 2014-2015: 198 applied, 177 accepted. Neither SAT nor ACT required. ACT 25/75 percentile: 29-31. High school rank: 60% in top tenth, 81% in top quarter, 96% in top half
Early decision deadline: N/A, notification date: N/A
Early action deadline: N/A, notification date: N/A
Application deadline (fall): 5/1
Undergraduate student body: 322 full time, 7 part time; 41% male, 59% female; 6% American Indian, 0% Asian, 6% black, 2% Hispanic, 12% multiracial, 7% Pacific Islander, 51% white, 14% international
Most popular majors: 12% Biological and Biomedical Sciences, 7% Foreign Languages, Literatures, and Linguistics, 9% Multi/Interdisciplinary Studies, 9% Social Sciences, 18% Visual and Performing Arts
Expenses: 2015-2016: $50,211; room/board: $13,660
Financial aid: (413) 528-7297; 74% of undergrads determined to have financial need; average aid package $37,991

Bay Path University

Longmeadow MA
(413) 565-1331
U.S. News ranking: Nat. Lib. Arts, second tier
Website: www.baypath.edu
Admissions email: admiss@baypath.edu
Private; founded 1897
Freshman admissions: less selective; 2014-2015: 893 applied, 563 accepted. Either SAT or ACT required. SAT 25/75 percentile: 840-1063. High school rank: 10% in top tenth, 39% in top quarter, 78% in top half
Early decision deadline: N/A, notification date: N/A
Early action deadline: 12/15, notification date: 1/2
Application deadline (fall): rolling
Undergraduate student body: 1,293 full time, 297 part time; 0% male, 100% female; 0% American Indian, 1% Asian, 14% black, 16% Hispanic, 2% multiracial, 0% Pacific Islander, 57% white, 0% international; 57% from in state; 50% live on campus; N/A of students in fraternities, N/A in sororities
Most popular majors: 27% Business, Management, Marketing, and Related Support Services, 9% Education, 10% Homeland Security, Law Enforcement, Firefighting and Related Protective Services, 16% Liberal Arts and Sciences, General Studies and Humanities, 23% Psychology
Expenses: 2015-2016: $31,785; room/board: $12,424
Financial aid: (413) 565-1261; 89% of undergrads determined to have financial need; average aid package $24,708

Bay State College

Boston MA
(617) 217-9000
U.S. News ranking: Reg. Coll. (N), second tier
Website: www.baystate.edu
Admissions email: N/A
For-profit; founded 1946
Freshman admissions: least selective; 2014-2015: N/A applied, N/A accepted. Neither SAT nor ACT required. ACT 25/75 percentile: N/A. High school rank: N/A
Early decision deadline: N/A, notification date: N/A
Early action deadline: N/A, notification date: N/A
Application deadline (fall): rolling
Undergraduate student body: 651 full time, 360 part time; 43% male, 57% female; N/A American Indian, N/A Asian, N/A black, N/A Hispanic, N/A multiracial, N/A Pacific Islander, N/A white, N/A international
Most popular majors: 19% Business Administration and Management, General, 7% Criminal Justice/Law Enforcement Administration, 9% Fashion Merchandising, 5% Music Management, 4% Registered Nursing/Registered Nurse
Expenses: 2015-2016: $26,780; room/board: $13,000
Financial aid: (617) 217-9186; 90% of undergrads determined to have financial need

Becker College[1]

Worcester MA
(877) 523-2537
U.S. News ranking: Reg. Coll. (N), second tier
Website: www.beckercollege.edu
Admissions email: admissions@beckercollege.edu
Private; founded 1784
Application deadline (fall): rolling
Undergraduate student body: N/A full time, N/A part time
Expenses: 2015-2016: $34,080; room/board: $12,400
Financial aid: (508) 791-9241; 85% of undergrads determined to have financial need; average aid package $21,776

Benjamin Franklin Institute of Technology[1]

Boston MA
(617) 423-4630
U.S. News ranking: Engineering, unranked
Website: www.bfit.edu
Admissions email: admissions@bfit.edu
Private
Application deadline (fall): N/A
Undergraduate student body: N/A full time, N/A part time
Expenses: 2014-2015: $16,950; room/board: $13,900
Financial aid: (617) 423-4630

Bentley University

Waltham MA
(781) 891-2244
U.S. News ranking: Reg. U. (N), No. 3
Website: www.bentley.edu
Admissions email: ugadmission@bentley.edu
Private; founded 1917
Freshman admissions: more selective; 2014-2015: 7,477 applied, 3,448 accepted. Either SAT or ACT required. SAT 25/75 percentile: 1150-1330. High school rank: 38% in top tenth, 75% in top quarter, 97% in top half
Early decision deadline: 11/1, notification date: 12/31
Early action deadline: N/A, notification date: N/A
Application deadline (fall): 1/7
Undergraduate student body: 4,170 full time, 94 part time; 60% male, 40% female; 0% American Indian, 8% Asian, 3% black, 7% Hispanic, 2% multiracial, 0% Pacific Islander, 60% white, 15% international; 46% from in state; 80% live on campus; 11% of students in fraternities, 11% in sororities
Most popular majors: 13% Accounting, 13% Business Administration and Management, General, 14% Business, Management, Marketing, and Related Support Services, Other, 14% Finance, General, 16% Marketing/Marketing Management, General
Expenses: 2015-2016: $44,085; room/board: $14,520
Financial aid: (781) 891-3441; 44% of undergrads determined to have financial need; average aid package $34,427

Berklee College of Music

Boston MA
(800) 237-5533
U.S. News ranking: Arts, unranked
Website: www.berklee.edu
Admissions email: admissions@berklee.edu
Private; founded 1945
Freshman admissions: N/A; 2014-2015: 6,037 applied, 2,111 accepted. Neither SAT nor ACT required. ACT 25/75 percentile: N/A. High school rank: N/A
Early decision deadline: N/A, notification date: N/A
Early action deadline: 11/1, notification date: 1/31
Application deadline (fall): 1/15
Undergraduate student body: 4,083 full time, 407 part time; 68% male, 32% female; 0% American Indian, 4% Asian, 5% black, 9% Hispanic, 5% multiracial, 0% Pacific Islander, 39% white, 30% international; 15% from in state; 28% live on campus; 0% of students in fraternities, 0% in sororities
Most popular majors: 2% Education, 3% Health Professions and Related Programs, 95% Visual and Performing Arts
Expenses: 2015-2016: $40,082; room/board: $17,546
Financial aid: (617) 747-2274; 47% of undergrads determined to have financial need; average aid package $8,365

Boston Architectural College

Boston MA
(617) 585-0123
U.S. News ranking: Arts, unranked
Website: www.the-bac.edu
Admissions email: admissions@the-bac.edu
Private; founded 1889
Freshman admissions: N/A; 2014-2015: 36 applied, 36 accepted. Neither SAT nor ACT required. ACT 25/75 percentile: N/A. High school rank: N/A
Early decision deadline: N/A, notification date: N/A
Early action deadline: N/A, notification date: N/A
Application deadline (fall): rolling
Undergraduate student body: 354 full time, 116 part time; 59% male, 41% female; 0% American Indian, 9% Asian, 6% black, 16% Hispanic, 4% multiracial, 0% Pacific Islander, 53% white, 3% international
Most popular majors: Information not available
Expenses: 2015-2016: $20,666; room/board: N/A
Financial aid: (617) 585-0125; 39% of undergrads determined to have financial need; average aid package $10,115

Boston College

Chestnut Hill MA
(617) 552-3100
U.S. News ranking: Nat. U., No. 30
Website: www.bc.edu
Admissions email: N/A
Private; founded 1863
Affiliation: Roman Catholic (Jesuit)
Freshman admissions: most selective; 2014-2015: 23,223 applied, 7,875 accepted. Either SAT or ACT required. SAT 25/75 percentile: 1270-1460. High school rank: 81% in top tenth, 95% in top quarter, 99% in top half
Early decision deadline: N/A, notification date: N/A
Early action deadline: 11/1, notification date: 12/25
Application deadline (fall): 1/1
Undergraduate student body: 9,154 full time, N/A part time; 46% male, 54% female; 0% American Indian, 10% Asian, 4% black, 10% Hispanic, 3% multiracial, 0% Pacific Islander, 62% white, 6% international; 25% from in state; 85% live on campus; 0% of students in fraternities, 0% in sororities
Most popular majors: 8% Biology/Biological Sciences, General, 9% Economics, General, 10% Finance, General, 7% Psychology, General, 9% Speech Communication and Rhetoric
Expenses: 2015-2016: $49,324; room/board: $13,496
Financial aid: (617) 552-3320; 41% of undergrads determined to have financial need; average aid package $38,790

Boston Conservatory[1]

Boston MA
(617) 912-9153
U.S. News ranking: Arts, unranked
Website: www.bostonconservatory.edu
Admissions email: admissions@bostonconservatory.edu
Private
Application deadline (fall): N/A
Undergraduate student body: N/A full time, N/A part time
Expenses: 2014-2015: $42,326; room/board: $17,180
Financial aid: (617) 912-9147

Boston University

Boston MA
(617) 353-2300
U.S. News ranking: Nat. U., No. 41
Website: www.bu.edu
Admissions email: admissions@bu.edu
Private; founded 1839
Freshman admissions: more selective; 2014-2015: 54,190 applied, 18,701 accepted. Either SAT or ACT required. SAT 25/75 percentile: 1190-1410. High school rank: 59% in top tenth, 89% in top quarter, 99% in top half
Early decision deadline: 11/1, notification date: 12/15
Early action deadline: N/A, notification date: N/A
Application deadline (fall): 1/1
Undergraduate student body: 16,619 full time, 1,398 part time; 40% male, 60% female; 0% American Indian, 13% Asian, 3% black, 10% Hispanic, 4% multiracial, 0% Pacific Islander, 46% white, 19% international; 26% from in state; 75% live on campus; 7% of students in fraternities, 11% in sororities
Most popular majors: 8% Biological and Biomedical Sciences, 19% Business, Management, Marketing, and Related Support Services, 15% Communication, Journalism, and Related Programs, 8% Health Professions and Related Programs, 16% Social Sciences
Expenses: 2015-2016: $48,436; room/board: $14,520
Financial aid: (617) 353-2965; 39% of undergrads determined to have financial need; average aid package $35,766

Brandeis University

Waltham MA
(781) 736-3500
U.S. News ranking: Nat. U., No. 34
Website: www.brandeis.edu
Admissions email: admissions@brandeis.edu
Private; founded 1948
Freshman admissions: most selective; 2014-2015: 10,004 applied, 3,523 accepted. Either SAT or ACT required. SAT 25/75 percentile: 1250-1480. High school rank: 71% in top tenth, 92% in top quarter, 98% in top half
Early decision deadline: 11/1, notification date: 12/15
Early action deadline: N/A, notification date: N/A
Application deadline (fall): 1/1
Undergraduate student body: 3,711 full time, 18 part time; 43% male, 57% female; 0% American Indian, 13% Asian, 5% black, 7% Hispanic, 3% multiracial, 0% Pacific Islander, 49% white, 18% international; 28% from in state; 77% live on campus; 0% of students in fraternities, 0% in sororities
Most popular majors: 11% Biology/Biological Sciences, General, 7% Business/Commerce, General, 9% Economics, General, 7% Health Policy Analysis, 7% Psychology, General
Expenses: 2015-2016: $49,598; room/board: $13,856
Financial aid: (781) 736-3700; 53% of undergrads determined to have financial need; average aid package $40,594

Bridgewater State University

Bridgewater MA
(508) 531-1237
U.S. News ranking: Reg. U. (N), No. 125
Website: www.bridgew.edu/admissions
Admissions email: admission@bridgew.edu
Public; founded 1840
Freshman admissions: less selective; 2014-2015: 5,799 applied, 4,599 accepted. Either SAT or ACT required. SAT 25/75 percentile: 890-1090. High school rank: N/A
Early decision deadline: N/A, notification date: N/A
Early action deadline: 11/15, notification date: 12/15
Application deadline (fall): rolling
Undergraduate student body: 8,019 full time, 1,609 part time; 41% male, 59% female; 0% American Indian, 2% Asian, 9% black, 6% Hispanic, 3% multiracial, 0% Pacific Islander, 78% white, 0% international; 96% from in state; 41% live on campus; N/A of students in fraternities, N/A in sororities
Most popular majors: 16% Business, Management, Marketing, and Related Support Services, 8% Communication, Journalism, and Related Programs, 18% Education, 11% Homeland Security, Law Enforcement, Firefighting and Related Protective Services, 11% Psychology
Expenses: 2015-2016: $8,474 in state, $14,614 out of state; room/board: $11,700
Financial aid: (508) 531-1341; 72% of undergrads determined to have financial need; average aid package $8,085

Cambridge College[1]

Cambridge MA
(800) 877-4723
U.S. News ranking: Reg. U. (N), unranked
Website: www.cambridgecollege.edu
Admissions email: N/A
Private; founded 1971
Application deadline (fall): rolling
Undergraduate student body: N/A full time, N/A part time
Expenses: 2014-2015: $13,392; room/board: N/A
Financial aid: (800) 877-4723

Clark University

Worcester MA
(508) 793-7431
U.S. News ranking: Nat. U., No. 75
Website: www.clarku.edu
Admissions email: admissions@clarku.edu
Private; founded 1887
Freshman admissions: more selective; 2014-2015: 7,304 applied, 3,946 accepted. Neither SAT nor ACT required. SAT 25/75 percentile: 1108-1333. High school rank: 37% in top tenth, 73% in top quarter, 96% in top half
Early decision deadline: 11/1, notification date: 12/15
Early action deadline: 11/1, notification date: 12/15
Application deadline (fall): 1/15
Undergraduate student body: 2,213 full time, 88 part time; 42% male, 58% female; 0% American Indian, 7% Asian, 4% black, 6% Hispanic, 2% multiracial, 0% Pacific Islander, 60% white, 14% international; 38% from in state; 70% live on campus; 0% of students in fraternities, 0% in sororities
Most popular majors: 7% Biology, General, 7% Business Administration, Management and Operations, 5% History, 6% Political Science and Government, 15% Psychology
Expenses: 2015-2016: $41,940; room/board: $8,200
Financial aid: (508) 793-7478; 59% of undergrads determined to have financial need; average aid package $33,231

College of Our Lady of the Elms

Chicopee MA
(800) 255-3567
U.S. News ranking: Reg. Coll. (N), No. 23
Website: www.elms.edu
Admissions email: admissions@elms.edu
Private
Affiliation: Roman Catholic, founded by Sisters of Saint Joseph of Springfield
Freshman admissions: less selective; 2014-2015: 851 applied, 672 accepted. Either SAT or ACT required. SAT 25/75 percentile: 840-1060. High school rank: N/A
Early decision deadline: N/A, notification date: N/A
Early action deadline: N/A, notification date: N/A
Application deadline (fall): rolling
Undergraduate student body: 1,005 full time, 366 part time; 24% male, 76% female; 1% American Indian, 3% Asian, 7% black, 9% Hispanic, 0% multiracial, 0% Pacific Islander, 52% white, 1% international; 80% from in state; 27% live on campus; 0% of students in fraternities, 0% in sororities
Most popular majors: 10% Business, Management, Marketing, and Related Support Services, 8% Education, 48% Health Professions and Related

Programs, 5% Psychology, 15% Public Administration and Social Service Professions
Expenses: 2015-2016: $32,280; room/board: $11,708
Financial aid: (413) 594-2761; 89% of undergrads determined to have financial need; average aid package $21,822

College of the Holy Cross

Worcester MA
(508) 793-2443
U.S. News ranking: Nat. Lib. Arts, No. 32
Website: www.holycross.edu
Admissions email: admissions@holycross.edu
Private; founded 1843
Affiliation: Roman Catholic (Jesuit)
Freshman admissions: more selective; 2014-2015: 5,302 applied, 2,298 accepted. Neither SAT nor ACT required. SAT 25/75 percentile: 1230-1380. High school rank: 56% in top tenth, 83% in top quarter, 98% in top half
Early decision deadline: 12/15, notification date: 1/15
Early action deadline: N/A, notification date: N/A
Application deadline (fall): 1/15
Undergraduate student body: 2,904 full time, 33 part time; 50% male, 50% female; 0% American Indian, 5% Asian, 4% black, 11% Hispanic, 4% multiracial, 0% Pacific Islander, 70% white, 1% international; 37% from in state; 91% live on campus; N/A of students in fraternities, N/A in sororities
Most popular majors: 11% English Language and Literature/Letters, 10% Foreign Languages, Literatures, and Linguistics, 10% History, 10% Psychology, 32% Social Sciences
Expenses: 2015-2016: $47,176; room/board: $12,748
Financial aid: (508) 793-2266; 55% of undergrads determined to have financial need; average aid package $35,279

Curry College

Milton MA
(800) 669-0686
U.S. News ranking: Reg. U. (N), second tier
Website: www.curry.edu
Admissions email: curryadm@curry.edu
Private; founded 1879
Freshman admissions: less selective; 2014-2015: 5,448 applied, 4,733 accepted. Neither SAT nor ACT required. SAT 25/75 percentile: 850-1040. High school rank: 5% in top tenth, 18% in top quarter, 53% in top half
Early decision deadline: N/A, notification date: N/A
Early action deadline: 12/1, notification date: 12/15
Application deadline (fall): rolling
Undergraduate student body: 2,103 full time, 797 part time; 37% male, 63% female; 0% American Indian, 2% Asian, 9% black, 5% Hispanic, 2% multiracial, 0% Pacific Islander, 69% white, 1% international; 78% from in state; 52% live on campus; 0% of students in fraternities, 0% in sororities
Most popular majors: 12% Business, Management, Marketing, and Related Support Services, 10% Communication, Journalism, and Related Programs, 39% Health Professions and Related Programs, 15% Homeland Security, Law Enforcement, Firefighting and Related Protective Services, 10% Psychology
Expenses: 2015-2016: $36,445; room/board: $13,900
Financial aid: (617) 333-2146; 75% of undergrads determined to have financial need; average aid package $24,327

Dean College

Franklin MA
(508) 541-1508
U.S. News ranking: Reg. Coll. (N), No. 31
Website: www.dean.edu
Admissions email: admission@dean.edu
Private; founded 1865
Freshman admissions: least selective; 2014-2015: 2,646 applied, 1,806 accepted. Neither SAT nor ACT required. SAT 25/75 percentile: 760-960. High school rank: N/A
Early decision deadline: N/A, notification date: N/A
Early action deadline: 12/1, notification date: 1/15
Application deadline (fall): rolling
Undergraduate student body: 1,069 full time, 223 part time; 48% male, 52% female; 0% American Indian, 3% Asian, 14% black, 5% Hispanic, 3% multiracial, 0% Pacific Islander, 44% white, 10% international; 53% from in state; 90% live on campus; 0% of students in fraternities, 0% in sororities
Most popular majors: 5% Arts, Entertainment,and Media Management, General, 28% Business Administration and Management, General, 33% Dance, General, 13% Drama and Dramatics/Theatre Arts, General, 11% Liberal Arts and Sciences/Liberal Studies
Expenses: 2015-2016: $35,420; room/board: $15,200
Financial aid: (508) 541-1519; 75% of undergrads determined to have financial need; average aid package $21,698

Eastern Nazarene College

Quincy MA
(617) 745-3711
U.S. News ranking: Nat. Lib. Arts, second tier
Website: www.enc.edu
Admissions email: info@enc.edu
Private; founded 1918
Affiliation: Nazarene
Freshman admissions: less selective; 2014-2015: 1,334 applied, 649 accepted. Either SAT or ACT required. SAT 25/75 percentile: 800-1050. High school rank: 7% in top tenth, 27% in top quarter, 55% in top half
Early decision deadline: N/A, notification date: N/A
Early action deadline: N/A, notification date: N/A
Application deadline (fall): rolling
Undergraduate student body: 1,045 full time, 17 part time; 33% male, 67% female; 1% American Indian, 2% Asian, 23% black, 12% Hispanic, 3% multiracial, 0% Pacific Islander, 54% white, 3% international; 51% from in state; 76% live on campus; 0% of students in fraternities, 0% in sororities
Most popular majors: Information not available
Expenses: 2015-2016: $29,880; room/board: $8,950
Financial aid: (617) 745-3869; 45% of undergrads determined to have financial need; average aid package $29,431

Emerson College

Boston MA
(617) 824-8600
U.S. News ranking: Reg. U. (N), No. 10
Website: www.emerson.edu
Admissions email: admission@emerson.edu
Private; founded 1880
Freshman admissions: more selective; 2014-2015: 8,709 applied, 4,283 accepted. Either SAT or ACT required. SAT 25/75 percentile: 1140-1330. High school rank: 37% in top tenth, 73% in top quarter, 95% in top half
Early decision deadline: N/A, notification date: N/A
Early action deadline: 11/1, notification date: 12/15
Application deadline (fall): 1/15
Undergraduate student body: 3,707 full time, 58 part time; 39% male, 61% female; 0% American Indian, 4% Asian, 3% black, 10% Hispanic, 5% multiracial, 0% Pacific Islander, 67% white, 5% international; 24% from in state; 58% live on campus; 2% of students in fraternities, 3% in sororities
Most popular majors: 16% Cinematography and Film/Video Production, 18% Creative Writing, 6% Drama and Dramatics/Theatre Arts, General, 16% Marketing/Marketing Management, General, 17% Radio and Television
Expenses: 2015-2016: $39,036; room/board: $15,700
Financial aid: (617) 824-8655; 53% of undergrads determined to have financial need; average aid package $20,840

Emmanuel College

Boston MA
(617) 735-9715
U.S. News ranking: Reg. U. (N), No. 66
Website: www.emmanuel.edu
Admissions email: enroll@emmanuel.edu
Private; founded 1919
Affiliation: Roman Catholic
Freshman admissions: selective; 2014-2015: 5,899 applied, 4,088 accepted. Neither SAT nor ACT required. SAT 25/75 percentile: 990-1190. High school rank: N/A
Early decision deadline: N/A, notification date: N/A
Early action deadline: 11/1, notification date: 12/15
Application deadline (fall): 2/15
Undergraduate student body: 1,817 full time, 265 part time; 26% male, 74% female; 0% American Indian, 3% Asian, 5% black, 7% Hispanic, 3% multiracial, 0% Pacific Islander, 72% white, 1% international; 56% from in state; 72% live on campus; 0% of students in fraternities, 0% in sororities
Most popular majors: 13% Biological and Biomedical Sciences, 15% Business, Management, Marketing, and Related Support Services, 8% Communication, Journalism, and Related Programs, 16% Psychology, 9% Social Sciences
Expenses: 2015-2016: $36,504; room/board: $13,920
Financial aid: (617) 735-9938; 81% of undergrads determined to have financial need; average aid package $27,346

Endicott College

Beverly MA
(978) 921-1000
U.S. News ranking: Reg. U. (N), No. 66
Website: www.endicott.edu
Admissions email: admission@endicott.edu
Private; founded 1939
Freshman admissions: selective; 2014-2015: 3,848 applied, 2,815 accepted. Neither SAT nor ACT required. SAT 25/75 percentile: 980-1170. High school rank: 13% in top tenth, 40% in top quarter, 78% in top half
Early decision deadline: N/A, notification date: N/A
Early action deadline: N/A, notification date: N/A
Application deadline (fall): 2/15
Undergraduate student body: 2,618 full time, 345 part time; 38% male, 62% female; 0% American Indian, 1% Asian, 3% black, 4% Hispanic, 2% multiracial, 0% Pacific Islander, 82% white, 1% international; 48% from in state; 86% live on campus; N/A of students in fraternities, N/A in sororities
Most popular majors: 28% Business, Management, Marketing, and Related Support Services, 7% Communication, Journalism, and Related Programs, 11% Health Professions and Related Programs, 14% Parks, Recreation, Leisure, and Fitness Studies, 9% Visual and Performing Arts
Expenses: 2015-2016: $30,492; room/board: $14,112
Financial aid: (978) 232-2070; 67% of undergrads determined to have financial need; average aid package $20,277

Fisher College

Boston MA
(617) 236-8818
U.S. News ranking: Reg. Coll. (N), second tier
Website: www.fisher.edu
Admissions email: admissions@fisher.edu
Private; founded 1903
Freshman admissions: least selective; 2014-2015: 2,774 applied, 1,819 accepted. Neither SAT nor ACT required. SAT 25/75 percentile: 710-940. High school rank: N/A
Early decision deadline: N/A, notification date: N/A
Early action deadline: N/A, notification date: N/A
Application deadline (fall): rolling
Undergraduate student body: 1,161 full time, 714 part time; 27% male, 73% female; 0% American Indian, 1% Asian, 10% black, 9% Hispanic, 1% multiracial, 0% Pacific Islander, 32% white, 8% international; 82% from in state; 16% live on campus; N/A of students in fraternities, N/A in sororities
Most popular majors: 42% Business Administration and Management, General, 6% Early Childhood Education and Teaching, 19% Health/Health Care Administration/Management, 5% Human Services, General, 15% Liberal Arts and Sciences/Liberal Studies
Expenses: 2015-2016: $28,942; room/board: $15,082
Financial aid: (617) 236-8821

Fitchburg State University

Fitchburg MA
(978) 665-3144
U.S. News ranking: Reg. U. (N), second tier
Website: www.fitchburgstate.edu
Admissions email: admissions@fitchburgstate.edu
Public; founded 1894
Freshman admissions: selective; 2014-2015: 3,814 applied, 2,758 accepted. Either SAT or ACT required. SAT 25/75 percentile: 900-1110. High school rank: N/A
Early decision deadline: N/A, notification date: N/A
Early action deadline: N/A, notification date: N/A
Application deadline (fall): rolling
Undergraduate student body: 3,419 full time, 793 part time; 44% male, 56% female; 0% American Indian, 2% Asian, 7% black, 10% Hispanic, 3% multiracial, 0% Pacific Islander, 74% white, 0% international; 92% from in state; 41% live on campus; 1% of students in fraternities, 1% in sororities
Most popular majors: 12% Business, Management, Marketing, and Related Support Services, 7% Homeland Security, Law Enforcement, Firefighting and Related Protective Services, 12% Multi/Interdisciplinary Studies, 8% Parks, Recreation, Leisure, and Fitness Studies, 16% Visual and Performing Arts
Expenses: 2014-2015: $9,260 in state, $15,340 out of state; room/board: $8,912
Financial aid: (978) 665-3156

Framingham State University

Framingham MA
(508) 626-4500
U.S. News ranking: Reg. U. (N), second tier
Website: www.framingham.edu
Admissions email: admissions@framingham.edu
Public; founded 1839
Freshman admissions: selective; 2014-2015: 5,207 applied, 3,241 accepted. Either SAT or ACT required. SAT 25/75 percentile: 920-1100. High school rank: 10% in top tenth, 26% in top quarter, 64% in top half
Early decision deadline: N/A, notification date: N/A
Early action deadline: 11/15, notification date: 12/15
Application deadline (fall): rolling
Undergraduate student body: 3,925 full time, 684 part time; 37% male, 63% female; 0% American

Indian, 3% Asian, 8% black, 9% Hispanic, 3% multiracial, 0% Pacific Islander, 74% white, 0% international; 96% from in state; 50% live on campus; N/A of students in fraternities, N/A in sororities
Most popular majors: 16% Business, Management, Marketing, and Related Support Services, 8% Communications Technologies/Technicians and Support Services, 11% Family and Consumer Sciences/Human Sciences, 12% Psychology, 16% Social Sciences
Expenses: 2014-2015: $8,320 in state, $14,400 out of state; room/board: $10,534
Financial aid: (508) 626-4534

Franklin W. Olin College of Engineering

Needham MA
(781) 292-2222
U.S. News ranking: Engineering, unranked
Website: www.olin.edu/
Admissions email: info@olin.edu
Private; founded 1997
Freshman admissions: more selective; 2014-2015: 983 applied, 118 accepted. Either SAT or ACT required. SAT 25/75 percentile: 1410-1550. High school rank: N/A
Early decision deadline: N/A, notification date: N/A
Early action deadline: N/A, notification date: N/A
Application deadline (fall): 1/1
Undergraduate student body: 348 full time, 22 part time; 51% male, 49% female; 0% American Indian, 15% Asian, 1% black, 4% Hispanic, 6% multiracial, 0% Pacific Islander, 56% white, 7% international; 15% from in state; 100% live on campus; 0% of students in fraternities, 0% in sororities
Most popular majors: 20% Electrical and Electronics Engineering, 48% Engineering, General, 32% Mechanical Engineering
Expenses: 2015-2016: $45,525; room/board: $15,600
Financial aid: N/A; 49% of undergrads determined to have financial need; average aid package $41,000

Gordon College

Wenham MA
(866) 464-6736
U.S. News ranking: Nat. Lib. Arts, No. 158
Website: www.gordon.edu
Admissions email: admissions@gordon.edu
Private; founded 1889
Affiliation: multi-denominational
Freshman admissions: selective; 2014-2015: 1,892 applied, 1,672 accepted. Either SAT or ACT required. SAT 25/75 percentile: 1030-1280. High school rank: 36% in top tenth, 67% in top quarter, 91% in top half
Early decision deadline: 11/1, notification date: 12/1
Early action deadline: 11/15, notification date: 12/1
Application deadline (fall): 8/1
Undergraduate student body: 1,697 full time, 39 part time; 38% male, 62% female; 0% American Indian, 4% Asian, 4% black, 7% Hispanic, 3% multiracial, 0% Pacific Islander, 75% white, 7% international; 34% from in state; 86% live on campus; N/A of students in fraternities, N/A in sororities
Most popular majors: 5% Biology/Biological Sciences, General, 8% Business Administration and Management, General, 7% English Language and Literature, General, 8% Psychology, General, 5% Speech Communication and Rhetoric
Expenses: 2015-2016: $35,386; room/board: $10,218
Financial aid: (978) 867-4246; 70% of undergrads determined to have financial need; average aid package $22,562

Hampshire College[1]

Amherst MA
(413) 559-5471
U.S. News ranking: Nat. Lib. Arts, unranked
Website: www.hampshire.edu
Admissions email: admissions@hampshire.edu
Private; founded 1965
Application deadline (fall): 1/15
Undergraduate student body: N/A full time, N/A part time
Expenses: 2014-2015: $48,065; room/board: $12,450
Financial aid: (413) 559-5484

Harvard University

Cambridge MA
(617) 495-1551
U.S. News ranking: Nat. U., No. 2
Website: www.college.harvard.edu
Admissions email: college@fas.harvard.edu
Private; founded 1636
Freshman admissions: most selective; 2014-2015: 34,295 applied, 2,045 accepted. Either SAT or ACT required. SAT 25/75 percentile: 1410-1600. High school rank: 95% in top tenth, 100% in top quarter, 100% in top half
Early decision deadline: N/A, notification date: N/A
Early action deadline: 11/1, notification date: 12/16
Application deadline (fall): 1/1
Undergraduate student body: 6,688 full time, 6 part time; 53% male, 47% female; 0% American Indian, 19% Asian, 7% black, 10% Hispanic, 7% multiracial, 0% Pacific Islander, 44% white, 11% international
Most popular majors: 14% Biology/Biological Sciences, General, 9% History, General, 8% Mathematics, General, 6% Physical Sciences, 33% Social Sciences, General
Expenses: 2015-2016: $45,278; room/board: $15,381
Financial aid: (617) 495-1581; 60% of undergrads determined to have financial need; average aid package $47,475

Lasell College

Newton MA
(617) 243-2225
U.S. News ranking: Reg. Coll. (N), No. 26
Website: www.lasell.edu
Admissions email: info@lasell.edu
Private; founded 1851
Freshman admissions: less selective; 2014-2015: 3,122 applied, 2,382 accepted. Either SAT or ACT required. SAT 25/75 percentile: 880-1070. High school rank: N/A
Early decision deadline: N/A, notification date: N/A
Early action deadline: 11/15, notification date: 12/1
Application deadline (fall): rolling
Undergraduate student body: 1,706 full time, 31 part time; 35% male, 65% female; 0% American Indian, 2% Asian, 6% black, 9% Hispanic, 3% multiracial, 0% Pacific Islander, 74% white, 4% international; 57% from in state; 79% live on campus; 0% of students in fraternities, 0% in sororities
Most popular majors: 12% Communication and Media Studies, 9% Fashion Merchandising, 8% Fashion/Apparel Design, 6% Marketing/Marketing Management, General, 6% Psychology, General
Expenses: 2015-2016: $32,000; room/board: $13,250
Financial aid: (617) 243-2227; 82% of undergrads determined to have financial need; average aid package $24,392

Lesley University

Cambridge MA
(617) 349-8800
U.S. News ranking: Reg. U. (N), No. 112
Website: www.lesley.edu
Admissions email: lcadmissions@lesley.edu
Private; founded 1909
Freshman admissions: selective; 2014-2015: 2,827 applied, 2,021 accepted. Either SAT or ACT required. SAT 25/75 percentile: 980-1190. High school rank: 11% in top tenth, 43% in top quarter, 79% in top half
Early decision deadline: N/A, notification date: N/A
Early action deadline: 12/1, notification date: 12/31
Application deadline (fall): rolling
Undergraduate student body: 1,307 full time, 185 part time; 22% male, 78% female; 0% American Indian, 4% Asian, 3% black, 10% Hispanic, 4% multiracial, 0% Pacific Islander, 71% white, 2% international; 58% from in state; 65% live on campus; N/A of students in fraternities, N/A in sororities
Most popular majors: 8% English Language and Literature/Letters, 10% Health Professions and Related Programs, 13% Liberal Arts and Sciences, General Studies and Humanities, 22% Psychology
Expenses: 2015-2016: $25,280; room/board: $15,430
Financial aid: (617) 349-8581; 68% of undergrads determined to have financial need; average aid package $14,007

Massachusetts College of Art and Design

Boston MA
(617) 879-7222
U.S. News ranking: Arts, unranked
Website: www.massart.edu
Admissions email: admissions@massart.edu
Public; founded 1873
Freshman admissions: N/A; 2014-2015: 1,345 applied, 981 accepted. Either SAT or ACT required. SAT 25/75 percentile: 950-1190. High school rank: N/A
Early decision deadline: N/A, notification date: N/A
Early action deadline: 12/1, notification date: 1/5
Application deadline (fall): 2/1
Undergraduate student body: 1,628 full time, 337 part time; 30% male, 70% female; 0% American Indian, 7% Asian, 3% black, 9% Hispanic, 2% multiracial, 0% Pacific Islander, 67% white, 4% international; 66% from in state; 38% live on campus; N/A of students in fraternities, N/A in sororities
Most popular majors: Information not available
Expenses: 2015-2016: $11,725 in state, $31,225 out of state; room/board: $13,000
Financial aid: (617) 879-7850; 61% of undergrads determined to have financial need; average aid package $10,544

Massachusetts College of Liberal Arts

North Adams MA
(413) 662-5410
U.S. News ranking: Nat. Lib. Arts, second tier
Website: www.mcla.edu
Admissions email: admissions@mcla.edu
Public; founded 1894
Freshman admissions: less selective; 2014-2015: 2,066 applied, 1,493 accepted. Either SAT or ACT required. SAT 25/75 percentile: 860-1090. High school rank: 8% in top tenth, 32% in top quarter, 76% in top half
Early decision deadline: N/A, notification date: N/A
Early action deadline: 12/1, notification date: 12/15
Application deadline (fall): rolling
Undergraduate student body: 1,378 full time, 184 part time; 37% male, 63% female; 0% American Indian, 2% Asian, 9% black, 7% Hispanic, 3% multiracial, N/A Pacific Islander, 75% white, N/A international; 75% from in state; 61% live on campus; N/A of students in fraternities, N/A in sororities
Most popular majors: 18% Business, Management, Marketing, and Related Support Services, 15% English Language and Literature/Letters, 13% Psychology, 13% Social Sciences, 11% Visual and Performing Arts
Expenses: 2015-2016: $9,475 in state, $18,420 out of state; room/board: $9,828
Financial aid: (413) 662-5219; 75% of undergrads determined to have financial need; average aid package $14,445

Massachusetts Institute of Technology

Cambridge MA
(617) 253-3400
U.S. News ranking: Nat. U., No. 7
Website: web.mit.edu/
Admissions email: admissions@mit.edu
Private; founded 1861
Freshman admissions: most selective; 2014-2015: 18,356 applied, 1,447 accepted. Either SAT or ACT required. SAT 25/75 percentile: 1420-1570. High school rank: 97% in top tenth, 100% in top quarter, 100% in top half
Early decision deadline: N/A, notification date: N/A
Early action deadline: 11/1, notification date: 12/20
Application deadline (fall): 1/1
Undergraduate student body: 4,476 full time, 36 part time; 54% male, 46% female; 0% American Indian, 25% Asian, 6% black, 16% Hispanic, 5% multiracial, 0% Pacific Islander, 37% white, 10% international; 9% from in state; 87% live on campus; 50% of students in fraternities, 32% in sororities
Most popular majors: 10% Biological and Biomedical Sciences, 23% Computer Science, 39% Engineering, 7% Mathematics, General, 8% Physical Sciences
Expenses: 2015-2016: $46,704; room/board: $13,730
Financial aid: (617) 253-4971; 59% of undergrads determined to have financial need; average aid package $42,353

Massachusetts Maritime Academy

Buzzards Bay MA
(800) 544-3411
U.S. News ranking: Reg. Coll. (N), No. 8
Website: www.maritime.edu
Admissions email: admissions@maritime.edu
Public; founded 1891
Freshman admissions: selective; 2014-2015: 810 applied, 499 accepted. Either SAT or ACT required. SAT 25/75 percentile: 1030-1190. High school rank: N/A
Early decision deadline: N/A, notification date: N/A
Early action deadline: 11/1, notification date: 12/15
Application deadline (fall): rolling
Undergraduate student body: 1,373 full time, 28 part time; 88% male, 12% female; 1% American Indian, 3% Asian, 2% black, 3% Hispanic, 0% multiracial, 0% Pacific Islander, 88% white, 1% international; 78% from in state; 96% live on campus; 0% of students in fraternities, 0% in sororities
Most popular majors: 68% Naval Architecture and Marine Engineering
Expenses: 2014-2015: $7,203 in state, $22,109 out of state; room/board: $11,120
Financial aid: (508) 830-5087

Merrimack College

North Andover MA
(978) 837-5100
U.S. News ranking: Reg. Coll. (N), No. 9
Website: www.merrimack.edu
Admissions email: Admission@Merrimack.edu
Private; founded 1947
Affiliation: Roman Catholic
Freshman admissions: selective; 2014-2015: 7,044 applied, 5,478 accepted. Neither SAT nor ACT required. SAT 25/75

percentile: 930-1120. High school rank: N/A
Early decision deadline: 11/15, notification date: 12/15
Early action deadline: 11/15, notification date: 12/15
Application deadline (fall): 2/15
Undergraduate student body: 2,877 full time, 174 part time; 49% male, 51% female; 0% American Indian, 1% Asian, 3% black, 6% Hispanic, 1% multiracial, 0% Pacific Islander, 69% white, 6% international; 72% from in state; 75% live on campus; 1% of students in fraternities, 5% in sororities
Most popular majors: 25% Business, Management, Marketing, and Related Support Services, 7% Engineering, 11% Family and Consumer Sciences/Human Sciences, 10% Health Professions and Related Programs, 7% Social Sciences
Expenses: 2015-2016: $37,270; room/board: $13,875
Financial aid: (978) 837-5196; 72% of undergrads determined to have financial need; average aid package $22,246

Montserrat College of Art

Beverly MA
(978) 921-4242
U.S. News ranking: Arts, unranked
Website: www.montserrat.edu
Admissions email: admissions@montserrrat.edu
Private; founded 1970
Freshman admissions: N/A; 2014-2015: N/A applied, N/A accepted. Neither SAT nor ACT required. ACT 25/75 percentile: N/A. High school rank: N/A
Early decision deadline: N/A, notification date: N/A
Early action deadline: N/A, notification date: N/A
Application deadline (fall): N/A
Undergraduate student body: 383 full time, 19 part time; 26% male, 74% female; N/A American Indian, N/A Asian, N/A black, N/A Hispanic, N/A multiracial, N/A Pacific Islander, N/A white, N/A international
Most popular majors: Information not available
Expenses: 2014-2015: $28,700; room/board: $9,700
Financial aid: (978) 921-4242

Mount Holyoke College

South Hadley MA
(413) 538-2023
U.S. News ranking: Nat. Lib. Arts, No. 35
Website: www.mtholyoke.edu
Admissions email: admission@mtholyoke.edu
Private; founded 1837
Freshman admissions: more selective; 2014-2015: 3,201 applied, 1,751 accepted. Neither SAT nor ACT required. SAT 25/75 percentile: 1220-1450. High school rank: 56% in top tenth, 82% in top quarter, 95% in top half
Early decision deadline: 11/15, notification date: 1/1
Early action deadline: N/A, notification date: N/A
Application deadline (fall): 1/15
Undergraduate student body: 2,161 full time, 28 part time; 0% male, 100% female; 0% American Indian, 10% Asian, 6% black, 8% Hispanic, 3% multiracial, 0% Pacific Islander, 47% white, 25% international; 23% from in state; 95% live on campus; 0% of students in fraternities, 0% in sororities
Most popular majors: 8% Biology/Biological Sciences, General, 10% Economics, General, 9% English Language and Literature, General, 9% International Relations and Affairs, 9% Psychology, General
Expenses: 2015-2016: $43,886; room/board: $12,860
Financial aid: (413) 538-2291; 67% of undergrads determined to have financial need; average aid package $36,761

Mount Ida College

Newton MA
(617) 928-4535
U.S. News ranking: Reg. Coll. (N), No. 38
Website: www.mountida.edu
Admissions email: admissions@mountida.edu
Private; founded 1899
Freshman admissions: less selective; 2014-2015: 2,024 applied, 1,384 accepted. Either SAT or ACT required. SAT 25/75 percentile: 780-990. High school rank: N/A
Early decision deadline: N/A, notification date: N/A
Early action deadline: N/A, notification date: N/A
Application deadline (fall): rolling
Undergraduate student body: 1,198 full time, 95 part time; 34% male, 66% female; 0% American Indian, 2% Asian, 11% black, 11% Hispanic, 3% multiracial, 0% Pacific Islander, 59% white, 6% international; 66% from in state; 83% live on campus; 0% of students in fraternities, 0% in sororities
Most popular majors: 8% Business Administration and Management, General, 13% Dental Hygiene/Hygienist, 7% Fashion Merchandising, 6% Psychology, General, 19% Veterinary/Animal Health Technology/Technician and Veterinary Assistant
Expenses: 2015-2016: $32,300; room/board: $13,000
Financial aid: (617) 928-4785; 81% of undergrads determined to have financial need; average aid package $21,136

National Graduate School of Quality Management[1]

Falmouth MA
(800) 838-2580
U.S. News ranking: Business, unranked
Website: www.ngs.edu
Admissions email: N/A
Private
Application deadline (fall): N/A
Undergraduate student body: N/A full time, N/A part time
Expenses: N/A
Financial aid: (800) 838-2580

Newbury College

Brookline MA
(617) 730-7007
U.S. News ranking: Reg. Coll. (N), unranked
Website: www.newbury.edu/
Admissions email: info@newbury.edu
Private; founded 1962
Freshman admissions: N/A; 2014-2015: 3,211 applied, 2,256 accepted. Neither SAT nor ACT required. SAT 25/75 percentile: 740-940. High school rank: N/A
Early decision deadline: N/A, notification date: N/A
Early action deadline: N/A, notification date: N/A
Application deadline (fall): rolling
Undergraduate student body: 800 full time, 74 part time; 43% male, 57% female; 0% American Indian, 6% Asian, 36% black, 14% Hispanic, 4% multiracial, 0% Pacific Islander, 37% white, 3% international; N/A from in state; 38% live on campus; N/A of students in fraternities, N/A in sororities
Most popular majors: 13% Business Administration and Management, General, 10% Corrections and Criminal Justice, Other, 9% Hospitality Administration/Management, General, 14% Psychology, General, 11% Restaurant, Culinary, and Catering Management/Manager
Expenses: 2015-2016: $31,408; room/board: $13,740
Financial aid: (617) 730-7100; 90% of undergrads determined to have financial need; average aid package $23,563

New England Conservatory of Music[1]

Boston MA
(617) 585-1101
U.S. News ranking: Arts, unranked
Website: www.newenglandconservatory.edu
Admissions email: admission@newenglandconservatory.edu
Private; founded 1867
Application deadline (fall): 12/1
Undergraduate student body: N/A full time, N/A part time
Expenses: 2015-2016: $43,055; room/board: $13,110
Financial aid: (617) 585-1110; 48% of undergrads determined to have financial need; average aid package $25,474

New England Institute of Art[1]

Brookline MA
(800) 903-4425
U.S. News ranking: Arts, unranked
Website: www.artinstitutes.edu/boston/
Admissions email: N/A
For-profit
Application deadline (fall): N/A
Undergraduate student body: N/A full time, N/A part time
Expenses: 2014-2015: $18,760; room/board: $18,225
Financial aid: N/A

Nichols College

Dudley MA
(800) 470-3379
U.S. News ranking: Reg. Coll. (N), No. 36
Website: www.nichols.edu/
Admissions email: admissions@nichols.edu
Private; founded 1815
Freshman admissions: less selective; 2014-2015: 2,457 applied, 1,875 accepted. Neither SAT nor ACT required. SAT 25/75 percentile: 840-1030. High school rank: 3% in top tenth, 13% in top quarter, 35% in top half
Early decision deadline: N/A, notification date: N/A
Early action deadline: 12/1, notification date: N/A
Application deadline (fall): rolling
Undergraduate student body: 1,180 full time, 150 part time; 61% male, 39% female; 0% American Indian, 2% Asian, 5% black, 7% Hispanic, 3% multiracial, 0% Pacific Islander, 81% white, 1% international; 66% from in state; 71% live on campus; 0% of students in fraternities, 0% in sororities
Most popular majors: 7% Accounting, 38% Business/Commerce, General, 9% Criminal Justice/Law Enforcement Administration, 6% Marketing/Marketing Management, General, 10% Sport and Fitness Administration/Management
Expenses: 2015-2016: $33,300; room/board: $12,600
Financial aid: (508) 213-2278; 84% of undergrads determined to have financial need; average aid package $24,699

Northeastern University

Boston MA
(617) 373-2200
U.S. News ranking: Nat. U., No. 47
Website: www.northeastern.edu/
Admissions email: admissions@neu.edu
Private; founded 1898
Freshman admissions: most selective; 2014-2015: 49,819 applied, 16,052 accepted. Either SAT or ACT required. SAT 25/75 percentile: 1340-1500. High school rank: 66% in top tenth, 92% in top quarter, 99% in top half
Early decision deadline: 11/1, notification date: 12/15
Early action deadline: 11/1, notification date: 12/31
Application deadline (fall): 1/1
Undergraduate student body: 13,492 full time, 18 part time; 49% male, 51% female; 0% American Indian, 11% Asian, 3% black, 7% Hispanic, 4% multiracial, 0% Pacific Islander, 49% white, 19% international; 32% from in state; N/A live on campus; N/A of students in fraternities, N/A in sororities
Most popular majors: 8% Biological and Biomedical Sciences, 21% Business, Management, Marketing, and Related Support Services, 15% Engineering, 15% Health Professions and Related Programs, 11% Social Sciences
Expenses: 2015-2016: $45,530; room/board: $15,000
Financial aid: (617) 373-3190; 38% of undergrads determined to have financial need; average aid package $26,669

Pine Manor College

Chestnut Hill MA
(617) 731-7104
U.S. News ranking: Nat. Lib. Arts, second tier
Website: www.pmc.edu
Admissions email: admission@pmc.edu
Private; founded 1911
Freshman admissions: least selective; 2014-2015: 908 applied, 616 accepted. Either SAT or ACT required. SAT 25/75 percentile: 680-880. High school rank: N/A
Early decision deadline: N/A, notification date: N/A
Early action deadline: N/A, notification date: N/A
Application deadline (fall): rolling
Undergraduate student body: 399 full time, 4 part time; 36% male, 64% female; 1% American Indian, 2% Asian, 28% black, 16% Hispanic, 8% multiracial, 0% Pacific Islander, 7% white, 28% international; 56% from in state; 64% live on campus; N/A of students in fraternities, N/A in sororities
Most popular majors: 20% Biology/Biological Sciences, General, 13% Education, General, 16% Management Science, 17% Psychology, General, 20% Social Sciences, General
Expenses: 2015-2016: $27,250; room/board: $12,980
Financial aid: (617) 731-7129; 89% of undergrads determined to have financial need; average aid package $25,405

Salem State University

Salem MA
(978) 542-6200
U.S. News ranking: Reg. U. (N), second tier
Website: www.salemstate.edu
Admissions email: admissions@salemstate.edu
Public; founded 1854
Freshman admissions: less selective; 2014-2015: 5,198 applied, 3,668 accepted. Either SAT or ACT required. SAT 25/75 percentile: 883-1080. High school rank: N/A
Early decision deadline: N/A, notification date: N/A
Early action deadline: 11/15, notification date: 12/1
Application deadline (fall): rolling
Undergraduate student body: 5,905 full time, 1,695 part time; 40% male, 60% female; 0% American Indian, 3% Asian, 9% black, 12% Hispanic, 2% multiracial, 0% Pacific Islander, 68% white, 4% international; 97% from in state; 30% live on campus; N/A of students in fraternities, N/A in sororities
Most popular majors: 22% Business, Management, Marketing, and Related Support Services, 9% Education, 13% Health Professions and Related Programs, 8% Homeland Security, Law Enforcement, Firefighting and Related Protective Services, 9% Psychology
Expenses: 2014-2015: $8,646 in state, $14,786 out of state; room/board: $11,758
Financial aid: (978) 542-6139

Simmons College

Boston MA
(800) 345-8468
U.S. News ranking: Reg. U. (N), No. 16
Website: www.simmons.edu

Admissions email: ugadm@simmons.edu
Private; founded 1899
Freshman admissions: more selective; 2014-2015: 3,999 applied, 2,086 accepted. Either SAT or ACT required. SAT 25/75 percentile: 1070-1260. High school rank: 30% in top tenth, 64% in top quarter, 92% in top half
Early decision deadline: N/A, notification date: N/A
Early action deadline: 11/1, notification date: 12/15
Application deadline (fall): 2/1
Undergraduate student body: 1,484 full time, 138 part time; 0% male, 100% female; 0% American Indian, 10% Asian, 6% black, 6% Hispanic, 3% multiracial, 0% Pacific Islander, 68% white, 3% international; 61% from in state; 60% live on campus; 0% of students in fraternities, 0% in sororities
Most popular majors: Information not available
Expenses: 2015-2016: $37,380; room/board: $14,040
Financial aid: (617) 521-2001; 78% of undergrads determined to have financial need; average aid package $27,847

Smith College

Northampton MA
(413) 585-2500
U.S. News ranking: Nat. Lib. Arts, No. 14
Website: www.smith.edu
Admissions email: admission@smith.edu
Private; founded 1871
Freshman admissions: more selective; 2014-2015: 4,466 applied, 1,885 accepted. Neither SAT nor ACT required. SAT 25/75 percentile: 1240-1470. High school rank: 62% in top tenth, 91% in top quarter, 100% in top half
Early decision deadline: 11/15, notification date: 12/15
Early action deadline: N/A, notification date: N/A
Application deadline (fall): 1/15
Undergraduate student body: 2,544 full time, 19 part time; 0% male, 100% female; 0% American Indian, 13% Asian, 5% black, 9% Hispanic, 4% multiracial, 0% Pacific Islander, 46% white, 14% international; 22% from in state; 95% live on campus; N/A of students in fraternities, N/A in sororities
Most popular majors: 11% Biological and Biomedical Sciences, 10% Foreign Languages, Literatures, and Linguistics, 9% Psychology, 24% Social Sciences, 8% Visual and Performing Arts
Expenses: 2015-2016: $46,288; room/board: $15,470
Financial aid: (413) 585-2530; 62% of undergrads determined to have financial need; average aid package $43,182

Springfield College

Springfield MA
(413) 748-3136
U.S. News ranking: Reg. U. (N), No. 29
Website: www.springfieldcollege.edu
Admissions email: admissions@springfiledcollege.edu
Private; founded 1885
Freshman admissions: selective; 2014-2015: 2,262 applied, 1,603 accepted. Either SAT or ACT required. SAT 25/75 percentile: 910-1170. High school rank: 18% in top tenth, 39% in top quarter, 70% in top half
Early decision deadline: 12/1, notification date: 2/1
Early action deadline: N/A, notification date: N/A
Application deadline (fall): 4/1
Undergraduate student body: 2,125 full time, 46 part time; 52% male, 48% female; 0% American Indian, 1% Asian, 5% black, 5% Hispanic, 1% multiracial, 0% Pacific Islander, 83% white, 2% international; 40% from in state; 85% live on campus; N/A of students in fraternities, N/A in sororities
Most popular majors: 6% Business, Management, Marketing, and Related Support Services, 11% Education, 34% Health Professions and Related Programs, 20% Parks, Recreation, Leisure, and Fitness Studies, 6% Psychology
Expenses: 2015-2016: $34,455; room/board: $11,540
Financial aid: (413) 748-3108; 82% of undergrads determined to have financial need; average aid package $24,673

Stonehill College

Easton MA
(508) 565-1373
U.S. News ranking: Nat. Lib. Arts, No. 116
Website: www.stonehill.edu
Admissions email: admission@stonehill.edu
Private; founded 1948
Affiliation: Roman Catholic
Freshman admissions: selective; 2014-2015: 6,006 applied, 4,622 accepted. Neither SAT nor ACT required. SAT 25/75 percentile: 1010-1220. High school rank: 29% in top tenth, 62% in top quarter, 89% in top half
Early decision deadline: 12/1, notification date: 12/31
Early action deadline: 11/1, notification date: 12/31
Application deadline (fall): 1/15
Undergraduate student body: 2,373 full time, 28 part time; 40% male, 60% female; 0% American Indian, 2% Asian, 4% black, 5% Hispanic, 2% multiracial, 0% Pacific Islander, 84% white, 1% international; 56% from in state; 92% live on campus; N/A of students in fraternities, N/A in sororities
Most popular majors: 10% Biological and Biomedical Sciences, 18% Business, Management, Marketing, and Related Support Services, 9% Communication, Journalism, and Related Programs, 10% Psychology, 14% Social Sciences
Expenses: 2015-2016: $38,550; room/board: $14,720
Financial aid: (508) 565-1088; 71% of undergrads determined to have financial need; average aid package $28,514

Suffolk University

Boston MA
(617) 573-8460
U.S. News ranking: Reg. U. (N), No. 58
Website: www.suffolk.edu
Admissions email: admission@suffolk.edu
Private; founded 1906
Freshman admissions: selective; 2014-2015: 8,921 applied, 7,486 accepted. Either SAT or ACT required. SAT 25/75 percentile: 890-1130. High school rank: 16% in top tenth, 41% in top quarter, 76% in top half
Early decision deadline: N/A, notification date: N/A
Early action deadline: 11/15, notification date: 12/15
Application deadline (fall): 7/30
Undergraduate student body: 5,130 full time, 366 part time; 45% male, 55% female; 0% American Indian, 8% Asian, 6% black, 12% Hispanic, 2% multiracial, 0% Pacific Islander, 39% white, 22% international; 66% from in state; 22% live on campus; N/A of students in fraternities, N/A in sororities
Most popular majors: 5% Biological and Biomedical Sciences, 38% Business, Management, Marketing, and Related Support Services, 16% Communication, Journalism, and Related Programs, 7% Psychology, 16% Social Sciences
Expenses: 2015-2016: $33,934; room/board: $14,648
Financial aid: (617) 573-8470; 61% of undergrads determined to have financial need; average aid package $26,333

Tufts University

Medford MA
(617) 627-3170
U.S. News ranking: Nat. U., No. 27
Website: www.tufts.edu
Admissions email: admissions.inquiry@ase.tufts.edu
Private; founded 1852
Freshman admissions: most selective; 2014-2015: 19,059 applied, 3,287 accepted. Either SAT or ACT required. SAT 25/75 percentile: 1360-1520. High school rank: 90% in top tenth, 99% in top quarter, 100% in top half
Early decision deadline: 11/1, notification date: 12/15
Early action deadline: N/A, notification date: N/A
Application deadline (fall): 1/1
Undergraduate student body: 5,127 full time, 50 part time; 49% male, 51% female; 0% American Indian, 11% Asian, 4% black, 7% Hispanic, 4% multiracial, 0% Pacific Islander, 57% white, 8% international; 23% from in state; 63% live on campus; 19% of students in fraternities, 17% in sororities
Most popular majors: Information not available
Expenses: 2015-2016: $50,604; room/board: $13,094
Financial aid: (617) 627-2000; 39% of undergrads determined to have financial need; average aid package $40,168

University of Massachusetts–Amherst

Amherst MA
(413) 545-0222
U.S. News ranking: Nat. U., No. 75
Website: www.umass.edu
Admissions email: mail@admissions.umass.edu
Public; founded 1863
Freshman admissions: more selective; 2014-2015: 37,183 applied, 22,804 accepted. Either SAT or ACT required. SAT 25/75 percentile: 1120-1310. High school rank: 33% in top tenth, 72% in top quarter, 98% in top half
Early decision deadline: N/A, notification date: N/A
Early action deadline: 11/1, notification date: 12/31
Application deadline (fall): 1/15
Undergraduate student body: 20,684 full time, 1,568 part time; 51% male, 49% female; 0% American Indian, 8% Asian, 4% black, 5% Hispanic, 2% multiracial, 0% Pacific Islander, 68% white, 3% international; 79% from in state; 65% live on campus; 8% of students in fraternities, 6% in sororities
Most popular majors: 10% Biological and Biomedical Sciences, 14% Business, Management, Marketing, and Related Support Services, 6% Multi/Interdisciplinary Studies, 9% Psychology, 11% Social Sciences
Expenses: 2015-2016: $14,356 in state, $30,689 out of state; room/board: $12,028
Financial aid: (413) 545-0801; 59% of undergrads determined to have financial need; average aid package $15,758

University of Massachusetts–Boston

Boston MA
(617) 287-6000
U.S. News ranking: Nat. U., second tier
Website: www.umb.edu
Admissions email: enrollment.info@umb.edu
Public; founded 1964
Freshman admissions: selective; 2014-2015: 8,453 applied, 5,981 accepted. SAT required. SAT 25/75 percentile: 950-1150. High school rank: N/A
Early decision deadline: N/A, notification date: N/A
Early action deadline: 12/15, notification date: N/A
Application deadline (fall): rolling
Undergraduate student body: 9,178 full time, 3,522 part time; 45% male, 55% female; 0% American Indian, 12% Asian, 16% black, 13% Hispanic, 2% multiracial, 0% Pacific Islander, 39% white, 12% international; 95% from in state; N/A live on campus; N/A of students in fraternities, N/A in sororities
Most popular majors: 6% Biological and Biomedical Sciences, 20% Business, Management, Marketing, and Related Support Services, 18% Health Professions and Related Programs, 7% Homeland Security, Law Enforcement, Firefighting and Related Protective Services, 12% Social Sciences
Expenses: 2014-2015: $11,966 in state, $28,390 out of state; room/board: N/A
Financial aid: (617) 287-6300; 67% of undergrads determined to have financial need; average aid package $15,227

University of Massachusetts–Dartmouth

North Dartmouth MA
(508) 999-8605
U.S. News ranking: Reg. U. (N), No. 83
Website: www.umassd.edu
Admissions email: admissions@umassd.edu
Public; founded 1895
Freshman admissions: selective; 2014-2015: 7,472 applied, 5,740 accepted. Either SAT or ACT required. SAT 25/75 percentile: 920-1130. High school rank: 13% in top tenth, 37% in top quarter, 73% in top half
Early decision deadline: N/A, notification date: N/A
Early action deadline: 11/15, notification date: 12/15
Application deadline (fall): rolling
Undergraduate student body: 6,361 full time, 1,093 part time; 52% male, 48% female; 0% American Indian, 3% Asian, 13% black, 8% Hispanic, 4% multiracial, 0% Pacific Islander, 66% white, 1% international; 95% from in state; 55% live on campus; 4% of students in fraternities, 8% in sororities
Most popular majors: 27% Business, Management, Marketing, and Related Support Services, 10% Engineering, 11% Health Professions and Related Programs, 8% Psychology, 12% Social Sciences
Expenses: 2014-2015: $11,681 in state, $18,363 out of state; room/board: $11,069
Financial aid: (508) 999-8632; 73% of undergrads determined to have financial need; average aid package $16,379

University of Massachusetts–Lowell

Lowell MA
(978) 934-3931
U.S. News ranking: Nat. U., No. 156
Website: www.uml.edu
Admissions email: admissions@uml.edu
Public; founded 1894
Freshman admissions: selective; 2014-2015: 9,394 applied, 5,825 accepted. Either SAT or ACT required. SAT 25/75 percentile: 1050-1240. High school rank: 23% in top tenth, 52% in top quarter, 83% in top half
Early decision deadline: N/A, notification date: N/A
Early action deadline: 11/1, notification date: 12/18
Application deadline (fall): 2/10
Undergraduate student body: 9,443 full time, 3,543 part time; 62% male, 38% female; 0% American Indian, 8% Asian, 6% black, 9% Hispanic, 3% multiracial, 0% Pacific Islander, 66% white, 2% international; 90% from in state; 38% live on campus; N/A

of students in fraternities, N/A in sororities
Most popular majors: 17% Business, Management, Marketing, and Related Support Services, 10% Computer and Information Sciences and Support Services, 15% Engineering, 11% Health Professions and Related Programs, 11% Homeland Security, Law Enforcement, Firefighting and Related Protective Services
Expenses: 2014-2015: $12,447 in state, $27,400 out of state; room/board: $11,278
Financial aid: (978) 934-4226; 64% of undergrads determined to have financial need; average aid package $14,892

Wellesley College

Wellesley MA
(781) 283-2270
U.S. News ranking: Nat. Lib. Arts, No. 4
Website: www.wellesley.edu
Admissions email: admission@wellesley.edu
Private; founded 1870
Freshman admissions: most selective; 2014-2015: 4,667 applied, 1,418 accepted. Either SAT or ACT required. SAT 25/75 percentile: 1290-1480. High school rank: 78% in top tenth, 97% in top quarter, 100% in top half
Early decision deadline: 11/1, notification date: 12/15
Early action deadline: N/A, notification date: N/A
Application deadline (fall): 1/15
Undergraduate student body: 2,177 full time, 146 part time; 3% male, 97% female; 0% American Indian, 24% Asian, 6% black, 9% Hispanic, 6% multiracial, 0% Pacific Islander, 42% white, 11% international; 16% from in state; 97% live on campus; N/A of students in fraternities, N/A in sororities
Most popular majors: 6% Biology/Biological Sciences, General, 16% Economics, General, 8% English Language and Literature, General, 7% Political Science and Government, General, 9% Psychology, General
Expenses: 2015-2016: $46,836; room/board: $14,504
Financial aid: (781) 283-2360; average aid package $42,400

Wentworth Institute of Technology

Boston MA
(617) 989-4000
U.S. News ranking: Reg. Coll. (N), No. 13
Website: www.wit.edu
Admissions email: admissions@wit.edu
Private; founded 1904
Freshman admissions: selective; 2014-2015: 5,316 applied, 4,393 accepted. Either SAT or ACT required. SAT 25/75 percentile: 1010-1220. High school rank: N/A
Early decision deadline: N/A, notification date: N/A
Early action deadline: N/A, notification date: N/A
Application deadline (fall): rolling
Undergraduate student body: 3,871 full time, 458 part time; 81% male, 19% female; 0% American Indian, 7% Asian, 5% black, 3% Hispanic, 6% multiracial, 0% Pacific Islander, 61% white, 6% international; 64% from in state; 49% live on campus; 0% of students in fraternities, 0% in sororities
Most popular majors: 21% Architecture and Related Services, 24% Business, Management, Marketing, and Related Support Services, 10% Computer and Information Sciences and Support Services, 8% Engineering, 29% Engineering Technologies and Engineering-Related Fields
Expenses: 2015-2016: $30,760; room/board: $13,390
Financial aid: (617) 989-4020; 74% of undergrads determined to have financial need; average aid package $19,628

Western New England University

Springfield MA
(413) 782-1321
U.S. News ranking: Reg. U. (N), No. 58
Website: www.wne.edu
Admissions email: learn@wne.edu
Private; founded 1919
Freshman admissions: selective; 2014-2015: 6,216 applied, 4,982 accepted. Either SAT or ACT required. SAT 25/75 percentile: 970-1170. High school rank: 19% in top tenth, 44% in top quarter, 76% in top half
Early decision deadline: N/A, notification date: N/A
Early action deadline: N/A, notification date: N/A
Application deadline (fall): rolling
Undergraduate student body: 2,576 full time, 156 part time; 60% male, 40% female; 0% American Indian, 3% Asian, 6% black, 8% Hispanic, 1% multiracial, 0% Pacific Islander, 74% white, 3% international; 48% from in state; 66% live on campus; N/A of students in fraternities, N/A in sororities
Most popular majors: 28% Business, Management, Marketing, and Related Support Services, 17% Engineering, 6% Homeland Security, Law Enforcement, Firefighting and Related Protective Services, 11% Psychology, General, 6% Sport and Fitness Administration/Management
Expenses: 2015-2016: $34,030; room/board: $12,894
Financial aid: (413) 796-2080; 80% of undergrads determined to have financial need; average aid package $23,667

Westfield State University

Westfield MA
(413) 572-5218
U.S. News ranking: Reg. U. (N), No. 116
Website: www.westfield.ma.edu
Admissions email: admissions@westfield.ma.edu
Public; founded 1838
Freshman admissions: selective; 2014-2015: 5,163 applied, 3,848 accepted. Either SAT or ACT required. SAT 25/75 percentile: 910-1090. High school rank: 6% in top tenth, 27% in top quarter, 66% in top half
Early decision deadline: N/A, notification date: N/A
Early action deadline: N/A, notification date: N/A
Application deadline (fall): 3/15
Undergraduate student body: 4,890 full time, 700 part time; 47% male, 53% female; 0% American Indian, 1% Asian, 4% black, 8% Hispanic, 4% multiracial, 0% Pacific Islander, 78% white, 0% international; 92% from in state; 54% live on campus; 0% of students in fraternities, 0% in sororities
Most popular majors: 14% Business, Management, Marketing, and Related Support Services, 11% Education, 13% Homeland Security, Law Enforcement, Firefighting and Related Protective Services, 14% Liberal Arts and Sciences, General Studies and Humanities, 9% Psychology
Expenses: 2014-2015: $8,548 in state, $14,628 out of state; room/board: $9,615
Financial aid: (413) 572-5218; 62% of undergrads determined to have financial need; average aid package $6,893

Wheaton College

Norton MA
(508) 286-8251
U.S. News ranking: Nat. Lib. Arts, No. 67
Website: www.wheatoncollege.edu
Admissions email: admission@wheatoncollege.edu
Private; founded 1834
Freshman admissions: more selective; 2014-2015: 4,047 applied, 2,818 accepted. Neither SAT nor ACT required. SAT 25/75 percentile: 1120-1350. High school rank: 34% in top tenth, 69% in top quarter, 91% in top half
Early decision deadline: 11/15, notification date: 12/15
Early action deadline: 11/15, notification date: 1/15
Application deadline (fall): 1/15
Undergraduate student body: 1,577 full time, 10 part time; 36% male, 64% female; 0% American Indian, 4% Asian, 6% black, 7% Hispanic, 3% multiracial, 0% Pacific Islander, 69% white, 10% international; 34% from in state; 96% live on campus; 0% of students in fraternities, 0% in sororities
Most popular majors: Information not available
Expenses: 2015-2016: $47,700; room/board: $12,165
Financial aid: (508) 286-8232; 65% of undergrads determined to have financial need; average aid package $36,669

Wheelock College

Boston MA
(617) 879-2206
U.S. News ranking: Reg. U. (N), No. 92
Website: www.wheelock.edu
Admissions email: undergrad@wheelock.edu
Private; founded 1888
Freshman admissions: less selective; 2014-2015: 1,458 applied, 1,276 accepted. Either SAT or ACT required. SAT 25/75 percentile: 850-1080. High school rank: 8% in top tenth, 35% in top quarter, 63% in top half
Early decision deadline: N/A, notification date: N/A
Early action deadline: 12/1, notification date: 12/20
Application deadline (fall): 5/1
Undergraduate student body: 836 full time, 33 part time; 12% male, 88% female; 0% American Indian, 3% Asian, 11% black, 12% Hispanic, 3% multiracial, 0% Pacific Islander, 60% white, 2% international; 61% from in state; 65% live on campus; N/A of students in fraternities, N/A in sororities
Most popular majors: 31% Education, 10% Family and Consumer Sciences/Human Sciences, 18% Psychology, 23% Public Administration and Social Service Professions
Expenses: 2015-2016: $33,835; room/board: $14,000
Financial aid: (617) 879-2206; 83% of undergrads determined to have financial need; average aid package $22,967

Williams College

Williamstown MA
(413) 597-2211
U.S. News ranking: Nat. Lib. Arts, No. 1
Website: www.williams.edu
Admissions email: admission@williams.edu
Private; founded 1793
Freshman admissions: most selective; 2014-2015: 6,316 applied, 1,220 accepted. Either SAT or ACT required. SAT 25/75 percentile: 1350-1560. High school rank: 95% in top tenth, 99% in top quarter, 100% in top half
Early decision deadline: 11/15, notification date: 12/15
Early action deadline: N/A, notification date: N/A
Application deadline (fall): 1/1
Undergraduate student body: 2,015 full time, 30 part time; 49% male, 51% female; 0% American Indian, 11% Asian, 7% black, 12% Hispanic, 7% multiracial, 0% Pacific Islander, 56% white, 7% international; 12% from in state; 94% live on campus; 0% of students in fraternities, 0% in sororities
Most popular majors: 16% Economics, General, 12% English Language and Literature, General, 13% History, General, 12% Political Science and Government, General, 13% Psychology, General
Expenses: 2015-2016: $50,070; room/board: $13,220
Financial aid: (413) 597-4181; 50% of undergrads determined to have financial need; average aid package $47,404

Worcester Polytechnic Institute

Worcester MA
(508) 831-5286
U.S. News ranking: Nat. U., No. 57
Website: admissions.wpi.edu
Admissions email: admissions@wpi.edu
Private; founded 1865
Freshman admissions: more selective; 2014-2015: 10,233 applied, 4,480 accepted. Neither SAT nor ACT required. SAT 25/75 percentile: 1210-1410. High school rank: 68% in top tenth, 92% in top quarter, 100% in top half
Early decision deadline: N/A, notification date: N/A
Early action deadline: 1/1, notification date: 2/10
Application deadline (fall): 2/1
Undergraduate student body: 4,096 full time, 139 part time; 68% male, 32% female; 0% American Indian, 5% Asian, 2% black, 8% Hispanic, 3% multiracial, 0% Pacific Islander, 62% white, 13% international; 42% from in state; 50% live on campus; 30% of students in fraternities, 48% in sororities
Most popular majors: 13% Bioengineering and Biomedical Engineering, 7% Chemical Engineering, 11% Electrical and Electronics Engineering, 6% Engineering, Other, 20% Mechanical Engineering
Expenses: 2015-2016: $45,590; room/board: $13,410
Financial aid: (508) 831-5469; 66% of undergrads determined to have financial need; average aid package $35,153

Worcester State University

Worcester MA
(508) 929-8040
U.S. News ranking: Reg. U. (N), No. 116
Website: www.worcester.edu
Admissions email: admissions@worcester.edu
Public; founded 1874
Freshman admissions: selective; 2014-2015: 4,158 applied, 2,549 accepted. Either SAT or ACT required. SAT 25/75 percentile: 890-1100. High school rank: N/A
Early decision deadline: N/A, notification date: N/A
Early action deadline: 11/15, notification date: 12/15
Application deadline (fall): 3/1
Undergraduate student body: 4,157 full time, 1,406 part time; 40% male, 60% female; 1% American Indian, 4% Asian, 7% black, 9% Hispanic, 2% multiracial, 0% Pacific Islander, 72% white, 1% international; 97% from in state; 25% live on campus; N/A of students in fraternities, N/A in sororities
Most popular majors: 17% Business, Management, Marketing, and Related Support Services, 7% Communication, Journalism, and Related Programs, 18% Health Professions and Related Programs, 10% Homeland Security, Law Enforcement, Firefighting and Related Protective Services, 7% Social Sciences
Expenses: 2014-2015: $8,557 in state, $14,637 out of state; room/board: $11,255
Financial aid: (508) 929-8056; 62% of undergrads determined to have financial need; average aid package $11,070

MICHIGAN

Adrian College

Adrian MI
(800) 877-2246
U.S. News ranking: Reg. Coll. (Mid.W), No. 19
Website: www.adrian.edu

Admissions email: admissions@adrian.edu
Private; founded 1859
Affiliation: The United Methodist Church
Freshman admissions: selective; 2014-2015: 5,153 applied, 3,189 accepted. Either SAT or ACT required. ACT 25/75 percentile: 19-24. High school rank: 26% in top tenth, 57% in top quarter, 81% in top half
Early decision deadline: N/A, notification date: N/A
Early action deadline: N/A, notification date: N/A
Application deadline (fall): rolling
Undergraduate student body: 1,546 full time, 76 part time; 52% male, 48% female; 0% American Indian, 1% Asian, 9% black, 5% Hispanic, 2% multiracial, 0% Pacific Islander, 75% white, 0% international; 82% from in state; 87% live on campus; 3% of students in fraternities, 5% in sororities
Most popular majors: 11% Biological and Biomedical Sciences, 22% Business, Management, Marketing, and Related Support Services, 11% Health Professions and Related Programs, 6% Homeland Security, Law Enforcement, Firefighting and Related Protective Services, 11% Visual and Performing Arts
Expenses: 2015-2016: $33,610; room/board: $10,220
Financial aid: (517) 264-3107; 87% of undergrads determined to have financial need; average aid package $26,296

Albion College

Albion MI
(800) 858-6770
U.S. News ranking: Nat. Lib. Arts, No. 100
Website: www.albion.edu/
Admissions email: admission@albion.edu
Private; founded 1835
Affiliation: United Methodist
Freshman admissions: more selective; 2014-2015: 4,886 applied, 2,970 accepted. Either SAT or ACT required. ACT 25/75 percentile: 22-27. High school rank: N/A
Early decision deadline: N/A, notification date: N/A
Early action deadline: 12/1, notification date: 1/15
Application deadline (fall): rolling
Undergraduate student body: 1,242 full time, 26 part time; 50% male, 50% female; 0% American Indian, 2% Asian, 4% black, 4% Hispanic, 3% multiracial, 0% Pacific Islander, 80% white, 2% international; 92% from in state; 90% live on campus; 53% of students in fraternities, 43% in sororities
Most popular majors: 7% Biochemistry, 14% Biology/Biological Sciences, General, 5% Communication, General, 5% Economics, General, 9% Psychology, General
Expenses: 2015-2016: $39,128; room/board: $11,066
Financial aid: (517) 629-0440; 73% of undergrads determined to have financial need; average aid package $29,076

Alma College

Alma MI
(800) 321-2562
U.S. News ranking: Nat. Lib. Arts, No. 143
Website: www.alma.edu
Admissions email: admissions@alma.edu
Private; founded 1886
Affiliation: Presbyterian
Freshman admissions: selective; 2014-2015: 2,338 applied, 1,683 accepted. Either SAT or ACT required. ACT 25/75 percentile: 21-27. High school rank: 23% in top tenth, 53% in top quarter, 83% in top half
Early decision deadline: N/A, notification date: N/A
Early action deadline: N/A, notification date: N/A
Application deadline (fall): rolling
Undergraduate student body: 1,353 full time, 43 part time; 45% male, 55% female; 1% American Indian, 1% Asian, 3% black, 4% Hispanic, 3% multiracial, 0% Pacific Islander, 84% white, 1% international; 91% from in state; 93% live on campus; 43% of students in fraternities, 38% in sororities
Most popular majors: 10% Biology, General, 19% Business Administration, Management and Operations, 17% Health and Physical Education/Fitness, 7% Psychology, General, 9% Teacher Education and Professional Development, Specific Levels and Methods
Expenses: 2015-2016: $35,806; room/board: $9,822
Financial aid: (989) 463-7347; 83% of undergrads determined to have financial need; average aid package $23,452

Andrews University

Berrien Springs MI
(800) 253-2874
U.S. News ranking: Nat. U., No. 175
Website: www.andrews.edu
Admissions email: enroll@andrews.edu
Private; founded 1874
Affiliation: Seventh-day Adventist
Freshman admissions: more selective; 2014-2015: 2,311 applied, 863 accepted. Either SAT or ACT required. ACT 25/75 percentile: 20-27. High school rank: 21% in top tenth, 44% in top quarter, 75% in top half
Early decision deadline: N/A, notification date: N/A
Early action deadline: N/A, notification date: N/A
Application deadline (fall): rolling
Undergraduate student body: 1,517 full time, 288 part time; 44% male, 56% female; 0% American Indian, 14% Asian, 20% black, 13% Hispanic, 3% multiracial, 0% Pacific Islander, 28% white, 20% international; 33% from in state; 62% live on campus; 0% of students in fraternities, 0% in sororities
Most popular majors: 7% Agriculture, Agriculture Operations, and Related Sciences, 7% Biological and Biomedical Sciences, 9% Business, Management, Marketing, and Related Support Services, 8% Education, 11% Visual and Performing Arts
Expenses: 2015-2016: $27,000; room/board: $8,532
Financial aid: (269) 471-3334; 60% of undergrads determined to have financial need; average aid package $27,265

Aquinas College

Grand Rapids MI
(616) 732-4460
U.S. News ranking: Reg. U. (Mid.W), No. 54
Website: www.aquinas.edu
Admissions email: admissions@aquinas.edu
Private; founded 1886
Affiliation: Roman Catholic
Freshman admissions: selective; 2014-2015: 2,572 applied, 1,674 accepted. Either SAT or ACT required. ACT 25/75 percentile: 21-26. High school rank: N/A
Early decision deadline: N/A, notification date: N/A
Early action deadline: N/A, notification date: N/A
Application deadline (fall): rolling
Undergraduate student body: 1,570 full time, 219 part time; 39% male, 61% female; 1% American Indian, 1% Asian, 3% black, 6% Hispanic, 2% multiracial, 0% Pacific Islander, 84% white, 1% international; 93% from in state; 54% live on campus; N/A of students in fraternities, N/A in sororities
Most popular majors: 7% Biological and Biomedical Sciences, 16% Business, Management, Marketing, and Related Support Services, 10% Psychology, 10% Social Sciences, 8% Visual and Performing Arts
Expenses: 2015-2016: $28,820; room/board: $8,558
Financial aid: (616) 632-2893; 80% of undergrads determined to have financial need; average aid package $20,213

Baker College of Flint[1]

Flint MI
(810) 766-4000
U.S. News ranking: Reg. Coll. (Mid.W), unranked
Website: www.baker.edu
Admissions email: troy.crowe@baker.edu
Private
Application deadline (fall): N/A
Undergraduate student body: N/A full time, N/A part time
Expenses: 2014-2015: $8,280; room/board: $5,400
Financial aid: (810) 766-4202

Calvin College

Grand Rapids MI
(616) 526-6106
U.S. News ranking: Nat. Lib. Arts, No. 120
Website: www.calvin.edu
Admissions email: admissions@calvin.edu
Private; founded 1876
Affiliation: Christian Reformed
Freshman admissions: more selective; 2014-2015: 3,679 applied, 2,691 accepted. Neither SAT nor ACT required. ACT 25/75 percentile: 23-29. High school rank: 32% in top tenth, 58% in top quarter, 85% in top half
Early decision deadline: N/A, notification date: N/A
Early action deadline: N/A, notification date: N/A
Application deadline (fall): 8/15
Undergraduate student body: 3,760 full time, 134 part time; 45% male, 55% female; 0% American Indian, 4% Asian, 2% black, 3% Hispanic, 3% multiracial, 0% Pacific Islander, 75% white, 10% international; 56% from in state; 60% live on campus; 0% of students in fraternities, 0% in sororities
Most popular majors: 7% Biology/Biological Sciences, General, 10% Business/Commerce, General, 5% Elementary Education and Teaching, 7% Engineering, General, 8% Registered Nursing/Registered Nurse
Expenses: 2015-2016: $30,660; room/board: $9,690
Financial aid: (616) 526-6137; 62% of undergrads determined to have financial need; average aid package $21,920

Central Michigan University

Mount Pleasant MI
(989) 774-3076
U.S. News ranking: Nat. U., No. 194
Website: www.cmich.edu
Admissions email: cmuadmit@cmich.edu
Public; founded 1892
Freshman admissions: selective; 2014-2015: 18,293 applied, 12,672 accepted. Either SAT or ACT required. ACT 25/75 percentile: 20-25. High school rank: 15% in top tenth, 39% in top quarter, 73% in top half
Early decision deadline: N/A, notification date: N/A
Early action deadline: N/A, notification date: N/A
Application deadline (fall): 7/1
Undergraduate student body: 18,059 full time, 2,735 part time; 44% male, 56% female; 1% American Indian, 1% Asian, 8% black, 3% Hispanic, 2% multiracial, 0% Pacific Islander, 80% white, 2% international; 96% from in state; 34% live on campus; 6% of students in fraternities, 10% in sororities
Most popular majors: 23% Business, Management, Marketing, and Related Support Services, 7% Communication, Journalism, and Related Programs, 11% Education, 9% Parks, Recreation, Leisure, and Fitness Studies, 7% Psychology
Expenses: 2015-2016: $11,850 in state, $23,670 out of state; room/board: $9,088
Financial aid: (989) 774-3674; 60% of undergrads determined to have financial need; average aid package $12,775

Cleary University[1]

Ann Arbor MI
(734) 332-4477
U.S. News ranking: Business, unranked
Website: www.cleary.edu
Admissions email: admissions@cleary.edu
Private; founded 1883
Application deadline (fall): N/A
Undergraduate student body: N/A full time, N/A part time
Expenses: 2015-2016: $14,760; room/board: $9,600
Financial aid: (800) 686-1883; 74% of undergrads determined to have financial need; average aid package $6,859

College for Creative Studies

Detroit MI
(313) 664-7425
U.S. News ranking: Arts, unranked
Website: www.collegeforcreativestudies.edu
Admissions email: admissions@collegeforcreativestudies.edu
Private; founded 1906
Freshman admissions: N/A; 2014-2015: N/A applied, N/A accepted. Either SAT or ACT required. ACT 25/75 percentile: 18-25. High school rank: N/A
Early decision deadline: N/A, notification date: N/A
Early action deadline: 12/1, notification date: 12/15
Application deadline (fall): 7/1
Undergraduate student body: 1,120 full time, 281 part time; 50% male, 50% female; 0% American Indian, 4% Asian, 9% black, 4% Hispanic, 4% multiracial, 0% Pacific Islander, 59% white, 7% international; 92% from in state; 38% live on campus; N/A of students in fraternities, N/A in sororities
Most popular majors: Information not available
Expenses: 2015-2016: $38,950; room/board: N/A
Financial aid: (313) 664-7495

Cornerstone University

Grand Rapids MI
(616) 222-1426
U.S. News ranking: Reg. U. (Mid.W), No. 108
Website: www.cornerstone.edu
Admissions email: admissions@cornerstone.edu
Private; founded 1941
Affiliation: Protestant
Freshman admissions: selective; 2014-2015: 2,394 applied, 1,648 accepted. Either SAT or ACT required. ACT 25/75 percentile: 20-25. High school rank: 13% in top tenth, 45% in top quarter, 76% in top half
Early decision deadline: N/A, notification date: N/A
Early action deadline: N/A, notification date: N/A
Application deadline (fall): 8/15
Undergraduate student body: 1,481 full time, 671 part time; 40% male, 60% female; 1% American Indian, 1% Asian, 12% black, 4% Hispanic, 0% multiracial, 0% Pacific Islander, 79% white, 2% international; 76% from in state; 91% live on campus; N/A of students in fraternities, N/A in sororities
Most popular majors: 14% Accounting, 12% Business Administration, Management and Operations, Other, 12% Kinesiology and Exercise Science, 16% Psychology, General, 13% Social Work
Expenses: 2015-2016: $26,100; room/board: $8,560
Financial aid: (616) 222-1424; 82% of undergrads determined to have financial need; average aid package $19,871

Davenport University

Grand Rapids MI
(866) 925-3884
U.S. News ranking: Reg. U. (Mid.W), second tier
Website: www.davenport.edu
Admissions email: Davenport.Admissions@davenport.edu
Private; founded 1866
Freshman admissions: selective; 2014-2015: 1,537 applied, 1,435 accepted. Neither SAT nor ACT required. Average composite ACT score: 21. High school rank: N/A
Early decision deadline: N/A, notification date: N/A
Early action deadline: N/A, notification date: N/A
Application deadline (fall): rolling
Undergraduate student body: 2,256 full time, 4,553 part time; 38% male, 62% female; 0% American Indian, 2% Asian, 15% black, 1% Hispanic, 3% multiracial, 0% Pacific Islander, 63% white, 2% international; 96% from in state; 5% live on campus; N/A of students in fraternities, N/A in sororities
Most popular majors: 8% Accounting, 17% Business Administration and Management, General, 5% Health/Health Care Administration/Management, 5% Marketing/Marketing Management, General, 6% Registered Nursing/Registered Nurse
Expenses: 2015-2016: $18,690; room/board: $8,912
Financial aid: (616) 451-3511

Eastern Michigan University

Ypsilanti MI
(734) 487-3060
U.S. News ranking: Reg. U. (Mid.W), No. 85
Website: www.emich.edu/
Admissions email: undergraduate.admissions@emich.edu
Public; founded 1849
Freshman admissions: selective; 2014-2015: 12,353 applied, 8,500 accepted. Either SAT or ACT required. ACT 25/75 percentile: 19-25. High school rank: 13% in top tenth, 39% in top quarter, 76% in top half
Early decision deadline: N/A, notification date: N/A
Early action deadline: N/A, notification date: N/A
Application deadline (fall): rolling
Undergraduate student body: 13,051 full time, 5,157 part time; 41% male, 59% female; 0% American Indian, 2% Asian, 20% black, 4% Hispanic, 3% multiracial, 0% Pacific Islander, 66% white, 2% international; 91% from in state; 23% live on campus; 4% of students in fraternities, 4% in sororities
Most popular majors: 20% Business, Management, Marketing, and Related Support Services, 12% Education, 13% Health Professions and Related Programs, 7% Psychology, 7% Social Sciences
Expenses: 2015-2016: $9,949 in state, $26,479 out of state; room/board: $9,344
Financial aid: (734) 487-0455; 70% of undergrads determined to have financial need; average aid package $9,291

Ferris State University

Big Rapids MI
(231) 591-2100
U.S. News ranking: Reg. U. (Mid.W), No. 61
Website: www.ferris.edu
Admissions email: admissions@ferris.edu
Public; founded 1884
Freshman admissions: selective; 2014-2015: 10,426 applied, 8,176 accepted. Either SAT or ACT required. ACT 25/75 percentile: 19-24. High school rank: N/A
Early decision deadline: N/A, notification date: N/A
Early action deadline: N/A, notification date: N/A
Application deadline (fall): 8/1
Undergraduate student body: 9,105 full time, 4,252 part time; 47% male, 53% female; 1% American Indian, 2% Asian, 8% black, 4% Hispanic, 3% multiracial, 0% Pacific Islander, 80% white, 2% international; 94% from in state; 26% live on campus; 4% of students in fraternities, 1% in sororities
Most popular majors: 5% Business Administration and Management, General, 9% Criminal Justice/Police Science, 4% Elementary Education and Teaching, 6% Pharmacy, 7% Registered Nursing/Registered Nurse
Expenses: 2015-2016: $10,970 in state, $17,562 out of state; room/board: $9,434
Financial aid: (231) 591-2110; 74% of undergrads determined to have financial need; average aid package $10,950

Finlandia University[1]

Hancock MI
(906) 487-7274
U.S. News ranking: Reg. Coll. (Mid.W), second tier
Website: www.finlandia.edu
Admissions email: N/A
Private
Application deadline (fall): N/A
Undergraduate student body: N/A full time, N/A part time
Expenses: 2014-2015: $21,480; room/board: $7,426
Financial aid: (906) 487-7240

Grace Bible College[1]

Grand Rapids MI
(616) 538-2330
U.S. News ranking: Reg. Coll. (Mid.W), second tier
Website: www.gbcol.edu
Admissions email: enrollment@gbcol.edu
Private
Application deadline (fall): N/A
Undergraduate student body: N/A full time, N/A part time
Expenses: 2014-2015: $12,239; room/board: $7,300
Financial aid: (800) 968-1887

Grand Valley State University

Allendale MI
(800) 748-0246
U.S. News ranking: Reg. U. (Mid.W), No. 26
Website: www.gvsu.edu
Admissions email: admissions@gvsu.edu
Public; founded 1960
Freshman admissions: selective; 2014-2015: 16,884 applied, 13,580 accepted. Either SAT or ACT required. ACT 25/75 percentile: 21-26. High school rank: 18% in top tenth, 48% in top quarter, 86% in top half
Early decision deadline: N/A, notification date: N/A
Early action deadline: N/A, notification date: N/A
Application deadline (fall): 5/1
Undergraduate student body: 19,084 full time, 2,552 part time; 42% male, 58% female; 0% American Indian, 2% Asian, 5% black, 5% Hispanic, 3% multiracial, 0% Pacific Islander, 83% white, 1% international; 94% from in state; 28% live on campus; N/A of students in fraternities, N/A in sororities
Most popular majors: 8% Biological and Biomedical Sciences, 18% Business, Management, Marketing, and Related Support Services, 11% Health Professions and Related Programs, 6% Psychology, 9% Social Sciences
Expenses: 2014-2015: $11,028 in state, $15,696 out of state; room/board: $8,420
Financial aid: (616) 331-3234; 61% of undergrads determined to have financial need; average aid package $9,357

Hillsdale College

Hillsdale MI
(517) 607-2327
U.S. News ranking: Nat. Lib. Arts, No. 67
Website: www.hillsdale.edu
Admissions email: admissions@hillsdale.edu
Private; founded 1844
Freshman admissions: more selective; 2014-2015: 1,833 applied, 972 accepted. Either SAT or ACT required. ACT 25/75 percentile: 27-31. High school rank: 50% in top tenth, 82% in top quarter, 97% in top half
Early decision deadline: 11/15, notification date: 12/1
Early action deadline: 12/15, notification date: 2/15
Application deadline (fall): 2/15
Undergraduate student body: 1,437 full time, 35 part time; 48% male, 52% female; N/A American Indian, N/A Asian, N/A black, N/A Hispanic, N/A multiracial, N/A Pacific Islander, N/A white, N/A international; 34% from in state; 74% live on campus; 26% of students in fraternities, 37% in sororities
Most popular majors: 15% Business, Management, Marketing, and Related Support Services, 12% English Language and Literature/Letters, 11% Foreign Languages, Literatures, and Linguistics, 10% History, 14% Social Sciences
Expenses: 2015-2016: $24,592; room/board: $9,760
Financial aid: (517) 607-2350; 54% of undergrads determined to have financial need; average aid package $16,245

Hope College

Holland MI
(616) 395-7850
U.S. News ranking: Nat. Lib. Arts, No. 100
Website: www.hope.edu
Admissions email: admissions@hope.edu
Private; founded 1866
Affiliation: Reformed Church in America
Freshman admissions: more selective; 2014-2015: 4,167 applied, 3,402 accepted. Either SAT or ACT required. ACT 25/75 percentile: 23-29. High school rank: 30% in top tenth, 62% in top quarter, 93% in top half
Early decision deadline: N/A, notification date: N/A
Early action deadline: N/A, notification date: N/A
Application deadline (fall): rolling
Undergraduate student body: 3,277 full time, 155 part time; 40% male, 60% female; 0% American Indian, 2% Asian, 2% black, 8% Hispanic, 2% multiracial, 0% Pacific Islander, 84% white, 2% international; 69% from in state; 81% live on campus; 12% of students in fraternities, 14% in sororities
Most popular majors: 7% Biology/Biological Sciences, General, 10% Business Administration and Management, General, 13% Education, General, 6% Health Services/Allied Health/Health Sciences, General, 10% Psychology, General
Expenses: 2015-2016: $30,550; room/board: $9,390
Financial aid: (616) 395-7765; 59% of undergrads determined to have financial need; average aid package $23,850

Kalamazoo College

Kalamazoo MI
(800) 253-3602
U.S. News ranking: Nat. Lib. Arts, No. 66
Website: www.kzoo.edu
Admissions email: admission@kzoo.edu
Private; founded 1833
Freshman admissions: more selective; 2014-2015: 2,366 applied, 1,648 accepted. Either SAT or ACT required. ACT 25/75 percentile: 25-30. High school rank: 35% in top tenth, 75% in top quarter, 96% in top half
Early decision deadline: 11/15, notification date: 12/1
Early action deadline: 11/15, notification date: 12/20
Application deadline (fall): 2/15
Undergraduate student body: 1,448 full time, 13 part time; 43% male, 57% female; 0% American Indian, 6% Asian, 5% black, 9% Hispanic, 5% multiracial, 0% Pacific Islander, 62% white, 6% international; 69% from in state; 66% live on campus; 0% of students in fraternities, 0% in sororities
Most popular majors: 12% Biological and Biomedical Sciences, 10% Business, Management, Marketing, and Related Support Services, 12% Physical Sciences, 10% Psychology, 17% Social Sciences
Expenses: 2015-2016: $42,846; room/board: $8,886
Financial aid: (269) 337-7192; 67% of undergrads determined to have financial need; average aid package $34,463

Kettering University

Flint MI
(800) 955-4464
U.S. News ranking: Reg. U. (Mid.W), No. 23
Website: www.kettering.edu
Admissions email: admissions@kettering.edu
Private; founded 1919
Freshman admissions: more selective; 2014-2015: 1,587 applied, 1,137 accepted. Either SAT or ACT required. ACT 25/75 percentile: 25-29. High school rank: 34% in top tenth, 71% in top quarter, 94% in top half
Early decision deadline: N/A, notification date: N/A
Early action deadline: N/A, notification date: N/A
Application deadline (fall): rolling
Undergraduate student body: 1,599 full time, 133 part time; 82% male, 18% female; 0% American Indian, 3% Asian, 4% black, 3% Hispanic, 3% multiracial, 0% Pacific Islander, 76% white, 5% international; 82% from in state; 35% live on campus; 41% of students in fraternities, 35% in sororities
Most popular majors: 3% Business, Management, Marketing, and Related Support Services, 7% Computer and Information Sciences and Support Services, 83% Engineering, 3% Mathematics and Statistics, 2% Physical Sciences
Expenses: 2014-2015: $36,980; room/board: $7,240
Financial aid: (810) 762-7859

Kuyper College[1]

Grand Rapids MI
(800) 511-3749
U.S. News ranking: Reg. Coll. (Mid.W), No. 69
Website: www.kuyper.edu
Admissions email: admissions@kuyper.edu
Private
Application deadline (fall): N/A
Undergraduate student body: N/A full time, N/A part time
Expenses: 2014-2015: $19,084; room/board: $7,050
Financial aid: (616) 222-3000

Lake Superior State University

Sault Ste. Marie MI
(906) 635-2231
U.S. News ranking: Reg. Coll. (Mid.W), No. 57
Website: www.lssu.edu
Admissions email: admissions@lssu.edu
Public; founded 1946
Freshman admissions: selective; 2014-2015: 1,538 applied, 1,401 accepted. Neither SAT nor ACT required. ACT 25/75 percentile: 21-25. High school rank: 11% in top tenth, 26% in top quarter, 72% in top half
Early decision deadline: N/A, notification date: N/A
Early action deadline: N/A, notification date: N/A
Application deadline (fall): rolling
Undergraduate student body: 1,966 full time, 462 part time; 50% male, 50% female; 8% American Indian, 1% Asian, 1% black, 2% Hispanic, 0% multiracial, 0% Pacific Islander, 79% white, 7% international
Most popular majors: 6% Biological and Biomedical Sciences, 15% Business, Management, Marketing, and Related Support Services, 5% Education, 17% Health Professions and Related Programs, 22% Homeland

More at usnews.com/college

Security, Law Enforcement, Firefighting and Related Protective Services
Expenses: 2014-2015: $10,253 in state, $15,317 out of state; room/board: $8,987
Financial aid: (906) 635-2678

Lawrence Technological University

Southfield MI
(248) 204-3160
U.S. News ranking: Reg. U. (Mid.W), No. 54
Website: www.ltu.edu
Admissions email: admissions@ltu.edu
Private; founded 1932
Freshman admissions: more selective; 2014-2015: 2,285 applied, 1,312 accepted. Either SAT or ACT required. ACT 25/75 percentile: 21-28. High school rank: 24% in top tenth, 50% in top quarter, 81% in top half
Early decision deadline: N/A, notification date: N/A
Early action deadline: N/A, notification date: N/A
Application deadline (fall): rolling
Undergraduate student body: 1,596 full time, 1,202 part time; 76% male, 24% female; 0% American Indian, 17% Asian, 6% black, 3% Hispanic, 0% multiracial, 0% Pacific Islander, 49% white, 6% international; 96% from in state; 24% live on campus; 8% of students in fraternities, 8% in sororities
Most popular majors: 35% Architecture, 9% Computer Science, 10% Engineering Technology, General, 29% Engineering, General, 1% Speech Communication and Rhetoric
Expenses: 2015-2016: $30,300; room/board: $9,470
Financial aid: (248) 204-2280; 61% of undergrads determined to have financial need; average aid package $23,689

Madonna University

Livonia MI
(734) 432-5339
U.S. News ranking: Reg. U. (Mid.W), No. 98
Website: www.madonna.edu
Admissions email: admissions@madonna.edu
Private; founded 1947
Affiliation: Roman Catholic
Freshman admissions: selective; 2014-2015: 838 applied, 491 accepted. Either SAT or ACT required. ACT 25/75 percentile: 19-26. High school rank: 14% in top tenth, 35% in top quarter, 72% in top half
Early decision deadline: N/A, notification date: N/A
Early action deadline: N/A, notification date: N/A
Application deadline (fall): rolling
Undergraduate student body: 1,561 full time, 1,473 part time; 33% male, 67% female; 0% American Indian, 1% Asian, 13% black, 4% Hispanic, 2% multiracial, 0% Pacific Islander, 64% white, 16% international; 99% from in state; 8% live on campus; N/A of students in fraternities, N/A in sororities
Most popular majors: 5% Biological and Biomedical Sciences, 20% Business, Management, Marketing, and Related Support Services, 25% Health Professions and Related Programs, 18% Homeland Security, Law Enforcement, Firefighting and Related Protective Services, 5% Public Administration and Social Service Professions
Expenses: 2015-2016: $18,740; room/board: $9,230
Financial aid: (734) 432-5662; 48% of undergrads determined to have financial need; average aid package $10,408

Marygrove College[1]

Detroit MI
(313) 927-1240
U.S. News ranking: Reg. U. (Mid.W), second tier
Website: www.marygrove.edu
Admissions email: info@marygrove.edu
Private
Affiliation: Roman Catholic
Application deadline (fall): rolling
Undergraduate student body: N/A full time, N/A part time
Expenses: 2014-2015: $20,336; room/board: $8,130
Financial aid: (313) 927-1692

Michigan State University

East Lansing MI
(517) 355-8332
U.S. News ranking: Nat. U., No. 75
Website: www.msu.edu/
Admissions email: admis@msu.edu
Public; founded 1855
Freshman admissions: more selective; 2014-2015: 33,211 applied, 21,950 accepted. Either SAT or ACT required. ACT 25/75 percentile: 23-28. High school rank: 31% in top tenth, 68% in top quarter, 95% in top half
Early decision deadline: N/A, notification date: N/A
Early action deadline: 10/17, notification date: 11/20
Application deadline (fall): rolling
Undergraduate student body: 35,341 full time, 3,445 part time; 50% male, 50% female; 0% American Indian, 4% Asian, 7% black, 4% Hispanic, 3% multiracial, 0% Pacific Islander, 68% white, 13% international; 89% from in state; 39% live on campus; 8% of students in fraternities, 7% in sororities
Most popular majors: 10% Biological and Biomedical Sciences, 17% Business, Management, Marketing, and Related Support Services, 11% Communication, Journalism, and Related Programs, 6% Engineering, 11% Social Sciences
Expenses: 2015-2016: $13,560 in state, $36,360 out of state; room/board: $9,474
Financial aid: (517) 353-5940; 48% of undergrads determined to have financial need; average aid package $12,712

Michigan Technological University

Houghton MI
(906) 487-2335
U.S. News ranking: Nat. U., No. 123
Website: www.mtu.edu
Admissions email: mtu4u@mtu.edu
Public; founded 1885
Freshman admissions: more selective; 2014-2015: 5,111 applied, 3,859 accepted. Either SAT or ACT required. ACT 25/75 percentile: 25-30. High school rank: 31% in top tenth, 65% in top quarter, 91% in top half
Early decision deadline: N/A, notification date: N/A
Early action deadline: N/A, notification date: N/A
Application deadline (fall): rolling
Undergraduate student body: 5,242 full time, 420 part time; 74% male, 26% female; 1% American Indian, 1% Asian, 1% black, 2% Hispanic, 2% multiracial, 0% Pacific Islander, 85% white, 5% international; 77% from in state; 48% live on campus; 6% of students in fraternities, 3% in sororities
Most popular majors: 5% Biological and Biomedical Sciences, 8% Business, Management, Marketing, and Related Support Services, 7% Computer and Information Sciences and Support Services, 59% Engineering, 4% Engineering Technologies and Engineering-Related Fields
Expenses: 2014-2015: $14,040 in state, $29,520 out of state; room/board: $9,516
Financial aid: (906) 487-2622; 65% of undergrads determined to have financial need; average aid package $13,900

Northern Michigan University

Marquette MI
(906) 227-2650
U.S. News ranking: Reg. U. (Mid.W), No. 85
Website: www.nmu.edu
Admissions email: admiss@nmu.edu
Public; founded 1899
Freshman admissions: selective; 2014-2015: 6,848 applied, 4,937 accepted. Either SAT or ACT required. ACT 25/75 percentile: 19-24. High school rank: N/A
Early decision deadline: N/A, notification date: N/A
Early action deadline: N/A, notification date: N/A
Application deadline (fall): rolling
Undergraduate student body: 7,002 full time, 999 part time; 46% male, 54% female; 2% American Indian, 1% Asian, 3% black, 3% Hispanic, 2% multiracial, 0% Pacific Islander, 86% white, 1% international; 81% from in state; 38% live on campus; N/A of students in fraternities, N/A in sororities
Most popular majors: 13% Business, Management, Marketing, and Related Support Services, 9% Education, 12% Health Professions and Related Programs, 7% Homeland Security, Law Enforcement, Firefighting and Related Protective Services, 9% Visual and Performing Arts
Expenses: 2014-2015: $9,984 in state, $15,216 out of state; room/board: $8,954
Financial aid: (906) 227-2327; 69% of undergrads determined to have financial need; average aid package $9,303

Northwood University

Midland MI
(989) 837-4273
U.S. News ranking: Business, unranked
Website: www.northwood.edu
Admissions email: miadmit@northwood.edu
Private; founded 1959
Freshman admissions: selective; 2014-2015: 1,417 applied, 990 accepted. Either SAT or ACT required. ACT 25/75 percentile: 19-24. High school rank: 11% in top tenth, 31% in top quarter, 63% in top half
Early decision deadline: N/A, notification date: N/A
Early action deadline: N/A, notification date: N/A
Application deadline (fall): rolling
Undergraduate student body: 1,363 full time, 53 part time; 63% male, 37% female; 0% American Indian, 1% Asian, 6% black, 3% Hispanic, 2% multiracial, 1% Pacific Islander, 73% white, 6% international; 87% from in state; 49% live on campus; 10% of students in fraternities, 17% in sororities
Most popular majors: 12% Accounting, 16% Business Administration and Management, General, 10% Finance, General, 20% Marketing/Marketing Management, General, 11% Sport and Fitness Administration/Management
Expenses: 2014-2015: $23,132; room/board: $9,310
Financial aid: (989) 837-4230

Oakland University

Rochester MI
(248) 370-3360
U.S. News ranking: Nat. U., second tier
Website: www.oakland.edu
Admissions email: visit@oakland.edu
Public; founded 1957
Freshman admissions: selective; 2014-2015: 12,403 applied, 8,354 accepted. Either SAT or ACT required. ACT 25/75 percentile: 20-26. High school rank: 16% in top tenth, 44% in top quarter, 81% in top half
Early decision deadline: N/A, notification date: N/A
Early action deadline: N/A, notification date: N/A
Application deadline (fall): rolling
Undergraduate student body: 12,454 full time, 4,481 part time; 42% male, 58% female; 0% American Indian, 4% Asian, 8% black, 3% Hispanic, 3% multiracial, 0% Pacific Islander, 75% white, 2% international; 99% from in state; 16% live on campus; 1% of students in fraternities, 2% in sororities
Most popular majors: 16% Business, Management, Marketing, and Related Support Services, 9% Communication, Journalism, and Related Programs, 7% Education, 24% Health Professions and Related Programs, 6% Psychology
Expenses: 2015-2016: $11,460 in state, $24,735 out of state; room/board: $8,894
Financial aid: (248) 370-2550; 66% of undergrads determined to have financial need; average aid package $12,835

Olivet College

Olivet MI
(269) 749-7635
U.S. News ranking: Reg. Coll. (Mid.W), No. 52
Website: www.olivetcollege.edu
Admissions email: admissions@olivetcollege.edu
Private; founded 1844
Affiliation: United Church of Christ
Freshman admissions: selective; 2014-2015: 3,017 applied, 1,853 accepted. Either SAT or ACT required. ACT 25/75 percentile: 18-23. High school rank: N/A
Early decision deadline: N/A, notification date: N/A
Early action deadline: N/A, notification date: N/A
Application deadline (fall): rolling
Undergraduate student body: 922 full time, 118 part time; 60% male, 40% female; 0% American Indian, 1% Asian, 11% black, 7% Hispanic, 3% multiracial, 0% Pacific Islander, 77% white, 1% international
Most popular majors: 14% Biology/Biological Sciences, General, 11% Business Administration and Management, General, 15% Criminal Justice/Safety Studies, 8% Insurance, 14% Sport and Fitness Administration/Management
Expenses: 2015-2016: $24,816; room/board: $8,400
Financial aid: (269) 749-7102; 93% of undergrads determined to have financial need; average aid package $18,131

Robert B. Miller College[1]

Battle Creek MI
(269) 660-8021
U.S. News ranking: Reg. Coll. (Mid.W), unranked
Website: www.millercollege.edu
Admissions email: N/A
Private
Application deadline (fall): N/A
Undergraduate student body: N/A full time, N/A part time
Expenses: N/A
Financial aid: (269) 660-8021

Rochester College

Rochester Hills MI
(248) 218-2031
U.S. News ranking: Reg. Coll. (Mid.W), No. 69
Website: www.rc.edu
Admissions email: admissions@rc.edu
Private; founded 1959
Affiliation: Church of Christ
Freshman admissions: selective; 2014-2015: 818 applied, 332 accepted. Neither SAT nor ACT required. ACT 25/75 percentile: 18-23. High school rank: N/A
Early decision deadline: N/A, notification date: N/A
Early action deadline: N/A, notification date: N/A
Application deadline (fall): rolling
Undergraduate student body: 735 full time, 368 part time; 40% male, 60% female; 0% American Indian, 1% Asian, 16% black, 2% Hispanic, 2% multiracial, 0% Pacific Islander, 59% white, 4% international; 95% from in state; 21% live on campus; N/A of students in fraternities, N/A in sororities

Most popular majors: 26% Business, Management, Marketing, and Related Support Services, 11% Communication, Journalism, and Related Programs, 25% Education, 12% Engineering, 24% Psychology
Expenses: 2015-2016: $22,129; room/board: $6,750
Financial aid: (248) 218-2028

Saginaw Valley State University

University Center MI
(989) 964-4200
U.S. News ranking: Reg. U. (Mid.W), second tier
Website: www.svsu.edu
Admissions email: admissions@svsu.edu
Public; founded 1963
Freshman admissions: selective; 2014-2015: 6,266 applied, 4,960 accepted. Either SAT or ACT required. ACT 25/75 percentile: 19-25. High school rank: 21% in top tenth, 43% in top quarter, 75% in top half
Early decision deadline: N/A, notification date: N/A
Early action deadline: N/A, notification date: N/A
Application deadline (fall): rolling
Undergraduate student body: 7,411 full time, 1,386 part time; 42% male, 58% female; 0% American Indian, 1% Asian, 11% black, 4% Hispanic, 2% multiracial, 0% Pacific Islander, 72% white, 5% international; 99% from in state; 31% live on campus; 3% of students in fraternities, 3% in sororities
Most popular majors: 5% Business Administration and Management, General, 8% Criminal Justice/Safety Studies, 6% Health/Medical Preparatory Programs, Other, 10% Registered Nursing/Registered Nurse, 7% Social Work
Expenses: 2014-2015: $8,691 in state, $20,409 out of state; room/board: N/A
Financial aid: (989) 964-4103; 67% of undergrads determined to have financial need

Siena Heights University

Adrian MI
(517) 264-7180
U.S. News ranking: Reg. U. (Mid.W), No. 92
Website: www.sienaheights.edu
Admissions email: admissions@sienaheights.edu
Private; founded 1919
Affiliation: Roman Catholic
Freshman admissions: selective; 2014-2015: 1,545 applied, 1,147 accepted. Either SAT or ACT required. ACT 25/75 percentile: 19-24. High school rank: 11% in top tenth, 38% in top quarter, 67% in top half
Early decision deadline: N/A, notification date: N/A
Early action deadline: N/A, notification date: N/A
Application deadline (fall): 8/1
Undergraduate student body: 1,245 full time, 1,157 part time; 44% male, 56% female; 0% American Indian, 1% Asian, 12% black, 4% Hispanic, 2% multiracial, 0% Pacific Islander, 67% white, 3% international; 84% from in state; 25% live on campus; 2% of students in fraternities, 2% in sororities
Most popular majors: 25% Business, Management, Marketing and Related Support Services, 26% Health Professions and Related Programs, 10% Homeland Security, Law Enforcement, Firefighting and Related Protective Services, 2% Liberal Arts and Sciences, General Studies and Humanities, 6% Public Administration and Social Service Professions
Expenses: 2015-2016: $23,750; room/board: $9,710
Financial aid: (517) 264-7130

Spring Arbor University

Spring Arbor MI
(800) 968-0011
U.S. News ranking: Reg. U. (Mid.W), No. 64
Website: www.arbor.edu/
Admissions email: admissions@arbor.edu
Private; founded 1873
Affiliation: Free Methodist
Freshman admissions: selective; 2014-2015: 2,630 applied, 1,752 accepted. Either SAT or ACT required. ACT 25/75 percentile: 19-25. High school rank: 16% in top tenth, 44% in top quarter, 76% in top half
Early decision deadline: N/A, notification date: N/A
Early action deadline: N/A, notification date: N/A
Application deadline (fall): 8/1
Undergraduate student body: 1,896 full time, 825 part time; 31% male, 69% female; 1% American Indian, 1% Asian, 11% black, 3% Hispanic, 2% multiracial, N/A Pacific Islander, 74% white, 1% international; 89% from in state; 71% live on campus; 0% of students in fraternities, 0% in sororities
Most popular majors: 6% Business Administration and Management, General, 8% Health and Physical Education/Fitness, General, 9% Psychology, General, 10% Social Work, 14% Teacher Education and Professional Development, Specific Subject Areas
Expenses: 2015-2016: $25,510; room/board: $8,870
Financial aid: (517) 750-6463; 86% of undergrads determined to have financial need; average aid package $21,899

University of Detroit Mercy

Detroit MI
(313) 993-1245
U.S. News ranking: Reg. U. (Mid.W), No. 23
Website: www.udmercy.edu
Admissions email: admissions@udmercy.edu
Private; founded 1877
Affiliation: Catholic
Freshman admissions: more selective; 2014-2015: 3,639 applied, 2,413 accepted. Either SAT or ACT required. ACT 25/75 percentile: 22-26. High school rank: 27% in top tenth, 55% in top quarter, 86% in top half
Early decision deadline: N/A, notification date: N/A
Early action deadline: N/A, notification date: N/A
Application deadline (fall): 3/1
Undergraduate student body: 2,102 full time, 660 part time; 35% male, 65% female; 1% American Indian, 4% Asian, 11% black, 3% Hispanic, 3% multiracial, 0% Pacific Islander, 59% white, 6% international; 93% from in state; 31% live on campus; 3% of students in fraternities, 5% in sororities
Most popular majors: 4% Architecture, 8% Biology/Biological Sciences, General, 4% Business Administration and Management, General, 4% Dental Hygiene/Hygienist, 47% Registered Nursing/Registered Nurse
Expenses: 2015-2016: $38,626; room/board: $8,870
Financial aid: (313) 993-3350; 74% of undergrads determined to have financial need; average aid package $29,470

University of Michigan–Ann Arbor

Ann Arbor MI
(734) 764-7433
U.S. News ranking: Nat. U., No. 29
Website: www.umich.edu
Admissions email: N/A
Public; founded 1817
Freshman admissions: most selective; 2014-2015: 49,776 applied, 16,047 accepted. Either SAT or ACT required. ACT 25/75 percentile: 29-33. High school rank: 73% in top tenth, 95% in top quarter, 99% in top half
Early decision deadline: N/A, notification date: N/A
Early action deadline: 11/1, notification date: 12/24
Application deadline (fall): 2/1
Undergraduate student body: 27,395 full time, 1,000 part time; 51% male, 49% female; 0% American Indian, 13% Asian, 4% black, 4% Hispanic, 3% multiracial, 0% Pacific Islander, 62% white, 7% international; 63% from in state; 34% live on campus; 17% of students in fraternities, 25% in sororities
Most popular majors: 6% Business Administration and Management, General, 7% Economics, General, 7% Experimental Psychology, 4% Neuroscience, 6% Political Science and Government, General
Expenses: 2014-2015: $14,336 in state, $43,377 out of state; room/board: $10,246
Financial aid: (734) 763-4119; 38% of undergrads determined to have financial need; average aid package $21,422

University of Michigan–Dearborn

Dearborn MI
(313) 593-5100
U.S. News ranking: Reg. U. (Mid.W), No. 36
Website: www.umd.umich.edu
Admissions email: admissions@umd.umich.edu
Public; founded 1959
Freshman admissions: more selective; 2014-2015: 5,174 applied, 3,292 accepted. Either SAT or ACT required. ACT 25/75 percentile: 21-27. High school rank: 28% in top tenth, 58% in top quarter, 90% in top half
Early decision deadline: N/A, notification date: N/A
Early action deadline: N/A, notification date: N/A
Application deadline (fall): rolling
Undergraduate student body: 4,843 full time, 2,328 part time; 51% male, 49% female; 0% American Indian, 6% Asian, 10% black, 6% Hispanic, 3% multiracial, 0% Pacific Islander, 70% white, 1% international; 96% from in state; N/A live on campus; 4% of students in fraternities, 5% in sororities
Most popular majors: 10% Biological and Biomedical Sciences, 19% Business, Management, Marketing, and Related Support Services, 12% Engineering, 11% Psychology, 9% Social Sciences
Expenses: 2015-2016: $11,524 in state, $23,866 out of state; room/board: N/A
Financial aid: (313) 593-5300; 66% of undergrads determined to have financial need; average aid package $9,031

University of Michigan–Flint

Flint MI
(810) 762-3300
U.S. News ranking: Reg. U. (Mid.W), No. 99
Website: www.umflint.edu
Admissions email: admissions@umflint.edu
Public; founded 1956
Freshman admissions: selective; 2014-2015: 3,160 applied, 2,485 accepted. Either SAT or ACT required. ACT 25/75 percentile: 18-24. High school rank: 17% in top tenth, 41% in top quarter, 77% in top half
Early decision deadline: N/A, notification date: N/A
Early action deadline: N/A, notification date: N/A
Application deadline (fall): 8/18
Undergraduate student body: 4,240 full time, 2,838 part time; 40% male, 60% female; 1% American Indian, 2% Asian, 13% black, 4% Hispanic, 3% multiracial, 0% Pacific Islander, 68% white, 6% international; 98% from in state; 4% live on campus; 5% of students in fraternities, 5% in sororities
Most popular majors: 7% Biological and Biomedical Sciences, 15% Business, Management, Marketing, and Related Support Services, 9% Education, 30% Health Professions and Related Programs, 7% Psychology
Expenses: 2015-2016: $10,458 in state, $19,980 out of state; room/board: $8,178
Financial aid: (810) 762-3444

Walsh College of Accountancy and Business Administration[1]

Troy MI
(248) 823-1610
U.S. News ranking: Business, unranked
Website: www.walshcollege.edu
Admissions email: admissions@walshcollege.edu
Private
Application deadline (fall): N/A
Undergraduate student body: N/A full time, N/A part time
Expenses: N/A
Financial aid: (248) 823-1665

Wayne State University

Detroit MI
(313) 577-3577
U.S. News ranking: Nat. U., second tier
Website: www.wayne.edu/
Admissions email: admissions@wayne.edu
Public; founded 1868
Freshman admissions: selective; 2014-2015: 12,199 applied, 9,433 accepted. Either SAT or ACT required. ACT 25/75 percentile: 20-26. High school rank: 21% in top tenth, 48% in top quarter, 79% in top half
Early decision deadline: N/A, notification date: N/A
Early action deadline: N/A, notification date: N/A
Application deadline (fall): rolling
Undergraduate student body: 12,030 full time, 6,317 part time; 45% male, 55% female; 0% American Indian, 8% Asian, 21% black, 4% Hispanic, 3% multiracial, 0% Pacific Islander, 55% white, 2% international; 99% from in state; 12% live on campus; N/A of students in fraternities, N/A in sororities
Most popular majors: 4% Accounting, 6% Biology/Biological Sciences, General, 5% Criminal Justice/Safety Studies, 4% Organizational Behavior Studies, 14% Psychology, General
Expenses: 2014-2015: $12,350 in state, $26,592 out of state; room/board: $9,713
Financial aid: (313) 577-3378; 76% of undergrads determined to have financial need; average aid package $10,591

Western Michigan University

Kalamazoo MI
(269) 387-2000
U.S. News ranking: Nat. U., No. 187
Website: www.wmich.edu
Admissions email: ask-wmu@wmich.edu
Public; founded 1903
Freshman admissions: selective; 2014-2015: 14,008 applied, 11,775 accepted. Either SAT or ACT required. ACT 25/75 percentile: 19-25. High school rank: 12% in top tenth, 33% in top quarter, 72% in top half
Early decision deadline: N/A, notification date: N/A
Early action deadline: N/A, notification date: N/A
Application deadline (fall): rolling
Undergraduate student body: 15,713 full time, 3,176 part time; 50% male, 50% female; 0% American Indian, 2% Asian, 12% black, 5% Hispanic, 3% multiracial, 0% Pacific Islander, 73% white, 3% international; 93% from in state; 28% live on campus; 5% of students in fraternities, 7% in sororities
Most popular majors: 20% Business, Management, Marketing, and Related Support Services, 9% Education, 6% Engineering, 10% Health Professions and Related Programs, 7% Multi/Interdisciplinary Studies

Expenses: 2014-2015: $10,685 in state, $24,917 out of state; room/board: $8,943
Financial aid: (269) 387-6000; 61% of undergrads determined to have financial need; average aid package $13,600

MINNESOTA

Augsburg College

Minneapolis MN
(612) 330-1001
U.S. News ranking: Reg. U. (Mid.W), No. 20
Website: www.augsburg.edu
Admissions email: admissions@augsburg.edu
Private; founded 1869
Affiliation: Lutheran
Freshman admissions: selective; 2014-2015: 2,826 applied, 1,922 accepted. Either SAT or ACT required. ACT 25/75 percentile: 20-26. High school rank: N/A
Early decision deadline: N/A, notification date: N/A
Early action deadline: N/A, notification date: N/A
Application deadline (fall): 8/15
Undergraduate student body: 2,002 full time, 618 part time; 46% male, 54% female; 1% American Indian, 8% Asian, 11% black, 5% Hispanic, 4% multiracial, 0% Pacific Islander, 58% white, 2% international; 80% from in state; 37% live on campus; N/A of students in fraternities, N/A in sororities
Most popular majors: 25% Business, Management, Marketing, and Related Support Services, 8% Communication, Journalism, and Related Programs, 9% Education, 10% Health Professions and Related Programs, 8% Social Sciences
Expenses: 2014-2015: $34,431; room/board: $9,106
Financial aid: (612) 330-1046

Bemidji State University

Bemidji MN
(218) 755-2040
U.S. News ranking: Reg. U. (Mid.W), No. 99
Website: www.bemidjistate.edu
Admissions email: admissions@bemidjistate.edu
Public; founded 1919
Freshman admissions: selective; 2014-2015: 2,132 applied, 1,994 accepted. Either SAT or ACT required. ACT 25/75 percentile: 19-24. High school rank: 5% in top tenth, 20% in top quarter, 56% in top half
Early decision deadline: N/A, notification date: N/A
Early action deadline: N/A, notification date: N/A
Application deadline (fall): rolling
Undergraduate student body: 3,504 full time, 1,193 part time; 44% male, 56% female; 3% American Indian, 1% Asian, 2% black, 2% Hispanic, 3% multiracial, 0% Pacific Islander, 85% white, 2% international; 90% from in state; 30% live on campus; N/A of students in fraternities, N/A in sororities
Most popular majors: 7% Biological and Biomedical Sciences, 21% Business, Management, Marketing, and Related Support Services, 14% Education, 13% Health Professions and Related Programs, 7% Homeland Security, Law Enforcement, Firefighting and Related Protective Services
Expenses: 2015-2016: $8,152 in state, $8,152 out of state; room/board: $7,694
Financial aid: (218) 755-4143; 63% of undergrads determined to have financial need; average aid package $9,502

Bethany Lutheran College

Mankato MN
(507) 344-7331
U.S. News ranking: Nat. Lib. Arts, second tier
Website: www.blc.edu
Admissions email: admiss@blc.edu
Private; founded 1927
Affiliation: Evangelical Lutheran Synod
Freshman admissions: selective; 2014-2015: 457 applied, 355 accepted. Either SAT or ACT required. ACT 25/75 percentile: 20-26. High school rank: 15% in top tenth, 35% in top quarter, 69% in top half
Early decision deadline: N/A, notification date: N/A
Early action deadline: N/A, notification date: N/A
Application deadline (fall): 7/1
Undergraduate student body: 503 full time, 30 part time; 47% male, 53% female; 1% American Indian, 0% Asian, 3% black, 3% Hispanic, 2% multiracial, 0% Pacific Islander, 87% white, 1% international; 74% from in state; 66% live on campus; N/A of students in fraternities, N/A in sororities
Most popular majors: 16% Biology/Biological Sciences, General, 18% Business Administration and Management, General, 18% Communication, General, 11% Social Sciences, General, 9% Visual and Performing Arts, General
Expenses: 2015-2016: $25,170; room/board: $7,710
Financial aid: (507) 344-7307; 82% of undergrads determined to have financial need; average aid package $20,936

Bethel University

St. Paul MN
(800) 255-8706
U.S. News ranking: Reg. U. (Mid.W), No. 23
Website: www.bethel.edu
Admissions email: undergrad-admissions@bethel.edu
Private; founded 1871
Affiliation: Converge Worldwide (former Baptist General Conference)
Freshman admissions: more selective; 2014-2015: 2,059 applied, 1,965 accepted. Either SAT or ACT required. ACT 25/75 percentile: 22-28. High school rank: 29% in top tenth, 57% in top quarter, 83% in top half
Early decision deadline: N/A, notification date: N/A
Early action deadline: N/A, notification date: N/A
Application deadline (fall): rolling
Undergraduate student body: 2,579 full time, 472 part time; 38% male, 62% female; 0% American Indian, 3% Asian, 5% black, 3% Hispanic, 2% multiracial, 0% Pacific Islander, 85% white, 0% international; 78% from in state; 71% live on campus; 0% of students in fraternities, 0% in sororities
Most popular majors: 7% Biological and Biomedical Sciences, 14% Business, Management, Marketing, and Related Support Services, 10% Communication, Journalism, and Related Programs, 13% Education, 13% Health Professions and Related Programs
Expenses: 2015-2016: $34,140; room/board: $9,770
Financial aid: (800) 255-8706; 74% of undergrads determined to have financial need; average aid package $24,292

Capella University[1]

Minneapolis MN
(888) 227-3552
U.S. News ranking: Nat. U., unranked
Website: www.capella.edu
Admissions email: admissionsoffice@capella.edu
For-profit
Application deadline (fall): N/A
Undergraduate student body: N/A full time, N/A part time
Expenses: 2014-2015: $12,816; room/board: $4,032
Financial aid: (612) 977-5233

Carleton College

Northfield MN
(507) 222-4190
U.S. News ranking: Nat. Lib. Arts, No. 8
Website: www.carleton.edu
Admissions email: admissions@carleton.edu
Private; founded 1866
Freshman admissions: most selective; 2014-2015: 6,297 applied, 1,434 accepted. Either SAT or ACT required. SAT 25/75 percentile: 1320-1510. High school rank: 70% in top tenth, 94% in top quarter, 99% in top half
Early decision deadline: 11/15, notification date: 12/15
Early action deadline: N/A, notification date: N/A
Application deadline (fall): 1/15
Undergraduate student body: 2,044 full time, 13 part time; 47% male, 53% female; 0% American Indian, 9% Asian, 4% black, 6% Hispanic, 5% multiracial, 0% Pacific Islander, 65% white, 9% international; 19% from in state; 96% live on campus; 0% of students in fraternities, 0% in sororities
Most popular majors: 14% Biological and Biomedical Sciences, 9% Mathematics and Statistics, 12% Physical Sciences, 20% Social Sciences, 9% Visual and Performing Arts
Expenses: 2015-2016: $49,263; room/board: $12,783
Financial aid: (507) 646-4138; 55% of undergrads determined to have financial need; average aid package $38,623

College of St. Benedict

St. Joseph MN
(320) 363-5060
U.S. News ranking: Nat. Lib. Arts, No. 90
Website: www.csbsju.edu
Admissions email: admissions@csbsju.edu
Private; founded 1913
Affiliation: Roman Catholic (Benedictine)
Freshman admissions: more selective; 2014-2015: 1,768 applied, 1,453 accepted. Either SAT or ACT required. ACT 25/75 percentile: 23-29. High school rank: 40% in top tenth, 70% in top quarter, 95% in top half
Early decision deadline: N/A, notification date: N/A
Early action deadline: 11/15, notification date: 12/15
Application deadline (fall): 1/15
Undergraduate student body: 1,992 full time, 28 part time; 0% male, 100% female; 1% American Indian, 6% Asian, 2% black, 5% Hispanic, 1% multiracial, 0% Pacific Islander, 81% white, 5% international; 84% from in state; 89% live on campus; 0% of students in fraternities, 0% in sororities
Most popular majors: 10% Biology/Biological Sciences, General, 9% Elementary Education and Teaching, 12% Psychology, General, 9% Registered Nursing/Registered Nurse, 9% Rhetoric and Composition
Expenses: 2015-2016: $40,846; room/board: $10,229
Financial aid: (320) 363-5388; 71% of undergrads determined to have financial need; average aid package $31,995

College of St. Scholastica

Duluth MN
(218) 723-6046
U.S. News ranking: Reg. U. (Mid.W), No. 33
Website: www.css.edu
Admissions email: admissions@css.edu
Private; founded 1912
Affiliation: Roman Catholic
Freshman admissions: selective; 2014-2015: 3,368 applied, 2,229 accepted. Either SAT or ACT required. ACT 25/75 percentile: 21-27. High school rank: 19% in top tenth, 50% in top quarter, 85% in top half
Early decision deadline: N/A, notification date: N/A
Early action deadline: N/A, notification date: N/A
Application deadline (fall): rolling
Undergraduate student body: 2,317 full time, 542 part time; 30% male, 70% female; 2% American Indian, 2% Asian, 3% black, 2% Hispanic, 2% multiracial, 0% Pacific Islander, 83% white, 4% international; 40% from in state; 53% live on campus; 0% of students in fraternities, 0% in sororities
Most popular majors: 12% Biological and Biomedical Sciences, 20% Business, Management, Marketing, and Related Support Services, 45% Health Professions and Related Programs, 5% Psychology, 6% Public Administration and Social Service Professions
Expenses: 2015-2016: $33,994; room/board: $8,932
Financial aid: (218) 723-6047; 78% of undergrads determined to have financial need; average aid package $21,774

Concordia College–Moorhead

Moorhead MN
(800) 699-9897
U.S. News ranking: Nat. Lib. Arts, No. 120
Website: www.concordiacollege.edu
Admissions email: admissions@cord.edu
Private; founded 1891
Affiliation: Evangelical Lutheran Church in America
Freshman admissions: more selective; 2014-2015: 2,948 applied, 1,895 accepted. Either SAT or ACT required. ACT 25/75 percentile: 23-28. High school rank: 30% in top tenth, 61% in top quarter, 89% in top half
Early decision deadline: N/A, notification date: N/A
Early action deadline: N/A, notification date: N/A
Application deadline (fall): rolling
Undergraduate student body: 2,332 full time, 49 part time; 40% male, 60% female; 1% American Indian, 2% Asian, 2% black, 2% Hispanic, 1% multiracial, 0% Pacific Islander, 84% white, 3% international; 72% from in state; 62% live on campus; 0% of students in fraternities, 0% in sororities
Most popular majors: 11% Biology, General, 11% Business Administration, Management and Operations, 8% Communication and Media Studies, 10% Education, General, 8% Health Services/Allied Health/Health Sciences, General
Expenses: 2015-2016: $35,464; room/board: $7,600
Financial aid: (218) 299-3010; 72% of undergrads determined to have financial need; average aid package $28,099

Concordia University–St. Paul

St. Paul MN
(651) 641-8230
U.S. News ranking: Reg. U. (Mid.W), No. 99
Website: www.csp.edu
Admissions email: admissions@csp.edu
Private; founded 1893
Affiliation: Lutheran Church-Missouri Synod
Freshman admissions: selective; 2014-2015: 1,435 applied, 764 accepted. ACT required. ACT 25/75 percentile: 18-24. High school rank: 12% in top tenth, 31% in top quarter, 66% in top half
Early decision deadline: N/A, notification date: N/A
Early action deadline: N/A, notification date: N/A
Application deadline (fall): rolling
Undergraduate student body: 1,374 full time, 1,046 part time; 41% male, 59% female; 1% American Indian, 6% Asian, 13% black, 4% Hispanic, 4% multiracial, 0% Pacific Islander, 64% white, 5% international; 74% from in state; 20% live on campus; 0%

of students in fraternities, 0% in sororities
Most popular majors: 41% Business, Management, Marketing, and Related Support Services, 7% Education, 8% Family and Consumer Sciences/ Human Sciences, 8% Homeland Security, Law Enforcement, Firefighting and Related Protective Services, 8% Parks, Recreation, Leisure, and Fitness Studies
Expenses: 2015-2016: $20,750; room/board: $8,300
Financial aid: (651) 603-6300; 77% of undergrads determined to have financial need; average aid package $13,706

Crown College[1]

St. Bonifacius MN
(952) 446-4142
U.S. News ranking: Reg. Coll. (Mid.W), second tier
Website: www.crown.edu
Admissions email: admissions@crown.edu
Private; founded 1916
Affiliation: Christian and Missionary Alliance
Application deadline (fall): 8/20
Undergraduate student body: N/A full time, N/A part time
Expenses: 2014-2015: $23,180; room/board: $7,860
Financial aid: (952) 446-4177

Dunwoody College of Technology

Minneapolis MN
(800) 292-4625
U.S. News ranking: Reg. Coll. (Mid.W), second tier
Website: www.dunwoody.edu
Admissions email: admissions@dunwoody.edu
Private; founded 1914
Freshman admissions: less selective; 2014-2015: 1,065 applied, N/A accepted. Neither SAT nor ACT required. ACT 25/75 percentile: N/A. High school rank: N/A
Early decision deadline: N/A, notification date: N/A
Early action deadline: N/A, notification date: N/A
Application deadline (fall): rolling
Undergraduate student body: 873 full time, 197 part time; 86% male, 14% female; 1% American Indian, 5% Asian, 7% black, 2% Hispanic, 5% multiracial, 0% Pacific Islander, 78% white, 0% international; 99% from in state; N/A live on campus; N/A of students in fraternities, N/A in sororities
Most popular majors: 50% Business Administration and Management, General, 25% Industrial Technology/Technician, 25% Interior Design
Expenses: 2015-2016: $22,938; room/board: N/A
Financial aid: N/A; 88% of undergrads determined to have financial need; average aid package $7,723

Gustavus Adolphus College

St. Peter MN
(507) 933-7676
U.S. News ranking: Nat. Lib. Arts, No. 79
Website: www.gac.edu
Admissions email: admission@gac.edu
Private; founded 1862
Affiliation: Lutheran - ELCA
Freshman admissions: more selective; 2014-2015: 5,199 applied, 3,175 accepted. Neither SAT nor ACT required. ACT 25/75 percentile: 24-30. High school rank: 31% in top tenth, 64% in top quarter, 94% in top half
Early decision deadline: N/A, notification date: N/A
Early action deadline: 11/1, notification date: 11/20
Application deadline (fall): rolling
Undergraduate student body: 2,425 full time, 31 part time; 46% male, 54% female; 0% American Indian, 4% Asian, 2% black, 3% Hispanic, 4% multiracial, 0% Pacific Islander, 83% white, 3% international; 81% from in state; 85% live on campus; 17% of students in fraternities, 19% in sororities
Most popular majors: 11% Biology/ Biological Sciences, General, 14% Business/Commerce, General, 6% Education, General, 8% Psychology, General, 6% Speech Communication and Rhetoric
Expenses: 2015-2016: $41,620; room/board: $9,176
Financial aid: (507) 933-7527; 71% of undergrads determined to have financial need; average aid package $33,738

Hamline University

St. Paul MN
(651) 523-2207
U.S. News ranking: Reg. U. (Mid.W), No. 12
Website: www.hamline.edu
Admissions email: admission@hamline.edu
Private; founded 1854
Affiliation: United Methodist
Freshman admissions: selective; 2014-2015: 3,417 applied, 2,378 accepted. Either SAT or ACT required. ACT 25/75 percentile: 21-27. High school rank: 15% in top tenth, 41% in top quarter, 80% in top half
Early decision deadline: 11/1, notification date: 11/15
Early action deadline: 12/1, notification date: N/A
Application deadline (fall): rolling
Undergraduate student body: 2,162 full time, 80 part time; 42% male, 58% female; 0% American Indian, 6% Asian, 6% black, 6% Hispanic, 6% multiracial, 0% Pacific Islander, 72% white, 1% international; 79% from in state; 42% live on campus; N/A of students in fraternities, N/A in sororities
Most popular majors: 12% Business, Management, Marketing, and Related Support Services, 7% Homeland Security, Law Enforcement, Firefighting and Related Protective Services, 8% Legal Professions and Studies, 12% Psychology, 15% Social Sciences
Expenses: 2015-2016: $37,886; room/board: $9,736
Financial aid: (651) 523-3000; 83% of undergrads determined to have financial need; average aid package $28,520

Macalester College

St. Paul MN
(651) 696-6357
U.S. News ranking: Nat. Lib. Arts, No. 23
Website: www.macalester.edu
Admissions email: admissions@macalester.edu
Private; founded 1874
Freshman admissions: most selective; 2014-2015: 6,463 applied, 2,349 accepted. Either SAT or ACT required. SAT 25/75 percentile: 1270-1465. High school rank: 65% in top tenth, 93% in top quarter, 100% in top half
Early decision deadline: 11/15, notification date: 12/15
Early action deadline: N/A, notification date: N/A
Application deadline (fall): 1/15
Undergraduate student body: 2,045 full time, 28 part time; 39% male, 61% female; 0% American Indian, 7% Asian, 2% black, 6% Hispanic, 5% multiracial, 0% Pacific Islander, 66% white, 13% international; 18% from in state; 62% live on campus; 0% of students in fraternities, 0% in sororities
Most popular majors: 12% Biological and Biomedical Sciences, 10% Foreign Languages, Literatures, and Linguistics, 8% Multi/ Interdisciplinary Studies, 7% Psychology, 27% Social Sciences
Expenses: 2015-2016: $48,887; room/board: $10,874
Financial aid: (651) 696-6214; 69% of undergrads determined to have financial need; average aid package $40,694

Martin Luther College[1]

New Ulm MN
(877) 652-1995
U.S. News ranking: Reg. Coll. (Mid.W), No. 38
Website: www.mlc-wels.edu
Admissions email: N/A
Private
Application deadline (fall): N/A
Undergraduate student body: N/A full time, N/A part time
Expenses: 2014-2015: $12,920; room/board: $5,100
Financial aid: (507) 354-8221

Metropolitan State University[1]

St. Paul MN
(651) 772-7600
U.S. News ranking: Reg. U. (Mid.W), second tier
Website: www.metrostate.edu
Admissions email: admissions@metrostate.edu
Public
Application deadline (fall): N/A
Undergraduate student body: N/A full time, N/A part time
Expenses: 2014-2015: $6,642 in state, $13,227 out of state; room/ board: $9,588
Financial aid: (651) 772-7670

Minneapolis College of Art and Design

Minneapolis MN
(612) 874-3760
U.S. News ranking: Arts, unranked
Website: www.mcad.edu
Admissions email: admissions@mcad.edu
Private; founded 1886
Freshman admissions: N/A; 2014-2015: 472 applied, 304 accepted. Either SAT or ACT required. ACT 25/75 percentile: 21-26. High school rank: N/A
Early decision deadline: N/A, notification date: N/A
Early action deadline: 12/1, notification date: 12/15
Application deadline (fall): 5/1
Undergraduate student body: 663 full time, 62 part time; 38% male, 62% female; 1% American Indian, 8% Asian, 4% black, 7% Hispanic, 0% multiracial, 0% Pacific Islander, 57% white, 3% international
Most popular majors: 7% Animation, Interactive Technology, Video Graphics and Special Effects, 18% Graphic Design, 30% Illustration, 8% Painting, 8% Photography
Expenses: 2015-2016: $35,326; room/board: N/A
Financial aid: (612) 874-3782; 79% of undergrads determined to have financial need; average aid package $22,825

Minnesota State University–Mankato

Mankato MN
(507) 389-1822
U.S. News ranking: Reg. U. (Mid.W), No. 75
Website: www.mnsu.edu
Admissions email: admissions@mnsu.edu
Public; founded 1867
Freshman admissions: selective; 2014-2015: 9,984 applied, 6,647 accepted. ACT required. ACT 25/75 percentile: 19-24. High school rank: 7% in top tenth, 24% in top quarter, 67% in top half
Early decision deadline: N/A, notification date: N/A
Early action deadline: N/A, notification date: N/A
Application deadline (fall): rolling
Undergraduate student body: 11,147 full time, 2,188 part time; 48% male, 52% female; 0% American Indian, 4% Asian, 5% black, 4% Hispanic, 2% multiracial, 0% Pacific Islander, 78% white, 5% international; 87% from in state; 20% live on campus; N/A of students in fraternities, N/A in sororities
Most popular majors: 20% Business, Management, Marketing, and Related Support Services, 7% Education, 15% Health Professions and Related Programs, 7% Homeland Security, Law Enforcement, Firefighting and Related Protective Services, 7% Parks, Recreation, Leisure, and Fitness Studies
Expenses: 2014-2015: $7,574 in state, $15,052 out of state; room/ board: $8,042
Financial aid: (507) 389-1866; 58% of undergrads determined to have financial need; average aid package $8,960

Minnesota State University–Moorhead

Moorhead MN
(800) 593-7246
U.S. News ranking: Reg. U. (Mid.W), No. 108
Website: www.mnstate.edu
Admissions email: admissions@mnstate.edu
Public; founded 1887
Freshman admissions: selective; 2014-2015: 2,992 applied, 2,519 accepted. Either SAT or ACT required. ACT 25/75 percentile: 20-25. High school rank: 9% in top tenth, 31% in top quarter, 67% in top half
Early decision deadline: N/A, notification date: N/A
Early action deadline: N/A, notification date: N/A
Application deadline (fall): 8/1
Undergraduate student body: 4,731 full time, 1,007 part time; 39% male, 61% female; 1% American Indian, 1% Asian, 3% black, 3% Hispanic, 2% multiracial, 0% Pacific Islander, 78% white, 7% international; 66% from in state; 25% live on campus; N/A of students in fraternities, N/A in sororities
Most popular majors: 15% Business, Management, Marketing, and Related Support Services, 7% Communication, Journalism, and Related Programs, 16% Education, 10% Health Professions and Related Programs, 11% Visual and Performing Arts
Expenses: 2015-2016: $7,854 in state, $14,752 out of state; room/ board: $7,798
Financial aid: (218) 477-2251; 58% of undergrads determined to have financial need

North Central University

Minneapolis MN
(800) 289-6222
U.S. News ranking: Reg. Coll. (Mid.W), No. 59
Website: www.northcentral.edu
Admissions email: admissions@northcentral.edu
Private; founded 1930
Affiliation: Assemblies of God
Freshman admissions: selective; 2014-2015: 942 applied, 521 accepted. Either SAT or ACT required. ACT 25/75 percentile: 19-25. High school rank: 13% in top tenth, 41% in top quarter, 69% in top half
Early decision deadline: N/A, notification date: N/A
Early action deadline: N/A, notification date: N/A
Application deadline (fall): 6/1
Undergraduate student body: 995 full time, 201 part time; 43% male, 57% female; 0% American Indian, 2% Asian, 4% black, 6% Hispanic, 4% multiracial, 0% Pacific Islander, 80% white, 1% international; 57% from in state; 80% live on campus; N/A of students in fraternities, N/A in sororities
Most popular majors: 9% Business Administration and Management, General, 10% Intercultural/ Multicultural and Diversity Studies, 8% Pastoral Studies/ Counseling, 9% Psychology, General, 9% Youth Ministry
Expenses: 2015-2016: $21,586; room/board: $6,584
Financial aid: (612) 343-4485; 84% of undergrads determined to have financial need; average aid package $15,951

Southwest Minnesota State University

Marshall MN
(507) 537-6286
U.S. News ranking: Reg. U. (Mid.W), second tier
Website: www.smsu.edu
Admissions email: N/A
Public; founded 1963
Freshman admissions: selective; 2014-2015: 1,839 applied, 1,231 accepted. ACT required. ACT 25/75 percentile: 19-23. High school rank: 7% in top tenth, 24% in top quarter, 59% in top half
Early decision deadline: N/A, notification date: N/A
Early action deadline: N/A, notification date: N/A
Application deadline (fall): 9/1
Undergraduate student body: 2,080 full time, 4,371 part time; 42% male, 58% female; 1% American Indian, 2% Asian, 4% black, 2% Hispanic, N/A multiracial, 0% Pacific Islander, 86% white, 4% international
Most popular majors: 29% Business, Management, Marketing, and Related Support Services, 19% Education, 8% Parks, Recreation, Leisure, and Fitness Studies, 6% Psychology, 5% Public Administration and Social Service Professions
Expenses: 2015-2016: $8,094 in state, $8,094 out of state; room/board: $7,544
Financial aid: (507) 537-6281; 70% of undergrads determined to have financial need; average aid package $8,638

St. Catherine University

St. Paul MN
(800) 945-4599
U.S. News ranking: Reg. U. (Mid.W), No. 15
Website: www.stkate.edu
Admissions email: admissions@stkate.edu
Private; founded 1905
Affiliation: Roman Catholic
Freshman admissions: selective; 2014-2015: 2,961 applied, 1,990 accepted. Either SAT or ACT required. ACT 25/75 percentile: 21-26. High school rank: 21% in top tenth, 60% in top quarter, 95% in top half
Early decision deadline: N/A, notification date: N/A
Early action deadline: N/A, notification date: N/A
Application deadline (fall): rolling
Undergraduate student body: 2,093 full time, 1,398 part time; 4% male, 96% female; 1% American Indian, 11% Asian, 10% black, 6% Hispanic, 2% multiracial, 0% Pacific Islander, 65% white, 1% international; 88% from in state; 43% live on campus; N/A of students in fraternities, N/A in sororities
Most popular majors: 5% Business Administration and Management, General, 5% Psychology, General, 5% Public Health Education and Promotion, 28% Registered Nursing/Registered Nurse, 7% Social Work
Expenses: 2015-2016: $35,514; room/board: $8,750
Financial aid: (651) 690-6540; 86% of undergrads determined to have financial need; average aid package $32,615

St. Cloud State University

St. Cloud MN
(320) 308-2244
U.S. News ranking: Reg. U. (Mid.W), No. 99
Website: www.stcloudstate.edu
Admissions email: scsu4u@stcloudstate.edu
Public; founded 1869
Freshman admissions: selective; 2014-2015: 5,941 applied, 4,883 accepted. Either SAT or ACT required. ACT 25/75 percentile: 19-24. High school rank: 7% in top tenth, 27% in top quarter, 67% in top half
Early decision deadline: N/A, notification date: N/A
Early action deadline: N/A, notification date: N/A
Application deadline (fall): 8/1
Undergraduate student body: 9,306 full time, 4,446 part time; 48% male, 52% female; 0% American Indian, 6% Asian, 6% black, 3% Hispanic, 3% multiracial, 0% Pacific Islander, 75% white, 6% international; 91% from in state; 18% live on campus; 1% of students in fraternities, 2% in sororities
Most popular majors: 22% Business Administration and Management, General, 10% Communication Sciences and Disorders, General, 11% Curriculum and Instruction, 8% Mass Communication/Media Studies, 8% Psychology, General
Expenses: 2014-2015: $7,553 in state, $15,195 out of state; room/board: $7,560
Financial aid: (320) 308-2047

St. John's University

Collegeville MN
(320) 363-5060
U.S. News ranking: Nat. Lib. Arts, No. 79
Website: www.csbsju.edu
Admissions email: admissions@csbsju.edu
Private; founded 1857
Affiliation: Roman Catholic (Benedictine)
Freshman admissions: more selective; 2014-2015: 1,469 applied, 1,157 accepted. Either SAT or ACT required. ACT 25/75 percentile: 23-28. High school rank: 16% in top tenth, 50% in top quarter, 83% in top half
Early decision deadline: N/A, notification date: N/A
Early action deadline: 11/15, notification date: 12/15
Application deadline (fall): 1/15
Undergraduate student body: 1,758 full time, 31 part time; 100% male, 0% female; 1% American Indian, 3% Asian, 3% black, 5% Hispanic, 1% multiracial, 0% Pacific Islander, 81% white, 6% international; 80% from in state; 87% live on campus; 0% of students in fraternities, 0% in sororities
Most popular majors: 11% Accounting, 11% Biology/Biological Sciences, General, 21% Business Administration and Management, General, 6% Political Science and Government, General, 8% Rhetoric and Composition
Expenses: 2015-2016: $40,226; room/board: $9,604
Financial aid: (320) 363-3664; 67% of undergrads determined to have financial need; average aid package $30,327

St. Mary's University of Minnesota

Winona MN
(507) 457-1700
U.S. News ranking: Nat. U., No. 180
Website: www.smumn.edu
Admissions email: admissions@smumn.edu
Private; founded 1912
Affiliation: Roman Catholic
Freshman admissions: selective; 2014-2015: 1,743 applied, 1,294 accepted. Either SAT or ACT required. ACT 25/75 percentile: 20-26. High school rank: 16% in top tenth, 35% in top quarter, 69% in top half
Early decision deadline: N/A, notification date: N/A
Early action deadline: N/A, notification date: N/A
Application deadline (fall): 5/1
Undergraduate student body: 1,298 full time, 606 part time; 47% male, 53% female; 0% American Indian, 2% Asian, 4% black, 6% Hispanic, 1% multiracial, 0% Pacific Islander, 55% white, 2% international; 54% from in state; 93% live on campus; 4% of students in fraternities, 3% in sororities
Most popular majors: 5% Accounting, 6% Business Administration and Management, General, 13% Business/Commerce, General, 8% Human Resources Management/Personnel Administration, General, 9% Marketing/Marketing Management, General
Expenses: 2015-2016: $31,335; room/board: $8,240
Financial aid: (507) 457-1438; 74% of undergrads determined to have financial need; average aid package $23,158

St. Olaf College

Northfield MN
(507) 786-3025
U.S. News ranking: Nat. Lib. Arts, No. 51
Website: wp.stolaf.edu/
Admissions email: admissions@stolaf.edu
Private; founded 1874
Affiliation: Lutheran
Freshman admissions: more selective; 2014-2015: 4,875 applied, 2,500 accepted. Either SAT or ACT required. ACT 25/75 percentile: 26-32. High school rank: 52% in top tenth, 79% in top quarter, 97% in top half
Early decision deadline: 11/15, notification date: 12/15
Early action deadline: N/A, notification date: N/A
Application deadline (fall): 1/15
Undergraduate student body: 2,989 full time, 45 part time; 42% male, 58% female; 0% American Indian, 6% Asian, 2% black, 5% Hispanic, 4% multiracial, 0% Pacific Islander, 77% white, 7% international; 48% from in state; 93% live on campus; N/A of students in fraternities, N/A in sororities
Most popular majors: 11% Biological and Biomedical Sciences, 9% Mathematics and Statistics, 9% Physical Sciences, 18% Social Sciences, 12% Visual and Performing Arts
Expenses: 2015-2016: $42,940; room/board: $9,790
Financial aid: (507) 646-3019; 66% of undergrads determined to have financial need; average aid package $33,883

University of Minnesota–Crookston

Crookston MN
(800) 232-6466
U.S. News ranking: Reg. Coll. (Mid.W), No. 48
Website: www.crk.umn.edu
Admissions email: UMCinfo@umn.edu
Public; founded 1966
Freshman admissions: selective; 2014-2015: 927 applied, 662 accepted. Either SAT or ACT required. ACT 25/75 percentile: 19-24. High school rank: 12% in top tenth, 31% in top quarter, 65% in top half
Early decision deadline: N/A, notification date: N/A
Early action deadline: N/A, notification date: N/A
Application deadline (fall): rolling
Undergraduate student body: 1,349 full time, 1,501 part time; 47% male, 53% female; 0% American Indian, 2% Asian, 7% black, 3% Hispanic, 1% multiracial, 0% Pacific Islander, 80% white, 4% international; 72% from in state; 31% live on campus; N/A of students in fraternities, N/A in sororities
Most popular majors: 20% Agriculture, Agriculture Operations, and Related Sciences, 36% Business, Management, Marketing, and Related Support Services, 7% Health Professions and Related Programs, 7% Multi/Interdisciplinary Studies, 12% Natural Resources and Conservation
Expenses: 2014-2015: $11,468 in state, $11,468 out of state; room/board: $7,350
Financial aid: (218) 281-8576; 70% of undergrads determined to have financial need; average aid package $11,205

University of Minnesota–Duluth

Duluth MN
(218) 726-7171
U.S. News ranking: Reg. U. (Mid.W), No. 36
Website: www.d.umn.edu
Admissions email: umdadmis@d.umn.edu
Public; founded 1947
Freshman admissions: selective; 2014-2015: 7,738 applied, 5,942 accepted. Either SAT or ACT required. ACT 25/75 percentile: 22-26. High school rank: 18% in top tenth, 45% in top quarter, 83% in top half
Early decision deadline: N/A, notification date: N/A
Early action deadline: N/A, notification date: N/A
Application deadline (fall): 8/1
Undergraduate student body: 8,869 full time, 1,118 part time; 54% male, 46% female; 1% American Indian, 3% Asian, 2% black, 2% Hispanic, 3% multiracial, 0% Pacific Islander, 86% white, 2% international; 90% from in state; 33% live on campus; N/A of students in fraternities, N/A in sororities
Most popular majors: 10% Biological and Biomedical Sciences, 16% Business, Management, Marketing, and Related Support Services, 11% Education, 9% Engineering, 11% Social Sciences
Expenses: 2014-2015: $12,802 in state, $16,467 out of state; room/board: $7,004
Financial aid: (218) 726-8000; 59% of undergrads determined to have financial need; average aid package $10,933

University of Minnesota–Morris

Morris MN
(888) 866-3382
U.S. News ranking: Nat. Lib. Arts, No. 136
Website: www.morris.umn.edu
Admissions email: admissions@morris.umn.edu
Public; founded 1959
Freshman admissions: more selective; 2014-2015: 2,867 applied, 1,823 accepted. Either SAT or ACT required. ACT 25/75 percentile: 22-28. High school rank: 27% in top tenth, 55% in top quarter, 90% in top half
Early decision deadline: N/A, notification date: N/A
Early action deadline: N/A, notification date: N/A
Application deadline (fall): 3/15
Undergraduate student body: 1,761 full time, 138 part time; 46% male, 54% female; 7% American Indian, 3% Asian, 1% black, 4% Hispanic, 11% multiracial, 0% Pacific Islander, 64% white, 10% international; 86% from in state; 52% live on campus; 1% of students in fraternities, 1% in sororities
Most popular majors: 11% Biological and Biomedical Sciences, 6% Education, 11% English Language and Literature/Letters, 10% Psychology, 7% Visual and Performing Arts
Expenses: 2015-2016: $12,846 in state, $12,846 out of state; room/board: $7,804
Financial aid: (320) 589-6035; 60% of undergrads determined to have financial need; average aid package $12,407

University of Minnesota–Twin Cities

Minneapolis MN
(800) 752-1000
U.S. News ranking: Nat. U., No. 69
Website: www.umn.edu
Admissions email: N/A
Public; founded 1851
Freshman admissions: more selective; 2014-2015: 44,761 applied, 20,300 accepted. Either SAT or ACT required. ACT 25/75 percentile: 26-30. High school rank: 47% in top tenth, 86% in top quarter, 99% in top half
Early decision deadline: N/A, notification date: N/A
Early action deadline: N/A, notification date: N/A
Application deadline (fall): rolling
Undergraduate student body: 28,904 full time, 5,447 part time; 49% male, 51% female; 0% American Indian, 9% Asian, 4% black, 3% Hispanic, 3%

multiracial, 0% Pacific Islander, 70% white, 9% international; 73% from in state; 23% live on campus; N/A of students in fraternities, N/A in sororities
Most popular majors: 9% Biological and Biomedical Sciences, 9% Business, Management, Marketing, and Related Support Services, 11% Engineering, 7% Psychology, 13% Social Sciences
Expenses: 2014-2015: $13,560 in state, $20,810 out of state; room/board: $8,920
Financial aid: (612) 624-1111; 50% of undergrads determined to have financial need; average aid package $12,397

University of Northwestern–St. Paul

St. Paul MN
(800) 827-6827
U.S. News ranking: Reg. Coll. (Mid.W), No. 16
Website: www.unwsp.edu
Admissions email: admissions@unwsp.edu
Private; founded 1902
Affiliation: Christian nondenominational
Freshman admissions: selective; 2014-2015: 1,356 applied, 1,110 accepted. Either SAT or ACT required. ACT 25/75 percentile: 21-27. High school rank: 27% in top tenth, 48% in top quarter, 79% in top half
Early decision deadline: N/A, notification date: N/A
Early action deadline: N/A, notification date: N/A
Application deadline (fall): 8/1
Undergraduate student body: 1,931 full time, 1,291 part time; 40% male, 60% female; 0% American Indian, 4% Asian, 3% black, 3% Hispanic, 2% multiracial, 0% Pacific Islander, 86% white, 0% international; 72% from in state; 64% live on campus; 0% of students in fraternities, 0% in sororities
Most popular majors: 6% Biology/Biological Sciences, General, 7% Elementary Education and Teaching, 7% Kinesiology and Exercise Science, 8% Psychology, General, 6% Registered Nursing/Registered Nurse
Expenses: 2015-2016: $28,390; room/board: $8,954
Financial aid: (651) 631-5212; 84% of undergrads determined to have financial need; average aid package $24,814

University of St. Thomas

St. Paul MN
(651) 962-6150
U.S. News ranking: Nat. U., No. 115
Website: www.stthomas.edu
Admissions email: admissions@stthomas.edu
Private; founded 1885
Affiliation: Roman Catholic
Freshman admissions: more selective; 2014-2015: 5,343 applied, 4,628 accepted. Either SAT or ACT required. ACT 25/75 percentile: 24-29. High school rank: 29% in top tenth, 58% in top quarter, 92% in top half
Early decision deadline: N/A, notification date: N/A
Early action deadline: N/A, notification date: N/A
Application deadline (fall): rolling
Undergraduate student body: 5,969 full time, 265 part time; 54% male, 46% female; 0% American Indian, 3% Asian, 2% black, 4% Hispanic, 3% multiracial, 0% Pacific Islander, 82% white, 3% international; 81% from in state; 41% live on campus; 0% of students in fraternities, 0% in sororities
Most popular majors: 8% Biological and Biomedical Sciences, 39% Business, Management, Marketing, and Related Support Services, 6% Engineering, 6% Philosophy and Religious Studies, 8% Social Sciences
Expenses: 2015-2016: $36,475; room/board: $9,420
Financial aid: (651) 962-6550; 57% of undergrads determined to have financial need; average aid package $24,513

Walden University[1]

Minneapolis MN
(866) 492-5336
U.S. News ranking: Nat. U., unranked
Website: www.waldenu.edu/
Admissions email: N/A
For-profit; founded 1970
Application deadline (fall): rolling
Undergraduate student body: N/A full time, N/A part time
Expenses: 2014-2015: $14,300; room/board: N/A
Financial aid: N/A

Winona State University

Winona MN
(507) 457-5100
U.S. News ranking: Reg. U. (Mid.W), No. 72
Website: www.winona.edu
Admissions email: admissions@winona.edu
Public; founded 1858
Freshman admissions: selective; 2014-2015: 7,099 applied, 4,475 accepted. Either SAT or ACT required. ACT 25/75 percentile: 20-25. High school rank: 9% in top tenth, 30% in top quarter, 67% in top half
Early decision deadline: N/A, notification date: N/A
Early action deadline: N/A, notification date: N/A
Application deadline (fall): rolling
Undergraduate student body: 7,202 full time, 907 part time; 38% male, 62% female; 0% American Indian, 2% Asian, 2% black, 2% Hispanic, 2% multiracial, 0% Pacific Islander, 88% white, 3% international; 69% from in state; 28% live on campus; N/A of students in fraternities, N/A in sororities
Most popular majors: 19% Business, Management, Marketing, and Related Support Services, 7% Communication, Journalism, and Related Programs, 16% Education, 17% Health Professions and Related Programs, 7% Parks, Recreation, Leisure, and Fitness Studies
Expenses: 2014-2015: $8,750 in state, $14,250 out of state; room/board: $7,890
Financial aid: (507) 457-5090

MISSISSIPPI

Alcorn State University

Alcorn State MS
(601) 877-6147
U.S. News ranking: Reg. U. (S), No. 68
Website: www.alcorn.edu
Admissions email: ebarnes@alcorn.edu
Public; founded 1871
Freshman admissions: less selective; 2014-2015: 2,078 applied, 1,630 accepted. Either SAT or ACT required. ACT 25/75 percentile: 16-20. High school rank: N/A in top tenth, N/A in top quarter, 68% in top half
Early decision deadline: N/A, notification date: N/A
Early action deadline: N/A, notification date: N/A
Application deadline (fall): rolling
Undergraduate student body: 2,570 full time, 436 part time; 36% male, 64% female; 0% American Indian, 0% Asian, 94% black, 0% Hispanic, 2% multiracial, 0% Pacific Islander, 2% white, 1% international; 87% from in state; 53% live on campus; N/A of students in fraternities, N/A in sororities
Most popular majors: 17% Biological and Biomedical Sciences, 8% Family and Consumer Sciences/Human Sciences, 11% Health Professions and Related Programs, 13% Liberal Arts and Sciences, General Studies and Humanities, 7% Public Administration and Social Service Professions
Expenses: 2014-2015: $6,200 in state, N/A out of state; room/board: $8,650
Financial aid: (601) 877-6190

Belhaven University

Jackson MS
(601) 968-5940
U.S. News ranking: Reg. U. (S), No. 58
Website: www.belhaven.edu
Admissions email: admission@belhaven.edu
Private; founded 1883
Affiliation: Presbyterian
Freshman admissions: selective; 2014-2015: 2,264 applied, 1,623 accepted. Either SAT or ACT required. ACT 25/75 percentile: 18-23. High school rank: 16% in top tenth, 37% in top quarter, 72% in top half
Early decision deadline: N/A, notification date: N/A
Early action deadline: N/A, notification date: N/A
Application deadline (fall): rolling
Undergraduate student body: 1,289 full time, 1,277 part time; 36% male, 64% female; 1% American Indian, 1% Asian, 29% black, 5% Hispanic, 3% multiracial, 0% Pacific Islander, 49% white, 7% international; 65% from in state; 43% live on campus; N/A of students in fraternities, N/A in sororities
Most popular majors: 30% Business, Management, Marketing, and Related Support Services, 9% Health Professions and Related Programs, 7% Parks, Recreation, Leisure, and Fitness Studies, 16% Social Sciences, 12% Visual and Performing Arts
Expenses: 2015-2016: $21,816; room/board: $8,000
Financial aid: (601) 968-5934; 83% of undergrads determined to have financial need; average aid package $21,316

Blue Mountain College

Blue Mountain MS
(662) 685-4161
U.S. News ranking: Reg. Coll. (S), No. 22
Website: www.bmc.edu
Admissions email: admissions@bmc.edu
Private; founded 1873
Affiliation: Southern Baptist
Freshman admissions: selective; 2014-2015: 298 applied, 164 accepted. Either SAT or ACT required. ACT 25/75 percentile: 17-26. High school rank: 25% in top tenth, 48% in top quarter, 80% in top half
Early decision deadline: N/A, notification date: N/A
Early action deadline: N/A, notification date: N/A
Application deadline (fall): rolling
Undergraduate student body: 463 full time, 57 part time; 41% male, 59% female; 0% American Indian, 1% Asian, 10% black, 2% Hispanic, 0% multiracial, 0% Pacific Islander, 85% white, 2% international; 79% from in state; 56% live on campus; 0% of students in fraternities, 0% in sororities
Most popular majors: 13% Bible/Biblical Studies, 9% Business Administration and Management, General, 36% Education, General, 9% History, General, 18% Psychology, General
Expenses: 2015-2016: $10,852; room/board: $5,424
Financial aid: (662) 685-4771; 81% of undergrads determined to have financial need; average aid package $10,156

Delta State University

Cleveland MS
(662) 846-4018
U.S. News ranking: Reg. U. (S), second tier
Website: www.deltastate.edu
Admissions email: admissions@deltastate.edu
Public; founded 1924
Freshman admissions: selective; 2014-2015: 494 applied, 455 accepted. ACT required. ACT 25/75 percentile: 18-22. High school rank: N/A
Early decision deadline: N/A, notification date: N/A
Early action deadline: N/A, notification date: N/A
Application deadline (fall): 8/1
Undergraduate student body: 2,308 full time, 470 part time; 39% male, 61% female; 0% American Indian, 1% Asian, 35% black, 1% Hispanic, 1% multiracial, 0% Pacific Islander, 59% white, 3% international
Most popular majors: Information not available
Expenses: 2015-2016: $6,112 in state, $6,112 out of state; room/board: $7,064
Financial aid: (662) 846-4670

Jackson State University

Jackson MS
(601) 979-2100
U.S. News ranking: Nat. U., second tier
Website: www.jsums.edu
Admissions email: admappl@jsums.edu
Public; founded 1877
Freshman admissions: less selective; 2014-2015: 9,543 applied, 2,486 accepted. Either SAT or ACT required. ACT 25/75 percentile: 17-21. High school rank: N/A in top tenth, N/A in top quarter, 75% in top half
Early decision deadline: N/A, notification date: N/A
Early action deadline: N/A, notification date: N/A
Application deadline (fall): 9/2
Undergraduate student body: 5,959 full time, 1,240 part time; 37% male, 63% female; 1% American Indian, 0% Asian, 92% black, 0% Hispanic, 1% multiracial, 0% Pacific Islander, 4% white, 2% international; 83% from in state; 31% live on campus; 2% of students in fraternities, 3% in sororities
Most popular majors: 8% Biological and Biomedical Sciences, 17% Business, Management, Marketing, and Related Support Services, 15% Education, 14% Multi/Interdisciplinary Studies, 6% Public Administration and Social Service Professions
Expenses: 2014-2015: $6,602 in state, $16,174 out of state; room/board: N/A
Financial aid: (601) 979-2227; 93% of undergrads determined to have financial need; average aid package $10,504

Millsaps College

Jackson MS
(601) 974-1050
U.S. News ranking: Nat. Lib. Arts, No. 93
Website: www.millsaps.edu
Admissions email: admissions@millsaps.edu
Private; founded 1890
Affiliation: United Methodist
Freshman admissions: more selective; 2014-2015: 2,861 applied, 1,636 accepted. Either SAT or ACT required. ACT 25/75 percentile: 23-29. High school rank: 36% in top tenth, 61% in top quarter, 84% in top half
Early decision deadline: N/A, notification date: N/A
Early action deadline: 11/15, notification date: 1/15
Application deadline (fall): 2/1
Undergraduate student body: 757 full time, 14 part time; 51% male, 49% female; 1% American Indian, 4% Asian, 11% black, 2% Hispanic, 1% multiracial, 0% Pacific Islander, 75% white, 4% international; 45% from in state; 87% live on campus; 59% of students in fraternities, 63% in sororities
Most popular majors: 18% Biological and Biomedical Sciences, 22% Business, Management, Marketing, and Related Support Services, 7% Physical Sciences, 11% Psychology, 10% Social Sciences
Expenses: 2015-2016: $35,510; room/board: $12,412

Financial aid: (601) 974-1220; 60% of undergrads determined to have financial need; average aid package $29,702

Mississippi College

Clinton MS
(601) 925-3800
U.S. News ranking: Reg. U. (S), No. 32
Website: www.mc.edu
Admissions email: enrollment-services@mc.edu
Private; founded 1826
Affiliation: Mississippi Baptist Convention
Freshman admissions: selective; 2014-2015: 2,124 applied, 1,339 accepted. Either SAT or ACT required. ACT 25/75 percentile: 21-28. High school rank: 30% in top tenth, 47% in top quarter, 61% in top half
Early decision deadline: N/A, notification date: N/A
Early action deadline: N/A, notification date: N/A
Application deadline (fall): rolling
Undergraduate student body: 2,669 full time, 315 part time; 42% male, 58% female; 0% American Indian, 2% Asian, 19% black, 3% Hispanic, 1% multiracial, 0% Pacific Islander, 66% white, 5% international; 78% from in state; 57% live on campus; 21% of students in fraternities, 32% in sororities
Most popular majors: 7% Accounting, 9% Business Administration and Management, General, 9% Elementary Education and Teaching, 9% Kinesiology and Exercise Science, 10% Registered Nursing/Registered Nurse
Expenses: 2015-2016: $16,114; room/board: $8,744
Financial aid: (601) 925-3319; 54% of undergrads determined to have financial need; average aid package $14,281

Mississippi State University

Mississippi State MS
(662) 325-2224
U.S. News ranking: Nat. U., No. 161
Website: www.msstate.edu
Admissions email: admit@admissions.msstate.edu
Public; founded 1878
Freshman admissions: more selective; 2014-2015: 10,766 applied, 7,646 accepted. Either SAT or ACT required. ACT 25/75 percentile: 21-28. High school rank: 28% in top tenth, 54% in top quarter, 81% in top half
Early decision deadline: N/A, notification date: N/A
Early action deadline: N/A, notification date: N/A
Application deadline (fall): rolling
Undergraduate student body: 15,146 full time, 1,390 part time; 52% male, 48% female; 1% American Indian, 1% Asian, 20% black, 2% Hispanic, 1% multiracial, 0% Pacific Islander, 72% white, 2% international; 74% from in state; 27% live on campus; 16% of students in fraternities, 25% in sororities
Most popular majors: 6% Biological and Biomedical Sciences, 18% Business, Management, Marketing, and Related Support Services, 18% Education, 12% Engineering, 5% Multi/Interdisciplinary Studies
Expenses: 2015-2016: $7,502 in state, $20,142 out of state; room/board: $9,068
Financial aid: (662) 325-2450; 62% of undergrads determined to have financial need; average aid package $13,557

Mississippi University for Women

Columbus MS
(662) 329-7106
U.S. News ranking: Reg. U. (S), No. 46
Website: www.muw.edu
Admissions email: admissions@muw.edu
Public; founded 1884
Freshman admissions: selective; 2014-2015: 720 applied, 674 accepted. Either SAT or ACT required. ACT 25/75 percentile: 18-23. High school rank: 29% in top tenth, 63% in top quarter, 91% in top half
Early decision deadline: N/A, notification date: N/A
Early action deadline: N/A, notification date: N/A
Application deadline (fall): rolling
Undergraduate student body: 2,065 full time, 462 part time; 19% male, 81% female; 0% American Indian, 1% Asian, 39% black, 1% Hispanic, 0% multiracial, 0% Pacific Islander, 56% white, 2% international; 91% from in state; 23% live on campus; 8% of students in fraternities, 12% in sororities
Most popular majors: 5% Business Administration and Management, General, 5% Elementary Education and Teaching, 6% Liberal Arts and Sciences/Liberal Studies, 5% Public Health Education and Promotion, 46% Registered Nursing/Registered Nurse
Expenses: 2015-2016: $5,781 in state, $15,847 out of state; room/board: $6,591
Financial aid: (662) 329-7114; 80% of undergrads determined to have financial need; average aid package $8,948

Mississippi Valley State University

Itta Bena MS
(662) 254-3344
U.S. News ranking: Reg. U. (S), second tier
Website: www.mvsu.edu
Admissions email: admsn@mvsu.edu
Public
Freshman admissions: less selective; 2014-2015: 7,655 applied, 1,250 accepted. Either SAT or ACT required. ACT 25/75 percentile: 15-19. High school rank: N/A
Early decision deadline: N/A, notification date: N/A
Early action deadline: N/A, notification date: N/A
Application deadline (fall): 8/17
Undergraduate student body: 1,652 full time, 237 part time; 43% male, 57% female; 0% American Indian, 1% Asian, 91% black, 1% Hispanic, N/A multiracial, N/A Pacific Islander, 3% white, N/A international; N/A from in state; 51% live on campus; 14% of students in fraternities, 20% in sororities
Most popular majors: 17% Business, Management, Marketing, and Related Support Services, 11% Education, 13% Education, 9% Homeland Security, Law Enforcement, Firefighting and Related Protective Services, 12% Mechanic and Repair Technologies/Technicians
Expenses: 2014-2015: $5,916 in state, N/A out of state; room/board: $7,167
Financial aid: (662) 254-3335

Rust College

Holly Springs MS
(662) 252-8000
U.S. News ranking: Nat. Lib. Arts, second tier
Website: www.rustcollege.edu
Admissions email: admissions@rustcollege.edu
Private; founded 1866
Affiliation: United Methodist
Freshman admissions: less selective; 2014-2015: 5,186 applied, 908 accepted. ACT required. ACT 25/75 percentile: 14-17. High school rank: N/A
Early decision deadline: N/A, notification date: N/A
Early action deadline: N/A, notification date: N/A
Application deadline (fall): rolling
Undergraduate student body: 908 full time, 55 part time; 42% male, 58% female; N/A American Indian, 0% Asian, 95% black, N/A Hispanic, N/A multiracial, N/A Pacific Islander, 0% white, 4% international
Most popular majors: Information not available
Expenses: 2015-2016: $9,500; room/board: $4,000
Financial aid: (662) 252-8000; 94% of undergrads determined to have financial need; average aid package $11,915

Tougaloo College

Tougaloo MS
(601) 977-7765
U.S. News ranking: Nat. Lib. Arts, second tier
Website: www.tougaloo.edu
Admissions email: information@mail.tougaloo.edu
Private; founded 1869
Affiliation: United Church Disciples of Christ
Freshman admissions: less selective; 2014-2015: 2,515 applied, 1,064 accepted. Either SAT or ACT required. ACT 25/75 percentile: 15-21. High school rank: 19% in top tenth, 25% in top quarter, 82% in top half
Early decision deadline: N/A, notification date: N/A
Early action deadline: 11/1, notification date: 12/1
Application deadline (fall): 7/1
Undergraduate student body: 872 full time, 28 part time; 35% male, 65% female; 0% American Indian, 0% Asian, 99% black, 0% Hispanic, 0% multiracial, 0% Pacific Islander, 0% white, 0% international; 81% from in state; 66% live on campus; 22% of students in fraternities, 43% in sororities
Most popular majors: 13% Biology/Biological Sciences, General, 8% Chemistry, General, 9% Economics, General, 17% Sociology
Expenses: 2015-2016: $10,600; room/board: $6,330
Financial aid: (601) 977-7769; 94% of undergrads determined to have financial need; average aid package $13,500

University of Mississippi

University MS
(662) 915-7226
U.S. News ranking: Nat. U., No. 140
Website: www.olemiss.edu
Admissions email: admissions@olemiss.edu
Public; founded 1844
Freshman admissions: selective; 2014-2015: 16,101 applied, 13,077 accepted. Neither SAT nor ACT required. ACT 25/75 percentile: 21-27. High school rank: 22% in top tenth, 47% in top quarter, 75% in top half
Early decision deadline: N/A, notification date: N/A
Early action deadline: N/A, notification date: N/A
Application deadline (fall): 9/1
Undergraduate student body: 16,665 full time, 1,436 part time; 44% male, 56% female; 0% American Indian, 2% Asian, 15% black, 3% Hispanic, 2% multiracial, 0% Pacific Islander, 77% white, 1% international; 60% from in state; 27% live on campus; 33% of students in fraternities, 41% in sororities
Most popular majors: 5% Accounting, 6% Elementary Education and Teaching, 5% Marketing/Marketing Management, General, 5% Psychology, General, 8% Registered Nursing/Registered Nurse
Expenses: 2015-2016: $7,444 in state, $20,674 out of state; room/board: $10,128
Financial aid: (662) 915-7175; 53% of undergrads determined to have financial need; average aid package $8,728

University of Southern Mississippi

Hattiesburg MS
(601) 266-5000
U.S. News ranking: Nat. U., second tier
Website: www.usm.edu/admissions
Admissions email: admissions@usm.edu
Public; founded 1910
Freshman admissions: selective; 2014-2015: 5,850 applied, 3,904 accepted. Either SAT or ACT required. ACT 25/75 percentile: 19-25. High school rank: 19% in top tenth, 44% in top quarter, 81% in top half
Early decision deadline: N/A, notification date: N/A
Early action deadline: N/A, notification date: N/A
Application deadline (fall): rolling
Undergraduate student body: 10,577 full time, 1,428 part time; 36% male, 64% female; 0% American Indian, 1% Asian, 30% black, 3% Hispanic, 2% multiracial, 0% Pacific Islander, 61% white, 1% international; 84% from in state; 26% live on campus; 11% of students in fraternities, 16% in sororities
Most popular majors: 5% Biology/Biological Sciences, General, 4% Business Administration and Management, General, 8% Elementary Education and Teaching, 7% Psychology, General, 7% Registered Nursing/Registered Nurse
Expenses: 2015-2016: $7,224 in state, $16,094 out of state; room/board: $7,640
Financial aid: (601) 266-4774; 83% of undergrads determined to have financial need; average aid package $9,831

William Carey University

Hattiesburg MS
(601) 318-6103
U.S. News ranking: Reg. U. (S), No. 41
Website: www.wmcarey.edu
Admissions email: admissions@wmcarey.edu
Private; founded 1892
Affiliation: Baptist
Freshman admissions: selective; 2014-2015: 787 applied, 409 accepted. Either SAT or ACT required. ACT 25/75 percentile: 20-27. High school rank: 28% in top tenth, 60% in top quarter, 82% in top half
Early decision deadline: N/A, notification date: N/A
Early action deadline: N/A, notification date: N/A
Application deadline (fall): rolling
Undergraduate student body: 1,874 full time, 402 part time; 35% male, 65% female; 1% American Indian, 1% Asian, 30% black, 2% Hispanic, 0% multiracial, 0% Pacific Islander, 61% white, 5% international; 85% from in state; 57% live on campus; 0% of students in fraternities, 2% in sororities
Most popular majors: 5% Biology/Biological Sciences, General, 11% Business Administration and Management, General, 18% Elementary Education and Teaching, 19% Psychology, General, 25% Registered Nursing/Registered Nurse
Expenses: 2015-2016: $11,700; room/board: $4,200
Financial aid: (601) 318-6153; 91% of undergrads determined to have financial need; average aid package $16,400

MISSOURI

Avila University[1]

Kansas City MO
(816) 501-2400
U.S. News ranking: Reg. U. (Mid.W), second tier
Website: www.Avila.edu
Admissions email: admissions@mail.avila.edu
Private
Application deadline (fall): N/A
Undergraduate student body: N/A full time, N/A part time
Expenses: 2014-2015: $25,700; room/board: $6,908
Financial aid: (816) 501-3600

Central Methodist University

Fayette MO
(660) 248-6251
U.S. News ranking: Reg. Coll. (Mid.W), No. 36
Website: www.centralmethodist.edu

Admissions email: admissions@centralmethodist.edu
Private; founded 1854
Affiliation: United Methodist
Freshman admissions: selective; 2014-2015: 1,533 applied, 928 accepted. Either SAT or ACT required. ACT 25/75 percentile: 20-25. High school rank: 15% in top tenth, 41% in top quarter, 77% in top half
Early decision deadline: N/A, notification date: N/A
Early action deadline: N/A, notification date: N/A
Application deadline (fall): rolling
Undergraduate student body: 1,149 full time, 36 part time; 48% male, 52% female; 1% American Indian, 0% Asian, 8% black, 3% Hispanic, 3% multiracial, 0% Pacific Islander, 81% white, 3% international; 86% from in state; 61% live on campus; 15% of students in fraternities, 13% in sororities
Most popular majors: 11% Biological and Biomedical Sciences, 7% Biological and Biomedical Sciences, 19% Education, 19% Health Professions and Related Programs, 10% Multi/Interdisciplinary Studies
Expenses: 2015-2016: $22,360; room/board: $7,340
Financial aid: (660) 248-6244; 83% of undergrads determined to have financial need; average aid package $24,015

College of the Ozarks

Point Lookout MO
(800) 222-0525
U.S. News ranking: Reg. Coll. (Mid.W), No. 4
Website: www.cofo.edu
Admissions email: admiss4@cofo.edu
Private; founded 1906
Affiliation: Evangelical Christian Interdenominational
Freshman admissions: selective; 2014-2015: 3,407 applied, 283 accepted. Either SAT or ACT required. ACT 25/75 percentile: 21-25. High school rank: 22% in top tenth, 52% in top quarter, 92% in top half
Early decision deadline: N/A, notification date: N/A
Early action deadline: N/A, notification date: N/A
Application deadline (fall): rolling
Undergraduate student body: 1,422 full time, 11 part time; 49% male, 51% female; 1% American Indian, 1% Asian, 1% black, 2% Hispanic, 2% multiracial, 0% Pacific Islander, 91% white, 2% international; 78% from in state; 81% live on campus; 0% of students in fraternities, 0% in sororities
Most popular majors: 11% Agriculture, Agriculture Operations, and Related Sciences, 16% Business, Management, Marketing, and Related Support Services, 14% Education, General, 3% Homeland Security, Law Enforcement, Firefighting and Related Protective Services, 3% Speech Communication and Rhetoric
Expenses: 2015-2016: $18,730; room/board: $6,500
Financial aid: (417) 334-6411; 94% of undergrads determined to have financial need; average aid package $19,237

Columbia College

Columbia MO
(573) 875-7352
U.S. News ranking: Reg. U. (Mid.W), unranked
Website: www.ccis.edu
Admissions email: admissions@ccis.edu
Private; founded 1851
Affiliation: Christian Church (Disciples of Christ)
Freshman admissions: N/A; 2014-2015: N/A applied, N/A accepted. Neither SAT nor ACT required. ACT 25/75 percentile: N/A. High school rank: N/A
Early decision deadline: N/A, notification date: N/A
Early action deadline: N/A, notification date: N/A
Application deadline (fall): rolling
Undergraduate student body: N/A full time, N/A part time; N/A male, N/A female; N/A American Indian, N/A Asian, N/A black, N/A Hispanic, N/A multiracial, N/A Pacific Islander, N/A white, N/A international
Most popular majors: Information not available
Expenses: 2014-2015: $7,115; room/board: N/A
Financial aid: (573) 875-7390

Culver-Stockton College

Canton MO
(800) 537-1883
U.S. News ranking: Reg. Coll. (Mid.W), No. 43
Website: www.culver.edu
Admissions email: admissions@culver.edu
Private; founded 1853
Affiliation: Christian Church (Disciples of Christ)
Freshman admissions: selective; 2014-2015: 2,372 applied, 1,369 accepted. Either SAT or ACT required. ACT 25/75 percentile: 19-23. High school rank: 11% in top tenth, 32% in top quarter, 64% in top half
Early decision deadline: N/A, notification date: N/A
Early action deadline: N/A, notification date: N/A
Application deadline (fall): rolling
Undergraduate student body: 892 full time, 65 part time; 52% male, 48% female; 0% American Indian, 0% Asian, 13% black, 5% Hispanic, 2% multiracial, 1% Pacific Islander, 74% white, 5% international; 55% from in state; 77% live on campus; 36% of students in fraternities, 39% in sororities
Most popular majors: 20% Business Administration and Management, General, 7% Criminal Justice/Law Enforcement Administration, 13% Psychology, General, 12% Registered Nursing/Registered Nurse, 10% Sport and Fitness Administration/Management
Expenses: 2015-2016: $24,900; room/board: $7,950
Financial aid: (573) 288-6307; 85% of undergrads determined to have financial need; average aid package $20,407

Drury University

Springfield MO
(417) 873-7205
U.S. News ranking: Reg. U. (Mid.W), No. 11
Website: www.drury.edu
Admissions email: druryad@drury.edu
Private; founded 1873
Affiliation: Christian Church (Disciples of Christ)
Freshman admissions: more selective; 2014-2015: 1,016 applied, 823 accepted. Either SAT or ACT required. ACT 25/75 percentile: 23-29. High school rank: 31% in top tenth, 62% in top quarter, 89% in top half
Early decision deadline: N/A, notification date: N/A
Early action deadline: N/A, notification date: N/A
Application deadline (fall): 5/1
Undergraduate student body: 1,425 full time, 29 part time; 48% male, 52% female; 0% American Indian, 2% Asian, 3% black, 4% Hispanic, 2% multiracial, 0% Pacific Islander, 78% white, 11% international; 85% from in state; 59% live on campus; 23% of students in fraternities, 28% in sororities
Most popular majors: 12% Biological and Biomedical Sciences, 17% Business, Management, Marketing, and Related Support Services, 9% Education, 11% Homeland Security, Law Enforcement, Firefighting and Related Protective Services, 21% Psychology
Expenses: 2015-2016: $24,905; room/board: $8,256
Financial aid: (417) 873-7312; 62% of undergrads determined to have financial need; average aid package $19,321

Evangel University

Springfield MO
(800) 382-6435
U.S. News ranking: Reg. Coll. (Mid.W), No. 55
Website: www.evangel.edu
Admissions email: admissions@evangel.edu
Private; founded 1955
Affiliation: Assemblies of God
Freshman admissions: selective; 2014-2015: 1,249 applied, 806 accepted. Either SAT or ACT required. ACT 25/75 percentile: 20-26. High school rank: N/A
Early decision deadline: N/A, notification date: N/A
Early action deadline: N/A, notification date: N/A
Application deadline (fall): rolling
Undergraduate student body: 1,603 full time, 191 part time; 46% male, 54% female; 1% American Indian, 2% Asian, 4% black, 5% Hispanic, 4% multiracial, N/A Pacific Islander, 76% white, 0% international; 57% from in state; 68% live on campus; N/A of students in fraternities, N/A in sororities
Most popular majors: Information not available
Expenses: 2015-2016: $21,316; room/board: $7,582
Financial aid: (417) 865-2815; 84% of undergrads determined to have financial need; average aid package $16,429

Fontbonne University

St. Louis MO
(314) 889-1400
U.S. News ranking: Reg. U. (Mid.W), No. 85
Website: www.fontbonne.edu
Admissions email: admissions@fontbonne.edu
Private; founded 1923
Affiliation: Roman Catholic
Freshman admissions: selective; 2014-2015: 393 applied, 367 accepted. Either SAT or ACT required. ACT 25/75 percentile: 20-25. High school rank: N/A
Early decision deadline: N/A, notification date: N/A
Early action deadline: N/A, notification date: N/A
Application deadline (fall): rolling
Undergraduate student body: 899 full time, 314 part time; 34% male, 66% female; 0% American Indian, 1% Asian, 16% black, 3% Hispanic, 2% multiracial, 0% Pacific Islander, 69% white, 8% international; 85% from in state; 14% live on campus; N/A of students in fraternities, N/A in sororities
Most popular majors: 20% Business Administration and Management, General, 5% Dietetics/Dietitian, 6% Psychology, General, 9% Special Education and Teaching, General, 7% Speech-Language Pathology/Pathologist
Expenses: 2015-2016: $23,790; room/board: $9,018
Financial aid: (314) 889-1414; 62% of undergrads determined to have financial need; average aid package $14,870

Hannibal-LaGrange University

Hannibal MO
(800) 454-1119
U.S. News ranking: Reg. Coll. (Mid.W), No. 62
Website: www.hlg.edu
Admissions email: admissions@hlg.edu
Private; founded 1858
Affiliation: Southern Baptist Convention
Freshman admissions: selective; 2014-2015: 899 applied, 544 accepted. Either SAT or ACT required. ACT 25/75 percentile: 19-25. High school rank: N/A
Early decision deadline: N/A, notification date: N/A
Early action deadline: N/A, notification date: N/A
Application deadline (fall): 8/27
Undergraduate student body: 799 full time, 311 part time; 43% male, 57% female; 0% American Indian, 0% Asian, 5% black, 2% Hispanic, 2% multiracial, 0% Pacific Islander, 80% white, 9% international; 71% from in state; 44% live on campus; N/A of students in fraternities, N/A in sororities
Most popular majors: 4% Business Administration and Management, General, 8% Criminal Justice/Safety Studies, 22% Elementary Education and Teaching, 12% Organizational Leadership, 18% Registered Nursing/Registered Nurse
Expenses: 2014-2015: $19,530; room/board: $7,110
Financial aid: (573) 221-3675

Harris-Stowe State University

St. Louis MO
(314) 340-3300
U.S. News ranking: Reg. Coll. (Mid.W), second tier
Website: www.hssu.edu
Admissions email: admissions@hssu.edu
Public; founded 1857
Freshman admissions: least selective; 2014-2015: 585 applied, 544 accepted. Either SAT or ACT required. ACT 25/75 percentile: 14-18. High school rank: 3% in top tenth, 15% in top quarter, 45% in top half
Early decision deadline: N/A, notification date: N/A
Early action deadline: N/A, notification date: N/A
Application deadline (fall): rolling
Undergraduate student body: 969 full time, 311 part time; 32% male, 68% female; 0% American Indian, 0% Asian, 83% black, 2% Hispanic, 2% multiracial, 0% Pacific Islander, 8% white, 1% international; 88% from in state; 23% live on campus; N/A of students in fraternities, N/A in sororities
Most popular majors: 15% Accounting, 6% Biology/Biological Sciences, General, 25% Business Administration and Management, General, 14% Criminal Justice/Safety Studies, 8% Education, General
Expenses: 2015-2016: $5,220 in state, $9,853 out of state; room/board: $9,250
Financial aid: (314) 340-3500; 91% of undergrads determined to have financial need; average aid package $9,259

Kansas City Art Institute[1]

Kansas City MO
(800) 522-5224
U.S. News ranking: Arts, unranked
Website: www.kcai.edu
Admissions email: admiss@kcai.edu
Private; founded 1885
Application deadline (fall): rolling
Undergraduate student body: N/A full time, N/A part time
Expenses: 2015-2016: $35,270; room/board: $10,240
Financial aid: (816) 802-3448; 83% of undergrads determined to have financial need

Lincoln University

Jefferson City MO
(573) 681-5599
U.S. News ranking: Reg. U. (Mid.W), second tier
Website: www.lincolnu.edu
Admissions email: enroll@lincolnu.edu
Public; founded 1866
Freshman admissions: less selective; 2014-2015: 3,940 applied, 2,139 accepted. Either SAT or ACT required. ACT 25/75 percentile: 15-21. High school rank: 5% in top tenth, 17% in top quarter, 48% in top half
Early decision deadline: N/A, notification date: N/A
Early action deadline: N/A, notification date: N/A
Application deadline (fall): rolling
Undergraduate student body: 2,032 full time, 945 part time; 44% male, 56% female; 0% American

Indian, 0% Asian, 49% black, 2% Hispanic, 2% multiracial, N/A Pacific Islander, 38% white, 2% international; 85% from in state; 27% live on campus; N/A of students in fraternities, N/A in sororities
Most popular majors: 9% Business Administration and Management, General, 8% Criminal Justice/ Law Enforcement Administration, 6% Elementary Education and Teaching, 6% Information Science/Studies, 12% Liberal Arts and Sciences/Liberal Studies
Expenses: 2015-2016: $7,042 in state, $13,432 out of state; room/ board: N/A
Financial aid: (573) 681-6156; 84% of undergrads determined to have financial need; average aid package $10,788

Lindenwood University

St. Charles MO
(636) 949-4949
U.S. News ranking: Reg. U. (Mid.W), No. 108
Website: www.lindenwood.edu
Admissions email: admissions@lindenwood.edu
Private; founded 1827
Affiliation: Presbyterian
Freshman admissions: selective; 2014-2015: 4,595 applied, 2,430 accepted. Either SAT or ACT required. ACT 25/75 percentile: 20-25. High school rank: 11% in top tenth, 33% in top quarter, 68% in top half
Early decision deadline: N/A, notification date: N/A
Early action deadline: N/A, notification date: N/A
Application deadline (fall): rolling
Undergraduate student body: 7,443 full time, 1,098 part time; 46% male, 54% female; 0% American Indian, 0% Asian, 14% black, 4% Hispanic, 3% multiracial, 0% Pacific Islander, 60% white, 12% international; 67% from in state; 53% live on campus; 2% of students in fraternities, 3% in sororities
Most popular majors: 24% Business/Commerce, General, 9% Criminal Justice/Safety Studies, 6% Elementary Education and Teaching, 6% Human Resources Management/Personnel Administration, General, 5% Psychology, General
Expenses: 2015-2016: $16,022; room/board: $7,934
Financial aid: (636) 949-4923; 58% of undergrads determined to have financial need; average aid package $10,874

Maryville University of St. Louis

St Louis MO
(800) 627-9855
U.S. News ranking: Nat. U., No. 161
Website: www.maryville.edu
Admissions email: admissions@maryville.edu
Private; founded 1872
Freshman admissions: more selective; 2014-2015: 1,576 applied, 1,134 accepted. Either SAT or ACT required. ACT 25/75 percentile: 23-27. High school rank: 28% in top tenth, 61% in top quarter, 89% in top half
Early decision deadline: N/A, notification date: N/A
Early action deadline: N/A, notification date: N/A
Application deadline (fall): 8/15
Undergraduate student body: 1,852 full time, 966 part time; 29% male, 71% female; 0% American Indian, 2% Asian, 8% black, 3% Hispanic, 2% multiracial, 0% Pacific Islander, 76% white, 3% international; 79% from in state; 24% live on campus; 0% of students in fraternities, 0% in sororities
Most popular majors: 4% Accounting, 7% Business/ Commerce, General, 6% Health Professions and Related Clinical Sciences, Other, 6% Psychology, General, 32% Registered Nursing/ Registered Nurse
Expenses: 2015-2016: $26,958; room/board: $10,552
Financial aid: (314) 529-9360; 70% of undergrads determined to have financial need; average aid package $22,814

Missouri Baptist University[1]

St. Louis MO
(314) 434-2290
U.S. News ranking: Reg. U. (Mid.W), second tier
Website: www.mobap.edu
Admissions email: admissions@mobap.edu
Private; founded 1964
Affiliation: Baptist
Application deadline (fall): rolling
Undergraduate student body: N/A full time, N/A part time
Expenses: 2014-2015: $22,760; room/board: $9,070
Financial aid: (314) 392-2366

Missouri Southern State University

Joplin MO
(417) 781-6778
U.S. News ranking: Reg. Coll. (Mid.W), second tier
Website: www.mssu.edu
Admissions email: admissions@mssu.edu
Public; founded 1937
Freshman admissions: selective; 2014-2015: 2,002 applied, 1,922 accepted. Either SAT or ACT required. ACT 25/75 percentile: 18-24. High school rank: 14% in top tenth, 37% in top quarter, 68% in top half
Early decision deadline: N/A, notification date: N/A
Early action deadline: N/A, notification date: N/A
Application deadline (fall): rolling
Undergraduate student body: 4,140 full time, 1,421 part time; 43% male, 57% female; 3% American Indian, 2% Asian, 7% black, 4% Hispanic, 1% multiracial, 0% Pacific Islander, 78% white, 2% international; 83% from in state; 13% live on campus; N/A of students in fraternities, N/A in sororities
Most popular majors: 23% Business, Management, Marketing, and Related Support Services, 11% Education, 14% Health Professions and Related Programs, 12% Homeland Security, Law Enforcement, Firefighting and Related Protective Services, 10% Liberal Arts and Sciences, General Studies and Humanities
Expenses: 2015-2016: $5,523 in state, $10,480 out of state; room/ board: $6,622
Financial aid: (417) 625-9325; 79% of undergrads determined to have financial need; average aid package $7,413

Missouri State University

Springfield MO
(800) 492-7900
U.S. News ranking: Reg. U. (Mid.W), No. 64
Website: www.missouristate.edu
Admissions email: info@missouristate.edu
Public; founded 1906
Freshman admissions: selective; 2014-2015: 8,044 applied, 6,840 accepted. Either SAT or ACT required. ACT 25/75 percentile: 21-26. High school rank: 24% in top tenth, 54% in top quarter, 85% in top half
Early decision deadline: N/A, notification date: N/A
Early action deadline: N/A, notification date: N/A
Application deadline (fall): 7/20
Undergraduate student body: 14,097 full time, 4,420 part time; 43% male, 57% female; 1% American Indian, 1% Asian, 4% black, 3% Hispanic, 3% multiracial, 0% Pacific Islander, 81% white, 5% international; 89% from in state; 27% live on campus; 23% of students in fraternities, 21% in sororities
Most popular majors: 27% Business, Management, Marketing, and Related Support Services, 6% Communication, Journalism, and Related Programs, 13% Education, 6% Health Professions and Related Programs, 8% Social Sciences
Expenses: 2015-2016: $7,060 in state, $13,930 out of state; room/ board: $7,868
Financial aid: (417) 836-5262; 63% of undergrads determined to have financial need; average aid package $8,892

Missouri University of Science & Technology

Rolla MO
(573) 341-4165
U.S. News ranking: Nat. U., No. 146
Website: www.mst.edu
Admissions email: admissions@mst.edu
Public; founded 1870
Freshman admissions: more selective; 2014-2015: 3,577 applied, 3,071 accepted. Either SAT or ACT required. ACT 25/75 percentile: 26-31. High school rank: 40% in top tenth, 72% in top quarter, 95% in top half
Early decision deadline: N/A, notification date: N/A
Early action deadline: N/A, notification date: N/A
Application deadline (fall): 7/1
Undergraduate student body: 5,825 full time, 697 part time; 77% male, 23% female; 0% American Indian, 3% Asian, 4% black, 2% Hispanic, 0% multiracial, 0% Pacific Islander, 81% white, 7% international; 81% from in state; 40% live on campus; 21% of students in fraternities, 19% in sororities
Most popular majors: 4% Biological and Biomedical Sciences, 9% Computer and Information Sciences and Support Services, 66% Engineering, 6% Physical Sciences, 3% Psychology
Expenses: 2015-2016: $9,628 in state, $26,152 out of state; room/ board: $9,715
Financial aid: (573) 341-4282; 58% of undergrads determined to have financial need; average aid package $15,253

Missouri Valley College[1]

Marshall MO
(660) 831-4114
U.S. News ranking: Reg. Coll. (Mid.W), second tier
Website: www.moval.edu
Admissions email: admissions@moval.edu
Private
Application deadline (fall): N/A
Undergraduate student body: N/A full time, N/A part time
Expenses: 2014-2015: $18,400; room/board: $7,700
Financial aid: (660) 831-4171

Missouri Western State University

St. Joseph MO
(816) 271-4266
U.S. News ranking: Reg. Coll. (Mid.W), second tier
Website: www.missouriwestern.edu
Admissions email: admission@missouriwestern.edu
Public; founded 1969
Freshman admissions: less selective; 2014-2015: 2,609 applied, 2,570 accepted. Neither SAT nor ACT required. ACT 25/75 percentile: 17-23. High school rank: 8% in top tenth, 26% in top quarter, 59% in top half
Early decision deadline: N/A, notification date: N/A
Early action deadline: N/A, notification date: N/A
Application deadline (fall): rolling
Undergraduate student body: 3,875 full time, 1,775 part time; 42% male, 58% female; 1% American Indian, 1% Asian, 12% black, 1% Hispanic, 3% multiracial, 0% Pacific Islander, 77% white, 1% international; 90% from in state; 26% live on campus; N/A of students in fraternities, N/A in sororities
Most popular majors: 6% Business Administration and Management, General, 8% Criminal Justice/ Safety Studies, 8% Elementary Education and Teaching, 6% Health and Physical Education/ Fitness, General, 12% Registered Nursing/Registered Nurse
Expenses: 2015-2016: $6,651 in state, $12,809 out of state; room/ board: $7,590
Financial aid: (816) 271-4361; 73% of undergrads determined to have financial need; average aid package $8,428

Northwest Missouri State University

Maryville MO
(800) 633-1175
U.S. News ranking: Reg. U. (Mid.W), No. 74
Website: www.nwmissouri.edu
Admissions email: admissions@nwmissouri.edu
Public; founded 1905
Freshman admissions: selective; 2014-2015: 4,516 applied, 3,334 accepted. Either SAT or ACT required. ACT 25/75 percentile: 20-25. High school rank: 14% in top tenth, 41% in top quarter, 77% in top half
Early decision deadline: N/A, notification date: N/A
Early action deadline: N/A, notification date: N/A
Application deadline (fall): rolling
Undergraduate student body: 4,980 full time, 511 part time; 45% male, 55% female; 0% American Indian, 1% Asian, 7% black, 3% Hispanic, 3% multiracial, 0% Pacific Islander, 81% white, 3% international; 71% from in state; 41% live on campus; 19% of students in fraternities, 18% in sororities
Most popular majors: 10% Agriculture, Agriculture Operations, and Related Sciences, 23% Business, Management, Marketing, and Related Support Services, 6% Communication, Journalism, and Related Programs, 19% Education, 10% Psychology
Expenses: 2015-2016: $8,459 in state, $14,780 out of state; room/ board: $8,484
Financial aid: (660) 562-1363; 69% of undergrads determined to have financial need; average aid package $9,380

Park University

Parkville MO
(800) 745-7275
U.S. News ranking: Reg. U. (Mid.W), second tier
Website: www.park.edu
Admissions email: admissions@mail.park.edu
Private; founded 1875
Freshman admissions: selective; 2014-2015: 1,098 applied, 721 accepted. ACT required. Average composite ACT score: 22. High school rank: 18% in top tenth, 34% in top quarter, 62% in top half
Early decision deadline: N/A, notification date: N/A
Early action deadline: N/A, notification date: N/A
Application deadline (fall): 8/1
Undergraduate student body: 1,180 full time, 8,712 part time; 53% male, 47% female; 1% American Indian, 2% Asian, 19% black, 13% Hispanic, 3% multiracial, 0% Pacific Islander, 60% white, 1% international
Most popular majors: 25% Business Administration and Management, General, 6% Criminal Justice/Law Enforcement Administration, 11% Human Resources Management/Personnel Administration, General, 7% Management Information Systems, General, 11% Social Psychology
Expenses: 2015-2016: $11,800; room/board: $7,672
Financial aid: (816) 584-6190; 55% of undergrads determined to have financial need; average aid package $10,589

Ranken Technical College[1]
Saint Louis MO
(866) 472-6536
U.S. News ranking: Reg. Coll. (Mid.W), unranked
Website: www.ranken.edu
Admissions email: N/A
Private
Application deadline (fall): N/A
Undergraduate student body: N/A full time, N/A part time
Expenses: 2014-2015: $14,457; room/board: $5,200
Financial aid: (314) 286-4862

Rockhurst University
Kansas City MO
(816) 501-4100
U.S. News ranking: Reg. U. (Mid.W), No. 18
Website: www.rockhurst.edu
Admissions email: admissions@rockhurst.edu
Private; founded 1910
Affiliation: Roman Catholic (Jesuit)
Freshman admissions: more selective; 2014-2015: 2,494 applied, 1,919 accepted. Either SAT or ACT required. ACT 25/75 percentile: 23-28. High school rank: 30% in top tenth, 58% in top quarter, 80% in top half
Early decision deadline: N/A, notification date: N/A
Early action deadline: N/A, notification date: N/A
Application deadline (fall): rolling
Undergraduate student body: 1,536 full time, 740 part time; 41% male, 59% female; 0% American Indian, 3% Asian, 4% black, 6% Hispanic, 2% multiracial, 0% Pacific Islander, 74% white, 1% international; 68% from in state; 52% live on campus; 30% of students in fraternities, 48% in sororities
Most popular majors: 11% Biological and Biomedical Sciences, 12% Business, Management, Marketing, and Related Support Services, 26% Health Professions and Related Programs, 8% Parks, Recreation, Leisure, and Fitness Studies, 12% Psychology
Expenses: 2015-2016: $34,790; room/board: $9,056
Financial aid: (816) 501-4100; 71% of undergrads determined to have financial need; average aid package $27,132

Saint Louis University
St. Louis MO
(314) 977-2500
U.S. News ranking: Nat. U., No. 96
Website: www.slu.edu
Admissions email: admission@slu.edu
Private; founded 1818
Affiliation: Roman Catholic
Freshman admissions: more selective; 2014-2015: 13,911 applied, 8,383 accepted. Either SAT or ACT required. ACT 25/75 percentile: 25-30. High school rank: 43% in top tenth, 72% in top quarter, 91% in top half
Early decision deadline: N/A, notification date: N/A
Early action deadline: N/A, notification date: N/A
Application deadline (fall): 8/20
Undergraduate student body: 7,703 full time, 861 part time; 42% male, 58% female; 0% American Indian, 8% Asian, 7% black, 5% Hispanic, 5% multiracial, 0% Pacific Islander, 66% white, 7% international; 37% from in state; 52% live on campus; 18% of students in fraternities, 26% in sororities
Most popular majors: 6% Biology/Biological Sciences, General, 5% Business Administration and Management, General, 5% Kinesiology and Exercise Science, 5% Psychology, General, 11% Registered Nursing/Registered Nurse
Expenses: 2015-2016: $39,226; room/board: $10,640
Financial aid: (314) 977-2350; 56% of undergrads determined to have financial need; average aid package $25,834

Southeast Missouri State University
Cape Girardeau MO
(573) 651-2590
U.S. News ranking: Reg. U. (Mid.W), No. 92
Website: www.semo.edu
Admissions email: admissions@semo.edu
Public; founded 1873
Freshman admissions: selective; 2014-2015: 4,750 applied, 4,027 accepted. Either SAT or ACT required. ACT 25/75 percentile: 20-25. High school rank: 15% in top tenth, 41% in top quarter, 74% in top half
Early decision deadline: N/A, notification date: N/A
Early action deadline: N/A, notification date: N/A
Application deadline (fall): 7/1
Undergraduate student body: 8,168 full time, 2,680 part time; 43% male, 57% female; 1% American Indian, 1% Asian, 10% black, 2% Hispanic, 0% multiracial, 0% Pacific Islander, 78% white, 7% international; 85% from in state; 31% live on campus; 14% of students in fraternities, 11% in sororities
Most popular majors: 7% Communication and Media Studies, 9% Liberal Arts and Sciences, General Studies and Humanities, 7% Registered Nursing, Nursing Administration, Nursing Research and Clinical Nursing, 8% Teacher Education and Professional Development, Specific Levels and Methods, 5% Teacher Education and Professional Development, Specific Subject Areas
Expenses: 2015-2016: $6,990 in state, $12,360 out of state; room/board: N/A
Financial aid: (573) 651-2253; 62% of undergrads determined to have financial need; average aid package $8,767

Southwest Baptist University[1]
Bolivar MO
(800) 526-5859
U.S. News ranking: Reg. U. (Mid.W), second tier
Website: www.sbuniv.edu
Admissions email: dcrowder@sbuniv.edu
Private
Application deadline (fall): N/A
Undergraduate student body: N/A full time, N/A part time
Expenses: 2014-2015: $20,840; room/board: $6,800
Financial aid: (417) 328-1822

Stephens College
Columbia MO
(800) 876-7207
U.S. News ranking: Reg. Coll. (Mid.W), No. 29
Website: www.stephens.edu
Admissions email: apply@stephens.edu
Private; founded 1833
Freshman admissions: selective; 2014-2015: 1,153 applied, 618 accepted. Either SAT or ACT required. ACT 25/75 percentile: 20-26. High school rank: 16% in top tenth, 41% in top quarter, 77% in top half
Early decision deadline: 11/15, notification date: 12/1
Early action deadline: 1/1, notification date: 1/15
Application deadline (fall): rolling
Undergraduate student body: 556 full time, 111 part time; 1% male, 99% female; 0% American Indian, 2% Asian, 16% black, 5% Hispanic, 6% multiracial, 1% Pacific Islander, 68% white, 0% international; 55% from in state; 65% live on campus; N/A of students in fraternities, N/A in sororities
Most popular majors: 9% Acting, 19% Fashion Merchandising, 6% Fashion/Apparel Design, 16% Health Information/Medical Records Administration/Administrator, 6% Marketing, Other
Expenses: 2014-2015: $28,510; room/board: $9,533
Financial aid: (573) 876-7106; 78% of undergrads determined to have financial need; average aid package $23,157

Truman State University
Kirksville MO
(660) 785-4114
U.S. News ranking: Reg. U. (Mid.W), No. 8
Website: www.truman.edu
Admissions email: admissions@truman.edu
Public; founded 1867
Freshman admissions: more selective; 2014-2015: 4,095 applied, 3,050 accepted. Either SAT or ACT required. ACT 25/75 percentile: 24-30. High school rank: 49% in top tenth, 80% in top quarter, 98% in top half
Early decision deadline: N/A, notification date: N/A
Early action deadline: N/A, notification date: N/A
Application deadline (fall): rolling
Undergraduate student body: 5,295 full time, 615 part time; 41% male, 59% female; 0% American Indian, 2% Asian, 4% black, 3% Hispanic, 3% multiracial, 0% Pacific Islander, 81% white, 7% international; 81% from in state; 49% live on campus; 23% of students in fraternities, 17% in sororities
Most popular majors: 10% Biology/Biological Sciences, General, 13% Business Administration and Management, General, 9% English Language and Literature, General, 12% Health and Physical Education/Fitness, General, 10% Psychology, General
Expenses: 2015-2016: $7,430 in state, $13,654 out of state; room/board: $8,480
Financial aid: (660) 785-4130; 53% of undergrads determined to have financial need; average aid package $11,917

University of Central Missouri
Warrensburg MO
(660) 543-4290
U.S. News ranking: Reg. U. (Mid.W), No. 75
Website: www.ucmo.edu
Admissions email: admit@ucmo.edu
Public; founded 1871
Freshman admissions: selective; 2014-2015: 4,612 applied, 3,595 accepted. Neither SAT nor ACT required. ACT 25/75 percentile: 19-24. High school rank: 11% in top tenth, 32% in top quarter, 67% in top half
Early decision deadline: N/A, notification date: N/A
Early action deadline: N/A, notification date: N/A
Application deadline (fall): 8/19
Undergraduate student body: 8,133 full time, 1,705 part time; 45% male, 55% female; 0% American Indian, 1% Asian, 8% black, 3% Hispanic, 3% multiracial, 0% Pacific Islander, 65% white, 3% international
Most popular majors: 14% Business, Management, Marketing, and Related Support Services, 17% Education, 7% Engineering Technologies and Engineering-Related Fields, 13% Health Professions and Related Programs, 9% Homeland Security, Law Enforcement, Firefighting and Related Protective Services
Expenses: 2015-2016: $7,322 in state, $13,767 out of state; room/board: $7,828
Financial aid: (660) 543-4040; 62% of undergrads determined to have financial need; average aid package $8,314

University of Missouri
Columbia MO
(573) 882-7786
U.S. News ranking: Nat. U., No. 103
Website: www.missouri.edu
Admissions email: mu4u@missouri.edu
Public; founded 1839
Freshman admissions: more selective; 2014-2015: 21,163 applied, 16,437 accepted. Either SAT or ACT required. ACT 25/75 percentile: 23-28. High school rank: 27% in top tenth, 57% in top quarter, 87% in top half
Early decision deadline: N/A, notification date: N/A
Early action deadline: N/A, notification date: N/A
Application deadline (fall): rolling
Undergraduate student body: 25,859 full time, 1,795 part time; 48% male, 52% female; 0% American Indian, 2% Asian, 8% black, 3% Hispanic, 3% multiracial, 0% Pacific Islander, 79% white, 3% international; 75% from in state; 21% live on campus; 23% of students in fraternities, 32% in sororities
Most popular majors: 15% Business, Management, Marketing, and Related Support Services, 12% Communication, Journalism, and Related Programs, 7% Engineering, 13% Health Professions and Related Programs, 7% Social Sciences
Expenses: 2015-2016: $9,509 in state, $25,166 out of state; room/board: $9,808
Financial aid: (573) 882-7506; 49% of undergrads determined to have financial need; average aid package $14,571

University of Missouri–Kansas City
Kansas City MO
(816) 235-1111
U.S. News ranking: Nat. U., No. 194
Website: www.umkc.edu
Admissions email: admit@umkc.edu
Public; founded 1929
Freshman admissions: more selective; 2014-2015: 4,377 applied, 2,786 accepted. Either SAT or ACT required. ACT 25/75 percentile: 21-27. High school rank: 29% in top tenth, 57% in top quarter, 84% in top half
Early decision deadline: N/A, notification date: N/A
Early action deadline: N/A, notification date: N/A
Application deadline (fall): rolling
Undergraduate student body: 6,817 full time, 3,645 part time; 43% male, 57% female; 0% American Indian, 6% Asian, 16% black, 7% Hispanic, 4% multiracial, 0% Pacific Islander, 57% white, 4% international; 78% from in state; 25% live on campus; 4% of students in fraternities, 6% in sororities
Most popular majors: 13% Business/Commerce, General, 6% Chemistry, General, 11% Liberal Arts and Sciences/Liberal Studies, 11% Registered Nursing/Registered Nurse, 6% Speech Communication and Rhetoric
Expenses: 2015-2016: $9,559 in state, $22,714 out of state; room/board: $9,772
Financial aid: (816) 235-1154; 67% of undergrads determined to have financial need; average aid package $9,709

University of Missouri–St. Louis
St. Louis MO
(314) 516-5451
U.S. News ranking: Nat. U., second tier
Website: www.umsl.edu
Admissions email: admissions@umsl.edu
Public; founded 1963
Freshman admissions: more selective; 2014-2015: 1,733 applied, 1,312 accepted. Either SAT or ACT required. ACT 25/75 percentile: 21-27. High school rank: 29% in top tenth, 59% in top quarter, 86% in top half
Early decision deadline: N/A, notification date: N/A
Early action deadline: N/A, notification date: N/A
Application deadline (fall): 8/26
Undergraduate student body: 6,071 full time, 7,816 part time; 42% male, 58% female; 0% American Indian, 5% Asian, 19% black, 3% Hispanic, 2% multiracial, 0% Pacific Islander, 62% white, 3% international; 89% from in state; 9% live on campus; 1% of students in fraternities, 1% in sororities

Most popular majors: 25% Business, Management, Marketing, and Related Support Services, 7% Communication, Journalism, and Related Programs, 11% Education, 12% Health Professions and Related Programs, 10% Social Sciences
Expenses: 2015-2016: $10,065 in state, $25,512 out of state; room/board: $9,052
Financial aid: (314) 516-5526; 71% of undergrads determined to have financial need; average aid package $10,702

Washington University in St. Louis

St. Louis MO
(800) 638-0700
U.S. News ranking: Nat. U., No. 15
Website: www.wustl.edu
Admissions email: admissions@wustl.edu
Private; founded 1853
Freshman admissions: most selective; 2014-2015: 29,211 applied, 5,004 accepted. Either SAT or ACT required. ACT 25/75 percentile: 32-34. High school rank: 92% in top tenth, 99% in top quarter, 100% in top half
Early decision deadline: 11/15, notification date: 12/15
Early action deadline: N/A, notification date: N/A
Application deadline (fall): 1/15
Undergraduate student body: 6,686 full time, 715 part time; 48% male, 52% female; 0% American Indian, 18% Asian, 5% black, 6% Hispanic, 4% multiracial, 0% Pacific Islander, 55% white, 8% international; 7% from in state; 79% live on campus; 25% of students in fraternities, 25% in sororities
Most popular majors: 11% Biological and Biomedical Sciences, 13% Business, Management, Marketing, and Related Support Services, 16% Engineering, 15% Pre-Medicine/Pre-Medical Studies, 16% Social Sciences
Expenses: 2015-2016: $48,093; room/board: $15,280
Financial aid: (888) 547-6670; 41% of undergrads determined to have financial need; average aid package $37,928

Webster University

St. Louis MO
(314) 246-7800
U.S. News ranking: Reg. U. (Mid.W), No. 26
Website: www.webster.edu
Admissions email: admit@webster.edu
Private; founded 1915
Freshman admissions: selective; 2014-2015: 1,863 applied, 1,038 accepted. Either SAT or ACT required. ACT 25/75 percentile: 21-27. High school rank: 17% in top tenth, 42% in top quarter, 73% in top half
Early decision deadline: N/A, notification date: N/A
Early action deadline: N/A, notification date: N/A
Application deadline (fall): 8/1
Undergraduate student body: 2,444 full time, 484 part time; 46% male, 54% female; 0% American Indian, 2% Asian, 13% black, 4% Hispanic, 3% multiracial, 0% Pacific Islander, 67% white, 4% international; 76% from in state; 25% live on campus; N/A of students in fraternities, 4% in sororities
Most popular majors: 4% Accounting, 16% Business Administration and Management, General, 5% Computer Science, 5% Education, General, 5% Psychology, General
Expenses: 2015-2016: $25,300; room/board: $10,860
Financial aid: (314) 968-6992; 87% of undergrads determined to have financial need; average aid package $18,287

Westminster College

Fulton MO
(800) 475-3361
U.S. News ranking: Nat. Lib. Arts, No. 148
Website: www.westminster-mo.edu
Admissions email: admissions@westminster-mo.edu
Private; founded 1851
Affiliation: Presbyterian
Freshman admissions: more selective; 2014-2015: 1,356 applied, 910 accepted. Either SAT or ACT required. ACT 25/75 percentile: 22-27. High school rank: 27% in top tenth, 48% in top quarter, 74% in top half
Early decision deadline: N/A, notification date: N/A
Early action deadline: N/A, notification date: N/A
Application deadline (fall): rolling
Undergraduate student body: 934 full time, 10 part time; 57% male, 43% female; 2% American Indian, 1% Asian, 8% black, 4% Hispanic, 1% multiracial, N/A Pacific Islander, 65% white, 16% international; 76% from in state; 85% live on campus; 48% of students in fraternities, 36% in sororities
Most popular majors: 13% Biological and Biomedical Sciences, 29% Business, Management, Marketing, and Related Support Services, 11% Education, 6% Multi/Interdisciplinary Studies, 10% Social Sciences
Expenses: 2015-2016: $23,480; room/board: $9,340
Financial aid: (573) 592-5364; 59% of undergrads determined to have financial need; average aid package $20,800

William Jewell College

Liberty MO
(888) 253-9355
U.S. News ranking: Nat. Lib. Arts, No. 158
Website: www.jewell.edu
Admissions email: admission@william.jewell.edu
Private; founded 1849
Freshman admissions: more selective; 2014-2015: 1,391 applied, 874 accepted. Neither SAT nor ACT required. ACT 25/75 percentile: 22-28. High school rank: 37% in top tenth, 60% in top quarter, 91% in top half
Early decision deadline: N/A, notification date: N/A
Early action deadline: N/A, notification date: N/A
Application deadline (fall): 8/15
Undergraduate student body: 1,019 full time, 24 part time; 40% male, 60% female; 0% American Indian, 1% Asian, 6% black, 3% Hispanic, 6% multiracial, 0% Pacific Islander, 77% white, 4% international; 63% from in state; 84% live on campus; 42% of students in fraternities, 39% in sororities
Most popular majors: 17% Business, Management, Marketing, and Related Support Services, 6% English Language and Literature/Letters, 31% Health Professions and Related Programs, 11% Psychology, 7% Social Sciences
Expenses: 2015-2016: $32,330; room/board: $8,880
Financial aid: (888) 253-9355; 71% of undergrads determined to have financial need; average aid package $26,735

William Woods University

Fulton MO
(573) 592-4221
U.S. News ranking: Reg. U. (Mid.W), No. 90
Website: www.williamwoods.edu
Admissions email: admissions@williamwoods.edu
Private; founded 1870
Affiliation: Disciples of Christ
Freshman admissions: selective; 2014-2015: 768 applied, 586 accepted. Either SAT or ACT required. ACT 25/75 percentile: 19-26. High school rank: 14% in top tenth, 39% in top quarter, 72% in top half
Early decision deadline: N/A, notification date: N/A
Early action deadline: N/A, notification date: N/A
Application deadline (fall): rolling
Undergraduate student body: 850 full time, 156 part time; 26% male, 74% female; 1% American Indian, 1% Asian, 4% black, 1% Hispanic, 2% multiracial, 0% Pacific Islander, 83% white, 0% international; 66% from in state; 65% live on campus; 26% of students in fraternities, 34% in sororities
Most popular majors: 15% Business Administration and Management, General, 8% Elementary Education and Teaching, 17% Equestrian/Equine Studies, 6% Sign Language Interpretation and Translation, 7% Sport and Fitness Administration/Management
Expenses: 2015-2016: $22,160; room/board: $8,960
Financial aid: (573) 592-4232; 63% of undergrads determined to have financial need; average aid package $17,991

MONTANA

Carroll College

Helena MT
(406) 447-4384
U.S. News ranking: Reg. Coll. (W), No. 1
Website: www.carroll.edu
Admissions email: admission@carroll.edu
Private; founded 1909
Affiliation: Roman Catholic
Freshman admissions: more selective; 2014-2015: 3,527 applied, 2,029 accepted. Either SAT or ACT required. ACT 25/75 percentile: 22-28. High school rank: 29% in top tenth, 64% in top quarter, 90% in top half
Early decision deadline: N/A, notification date: N/A
Early action deadline: 12/1, notification date: 1/1
Application deadline (fall): 5/1
Undergraduate student body: 1,386 full time, 44 part time; 42% male, 58% female; 1% American Indian, 1% Asian, 1% black, 5% Hispanic, 2% multiracial, 0% Pacific Islander, 80% white, 1% international; 46% from in state; 57% live on campus; N/A of students in fraternities, N/A in sororities
Most popular majors: 16% Biological and Biomedical Sciences, 12% Business, Management, Marketing, and Related Support Services, 8% Communication, Journalism, and Related Programs, 26% Health Professions and Related Programs, 6% Psychology
Expenses: 2015-2016: $30,714; room/board: $9,218
Financial aid: (406) 447-5423; 66% of undergrads determined to have financial need; average aid package $21,719

Montana State University

Bozeman MT
(406) 994-2452
U.S. News ranking: Nat. U., second tier
Website: www.montana.edu
Admissions email: admissions@montana.edu
Public; founded 1893
Freshman admissions: selective; 2014-2015: 13,799 applied, 11,570 accepted. Either SAT or ACT required. ACT 25/75 percentile: 21-28. High school rank: 19% in top tenth, 42% in top quarter, 74% in top half
Early decision deadline: N/A, notification date: N/A
Early action deadline: N/A, notification date: N/A
Application deadline (fall): rolling
Undergraduate student body: 11,236 full time, 2,135 part time; 54% male, 46% female; 1% American Indian, 1% Asian, 1% black, 3% Hispanic, 3% multiracial, 0% Pacific Islander, 85% white, 3% international; 63% from in state; 25% live on campus; 2% of students in fraternities, 2% in sororities
Most popular majors: 9% Business/Commerce, General, 3% Cell/Cellular Biology and Histology, 4% Elementary Education and Teaching, 4% Mechanical Engineering
Expenses: 2015-2016: $6,968 in state, $21,961 out of state; room/board: $8,650
Financial aid: (406) 994-2845; 54% of undergrads determined to have financial need; average aid package $12,022

Montana State University–Billings

Billings MT
(406) 657-2158
U.S. News ranking: Reg. U. (W), second tier
Website: www.msubillings.edu
Admissions email: admissions@msubillings.edu
Public; founded 1927
Freshman admissions: selective; 2014-2015: 1,602 applied, 1,597 accepted. Neither SAT nor ACT required. ACT 25/75 percentile: 18-23. High school rank: 9% in top tenth, 27% in top quarter, 63% in top half
Early decision deadline: N/A, notification date: N/A
Early action deadline: N/A, notification date: N/A
Application deadline (fall): rolling
Undergraduate student body: 3,044 full time, 1,309 part time; 38% male, 62% female; 4% American Indian, 1% Asian, 1% black, 5% Hispanic, 2% multiracial, 0% Pacific Islander, 81% white, 3% international; 89% from in state; 12% live on campus; N/A of students in fraternities, N/A in sororities
Most popular majors: 19% Business/Commerce, General, 8% Communication, Journalism, and Related Programs, 23% Education, 9% Liberal Arts and Sciences/Liberal Studies, 8% Psychology, General
Expenses: 2015-2016: $5,780 in state, $17,342 out of state; room/board: $6,980
Financial aid: (406) 657-2188; 63% of undergrads determined to have financial need; average aid package $9,981

Montana State University–Northern[1]

Havre MT
(406) 265-3704
U.S. News ranking: Reg. Coll. (W), second tier
Website: www.msun.edu
Admissions email: admissions@msun.edu
Public
Application deadline (fall): N/A
Undergraduate student body: N/A full time, N/A part time
Expenses: 2014-2015: $5,480 in state, $17,312 out of state; room/board: $6,198
Financial aid: (406) 265-3787

Montana Tech of the University of Montana

Butte MT
(406) 496-4256
U.S. News ranking: Reg. Coll. (W), No. 5
Website: www.mtech.edu
Admissions email: enrollment@mtech.edu
Public; founded 1893
Freshman admissions: more selective; 2014-2015: 952 applied, 861 accepted. Either SAT or ACT required. ACT 25/75 percentile: 22-27. High school rank: 24% in top tenth, 57% in top quarter, 85% in top half
Early decision deadline: N/A, notification date: N/A
Early action deadline: N/A, notification date: N/A
Application deadline (fall): rolling
Undergraduate student body: 2,219 full time, 532 part time; 60% male, 40% female; 2% American Indian, 1% Asian, 1% black, 2% Hispanic, 0% multiracial, 0% Pacific Islander, 81% white, 9% international; 85% from in state; 12% live on campus; N/A of students in fraternities, N/A in sororities
Most popular majors: 10% Business/Commerce, General,

14% Engineering, General, 8% Environmental/Environmental Health Engineering, 22% Petroleum Engineering, 8% Registered Nursing/Registered Nurse
Expenses: 2015-2016: $6,797 in state, $20,512 out of state; room/board: $8,562
Financial aid: (406) 496-4212; 60% of undergrads determined to have financial need; average aid package $11,296

Rocky Mountain College

Billings MT
(406) 657-1026
U.S. News ranking: Reg. Coll. (W), No. 15
Website: www.rocky.edu
Admissions email: admissions@rocky.edu
Private; founded 1878
Affiliation: United Church of Christ, Methodist, and Presbyterian
Freshman admissions: selective; 2014-2015: 1,466 applied, 960 accepted. Either SAT or ACT required. ACT 25/75 percentile: 20-26. High school rank: 16% in top tenth, 49% in top quarter, 77% in top half
Early decision deadline: N/A, notification date: N/A
Early action deadline: N/A, notification date: N/A
Application deadline (fall): rolling
Undergraduate student body: 884 full time, 55 part time; 52% male, 48% female; 2% American Indian, 1% Asian, 3% black, 5% Hispanic, 5% multiracial, 1% Pacific Islander, 77% white, 4% international; 55% from in state; 47% live on campus; N/A of students in fraternities, N/A in sororities
Most popular majors: 8% Airline/Commercial/Professional Pilot and Flight Crew, 9% Biology/Biological Sciences, General, 19% Business Administration and Management, General, 11% Equestrian/Equine Studies, 9% Kinesiology and Exercise Science
Expenses: 2014-2015: $24,530; room/board: $7,712
Financial aid: (406) 657-1031

University of Great Falls

Great Falls MT
(406) 791-5200
U.S. News ranking: Reg. Coll. (W), No. 29
Website: www.ugf.edu
Admissions email: enroll@ugf.edu
Private; founded 1932
Affiliation: Roman Catholic
Freshman admissions: least selective; 2014-2015: N/A applied, N/A accepted. Either SAT or ACT required. ACT 25/75 percentile: N/A. High school rank: N/A
Early decision deadline: N/A, notification date: N/A
Early action deadline: N/A, notification date: N/A
Application deadline (fall): 9/1
Undergraduate student body: 627 full time, 416 part time; 30% male, 70% female; 2% American Indian, 3% Asian, 2% black, 7% Hispanic, 1% multiracial, 1% Pacific Islander, 79% white, 0% international; 38% from in state; 38% live on campus; 0% of students in fraternities, 0% in sororities
Most popular majors: 9% Biological and Biomedical Sciences, 8% Business, Management, Marketing, and Related Support Services, 12% Education, 29% Health Professions and Related Programs, 8% Social Sciences
Expenses: 2015-2016: $21,556; room/board: $6,800
Financial aid: (406) 791-5235; 76% of undergrads determined to have financial need; average aid package $18,476

University of Montana

Missoula MT
(800) 462-8636
U.S. News ranking: Nat. U., second tier
Website: www.umt.edu
Admissions email: admiss@umontana.edu
Public; founded 1893
Freshman admissions: selective; 2014-2015: 4,583 applied, 4,317 accepted. Either SAT or ACT required. ACT 25/75 percentile: 20-26. High school rank: 18% in top tenth, 42% in top quarter, 73% in top half
Early decision deadline: N/A, notification date: N/A
Early action deadline: N/A, notification date: N/A
Application deadline (fall): rolling
Undergraduate student body: 8,089 full time, 1,358 part time; 47% male, 53% female; 3% American Indian, 1% Asian, 1% black, 4% Hispanic, 4% multiracial, 0% Pacific Islander, 80% white, 3% international; 73% from in state; 30% live on campus; 6% of students in fraternities, 6% in sororities
Most popular majors: 16% Business, Management, Marketing, and Related Support Services, 8% Communication, Journalism, and Related Programs, 8% Psychology, 13% Social Sciences, 9% Visual and Performing Arts
Expenses: 2015-2016: $6,389 in state, $23,845 out of state; room/board: $8,406
Financial aid: (406) 243-5373; 60% of undergrads determined to have financial need; average aid package $10,458

University of Montana–Western

Dillon MT
(877) 683-7331
U.S. News ranking: Reg. Coll. (W), No. 20
Website: www.umwestern.edu
Admissions email: admissions@umwestern.edu
Public; founded 1893
Freshman admissions: less selective; 2014-2015: 569 applied, 405 accepted. Either SAT or ACT required. ACT 25/75 percentile: 17-22. High school rank: 6% in top tenth, 17% in top quarter, 51% in top half
Early decision deadline: N/A, notification date: N/A
Early action deadline: N/A, notification date: N/A
Application deadline (fall): rolling
Undergraduate student body: 1,163 full time, 307 part time; 41% male, 59% female; 2% American Indian, 1% Asian, 1% black, 2% Hispanic, 1% multiracial, 0% Pacific Islander, 83% white, 0% international; 77% from in state; 24% live on campus; N/A of students in fraternities, N/A in sororities
Most popular majors: 4% Biology/Biological Sciences, General, 17% Business/Commerce, General, 3% Early Childhood Education and Teaching, 16% Elementary Education and Teaching, 9% Secondary Education and Teaching
Expenses: 2015-2016: $5,423 in state, $15,265 out of state; room/board: $6,994
Financial aid: (406) 683-7511; 65% of undergrads determined to have financial need; average aid package $3,394

NEBRASKA

Bellevue University[1]

Bellevue NE
(800) 756-7920
U.S. News ranking: Reg. U. (Mid.W), unranked
Website: www.bellevue.edu
Admissions email: info@bellevue.edu
Private
Application deadline (fall): N/A
Undergraduate student body: N/A full time, N/A part time
Expenses: 2014-2015: $7,950; room/board: N/A
Financial aid: (402) 293-3763

Chadron State College

Chadron NE
(308) 432-6263
U.S. News ranking: Reg. Coll. (Mid.W), unranked
Website: www.csc.edu
Admissions email: inquire@csc.edu
Public; founded 1911
Freshman admissions: N/A; 2014-2015: N/A applied, N/A accepted. Neither SAT nor ACT required. ACT 25/75 percentile: N/A. High school rank: N/A
Early decision deadline: N/A, notification date: N/A
Early action deadline: N/A, notification date: N/A
Application deadline (fall): N/A
Undergraduate student body: 1,837 full time, 616 part time; 42% male, 58% female; 1% American Indian, 1% Asian, 4% black, 6% Hispanic, 3% multiracial, 0% Pacific Islander, 75% white, 2% international
Most popular majors: Information not available
Expenses: 2014-2015: $5,668 in state, $5,698 out of state; room/board: $5,760
Financial aid: (308) 432-6230

College of St. Mary

Omaha NE
(402) 399-2407
U.S. News ranking: Reg. U. (Mid.W), No. 75
Website: www.csm.edu
Admissions email: enroll@csm.edu
Private; founded 1923
Affiliation: Catholic
Freshman admissions: selective; 2014-2015: N/A applied, N/A accepted. Either SAT or ACT required. ACT 25/75 percentile: 20-25. High school rank: 21% in top tenth, 52% in top quarter, 87% in top half
Early decision deadline: N/A, notification date: N/A
Early action deadline: N/A, notification date: N/A
Application deadline (fall): rolling
Undergraduate student body: 679 full time, 91 part time; 1% male, 99% female; 1% American Indian, 2% Asian, 6% black, 11% Hispanic, 2% multiracial, 0% Pacific Islander, 76% white, 1% international; 79% from in state; 34% live on campus; N/A of students in fraternities, N/A in sororities
Most popular majors: 7% Biological and Biomedical Sciences, 10% Business, Management, Marketing, and Related Support Services, 8% Education, 49% Health Professions and Related Programs, 8% Psychology
Expenses: 2015-2016: $28,964; room/board: $7,400
Financial aid: (402) 399-2362; 93% of undergrads determined to have financial need; average aid package $19,862

Concordia University

Seward NE
(800) 535-5494
U.S. News ranking: Reg. U. (Mid.W), No. 44
Website: www.cune.edu
Admissions email: admiss@cune.edu
Private; founded 1894
Affiliation: Lutheran Church-Missouri Synod
Freshman admissions: selective; 2014-2015: 1,428 applied, 1,094 accepted. Either SAT or ACT required. ACT 25/75 percentile: 20-27. High school rank: 17% in top tenth, 43% in top quarter, 75% in top half
Early decision deadline: N/A, notification date: N/A
Early action deadline: N/A, notification date: N/A
Application deadline (fall): 8/1
Undergraduate student body: 1,186 full time, 421 part time; 49% male, 51% female; 0% American Indian, 1% Asian, 4% black, 4% Hispanic, 1% multiracial, 0% Pacific Islander, 87% white, 1% international; 46% from in state; 70% live on campus; N/A of students in fraternities, N/A in sororities
Most popular majors: 6% Biological and Biomedical Sciences, 33% Education, 9% Parks, Recreation, Leisure, and Fitness Studies, 13% Physical Sciences, 9% Visual and Performing Arts
Expenses: 2015-2016: $27,110; room/board: $7,260
Financial aid: (402) 643-7270; 73% of undergrads determined to have financial need; average aid package $20,709

Creighton University

Omaha NE
(800) 282-5835
U.S. News ranking: Reg. U. (Mid.W), No. 1
Website: www.creighton.edu
Admissions email: admissions@creighton.edu
Private; founded 1878
Affiliation: Roman Catholic (Jesuit)
Freshman admissions: more selective; 2014-2015: 8,398 applied, 6,103 accepted. Either SAT or ACT required. ACT 25/75 percentile: 24-29. High school rank: 38% in top tenth, 72% in top quarter, 93% in top half
Early decision deadline: N/A, notification date: N/A
Early action deadline: N/A, notification date: N/A
Application deadline (fall): 2/15
Undergraduate student body: 3,842 full time, 223 part time; 42% male, 58% female; 0% American Indian, 9% Asian, 3% black, 7% Hispanic, 4% multiracial, 0% Pacific Islander, 73% white, 3% international; 28% from in state; 60% live on campus; 28% of students in fraternities, 46% in sororities
Most popular majors: 10% Biological and Biomedical Sciences, 17% Business, Management, Marketing, and Related Support Services, 24% Health Professions and Related Programs, 7% Psychology, 9% Social Sciences
Expenses: 2015-2016: $36,422; room/board: $10,294
Financial aid: (402) 280-2731; 53% of undergrads determined to have financial need; average aid package $28,375

Doane College

Crete NE
(402) 826-8222
U.S. News ranking: Nat. Lib. Arts, No. 158
Website: www.doane.edu
Admissions email: admissions@doane.edu
Private; founded 1872
Freshman admissions: selective; 2014-2015: 1,627 applied, 1,291 accepted. ACT required. ACT 25/75 percentile: 21-25. High school rank: 17% in top tenth, 42% in top quarter, 76% in top half
Early decision deadline: N/A, notification date: N/A
Early action deadline: N/A, notification date: N/A
Application deadline (fall): rolling
Undergraduate student body: 1,057 full time, 10 part time; 50% male, 50% female; 0% American Indian, 1% Asian, 4% black, 6% Hispanic, 2% multiracial, 0% Pacific Islander, 82% white, 2% international; 80% from in state; 78% live on campus; 17% of students in fraternities, 22% in sororities
Most popular majors: 13% Biological and Biomedical Sciences, 9% Business, Management, Marketing, and Related Support Services, 23% Education, 9% Psychology, 10% Visual and Performing Arts
Expenses: 2015-2016: $28,790; room/board: $8,350
Financial aid: (402) 826-8260; 76% of undergrads determined to have financial need; average aid package $21,187

Grace University[1]

Omaha NE
(402) 449-2831
U.S. News ranking: Reg. Coll. (Mid.W), second tier
Website: www.graceuniversity.edu
Admissions email: admissions@graceuniversity.edu
Private
Application deadline (fall): N/A
Undergraduate student body: N/A full time, N/A part time

More at usnews.com/college

Expenses: 2014-2015: $19,290; room/board: $6,880
Financial aid: (402) 449-2810

Hastings College

Hastings NE
(800) 532-7642
U.S. News ranking: Reg. Coll. (Mid.W), No. 14
Website: www.hastings.edu
Admissions email: hcadmissions@hastings.edu
Private; founded 1882
Affiliation: Presbyterian Church (USA)
Freshman admissions: selective; 2014-2015: 1,542 applied, 1,074 accepted. Either SAT or ACT required. ACT 25/75 percentile: 20-27. High school rank: 20% in top tenth, 45% in top quarter, 80% in top half
Early decision deadline: N/A, notification date: N/A
Early action deadline: N/A, notification date: N/A
Application deadline (fall): rolling
Undergraduate student body: 1,129 full time, 54 part time; 51% male, 49% female; 1% American Indian, 1% Asian, 3% black, 6% Hispanic, 3% multiracial, 0% Pacific Islander, 83% white, 2% international; 68% from in state; 70% live on campus; 27% of students in fraternities, 27% in sororities
Most popular majors: 8% Biological and Biomedical Sciences, 15% Business, Management, Marketing, and Related Support Services, 28% Education, 8% Social Sciences, 7% Visual and Performing Arts
Expenses: 2015-2016: $27,300; room/board: $8,080
Financial aid: (402) 461-7391; 75% of undergrads determined to have financial need; average aid package $21,139

Midland University

Fremont NE
(402) 941-6501
U.S. News ranking: Reg. Coll. (Mid.W), No. 60
Website: www.midlandu.edu/
Admissions email: admissions@midlandu.edu
Private; founded 1883
Affiliation: Lutheran
Freshman admissions: selective; 2014-2015: 1,866 applied, 1,123 accepted. Either SAT or ACT required. ACT 25/75 percentile: 17-26. High school rank: N/A
Early decision deadline: N/A, notification date: N/A
Early action deadline: N/A, notification date: N/A
Application deadline (fall): rolling
Undergraduate student body: 1,191 full time, 45 part time; 51% male, 49% female; 0% American Indian, 1% Asian, 5% black, 3% Hispanic, 7% multiracial, 1% Pacific Islander, 65% white, 5% international; N/A from in state; 52% live on campus; 11% of students in fraternities, 10% in sororities
Most popular majors: 33% Business/Commerce, General, 9% Criminal Justice/Police Science, 13% Education, Other, 19% Nursing Science, 8% Sport and Fitness Administration/Management

Expenses: 2014-2015: $28,150; room/board: $7,250
Financial aid: (402) 941-6520

Nebraska Wesleyan University

Lincoln NE
(402) 465-2218
U.S. News ranking: Nat. Lib. Arts, No. 143
Website: www.nebrwesleyan.edu/undergraduate-admissions
Admissions email: admissions@nebrwesleyan.edu
Private; founded 1887
Affiliation: United Methodist
Freshman admissions: more selective; 2014-2015: 1,775 applied, 1,387 accepted. Either SAT or ACT required. ACT 25/75 percentile: 22-27. High school rank: 21% in top tenth, 54% in top quarter, 81% in top half
Early decision deadline: 12/1, notification date: N/A
Early action deadline: N/A, notification date: N/A
Application deadline (fall): 8/15
Undergraduate student body: 1,511 full time, 321 part time; 38% male, 62% female; 0% American Indian, 2% Asian, 3% black, 5% Hispanic, 2% multiracial, 0% Pacific Islander, 84% white, 1% international; 86% from in state; 53% live on campus; 16% of students in fraternities, 24% in sororities
Most popular majors: 10% Biological and Biomedical Sciences, 16% Business, Management, Marketing, and Related Support Services, 16% Health Professions and Related Programs, 8% Psychology, 10% Visual and Performing Arts
Expenses: 2015-2016: $29,800; room/board: $8,340
Financial aid: (402) 465-2212; 72% of undergrads determined to have financial need; average aid package $20,839

Peru State College[1]

Peru NE
(402) 872-2221
U.S. News ranking: Reg. U. (Mid.W), unranked
Website: www.peru.edu
Admissions email: admissions@peru.edu
Public
Application deadline (fall): N/A
Undergraduate student body: N/A full time, N/A part time
Expenses: 2014-2015: $6,272 in state, N/A out of state; room/board: $7,232
Financial aid: (402) 872-2228

Union College

Lincoln NE
(800) 228-4600
U.S. News ranking: Reg. Coll. (Mid.W), No. 48
Website: www.ucollege.edu
Admissions email: ucenroll@ucollege.edu
Private; founded 1891
Affiliation: Seventh-day Adventist
Freshman admissions: selective; 2014-2015: 1,260 applied, 657 accepted. Either SAT or ACT required. ACT 25/75 percentile: 19-25. High school rank: 10% in top tenth, 29% in top quarter, 76% in top half
Early decision deadline: N/A, notification date: N/A
Early action deadline: N/A, notification date: N/A
Application deadline (fall): rolling
Undergraduate student body: 712 full time, 85 part time; 41% male, 59% female; 1% American Indian, 3% Asian, 7% black, 16% Hispanic, 5% multiracial, 1% Pacific Islander, 60% white, 7% international; 29% from in state; 73% live on campus; 0% of students in fraternities, 0% in sororities
Most popular majors: 7% Biological and Biomedical Sciences, 19% Business, Management, Marketing, and Related Support Services, 9% Education, 34% Health Professions and Related Programs, 5% Theology and Religious Vocations
Expenses: 2015-2016: $21,970; room/board: $6,730
Financial aid: (402) 486-2505; 88% of undergrads determined to have financial need; average aid package $15,499

University of Nebraska–Kearney

Kearney NE
(308) 865-8526
U.S. News ranking: Reg. U. (Mid.W), No. 46
Website: www.unk.edu
Admissions email: admissionsug@unk.edu
Public; founded 1903
Freshman admissions: selective; 2014-2015: 2,706 applied, 2,276 accepted. Either SAT or ACT required. ACT 25/75 percentile: 20-25. High school rank: 18% in top tenth, 42% in top quarter, 76% in top half
Early decision deadline: N/A, notification date: N/A
Early action deadline: N/A, notification date: N/A
Application deadline (fall): 9/1
Undergraduate student body: 4,668 full time, 606 part time; 43% male, 57% female; 0% American Indian, 1% Asian, 2% black, 10% Hispanic, 1% multiracial, 0% Pacific Islander, 79% white, 6% international; 92% from in state; 35% live on campus; 12% of students in fraternities, 14% in sororities
Most popular majors: 14% Business Administration and Management, General, 14% Elementary Education and Teaching, 7% Operations Management and Supervision, 8% Parks, Recreation and Leisure Studies, 4% Psychology, General
Expenses: 2015-2016: $6,724 in state, $12,994 out of state; room/board: $9,230
Financial aid: (308) 865-8520; 64% of undergrads determined to have financial need; average aid package $10,645

University of Nebraska–Lincoln

Lincoln NE
(800) 742-8800
U.S. News ranking: Nat. U., No. 103
Website: www.unl.edu
Admissions email: Admissions@unl.edu
Public; founded 1869
Freshman admissions: more selective; 2014-2015: 11,865 applied, 8,293 accepted. Either SAT or ACT required. ACT 25/75 percentile: 22-28. High school rank: 24% in top tenth, 51% in top quarter, 83% in top half
Early decision deadline: N/A, notification date: N/A
Early action deadline: N/A, notification date: N/A
Application deadline (fall): 5/1
Undergraduate student body: 18,660 full time, 1,319 part time; 53% male, 47% female; 0% American Indian, 2% Asian, 3% black, 5% Hispanic, 3% multiracial, 0% Pacific Islander, 78% white, 8% international; 79% from in state; 43% live on campus; 19% of students in fraternities, 23% in sororities
Most popular majors: 8% Agriculture, Agriculture Operations, and Related Sciences, 23% Business, Management, Marketing, and Related Support Services, 8% Education, 10% Engineering, 8% Family and Consumer Sciences/Human Sciences
Expenses: 2015-2016: $8,382 in state, $22,790 out of state; room/board: $8,382
Financial aid: (402) 472-2030; 47% of undergrads determined to have financial need; average aid package $12,825

University of Nebraska–Omaha

Omaha NE
(402) 554-2393
U.S. News ranking: Nat. U., second tier
Website: www.unomaha.edu
Admissions email: unoadm@unomaha.edu
Public; founded 1908
Freshman admissions: selective; 2014-2015: 5,750 applied, 4,514 accepted. Either SAT or ACT required. ACT 25/75 percentile: 19-26. High school rank: 14% in top tenth, 38% in top quarter, 70% in top half
Early decision deadline: N/A, notification date: N/A
Early action deadline: N/A, notification date: N/A
Application deadline (fall): 8/1
Undergraduate student body: 9,417 full time, 2,804 part time; 49% male, 51% female; 0% American Indian, 3% Asian, 7% black, 10% Hispanic, 4% multiracial, 0% Pacific Islander, 70% white, 3% international; 92% from in state; 13% live on campus; 2% of students in fraternities, 2% in sororities
Most popular majors: 5% Business Administration and Management, General, 9% Criminal Justice/Safety Studies, 4% Elementary Education and Teaching, 4% Finance, General, 5% Psychology, General
Expenses: 2015-2016: $6,898 in state, $18,610 out of state; room/board: $8,742
Financial aid: (402) 554-2327; 62% of undergrads determined to have financial need; average aid package $11,854

Wayne State College

Wayne NE
(800) 228-9972
U.S. News ranking: Reg. U. (Mid.W), No. 75
Website: www.wsc.edu
Admissions email: admit1@wsc.edu
Public; founded 1909
Freshman admissions: selective; 2014-2015: 2,060 applied, 2,060 accepted. Neither SAT nor ACT required. ACT 25/75 percentile: 18-24. High school rank: 10% in top tenth, 29% in top quarter, 60% in top half
Early decision deadline: N/A, notification date: N/A
Early action deadline: N/A, notification date: N/A
Application deadline (fall): rolling
Undergraduate student body: 2,693 full time, 276 part time; 43% male, 57% female; 1% American Indian, 1% Asian, 3% black, 7% Hispanic, 2% multiracial, 0% Pacific Islander, 81% white, 0% international; 88% from in state; 47% live on campus; N/A of students in fraternities, N/A in sororities
Most popular majors: 15% Business, Management, Marketing, and Related Support Services, 31% Education, 8% Homeland Security, Law Enforcement, Firefighting and Related Protective Services, 7% Parks, Recreation, Leisure, and Fitness Studies, 8% Psychology
Expenses: 2015-2016: $6,042 in state, $10,632 out of state; room/board: $6,760
Financial aid: (402) 375-7230; 68% of undergrads determined to have financial need; average aid package $8,034

York College

York NE
(800) 950-9675
U.S. News ranking: Reg. Coll. (Mid.W), No. 69
Website: www.york.edu
Admissions email: enroll@york.edu
Private; founded 1890
Affiliation: Church of Christ
Freshman admissions: selective; 2014-2015: 650 applied, 300 accepted. Either SAT or ACT required. ACT 25/75 percentile: 18-22. High school rank: 10% in top tenth, 25% in top quarter, 60% in top half
Early decision deadline: N/A, notification date: N/A
Early action deadline: N/A, notification date: N/A
Application deadline (fall): 8/31
Undergraduate student body: 377 full time, 25 part time; 56% male, 44% female; 1% American Indian, 1% Asian, 16% black, 16% Hispanic, 0% multiracial, 0% Pacific Islander, 66% white, 0% international; 20% from in state; N/A live on campus; N/A of students in fraternities, N/A in sororities
Most popular majors: 5% Biology/Biological Sciences, General, 30% Business Administration and Management, 20% Liberal Arts and Sciences/Liberal Studies, 15% Psychology, General, 30% Special Education and Teaching, General
Expenses: 2015-2016: $17,200; room/board: $6,400

Financial aid: (402) 363-5624; 84% of undergrads determined to have financial need; average aid package $13,800

NEVADA

College of Southern Nevada

Las Vegas NV
(702) 651-5610
U.S. News ranking: Reg. Coll. (W), unranked
Website: www.csn.edu
Admissions email: N/A
Public; founded 1971
Freshman admissions: N/A; 2014-2015: N/A applied, N/A accepted. Neither SAT nor ACT required. ACT 25/75 percentile: N/A. High school rank: N/A
Early decision deadline: N/A, notification date: N/A
Early action deadline: N/A, notification date: N/A
Application deadline (fall): rolling
Undergraduate student body: 9,289 full time, 26,654 part time; 44% male, 56% female; 1% American Indian, 9% Asian, 12% black, 27% Hispanic, 5% multiracial, 2% Pacific Islander, 36% white, 1% international
Most popular majors: Information not available
Expenses: 2014-2015: $2,700 in state, $9,345 out of state; room/board: $7,464
Financial aid: (702) 651-5660

Great Basin College[1]

Elko NV
(775) 753-2102
U.S. News ranking: Reg. Coll. (W), unranked
Website: www.gbcnv.edu
Admissions email: N/A
Public
Application deadline (fall): N/A
Undergraduate student body: N/A full time, N/A part time
Expenses: 2014-2015: $2,700 in state, $9,345 out of state; room/board: $5,450
Financial aid: (775) 753-2399

Nevada State College

Henderson NV
(702) 992-2130
U.S. News ranking: Reg. Coll. (W), second tier
Website: nsc.nevada.edu
Admissions email: N/A
Public; founded 2002
Freshman admissions: less selective; 2014-2015: 3,249 applied, 2,012 accepted. Neither SAT nor ACT required. ACT 25/75 percentile: N/A. High school rank: N/A
Early decision deadline: N/A, notification date: N/A
Early action deadline: N/A, notification date: N/A
Application deadline (fall): rolling
Undergraduate student body: 1,200 full time, 2,349 part time; 24% male, 76% female; 0% American Indian, 10% Asian, 11% black, 22% Hispanic, 4% multiracial, 2% Pacific Islander, 44% white, N/A international
Most popular majors: Information not available
Expenses: 2014-2015: $4,482 in state, $14,758 out of state; room/board: $10,260
Financial aid: (702) 992-2150

Sierra Nevada College[1]

Incline Village NV
(866) 412-4636
U.S. News ranking: Reg. U. (W), second tier
Website: www.sierranevada.edu
Admissions email: admissions@sierranevada.edu
Private; founded 1969
Application deadline (fall): 8/28
Undergraduate student body: N/A full time, N/A part time
Expenses: 2015-2016: $29,994; room/board: $12,066
Financial aid: (775) 831-1314; 68% of undergrads determined to have financial need; average aid package $20,307

University of Nevada–Las Vegas

Las Vegas NV
(702) 774-8658
U.S. News ranking: Nat. U., second tier
Website: www.unlv.edu
Admissions email: undergraduate.recruitment@unlv.edu
Public; founded 1957
Freshman admissions: selective; 2014-2015: 7,408 applied, 6,437 accepted. Either SAT or ACT required. SAT 25/75 percentile: 880-1110. High school rank: 21% in top tenth, 51% in top quarter, 83% in top half
Early decision deadline: N/A, notification date: N/A
Early action deadline: N/A, notification date: N/A
Application deadline (fall): 7/1
Undergraduate student body: 17,444 full time, 6,369 part time; 45% male, 55% female; 0% American Indian, 15% Asian, 8% black, 25% Hispanic, 9% multiracial, 1% Pacific Islander, 37% white, 4% international; 87% from in state; 7% live on campus; 8% of students in fraternities, 8% in sororities
Most popular majors: 6% Biological and Biomedical Sciences, 35% Business, Management, Marketing, and Related Support Services, 7% Psychology, 7% Social Sciences, 5% Visual and Performing Arts
Expenses: 2015-2016: $6,943 in state, $20,852 out of state; room/board: $10,730
Financial aid: (702) 895-3424; 63% of undergrads determined to have financial need; average aid package $11,044

University of Nevada–Reno

Reno NV
(775) 784-4700
U.S. News ranking: Nat. U., No. 187
Website: www.unr.edu
Admissions email: asknevada@unr.edu
Public; founded 1864
Freshman admissions: selective; 2014-2015: 8,832 applied, 7,408 accepted. Either SAT or ACT required. SAT 25/75 percentile: 960-1190. High school rank: 23% in top tenth, 55% in top quarter, 87% in top half
Early decision deadline: N/A, notification date: N/A
Early action deadline: N/A, notification date: N/A
Application deadline (fall): 4/30
Undergraduate student body: 13,999 full time, 2,840 part time; 48% male, 52% female; 1% American Indian, 7% Asian, 4% black, 18% Hispanic, 6% multiracial, 0% Pacific Islander, 62% white, 1% international; 73% from in state; 16% live on campus; N/A of students in fraternities, N/A in sororities
Most popular majors: 11% Biological and Biomedical Sciences, 14% Business, Management, Marketing, and Related Support Services, 10% Engineering, 12% Health Professions and Related Programs, 11% Social Sciences
Expenses: 2015-2016: $6,902 in state, $20,812 out of state; room/board: $10,240
Financial aid: (775) 784-4666; 53% of undergrads determined to have financial need; average aid package $9,081

Western Nevada College[1]

Carson City NV
(775) 445-3000
U.S. News ranking: Reg. Coll. (W), unranked
Website: www.wnc.edu
Admissions email: N/A
Public; founded 1971
Application deadline (fall): rolling
Undergraduate student body: N/A full time, N/A part time
Expenses: 2014-2015: $2,700 in state, $9,345 out of state; room/board: $9,220
Financial aid: (775) 445-3264

NEW HAMPSHIRE

Colby-Sawyer College[1]

New London NH
(800) 272-1015
U.S. News ranking: Reg. Coll. (N), unranked
Website: www.colby-sawyer.edu
Admissions email: admissions@colby-sawyer.edu
Private
Application deadline (fall): N/A
Undergraduate student body: N/A full time, N/A part time
Expenses: 2014-2015: $38,040; room/board: $12,750
Financial aid: (603) 526-3717

Daniel Webster College[1]

Nashua NH
(800) 325-6876
U.S. News ranking: Reg. Coll. (N), second tier
Website: www.dwc.edu
Admissions email: admissions@dwc.edu
Private; founded 1965
Application deadline (fall): rolling
Undergraduate student body: N/A full time, N/A part time
Expenses: 2014-2015: $15,630; room/board: $10,970
Financial aid: (603) 577-6590

Dartmouth College

Hanover NH
(603) 646-2875
U.S. News ranking: Nat. U., No. 12
Website: www.dartmouth.edu
Admissions email: admissions.office@dartmouth.edu
Private; founded 1769
Freshman admissions: most selective; 2014-2015: 19,296 applied, 2,220 accepted. Either SAT or ACT required. SAT 25/75 percentile: 1360-1550. High school rank: 93% in top tenth, 99% in top quarter, 100% in top half
Early decision deadline: 11/1, notification date: 12/15
Early action deadline: N/A, notification date: N/A
Application deadline (fall): 1/1
Undergraduate student body: 4,228 full time, 61 part time; 51% male, 49% female; 2% American Indian, 14% Asian, 7% black, 8% Hispanic, 5% multiracial, 0% Pacific Islander, 48% white, 8% international; 3% from in state; 88% live on campus; 46% of students in fraternities, 44% in sororities
Most popular majors: 13% Economics, General, 7% Engineering, General, 6% History, General, 9% Political Science and Government, General, 6% Psychology, General
Expenses: 2015-2016: $49,506; room/board: $14,238
Financial aid: (603) 646-2451; 51% of undergrads determined to have financial need; average aid package $45,258

Franklin Pierce University

Rindge NH
(800) 437-0048
U.S. News ranking: Reg. U. (N), second tier
Website: www.franklinpierce.edu/
Admissions email: admissions@franklinpierce.edu
Private; founded 1962
Freshman admissions: less selective; 2014-2015: 3,604 applied, 3,038 accepted. Either SAT or ACT required. SAT 25/75 percentile: 850-1050. High school rank: 10% in top tenth, 28% in top quarter, 54% in top half
Early decision deadline: N/A, notification date: N/A
Early action deadline: N/A, notification date: N/A
Application deadline (fall): rolling
Undergraduate student body: 1,465 full time, 206 part time; 44% male, 56% female; 0% American Indian, 1% Asian, 5% black, 3% Hispanic, 4% multiracial, 0% Pacific Islander, 75% white, 2% international; 19% from in state; 85% live on campus; 0% of students in fraternities, 0% in sororities
Most popular majors: 8% Biological and Biomedical Sciences, 19% Business, Management, Marketing, and Related Support Services, 7% Education, 14% Health Professions and Related Programs, 5% Visual and Performing Arts
Expenses: 2014-2015: $31,782; room/board: $12,060
Financial aid: (603) 899-4186

Granite State College

Concord NH
(603) 513-1391
U.S. News ranking: Nat. Lib. Arts, unranked
Website: www.granite.edu
Admissions email: gsc.admissions@granite.edu
Public; founded 1972
Freshman admissions: N/A; 2014-2015: 253 applied, 253 accepted. Neither SAT nor ACT required. ACT 25/75 percentile: N/A. High school rank: N/A
Early decision deadline: N/A, notification date: N/A
Early action deadline: N/A, notification date: N/A
Application deadline (fall): rolling
Undergraduate student body: 1,046 full time, 824 part time; 26% male, 74% female; 0% American Indian, 1% Asian, 2% black, 2% Hispanic, 2% multiracial, 0% Pacific Islander, 84% white, 0% international; 89% from in state; 0% live on campus; 0% of students in fraternities, 0% in sororities
Most popular majors: 26% Business Administration and Management, General, 11% Education, 13% Liberal Arts and Sciences/Liberal Studies, 20% Multi/Interdisciplinary Studies, Other, 21% Psychology, General
Expenses: 2014-2015: $8,775 in state, $9,675 out of state; room/board: N/A
Financial aid: (603) 228-3000

Keene State College

Keene NH
(603) 358-2276
U.S. News ranking: Reg. U. (N), No. 76
Website: www.keene.edu
Admissions email: admissions@keene.edu
Public; founded 1909
Freshman admissions: less selective; 2014-2015: 6,484 applied, 5,096 accepted. Either SAT or ACT required. SAT 25/75 percentile: 870-1060. High school rank: 3% in top tenth, 18% in top quarter, 54% in top half
Early decision deadline: N/A, notification date: N/A
Early action deadline: N/A, notification date: N/A
Application deadline (fall): 4/1
Undergraduate student body: 4,569 full time, 272 part time; 43% male, 57% female; 0% American Indian, 1% Asian, 1% black, 3% Hispanic, 2% multiracial, 0% Pacific Islander, 85% white, 0% international; 46% from in state; 57% live on campus; 4% of students in fraternities, 4% in sororities
Most popular majors: 17% Education, 11% Engineering Technologies and Engineering-Related Fields, 10% Health Professions and Related Programs, 11% Psychology, 10% Social Sciences
Expenses: 2015-2016: $12,938 in state, $21,408 out of state; room/board: $9,712
Financial aid: (603) 358-2280; 67% of undergrads determined to have financial need; average aid package $10,785

Mount Washington College[1]

Manchester NH
(888) 971-2190
U.S. News ranking: Reg. Coll. (N), unranked
Website: www.mountwashington.edu

Admissions email: N/A
For-profit
Application deadline (fall): N/A
Undergraduate student body: N/A full time, N/A part time
Expenses: 2014-2015: $9,000; room/board: $5,648
Financial aid: N/A

New England College

Henniker NH
(800) 521-7642
U.S. News ranking: Reg. U. (N), second tier
Website: www.nec.edu
Admissions email: admission@nec.edu
Private; founded 1946
Freshman admissions: least selective; 2014-2015: 5,563 applied, 5,337 accepted. Neither SAT nor ACT required. SAT 25/75 percentile: 770-1000. High school rank: 6% in top tenth, 14% in top quarter, 43% in top half
Early decision deadline: N/A, notification date: N/A
Early action deadline: N/A, notification date: N/A
Application deadline (fall): rolling
Undergraduate student body: 1,690 full time, 39 part time; 43% male, 57% female; 1% American Indian, 2% Asian, 22% black, 8% Hispanic, 1% multiracial, 0% Pacific Islander, 56% white, 3% international; 27% from in state; 31% live on campus; 7% of students in fraternities, 8% in sororities
Most popular majors: 11% Biological and Biomedical Sciences, 13% Business, Management, Marketing, and Related Support Services, 11% Multi/Interdisciplinary Studies, 16% Parks, Recreation, Leisure, and Fitness Studies, 11% Psychology
Expenses: 2015-2016: $34,606; room/board: $13,268
Financial aid: (603) 428-2414; 79% of undergrads determined to have financial need; average aid package $22,768

Plymouth State University

Plymouth NH
(603) 535-2237
U.S. News ranking: Reg. U. (N), No. 100
Website: www.plymouth.edu
Admissions email: plymouthadmit@plymouth.edu
Public; founded 1871
Freshman admissions: less selective; 2014-2015: 4,783 applied, 3,597 accepted. Neither SAT nor ACT required. SAT 25/75 percentile: 890-1060. High school rank: 6% in top tenth, 20% in top quarter, 54% in top half
Early decision deadline: N/A, notification date: N/A
Early action deadline: N/A, notification date: N/A
Application deadline (fall): 4/1
Undergraduate student body: 3,508 full time, 279 part time; 53% male, 47% female; 0% American Indian, 2% Asian, 2% black, 3% Hispanic, 2% multiracial, 0% Pacific Islander, 80% white, 2% international; 60% from in state; 48% live on campus; 0% of students in fraternities, 2% in sororities
Most popular majors: 20% Business, Management, Marketing, and Related Support Services, 15% Education, 7% Homeland Security, Law Enforcement, Firefighting and Related Protective Services, 8% Parks, Recreation, Leisure, and Fitness Studies, 7% Visual and Performing Arts
Expenses: 2014-2015: $12,677 in state, $20,587 out of state; room/board: $10,728
Financial aid: (603) 535-2338; 67% of undergrads determined to have financial need; average aid package $10,378

Rivier University[1]

Nashua NH
(603) 888-1311
U.S. News ranking: Reg. U. (N), second tier
Website: rivier.edu
Admissions email: admissions@rivier.edu
Private
Application deadline (fall): rolling
Undergraduate student body: N/A full time, N/A part time
Expenses: 2014-2015: $28,900; room/board: $10,940
Financial aid: (603) 897-8533

Southern New Hampshire University

Manchester NH
(603) 645-9611
U.S. News ranking: Reg. U. (N), No. 131
Website: www.snhu.edu
Admissions email: admission@snhu.edu
Private; founded 1932
Freshman admissions: less selective; 2014-2015: 4,199 applied, 3,536 accepted. Neither SAT nor ACT required. SAT 25/75 percentile: 870-1060. High school rank: 10% in top tenth, 20% in top quarter, 66% in top half
Early decision deadline: N/A, notification date: N/A
Early action deadline: 11/15, notification date: 12/15
Application deadline (fall): rolling
Undergraduate student body: 2,961 full time, 937 part time; 46% male, 54% female; 0% American Indian, 1% Asian, 2% black, 3% Hispanic, 1% multiracial, 0% Pacific Islander, 60% white, 9% international; 44% from in state; 67% live on campus; 4% of students in fraternities, 5% in sororities
Most popular majors: 24% Business Administration and Management, General, 6% Computer and Information Sciences, General, 5% Elementary Education and Teaching, 6% Organizational Communication, General, 10% Psychology, General
Expenses: 2015-2016: $30,766; room/board: $11,798
Financial aid: (603) 645-9645; 72% of undergrads determined to have financial need; average aid package $19,958

St. Anselm College

Manchester NH
(603) 641-7500
U.S. News ranking: Nat. Lib. Arts, No. 112
Website: www.anselm.edu
Admissions email: admission@anselm.edu
Private; founded 1889
Affiliation: Roman Catholic (Benedictine)
Freshman admissions: selective; 2014-2015: 3,568 applied, 2,715 accepted. Neither SAT nor ACT required. SAT 25/75 percentile: 1050-1230. High school rank: 27% in top tenth, 58% in top quarter, 90% in top half
Early decision deadline: N/A, notification date: N/A
Early action deadline: 11/15, notification date: 1/15
Application deadline (fall): 2/1
Undergraduate student body: 1,915 full time, 53 part time; 40% male, 60% female; 0% American Indian, 1% Asian, 2% black, 3% Hispanic, 2% multiracial, 0% Pacific Islander, 80% white, 1% international; 24% from in state; 90% live on campus; 0% of students in fraternities, 0% in sororities
Most popular majors: 9% Business/Commerce, General, 11% Criminology, 6% Psychology, General, 20% Registered Nursing/Registered Nurse, 8% Speech Communication and Rhetoric
Expenses: 2015-2016: $37,694; room/board: $13,334
Financial aid: (603) 641-7110; 72% of undergrads determined to have financial need; average aid package $27,727

Thomas More College of Liberal Arts[1]

Merrimack NH
(800) 880-8308
U.S. News ranking: Nat. Lib. Arts, unranked
Website: www.thomasmorecollege.edu
Admissions email: admissions@thomasmorecollege.edu
Private
Affiliation: Roman Catholic
Application deadline (fall): rolling
Undergraduate student body: N/A full time, N/A part time
Expenses: 2015-2016: $20,400; room/board: $9,500
Financial aid: (800) 880-8308; 86% of undergrads determined to have financial need; average aid package $11,747

University of New Hampshire

Durham NH
(603) 862-1360
U.S. News ranking: Nat. U., No. 103
Website: www.unh.edu
Admissions email: admissions@unh.edu
Public; founded 1866
Freshman admissions: selective; 2014-2015: 18,420 applied, 14,740 accepted. Either SAT or ACT required. SAT 25/75 percentile: 1000-1200. High school rank: 17% in top tenth, 48% in top quarter, 87% in top half
Early decision deadline: N/A, notification date: N/A
Early action deadline: 11/15, notification date: 1/15
Application deadline (fall): 2/1
Undergraduate student body: 12,377 full time, 463 part time; 46% male, 54% female; 0% American Indian, 2% Asian, 1% black, 3% Hispanic, 2% multiracial, 0% Pacific Islander, 81% white, 2% international; 51% from in state; 56% live on campus; 12% of students in fraternities, 12% in sororities
Most popular majors: 4% Biomedical Sciences, General, 17% Business Administration and Management, General, 4% Mechanical Engineering, 5% Psychology, General, 4% Speech Communication and Rhetoric
Expenses: 2014-2015: $16,552 in state, $29,532 out of state; room/board: $10,360
Financial aid: (603) 862-3600; 68% of undergrads determined to have financial need; average aid package $22,877

NEW JERSEY

Berkeley College

Woodland Park NJ
(800) 446-5400
U.S. News ranking: Business, unranked
Website: www.berkeleycollege.edu
Admissions email: admissions@berkeleycollege.edu
For-profit; founded 1931
Freshman admissions: less selective; 2014-2015: 2,456 applied, 2,395 accepted. Neither SAT nor ACT required. ACT 25/75 percentile: N/A. High school rank: N/A
Early decision deadline: N/A, notification date: N/A
Early action deadline: N/A, notification date: N/A
Application deadline (fall): rolling
Undergraduate student body: 3,066 full time, 593 part time; 28% male, 72% female; 0% American Indian, 2% Asian, 21% black, 34% Hispanic, 0% multiracial, 0% Pacific Islander, 18% white, 1% international
Most popular majors: 10% Accounting, 27% Business Administration and Management, General, 28% Criminal Justice/Law Enforcement Administration, 11% Fashion Merchandising, 10% Health/Health Care Administration/Management
Expenses: 2015-2016: $24,300; room/board: N/A
Financial aid: (973) 278-5400

Bloomfield College

Bloomfield NJ
(800) 848-4555
U.S. News ranking: Nat. Lib. Arts, second tier
Website: www.bloomfield.edu
Admissions email: admission@bloomfield.edu
Private; founded 1868
Affiliation: Presbyterian
Freshman admissions: least selective; 2014-2015: 3,079 applied, 1,952 accepted. Either SAT or ACT required. SAT 25/75 percentile: 730-910. High school rank: 6% in top tenth, 24% in top quarter, 54% in top half
Early decision deadline: N/A, notification date: N/A
Early action deadline: 12/1, notification date: 12/23
Application deadline (fall): 8/1
Undergraduate student body: 1,755 full time, 252 part time; 36% male, 64% female; 1% American Indian, 3% Asian, 52% black, 25% Hispanic, 1% multiracial, 0% Pacific Islander, 11% white, 3% international; 95% from in state; 28% live on campus; 1% of students in fraternities, 1% in sororities
Most popular majors: 15% Business, Management, Marketing, and Related Support Services, 14% Health Professions and Related Programs, 15% Psychology, 15% Social Sciences, 18% Visual and Performing Arts
Expenses: 2015-2016: $27,800; room/board: $11,300
Financial aid: (973) 748-9000; 92% of undergrads determined to have financial need; average aid package $20,634

Caldwell University

Caldwell NJ
(973) 618-3500
U.S. News ranking: Reg. U. (N), No. 103
Website: www.caldwell.edu
Admissions email: admissions@caldwell.edu
Private; founded 1939
Affiliation: Roman Catholic
Freshman admissions: less selective; 2014-2015: 3,132 applied, 2,008 accepted. Either SAT or ACT required. SAT 25/75 percentile: 830-1070. High school rank: 7% in top tenth, 37% in top quarter, 75% in top half
Early decision deadline: N/A, notification date: N/A
Early action deadline: 12/1, notification date: 1/1
Application deadline (fall): rolling
Undergraduate student body: 1,352 full time, 243 part time; 30% male, 70% female; 0% American Indian, 5% Asian, 15% black, 16% Hispanic, 2% multiracial, 0% Pacific Islander, 42% white, 4% international; 89% from in state; 37% live on campus; N/A of students in fraternities, N/A in sororities
Most popular majors: 15% Business Administration and Management, General, 11% English Language and Literature, General, 11% Health Professions and Related Programs, 23% Psychology, General
Expenses: 2015-2016: $31,200; room/board: $12,140
Financial aid: (973) 618-3221; 80% of undergrads determined to have financial need; average aid package $22,000

Centenary College

Hackettstown NJ
(800) 236-8679
U.S. News ranking: Reg. U. (N), second tier
Website: www.centenarycollege.edu
Admissions email: admissions@centenarycollege.edu
Private; founded 1867
Affiliation: United Methodist
Freshman admissions: less selective; 2014-2015: 1,183 applied, 966 accepted. Either SAT or ACT required. SAT 25/75 percentile: 820-1040. High school rank: 12% in top tenth, 31% in top quarter, 62% in top half
Early decision deadline: N/A, notification date: N/A
Early action deadline: N/A, notification date: N/A
Application deadline (fall): 8/15

Undergraduate student body: 1,524 full time, 88 part time; 37% male, 63% female; 0% American Indian, 1% Asian, 11% black, 7% Hispanic, 0% multiracial, 0% Pacific Islander, 57% white, 2% international
Most popular majors: Information not available
Expenses: 2015-2016: $31,754; room/board: $10,730
Financial aid: (908) 852-1400; 80% of undergrads determined to have financial need; average aid package $25,658

College of New Jersey

Ewing NJ
(609) 771-2131
U.S. News ranking: Reg. U. (N), No. 3
Website: www.tcnj.edu
Admissions email: admiss@tcnj.edu
Public; founded 1855
Freshman admissions: more selective; 2014-2015: 10,937 applied, 5,356 accepted. Either SAT or ACT required. SAT 25/75 percentile: 1120-1310. High school rank: 49% in top tenth, 85% in top quarter, 99% in top half
Early decision deadline: 11/15, notification date: 12/15
Early action deadline: N/A, notification date: N/A
Application deadline (fall): 1/15
Undergraduate student body: 6,482 full time, 261 part time; 43% male, 57% female; 0% American Indian, 10% Asian, 5% black, 12% Hispanic, 1% multiracial, 0% Pacific Islander, 66% white, 0% international; 93% from in state; 60% live on campus; 14% of students in fraternities, 11% in sororities
Most popular majors: 6% Biology/Biological Sciences, General, 16% Business Administration and Management, General, 8% Engineering, General, 9% Psychology, General, 22% Teacher Education and Professional Development, Specific Levels and Methods
Expenses: 2014-2015: $15,024 in state, $25,637 out of state; room/board: $11,677
Financial aid: (609) 771-2211; 53% of undergrads determined to have financial need; average aid package $11,106

College of St. Elizabeth

Morristown NJ
(973) 290-4700
U.S. News ranking: Reg. U. (N), No. 112
Website: www.cse.edu
Admissions email: apply@cse.edu
Private; founded 1899
Affiliation: Catholic
Freshman admissions: least selective; 2014-2015: 2,959 applied, 1,704 accepted. Either SAT or ACT required. SAT 25/75 percentile: 750-905. High school rank: N/A
Early decision deadline: N/A, notification date: N/A
Early action deadline: N/A, notification date: N/A
Application deadline (fall): rolling
Undergraduate student body: 560 full time, 335 part time; 6% male, 94% female; 0% American Indian, 3% Asian, 27% black, 17% Hispanic, 1% multiracial, 0% Pacific Islander, 36% white, 4% international; 95% from in state; 39% live on campus; 0% of students in fraternities, 0% in sororities
Most popular majors: 11% Business Administration and Management, General, 7% Dietetics/Dietitian, 12% Legal Professions and Studies, Other, 7% Psychology, General, 38% Registered Nursing/Registered Nurse
Expenses: 2015-2016: $31,679; room/board: $12,744
Financial aid: (973) 290-4445; 89% of undergrads determined to have financial need; average aid package $30,990

Drew University

Madison NJ
(973) 408-3739
U.S. News ranking: Nat. Lib. Arts, No. 112
Website: www.drew.edu
Admissions email: cadm@drew.edu
Private; founded 1867
Affiliation: Methodist
Freshman admissions: selective; 2014-2015: 3,413 applied, 2,395 accepted. Neither SAT nor ACT required. SAT 25/75 percentile: 1000-1220. High school rank: 28% in top tenth, 54% in top quarter, 83% in top half
Early decision deadline: 12/1, notification date: 12/15
Early action deadline: N/A, notification date: N/A
Application deadline (fall): 2/15
Undergraduate student body: 1,357 full time, 60 part time; 38% male, 62% female; 0% American Indian, 6% Asian, 10% black, 12% Hispanic, 4% multiracial, 0% Pacific Islander, 54% white, 5% international; 69% from in state; 74% live on campus; 0% of students in fraternities, 0% in sororities
Most popular majors: 7% Biology/Biological Sciences, General, 9% Business Administration and Management, General, 9% Economics, General, 7% Political Science and Government, General, 9% Psychology, General
Expenses: 2015-2016: $46,384; room/board: $12,672
Financial aid: (973) 408-3112; 72% of undergrads determined to have financial need; average aid package $36,468

Fairleigh Dickinson University

Teaneck NJ
(800) 338-8803
U.S. News ranking: Reg. U. (N), No. 83
Website: www.fdu.edu
Admissions email: admissions@fdu.edu
Private; founded 1942
Freshman admissions: selective; 2014-2015: 10,345 applied, 6,502 accepted. Either SAT or ACT required. SAT 25/75 percentile: 890-1090. High school rank: 14% in top tenth, 36% in top quarter, 70% in top half
Early decision deadline: N/A, notification date: N/A
Early action deadline: N/A, notification date: N/A
Application deadline (fall): rolling
Undergraduate student body: 4,927 full time, 3,523 part time; 43% male, 57% female; 0% American Indian, 5% Asian, 13% black, 27% Hispanic, 2% multiracial, 0% Pacific Islander, 38% white, 5% international; 86% from in state; 35% live on campus; N/A of students in fraternities, N/A in sororities
Most popular majors: 17% Business, Management, Marketing, and Related Support Services, 7% Health Professions and Related Programs, 34% Liberal Arts and Sciences, General Studies and Humanities, 9% Psychology, 5% Visual and Performing Arts
Expenses: 2014-2015: $35,880; room/board: $12,708
Financial aid: (201) 692-2823

Felician College

Lodi NJ
(201) 559-6131
U.S. News ranking: Reg. U. (N), second tier
Website: www.felician.edu
Admissions email: admissions@felician.edu
Private; founded 1942
Affiliation: Roman Catholic
Freshman admissions: least selective; 2014-2015: 1,667 applied, 1,403 accepted. Either SAT or ACT required. SAT 25/75 percentile: 790-960. High school rank: 7% in top tenth, 23% in top quarter, 59% in top half
Early decision deadline: N/A, notification date: N/A
Early action deadline: N/A, notification date: N/A
Application deadline (fall): rolling
Undergraduate student body: 1,390 full time, 244 part time; 27% male, 73% female; 0% American Indian, 7% Asian, 20% black, 26% Hispanic, 1% multiracial, 0% Pacific Islander, 35% white, 3% international; 92% from in state; 22% live on campus; N/A of students in fraternities, N/A in sororities
Most popular majors: 7% Biological and Biomedical Sciences, 12% Business, Management, Marketing, and Related Support Services, 6% Education, 48% Health Professions and Related Programs, 7% Multi/Interdisciplinary Studies
Expenses: 2014-2015: $30,615; room/board: $11,650
Financial aid: (201) 559-6010; 88% of undergrads determined to have financial need; average aid package $26,716

Georgian Court University

Lakewood NJ
(800) 458-8422
U.S. News ranking: Reg. U. (N), No. 131
Website: www.georgian.edu
Admissions email: admissions@georgian.edu
Private; founded 1908
Affiliation: Roman Catholic
Freshman admissions: less selective; 2014-2015: 1,290 applied, 878 accepted. Either SAT or ACT required. SAT 25/75 percentile: 840-1050. High school rank: 6% in top tenth, 29% in top quarter, 66% in top half
Early decision deadline: N/A, notification date: N/A
Early action deadline: 11/15, notification date: 12/30
Application deadline (fall): 8/1
Undergraduate student body: 1,299 full time, 322 part time; 24% male, 76% female; 0% American Indian, 2% Asian, 14% black, 11% Hispanic, 2% multiracial, 0% Pacific Islander, 56% white, 1% international; 95% from in state; 28% live on campus; 0% of students in fraternities, 0% in sororities
Most popular majors: 10% Business, Management, Marketing, and Related Support Services, 13% English Language and Literature/Letters, 10% Health Professions and Related Programs, 30% Psychology, 6% Visual and Performing Arts
Expenses: 2015-2016: $31,618; room/board: $10,808
Financial aid: (732) 364-2200; 83% of undergrads determined to have financial need; average aid package $26,664

Kean University

Union NJ
(908) 737-7100
U.S. News ranking: Reg. U. (N), second tier
Website: www.kean.edu
Admissions email: admitme@kean.edu
Public; founded 1855
Freshman admissions: less selective; 2014-2015: 5,718 applied, 4,023 accepted. Either SAT or ACT required. SAT 25/75 percentile: 820-1000. High school rank: 8% in top tenth, 26% in top quarter, 64% in top half
Early decision deadline: N/A, notification date: N/A
Early action deadline: N/A, notification date: N/A
Application deadline (fall): 5/31
Undergraduate student body: 9,283 full time, 2,704 part time; 40% male, 60% female; 0% American Indian, 6% Asian, 20% black, 25% Hispanic, 2% multiracial, 0% Pacific Islander, 38% white, 1% international; 98% from in state; 14% live on campus; N/A of students in fraternities, N/A in sororities
Most popular majors: 5% Biology/Biological Sciences, General, 7% Business Administration and Management, General, 6% Criminal Justice/Law Enforcement Administration, 16% Psychology, General, 6% Speech Communication and Rhetoric
Expenses: 2014-2015: $11,244 in state, $17,653 out of state; room/board: $12,200
Financial aid: (908) 737-3190; 72% of undergrads determined to have financial need; average aid package $10,300

Monmouth University

West Long Branch NJ
(800) 543-9671
U.S. News ranking: Reg. U. (N), No. 36
Website: www.monmouth.edu
Admissions email: admission@monmouth.edu
Private; founded 1933
Freshman admissions: selective; 2014-2015: 7,691 applied, 5,706 accepted. Either SAT or ACT required. SAT 25/75 percentile: 960-1140. High school rank: 19% in top tenth, 49% in top quarter, 81% in top half
Early decision deadline: N/A, notification date: N/A
Early action deadline: 12/1, notification date: 1/15
Application deadline (fall): 3/1
Undergraduate student body: 4,370 full time, 264 part time; 41% male, 59% female; 0% American Indian, 3% Asian, 5% black, 10% Hispanic, 2% multiracial, 0% Pacific Islander, 76% white, 1% international; 88% from in state; 42% live on campus; 14% of students in fraternities, 15% in sororities
Most popular majors: 24% Business, Management, Marketing, and Related Support Services, 12% Communication, Journalism, and Related Programs, 12% Education, 9% Homeland Security, Law Enforcement, Firefighting and Related Protective Services, 7% Psychology
Expenses: 2015-2016: $33,728; room/board: $12,506
Financial aid: (732) 571-3463; 71% of undergrads determined to have financial need; average aid package $24,858

Montclair State University

Montclair NJ
(973) 655-4444
U.S. News ranking: Reg. U. (N), No. 34
Website: www.montclair.edu
Admissions email: undergraduate.admissions@montclair.edu
Public; founded 1908
Freshman admissions: selective; 2014-2015: 12,462 applied, 8,328 accepted. Neither SAT nor ACT required. SAT 25/75 percentile: 880-1070. High school rank: 12% in top tenth, 37% in top quarter, 78% in top half
Early decision deadline: N/A, notification date: N/A
Early action deadline: N/A, notification date: N/A
Application deadline (fall): 3/1
Undergraduate student body: 13,879 full time, 2,006 part time; 39% male, 61% female; 0% American Indian, 5% Asian, 10% black, 24% Hispanic, 4% multiracial, 0% Pacific Islander, 46% white, 2% international; 97% from in state; 31% live on campus; 3% of students in fraternities, 3% in sororities
Most popular majors: 5% Biology/Biological Sciences, General, 14% Business Administration and Management, General, 6% English Language and Literature, General, 6% Family and Consumer Sciences/Human Sciences, General, 12% Psychology, General
Expenses: 2015-2016: $11,771 in state, $20,318 out of state; room/board: $13,884
Financial aid: (973) 655-4461; 71% of undergrads determined to have financial need; average aid package $15,921

New Jersey City University

Jersey City NJ
(888) 441-6528
U.S. News ranking: Reg. U. (N), second tier
Website: www.njcu.edu/

Admissions email: admissions@njcu.edu
Public; founded 1927
Freshman admissions: less selective; 2014-2015: 2,618 applied, 2,005 accepted. Either SAT or ACT required. SAT 25/75 percentile: 800-980. High school rank: 13% in top tenth, 33% in top quarter, 61% in top half
Early decision deadline: N/A, notification date: N/A
Early action deadline: N/A, notification date: N/A
Undergraduate student body: 4,689 full time, 1,540 part time; 39% male, 61% female; 0% American Indian, 9% Asian, 21% black, 35% Hispanic, 1% multiracial, 0% Pacific Islander, 25% white, 1% international; 99% from in state; 4% live on campus; 1% of students in fraternities, 1% in sororities
Most popular majors: 8% Business Administration and Management, General, 9% Corrections and Criminal Justice, Other, 11% Psychology, General, 16% Registered Nursing, Nursing Administration, Nursing Research and Clinical Nursing, Other, 6% Sociology
Expenses: 2014-2015: $10,852 in state, $19,424 out of state; room/board: $10,604
Financial aid: (201) 200-3173; 87% of undergrads determined to have financial need; average aid package $15,970

New Jersey Institute of Technology

Newark NJ
(973) 596-3300
U.S. News ranking: Nat. U., No. 140
Website: www.njit.edu
Admissions email: admissions@njit.edu
Public; founded 1881
Freshman admissions: more selective; 2014-2015: 4,765 applied, 3,025 accepted. Either SAT or ACT required. SAT 25/75 percentile: 1080-1300. High school rank: 26% in top tenth, 54% in top quarter, 86% in top half
Early decision deadline: N/A, notification date: N/A
Early action deadline: N/A, notification date: N/A
Application deadline (fall): 3/1
Undergraduate student body: 5,923 full time, 1,627 part time; 77% male, 23% female; 0% American Indian, 21% Asian, 9% black, 20% Hispanic, 3% multiracial, 0% Pacific Islander, 31% white, 4% international; 94% from in state; 23% live on campus; 6% of students in fraternities, 3% in sororities
Most popular majors: 10% Architecture and Related Services, 7% Business, Management, Marketing, and Related Support Services, 14% Computer and Information Sciences and Support Services, 41% Engineering, 15% Engineering Technologies and Engineering-Related Fields
Expenses: 2014-2015: $15,648 in state, $29,288 out of state; room/board: $13,280
Financial aid: (973) 596-3479; 71% of undergrads determined to have financial need; average aid package $14,403

Princeton University

Princeton NJ
(609) 258-3060
U.S. News ranking: Nat. U., No. 1
Website: www.princeton.edu
Admissions email: uaoffice@princeton.edu
Private; founded 1746
Freshman admissions: most selective; 2014-2015: 26,641 applied, 1,983 accepted. Either SAT or ACT required. SAT 25/75 percentile: 1400-1600. High school rank: 96% in top tenth, 99% in top quarter, 100% in top half
Early decision deadline: N/A, notification date: N/A
Early action deadline: 11/1, notification date: 12/15
Application deadline (fall): 1/1
Undergraduate student body: 5,275 full time, 116 part time; 51% male, 49% female; 0% American Indian, 21% Asian, 8% black, 8% Hispanic, 4% multiracial, 0% Pacific Islander, 46% white, 11% international; 18% from in state; 98% live on campus; 0% of students in fraternities, 0% in sororities
Most popular majors: 7% Computer Engineering, General, 6% Ecology and Evolutionary Biology, 11% Economics, General, 9% Political Science and Government, General, 7% Public Policy Analysis, General
Expenses: 2015-2016: $43,450; room/board: $14,160
Financial aid: (609) 258-3330; 59% of undergrads determined to have financial need; average aid package $44,047

Ramapo College of New Jersey

Mahwah NJ
(201) 684-7300
U.S. News ranking: Reg. U. (N), No. 26
Website: www.ramapo.edu
Admissions email: admissions@ramapo.edu
Public; founded 1969
Freshman admissions: selective; 2014-2015: 6,699 applied, 3,572 accepted. Either SAT or ACT required. SAT 25/75 percentile: 980-1200. High school rank: 10% in top tenth, 26% in top quarter, 51% in top half
Early decision deadline: 11/1, notification date: 12/5
Early action deadline: N/A, notification date: N/A
Application deadline (fall): 3/1
Undergraduate student body: 5,044 full time, 666 part time; 45% male, 55% female; 0% American Indian, 6% Asian, 6% black, 14% Hispanic, 1% multiracial, 0% Pacific Islander, 63% white, 1% international; 95% from in state; 48% live on campus; 5% of students in fraternities, 5% in sororities
Most popular majors: 6% Accounting, 15% Business/Commerce, General, 7% Nursing Science, 16% Psychology, General, 12% Speech Communication and Rhetoric
Expenses: 2015-2016: $13,698 in state, $22,563 out of state; room/board: $11,640
Financial aid: (201) 684-7549; 60% of undergrads determined to have financial need; average aid package $11,637

Rider University

Lawrenceville NJ
(609) 896-5042
U.S. News ranking: Reg. U. (N), No. 22
Website: www.rider.edu
Admissions email: admissions@rider.edu
Private; founded 1865
Freshman admissions: selective; 2014-2015: 9,366 applied, 6,641 accepted. Either SAT or ACT required. SAT 25/75 percentile: 930-1120. High school rank: 17% in top tenth, 47% in top quarter, 82% in top half
Early decision deadline: N/A, notification date: N/A
Early action deadline: 11/15, notification date: 12/15
Application deadline (fall): rolling
Undergraduate student body: 3,822 full time, 502 part time; 41% male, 59% female; 0% American Indian, 4% Asian, 11% black, 11% Hispanic, 3% multiracial, 0% Pacific Islander, 64% white, 3% international; 77% from in state; 57% live on campus; 4% of students in fraternities, 9% in sororities
Most popular majors: 11% Accounting, 7% Business Administration and Management, General, 10% Elementary Education and Teaching, 4% Finance, General, 9% Psychology, General
Expenses: 2015-2016: $38,360; room/board: $13,770
Financial aid: (609) 896-5360; 73% of undergrads determined to have financial need; average aid package $25,946

Rowan University

Glassboro NJ
(856) 256-4200
U.S. News ranking: Reg. U. (N), No. 19
Website: www.rowan.edu
Admissions email: admissions@rowan.edu
Public; founded 1923
Freshman admissions: selective; 2014-2015: 10,078 applied, 6,600 accepted. Either SAT or ACT required. SAT 25/75 percentile: 1010-1220. High school rank: N/A
Early decision deadline: N/A, notification date: N/A
Early action deadline: N/A, notification date: N/A
Application deadline (fall): 3/1
Undergraduate student body: 10,499 full time, 1,523 part time; 53% male, 47% female; 0% American Indian, 6% Asian, 9% black, 9% Hispanic, 3% multiracial, 0% Pacific Islander, 69% white, 1% international; 95% from in state; 36% live on campus; 5% of students in fraternities, 4% in sororities
Most popular majors: 13% Business, Management, Marketing, and Related Support Services, 10% Communication, Journalism, and Related Programs, 14% Education, 7% Homeland Security, Law Enforcement, Firefighting and Related Protective Services, 8% Psychology
Expenses: 2015-2016: $12,864 in state, $20,978 out of state; room/board: $11,646
Financial aid: (856) 256-4250; 64% of undergrads determined to have financial need; average aid package $8,771

Rutgers, The State University of New Jersey–Camden

Camden NJ
(856) 225-6104
U.S. News ranking: Reg. U. (N), No. 36
Website: www.rutgers.edu/
Admissions email: camden@ugadm.rutgers.edu
Public; founded 1927
Freshman admissions: selective; 2014-2015: 6,550 applied, 3,955 accepted. Either SAT or ACT required. SAT 25/75 percentile: 920-1130. High school rank: 17% in top tenth, 45% in top quarter, 81% in top half
Early decision deadline: N/A, notification date: N/A
Early action deadline: N/A, notification date: N/A
Application deadline (fall): rolling
Undergraduate student body: 3,990 full time, 867 part time; 44% male, 56% female; 0% American Indian, 9% Asian, 17% black, 12% Hispanic, 4% multiracial, 0% Pacific Islander, 55% white, 1% international; 98% from in state; 9% live on campus; N/A of students in fraternities, N/A in sororities
Most popular majors: 8% Accounting, 7% Biology/Biological Sciences, General, 9% Business Administration and Management, General, 9% Criminal Justice/Safety Studies, 14% Psychology, General
Expenses: 2015-2016: $14,000 in state, $28,890 out of state; room/board: $11,710
Financial aid: (856) 225-6039; 78% of undergrads determined to have financial need; average aid package $12,618

Rutgers, The State University of New Jersey–Newark

Newark NJ
(973) 353-5205
U.S. News ranking: Nat. U., No. 140
Website: rutgers-newark.rutgers.edu
Admissions email: admissions@ugadm.rutgers.edu
Public; founded 1908
Freshman admissions: selective; 2014-2015: 10,332 applied, 6,483 accepted. Either SAT or ACT required. SAT 25/75 percentile: 940-1130. High school rank: 20% in top tenth, 51% in top quarter, 83% in top half
Early decision deadline: N/A, notification date: N/A
Early action deadline: N/A, notification date: N/A
Application deadline (fall): rolling
Undergraduate student body: 5,943 full time, 1,465 part time; 49% male, 51% female; 0% American Indian, 21% Asian, 19% black, 26% Hispanic, 3% multiracial, 0% Pacific Islander, 26% white, 3% international; 98% from in state; 9% live on campus; N/A of students in fraternities, N/A in sororities
Most popular majors: 14% Accounting, 12% Criminal Justice/Safety Studies, 9% Finance, General, 11% Psychology, General, 10% Registered Nursing/Registered Nurse
Expenses: 2015-2016: $13,597 in state, $28,987 out of state; room/board: $12,841
Financial aid: (973) 353-5151; 83% of undergrads determined to have financial need; average aid package $13,705

Rutgers, The State University of New Jersey–New Brunswick

Piscataway NJ
(732) 932-4636
U.S. News ranking: Nat. U., No. 72
Website: www.rutgers.edu
Admissions email: admissions@ugadm.rutgers.edu
Public; founded 1766
Freshman admissions: more selective; 2014-2015: 31,941 applied, 19,324 accepted. Either SAT or ACT required. SAT 25/75 percentile: 1090-1340. High school rank: 39% in top tenth, 74% in top quarter, 96% in top half
Early decision deadline: N/A, notification date: N/A
Early action deadline: N/A, notification date: N/A
Application deadline (fall): rolling
Undergraduate student body: 32,411 full time, 2,133 part time; 50% male, 50% female; 0% American Indian, 26% Asian, 7% black, 13% Hispanic, 3% multiracial, 0% Pacific Islander, 43% white, 6% international; 94% from in state; 48% live on campus; N/A of students in fraternities, N/A in sororities
Most popular majors: 9% Biological and Biomedical Sciences, 13% Business, Management, Marketing, and Related Support Services, 9% Communication, Journalism, and Related Programs, 9% Psychology, 11% Social Sciences
Expenses: 2015-2016: $14,131 in state, $29,521 out of state; room/board: $12,054
Financial aid: (732) 932-7057; 55% of undergrads determined to have financial need; average aid package $13,376

Seton Hall University

South Orange NJ
(973) 761-9332
U.S. News ranking: Nat. U., No. 123
Website: www.shu.edu
Admissions email: thehall@shu.edu
Private; founded 1856
Affiliation: Roman Catholic
Freshman admissions: more selective; 2014-2015: 12,808 applied, 9,675 accepted. Either SAT or ACT required. SAT 25/75 percentile: 1040-1220. High school rank: 38% in top tenth, 69% in top quarter, 90% in top half
Early decision deadline: N/A, notification date: N/A
Early action deadline: 11/15, notification date: 12/30
Application deadline (fall): rolling
Undergraduate student body: 5,348 full time, 469 part time; 42% male, 58% female; 0% American Indian, 9% Asian, 12% black, 18% Hispanic, 3% multiracial, 0% Pacific Islander, 50% white, 2% international; 76% from in

state; 42% live on campus; 9% of students in fraternities, 11% in sororities
Most popular majors: 8% Biology/ Biological Sciences, General, 6% Finance, General, 6% Humanities/Humanistic Studies, 7% International Relations and Affairs, 19% Registered Nursing/ Registered Nurse
Expenses: 2014-2015: $36,926; room/board: $13,742
Financial aid: (973) 761-9350

Stevens Institute of Technology
Hoboken NJ
(201) 216-5194
U.S. News ranking: Nat. U., No. 75
Website: www.stevens.edu
Admissions email: admissions@stevens.edu
Private; founded 1870
Freshman admissions: more selective; 2014-2015: 5,190 applied, 2,272 accepted. Either SAT or ACT required. SAT 25/75 percentile: 1255-1425. High school rank: 70% in top tenth, 91% in top quarter, 100% in top half
Early decision deadline: 11/15, notification date: 12/15
Early action deadline: N/A, notification date: N/A
Application deadline (fall): 2/1
Undergraduate student body: 2,842 full time, 50 part time; 71% male, 29% female; 0% American Indian, 10% Asian, 2% black, 9% Hispanic, N/A multiracial, N/A Pacific Islander, 64% white, 4% international; 61% from in state; 74% live on campus; 25% of students in fraternities, 25% in sororities
Most popular majors: Information not available
Expenses: 2015-2016: $47,190; room/board: $14,124
Financial aid: (201) 216-5555

Stockton University
Galloway NJ
(609) 652-4261
U.S. News ranking: Reg. U. (N), No. 53
Website: www.stockton.edu
Admissions email: admissions@stockton.edu
Public; founded 1969
Freshman admissions: selective; 2014-2015: 5,229 applied, 3,386 accepted. Either SAT or ACT required. SAT 25/75 percentile: 980-1200. High school rank: 23% in top tenth, 54% in top quarter, 91% in top half
Early decision deadline: N/A, notification date: N/A
Early action deadline: N/A, notification date: N/A
Application deadline (fall): 5/1
Undergraduate student body: 7,170 full time, 544 part time; 41% male, 59% female; 0% American Indian, 5% Asian, 6% black, 10% Hispanic, 3% multiracial, 0% Pacific Islander, 73% white, 0% international; 99% from in state; 38% live on campus; 6% of students in fraternities, 5% in sororities
Most popular majors: 6% Audiology/Audiologist and Speech-Language Pathology/ Pathologist, 9% Biology/Biological Sciences, General, 15% Business Administration and Management, General, 9% Criminology, 12% Psychology, General
Expenses: 2014-2015: $12,568 in state, $19,089 out of state; room/board: $11,164
Financial aid: (609) 652-4201; 71% of undergrads determined to have financial need; average aid package $15,871

St. Peter's University
Jersey City NJ
(201) 761-7100
U.S. News ranking: Reg. U. (N), No. 92
Website: www.spc.edu
Admissions email: admissions@spc.edu
Private; founded 1872
Affiliation: Roman Catholic (Jesuit)
Freshman admissions: less selective; 2014-2015: 5,993 applied, 3,410 accepted. Either SAT or ACT required. SAT 25/75 percentile: 810-990. High school rank: 12% in top tenth, 39% in top quarter, 72% in top half
Early decision deadline: N/A, notification date: N/A
Early action deadline: 12/1, notification date: 1/31
Application deadline (fall): rolling
Undergraduate student body: 2,165 full time, 341 part time; 38% male, 62% female; 0% American Indian, 8% Asian, 30% black, 34% Hispanic, 1% multiracial, 1% Pacific Islander, 22% white, 2% international; 88% from in state; 31% live on campus; N/A of students in fraternities, N/A in sororities
Most popular majors: 8% Biological and Biomedical Sciences, 22% Business, Management, Marketing, and Related Support Services, 9% Health Professions and Related Programs, 10% Homeland Security, Law Enforcement, Firefighting and Related Protective Services, 11% Social Sciences
Expenses: 2015-2016: $34,197; room/board: $14,468
Financial aid: (201) 915-4929; 90% of undergrads determined to have financial need; average aid package $27,243

Thomas Edison State College[1]
Trenton NJ
(888) 442-8372
U.S. News ranking: Reg. U. (N), unranked
Website: www.tesc.edu
Admissions email: admissions@tesc.edu
Public; founded 1972
Application deadline (fall): rolling
Undergraduate student body: N/A full time, N/A part time
Expenses: 2014-2015: $5,996 in state, $8,772 out of state; room/ board: N/A
Financial aid: (609) 633-9658

William Paterson University of New Jersey
Wayne NJ
(973) 720-2125
U.S. News ranking: Reg. U. (N), No. 104
Website: www.wpunj.edu/
Admissions email: admissions@wpunj.edu
Public; founded 1855
Freshman admissions: selective; 2014-2015: 9,634 applied, 7,187 accepted. Either SAT or ACT required. SAT 25/75 percentile: 890-1070. High school rank: N/A
Early decision deadline: N/A, notification date: N/A
Early action deadline: 12/1, notification date: 1/15
Application deadline (fall): 6/1
Undergraduate student body: 7,883 full time, 1,736 part time; 45% male, 55% female; 0% American Indian, 7% Asian, 15% black, 26% Hispanic, 3% multiracial, 0% Pacific Islander, 45% white, 1% international; 98% from in state; 23% live on campus; 2% of students in fraternities, 2% in sororities
Most popular majors: 18% Business, Management, Marketing, and Related Support Services, 13% Communication, Journalism, and Related Programs, 9% Education, 11% Psychology, 12% Social Sciences
Expenses: 2015-2016: $12,365 in state, $20,125 out of state; room/board: $10,885
Financial aid: (973) 720-2202; 74% of undergrads determined to have financial need; average aid package $10,356

NEW MEXICO

Eastern New Mexico University[1]
Portales NM
(505) 562-2178
U.S. News ranking: Reg. U. (W), second tier
Website: www.enmu.edu
Admissions email: admissions.office@enmu.edu
Public
Application deadline (fall): N/A
Undergraduate student body: N/A full time, N/A part time
Expenses: 2014-2015: $4,858 in state, $10,633 out of state; room/ board: $6,452
Financial aid: (800) 367-3668

New Mexico Highlands University
Las Vegas NM
(505) 454-3439
U.S. News ranking: Reg. U. (W), unranked
Website: www.nmhu.edu
Admissions email: admissions@nmhu.edu
Public; founded 1893
Freshman admissions: N/A; 2014-2015: 1,389 applied, 1,389 accepted. Neither SAT nor ACT required. ACT 25/75 percentile: 15-20. High school rank: 3% in top tenth, 13% in top quarter, 42% in top half
Early decision deadline: N/A, notification date: N/A
Early action deadline: N/A, notification date: N/A
Application deadline (fall): rolling
Undergraduate student body: 1,510 full time, 765 part time; 54% male, 46% female; 7% American Indian, 1% Asian, 5% black, 58% Hispanic, 1% multiracial, 1% Pacific Islander, 19% white, 5% international; 85% from in state; 24% live on campus; 1% of students in fraternities, 1% in sororities
Most popular majors: 17% Business, Management, Marketing, and Related Support Services, 40% Education, 28% Health Professions and Related Programs, 7% Homeland Security, Law Enforcement, Firefighting and Related Protective Services, 6% Psychology
Expenses: 2015-2016: $4,800 in state, $7,530 out of state; room/ board: $5,982
Financial aid: (505) 454-3430; 77% of undergrads determined to have financial need; average aid package $1,847

New Mexico Institute of Mining and Technology
Socorro NM
(505) 835-5424
U.S. News ranking: Reg. U. (W), No. 25
Website: www.nmt.edu
Admissions email: admission@admin.nmt.edu
Public; founded 1889
Freshman admissions: more selective; 2014-2015: 1,003 applied, 365 accepted. Either SAT or ACT required. ACT 25/75 percentile: 23-29. High school rank: 36% in top tenth, 64% in top quarter, 86% in top half
Early decision deadline: N/A, notification date: N/A
Early action deadline: N/A, notification date: N/A
Application deadline (fall): 8/1
Undergraduate student body: 1,443 full time, 190 part time; 70% male, 30% female; 3% American Indian, 3% Asian, 2% black, 28% Hispanic, 4% multiracial, 0% Pacific Islander, 56% white, 4% international; 84% from in state; N/A live on campus; N/A of students in fraternities, N/A in sororities
Most popular majors: 11% Chemical Engineering, 7% Civil Engineering, General, 7% Electrical and Electronics Engineering, 20% Mechanical Engineering, 12% Petroleum Engineering
Expenses: 2015-2016: $6,613 in state, $19,137 out of state; room/ board: $7,586
Financial aid: (505) 835-5333; 53% of undergrads determined to have financial need; average aid package $11,495

New Mexico State University
Las Cruces NM
(505) 646-3121
U.S. News ranking: Nat. U., No. 199
Website: www.nmsu.edu
Admissions email: admissions@nmsu.edu
Public; founded 1888
Freshman admissions: selective; 2014-2015: 7,101 applied, 4,942 accepted. Either SAT or ACT required. ACT 25/75 percentile: 18-24. High school rank: 19% in top tenth, 46% in top quarter, 77% in top half
Early decision deadline: N/A, notification date: N/A
Early action deadline: N/A, notification date: N/A
Application deadline (fall): rolling
Undergraduate student body: 10,668 full time, 2,116 part time; 47% male, 53% female; 2% American Indian, 1% Asian, 3% black, 54% Hispanic, 2% multiracial, 0% Pacific Islander, 31% white, 4% international; 75% from in state; 19% live on campus; 2% of students in fraternities, 2% in sororities
Most popular majors: 3% Biology/ Biological Sciences, General, 7% Criminal Justice/Safety Studies, 6% Liberal Arts and Sciences/ Liberal Studies, 4% Psychology, General, 5% Registered Nursing/ Registered Nurse
Expenses: 2015-2016: $6,729 in state, $21,234 out of state; room/ board: $7,572
Financial aid: (505) 646-4105; 68% of undergrads determined to have financial need; average aid package $12,505

Northern New Mexico University[1]
Espanola NM
(505) 747-2111
U.S. News ranking: Reg. Coll. (W), unranked
Website: nnmc.edu
Admissions email: N/A
Public
Application deadline (fall): N/A
Undergraduate student body: N/A full time, N/A part time
Expenses: 2014-2015: $3,961 in state, $11,523 out of state; room/ board: $7,920
Financial aid: (505) 747-2128

Santa Fe University of Art and Design
Santa Fe NM
(505) 473-6937
U.S. News ranking: Arts, unranked
Website: www.santafeuniversity.edu
Admissions email: admissions@santafeuniversity.edu
For-profit; founded 1859
Freshman admissions: N/A; 2014-2015: 608 applied, 608 accepted. Neither SAT nor ACT required. ACT 25/75 percentile: N/A. High school rank: N/A
Early decision deadline: N/A, notification date: N/A
Early action deadline: N/A, notification date: N/A
Application deadline (fall): rolling
Undergraduate student body: 918 full time, 32 part time; 46% male, 54% female; 3% American Indian, 2% Asian, 7% black, 28% Hispanic, 8% multiracial, 2% Pacific Islander, 45% white, 5% international; 22% from in state; N/A live on campus; 0% of students in fraternities, 0% in sororities
Most popular majors: 21% Cinematography and Film/Video Production, 12% Creative Writing, 23% Drama and Dramatics/ Theatre Arts, General, 14% Graphic Design, 11% Photography
Expenses: 2015-2016: $31,346; room/board: $8,946
Financial aid: (505) 473-6454

St. John's College
Santa Fe NM
(505) 984-6060
U.S. News ranking: Nat. Lib. Arts, No. 100
Website: www.sjc.edu/admissions-and-aid

Admissions email: santafe.admissions@sjc.edu
Private; founded 1964
Freshman admissions: more selective; 2014-2015: 198 applied, 185 accepted. Neither SAT nor ACT required. SAT 25/75 percentile: 1210-1450. High school rank: 32% in top tenth, 46% in top quarter, 86% in top half
Early decision deadline: N/A, notification date: N/A
Early action deadline: 1/15, notification date: 2/15
Application deadline (fall): rolling
Undergraduate student body: 337 full time, 3 part time; 56% male, 44% female; 0% American Indian, 2% Asian, 1% black, 10% Hispanic, 7% multiracial, 0% Pacific Islander, 61% white, 16% international; 9% from in state; 85% live on campus; 0% of students in fraternities, 0% in sororities
Most popular majors: 100% Liberal Arts and Sciences/Liberal Studies
Expenses: 2015-2016: $49,194; room/board: $10,890
Financial aid: (505) 984-6073; 88% of undergrads determined to have financial need; average aid package $40,191

University of New Mexico

Albuquerque NM
(505) 277-8900
U.S. News ranking: Nat. U., No. 180
Website: www.unm.edu
Admissions email: apply@unm.edu
Public; founded 1889
Freshman admissions: selective; 2014-2015: 12,574 applied, 5,796 accepted. Either SAT or ACT required. ACT 25/75 percentile: 20-25. High school rank: N/A
Early decision deadline: N/A, notification date: N/A
Early action deadline: N/A, notification date: N/A
Application deadline (fall): rolling
Undergraduate student body: 16,384 full time, 4,473 part time; 45% male, 55% female; 6% American Indian, 3% Asian, 3% black, 46% Hispanic, 3% multiracial, 0% Pacific Islander, 36% white, 1% international; 90% from in state; 8% live on campus; 5% of students in fraternities, 6% in sororities
Most popular majors: 8% Biological and Biomedical Sciences, 14% Business, Management, Marketing, and Related Support Services, 9% Education, 11% Psychology, 8% Social Sciences
Expenses: 2014-2015: $6,846 in state, $20,664 out of state; room/board: $8,580
Financial aid: (505) 277-3012

University of the Southwest[1]

Hobbs NM
(575) 392-6563
U.S. News ranking: Reg. Coll. (W), second tier
Website: www.usw.edu
Admissions email: admissions@usw.edu
Private; founded 1962
Application deadline (fall): rolling
Undergraduate student body: N/A full time, N/A part time
Expenses: 2014-2015: $14,616; room/board: $6,960
Financial aid: (505) 392-6561

Western New Mexico University[1]

Silver City NM
(505) 538-6127
U.S. News ranking: Reg. U. (W), unranked
Website: www.wnmu.edu
Admissions email: admissions@wnmu.edu
Public; founded 1893
Application deadline (fall): 8/1
Undergraduate student body: N/A full time, N/A part time
Expenses: 2014-2015: $5,346 in state, $13,184 out of state; room/board: $10,256
Financial aid: (575) 538-6173

NEW YORK

Adelphi University

Garden City NY
(800) 233-5744
U.S. News ranking: Nat. U., No. 153
Website: www.adelphi.edu
Admissions email: admissions@adelphi.edu
Private; founded 1896
Freshman admissions: selective; 2014-2015: 8,806 applied, 6,377 accepted. Neither SAT nor ACT required. SAT 25/75 percentile: 1010-1220. High school rank: 29% in top tenth, 62% in top quarter, 88% in top half
Early decision deadline: N/A, notification date: N/A
Early action deadline: 12/1, notification date: 12/31
Application deadline (fall): rolling
Undergraduate student body: 4,589 full time, 482 part time; 30% male, 70% female; 0% American Indian, 8% Asian, 10% black, 14% Hispanic, 2% multiracial, 0% Pacific Islander, 54% white, 4% international; 93% from in state; 23% live on campus; 15% of students in fraternities, 10% in sororities
Most popular majors: 15% Business, Management, Marketing, and Related Support Services, 11% Education, 28% Health Professions and Related Programs, 6% Psychology, 7% Social Sciences
Expenses: 2015-2016: $34,034; room/board: $14,210
Financial aid: (516) 877-3365; 72% of undergrads determined to have financial need; average aid package $20,900

Alfred University

Alfred NY
(800) 541-9229
U.S. News ranking: Reg. U. (N), No. 47
Website: www.alfred.edu
Admissions email: admissions@alfred.edu
Private; founded 1836
Freshman admissions: selective; 2014-2015: 3,482 applied, 2,418 accepted. Either SAT or ACT required. SAT 25/75 percentile: 950-1170. High school rank: 12% in top tenth, 41% in top quarter, 78% in top half
Early decision deadline: 12/1, notification date: 12/15
Early action deadline: N/A, notification date: N/A
Application deadline (fall): rolling
Undergraduate student body: 1,840 full time, 80 part time; 51% male, 49% female; 0% American Indian, 2% Asian, 8% black, 7% Hispanic, 3% multiracial, 0% Pacific Islander, 66% white, 3% international; 78% from in state; 73% live on campus; 0% of students in fraternities, 0% in sororities
Most popular majors: 5% Biological and Biomedical Sciences, 11% Business, Management, Marketing, and Related Support Services, 16% Engineering, 8% Psychology, 32% Visual and Performing Arts
Expenses: 2015-2016: $30,200; room/board: $11,960
Financial aid: (607) 871-2159; 87% of undergrads determined to have financial need; average aid package $28,564

Bard College

Annandale on Hudson NY
(845) 758-7472
U.S. News ranking: Nat. Lib. Arts, No. 45
Website: www.bard.edu
Admissions email: admission@bard.edu
Private; founded 1860
Freshman admissions: more selective; 2014-2015: 6,960 applied, 3,105 accepted. Neither SAT nor ACT required. SAT 25/75 percentile: 1170-1390. High school rank: 60% in top tenth, 95% in top quarter, 99% in top half
Early decision deadline: N/A, notification date: N/A
Early action deadline: 11/1, notification date: 1/1
Application deadline (fall): 1/1
Undergraduate student body: 1,987 full time, 72 part time; 45% male, 55% female; 1% American Indian, 6% Asian, 7% black, 1% Hispanic, 0% multiracial, 0% Pacific Islander, 63% white, 11% international; 33% from in state; 73% live on campus; 0% of students in fraternities, 0% in sororities
Most popular majors: 14% English Language and Literature/Letters, 5% Foreign Languages, Literatures, and Linguistics, 5% Philosophy and Religious Studies, 16% Social Sciences, 31% Visual and Performing Arts
Expenses: 2015-2016: $49,906; room/board: $14,118
Financial aid: (845) 758-7525; 70% of undergrads determined to have financial need; average aid package $40,938

Barnard College

New York NY
(212) 854-2014
U.S. News ranking: Nat. Lib. Arts, No. 29
Website: www.barnard.edu
Admissions email: admissions@barnard.edu
Private; founded 1889
Freshman admissions: most selective; 2014-2015: 5,676 applied, 1,349 accepted. Either SAT or ACT required. SAT 25/75 percentile: 1250-1440. High school rank: 82% in top tenth, 97% in top quarter, 100% in top half
Early decision deadline: 11/1, notification date: 12/15
Early action deadline: N/A, notification date: N/A
Application deadline (fall): 1/1
Undergraduate student body: 2,537 full time, 36 part time; 0% male, 100% female; 0% American Indian, 14% Asian, 7% black, 11% Hispanic, 5% multiracial, 0% Pacific Islander, 55% white, 7% international; 37% from in state; 91% live on campus; N/A of students in fraternities, N/A in sororities
Most popular majors: 10% Biological and Biomedical Sciences, 9% English Language and Literature/Letters, 10% Psychology, 30% Social Sciences, 12% Visual and Performing Arts
Expenses: 2015-2016: $47,631; room/board: $15,110
Financial aid: (212) 854-2154; 41% of undergrads determined to have financial need; average aid package $44,040

Berkeley College

New York NY
(212) 986-4343
U.S. News ranking: Business, unranked
Website: www.berkeleycollege.edu
Admissions email: admissions@berkeleycollege.edu
For-profit; founded 1931
Freshman admissions: less selective; 2014-2015: 889 applied, 810 accepted. Neither SAT nor ACT required. ACT 25/75 percentile: N/A. High school rank: N/A
Early decision deadline: N/A, notification date: N/A
Early action deadline: N/A, notification date: N/A
Application deadline (fall): rolling
Undergraduate student body: 3,946 full time, 533 part time; 36% male, 64% female; 0% American Indian, 3% Asian, 27% black, 21% Hispanic, 0% multiracial, 0% Pacific Islander, 8% white, 17% international
Most popular majors: 26% Business Administration and Management, General, 16% Criminal Justice/Law Enforcement Administration, 17% Fashion Merchandising, 10% Health/Health Care Administration/Management, 10% International Business/Trade/Commerce
Expenses: 2015-2016: $24,300; room/board: $12,600
Financial aid: (212) 986-4343

Binghamton University–SUNY

Binghamton NY
(607) 777-2171
U.S. News ranking: Nat. U., No. 89
Website: www.binghamton.edu
Admissions email: admit@binghamton.edu
Public; founded 1946
Freshman admissions: more selective; 2014-2015: 28,518 applied, 12,564 accepted. Either SAT or ACT required. SAT 25/75 percentile: 1210-1370. High school rank: 48% in top tenth, 83% in top quarter, 97% in top half
Early decision deadline: N/A, notification date: N/A
Early action deadline: 11/15, notification date: 1/15
Application deadline (fall): rolling
Undergraduate student body: 12,908 full time, 504 part time; 52% male, 48% female; 0% American Indian, 14% Asian, 5% black, 10% Hispanic, 2% multiracial, 0% Pacific Islander, 55% white, 10% international; 90% from in state; 52% live on campus; 12% of students in fraternities, 10% in sororities
Most popular majors: 8% Biology/Biological Sciences, General, 13% Business Administration and Management, General, 10% Engineering, General, 7% English Language and Literature, General, 12% Psychology, General
Expenses: 2015-2016: $9,044 in state, $22,164 out of state; room/board: $13,198
Financial aid: (607) 777-2428; 49% of undergrads determined to have financial need; average aid package $12,449

Boricua College[1]

New York NY
(212) 694-1000
U.S. News ranking: Reg. Coll. (N), unranked
Website: www.boricuacollege.edu/
Admissions email: acruz@boricuacollege.edu
Private; founded 1973
Application deadline (fall): rolling
Undergraduate student body: N/A full time, N/A part time
Expenses: 2014-2015: $10,625; room/board: $5,750
Financial aid: (212) 694-1000

Briarcliffe College[1]

Bethpage NY
(888) 348-4999
U.S. News ranking: Reg. Coll. (N), unranked
Website: www.briarcliffe.edu
Admissions email: N/A
For-profit
Application deadline (fall): N/A
Undergraduate student body: N/A full time, N/A part time
Expenses: 2014-2015: $14,677; room/board: $7,992
Financial aid: N/A

Canisius College

Buffalo NY
(800) 843-1517
U.S. News ranking: Reg. U. (N), No. 34
Website: www.canisius.edu
Admissions email: admissions@canisius.edu
Private; founded 1870
Affiliation: Roman Catholic
Freshman admissions: selective; 2014-2015: 3,667 applied, 2,942 accepted. Either SAT or ACT required. SAT 25/75 percentile: 970-1180. High school rank: 20% in top tenth, 52% in top quarter, 84% in top half
Early decision deadline: N/A, notification date: N/A
Early action deadline: N/A, notification date: N/A
Application deadline (fall): rolling
Undergraduate student body: 2,725 full time, 143 part time; 47% male, 53% female; 0% American Indian, 2% Asian, 7% black, 5% Hispanic, 2% multiracial, 0% Pacific Islander, 74% white, 4% international; 91% from in state; 46% live on campus; 1% of students in fraternities, 1% in sororities

Most popular majors: 10% Biological and Biomedical Sciences, 31% Business, Management, Marketing, and Related Support Services, 9% Communication, Journalism, and Related Programs, 9% Psychology, 13% Social Sciences
Expenses: 2015-2016: $34,690; room/board: $12,766
Financial aid: (716) 888-2300; 75% of undergrads determined to have financial need; average aid package $29,284

Cazenovia College
Cazenovia NY
(800) 654-3210
U.S. News ranking: Reg. Coll. (N), No. 24
Website: www.cazenovia.edu
Admissions email: admission@cazenovia.edu
Private; founded 1824
Freshman admissions: less selective; 2014-2015: 2,382 applied, 1,815 accepted. Neither SAT nor ACT required. SAT 25/75 percentile: 830-1060. High school rank: 12% in top tenth, 34% in top quarter, 68% in top half
Early decision deadline: N/A, notification date: N/A
Early action deadline: N/A, notification date: N/A
Application deadline (fall): rolling
Undergraduate student body: 963 full time, 128 part time; 28% male, 72% female; 1% American Indian, 1% Asian, 7% black, 6% Hispanic, 4% multiracial, 0% Pacific Islander, 67% white, 0% international; 85% from in state; 94% live on campus; N/A of students in fraternities, N/A in sororities
Most popular majors: 21% Business, Management, Marketing, and Related Support Services, 21% Public Administration and Social Service Professions, 27% Visual and Performing Arts
Expenses: 2015-2016: $31,754; room/board: $12,826
Financial aid: (315) 655-7887; 91% of undergrads determined to have financial need; average aid package $29,600

Clarkson University
Potsdam NY
(800) 527-6577
U.S. News ranking: Nat. U., No. 115
Website: www.clarkson.edu
Admissions email: admission@clarkson.edu
Private; founded 1896
Freshman admissions: more selective; 2014-2015: 7,401 applied, 4,599 accepted. Either SAT or ACT required. SAT 25/75 percentile: 1090-1290. High school rank: 41% in top tenth, 76% in top quarter, 96% in top half
Early decision deadline: 12/1, notification date: 1/1
Early action deadline: N/A, notification date: N/A
Application deadline (fall): 1/15
Undergraduate student body: 3,166 full time, 81 part time; 70% male, 30% female; 0% American Indian, 3% Asian, 2% black, 5% Hispanic, 2% multiracial, 0% Pacific Islander, 83% white, 2% international; 75% from in state; 83% live on campus; 14% of students in fraternities, 14% in sororities
Most popular majors: 8% Biology/Biological Sciences, General, 21% Business Administration and Management, General, 55% Engineering, General, 4% Psychology, General
Expenses: 2015-2016: $44,630; room/board: $14,132
Financial aid: (315) 268-6479; 84% of undergrads determined to have financial need; average aid package $40,409

Colgate University
Hamilton NY
(315) 228-7401
U.S. News ranking: Nat. Lib. Arts, No. 19
Website: www.colgate.edu
Admissions email: admission@mail.colgate.edu
Private; founded 1819
Freshman admissions: more selective; 2014-2015: 8,717 applied, 2,287 accepted. Either SAT or ACT required. SAT 25/75 percentile: 1280-1470. High school rank: 72% in top tenth, 92% in top quarter, 98% in top half
Early decision deadline: 11/15, notification date: 12/15
Early action deadline: N/A, notification date: N/A
Application deadline (fall): 1/15
Undergraduate student body: 2,863 full time, 12 part time; 46% male, 54% female; 0% American Indian, 4% Asian, 4% black, 8% Hispanic, 4% multiracial, 0% Pacific Islander, 67% white, 9% international; 27% from in state; 90% live on campus; 13% of students in fraternities, 19% in sororities
Most popular majors: 11% Economics, General, 10% English Language and Literature, General, 9% History, General, 6% International Relations and Affairs, 9% Political Science and Government, General
Expenses: 2015-2016: $49,970; room/board: $12,570
Financial aid: (315) 228-7431; 35% of undergrads determined to have financial need; average aid package $45,594

College at Brockport–SUNY
Brockport NY
(585) 395-2751
U.S. News ranking: Reg. U. (N), No. 58
Website: www.brockport.edu
Admissions email: admit@brockport.edu
Public; founded 1835
Freshman admissions: selective; 2014-2015: 9,769 applied, 4,782 accepted. Either SAT or ACT required. SAT 25/75 percentile: 950-1150. High school rank: 14% in top tenth, 44% in top quarter, 83% in top half
Early decision deadline: N/A, notification date: N/A
Early action deadline: N/A, notification date: N/A
Application deadline (fall): 8/1
Undergraduate student body: 6,304 full time, 736 part time; 45% male, 55% female; 0% American Indian, 2% Asian, 9% black, 5% Hispanic, 2% multiracial, 0% Pacific Islander, 72% white, 2% international; 1% from in state; 38% live on campus; 1% of students in fraternities, 2% in sororities
Most popular majors: 15% Business, Management, Marketing, and Related Support Services, 18% Health Professions and Related Programs, 8% Homeland Security, Law Enforcement, Firefighting and Related Protective Services, 9% Parks, Recreation, Leisure, and Fitness Studies, 7% Psychology
Expenses: 2015-2016: $7,904 in state, $17,254 out of state; room/board: $11,540
Financial aid: (585) 395-2501; 70% of undergrads determined to have financial need; average aid package $10,388

College of Mount St. Vincent
Riverdale NY
(718) 405-3267
U.S. News ranking: Reg. U. (N), No. 112
Website: www.mountsaintvincent.edu
Admissions email: admissions.office@mountsaintvincent.edu
Private; founded 1847
Affiliation: Roman Catholic
Freshman admissions: less selective; 2014-2015: 2,590 applied, 2,266 accepted. Either SAT or ACT required. SAT 25/75 percentile: 840-1010. High school rank: 2% in top tenth, 9% in top quarter, 39% in top half
Early decision deadline: N/A, notification date: N/A
Early action deadline: 11/1, notification date: 12/1
Application deadline (fall): rolling
Undergraduate student body: 1,523 full time, 106 part time; 31% male, 69% female; 0% American Indian, 10% Asian, 15% black, 35% Hispanic, 6% multiracial, 0% Pacific Islander, 28% white, 2% international; 86% from in state; 53% live on campus; 0% of students in fraternities, 0% in sororities
Most popular majors: 10% Business/Commerce, General, 7% Psychology, General, 51% Registered Nursing/Registered Nurse, 8% Sociology, 8% Speech Communication and Rhetoric
Expenses: 2015-2016: $22,490; room/board: $8,040
Financial aid: (718) 405-3290; 87% of undergrads determined to have financial need; average aid package $19,829

College of New Rochelle
New Rochelle NY
(800) 933-5923
U.S. News ranking: Reg. U. (N), No. 116
Website: www.cnr.edu
Admissions email: admission@cnr.edu
Private; founded 1904
Affiliation: Roman Catholic
Freshman admissions: selective; 2014-2015: 2,312 applied, 658 accepted. Either SAT or ACT required. SAT 25/75 percentile: 880-1030. High school rank: N/A
Early decision deadline: N/A, notification date: N/A
Early action deadline: N/A, notification date: N/A
Application deadline (fall): rolling
Undergraduate student body: 473 full time, 41 part time; 7% male, 93% female; 1% American Indian, 7% Asian, 36% black, 30% Hispanic, 1% multiracial, 1% Pacific Islander, 15% white, 1% international; 91% from in state; 38% live on campus; 0% of students in fraternities, 0% in sororities
Most popular majors: 8% Biology/Biological Sciences, General, 6% English Language and Literature, General, 14% Psychology, General, 50% Registered Nursing/Registered Nurse, 7% Social Work
Expenses: 2015-2016: $33,600; room/board: $12,700
Financial aid: (914) 654-5224; 95% of undergrads determined to have financial need; average aid package $22,358

College of St. Rose
Albany NY
(518) 454-5150
U.S. News ranking: Reg. U. (N), No. 53
Website: www.strose.edu
Admissions email: admit@strose.edu
Private; founded 1920
Freshman admissions: selective; 2014-2015: 5,525 applied, 4,215 accepted. Neither SAT nor ACT required. SAT 25/75 percentile: 940-1150. High school rank: 11% in top tenth, 34% in top quarter, 73% in top half
Early decision deadline: N/A, notification date: N/A
Early action deadline: 12/1, notification date: 12/15
Application deadline (fall): 5/1
Undergraduate student body: 2,533 full time, 240 part time; 34% male, 66% female; 0% American Indian, 2% Asian, 8% black, 6% Hispanic, 6% multiracial, 0% Pacific Islander, 72% white, 1% international; 88% from in state; 46% live on campus; 0% of students in fraternities, 0% in sororities
Most popular majors: 16% Business, Management, Marketing, and Related Support Services, 9% Communication, Journalism, and Related Programs, 30% Education, 6% Psychology, 9% Visual and Performing Arts
Expenses: 2015-2016: $29,826; room/board: $11,878
Financial aid: (518) 458-5424; 84% of undergrads determined to have financial need; average aid package $18,419

Columbia University
New York NY
(212) 854-2522
U.S. News ranking: Nat. U., No. 4
Website: www.columbia.edu
Admissions email: ugrad-ask@columbia.edu
Private; founded 1754
Freshman admissions: most selective; 2014-2015: 32,967 applied, 2,291 accepted. Either SAT or ACT required. SAT 25/75 percentile: 1390-1570. High school rank: 93% in top tenth, 99% in top quarter, 100% in top half
Early decision deadline: 11/1, notification date: 12/15
Early action deadline: N/A, notification date: N/A
Application deadline (fall): 1/1
Undergraduate student body: 6,170 full time, N/A part time; 52% male, 48% female; 2% American Indian, 22% Asian, 12% black, 12% Hispanic, N/A multiracial, N/A Pacific Islander, 35% white, 13% international; 24% from in state; 94% live on campus; 19% of students in fraternities, 9% in sororities
Most popular majors: 10% Biological and Biomedical Sciences, 22% Engineering, 5% Mathematics and Statistics, 5% Psychology, 20% Social Sciences
Expenses: 2014-2015: $51,008; room/board: $12,432
Financial aid: (212) 854-3711; 49% of undergrads determined to have financial need; average aid package $46,516

Concordia College
Bronxville NY
(800) 937-2655
U.S. News ranking: Reg. Coll. (N), No. 40
Website: www.concordia-ny.edu
Admissions email: admission@concordia-ny.edu
Private; founded 1881
Affiliation: Lutheran
Freshman admissions: least selective; 2014-2015: 983 applied, 724 accepted. Either SAT or ACT required. ACT 25/75 percentile: N/A. High school rank: N/A
Early decision deadline: N/A, notification date: N/A
Early action deadline: 11/15, notification date: 12/15
Application deadline (fall): 8/15
Undergraduate student body: 835 full time, 109 part time; 32% male, 68% female; 0% American Indian, 3% Asian, 22% black, 22% Hispanic, 2% multiracial, 0% Pacific Islander, 36% white, 13% international
Most popular majors: Information not available
Expenses: 2014-2015: $28,770; room/board: $10,265
Financial aid: (914) 337-9300

Cooper Union
New York NY
(212) 353-4120
U.S. News ranking: Reg. Coll. (N), No. 2
Website: www.cooper.edu
Admissions email: admissions@cooper.edu
Private; founded 1859
Freshman admissions: most selective; 2014-2015: 2,536 applied, 382 accepted. Either SAT or ACT required. SAT 25/75 percentile: 1250-1500. High school rank: 88% in top tenth, 90% in top quarter, 95% in top half
Early decision deadline: 12/1, notification date: 12/22
Early action deadline: N/A, notification date: N/A
Application deadline (fall): 1/1
Undergraduate student body: 866 full time, 10 part time; 66% male, 34% female; 1% American Indian, 20% Asian, 5% black, 10% Hispanic, 2% multiracial, 0% Pacific Islander, 33% white, 14% international; 52% from in state; 20% live on campus; 5% of students in fraternities, N/A in sororities
Most popular majors: 15% Architecture and Related Services,

56% Engineering, 29% Visual and Performing Arts
Expenses: 2015-2016: $42,650; room/board: $11,560
Financial aid: (212) 353-4113; 32% of undergrads determined to have financial need; average aid package $39,600

Cornell University

Ithaca NY
(607) 255-5241
U.S. News ranking: Nat. U., No. 15
Website: www.cornell.edu
Admissions email: admissions@cornell.edu
Private; founded 1865
Freshman admissions: most selective; 2014-2015: 43,037 applied, 6,105 accepted. Either SAT or ACT required. SAT 25/75 percentile: 1330-1510. High school rank: 87% in top tenth, 98% in top quarter, 99% in top half
Early decision deadline: 11/1, notification date: 12/15
Early action deadline: N/A, notification date: N/A
Application deadline (fall): 1/2
Undergraduate student body: 14,453 full time, N/A part time; 49% male, 51% female; 0% American Indian, 17% Asian, 6% black, 12% Hispanic, 4% multiracial, 0% Pacific Islander, 42% white, 10% international; 36% from in state; 55% live on campus; 27% of students in fraternities, 23% in sororities
Most popular majors: 13% Agriculture, Agriculture Operations, and Related Sciences, 13% Biological and Biomedical Sciences, 13% Business, Management, Marketing, and Related Support Services, 16% Engineering, 11% Social Sciences
Expenses: 2015-2016: $49,116; room/board: $13,678
Financial aid: (607) 255-5145; 47% of undergrads determined to have financial need; average aid package $43,416

CUNY–Baruch College

New York NY
(646) 312-1400
U.S. News ranking: Reg. U. (N), No. 32
Website: www.baruch.cuny.edu
Admissions email: admissions@baruch.cuny.edu
Public; founded 1919
Freshman admissions: more selective; 2014-2015: 19,768 applied, 5,516 accepted. Either SAT or ACT required. SAT 25/75 percentile: 1120-1330. High school rank: 48% in top tenth, 78% in top quarter, 95% in top half
Early decision deadline: 12/13, notification date: 1/7
Early action deadline: N/A, notification date: N/A
Application deadline (fall): 2/1
Undergraduate student body: 10,865 full time, 3,992 part time; 51% male, 49% female; 0% American Indian, 33% Asian, 9% black, 19% Hispanic, 1% multiracial, 0% Pacific Islander, 25% white, 12% international; 96% from in state; 2% live on campus; 0% of students in fraternities, 0% in sororities
Most popular majors: 20% Accounting, 8% Business Administration and Management, General, 8% Business/Corporate Communications, 23% Finance, General, 10% Sales, Distribution, and Marketing Operations, General
Expenses: 2015-2016: $7,301 in state, $17,771 out of state; room/board: $12,990
Financial aid: (646) 312-1360; 62% of undergrads determined to have financial need; average aid package $8,549

CUNY–Brooklyn College

Brooklyn NY
(718) 951-5001
U.S. News ranking: Reg. U. (N), No. 83
Website: www.brooklyn.cuny.edu
Admissions email: adminqry@brooklyn.cuny.edu
Public; founded 1930
Freshman admissions: selective; 2014-2015: 20,260 applied, 7,158 accepted. Either SAT or ACT required. SAT 25/75 percentile: 970-1160. High school rank: 18% in top tenth, 49% in top quarter, 76% in top half
Early decision deadline: N/A, notification date: N/A
Early action deadline: N/A, notification date: N/A
Undergraduate student body: 9,897 full time, 4,218 part time; 41% male, 59% female; 0% American Indian, 18% Asian, 22% black, 20% Hispanic, 1% multiracial, 0% Pacific Islander, 35% white, 3% international; 98% from in state; 0% live on campus; 3% of students in fraternities, 3% in sororities
Most popular majors: 11% Accounting, 17% Business Administration and Management, General, 6% Early Childhood Education and Teaching, 4% Elementary Education and Teaching, 15% Psychology, General
Expenses: 2015-2016: $6,835 in state, $17,305 out of state; room/board: N/A
Financial aid: (718) 951-5045; 89% of undergrads determined to have financial need; average aid package $7,500

CUNY–City College

New York NY
(212) 650-6977
U.S. News ranking: Reg. U. (N), No. 66
Website: www.ccny.cuny.edu
Admissions email: admissions@ccny.cuny.edu
Public; founded 1847
Freshman admissions: selective; 2014-2015: 24,497 applied, 8,492 accepted. SAT required. SAT 25/75 percentile: 980-1220. High school rank: N/A
Early decision deadline: N/A, notification date: N/A
Early action deadline: N/A, notification date: N/A
Application deadline (fall): 1/15
Undergraduate student body: 9,309 full time, 2,900 part time; 49% male, 51% female; 0% American Indian, 23% Asian, 20% black, 31% Hispanic, 0% multiracial, 0% Pacific Islander, 19% white, 7% international; 99% from in state; N/A live on campus; N/A of students in fraternities, N/A in sororities
Most popular majors: 8% Biological and Biomedical Sciences, 13% Engineering, 15% Psychology, 11% Social Sciences, 10% Visual and Performing Arts
Expenses: 2015-2016: $6,472 in state, $15,742 out of state; room/board: N/A
Financial aid: (212) 650-5819; 81% of undergrads determined to have financial need; average aid package $8,878

CUNY–College of Staten Island

Staten Island NY
(718) 982-2010
U.S. News ranking: Reg. U. (N), second tier
Website: www.csi.cuny.edu
Admissions email: admissions@csi.cuny.edu
Public; founded 1976
Freshman admissions: less selective; 2014-2015: 13,084 applied, 13,084 accepted. Either SAT or ACT required. SAT 25/75 percentile: 910-1100. High school rank: N/A
Early decision deadline: N/A, notification date: N/A
Early action deadline: N/A, notification date: N/A
Application deadline (fall): rolling
Undergraduate student body: 10,043 full time, 3,300 part time; 45% male, 55% female; 0% American Indian, 12% Asian, 15% black, 17% Hispanic, 0% multiracial, 0% Pacific Islander, 54% white, 2% international; 99% from in state; 3% live on campus; 0% of students in fraternities, 0% in sororities
Most popular majors: 17% Business, Management, Marketing, and Related Support Services, 7% Education, 11% Health Professions and Related Programs, 17% Psychology, 13% Social Sciences
Expenses: 2015-2016: $6,809 in state, $17,279 out of state; room/board: $16,832
Financial aid: (718) 982-2030; 74% of undergrads determined to have financial need; average aid package $4,969

CUNY–Hunter College

New York NY
(212) 772-4490
U.S. News ranking: Reg. U. (N), No. 47
Website: www.hunter.cuny.edu
Admissions email: admissions@hunter.cuny.edu
Public; founded 1870
Freshman admissions: more selective; 2014-2015: 31,100 applied, 10,836 accepted. Either SAT or ACT required. SAT 25/75 percentile: 1060-1270. High school rank: 24% in top tenth, 57% in top quarter, 87% in top half
Early decision deadline: N/A, notification date: N/A
Early action deadline: N/A, notification date: N/A
Application deadline (fall): 3/15
Undergraduate student body: 12,142 full time, 4,737 part time; 36% male, 64% female; 0% American Indian, 27% Asian, 11% black, 20% Hispanic, 0% multiracial, 0% Pacific Islander, 36% white, 6% international
Most popular majors: 11% English Language and Literature/Letters, 8% Health Professions and Related Programs, 23% Psychology, 17% Social Sciences, 8% Visual and Performing Arts
Expenses: 2015-2016: $6,480 in state, $15,750 out of state; room/board: $10,573
Financial aid: (212) 772-4820; 83% of undergrads determined to have financial need; average aid package $8,495

CUNY–John Jay College of Criminal Justice

New York NY
(212) 237-8866
U.S. News ranking: Reg. U. (N), No. 125
Website: www.jjay.cuny.edu/
Admissions email: admissions@jjay.cuny.edu
Public; founded 1965
Freshman admissions: less selective; 2014-2015: 13,884 applied, 7,085 accepted. Either SAT or ACT required. SAT 25/75 percentile: 860-1040. High school rank: N/A
Early decision deadline: N/A, notification date: N/A
Early action deadline: N/A, notification date: N/A
Application deadline (fall): 5/31
Undergraduate student body: 10,225 full time, 3,080 part time; 43% male, 57% female; 0% American Indian, 12% Asian, 20% black, 40% Hispanic, 0% multiracial, 0% Pacific Islander, 25% white, 3% international; 94% from in state; N/A live on campus; N/A of students in fraternities, N/A in sororities
Most popular majors: 49% Criminal Justice/Law Enforcement Administration, 22% Forensic Psychology, 4% Humanities/Humanistic Studies, 5% Legal Studies, General, 15% Social Sciences, Other
Expenses: 2014-2015: $6,359 in state, $16,379 out of state; room/board: N/A
Financial aid: (212) 237-8151; 71% of undergrads determined to have financial need; average aid package $9,445

CUNY–Lehman College

Bronx NY
(718) 960-8131
U.S. News ranking: Reg. U. (N), No. 116
Website: www.lehman.cuny.edu
Admissions email: undergraduate.admissions@lehman.cuny.edu
Public; founded 1968
Freshman admissions: less selective; 2014-2015: 14,605 applied, 4,224 accepted. Either SAT or ACT required. SAT 25/75 percentile: 870-1020. High school rank: N/A
Early decision deadline: N/A, notification date: N/A
Early action deadline: N/A, notification date: N/A
Application deadline (fall): 10/1
Undergraduate student body: 5,925 full time, 4,401 part time; 32% male, 68% female; 0% American Indian, 6% Asian, 32% black, 49% Hispanic, N/A multiracial, N/A Pacific Islander, 9% white, 3% international
Most popular majors: 2% English Language and Literature/Letters, 3% Health Professions and Related Programs, 6% Psychology, 8% Public Administration and Social Service Professions, 8% Social Sciences
Expenses: 2015-2016: $6,230 in state, $13,040 out of state; room/board: N/A
Financial aid: (718) 960-8545; 88% of undergrads determined to have financial need; average aid package $4,650

CUNY–Medgar Evers College

Brooklyn NY
(718) 270-6024
U.S. News ranking: Reg. Coll. (N), second tier
Website: www.mec.cuny.edu
Admissions email: enroll@mec.cuny.edu
Public; founded 1969
Freshman admissions: least selective; 2014-2015: 9,573 applied, 8,737 accepted. Neither SAT nor ACT required. SAT 25/75 percentile: 680-870. High school rank: N/A
Early decision deadline: N/A, notification date: N/A
Early action deadline: N/A, notification date: N/A
Application deadline (fall): rolling
Undergraduate student body: 4,324 full time, 2,377 part time; 29% male, 71% female; 1% American Indian, 2% Asian, 71% black, 11% Hispanic, 0% multiracial, 0% Pacific Islander, 1% white, 1% international
Most popular majors: 9% Biology/Biological Sciences, General, 37% Business/Commerce, General, 15% Health Professions and Related Programs, 13% Psychology, General, 7% Public Administration and Social Service Professions
Expenses: 2015-2016: $6,225 in state, $16,245 out of state; room/board: N/A
Financial aid: (718) 270-6038

CUNY–New York City College of Technology

Brooklyn NY
(718) 260-5500
U.S. News ranking: Reg. Coll. (N), second tier
Website: www.citytech.cuny.edu
Admissions email: admissions@citytech.cuny.edu
Public; founded 1946
Freshman admissions: least selective; 2014-2015: 17,293 applied, 12,586 accepted. Neither SAT nor ACT required. SAT 25/75 percentile: 740-950. High school rank: N/A
Early decision deadline: N/A, notification date: N/A
Early action deadline: N/A, notification date: N/A
Application deadline (fall): 2/1
Undergraduate student body: 10,587 full time, 6,787 part time; 56% male, 44% female; 0% American Indian, 21% Asian, 32% black, 29% Hispanic, 0% multiracial, 0% Pacific Islander, 13% white, 5% international; 97% from in state; 0% live on campus; 0% of students in fraternities, 0% in sororities
Most popular majors: 9% Architectural Technology/

Technician, 10% Design and Visual Communications, General, 14% Hospitality Administration/ Management, General, 16% Information Science/Studies, 14% Registered Nursing/Registered Nurse
Expenses: 2014-2015: $6,369 in state, $13,179 out of state; room/ board: $13,554
Financial aid: (718) 260-5700

CUNY–Queens College
Flushing NY
(718) 997-5600
U.S. News ranking: Reg. U. (N), No. 47
Website: www.qc.edu/
Admissions email: applyto@ uapc.cuny.edu
Public; founded 1937
Freshman admissions: selective; 2014-2015: 18,289 applied, 7,283 accepted. Either SAT or ACT required. SAT 25/75 percentile: 1020-1180. High school rank: 35% in top tenth, 65% in top quarter, 99% in top half
Early decision deadline: N/A, notification date: N/A
Early action deadline: N/A, notification date: N/A
Application deadline (fall): 2/1
Undergraduate student body: 11,079 full time, 4,694 part time; 44% male, 56% female; 0% American Indian, 25% Asian, 8% black, 28% Hispanic, 1% multiracial, 1% Pacific Islander, 32% white, 5% international; 99% from in state; 3% live on campus; N/A of students in fraternities, N/A in sororities
Most popular majors: 14% Accounting, 9% Economics, General, 5% English Language and Literature, General, 16% Psychology, General, 9% Sociology
Expenses: 2015-2016: $6,938 in state, $17,408 out of state; room/ board: N/A
Financial aid: (718) 997-5101; 73% of undergrads determined to have financial need; average aid package $7,469

CUNY–York College[1]
Jamaica NY
(718) 262-2165
U.S. News ranking: Reg. Coll. (N), second tier
Website: www.york.cuny.edu
Admissions email: admissions@ york.cuny.edu
Public; founded 1966
Application deadline (fall): 6/1
Undergraduate student body: N/A full time, N/A part time
Expenses: 2014-2015: $6,396 in state, $16,416 out of state; room/ board: N/A
Financial aid: (718) 262-2230

Daemen College
Amherst NY
(800) 462-7652
U.S. News ranking: Reg. U. (N), second tier
Website: www.daemen.edu
Admissions email: admissions@ daemen.edu
Private; founded 1947
Freshman admissions: selective; 2014-2015: 2,849 applied, 1,564 accepted. Neither SAT nor ACT required. SAT 25/75 percentile: 920-1130. High school rank: 19% in top tenth, 54% in top quarter, 86% in top half
Early decision deadline: N/A, notification date: N/A
Early action deadline: N/A, notification date: N/A
Application deadline (fall): rolling
Undergraduate student body: 1,677 full time, 368 part time; 28% male, 72% female; 0% American Indian, 2% Asian, 12% black, 6% Hispanic, 1% multiracial, 0% Pacific Islander, 74% white, 1% international; 95% from in state; 35% live on campus; N/A of students in fraternities, N/A in sororities
Most popular majors: 10% Business Administration and Management, General, 5% Elementary Education and Teaching, 18% Natural Sciences, 9% Physician Assistant, 32% Registered Nursing/Registered Nurse
Expenses: 2015-2016: $25,995; room/board: $12,050
Financial aid: (716) 839-8254

Dominican College
Orangeburg NY
(845) 359-3533
U.S. News ranking: Reg. U. (N), second tier
Website: www.dc.edu
Admissions email: admissions@ dc.edu
Private; founded 1952
Freshman admissions: less selective; 2014-2015: 2,385 applied, 1,498 accepted. Either SAT or ACT required. SAT 25/75 percentile: 780-960. High school rank: N/A
Early decision deadline: N/A, notification date: N/A
Early action deadline: N/A, notification date: N/A
Application deadline (fall): rolling
Undergraduate student body: 1,269 full time, 214 part time; 36% male, 64% female; 0% American Indian, 8% Asian, 16% black, 27% Hispanic, 2% multiracial, 0% Pacific Islander, 33% white, 1% international
Most popular majors: 16% Business, Management, Marketing, and Related Support Services, 8% Education, 28% Health Professions and Related Programs, 6% Homeland Security, Law Enforcement, Firefighting and Related Protective Services, 25% Social Sciences
Expenses: 2015-2016: $26,450; room/board: $12,120
Financial aid: (845) 359-7800; 77% of undergrads determined to have financial need; average aid package $19,805

Dowling College
Oakdale Long Island NY
(631) 244-3030
U.S. News ranking: Reg. U. (N), second tier
Website: www.dowling.edu
Admissions email: admissions@ dowling.edu
Private; founded 1955
Freshman admissions: less selective; 2014-2015: 1,885 applied, 1,477 accepted. Neither SAT nor ACT required. ACT 25/75 percentile: N/A. High school rank: N/A
Early decision deadline: N/A, notification date: N/A
Early action deadline: N/A, notification date: N/A
Application deadline (fall): rolling
Undergraduate student body: 1,087 full time, 696 part time; 47% male, 53% female; 0% American Indian, 0% Asian, 10% black, 7% Hispanic, N/A multiracial, 0% Pacific Islander, 39% white, 4% international; 93% from in state; 15% live on campus; N/A of students in fraternities, N/A in sororities
Most popular majors: Information not available
Expenses: 2014-2015: $29,100; room/board: $10,770
Financial aid: (631) 244-3303; 73% of undergrads determined to have financial need; average aid package $19,348

D'Youville College
Buffalo NY
(716) 829-7600
U.S. News ranking: Reg. U. (N), second tier
Website: www.dyc.edu
Admissions email: admissions@ dyc.edu
Private; founded 1908
Freshman admissions: selective; 2014-2015: 1,107 applied, 940 accepted. Either SAT or ACT required. SAT 25/75 percentile: 910-1120. High school rank: 16% in top tenth, 51% in top quarter, 83% in top half
Early decision deadline: N/A, notification date: N/A
Early action deadline: N/A, notification date: N/A
Application deadline (fall): rolling
Undergraduate student body: 1,505 full time, 458 part time; 27% male, 73% female; 1% American Indian, 3% Asian, 8% black, 5% Hispanic, 2% multiracial, 0% Pacific Islander, 74% white, 6% international; 95% from in state; 17% live on campus; 0% of students in fraternities, 0% in sororities
Most popular majors: 9% Biological and Biomedical Sciences, 11% Business, Management, Marketing, and Related Support Services, 65% Health Professions and Related Programs, 9% Multi/ Interdisciplinary Studies, 3% Social Sciences
Expenses: 2015-2016: $24,370; room/board: $11,180
Financial aid: (716) 829-7500; 82% of undergrads determined to have financial need; average aid package $17,951

Elmira College
Elmira NY
(800) 935-6472
U.S. News ranking: Reg. Coll. (N), No. 11
Website: www.elmira.edu
Admissions email: admissions@ elmira.edu
Private; founded 1855
Freshman admissions: selective; 2014-2015: 2,310 applied, 1,899 accepted. Either SAT or ACT required. SAT 25/75 percentile: 940-1180. High school rank: N/A
Early decision deadline: 11/15, notification date: 12/15
Early action deadline: N/A, notification date: N/A
Application deadline (fall): rolling
Undergraduate student body: 1,177 full time, 188 part time; 30% male, 70% female; 1% American Indian, 2% Asian, 4% black, 3% Hispanic, 3% multiracial, 0% Pacific Islander, 67% white, 5% international; 64% from in state; 90% live on campus; 0% of students in fraternities, 0% in sororities
Most popular majors: 9% Biology/ Biological Sciences, General, 13% Business Administration and Management, General, 19% Education, 11% Psychology, General, 12% Registered Nursing/ Registered Nurse
Expenses: 2015-2016: $39,950; room/board: $12,000
Financial aid: (607) 735-1728; 82% of undergrads determined to have financial need; average aid package $30,559

Excelsior College[1]
Albany NY
(518) 464-8500
U.S. News ranking: Reg. U. (N), unranked
Website: www.excelsior.edu
Admissions email: admissions@ excelsior.edu
Private; founded 1971
Application deadline (fall): rolling
Undergraduate student body: N/A full time, N/A part time
Expenses: N/A
Financial aid: (518) 464-8500

Farmingdale State College–SUNY
Farmingdale NY
(631) 420-2200
U.S. News ranking: Reg. Coll. (N), No. 32
Website: www.farmingdale.edu
Admissions email: admissions@ farmingdale.edu
Public; founded 1912
Freshman admissions: selective; 2014-2015: 5,183 applied, 2,418 accepted. Either SAT or ACT required. SAT 25/75 percentile: 900-1060. High school rank: 4% in top tenth, 24% in top quarter, 65% in top half
Early decision deadline: N/A, notification date: N/A
Early action deadline: N/A, notification date: N/A
Application deadline (fall): 6/1
Undergraduate student body: 6,287 full time, 2,107 part time; 57% male, 43% female; 0% American Indian, 7% Asian, 10% black, 16% Hispanic, 2% multiracial, 1% Pacific Islander, 60% white, 3% international; 100% from in state; 8% live on campus; 2% of students in fraternities, 4% in sororities
Most popular majors: 29% Business, Management, Marketing, and Related Support Services, 14% Engineering Technologies and Engineering-Related Fields, 9% Health Professions and Related Programs, 10% Homeland Security, Law Enforcement, Firefighting and Related Protective Services, 9% Multi/Interdisciplinary Studies
Expenses: 2015-2016: $7,808 in state, $17,658 out of state; room/ board: $12,500
Financial aid: (631) 420-2328; 55% of undergrads determined to have financial need; average aid package $7,717

Fashion Institute of Technology
New York NY
(212) 217-3760
U.S. News ranking: Reg. U. (N), unranked
Website: www.fitnyc.edu
Admissions email: FITinfo@ fitnyc.edu
Public; founded 1944
Freshman admissions: N/A; 2014-2015: 4,729 applied, 2,094 accepted. Neither SAT nor ACT required. ACT 25/75 percentile: N/A. High school rank: N/A
Early decision deadline: N/A, notification date: N/A
Early action deadline: N/A, notification date: N/A
Application deadline (fall): 1/1
Undergraduate student body: 7,454 full time, 2,113 part time; 15% male, 85% female; 0% American Indian, 9% Asian, 9% black, 17% Hispanic, 4% multiracial, 0% Pacific Islander, 47% white, 14% international; 68% from in state; 22% live on campus; 0% of students in fraternities, 0% in sororities
Most popular majors: 37% Business, Management, Marketing, and Related Support Services, 17% Communication, Journalism, and Related Programs, 2% Communications Technologies/Technicians and Support Services, 4% Family and Consumer Sciences/Human Sciences, 40% Visual and Performing Arts
Expenses: 2014-2015: $6,870 in state, $18,510 out of state; room/ board: $13,162
Financial aid: (212) 217-7439; 53% of undergrads determined to have financial need; average aid package $11,882

Five Towns College
Dix Hills NY
(631) 424-7000
U.S. News ranking: Reg. Coll. (N), second tier
Website: www.ftc.edu
Admissions email: admissions@ ftc.edu
For-profit; founded 1972
Freshman admissions: less selective; 2014-2015: 335 applied, 188 accepted. Either SAT or ACT required. SAT 25/75 percentile: 760-1000. High school rank: 24% in top tenth, 39% in top quarter, 71% in top half
Early decision deadline: 10/15, notification date: 11/1
Early action deadline: N/A, notification date: N/A
Application deadline (fall): rolling
Undergraduate student body: 618 full time, 31 part time; 66% male, 34% female; 0% American Indian, 4% Asian, 21% black, 15% Hispanic, 6% multiracial, 0% Pacific Islander, 50% white, 0% international; 93% from in state; 23% live on campus; 0% of students in fraternities, 0% in sororities
Most popular majors: 45% Business, Management, Marketing, and Related Support Services, 13% Education, 42% Visual and Performing Arts
Expenses: 2015-2016: $22,500; room/board: $12,270

Financial aid: (631) 424-7000; 85% of undergrads determined to have financial need; average aid package $14,472

Fordham University

New York NY
(800) 367-3426
U.S. News ranking: Nat. U., No. 66
Website: www.fordham.edu
Admissions email: enroll@fordham.edu
Private; founded 1841
Affiliation: Roman Catholic
Freshman admissions: more selective; 2014-2015: 40,912 applied, 19,685 accepted. Either SAT or ACT required. SAT 25/75 percentile: 1150-1350. High school rank: 47% in top tenth, 80% in top quarter, 97% in top half
Early decision deadline: N/A, notification date: N/A
Early action deadline: 11/1, notification date: 12/20
Application deadline (fall): 1/1
Undergraduate student body: 8,058 full time, 575 part time; 45% male, 55% female; 0% American Indian, 9% Asian, 5% black, 14% Hispanic, 3% multiracial, 0% Pacific Islander, 60% white, 6% international; 47% from in state; 55% live on campus; N/A of students in fraternities, N/A in sororities
Most popular majors: 6% Accounting, 14% Business Administration and Management, General, 5% English Language and Literature, General, 7% Psychology, General, 13% Speech Communication and Rhetoric
Expenses: 2014-2015: $45,623; room/board: $15,965
Financial aid: (718) 817-3800

Hamilton College

Clinton NY
(800) 843-2655
U.S. News ranking: Nat. Lib. Arts, No. 14
Website: www.hamilton.edu
Admissions email: admission@hamilton.edu
Private; founded 1812
Freshman admissions: most selective; 2014-2015: 5,071 applied, 1,336 accepted. Either SAT or ACT required. SAT 25/75 percentile: 1310-1470. High school rank: 75% in top tenth, 94% in top quarter, 99% in top half
Early decision deadline: 11/15, notification date: 12/15
Early action deadline: N/A, notification date: N/A
Application deadline (fall): 1/1
Undergraduate student body: 1,894 full time, 6 part time; 48% male, 52% female; 0% American Indian, 7% Asian, 4% black, 8% Hispanic, 3% multiracial, 0% Pacific Islander, 64% white, 5% international; 30% from in state; 97% live on campus; 28% of students in fraternities, 21% in sororities
Most popular majors: 6% Biology/Biological Sciences, General, 9% Economics, General, 8% International Relations and Affairs, 6% Mathematics, General, 7% Psychology, General
Expenses: 2015-2016: $49,500; room/board: $12,570

Financial aid: (315) 859-4434; 47% of undergrads determined to have financial need; average aid package $43,256

Hartwick College

Oneonta NY
(607) 431-4150
U.S. News ranking: Nat. Lib. Arts, No. 164
Website: www.hartwick.edu
Admissions email: admissions@hartwick.edu
Private; founded 1797
Freshman admissions: selective; 2014-2015: 5,036 applied, 4,510 accepted. Neither SAT nor ACT required. SAT 25/75 percentile: 1010-1200. High school rank: 15% in top tenth, 45% in top quarter, 79% in top half
Early decision deadline: 11/15, notification date: 11/25
Early action deadline: N/A, notification date: N/A
Application deadline (fall): rolling
Undergraduate student body: 1,507 full time, 33 part time; 39% male, 61% female; 0% American Indian, 2% Asian, 8% black, 7% Hispanic, 0% multiracial, 0% Pacific Islander, 68% white, 3% international; 73% from in state; 81% live on campus; 10% of students in fraternities, 8% in sororities
Most popular majors: 13% Biology/Biological Sciences, General, 19% Business Administration and Management, General, 5% Psychology, General, 14% Registered Nursing, Nursing Administration, Nursing Research and Clinical Nursing, 18% Sociology
Expenses: 2015-2016: $41,440; room/board: $11,120
Financial aid: (607) 431-4130; 82% of undergrads determined to have financial need; average aid package $32,197

Hilbert College[1]

Hamburg NY
(716) 649-7900
U.S. News ranking: Reg. Coll. (N), unranked
Website: www.hilbert.edu/
Admissions email: admissions@hilbert.edu
Private
Application deadline (fall): N/A
Undergraduate student body: N/A full time, N/A part time
Expenses: 2014-2015: $19,940; room/board: $8,890
Financial aid: (716) 649-7900

Hobart and William Smith Colleges

Geneva NY
(315) 781-3622
U.S. News ranking: Nat. Lib. Arts, No. 61
Website: www.hws.edu
Admissions email: admissions@hws.edu
Private; founded 1822
Freshman admissions: more selective; 2014-2015: 5,093 applied, 2,528 accepted. Neither SAT nor ACT required. SAT 25/75 percentile: 1140-1320. High school rank: 30% in top tenth, 70% in top quarter, 90% in top half
Early decision deadline: 11/15, notification date: 12/15
Early action deadline: N/A, notification date: N/A
Application deadline (fall): 2/1
Undergraduate student body: 2,362 full time, 59 part time; 48% male, 52% female; 1% American Indian, 3% Asian, 5% black, 6% Hispanic, 0% multiracial, 0% Pacific Islander, 70% white, 5% international; 42% from in state; 90% live on campus; 20% of students in fraternities, N/A in sororities
Most popular majors: 6% Biology/Biological Sciences, General, 7% Economics, General, 7% English Language and Literature, General, 10% Mass Communication/Media Studies, 8% Psychology, General
Expenses: 2015-2016: $49,677; room/board: $12,583
Financial aid: (315) 781-3315; 66% of undergrads determined to have financial need; average aid package $33,069

Hofstra University

Hempstead NY
(516) 463-6700
U.S. News ranking: Nat. U., No. 135
Website: www.hofstra.edu
Admissions email: admission@hofstra.edu
Private; founded 1935
Freshman admissions: selective; 2014-2015: 26,388 applied, 16,258 accepted. Neither SAT nor ACT required. SAT 25/75 percentile: 1050-1230. High school rank: 28% in top tenth, 57% in top quarter, 86% in top half
Early decision deadline: N/A, notification date: N/A
Early action deadline: 11/15, notification date: 12/15
Application deadline (fall): rolling
Undergraduate student body: 6,474 full time, 430 part time; 46% male, 54% female; 0% American Indian, 9% Asian, 9% black, 14% Hispanic, 2% multiracial, 1% Pacific Islander, 56% white, 4% international; 65% from in state; 47% live on campus; 5% of students in fraternities, 7% in sororities
Most popular majors: 6% Accounting, 5% Business Administration and Management, General, 6% Marketing/Marketing Management, General, 8% Psychology, General, 5% Public Relations/Image Management
Expenses: 2015-2016: $40,460; room/board: $13,530
Financial aid: (516) 463-6680; 68% of undergrads determined to have financial need; average aid package $26,000

Houghton College

Houghton NY
(800) 777-2556
U.S. News ranking: Nat. Lib. Arts, No. 136
Website: www.houghton.edu
Admissions email: admission@houghton.edu
Private; founded 1883
Affiliation: The Wesleyan Church
Freshman admissions: selective; 2014-2015: 792 applied, 743 accepted. Either SAT or ACT required. SAT 25/75 percentile: 980-1260. High school rank: 23% in top tenth, 55% in top quarter, 81% in top half
Early decision deadline: N/A, notification date: N/A
Early action deadline: N/A, notification date: N/A
Application deadline (fall): rolling
Undergraduate student body: 994 full time, 54 part time; 35% male, 65% female; 0% American Indian, 2% Asian, 2% black, 2% Hispanic, 4% multiracial, 0% Pacific Islander, 79% white, 9% international; 62% from in state; 85% live on campus; 0% of students in fraternities, 0% in sororities
Most popular majors: 8% Area, Ethnic, Cultural, Gender, and Group Studies, 21% Business, Management, Marketing, and Related Support Services, 14% Education, 7% English Language and Literature/Letters, 9% Visual and Performing Arts
Expenses: 2015-2016: $29,458; room/board: $8,498
Financial aid: (585) 567-9328; 81% of undergrads determined to have financial need; average aid package $19,967

Iona College

New Rochelle NY
(914) 633-2502
U.S. News ranking: Reg. U. (N), No. 79
Website: www.iona.edu/info
Admissions email: admissions@iona.edu
Private; founded 1940
Affiliation: Roman Catholic
Freshman admissions: less selective; 2014-2015: 7,818 applied, 6,778 accepted. Either SAT or ACT required. SAT 25/75 percentile: 920-1110. High school rank: 8% in top tenth, 29% in top quarter, 58% in top half
Early decision deadline: N/A, notification date: N/A
Early action deadline: 12/1, notification date: 12/19
Application deadline (fall): 2/15
Undergraduate student body: 2,994 full time, 307 part time; 47% male, 53% female; 0% American Indian, 2% Asian, 8% black, 21% Hispanic, 2% multiracial, 0% Pacific Islander, 58% white, 2% international; 75% from in state; 43% live on campus; 7% of students in fraternities, 13% in sororities
Most popular majors: 33% Business, Management, Marketing, and Related Support Services, 15% Communication, Journalism, and Related Programs, 6% Health Professions and Related Programs, 10% Psychology, 6% Social Sciences
Expenses: 2015-2016: $35,324; room/board: $13,980
Financial aid: (914) 633-2497; 81% of undergrads determined to have financial need; average aid package $21,845

Ithaca College

Ithaca NY
(800) 429-4274
U.S. News ranking: Reg. U. (N), No. 9
Website: www.ithaca.edu
Admissions email: admission@ithaca.edu
Private; founded 1892
Freshman admissions: more selective; 2014-2015: 18,207 applied, 10,763 accepted. Neither SAT nor ACT required. SAT 25/75 percentile: 1100-1300. High school rank: 29% in top tenth, 68% in top quarter, 92% in top half
Early decision deadline: 11/1, notification date: 12/15
Early action deadline: 12/1, notification date: 2/1
Application deadline (fall): 2/1
Undergraduate student body: 6,012 full time, 112 part time; 43% male, 57% female; 0% American Indian, 4% Asian, 5% black, 8% Hispanic, 3% multiracial, 0% Pacific Islander, 71% white, 2% international; 45% from in state; 70% live on campus; 1% of students in fraternities, 1% in sororities
Most popular majors: 10% Business, Management, Marketing, and Related Support Services, 22% Communication, Journalism, and Related Programs, 13% Health Professions and Related Programs, 7% Social Sciences, 18% Visual and Performing Arts
Expenses: 2015-2016: $40,658; room/board: $14,674
Financial aid: (607) 274-3131; 68% of undergrads determined to have financial need; average aid package $33,300

Juilliard School

New York NY
(212) 799-5000
U.S. News ranking: Arts, unranked
Website: www.juilliard.edu
Admissions email: admissions@juilliard.edu
Private; founded 1905
Freshman admissions: N/A; 2014-2015: 2,385 applied, 201 accepted. Neither SAT nor ACT required. ACT 25/75 percentile: N/A. High school rank: N/A
Early decision deadline: N/A, notification date: N/A
Early action deadline: N/A, notification date: N/A
Application deadline (fall): 12/1
Undergraduate student body: 509 full time, 61 part time; 56% male, 44% female; 0% American Indian, 13% Asian, 5% black, 6% Hispanic, 6% multiracial, 0% Pacific Islander, 43% white, 26% international; 68% from in state; 61% live on campus; 0% of students in fraternities, 0% in sororities
Most popular majors: Information not available
Expenses: 2015-2016: $40,170; room/board: $14,790
Financial aid: (212) 799-5000; 77% of undergrads determined to have financial need; average aid package $34,916

Keuka College

Keuka Park NY
(315) 279-5254
U.S. News ranking: Reg. U. (N), second tier
Website: www.keuka.edu
Admissions email: admissions@mail.keuka.edu
Private; founded 1890
Affiliation: American Baptist
Freshman admissions: less selective; 2014-2015: 1,371 applied, 1,136 accepted. Neither SAT nor ACT required. SAT 25/75 percentile: 875-1050. High

school rank: 8% in top tenth, 26% in top quarter, 71% in top half
Early decision deadline: N/A, notification date: N/A
Early action deadline: N/A, notification date: N/A
Application deadline (fall): rolling
Undergraduate student body: 1,355 full time, 448 part time; 25% male, 75% female; 1% American Indian, 3% Asian, 8% black, 3% Hispanic, 1% multiracial, 0% Pacific Islander, 77% white, N/A international; 94% from in state; 80% live on campus; N/A of students in fraternities, N/A in sororities
Most popular majors: 27% Business, Management, Marketing, and Related Support Services, 14% Education, 24% Health Professions and Related Programs, 12% Homeland Security, Law Enforcement, Firefighting and Related Protective Services, 9% Public Administration and Social Service Professions
Expenses: 2015-2016: $28,692; room/board: $11,070
Financial aid: (315) 279-5232; 89% of undergrads determined to have financial need; average aid package $18,697

The King's College

New York NY
(212) 659-3610
U.S. News ranking: Nat. Lib. Arts, second tier
Website: www.tkc.edu/
Admissions email: admissions@tkc.edu
Private; founded 1938
Affiliation: Christian nondenominational
Freshman admissions: selective; 2014-2015: 4,589 applied, 3,230 accepted. Either SAT or ACT required. SAT 25/75 percentile: 1000-1220. High school rank: N/A
Early decision deadline: N/A, notification date: N/A
Early action deadline: 11/15, notification date: 12/15
Application deadline (fall): rolling
Undergraduate student body: 474 full time, 13 part time; 39% male, 61% female; 1% American Indian, 3% Asian, 4% black, 11% Hispanic, 4% multiracial, 0% Pacific Islander, 73% white, 4% international; 9% from in state; N/A live on campus; 0% of students in fraternities, 0% in sororities
Most popular majors: 14% Business, Management, Marketing, and Related Support Services, 17% Education, 7% Engineering Technologies and Engineering-Related Fields, 13% Health Professions and Related Programs, 9% Homeland Security, Law Enforcement, Firefighting and Related Protective Services
Expenses: 2015-2016: $33,270; room/board: N/A
Financial aid: (212) 659-7200; 73% of undergrads determined to have financial need; average aid package $25,931

Le Moyne College

Syracuse NY
(315) 445-4300
U.S. News ranking: Reg. U. (N), No. 19
Website: www.lemoyne.edu
Admissions email: admission@lemoyne.edu
Private; founded 1946
Affiliation: Roman Catholic (Jesuit)
Freshman admissions: selective; 2014-2015: 6,353 applied, 4,124 accepted. Either SAT or ACT required. SAT 25/75 percentile: 950-1160. High school rank: 21% in top tenth, 50% in top quarter, 85% in top half
Early decision deadline: N/A, notification date: N/A
Early action deadline: 11/15, notification date: 12/15
Application deadline (fall): rolling
Undergraduate student body: 2,500 full time, 349 part time; 42% male, 58% female; 0% American Indian, 3% Asian, 6% black, 5% Hispanic, 2% multiracial, 0% Pacific Islander, 79% white, 1% international; 94% from in state; 61% live on campus; 0% of students in fraternities, 0% in sororities
Most popular majors: 7% Accounting, 13% Biology/Biological Sciences, General, 7% English Language and Literature, General, 18% Psychology, General, 6% Sociology
Expenses: 2015-2016: $32,250; room/board: $12,540
Financial aid: (315) 445-4400; 83% of undergrads determined to have financial need; average aid package $24,207

LIM College

New York NY
(800) 677-1323
U.S. News ranking: Business, unranked
Website: www.limcollege.edu/html/home.htm
Admissions email: admissions@limcollege.edu
For-profit; founded 1939
Freshman admissions: less selective; 2014-2015: 1,387 applied, 1,030 accepted. Either SAT or ACT required. SAT 25/75 percentile: 820-1020. High school rank: N/A
Early decision deadline: N/A, notification date: N/A
Early action deadline: 11/15, notification date: 12/15
Application deadline (fall): rolling
Undergraduate student body: 1,424 full time, 128 part time; 8% male, 92% female; 0% American Indian, 5% Asian, 15% black, 17% Hispanic, 1% multiracial, 0% Pacific Islander, 55% white, 3% international; 40% from in state; 24% live on campus; N/A of students in fraternities, N/A in sororities
Most popular majors: 8% Business Administration and Management, General, 8% Design and Visual Communications, General, 60% Fashion Merchandising, 24% Marketing/Marketing Management, General
Expenses: 2015-2016: $24,825; room/board: $19,850
Financial aid: (800) 677-1323; 67% of undergrads determined to have financial need; average aid package $9,693

LIU Post

Brookville NY
(516) 299-2900
U.S. News ranking: Reg. U. (N), second tier
Website: www.liu.edu
Admissions email: post-enroll@liu.edu
Private; founded 1954
Freshman admissions: less selective; 2014-2015: 6,555 applied, 5,437 accepted. Either SAT or ACT required. SAT 25/75 percentile: 840-1053. High school rank: N/A
Early decision deadline: N/A, notification date: N/A
Early action deadline: 12/1, notification date: 12/31
Application deadline (fall): rolling
Undergraduate student body: 3,387 full time, 3,730 part time; 42% male, 58% female; 0% American Indian, 4% Asian, 11% black, 13% Hispanic, 2% multiracial, 0% Pacific Islander, 47% white, 11% international; 93% from in state; 31% live on campus; 1% of students in fraternities, 2% in sororities
Most popular majors: 5% Accounting, 13% Business Administration and Management, General, 8% Criminal Justice/Law Enforcement Administration, 6% Elementary Education and Teaching, 8% Psychology, General
Expenses: 2015-2016: $35,546; room/board: $13,138
Financial aid: (516) 299-2338; 73% of undergrads determined to have financial need; average aid package $21,023

Manhattan College

Riverdale NY
(718) 862-7200
U.S. News ranking: Reg. U. (N), No. 17
Website: www.manhattan.edu
Admissions email: admit@manhattan.edu
Private; founded 1853
Affiliation: Roman Catholic
Freshman admissions: selective; 2014-2015: 8,199 applied, 5,456 accepted. SAT required. SAT 25/75 percentile: 990-1190. High school rank: 23% in top tenth, 52% in top quarter, 85% in top half
Early decision deadline: 11/15, notification date: 12/15
Early action deadline: N/A, notification date: N/A
Application deadline (fall): rolling
Undergraduate student body: 3,276 full time, 195 part time; 56% male, 44% female; 0% American Indian, 4% Asian, 4% black, 19% Hispanic, 2% multiracial, 0% Pacific Islander, 56% white, 3% international; 72% from in state; 56% live on campus; 2% of students in fraternities, 5% in sororities
Most popular majors: 22% Business, Management, Marketing, and Related Support Services, 6% Communication, Journalism, and Related Programs, 13% Education, 27% Engineering, 7% Psychology
Expenses: 2014-2015: $37,188; room/board: $13,740
Financial aid: (718) 862-7100

Manhattan School of Music

New York NY
(212) 749-2802
U.S. News ranking: Arts, unranked
Website: www.msmnyc.edu
Admissions email: admission@msmnyc.edu
Private; founded 1917
Freshman admissions: N/A; 2014-2015: 897 applied, 402 accepted. Neither SAT nor ACT required. ACT 25/75 percentile: N/A. High school rank: N/A
Early decision deadline: N/A, notification date: N/A
Early action deadline: N/A, notification date: N/A
Application deadline (fall): rolling
Undergraduate student body: 385 full time, 4 part time; 45% male, 55% female; 0% American Indian, 7% Asian, 2% black, 7% Hispanic, 5% multiracial, 0% Pacific Islander, 32% white, 43% international; 58% from in state; 68% live on campus; 0% of students in fraternities, 0% in sororities
Most popular majors: 20% Keyboard Instruments, 9% Music, General, 21% Stringed Instruments, 36% Voice and Opera, 5% Woodwind Instruments
Expenses: 2015-2016: $42,500; room/board: $12,260
Financial aid: (212) 749-2802; 38% of undergrads determined to have financial need; average aid package $23,083

Manhattanville College

Purchase NY
(914) 323-5464
U.S. News ranking: Reg. U. (N), No. 92
Website: www.mville.edu
Admissions email: admissions@mville.edu
Private; founded 1841
Freshman admissions: selective; 2014-2015: 3,929 applied, 2,902 accepted. Neither SAT nor ACT required. SAT 25/75 percentile: 970-1160. High school rank: N/A
Early decision deadline: N/A, notification date: N/A
Early action deadline: 12/1, notification date: 12/20
Application deadline (fall): rolling
Undergraduate student body: 1,708 full time, 90 part time; 36% male, 64% female; 0% American Indian, 1% Asian, 8% black, 13% Hispanic, 2% multiracial, 0% Pacific Islander, 29% white, 9% international; 70% from in state; 64% live on campus; 0% of students in fraternities, 0% in sororities
Most popular majors: 18% Business Administration and Management, General, 12% Psychology, General, 16% Social Sciences, General, 9% Speech Communication and Rhetoric, 12% Visual and Performing Arts, General
Expenses: 2014-2015: $36,220; room/board: $14,520
Financial aid: (914) 323-5357

Marist College

Poughkeepsie NY
(845) 575-3226
U.S. News ranking: Reg. U. (N), No. 13
Website: www.marist.edu
Admissions email: admissions@marist.edu
Private; founded 1929
Freshman admissions: selective; 2014-2015: 9,751 applied, 3,755 accepted. Neither SAT nor ACT required. SAT 25/75 percentile: 1090-1270. High school rank: 30% in top tenth, 58% in top quarter, 87% in top half
Early decision deadline: 11/1, notification date: 12/15
Early action deadline: 11/15, notification date: 1/30
Application deadline (fall): 2/1
Undergraduate student body: 4,876 full time, 640 part time; 41% male, 59% female; 0% American Indian, 3% Asian, 4% black, 9% Hispanic, 2% multiracial, 0% Pacific Islander, 78% white, 2% international; 57% from in state; 73% live on campus; 3% of students in fraternities, 3% in sororities
Most popular majors: 21% Business, Management, Marketing, and Related Support Services, 19% Communication, Journalism, and Related Programs, 5% Computer and Information Sciences and Support Services, 15% Psychology, 10% Visual and Performing Arts
Expenses: 2015-2016: $33,750; room/board: $14,850
Financial aid: (845) 575-3230; 58% of undergrads determined to have financial need; average aid package $18,969

Marymount Manhattan College

New York NY
(212) 517-0430
U.S. News ranking: Nat. Lib. Arts, second tier
Website: www.mmm.edu
Admissions email: admissions@mmm.edu
Private; founded 1936
Freshman admissions: selective; 2014-2015: 4,385 applied, 3,226 accepted. Either SAT or ACT required. SAT 25/75 percentile: 940-1170. High school rank: N/A
Early decision deadline: N/A, notification date: N/A
Early action deadline: N/A, notification date: N/A
Application deadline (fall): rolling
Undergraduate student body: 1,640 full time, 218 part time; 23% male, 77% female; 1% American Indian, 3% Asian, 10% black, 17% Hispanic, 1% multiracial, 0% Pacific Islander, 57% white, 5% international; 40% from in state; 36% live on campus; 0% of students in fraternities, 0% in sororities
Most popular majors: 8% Business, Management, Marketing, and Related Support Services, 16% Communication, Journalism, and Related Programs, 5% Health Professions and Related Programs, 6% Psychology, 43% Visual and Performing Arts
Expenses: 2015-2016: $28,700; room/board: $15,500
Financial aid: (212) 517-0480

More at usnews.com/college

Medaille College[1]

Buffalo NY
(716) 880-2200
U.S. News ranking: Reg. U. (N), second tier
Website: www.medaille.edu
Admissions email: admissionsug@medaille.edu
Private; founded 1937
Application deadline (fall): rolling
Undergraduate student body: N/A full time, N/A part time
Expenses: 2014-2015: $25,002; room/board: $11,866
Financial aid: (716) 880-2256

Mercy College

Dobbs Ferry NY
(877) 637-2946
U.S. News ranking: Reg. U. (N), unranked
Website: www.mercy.edu
Admissions email: admissions@mercy.edu
Private; founded 1950
Freshman admissions: N/A; 2014-2015: 5,728 applied, 4,118 accepted. Neither SAT nor ACT required. ACT 25/75 percentile: N/A. High school rank: N/A
Early decision deadline: N/A, notification date: N/A
Early action deadline: N/A, notification date: N/A
Application deadline (fall): rolling
Undergraduate student body: 5,289 full time, 2,650 part time; 31% male, 69% female; 0% American Indian, 3% Asian, 27% black, 36% Hispanic, 2% multiracial, 0% Pacific Islander, 27% white, 1% international; 93% from in state; 8% live on campus; N/A of students in fraternities, N/A in sororities
Most popular majors: 14% Business, Management, Marketing, and Related Support Services, 22% Health Professions and Related Programs, 8% Homeland Security, Law Enforcement, Firefighting and Related Protective Services, 12% Psychology, 26% Social Sciences
Expenses: 2015-2016: $18,076; room/board: $13,200
Financial aid: (914) 378-3421; 87% of undergrads determined to have financial need; average aid package $13,707

Metropolitan College of New York

New York NY
(800) 338-4465
U.S. News ranking: Reg. U. (N), second tier
Website: www.metropolitan.edu/
Admissions email: N/A
Private
Freshman admissions: less selective; 2014-2015: 251 applied, 109 accepted. Neither SAT nor ACT required. ACT 25/75 percentile: N/A. High school rank: N/A
Early decision deadline: N/A, notification date: N/A
Early action deadline: N/A, notification date: N/A
Application deadline (fall): rolling
Undergraduate student body: 806 full time, 91 part time; 28% male, 72% female; 1% American Indian, 2% Asian, 60% black, 20% Hispanic, 1% multiracial, 0% Pacific Islander, 4% white, 2% international
Most popular majors: 36% Business/Commerce, General, 43% Community Organization and Advocacy, 18% Health Information/Medical Records Administration/Administrator, 3% Urban Studies/Affairs
Expenses: 2015-2016: $17,490; room/board: N/A
Financial aid: (212) 343-1234; 95% of undergrads determined to have financial need; average aid package $16,033

Molloy College

Rockville Centre NY
(516) 323-4000
U.S. News ranking: Reg. U. (N), No. 36
Website: www.molloy.edu
Admissions email: admissions@molloy.edu
Private; founded 1955
Affiliation: Roman Catholic
Freshman admissions: selective; 2014-2015: 3,277 applied, 2,471 accepted. Either SAT or ACT required. SAT 25/75 percentile: 980-1140. High school rank: 34% in top tenth, 54% in top quarter, 93% in top half
Early decision deadline: N/A, notification date: N/A
Early action deadline: 12/1, notification date: 12/15
Application deadline (fall): rolling
Undergraduate student body: 2,679 full time, 657 part time; 25% male, 75% female; 0% American Indian, 7% Asian, 12% black, 14% Hispanic, 1% multiracial, 1% Pacific Islander, 63% white, 0% international; 98% from in state; 8% live on campus; N/A of students in fraternities, N/A in sororities
Most popular majors: 7% Business, Management, Marketing, and Related Support Services, 10% Education, 53% Health Professions and Related Programs, 7% Homeland Security, Law Enforcement, Firefighting and Related Protective Services, 5% Public Administration and Social Service Professions
Expenses: 2015-2016: $28,030; room/board: $13,940
Financial aid: (516) 256-2217; 75% of undergrads determined to have financial need; average aid package $15,670

Monroe College

Bronx NY
(800) 556-6676
U.S. News ranking: Reg. U. (N), second tier
Website: www.monroecollege.edu
Admissions email: N/A
For-profit; founded 1933
Freshman admissions: less selective; 2014-2015: 4,251 applied, 1,712 accepted. Neither SAT nor ACT required. SAT 25/75 percentile: 710-960. High school rank: N/A
Early decision deadline: N/A, notification date: N/A
Early action deadline: 12/15, notification date: 1/31
Application deadline (fall): rolling
Undergraduate student body: 4,769 full time, 1,729 part time; 36% male, 64% female; 0% American Indian, 1% Asian, 43% black, 40% Hispanic, 0% multiracial, 0% Pacific Islander, 3% white, 8% international; 90% from in state; 15% live on campus; 0% of students in fraternities, 0% in sororities
Most popular majors: 13% Accounting, 20% Business Administration and Management, General, 27% Criminal Justice/Law Enforcement Administration, 13% Health Services Administration, 11% Hospitality Administration/Management, General
Expenses: 2015-2016: $14,148; room/board: $9,400
Financial aid: N/A; 93% of undergrads determined to have financial need; average aid package $12,681

Morrisville State College

Morrisville NY
(315) 684-6046
U.S. News ranking: Reg. Coll. (N), No. 33
Website: www.morrisville.edu
Admissions email: admissions@morrisville.edu
Public; founded 1908
Freshman admissions: less selective; 2014-2015: 4,088 applied, 2,297 accepted. Neither SAT nor ACT required. SAT 25/75 percentile: 840-1000. High school rank: 7% in top tenth, 25% in top quarter, 60% in top half
Early decision deadline: N/A, notification date: N/A
Early action deadline: N/A, notification date: N/A
Application deadline (fall): rolling
Undergraduate student body: 2,505 full time, 405 part time; 52% male, 48% female; 1% American Indian, 1% Asian, 19% black, 7% Hispanic, 2% multiracial, 0% Pacific Islander, 68% white, 1% international; 95% from in state; 56% live on campus; 0% of students in fraternities, 0% in sororities
Most popular majors: 22% Agriculture, Agriculture Operations, and Related Sciences, 15% Business, Management, Marketing, and Related Support Services, 14% Health Professions and Related Programs, 13% Liberal Arts and Sciences, General Studies and Humanities, 9% Mechanic and Repair Technologies/Technicians
Expenses: 2015-2016: $7,970 in state, $13,040 out of state; room/board: $13,370
Financial aid: (315) 684-6289; 86% of undergrads determined to have financial need; average aid package $10,028

Mount St. Mary College

Newburgh NY
(845) 569-3488
U.S. News ranking: Reg. U. (N), No. 106
Website: www.msmc.edu
Admissions email: admissions@msmc.edu
Private; founded 1959
Affiliation: Roman Catholic
Freshman admissions: selective; 2014-2015: 3,742 applied, 3,316 accepted. Either SAT or ACT required. SAT 25/75 percentile: 910-1100. High school rank: 10% in top tenth, 37% in top quarter, 75% in top half
Early decision deadline: N/A, notification date: N/A
Early action deadline: N/A, notification date: N/A
Application deadline (fall): 8/15
Undergraduate student body: 1,712 full time, 411 part time; 29% male, 71% female; 1% American Indian, 2% Asian, 8% black, 13% Hispanic, 1% multiracial, 0% Pacific Islander, 63% white, 0% international; 89% from in state; 46% live on campus; 0% of students in fraternities, 0% in sororities
Most popular majors: 17% Business, Management, Marketing, and Related Support Services, 25% Health Professions and Related Programs, 8% History, 6% Mathematics and Statistics, 10% Psychology
Expenses: 2015-2016: $28,233; room/board: $13,828
Financial aid: (845) 569-3298; 81% of undergrads determined to have financial need; average aid package $17,529

Nazareth College

Rochester NY
(585) 389-2860
U.S. News ranking: Reg. U. (N), No. 29
Website: www.naz.edu
Admissions email: admissions@naz.edu
Private; founded 1924
Freshman admissions: selective; 2014-2015: 4,185 applied, 2,950 accepted. Neither SAT nor ACT required. SAT 25/75 percentile: 980-1190. High school rank: 23% in top tenth, 56% in top quarter, 86% in top half
Early decision deadline: 11/15, notification date: 12/15
Early action deadline: N/A, notification date: N/A
Application deadline (fall): 2/1
Undergraduate student body: 1,931 full time, 126 part time; 29% male, 71% female; 0% American Indian, 3% Asian, 7% black, 4% Hispanic, 2% multiracial, 0% Pacific Islander, 74% white, 2% international; 92% from in state; 53% live on campus; 0% of students in fraternities, 0% in sororities
Most popular majors: 13% Business, Management, Marketing, and Related Support Services, 15% Education, 17% Health Professions and Related Programs, 8% Psychology, 9% Visual and Performing Arts
Expenses: 2015-2016: $31,520; room/board: $12,918
Financial aid: (585) 389-2310; 82% of undergrads determined to have financial need; average aid package $24,940

New School

New York NY
(800) 292-3040
U.S. News ranking: Nat. U., No. 127
Website: www.newschool.edu
Admissions email: admission@newschool.edu
Private; founded 1919
Freshman admissions: selective; 2014-2015: 5,622 applied, 3,705 accepted. Neither SAT nor ACT required. SAT 25/75 percentile: 990-1240. High school rank: 15% in top tenth, 42% in top quarter, 74% in top half
Early decision deadline: 11/1, notification date: 12/30
Early action deadline: N/A, notification date: N/A
Application deadline (fall): 1/15
Undergraduate student body: 5,885 full time, 810 part time; 28% male, 72% female; 0% American Indian, 10% Asian, 5% black, 11% Hispanic, 3% multiracial, 0% Pacific Islander, 34% white, 32% international; 32% from in state; 23% live on campus; 0% of students in fraternities, 0% in sororities
Most popular majors: 7% English Language and Literature/Letters, 8% Liberal Arts and Sciences, General Studies and Humanities, 5% Psychology, 11% Social Sciences, 69% Visual and Performing Arts
Expenses: 2015-2016: $42,977; room/board: $17,235
Financial aid: (212) 229-8930; 46% of undergrads determined to have financial need; average aid package $24,505

New York Institute of Technology

Old Westbury NY
(516) 686-7520
U.S. News ranking: Reg. U. (N), No. 41
Website: www.nyit.edu
Admissions email: admissions@nyit.edu
Private; founded 1955
Freshman admissions: more selective; 2014-2015: 8,394 applied, 5,375 accepted. Either SAT or ACT required. SAT 25/75 percentile: 1040-1270. High school rank: 22% in top tenth, 52% in top quarter, 88% in top half
Early decision deadline: N/A, notification date: N/A
Early action deadline: 12/1, notification date: 12/31
Application deadline (fall): rolling
Undergraduate student body: 3,722 full time, 569 part time; 63% male, 37% female; 0% American Indian, 13% Asian, 7% black, 13% Hispanic, 1% multiracial, 0% Pacific Islander, 19% white, 18% international; 90% from in state; 21% live on campus; 3% of students in fraternities, 4% in sororities
Most popular majors: 17% Architecture and Related Services, 11% Biological and Biomedical Sciences, 12% Business, Management, Marketing, and Related Support Services, 10% Communication, Journalism, and Related Programs, 14% Engineering
Expenses: 2015-2016: $33,480; room/board: $13,090
Financial aid: (516) 686-7680; 69% of undergrads determined to have financial need; average aid package $19,693

New York University

New York NY
(212) 998-4500
U.S. News ranking: Nat. U., No. 32
Website: www.nyu.edu
Admissions email: admissions@nyu.edu
Private; founded 1831
Freshman admissions: more selective; 2014-2015: 50,804 applied, 18,010 accepted. Either SAT or ACT required. SAT 25/75 percentile: 1240-1450. High

school rank: 54% in top tenth, 85% in top quarter, 98% in top half
Early decision deadline: 11/1, notification date: 12/15
Early action deadline: N/A, notification date: N/A
Application deadline (fall): 1/1
Undergraduate student body: 23,715 full time, 1,270 part time; 43% male, 57% female; 0% American Indian, 20% Asian, 5% black, 12% Hispanic, 4% multiracial, 0% Pacific Islander, 36% white, 15% international; 36% from in state; 44% live on campus; 7% of students in fraternities, 6% in sororities
Most popular majors: 13% Business, Management, Marketing, and Related Support Services, 7% Health Professions and Related Programs, 10% Liberal Arts and Sciences, General Studies and Humanities, 16% Social Sciences, 21% Visual and Performing Arts
Expenses: 2014-2015: $46,170; room/board: $16,782
Financial aid: (212) 998-4444; 56% of undergrads determined to have financial need; average aid package $29,271

Niagara University

Niagara University NY
(716) 286-8700
U.S. News ranking: Reg. U. (N), No. 47
Website: www.niagara.edu
Admissions email: admissions@niagara.edu
Private; founded 1856
Affiliation: Roman Catholic (Vincentian)
Freshman admissions: selective; 2014-2015: 3,565 applied, 2,348 accepted. Either SAT or ACT required. SAT 25/75 percentile: 940-1130. High school rank: 19% in top tenth, 44% in top quarter, 76% in top half
Early decision deadline: N/A, notification date: N/A
Early action deadline: N/A, notification date: N/A
Application deadline (fall): rolling
Undergraduate student body: 2,833 full time, 343 part time; 39% male, 61% female; 1% American Indian, 2% Asian, 6% black, 4% Hispanic, 2% multiracial, 0% Pacific Islander, 71% white, 9% international; 91% from in state; 55% live on campus; 3% of students in fraternities, 4% in sororities
Most popular majors: 5% Biological and Biomedical Sciences, 28% Business, Management, Marketing, and Related Support Services, 34% Education, 5% Health Professions and Related Programs, 9% Homeland Security, Law Enforcement, Firefighting and Related Protective Services
Expenses: 2015-2016: $29,900; room/board: $12,300
Financial aid: (716) 286-8686; 76% of undergrads determined to have financial need; average aid package $23,602

Nyack College

Nyack NY
(800) 336-9225
U.S. News ranking: Reg. U. (N), second tier
Website: www.nyack.edu
Admissions email: admissions@nyack.edu
Private; founded 1882
Affiliation: Christian & Missionary Alliance
Freshman admissions: least selective; 2014-2015: 625 applied, 621 accepted. Neither SAT nor ACT required. SAT 25/75 percentile: 760-1010. High school rank: 9% in top tenth, 27% in top quarter, 57% in top half
Early decision deadline: N/A, notification date: N/A
Early action deadline: N/A, notification date: N/A
Application deadline (fall): rolling
Undergraduate student body: 1,416 full time, 289 part time; 38% male, 62% female; 0% American Indian, 8% Asian, 30% black, 29% Hispanic, 2% multiracial, 0% Pacific Islander, 22% white, 6% international; 66% from in state; N/A live on campus; 0% of students in fraternities, 0% in sororities
Most popular majors: 5% Business Administration and Management, General, 12% Multi/Interdisciplinary Studies, General, 34% Organizational Behavior Studies, 8% Psychology, General, 6% Registered Nursing/Registered Nurse
Expenses: 2015-2016: $24,300; room/board: $8,950
Financial aid: (845) 358-1710; 83% of undergrads determined to have financial need; average aid package $20,230

Pace University

New York NY
(212) 346-1323
U.S. News ranking: Nat. U., No. 180
Website: www.pace.edu
Admissions email: infoctr@pace.edu
Private; founded 1906
Freshman admissions: selective; 2014-2015: 15,722 applied, 13,362 accepted. Neither SAT nor ACT required. SAT 25/75 percentile: 950-1150. High school rank: 14% in top tenth, 39% in top quarter, 75% in top half
Early decision deadline: N/A, notification date: N/A
Early action deadline: 12/1, notification date: 1/1
Application deadline (fall): 2/15
Undergraduate student body: 7,262 full time, 1,432 part time; 41% male, 59% female; 0% American Indian, 9% Asian, 11% black, 15% Hispanic, 4% multiracial, 0% Pacific Islander, 50% white, 9% international; 59% from in state; 40% live on campus; 4% of students in fraternities, 5% in sororities
Most popular majors: 32% Business, Management, Marketing, and Related Support Services, 13% Communication, Journalism, and Related Programs, 10% Health Professions and Related Programs, 9% Psychology, 7% Visual and Performing Arts
Expenses: 2015-2016: $41,325; room/board: $15,010
Financial aid: (212) 346-1300; 72% of undergrads determined to have financial need; average aid package $29,194

Paul Smith's College[1]

Paul Smiths NY
(800) 421-2605
U.S. News ranking: Reg. Coll. (N), No. 44
Website: www.paulsmiths.edu
Admissions email: admiss@paulsmiths.edu
Private
Application deadline (fall): N/A
Undergraduate student body: N/A full time, N/A part time
Expenses: 2014-2015: $26,146; room/board: $10,568
Financial aid: (518) 327-6220

Plaza College

Forest Hills NY
(718) 779-1430
U.S. News ranking: Reg. Coll. (N), unranked
Website: www.plazacollege.edu
Admissions email: N/A
For-profit; founded 1916
Freshman admissions: N/A; 2014-2015: N/A applied, N/A accepted. Neither SAT nor ACT required. ACT 25/75 percentile: N/A. High school rank: N/A
Early decision deadline: N/A, notification date: N/A
Early action deadline: N/A, notification date: N/A
Application deadline (fall): rolling
Undergraduate student body: N/A full time, N/A part time; N/A male, N/A female; N/A American Indian, N/A Asian, N/A black, N/A Hispanic, N/A multiracial, N/A Pacific Islander, N/A white, N/A international
Most popular majors: Information not available
Expenses: 2014-2015: $11,350; room/board: $5,900
Financial aid: (718) 779-1430

Pratt Institute

Brooklyn NY
(718) 636-3514
U.S. News ranking: Reg. U. (N), No. 18
Website: www.pratt.edu
Admissions email: admissions@pratt.edu
Private; founded 1887
Freshman admissions: selective; 2014-2015: 4,679 applied, 2,964 accepted. Either SAT or ACT required. SAT 25/75 percentile: 1060-1290. High school rank: N/A
Early decision deadline: N/A, notification date: N/A
Early action deadline: 11/1, notification date: 12/22
Application deadline (fall): 1/5
Undergraduate student body: 3,034 full time, 109 part time; 32% male, 68% female; 0% American Indian, 17% Asian, 4% black, 10% Hispanic, 1% multiracial, 0% Pacific Islander, 42% white, 25% international
Most popular majors: Information not available
Expenses: 2015-2016: $46,586; room/board: $11,496
Financial aid: (718) 636-3599

Purchase College–SUNY

Purchase NY
(914) 251-6300
U.S. News ranking: Nat. Lib. Arts, No. 171
Website: www.purchase.edu
Admissions email: admissions@purchase.edu
Public; founded 1967
Freshman admissions: selective; 2014-2015: 6,955 applied, 2,839 accepted. Either SAT or ACT required. SAT 25/75 percentile: 990-1210. High school rank: N/A
Early decision deadline: N/A, notification date: N/A
Early action deadline: 11/15, notification date: 12/15
Application deadline (fall): 7/15
Undergraduate student body: 3,838 full time, 350 part time; 45% male, 55% female; 0% American Indian, 3% Asian, 9% black, 17% Hispanic, 5% multiracial, 0% Pacific Islander, 56% white, 2% international; 85% from in state; 66% live on campus; N/A of students in fraternities, N/A in sororities
Most popular majors: Information not available
Expenses: 2015-2016: $8,233 in state, $18,083 out of state; room/board: $12,436
Financial aid: (914) 251-6350; 63% of undergrads determined to have financial need; average aid package $9,445

Rensselaer Polytechnic Institute

Troy NY
(518) 276-6216
U.S. News ranking: Nat. U., No. 41
Website: www.rpi.edu
Admissions email: admissions@rpi.edu
Private; founded 1824
Freshman admissions: most selective; 2014-2015: 18,602 applied, 6,976 accepted. Either SAT or ACT required. SAT 25/75 percentile: 1300-1490. High school rank: 69% in top tenth, 95% in top quarter, 99% in top half
Early decision deadline: 11/1, notification date: 12/13
Early action deadline: N/A, notification date: N/A
Application deadline (fall): 1/15
Undergraduate student body: 5,598 full time, 20 part time; 69% male, 31% female; 0% American Indian, 10% Asian, 3% black, 7% Hispanic, 7% multiracial, 0% Pacific Islander, 62% white, 9% international; 33% from in state; 57% live on campus; 30% of students in fraternities, 16% in sororities
Most popular majors: 6% Biological and Biomedical Sciences, 6% Business, Management, Marketing, and Related Support Services, 10% Computer and Information Sciences and Support Services, 53% Engineering, 5% Physical Sciences
Expenses: 2015-2016: $49,341; room/board: $14,095
Financial aid: (518) 276-6813; 63% of undergrads determined to have financial need; average aid package $34,359

Roberts Wesleyan College

Rochester NY
(585) 594-6400
U.S. News ranking: Reg. U. (N), No. 83
Website: www.roberts.edu
Admissions email: admissions@roberts.edu
Private; founded 1866
Affiliation: Free Methodist
Freshman admissions: selective; 2014-2015: 915 applied, 631 accepted. Either SAT or ACT required. SAT 25/75 percentile: 950-1160. High school rank: 18% in top tenth, 42% in top quarter, 80% in top half
Early decision deadline: N/A, notification date: N/A
Early action deadline: N/A, notification date: N/A
Application deadline (fall): 8/20
Undergraduate student body: 1,220 full time, 116 part time; 32% male, 68% female; 1% American Indian, 1% Asian, 11% black, 6% Hispanic, 3% multiracial, 0% Pacific Islander, 73% white, 3% international; 92% from in state; 65% live on campus; 0% of students in fraternities, 0% in sororities
Most popular majors: Information not available
Expenses: 2015-2016: $28,630; room/board: $10,038
Financial aid: (585) 594-6150; 86% of undergrads determined to have financial need; average aid package $21,573

Rochester Institute of Technology

Rochester NY
(585) 475-6631
U.S. News ranking: Reg. U. (N), No. 7
Website: www.rit.edu
Admissions email: admissions@rit.edu
Private; founded 1829
Freshman admissions: more selective; 2014-2015: 17,936 applied, 10,307 accepted. Either SAT or ACT required. SAT 25/75 percentile: 1110-1320. High school rank: 32% in top tenth, 67% in top quarter, 95% in top half
Early decision deadline: 12/1, notification date: 1/15
Early action deadline: N/A, notification date: N/A
Application deadline (fall): rolling
Undergraduate student body: 12,211 full time, 1,249 part time; 68% male, 32% female; 0% American Indian, 7% Asian, 5% black, 7% Hispanic, 3% multiracial, 0% Pacific Islander, 64% white, 6% international; 56% from in state; 57% live on campus; 5% of students in fraternities, 6% in sororities
Most popular majors: 10% Business, Management, Marketing, and Related Support Services, 17% Computer and Information Sciences and Support Services, 18% Engineering, 10% Engineering Technologies and Engineering-Related Fields, 15% Visual and Performing Arts
Expenses: 2015-2016: $37,124; room/board: $11,918
Financial aid: (585) 475-2186; 74% of undergrads determined to have financial need; average aid package $24,500

The Sage Colleges

Troy NY
(888) 837-9724
U.S. News ranking: Reg. U. (N), No. 100
Website: www.sage.edu
Admissions email: tscadm@sage.edu
Private; founded 1916
Freshman admissions: selective; 2014-2015: 2,307 applied, 1,265 accepted. Neither SAT nor ACT required. SAT 25/75 percentile: 830-1090. High school rank: 18% in top tenth, 48% in top quarter, 82% in top half
Early decision deadline: N/A, notification date: N/A
Early action deadline: N/A, notification date: N/A
Application deadline (fall): rolling
Undergraduate student body: 1,464 full time, 246 part time; 22% male, 78% female; 0% American Indian, 3% Asian, 13% black, 10% Hispanic, 2% multiracial, 0% Pacific Islander, 62% white, 0% international; 93% from in state; 55% live on campus; N/A of students in fraternities, N/A in sororities
Most popular majors: 8% Biological and Biomedical Sciences, 11% Business, Management, Marketing, and Related Support Services, 21% Health Professions and Related Programs, 11% Social Sciences, 12% Visual and Performing Arts
Expenses: 2015-2016: $28,400; room/board: $12,220
Financial aid: (518) 244-2215; 92% of undergrads determined to have financial need

Sarah Lawrence College

Bronxville NY
(914) 395-2510
U.S. News ranking: Nat. Lib. Arts, No. 57
Website: www.slc.edu
Admissions email: slcadmit@sarahlawrence.edu
Private; founded 1926
Freshman admissions: more selective; 2014-2015: 2,392 applied, 1,271 accepted. Neither SAT nor ACT required. SAT 25/75 percentile: 1160-1380. High school rank: 41% in top tenth, 77% in top quarter, 96% in top half
Early decision deadline: 11/1, notification date: 12/15
Early action deadline: N/A, notification date: N/A
Application deadline (fall): 1/15
Undergraduate student body: 1,415 full time, 22 part time; 29% male, 71% female; 0% American Indian, 4% Asian, 4% black, 9% Hispanic, 6% multiracial, 0% Pacific Islander, 57% white, 13% international; 21% from in state; 81% live on campus; N/A of students in fraternities, N/A in sororities
Most popular majors: 100% Liberal Arts and Sciences, General Studies and Humanities
Expenses: 2015-2016: $51,034; room/board: $14,208
Financial aid: (914) 395-2570; 73% of undergrads determined to have financial need; average aid package $35,368

School of Visual Arts

New York NY
(212) 592-2100
U.S. News ranking: Arts, unranked
Website: www.schoolofvisualarts.edu/
Admissions email: admissions@sva.edu
For-profit; founded 1947
Freshman admissions: N/A; 2014-2015: 3,431 applied, 2,634 accepted. Either SAT or ACT required. SAT 25/75 percentile: 910-1160. High school rank: N/A
Early decision deadline: N/A, notification date: N/A
Early action deadline: 12/1, notification date: N/A
Application deadline (fall): rolling
Undergraduate student body: 3,435 full time, 243 part time; 38% male, 62% female; 1% American Indian, 14% Asian, 6% black, 6% Hispanic, 0% multiracial, 1% Pacific Islander, 38% white, 33% international; 52% from in state; 31% live on campus; 0% of students in fraternities, 0% in sororities
Most popular majors: Information not available
Expenses: 2014-2015: $33,560; room/board: $17,000
Financial aid: (212) 592-2030

Siena College

Loudonville NY
(888) 287-4362
U.S. News ranking: Nat. Lib. Arts, No. 112
Website: www.siena.edu
Admissions email: admissions@siena.edu
Private; founded 1937
Affiliation: Roman Catholic
Freshman admissions: selective; 2014-2015: 8,647 applied, 5,013 accepted. Neither SAT nor ACT required. SAT 25/75 percentile: 1020-1220. High school rank: 23% in top tenth, 53% in top quarter, 87% in top half
Early decision deadline: 12/1, notification date: 12/15
Early action deadline: 12/1, notification date: 1/1
Application deadline (fall): 2/15
Undergraduate student body: 2,990 full time, 149 part time; 48% male, 52% female; 0% American Indian, 4% Asian, 3% black, 7% Hispanic, 3% multiracial, 0% Pacific Islander, 80% white, 2% international; 81% from in state; 78% live on campus; 0% of students in fraternities, 0% in sororities
Most popular majors: 14% Accounting, 7% Biology/Biological Sciences, General, 7% Finance, General, 17% Marketing/Marketing Management, General, 11% Psychology, General
Expenses: 2015-2016: $33,415; room/board: $13,595
Financial aid: (518) 783-2427; 73% of undergrads determined to have financial need; average aid package $26,600

Skidmore College

Saratoga Springs NY
(518) 580-5570
U.S. News ranking: Nat. Lib. Arts, No. 38
Website: www.skidmore.edu
Admissions email: admissions@skidmore.edu
Private; founded 1903
Freshman admissions: more selective; 2014-2015: 8,669 applied, 3,237 accepted. Either SAT or ACT required. SAT 25/75 percentile: 1130-1350. High school rank: 43% in top tenth, 78% in top quarter, 96% in top half
Early decision deadline: 11/15, notification date: 12/15
Early action deadline: N/A, notification date: N/A
Application deadline (fall): 1/15
Undergraduate student body: 2,609 full time, 23 part time; 41% male, 59% female; 0% American Indian, 6% Asian, 4% black, 8% Hispanic, 4% multiracial, 0% Pacific Islander, 63% white, 8% international; 33% from in state; 89% live on campus; 0% of students in fraternities, 0% in sororities
Most popular majors: 10% Business, Management, Marketing, and Related Support Services, 7% English Language and Literature/Letters, 11% Psychology, 15% Social Sciences, 16% Visual and Performing Arts
Expenses: 2015-2016: $48,970; room/board: $13,072
Financial aid: (518) 580-5750; 45% of undergrads determined to have financial need; average aid package $41,800

St. Bonaventure University

St. Bonaventure NY
(800) 462-5050
U.S. News ranking: Reg. U. (N), No. 24
Website: www.sbu.edu
Admissions email: admissions@sbu.edu
Private; founded 1858
Affiliation: Roman Catholic
Freshman admissions: selective; 2014-2015: 2,682 applied, 1,889 accepted. Either SAT or ACT required. SAT 25/75 percentile: 940-1160. High school rank: 18% in top tenth, 43% in top quarter, 74% in top half
Early decision deadline: N/A, notification date: N/A
Early action deadline: N/A, notification date: N/A
Application deadline (fall): 7/1
Undergraduate student body: 1,725 full time, 46 part time; 50% male, 50% female; 0% American Indian, 4% Asian, 5% black, 7% Hispanic, 2% multiracial, 0% Pacific Islander, 70% white, 2% international; 75% from in state; 76% live on campus; 0% of students in fraternities, 0% in sororities
Most popular majors: 8% Biology/Biological Sciences, General, 15% Journalism, 25% Marketing/Marketing Management, General, 7% Psychology, General, 11% Special Education and Teaching, General
Expenses: 2015-2016: $31,389; room/board: $11,128
Financial aid: (716) 375-2528; 74% of undergrads determined to have financial need; average aid package $23,568

St. Francis College

Brooklyn Heights NY
(718) 489-5200
U.S. News ranking: Reg. Coll. (N), No. 21
Website: www.sfc.edu
Admissions email: admissions@stfranciscollege.edu
Private; founded 1884
Freshman admissions: less selective; 2014-2015: 2,513 applied, 1,936 accepted. Either SAT or ACT required. SAT 25/75 percentile: 830-1040. High school rank: N/A
Early decision deadline: N/A, notification date: N/A
Early action deadline: N/A, notification date: N/A
Application deadline (fall): rolling
Undergraduate student body: 2,414 full time, 257 part time; 44% male, 56% female; 0% American Indian, 4% Asian, 20% black, 20% Hispanic, 2% multiracial, 1% Pacific Islander, 39% white, 5% international; 96% from in state; 6% live on campus; 5% of students in fraternities, 1% in sororities
Most popular majors: 16% Business Administration, Management and Operations, 14% Communication and Media Studies, 10% Education, General, 12% Health Professions and Related Clinical Sciences, Other, 8% Psychology, General
Expenses: 2015-2016: $23,800; room/board: $14,250
Financial aid: (718) 489-5255; 73% of undergrads determined to have financial need; average aid package $14,255

St. John Fisher College

Rochester NY
(585) 385-8064
U.S. News ranking: Nat. U., No. 146
Website: www.sjfc.edu
Admissions email: admissions@sjfc.edu
Private; founded 1948
Affiliation: Roman Catholic
Freshman admissions: selective; 2014-2015: 3,836 applied, 2,605 accepted. Either SAT or ACT required. SAT 25/75 percentile: 970-1160. High school rank: 18% in top tenth, 54% in top quarter, 92% in top half
Early decision deadline: 12/1, notification date: 1/15
Early action deadline: N/A, notification date: N/A
Application deadline (fall): rolling
Undergraduate student body: 2,661 full time, 196 part time; 40% male, 60% female; 0% American Indian, 3% Asian, 4% black, 4% Hispanic, 2% multiracial, 0% Pacific Islander, 84% white, 0% international; 100% from in state; 50% live on campus; 0% of students in fraternities, 0% in sororities
Most popular majors: 7% Biological and Biomedical Sciences, 28% Business, Management, Marketing, and Related Support Services, 8% Education, 21% Health Professions and Related Programs, 8% Psychology
Expenses: 2015-2016: $30,690; room/board: $11,460
Financial aid: (585) 385-8042; 82% of undergrads determined to have financial need; average aid package $20,935

St. John's University

Queens NY
(718) 990-2000
U.S. News ranking: Nat. U., No. 153
Website: www.stjohns.edu/
Admissions email: admission@stjohns.edu
Private; founded 1870
Affiliation: Roman Catholic
Freshman admissions: selective; 2014-2015: 44,597 applied, 27,883 accepted. Either SAT or ACT required. SAT 25/75 percentile: 990-1210. High school rank: 19% in top tenth, 43% in top quarter, 77% in top half
Early decision deadline: N/A, notification date: N/A
Early action deadline: N/A, notification date: N/A
Application deadline (fall): rolling
Undergraduate student body: 10,720 full time, 5,045 part time; 45% male, 55% female; 0% American Indian, 18% Asian, 19% black, 15% Hispanic, 4% multiracial, 0% Pacific Islander, 34% white, 5% international; 70% from in state; 29% live on campus; 10% of students in fraternities, 9% in sororities
Most popular majors: 19% Business, Management, Marketing, and Related Support Services, 11% Communication, Journalism, and Related Programs, 9% Health Professions and Related Programs, 9% Homeland Security, Law Enforcement, Firefighting and Related Protective Services, 7% Psychology
Expenses: 2015-2016: $38,680; room/board: $16,390
Financial aid: (718) 990-2000; 82% of undergrads determined to have financial need; average aid package $27,001

St. Joseph's College New York

Brooklyn NY
(718) 940-5800
U.S. News ranking: Reg. U. (N), No. 74
Website: www.sjcny.edu
Admissions email: longislandas@sjcny.edu
Private; founded 1916
Freshman admissions: selective; 2014-2015: 3,024 applied, 2,139 accepted. Either SAT or ACT required. SAT 25/75 percentile: 920-1130. High school rank: N/A
Early decision deadline: N/A, notification date: N/A
Early action deadline: N/A, notification date: N/A
Application deadline (fall): rolling
Undergraduate student body: 3,260 full time, 878 part time; 34% male, 66% female; 1% American Indian, 3% Asian, 10% black, 12% Hispanic, 1% multiracial, 0% Pacific Islander, 63% white, 0% international; 98% from in state; 0% live on campus; N/A of students in fraternities, N/A in sororities
Most popular majors: 13% Business Administration and Management, General, 6% Practical Nursing, Vocational

Nursing and Nursing Assistants, Other, 9% Psychology, General, 8% Rhetoric and Composition, 18% Special Education and Teaching, General
Expenses: 2015-2016: $24,130; room/board: N/A
Financial aid: (718) 636-6808; 77% of undergrads determined to have financial need; average aid package $12,729

St. Lawrence University

Canton NY
(315) 229-5261
U.S. News ranking: Nat. Lib. Arts, No. 60
Website: www.stlawu.edu
Admissions email: admissions@stlawu.edu
Private; founded 1856
Freshman admissions: more selective; 2014-2015: 4,328 applied, 2,062 accepted. Neither SAT nor ACT required. SAT 25/75 percentile: 1110-1290. High school rank: 37% in top tenth, 78% in top quarter, 97% in top half
Early decision deadline: 11/1, notification date: N/A
Early action deadline: N/A, notification date: N/A
Application deadline (fall): 2/1
Undergraduate student body: 2,371 full time, 35 part time; 46% male, 54% female; 0% American Indian, 2% Asian, 3% black, 4% Hispanic, 2% multiracial, 0% Pacific Islander, 79% white, 8% international; 42% from in state; 98% live on campus; 10% of students in fraternities, 19% in sororities
Most popular majors: 14% Biological and Biomedical Sciences, 6% Mathematics and Statistics, 6% Physical Sciences, 8% Psychology, 30% Social Sciences
Expenses: 2015-2016: $49,420; room/board: $12,731
Financial aid: (315) 229-5265; 55% of undergrads determined to have financial need; average aid package $38,322

Stony Brook University–SUNY

Stony Brook NY
(631) 632-6868
U.S. News ranking: Nat. U., No. 89
Website: www.stonybrook.edu
Admissions email: enroll@stonybrook.edu
Public; founded 1957
Freshman admissions: more selective; 2014-2015: 33,714 applied, 13,938 accepted. Either SAT or ACT required. SAT 25/75 percentile: 1150-1350. High school rank: 48% in top tenth, 82% in top quarter, 97% in top half
Early decision deadline: N/A, notification date: N/A
Early action deadline: N/A, notification date: N/A
Application deadline (fall): rolling
Undergraduate student body: 15,385 full time, 1,095 part time; 54% male, 46% female; 0% American Indian, 24% Asian, 6% black, 11% Hispanic, 2% multiracial, 0% Pacific Islander, 38% white, 11% international; 92% from in state; 60% live on campus; 3% of students in fraternities, 3% in sororities
Most popular majors: 9% Biology/Biological Sciences, General, 8% Business Administration and Management, General, 11% Health Services/Allied Health/Health Sciences, General, 11% Psychology, General, 8% Registered Nursing/Registered Nurse
Expenses: 2015-2016: $8,855 in state, $23,935 out of state; room/board: $12,032
Financial aid: (631) 632-6840; 58% of undergrads determined to have financial need; average aid package $12,700

St. Thomas Aquinas College

Sparkill NY
(845) 398-4100
U.S. News ranking: Reg. U. (N), No. 109
Website: www.stac.edu
Admissions email: admissions@stac.edu
Private; founded 1952
Freshman admissions: less selective; 2014-2015: 1,423 applied, 1,150 accepted. Either SAT or ACT required. SAT 25/75 percentile: 837-1082. High school rank: 10% in top tenth, 29% in top quarter, 58% in top half
Early decision deadline: 12/15, notification date: 3/1
Early action deadline: N/A, notification date: N/A
Application deadline (fall): rolling
Undergraduate student body: 1,147 full time, 633 part time; 45% male, 55% female; 0% American Indian, 3% Asian, 8% black, 20% Hispanic, 2% multiracial, 0% Pacific Islander, 55% white, 2% international; 78% from in state; 35% live on campus; 0% of students in fraternities, 0% in sororities
Most popular majors: 17% Business Administration and Management, General, 13% Criminal Justice/Law Enforcement Administration, 12% Education/Teaching of Individuals in Early Childhood Special Education Programs, 15% Psychology, General, 10% Visual and Performing Arts, General
Expenses: 2015-2016: $28,740; room/board: $12,030
Financial aid: (845) 398-4097; 76% of undergrads determined to have financial need; average aid package $15,315

SUNY Buffalo State

Buffalo NY
(716) 878-4017
U.S. News ranking: Reg. U. (N), No. 122
Website: www.buffalostate.edu
Admissions email: admissions@buffalostate.edu
Public; founded 1871
Freshman admissions: less selective; 2014-2015: 12,589 applied, 7,748 accepted. Either SAT or ACT required. SAT 25/75 percentile: 820-1010. High school rank: 8% in top tenth, 30% in top quarter, 64% in top half
Early decision deadline: N/A, notification date: N/A
Early action deadline: N/A, notification date: N/A
Application deadline (fall): rolling
Undergraduate student body: 8,327 full time, 1,148 part time; 43% male, 57% female; 0% American Indian, 2% Asian, 26% black, 12% Hispanic, 3% multiracial, 0% Pacific Islander, 54% white, 2% international; 98% from in state; 33% live on campus; 1% of students in fraternities, 1% in sororities
Most popular majors: 13% Business, Management, Marketing, and Related Support Services, 18% Education, 9% Homeland Security, Law Enforcement, Firefighting and Related Protective Services, 9% Social Sciences, 7% Visual and Performing Arts
Expenses: 2015-2016: $7,669 in state, $17,519 out of state; room/board: $12,404
Financial aid: (716) 878-4901; 88% of undergrads determined to have financial need; average aid package $12,749

SUNY College–Cortland

Cortland NY
(607) 753-4711
U.S. News ranking: Reg. U. (N), No. 74
Website: www.cortland.edu/admissions
Admissions email: admissions@cortland.edu
Public; founded 1868
Freshman admissions: selective; 2014-2015: 11,221 applied, 5,494 accepted. Neither SAT nor ACT required. SAT 25/75 percentile: 970-1130. High school rank: 14% in top tenth, 52% in top quarter, 95% in top half
Early decision deadline: N/A, notification date: N/A
Early action deadline: 11/15, notification date: 1/1
Application deadline (fall): rolling
Undergraduate student body: 6,203 full time, 114 part time; 43% male, 57% female; 0% American Indian, 1% Asian, 5% black, 11% Hispanic, 2% multiracial, 0% Pacific Islander, 74% white, 1% international; 96% from in state; N/A live on campus; N/A of students in fraternities, N/A in sororities
Most popular majors: 7% Business, Management, Marketing, and Related Support Services, 29% Education, 8% Health Professions and Related Programs, 16% Parks, Recreation, Leisure, and Fitness Studies, 10% Social Sciences
Expenses: 2014-2015: $7,719 in state, $17,369 out of state; room/board: $12,040
Financial aid: (607) 753-4717

SUNY College of Agriculture and Technology–Cobleskill

Cobleskill NY
(518) 255-5525
U.S. News ranking: Reg. Coll. (N), No. 28
Website: www.cobleskill.edu
Admissions email: admissionsoffice@cobleskill.edu
Public; founded 1911
Freshman admissions: least selective; 2014-2015: 3,139 applied, 2,294 accepted. Neither SAT nor ACT required. SAT 25/75 percentile: 740-1010. High school rank: 5% in top tenth, 19% in top quarter, 51% in top half
Early decision deadline: N/A, notification date: N/A
Early action deadline: N/A, notification date: N/A
Application deadline (fall): rolling
Undergraduate student body: 2,413 full time, 119 part time; 48% male, 52% female; 0% American Indian, 1% Asian, 12% black, 7% Hispanic, 0% multiracial, 0% Pacific Islander, 73% white, 2% international; 77% from in state; 59% live on campus; 0% of students in fraternities, 0% in sororities
Most popular majors: 46% Agriculture, Agriculture Operations, and Related Sciences, 14% Business, Management, Marketing, and Related Support Services, 5% Computer and Information Sciences and Support Services, 13% Natural Resources and Conservation, 4% Personal and Culinary Services
Expenses: 2015-2016: $8,231 in state, $18,071 out of state; room/board: $12,948
Financial aid: (518) 255-5623; 76% of undergrads determined to have financial need; average aid package $8,475

SUNY College of Environmental Science and Forestry

Syracuse NY
(315) 470-6600
U.S. News ranking: Nat. U., No. 89
Website: www.esf.edu
Admissions email: esfinfo@esf.edu
Public; founded 1911
Freshman admissions: more selective; 2014-2015: 1,596 applied, 816 accepted. Either SAT or ACT required. SAT 25/75 percentile: 1090-1280. High school rank: 28% in top tenth, 68% in top quarter, 96% in top half
Early decision deadline: 12/1, notification date: 1/15
Early action deadline: N/A, notification date: N/A
Application deadline (fall): rolling
Undergraduate student body: 1,677 full time, 179 part time; 55% male, 45% female; 0% American Indian, 3% Asian, 2% black, 4% Hispanic, 3% multiracial, 0% Pacific Islander, 83% white, 2% international; 83% from in state; 35% live on campus; 5% of students in fraternities, 5% in sororities
Most popular majors: 13% Engineering, General, 41% Environmental Biology, 18% Environmental Science, 14% Natural Resources Management and Policy
Expenses: 2015-2016: $7,770 in state, $17,620 out of state; room/board: $14,490
Financial aid: (315) 470-6706; 70% of undergrads determined to have financial need; average aid package $15,000

SUNY College of Technology–Alfred

Alfred NY
(800) 425-3733
U.S. News ranking: Reg. Coll. (N), No. 19
Website: www.alfredstate.edu/alfred/Default.asp
Admissions email: admissions@alfredstate.edu
Public; founded 1908
Freshman admissions: less selective; 2014-2015: 5,849 applied, 3,210 accepted. Neither SAT nor ACT required. SAT 25/75 percentile: 840-1090. High school rank: N/A
Early decision deadline: N/A, notification date: N/A
Early action deadline: N/A, notification date: N/A
Application deadline (fall): rolling
Undergraduate student body: 3,329 full time, 332 part time; 61% male, 39% female; 0% American Indian, 2% Asian, 8% black, 6% Hispanic, 2% multiracial, 0% Pacific Islander, 78% white, 0% international; 96% from in state; 66% live on campus; 7% of students in fraternities, 7% in sororities
Most popular majors: 23% Business, Management, Marketing, and Related Support Services, 9% Communication, Journalism, and Related Programs, 12% Computer and Information Sciences and Support Services, 39% Engineering Technologies and Engineering-Related Fields, 9% Visual and Performing Arts
Expenses: 2015-2016: $8,057 in state, $17,907 out of state; room/board: $11,430
Financial aid: (607) 587-4251; 83% of undergrads determined to have financial need; average aid package $10,970

SUNY College of Technology–Canton

Canton NY
(800) 388-7123
U.S. News ranking: Reg. Coll. (N), No. 44
Website: www.canton.edu/
Admissions email: admissions@canton.edu
Public; founded 1906
Freshman admissions: less selective; 2014-2015: 3,119 applied, 2,516 accepted. Neither SAT nor ACT required. SAT 25/75 percentile: 780-1020. High school rank: 3% in top tenth, 16% in top quarter, 48% in top half
Early decision deadline: N/A, notification date: N/A
Early action deadline: N/A, notification date: N/A
Application deadline (fall): rolling
Undergraduate student body: 2,793 full time, 485 part time; 45% male, 55% female; 2% American Indian, 1% Asian, 14% black, 9% Hispanic, 2% multiracial, 0% Pacific Islander, 68% white, 1% international; 97% from in state; 40% live on campus; 2% of students in fraternities, 1% in sororities
Most popular majors: 11% Business Administration and Management, General, 11% Corrections and Criminal Justice, Other, 11% Finance, General, 15% Legal Assistant/Paralegal, 10% Registered Nursing/Registered Nurse

Expenses: 2015-2016: $7,938 in state, $17,788 out of state; room/board: $11,700
Financial aid: (315) 386-7616; 85% of undergrads determined to have financial need; average aid package $10,516

SUNY College of Technology–Delhi

Delhi NY
(607) 746-4550
U.S. News ranking: Reg. Coll. (N), No. 28
Website: www.delhi.edu/
Admissions email: enroll@delhi.edu
Public; founded 1913
Freshman admissions: less selective; 2014-2015: 5,134 applied, 3,490 accepted. Neither SAT nor ACT required. ACT 25/75 percentile: 18-22. High school rank: 3% in top tenth, 13% in top quarter, 44% in top half
Early decision deadline: N/A, notification date: N/A
Early action deadline: N/A, notification date: N/A
Application deadline (fall): rolling
Undergraduate student body: 2,691 full time, 923 part time; 45% male, 55% female; 1% American Indian, 3% Asian, 17% black, 14% Hispanic, 0% multiracial, 0% Pacific Islander, 60% white, 0% international; 96% from in state; N/A live on campus; N/A of students in fraternities, N/A in sororities
Most popular majors: 5% Architecture and Related Services, 47% Business, Management, Marketing, and Related Support Services, 37% Health Professions and Related Programs, 4% Homeland Security, Law Enforcement, Firefighting and Related Protective Services, 7% Personal and Culinary Services
Expenses: 2014-2015: $7,740 in state, $17,390 out of state; room/board: $10,970
Financial aid: (607) 746-4570; average aid package $3,533

SUNY College–Old Westbury

Old Westbury NY
(516) 876-3073
U.S. News ranking: Nat. Lib. Arts, second tier
Website: www.oldwestbury.edu
Admissions email: enroll@oldwestbury.edu
Public; founded 1965
Freshman admissions: less selective; 2014-2015: 3,490 applied, 2,176 accepted. Either SAT or ACT required. SAT 25/75 percentile: 910-1080. High school rank: N/A
Early decision deadline: N/A, notification date: N/A
Early action deadline: N/A, notification date: N/A
Application deadline (fall): rolling
Undergraduate student body: 3,670 full time, 645 part time; 42% male, 58% female; 0% American Indian, 10% Asian, 31% black, 21% Hispanic, 3% multiracial, 1% Pacific Islander, 31% white, 1% international; 98% from in state; 20% live on campus; 2% of students in fraternities, 2% in sororities
Most popular majors: Information not available
Expenses: 2014-2015: $8,436 in state, $18,086 out of state; room/board: $10,390
Financial aid: (516) 876-3222

SUNY College–Oneonta

Oneonta NY
(607) 436-2524
U.S. News ranking: Reg. U. (N), No. 47
Website: www.oneonta.edu
Admissions email: admissions@oneonta.edu
Public; founded 1889
Freshman admissions: selective; 2014-2015: 11,586 applied, 5,779 accepted. Either SAT or ACT required. SAT 25/75 percentile: 1000-1170. High school rank: 20% in top tenth, 54% in top quarter, 92% in top half
Early decision deadline: N/A, notification date: N/A
Early action deadline: 11/15, notification date: 12/1
Application deadline (fall): rolling
Undergraduate student body: 5,727 full time, 109 part time; 39% male, 61% female; 0% American Indian, 2% Asian, 3% black, 10% Hispanic, 2% multiracial, 0% Pacific Islander, 79% white, 1% international; 98% from in state; 57% live on campus; 1% of students in fraternities, 1% in sororities
Most popular majors: 9% Business, Management, Marketing, and Related Support Services, 11% Communication, Journalism, and Related Programs, 16% Education, 11% Family and Consumer Sciences/Human Sciences, 12% Visual and Performing Arts
Expenses: 2015-2016: $7,520 in state, $17,170 out of state; room/board: $11,530
Financial aid: (607) 436-2532; 57% of undergrads determined to have financial need; average aid package $9,652

SUNY College–Potsdam

Potsdam NY
(315) 267-2180
U.S. News ranking: Reg. U. (N), No. 92
Website: www.potsdam.edu
Admissions email: admissions@potsdam.edu
Public; founded 1816
Freshman admissions: selective; 2014-2015: 5,155 applied, 3,484 accepted. Neither SAT nor ACT required. SAT 25/75 percentile: 900-1140. High school rank: 9% in top tenth, 32% in top quarter, 59% in top half
Early decision deadline: N/A, notification date: N/A
Early action deadline: N/A, notification date: N/A
Application deadline (fall): rolling
Undergraduate student body: 3,573 full time, 108 part time; 44% male, 56% female; 2% American Indian, 2% Asian, 8% black, 10% Hispanic, 3% multiracial, 0% Pacific Islander, 69% white, 1% international; 97% from in state; 61% live on campus; 4% of students in fraternities, 6% in sororities
Most popular majors: 8% Business, Management, Marketing, and Related Support Services, 23% Education, 8% Psychology, 9% Social Sciences, 13% Visual and Performing Arts
Expenses: 2014-2015: $7,553 in state, $17,203 out of state; room/board: $11,370
Financial aid: (315) 267-2162; 74% of undergrads determined to have financial need; average aid package $14,253

SUNY Empire State College

Saratoga Springs NY
(518) 587-2100
U.S. News ranking: Reg. U. (N), unranked
Website: www.esc.edu
Admissions email: admissions@esc.edu
Public; founded 1971
Freshman admissions: N/A; 2014-2015: 1,308 applied, 1,061 accepted. Neither SAT nor ACT required. ACT 25/75 percentile: N/A. High school rank: N/A
Early decision deadline: N/A, notification date: N/A
Early action deadline: N/A, notification date: N/A
Application deadline (fall): rolling
Undergraduate student body: 4,249 full time, 6,629 part time; 39% male, 61% female; 1% American Indian, 2% Asian, 15% black, 11% Hispanic, 2% multiracial, 0% Pacific Islander, 63% white, 3% international; 94% from in state; 0% live on campus; 0% of students in fraternities, 0% in sororities
Most popular majors: 35% Business/Commerce, General, 24% Community Organization and Advocacy, 6% English Language and Literature/Letters, Other, 6% Physical Sciences, Other, 7% Psychology, General
Expenses: 2014-2015: $6,665 in state, $16,315 out of state; room/board: $11,600
Financial aid: (518) 587-2100

SUNY–Fredonia

Fredonia NY
(800) 252-1212
U.S. News ranking: Reg. U. (N), No. 66
Website: www.fredonia.edu
Admissions email: admissions.office@fredonia.edu
Public; founded 1826
Freshman admissions: selective; 2014-2015: 6,095 applied, 3,244 accepted. Either SAT or ACT required. SAT 25/75 percentile: 940-1140. High school rank: 16% in top tenth, 39% in top quarter, 75% in top half
Early decision deadline: 11/1, notification date: 12/1
Early action deadline: N/A, notification date: N/A
Application deadline (fall): rolling
Undergraduate student body: 4,821 full time, 120 part time; 46% male, 54% female; 0% American Indian, 1% Asian, 6% black, 6% Hispanic, 2% multiracial, 0% Pacific Islander, 78% white, 3% international; 98% from in state; 50% live on campus; 1% of students in fraternities, 1% in sororities
Most popular majors: 16% Business, Management, Marketing, and Related Support Services, 9% Communication, Journalism, and Related Programs, 19% Education, 6% Multi/Interdisciplinary Studies, 6% Psychology
Expenses: 2015-2016: $8,150 in state, $18,000 out of state; room/board: $12,500
Financial aid: (716) 673-3253; 69% of undergrads determined to have financial need; average aid package $10,689

SUNY–Geneseo

Geneseo NY
(585) 245-5571
U.S. News ranking: Reg. U. (N), No. 14
Website: www.geneseo.edu
Admissions email: admissions@geneseo.edu
Public; founded 1871
Freshman admissions: more selective; 2014-2015: 9,305 applied, 5,502 accepted. Either SAT or ACT required. SAT 25/75 percentile: 1120-1320. High school rank: 37% in top tenth, 76% in top quarter, 97% in top half
Early decision deadline: 11/15, notification date: 12/15
Early action deadline: N/A, notification date: N/A
Application deadline (fall): 1/1
Undergraduate student body: 5,455 full time, 98 part time; 42% male, 58% female; 0% American Indian, 6% Asian, 3% black, 7% Hispanic, 3% multiracial, 0% Pacific Islander, 75% white, 2% international; 98% from in state; 56% live on campus; 18% of students in fraternities, 25% in sororities
Most popular majors: 15% Biological and Biomedical Sciences, 12% Business, Management, Marketing, and Related Support Services, 8% Education, 12% Psychology, 16% Social Sciences
Expenses: 2015-2016: $8,113 in state, $17,963 out of state; room/board: $11,980
Financial aid: (585) 245-5731; 50% of undergrads determined to have financial need; average aid package $10,672

SUNY Maritime College

Throggs Neck NY
(718) 409-7221
U.S. News ranking: Reg. Coll. (N), No. 17
Website: www.sunymaritime.edu
Admissions email: admissions@sunymaritime.edu
Public; founded 1874
Freshman admissions: selective; 2014-2015: 1,795 applied, 945 accepted. Either SAT or ACT required. SAT 25/75 percentile: 1020-1190. High school rank: 8% in top tenth, 44% in top quarter, 81% in top half
Early decision deadline: 11/1, notification date: 12/15
Early action deadline: N/A, notification date: N/A
Application deadline (fall): 1/31
Undergraduate student body: 1,591 full time, 50 part time; 90% male, 10% female; 0% American Indian, 4% Asian, 4% black, 10% Hispanic, 1% multiracial, 0% Pacific Islander, 72% white, 3% international; 74% from in state; 84% live on campus; N/A of students in fraternities, N/A in sororities
Most popular majors: 21% Business, Management, Marketing, and Related Support Services, Other, 6% Industrial Engineering, 8% Mechanical Engineering, 22% Naval Architecture and Marine Engineering, 32% Transportation/Mobility Management
Expenses: 2015-2016: $7,809 in state, $17,659 out of state; room/board: $11,516
Financial aid: (718) 409-7254; 52% of undergrads determined to have financial need; average aid package $7,538

SUNY–New Paltz

New Paltz NY
(845) 257-3200
U.S. News ranking: Reg. U. (N), No. 24
Website: www.newpaltz.edu
Admissions email: admissions@newpaltz.edu
Public; founded 1828
Freshman admissions: selective; 2014-2015: 13,726 applied, 5,755 accepted. Either SAT or ACT required. SAT 25/75 percentile: 1030-1200. High school rank: 33% in top tenth, 80% in top quarter, 98% in top half
Early decision deadline: N/A, notification date: N/A
Early action deadline: 11/15, notification date: 12/15
Application deadline (fall): 4/1
Undergraduate student body: 6,097 full time, 545 part time; 38% male, 62% female; 0% American Indian, 5% Asian, 6% black, 16% Hispanic, 2% multiracial, 0% Pacific Islander, 65% white, 2% international; 97% from in state; 43% live on campus; 1% of students in fraternities, 2% in sororities
Most popular majors: 15% Business, Management, Marketing, and Related Support Services, 11% Communication, Journalism, and Related Programs, 13% Education, 13% Social Sciences, 12% Visual and Performing Arts
Expenses: 2014-2015: $7,408 in state, $17,058 out of state; room/board: $10,895
Financial aid: (845) 257-3250; 57% of undergrads determined to have financial need; average aid package $10,590

SUNY–Oswego

Oswego NY
(315) 312-2250
U.S. News ranking: Reg. U. (N), No. 58
Website: www.oswego.edu
Admissions email: admiss@oswego.edu
Public; founded 1861
Freshman admissions: selective; 2014-2015: 11,022 applied, 5,331 accepted. Either SAT or ACT required. SAT 25/75 percentile: 1020-1190. High school rank: 14% in top tenth, 53% in top quarter, 86% in top half
Early decision deadline: 11/30, notification date: 12/15
Early action deadline: N/A, notification date: N/A
Application deadline (fall): rolling

Undergraduate student body: 6,880 full time, 313 part time; 49% male, 51% female; 0% American Indian, 2% Asian, 7% black, 9% Hispanic, 2% multiracial, 0% Pacific Islander, 78% white, 2% international; 98% from in state; 60% live on campus; 3% of students in fraternities, 3% in sororities
Most popular majors: 22% Business, Management, Marketing, and Related Support Services, 13% Communication, Journalism, and Related Programs, 15% Education, 6% Homeland Security, Law Enforcement, Firefighting and Related Protective Services, 10% Psychology
Expenses: 2015-2016: $7,881 in state, $17,731 out of state; room/board: $12,690
Financial aid: (315) 312-2248; 66% of undergrads determined to have financial need; average aid package $10,395

SUNY–Plattsburgh

Plattsburgh NY
(888) 673-0012
U.S. News ranking: Reg. U. (N), No. 76
Website: www.plattsburgh.edu
Admissions email: admissions@plattsburgh.edu
Public; founded 1889
Freshman admissions: selective; 2014-2015: 8,452 applied, 4,045 accepted. Either SAT or ACT required. SAT 25/75 percentile: 970-1160. High school rank: 12% in top tenth, 40% in top quarter, 77% in top half
Early decision deadline: N/A, notification date: N/A
Early action deadline: N/A, notification date: N/A
Application deadline (fall): rolling
Undergraduate student body: 5,143 full time, 422 part time; 44% male, 56% female; 0% American Indian, 2% Asian, 7% black, 10% Hispanic, 2% multiracial, 0% Pacific Islander, 69% white, 6% international; 97% from in state; 46% live on campus; 18% of students in fraternities, 16% in sororities
Most popular majors: 25% Business, Management, Marketing, and Related Support Services, 8% Communication, Journalism, and Related Programs, 7% Education, 8% Homeland Security, Law Enforcement, Firefighting and Related Protective Services, 8% Psychology
Expenses: 2015-2016: $7,850 in state, $17,700 out of state; room/board: $11,270
Financial aid: (518) 564-4061; 64% of undergrads determined to have financial need; average aid package $12,593

SUNY Polytechnic Institute

Utica NY
(315) 792-7500
U.S. News ranking: Reg. U. (N), No. 122
Website: www.sunypoly.edu
Admissions email: admissions@sunyit.edu
Public; founded 1966
Freshman admissions: selective; 2014-2015: 2,233 applied, 1,263 accepted. Either SAT or ACT required. SAT 25/75 percentile: 920-1260. High school rank: 17% in top tenth, 43% in top quarter, 83% in top half
Early decision deadline: N/A, notification date: N/A
Early action deadline: 11/15, notification date: 12/15
Application deadline (fall): 7/15
Undergraduate student body: 1,646 full time, 388 part time; 60% male, 40% female; 0% American Indian, 3% Asian, 8% black, 7% Hispanic, 2% multiracial, 0% Pacific Islander, 79% white, 1% international; 99% from in state; 28% live on campus; 0% of students in fraternities, 0% in sororities
Most popular majors: 18% Business Administration and Management, General, 6% Health Information/Medical Records Administration/Administrator, 7% Mechanical Engineering/Mechanical Technology/Technician, 9% Psychology, General, 14% Registered Nursing/Registered Nurse
Expenses: 2015-2016: $7,870 in state, $17,720 out of state; room/board: $12,870
Financial aid: (315) 792-7210; 71% of undergrads determined to have financial need; average aid package $9,820

Syracuse University

Syracuse NY
(315) 443-3611
U.S. News ranking: Nat. U., No. 61
Website: syr.edu
Admissions email: orange@syr.edu
Private; founded 1870
Freshman admissions: more selective; 2014-2015: 26,790 applied, 14,260 accepted. Either SAT or ACT required. SAT 25/75 percentile: 1070-1280. High school rank: 37% in top tenth, 71% in top quarter, 93% in top half
Early decision deadline: 11/15, notification date: 1/1
Early action deadline: N/A, notification date: N/A
Application deadline (fall): 1/1
Undergraduate student body: 14,532 full time, 692 part time; 45% male, 55% female; 1% American Indian, 8% Asian, 9% black, 11% Hispanic, 3% multiracial, 0% Pacific Islander, 55% white, 11% international; 43% from in state; 75% live on campus; 24% of students in fraternities, 28% in sororities
Most popular majors: 16% Business, Management, Marketing, and Related Support Services, 14% Communication, Journalism, and Related Programs, 9% Engineering, 11% Social Sciences, 11% Visual and Performing Arts
Expenses: 2015-2016: $43,318; room/board: $14,880
Financial aid: (315) 443-1513; 57% of undergrads determined to have financial need; average aid package $34,620

Touro College

New York NY
(212) 463-0400
U.S. News ranking: Reg. U. (N), second tier
Website: www.touro.edu/
Admissions email: lasadmit@touro.edu
Private; founded 1971
Affiliation: Jewish
Freshman admissions: less selective; 2014-2015: 1,355 applied, 503 accepted. Neither SAT nor ACT required. SAT 25/75 percentile: 830-1180. High school rank: N/A
Early decision deadline: N/A, notification date: N/A
Early action deadline: N/A, notification date: N/A
Application deadline (fall): rolling
Undergraduate student body: 4,849 full time, 1,636 part time; 31% male, 69% female; 0% American Indian, 3% Asian, 16% black, 8% Hispanic, 0% multiracial, 0% Pacific Islander, 62% white, 6% international; 88% from in state; 0% live on campus; 0% of students in fraternities, 0% in sororities
Most popular majors: 9% Biology/Biological Sciences, General, 9% Business/Commerce, General, 16% Health Services/Allied Health/Health Sciences, General, 22% Multi/Interdisciplinary Studies, General, 22% Psychology, General
Expenses: 2015-2016: $16,500; room/board: $11,970
Financial aid: (718) 252-7800; 70% of undergrads determined to have financial need; average aid package $7,511

Union College

Schenectady NY
(888) 843-6688
U.S. News ranking: Nat. Lib. Arts, No. 38
Website: www.union.edu
Admissions email: admissions@union.edu
Private; founded 1795
Freshman admissions: more selective; 2014-2015: 5,406 applied, 2,223 accepted. Neither SAT nor ACT required. SAT 25/75 percentile: 1210-1400. High school rank: 70% in top tenth, 87% in top quarter, 98% in top half
Early decision deadline: 11/15, notification date: 12/15
Early action deadline: N/A, notification date: N/A
Application deadline (fall): 1/15
Undergraduate student body: 2,228 full time, 14 part time; 54% male, 46% female; 0% American Indian, 6% Asian, 4% black, 7% Hispanic, 2% multiracial, 0% Pacific Islander, 75% white, 7% international; 30% from in state; 87% live on campus; 39% of students in fraternities, 43% in sororities
Most popular majors: 7% Biological and Biomedical Sciences, 7% Engineering, 9% Psychology, 14% Social Sciences, 7% Social Sciences
Expenses: 2015-2016: $50,013; room/board: $12,261
Financial aid: (518) 388-6123; 51% of undergrads determined to have financial need; average aid package $39,479

United States Merchant Marine Academy

Kings Point NY
(516) 773-5391
U.S. News ranking: Reg. Coll. (N), No. 3
Website: www.usmma.edu
Admissions email: admissions@usmma.edu
Public; founded 1943
Freshman admissions: more selective; 2014-2015: 1,696 applied, 378 accepted. Either SAT or ACT required. ACT 25/75 percentile: 26-30. High school rank: 35% in top tenth, 68% in top quarter, 93% in top half
Early decision deadline: N/A, notification date: N/A
Early action deadline: N/A, notification date: N/A
Application deadline (fall): 3/1
Undergraduate student body: 939 full time, 0 part time; 84% male, 16% female; 1% American Indian, 7% Asian, 3% black, 10% Hispanic, 0% multiracial, 0% Pacific Islander, 76% white, 1% international; 11% from in state; 100% live on campus; 0% of students in fraternities, 0% in sororities
Most popular majors: 19% Engineering, General, 13% Engineering, Other, 10% Marine Transportation, Other, 27% Systems Engineering, 26% Transportation and Materials Moving, Other
Expenses: 2015-2016: $1,107 in state, $1,107 out of state; room/board: $0
Financial aid: (516) 773-5295; 9% of undergrads determined to have financial need; average aid package $6,532

United States Military Academy

West Point NY
(845) 938-4041
U.S. News ranking: Nat. Lib. Arts, No. 22
Website: www.usma.edu
Admissions email: admissions@usma.edu
Public; founded 1802
Freshman admissions: more selective; 2014-2015: 14,977 applied, 1,418 accepted. Either SAT or ACT required. SAT 25/75 percentile: 1160-1390. High school rank: 52% in top tenth, 78% in top quarter, 95% in top half
Early decision deadline: N/A, notification date: N/A
Early action deadline: N/A, notification date: N/A
Application deadline (fall): 2/28
Undergraduate student body: 4,414 full time, 0 part time; 83% male, 17% female; 1% American Indian, 6% Asian, 9% black, 11% Hispanic, 3% multiracial, 0% Pacific Islander, 67% white, 1% international; 7% from in state; 100% live on campus; 0% of students in fraternities, 0% in sororities
Most popular majors: 6% Computer and Information Sciences and Support Services, 25% Engineering, 5% Engineering Technologies and Engineering-Related Fields, 10% Foreign Languages, Literatures, and Linguistics, 20% Social Sciences
Expenses: N/A
Financial aid: (845) 938-4262; 0% of undergrads determined to have financial need; average aid package $0

University at Albany–SUNY

Albany NY
(518) 442-5435
U.S. News ranking: Nat. U., No. 129
Website: www.albany.edu
Admissions email: ugadmissions@albany.edu
Public; founded 1844
Freshman admissions: selective; 2014-2015: 21,755 applied, 12,148 accepted. Either SAT or ACT required. SAT 25/75 percentile: 1010-1180. High school rank: 18% in top tenth, 49% in top quarter, 88% in top half
Early decision deadline: N/A, notification date: N/A
Early action deadline: 11/15, notification date: 11/15
Application deadline (fall): 3/1
Undergraduate student body: 12,191 full time, 738 part time; 52% male, 48% female; 0% American Indian, 8% Asian, 15% black, 14% Hispanic, 3% multiracial, 0% Pacific Islander, 51% white, 6% international; 94% from in state; 58% live on campus; 1% of students in fraternities, 2% in sororities
Most popular majors: 13% Biological and Biomedical Sciences, 12% Business, Management, Marketing, and Related Support Services, 14% English Language and Literature/Letters, 10% Psychology, 26% Social Sciences
Expenses: 2015-2016: $8,996 in state, $22,116 out of state; room/board: $12,422
Financial aid: (518) 442-5757; 64% of undergrads determined to have financial need; average aid package $10,639

University at Buffalo–SUNY

Buffalo NY
(716) 645-6900
U.S. News ranking: Nat. U., No. 99
Website: www.buffalo.edu
Admissions email: ub-admissions@buffalo.edu
Public; founded 1846
Freshman admissions: more selective; 2014-2015: 24,444 applied, 14,128 accepted. Either SAT or ACT required. SAT 25/75 percentile: 1050-1250. High school rank: 29% in top tenth, 63% in top quarter, 93% in top half
Early decision deadline: 11/1, notification date: 12/15
Early action deadline: N/A, notification date: N/A
Application deadline (fall): rolling
Undergraduate student body: 18,164 full time, 1,665 part time; 54% male, 46% female; 0% American Indian, 14% Asian, 7% black, 6% Hispanic, 2% multiracial, 0% Pacific Islander, 49% white, 16% international; 97% from in state; 35% live on campus; 2% of students in fraternities, 2% in sororities
Most popular majors: 8% Biological and Biomedical Sciences, 17% Business, Management, Marketing, and Related Support Services, 14% Engineering, 12% Psychology, 17% Social Sciences
Expenses: 2015-2016: $8,870 in state, $22,290 out of state; room/board: $12,761

Financial aid: (866) 838-7257; 77% of undergrads determined to have financial need; average aid package $9,494

University of Rochester

Rochester NY
(585) 275-3221
U.S. News ranking: Nat. U., No. 33
Website: www.rochester.edu
Admissions email: admit@admissions.rochester.edu
Private; founded 1850
Freshman admissions: most selective; 2014-2015: 17,410 applied, 6,344 accepted. Neither SAT nor ACT required. SAT 25/75 percentile: 1240-1450. High school rank: 72% in top tenth, 93% in top quarter, 100% in top half
Early decision deadline: 11/1, notification date: 12/15
Early action deadline: N/A, notification date: N/A
Application deadline (fall): 1/5
Undergraduate student body: 5,942 full time, 324 part time; 49% male, 51% female; 0% American Indian, 11% Asian, 5% black, 6% Hispanic, 3% multiracial, 0% Pacific Islander, 51% white, 17% international; 41% from in state; 90% live on campus; 20% of students in fraternities, 26% in sororities
Most popular majors: 13% Biological and Biomedical Sciences, 12% Engineering, 14% Health Professions and Related Programs, 10% Psychology, 15% Social Sciences
Expenses: 2015-2016: $48,290; room/board: $14,366
Financial aid: (585) 275-3226; 52% of undergrads determined to have financial need; average aid package $40,149

Utica College

Utica NY
(315) 792-3006
U.S. News ranking: Reg. U. (N), No. 116
Website: www.utica.edu
Admissions email: admiss@utica.edu
Private; founded 1946
Freshman admissions: less selective; 2014-2015: 3,677 applied, 2,998 accepted. Neither SAT nor ACT required. SAT 25/75 percentile: 870-1070. High school rank: 9% in top tenth, 30% in top quarter, 63% in top half
Early decision deadline: 11/15, notification date: 12/15
Early action deadline: 11/15, notification date: 12/15
Application deadline (fall): rolling
Undergraduate student body: 2,216 full time, 705 part time; 40% male, 60% female; 1% American Indian, 3% Asian, 11% black, 8% Hispanic, 3% multiracial, 0% Pacific Islander, 66% white, 3% international; 90% from in state; 44% live on campus; 2% of students in fraternities, 2% in sororities
Most popular majors: 4% Biological and Biomedical Sciences, 8% Business, Management, Marketing, and Related Support Services, 45% Health Professions and Related Programs, 17% Homeland Security, Law Enforcement, Firefighting and Related Protective Services, 5% Liberal Arts and Sciences, General Studies and Humanities
Expenses: 2014-2015: $33,736; room/board: $11,934
Financial aid: (315) 792-3179; 87% of undergrads determined to have financial need; average aid package $25,627

Vassar College

Poughkeepsie NY
(845) 437-7300
U.S. News ranking: Nat. Lib. Arts, No. 12
Website: www.vassar.edu
Admissions email: admission@vassar.edu
Private; founded 1861
Freshman admissions: most selective; 2014-2015: 7,784 applied, 1,832 accepted. Either SAT or ACT required. SAT 25/75 percentile: 1320-1490. High school rank: 70% in top tenth, 95% in top quarter, 100% in top half
Early decision deadline: 11/15, notification date: 12/15
Early action deadline: N/A, notification date: N/A
Application deadline (fall): 1/1
Undergraduate student body: 2,394 full time, 24 part time; 44% male, 56% female; 0% American Indian, 11% Asian, 6% black, 11% Hispanic, 6% multiracial, 0% Pacific Islander, 59% white, 7% international; 27% from in state; 96% live on campus; 0% of students in fraternities, 0% in sororities
Most popular majors: 10% Biological and Biomedical Sciences, 8% English Language and Literature/Letters, 9% Foreign Languages, Literatures, and Linguistics, 28% Social Sciences, 11% Visual and Performing Arts
Expenses: 2015-2016: $51,300; room/board: $11,980
Financial aid: (845) 437-5320; 59% of undergrads determined to have financial need; average aid package $47,836

Vaughn College of Aeronautics and Technology

Flushing NY
(718) 429-6600
U.S. News ranking: Reg. Coll. (N), No. 26
Website: www.vaughn.edu
Admissions email: admitme@vaughn.edu
Private; founded 1932
Freshman admissions: selective; 2014-2015: 813 applied, 608 accepted. SAT required. SAT 25/75 percentile: 891-1093. High school rank: N/A
Early decision deadline: N/A, notification date: N/A
Early action deadline: N/A, notification date: N/A
Application deadline (fall): rolling
Undergraduate student body: 1,261 full time, 344 part time; 87% male, 13% female; 0% American Indian, 12% Asian, 22% black, 38% Hispanic, 5% multiracial, 3% Pacific Islander, 13% white, 2% international; 89% from in state; 11% live on campus; 0% of students in fraternities, 0% in sororities
Most popular majors: Information not available
Expenses: 2015-2016: $22,740; room/board: $12,860
Financial aid: (718) 429-6600; 85% of undergrads determined to have financial need; average aid package $30,858

Wagner College

Staten Island NY
(718) 390-3411
U.S. News ranking: Reg. U. (N), No. 26
Website: www.wagner.edu
Admissions email: adm@wagner.edu
Private; founded 1883
Freshman admissions: selective; 2014-2015: 2,764 applied, 1,995 accepted. Neither SAT nor ACT required. SAT 25/75 percentile: 1060-1270. High school rank: 16% in top tenth, 73% in top quarter, 92% in top half
Early decision deadline: 12/1, notification date: 1/2
Early action deadline: N/A, notification date: N/A
Application deadline (fall): 2/15
Undergraduate student body: 1,751 full time, 58 part time; 37% male, 63% female; 0% American Indian, 3% Asian, 7% black, 10% Hispanic, 2% multiracial, 0% Pacific Islander, 67% white, 2% international; 48% from in state; 70% live on campus; 10% of students in fraternities, 7% in sororities
Most popular majors: 31% Biological and Biomedical Sciences, 15% Business, Management, Marketing, and Related Support Services, 8% Psychology, 10% Social Sciences, 18% Visual and Performing Arts
Expenses: 2015-2016: $42,480; room/board: $13,000
Financial aid: (718) 390-3183; 65% of undergrads determined to have financial need; average aid package $27,083

Webb Institute

Glen Cove NY
(516) 671-8355
U.S. News ranking: Engineering, unranked
Website: www.webb.edu
Admissions email: admissions@webb.edu
Private; founded 1889
Freshman admissions: most selective; 2014-2015: 97 applied, 32 accepted. SAT required. SAT 25/75 percentile: 1320-1520. High school rank: 71% in top tenth, 92% in top quarter, 100% in top half
Early decision deadline: 10/15, notification date: 12/15
Early action deadline: N/A, notification date: N/A
Application deadline (fall): 2/15
Undergraduate student body: 90 full time, N/A part time; 87% male, 13% female; N/A American Indian, 9% Asian, N/A black, N/A Hispanic, 4% multiracial, N/A Pacific Islander, 84% white, 1% international; 28% from in state; 100% live on campus; N/A of students in fraternities, N/A in sororities
Most popular majors: Information not available
Expenses: 2015-2016: $46,000; room/board: $14,050
Financial aid: (516) 671-2213; 29% of undergrads determined to have financial need; average aid package $49,000

Wells College

Aurora NY
(800) 952-9355
U.S. News ranking: Nat. Lib. Arts, No. 136
Website: www.wells.edu
Admissions email: admissions@wells.edu
Private; founded 1868
Freshman admissions: selective; 2014-2015: 2,222 applied, 1,295 accepted. Either SAT or ACT required. SAT 25/75 percentile: 930-1070. High school rank: N/A
Early decision deadline: 12/15, notification date: 1/15
Early action deadline: 12/15, notification date: 1/15
Undergraduate student body: 525 full time, 26 part time; 34% male, 66% female; 1% American Indian, 2% Asian, 13% black, 9% Hispanic, 2% multiracial, 0% Pacific Islander, 66% white, 2% international; 75% from in state; N/A live on campus; N/A of students in fraternities, N/A in sororities
Most popular majors: Information not available
Expenses: 2015-2016: $37,500; room/board: $13,000
Financial aid: (315) 364-3289; 92% of undergrads determined to have financial need; average aid package $31,365

Yeshiva University

New York NY
(212) 960-5277
U.S. News ranking: Nat. U., No. 52
Website: www.yu.edu
Admissions email: yuadmit@ymail.yu.edu
Private; founded 1886
Freshman admissions: more selective; 2014-2015: 1,703 applied, 1,393 accepted. Either SAT or ACT required. SAT 25/75 percentile: 1120-1360. High school rank: 39% in top tenth, 63% in top quarter, 81% in top half
Early decision deadline: 11/1, notification date: 12/15
Early action deadline: N/A, notification date: N/A
Application deadline (fall): 2/1
Undergraduate student body: 2,767 full time, 50 part time; 54% male, 46% female; 0% American Indian, 0% Asian, 0% black, 0% Hispanic, 0% multiracial, 0% Pacific Islander, 94% white, 5% international; 34% from in state; 66% live on campus; 0% of students in fraternities, 0% in sororities
Most popular majors: 12% Accounting, 15% Biology/Biological Sciences, General, 7% Hebrew Language and Literature, 6% Multi/Interdisciplinary Studies, Other, 13% Psychology, General
Expenses: 2015-2016: $39,530; room/board: $11,250
Financial aid: (212) 960-5399; 55% of undergrads determined to have financial need; average aid package $32,105

NORTH CAROLINA

Appalachian State University

Boone NC
(828) 262-2120
U.S. News ranking: Reg. U. (S), No. 10
Website: www.appstate.edu
Admissions email: admissions@appstate.edu
Public; founded 1899
Freshman admissions: selective; 2014-2015: 13,506 applied, 8,463 accepted. Either SAT or ACT required. SAT 25/75 percentile: 1060-1240. High school rank: 19% in top tenth, 56% in top quarter, 91% in top half
Early decision deadline: N/A, notification date: N/A
Early action deadline: N/A, notification date: N/A
Application deadline (fall): 3/15
Undergraduate student body: 15,312 full time, 943 part time; 46% male, 54% female; 0% American Indian, 2% Asian, 3% black, 4% Hispanic, 3% multiracial, 0% Pacific Islander, 86% white, 1% international; 92% from in state; 34% live on campus; 8% of students in fraternities, 13% in sororities
Most popular majors: 18% Business, Management, Marketing, and Related Support Services, 14% Education, 7% Parks, Recreation, Leisure, and Fitness Studies, 7% Psychology, 7% Social Sciences
Expenses: 2014-2015: $6,553 in state, $19,720 out of state; room/board: $7,675
Financial aid: (828) 262-2190; 51% of undergrads determined to have financial need; average aid package $9,551

Barton College

Wilson NC
(800) 345-4973
U.S. News ranking: Reg. Coll. (S), No. 22
Website: www.barton.edu
Admissions email: enroll@barton.edu
Private; founded 1902
Affiliation: Christian Church (Disciples of Christ)
Freshman admissions: selective; 2014-2015: 3,097 applied, 1,191 accepted. Either SAT or ACT required. SAT 25/75 percentile: 860-1050. High school rank: 17% in top tenth, 41% in top quarter, 75% in top half
Early decision deadline: N/A, notification date: N/A
Early action deadline: N/A, notification date: N/A
Application deadline (fall): rolling
Undergraduate student body: 892 full time, 118 part time; 31% male, 69% female; 1% American Indian, 1% Asian, 21% black, 6% Hispanic, 3% multiracial, 0% Pacific Islander, 61% white, 3% international
Most popular majors: Information not available
Expenses: 2015-2016: $27,940; room/board: $9,264
Financial aid: (252) 399-6323; 88% of undergrads determined to have financial need; average aid package $20,605

Belmont Abbey College

Belmont NC
(704) 461-6665
U.S. News ranking: Reg. Coll. (S), No. 39
Website: www.belmontabbeycollege.edu
Admissions email: admissions@bac.edu
Private; founded 1876
Affiliation: Roman Catholic
Freshman admissions: less selective; 2014-2015: 1,950 applied, 1,350 accepted. Neither SAT nor ACT required. SAT 25/75 percentile: 890-1120. High school rank: 5% in top tenth, 15% in top quarter, 61% in top half
Early decision deadline: N/A, notification date: N/A
Early action deadline: N/A, notification date: N/A
Application deadline (fall): 8/1
Undergraduate student body: 1,452 full time, 108 part time; 43% male, 57% female; 0% American Indian, 1% Asian, 25% black, 1% Hispanic, 0% multiracial, N/A Pacific Islander, 41% white, 1% international; 72% from in state; 42% live on campus; 2% of students in fraternities, 3% in sororities
Most popular majors: Information not available
Expenses: 2015-2016: $18,500; room/board: $10,390
Financial aid: (704) 825-6718; 75% of undergrads determined to have financial need; average aid package $12,140

Bennett College

Greensboro NC
(336) 370-8624
U.S. News ranking: Nat. Lib. Arts, second tier
Website: www.bennett.edu
Admissions email: admiss@bennett.edu
Private; founded 1873
Affiliation: United Methodist
Freshman admissions: least selective; 2014-2015: 1,560 applied, 1,432 accepted. Either SAT or ACT required. SAT 25/75 percentile: 680-845. High school rank: 4% in top tenth, 14% in top quarter, 54% in top half
Early decision deadline: N/A, notification date: N/A
Early action deadline: N/A, notification date: N/A
Application deadline (fall): rolling
Undergraduate student body: 545 full time, 88 part time; 0% male, 100% female; 0% American Indian, 0% Asian, 89% black, 3% Hispanic, 2% multiracial, 0% Pacific Islander, 0% white, 0% international; 44% from in state; 59% live on campus; 0% of students in fraternities, 5% in sororities
Most popular majors: 13% Biology/Biological Sciences, General, 12% Business Administration and Management, General, 10% Journalism, Other, 21% Multi/Interdisciplinary Studies, Other, 14% Psychology, General
Expenses: 2014-2015: $17,130; room/board: $7,576
Financial aid: (336) 517-2205; 97% of undergrads determined to have financial need; average aid package $14,040

Brevard College

Brevard NC
(828) 884-8300
U.S. News ranking: Nat. Lib. Arts, second tier
Website: www.brevard.edu
Admissions email: admissions@brevard.edu
Private; founded 1853
Affiliation: Methodist
Freshman admissions: selective; 2014-2015: 2,858 applied, 1,235 accepted. Neither SAT nor ACT required. SAT 25/75 percentile: 840-1050. High school rank: 6% in top tenth, 24% in top quarter, 62% in top half
Early decision deadline: N/A, notification date: N/A
Early action deadline: N/A, notification date: N/A
Application deadline (fall): rolling
Undergraduate student body: 697 full time, 8 part time; 58% male, 42% female; 1% American Indian, 1% Asian, 10% black, 2% Hispanic, 3% multiracial, 0% Pacific Islander, 71% white, 6% international; 58% from in state; 76% live on campus; 0% of students in fraternities, 0% in sororities
Most popular majors: 16% Business/Commerce, General, 9% Multi/Interdisciplinary Studies, 26% Parks, Recreation and Leisure Studies, 12% Psychology, General, 12% Visual and Performing Arts
Expenses: 2014-2015: $26,170; room/board: $9,100
Financial aid: (828) 884-8287

Campbell University

Buies Creek NC
(910) 893-1320
U.S. News ranking: Reg. U. (S), No. 24
Website: www.campbell.edu
Admissions email: adm@mailcenter.campbell.edu
Private; founded 1887
Affiliation: Baptist
Freshman admissions: selective; 2014-2015: 6,770 applied, 4,608 accepted. Either SAT or ACT required. SAT 25/75 percentile: 802-1248. High school rank: 24% in top tenth, 53% in top quarter, 86% in top half
Early decision deadline: N/A, notification date: N/A
Early action deadline: N/A, notification date: N/A
Application deadline (fall): rolling
Undergraduate student body: 3,449 full time, 849 part time; 48% male, 52% female; 1% American Indian, 2% Asian, 18% black, 7% Hispanic, 2% multiracial, 0% Pacific Islander, 57% white, 2% international; N/A from in state; 28% live on campus; N/A of students in fraternities, N/A in sororities
Most popular majors: 11% Business Administration and Management, General, 6% Information Technology, 7% Psychology, General, 9% Science Technologies/Technicians, Other, 8% Social Sciences, General
Expenses: 2015-2016: $28,820; room/board: $10,250
Financial aid: (910) 893-1310; 82% of undergrads determined to have financial need; average aid package $23,802

Catawba College

Salisbury NC
(800) 228-2922
U.S. News ranking: Reg. Coll. (S), No. 15
Website: www.catawba.edu
Admissions email: admission@catawba.edu
Private; founded 1851
Affiliation: United Church of Christ
Freshman admissions: less selective; 2014-2015: 3,694 applied, 1,326 accepted. Neither SAT nor ACT required. SAT 25/75 percentile: 860-1090. High school rank: 10% in top tenth, 36% in top quarter, 73% in top half
Early decision deadline: N/A, notification date: N/A
Early action deadline: N/A, notification date: N/A
Application deadline (fall): rolling
Undergraduate student body: 1,231 full time, 78 part time; 47% male, 53% female; 1% American Indian, 1% Asian, 21% black, 4% Hispanic, 2% multiracial, 0% Pacific Islander, 69% white, 3% international; 80% from in state; 71% live on campus; N/A of students in fraternities, N/A in sororities
Most popular majors: 28% Business, Management, Marketing, and Related Support Services, 5% Communication, Journalism, and Related Programs, 19% Education, 13% Parks, Recreation, Leisure, and Fitness Studies, 7% Visual and Performing Arts
Expenses: 2015-2016: $28,730; room/board: $10,360
Financial aid: (704) 637-4416; 84% of undergrads determined to have financial need; average aid package $21,799

Chowan University

Murfreesboro NC
(252) 398-1236
U.S. News ranking: Reg. Coll. (S), second tier
Website: www.chowan.edu
Admissions email: admission@chowan.edu
Private; founded 1848
Affiliation: Baptist
Freshman admissions: least selective; 2014-2015: 4,225 applied, 2,527 accepted. Either SAT or ACT required. SAT 25/75 percentile: 710-880. High school rank: 2% in top tenth, 11% in top quarter, 35% in top half
Early decision deadline: N/A, notification date: N/A
Early action deadline: N/A, notification date: N/A
Application deadline (fall): rolling
Undergraduate student body: 1,408 full time, 70 part time; 49% male, 51% female; 1% American Indian, 0% Asian, 71% black, 3% Hispanic, 3% multiracial, 0% Pacific Islander, 18% white, 2% international; 53% from in state; 85% live on campus; 15% of students in fraternities, 15% in sororities
Most popular majors: 14% Biomedical Sciences, General, 15% Health and Physical Education/Fitness, General, 13% Multi/Interdisciplinary Studies, General, 12% Psychology, General, 14% Social Sciences, General
Expenses: 2015-2016: $23,400; room/board: $8,360
Financial aid: (252) 398-1229; 67% of undergrads determined to have financial need; average aid package $26,494

Davidson College

Davidson NC
(800) 768-0380
U.S. News ranking: Nat. Lib. Arts, No. 9
Website: www.davidson.edu
Admissions email: admission@davidson.edu
Private; founded 1837
Affiliation: Presbyterian Church (USA)
Freshman admissions: most selective; 2014-2015: 5,560 applied, 1,205 accepted. Either SAT or ACT required. SAT 25/75 percentile: 1230-1440. High school rank: 74% in top tenth, 97% in top quarter, 99% in top half
Early decision deadline: 11/15, notification date: 12/15
Early action deadline: N/A, notification date: N/A
Application deadline (fall): 1/2
Undergraduate student body: 1,770 full time, 0 part time; 49% male, 51% female; 1% American Indian, 6% Asian, 6% black, 7% Hispanic, 4% multiracial, 0% Pacific Islander, 69% white, 6% international; 23% from in state; 93% live on campus; 16% of students in fraternities, 1% in sororities
Most popular majors: 10% Biology/Biological Sciences, General, 11% Economics, General, 8% English Language and Literature, General, 13% Political Science and Government, General, 10% Psychology, General
Expenses: 2015-2016: $46,966; room/board: $13,153
Financial aid: (704) 894-2232; 49% of undergrads determined to have financial need; average aid package $38,522

Duke University

Durham NC
(919) 684-3214
U.S. News ranking: Nat. U., No. 8
Website: www.duke.edu/
Admissions email: N/A
Private; founded 1838
Affiliation: Methodist
Freshman admissions: most selective; 2014-2015: 31,523 applied, 3,596 accepted. Either SAT or ACT required. SAT 25/75 percentile: 1370-1550. High school rank: 91% in top tenth, 98% in top quarter, 100% in top half
Early decision deadline: 11/1, notification date: 12/15
Early action deadline: N/A, notification date: N/A
Application deadline (fall): 1/2
Undergraduate student body: 6,601 full time, 25 part time; 50% male, 50% female; 1% American Indian, 21% Asian, 10% black, 7% Hispanic, 2% multiracial, 0% Pacific Islander, 48% white, 10% international; 14% from in state; 82% live on campus; 30% of students in fraternities, 39% in sororities
Most popular majors: 6% Bioengineering and Biomedical Engineering, 9% Biology/Biological Sciences, General, 11% Economics, General, 7% Psychology, General, 9% Public Policy Analysis, General
Expenses: 2015-2016: $49,341; room/board: $12,886
Financial aid: (919) 684-6225; 45% of undergrads determined to have financial need; average aid package $44,635

East Carolina University

Greenville NC
(252) 328-6640
U.S. News ranking: Nat. U., No. 194
Website: www.ecu.edu
Admissions email: admis@ecu.edu
Public; founded 1907
Freshman admissions: selective; 2014-2015: 14,223 applied, 10,992 accepted. Either SAT or ACT required. SAT 25/75 percentile: 950-1110. High school rank: 13% in top tenth, 40% in top quarter, 78% in top half
Early decision deadline: N/A, notification date: N/A
Early action deadline: N/A, notification date: N/A
Application deadline (fall): 3/15
Undergraduate student body: 18,903 full time, 3,349 part time; 41% male, 59% female; 1% American Indian, 3% Asian, 16% black, 6% Hispanic, 3% multiracial, 0% Pacific Islander, 69% white, 0% international; 88% from in state; 25% live on campus; 11% of students in fraternities, 13% in sororities
Most popular majors: 6% Biological and Biomedical Sciences, 16% Business, Management, Marketing, and Related Support Services, 6% Communication, Journalism, and Related Programs, 12% Education, 17% Health Professions and Related Programs
Expenses: 2015-2016: $6,550 in state, $22,124 out of state; room/board: $9,319
Financial aid: (252) 328-6610; 63% of undergrads determined to have financial need; average aid package $10,661

Elizabeth City State University[1]

Elizabeth City NC
(252) 335-3305
U.S. News ranking: Reg. Coll. (S), No. 30
Website: www.ecsu.edu
Admissions email: admissions@mail.ecsu.edu
Public; founded 1891
Application deadline (fall): 6/30
Undergraduate student body: N/A full time, N/A part time
Expenses: 2014-2015: $4,497 in state, $16,172 out of state; room/board: $7,213
Financial aid: (252) 335-3282

Elon University

Elon NC
(800) 334-8448
U.S. News ranking: Reg. U. (S), No. 1
Website: www.elon.edu
Admissions email: admissions@elon.edu
Private; founded 1889
Freshman admissions: more selective; 2014-2015: 10,443 applied, 5,632 accepted. Either SAT or ACT required. SAT 25/75 percentile: 1130-1320. High

school rank: 25% in top tenth, 62% in top quarter, 91% in top half
Early decision deadline: 11/1, notification date: 12/1
Early action deadline: 11/10, notification date: 12/20
Application deadline (fall): 1/10
Undergraduate student body: 5,638 full time, 144 part time; 41% male, 59% female; 0% American Indian, 2% Asian, 6% black, 5% Hispanic, 2% multiracial, 0% Pacific Islander, 82% white, 2% international; 21% from in state; 62% live on campus; 22% of students in fraternities, 39% in sororities
Most popular majors: 24% Business/Commerce, General, 19% Communication and Media Studies, 4% Kinesiology and Exercise Science, 4% Political Science and Government, General, 7% Psychology, General
Expenses: 2015-2016: $32,172; room/board: $10,998
Financial aid: (336) 278-7640; 34% of undergrads determined to have financial need; average aid package $17,306

Fayetteville State University

Fayetteville NC
(910) 672-1371
U.S. News ranking: Reg. U. (S), No. 84
Website: www.uncfsu.edu
Admissions email: admissions@uncfsu.edu
Public; founded 1867
Freshman admissions: less selective; 2014-2015: 4,110 applied, 2,068 accepted. Either SAT or ACT required. SAT 25/75 percentile: 810-960. High school rank: 9% in top tenth, 26% in top quarter, 62% in top half
Early decision deadline: N/A, notification date: N/A
Early action deadline: N/A, notification date: N/A
Application deadline (fall): 6/30
Undergraduate student body: 3,935 full time, 1,312 part time; 31% male, 69% female; 3% American Indian, 1% Asian, 66% black, 6% Hispanic, 0% multiracial, 0% Pacific Islander, 17% white, 0% international; 96% from in state; 28% live on campus; 1% of students in fraternities, 1% in sororities
Most popular majors: Information not available
Expenses: 2015-2016: $5,265 in state, $16,873 out of state; room/board: N/A
Financial aid: (910) 672-1325; 89% of undergrads determined to have financial need; average aid package $10,666

Gardner-Webb University

Boiling Springs NC
(800) 253-6472
U.S. News ranking: Reg. U. (S), No. 41
Website: www.gardner-webb.edu
Admissions email: admissions@gardner-webb.edu
Private; founded 1905
Affiliation: Baptist
Freshman admissions: selective; 2014-2015: 3,363 applied, 2,242 accepted. Either SAT or ACT required. SAT 25/75 percentile: 900-1130. High school rank: 29% in top tenth, 53% in top quarter, 81% in top half
Early decision deadline: N/A, notification date: N/A
Early action deadline: N/A, notification date: N/A
Application deadline (fall): rolling
Undergraduate student body: 2,122 full time, 566 part time; 34% male, 66% female; 1% American Indian, 1% Asian, 18% black, 3% Hispanic, 0% multiracial, 0% Pacific Islander, 69% white, 1% international; 79% from in state; 49% live on campus; 0% of students in fraternities, 0% in sororities
Most popular majors: 23% Business, Management, Marketing, and Related Support Services, 6% Education, 18% Health Professions and Related Programs, 6% Homeland Security, Law Enforcement, Firefighting and Related Protective Services, 22% Psychology
Expenses: 2015-2016: $28,280; room/board: $9,280
Financial aid: (704) 406-4243; 80% of undergrads determined to have financial need; average aid package $21,535

Greensboro College[1]

Greensboro NC
(336) 272-7102
U.S. News ranking: Reg. Coll. (S), second tier
Website: www.gborocollege.edu
Admissions email: admissions@gborocollege.edu
Private
Application deadline (fall): N/A
Undergraduate student body: N/A full time, N/A part time
Expenses: 2014-2015: $26,850; room/board: $10,100
Financial aid: (336) 272-7102

Guilford College

Greensboro NC
(800) 992-7759
U.S. News ranking: Nat. Lib. Arts, No. 158
Website: www.guilford.edu
Admissions email: admission@guilford.edu
Private; founded 1837
Affiliation: Quaker
Freshman admissions: selective; 2014-2015: 3,001 applied, 1,866 accepted. Neither SAT nor ACT required. SAT 25/75 percentile: 910-1170. High school rank: 12% in top tenth, 34% in top quarter, 71% in top half
Early decision deadline: N/A, notification date: N/A
Early action deadline: 12/15, notification date: 1/1
Application deadline (fall): 8/10
Undergraduate student body: 1,778 full time, 359 part time; 47% male, 53% female; 0% American Indian, 2% Asian, 23% black, 6% Hispanic, 3% multiracial, 0% Pacific Islander, 63% white, 2% international; 54% from in state; 74% live on campus; N/A of students in fraternities, N/A in sororities
Most popular majors: 7% Biological and Biomedical Sciences, 19% Business, Management, Marketing, and Related Support Services, 12% Homeland Security, Law Enforcement, Firefighting and Related Protective Services, 11% Psychology, 6% Social Sciences
Expenses: 2015-2016: $34,090; room/board: $9,556
Financial aid: (336) 316-2165; 76% of undergrads determined to have financial need; average aid package $20,011

High Point University

High Point NC
(800) 345-6993
U.S. News ranking: Reg. Coll. (S), No. 1
Website: www.highpoint.edu
Admissions email: admiss@highpoint.edu
Private; founded 1924
Affiliation: United Methodist
Freshman admissions: selective; 2014-2015: 7,410 applied, 5,942 accepted. Either SAT or ACT required. SAT 25/75 percentile: 1009-1192. High school rank: 22% in top tenth, 48% in top quarter, 80% in top half
Early decision deadline: 11/1, notification date: 11/23
Early action deadline: 11/8, notification date: 12/17
Application deadline (fall): 7/1
Undergraduate student body: 4,164 full time, 44 part time; 40% male, 60% female; 0% American Indian, 1% Asian, 5% black, 4% Hispanic, 4% multiracial, 0% Pacific Islander, 81% white, 2% international; 22% from in state; 92% live on campus; 6% of students in fraternities, 20% in sororities
Most popular majors: 5% Biology/Biological Sciences, General, 21% Business Administration and Management, General, 19% Communication, General, 5% Kinesiology and Exercise Science, 5% Organizational Behavior Studies
Expenses: 2015-2016: $32,430; room/board: $12,200
Financial aid: (336) 841-9128; 50% of undergrads determined to have financial need; average aid package $14,668

Johnson C. Smith University

Charlotte NC
(704) 378-1010
U.S. News ranking: Nat. Lib. Arts, second tier
Website: www.jcsu.edu
Admissions email: admissions@jcsu.edu
Private; founded 1867
Freshman admissions: least selective; 2014-2015: 3,801 applied, 1,606 accepted. Either SAT or ACT required. SAT 25/75 percentile: 720-900. High school rank: 4% in top tenth, 17% in top quarter, 45% in top half
Early decision deadline: N/A, notification date: N/A
Early action deadline: N/A, notification date: N/A
Application deadline (fall): rolling
Undergraduate student body: 1,318 full time, 57 part time; 39% male, 61% female; 0% American Indian, 0% Asian, 73% black, 6% Hispanic, 2% multiracial, 0% Pacific Islander, 0% white, 3% international; 59% from in state; 62% live on campus; 8% of students in fraternities, 7% in sororities
Most popular majors: 21% Business Administration and Management, General, 8% Criminology, 11% Mass Communication/Media Studies, 9% Social Work, 9% Sport and Fitness Administration/Management
Expenses: 2015-2016: $18,336; room/board: $7,100
Financial aid: (704) 378-1035; 88% of undergrads determined to have financial need; average aid package $15,885

Lees-McRae College

Banner Elk NC
(828) 898-8723
U.S. News ranking: Reg. Coll. (S), No. 60
Website: www.lmc.edu
Admissions email: admissions@lmc.edu
Private; founded 1900
Affiliation: Presbyterian Church (U.S.A.)
Freshman admissions: less selective; 2014-2015: 1,514 applied, 938 accepted. Neither SAT nor ACT required. SAT 25/75 percentile: 840-1060. High school rank: 6% in top tenth, 22% in top quarter, 50% in top half
Early decision deadline: N/A, notification date: N/A
Early action deadline: N/A, notification date: N/A
Application deadline (fall): rolling
Undergraduate student body: 930 full time, 10 part time; 34% male, 66% female; 0% American Indian, 1% Asian, 7% black, 2% Hispanic, 1% multiracial, 0% Pacific Islander, 58% white, 2% international; 75% from in state; 64% live on campus; N/A of students in fraternities, N/A in sororities
Most popular majors: Information not available
Expenses: 2015-2016: $24,854; room/board: $10,096
Financial aid: (828) 898-8793; 80% of undergrads determined to have financial need; average aid package $22,736

Lenoir-Rhyne University

Hickory NC
(828) 328-7300
U.S. News ranking: Reg. Coll. (S), No. 13
Website: www.lr.edu
Admissions email: admission@lr.edu
Private; founded 1891
Affiliation: Evangelical Lutheran Church in America
Freshman admissions: selective; 2014-2015: 4,488 applied, 2,953 accepted. Either SAT or ACT required. SAT 25/75 percentile: 870-1090. High school rank: 16% in top tenth, 39% in top quarter, 74% in top half
Early decision deadline: N/A, notification date: N/A
Early action deadline: 11/7, notification date: 11/21
Application deadline (fall): rolling
Undergraduate student body: 1,334 full time, 190 part time; 43% male, 57% female; 1% American Indian, 2% Asian, 15% black, 3% Hispanic, 3% multiracial, 0% Pacific Islander, 72% white, 1% international; 79% from in state; 53% live on campus; 8% of students in fraternities, 14% in sororities
Most popular majors: 15% Business, Management, Marketing, and Related Support Services, 8% Education, 15% Health Professions and Related Programs, 17% Parks, Recreation, Leisure, and Fitness Studies, 9% Psychology
Expenses: 2015-2016: $32,140; room/board: $11,060
Financial aid: (828) 328-7304; 88% of undergrads determined to have financial need; average aid package $25,809

Livingstone College

Salisbury NC
(704) 216-6001
U.S. News ranking: Reg. Coll. (S), second tier
Website: www.livingstone.edu/
Admissions email: admissions@livingstone.edu
Private; founded 1879
Affiliation: African Methodist Episcopal Zion
Freshman admissions: least selective; 2014-2015: 4,420 applied, 2,834 accepted. Either SAT or ACT required. SAT 25/75 percentile: 645-800. High school rank: 2% in top tenth, 6% in top quarter, 25% in top half
Early decision deadline: N/A, notification date: N/A
Early action deadline: N/A, notification date: N/A
Application deadline (fall): rolling
Undergraduate student body: 1,293 full time, 8 part time; 53% male, 47% female; 1% American Indian, 0% Asian, 88% black, 1% Hispanic, N/A multiracial, N/A Pacific Islander, 0% white, 1% international; 64% from in state; 83% live on campus; 3% of students in fraternities, 3% in sororities
Most popular majors: 19% Business Administration and Management, General, 14% Criminal Justice/Safety Studies, 6% Psychology, General, 12% Social Work, 3% Sociology
Expenses: 2015-2016: $17,246; room/board: $6,596
Financial aid: (704) 216-6069; 98% of undergrads determined to have financial need; average aid package $13,718

Mars Hill University

Mars Hill NC
(866) 642-4968
U.S. News ranking: Reg. Coll. (S), No. 36
Website: www.mhc.edu
Admissions email: admissions@mhc.edu
Private; founded 1856
Freshman admissions: less selective; 2014-2015: 3,142 applied, 1,951 accepted. Either SAT or ACT required. SAT 25/75 percentile: 810-1030. High school rank: 8% in top tenth, 27% in top quarter, 60% in top half
Early decision deadline: N/A, notification date: N/A
Early action deadline: N/A, notification date: N/A
Application deadline (fall): rolling
Undergraduate student body: 1,335 full time, 83 part time; 50% male, 50% female; 2% American Indian, 0% Asian, 22% black, 3% Hispanic, 0% multiracial, 0% Pacific Islander, 69% white, 0% international; 73% from in state; 71% live on campus; 4%

of students in fraternities, 11% in sororities
Most popular majors: 19% Business Administration and Management, General, 14% Elementary Education and Teaching, 6% Physical Education Teaching and Coaching, 6% Psychology, General, 12% Social Work
Expenses: 2014-2015: $27,590; room/board: $8,614
Financial aid: (828) 689-1103

Meredith College

Raleigh NC
(919) 760-8581
U.S. News ranking: Reg. Coll. (S), No. 5
Website: www.meredith.edu
Admissions email: admissions@meredith.edu
Private; founded 1891
Freshman admissions: selective; 2014-2015: 1,797 applied, 1,101 accepted. Either SAT or ACT required. SAT 25/75 percentile: 920-1130. High school rank: 18% in top tenth, 46% in top quarter, 83% in top half
Early decision deadline: 10/30, notification date: 11/15
Early action deadline: N/A, notification date: N/A
Application deadline (fall): rolling
Undergraduate student body: 1,571 full time, 73 part time; 0% male, 100% female; 1% American Indian, 3% Asian, 11% black, 4% Hispanic, 3% multiracial, 0% Pacific Islander, 72% white, 4% international; 88% from in state; 61% live on campus; N/A of students in fraternities, N/A in sororities
Most popular majors: 10% Biology/Biological Sciences, General, 6% Business Administration and Management, General, 6% Child Development, 6% Interior Design, 10% Psychology, General
Expenses: 2015-2016: $33,730; room/board: $10,040
Financial aid: (919) 760-8565; 75% of undergrads determined to have financial need; average aid package $23,739

Methodist University

Fayetteville NC
(910) 630-7027
U.S. News ranking: Reg. Coll. (S), No. 38
Website: www.methodist.edu
Admissions email: admissions@methodist.edu
Private
Freshman admissions: selective; 2014-2015: 4,380 applied, 2,506 accepted. Either SAT or ACT required. SAT 25/75 percentile: 870-1080. High school rank: 11% in top tenth, 33% in top quarter, 71% in top half
Early decision deadline: N/A, notification date: N/A
Early action deadline: N/A, notification date: N/A
Application deadline (fall): rolling
Undergraduate student body: 1,994 full time, 234 part time; 54% male, 46% female; 1% American Indian, 1% Asian, 20% black, 8% Hispanic, 4% multiracial, 0% Pacific Islander, 51% white, 6% international
Most popular majors: Information not available
Expenses: 2015-2016: $30,200; room/board: $11,344
Financial aid: (910) 630-7193; 79% of undergrads determined to have financial need; average aid package $18,364

Mid-Atlantic Christian University

Elizabeth City NC
(866) 996-6228
U.S. News ranking: Reg. Coll. (S), unranked
Website: www.macuniversity.edu
Admissions email: admissions@macuniversity.edu
Private; founded 1948
Affiliation: Christian Church/Church of Christ/Restoration Movement
Freshman admissions: N/A; 2014-2015: N/A applied, 95 accepted. Either SAT or ACT required. SAT 25/75 percentile: 778-943. High school rank: 3% in top tenth, 15% in top quarter, 48% in top half
Early decision deadline: N/A, notification date: N/A
Early action deadline: N/A, notification date: N/A
Application deadline (fall): rolling
Undergraduate student body: 148 full time, 46 part time; 40% male, 60% female; N/A American Indian, N/A Asian, N/A black, N/A Hispanic, N/A multiracial, N/A Pacific Islander, N/A white, N/A international
Most popular majors: 0% Business, Management, Marketing, and Related Support Services, 0% Foreign Languages, Literatures, and Linguistics, 11% Psychology, 78% Theology and Religious Vocations
Expenses: 2015-2016: $13,745; room/board: $8,200
Financial aid: N/A; 96% of undergrads determined to have financial need; average aid package $12,224

Montreat College

Montreat NC
(800) 622-6968
U.S. News ranking: Reg. U. (S), No. 93
Website: www.montreat.edu
Admissions email: admissions@montreat.edu
Private; founded 1916
Affiliation: Non-denominational Christian
Freshman admissions: selective; 2014-2015: 799 applied, 368 accepted. Either SAT or ACT required. SAT 25/75 percentile: 820-1080. High school rank: 15% in top tenth, 40% in top quarter, 76% in top half
Early decision deadline: N/A, notification date: N/A
Early action deadline: N/A, notification date: N/A
Application deadline (fall): rolling
Undergraduate student body: 444 full time, 291 part time; 46% male, 54% female; 2% American Indian, 2% Asian, 21% black, 2% Hispanic, 3% multiracial, 0% Pacific Islander, 57% white, 6% international; 77% from in state; 80% live on campus; N/A of students in fraternities, N/A in sororities
Most popular majors: 8% Biological and Biomedical Sciences, 62% Business, Management, Marketing, and Related Support Services, 7% Communication, Journalism, and Related Programs, 7% Parks, Recreation, Leisure, and Fitness Studies, 16% Psychology
Expenses: 2015-2016: $25,720; room/board: $8,266
Financial aid: (800) 545-4656; 82% of undergrads determined to have financial need; average aid package $18,198

North Carolina A&T State University

Greensboro NC
(336) 334-7946
U.S. News ranking: Nat. U., second tier
Website: www.ncat.edu
Admissions email: uadmit@ncat.edu
Public; founded 1891
Freshman admissions: less selective; 2014-2015: 7,491 applied, 4,314 accepted. Either SAT or ACT required. SAT 25/75 percentile: 830-990. High school rank: 11% in top tenth, 34% in top quarter, 74% in top half
Early decision deadline: N/A, notification date: N/A
Early action deadline: N/A, notification date: N/A
Application deadline (fall): 6/15
Undergraduate student body: 8,423 full time, 780 part time; 45% male, 55% female; 0% American Indian, 1% Asian, 81% black, 2% Hispanic, 3% multiracial, 0% Pacific Islander, 4% white, 2% international; 80% from in state; 42% live on campus; 45% of students in fraternities, 45% in sororities
Most popular majors: 10% Business, Management, Marketing, and Related Support Services, 6% Communication, Journalism, and Related Programs, 12% Engineering, 9% Liberal Arts and Sciences, General Studies and Humanities, 9% Psychology
Expenses: 2015-2016: $5,872 in state, $18,632 out of state; room/board: $6,755
Financial aid: (336) 334-7973; 87% of undergrads determined to have financial need; average aid package $14,160

North Carolina Central University

Durham NC
(919) 530-6298
U.S. News ranking: Reg. U. (S), No. 65
Website: www.nccu.edu
Admissions email: admissions@nccu.edu
Public; founded 1910
Freshman admissions: less selective; 2014-2015: 11,246 applied, 4,860 accepted. Either SAT or ACT required. SAT 25/75 percentile: 810-950. High school rank: 6% in top tenth, 24% in top quarter, 66% in top half
Early decision deadline: N/A, notification date: N/A
Early action deadline: N/A, notification date: N/A
Application deadline (fall): rolling
Undergraduate student body: 5,035 full time, 882 part time; 34% male, 66% female; 0% American Indian, 1% Asian, 83% black, 3% Hispanic, 4% multiracial, 0% Pacific Islander, 6% white, 0% international; 91% from in state; 44% live on campus; N/A of students in fraternities, N/A in sororities
Most popular majors: 8% Business Administration and Management, General, 12% Criminal Justice/Safety Studies, 11% Family and Consumer Sciences/Human Sciences, General, 7% Mass Communication/Media Studies, 8% Psychology, General
Expenses: 2015-2016: $5,755 in state, $17,793 out of state; room/board: $8,165
Financial aid: (919) 530-6180

North Carolina State University–Raleigh

Raleigh NC
(919) 515-2434
U.S. News ranking: Nat. U., No. 89
Website: admissions.ncsu.edu
Admissions email: undergrad-admissions@ncsu.edu
Public; founded 1887
Freshman admissions: more selective; 2014-2015: 20,208 applied, 10,390 accepted. Either SAT or ACT required. SAT 25/75 percentile: 1160-1330. High school rank: 52% in top tenth, 86% in top quarter, 99% in top half
Early decision deadline: N/A, notification date: N/A
Early action deadline: 11/1, notification date: 1/30
Application deadline (fall): 1/15
Undergraduate student body: 21,402 full time, 3,071 part time; 56% male, 44% female; 0% American Indian, 5% Asian, 7% black, 4% Hispanic, 4% multiracial, 0% Pacific Islander, 75% white, 3% international; 90% from in state; 32% live on campus; 11% of students in fraternities, 17% in sororities
Most popular majors: 7% Agriculture, Agriculture Operations, and Related Sciences, 10% Biological and Biomedical Sciences, 14% Business, Management, Marketing, and Related Support Services, 23% Engineering, 6% Social Sciences
Expenses: 2015-2016: $8,581 in state, $24,932 out of state; room/board: $10,311
Financial aid: (919) 515-2421; 51% of undergrads determined to have financial need; average aid package $13,174

North Carolina Wesleyan College

Rocky Mount NC
(800) 488-6292
U.S. News ranking: Reg. Coll. (S), No. 63
Website: www.ncwc.edu
Admissions email: adm@ncwc.edu
Private; founded 1956
Affiliation: Methodist
Freshman admissions: less selective; 2014-2015: 2,683 applied, 1,429 accepted. Neither SAT nor ACT required. SAT 25/75 percentile: 756-1144. High school rank: 8% in top tenth, 26% in top quarter, 61% in top half
Early decision deadline: N/A, notification date: N/A
Early action deadline: N/A, notification date: N/A
Application deadline (fall): rolling
Undergraduate student body: 1,530 full time, 342 part time; 42% male, 58% female; 1% American Indian, 1% Asian, 48% black, 2% Hispanic, 2% multiracial, 0% Pacific Islander, 30% white, 4% international; 87% from in state; 32% live on campus; N/A of students in fraternities, N/A in sororities
Most popular majors: 11% Accounting, 31% Business Administration and Management, General, 8% Computer and Information Sciences, General, 23% Criminal Justice/Law Enforcement Administration, 18% Psychology, General
Expenses: 2015-2016: $28,250; room/board: $9,594
Financial aid: (252) 985-5200; 90% of undergrads determined to have financial need; average aid package $17,878

Pfeiffer University

Misenheimer NC
(800) 338-2060
U.S. News ranking: Reg. U. (S), No. 76
Website: www.pfeiffer.edu
Admissions email: admissions@pfeiffer.edu
Private; founded 1885
Affiliation: Methodist
Freshman admissions: selective; 2014-2015: 1,518 applied, 717 accepted. Either SAT or ACT required. ACT 25/75 percentile: 17-21. High school rank: 9% in top tenth, 31% in top quarter, 70% in top half
Early decision deadline: N/A, notification date: N/A
Early action deadline: N/A, notification date: N/A
Application deadline (fall): rolling
Undergraduate student body: 844 full time, 114 part time; 41% male, 59% female; 0% American Indian, 1% Asian, 17% black, 4% Hispanic, 1% multiracial, 0% Pacific Islander, 55% white, 6% international; 79% from in state; 53% live on campus; 0% of students in fraternities, 0% in sororities
Most popular majors: 20% Business Administration and Management, General, 9% Criminal Justice/Safety Studies, 5% Elementary Education and Teaching, 6% Kinesiology and Exercise Science, 6% Registered Nursing/Registered Nurse
Expenses: 2015-2016: $27,125; room/board: $10,525
Financial aid: (800) 338-2060; 88% of undergrads determined to have financial need; average aid package $23,152

Queens University of Charlotte

Charlotte NC
(800) 849-0202
U.S. News ranking: Reg. U. (S), No. 20
Website: www.queens.edu
Admissions email: admissions@queens.edu
Private; founded 1857
Affiliation: Presbyterian
Freshman admissions: selective; 2014-2015: 1,958 applied, 1,536 accepted. Either SAT or ACT required. SAT 25/75 percentile: 920-1160. High school rank: 16% in top tenth, 46% in top quarter, 81% in top half
Early decision deadline: N/A, notification date: N/A
Early action deadline: 12/1, notification date: 12/15
Application deadline (fall): 9/8

Undergraduate student body: 1,369 full time, 296 part time; 30% male, 70% female; 0% American Indian, 3% Asian, 18% black, 6% Hispanic, 1% multiracial, 0% Pacific Islander, 55% white, 7% international; 59% from in state; 71% live on campus; 10% of students in fraternities, 21% in sororities
Most popular majors: 16% Business, Management, Marketing, and Related Support Services, 9% Communication, Journalism, and Related Programs, 6% English Language and Literature/Letters, 28% Health Professions and Related Programs, 7% Psychology
Expenses: 2015-2016: $32,330; room/board: $10,840
Financial aid: (704) 337-2225; 69% of undergrads determined to have financial need; average aid package $22,563

Salem College

Winston-Salem NC
(336) 721-2621
U.S. News ranking: Nat. Lib. Arts, No. 136
Website: www.salem.edu
Admissions email: admissions@salem.edu
Private; founded 1772
Affiliation: Moravian Church in America
Freshman admissions: more selective; 2014-2015: 929 applied, 556 accepted. Either SAT or ACT required. ACT 25/75 percentile: 21-27. High school rank: 40% in top tenth, 76% in top quarter, 97% in top half
Early decision deadline: N/A, notification date: N/A
Early action deadline: N/A, notification date: N/A
Application deadline (fall): rolling
Undergraduate student body: 773 full time, 172 part time; 4% male, 96% female; 1% American Indian, 4% Asian, 23% black, 12% Hispanic, 4% multiracial, 0% Pacific Islander, 53% white, 1% international; 73% from in state; 56% live on campus; N/A of students in fraternities, N/A in sororities
Most popular majors: 10% Business Administration and Management, General, 6% Communication, General, 17% Education, General, 8% Psychology, General, 9% Sociology
Expenses: 2014-2015: $25,356; room/board: $11,764
Financial aid: (336) 721-2808; 88% of undergrads determined to have financial need; average aid package $32,357

Shaw University[1]

Raleigh NC
(800) 214-6683
U.S. News ranking: Reg. Coll. (S), second tier
Website: www.shawu.edu
Admissions email: admission@shawu.edu
Private; founded 1865
Affiliation: Baptist
Application deadline (fall): 7/30
Undergraduate student body: N/A full time, N/A part time
Expenses: 2014-2015: $16,480; room/board: $8,158
Financial aid: (919) 546-8240

St. Augustine's University

Raleigh NC
(919) 516-4012
U.S. News ranking: Reg. Coll. (S), second tier
Website: www.st-aug.edu
Admissions email: admissions@st-aug.edu
Private; founded 1867
Affiliation: Episcopal
Freshman admissions: least selective; 2014-2015: 2,233 applied, 1,653 accepted. Either SAT or ACT required. SAT 25/75 percentile: 665-790. High school rank: N/A
Early decision deadline: N/A, notification date: N/A
Early action deadline: N/A, notification date: N/A
Application deadline (fall): rolling
Undergraduate student body: 1,003 full time, 13 part time; 51% male, 49% female; 0% American Indian, 0% Asian, 95% black, 1% Hispanic, N/A multiracial, N/A Pacific Islander, 1% white, 2% international; 56% from in state; 75% live on campus; N/A of students in fraternities, N/A in sororities
Most popular majors: 22% Business, Management, Marketing, and Related Support Services, 7% Communication, Journalism, and Related Programs, 11% Health Professions and Related Programs, 14% Homeland Security, Law Enforcement, Firefighting and Related Protective Services, 14% Liberal Arts and Sciences, General Studies and Humanities
Expenses: 2015-2016: $17,890; room/board: $7,692
Financial aid: (919) 516-4131; 61% of undergrads determined to have financial need; average aid package $5,134

University of Mount Olive

Mount Olive NC
(919) 658-2502
U.S. News ranking: Reg. Coll. (S), No. 51
Website: www.umo.edu/
Admissions email: admissions@umo.edu
Private; founded 1951
Affiliation: Original Free Will Baptist
Freshman admissions: less selective; 2014-2015: 2,143 applied, 1,004 accepted. Neither SAT nor ACT required. SAT 25/75 percentile: 805-1020. High school rank: N/A
Early decision deadline: N/A, notification date: N/A
Early action deadline: N/A, notification date: N/A
Application deadline (fall): rolling
Undergraduate student body: 1,373 full time, 2,033 part time; 34% male, 66% female; 0% American Indian, 1% Asian, 33% black, 6% Hispanic, 0% multiracial, 0% Pacific Islander, 49% white, 3% international; 93% from in state; N/A live on campus; N/A of students in fraternities, N/A in sororities
Most popular majors: 29% Business, Management, Marketing, and Related Support Services, 19% Education, 20% Health Professions and Related Programs, 13% Homeland Security, Law Enforcement, Firefighting and Related Protective Services, 5% Parks, Recreation, Leisure, and Fitness Studies
Expenses: 2014-2015: $17,800; room/board: $7,295
Financial aid: (919) 658-2502

University of North Carolina–Asheville

Asheville NC
(828) 251-6481
U.S. News ranking: Nat. Lib. Arts, No. 148
Website: www.unca.edu
Admissions email: admissions@unca.edu
Public; founded 1927
Freshman admissions: more selective; 2014-2015: 3,109 applied, 2,280 accepted. Either SAT or ACT required. SAT 25/75 percentile: 1100-1290. High school rank: 21% in top tenth, 54% in top quarter, 90% in top half
Early decision deadline: N/A, notification date: N/A
Early action deadline: 11/15, notification date: 12/15
Application deadline (fall): 2/15
Undergraduate student body: 3,183 full time, 621 part time; 44% male, 56% female; 0% American Indian, 2% Asian, 3% black, 5% Hispanic, 3% multiracial, 0% Pacific Islander, 82% white, 0% international; 89% from in state; 41% live on campus; 2% of students in fraternities, 2% in sororities
Most popular majors: 6% Art/Art Studies, General, 8% Business Administration and Management, General, 8% Environmental Studies, 7% Liberal Arts and Sciences/Liberal Studies, 14% Psychology, General
Expenses: 2015-2016: $6,485 in state, $22,099 out of state; room/board: $8,332
Financial aid: (828) 251-6535; 59% of undergrads determined to have financial need; average aid package $11,633

University of North Carolina–Chapel Hill

Chapel Hill NC
(919) 966-3621
U.S. News ranking: Nat. U., No. 30
Website: www.unc.edu
Admissions email: unchelp@admissions.unc.edu
Public; founded 1789
Freshman admissions: most selective; 2014-2015: 31,332 applied, 8,929 accepted. Either SAT or ACT required. SAT 25/75 percentile: 1210-1400. High school rank: 78% in top tenth, 96% in top quarter, 99% in top half
Early decision deadline: N/A, notification date: N/A
Early action deadline: 10/15, notification date: 1/31
Application deadline (fall): 1/10
Undergraduate student body: 17,570 full time, 780 part time; 42% male, 58% female; 1% American Indian, 9% Asian, 8% black, 7% Hispanic, 4% multiracial, 0% Pacific Islander, 65% white, 2% international; 83% from in state; 53% live on campus; 18% of students in fraternities, 18% in sororities
Most popular majors: 6% Area Studies, 8% Biology, General, 10% Communication and Media Studies, 6% Economics, 9% Psychology, General
Expenses: 2015-2016: $8,562 in state, $33,644 out of state; room/board: $10,902
Financial aid: (919) 962-8396; 45% of undergrads determined to have financial need; average aid package $18,725

University of North Carolina–Charlotte

Charlotte NC
(704) 687-5507
U.S. News ranking: Nat. U., No. 194
Website: www.uncc.edu/
Admissions email: admissions@uncc.edu
Public; founded 1946
Freshman admissions: selective; 2014-2015: 15,610 applied, 10,004 accepted. Either SAT or ACT required. SAT 25/75 percentile: 1000-1170. High school rank: 23% in top tenth, 56% in top quarter, 88% in top half
Early decision deadline: N/A, notification date: N/A
Early action deadline: N/A, notification date: N/A
Application deadline (fall): 7/1
Undergraduate student body: 18,983 full time, 3,233 part time; 52% male, 48% female; 0% American Indian, 5% Asian, 17% black, 8% Hispanic, 4% multiracial, 0% Pacific Islander, 60% white, 2% international; 94% from in state; 23% live on campus; 2% of students in fraternities, 5% in sororities
Most popular majors: 18% Business, Management, Marketing, and Related Support Services, 8% Engineering, 8% Health Professions and Related Programs, 7% Psychology, 9% Social Sciences
Expenses: 2015-2016: $6,384 in state, $19,555 out of state; room/board: $11,646
Financial aid: (704) 687-2461; 80% of undergrads determined to have financial need; average aid package $9,749

University of North Carolina–Greensboro

Greensboro NC
(336) 334-5243
U.S. News ranking: Nat. U., No. 187
Website: www.uncg.edu/
Admissions email: admissions@uncg.edu
Public; founded 1891
Freshman admissions: selective; 2014-2015: 9,852 applied, 5,909 accepted. Either SAT or ACT required. SAT 25/75 percentile: 940-1100. High school rank: 16% in top tenth, 43% in top quarter, 82% in top half
Early decision deadline: N/A, notification date: N/A
Early action deadline: N/A, notification date: N/A
Application deadline (fall): 3/1
Undergraduate student body: 12,773 full time, 2,400 part time; 34% male, 66% female; 0% American Indian, 5% Asian, 27% black, 7% Hispanic, 4% multiracial, 0% Pacific Islander, 55% white, 2% international; 94% from in state; 33% live on campus; 4% of students in fraternities, 4% in sororities
Most popular majors: 18% Business, Management, Marketing, and Related Support Services, 10% Education, 11% Health Professions and Related Programs, 8% Social Sciences, 8% Visual and Performing Arts
Expenses: 2015-2016: $6,733 in state, $21,595 out of state; room/board: $8,252
Financial aid: (336) 334-5702; 74% of undergrads determined to have financial need; average aid package $9,757

University of North Carolina–Pembroke

Pembroke NC
(910) 521-6262
U.S. News ranking: Reg. U. (S), No. 93
Website: www.uncp.edu
Admissions email: admissions@uncp.edu
Public; founded 1887
Freshman admissions: less selective; 2014-2015: 4,035 applied, 2,956 accepted. Either SAT or ACT required. SAT 25/75 percentile: 850-1000. High school rank: 11% in top tenth, 34% in top quarter, 72% in top half
Early decision deadline: N/A, notification date: N/A
Early action deadline: N/A, notification date: N/A
Application deadline (fall): 7/31
Undergraduate student body: 4,400 full time, 1,111 part time; 39% male, 61% female; 15% American Indian, 2% Asian, 36% black, 5% Hispanic, 2% multiracial, 0% Pacific Islander, 38% white, 1% international; 96% from in state; 40% live on campus; 7% of students in fraternities, 4% in sororities
Most popular majors: 9% Biology/Biological Sciences, General, 11% Business Administration and Management, General, 12% Criminal Justice/Safety Studies, 11% Health and Physical Education/Fitness, General, 8% Sociology
Expenses: 2015-2016: $5,534 in state, $15,982 out of state; room/board: $8,782
Financial aid: (910) 521-6255; 82% of undergrads determined to have financial need; average aid package $9,948

University of North Carolina School of the Arts

Winston-Salem NC
(336) 770-3291
U.S. News ranking: Arts, unranked
Website: www.uncsa.edu
Admissions email: admissions@uncsa.edu
Public; founded 1963
Freshman admissions: N/A; 2014-2015: 868 applied, 375 accepted. Either SAT or ACT required. SAT 25/75 percentile:

1010-1230. High school rank: 12% in top tenth, 46% in top quarter, 77% in top half
Early decision deadline: N/A, notification date: N/A
Early action deadline: N/A, notification date: N/A
Application deadline (fall): 3/15
Undergraduate student body: 845 full time, 9 part time; 52% male, 48% female; 1% American Indian, 1% Asian, 8% black, 8% Hispanic, 5% multiracial, 0% Pacific Islander, 73% white, 2% international; 50% from in state; 63% live on campus; N/A of students in fraternities, N/A in sororities
Most popular majors: 36% Cinematography and Film/Video Production, 16% Dance, General, 16% Drama and Dramatics/ Theatre Arts, General, 11% Music Performance, General, 21% Technical Theatre/Theatre Design and Technology
Expenses: 2015-2016: $8,983 in state, $24,403 out of state; room/ board: $8,570
Financial aid: (336) 770-3297; 63% of undergrads determined to have financial need; average aid package $13,157

University of orth Carolina–Wilmington

Wilmington NC
(910) 962-3243
U.S. News ranking: Reg. U. (S), No. 16
Website: www.uncw.edu
Admissions email: admissions@uncw.edu
Public; founded 1947
Freshman admissions: more selective; 2014-2015: 11,523 applied, 6,747 accepted. Either SAT or ACT required. SAT 25/75 percentile: 1110-1270. High school rank: 27% in top tenth, 69% in top quarter, 95% in top half
Early decision deadline: N/A, notification date: N/A
Early action deadline: 11/1, notification date: 1/20
Application deadline (fall): 2/1
Undergraduate student body: 11,690 full time, 1,262 part time; 39% male, 61% female; 0% American Indian, 2% Asian, 5% black, 7% Hispanic, 3% multiracial, 0% Pacific Islander, 79% white, 1% international; 85% from in state; 32% live on campus; 5% of students in fraternities, 8% in sororities
Most popular majors: 5% Biological and Biomedical Sciences, 19% Business, Management, Marketing, and Related Support Services, 6% Communication, Journalism, and Related Programs, 5% Education, 9% Psychology
Expenses: 2015-2016: $6,647 in state, $20,513 out of state; room/ board: $9,862
Financial aid: (910) 962-3177; 56% of undergrads determined to have financial need; average aid package $10,163

Wake Forest University

Winston-Salem NC
(336) 758-5201
U.S. News ranking: Nat. U., No. 27
Website: www.wfu.edu
Admissions email: admissions@wfu.edu
Private; founded 1834
Freshman admissions: most selective; 2014-2015: 11,119 applied, 3,826 accepted. Neither SAT nor ACT required. SAT 25/75 percentile: 1210-1420. High school rank: 77% in top tenth, 93% in top quarter, 99% in top half
Early decision deadline: 11/15, notification date: N/A
Early action deadline: N/A, notification date: N/A
Application deadline (fall): 1/1
Undergraduate student body: 4,804 full time, 63 part time; 47% male, 53% female; 0% American Indian, 5% Asian, 6% black, 6% Hispanic, 3% multiracial, 0% Pacific Islander, 74% white, 6% international; 21% from in state; 77% live on campus; 39% of students in fraternities, 58% in sororities
Most popular majors: 10% Biological and Biomedical Sciences, 24% Business, Management, Marketing, and Related Support Services, 10% Communication, Journalism, and Related Programs, 9% Psychology, 19% Social Sciences
Expenses: 2015-2016: $47,682; room/board: $12,996
Financial aid: (336) 758-5154; 35% of undergrads determined to have financial need; average aid package $40,534

Warren Wilson College

Asheville NC
(800) 934-3536
U.S. News ranking: Nat. Lib. Arts, No. 164
Website: www.warren-wilson.edu
Admissions email: admit@warren-wilson.edu
Private; founded 1894
Freshman admissions: selective; 2014-2015: 1,176 applied, 844 accepted. Neither SAT nor ACT required. SAT 25/75 percentile: 1010-1220. High school rank: 28% in top tenth, 52% in top quarter, 80% in top half
Early decision deadline: 11/15, notification date: 12/1
Early action deadline: 11/1, notification date: 12/1
Application deadline (fall): 2/1
Undergraduate student body: 817 full time, 7 part time; 38% male, 62% female; 1% American Indian, 1% Asian, 4% black, 6% Hispanic, 4% multiracial, 0% Pacific Islander, 82% white, 2% international; 24% from in state; 90% live on campus; 0% of students in fraternities, 0% in sororities
Most popular majors: 8% Creative Writing, 23% Environmental Studies, 7% History, General, 8% International/Global Studies, 9% Psychology, General
Expenses: 2015-2016: $32,560; room/board: $9,900
Financial aid: (828) 771-2082; 76% of undergrads determined to have financial need; average aid package $28,482

Western Carolina University

Cullowhee NC
(828) 227-7317
U.S. News ranking: Reg. U. (S), No. 32
Website: www.wcu.edu
Admissions email: admiss@email.wcu.edu
Public; founded 1889
Freshman admissions: selective; 2014-2015: 15,397 applied, 6,637 accepted. Either SAT or ACT required. SAT 25/75 percentile: 930-1120. High school rank: 13% in top tenth, 39% in top quarter, 79% in top half
Early decision deadline: N/A, notification date: N/A
Early action deadline: 11/15, notification date: 12/15
Application deadline (fall): 3/1
Undergraduate student body: 7,373 full time, 1,414 part time; 46% male, 54% female; 1% American Indian, 1% Asian, 6% black, 5% Hispanic, 3% multiracial, 0% Pacific Islander, 80% white, 2% international; 93% from in state; 42% live on campus; N/A of students in fraternities, N/A in sororities
Most popular majors: 16% Business, Management, Marketing, and Related Support Services, 10% Education, 19% Health Professions and Related Programs, 8% Homeland Security, Law Enforcement, Firefighting and Related Protective Services, 6% Psychology
Expenses: 2015-2016: $6,903 in state, $17,296 out of state; room/ board: N/A
Financial aid: (828) 227-7290; 69% of undergrads determined to have financial need; average aid package $9,507

William Peace University[1]

Raleigh NC
(919) 508-2214
U.S. News ranking: Nat. Lib. Arts, second tier
Website: www.peace.edu
Admissions email: admissions@peace.edu
Private; founded 1857
Affiliation: Presbyterian Church (USA)
Application deadline (fall): rolling
Undergraduate student body: N/A full time, N/A part time
Expenses: 2014-2015: $24,650; room/board: $9,600
Financial aid: (919) 508-2249

Wingate University

Wingate NC
(800) 755-5550
U.S. News ranking: Reg. U. (S), No. 37
Website: www.wingate.edu/admissions
Admissions email: admit@wingate.edu
Private; founded 1896
Freshman admissions: selective; 2014-2015: 6,601 applied, 4,955 accepted. Either SAT or ACT required. SAT 25/75 percentile: 907-1110. High school rank: 16% in top tenth, 45% in top quarter, 82% in top half
Early decision deadline: N/A, notification date: N/A
Early action deadline: N/A, notification date: N/A
Application deadline (fall): rolling
Undergraduate student body: 1,891 full time, 61 part time; 41% male, 59% female; 1% American Indian, 2% Asian, 15% black, 3% Hispanic, 5% multiracial, 0% Pacific Islander, 64% white, 4% international; 81% from in state; 76% live on campus; 4% of students in fraternities, 10% in sororities
Most popular majors: 11% Biological and Biomedical Sciences, 18% Business, Management, Marketing, and Related Support Services, 12% Communication, Journalism, and Related Programs, 10% Parks, Recreation, Leisure, and Fitness Studies, 10% Psychology
Expenses: 2015-2016: $28,110; room/board: $10,600
Financial aid: (704) 233-8209; 83% of undergrads determined to have financial need; average aid package $23,009

Winston-Salem State University[1]

Winston-Salem NC
(336) 750-2070
U.S. News ranking: Reg. U. (S), No. 84
Website: www.wssu.edu
Admissions email: admissions@wssu.edu
Public; founded 1892
Application deadline (fall): 3/15
Undergraduate student body: N/A full time, N/A part time
Expenses: 2014-2015: $5,583 in state, $15,113 out of state; room/ board: $8,621
Financial aid: (336) 750-3280

NORTH DAKOTA

Bismarck State College

Bismarck ND
(701) 224-2459
U.S. News ranking: Reg. Coll. (Mid.W), second tier
Website: www.bismarckstate.edu
Admissions email: bsc.admissions@bismarckstate.edu
Public; founded 1959
Freshman admissions: less selective; 2014-2015: 1,171 applied, 1,171 accepted. Neither SAT nor ACT required. ACT 25/75 percentile: 17-22. High school rank: N/A
Early decision deadline: N/A, notification date: N/A
Early action deadline: N/A, notification date: N/A
Application deadline (fall): rolling
Undergraduate student body: 2,303 full time, 1,699 part time; 57% male, 43% female; 1% American Indian, 1% Asian, 3% black, 2% Hispanic, 3% multiracial, 0% Pacific Islander, 88% white, 0% international; 73% from in state; 9% live on campus; 0% of students in fraternities, 0% in sororities
Most popular majors: 100% Business, Management, Marketing, and Related Support Services
Expenses: 2014-2015: $4,222 in state, $10,084 out of state; room/ board: $6,801
Financial aid: (701) 224-5494

Dickinson State University

Dickinson ND
(701) 483-2175
U.S. News ranking: Reg. Coll. (Mid.W), second tier
Website: www.dickinsonstate.com
Admissions email: dsu.hawks@dsu.nodak.edu
Public
Freshman admissions: selective; 2014-2015: 467 applied, 285 accepted. Neither SAT nor ACT required. ACT 25/75 percentile: 18-23. High school rank: N/A
Early decision deadline: N/A, notification date: N/A
Early action deadline: 4/15, notification date: N/A
Application deadline (fall): 8/1
Undergraduate student body: 980 full time, 495 part time; 40% male, 60% female; 1% American Indian, 1% Asian, 4% black, 4% Hispanic, 3% multiracial, 0% Pacific Islander, 79% white, 5% international; 72% from in state; 19% live on campus; 0% of students in fraternities, 0% in sororities
Most popular majors: 38% Business, Management, Marketing, and Related Support Services, 18% Education, 7% Multi/Interdisciplinary Studies, 7% Parks, Recreation, Leisure, and Fitness Studies, 1% Psychology
Expenses: 2014-2015: $6,050 in state, $8,495 out of state; room/ board: $5,850
Financial aid: (701) 483-2371; 54% of undergrads determined to have financial need; average aid package $13,818

Mayville State University

Mayville ND
(701) 788-4667
U.S. News ranking: Reg. Coll. (Mid.W), No. 62
Website: www.mayvillestate.edu
Admissions email: masuadmissions@mayvillestate.edu
Public; founded 1889
Freshman admissions: selective; 2014-2015: 413 applied, 236 accepted. Either SAT or ACT required. ACT 25/75 percentile: 17-22. High school rank: N/A
Early decision deadline: N/A, notification date: N/A
Early action deadline: N/A, notification date: N/A
Application deadline (fall): rolling
Undergraduate student body: 635 full time, 421 part time; 44% male, 56% female; 2% American Indian, 0% Asian, 7% black, 5% Hispanic, 3% multiracial, 0% Pacific Islander, 80% white, 3% international; 59% from in state; 43% live on campus; 0% of students in fraternities, 0% in sororities
Most popular majors: 27% Business Administration and Management, General, 7% Early Childhood Education and Teaching, 13% Elementary Education and Teaching, 15% General Studies, 7% Physical Education Teaching and Coaching
Expenses: 2015-2016: $6,380 in state, $8,845 out of state; room/ board: $5,904

Financial aid: (701) 788-4767; 63% of undergrads determined to have financial need; average aid package $14,270

Minot State University

Minot ND
(701) 858-3350
U.S. News ranking: Reg. U. (Mid.W), No. 112
Website: www.minotstateu.edu
Admissions email: askmsu@minotstateu.edu
Public; founded 1913
Freshman admissions: selective; 2014-2015: 775 applied, 447 accepted. Either SAT or ACT required. ACT 25/75 percentile: 20-25. High school rank: 13% in top tenth, 31% in top quarter, 68% in top half
Early decision deadline: N/A, notification date: N/A
Early action deadline: N/A, notification date: N/A
Application deadline (fall): rolling
Undergraduate student body: 2,075 full time, 1,041 part time; 40% male, 60% female; 2% American Indian, 1% Asian, 4% black, 5% Hispanic, 3% multiracial, 0% Pacific Islander, 67% white, 15% international; 83% from in state; 17% live on campus; N/A of students in fraternities, N/A in sororities
Most popular majors: 29% Business Administration and Management, General, 6% Criminal Justice/Safety Studies, 14% Elementary Education and Teaching, 20% Registered Nursing/Registered Nurse, 9% Social Work
Expenses: 2015-2016: $6,390 in state, $6,390 out of state; room/board: $5,936
Financial aid: (701) 858-3375; 46% of undergrads determined to have financial need; average aid package $10,024

North Dakota State University

Fargo ND
(701) 231-8643
U.S. News ranking: Nat. U., No. 185
Website: www.ndsu.edu
Admissions email: NDSU.Admission@ndsu.edu
Public; founded 1890
Freshman admissions: selective; 2014-2015: 5,713 applied, 4,727 accepted. Either SAT or ACT required. ACT 25/75 percentile: 21-26. High school rank: 17% in top tenth, 42% in top quarter, 74% in top half
Early decision deadline: N/A, notification date: N/A
Early action deadline: N/A, notification date: N/A
Application deadline (fall): 8/1
Undergraduate student body: 10,865 full time, 1,259 part time; 55% male, 45% female; 1% American Indian, 1% Asian, 2% black, 2% Hispanic, 2% multiracial, 0% Pacific Islander, 87% white, 3% international; 43% from in state; 33% live on campus; 2% of students in fraternities, 3% in sororities
Most popular majors: 9% Agriculture, Agriculture Operations, and Related Sciences, 15% Business, Management, Marketing, and Related Support Services, 13% Engineering, 8% Family and Consumer Sciences/Human Sciences, 11% Health Professions and Related Programs
Expenses: 2014-2015: $7,820 in state, $11,169 out of state; room/board: $7,484
Financial aid: (800) 726-3188; 51% of undergrads determined to have financial need; average aid package $11,264

University of Jamestown

Jamestown ND
(701) 252-3467
U.S. News ranking: Reg. Coll. (Mid.W), No. 36
Website: www.jc.edu
Admissions email: admissions@jc.edu
Private; founded 1884
Affiliation: Presbyterian
Freshman admissions: selective; 2014-2015: 839 applied, 540 accepted. Either SAT or ACT required. ACT 25/75 percentile: 20-25. High school rank: 22% in top tenth, 45% in top quarter, 78% in top half
Early decision deadline: N/A, notification date: N/A
Early action deadline: N/A, notification date: N/A
Application deadline (fall): rolling
Undergraduate student body: 839 full time, 53 part time; 46% male, 54% female; 2% American Indian, 1% Asian, 5% black, 6% Hispanic, N/A multiracial, 0% Pacific Islander, 80% white, 7% international; 51% from in state; 76% live on campus; N/A of students in fraternities, N/A in sororities
Most popular majors: 6% Biology/Biological Sciences, General, 20% Business Administration and Management, General, 6% Criminal Justice/Police Science, 19% Elementary Education and Teaching, 20% Registered Nursing, Nursing Administration, Nursing Research and Clinical Nursing
Expenses: 2015-2016: $19,870; room/board: $6,860
Financial aid: (701) 252-3467; 66% of undergrads determined to have financial need; average aid package $14,396

University of Mary

Bismarck ND
(701) 355-8030
U.S. News ranking: Reg. U. (Mid.W), second tier
Website: www.umary.edu
Admissions email: marauder@umary.edu
Private; founded 1959
Affiliation: Christian, Catholic, and Benedictine.
Freshman admissions: selective; 2014-2015: 1,109 applied, 873 accepted. Either SAT or ACT required. ACT 25/75 percentile: 20-25. High school rank: N/A
Early decision deadline: N/A, notification date: N/A
Early action deadline: N/A, notification date: N/A
Application deadline (fall): rolling
Undergraduate student body: 1,727 full time, 309 part time; 35% male, 65% female; 2% American Indian, 1% Asian, 3% black, 3% Hispanic, 1% multiracial, 0% Pacific Islander, 84% white, 1% international; 43% from in state; 52% live on campus; 0% of students in fraternities, 0% in sororities
Most popular majors: 29% Communication Sciences and Disorders, General, 5% General Studies, 7% Nursing Administration, 8% Nursing Administration, 4% Organizational Leadership
Expenses: 2014-2015: $15,665; room/board: $5,931
Financial aid: (701) 355-8079

University of North Dakota

Grand Forks ND
(800) 225-5863
U.S. News ranking: Nat. U., No. 180
Website: und.edu
Admissions email: admissions@und.edu
Public; founded 1883
Freshman admissions: selective; 2014-2015: 4,642 applied, 3,992 accepted. Either SAT or ACT required. ACT 25/75 percentile: 21-26. High school rank: 17% in top tenth, 39% in top quarter, 76% in top half
Early decision deadline: N/A, notification date: N/A
Early action deadline: N/A, notification date: N/A
Application deadline (fall): rolling
Undergraduate student body: 9,079 full time, 2,458 part time; 57% male, 43% female; 2% American Indian, 2% Asian, 2% black, 3% Hispanic, 3% multiracial, 0% Pacific Islander, 80% white, 6% international; 40% from in state; 28% live on campus; 10% of students in fraternities, 11% in sororities
Most popular majors: 6% Airline/Commercial/Professional Pilot and Flight Crew, 5% Communication and Media Studies, 7% General Studies, 6% Psychology, General, 7% Registered Nursing/Registered Nurse
Expenses: 2014-2015: $7,741 in state, $18,409 out of state; room/board: $6,746
Financial aid: (701) 777-3121

Valley City State University

Valley City ND
(701) 845-7101
U.S. News ranking: Reg. Coll. (Mid.W), No. 43
Website: www.vcsu.edu
Admissions email: enrollment.services@vcsu.edu
Public; founded 1890
Freshman admissions: selective; 2014-2015: 370 applied, 334 accepted. Either SAT or ACT required. ACT 25/75 percentile: 19-25. High school rank: 7% in top tenth, 25% in top quarter, 58% in top half
Early decision deadline: N/A, notification date: N/A
Early action deadline: N/A, notification date: N/A
Application deadline (fall): rolling
Undergraduate student body: 779 full time, 455 part time; 42% male, 58% female; 1% American Indian, 0% Asian, 4% black, 5% Hispanic, 3% multiracial, 0% Pacific Islander, 82% white, 4% international; 65% from in state; 35% live on campus; 1% of students in fraternities, 1% in sororities
Most popular majors: 5% Biology/Biological Sciences, General, 12% Business Administration and Management, General, 45% Elementary Education and Teaching, 4% Health and Physical Education/Fitness, General, 4% Wildlife, Fish and Wildlands Science and Management
Expenses: 2015-2016: $6,799 in state, $15,405 out of state; room/board: $6,175
Financial aid: (701) 845-7412; 67% of undergrads determined to have financial need; average aid package $9,366

OHIO

Antioch University

Yellow Springs OH
(937) 769-1818
U.S. News ranking: Reg. U. (Mid.W), unranked
Website: midwest.antioch.edu
Admissions email: admission.aum@antioch.edu
Private; founded 1852
Freshman admissions: N/A; 2014-2015: 0 applied, 0 accepted. Neither SAT nor ACT required. ACT 25/75 percentile: N/A. High school rank: N/A
Early decision deadline: N/A, notification date: N/A
Early action deadline: N/A, notification date: N/A
Application deadline (fall): rolling
Undergraduate student body: 39 full time, 77 part time; 29% male, 71% female; 2% American Indian, 1% Asian, 14% black, 1% Hispanic, 0% multiracial, 0% Pacific Islander, 53% white, 0% international; 100% from in state; 0% live on campus; 0% of students in fraternities, 0% in sororities
Most popular majors: 23% Business Administration and Management, General, 30% Elementary Education and Teaching, 11% Health and Wellness, General, 17% Human Services, General, 9% Humanities/Humanistic Studies
Expenses: N/A
Financial aid: N/A

Art Academy of Cincinnati

Cincinnati OH
(513) 562-8740
U.S. News ranking: Arts, unranked
Website: www.artacademy.edu
Admissions email: admissions@artacademy.edu
Private; founded 1869
Freshman admissions: N/A; 2014-2015: 493 applied, 120 accepted. Either SAT or ACT required. ACT 25/75 percentile: 18-23. High school rank: N/A
Early decision deadline: N/A, notification date: N/A
Early action deadline: N/A, notification date: N/A
Application deadline (fall): rolling
Undergraduate student body: 198 full time, 11 part time; 39% male, 61% female; 0% American Indian, 3% Asian, 8% black, 5% Hispanic, 3% multiracial, 1% Pacific Islander, 80% white, 1% international; N/A from in state; 20% live on campus; N/A of students in fraternities, N/A in sororities
Most popular majors: 14% Design and Visual Communications, General, 16% Drawing, 23% Illustration, 16% Photography, 9% Sculpture
Expenses: 2014-2015: $26,376; room/board: $6,400
Financial aid: (513) 562-8751

Ashland University

Ashland OH
(419) 289-5052
U.S. News ranking: Nat. U., No. 199
Website: www.ashland.edu/admissions
Admissions email: enrollme@ashland.edu
Private; founded 1878
Affiliation: Brethren Church
Freshman admissions: selective; 2014-2015: 3,184 applied, 2,288 accepted. Either SAT or ACT required. ACT 25/75 percentile: 20-25. High school rank: 18% in top tenth, 43% in top quarter, 78% in top half
Early decision deadline: N/A, notification date: N/A
Early action deadline: N/A, notification date: N/A
Application deadline (fall): rolling
Undergraduate student body: 2,562 full time, 1,206 part time; 47% male, 53% female; 0% American Indian, 0% Asian, 5% black, 3% Hispanic, 2% multiracial, 0% Pacific Islander, 85% white, 3% international; 93% from in state; 64% live on campus; 13% of students in fraternities, 21% in sororities
Most popular majors: 4% Business Administration and Management, General, 9% Early Childhood Education and Teaching, 5% Education/Teaching of Individuals in Early Childhood Special Education Programs, 6% Junior High/Intermediate/Middle School Education and Teaching, 13% Nursing Practice
Expenses: 2015-2016: $20,242; room/board: $9,602
Financial aid: (419) 289-5002; 76% of undergrads determined to have financial need; average aid package $17,689

Baldwin Wallace University

Berea OH
(440) 826-2222
U.S. News ranking: Reg. U. (Mid.W), No. 13
Website: www.bw.edu
Admissions email: admission@bw.edu
Private; founded 1845
Affiliation: United Methodist
Freshman admissions: selective; 2014-2015: 4,224 applied, 2,702 accepted. Neither SAT nor ACT required. ACT 25/75 percentile: 20-25. High school rank: 22% in top tenth, 46% in top quarter, 77% in top half
Early decision deadline: N/A, notification date: N/A
Early action deadline: N/A, notification date: N/A
Application deadline (fall): rolling
Undergraduate student body: 2,969 full time, 393 part time; 44% male, 56% female; 0% American Indian, 1% Asian, 9% black, 5% Hispanic, 4% multiracial, 0%

Pacific Islander, 79% white, 1% international; 81% from in state; 63% live on campus; 13% of students in fraternities, 20% in sororities
Most popular majors: 8% Biological and Biomedical Sciences, 22% Business, Management, Marketing, and Related Support Services, 9% Education, 11% Health Professions and Related Programs, 10% Visual and Performing Arts
Expenses: 2015-2016: $29,908; room/board: $8,370
Financial aid: (440) 826-2108; 80% of undergrads determined to have financial need; average aid package $21,666

Bluffton University

Bluffton OH
(800) 488-3257
U.S. News ranking: Reg. Coll. (Mid.W), No. 27
Website: www.bluffton.edu
Admissions email: admissions@bluffton.edu
Private; founded 1899
Affiliation: Mennonite Church USA
Freshman admissions: selective; 2014-2015: 2,315 applied, 1,297 accepted. Either SAT or ACT required. ACT 25/75 percentile: 19-25. High school rank: 14% in top tenth, 36% in top quarter, 71% in top half
Early decision deadline: N/A, notification date: N/A
Early action deadline: N/A, notification date: N/A
Application deadline (fall): 8/15
Undergraduate student body: 796 full time, 201 part time; 50% male, 50% female; 0% American Indian, 0% Asian, 6% black, 4% Hispanic, 2% multiracial, 0% Pacific Islander, 85% white, 0% international; 86% from in state; 84% live on campus; 0% of students in fraternities, 0% in sororities
Most popular majors: 39% Business Administration and Management, General, 16% Early Childhood Education and Teaching, 4% Foods, Nutrition, and Wellness Studies, General, 8% Social Work, 10% Sport and Fitness Administration/ Management
Expenses: 2015-2016: $30,168; room/board: $9,890
Financial aid: (419) 358-3266; 85% of undergrads determined to have financial need; average aid package $27,372

Bowling Green State University

Bowling Green OH
(419) 372-2478
U.S. News ranking: Nat. U., No. 185
Website: www.bgsu.edu
Admissions email: choosebgsu@bgsu.edu
Public; founded 1910
Freshman admissions: selective; 2014-2015: 14,509 applied, 7,743 accepted. Either SAT or ACT required. ACT 25/75 percentile: 20-25. High school rank: 13% in top tenth, 35% in top quarter, 70% in top half
Early decision deadline: N/A, notification date: N/A
Early action deadline: N/A, notification date: N/A
Application deadline (fall): 7/15
Undergraduate student body: 12,993 full time, 1,106 part time; 44% male, 56% female; 0% American Indian, 1% Asian, 10% black, 4% Hispanic, 3% multiracial, 0% Pacific Islander, 77% white, 2% international; 88% from in state; 42% live on campus; 12% of students in fraternities, 13% in sororities
Most popular majors: 4% Biology/ Biological Sciences, General, 4% Kindergarten/Preschool Education and Teaching, 4% Liberal Arts and Sciences/Liberal Studies, 4% Psychology, General, 4% Teacher Education, Multiple Levels
Expenses: 2014-2015: $10,726 in state, $18,034 out of state; room/board: $8,244
Financial aid: (419) 372-2651; 66% of undergrads determined to have financial need; average aid package $13,928

Capital University

Columbus OH
(866) 544-6175
U.S. News ranking: Reg. U. (Mid.W), No. 36
Website: www.capital.edu
Admissions email: admission@capital.edu
Private; founded 1830
Affiliation: Lutheran
Freshman admissions: selective; 2014-2015: 3,654 applied, 2,666 accepted. Either SAT or ACT required. ACT 25/75 percentile: 21-27. High school rank: 17% in top tenth, 44% in top quarter, 76% in top half
Early decision deadline: N/A, notification date: N/A
Early action deadline: N/A, notification date: N/A
Application deadline (fall): 5/1
Undergraduate student body: 2,454 full time, 288 part time; 42% male, 58% female; 0% American Indian, 1% Asian, 9% black, 4% Hispanic, 4% multiracial, 0% Pacific Islander, 77% white, 2% international; 90% from in state; 59% live on campus; 9% of students in fraternities, 11% in sororities
Most popular majors: 14% Business, Management, Marketing, and Related Support Services, 14% Education, 18% Health Professions and Related Programs, 8% Social Sciences, 9% Visual and Performing Arts
Expenses: 2015-2016: $32,830; room/board: $9,422
Financial aid: (614) 236-6511; 81% of undergrads determined to have financial need; average aid package $26,007

Case Western Reserve University

Cleveland OH
(216) 368-4450
U.S. News ranking: Nat. U., No. 37
Website: www.case.edu
Admissions email: admission@case.edu
Private; founded 1826
Freshman admissions: most selective; 2014-2015: 21,733 applied, 8,326 accepted. Either SAT or ACT required. SAT 25/75 percentile: 1270-1470. High school rank: 68% in top tenth, 92% in top quarter, 99% in top half
Early decision deadline: 11/1, notification date: 12/15
Early action deadline: 11/1, notification date: 12/15
Application deadline (fall): 1/15
Undergraduate student body: 4,766 full time, 145 part time; 54% male, 46% female; 0% American Indian, 19% Asian, 4% black, 6% Hispanic, 4% multiracial, 0% Pacific Islander, 53% white, 9% international; 33% from in state; 82% live on campus; 34% of students in fraternities, 35% in sororities
Most popular majors: 10% Bioengineering and Biomedical Engineering, 9% Biology/Biological Sciences, General, 8% Mechanical Engineering, 7% Psychology, General, 6% Registered Nursing/ Registered Nurse
Expenses: 2015-2016: $44,560; room/board: $13,850
Financial aid: (216) 368-3866; 56% of undergrads determined to have financial need; average aid package $37,356

Cedarville University

Cedarville OH
(800) 233-2784
U.S. News ranking: Reg. Coll. (Mid.W), No. 9
Website: www.cedarville.edu
Admissions email: admissions@cedarville.edu
Private; founded 1887
Affiliation: Baptist
Freshman admissions: more selective; 2014-2015: 3,003 applied, 2,237 accepted. Either SAT or ACT required. ACT 25/75 percentile: 23-29. High school rank: 35% in top tenth, 65% in top quarter, 89% in top half
Early decision deadline: N/A, notification date: N/A
Early action deadline: N/A, notification date: N/A
Application deadline (fall): 8/1
Undergraduate student body: 3,028 full time, 275 part time; 48% male, 52% female; 0% American Indian, 2% Asian, 2% black, 2% Hispanic, 3% multiracial, 0% Pacific Islander, 87% white, 2% international; 38% from in state; 83% live on campus; 0% of students in fraternities, 0% in sororities
Most popular majors: 11% Business, Management, Marketing, and Related Support Services, 8% Communication, Journalism, and Related Programs, 11% Education, 20% Health Professions and Related Programs, 8% Theology and Religious Vocations
Expenses: 2015-2016: $27,206; room/board: $6,542
Financial aid: (937) 766-7866; 68% of undergrads determined to have financial need; average aid package $17,006

Central State University

Wilberforce OH
(937) 376-6348
U.S. News ranking: Reg. Coll. (Mid.W), second tier
Website: www.centralstate.edu
Admissions email: admissions@centralstate.edu
Public; founded 1887
Freshman admissions: less selective; 2014-2015: 5,944 applied, 2,242 accepted. Either SAT or ACT required. ACT 25/75 percentile: 15-18. High school rank: 7% in top tenth, 21% in top quarter, 49% in top half
Early decision deadline: N/A, notification date: N/A
Early action deadline: N/A, notification date: N/A
Application deadline (fall): rolling
Undergraduate student body: 1,576 full time, 157 part time; 46% male, 54% female; 0% American Indian, N/A Asian, 95% black, 1% Hispanic, 1% multiracial, N/A Pacific Islander, 1% white, 0% international; 58% from in state; 62% live on campus; 1% of students in fraternities, 1% in sororities
Most popular majors: 23% Business, Management, Marketing, and Related Support Services, 15% Communication, Journalism, and Related Programs, 12% Education, 13% Homeland Security, Law Enforcement, Firefighting and Related Protective Services, 11% Psychology
Expenses: 2015-2016: $7,938 in state, $14,206 out of state; room/board: $9,644
Financial aid: (937) 376-6579

Cleveland Institute of Art

Cleveland OH
(216) 421-7418
U.S. News ranking: Arts, unranked
Website: www.cia.edu
Admissions email: admissions@cia.edu
Private; founded 1882
Freshman admissions: N/A; 2014-2015: 715 applied, 479 accepted. Either SAT or ACT required. ACT 25/75 percentile: 19-26. High school rank: 15% in top tenth, 36% in top quarter, 64% in top half
Early decision deadline: N/A, notification date: N/A
Early action deadline: 12/1, notification date: 12/15
Application deadline (fall): rolling
Undergraduate student body: 551 full time, 8 part time; 45% male, 55% female; 0% American Indian, 3% Asian, 10% black, 6% Hispanic, 3% multiracial, 0% Pacific Islander, 70% white, 7% international; 63% from in state; 33% live on campus; 4% of students in fraternities, 4% in sororities
Most popular majors: 8% Graphic Design, 16% Illustration, 10% Industrial and Product Design, 9% Painting, 8% Photography
Expenses: 2015-2016: $38,487; room/board: $11,454
Financial aid: (216) 421-7425; 81% of undergrads determined to have financial need; average aid package $26,973

Cleveland Institute of Music

Cleveland OH
(216) 795-3107
U.S. News ranking: Arts, unranked
Website: www.cim.edu/
Admissions email: admission@cim.edu
Private; founded 1920
Freshman admissions: N/A; 2014-2015: 429 applied, 201 accepted. Neither SAT nor ACT required. ACT 25/75 percentile: N/A. High school rank: N/A
Early decision deadline: N/A, notification date: N/A
Early action deadline: N/A, notification date: N/A
Application deadline (fall): 12/1
Undergraduate student body: 236 full time, 2 part time; 49% male, 51% female; 0% American Indian, 3% Asian, 2% black, 2% Hispanic, 0% multiracial, 0% Pacific Islander, 12% white, 17% international; 55% from in state; 42% live on campus; 0% of students in fraternities, 0% in sororities
Most popular majors: Information not available
Expenses: 2014-2015: $46,027; room/board: $13,613
Financial aid: (216) 791-5000

Cleveland State University

Cleveland OH
(216) 687-2100
U.S. News ranking: Nat. U., second tier
Website: www.csuohio.edu
Admissions email: admissions@csuohio.edu
Public; founded 1964
Freshman admissions: selective; 2014-2015: 6,288 applied, 4,222 accepted. Either SAT or ACT required. ACT 25/75 percentile: 19-25. High school rank: 12% in top tenth, 34% in top quarter, 68% in top half
Early decision deadline: N/A, notification date: N/A
Early action deadline: 5/1, notification date: N/A
Application deadline (fall): 8/16
Undergraduate student body: 8,674 full time, 3,520 part time; 46% male, 54% female; 0% American Indian, 3% Asian, 18% black, 5% Hispanic, 3% multiracial, 0% Pacific Islander, 63% white, 5% international; 96% from in state; 8% live on campus; 1% of students in fraternities, 1% in sororities
Most popular majors: Information not available
Expenses: 2015-2016: $9,848 in state, $13,156 out of state; room/board: $12,462
Financial aid: (216) 687-2054; 77% of undergrads determined to have financial need; average aid package $8,935

College of Wooster

Wooster OH
(800) 877-9905
U.S. News ranking: Nat. Lib. Arts, No. 61
Website: www.wooster.edu/
Admissions email: admissions@wooster.edu
Private; founded 1866
Freshman admissions: more selective; 2014-2015: 5,497 applied, 3,248 accepted. Either SAT or ACT required. ACT 25/75 percentile: 25-30. High school rank: 41% in top tenth, 71% in top quarter, 92% in top half
Early decision deadline: 11/1, notification date: 11/15
Early action deadline: 11/15, notification date: 12/31
Application deadline (fall): 2/15
Undergraduate student body: 2,024 full time, 42 part time; 45% male, 55% female; 1% American

Indian, 4% Asian, 8% black, 5% Hispanic, 0% multiracial, 0% Pacific Islander, 70% white, 8% international; 39% from in state; 99% live on campus; 15% of students in fraternities, 21% in sororities
Most popular majors: 13% Biological and Biomedical Sciences, 8% History, 6% Philosophy and Religious Studies, 7% Physical Sciences, 26% Social Sciences
Expenses: 2015-2016: $44,950; room/board: $10,650
Financial aid: (330) 263-2317; 60% of undergrads determined to have financial need; average aid package $39,304

Columbus College of Art and Design

Columbus OH
(614) 222-3261
U.S. News ranking: Arts, unranked
Website: www.ccad.edu
Admissions email: admissions@ccad.edu
Private; founded 1879
Freshman admissions: N/A; 2014-2015: 657 applied, 581 accepted. Neither SAT nor ACT required. ACT 25/75 percentile: 19-25. High school rank: N/A
Early decision deadline: N/A, notification date: N/A
Early action deadline: 12/1, notification date: 12/20
Application deadline (fall): 8/22
Undergraduate student body: 1,141 full time, 173 part time; 34% male, 66% female; 0% American Indian, 3% Asian, 9% black, 4% Hispanic, 5% multiracial, 0% Pacific Islander, 68% white, 7% international; 75% from in state; 34% live on campus; N/A of students in fraternities, N/A in sororities
Most popular majors: Information not available
Expenses: 2015-2016: $33,290; room/board: $8,390
Financial aid: (614) 222-3295; 81% of undergrads determined to have financial need; average aid package $20,892

Defiance College

Defiance OH
(800) 520-4632
U.S. News ranking: Reg. Coll. (Mid.W), No. 41
Website: www.defiance.edu
Admissions email: admissions@defiance.edu
Private; founded 1850
Affiliation: United Church of Christ
Freshman admissions: selective; 2014-2015: 1,671 applied, 1,081 accepted. Either SAT or ACT required. ACT 25/75 percentile: 18-23. High school rank: 12% in top tenth, 29% in top quarter, 57% in top half
Early decision deadline: N/A, notification date: N/A
Early action deadline: N/A, notification date: N/A
Application deadline (fall): rolling
Undergraduate student body: 690 full time, 134 part time; 52% male, 48% female; 1% American Indian, 1% Asian, 12% black, 5% Hispanic, 1% multiracial, 0% Pacific Islander, 77% white, 2% international; 72% from in state; 50% live on campus; 6% of students in fraternities, 6% in sororities
Most popular majors: 22% Business Administration and Management, General, 18% Criminal Justice/Police Science, 14% Education, General, 8% Social Work, 14% Sport and Fitness Administration/Management
Expenses: 2015-2016: $31,082; room/board: $9,850
Financial aid: (419) 783-2376; 89% of undergrads determined to have financial need; average aid package $22,522

Denison University

Granville OH
(740) 587-6276
U.S. News ranking: Nat. Lib. Arts, No. 55
Website: www.denison.edu
Admissions email: admissions@denison.edu
Private; founded 1831
Freshman admissions: more selective; 2014-2015: 4,898 applied, 2,481 accepted. Neither SAT nor ACT required. ACT 25/75 percentile: 26-31. High school rank: 45% in top tenth, 87% in top quarter, 100% in top half
Early decision deadline: 11/15, notification date: N/A
Early action deadline: N/A, notification date: N/A
Application deadline (fall): 1/15
Undergraduate student body: 2,263 full time, 17 part time; 42% male, 58% female; 0% American Indian, 4% Asian, 7% black, 10% Hispanic, 4% multiracial, 0% Pacific Islander, 67% white, 7% international; 24% from in state; 99% live on campus; 30% of students in fraternities, 46% in sororities
Most popular majors: 9% Biological and Biomedical Sciences, 11% Communication, Journalism, and Related Programs, 8% English Language and Literature/Letters, 9% Psychology, 26% Social Sciences
Expenses: 2015-2016: $47,290; room/board: $11,570
Financial aid: (740) 587-6279; 53% of undergrads determined to have financial need; average aid package $40,637

Franciscan University of Steubenville

Steubenville OH
(740) 283-6226
U.S. News ranking: Reg. U. (Mid.W), No. 20
Website: www.franciscan.edu
Admissions email: admissions@franciscan.edu
Private; founded 1946
Affiliation: Roman Catholic
Freshman admissions: more selective; 2014-2015: 1,816 applied, 1,418 accepted. Either SAT or ACT required. ACT 25/75 percentile: 23-29. High school rank: 30% in top tenth, 60% in top quarter, 86% in top half
Early decision deadline: N/A, notification date: N/A
Early action deadline: N/A, notification date: N/A
Application deadline (fall): rolling
Undergraduate student body: 2,002 full time, 133 part time; 38% male, 62% female; 0% American Indian, 2% Asian, 0% black, 10% Hispanic, 2% multiracial, 0% Pacific Islander, 83% white, 1% international; 19% from in state; 83% live on campus; 0% of students in fraternities, 0% in sororities
Most popular majors: 10% Business Administration and Management, General, 7% Psychology, General, 10% Registered Nursing/Registered Nurse, 7% Speech Communication and Rhetoric, 27% Theology/Theological Studies
Expenses: 2015-2016: $24,780; room/board: $8,300
Financial aid: (740) 283-6226; 62% of undergrads determined to have financial need; average aid package $13,829

Franklin University[1]

Columbus OH
(614) 341-6256
U.S. News ranking: Business, unranked
Website: www.franklin.edu
Admissions email: info@franklin.edu
Private; founded 1902
Application deadline (fall): rolling
Undergraduate student body: N/A full time, N/A part time
Expenses: 2014-2015: $11,161; room/board: $13,870
Financial aid: (614) 797-4700

Heidelberg University

Tiffin OH
(419) 448-2330
U.S. News ranking: Reg. U. (Mid.W), No. 49
Website: www.heidelberg.edu
Admissions email: adminfo@heidelberg.edu
Private; founded 1850
Affiliation: United Church of Christ
Freshman admissions: selective; 2014-2015: 1,616 applied, 1,213 accepted. Either SAT or ACT required. ACT 25/75 percentile: 19-25. High school rank: N/A
Early decision deadline: N/A, notification date: N/A
Early action deadline: N/A, notification date: N/A
Application deadline (fall): 8/1
Undergraduate student body: 1,069 full time, 34 part time; 51% male, 49% female; 0% American Indian, 1% Asian, 5% black, 3% Hispanic, 3% multiracial, 0% Pacific Islander, 74% white, 0% international; 85% from in state; 79% live on campus; 18% of students in fraternities, 36% in sororities
Most popular majors: 7% Biological and Biomedical Sciences, 15% Business, Management, Marketing, and Related Support Services, 10% Psychology, 9% Social Sciences, 5% Visual and Performing Arts
Expenses: 2015-2016: $28,500; room/board: $9,600
Financial aid: (419) 448-2293; 88% of undergrads determined to have financial need; average aid package $23,339

Hiram College

Hiram OH
(800) 362-5280
U.S. News ranking: Nat. Lib. Arts, No. 154
Website: www.hiram.edu
Admissions email: admission@hiram.edu
Private; founded 1850
Freshman admissions: selective; 2014-2015: 2,136 applied, 1,326 accepted. Either SAT or ACT required. ACT 25/75 percentile: 18-25. High school rank: 15% in top tenth, 34% in top quarter, 65% in top half
Early decision deadline: N/A, notification date: N/A
Early action deadline: N/A, notification date: N/A
Application deadline (fall): rolling
Undergraduate student body: 1,068 full time, 167 part time; 47% male, 53% female; 0% American Indian, 1% Asian, 16% black, 4% Hispanic, 2% multiracial, 0% Pacific Islander, 68% white, 3% international; 84% from in state; 80% live on campus; 9% of students in fraternities, 12% in sororities
Most popular majors: 15% Biological and Biomedical Sciences, 29% Business, Management, Marketing, and Related Support Services, 9% Health Professions and Related Programs, 7% Psychology, 9% Social Sciences
Expenses: 2015-2016: $31,530; room/board: $10,190
Financial aid: (330) 569-5107

John Carroll University

University Heights OH
(216) 397-4294
U.S. News ranking: Reg. U. (Mid.W), No. 7
Website: www.jcu.edu
Admissions email: admission@jcu.edu
Private; founded 1886
Affiliation: Roman Catholic (Jesuit)
Freshman admissions: selective; 2014-2015: 3,873 applied, 3,211 accepted. Either SAT or ACT required. ACT 25/75 percentile: 22-27. High school rank: 20% in top tenth, 44% in top quarter, 79% in top half
Early decision deadline: N/A, notification date: N/A
Early action deadline: N/A, notification date: N/A
Application deadline (fall): 2/1
Undergraduate student body: 3,022 full time, 103 part time; 53% male, 47% female; 0% American Indian, 2% Asian, 4% black, 3% Hispanic, 2% multiracial, 0% Pacific Islander, 85% white, 2% international; 69% from in state; 57% live on campus; 11% of students in fraternities, 23% in sororities
Most popular majors: 8% Biological and Biomedical Sciences, 28% Business, Management, Marketing, and Related Support Services, 12% Communication, Journalism, and Related Programs, 9% Psychology, 13% Social Sciences
Expenses: 2015-2016: $37,180; room/board: $10,920
Financial aid: (216) 397-4248; 73% of undergrads determined to have financial need; average aid package $28,538

Kent State University

Kent OH
(330) 672-2444
U.S. News ranking: Nat. U., No. 175
Website: www.kent.edu
Admissions email: kentadm@kent.edu
Public; founded 1910
Freshman admissions: selective; 2014-2015: 16,125 applied, 13,607 accepted. Either SAT or ACT required. ACT 25/75 percentile: 20-25. High school rank: 15% in top tenth, 40% in top quarter, 77% in top half
Early decision deadline: N/A, notification date: N/A
Early action deadline: N/A, notification date: N/A
Application deadline (fall): 5/1
Undergraduate student body: 20,334 full time, 2,994 part time; 41% male, 59% female; 0% American Indian, 1% Asian, 9% black, 3% Hispanic, 3% multiracial, 0% Pacific Islander, 75% white, 6% international; 87% from in state; 28% live on campus; 8% of students in fraternities, 10% in sororities
Most popular majors: 19% Business, Management, Marketing, and Related Support Services, 9% Communication, Journalism, and Related Programs, 9% Education, 18% Health Professions and Related Programs, 6% Psychology
Expenses: 2015-2016: $10,012 in state, $18,212 out of state; room/board: $10,334
Financial aid: (330) 672-2972; 66% of undergrads determined to have financial need; average aid package $8,888

Kenyon College

Gambier OH
(740) 427-5776
U.S. News ranking: Nat. Lib. Arts, No. 25
Website: www.kenyon.edu
Admissions email: admissions@kenyon.edu
Private; founded 1824
Freshman admissions: more selective; 2014-2015: 6,635 applied, 1,663 accepted. Either SAT or ACT required. SAT 25/75 percentile: 1230-1420. High school rank: 65% in top tenth, 86% in top quarter, 99% in top half
Early decision deadline: 11/15, notification date: 12/15
Early action deadline: N/A, notification date: N/A
Application deadline (fall): 1/15
Undergraduate student body: 1,650 full time, 12 part time; 45% male, 55% female; 1% American Indian, 5% Asian, 4% black, 6% Hispanic, 4% multiracial, 0% Pacific Islander, 74% white, 4% international; 22% from in state; 100% live on campus; 22% of students in fraternities, 13% in sororities
Most popular majors: 13% Economics, General, 12% English Language and Literature, General, 7% International/Global Studies, 11% Political Science and Government, General, 8% Psychology, General
Expenses: 2015-2016: $49,140; room/board: $11,960

Financial aid: (740) 427-5430; 41% of undergrads determined to have financial need; average aid package $40,946

Lake Erie College

Painesville OH
(800) 916-0904
U.S. News ranking: Reg. U. (Mid.W), second tier
Website: www.lec.edu
Admissions email: admissions@lec.edu
Private; founded 1856
Freshman admissions: selective; 2014-2015: 891 applied, 618 accepted. Either SAT or ACT required. ACT 25/75 percentile: 18-23. High school rank: N/A
Early decision deadline: N/A, notification date: N/A
Early action deadline: N/A, notification date: N/A
Application deadline (fall): 8/1
Undergraduate student body: 802 full time, 101 part time; 50% male, 50% female; 0% American Indian, 0% Asian, 12% black, 2% Hispanic, 2% multiracial, N/A Pacific Islander, 77% white, 3% international; 74% from in state; 63% live on campus; N/A of students in fraternities, N/A in sororities
Most popular majors: 16% Biology/Biological Sciences, General, 12% Business Administration and Management, General, 5% Early Childhood Education and Teaching, 6% Marketing/Marketing Management, General, 5% Psychology, General
Expenses: 2015-2016: $29,162; room/board: $9,178
Financial aid: (440) 375-7100; 83% of undergrads determined to have financial need; average aid package $22,717

Lourdes University

Sylvania OH
(419) 885-5291
U.S. News ranking: Reg. U. (Mid.W), second tier
Website: www.lourdes.edu
Admissions email: admissionslcadmits@lourdes.edu
Private; founded 1958
Affiliation: Roman Catholic
Freshman admissions: selective; 2014-2015: 1,024 applied, 662 accepted. Either SAT or ACT required. ACT 25/75 percentile: 18-22. High school rank: 3% in top tenth, 33% in top quarter, 60% in top half
Early decision deadline: N/A, notification date: N/A
Early action deadline: N/A, notification date: N/A
Application deadline (fall): rolling
Undergraduate student body: 1,016 full time, 466 part time; 30% male, 70% female; 1% American Indian, 1% Asian, 14% black, 7% Hispanic, 3% multiracial, 0% Pacific Islander, 72% white, 0% international
Most popular majors: 8% Accounting and Related Services, 10% Business Administration, Management and Operations, 10% Multi/Interdisciplinary Studies, Other, 29% Registered Nursing, Nursing Administration, Nursing Research and Clinical Nursing, 8% Social Work
Expenses: 2014-2015: $18,353; room/board: $8,800
Financial aid: (419) 824-3732

Malone University

Canton OH
(330) 471-8145
U.S. News ranking: Reg. U. (Mid.W), No. 61
Website: www.malone.edu
Admissions email: admissions@malone.edu
Private; founded 1892
Affiliation: Evangelical Friends
Freshman admissions: selective; 2014-2015: 1,327 applied, 952 accepted. Either SAT or ACT required. ACT 25/75 percentile: 20-25. High school rank: 18% in top tenth, 44% in top quarter, 76% in top half
Early decision deadline: N/A, notification date: N/A
Early action deadline: N/A, notification date: N/A
Application deadline (fall): rolling
Undergraduate student body: 1,332 full time, 233 part time; 41% male, 59% female; 0% American Indian, 1% Asian, 8% black, 2% Hispanic, 2% multiracial, 0% Pacific Islander, 84% white, 1% international; 86% from in state; 56% live on campus; 0% of students in fraternities, 0% in sororities
Most popular majors: 9% Business Administration and Management, General, 15% Business Administration, Management and Operations, Other, 6% Early Childhood Education and Teaching, 4% Kinesiology and Exercise Science, 14% Registered Nursing/Registered Nurse
Expenses: 2015-2016: $27,960; room/board: $8,948
Financial aid: (330) 471-8159; 80% of undergrads determined to have financial need; average aid package $21,583

Marietta College[1]

Marietta OH
(800) 331-7896
U.S. News ranking: Reg. Coll. (Mid.W), No. 5
Website: www.marietta.edu
Admissions email: admit@marietta.edu
Private; founded 1797
Application deadline (fall): 4/15
Undergraduate student body: N/A full time, N/A part time
Expenses: 2014-2015: $33,490; room/board: $10,395
Financial aid: (740) 376-4712

Miami University–Oxford

Oxford OH
(513) 529-2531
U.S. News ranking: Nat. U., No. 82
Website: www.MiamiOH.edu
Admissions email: admission@MiamiOH.edu
Public; founded 1809
Freshman admissions: more selective; 2014-2015: 25,301 applied, 16,657 accepted. Either SAT or ACT required. ACT 25/75 percentile: 25-30. High school rank: 34% in top tenth, 68% in top quarter, 94% in top half
Early decision deadline: 11/15, notification date: 12/15
Early action deadline: 12/1, notification date: 2/1
Application deadline (fall): 2/1
Undergraduate student body: 15,311 full time, 502 part time; 49% male, 51% female; 0% American Indian, 2% Asian, 3% black, 3% Hispanic, 3% multiracial, 0% Pacific Islander, 80% white, 7% international; 66% from in state; 47% live on campus; 22% of students in fraternities, 31% in sororities
Most popular majors: 7% Biological and Biomedical Sciences, 24% Business, Management, Marketing, and Related Support Services, 9% Education, 6% Parks, Recreation, Leisure, and Fitness Studies, 9% Social Sciences
Expenses: 2014-2015: $14,287 in state, $30,394 out of state; room/board: $11,109
Financial aid: (513) 529-8734; 37% of undergrads determined to have financial need; average aid package $12,727

Mount St. Joseph University

Cincinnati OH
(513) 244-4531
U.S. News ranking: Reg. U. (Mid.W), No. 68
Website: www.msj.edu
Admissions email: admission@mail.msj.edu
Private; founded 1920
Affiliation: Catholic
Freshman admissions: selective; 2014-2015: 1,010 applied, 885 accepted. Either SAT or ACT required. ACT 25/75 percentile: 19-24. High school rank: 9% in top tenth, 34% in top quarter, 59% in top half
Early decision deadline: N/A, notification date: N/A
Early action deadline: N/A, notification date: N/A
Application deadline (fall): 8/1
Undergraduate student body: 1,142 full time, 515 part time; 38% male, 62% female; 0% American Indian, 1% Asian, 11% black, 2% Hispanic, 2% multiracial, 0% Pacific Islander, 80% white, 0% international; 84% from in state; 24% live on campus; N/A of students in fraternities, N/A in sororities
Most popular majors: 11% Business Administration and Management, General, 8% Early Childhood Education and Teaching, 9% General Studies, 28% Registered Nursing/Registered Nurse, 9% Visual and Performing Arts, General
Expenses: 2015-2016: $27,500; room/board: $8,810
Financial aid: (513) 244-4418; 79% of undergrads determined to have financial need; average aid package $18,934

Mount Vernon Nazarene University

Mount Vernon OH
(866) 462-6868
U.S. News ranking: Reg. U. (Mid.W), No. 61
Website: www.gotomvnu.com
Admissions email: admissions@mvnu.edu
Private; founded 1968
Affiliation: Nazarene
Freshman admissions: selective; 2014-2015: 1,020 applied, 775 accepted. Either SAT or ACT required. ACT 25/75 percentile: 20-25. High school rank: 22% in top tenth, 44% in top quarter, 71% in top half
Early decision deadline: N/A, notification date: N/A
Early action deadline: N/A, notification date: N/A
Application deadline (fall): 7/15
Undergraduate student body: 1,394 full time, 379 part time; 37% male, 63% female; 0% American Indian, 0% Asian, 4% black, 2% Hispanic, 1% multiracial, 0% Pacific Islander, 83% white, 1% international; 87% from in state; 56% live on campus; 0% of students in fraternities, 0% in sororities
Most popular majors: 40% Business, Management, Marketing, and Related Support Services, 13% Education, 4% Health Professions and Related Programs, 15% Public Administration and Social Service Professions
Expenses: 2014-2015: $24,650; room/board: $7,260
Financial aid: (740) 392-6868

Muskingum University

New Concord OH
(740) 826-8137
U.S. News ranking: Reg. U. (Mid.W), No. 50
Website: www.muskingum.edu
Admissions email: adminfo@muskingum.edu
Private; founded 1837
Affiliation: Presbyterian Church (USA)
Freshman admissions: selective; 2014-2015: 2,012 applied, 1,568 accepted. Either SAT or ACT required. ACT 25/75 percentile: 19-24. High school rank: 18% in top tenth, 37% in top quarter, 69% in top half
Early decision deadline: N/A, notification date: N/A
Early action deadline: N/A, notification date: N/A
Application deadline (fall): 8/1
Undergraduate student body: 1,387 full time, 337 part time; 45% male, 55% female; 0% American Indian, 1% Asian, 5% black, 2% Hispanic, 2% multiracial, 0% Pacific Islander, 79% white, 4% international; 91% from in state; 71% live on campus; 20% of students in fraternities, 35% in sororities
Most popular majors: 6% Biological and Biomedical Sciences, 16% Business, Management, Marketing, and Related Support Services, 19% Education, 12% Health Professions and Related Programs, 7% Psychology
Expenses: 2015-2016: $25,932; room/board: $10,190
Financial aid: (740) 826-8139; 85% of undergrads determined to have financial need; average aid package $24,104

Notre Dame College of Ohio[1]

Cleveland OH
(216) 373-5355
U.S. News ranking: Reg. Coll. (Mid.W), second tier
Website: www.notredamecollege.edu
Admissions email: admissions@ndc.edu
Private; founded 1922
Affiliation: Roman Catholic
Application deadline (fall): rolling
Undergraduate student body: N/A full time, N/A part time
Expenses: 2014-2015: $26,844; room/board: $8,858
Financial aid: (216) 373-5263

Oberlin College

Oberlin OH
(440) 775-8411
U.S. News ranking: Nat. Lib. Arts, No. 23
Website: www.oberlin.edu
Admissions email: college.admissions@oberlin.edu
Private; founded 1833
Freshman admissions: more selective; 2014-2015: 7,227 applied, 2,365 accepted. Either SAT or ACT required. SAT 25/75 percentile: 1260-1450. High school rank: 61% in top tenth, 91% in top quarter, 100% in top half
Early decision deadline: 11/15, notification date: 12/10
Early action deadline: N/A, notification date: N/A
Application deadline (fall): 1/15
Undergraduate student body: 2,920 full time, 41 part time; 45% male, 55% female; 0% American Indian, 4% Asian, 5% black, 7% Hispanic, 6% multiracial, 0% Pacific Islander, 70% white, 7% international; 8% from in state; 91% live on campus; 0% of students in fraternities, 0% in sororities
Most popular majors: 8% Biology, General, 7% History, General, 14% Music Performance, General, 6% Neuroscience, 10% Political Science and Government
Expenses: 2015-2016: $50,586; room/board: $13,630
Financial aid: (440) 775-8142; 48% of undergrads determined to have financial need; average aid package $37,294

Ohio Christian University

Circleville OH
(877) 762-8669
U.S. News ranking: Reg. Coll. (Mid.W), No. 62
Website: www.ohiochristian.edu/
Admissions email: enroll@ohiochristian.edu
Private; founded 1948
Affiliation: Protestant
Freshman admissions: less selective; 2014-2015: 844 applied, 552 accepted. Either SAT or ACT required. ACT 25/75 percentile: 17-22. High school rank: N/A
Early decision deadline: N/A, notification date: N/A
Early action deadline: N/A, notification date: N/A
Application deadline (fall): N/A
Undergraduate student body: 1,613 full time, 2,125 part time; 37% male, 63% female; 0% American Indian, 0% Asian, 13% black, 1% Hispanic, 1% multiracial, 0% Pacific Islander, 32% white, 0% international
Most popular majors: Information not available
Expenses: 2014-2015: $17,720; room/board: $7,498
Financial aid: (740) 477-7758

More at usnews.com/college

Ohio Dominican University

Columbus OH
(614) 251-4500
U.S. News ranking: Reg. U. (Mid.W), No. 85
Website: www.ohiodominican.edu
Admissions email: admissions@ohiodominican.edu
Private; founded 1911
Affiliation: Roman Catholic
Freshman admissions: selective; 2014-2015: 2,317 applied, 1,079 accepted. Either SAT or ACT required. ACT 25/75 percentile: 19-24. High school rank: 19% in top tenth, 42% in top quarter, 75% in top half
Early decision deadline: N/A, notification date: N/A
Early action deadline: N/A, notification date: N/A
Application deadline (fall): rolling
Undergraduate student body: 1,292 full time, 573 part time; 46% male, 54% female; 0% American Indian, 1% Asian, 26% black, 3% Hispanic, 5% multiracial, 0% Pacific Islander, 61% white, 1% international; 96% from in state; 40% live on campus; N/A of students in fraternities, N/A in sororities
Most popular majors: 6% Biology/Biological Sciences, General, 34% Business Administration and Management, General, 4% Criminalistics and Criminal Science, 17% Elementary Education and Teaching, 5% Sport and Fitness Administration/Management
Expenses: 2014-2015: $29,430; room/board: $10,378
Financial aid: (614) 251-4778

Ohio Northern University

Ada OH
(888) 408-4668
U.S. News ranking: Reg. Coll. (Mid.W), No. 2
Website: www.onu.edu
Admissions email: admissions-ug@onu.edu
Private; founded 1871
Affiliation: Methodist
Freshman admissions: more selective; 2014-2015: 3,337 applied, 2,289 accepted. Either SAT or ACT required. ACT 25/75 percentile: 23-29. High school rank: 35% in top tenth, 62% in top quarter, 90% in top half
Early decision deadline: N/A, notification date: N/A
Early action deadline: N/A, notification date: N/A
Application deadline (fall): 8/15
Undergraduate student body: 2,262 full time, 592 part time; 52% male, 48% female; 0% American Indian, 1% Asian, 4% black, 1% Hispanic, 3% multiracial, 0% Pacific Islander, 84% white, 4% international; 87% from in state; 63% live on campus; 14% of students in fraternities, 20% in sororities
Most popular majors: 10% Business, Management, Marketing, and Related Support Services, 7% Communication, Journalism, and Related Programs, 14% Education, 7% Engineering, 14% Visual and Performing Arts
Expenses: 2015-2016: $28,810; room/board: $10,890
Financial aid: (419) 772-2272

Ohio State University–Columbus

Columbus OH
(614) 292-3980
U.S. News ranking: Nat. U., No. 52
Website: www.osu.edu
Admissions email: askabuckeye@osu.edu
Public; founded 1870
Freshman admissions: more selective; 2014-2015: 36,788 applied, 19,484 accepted. Either SAT or ACT required. ACT 25/75 percentile: 27-31. High school rank: 61% in top tenth, 94% in top quarter, 99% in top half
Early decision deadline: N/A, notification date: N/A
Early action deadline: 11/1, notification date: 1/15
Application deadline (fall): 2/1
Undergraduate student body: 40,613 full time, 4,128 part time; 52% male, 48% female; 0% American Indian, 6% Asian, 6% black, 3% Hispanic, 3% multiracial, 0% Pacific Islander, 72% white, 8% international; 84% from in state; 25% live on campus; N/A of students in fraternities, N/A in sororities
Most popular majors: 3% Accounting, 4% Biology/Biological Sciences, General, 4% Finance, General, 6% Psychology, General, 4% Speech Communication and Rhetoric
Expenses: 2014-2015: $10,037 in state, $26,537 out of state; room/board: $9,850
Financial aid: (614) 292-0300; 50% of undergrads determined to have financial need; average aid package $12,473

Ohio University

Athens OH
(740) 593-4100
U.S. News ranking: Nat. U., No. 135
Website: www.ohio.edu
Admissions email: admissions@ohio.edu
Public; founded 1804
Freshman admissions: selective; 2014-2015: 20,934 applied, 15,548 accepted. Either SAT or ACT required. ACT 25/75 percentile: 22-26. High school rank: 15% in top tenth, 43% in top quarter, 82% in top half
Early decision deadline: N/A, notification date: N/A
Early action deadline: N/A, notification date: N/A
Undergraduate student body: 17,019 full time, 6,552 part time; 40% male, 60% female; 0% American Indian, 1% Asian, 5% black, 3% Hispanic, 3% multiracial, 0% Pacific Islander, 83% white, 4% international; 85% from in state; 45% live on campus; 9% of students in fraternities, 10% in sororities
Most popular majors: 3% Health/Health Care Administration/Management, 3% Liberal Arts and Sciences, General Studies and Humanities, Other, 35% Registered Nursing/Registered Nurse, 3% Secondary Education and Teaching, 4% Speech Communication and Rhetoric
Expenses: 2015-2016: $11,548 in state, $20,512 out of state; room/board: $11,934
Financial aid: (740) 593-4141; 60% of undergrads determined to have financial need; average aid package $8,397

Ohio Wesleyan University

Delaware OH
(740) 368-3020
U.S. News ranking: Nat. Lib. Arts, No. 108
Website: web.owu.edu
Admissions email: owuadmit@owu.edu
Private; founded 1842
Affiliation: Methodist
Freshman admissions: more selective; 2014-2015: 3,981 applied, 2,958 accepted. Neither SAT nor ACT required. ACT 25/75 percentile: 22-28. High school rank: 24% in top tenth, 56% in top quarter, 88% in top half
Early decision deadline: 11/15, notification date: 11/30
Early action deadline: 1/15, notification date: N/A
Application deadline (fall): 3/1
Undergraduate student body: 1,717 full time, 17 part time; 46% male, 54% female; 0% American Indian, 2% Asian, 7% black, 4% Hispanic, 5% multiracial, 0% Pacific Islander, 72% white, 7% international; 46% from in state; 96% live on campus; 46% of students in fraternities, 34% in sororities
Most popular majors: 14% Biological and Biomedical Sciences, 11% Business, Management, Marketing, and Related Support Services, 8% English Language and Literature/Letters, 8% Psychology, 16% Social Sciences
Expenses: 2015-2016: $43,230; room/board: $11,540
Financial aid: (740) 368-3050; 68% of undergrads determined to have financial need; average aid package $33,962

Otterbein University

Westerville OH
(614) 823-1500
U.S. News ranking: Reg. U. (Mid.W), No. 13
Website: www.otterbein.edu
Admissions email: UOtterB@Otterbein.edu
Private; founded 1847
Affiliation: United Methodist
Freshman admissions: more selective; 2014-2015: 2,584 applied, 1,946 accepted. Either SAT or ACT required. ACT 25/75 percentile: 21-26. High school rank: 26% in top tenth, 55% in top quarter, 84% in top half
Early decision deadline: N/A, notification date: N/A
Early action deadline: N/A, notification date: N/A
Application deadline (fall): rolling
Undergraduate student body: 2,128 full time, 214 part time; 39% male, 61% female; 0% American Indian, 1% Asian, 5% black, 2% Hispanic, 3% multiracial, 0% Pacific Islander, 71% white, 2% international; 88% from in state; 62% live on campus; 27% of students in fraternities, 25% in sororities
Most popular majors: 13% Business, Management, Marketing, and Related Support Services, 8% Communication, Journalism, and Related Programs, 14% Education, 19% Health Professions and Related Programs, 15% Visual and Performing Arts
Expenses: 2015-2016: $31,624; room/board: $9,652
Financial aid: (614) 823-1502; 65% of undergrads determined to have financial need; average aid package $23,224

Shawnee State University

Portsmouth OH
(800) 959-2778
U.S. News ranking: Nat. Lib. Arts, second tier
Website: www.shawnee.edu
Admissions email: To_SSU@shawnee.edu
Public; founded 1986
Freshman admissions: selective; 2014-2015: 3,686 applied, 2,733 accepted. Either SAT or ACT required. ACT 25/75 percentile: 18-24. High school rank: 12% in top tenth, 33% in top quarter, 63% in top half
Early decision deadline: N/A, notification date: N/A
Early action deadline: N/A, notification date: N/A
Application deadline (fall): rolling
Undergraduate student body: 3,309 full time, 805 part time; 43% male, 57% female; 1% American Indian, 0% Asian, 6% black, 1% Hispanic, 2% multiracial, 0% Pacific Islander, 87% white, 1% international; 89% from in state; 24% live on campus; 1% of students in fraternities, 1% in sororities
Most popular majors: 9% Art/Art Studies, General, 8% Biology/Biological Sciences, General, 22% Business Administration and Management, General, 8% Psychology, General, 8% Sociology
Expenses: 2014-2015: $7,364 in state, $12,617 out of state; room/board: $9,552
Financial aid: (740) 351-4243

Tiffin University

Tiffin OH
(419) 448-3423
U.S. News ranking: Reg. U. (Mid.W), No. 68
Website: www.tiffin.edu
Admissions email: admiss@tiffin.edu
Private; founded 1888
Freshman admissions: less selective; 2014-2015: 4,384 applied, 2,367 accepted. Either SAT or ACT required. ACT 25/75 percentile: 17-22. High school rank: N/A
Early decision deadline: N/A, notification date: N/A
Early action deadline: N/A, notification date: N/A
Application deadline (fall): rolling
Undergraduate student body: 1,964 full time, 1,050 part time; 46% male, 54% female; 0% American Indian, 0% Asian, 17% black, 3% Hispanic, 2% multiracial, 0% Pacific Islander, 44% white, 7% international; 66% from in state; 25% live on campus; 1% of students in fraternities, 1% in sororities
Most popular majors: Information not available
Expenses: 2015-2016: $22,165; room/board: $10,196
Financial aid: (419) 448-3357; 89% of undergrads determined to have financial need; average aid package $17,005

Union Institute and University

Cincinnati OH
(513) 487-1239
U.S. News ranking: Nat. U., unranked
Website: www.myunion.edu
Admissions email: admissions@myunion.edu
Private; founded 1694
Freshman admissions: N/A; 2014-2015: N/A applied, N/A accepted. Neither SAT nor ACT required. ACT 25/75 percentile: N/A. High school rank: N/A
Early decision deadline: N/A, notification date: N/A
Early action deadline: N/A, notification date: N/A
Application deadline (fall): N/A
Undergraduate student body: 560 full time, 525 part time; 48% male, 52% female; 0% American Indian, 1% Asian, 19% black, 26% Hispanic, 3% multiracial, 0% Pacific Islander, 42% white, 0% international
Most popular majors: Information not available
Expenses: 2014-2015: $11,904; room/board: $11,508
Financial aid: (513) 487-1127

University of Akron

Akron OH
(330) 972-7077
U.S. News ranking: Nat. U., second tier
Website: www.uakron.edu
Admissions email: admissions@uakron.edu
Public; founded 1870
Freshman admissions: selective; 2014-2015: 13,109 applied, 12,546 accepted. Either SAT or ACT required. ACT 25/75 percentile: 19-26. High school rank: 16% in top tenth, 38% in top quarter, 66% in top half
Early decision deadline: N/A, notification date: N/A
Early action deadline: 11/1, notification date: 12/15
Application deadline (fall): 7/1
Undergraduate student body: 15,512 full time, 4,211 part time; 52% male, 48% female; 0% American Indian, 2% Asian, 13% black, 2% Hispanic, 3% multiracial, 0% Pacific Islander, 74% white, 2% international; 96% from in state; 14% live on campus; 4% of students in fraternities, 4% in sororities
Most popular majors: 20% Business, Management, Marketing, and Related Support Services, 7% Communication, Journalism, and Related Programs, 11% Education, 9% Engineering, 15% Health Professions and Related Programs
Expenses: 2015-2016: $10,509 in state, $19,040 out of state; room/board: $11,322
Financial aid: (330) 972-7032; 72% of undergrads determined to have financial need; average aid package $7,235

University of Cincinnati

Cincinnati OH
(513) 556-1100
U.S. News ranking: Nat. U., No. 140
Website: www.uc.edu
Admissions email: admissions@uc.edu
Public; founded 1819
Freshman admissions: selective; 2014-2015: 16,593 applied, 12,611 accepted. Either SAT or ACT required. ACT 25/75 percentile: 23-28. High school rank: 20% in top tenth, 48% in top quarter, 83% in top half
Early decision deadline: N/A, notification date: N/A
Early action deadline: N/A, notification date: N/A
Application deadline (fall): 2/1
Undergraduate student body: 20,788 full time, 3,619 part time; 50% male, 50% female; 0% American Indian, 3% Asian, 7% black, 3% Hispanic, 3% multiracial, 0% Pacific Islander, 76% white, 4% international; 89% from in state; 24% live on campus; N/A of students in fraternities, N/A in sororities
Most popular majors: 16% Business, Management, Marketing, and Related Support Services, 7% Communication, Journalism, and Related Programs, 10% Engineering, 15% Health Professions and Related Programs, 8% Visual and Performing Arts
Expenses: 2015-2016: $11,000 in state, $26,334 out of state; room/board: $10,750
Financial aid: (513) 556-6982; 56% of undergrads determined to have financial need; average aid package $8,470

University of Cincinnati–UC Blue Ash College[1]

Cincinnati OH
(513) 745-5700
U.S. News ranking: Reg. Coll. (Mid.W), unranked
Website: www.rwc.uc.edu/
Admissions email: N/A
Public
Application deadline (fall): N/A
Undergraduate student body: N/A full time, N/A part time
Expenses: 2014-2015: $6,010 in state, $14,808 out of state; room/board: $11,438
Financial aid: (513) 745-5700

University of Dayton

Dayton OH
(937) 229-4411
U.S. News ranking: Nat. U., No. 108
Website: www.udayton.edu
Admissions email: admission@udayton.edu
Private; founded 1850
Affiliation: Roman Catholic (Marianist)
Freshman admissions: more selective; 2014-2015: 16,974 applied, 10,016 accepted. Either SAT or ACT required. ACT 25/75 percentile: 24-29. High school rank: 24% in top tenth, 54% in top quarter, 87% in top half
Early decision deadline: N/A, notification date: N/A
Early action deadline: 12/15, notification date: 2/1
Application deadline (fall): 3/1
Undergraduate student body: 7,898 full time, 631 part time; 53% male, 47% female; 0% American Indian, 1% Asian, 3% black, 3% Hispanic, 1% multiracial, 0% Pacific Islander, 79% white, 11% international; 53% from in state; 71% live on campus; 13% of students in fraternities, 20% in sororities
Most popular majors: 28% Business, Management, Marketing, and Related Support Services, 7% Communication, Journalism, and Related Programs, 9% Education, 12% Engineering, 7% Health Professions and Related Programs
Expenses: 2015-2016: $39,090; room/board: $12,190
Financial aid: (937) 229-4311; 52% of undergrads determined to have financial need; average aid package $23,498

University of Findlay

Findlay OH
(800) 548-0932
U.S. News ranking: Reg. U. (Mid.W), No. 54
Website: www.findlay.edu
Admissions email: admissions@findlay.edu
Private; founded 1882
Affiliation: Churches of God General Conference
Freshman admissions: more selective; 2014-2015: 2,715 applied, 1,954 accepted. Either SAT or ACT required. ACT 25/75 percentile: 20-25. High school rank: 42% in top tenth, 45% in top quarter, 89% in top half
Early decision deadline: N/A, notification date: N/A
Early action deadline: N/A, notification date: N/A
Application deadline (fall): rolling
Undergraduate student body: 2,613 full time, 1,354 part time; 38% male, 62% female; 0% American Indian, 1% Asian, 4% black, 1% Hispanic, 2% multiracial, 0% Pacific Islander, 80% white, 11% international; N/A from in state; 40% live on campus; 2% of students in fraternities, 2% in sororities
Most popular majors: 12% Agriculture, Agriculture Operations, and Related Sciences, 5% Biological and Biomedical Sciences, 17% Business, Management, Marketing, and Related Support Services, 8% Education, 26% Health Professions and Related Programs
Expenses: 2015-2016: $31,508; room/board: $9,442
Financial aid: (419) 434-4792; 49% of undergrads determined to have financial need; average aid package $23,147

University of Mount Union

Alliance OH
(330) 823-2590
U.S. News ranking: Reg. Coll. (Mid.W), No. 8
Website: www.mountunion.edu/
Admissions email: admission@mountunion.edu
Private; founded 1846
Affiliation: United Methodist
Freshman admissions: selective; 2014-2015: 2,529 applied, 1,860 accepted. Either SAT or ACT required. ACT 25/75 percentile: 21-25. High school rank: 18% in top tenth, 44% in top quarter, 77% in top half
Early decision deadline: N/A, notification date: N/A
Early action deadline: N/A, notification date: N/A
Application deadline (fall): rolling
Undergraduate student body: 2,126 full time, 48 part time; 51% male, 49% female; 0% American Indian, 1% Asian, 6% black, 2% Hispanic, 4% multiracial, 0% Pacific Islander, 83% white, 3% international; 85% from in state; 74% live on campus; 20% of students in fraternities, 40% in sororities
Most popular majors: 16% Business, Management, Marketing, and Related Support Services, 13% Education, 10% Health Professions and Related Programs, 12% Parks, Recreation, Leisure, and Fitness Studies, 5% Psychology
Expenses: 2015-2016: $28,550; room/board: $9,540
Financial aid: (877) 543-9185; 79% of undergrads determined to have financial need; average aid package $21,734

University of Northwestern Ohio[1]

Lima OH
(419) 998-3120
U.S. News ranking: Reg. Coll. (Mid.W), unranked
Website: www.unoh.edu/
Admissions email: info@unoh.edu
Private
Application deadline (fall): N/A
Undergraduate student body: N/A full time, N/A part time
Expenses: 2014-2015: $9,725; room/board: $6,750
Financial aid: (419) 998-3140

University of Rio Grande

Rio Grande OH
(740) 245-7208
U.S. News ranking: Reg. U. (Mid.W), unranked
Website: www.rio.edu
Admissions email: admissions@rio.edu
Private; founded 1876
Freshman admissions: N/A; 2014-2015: 1,734 applied, 1,280 accepted. Neither SAT nor ACT required. Average composite ACT score: 19. High school rank: 5% in top tenth, 20% in top quarter, 49% in top half
Early decision deadline: N/A, notification date: N/A
Early action deadline: N/A, notification date: N/A
Application deadline (fall): rolling
Undergraduate student body: 1,719 full time, 387 part time; 36% male, 64% female; 0% American Indian, 0% Asian, 6% black, 1% Hispanic, 0% multiracial, 0% Pacific Islander, 84% white, 1% international; 98% from in state; 17% live on campus; 2% of students in fraternities, 1% in sororities
Most popular majors: Information not available
Expenses: 2014-2015: $21,930; room/board: $9,450
Financial aid: (740) 245-7218; 95% of undergrads determined to have financial need; average aid package $7,030

University of Toledo

Toledo OH
(419) 530-8888
U.S. News ranking: Nat. U., second tier
Website: www.utoledo.edu
Admissions email: enroll@utnet.utoledo.edu
Public; founded 1872
Freshman admissions: selective; 2014-2015: 10,394 applied, 9,846 accepted. Either SAT or ACT required. ACT 25/75 percentile: 19-25. High school rank: 17% in top tenth, 41% in top quarter, 70% in top half
Early decision deadline: N/A, notification date: N/A
Early action deadline: N/A, notification date: N/A
Application deadline (fall): rolling
Undergraduate student body: 12,806 full time, 3,284 part time; 52% male, 48% female; 0% American Indian, 2% Asian, 14% black, 4% Hispanic, 3% multiracial, 0% Pacific Islander, 69% white, 6% international; 83% from in state; 20% live on campus; 8% of students in fraternities, 8% in sororities
Most popular majors: 19% Business, Management, Marketing, and Related Support Services, 8% Education, 12% Engineering, 17% Health Professions and Related Programs, 5% Multi/Interdisciplinary Studies
Expenses: 2015-2016: $9,568 in state, $18,906 out of state; room/board: $10,492
Financial aid: (419) 530-8700; 66% of undergrads determined to have financial need; average aid package $11,172

Urbana University[1]

Urbana OH
(937) 484-1356
U.S. News ranking: Reg. Coll. (Mid.W), unranked
Website: www.urbana.edu
Admissions email: admiss@urbana.edu
Private
Application deadline (fall): N/A
Undergraduate student body: N/A full time, N/A part time
Expenses: 2014-2015: $22,012; room/board: $8,542
Financial aid: (937) 484-1355

Ursuline College

Pepper Pike OH
(440) 449-4203
U.S. News ranking: Reg. U. (Mid.W), No. 50
Website: www.ursuline.edu
Admissions email: admission@ursuline.edu
Private; founded 1871
Affiliation: Roman Catholic
Freshman admissions: selective; 2014-2015: 374 applied, 245 accepted. Either SAT or ACT required. ACT 25/75 percentile: 18-25. High school rank: 12% in top tenth, 31% in top quarter, 76% in top half
Early decision deadline: N/A, notification date: N/A
Early action deadline: N/A, notification date: N/A
Application deadline (fall): 2/1
Undergraduate student body: 485 full time, 221 part time; 8% male, 92% female; 0% American Indian, 1% Asian, 26% black, 3% Hispanic, 3% multiracial, 0% Pacific Islander, 65% white, 1% international; 92% from in state; 23% live on campus; 0% of students in fraternities, 0% in sororities
Most popular majors: 14% Business, Management, Marketing, and Related Support Services, 3% Communication, Journalism, and Related Programs, 63% Health Professions and Related Programs, 6% Psychology, 4% Visual and Performing Arts
Expenses: 2015-2016: $28,520; room/board: $9,108
Financial aid: (440) 646-8309; 73% of undergrads determined to have financial need; average aid package $21,524

Walsh University

North Canton OH
(800) 362-9846
U.S. News ranking: Reg. U. (Mid.W), No. 54
Website: www.walsh.edu
Admissions email: admissions@walsh.edu
Private; founded 1958
Affiliation: Roman Catholic
Freshman admissions: selective; 2014-2015: 1,480 applied, 1,194 accepted. Either SAT or ACT required. ACT 25/75 percentile: 20-25. High school rank: 16% in top tenth, 45% in top quarter, 76% in top half
Early decision deadline: N/A, notification date: N/A
Early action deadline: N/A, notification date: N/A
Application deadline (fall): 8/15
Undergraduate student body: 1,895 full time, 430 part time; 38% male, 62% female; 0% American Indian, 0% Asian, 7% black, 3% Hispanic, 3% multiracial, 0% Pacific Islander, 77% white, 2% international; 94% from in state; 48% live on campus; 0% of students in fraternities, 0% in sororities
Most popular majors: 10% Biological and Biomedical Sciences, 37% Business, Management, Marketing, and Related Support Services, 15% Education, 18% Health Professions and Related Programs, 5% Psychology
Expenses: 2015-2016: $27,710; room/board: $9,920
Financial aid: (330) 490-7150; 83% of undergrads determined to have financial need; average aid package $22,734

Wilberforce University[1]

Wilberforce OH
(800) 367-8568
U.S. News ranking: Reg. Coll. (Mid.W), second tier
Website: www.wilberforce.edu
Admissions email: admissions@wilberforce.edu
Private
Application deadline (fall): N/A
Undergraduate student body: N/A full time, N/A part time
Expenses: 2014-2015: $15,140; room/board: $6,456
Financial aid: (800) 367-8565

Wilmington College[1]
Wilmington OH
(937) 382-6661
U.S. News ranking: Reg. Coll. (Mid.W), No. 54
Website: www2.wilmington.edu
Admissions email: admission@wilmington.edu
Private; founded 1870
Affiliation: Religious Society of Friends
Undergraduate student body: N/A full time, N/A part time
Expenses: 2014-2015: $29,120; room/board: $9,392
Financial aid: (937) 382-6661

Wittenberg University
Springfield OH
(937) 327-6314
U.S. News ranking: Nat. Lib. Arts, No. 148
Website: www5.wittenberg.edu
Admissions email: admission@wittenberg.edu
Private; founded 1845
Affiliation: Lutheran
Freshman admissions: selective; 2014-2015: 4,850 applied, 4,432 accepted. Neither SAT nor ACT required. ACT 25/75 percentile: 22-28. High school rank: 22% in top tenth, 46% in top quarter, 77% in top half
Early decision deadline: 11/15, notification date: 12/15
Early action deadline: 12/1, notification date: 1/1
Application deadline (fall): rolling
Undergraduate student body: 1,850 full time, 98 part time; 43% male, 57% female; 0% American Indian, 1% Asian, 7% black, 3% Hispanic, 5% multiracial, 0% Pacific Islander, 81% white, 2% international; 72% from in state; 86% live on campus; 26% of students in fraternities, 33% in sororities
Most popular majors: 11% Biological and Biomedical Sciences, 13% Business, Management, Marketing, and Related Support Services, 11% Education, 7% English Language and Literature/Letters, 12% Psychology
Expenses: 2015-2016: $38,030; room/board: $10,028
Financial aid: (937) 327-7321; 78% of undergrads determined to have financial need; average aid package $31,787

Wright State University
Dayton OH
(937) 775-5700
U.S. News ranking: Nat. U., second tier
Website: www.wright.edu
Admissions email: admissions@wright.edu
Public; founded 1964
Freshman admissions: selective; 2014-2015: 5,237 applied, 5,067 accepted. Either SAT or ACT required. ACT 25/75 percentile: 18-25. High school rank: 15% in top tenth, 36% in top quarter, 67% in top half
Early decision deadline: N/A, notification date: N/A
Early action deadline: N/A, notification date: N/A
Application deadline (fall): rolling
Undergraduate student body: 9,937 full time, 2,745 part time; 49% male, 51% female; 0% American Indian, 2% Asian, 13% black, 3% Hispanic, 4% multiracial, 0% Pacific Islander, 72% white, 6% international; 97% from in state; 19% live on campus; 3% of students in fraternities, 6% in sororities
Most popular majors: 3% Accounting, 5% Biology/Biological Sciences, General, 6% Mechanical Engineering, 5% Psychology, General, 8% Registered Nursing/Registered Nurse
Expenses: 2015-2016: $8,730 in state, $17,098 out of state; room/board: N/A
Financial aid: (937) 873-5721; 64% of undergrads determined to have financial need; average aid package $10,400

Xavier University
Cincinnati OH
(877) 982-3648
U.S. News ranking: Reg. U. (Mid.W), No. 6
Website: www.xavier.edu
Admissions email: xuadmit@xavier.edu
Private; founded 1831
Affiliation: Roman Catholic (Jesuit)
Freshman admissions: selective; 2014-2015: 11,605 applied, 8,489 accepted. Either SAT or ACT required. ACT 25/75 percentile: 22-27. High school rank: 20% in top tenth, 48% in top quarter, 84% in top half
Early decision deadline: N/A, notification date: N/A
Early action deadline: N/A, notification date: N/A
Application deadline (fall): rolling
Undergraduate student body: 4,270 full time, 363 part time; 46% male, 54% female; 0% American Indian, 2% Asian, 10% black, 5% Hispanic, 4% multiracial, 0% Pacific Islander, 72% white, 2% international; 51% from in state; 52% live on campus; N/A of students in fraternities, N/A in sororities
Most popular majors: 7% Biological and Biomedical Sciences, 29% Business, Management, Marketing, and Related Support Services, 10% Health Professions and Related Programs, 12% Liberal Arts and Sciences, General Studies and Humanities, 6% Social Sciences
Expenses: 2015-2016: $35,080; room/board: $11,380
Financial aid: (513) 745-3142; 60% of undergrads determined to have financial need; average aid package $20,540

Youngstown State University
Youngstown OH
(877) 468-6978
U.S. News ranking: Reg. U. (Mid.W), second tier
Website: www.ysu.edu
Admissions email: enroll@ysu.edu
Public; founded 1908
Freshman admissions: selective; 2014-2015: 3,784 applied, 3,152 accepted. Either SAT or ACT required. ACT 25/75 percentile: 18-24. High school rank: 11% in top tenth, 30% in top quarter, 60% in top half
Early decision deadline: N/A, notification date: N/A
Early action deadline: N/A, notification date: N/A
Application deadline (fall): 8/1
Undergraduate student body: 8,810 full time, 2,538 part time; 47% male, 53% female; 0% American Indian, 1% Asian, 12% black, 3% Hispanic, 2% multiracial, 0% Pacific Islander, 76% white, 1% international; 88% from in state; 10% live on campus; 1% of students in fraternities, 2% in sororities
Most popular majors: 4% Accounting, 6% Criminal Justice/Safety Studies, 6% General Studies, 6% Registered Nursing/Registered Nurse, 5% Social Work
Expenses: 2015-2016: $8,317 in state, $14,317 out of state; room/board: $8,645
Financial aid: (330) 941-3399; 76% of undergrads determined to have financial need; average aid package $8,877

OKLAHOMA

Bacone College
Muskogee OK
(888) 682-5514
U.S. News ranking: Reg. Coll. (W), second tier
Website: www.bacone.edu/
Admissions email: admissions@bacone.edu
Private
Freshman admissions: less selective; 2014-2015: N/A applied, N/A accepted. Either SAT or ACT required. ACT 25/75 percentile: 16-19. High school rank: N/A
Early decision deadline: N/A, notification date: N/A
Early action deadline: N/A, notification date: N/A
Application deadline (fall): rolling
Undergraduate student body: 861 full time, 107 part time; 63% male, 37% female; 25% American Indian, 3% Asian, 32% black, 9% Hispanic, 3% multiracial, 1% Pacific Islander, 19% white, 0% international; N/A from in state; 67% live on campus; N/A of students in fraternities, N/A in sororities
Most popular majors: 5% Business Administration and Management, General, 9% Criminal Justice/Police Science, 3% Health and Physical Education/Fitness, General, 8% Kinesiology and Exercise Science, 8% Sport and Fitness Administration/Management
Expenses: 2014-2015: $14,050; room/board: $9,750
Financial aid: (888) 682-5514

Cameron University
Lawton OK
(580) 581-2289
U.S. News ranking: Reg. U. (W), second tier
Website: www.cameron.edu
Admissions email: admissions@cameron.edu
Public; founded 1908
Freshman admissions: less selective; 2014-2015: 1,114 applied, 1,110 accepted. Neither SAT nor ACT required. ACT 25/75 percentile: 17-23. High school rank: 3% in top tenth, 13% in top quarter, 40% in top half
Early decision deadline: N/A, notification date: N/A
Early action deadline: N/A, notification date: N/A
Application deadline (fall): rolling
Undergraduate student body: 3,399 full time, 1,655 part time; 40% male, 60% female; 6% American Indian, 2% Asian, 16% black, 12% Hispanic, 8% multiracial, 1% Pacific Islander, 49% white, 5% international; 87% from in state; 10% live on campus; 1% of students in fraternities, 1% in sororities
Most popular majors: 11% Business Administration and Management, General, 11% Corrections and Criminal Justice, Other, 8% Elementary Education and Teaching, 6% General Studies, 11% Psychology, General
Expenses: 2014-2015: $5,340 in state, $13,380 out of state; room/board: $4,664
Financial aid: (580) 581-2293; 69% of undergrads determined to have financial need; average aid package $9,682

East Central University[1]
Ada OK
(580) 559-5239
U.S. News ranking: Reg. U. (W), second tier
Website: www.ecok.edu
Admissions email: parmstro@ecok.edu
Public
Application deadline (fall): N/A
Undergraduate student body: N/A full time, N/A part time
Expenses: 2014-2015: $5,599 in state, $13,512 out of state; room/board: $5,158
Financial aid: (580) 559-5242

Langston University
Langston OK
(405) 466-3231
U.S. News ranking: Reg. U. (W), unranked
Website: www.lunet.edu
Admissions email: admission@speedy.lunet.edu
Public
Freshman admissions: N/A; 2014-2015: 9,115 applied, 5,527 accepted. Neither SAT nor ACT required. Average composite ACT score: 16. High school rank: N/A
Early decision deadline: N/A, notification date: N/A
Early action deadline: N/A, notification date: N/A
Application deadline (fall): rolling
Undergraduate student body: 1,851 full time, 208 part time; 39% male, 61% female; 2% American Indian, 0% Asian, 85% black, 1% Hispanic, 0% multiracial, 0% Pacific Islander, 7% white, 0% international
Most popular majors: 10% Business, Management, Marketing, and Related Support Services, 21% Health Professions and Related Programs, 4% Homeland Security, Law Enforcement, Firefighting and Related Protective Services, 4% Liberal Arts and Sciences, General Studies and Humanities, 4% Psychology
Expenses: 2014-2015: $4,802 in state, $11,788 out of state; room/board: $9,234
Financial aid: (405) 466-3282; 92% of undergrads determined to have financial need; average aid package $14,990

Mid-America Christian University[1]
Oklahoma City OK
(888) 436-3035
U.S. News ranking: Reg. Coll. (W), unranked
Website: www.macu.edu
Admissions email: info@macu.edu
Private
Application deadline (fall): N/A
Undergraduate student body: N/A full time, N/A part time
Expenses: 2014-2015: $16,230; room/board: $6,430
Financial aid: (405) 691-3800

Northeastern State University
Tahlequah OK
(918) 444-2200
U.S. News ranking: Reg. U. (W), second tier
Website: www.nsuok.edu
Admissions email: nsuinfo@nsuok.edu
Public; founded 1846
Freshman admissions: selective; 2014-2015: 1,957 applied, 1,468 accepted. ACT required. ACT 25/75 percentile: 19-24. High school rank: 22% in top tenth, 46% in top quarter, 83% in top half
Early decision deadline: N/A, notification date: N/A
Early action deadline: N/A, notification date: N/A
Application deadline (fall): rolling
Undergraduate student body: 5,054 full time, 2,063 part time; 39% male, 61% female; 22% American Indian, 2% Asian, 5% black, 4% Hispanic, 14% multiracial, 0% Pacific Islander, 50% white, 1% international; 95% from in state; 19% live on campus; 2% of students in fraternities, 1% in sororities
Most popular majors: 6% Biology/Biological Sciences, General, 9% Criminal Justice/Law Enforcement Administration, 7% Elementary Education and Teaching, 6% General Studies, 9% Psychology, General
Expenses: 2015-2016: $5,442 in state, $13,013 out of state; room/board: $7,252
Financial aid: (918) 456-5511; 69% of undergrads determined to have financial need; average aid package $12,446

Northwestern Oklahoma State University
Alva OK
(580) 327-8545
U.S. News ranking: Reg. U. (W), second tier
Website: www.nwosu.edu
Admissions email: recruit@nwosu.edu
Public; founded 1897
Freshman admissions: selective; 2014-2015: 871 applied, 564 accepted. Either SAT or ACT required. ACT 25/75 percentile: 18-22. High school rank: 9% in top tenth, 26% in top quarter, 63% in top half
Early decision deadline: N/A, notification date: N/A
Early action deadline: N/A, notification date: N/A
Application deadline (fall): rolling
Undergraduate student body: 1,563 full time, 450 part time; 43%

male, 57% female; 7% American Indian, 1% Asian, 7% black, 7% Hispanic, 1% multiracial, 0% Pacific Islander, 64% white, 7% international; 82% from in state; 51% live on campus; N/A of students in fraternities, N/A in sororities
Most popular majors: 7% Biology/ Biological Sciences, General, 12% Business Administration and Management, General, 9% Parks, Recreation, Leisure, and Fitness Studies, Other, 8% Psychology, General, 15% Registered Nursing/ Registered Nurse
Expenses: 2014-2015: $5,843 in state, $12,293 out of state; room/ board: $4,230
Financial aid: (580) 327-8542; 60% of undergrads determined to have financial need

Oklahoma Baptist University

Shawnee OK
(405) 585-5000
U.S. News ranking: Reg. Coll. (W), No. 4
Website: www.okbu.edu
Admissions email: admissions@okbu.edu
Private; founded 1910
Affiliation: Southern Baptist Convention
Freshman admissions: more selective; 2014-2015: 5,984 applied, 3,619 accepted. Either SAT or ACT required. ACT 25/75 percentile: 21-27. High school rank: 23% in top tenth, 49% in top quarter, 89% in top half
Early decision deadline: N/A, notification date: N/A
Early action deadline: N/A, notification date: N/A
Application deadline (fall): 8/1
Undergraduate student body: 1,808 full time, 113 part time; 41% male, 59% female; 5% American Indian, 1% Asian, 6% black, 2% Hispanic, 8% multiracial, 0% Pacific Islander, 70% white, 4% international; 56% from in state; 68% live on campus; 2% of students in fraternities, 11% in sororities
Most popular majors: 9% Business, Management, Marketing, and Related Support Services, 16% Education, 22% Health Professions and Related Programs, 6% Psychology, 12% Theology and Religious Vocations
Expenses: 2015-2016: $24,000; room/board: $6,780
Financial aid: (405) 878-2016; 72% of undergrads determined to have financial need; average aid package $21,522

Oklahoma Christian University

Oklahoma City OK
(405) 425-5050
U.S. News ranking: Reg. U. (W), No. 42
Website: www.oc.edu/
Admissions email: info@oc.edu
Private; founded 1950
Affiliation: Church of Christ
Freshman admissions: selective; 2014-2015: 2,159 applied, 1,382 accepted. Either SAT or ACT required. ACT 25/75 percentile: 22-28. High school rank: 27% in top tenth, 52% in top quarter, 79% in top half
Early decision deadline: N/A, notification date: N/A
Early action deadline: N/A, notification date: N/A
Application deadline (fall): rolling
Undergraduate student body: 1,892 full time, 81 part time; 52% male, 48% female; 2% American Indian, 1% Asian, 5% black, 6% Hispanic, 6% multiracial, 0% Pacific Islander, 70% white, 10% international; 41% from in state; 81% live on campus; 36% of students in fraternities, 38% in sororities
Most popular majors: 18% Business, Management, Marketing, and Related Support Services, 8% Communication, Journalism, and Related Programs, 10% Education, 13% Engineering, 7% Health Professions and Related Programs
Expenses: 2014-2015: $19,120; room/board: $6,670
Financial aid: (405) 425-5190

Oklahoma City University

Oklahoma City OK
(405) 208-5050
U.S. News ranking: Reg. U. (W), No. 23
Website: www.okcu.edu
Admissions email: uadmissions@okcu.edu
Private; founded 1904
Affiliation: United Methodist
Freshman admissions: more selective; 2014-2015: 1,505 applied, 1,020 accepted. Either SAT or ACT required. ACT 25/75 percentile: 23-28. High school rank: 40% in top tenth, 64% in top quarter, 90% in top half
Early decision deadline: N/A, notification date: N/A
Early action deadline: N/A, notification date: N/A
Application deadline (fall): rolling
Undergraduate student body: 1,578 full time, 203 part time; 37% male, 63% female; 2% American Indian, 2% Asian, 5% black, 8% Hispanic, 8% multiracial, 0% Pacific Islander, 61% white, 13% international; 52% from in state; 52% live on campus; 30% of students in fraternities, 17% in sororities
Most popular majors: 13% Business, Management, Marketing, and Related Support Services, 6% Education, 20% Health Professions and Related Programs, 12% Liberal Arts and Sciences, General Studies and Humanities, 16% Visual and Performing Arts
Expenses: 2015-2016: $30,726; room/board: $9,682
Financial aid: (405) 208-5211

Oklahoma Panhandle State University

Goodwell OK
(800) 664-6778
U.S. News ranking: Reg. Coll. (W), second tier
Website: www.opsu.edu
Admissions email: opsu@opsu.edu
Public; founded 1909
Freshman admissions: less selective; 2014-2015: 726 applied, 432 accepted. Neither SAT nor ACT required. ACT 25/75 percentile: 17-21. High school rank: N/A
Early decision deadline: N/A, notification date: N/A
Early action deadline: N/A, notification date: N/A
Application deadline (fall): rolling
Undergraduate student body: 964 full time, 334 part time; 45% male, 55% female; 4% American Indian, 1% Asian, 12% black, 16% Hispanic, 2% multiracial, 0% Pacific Islander, 60% white, 2% international
Most popular majors: Information not available
Expenses: 2014-2015: $6,777 in state, $8,293 out of state; room/ board: $4,200
Financial aid: (580) 349-1580

Oklahoma State University

Stillwater OK
(405) 744-5358
U.S. News ranking: Nat. U., No. 149
Website: osu.okstate.edu
Admissions email: admissions@okstate.edu
Public; founded 1890
Freshman admissions: more selective; 2014-2015: 12,259 applied, 9,188 accepted. Either SAT or ACT required. ACT 25/75 percentile: 22-28. High school rank: 26% in top tenth, 54% in top quarter, 85% in top half
Early decision deadline: N/A, notification date: N/A
Early action deadline: N/A, notification date: N/A
Application deadline (fall): rolling
Undergraduate student body: 18,156 full time, 2,665 part time; 51% male, 49% female; 5% American Indian, 2% Asian, 5% black, 6% Hispanic, 8% multiracial, 0% Pacific Islander, 71% white, 3% international; 73% from in state; 45% live on campus; 19% of students in fraternities, 28% in sororities
Most popular majors: 8% Agriculture, Agriculture Operations, and Related Sciences, 6% Biological and Biomedical Sciences, 26% Business, Management, Marketing, and Related Support Services, 10% Engineering, 7% Family and Consumer Sciences/Human Sciences
Expenses: 2014-2015: $7,442 in state, $20,027 out of state; room/ board: $7,390
Financial aid: (405) 744-6604; 51% of undergrads determined to have financial need; average aid package $13,222

Oklahoma State University Institute of Technology–Okmulgee

Okmulgee OK
(918) 293-4680
U.S. News ranking: Reg. Coll. (W), No. 30
Website: www.osuit.edu/admissions
Admissions email: osuit.admissions@okstate.edu
Public; founded 1946
Freshman admissions: less selective; 2014-2015: 1,805 applied, 843 accepted. Either SAT or ACT required. ACT 25/75 percentile: 16-21. High school rank: 3% in top tenth, 14% in top quarter, 48% in top half
Early decision deadline: N/A, notification date: N/A
Early action deadline: N/A, notification date: N/A
Application deadline (fall): rolling
Undergraduate student body: 1,995 full time, 1,384 part time; 64% male, 36% female; 15% American Indian, 1% Asian, 5% black, 6% Hispanic, 8% multiracial, 0% Pacific Islander, 60% white, 1% international; 88% from in state; 28% live on campus; N/A of students in fraternities, N/A in sororities
Most popular majors: 9% Civil Engineering Technology/ Technician, 54% Computer and Information Systems Security/ Information Assurance, 37% Instrumentation Technology/ Technician
Expenses: 2015-2016: $21,003 in state, $27,200 out of state; room/board: $6,000
Financial aid: (800) 722-4471; 75% of undergrads determined to have financial need; average aid package $7,550

Oklahoma State University–Oklahoma City

Oklahoma City OK
(405) 945-3224
U.S. News ranking: Reg. Coll. (W), unranked
Website: www.osuokc.edu/
Admissions email: admissions@osuokc.edu
Public; founded 1961
Freshman admissions: N/A; 2014-2015: 2,417 applied, 2,417 accepted. Neither SAT nor ACT required. ACT 25/75 percentile: N/A. High school rank: N/A
Early decision deadline: N/A, notification date: N/A
Early action deadline: N/A, notification date: N/A
Application deadline (fall): rolling
Undergraduate student body: 2,175 full time, 4,537 part time; 39% male, 61% female; 4% American Indian, 3% Asian, 16% black, 10% Hispanic, 9% multiracial, N/A Pacific Islander, 55% white, N/A international; 93% from in state; N/A live on campus; N/A of students in fraternities, N/A in sororities
Most popular majors: Information not available
Expenses: 2014-2015: $3,539 in state, $9,614 out of state; room/ board: N/A
Financial aid: (405) 945-3319

Oklahoma Wesleyan University

Bartlesville OK
(866) 222-8226
U.S. News ranking: Reg. Coll. (W), No. 12
Website: www.okwu.edu
Admissions email: admissions@okwu.edu
Private; founded 1972
Affiliation: The Wesleyan Church
Freshman admissions: selective; 2014-2015: 2,587 applied, 1,622 accepted. Either SAT or ACT required. ACT 25/75 percentile: 18-25. High school rank: N/A
Early decision deadline: N/A, notification date: N/A
Early action deadline: N/A, notification date: N/A
Application deadline (fall): rolling
Undergraduate student body: 602 full time, 603 part time; 37% male, 63% female; 4% American Indian, 0% Asian, 7% black, 12% Hispanic, 7% multiracial, 0% Pacific Islander, 58% white, 10% international
Most popular majors: 9% Business Administration and Management, General, 11% Business, Management, Marketing, and Related Support Services, Other, 5% Business/Managerial Economics, 38% Nursing Science, 6% Theological and Ministerial Studies, Other
Expenses: 2015-2016: $24,108; room/board: $7,862
Financial aid: (918) 335-6282; 75% of undergrads determined to have financial need; average aid package $16,533

Oral Roberts University

Tulsa OK
(800) 678-8876
U.S. News ranking: Reg. U. (W), No. 50
Website: www.oru.edu
Admissions email: admissions@oru.edu
Private; founded 1963
Affiliation: Christian interdenominational
Freshman admissions: selective; 2014-2015: 1,539 applied, 689 accepted. Either SAT or ACT required. ACT 25/75 percentile: 19-25. High school rank: 18% in top tenth, 44% in top quarter, 72% in top half
Early decision deadline: N/A, notification date: N/A
Early action deadline: N/A, notification date: N/A
Application deadline (fall): rolling
Undergraduate student body: 2,409 full time, 669 part time; 43% male, 57% female; 3% American Indian, 2% Asian, 15% black, 9% Hispanic, 5% multiracial, 0% Pacific Islander, 49% white, 6% international; 47% from in state; 89% live on campus; 0% of students in fraternities, 0% in sororities
Most popular majors: 18% Business, Management, Marketing, and Related Support Services, 9% Communication, Journalism, and Related Programs, 9% Health Professions and Related Programs, 14% Theology and Religious Vocations, 8% Visual and Performing Arts
Expenses: 2015-2016: $24,792; room/board: $10,348
Financial aid: (918) 495-7088; 72% of undergrads determined to have financial need; average aid package $22,392

Rogers State University

Claremore OK
(918) 343-7545
U.S. News ranking: Reg. Coll. (W), second tier
Website: www.rsu.edu/
Admissions email: info@rsu.edu
Public; founded 1909
Freshman admissions: least selective; 2014-2015: 1,057 applied, 814 accepted. Either SAT or ACT required. ACT 25/75

percentile: 16-19. High school rank: 4% in top tenth, 14% in top quarter, 35% in top half
Early decision deadline: N/A, notification date: N/A
Early action deadline: N/A, notification date: N/A
Application deadline (fall): rolling
Undergraduate student body: 2,407 full time, 1,612 part time; 37% male, 63% female; 13% American Indian, 1% Asian, 2% black, 5% Hispanic, 18% multiracial, 0% Pacific Islander, 60% white, 1% international
Most popular majors: 11% Biological and Biomedical Sciences, 26% Business, Management, Marketing, and Related Support Services, 7% Health Professions and Related Programs, 8% Multi/ Interdisciplinary Studies, 8% Social Sciences
Expenses: 2014-2015: $5,725 in state, $12,766 out of state; room/ board: $8,190
Financial aid: (918) 343-7553; 56% of undergrads determined to have financial need; average aid package $9,637

Southeastern Oklahoma State University

Durant OK
(580) 745-2060
U.S. News ranking: Reg. U. (W), second tier
Website: www.se.edu
Admissions email: admissions@se.edu
Public; founded 1909
Freshman admissions: less selective; 2014-2015: 980 applied, 771 accepted. Either SAT or ACT required. ACT 25/75 percentile: 18-22. High school rank: 13% in top tenth, 34% in top quarter, 71% in top half
Early decision deadline: N/A, notification date: N/A
Early action deadline: N/A, notification date: N/A
Application deadline (fall): rolling
Undergraduate student body: 2,703 full time, 765 part time; 45% male, 55% female; 30% American Indian, 1% Asian, 7% black, 4% Hispanic, 0% multiracial, 0% Pacific Islander, 55% white, 3% international; 74% from in state; 16% live on campus; N/A of students in fraternities, N/A in sororities
Most popular majors: 14% Business, Management, Marketing, and Related Support Services, 15% Education, 15% Engineering Technologies and Engineering-Related Fields, 11% Liberal Arts and Sciences, General Studies and Humanities, 7% Psychology
Expenses: 2014-2015: $6,580 in state, $14,290 out of state; room/ board: $6,143
Financial aid: (580) 745-2186; 74% of undergrads determined to have financial need; average aid package $10,559

Southern Nazarene University

Bethany OK
(405) 491-6324
U.S. News ranking: Reg. U. (W), No. 83
Website: www.snu.edu
Admissions email: admissions@snu.edu
Private; founded 1899
Affiliation: Nazarene
Freshman admissions: selective; 2014-2015: 834 applied, 311 accepted. Either SAT or ACT required. ACT 25/75 percentile: N/A. High school rank: N/A
Early decision deadline: N/A, notification date: N/A
Early action deadline: N/A, notification date: N/A
Application deadline (fall): 8/6
Undergraduate student body: 1,645 full time, N/A part time; 48% male, 52% female; N/A American Indian, N/A Asian, N/A black, N/A Hispanic, N/A multiracial, N/A Pacific Islander, N/A white, N/A international
Most popular majors: Information not available
Expenses: 2014-2015: $22,680; room/board: $7,970
Financial aid: (405) 491-6310

Southwestern Christian University[1]

Bethany OK
(405) 789-7661
U.S. News ranking: Reg. Coll. (W), No. 28
Website: www.swcu.edu/
Admissions email: admissions@swcu.edu
Private; founded 1946
Affiliation: Pentecostal
Application deadline (fall): rolling
Undergraduate student body: N/A full time, N/A part time
Expenses: 2014-2015: $12,470; room/board: $6,600
Financial aid: N/A

Southwestern Oklahoma State University

Weatherford OK
(580) 774-3782
U.S. News ranking: Reg. U. (W), second tier
Website: www.swosu.edu
Admissions email: admissions@swosu.edu
Public; founded 1901
Freshman admissions: selective; 2014-2015: 2,632 applied, 2,244 accepted. Either SAT or ACT required. ACT 25/75 percentile: 19-24. High school rank: 23% in top tenth, 46% in top quarter, 77% in top half
Early decision deadline: N/A, notification date: N/A
Early action deadline: N/A, notification date: N/A
Application deadline (fall): rolling
Undergraduate student body: 3,396 full time, 844 part time; 41% male, 59% female; 4% American Indian, 2% Asian, 6% black, 8% Hispanic, 8% multiracial, 0% Pacific Islander, 67% white, 4% international; 90% from in state; 25% live on campus; 3% of students in fraternities, 4% in sororities
Most popular majors: 14% Business, Management, Marketing, and Related Support Services, 15% Education, 4% Engineering Technologies and Engineering-Related Fields, 32% Health Professions and Related Programs, 9% Parks, Recreation, Leisure, and Fitness Studies
Expenses: 2015-2016: $5,820 in state, $12,270 out of state; room/ board: $5,080
Financial aid: (580) 774-3786; 61% of undergrads determined to have financial need; average aid package $5,568

St. Gregory's University

Shawnee OK
(405) 878-5444
U.S. News ranking: Reg. Coll. (W), No. 27
Website: www.stgregorys.edu
Admissions email: admissions@stgregorys.edu
Private; founded 1915
Affiliation: Roman Catholic–Benedictine
Freshman admissions: less selective; 2014-2015: 587 applied, 367 accepted. Either SAT or ACT required. ACT 25/75 percentile: 19-23. High school rank: N/A
Early decision deadline: N/A, notification date: N/A
Early action deadline: N/A, notification date: N/A
Application deadline (fall): N/A
Undergraduate student body: 503 full time, 117 part time; 47% male, 53% female; 8% American Indian, 1% Asian, 8% black, 13% Hispanic, 9% multiracial, 0% Pacific Islander, 48% white, 4% international
Most popular majors: Information not available
Expenses: 2015-2016: $20,280; room/board: $4,085
Financial aid: (405) 878-5412

University of Central Oklahoma

Edmond OK
(405) 974-2727
U.S. News ranking: Reg. U. (W), No. 81
Website: www.uco.edu/em/become-a-broncho/index.asp
Admissions email: onestop@uco.edu
Public; founded 1890
Freshman admissions: selective; 2014-2015: 4,537 applied, 4,098 accepted. Either SAT or ACT required. ACT 25/75 percentile: 18-24. High school rank: 13% in top tenth, 21% in top quarter, 70% in top half
Early decision deadline: N/A, notification date: N/A
Early action deadline: N/A, notification date: N/A
Application deadline (fall): rolling
Undergraduate student body: 10,726 full time, 4,272 part time; 42% male, 58% female; 4% American Indian, 3% Asian, 9% black, 8% Hispanic, 8% multiracial, 0% Pacific Islander, 58% white, 8% international; 97% from in state; 9% live on campus; 3% of students in fraternities, 5% in sororities
Most popular majors: 6% Business Administration and Management, General, 4% Finance, General, 12% General Studies, 4% Psychology, General, 5% Registered Nursing/Registered Nurse
Expenses: 2014-2015: $5,437 in state, $13,552 out of state; room/ board: $6,940
Financial aid: (405) 974-3334

University of Oklahoma

Norman OK
(405) 325-2252
U.S. News ranking: Nat. U., No. 108
Website: www.ou.edu
Admissions email: admrec@ou.edu
Public; founded 1890
Freshman admissions: more selective; 2014-2015: 11,331 applied, 9,216 accepted. Either SAT or ACT required. ACT 25/75 percentile: 23-29. High school rank: 35% in top tenth, 65% in top quarter, 91% in top half
Early decision deadline: N/A, notification date: N/A
Early action deadline: N/A, notification date: N/A
Application deadline (fall): 4/1
Undergraduate student body: 18,764 full time, 3,080 part time; 50% male, 50% female; 4% American Indian, 6% Asian, 5% black, 9% Hispanic, 7% multiracial, 0% Pacific Islander, 63% white, 4% international; 68% from in state; 32% live on campus; 26% of students in fraternities, 30% in sororities
Most popular majors: 3% Business, Management, Marketing, and Related Support Services, 7% Health Professions and Related Programs, 10% Multi/ Interdisciplinary Studies, 3% Psychology
Expenses: 2014-2015: $7,695 in state, $20,469 out of state; room/ board: $9,126
Financial aid: (405) 325-4521; 47% of undergrads determined to have financial need; average aid package $12,556

University of Science and Arts of Oklahoma

Chickasha OK
(405) 574-1357
U.S. News ranking: Nat. Lib. Arts, second tier
Website: www.usao.edu
Admissions email: usao-admissions@usao.edu
Public; founded 1908
Freshman admissions: selective; 2014-2015: 567 applied, 383 accepted. Either SAT or ACT required. ACT 25/75 percentile: 20-25. High school rank: 27% in top tenth, 49% in top quarter, 83% in top half
Early decision deadline: N/A, notification date: N/A
Early action deadline: N/A, notification date: N/A
Application deadline (fall): 8/30
Undergraduate student body: 801 full time, 103 part time; 36% male, 64% female; 10% American Indian, 1% Asian, 5% black, 7% Hispanic, 6% multiracial, N/A Pacific Islander, 63% white, 8% international; 86% from in state; 47% live on campus; 2% of students in fraternities, 13% in sororities
Most popular majors: Information not available
Expenses: 2015-2016: $6,570 in state, $16,020 out of state; room/ board: $5,720
Financial aid: (405) 574-1240; 66% of undergrads determined to have financial need; average aid package $10,607

University of Tulsa

Tulsa OK
(918) 631-2307
U.S. News ranking: Nat. U., No. 86
Website: utulsa.edu
Admissions email: admission@utulsa.edu
Private; founded 1894
Affiliation: Presbyterian
Freshman admissions: most selective; 2014-2015: 7,636 applied, 3,074 accepted. Either SAT or ACT required. ACT 25/75 percentile: 26-32. High school rank: 75% in top tenth, 92% in top quarter, 98% in top half
Early decision deadline: N/A, notification date: N/A
Early action deadline: 11/1, notification date: 12/15
Application deadline (fall): rolling
Undergraduate student body: 3,362 full time, 111 part time; 58% male, 42% female; 4% American Indian, 3% Asian, 4% black, 4% Hispanic, 1% multiracial, 0% Pacific Islander, 55% white, 27% international; 55% from in state; 73% live on campus; 21% of students in fraternities, 23% in sororities
Most popular majors: 7% Biological and Biomedical Sciences, 22% Business, Management, Marketing, and Related Support Services, 20% Engineering, 6% Social Sciences, 7% Visual and Performing Arts
Expenses: 2015-2016: $36,962; room/board: $10,630
Financial aid: (918) 631-2526; 40% of undergrads determined to have financial need; average aid package $26,493

OREGON

Art Institute of Portland[1]

Portland OR
(888) 228-6528
U.S. News ranking: Arts, unranked
Website: www.artinstitutes.edu/portland/
Admissions email: N/A
For-profit
Application deadline (fall): N/A
Undergraduate student body: N/A full time, N/A part time
Expenses: 2014-2015: $17,416; room/board: $9,522
Financial aid: N/A

Concordia University[1]

Portland OR
(503) 280-8501
U.S. News ranking: Reg. U. (W), second tier
Website: www.cu-portland.edu
Admissions email: admissions@cu-portland.edu
Private; founded 1905
Affiliation: Lutheran
Application deadline (fall): 7/1
Undergraduate student body: N/A full time, N/A part time
Expenses: 2014-2015: $27,420; room/board: $7,580
Financial aid: (503) 280-8514

Corban University

Salem OR
(800) 845-3005
U.S. News ranking: Reg. Coll. (W), No. 5
Website: www.corban.edu

Admissions email: admissions@corban.edu
Private; founded 1935
Affiliation: Evangelical
Freshman admissions: selective; 2014-2015: 2,678 applied, 1,001 accepted. Either SAT or ACT required. SAT 25/75 percentile: 895-1140. High school rank: 26% in top tenth, 58% in top quarter, 88% in top half
Early decision deadline: N/A, notification date: N/A
Early action deadline: N/A, notification date: N/A
Application deadline (fall): 8/1
Undergraduate student body: 871 full time, 153 part time; 40% male, 60% female; 1% American Indian, 3% Asian, 1% black, 3% Hispanic, 6% multiracial, 1% Pacific Islander, 78% white, 2% international; 50% from in state; 63% live on campus; N/A of students in fraternities, N/A in sororities
Most popular majors: Information not available
Expenses: 2015-2016: $29,640; room/board: $9,240
Financial aid: (503) 375-7006; 80% of undergrads determined to have financial need; average aid package $20,591

Eastern Oregon University

La Grande OR
(541) 962-3393
U.S. News ranking: Reg. U. (W), second tier
Website: www.eou.edu
Admissions email: admissions@eou.edu
Public; founded 1929
Freshman admissions: less selective; 2014-2015: 1,530 applied, 982 accepted. Either SAT or ACT required. SAT 25/75 percentile: 820-1050. High school rank: 9% in top tenth, 36% in top quarter, 74% in top half
Early decision deadline: N/A, notification date: N/A
Early action deadline: 2/1, notification date: N/A
Application deadline (fall): 9/1
Undergraduate student body: 1,956 full time, 1,392 part time; 37% male, 63% female; 3% American Indian, 2% Asian, 3% black, 6% Hispanic, 2% multiracial, 1% Pacific Islander, 76% white, 2% international; 72% from in state; 10% live on campus; 0% of students in fraternities, 0% in sororities
Most popular majors: 34% Business, Management, Marketing, and Related Support Services, 12% Education, 5% Homeland Security, Law Enforcement, Firefighting and Related Protective Services, 17% Liberal Arts and Sciences, General Studies and Humanities, 5% Psychology
Expenses: 2014-2015: $7,440 in state, $17,520 out of state; room/board: $9,642
Financial aid: (541) 962-3551

George Fox University

Newberg OR
(800) 765-4369
U.S. News ranking: Reg. U. (W), No. 28
Website: www.georgefox.edu
Admissions email: admissions@georgefox.edu
Private; founded 1891
Affiliation: Evangelical Friends
Freshman admissions: selective; 2014-2015: 2,777 applied, 2,122 accepted. Either SAT or ACT required. SAT 25/75 percentile: 960-1210. High school rank: 28% in top tenth, 57% in top quarter, 85% in top half
Early decision deadline: N/A, notification date: N/A
Early action deadline: 11/15, notification date: 12/15
Application deadline (fall): rolling
Undergraduate student body: 2,250 full time, 265 part time; 44% male, 56% female; 0% American Indian, 4% Asian, 2% black, 9% Hispanic, 6% multiracial, 0% Pacific Islander, 70% white, 6% international; N/A from in state; 54% live on campus; 0% of students in fraternities, 0% in sororities
Most popular majors: 27% Business, Management, Marketing, and Related Support Services, 7% Engineering, 8% Health Professions and Related Programs, 9% Multi/Interdisciplinary Studies, 7% Visual and Performing Arts
Expenses: 2014-2015: $31,866; room/board: $9,864
Financial aid: (503) 554-2290

Lewis & Clark College

Portland OR
(800) 444-4111
U.S. News ranking: Nat. Lib. Arts, No. 72
Website: www.lclark.edu
Admissions email: admissions@lclark.edu
Private; founded 1867
Freshman admissions: more selective; 2014-2015: 6,243 applied, 4,159 accepted. Neither SAT nor ACT required. SAT 25/75 percentile: 1190-1380. High school rank: 38% in top tenth, 79% in top quarter, 96% in top half
Early decision deadline: 11/1, notification date: 12/15
Early action deadline: 11/1, notification date: 12/31
Application deadline (fall): 3/1
Undergraduate student body: 2,156 full time, 23 part time; 41% male, 59% female; 1% American Indian, 7% Asian, 2% black, 9% Hispanic, 1% multiracial, 0% Pacific Islander, 68% white, 5% international; 20% from in state; 65% live on campus; 0% of students in fraternities, 0% in sororities
Most popular majors: 8% Area, Ethnic, Cultural, Gender, and Group Studies, 9% Biological and Biomedical Sciences, 17% Psychology, 21% Social Sciences, 9% Visual and Performing Arts
Expenses: 2015-2016: $45,104; room/board: $11,218
Financial aid: (503) 768-7090; 60% of undergrads determined to have financial need; average aid package $36,865

Linfield College

McMinnville OR
(800) 640-2287
U.S. News ranking: Nat. Lib. Arts, No. 120
Website: www.linfield.edu
Admissions email: admission@linfield.edu
Private; founded 1858
Affiliation: American Baptist
Freshman admissions: selective; 2014-2015: 2,054 applied, 1,926 accepted. Either SAT or ACT required. SAT 25/75 percentile: 960-1200. High school rank: 27% in top tenth, 56% in top quarter, 94% in top half
Early decision deadline: N/A, notification date: N/A
Early action deadline: 11/15, notification date: 1/15
Application deadline (fall): rolling
Undergraduate student body: 1,644 full time, 39 part time; 38% male, 62% female; 1% American Indian, 6% Asian, 2% black, 10% Hispanic, 11% multiracial, 1% Pacific Islander, 64% white, 4% international; 50% from in state; 78% live on campus; 26% of students in fraternities, 23% in sororities
Most popular majors: 6% Biological and Biomedical Sciences, 22% Business, Management, Marketing, and Related Support Services, 6% Communication, Journalism, and Related Programs, 8% Parks, Recreation, Leisure, and Fitness Studies, 15% Social Sciences
Expenses: 2015-2016: $38,684; room/board: $11,410
Financial aid: (503) 883-2225; 75% of undergrads determined to have financial need; average aid package $30,438

Marylhurst University[1]

Marylhurst OR
(503) 699-6268
U.S. News ranking: Reg. U. (W), unranked
Website: www.marylhurst.edu
Admissions email: admissions@marylhurst.edu
Private
Application deadline (fall): N/A
Undergraduate student body: N/A full time, N/A part time
Expenses: 2014-2015: $20,295; room/board: $10,200
Financial aid: (503) 699-6253

Northwest Christian University

Eugene OR
(541) 684-7201
U.S. News ranking: Reg. Coll. (W), No. 22
Website: www.nwcu.edu
Admissions email: admissions@nwcu.edu
Private; founded 1895
Affiliation: Christian Church (Disciples of Christ)
Freshman admissions: less selective; 2014-2015: 356 applied, 256 accepted. Either SAT or ACT required. SAT 25/75 percentile: 888-1103. High school rank: N/A
Early decision deadline: N/A, notification date: N/A
Early action deadline: N/A, notification date: N/A
Application deadline (fall): rolling
Undergraduate student body: 395 full time, 101 part time; 39% male, 61% female; 3% American Indian, 2% Asian, 2% black, 9% Hispanic, 3% multiracial, 0% Pacific Islander, 79% white, 0% international; 75% from in state; 28% live on campus; 0% of students in fraternities, 0% in sororities
Most popular majors: 7% Biological and Biomedical Sciences, 29% Business, Management, Marketing, and Related Support Services, 22% Education, 9% Multi/Interdisciplinary Studies, 19% Psychology
Expenses: 2015-2016: $27,270; room/board: $8,400
Financial aid: (541) 684-7203; 87% of undergrads determined to have financial need; average aid package $20,379

Oregon College of Art and Craft

Portland OR
(800) 390-0632
U.S. News ranking: Arts, unranked
Website: www.ocac.edu/
Admissions email: admissions@ocac.edu
Private; founded 1907
Freshman admissions: N/A; 2014-2015: 184 applied, 93 accepted. Neither SAT nor ACT required. SAT 25/75 percentile: 920-1150. High school rank: 7% in top tenth, 27% in top quarter, 50% in top half
Early decision deadline: N/A, notification date: N/A
Early action deadline: N/A, notification date: N/A
Application deadline (fall): rolling
Undergraduate student body: 122 full time, 25 part time; 17% male, 83% female; 1% American Indian, 2% Asian, 1% black, 12% Hispanic, 13% multiracial, 1% Pacific Islander, 64% white, 0% international; 41% from in state; 14% live on campus; N/A of students in fraternities, N/A in sororities
Most popular majors: Information not available
Expenses: N/A
Financial aid: N/A

Oregon Institute of Technology

Klamath Falls OR
(541) 885-1155
U.S. News ranking: Reg. Coll. (W), No. 5
Website: www.oit.edu
Admissions email: oit@oit.edu
Public; founded 1947
Freshman admissions: selective; 2014-2015: 2,551 applied, 1,014 accepted. Either SAT or ACT required. ACT 25/75 percentile: 19-26. High school rank: 14% in top tenth, 54% in top quarter, 87% in top half
Early decision deadline: N/A, notification date: N/A
Early action deadline: N/A, notification date: N/A
Application deadline (fall): 9/7
Undergraduate student body: 2,317 full time, 1,733 part time; 54% male, 46% female; 1% American Indian, 5% Asian, 1% black, 8% Hispanic, 5% multiracial, 1% Pacific Islander, 73% white, 3% international; 76% from in state; 16% live on campus; 0% of students in fraternities, N/A in sororities
Most popular majors: 7% Business, Management, Marketing, and Related Support Services, 15% Engineering, 13% Engineering Technologies and Engineering-Related Fields, 48% Health Professions and Related Programs, 6% Psychology
Expenses: 2015-2016: $8,684 in state, $23,700 out of state; room/board: $9,059
Financial aid: (541) 885-1280; 74% of undergrads determined to have financial need; average aid package $7,623

Oregon State University

Corvallis OR
(541) 737-4411
U.S. News ranking: Nat. U., No. 135
Website: oregonstate.edu
Admissions email: osuadmit@oregonstate.edu
Public; founded 1868
Freshman admissions: selective; 2014-2015: 14,115 applied, 10,975 accepted. Either SAT or ACT required. SAT 25/75 percentile: 980-1230. High school rank: 27% in top tenth, 57% in top quarter, 89% in top half
Early decision deadline: N/A, notification date: N/A
Early action deadline: 11/1, notification date: 12/20
Application deadline (fall): 9/1
Undergraduate student body: 18,477 full time, 5,426 part time; 54% male, 46% female; 1% American Indian, 7% Asian, 1% black, 8% Hispanic, 6% multiracial, 0% Pacific Islander, 68% white, 6% international; 73% from in state; 18% live on campus; 13% of students in fraternities, 18% in sororities
Most popular majors: 7% Agriculture, Agriculture Operations, and Related Sciences, 14% Business, Management, Marketing, and Related Support Services, 15% Engineering, 11% Family and Consumer Sciences/Human Sciences, 7% Natural Resources and Conservation
Expenses: 2015-2016: $10,107 in state, $28,767 out of state; room/board: $11,691
Financial aid: (541) 737-2241; 57% of undergrads determined to have financial need; average aid package $12,913

Pacific Northwest College of Art[1]

Portland OR
(800) 818-7622
U.S. News ranking: Arts, unranked
Website: www.pnca.edu
Admissions email: admissions@pnca.edu
Private
Application deadline (fall): N/A
Undergraduate student body: N/A full time, N/A part time
Expenses: 2014-2015: $33,714; room/board: $10,324
Financial aid: (503) 821-8976

Pacific University

Forest Grove OR
(800) 677-6712
U.S. News ranking: Reg. U. (W), No. 25
Website: www.pacificu.edu
Admissions email: admissions@pacificu.edu
Private; founded 1849
Freshman admissions: selective; 2014-2015: 2,665 applied, 2,144 accepted. Either SAT or ACT required. SAT 25/75

percentile: 980-1200. High school rank: N/A
Early decision deadline: N/A, notification date: N/A
Early action deadline: N/A, notification date: N/A
Application deadline (fall): 8/15
Undergraduate student body: 1,797 full time, 43 part time; 41% male, 59% female; 1% American Indian, 12% Asian, 2% black, 11% Hispanic, 13% multiracial, 2% Pacific Islander, 53% white, 2% international; 48% from in state; 98% live on campus; 6% of students in fraternities, 9% in sororities
Most popular majors: Information not available
Expenses: 2015-2016: $39,858; room/board: $11,448
Financial aid: (503) 352-2222; 73% of undergrads determined to have financial need; average aid package $32,277

Portland State University

Portland OR
(503) 725-3511
U.S. News ranking: Nat. U., second tier
Website: www.pdx.edu
Admissions email: admissions@pdx.edu
Public; founded 1946
Freshman admissions: selective; 2014-2015: 4,936 applied, 4,184 accepted. Neither SAT nor ACT required. SAT 25/75 percentile: 910-1160. High school rank: 13% in top tenth, 40% in top quarter, 80% in top half
Early decision deadline: N/A, notification date: N/A
Early action deadline: N/A, notification date: N/A
Application deadline (fall): rolling
Undergraduate student body: 14,561 full time, 7,575 part time; 48% male, 52% female; 1% American Indian, 8% Asian, 3% black, 11% Hispanic, 6% multiracial, 1% Pacific Islander, 60% white, 5% international; 86% from in state; 10% live on campus; 1% of students in fraternities, 1% in sororities
Most popular majors: 16% Business, Management, Marketing, and Related Support Services, 8% Health Professions and Related Programs, 7% Liberal Arts and Sciences, General Studies and Humanities, 7% Psychology, 17% Social Sciences
Expenses: 2014-2015: $7,794 in state, $23,319 out of state; room/board: $10,119
Financial aid: (503) 725-3461; 67% of undergrads determined to have financial need; average aid package $9,509

Reed College[1]

Portland OR
(503) 777-7511
U.S. News ranking: Nat. Lib. Arts, No. 93
Website: www.reed.edu/
Admissions email: admission@reed.edu
Private
Application deadline (fall): N/A
Undergraduate student body: N/A full time, N/A part time
Expenses: 2014-2015: $47,760; room/board: $12,200
Financial aid: (503) 777-7223

Southern Oregon University

Ashland OR
(541) 552-6411
U.S. News ranking: Reg. U. (W), No. 73
Website: www.sou.edu
Admissions email: admissions@sou.edu
Public; founded 1926
Freshman admissions: selective; 2014-2015: 2,209 applied, 2,064 accepted. Either SAT or ACT required. SAT 25/75 percentile: 910-1150. High school rank: N/A
Early decision deadline: N/A, notification date: N/A
Early action deadline: N/A, notification date: N/A
Application deadline (fall): rolling
Undergraduate student body: 3,678 full time, 1,569 part time; 42% male, 58% female; 1% American Indian, 2% Asian, 3% black, 10% Hispanic, 8% multiracial, 0% Pacific Islander, 63% white, 3% international; 66% from in state; 26% live on campus; 0% of students in fraternities, 0% in sororities
Most popular majors: 17% Business, Management, Marketing, and Related Support Services, 8% Education, 10% Psychology, 8% Social Sciences, 13% Visual and Performing Arts
Expenses: 2014-2015: $7,701 in state, $21,279 out of state; room/board: $11,682
Financial aid: (541) 552-6754

University of Oregon

Eugene OR
(800) 232-3825
U.S. News ranking: Nat. U., No. 103
Website: www.uoregon.edu
Admissions email: uoadmit@uoregon.edu
Public; founded 1876
Freshman admissions: selective; 2014-2015: 21,359 applied, 15,997 accepted. Either SAT or ACT required. SAT 25/75 percentile: 990-1230. High school rank: 23% in top tenth, 66% in top quarter, 93% in top half
Early decision deadline: N/A, notification date: N/A
Early action deadline: 11/1, notification date: 12/15
Application deadline (fall): 1/15
Undergraduate student body: 18,673 full time, 1,886 part time; 48% male, 52% female; 1% American Indian, 5% Asian, 2% black, 9% Hispanic, 6% multiracial, 0% Pacific Islander, 62% white, 13% international; 59% from in state; 19% live on campus; 14% of students in fraternities, 19% in sororities
Most popular majors: 11% Business/Commerce, General, 5% Economics, General, 5% Physiology, General, 8% Psychology, General, 6% Social Sciences, General
Expenses: 2014-2015: $9,918 in state, $30,888 out of state; room/board: $11,442
Financial aid: (541) 346-3221; 46% of undergrads determined to have financial need; average aid package $10,046

University of Portland

Portland OR
(888) 627-5601
U.S. News ranking: Reg. U. (W), No. 7
Website: www.up.edu
Admissions email: admission@up.edu
Private; founded 1901
Affiliation: Roman Catholic
Freshman admissions: more selective; 2014-2015: 11,099 applied, 6,986 accepted. Either SAT or ACT required. SAT 25/75 percentile: 1080-1310. High school rank: 35% in top tenth, 73% in top quarter, 94% in top half
Early decision deadline: N/A, notification date: N/A
Early action deadline: N/A, notification date: N/A
Application deadline (fall): 2/1
Undergraduate student body: 3,609 full time, 71 part time; 42% male, 58% female; 0% American Indian, 10% Asian, 1% black, 11% Hispanic, 9% multiracial, 2% Pacific Islander, 62% white, 3% international; 32% from in state; 57% live on campus; 0% of students in fraternities, 0% in sororities
Most popular majors: 11% Biological and Biomedical Sciences, 17% Business, Management, Marketing, and Related Support Services, 12% Engineering, 18% Health Professions and Related Programs, 7% Social Sciences
Expenses: 2015-2016: $40,250; room/board: $13,666
Financial aid: (503) 943-7311; 62% of undergrads determined to have financial need; average aid package $28,729

Warner Pacific College

Portland OR
(503) 517-1020
U.S. News ranking: Reg. Coll. (W), No. 10
Website: www.warnerpacific.edu
Admissions email: admissions@warnerpacific.edu
Private; founded 1937
Affiliation: Church of God
Freshman admissions: less selective; 2014-2015: 476 applied, 299 accepted. Either SAT or ACT required. SAT 25/75 percentile: 815-1020. High school rank: 14% in top tenth, 18% in top quarter, 62% in top half
Early decision deadline: N/A, notification date: N/A
Early action deadline: N/A, notification date: N/A
Application deadline (fall): rolling
Undergraduate student body: 522 full time, 30 part time; 44% male, 56% female; 1% American Indian, 4% Asian, 10% black, 17% Hispanic, 5% multiracial, 2% Pacific Islander, 54% white, 1% international; 68% from in state; 44% live on campus; 0% of students in fraternities, 0% in sororities
Most popular majors: 11% Biological and Biomedical Sciences, 26% Business, Management, Marketing, and Related Support Services, 14% Education, 12% Family and Consumer Sciences/Human Sciences, 8% Mechanic and Repair Technologies/Technicians
Expenses: 2015-2016: $21,460; room/board: $8,560
Financial aid: (503) 517-1017; 82% of undergrads determined to have financial need; average aid package $17,590

Western Oregon University

Monmouth OR
(503) 838-8211
U.S. News ranking: Reg. U. (W), No. 77
Website: www.wou.edu
Admissions email: wolfgram@wou.edu
Public; founded 1856
Freshman admissions: selective; 2014-2015: 2,887 applied, 2,562 accepted. Either SAT or ACT required. SAT 25/75 percentile: 860-1180. High school rank: 11% in top tenth, 35% in top quarter, 74% in top half
Early decision deadline: N/A, notification date: N/A
Early action deadline: N/A, notification date: N/A
Application deadline (fall): rolling
Undergraduate student body: 4,195 full time, 735 part time; 42% male, 58% female; 2% American Indian, 4% Asian, 4% black, 8% Hispanic, 0% multiracial, 3% Pacific Islander, 68% white, 6% international; 79% from in state; 24% live on campus; 1% of students in fraternities, 1% in sororities
Most popular majors: 10% Business/Commerce, General, 14% Criminal Justice/Law Enforcement Administration, 13% Education, General, 12% Health and Wellness, General, 11% Psychology, General
Expenses: 2015-2016: $8,796 in state, $22,056 out of state; room/board: $9,638
Financial aid: (503) 838-8475; 82% of undergrads determined to have financial need; average aid package $9,853

Willamette University

Salem OR
(877) 542-2787
U.S. News ranking: Nat. Lib. Arts, No. 67
Website: www.willamette.edu
Admissions email: LIBARTS@willamette.edu
Private; founded 1842
Affiliation: United Methodist
Freshman admissions: more selective; 2014-2015: 5,729 applied, 4,658 accepted. Either SAT or ACT required. SAT 25/75 percentile: 1080-1320. High school rank: 40% in top tenth, 72% in top quarter, 96% in top half
Early decision deadline: N/A, notification date: N/A
Early action deadline: 12/1, notification date: 1/15
Application deadline (fall): 2/1
Undergraduate student body: 2,042 full time, 333 part time; 44% male, 56% female; 1% American Indian, 8% Asian, 2% black, 11% Hispanic, 9% multiracial, 0% Pacific Islander, 62% white, 2% international; 27% from in state; 64% live on campus; 26% of students in fraternities, 25% in sororities
Most popular majors: 10% Area, Ethnic, Cultural, Gender, and Group Studies, 17% Biological and Biomedical Sciences, 9% Physical Sciences, 25% Social Sciences, 14% Visual and Performing Arts
Expenses: 2015-2016: $45,616; room/board: $11,200
Financial aid: (503) 370-6273; 62% of undergrads determined to have financial need; average aid package $33,934

PENNSYLVANIA

Albright College

Reading PA
(800) 252-1856
U.S. News ranking: Nat. Lib. Arts, second tier
Website: www.albright.edu
Admissions email: admission@alb.edu
Private; founded 1856
Affiliation: United Methodist
Freshman admissions: selective; 2014-2015: 7,604 applied, 3,807 accepted. Neither SAT nor ACT required. SAT 25/75 percentile: 960-1150. High school rank: 23% in top tenth, 49% in top quarter, 78% in top half
Early decision deadline: N/A, notification date: N/A
Early action deadline: N/A, notification date: N/A
Application deadline (fall): rolling
Undergraduate student body: 2,330 full time, 30 part time; 41% male, 59% female; 1% American Indian, 4% Asian, 19% black, 10% Hispanic, 1% multiracial, 0% Pacific Islander, 60% white, 3% international; 60% from in state; 72% live on campus; 6% of students in fraternities, 11% in sororities
Most popular majors: 8% Biological and Biomedical Sciences, 14% Business, Management, Marketing, and Related Support Services, 10% Psychology, 20% Social Sciences, 13% Visual and Performing Arts
Expenses: 2015-2016: $39,850; room/board: $10,770
Financial aid: (610) 921-7515; 90% of undergrads determined to have financial need; average aid package $32,847

Allegheny College

Meadville PA
(800) 521-5293
U.S. News ranking: Nat. Lib. Arts, No. 72
Website: www.allegheny.edu
Admissions email: admissions@allegheny.edu
Private; founded 1815
Affiliation: United Methodist
Freshman admissions: more selective; 2014-2015: 3,857 applied, 2,768 accepted. Either SAT or ACT required. SAT 25/75 percentile: 1050-1270. High school rank: 43% in top tenth, 73% in top quarter, 95% in top half
Early decision deadline: 11/1, notification date: 12/15
Early action deadline: N/A, notification date: N/A
Application deadline (fall): 2/15
Undergraduate student body: 1,979 full time, 44 part time; 45% male, 55% female; 0% American Indian, 2% Asian, 5% black, 6% Hispanic, 4% multiracial, 0% Pacific Islander, 79% white, 2%

international; 54% from in state; 91% live on campus; 27% of students in fraternities, 30% in sororities
Most popular majors: 12% Biology/ Biological Sciences, General, 9% Economics, General, 10% English Language and Literature, General, 8% Political Science and Government, General, 16% Psychology, General
Expenses: 2015-2016: $42,470; room/board: $10,740
Financial aid: (800) 835-7780; 74% of undergrads determined to have financial need; average aid package $33,833

Alvernia University

Reading PA
(610) 796-8220
U.S. News ranking: Reg. U. (N), No. 109
Website: www.alvernia.edu
Admissions email: admissions@ alvernia.edu
Private; founded 1958
Affiliation: Roman Catholic
Freshman admissions: less selective; 2014-2015: 1,747 applied, 1,305 accepted. Either SAT or ACT required. SAT 25/75 percentile: 870-1070. High school rank: 11% in top tenth, 32% in top quarter, 67% in top half
Early decision deadline: N/A, notification date: N/A
Early action deadline: N/A, notification date: N/A
Application deadline (fall): rolling
Undergraduate student body: 1,798 full time, 644 part time; 26% male, 74% female; 0% American Indian, 1% Asian, 14% black, 8% Hispanic, 1% multiracial, 0% Pacific Islander, 70% white, 0% international; 76% from in state; 59% live on campus; 0% of students in fraternities, 0% in sororities
Most popular majors: 17% Business, Management, Marketing, and Related Support Services, 6% Education, 38% Health Professions and Related Programs, 12% Homeland Security, Law Enforcement, Firefighting and Related Protective Services, 6% Psychology
Expenses: 2015-2016: $31,100; room/board: $10,820
Financial aid: (610) 796-8356; 88% of undergrads determined to have financial need; average aid package $19,156

Arcadia University

Glenside PA
(215) 572-2910
U.S. News ranking: Reg. U. (N), No. 41
Website: www.arcadia.edu
Admissions email: admiss@ arcadia.edu
Private; founded 1853
Freshman admissions: selective; 2014-2015: 9,634 applied, 5,665 accepted. Either SAT or ACT required. SAT 25/75 percentile: 1000-1200. High school rank: 28% in top tenth, 60% in top quarter, 88% in top half
Early decision deadline: N/A, notification date: N/A
Early action deadline: N/A, notification date: N/A
Application deadline (fall): rolling
Undergraduate student body: 2,367 full time, 227 part time; 31% male, 69% female; 0% American Indian, 5% Asian, 9% black, 7% Hispanic, 4% multiracial, 0% Pacific Islander, 69% white, 3% international; 61% from in state; 54% live on campus; 0% of students in fraternities, 0% in sororities
Most popular majors: Information not available
Expenses: 2015-2016: $39,560; room/board: $13,200
Financial aid: (215) 572-2980; 76% of undergrads determined to have financial need; average aid package $28,791

Art Institute of Pittsburgh[1]

Pittsburgh PA
(800) 275-2470
U.S. News ranking: Arts, unranked
Website: www.artinstitutes.edu/ pittsburgh/Admissions
Admissions email: aip@aii.edu
For-profit
Application deadline (fall): N/A
Undergraduate student body: N/A full time, N/A part time
Expenses: 2014-2015: $17,632; room/board: $9,450
Financial aid: N/A

Bloomsburg University of Pennsylvania

Bloomsburg PA
(570) 389-4316
U.S. News ranking: Reg. U. (N), No. 104
Website: www.bloomu.edu
Admissions email: buadmiss@ bloomu.edu
Public; founded 1839
Freshman admissions: less selective; 2014-2015: 10,043 applied, 8,819 accepted. Either SAT or ACT required. SAT 25/75 percentile: 880-1070. High school rank: 9% in top tenth, 27% in top quarter, 64% in top half
Early decision deadline: N/A, notification date: N/A
Early action deadline: N/A, notification date: 5/1
Application deadline (fall): rolling
Undergraduate student body: 8,630 full time, 689 part time; 43% male, 57% female; 0% American Indian, 1% Asian, 8% black, 5% Hispanic, 2% multiracial, 0% Pacific Islander, 81% white, 1% international; 90% from in state; 43% live on campus; N/A of students in fraternities, N/A in sororities
Most popular majors: 15% Business Administration, Management and Operations, 6% Psychology, General, 7% Public Relations, Advertising, and Applied Communication, 6% Special Education and Teaching, 5% Teacher Education and Professional Development, Specific Levels and Methods
Expenses: 2015-2016: $9,326 in state, $19,916 out of state; room/ board: $8,480
Financial aid: (570) 389-4297; 65% of undergrads determined to have financial need; average aid package $8,750

Bryn Athyn College of the New Church[1]

Bryn Athyn PA
(267) 502-6000
U.S. News ranking: Nat. Lib. Arts, second tier
Website: www.brynathyn.edu
Admissions email: admissions@ brynathyn.edu
Private; founded 1877
Affiliation: General Church of the New Jerusalem
Application deadline (fall): rolling
Undergraduate student body: N/A full time, N/A part time
Expenses: 2014-2015: $18,610; room/board: $10,773
Financial aid: (267) 502-2630

Bryn Mawr College

Bryn Mawr PA
(610) 526-5152
U.S. News ranking: Nat. Lib. Arts, No. 25
Website: www.brynmawr.edu
Admissions email: admissions@ brynmawr.edu
Private; founded 1885
Freshman admissions: more selective; 2014-2015: 2,706 applied, 1,095 accepted. Neither SAT nor ACT required. SAT 25/75 percentile: 1200-1440. High school rank: 65% in top tenth, 88% in top quarter, 99% in top half
Early decision deadline: 11/15, notification date: 12/15
Early action deadline: N/A, notification date: N/A
Application deadline (fall): 1/15
Undergraduate student body: 1,291 full time, 17 part time; 0% male, 100% female; 0% American Indian, 12% Asian, 5% black, 9% Hispanic, 5% multiracial, 0% Pacific Islander, 36% white, 24% international; 19% from in state; 91% live on campus; 0% of students in fraternities, 0% in sororities
Most popular majors: 9% English Language and Literature, General, 10% Foreign Languages and Literatures, General, 12% Mathematics, General, 9% Psychology, General, 24% Social Sciences, General
Expenses: 2015-2016: $47,140; room/board: $14,850
Financial aid: (610) 526-5245; 53% of undergrads determined to have financial need; average aid package $42,369

Bucknell University

Lewisburg PA
(570) 577-3000
U.S. News ranking: Nat. Lib. Arts, No. 32
Website: www.bucknell.edu
Admissions email: admissions@ bucknell.edu
Private; founded 1846
Freshman admissions: more selective; 2014-2015: 7,864 applied, 2,416 accepted. Either SAT or ACT required. SAT 25/75 percentile: 1210-1400. High school rank: 68% in top tenth, 91% in top quarter, 99% in top half
Early decision deadline: 11/15, notification date: 12/15
Early action deadline: N/A, notification date: N/A
Application deadline (fall): 1/15
Undergraduate student body: 3,538 full time, 27 part time; 48% male, 52% female; 0% American Indian, 4% Asian, 3% black, 5% Hispanic, 3% multiracial, 0% Pacific Islander, 79% white, 5% international; 23% from in state; 86% live on campus; 41% of students in fraternities, 47% in sororities
Most popular majors: 8% Biology/ Biological Sciences, General, 10% Business Administration and Management, General, 8% Economics, General, 6% Political Science and Government, General, 6% Psychology, General
Expenses: 2015-2016: $50,152; room/board: $12,216
Financial aid: (570) 577-1331; 42% of undergrads determined to have financial need; average aid package $30,000

Cabrini College

Radnor PA
(610) 902-8552
U.S. News ranking: Reg. U. (N), second tier
Website: www.cabrini.edu
Admissions email: admit@cabrini.edu
Private; founded 1957
Affiliation: Roman Catholic
Freshman admissions: least selective; 2014-2015: 2,257 applied, 1,699 accepted. Neither SAT nor ACT required. SAT 25/75 percentile: 790-990. High school rank: 5% in top tenth, 17% in top quarter, 45% in top half
Early decision deadline: N/A, notification date: N/A
Early action deadline: N/A, notification date: N/A
Application deadline (fall): rolling
Undergraduate student body: 1,283 full time, 123 part time; 38% male, 62% female; 0% American Indian, 1% Asian, 16% black, 6% Hispanic, 3% multiracial, 0% Pacific Islander, 68% white, 0% international; 67% from in state; 66% live on campus; N/A of students in fraternities, N/A in sororities
Most popular majors: 22% Business, Management, Marketing, and Related Support Services, Other, 14% Education, General, 9% Psychology, General, 9% Social Sciences, General, 10% Speech Communication and Rhetoric
Expenses: 2015-2016: $29,842; room/board: $12,226
Financial aid: (610) 902-8420; 84% of undergrads determined to have financial need; average aid package $24,495

Cairn University

Langhorne PA
(215) 702-4235
U.S. News ranking: Reg. U. (N), No. 106
Website: cairn.edu/
Admissions email: admissions@cairn.edu
Private; founded 1913
Affiliation: Evangelical
Freshman admissions: less selective; 2014-2015: 318 applied, 311 accepted. Either SAT or ACT required. SAT 25/75 percentile: 870-1110. High school rank: 14% in top tenth, 31% in top quarter, 60% in top half
Early decision deadline: N/A, notification date: N/A
Early action deadline: N/A, notification date: N/A
Application deadline (fall): rolling
Undergraduate student body: 771 full time, 46 part time; 46% male, 54% female; 0% American Indian, 3% Asian, 12% black, 7% Hispanic, 2% multiracial, 0% Pacific Islander, 73% white, 2% international; 57% from in state; 60% live on campus; 0% of students in fraternities, 0% in sororities
Most popular majors: 6% Business, Management, Marketing, and Related Support Services, 15% Education, 64% Philosophy and Religious Studies, 9% Public Administration and Social Service Professions, 3% Visual and Performing Arts
Expenses: 2015-2016: $23,920; room/board: $9,350
Financial aid: (215) 702-4246; 82% of undergrads determined to have financial need; average aid package $18,367

California University of Pennsylvania

California PA
(724) 938-4404
U.S. News ranking: Reg. U. (N), second tier
Website: www.calu.edu/
Admissions email: inquiry@calu.edu
Public
Freshman admissions: less selective; 2014-2015: 3,714 applied, 2,752 accepted. SAT required. SAT 25/75 percentile: 840-1030. High school rank: 6% in top tenth, 24% in top quarter, 58% in top half
Early decision deadline: N/A, notification date: N/A
Early action deadline: N/A, notification date: N/A
Application deadline (fall): 8/22
Undergraduate student body: 5,330 full time, 746 part time; 48% male, 52% female; 0% American Indian, 1% Asian, 11% black, 3% Hispanic, 3% multiracial, 0% Pacific Islander, 78% white, 1% international; 90% from in state; 33% live on campus; 8% of students in fraternities, 6% in sororities
Most popular majors: 13% Business, Management, Marketing, and Related Support Services, 9% Education, 11% Health Professions and Related Programs, 3% Homeland Security, Law Enforcement, Firefighting and Related Protective Services, 12% Parks, Recreation, Leisure, and Fitness Studies
Expenses: 2014-2015: $9,556 in state, $12,966 out of state; room/ board: $10,086
Financial aid: (724) 938-4415

Carlow University[1]

Pittsburgh PA
(412) 578-6059
U.S. News ranking: Reg. U. (N), second tier
Website: www.carlow.edu
Admissions email: admissions@carlow.edu
Private
Application deadline (fall): N/A
Undergraduate student body: N/A full time, N/A part time
Expenses: 2014-2015: $26,178; room/board: $10,314
Financial aid: (412) 578-6058

More at usnews.com/college

Carnegie Mellon University

Pittsburgh PA
(412) 268-2082
U.S. News ranking: Nat. U., No. 23
Website: www.cmu.edu
Admissions email: undergraduate-admissions@andrew.cmu.edu
Private; founded 1900
Freshman admissions: most selective; 2014-2015: 19,812 applied, 4,874 accepted. Either SAT or ACT required. SAT 25/75 percentile: 1340-1540. High school rank: 79% in top tenth, 94% in top quarter, 99% in top half
Early decision deadline: 11/1, notification date: 12/15
Early action deadline: N/A, notification date: N/A
Application deadline (fall): 1/1
Undergraduate student body: 6,104 full time, 205 part time; 56% male, 44% female; 0% American Indian, 25% Asian, 5% black, 7% Hispanic, 4% multiracial, 0% Pacific Islander, 33% white, 21% international; 16% from in state; 61% live on campus; 21% of students in fraternities, 20% in sororities
Most popular majors: 5% Chemical Engineering, 12% Computer Science, 9% Electrical and Electronics Engineering, 8% Mechanical Engineering, 7% Systems Science and Theory
Expenses: 2015-2016: $50,410; room/board: $12,830
Financial aid: (412) 268-8186; 46% of undergrads determined to have financial need; average aid package $36,001

Cedar Crest College

Allentown PA
(800) 360-1222
U.S. News ranking: Reg. Coll. (N), No. 14
Website: www.cedarcrest.edu
Admissions email: cccadmis@cedarcrest.edu
Private; founded 1867
Freshman admissions: less selective; 2014-2015: 1,246 applied, 652 accepted. Either SAT or ACT required. SAT 25/75 percentile: 888-1120. High school rank: 22% in top tenth, 44% in top quarter, 86% in top half
Early decision deadline: N/A, notification date: N/A
Early action deadline: N/A, notification date: N/A
Application deadline (fall): rolling
Undergraduate student body: 719 full time, 623 part time; 7% male, 93% female; 0% American Indian, 3% Asian, 10% black, 13% Hispanic, 1% multiracial, 0% Pacific Islander, 67% white, 2% international; 87% from in state; 25% live on campus; N/A of students in fraternities, N/A in sororities
Most popular majors: 8% Biological and Biomedical Sciences, 8% Business, Management, Marketing, and Related Support Services, 43% Health Professions and Related Programs, 9% Psychology, 8% Public Administration and Social Service Professions
Expenses: 2015-2016: $35,600; room/board: $10,765
Financial aid: (610) 740-3785; 92% of undergrads determined to have financial need; average aid package $26,519

Central Penn College[1]

Summerdale PA
(800) 759-2727
U.S. News ranking: Reg. Coll. (N), unranked
Website: www.centralpenn.edu
Admissions email: admissions@centralpenn.edu
For-profit
Application deadline (fall): N/A
Undergraduate student body: N/A full time, N/A part time
Expenses: 2014-2015: $16,659; room/board: $6,675
Financial aid: (800) 759-2727

Chatham University

Pittsburgh PA
(800) 837-1290
U.S. News ranking: Reg. U. (N), No. 53
Website: www.chatham.edu
Admissions email: admissions@chatham.edu
Private; founded 1869
Freshman admissions: selective; 2014-2015: 619 applied, 330 accepted. Neither SAT nor ACT required. SAT 25/75 percentile: 915-1160. High school rank: 26% in top tenth, 54% in top quarter, 85% in top half
Early decision deadline: N/A, notification date: N/A
Early action deadline: N/A, notification date: N/A
Application deadline (fall): 8/1
Undergraduate student body: 562 full time, 370 part time; 11% male, 89% female; 0% American Indian, 3% Asian, 12% black, 4% Hispanic, 3% multiracial, N/A Pacific Islander, 69% white, 5% international; 81% from in state; 44% live on campus; N/A of students in fraternities, N/A in sororities
Most popular majors: 11% Biological and Biomedical Sciences, 6% Business, Management, Marketing, and Related Support Services, 25% Health Professions and Related Programs, 12% Psychology, 11% Visual and Performing Arts
Expenses: 2015-2016: $34,440; room/board: $10,720
Financial aid: (412) 365-1777; 81% of undergrads determined to have financial need; average aid package $23,512

Chestnut Hill College

Philadelphia PA
(215) 248-7001
U.S. News ranking: Reg. U. (N), No. 131
Website: www.chc.edu
Admissions email: chcapply@chc.edu
Private; founded 1924
Affiliation: Roman Catholic
Freshman admissions: selective; 2014-2015: 1,916 applied, 1,179 accepted. Either SAT or ACT required. SAT 25/75 percentile: 850-1080. High school rank: 8% in top tenth, 28% in top quarter, 59% in top half
Early decision deadline: N/A, notification date: N/A
Early action deadline: N/A, notification date: N/A
Application deadline (fall): rolling
Undergraduate student body: 1,180 full time, 311 part time; 33% male, 67% female; 0% American Indian, 2% Asian, 36% black, 9% Hispanic, 3% multiracial, 0% Pacific Islander, 41% white, 2% international; 76% from in state; 38% live on campus; 0% of students in fraternities, 0% in sororities
Most popular majors: 23% Business, Management, Marketing, and Related Support Services, 11% Education, 13% Homeland Security, Law Enforcement, Firefighting and Related Protective Services, 10% Psychology, 20% Public Administration and Social Service Professions
Expenses: 2015-2016: $33,130; room/board: $10,200
Financial aid: (215) 248-7182; 87% of undergrads determined to have financial need; average aid package $21,138

Cheyney University of Pennsylvania[1]

Cheyney PA
(610) 399-2275
U.S. News ranking: Reg. U. (N), second tier
Website: www.cheyney.edu
Admissions email: abrown@cheyney.edu
Public; founded 1837
Application deadline (fall): rolling
Undergraduate student body: N/A full time, N/A part time
Expenses: 2014-2015: $8,842 in state, $13,148 out of state; room/board: $11,270
Financial aid: (610) 399-2302

Clarion University of Pennsylvania

Clarion PA
(814) 393-2306
U.S. News ranking: Reg. U. (N), second tier
Website: www.clarion.edu
Admissions email: admissions@clarion.edu
Public; founded 1867
Freshman admissions: less selective; 2014-2015: 2,208 applied, 2,047 accepted. Either SAT or ACT required. SAT 25/75 percentile: 830-1030. High school rank: 9% in top tenth, 27% in top quarter, 59% in top half
Early decision deadline: N/A, notification date: N/A
Early action deadline: N/A, notification date: N/A
Application deadline (fall): rolling
Undergraduate student body: 4,018 full time, 893 part time; 37% male, 63% female; 0% American Indian, 1% Asian, 7% black, 2% Hispanic, 3% multiracial, 0% Pacific Islander, 84% white, 1% international; 93% from in state; 41% live on campus; 0% of students in fraternities, 1% in sororities
Most popular majors: 14% Business, Management, Marketing, and Related Support Services, 8% Communication, Journalism, and Related Programs, 10% Education, 23% Health Professions and Related Programs, 12% Liberal Arts and Sciences, General Studies and Humanities
Expenses: 2014-2015: $9,788 in state, $13,198 out of state; room/board: $8,294
Financial aid: (814) 393-2315; 78% of undergrads determined to have financial need; average aid package $9,440

Curtis Institute of Music[1]

Philadelphia PA
(215) 717-3117
U.S. News ranking: Arts, unranked
Website: www.curtis.edu
Admissions email: admissions@curtis.edu
Private; founded 1924
Application deadline (fall): 12/12
Undergraduate student body: N/A full time, N/A part time
Expenses: 2014-2015: $2,475; room/board: $14,363
Financial aid: (215) 717-3165

Delaware Valley University

Doylestown PA
(215) 489-2211
U.S. News ranking: Reg. Coll. (N), No. 18
Website: www.delval.edu
Admissions email: admitme@delval.edu
Private; founded 1896
Freshman admissions: less selective; 2014-2015: 1,888 applied, 1,430 accepted. Either SAT or ACT required. SAT 25/75 percentile: 870-1110. High school rank: 11% in top tenth, 29% in top quarter, 62% in top half
Early decision deadline: N/A, notification date: N/A
Early action deadline: N/A, notification date: N/A
Application deadline (fall): rolling
Undergraduate student body: 1,682 full time, 178 part time; 38% male, 62% female; 1% American Indian, 1% Asian, 8% black, 8% Hispanic, 1% multiracial, 0% Pacific Islander, 78% white, 1% international; 59% from in state; 57% live on campus; 2% of students in fraternities, 3% in sororities
Most popular majors: 46% Agriculture, Agriculture Operations, and Related Sciences, 16% Biological and Biomedical Sciences, 16% Business, Management, Marketing, and Related Support Services, 6% Homeland Security, Law Enforcement, Firefighting and Related Protective Services, 10% Natural Resources and Conservation
Expenses: 2015-2016: $35,256; room/board: $12,618
Financial aid: (215) 489-2272; 80% of undergrads determined to have financial need; average aid package $22,896

DeSales University

Center Valley PA
(610) 282-4443
U.S. News ranking: Reg. U. (N), No. 71
Website: www.desales.edu
Admissions email: admiss@desales.edu
Private; founded 1964
Affiliation: Roman Catholic
Freshman admissions: selective; 2014-2015: 2,658 applied, 2,117 accepted. Either SAT or ACT required. SAT 25/75 percentile: 890-1150. High school rank: 13% in top tenth, 44% in top quarter, 71% in top half
Early decision deadline: N/A, notification date: N/A
Early action deadline: N/A, notification date: N/A
Application deadline (fall): 8/1
Undergraduate student body: 1,784 full time, 597 part time; 40% male, 60% female; 1% American Indian, 3% Asian, 4% black, 10% Hispanic, 0% multiracial, 0% Pacific Islander, 76% white, 0% international; 77% from in state; 67% live on campus; 0% of students in fraternities, 0% in sororities
Most popular majors: 23% Business, Management, Marketing, and Related Support Services, 23% Health Professions and Related Programs, 8% Parks, Recreation, Leisure, and Fitness Studies, 9% Psychology, 11% Visual and Performing Arts
Expenses: 2015-2016: $33,350; room/board: $12,050
Financial aid: (610) 282-1100; 80% of undergrads determined to have financial need; average aid package $23,059

Dickinson College

Carlisle PA
(800) 644-1773
U.S. News ranking: Nat. Lib. Arts, No. 40
Website: www.dickinson.edu
Admissions email: admissions@dickinson.edu
Private; founded 1783
Freshman admissions: more selective; 2014-2015: 5,700 applied, 2,742 accepted. Neither SAT nor ACT required. SAT 25/75 percentile: 1190-1370. High school rank: 46% in top tenth, 80% in top quarter, 97% in top half
Early decision deadline: 11/15, notification date: 12/15
Early action deadline: 12/1, notification date: 2/1
Application deadline (fall): 2/1
Undergraduate student body: 2,332 full time, 32 part time; 42% male, 58% female; 0% American Indian, 2% Asian, 4% black, 6% Hispanic, 3% multiracial, 0% Pacific Islander, 74% white, 8% international; 23% from in state; 94% live on campus; 14% of students in fraternities, 18% in sororities
Most popular majors: 7% Biology/Biological Sciences, General, 6% English Language and Literature, General, 11% International Business/Trade/Commerce, 10% Political Science and Government, General, 6% Psychology, General
Expenses: 2015-2016: $49,464; room/board: $12,362
Financial aid: (717) 245-1308; 55% of undergrads determined to have financial need; average aid package $38,290

Drexel University

Philadelphia PA
(800) 237-3935
U.S. News ranking: Nat. U., No. 99
Website: www.drexel.edu
Admissions email: enroll@drexel.edu
Private; founded 1891
Freshman admissions: more selective; 2014-2015: 47,477 applied, 36,088 accepted. Either

SAT or ACT required. SAT 25/75 percentile: 1090-1300. High school rank: 29% in top tenth, 61% in top quarter, 90% in top half
Early decision deadline: N/A, notification date: N/A
Early action deadline: 11/1, notification date: 12/15
Application deadline (fall): 1/15
Undergraduate student body: 11,975 full time, 2,528 part time; 52% male, 48% female; 0% American Indian, 13% Asian, 7% black, 6% Hispanic, 3% multiracial, 1% Pacific Islander, 55% white, 13% international; 47% from in state; 26% live on campus; 12% of students in fraternities, 11% in sororities
Most popular majors: 19% Business, Management, Marketing, and Related Support Services, 6% Computer and Information Sciences and Support Services, 18% Engineering, 24% Health Professions and Related Programs, 11% Visual and Performing Arts
Expenses: 2015-2016: $48,791; room/board: $14,367
Financial aid: (215) 895-2537; 57% of undergrads determined to have financial need; average aid package $25,190

Duquesne University
Pittsburgh PA
(412) 396-6222
U.S. News ranking: Nat. U., No. 115
Website: www.duq.edu
Admissions email: admissions@duq.edu
Private; founded 1878
Affiliation: Roman Catholic
Freshman admissions: selective; 2014-2015: 6,534 applied, 4,774 accepted. Neither SAT nor ACT required. SAT 25/75 percentile: 1040-1230. High school rank: 30% in top tenth, 58% in top quarter, 89% in top half
Early decision deadline: 11/1, notification date: 11/15
Early action deadline: 12/1, notification date: 1/15
Application deadline (fall): 7/1
Undergraduate student body: 5,747 full time, 248 part time; 39% male, 61% female; 0% American Indian, 2% Asian, 4% black, 3% Hispanic, 2% multiracial, 0% Pacific Islander, 83% white, 4% international; 74% from in state; 59% live on campus; 16% of students in fraternities, 24% in sororities
Most popular majors: 8% Biological and Biomedical Sciences, 24% Business, Management, Marketing, and Related Support Services, 7% Communication, Journalism, and Related Programs, 25% Health Professions and Related Programs, 8% Social Sciences
Expenses: 2015-2016: $33,778; room/board: $11,418
Financial aid: (412) 396-6607; 68% of undergrads determined to have financial need; average aid package $24,480

Eastern University
St. Davids PA
(610) 341-5967
U.S. News ranking: Reg. U. (N), No. 83
Website: www.eastern.edu
Admissions email: ugadm@eastern.edu
Private; founded 1952
Affiliation: American Baptist
Freshman admissions: selective; 2014-2015: 1,711 applied, 1,156 accepted. Either SAT or ACT required. SAT 25/75 percentile: 910-1150. High school rank: 20% in top tenth, 51% in top quarter, 79% in top half
Early decision deadline: N/A, notification date: N/A
Early action deadline: N/A, notification date: N/A
Application deadline (fall): rolling
Undergraduate student body: 1,992 full time, 410 part time; 29% male, 71% female; 1% American Indian, 2% Asian, 22% black, 16% Hispanic, 0% multiracial, 0% Pacific Islander, 51% white, 2% international; 56% from in state; 75% live on campus; N/A of students in fraternities, N/A in sororities
Most popular majors: 8% Business Administration and Management, General, 18% Early Childhood Education and Teaching, 6% Nursing Practice, 6% Organizational Leadership, 7% Psychology, General
Expenses: 2015-2016: $30,590; room/board: $10,188
Financial aid: (610) 341-5842; 93% of undergrads determined to have financial need; average aid package $18,517

East Stroudsburg University of Pennsylvania[1]
East Stroudsburg PA
(570) 422-3542
U.S. News ranking: Reg. U. (N), No. 131
Website: www.esu.edu
Admissions email: undergrads@po-box.esu.edu
Public; founded 1893
Application deadline (fall): 4/1
Undergraduate student body: N/A full time, N/A part time
Expenses: 2014-2015: $9,376 in state, $19,606 out of state; room/board: $7,980
Financial aid: (570) 422-2800

Edinboro University of Pennsylvania
Edinboro PA
(888) 846-2676
U.S. News ranking: Reg. U. (N), second tier
Website: www.edinboro.edu
Admissions email: eup_admissions@edinboro.edu
Public; founded 1857
Freshman admissions: less selective; 2014-2015: 3,143 applied, 3,121 accepted. Either SAT or ACT required. SAT 25/75 percentile: 820-1050. High school rank: 7% in top tenth, 24% in top quarter, 56% in top half
Early decision deadline: N/A, notification date: N/A
Early action deadline: N/A, notification date: N/A
Application deadline (fall): rolling
Undergraduate student body: 5,086 full time, 499 part time; 42% male, 58% female; 0% American Indian, 1% Asian, 9% black, 3% Hispanic, 3% multiracial, 0% Pacific Islander, 82% white, 2% international; 88% from in state; 63% live on campus; 1% of students in fraternities, 1% in sororities
Most popular majors: 8% Business, Management, Marketing, and Related Support Services, 8% Communication, Journalism, and Related Programs, 9% Education, 11% Health Professions and Related Programs, 16% Visual and Performing Arts
Expenses: 2015-2016: $9,256 in state, $12,666 out of state; room/board: $8,612
Financial aid: (814) 732-5555

Elizabethtown College
Elizabethtown PA
(717) 361-1400
U.S. News ranking: Reg. Coll. (N), No. 4
Website: www.etown.edu
Admissions email: admissions@etown.edu
Private; founded 1899
Affiliation: Brethren
Freshman admissions: selective; 2014-2015: 3,468 applied, 2,456 accepted. Either SAT or ACT required. SAT 25/75 percentile: 1020-1240. High school rank: 31% in top tenth, 64% in top quarter, 92% in top half
Early decision deadline: N/A, notification date: N/A
Early action deadline: N/A, notification date: N/A
Application deadline (fall): rolling
Undergraduate student body: 1,749 full time, 39 part time; 37% male, 63% female; 0% American Indian, 2% Asian, 3% black, 4% Hispanic, 2% multiracial, 0% Pacific Islander, 86% white, 4% international; 67% from in state; 87% live on campus; 0% of students in fraternities, 0% in sororities
Most popular majors: 11% Biological and Biomedical Sciences, 13% Business, Management, Marketing, and Related Support Services, 9% Education, 10% Health Professions and Related Programs, 10% Social Sciences
Expenses: 2015-2016: $41,710; room/board: $10,140
Financial aid: (717) 361-1404; 75% of undergrads determined to have financial need; average aid package $27,722

Franklin and Marshall College
Lancaster PA
(717) 291-3953
U.S. News ranking: Nat. Lib. Arts, No. 40
Website: www.fandm.edu
Admissions email: admission@fandm.edu
Private; founded 1787
Freshman admissions: more selective; 2014-2015: 5,472 applied, 2,130 accepted. Neither SAT nor ACT required. SAT 25/75 percentile: 1220-1390. High school rank: 62% in top tenth, 88% in top quarter, 98% in top half
Early decision deadline: 11/15, notification date: 12/15
Early action deadline: N/A, notification date: N/A
Application deadline (fall): 1/15
Undergraduate student body: 2,174 full time, 35 part time; 49% male, 51% female; 0% American Indian, 5% Asian, 6% black, 8% Hispanic, 2% multiracial, 0% Pacific Islander, 60% white, 14% international; 24% from in state; 97% live on campus; 24% of students in fraternities, 36% in sororities
Most popular majors: 5% Biology/Biological Sciences, General, 10% Business/Commerce, General, 7% Economics, General, 11% Political Science and Government, General, 5% Sociology
Expenses: 2015-2016: $50,400; room/board: $12,770
Financial aid: (717) 291-3991; 52% of undergrads determined to have financial need; average aid package $43,852

Gannon University
Erie PA
(814) 871-7240
U.S. News ranking: Reg. U. (N), No. 58
Website: www.gannon.edu
Admissions email: admissions@gannon.edu
Private; founded 1925
Affiliation: Roman Catholic
Freshman admissions: selective; 2014-2015: 4,097 applied, 3,182 accepted. Either SAT or ACT required. SAT 25/75 percentile: 930-1130. High school rank: 17% in top tenth, 45% in top quarter, 78% in top half
Early decision deadline: N/A, notification date: N/A
Early action deadline: N/A, notification date: N/A
Application deadline (fall): rolling
Undergraduate student body: 2,593 full time, 612 part time; 43% male, 57% female; 0% American Indian, 2% Asian, 5% black, 3% Hispanic, 2% multiracial, 0% Pacific Islander, 79% white, 8% international; 73% from in state; 43% live on campus; 18% of students in fraternities, 19% in sororities
Most popular majors: 9% Biological and Biomedical Sciences, 13% Business, Management, Marketing, and Related Support Services, 33% Health Professions and Related Programs, 6% Homeland Security, Law Enforcement, Firefighting and Related Protective Services, 10% Parks, Recreation, Leisure, and Fitness Studies
Expenses: 2015-2016: $29,258; room/board: $11,710
Financial aid: (814) 871-7337; 79% of undergrads determined to have financial need; average aid package $23,719

Geneva College
Beaver Falls PA
(724) 847-6500
U.S. News ranking: Reg. Coll. (N), No. 16
Website: www.geneva.edu
Admissions email: admissions@geneva.edu
Private; founded 1848
Affiliation: Reformed Presbyterian Church of North America
Freshman admissions: selective; 2014-2015: 1,537 applied, 1,091 accepted. Either SAT or ACT required. SAT 25/75 percentile: 920-1190. High school rank: 21% in top tenth, 51% in top quarter, 75% in top half
Early decision deadline: N/A, notification date: N/A
Early action deadline: N/A, notification date: N/A
Application deadline (fall): rolling
Undergraduate student body: 1,350 full time, 67 part time; 50% male, 50% female; 0% American Indian, 0% Asian, 9% black, 1% Hispanic, 2% multiracial, 0% Pacific Islander, 86% white, 1% international; 71% from in state; 72% live on campus; 0% of students in fraternities, 0% in sororities
Most popular majors: 16% Business, Management, Marketing, and Related Support Services, 9% Education, 13% Engineering, 7% Public Administration and Social Service Professions, 8% Theology and Religious Vocations
Expenses: 2015-2016: $25,450; room/board: $9,630
Financial aid: (724) 847-6530; 84% of undergrads determined to have financial need; average aid package $19,305

Gettysburg College
Gettysburg PA
(800) 431-0803
U.S. News ranking: Nat. Lib. Arts, No. 48
Website: www.gettysburg.edu
Admissions email: admiss@gettysburg.edu
Private; founded 1832
Affiliation: Lutheran
Freshman admissions: more selective; 2014-2015: 4,915 applied, 2,233 accepted. Either SAT or ACT required. SAT 25/75 percentile: 1210-1360. High school rank: 70% in top tenth, 88% in top quarter, 99% in top half
Early decision deadline: 11/15, notification date: 12/15
Early action deadline: N/A, notification date: N/A
Application deadline (fall): 1/15
Undergraduate student body: 2,429 full time, 22 part time; 48% male, 52% female; 0% American Indian, 2% Asian, 4% black, 5% Hispanic, 3% multiracial, 0% Pacific Islander, 80% white, 4% international; 27% from in state; 93% live on campus; 31% of students in fraternities, 31% in sororities
Most popular majors: 13% Biology/Biological Sciences, General, 8% Business/Commerce, General, 6% English Language and Literature, General, 7% History, General, 21% Social Sciences, General
Expenses: 2015-2016: $49,140; room/board: $11,730
Financial aid: (717) 337-6611; 61% of undergrads determined to have financial need; average aid package $37,087

Gratz College[1]
Melrose Park PA
(215) 635-7300
U.S. News ranking: Reg. U. (N), unranked
Website: www.gratzcollege.edu

More at usnews.com/college

Admissions email: admissions@gratz.edu
Private
Affiliation: Jewish
Application deadline (fall): N/A
Undergraduate student body: N/A full time, N/A part time
Expenses: N/A
Financial aid: (215) 635-7300

Grove City College

Grove City PA
(724) 458-2100
U.S. News ranking: Nat. Lib. Arts, No. 134
Website: www.gcc.edu
Admissions email: admissions@gcc.edu
Private; founded 1876
Affiliation: Presbyterian
Freshman admissions: more selective; 2014-2015: 1,492 applied, 1,306 accepted. Either SAT or ACT required. SAT 25/75 percentile: 1070-1334. High school rank: 45% in top tenth, 79% in top quarter, 93% in top half
Early decision deadline: 11/1, notification date: 12/15
Early action deadline: N/A, notification date: N/A
Application deadline (fall): 2/1
Undergraduate student body: 2,465 full time, 44 part time; 49% male, 51% female; 0% American Indian, 2% Asian, 1% black, 1% Hispanic, 2% multiracial, 0% Pacific Islander, 93% white, 1% international; 51% from in state; 95% live on campus; 17% of students in fraternities, 17% in sororities
Most popular majors: 7% General Literature, 6% Mechanical Engineering, 5% Molecular Biology, 6% Psychology, General, 7% Speech Communication and Rhetoric
Expenses: 2015-2016: $16,154; room/board: $8,802
Financial aid: (724) 458-3300; 43% of undergrads determined to have financial need; average aid package $6,777

Gwynedd Mercy University

Gwynedd Valley PA
(215) 681-5510
U.S. News ranking: Reg. U. (N), No. 131
Website: https://www.gmercyu.edu/
Admissions email: admissions@gmercyu.edu
Private; founded 1948
Affiliation: Roman Catholic
Freshman admissions: less selective; 2014-2015: 1,016 applied, 776 accepted. Either SAT or ACT required. SAT 25/75 percentile: 860-1060. High school rank: 8% in top tenth, 25% in top quarter, 59% in top half
Early decision deadline: N/A, notification date: N/A
Early action deadline: N/A, notification date: N/A
Application deadline (fall): 8/20
Undergraduate student body: 1,808 full time, 175 part time; 25% male, 75% female; 1% American Indian, 4% Asian, 24% black, 5% Hispanic, 0% multiracial, 0% Pacific Islander, 59% white, 0% international; 90% from in state; 21% live on campus; 0% of students in fraternities, 0% in sororities
Most popular majors: 33% Business, Management, Marketing, and Related Support Services, 10% Education, 42% Health Professions and Related Programs, 3% Homeland Security, Law Enforcement, Firefighting and Related Protective Services, 4% Psychology
Expenses: 2015-2016: $31,360; room/board: $11,010
Financial aid: (215) 641-5570; 73% of undergrads determined to have financial need; average aid package $21,574

Harrisburg University of Science and Technology

Harrisburg PA
(717) 901-5150
U.S. News ranking: Nat. Lib. Arts, second tier
Website: www.harrisburgu.edu
Admissions email: admissions@harrisburgu.edu
Private; founded 2001
Freshman admissions: less selective; 2014-2015: N/A applied, N/A accepted. Neither SAT nor ACT required. SAT 25/75 percentile: 830-1050. High school rank: N/A
Early decision deadline: N/A, notification date: N/A
Early action deadline: N/A, notification date: N/A
Application deadline (fall): rolling
Undergraduate student body: 283 full time, 30 part time; 57% male, 43% female; 1% American Indian, 5% Asian, 35% black, 9% Hispanic, 5% multiracial, 0% Pacific Islander, 42% white, 1% international
Most popular majors: 50% Computer and Information Sciences, General, 35% Natural Sciences
Expenses: 2015-2016: $23,900; room/board: $9,700
Financial aid: N/A; 94% of undergrads determined to have financial need; average aid package $19,000

Haverford College

Haverford PA
(610) 896-1350
U.S. News ranking: Nat. Lib. Arts, No. 12
Website: www.haverford.edu
Admissions email: admission@haverford.edu
Private; founded 1833
Freshman admissions: most selective; 2014-2015: 3,496 applied, 863 accepted. Either SAT or ACT required. SAT 25/75 percentile: 1330-1490. High school rank: 94% in top tenth, 98% in top quarter, 100% in top half
Early decision deadline: 11/15, notification date: 12/15
Early action deadline: N/A, notification date: N/A
Application deadline (fall): 1/15
Undergraduate student body: 1,189 full time, 5 part time; 47% male, 53% female; 0% American Indian, 9% Asian, 6% black, 9% Hispanic, 6% multiracial, 0% Pacific Islander, 64% white, 6% international; 12% from in state; 98% live on campus; 0% of students in fraternities, 0% in sororities
Most popular majors: 9% Biology/Biological Sciences, General, 10% Foreign Languages and Literatures, General, 11% Physical Sciences, 10% Psychology, General
Expenses: 2015-2016: $49,098; room/board: $14,888
Financial aid: (610) 896-1350; 51% of undergrads determined to have financial need; average aid package $42,851

Holy Family University

Philadelphia PA
(215) 637-3050
U.S. News ranking: Reg. U. (N), No. 125
Website: www.holyfamily.edu
Admissions email: admissions@holyfamily.edu
Private; founded 1954
Affiliation: Roman Catholic
Freshman admissions: less selective; 2014-2015: 1,092 applied, 800 accepted. Either SAT or ACT required. SAT 25/75 percentile: 830-1020. High school rank: 6% in top tenth, 28% in top quarter, 60% in top half
Early decision deadline: N/A, notification date: N/A
Early action deadline: N/A, notification date: N/A
Application deadline (fall): rolling
Undergraduate student body: 1,337 full time, 648 part time; 27% male, 73% female; 0% American Indian, 4% Asian, 8% black, 7% Hispanic, 0% multiracial, 0% Pacific Islander, 63% white, 0% international; 86% from in state; 13% live on campus; 0% of students in fraternities, 0% in sororities
Most popular majors: 18% Business, Management, Marketing, and Related Support Services, 11% Education, 38% Health Professions and Related Programs, 8% Homeland Security, Law Enforcement, Firefighting and Related Protective Services, 11% Psychology
Expenses: 2015-2016: $29,168; room/board: $13,576
Financial aid: (215) 637-5538; 88% of undergrads determined to have financial need; average aid package $20,394

Immaculata University

Immaculata PA
(877) 428-6329
U.S. News ranking: Nat. U., No. 161
Website: www.immaculata.edu
Admissions email: admiss@immaculata.edu
Private; founded 1920
Affiliation: Roman Catholic
Freshman admissions: less selective; 2014-2015: 1,729 applied, 1,313 accepted. Either SAT or ACT required. SAT 25/75 percentile: 870-1060. High school rank: N/A
Early decision deadline: N/A, notification date: N/A
Early action deadline: N/A, notification date: N/A
Application deadline (fall): rolling
Undergraduate student body: 1,107 full time, 1,031 part time; 25% male, 75% female; 0% American Indian, 2% Asian, 15% black, 5% Hispanic, 2% multiracial, 0% Pacific Islander, 73% white, 1% international; 74% from in state; 23% live on campus; 2% of students in fraternities, 6% in sororities
Most popular majors: 18% Business, Management, Marketing, and Related Support Services, 5% Education, 58% Health Professions and Related Programs, 3% Parks, Recreation, Leisure, and Fitness Studies, 5% Psychology
Expenses: 2015-2016: $33,280; room/board: $13,210
Financial aid: (610) 647-4400

Indiana University of Pennsylvania

Indiana PA
(800) 442-6830
U.S. News ranking: Nat. U., second tier
Website: www.iup.edu
Admissions email: admissions-inquiry@iup.edu
Public; founded 1875
Freshman admissions: less selective; 2014-2015: 8,754 applied, 8,293 accepted. Either SAT or ACT required. SAT 25/75 percentile: 860-1060. High school rank: 8% in top tenth, 26% in top quarter, 60% in top half
Early decision deadline: N/A, notification date: N/A
Early action deadline: N/A, notification date: N/A
Application deadline (fall): rolling
Undergraduate student body: 11,288 full time, 842 part time; 46% male, 54% female; 0% American Indian, 1% Asian, 11% black, 4% Hispanic, 3% multiracial, 0% Pacific Islander, 77% white, 3% international; 94% from in state; 32% live on campus; 7% of students in fraternities, 8% in sororities
Most popular majors: 24% Business, Management, Marketing, and Related Support Services, 7% Communication, Journalism, and Related Programs, 8% Health Professions and Related Programs, 17% Social Sciences, 6% Visual and Performing Arts
Expenses: 2014-2015: $9,470 in state, $19,700 out of state; room/board: $11,346
Financial aid: (724) 357-2218; 71% of undergrads determined to have financial need; average aid package $9,270

Juniata College

Huntingdon PA
(877) 586-4282
U.S. News ranking: Nat. Lib. Arts, No. 105
Website: www.juniata.edu
Admissions email: admissions@juniata.edu
Private; founded 1876
Freshman admissions: selective; 2014-2015: 2,207 applied, 1,637 accepted. Neither SAT nor ACT required. SAT 25/75 percentile: 1040-1250. High school rank: 33% in top tenth, 64% in top quarter, 91% in top half
Early decision deadline: 11/15, notification date: 12/23
Early action deadline: N/A, notification date: N/A
Application deadline (fall): 2/15
Undergraduate student body: 1,547 full time, 68 part time; 46% male, 54% female; N/A American Indian, 3% Asian, 3% black, 4% Hispanic, 3% multiracial, N/A Pacific Islander, 72% white, 8% international; 64% from in state; 82% live on campus; 0% of students in fraternities, 0% in sororities
Most popular majors: 15% Biological and Biomedical Sciences, 13% Business, Management, Marketing, and Related Support Services, 7% Communication, Journalism, and Related Programs, 7% Education, 11% Natural Resources and Conservation
Expenses: 2015-2016: $40,600; room/board: $11,140
Financial aid: (814) 641-3142; 70% of undergrads determined to have financial need; average aid package $30,563

Keystone College

La Plume PA
(570) 945-8000
U.S. News ranking: Reg. Coll. (N), No. 44
Website: www.keystone.edu
Admissions email: admissions@keystone.edu
Private; founded 1868
Freshman admissions: less selective; 2014-2015: 981 applied, 903 accepted. Either SAT or ACT required. SAT 25/75 percentile: 810-1030. High school rank: 5% in top tenth, 17% in top quarter, 45% in top half
Early decision deadline: N/A, notification date: N/A
Early action deadline: N/A, notification date: N/A
Application deadline (fall): 6/1
Undergraduate student body: 1,231 full time, 229 part time; 41% male, 59% female; 0% American Indian, 1% Asian, 6% black, 7% Hispanic, 1% multiracial, 0% Pacific Islander, 76% white, 0% international; 86% from in state; 30% live on campus; 0% of students in fraternities, 0% in sororities
Most popular majors: 25% Business, Management, Marketing, and Related Support Services, 15% Education, 12% Homeland Security, Law Enforcement, Firefighting and Related Protective Services, 12% Parks, Recreation, Leisure, and Fitness Studies, 7% Visual and Performing Arts
Expenses: 2015-2016: $24,300; room/board: $10,050
Financial aid: (877) 426-5534; 91% of undergrads determined to have financial need; average aid package $17,679

King's College

Wilkes-Barre PA
(888) 546-4772
U.S. News ranking: Reg. U. (N), No. 53
Website: www.kings.edu
Admissions email: admissions@kings.edu
Private; founded 1946
Affiliation: Catholic
Freshman admissions: selective; 2014-2015: 3,150 applied, 2,119 accepted. Neither SAT nor ACT required. SAT 25/75 percentile: 920-1140. High school rank: 14% in top tenth, 39% in top quarter, 67% in top half
Early decision deadline: N/A, notification date: N/A

Early action deadline: 12/15, notification date: N/A
Application deadline (fall): rolling
Undergraduate student body: 1,811 full time, 191 part time; 52% male, 48% female; 0% American Indian, 2% Asian, 3% black, 6% Hispanic, 2% multiracial, 0% Pacific Islander, 79% white, 1% international; 71% from in state; 51% live on campus; 0% of students in fraternities, 0% in sororities
Most popular majors: 8% Accounting, 8% Biology/Biological Sciences, General, 8% Business/ Commerce, General, 9% Criminal Justice/Safety Studies, 11% Elementary Education and Teaching
Expenses: 2015-2016: $33,090; room/board: $11,958
Financial aid: (570) 208-5868; 82% of undergrads determined to have financial need; average aid package $22,682

Kutztown University of Pennsylvania

Kutztown PA
(610) 683-4060
U.S. News ranking: Reg. U. (N), No. 131
Website: www.kutztown.edu
Admissions email: admissions@ kutztown.edu
Public; founded 1866
Freshman admissions: less selective; 2014-2015: 8,061 applied, 6,388 accepted. Either SAT or ACT required. SAT 25/75 percentile: 870-1060. High school rank: 5% in top tenth, 17% in top quarter, 52% in top half
Early decision deadline: N/A, notification date: N/A
Early action deadline: N/A, notification date: N/A
Application deadline (fall): rolling
Undergraduate student body: 8,043 full time, 526 part time; 44% male, 56% female; 0% American Indian, 1% Asian, 8% black, 7% Hispanic, 2% multiracial, 0% Pacific Islander, 79% white, 1% international; 89% from in state; 43% live on campus; 3% of students in fraternities, 8% in sororities
Most popular majors: 20% Business Administration and Management, General, 7% Criminal Justice/Safety Studies, 6% Early Childhood Education and Teaching, 5% English Language and Literature, General, 9% Psychology, General
Expenses: 2014-2015: $8,833 in state, $19,063 out of state; room/ board: $8,430
Financial aid: (610) 683-4077; 70% of undergrads determined to have financial need; average aid package $8,198

Lafayette College

Easton PA
(610) 330-5100
U.S. News ranking: Nat. Lib. Arts, No. 37
Website: www.lafayette.edu
Admissions email: admissions@ lafayette.edu
Private; founded 1826
Freshman admissions: more selective; 2014-2015: 7,796 applied, 2,319 accepted. Either SAT or ACT required. SAT 25/75 percentile: 1200-1400. High school rank: 63% in top tenth, 88% in top quarter, 97% in top half
Early decision deadline: 11/15, notification date: 12/15
Early action deadline: N/A, notification date: N/A
Application deadline (fall): 1/15
Undergraduate student body: 2,446 full time, 57 part time; 53% male, 47% female; 0% American Indian, 3% Asian, 5% black, 7% Hispanic, 2% multiracial, 0% Pacific Islander, 68% white, 8% international; 20% from in state; 93% live on campus; 17% of students in fraternities, 35% in sororities
Most popular majors: 10% Biological and Biomedical Sciences, 16% Engineering, 6% English Language and Literature/ Letters, 9% Psychology, 34% Social Sciences
Expenses: 2015-2016: $47,010; room/board: $13,920
Financial aid: (610) 330-5055; 37% of undergrads determined to have financial need; average aid package $41,206

La Roche College

Pittsburgh PA
(800) 838-4572
U.S. News ranking: Reg. Coll. (N), No. 34
Website: www.laroche.edu
Admissions email: admissions@ laroche.edu
Private; founded 1963
Affiliation: Roman Catholic
Freshman admissions: less selective; 2014-2015: 990 applied, 930 accepted. Either SAT or ACT required. SAT 25/75 percentile: 840-1010. High school rank: 14% in top tenth, 37% in top quarter, 74% in top half
Early decision deadline: N/A, notification date: N/A
Early action deadline: N/A, notification date: N/A
Application deadline (fall): rolling
Undergraduate student body: 1,065 full time, 240 part time; 45% male, 55% female; 0% American Indian, 1% Asian, 7% black, 2% Hispanic, 1% multiracial, 0% Pacific Islander, 62% white, 14% international; 94% from in state; 39% live on campus; N/A of students in fraternities, N/A in sororities
Most popular majors: 6% Accounting, 7% Business Administration, Management and Operations, Other, 8% Criminal Justice/Safety Studies, 9% Medical Radiologic Technology/ Science - Radiation Therapist, 11% Psychology, General
Expenses: 2015-2016: $26,250; room/board: $10,630
Financial aid: (412) 536-1120; 72% of undergrads determined to have financial need; average aid package $26,801

La Salle University

Philadelphia PA
(215) 951-1500
U.S. News ranking: Reg. U. (N), No. 26
Website: www.lasalle.edu
Admissions email: admiss@lasalle.edu
Private; founded 1863
Affiliation: Roman Catholic
Freshman admissions: selective; 2014-2015: 5,778 applied, 4,520 accepted. Either SAT or ACT required. SAT 25/75 percentile: 900-1100. High school rank: 15% in top tenth, 35% in top quarter, 68% in top half
Early decision deadline: N/A, notification date: N/A
Early action deadline: 11/15, notification date: 12/15
Application deadline (fall): rolling
Undergraduate student body: 3,583 full time, 739 part time; 36% male, 64% female; 0% American Indian, 5% Asian, 19% black, 10% Hispanic, 6% multiracial, 0% Pacific Islander, 55% white, 2% international; 67% from in state; 56% live on campus; 6% of students in fraternities, 13% in sororities
Most popular majors: 7% Accounting, 6% Marketing, 25% Nursing Science, 7% Psychology, General, 8% Speech Communication and Rhetoric
Expenses: 2015-2016: $41,100; room/board: $14,120
Financial aid: (215) 951-1070; 82% of undergrads determined to have financial need; average aid package $30,065

Lebanon Valley College

Annville PA
(717) 867-6181
U.S. News ranking: Reg. Coll. (N), No. 6
Website: www.lvc.edu
Admissions email: admission@ lvc.edu
Private; founded 1866
Affiliation: Methodist
Freshman admissions: selective; 2014-2015: 3,643 applied, 2,570 accepted. Neither SAT nor ACT required. SAT 25/75 percentile: 970-1210. High school rank: 32% in top tenth, 66% in top quarter, 91% in top half
Early decision deadline: 11/1, notification date: 12/1
Early action deadline: N/A, notification date: N/A
Application deadline (fall): rolling
Undergraduate student body: 1,573 full time, 110 part time; 46% male, 54% female; 0% American Indian, 2% Asian, 3% black, 5% Hispanic, 2% multiracial, 0% Pacific Islander, 83% white, 0% international; 80% from in state; 80% live on campus; 6% of students in fraternities, 5% in sororities
Most popular majors: 15% Business, Management, Marketing, and Related Support Services, 20% Education, 10% Health Professions and Related Programs, 12% Social Sciences, 9% Visual and Performing Arts
Expenses: 2015-2016: $39,030; room/board: $10,510
Financial aid: (717) 867-6126; 85% of undergrads determined to have financial need; average aid package $28,025

Lehigh University

Bethlehem PA
(610) 758-3100
U.S. News ranking: Nat. U., No. 47
Website: www.lehigh.edu
Admissions email: admissions@ lehigh.edu
Private; founded 1865
Freshman admissions: more selective; 2014-2015: 11,512 applied, 3,945 accepted. Either SAT or ACT required. SAT 25/75 percentile: 1230-1410. High school rank: 62% in top tenth, 89% in top quarter, 99% in top half
Early decision deadline: 11/15, notification date: 12/15
Early action deadline: N/A, notification date: N/A
Application deadline (fall): 1/1
Undergraduate student body: 4,984 full time, 78 part time; 55% male, 45% female; 0% American Indian, 8% Asian, 4% black, 8% Hispanic, 3% multiracial, 0% Pacific Islander, 67% white, 7% international; 27% from in state; 67% live on campus; 40% of students in fraternities, 45% in sororities
Most popular majors: 5% Accounting, 12% Finance, General, 4% Industrial Engineering, 5% Marketing/ Marketing Management, General, 9% Mechanical Engineering
Expenses: 2015-2016: $46,230; room/board: $12,280
Financial aid: (610) 758-3181; 41% of undergrads determined to have financial need; average aid package $38,996

Lincoln University

Lincoln University PA
(800) 790-0191
U.S. News ranking: Reg. U. (N), second tier
Website: www.lincoln.edu
Admissions email: admiss@ lu.lincoln.edu
Public; founded 1854
Freshman admissions: less selective; 2014-2015: 5,181 applied, 1,406 accepted. Either SAT or ACT required. SAT 25/75 percentile: 772-940. High school rank: 6% in top tenth, 23% in top quarter, 44% in top half
Early decision deadline: N/A, notification date: N/A
Early action deadline: N/A, notification date: N/A
Application deadline (fall): rolling
Undergraduate student body: 1,428 full time, 161 part time; 39% male, 61% female; 0% American Indian, 0% Asian, 81% black, 2% Hispanic, 1% multiracial, 0% Pacific Islander, 2% white, 4% international; 45% from in state; 84% live on campus; 1% of students in fraternities, 2% in sororities
Most popular majors: 8% Biology/ Biological Sciences, General, 9% Business Administration and Management, General, 12% Criminal Justice/Safety Studies, 7% Health and Physical Education/Fitness, General, 11% Human Services, General
Expenses: 2015-2016: $11,606 in state, $16,398 out of state; room/board: $8,900
Financial aid: (800) 561-2606; 94% of undergrads determined to have financial need; average aid package $8,714

Lock Haven University of Pennsylvania

Lock Haven PA
(570) 893-2027
U.S. News ranking: Reg. U. (N), second tier
Website: www.lhup.edu
Admissions email: admissions@ lhup.edu
Public; founded 1870
Freshman admissions: less selective; 2014-2015: 3,436 applied, 3,209 accepted. Either SAT or ACT required. SAT 25/75 percentile: 850-1050. High school rank: 9% in top tenth, 30% in top quarter, 61% in top half
Early decision deadline: N/A, notification date: N/A
Early action deadline: N/A, notification date: N/A
Application deadline (fall): rolling
Undergraduate student body: 4,165 full time, 356 part time; 44% male, 56% female; 0% American Indian, 1% Asian, 9% black, 2% Hispanic, 1% multiracial, 0% Pacific Islander, 85% white, 0% international; 94% from in state; 36% live on campus; 3% of students in fraternities, 4% in sororities
Most popular majors: 12% Criminal Justice/Law Enforcement Administration, 7% Early Childhood Education and Teaching, 12% Health Professions and Related Clinical Sciences, Other, 6% Psychology, General, 7% Sport and Fitness Administration/Management
Expenses: 2014-2015: $9,276 in state, $17,506 out of state; room/ board: $8,752
Financial aid: (570) 893-2344; 63% of undergrads determined to have financial need; average aid package $8,511

Lycoming College

Williamsport PA
(800) 345-3920
U.S. News ranking: Nat. Lib. Arts, No. 164
Website: www.lycoming.edu
Admissions email: admissions@ lycoming.edu
Private; founded 1812
Affiliation: Methodist
Freshman admissions: selective; 2014-2015: 1,782 applied, 1,287 accepted. Neither SAT nor ACT required. SAT 25/75 percentile: 930-1153. High school rank: 20% in top tenth, 45% in top quarter, 83% in top half
Early decision deadline: N/A, notification date: N/A
Early action deadline: N/A, notification date: N/A
Application deadline (fall): 3/1
Undergraduate student body: 1,331 full time, 26 part time; 46% male, 54% female; 0% American Indian, 1% Asian, 7% black, 4% Hispanic, 3% multiracial, 0% Pacific Islander, 76% white, 4% international; 66% from in state; 87% live on campus; 12% of students in fraternities, 20% in sororities
Most popular majors: 12% Biological and Biomedical Sciences, 19% Business, Management, Marketing, and Related Support Services, 11% Psychology, 13% Social Sciences, 12% Visual and Performing Arts
Expenses: 2015-2016: $35,900; room/board: $10,884
Financial aid: (570) 321-4040; 82% of undergrads determined to have financial need; average aid package $30,635

More at usnews.com/college

Mansfield University of Pennsylvania

Mansfield PA
(800) 577-6826
U.S. News ranking: Reg. U. (N), No. 131
Website: www.mansfield.edu
Admissions email: admissns@mansfield.edu
Public; founded 1857
Freshman admissions: less selective; 2014-2015: 1,936 applied, 1,756 accepted. Neither SAT nor ACT required. SAT 25/75 percentile: 850-1050. High school rank: 9% in top tenth, 30% in top quarter, 66% in top half
Early decision deadline: N/A, notification date: N/A
Early action deadline: N/A, notification date: N/A
Application deadline (fall): rolling
Undergraduate student body: 2,341 full time, 246 part time; 40% male, 60% female; 0% American Indian, 1% Asian, 9% black, 3% Hispanic, 2% multiracial, 0% Pacific Islander, 82% white, 1% international; 83% from in state; 52% live on campus; N/A of students in fraternities, N/A in sororities
Most popular majors: 9% Business, Management, Marketing, and Related Support Services, 11% Health Professions and Related Programs, 9% Psychology, 8% Social Sciences, 12% Visual and Performing Arts
Expenses: 2014-2015: $9,526 in state, $19,756 out of state; room/board: $10,582
Financial aid: (570) 662-4878; 81% of undergrads determined to have financial need; average aid package $9,650

Marywood University

Scranton PA
(570) 348-6234
U.S. News ranking: Reg. U. (N), No. 41
Website: www.marywood.edu
Admissions email: YourFuture@marywood.edu
Private; founded 1915
Affiliation: Roman Catholic
Freshman admissions: selective; 2014-2015: 2,111 applied, 1,566 accepted. Either SAT or ACT required. SAT 25/75 percentile: 930-1130. High school rank: 18% in top tenth, 45% in top quarter, 84% in top half
Early decision deadline: N/A, notification date: N/A
Early action deadline: N/A, notification date: N/A
Application deadline (fall): rolling
Undergraduate student body: 1,836 full time, 167 part time; 34% male, 66% female; 0% American Indian, 2% Asian, 2% black, 6% Hispanic, 2% multiracial, 0% Pacific Islander, 79% white, 1% international; 70% from in state; 43% live on campus; 0% of students in fraternities, 9% in sororities
Most popular majors: 7% Architecture and Related Services, 10% Business, Management, Marketing, and Related Support Services, 11% Education, 22% Health Professions and Related Programs, 12% Visual and Performing Arts
Expenses: 2015-2016: $32,692; room/board: $13,900
Financial aid: (570) 348-6225; 86% of undergrads determined to have financial need; average aid package $23,187

Mercyhurst University

Erie PA
(814) 824-2202
U.S. News ranking: Reg. U. (N), No. 41
Website: www.mercyhurst.edu
Admissions email: admug@mercyhurst.edu
Private; founded 1926
Affiliation: Roman Catholic
Freshman admissions: selective; 2014-2015: 2,610 applied, 2,097 accepted. Neither SAT nor ACT required. SAT 25/75 percentile: 880-1210. High school rank: 15% in top tenth, 16% in top quarter, 75% in top half
Early decision deadline: N/A, notification date: N/A
Early action deadline: N/A, notification date: N/A
Application deadline (fall): rolling
Undergraduate student body: 2,477 full time, 96 part time; 44% male, 56% female; 0% American Indian, 1% Asian, 3% black, 3% Hispanic, 0% multiracial, 0% Pacific Islander, 41% white, 9% international; 58% from in state; 64% live on campus; 0% of students in fraternities, 0% in sororities
Most popular majors: 8% Biological and Biomedical Sciences, 23% Business, Management, Marketing, and Related Support Services, 8% Education, 10% Homeland Security, Law Enforcement, Firefighting and Related Protective Services, 11% Military Technologies and Applied Sciences
Expenses: 2015-2016: $33,314; room/board: $11,232
Financial aid: (814) 824-2288; 74% of undergrads determined to have financial need; average aid package $25,677

Messiah College

Mechanicsburg PA
(717) 691-6000
U.S. News ranking: Reg. Coll. (N), No. 5
Website: www.messiah.edu
Admissions email: admiss@messiah.edu
Private; founded 1909
Affiliation: Christian interdenominational
Freshman admissions: selective; 2014-2015: 2,472 applied, 1,977 accepted. Either SAT or ACT required. SAT 25/75 percentile: 1010-1240. High school rank: 29% in top tenth, 63% in top quarter, 89% in top half
Early decision deadline: N/A, notification date: N/A
Early action deadline: N/A, notification date: N/A
Application deadline (fall): rolling
Undergraduate student body: 2,680 full time, 109 part time; 40% male, 60% female; 0% American Indian, 2% Asian, 2% black, 4% Hispanic, 3% multiracial, 0% Pacific Islander, 85% white, 3% international; 63% from in state; 86% live on campus; 0% of students in fraternities, 0% in sororities
Most popular majors: 6% Business Administration and Management, General, 4% Elementary Education and Teaching, 4% Engineering, General, 6% Psychology, General, 7% Registered Nursing/Registered Nurse
Expenses: 2015-2016: $32,240; room/board: $9,630
Financial aid: (717) 691-6007; 72% of undergrads determined to have financial need; average aid package $22,327

Millersville University of Pennsylvania

Millersville PA
(717) 871-4625
U.S. News ranking: Reg. U. (N), No. 83
Website: www.millersville.edu
Admissions email: Admissions@millersville.edu
Public; founded 1855
Freshman admissions: selective; 2014-2015: 6,184 applied, 4,249 accepted. Either SAT or ACT required. SAT 25/75 percentile: 920-1110. High school rank: 13% in top tenth, 37% in top quarter, 73% in top half
Early decision deadline: N/A, notification date: N/A
Early action deadline: N/A, notification date: N/A
Application deadline (fall): rolling
Undergraduate student body: 6,358 full time, 813 part time; 45% male, 55% female; 0% American Indian, 2% Asian, 10% black, 8% Hispanic, 2% multiracial, 0% Pacific Islander, 77% white, 0% international; 95% from in state; 33% live on campus; 2% of students in fraternities, 4% in sororities
Most popular majors: 8% Biological and Biomedical Sciences, 11% Business, Management, Marketing, and Related Support Services, 13% Education, 9% Psychology, 12% Social Sciences
Expenses: 2014-2015: $10,268 in state, $23,648 out of state; room/board: $11,380
Financial aid: (717) 872-3026; 69% of undergrads determined to have financial need; average aid package $8,592

Misericordia University

Dallas PA
(570) 674-6264
U.S. News ranking: Reg. U. (N), No. 47
Website: www.misericordia.edu/
Admissions email: admiss@misericordia.edu
Private; founded 1924
Affiliation: Roman Catholic
Freshman admissions: selective; 2014-2015: 2,050 applied, 1,465 accepted. Either SAT or ACT required. SAT 25/75 percentile: 970-1170. High school rank: 30% in top tenth, 60% in top quarter, 84% in top half
Early decision deadline: N/A, notification date: N/A
Early action deadline: N/A, notification date: N/A
Application deadline (fall): rolling
Undergraduate student body: 1,773 full time, 692 part time; 32% male, 68% female; 0% American Indian, 1% Asian, 2% black, 3% Hispanic, 1% multiracial, 0% Pacific Islander, 93% white, 0% international; 76% from in state; 43% live on campus; 0% of students in fraternities, 0% in sororities
Most popular majors: 10% Business Administration and Management, General, 11% Health Services/Allied Health/Health Sciences, General, 8% Health/Health Care Administration/Management, 7% Psychology, General, 14% Registered Nursing/Registered Nurse
Expenses: 2015-2016: $29,840; room/board: $12,460
Financial aid: (570) 674-6280; 79% of undergrads determined to have financial need; average aid package $20,002

Moore College of Art & Design

Philadelphia PA
(215) 965-4015
U.S. News ranking: Arts, unranked
Website: www.moore.edu
Admissions email: admiss@moore.edu
Private
Freshman admissions: N/A; 2014-2015: 612 applied, 367 accepted. Neither SAT nor ACT required. SAT 25/75 percentile: 850-1100. High school rank: N/A
Early decision deadline: N/A, notification date: N/A
Early action deadline: N/A, notification date: N/A
Application deadline (fall): 8/1
Undergraduate student body: 393 full time, 19 part time; 0% male, 100% female; 0% American Indian, 3% Asian, 16% black, 7% Hispanic, 5% multiracial, 0% Pacific Islander, 64% white, 2% international
Most popular majors: 21% Fashion/Apparel Design, 13% Fine/Studio Arts, General, 15% Graphic Design, 17% Illustration, 10% Interior Design
Expenses: 2014-2015: $35,410; room/board: $13,304
Financial aid: (215) 965-4042

Moravian College

Bethlehem PA
(610) 861-1320
U.S. News ranking: Nat. Lib. Arts, No. 148
Website: www.moravian.edu
Admissions email: admissions@moravian.edu
Private; founded 1742
Affiliation: Moravian Church
Freshman admissions: selective; 2014-2015: 1,536 applied, 1,324 accepted. Either SAT or ACT required. SAT 25/75 percentile: 910-1130. High school rank: 17% in top tenth, 45% in top quarter, 77% in top half
Early decision deadline: 1/15, notification date: 1/29
Early action deadline: N/A, notification date: N/A
Application deadline (fall): 3/1
Undergraduate student body: 1,481 full time, 131 part time; 41% male, 59% female; 0% American Indian, 2% Asian, 4% black, 9% Hispanic, 2% multiracial, 0% Pacific Islander, 75% white, 3% international; 67% from in state; 70% live on campus; 19% of students in fraternities, 27% in sororities
Most popular majors: 17% Business, Management, Marketing, and Related Support Services, 12% Health Professions and Related Programs, 9% Psychology, 14% Social Sciences, 12% Visual and Performing Arts
Expenses: 2015-2016: $38,132; room/board: $11,636
Financial aid: (610) 861-1330; 83% of undergrads determined to have financial need; average aid package $28,034

Mount Aloysius College

Cresson PA
(814) 886-6383
U.S. News ranking: Reg. Coll. (N), No. 42
Website: www.mtaloy.edu
Admissions email: admissions@mtaloy.edu
Private; founded 1853
Affiliation: Roman Catholic (Sisters of Mercy)
Freshman admissions: least selective; 2014-2015: 1,572 applied, 1,163 accepted. Either SAT or ACT required. SAT 25/75 percentile: 840-1010. High school rank: N/A
Early decision deadline: N/A, notification date: N/A
Early action deadline: N/A, notification date: N/A
Application deadline (fall): rolling
Undergraduate student body: 1,251 full time, 543 part time; 28% male, 72% female; 0% American Indian, 0% Asian, 3% black, 1% Hispanic, N/A multiracial, N/A Pacific Islander, 78% white, 1% international
Most popular majors: Information not available
Expenses: 2014-2015: $20,790; room/board: $9,186
Financial aid: (814) 886-6357; 92% of undergrads determined to have financial need; average aid package $14,510

Muhlenberg College

Allentown PA
(484) 664-3200
U.S. News ranking: Nat. Lib. Arts, No. 72
Website: www.muhlenberg.edu
Admissions email: admissions@muhlenberg.edu
Private; founded 1848
Affiliation: Lutheran
Freshman admissions: more selective; 2014-2015: 4,714 applied, 2,489 accepted. Neither SAT nor ACT required. SAT 25/75 percentile: 1120-1330. High school rank: 43% in top tenth, 74% in top quarter, 92% in top half
Early decision deadline: 2/15, notification date: 12/1
Early action deadline: N/A, notification date: N/A
Application deadline (fall): 2/15
Undergraduate student body: 2,299 full time, 141 part time; 40% male, 60% female; 0% American Indian, 3% Asian, 3% black, 6% Hispanic, 2% multiracial, 0% Pacific Islander, 77% white, 1% international; 28% from in state; 92% live on campus; 11% of students in fraternities, 20% in sororities
Most popular majors: 12% Business Administration and Management, General, 9% Crafts/Craft Design, Folk Art and Artisanry, 5% Finance, General, 9% Psychology, General, 9%

Speech Communication and Rhetoric
Expenses: 2015-2016: $45,875; room/board: $10,650
Financial aid: (484) 664-3174; 52% of undergrads determined to have financial need; average aid package $29,709

Neumann University

Aston PA
(610) 558-5616
U.S. News ranking: Reg. U. (N), second tier
Website: www.neumann.edu
Admissions email: neumann@neumann.edu
Private; founded 1965
Affiliation: Roman Catholic
Freshman admissions: least selective; 2014-2015: 1,964 applied, 1,847 accepted. Either SAT or ACT required. SAT 25/75 percentile: 760-950. High school rank: N/A
Early decision deadline: N/A, notification date: N/A
Early action deadline: N/A, notification date: N/A
Application deadline (fall): rolling
Undergraduate student body: 1,992 full time, 570 part time; 35% male, 65% female; 0% American Indian, 1% Asian, 22% black, 3% Hispanic, 2% multiracial, 0% Pacific Islander, 53% white, 1% international; 68% from in state; 30% live on campus; 0% of students in fraternities, 0% in sororities
Most popular majors: 10% Criminal Justice/Safety Studies, 11% Education/Teaching of Individuals in Elementary Special Education Programs, 19% Liberal Arts and Sciences/Liberal Studies, 10% Psychology, General, 15% Registered Nursing, Nursing Administration, Nursing Research and Clinical Nursing, Other
Expenses: 2014-2015: $25,860; room/board: $11,800
Financial aid: (610) 558-5521

Peirce College

Philadelphia PA
(888) 467-3472
U.S. News ranking: Reg. Coll. (N), unranked
Website: www.peirce.edu
Admissions email: info@peirce.edu
Private; founded 1865
Freshman admissions: N/A; 2014-2015: N/A applied, N/A accepted. Neither SAT nor ACT required. ACT 25/75 percentile: N/A. High school rank: N/A
Early decision deadline: N/A, notification date: N/A
Early action deadline: N/A, notification date: N/A
Application deadline (fall): rolling
Undergraduate student body: 347 full time, 1,424 part time; 28% male, 72% female; 0% American Indian, 2% Asian, 69% black, 7% Hispanic, 1% multiracial, 0% Pacific Islander, 19% white, 0% international; 92% from in state; N/A live on campus; N/A of students in fraternities, N/A in sororities
Most popular majors: 62% Business, Management, Marketing, and Related Support Services, 19% Computer and Information Sciences and Support Services, 2% Health Professions and Related Programs, 17% Legal Professions and Studies
Expenses: 2014-2015: $13,800; room/board: $6,190
Financial aid: (215) 670-9370

Pennsylvania College of Art and Design

Lancaster PA
(717) 396-7833
U.S. News ranking: Arts, unranked
Website: www.pcad.edu
Admissions email: N/A
Private; founded 1982
Freshman admissions: N/A; 2014-2015: 350 applied, 138 accepted. Neither SAT nor ACT required. ACT 25/75 percentile: N/A. High school rank: N/A
Early decision deadline: N/A, notification date: N/A
Early action deadline: N/A, notification date: N/A
Application deadline (fall): rolling
Undergraduate student body: 198 full time, 8 part time; 28% male, 72% female; 0% American Indian, 2% Asian, 4% black, 4% Hispanic, 4% multiracial, 0% Pacific Islander, 77% white, 0% international
Most popular majors: 100% Visual and Performing Arts
Expenses: 2014-2015: $22,000; room/board: $7,000
Financial aid: (800) 689-0379

Pennsylvania College of Technology

Williamsport PA
(570) 327-4761
U.S. News ranking: Reg. Coll. (N), No. 37
Website: www.pct.edu
Admissions email: admissions@pct.edu
Public; founded 1941
Freshman admissions: least selective; 2014-2015: 4,640 applied, 4,091 accepted. Neither SAT nor ACT required. ACT 25/75 percentile: N/A. High school rank: 4% in top tenth, 16% in top quarter, 45% in top half
Early decision deadline: N/A, notification date: N/A
Early action deadline: N/A, notification date: N/A
Application deadline (fall): 7/1
Undergraduate student body: 4,772 full time, 851 part time; 64% male, 36% female; 0% American Indian, 1% Asian, 3% black, 3% Hispanic, 2% multiracial, 0% Pacific Islander, 86% white, 1% international; 90% from in state; 30% live on campus; N/A of students in fraternities, N/A in sororities
Most popular majors: 8% Adult Health Nurse/Nursing, 9% Building/Construction Site Management/Manager, 7% Business Administration, Management and Operations, Other, 5% Health and Medical Administrative Services, Other, 6% Physician Assistant
Expenses: 2015-2016: $15,900 in state, $22,590 out of state; room/board: $10,288
Financial aid: (570) 327-4766; 87% of undergrads determined to have financial need

Pennsylvania State University–University Park

University Park PA
(814) 865-5471
U.S. News ranking: Nat. U., No. 47
Website: www.psu.edu
Admissions email: admissions@psu.edu
Public; founded 1855
Freshman admissions: more selective; 2014-2015: 50,299 applied, 25,295 accepted. Either SAT or ACT required. SAT 25/75 percentile: 1090-1290. High school rank: 40% in top tenth, 82% in top quarter, 99% in top half
Early decision deadline: N/A, notification date: N/A
Early action deadline: N/A, notification date: N/A
Application deadline (fall): rolling
Undergraduate student body: 39,357 full time, 1,184 part time; 54% male, 46% female; 0% American Indian, 6% Asian, 4% black, 5% Hispanic, 2% multiracial, 0% Pacific Islander, 71% white, 10% international; 69% from in state; 35% live on campus; 17% of students in fraternities, 19% in sororities
Most popular majors: 15% Business, Management, Marketing, and Related Support Services, 9% Communication, Journalism, and Related Programs, 15% Engineering, 6% Health Professions and Related Programs, 8% Social Sciences
Expenses: 2015-2016: $17,514 in state, $31,346 out of state; room/board: $10,920
Financial aid: (814) 865-6301; 48% of undergrads determined to have financial need; average aid package $11,213

Philadelphia University

Philadelphia PA
(215) 951-2800
U.S. News ranking: Reg. U. (N), No. 58
Website: www.philau.edu
Admissions email: admissions@philau.edu
Private; founded 1884
Freshman admissions: selective; 2014-2015: 4,767 applied, 3,048 accepted. Either SAT or ACT required. SAT 25/75 percentile: 970-1180. High school rank: 17% in top tenth, 46% in top quarter, 78% in top half
Early decision deadline: N/A, notification date: N/A
Early action deadline: N/A, notification date: N/A
Application deadline (fall): rolling
Undergraduate student body: 2,557 full time, 349 part time; 34% male, 66% female; 0% American Indian, 5% Asian, 14% black, 7% Hispanic, 2% multiracial, 0% Pacific Islander, 59% white, 4% international
Most popular majors: 18% Architecture and Related Services, 33% Business, Management, Marketing, and Related Support Services, 12% Health Professions and Related Programs, 6% Psychology, 22% Visual and Performing Arts
Expenses: 2015-2016: $36,520; room/board: $12,140
Financial aid: (215) 951-2940; 78% of undergrads determined to have financial need; average aid package $25,116

Point Park University

Pittsburgh PA
(800) 321-0129
U.S. News ranking: Reg. U. (N), No. 112
Website: www.pointpark.edu
Admissions email: enroll@pointpark.edu
Private; founded 1960
Freshman admissions: selective; 2014-2015: 3,469 applied, 2,454 accepted. Either SAT or ACT required. SAT 25/75 percentile: 880-1100. High school rank: 9% in top tenth, 31% in top quarter, 68% in top half
Early decision deadline: N/A, notification date: N/A
Early action deadline: N/A, notification date: N/A
Application deadline (fall): rolling
Undergraduate student body: 2,616 full time, 546 part time; 44% male, 56% female; 0% American Indian, 2% Asian, 16% black, 4% Hispanic, 4% multiracial, 0% Pacific Islander, 70% white, 4% international; 76% from in state; 33% live on campus; N/A of students in fraternities, N/A in sororities
Most popular majors: 9% Business Administration and Management, General, 9% Business, Management, Marketing, and Related Support Services, Other, 6% Cinematography and Film/Video Production, 8% Dance, General, 11% Drama and Dramatics/Theatre Arts, General
Expenses: 2015-2016: $28,250; room/board: $10,620
Financial aid: (412) 392-3930; 91% of undergrads determined to have financial need; average aid package $21,099

Robert Morris University

Moon Township PA
(412) 397-5200
U.S. News ranking: Reg. U. (N), No. 66
Website: www.rmu.edu
Admissions email: admissions@rmu.edu
Private; founded 1921
Freshman admissions: selective; 2014-2015: 6,064 applied, 4,621 accepted. Either SAT or ACT required. SAT 25/75 percentile: 950-1160. High school rank: 19% in top tenth, 48% in top quarter, 80% in top half
Early decision deadline: N/A, notification date: N/A
Early action deadline: N/A, notification date: N/A
Application deadline (fall): rolling
Undergraduate student body: 3,968 full time, 606 part time; 56% male, 44% female; 0% American Indian, 1% Asian, 6% black, 2% Hispanic, 2% multiracial, 0% Pacific Islander, 75% white, 10% international; 87% from in state; 53% live on campus; 14% of students in fraternities, 18% in sororities
Most popular majors: 9% Accounting, 8% Business Administration and Management, General, 7% Engineering, General, 6% Marketing/Marketing Management, General, 7% Registered Nursing/Registered Nurse
Expenses: 2015-2016: $27,194; room/board: $12,130
Financial aid: (412) 262-8545; 77% of undergrads determined to have financial need; average aid package $20,822

Rosemont College

Rosemont PA
(800) 331-0708
U.S. News ranking: Reg. U. (N), No. 116
Website: www.rosemont.edu
Admissions email: admissions@rosemont.edu
Private; founded 1921
Affiliation: Roman Catholic
Freshman admissions: less selective; 2014-2015: 800 applied, 463 accepted. Either SAT or ACT required. SAT 25/75 percentile: 800-1063. High school rank: 26% in top tenth, 49% in top quarter, 77% in top half
Early decision deadline: N/A, notification date: N/A
Early action deadline: N/A, notification date: N/A
Application deadline (fall): rolling
Undergraduate student body: 442 full time, 80 part time; 34% male, 66% female; 0% American Indian, 5% Asian, 38% black, 6% Hispanic, 3% multiracial, 0% Pacific Islander, 43% white, 1% international; 73% from in state; 72% live on campus; 0% of students in fraternities, 0% in sororities
Most popular majors: 9% Biology/Biological Sciences, General, 37% Business/Commerce, General, 12% Education, General, 7% Social Sciences, General, 7% Visual and Performing Arts, General
Expenses: 2015-2016: $32,500; room/board: $13,400
Financial aid: (610) 527-0200; 31% of undergrads determined to have financial need; average aid package $30,540

Saint Vincent College

Latrobe PA
(800) 782-5549
U.S. News ranking: Nat. Lib. Arts, No. 154
Website: www.stvincent.edu
Admissions email: admission@stvincent.edu
Private; founded 1846
Affiliation: Roman Catholic
Freshman admissions: selective; 2014-2015: 1,891 applied, 1,360 accepted. Either SAT or ACT required. SAT 25/75 percentile: 910-1160. High school rank: 25% in top tenth, 52% in top quarter, 78% in top half
Early decision deadline: N/A, notification date: N/A
Early action deadline: N/A, notification date: N/A
Application deadline (fall): 5/1
Undergraduate student body: 1,560 full time, 66 part time; 52% male, 48% female; 0% American Indian, 2% Asian, 5% black, 4% Hispanic, 1% multiracial, 0% Pacific Islander, 84% white, 1% international; 83% from in state; 73% live on campus; 0% of students in fraternities, 0% in sororities
Most popular majors: 13% Biological and Biomedical

Sciences, 18% Business, Management, Marketing, and Related Support Services, 9% Communication, Journalism, and Related Programs, 13% Education, 7% Psychology
Expenses: 2015-2016: $32,380; room/board: $10,292
Financial aid: (724) 537-4540; 80% of undergrads determined to have financial need; average aid package $27,394

Seton Hill University

Greensburg PA
(724) 838-4255
U.S. News ranking: Reg. Coll. (N), No. 10
Website: www.setonhill.edu
Admissions email: dmit@setonhill.edu
Private; founded 1883
Affiliation: Roman Catholic
Freshman admissions: selective; 2014-2015: 2,248 applied, 1,554 accepted. Neither SAT nor ACT required. SAT 25/75 percentile: 940-1180. High school rank: 27% in top tenth, 51% in top quarter, 83% in top half
Early decision deadline: N/A, notification date: N/A
Early action deadline: N/A, notification date: N/A
Application deadline (fall): 8/15
Undergraduate student body: 1,427 full time, 155 part time; 35% male, 65% female; 0% American Indian, 1% Asian, 8% black, 3% Hispanic, 2% multiracial, 0% Pacific Islander, 81% white, 4% international; 77% from in state; 59% live on campus; 0% of students in fraternities, 0% in sororities
Most popular majors: 8% Biological and Biomedical Sciences, 23% Business, Management, Marketing, and Related Support Services, 8% Education, 7% Health Professions and Related Programs, 7% Visual and Performing Arts
Expenses: 2015-2016: $32,420; room/board: $10,868
Financial aid: (724) 838-4293

Shippensburg University of Pennsylvania

Shippensburg PA
(717) 477-1231
U.S. News ranking: Reg. U. (N), No. 92
Website: www.ship.edu
Admissions email: admiss@ship.edu
Public; founded 1871
Freshman admissions: less selective; 2014-2015: 6,319 applied, 5,253 accepted. Either SAT or ACT required. SAT 25/75 percentile: 890-1080. High school rank: 7% in top tenth, 25% in top quarter, 59% in top half
Early decision deadline: N/A, notification date: N/A
Early action deadline: N/A, notification date: N/A
Application deadline (fall): rolling
Undergraduate student body: 5,956 full time, 349 part time; 51% male, 49% female; 0% American Indian, 1% Asian, 9% black, 5% Hispanic, 3% multiracial, 0% Pacific Islander, 79% white, 0% international; 93% from in state; 36% live on campus; 8% of students in fraternities, 11% in sororities
Most popular majors: 6% Biology/Biological Sciences, General, 7% Business Administration and Management, General, 7% Criminal Justice/Safety Studies, 7% Early Childhood Education and Teaching, 9% Psychology, General
Expenses: 2014-2015: $9,774 in state, $18,300 out of state; room/board: $11,160
Financial aid: (717) 477-1131; 69% of undergrads determined to have financial need; average aid package $8,351

Slippery Rock University of Pennsylvania

Slippery Rock PA
(800) 929-4778
U.S. News ranking: Reg. U. (N), No. 79
Website: www.sru.edu
Admissions email: asktherock@sru.edu
Public; founded 1889
Freshman admissions: selective; 2014-2015: 5,775 applied, 3,810 accepted. Either SAT or ACT required. SAT 25/75 percentile: 910-1080. High school rank: 12% in top tenth, 36% in top quarter, 76% in top half
Early decision deadline: N/A, notification date: N/A
Early action deadline: N/A, notification date: N/A
Application deadline (fall): rolling
Undergraduate student body: 7,059 full time, 528 part time; 43% male, 57% female; 0% American Indian, 1% Asian, 5% black, 2% Hispanic, 3% multiracial, 0% Pacific Islander, 86% white, 1% international; 90% from in state; 37% live on campus; 2% of students in fraternities, 1% in sororities
Most popular majors: 14% Business, Management, Marketing, and Related Support Services, 8% Education, 21% Health Professions and Related Programs, 9% Parks, Recreation, Leisure, and Fitness Studies, 7% Social Sciences
Expenses: 2014-2015: $9,309 in state, $12,719 out of state; room/board: $9,794
Financial aid: (724) 738-2044; 70% of undergrads determined to have financial need; average aid package $8,831

St. Francis University

Loretto PA
(814) 472-3100
U.S. News ranking: Reg. U. (N), No. 41
Website: www.francis.edu/undergraduate_admissions
Admissions email: admissions@francis.edu
Private; founded 1847
Affiliation: Roman Catholic
Freshman admissions: selective; 2014-2015: 1,640 applied, 1,127 accepted. Either SAT or ACT required. SAT 25/75 percentile: 920-1130. High school rank: 24% in top tenth, 54% in top quarter, 82% in top half
Early decision deadline: N/A, notification date: N/A
Early action deadline: N/A, notification date: N/A
Application deadline (fall): 7/30
Undergraduate student body: 1,605 full time, 117 part time; 37% male, 63% female; 0% American Indian, 1% Asian, 6% black, 2% Hispanic, 1% multiracial, 0% Pacific Islander, 79% white, 5% international
Most popular majors: Information not available
Expenses: 2014-2015: $31,078; room/board: $10,760
Financial aid: (814) 472-3010

St. Joseph's University

Philadelphia PA
(610) 660-1300
U.S. News ranking: Reg. U. (N), No. 15
Website: www.sju.edu
Admissions email: admit@sju.edu
Private; founded 1851
Affiliation: Roman Catholic (Jesuit)
Freshman admissions: selective; 2014-2015: 8,462 applied, 7,160 accepted. Neither SAT nor ACT required. SAT 25/75 percentile: 1030-1220. High school rank: 16% in top tenth, 44% in top quarter, 78% in top half
Early decision deadline: N/A, notification date: N/A
Early action deadline: 11/15, notification date: 12/25
Application deadline (fall): 2/1
Undergraduate student body: 4,671 full time, 841 part time; 46% male, 54% female; 0% American Indian, 3% Asian, 7% black, 6% Hispanic, 2% multiracial, 0% Pacific Islander, 80% white, 2% international; 47% from in state; 59% live on campus; 6% of students in fraternities, 22% in sororities
Most popular majors: 8% Accounting, 8% Finance, General, 9% Marketing/Marketing Management, General, 14% Special Products Marketing Operations
Expenses: 2015-2016: $42,180; room/board: $14,928
Financial aid: (610) 660-1556; 58% of undergrads determined to have financial need; average aid package $25,302

Susquehanna University

Selinsgrove PA
(800) 326-9672
U.S. News ranking: Nat. Lib. Arts, No. 120
Website: www.susqu.edu
Admissions email: suadmiss@susqu.edu
Private; founded 1858
Affiliation: Lutheran
Freshman admissions: selective; 2014-2015: 4,510 applied, 3,527 accepted. Neither SAT nor ACT required. SAT 25/75 percentile: 1020-1210. High school rank: 28% in top tenth, 54% in top quarter, 85% in top half
Early decision deadline: 11/15, notification date: 12/1
Early action deadline: 11/1, notification date: 12/1
Application deadline (fall): rolling
Undergraduate student body: 2,008 full time, 76 part time; 45% male, 55% female; 0% American Indian, 2% Asian, 5% black, 6% Hispanic, 3% multiracial, 0% Pacific Islander, 83% white, 2% international; 49% from in state; 90% live on campus; 19% of students in fraternities, 14% in sororities
Most popular majors: 19% Business/Commerce, General, 6% Creative Writing, 7% Liberal Arts and Sciences/Liberal Studies, 8% Psychology, General, 13% Speech Communication and Rhetoric
Expenses: 2015-2016: $42,040; room/board: $11,170
Financial aid: (570) 372-4450; 76% of undergrads determined to have financial need; average aid package $30,817

Swarthmore College

Swarthmore PA
(610) 328-8300
U.S. News ranking: Nat. Lib. Arts, No. 3
Website: www.swarthmore.edu
Admissions email: admissions@swarthmore.edu
Private; founded 1864
Freshman admissions: most selective; 2014-2015: 5,540 applied, 943 accepted. Either SAT or ACT required. SAT 25/75 percentile: 1360-1540. High school rank: 88% in top tenth, 98% in top quarter, 100% in top half
Early decision deadline: 11/15, notification date: 12/15
Early action deadline: N/A, notification date: N/A
Application deadline (fall): 1/1
Undergraduate student body: 1,534 full time, 8 part time; 49% male, 51% female; 0% American Indian, 16% Asian, 6% black, 13% Hispanic, 8% multiracial, 0% Pacific Islander, 42% white, 10% international; 13% from in state; 93% live on campus; 12% of students in fraternities, 5% in sororities
Most popular majors: 12% Biological and Biomedical Sciences, 10% Computer and Information Sciences and Support Services, 6% Mathematics and Statistics, 7% Psychology, 26% Social Sciences
Expenses: 2015-2016: $47,442; room/board: $13,958
Financial aid: (610) 328-8358; 51% of undergrads determined to have financial need; average aid package $41,989

Temple University

Philadelphia PA
(215) 204-7200
U.S. News ranking: Nat. U., No. 115
Website: www.temple.edu
Admissions email: askanowl@temple.edu
Public; founded 1884
Freshman admissions: selective; 2014-2015: 26,496 applied, 16,357 accepted. Neither SAT nor ACT required. SAT 25/75 percentile: 1010-1230. High school rank: 21% in top tenth, 51% in top quarter, 87% in top half
Early decision deadline: N/A, notification date: N/A
Early action deadline: 11/1, notification date: 1/10
Application deadline (fall): 3/1
Undergraduate student body: 24,990 full time, 3,297 part time; 49% male, 51% female; 0% American Indian, 10% Asian, 13% black, 6% Hispanic, 3% multiracial, 0% Pacific Islander, 58% white, 5% international; 78% from in state; 19% live on campus; 1% of students in fraternities, 2% in sororities
Most popular majors: 21% Business, Management, Marketing, and Related Support Services, 12% Communication, Journalism, and Related Programs, 6% Education, 6% Psychology, 10% Visual and Performing Arts
Expenses: 2015-2016: $15,096 in state, $25,122 out of state; room/board: $10,738
Financial aid: (215) 204-8760; 70% of undergrads determined to have financial need; average aid package $16,611

Thiel College

Greenville PA
(800) 248-4435
U.S. News ranking: Reg. Coll. (N), No. 34
Website: www.thiel.edu
Admissions email: admission@thiel.edu
Private; founded 1866
Affiliation: Lutheran
Freshman admissions: less selective; 2014-2015: 2,465 applied, 1,713 accepted. Either SAT or ACT required. SAT 25/75 percentile: 860-1060. High school rank: 12% in top tenth, 35% in top quarter, 64% in top half
Early decision deadline: N/A, notification date: N/A
Early action deadline: N/A, notification date: N/A
Application deadline (fall): rolling
Undergraduate student body: 1,039 full time, 35 part time; 53% male, 47% female; 0% American Indian, 0% Asian, 9% black, 2% Hispanic, 2% multiracial, 0% Pacific Islander, 75% white, 4% international; 61% from in state; 91% live on campus; 25% of students in fraternities, 39% in sororities
Most popular majors: 11% Biological and Biomedical Sciences, 25% Business, Management, Marketing, and Related Support Services, 6% Education, 12% Homeland Security, Law Enforcement, Firefighting and Related Protective Services, 11% Psychology
Expenses: 2015-2016: $28,868; room/board: $11,336
Financial aid: (724) 589-2178; 86% of undergrads determined to have financial need; average aid package $23,041

University of Pennsylvania

Philadelphia PA
(215) 898-7507
U.S. News ranking: Nat. U., No. 9
Website: www.upenn.edu
Admissions email: info@admissions.ugao.upenn.edu
Private; founded 1740
Freshman admissions: most selective; 2014-2015: 35,866 applied, 3,718 accepted. Either SAT or ACT required. SAT 25/75 percentile: 1360-1550. High school rank: 93% in top tenth, 98% in top quarter, 100% in top half
Early decision deadline: 11/1, notification date: 12/15
Early action deadline: N/A, notification date: N/A

Application deadline (fall): 1/1
Undergraduate student body: 9,437 full time, 309 part time; 50% male, 50% female; 0% American Indian, 20% Asian, 7% black, 10% Hispanic, 4% multiracial, 0% Pacific Islander, 45% white, 11% international; 19% from in state; 54% live on campus; 30% of students in fraternities, 27% in sororities
Most popular majors: 9% Biological and Biomedical Sciences, 21% Business, Management, Marketing, and Related Support Services, 9% Engineering, 10% Health Professions and Related Programs, 16% Social Sciences
Expenses: 2015-2016: $49,536; room/board: $13,990
Financial aid: (215) 898-1988; 48% of undergrads determined to have financial need; average aid package $42,419

University of Pittsburgh

Pittsburgh PA
(412) 624-7488
U.S. News ranking: Nat. U., No. 66
Website: www.oafa.pitt.edu/
Admissions email: oafa@pitt.edu
Public; founded 1787
Freshman admissions: more selective; 2014-2015: 30,629 applied, 16,271 accepted. Either SAT or ACT required. SAT 25/75 percentile: 1180-1360. High school rank: 54% in top tenth, 87% in top quarter, 99% in top half
Early decision deadline: N/A, notification date: N/A
Early action deadline: N/A, notification date: N/A
Application deadline (fall): rolling
Undergraduate student body: 17,694 full time, 1,063 part time; 49% male, 51% female; 0% American Indian, 8% Asian, 5% black, 3% Hispanic, 3% multiracial, 0% Pacific Islander, 76% white, 4% international; 73% from in state; 43% live on campus; 11% of students in fraternities, 10% in sororities
Most popular majors: 15% Business, Management, Marketing, and Related Support Services, 11% Engineering, 12% Health Professions and Related Programs, 9% Psychology, 12% Social Sciences
Expenses: 2015-2016: $18,192 in state, $28,958 out of state; room/board: $10,900
Financial aid: (412) 624-7488; 55% of undergrads determined to have financial need; average aid package $13,044

University of Scranton

Scranton PA
(570) 941-7540
U.S. News ranking: Reg. U. (N), No. 8
Website: www.scranton.edu
Admissions email: admissions@scranton.edu
Private; founded 1888
Affiliation: Roman Catholic (Jesuit)
Freshman admissions: selective; 2014-2015: 9,404 applied, 7,266 accepted. Either SAT or ACT required. SAT 25/75 percentile: 1040-1210. High school rank: 24% in top tenth, 57% in top quarter, 86% in top half
Early decision deadline: N/A, notification date: N/A
Early action deadline: 11/15, notification date: 12/15
Application deadline (fall): 3/1
Undergraduate student body: 3,844 full time, 154 part time; 43% male, 57% female; 0% American Indian, 2% Asian, 2% black, 8% Hispanic, 3% multiracial, 0% Pacific Islander, 82% white, 0% international; 40% from in state; 64% live on campus; 0% of students in fraternities, 0% in sororities
Most popular majors: 6% Accounting, 7% Biology/Biological Sciences, General, 6% Human Services, General, 6% Kinesiology and Exercise Science, 7% Registered Nursing/Registered Nurse
Expenses: 2015-2016: $41,044; room/board: $13,918
Financial aid: (570) 941-7700; 72% of undergrads determined to have financial need; average aid package $25,070

University of the Arts

Philadelphia PA
(215) 717-6049
U.S. News ranking: Arts, unranked
Website: www.uarts.edu
Admissions email: admissions@uarts.edu
Private; founded 1876
Freshman admissions: N/A; 2014-2015: 1,494 applied, 1,039 accepted. Either SAT or ACT required. SAT 25/75 percentile: 880-1140. High school rank: N/A
Early decision deadline: N/A, notification date: N/A
Early action deadline: N/A, notification date: N/A
Application deadline (fall): rolling
Undergraduate student body: 1,711 full time, 43 part time; 41% male, 59% female; 0% American Indian, 3% Asian, 12% black, 10% Hispanic, 4% multiracial, 1% Pacific Islander, 62% white, 5% international; 38% from in state; 32% live on campus; 0% of students in fraternities, 0% in sororities
Most popular majors: 16% Dance, General, 8% Film/Video and Photographic Arts, Other, 8% Graphic Design, 10% Illustration, 8% Photography
Expenses: 2015-2016: $39,908; room/board: $14,552
Financial aid: (215) 717-6170

University of Valley Forge[1]

Phoenixville PA
(800) 432-8322
U.S. News ranking: Reg. Coll. (N), No. 44
Website: www.valleyforge.edu/
Admissions email: admissions@valleyforge.edu
Private
Application deadline (fall): N/A
Undergraduate student body: N/A full time, N/A part time
Expenses: 2014-2015: $20,394; room/board: $8,116
Financial aid: (610) 917-1498

Ursinus College

Collegeville PA
(610) 409-3200
U.S. News ranking: Nat. Lib. Arts, No. 93
Website: www.ursinus.edu
Admissions email: Admissions@Ursinus.edu
Private; founded 1869
Freshman admissions: selective; 2014-2015: 2,672 applied, 2,222 accepted. Neither SAT nor ACT required. SAT 25/75 percentile: 1050-1260. High school rank: 24% in top tenth, 54% in top quarter, 88% in top half
Early decision deadline: 1/15, notification date: 1/30
Early action deadline: 12/1, notification date: 1/15
Application deadline (fall): rolling
Undergraduate student body: 1,662 full time, 19 part time; 48% male, 52% female; 0% American Indian, 5% Asian, 6% black, 6% Hispanic, 4% multiracial, 0% Pacific Islander, 75% white, 2% international; 54% from in state; 96% live on campus; 18% of students in fraternities, 24% in sororities
Most popular majors: 27% Biological and Biomedical Sciences, 5% Communication, Journalism, and Related Programs, 5% Physical Sciences, 11% Psychology, 22% Social Sciences
Expenses: 2015-2016: $47,700; room/board: $11,900
Financial aid: (610) 409-3600; 72% of undergrads determined to have financial need; average aid package $34,458

Villanova University

Villanova PA
(610) 519-4000
U.S. News ranking: Reg. U. (N), No. 1
Website: www.villanova.edu
Admissions email: gotovu@villanova.edu
Private; founded 1842
Affiliation: Roman Catholic
Freshman admissions: more selective; 2014-2015: 15,705 applied, 7,748 accepted. Either SAT or ACT required. SAT 25/75 percentile: 1220-1400. High school rank: 55% in top tenth, 87% in top quarter, 98% in top half
Early decision deadline: N/A, notification date: N/A
Early action deadline: 11/1, notification date: 12/20
Application deadline (fall): 1/15
Undergraduate student body: 6,553 full time, 565 part time; 48% male, 52% female; 0% American Indian, 7% Asian, 5% black, 7% Hispanic, 2% multiracial, 0% Pacific Islander, 76% white, 2% international; 19% from in state; 70% live on campus; 19% of students in fraternities, 41% in sororities
Most popular majors: 32% Business, Management, Marketing, and Related Support Services, 8% Communication, Journalism, and Related Programs, 10% Engineering, 10% Health Professions and Related Programs, 10% Social Sciences
Expenses: 2015-2016: $47,616; room/board: $12,680
Financial aid: (610) 519-4010; 50% of undergrads determined to have financial need; average aid package $33,845

Washington and Jefferson College

Washington PA
(724) 223-6025
U.S. News ranking: Nat. Lib. Arts, No. 100
Website: www.washjeff.edu
Admissions email: admission@washjeff.edu
Private; founded 1781
Freshman admissions: more selective; 2014-2015: 7,094 applied, 2,955 accepted. Neither SAT nor ACT required. SAT 25/75 percentile: 1040-1230. High school rank: 31% in top tenth, 63% in top quarter, 91% in top half
Early decision deadline: 12/1, notification date: 12/15
Early action deadline: 1/15, notification date: 2/15
Application deadline (fall): 3/1
Undergraduate student body: 1,354 full time, 8 part time; 51% male, 49% female; 0% American Indian, 3% Asian, 3% black, 3% Hispanic, 3% multiracial, 0% Pacific Islander, 84% white, 2% international; 77% from in state; 94% live on campus; 37% of students in fraternities, 40% in sororities
Most popular majors: 10% Accounting, 14% Business/Commerce, General, 5% Economics, General, 5% English Language and Literature, General, 12% Psychology, General
Expenses: 2015-2016: $43,226; room/board: $11,406
Financial aid: (724) 223-6019; 78% of undergrads determined to have financial need; average aid package $31,274

Waynesburg University

Waynesburg PA
(800) 225-7393
U.S. News ranking: Reg. U. (N), No. 100
Website: www.waynesburg.edu/
Admissions email: admissions@waynesburg.edu
Private; founded 1849
Affiliation: Presbyterian
Freshman admissions: selective; 2014-2015: 1,448 applied, 1,210 accepted. SAT required. SAT 25/75 percentile: 900-1090. High school rank: 15% in top tenth, 46% in top quarter, 86% in top half
Early decision deadline: N/A, notification date: N/A
Early action deadline: N/A, notification date: N/A
Application deadline (fall): rolling
Undergraduate student body: 1,414 full time, 114 part time; 39% male, 61% female; 0% American Indian, 0% Asian, 4% black, 1% Hispanic, 1% multiracial, 0% Pacific Islander, 92% white, 0% international; 80% from in state; 67% live on campus; N/A of students in fraternities, N/A in sororities
Most popular majors: 13% Business Administration and Management, General, 7% Criminal Justice/Law Enforcement Administration, 8% Elementary Education and Teaching, 28% Registered Nursing/Registered Nurse, 7% Speech Communication and Rhetoric
Expenses: 2015-2016: $22,030; room/board: $9,170
Financial aid: (724) 852-3208; 84% of undergrads determined to have financial need; average aid package $16,528

West Chester University of Pennsylvania

West Chester PA
(610) 436-3414
U.S. News ranking: Reg. U. (N), No. 71
Website: www.wcupa.edu/
Admissions email: ugadmiss@wcupa.edu
Public; founded 1871
Freshman admissions: selective; 2014-2015: 13,291 applied, 7,108 accepted. Either SAT or ACT required. SAT 25/75 percentile: 990-1160. High school rank: 13% in top tenth, 39% in top quarter, 80% in top half
Early decision deadline: N/A, notification date: N/A
Early action deadline: N/A, notification date: N/A
Application deadline (fall): rolling
Undergraduate student body: 12,582 full time, 1,262 part time; 40% male, 60% female; 0% American Indian, 2% Asian, 10% black, 5% Hispanic, 3% multiracial, 0% Pacific Islander, 80% white, 0% international; 88% from in state; 36% live on campus; 12% of students in fraternities, 16% in sororities
Most popular majors: 17% Business, Management, Marketing, and Related Support Services, 12% Education, 8% English Language and Literature/Letters, 15% Health Professions and Related Programs, 8% Liberal Arts and Sciences, General Studies and Humanities
Expenses: 2014-2015: $9,144 in state, $19,374 out of state; room/board: $8,042
Financial aid: (610) 436-2627; 61% of undergrads determined to have financial need; average aid package $7,704

Westminster College

New Wilmington PA
(800) 942-8033
U.S. News ranking: Nat. Lib. Arts, No. 125
Website: www.westminster.edu
Admissions email: admis@westminster.edu
Private; founded 1852
Affiliation: Presbyterian Church (USA)
Freshman admissions: selective; 2014-2015: 2,082 applied, 1,950 accepted. Either SAT or ACT required. SAT 25/75 percentile: 940-1160. High school rank: 22% in top tenth, 62% in top quarter, 93% in top half
Early decision deadline: N/A, notification date: N/A
Early action deadline: 11/15, notification date: 12/1
Application deadline (fall): 1/5
Undergraduate student body: 1,115 full time, 23 part time; 42% male, 58% female; 0% American Indian, 1% Asian, 3% black, 1% Hispanic, 2% multiracial, 0%

Pacific Islander, 79% white, 0% international
Most popular majors: 12% Biological and Biomedical Sciences, 19% Business, Management, Marketing, and Related Support Services, 9% Communication, Journalism, and Related Programs, 17% Education, 11% Social Sciences
Expenses: 2015-2016: $34,105; room/board: $10,370
Financial aid: (724) 946-7102; 80% of undergrads determined to have financial need; average aid package $25,855

Widener University

Chester PA
(610) 499-4126
U.S. News ranking: Nat. U., No. 187
Website: www.widener.edu
Admissions email: admissions.office@widener.edu
Private; founded 1821
Freshman admissions: selective; 2014-2015: 5,501 applied, 3,576 accepted. Either SAT or ACT required. SAT 25/75 percentile: 920-1130. High school rank: 12% in top tenth, 36% in top quarter, 73% in top half
Early decision deadline: N/A, notification date: N/A
Early action deadline: N/A, notification date: N/A
Application deadline (fall): rolling
Undergraduate student body: 2,883 full time, 554 part time; 44% male, 56% female; 0% American Indian, 4% Asian, 13% black, 5% Hispanic, 3% multiracial, 0% Pacific Islander, 70% white, 4% international; 60% from in state; 47% live on campus; 10% of students in fraternities, 9% in sororities
Most popular majors: 20% Business, Management, Marketing, and Related Support Services, 5% Education, 12% Engineering, 26% Health Professions and Related Programs, 10% Psychology
Expenses: 2015-2016: $41,224; room/board: $13,092
Financial aid: (610) 499-4174; 80% of undergrads determined to have financial need; average aid package $29,545

Wilkes University

Wilkes-Barre PA
(570) 408-4400
U.S. News ranking: Reg. U. (N), No. 83
Website: www.wilkes.edu
Admissions email: admissions@wilkes.edu
Private; founded 1933
Freshman admissions: selective; 2014-2015: 2,812 applied, 2,211 accepted. Either SAT or ACT required. SAT 25/75 percentile: 930-1160. High school rank: 25% in top tenth, 53% in top quarter, 82% in top half
Early decision deadline: N/A, notification date: N/A
Early action deadline: N/A, notification date: N/A
Application deadline (fall): rolling
Undergraduate student body: 2,217 full time, 143 part time; 53% male, 47% female; 0% American Indian, 2% Asian, 3% black, 6% Hispanic, 4% multiracial, 0% Pacific Islander, 74% white, 9% international; 84% from in state; 41% live on campus; 0% of students in fraternities, 0% in sororities
Most popular majors: 17% Business, Management, Marketing, and Related Support Services, 7% Communication, Journalism, and Related Programs, 9% Engineering, 15% Health Professions and Related Programs, 7% Psychology
Expenses: 2015-2016: $32,356; room/board: $13,266
Financial aid: (570) 408-4346; 81% of undergrads determined to have financial need; average aid package $24,265

Wilson College

Chambersburg PA
(800) 421-8402
U.S. News ranking: Reg. Coll. (N), No. 21
Website: www.wilson.edu
Admissions email: admissions@wilson.edu
Private; founded 1869
Affiliation: Presbyterian Church (USA)
Freshman admissions: selective; 2014-2015: 748 applied, 234 accepted. Neither SAT nor ACT required. SAT 25/75 percentile: 870-1090. High school rank: 8% in top tenth, 34% in top quarter, 69% in top half
Early decision deadline: N/A, notification date: N/A
Early action deadline: N/A, notification date: N/A
Application deadline (fall): rolling
Undergraduate student body: 365 full time, 242 part time; 14% male, 86% female; 0% American Indian, 1% Asian, 5% black, 2% Hispanic, 2% multiracial, 0% Pacific Islander, 63% white, 7% international; 75% from in state; 50% live on campus; 0% of students in fraternities, 0% in sororities
Most popular majors: 7% Biology/Biological Sciences, General, 8% Elementary Education and Teaching, 6% English Language and Literature, General, 6% Equestrian/Equine Studies, 33% Veterinary/Animal Health Technology/Technician and Veterinary Assistant
Expenses: 2015-2016: $24,392; room/board: $10,912
Financial aid: (717) 262-2016; 90% of undergrads determined to have financial need; average aid package $23,120

York College of Pennsylvania

York PA
(717) 849-1600
U.S. News ranking: Reg. U. (N), No. 83
Website: www.ycp.edu
Admissions email: admissions@ycp.edu
Private; founded 1787
Freshman admissions: selective; 2014-2015: 15,270 applied, 6,946 accepted. Either SAT or ACT required. SAT 25/75 percentile: 950-1150. High school rank: 13% in top tenth, 42% in top quarter, 78% in top half
Early decision deadline: N/A, notification date: N/A
Early action deadline: N/A, notification date: N/A
Application deadline (fall): rolling
Undergraduate student body: 4,340 full time, 513 part time; 44% male, 56% female; 0% American Indian, 2% Asian, 6% black, 6% Hispanic, 3% multiracial, 0% Pacific Islander, 83% white, 0% international; 54% from in state; 55% live on campus; 9% of students in fraternities, 12% in sororities
Most popular majors: 19% Business, Management, Marketing, and Related Support Services, 7% Communication, Journalism, and Related Programs, 9% Education, 16% Health Professions and Related Programs, 10% Homeland Security, Law Enforcement, Firefighting and Related Protective Services
Expenses: 2015-2016: $18,240; room/board: $10,160
Financial aid: (717) 849-1682; 68% of undergrads determined to have financial need; average aid package $13,707

RHODE ISLAND

Brown University

Providence RI
(401) 863-2378
U.S. News ranking: Nat. U., No. 14
Website: www.brown.edu
Admissions email: admission@brown.edu
Private; founded 1764
Freshman admissions: most selective; 2014-2015: 30,431 applied, 2,661 accepted. Either SAT or ACT required. SAT 25/75 percentile: 1330-1550. High school rank: 92% in top tenth, 98% in top quarter, 100% in top half
Early decision deadline: 11/1, notification date: 12/15
Early action deadline: N/A, notification date: N/A
Application deadline (fall): 1/1
Undergraduate student body: 6,255 full time, 293 part time; 48% male, 52% female; 0% American Indian, 13% Asian, 7% black, 11% Hispanic, 5% multiracial, 0% Pacific Islander, 44% white, 12% international; 5% from in state; 78% live on campus; 22% of students in fraternities, 10% in sororities
Most popular majors: 10% Biology/Biological Sciences, General, 4% Computer Science, 10% Economics, General, 4% History, General, 4% Neuroscience
Expenses: 2015-2016: $49,346; room/board: $12,700
Financial aid: (401) 863-2721; 45% of undergrads determined to have financial need; average aid package $42,468

Bryant University

Smithfield RI
(800) 622-7001
U.S. News ranking: Reg. U. (N), No. 11
Website: www.bryant.edu
Admissions email: admission@bryant.edu
Private; founded 1863
Freshman admissions: selective; 2014-2015: 6,227 applied, 4,675 accepted. Neither SAT nor ACT required. SAT 25/75 percentile: 1065-1240. High school rank: 20% in top tenth, 52% in top quarter, 87% in top half
Early decision deadline: 12/15, notification date: 1/9
Early action deadline: 12/2, notification date: 1/15
Application deadline (fall): 2/2
Undergraduate student body: 3,232 full time, 88 part time; 58% male, 42% female; 0% American Indian, 4% Asian, 4% black, 7% Hispanic, 1% multiracial, 0% Pacific Islander, 73% white, 8% international; 13% from in state; 82% live on campus; 7% of students in fraternities, 11% in sororities
Most popular majors: 73% Business, Management, Marketing, and Related Support Services, 5% Communication, Journalism, and Related Programs, 5% Mathematics and Statistics, 4% Multi/Interdisciplinary Studies, 3% Social Sciences
Expenses: 2015-2016: $39,808; room/board: $14,270
Financial aid: (401) 232-6020; 63% of undergrads determined to have financial need; average aid package $21,753

Johnson & Wales University

Providence RI
(800) 342-5598
U.S. News ranking: Reg. U. (N), No. 58
Website: www.jwu.edu
Admissions email: admissions.pvd@jwu.edu
Private; founded 1914
Freshman admissions: less selective; 2014-2015: 11,899 applied, 9,656 accepted. Neither SAT nor ACT required. ACT 25/75 percentile: N/A. High school rank: N/A
Early decision deadline: N/A, notification date: N/A
Early action deadline: N/A, notification date: N/A
Application deadline (fall): rolling
Undergraduate student body: 8,529 full time, 644 part time; 41% male, 59% female; 0% American Indian, 1% Asian, 11% black, 11% Hispanic, 6% multiracial, 0% Pacific Islander, 57% white, 8% international; 19% from in state; 44% live on campus; N/A of students in fraternities, N/A in sororities
Most popular majors: 6% Business Administration and Management, General, 6% Culinary Arts/Chef Training, 18% Foodservice Systems Administration/Management, 8% Hotel/Motel Administration/Management, 10% Parks, Recreation and Leisure Facilities Management, General
Expenses: 2015-2016: $29,576; room/board: $11,226
Financial aid: (401) 598-1468; 75% of undergrads determined to have financial need; average aid package $19,208

New England Institute of Technology

East Greenwich RI
(401) 467-7744
U.S. News ranking: Reg. Coll. (N), unranked
Website: www.neit.edu/
Admissions email: NEITAdmissions@neit.edu
Private; founded 1940
Freshman admissions: N/A; 2014-2015: N/A applied, N/A accepted. Neither SAT nor ACT required. ACT 25/75 percentile: N/A. High school rank: N/A
Early decision deadline: N/A, notification date: N/A
Early action deadline: N/A, notification date: N/A
Application deadline (fall): rolling
Undergraduate student body: 2,417 full time, 424 part time; 68% male, 32% female; 1% American Indian, 2% Asian, 5% black, 10% Hispanic, 1% multiracial, 0% Pacific Islander, 68% white, 4% international
Most popular majors: Information not available
Expenses: 2015-2016: $23,031; room/board: N/A
Financial aid: (800) 736-7744

Providence College

Providence RI
(401) 865-2535
U.S. News ranking: Reg. U. (N), No. 2
Website: www.providence.edu
Admissions email: pcadmiss@providence.edu
Private; founded 1917
Affiliation: Roman Catholic
Freshman admissions: more selective; 2014-2015: 8,976 applied, 5,660 accepted. Neither SAT nor ACT required. SAT 25/75 percentile: 1040-1250. High school rank: 34% in top tenth, 65% in top quarter, 94% in top half
Early decision deadline: 12/1, notification date: 1/1
Early action deadline: 11/1, notification date: 11/1
Application deadline (fall): 1/15
Undergraduate student body: 3,866 full time, 310 part time; 43% male, 57% female; 0% American Indian, 1% Asian, 4% black, 8% Hispanic, 2% multiracial, 0% Pacific Islander, 77% white, 2% international; 13% from in state; 72% live on campus; N/A of students in fraternities, N/A in sororities
Most popular majors: 7% Biological and Biomedical Sciences, 34% Business, Management, Marketing, and Related Support Services, 7% Health Professions and Related Programs, 7% Psychology, 11% Social Sciences
Expenses: 2015-2016: $45,400; room/board: $13,390
Financial aid: (401) 865-2286; 55% of undergrads determined to have financial need; average aid package $27,800

Rhode Island College

Providence RI
(800) 669-5760
U.S. News ranking: Reg. U. (N), No. 131
Website: www.ric.edu
Admissions email: admissions@ric.edu
Public; founded 1854
Freshman admissions: less selective; 2014-2015: 4,837 applied, 3,166 accepted. Either SAT or ACT required. SAT 25/75 percentile: 810-1030. High school rank: 10% in top tenth, 34% in top quarter, 76% in top half
Early decision deadline: N/A, notification date: N/A
Early action deadline: N/A, notification date: N/A
Application deadline (fall): 3/15

Undergraduate student body: 5,616 full time, 1,902 part time; 33% male, 67% female; 0% American Indian, 3% Asian, 8% black, 14% Hispanic, 2% multiracial, 0% Pacific Islander, 63% white, 0% international; 85% from in state; 15% live on campus; N/A of students in fraternities, N/A in sororities
Most popular majors: 14% Business, Management, Marketing, and Related Support Services, 13% Education, 16% Health Professions and Related Programs, 11% Psychology, 8% Social Sciences
Expenses: 2015-2016: $8,197 in state, $19,858 out of state; room/board: $10,394
Financial aid: (401) 456-8033; 69% of undergrads determined to have financial need; average aid package $8,999

Rhode Island School of Design

Providence RI
(401) 454-6300
U.S. News ranking: Arts, unranked
Website: www.risd.edu
Admissions email: admissions@risd.edu
Private; founded 1877
Freshman admissions: N/A; 2014-2015: 2,408 applied, 993 accepted. Either SAT or ACT required. SAT 25/75 percentile: 1110-1380. High school rank: N/A
Early decision deadline: 11/1, notification date: 12/7
Early action deadline: N/A, notification date: N/A
Application deadline (fall): 2/1
Undergraduate student body: 2,014 full time, N/A part time; 33% male, 67% female; 0% American Indian, 18% Asian, 2% black, 8% Hispanic, 4% multiracial, 0% Pacific Islander, 32% white, 26% international; 6% from in state; 60% live on campus; 0% of students in fraternities, 0% in sororities
Most popular majors: 11% Architecture, 11% Graphic Design, 17% Illustration, 14% Industrial and Product Design, 10% Painting
Expenses: 2015-2016: $45,840; room/board: $12,600
Financial aid: (401) 454-6636; 39% of undergrads determined to have financial need; average aid package $28,778

Roger Williams University

Bristol RI
(401) 254-3500
U.S. News ranking: Reg. U. (N), No. 36
Website: www.rwu.edu
Admissions email: admit@rwu.edu
Private; founded 1956
Freshman admissions: selective; 2014-2015: 9,913 applied, 7,726 accepted. Neither SAT nor ACT required. SAT 25/75 percentile: 1030-1200. High school rank: 15% in top tenth, 44% in top quarter, 81% in top half
Early decision deadline: N/A, notification date: N/A
Early action deadline: 11/1, notification date: 12/15
Application deadline (fall): 2/1
Undergraduate student body: 4,030 full time, 580 part time; 50% male, 50% female; 1% American Indian, 2% Asian, 2% black, 5% Hispanic, 0% multiracial, 0% Pacific Islander, 73% white, 5% international; 18% from in state; 77% live on campus; 0% of students in fraternities, 0% in sororities
Most popular majors: 12% Architecture and Related Services, 20% Business, Management, Marketing, and Related Support Services, 7% Communication, Journalism, and Related Programs, 10% Homeland Security, Law Enforcement, Firefighting and Related Protective Services, 9% Psychology
Expenses: 2015-2016: $31,800; room/board: $14,846
Financial aid: (401) 254-3100; 61% of undergrads determined to have financial need; average aid package $20,466

Salve Regina University

Newport RI
(888) 467-2583
U.S. News ranking: Reg. U. (N), No. 36
Website: www.salve.edu
Admissions email: sruadmis@salve.edu
Private; founded 1934
Affiliation: Roman Catholic
Freshman admissions: selective; 2014-2015: 4,810 applied, 3,412 accepted. Neither SAT nor ACT required. SAT 25/75 percentile: 1010-1180. High school rank: 16% in top tenth, 45% in top quarter, 79% in top half
Early decision deadline: N/A, notification date: N/A
Early action deadline: 11/1, notification date: 12/25
Application deadline (fall): rolling
Undergraduate student body: 1,959 full time, 162 part time; 30% male, 70% female; 0% American Indian, 1% Asian, 2% black, 7% Hispanic, 2% multiracial, 0% Pacific Islander, 78% white, 2% international; 22% from in state; 58% live on campus; 0% of students in fraternities, 0% in sororities
Most popular majors: 7% Biology/Biological Sciences, General, 9% Criminal Justice/Law Enforcement Administration, 8% Marketing/Marketing Management, General, 8% Psychology, General, 15% Registered Nursing/Registered Nurse
Expenses: 2015-2016: $36,740; room/board: $13,250
Financial aid: (401) 341-2901; 81% of undergrads determined to have financial need; average aid package $24,568

University of Rhode Island

Kingston RI
(401) 874-7100
U.S. News ranking: Nat. U., No. 161
Website: www.uri.edu
Admissions email: admission@uri.edu
Public; founded 1892
Freshman admissions: selective; 2014-2015: 20,928 applied, 15,846 accepted. Either SAT or ACT required. SAT 25/75 percentile: 1010-1200. High school rank: 19% in top tenth, 49% in top quarter, 86% in top half
Early decision deadline: N/A, notification date: N/A
Early action deadline: 12/1, notification date: 1/31
Application deadline (fall): 2/1
Undergraduate student body: 12,139 full time, 1,450 part time; 46% male, 54% female; 0% American Indian, 3% Asian, 5% black, 9% Hispanic, 3% multiracial, 0% Pacific Islander, 70% white, 1% international; 56% from in state; 45% live on campus; 5% of students in fraternities, 7% in sororities
Most popular majors: 5% Human Development and Family Studies, General, 5% Kinesiology and Exercise Science, 7% Psychology, General, 8% Registered Nursing/Registered Nurse, 7% Speech Communication and Rhetoric
Expenses: 2014-2015: $12,506 in state, $28,072 out of state; room/board: $11,496
Financial aid: (401) 874-9500; 83% of undergrads determined to have financial need; average aid package $15,819

SOUTH CAROLINA

Allen University

Columbia SC
(803) 376-5735
U.S. News ranking: Nat. Lib. Arts, second tier
Website: www.allenuniversity.edu
Admissions email: admissions@allenuniversity.edu
Private; founded 1870
Affiliation: African Methodist Episcopal
Freshman admissions: less selective; 2014-2015: 2,784 applied, 1,195 accepted. Neither SAT nor ACT required. Average composite ACT score: 16. High school rank: N/A
Early decision deadline: N/A, notification date: N/A
Early action deadline: N/A, notification date: N/A
Application deadline (fall): rolling
Undergraduate student body: 660 full time, 18 part time; 44% male, 56% female; 0% American Indian, 0% Asian, 96% black, 1% Hispanic, 0% multiracial, 0% Pacific Islander, 1% white, 3% international; 91% from in state; 15% live on campus; 26% of students in fraternities, 73% in sororities
Most popular majors: Information not available
Expenses: 2015-2016: $12,970; room/board: $6,560
Financial aid: (803) 376-5736; 100% of undergrads determined to have financial need; average aid package $11,674

Anderson University

Anderson SC
(864) 231-5607
U.S. News ranking: Reg. Coll. (S), No. 16
Website: www.andersonuniversity.edu
Admissions email: admission@andersonuniversity.edu
Private; founded 1911
Affiliation: South Carolina Baptist Convention
Freshman admissions: selective; 2014-2015: 2,958 applied, 1,852 accepted. Either SAT or ACT required. SAT 25/75 percentile: 920-1170. High school rank: 42% in top tenth, 63% in top quarter, 89% in top half
Early decision deadline: N/A, notification date: N/A
Early action deadline: N/A, notification date: N/A
Application deadline (fall): rolling
Undergraduate student body: 2,286 full time, 490 part time; 32% male, 68% female; 1% American Indian, 1% Asian, 9% black, 3% Hispanic, 0% multiracial, 1% Pacific Islander, 80% white, 2% international; 81% from in state; 51% live on campus; 0% of students in fraternities, 0% in sororities
Most popular majors: 28% Business, Management, Marketing, and Related Support Services, 17% Education, 6% Homeland Security, Law Enforcement, Firefighting and Related Protective Services, 7% Parks, Recreation, Leisure, and Fitness Studies, 13% Visual and Performing Arts
Expenses: 2015-2016: $24,860; room/board: $8,860
Financial aid: (864) 231-2070; 82% of undergrads determined to have financial need; average aid package $18,123

Benedict College

Columbia SC
(803) 253-5143
U.S. News ranking: Reg. Coll. (S), second tier
Website: www.benedict.edu
Admissions email: admissions@benedict.edu
Private; founded 1870
Affiliation: Baptist
Freshman admissions: least selective; 2014-2015: 8,624 applied, 6,258 accepted. Neither SAT nor ACT required. Average composite ACT score: 17. High school rank: N/A
Early decision deadline: N/A, notification date: N/A
Early action deadline: N/A, notification date: N/A
Application deadline (fall): rolling
Undergraduate student body: 2,405 full time, 39 part time; 50% male, 50% female; N/A American Indian, N/A Asian, 99% black, 0% Hispanic, N/A multiracial, 0% Pacific Islander, 0% white, N/A international
Most popular majors: 0% Biology/Biological Sciences, General
Expenses: 2014-2015: $18,288; room/board: $8,104
Financial aid: (803) 253-5105

Charleston Southern University

Charleston SC
(843) 863-7050
U.S. News ranking: Reg. U. (S), No. 93
Website: www.csuniv.edu
Admissions email: enroll@csuniv.edu
Private; founded 1964
Affiliation: Baptist
Freshman admissions: selective; 2014-2015: 4,197 applied, 2,463 accepted. Either SAT or ACT required. SAT 25/75 percentile: 890-1080. High school rank: 14% in top tenth, 51% in top quarter, 76% in top half
Early decision deadline: N/A, notification date: N/A
Early action deadline: N/A, notification date: N/A
Application deadline (fall): rolling
Undergraduate student body: 2,638 full time, 329 part time; 37% male, 63% female; 1% American Indian, 1% Asian, 28% black, 3% Hispanic, 2% multiracial, 0% Pacific Islander, 60% white, 1% international; 85% from in state; 40% live on campus; N/A of students in fraternities, N/A in sororities
Most popular majors: 8% Criminal Justice/Law Enforcement Administration, 9% Health and Physical Education/Fitness, General, 6% Non-Profit/Public/Organizational Management, 10% Psychology, General, 9% Registered Nursing/Registered Nurse
Expenses: 2015-2016: $23,440; room/board: $9,270
Financial aid: (843) 863-7050

The Citadel

Charleston SC
(843) 953-5230
U.S. News ranking: Reg. U. (S), No. 3
Website: www.citadel.edu/root/
Admissions email: admissions@citadel.edu
Public; founded 1842
Freshman admissions: selective; 2014-2015: 2,625 applied, 1,983 accepted. Either SAT or ACT required. SAT 25/75 percentile: 990-1190. High school rank: 12% in top tenth, 33% in top quarter, 74% in top half
Early decision deadline: N/A, notification date: N/A
Early action deadline: N/A, notification date: N/A
Application deadline (fall): rolling
Undergraduate student body: 2,531 full time, 232 part time; 90% male, 10% female; 1% American Indian, 2% Asian, 8% black, 7% Hispanic, 3% multiracial, 0% Pacific Islander, 77% white, 1% international; 58% from in state; 100% live on campus; 0% of students in fraternities, 0% in sororities
Most popular majors: 28% Business Administration and Management, General, 16% Criminal Justice/Law Enforcement Administration, 14% Engineering, General, 7% Secondary Education and Teaching, 10% Social Sciences, General
Expenses: 2014-2015: $12,568 in state, $32,176 out of state; room/board: $6,381
Financial aid: (843) 953-5187; 58% of undergrads determined to have financial need; average aid package $14,819

Claflin University

Orangeburg SC
(803) 535-5340
U.S. News ranking: Nat. Lib. Arts, No. 174
Website: www.claflin.edu
Admissions email: mike.zeigler@claflin.edu
Private; founded 1869
Affiliation: United Methodist

Freshman admissions: least selective; 2014-2015: 5,237 applied, 2,292 accepted. Either SAT or ACT required. SAT 25/75 percentile: 700-880. High school rank: 10% in top tenth, 26% in top quarter, 63% in top half
Early decision deadline: N/A, notification date: N/A
Early action deadline: N/A, notification date: N/A
Application deadline (fall): rolling
Undergraduate student body: 1,751 full time, 52 part time; 35% male, 65% female; 1% American Indian, 1% Asian, 91% black, 2% Hispanic, 0% multiracial, 0% Pacific Islander, 1% white, 4% international; 82% from in state; 59% live on campus; 3% of students in fraternities, 6% in sororities
Most popular majors: 8% Biology/Biological Sciences, General, 9% Business Administration and Management, General, 9% Criminal Justice/Law Enforcement Administration, 10% Mass Communication/Media Studies, 12% Sociology
Expenses: 2015-2016: $15,650; room/board: $10,794
Financial aid: (803) 535-5334; 93% of undergrads determined to have financial need; average aid package $14,722

Clemson University

Clemson SC
(864) 656-2287
U.S. News ranking: Nat. U., No. 61
Website: www.clemson.edu
Admissions email: cuadmissions@clemson.edu
Public; founded 1889
Freshman admissions: more selective; 2014-2015: 20,755 applied, 10,967 accepted. Either SAT or ACT required. SAT 25/75 percentile: 1160-1350. High school rank: 53% in top tenth, 85% in top quarter, 97% in top half
Early decision deadline: N/A, notification date: N/A
Early action deadline: N/A, notification date: N/A
Application deadline (fall): 5/1
Undergraduate student body: 16,572 full time, 688 part time; 53% male, 47% female; 0% American Indian, 2% Asian, 6% black, 3% Hispanic, 2% multiracial, 0% Pacific Islander, 83% white, 1% international; 69% from in state; 41% live on campus; 10% of students in fraternities, 15% in sororities
Most popular majors: 9% Biological and Biomedical Sciences, 18% Business, Management, Marketing, and Related Support Services, 19% Engineering, 7% Health Professions and Related Programs, 7% Social Sciences
Expenses: 2015-2016: $14,240 in state, $32,796 out of state; room/board: $8,718
Financial aid: (864) 656-2280; 46% of undergrads determined to have financial need; average aid package $10,812

Coastal Carolina University

Conway SC
(843) 349-2170
U.S. News ranking: Reg. U. (S), No. 63
Website: www.coastal.edu
Admissions email: admissions@coastal.edu
Public; founded 1954
Freshman admissions: selective; 2014-2015: 14,799 applied, 9,412 accepted. Either SAT or ACT required. SAT 25/75 percentile: 910-1090. High school rank: 8% in top tenth, 29% in top quarter, 67% in top half
Early decision deadline: N/A, notification date: N/A
Early action deadline: N/A, notification date: N/A
Application deadline (fall): 8/1
Undergraduate student body: 8,502 full time, 862 part time; 46% male, 54% female; 0% American Indian, 1% Asian, 20% black, 4% Hispanic, 4% multiracial, 0% Pacific Islander, 70% white, 1% international; 50% from in state; 39% live on campus; 2% of students in fraternities, 5% in sororities
Most popular majors: 9% Business Administration and Management, General, 6% Kinesiology and Exercise Science, 6% Liberal Arts and Sciences/Liberal Studies, 6% Marketing/Marketing Management, General, 8% Speech Communication and Rhetoric
Expenses: 2014-2015: $10,140 in state, $23,480 out of state; room/board: $8,440
Financial aid: (843) 349-2313; 72% of undergrads determined to have financial need; average aid package $9,964

Coker College

Hartsville SC
(843) 383-8050
U.S. News ranking: Reg. Coll. (S), No. 20
Website: www.coker.edu
Admissions email: admissions@coker.edu
Private; founded 1908
Freshman admissions: selective; 2014-2015: 1,393 applied, 709 accepted. Either SAT or ACT required. SAT 25/75 percentile: 910-1108. High school rank: 7% in top tenth, 18% in top quarter, 53% in top half
Early decision deadline: N/A, notification date: N/A
Early action deadline: N/A, notification date: N/A
Application deadline (fall): 8/1
Undergraduate student body: 967 full time, 198 part time; 38% male, 62% female; 1% American Indian, 0% Asian, 35% black, 3% Hispanic, 0% multiracial, 0% Pacific Islander, 52% white, 1% international
Most popular majors: 18% Business Administration and Management, General, 10% Criminology, 9% Psychology, General, 9% Social Work, 9% Sport and Fitness Administration/Management
Expenses: 2015-2016: $26,568; room/board: $8,242
Financial aid: (843) 383-8055; 73% of undergrads determined to have financial need; average aid package $19,754

College of Charleston

Charleston SC
(843) 953-5670
U.S. News ranking: Reg. U. (S), No. 11
Website: www.cofc.edu
Admissions email: admissions@cofc.edu
Public; founded 1770
Freshman admissions: selective; 2014-2015: 11,179 applied, 8,722 accepted. Either SAT or ACT required. SAT 25/75 percentile: 1030-1230. High school rank: 21% in top tenth, 55% in top quarter, 90% in top half
Early decision deadline: N/A, notification date: N/A
Early action deadline: 11/1, notification date: 1/1
Application deadline (fall): 4/1
Undergraduate student body: 9,608 full time, 832 part time; 37% male, 63% female; 0% American Indian, 2% Asian, 7% black, 4% Hispanic, 4% multiracial, 0% Pacific Islander, 81% white, 1% international; 64% from in state; 31% live on campus; 19% of students in fraternities, 23% in sororities
Most popular majors: 12% Biological and Biomedical Sciences, 23% Business, Management, Marketing, and Related Support Services, 9% Communication, Journalism, and Related Programs, 10% Social Sciences, 9% Visual and Performing Arts
Expenses: 2015-2016: $11,360 in state, $28,904 out of state; room/board: N/A
Financial aid: (843) 953-5540; 48% of undergrads determined to have financial need; average aid package $13,248

Columbia College

Columbia SC
(800) 277-1301
U.S. News ranking: Reg. U. (S), No. 37
Website: www.columbiasc.edu
Admissions email: admissions@columbiasc.edu
Private; founded 1854
Affiliation: United Methodist
Freshman admissions: selective; 2014-2015: 420 applied, 332 accepted. Either SAT or ACT required. SAT 25/75 percentile: 900-1140. High school rank: 22% in top tenth, 52% in top quarter, 81% in top half
Early decision deadline: N/A, notification date: N/A
Early action deadline: N/A, notification date: N/A
Application deadline (fall): rolling
Undergraduate student body: 794 full time, 326 part time; 14% male, 86% female; 0% American Indian, 1% Asian, 37% black, 5% Hispanic, 4% multiracial, 0% Pacific Islander, 51% white, 2% international; 93% from in state; 37% live on campus; 0% of students in fraternities, 0% in sororities
Most popular majors: 10% Behavioral Sciences, 7% Biology/Biological Sciences, General, 7% Business Administration and Management, General, 8% Human Development, Family Studies, and Related Services, Other, 14% Psychology, General

Expenses: 2015-2016: $28,100; room/board: $7,400
Financial aid: (803) 786-3612; 86% of undergrads determined to have financial need; average aid package $22,390

Columbia International University

Columbia SC
(800) 777-2227
U.S. News ranking: Reg. U. (S), No. 35
Website: www.ciu.edu
Admissions email: N/A
Private; founded 1923
Affiliation: Evangelical multi-denominational
Freshman admissions: selective; 2014-2015: 569 applied, 189 accepted. Either SAT or ACT required. SAT 25/75 percentile: 980-1190. High school rank: 12% in top tenth, 34% in top quarter, 75% in top half
Early decision deadline: N/A, notification date: N/A
Early action deadline: N/A, notification date: N/A
Application deadline (fall): 8/1
Undergraduate student body: 497 full time, 63 part time; 49% male, 51% female; 0% American Indian, 2% Asian, 13% black, 3% Hispanic, 2% multiracial, 0% Pacific Islander, 72% white, 4% international; 59% from in state; 60% live on campus; N/A of students in fraternities, N/A in sororities
Most popular majors: 10% General Studies, 8% Humanities/Humanistic Studies, 10% Mass Communication/Media Studies, 14% Psychology, General, 13% Youth Ministry
Expenses: 2014-2015: $19,480; room/board: $7,310
Financial aid: (803) 754-4100

Converse College

Spartanburg SC
(864) 596-9040
U.S. News ranking: Reg. U. (S), No. 25
Website: www.converse.edu
Admissions email: info@converse.edu
Private; founded 1889
Freshman admissions: selective; 2014-2015: 1,697 applied, 909 accepted. Either SAT or ACT required. SAT 25/75 percentile: 930-1150. High school rank: 20% in top tenth, 48% in top quarter, 85% in top half
Early decision deadline: N/A, notification date: N/A
Early action deadline: N/A, notification date: N/A
Application deadline (fall): rolling
Undergraduate student body: 750 full time, 73 part time; 0% male, 100% female; 0% American Indian, 0% Asian, 9% black, 6% Hispanic, 4% multiracial, 0% Pacific Islander, 63% white, 1% international
Most popular majors: 10% Biological and Biomedical Sciences, 8% Business, Management, Marketing, and Related Support Services, 23% Education, 19% Psychology, 13% Visual and Performing Arts
Expenses: 2015-2016: $16,850; room/board: $9,995

Financial aid: (864) 596-9019; 81% of undergrads determined to have financial need; average aid package $14,940

Erskine College

Due West SC
(864) 379-8838
U.S. News ranking: Nat. Lib. Arts, second tier
Website: www.erskine.edu
Admissions email: admissions@erskine.edu
Private; founded 1839
Affiliation: Associate Reformed Presbyterian
Freshman admissions: selective; 2014-2015: 913 applied, 553 accepted. Either SAT or ACT required. SAT 25/75 percentile: 900-1140. High school rank: 15% in top tenth, 30% in top quarter, 68% in top half
Early decision deadline: N/A, notification date: N/A
Early action deadline: N/A, notification date: N/A
Application deadline (fall): rolling
Undergraduate student body: 571 full time, 20 part time; 52% male, 48% female; 0% American Indian, 1% Asian, 11% black, 3% Hispanic, 0% multiracial, 0% Pacific Islander, 66% white, 0% international; 69% from in state; 92% live on campus; 0% of students in fraternities, 0% in sororities
Most popular majors: 21% Biological and Biomedical Sciences, 13% Business, Management, Marketing, and Related Support Services, 6% English Language and Literature/Letters, 12% Parks, Recreation, Leisure, and Fitness Studies, 7% Physical Sciences
Expenses: 2015-2016: $33,315; room/board: $10,500
Financial aid: (864) 379-8832; 100% of undergrads determined to have financial need; average aid package $22,315

Francis Marion University

Florence SC
(843) 661-1231
U.S. News ranking: Reg. U. (S), No. 76
Website: www.fmarion.edu
Admissions email: admissions@fmarion.edu
Public; founded 1970
Freshman admissions: less selective; 2014-2015: 3,759 applied, 2,222 accepted. Either SAT or ACT required. ACT 25/75 percentile: 17-21. High school rank: 16% in top tenth, 46% in top quarter, 83% in top half
Early decision deadline: N/A, notification date: N/A
Early action deadline: N/A, notification date: N/A
Application deadline (fall): 8/15
Undergraduate student body: 3,168 full time, 437 part time; 31% male, 69% female; 0% American Indian, 1% Asian, 49% black, 2% Hispanic, 1% multiracial, 0% Pacific Islander, 45% white, 2% international; 96% from in state; 39% live on campus; 1% of students in fraternities, 1% in sororities
Most popular majors: 14% Biological and Biomedical Sciences, 18% Business,

Management, Marketing, and Related Support Services, 16% Health Professions and Related Programs, 10% Psychology, 9% Social Sciences
Expenses: 2015-2016: $532 in state, $19,668 out of state; room/board: $7,472
Financial aid: (843) 661-1190; 81% of undergrads determined to have financial need; average aid package $11,317

Furman University

Greenville SC
(864) 294-2034
U.S. News ranking: Nat. Lib. Arts, No. 51
Website: www.furman.edu/
Admissions email: admissions@furman.edu
Private; founded 1826
Freshman admissions: more selective; 2014-2015: 4,583 applied, 3,149 accepted. Neither SAT nor ACT required. SAT 25/75 percentile: 1130-1340. High school rank: 38% in top tenth, 72% in top quarter, 92% in top half
Early decision deadline: 11/1, notification date: 11/30
Early action deadline: 11/15, notification date: 2/1
Application deadline (fall): 1/15
Undergraduate student body: 2,698 full time, 112 part time; 43% male, 57% female; 0% American Indian, 2% Asian, 5% black, 4% Hispanic, 3% multiracial, 0% Pacific Islander, 80% white, 5% international; 28% from in state; 94% live on campus; 41% of students in fraternities, 54% in sororities
Most popular majors: 8% Business Administration, Management and Operations, 6% Communication and Media Studies, 9% Health Professions and Related Clinical Sciences, Other, 6% History, 11% Political Science and Government
Expenses: 2015-2016: $46,012; room/board: $11,522
Financial aid: (864) 294-2204; 43% of undergrads determined to have financial need; average aid package $35,321

Lander University

Greenwood SC
(864) 388-8307
U.S. News ranking: Reg. Coll. (S), No. 44
Website: www.lander.edu
Admissions email: admissions@lander.edu
Public; founded 1872
Freshman admissions: selective; 2014-2015: 2,963 applied, 1,712 accepted. Either SAT or ACT required. SAT 25/75 percentile: 840-1040. High school rank: 12% in top tenth, 40% in top quarter, 77% in top half
Early decision deadline: N/A, notification date: N/A
Early action deadline: N/A, notification date: N/A
Application deadline (fall): rolling
Undergraduate student body: 2,524 full time, 193 part time; 31% male, 69% female; 0% American Indian, 2% Asian, 32% black, 1% Hispanic, 2% multiracial, 0% Pacific Islander, 59% white, 1% international; 94% from in state; 48% live on campus; 1% of students in fraternities, 7% in sororities
Most popular majors: 20% Business Administration and Management, General, 7% Humanities/Humanistic Studies, 10% Kinesiology and Exercise Science, 7% Psychology, General, 8% Registered Nursing/Registered Nurse
Expenses: 2014-2015: $10,428 in state, $19,748 out of state; room/board: $8,000
Financial aid: (864) 388-8340

Limestone College

Gaffney SC
(864) 488-4554
U.S. News ranking: Reg. Coll. (S), No. 73
Website: www.limestone.edu
Admissions email: admiss@limestone.edu
Private; founded 1845
Affiliation: Christian nondenominational
Freshman admissions: selective; 2014-2015: 3,154 applied, 1,640 accepted. Either SAT or ACT required. SAT 25/75 percentile: 960-1100. High school rank: 7% in top tenth, 19% in top quarter, 52% in top half
Early decision deadline: N/A, notification date: N/A
Early action deadline: N/A, notification date: N/A
Application deadline (fall): 8/22
Undergraduate student body: 1,171 full time, 17 part time; 61% male, 39% female; 0% American Indian, 0% Asian, 32% black, 4% Hispanic, 3% multiracial, 0% Pacific Islander, 51% white, 9% international; N/A from in state; 64% live on campus; 0% of students in fraternities, 0% in sororities
Most popular majors: 28% Business, Management, Marketing, and Related Support Services, 11% Education, 9% Homeland Security, Law Enforcement, Firefighting and Related Protective Services, 10% Liberal Arts and Sciences, General Studies and Humanities, 20% Parks, Recreation, Leisure, and Fitness Studies
Expenses: 2015-2016: $23,900; room/board: $8,100
Financial aid: (864) 488-8231; 67% of undergrads determined to have financial need; average aid package $17,083

Morris College[1]

Sumter SC
(803) 934-3225
U.S. News ranking: Reg. Coll. (S), unranked
Website: www.morris.edu
Admissions email: dcalhoun@morris.edu
Private
Application deadline (fall): N/A
Undergraduate student body: N/A full time, N/A part time
Expenses: 2014-2015: $12,317; room/board: $5,028
Financial aid: (803) 934-3238

Newberry College

Newberry SC
(800) 845-4955
U.S. News ranking: Reg. Coll. (S), No. 41
Website: www.newberry.edu/
Admissions email: admissions@newberry.edu
Private; founded 1856
Affiliation: Evangelical Lutheran Church of America
Freshman admissions: less selective; 2014-2015: 996 applied, 571 accepted. Either SAT or ACT required. SAT 25/75 percentile: 830-1050. High school rank: 11% in top tenth, 25% in top quarter, 63% in top half
Early decision deadline: N/A, notification date: N/A
Early action deadline: N/A, notification date: N/A
Application deadline (fall): rolling
Undergraduate student body: 1,049 full time, 44 part time; 53% male, 47% female; 0% American Indian, 1% Asian, 26% black, 4% Hispanic, 3% multiracial, 0% Pacific Islander, 59% white, 4% international; 77% from in state; 77% live on campus; 16% of students in fraternities, 24% in sororities
Most popular majors: 21% Business Administration and Management, General, 15% Education, General, 10% Parks, Recreation and Leisure Studies, 10% Psychology, General, 7% Registered Nursing/Registered Nurse
Expenses: 2015-2016: $25,000; room/board: $9,550
Financial aid: (803) 321-5120; 94% of undergrads determined to have financial need; average aid package $23,322

North Greenville University

Tigerville SC
(864) 977-7001
U.S. News ranking: Reg. Coll. (S), No. 27
Website: www.ngu.edu
Admissions email: admissions@ngu.edu
Private; founded 1892
Affiliation: Southern Baptist Convention
Freshman admissions: selective; 2014-2015: 1,776 applied, 1,056 accepted. Either SAT or ACT required. ACT 25/75 percentile: 22-30. High school rank: 24% in top tenth, 37% in top quarter, 75% in top half
Early decision deadline: N/A, notification date: N/A
Early action deadline: N/A, notification date: N/A
Application deadline (fall): rolling
Undergraduate student body: 2,063 full time, 256 part time; 51% male, 49% female; 0% American Indian, 0% Asian, 8% black, 3% Hispanic, 1% multiracial, 0% Pacific Islander, 83% white, 0% international; 77% from in state; 68% live on campus; 0% of students in fraternities, 0% in sororities
Most popular majors: 15% Business, Management, Marketing, and Related Support Services, 14% Education, 17% Liberal Arts and Sciences, General Studies and Humanities, 14% Parks, Recreation, Leisure, and Fitness Studies, 12% Theology and Religious Vocations
Expenses: 2015-2016: $16,290; room/board: $9,640
Financial aid: (864) 977-7058; 59% of undergrads determined to have financial need; average aid package $5,812

Presbyterian College

Clinton SC
(864) 833-8230
U.S. News ranking: Nat. Lib. Arts, No. 127
Website: www.presby.edu
Admissions email: admissions@presby.edu
Private; founded 1880
Affiliation: Presbyterian Church (USA)
Freshman admissions: selective; 2014-2015: 1,506 applied, 809 accepted. Neither SAT nor ACT required. SAT 25/75 percentile: 970-1210. High school rank: 29% in top tenth, 58% in top quarter, 90% in top half
Early decision deadline: 11/1, notification date: 12/1
Early action deadline: 11/15, notification date: 12/15
Application deadline (fall): 6/30
Undergraduate student body: 1,078 full time, 68 part time; 45% male, 55% female; 0% American Indian, 1% Asian, 12% black, 2% Hispanic, 2% multiracial, 0% Pacific Islander, 81% white, 1% international; 62% from in state; 97% live on campus; 38% of students in fraternities, 47% in sororities
Most popular majors: 14% Biological and Biomedical Sciences, 23% Business, Management, Marketing, and Related Support Services, 7% History, 11% Psychology, 8% Social Sciences
Expenses: 2015-2016: $36,130; room/board: $9,750
Financial aid: (864) 833-8289

South Carolina State University

Orangeburg SC
(803) 536-7185
U.S. News ranking: Nat. U., No. 194
Website: www.scsu.edu
Admissions email: admissions@scsu.edu
Public; founded 1896
Freshman admissions: least selective; 2014-2015: 2,911 applied, 2,461 accepted. Either SAT or ACT required. ACT 25/75 percentile: 15-18. High school rank: 6% in top tenth, 35% in top quarter, 47% in top half
Early decision deadline: N/A, notification date: N/A
Early action deadline: N/A, notification date: N/A
Application deadline (fall): 7/31
Undergraduate student body: 2,581 full time, 210 part time; 49% male, 51% female; 0% American Indian, 1% Asian, 95% black, 1% Hispanic, 0% multiracial, 0% Pacific Islander, 2% white, 0% international; 80% from in state; 64% live on campus; 20% of students in fraternities, 20% in sororities
Most popular majors: 9% Biology/Biological Sciences, General, 7% Criminal Justice/Law Enforcement Administration, 10% Family and Consumer Sciences/Human Sciences, General, 8% Registered Nursing/Registered Nurse, 8% Social Work
Expenses: 2015-2016: $10,088 in state, $19,856 out of state; room/board: $9,402
Financial aid: (803) 536-7067

Southern Wesleyan University[1]

Central SC
(864) 644-5550
U.S. News ranking: Reg. U. (S), second tier
Website: www.swu.edu
Admissions email: admissions@swu.edu
Private
Application deadline (fall): N/A
Undergraduate student body: N/A full time, N/A part time
Expenses: 2014-2015: $22,950; room/board: $8,710
Financial aid: (864) 644-5500

University of South Carolina

Columbia SC
(803) 777-7700
U.S. News ranking: Nat. U., No. 108
Website: www.sc.edu
Admissions email: admissions-ugrad@sc.edu
Public; founded 1801
Freshman admissions: more selective; 2014-2015: 23,341 applied, 15,219 accepted. Either SAT or ACT required. SAT 25/75 percentile: 1110-1300. High school rank: 29% in top tenth, 64% in top quarter, 93% in top half
Early decision deadline: N/A, notification date: N/A
Early action deadline: 10/15, notification date: 12/20
Application deadline (fall): 12/1
Undergraduate student body: 23,177 full time, 1,686 part time; 46% male, 54% female; 0% American Indian, 3% Asian, 10% black, 4% Hispanic, 3% multiracial, 0% Pacific Islander, 77% white, 1% international; 64% from in state; 29% live on campus; 16% of students in fraternities, 30% in sororities
Most popular majors: 6% Biology, General, 5% Business Administration, Management and Operations, 5% Physiology, Pathology and Related Sciences, 5% Public Relations, Advertising, and Applied Communication, 6% Research and Experimental Psychology
Expenses: 2014-2015: $11,158 in state, $29,440 out of state; room/board: $9,248
Financial aid: (803) 777-8134; 53% of undergrads determined to have financial need; average aid package $10,148

University of South Carolina–Aiken

Aiken SC
(803) 641-3366
U.S. News ranking: Reg. Coll. (S), No. 18
Website: web.usca.edu/
Admissions email: admit@sc.edu
Public; founded 1961
Freshman admissions: selective; 2014-2015: 2,102 applied, 1,376 accepted. Either SAT or ACT required. SAT 25/75 percentile: 860-1080. High school rank: 14% in top tenth, 43% in top quarter, 78% in top half
Early decision deadline: N/A, notification date: N/A
Early action deadline: N/A, notification date: N/A
Application deadline (fall): 8/1

More at usnews.com/college

Undergraduate student body: 2,493 full time, 763 part time; 38% male, 62% female; 0% American Indian, 1% Asian, 26% black, 4% Hispanic, 4% multiracial, 0% Pacific Islander, 59% white, 3% international; 88% from in state; 30% live on campus; 8% of students in fraternities, 7% in sororities
Most popular majors: 23% Business, Management, Marketing, and Related Support Services, 11% Education, 15% Health Professions and Related Programs, 12% Parks, Recreation, Leisure, and Fitness Studies, 8% Social Sciences
Expenses: 2014-2015: $9,602 in state, $18,926 out of state; room/board: $7,110
Financial aid: (803) 641-3476; 61% of undergrads determined to have financial need; average aid package $10,374

University of South Carolina–Beaufort

Bluffton SC
(843) 208-8000
U.S. News ranking: Reg. Coll. (S), No. 58
Website: www.uscb.edu
Admissions email: admissions@uscb.edu
Public; founded 1959
Freshman admissions: less selective; 2014-2015: 1,684 applied, 964 accepted. Either SAT or ACT required. SAT 25/75 percentile: 840-1030. High school rank: 5% in top tenth, 25% in top quarter, 64% in top half
Early decision deadline: N/A, notification date: N/A
Early action deadline: N/A, notification date: N/A
Application deadline (fall): rolling
Undergraduate student body: 1,435 full time, 359 part time; 38% male, 62% female; 0% American Indian, 2% Asian, 20% black, 6% Hispanic, 3% multiracial, 0% Pacific Islander, 60% white, 1% international; 80% from in state; N/A live on campus; N/A of students in fraternities, N/A in sororities
Most popular majors: 23% Business Administration and Management, General, 14% Hospitality Administration/Management, General, 14% Psychology, General, 12% Registered Nursing/Registered Nurse, 8% Social Sciences, General
Expenses: 2015-2016: $9,818 in state, $19,994 out of state; room/board: $8,297
Financial aid: (843) 521-3104

University of South Carolina–Upstate

Spartanburg SC
(864) 503-5246
U.S. News ranking: Reg. Coll. (S), No. 33
Website: www.uscupstate.edu/
Admissions email: admissions@uscupstate.edu
Public; founded 1967
Freshman admissions: less selective; 2014-2015: 3,995 applied, 2,098 accepted. Either SAT or ACT required. SAT 25/75 percentile: 850-1040. High school rank: 10% in top tenth, 37% in top quarter, 75% in top half
Early decision deadline: N/A, notification date: N/A
Early action deadline: N/A, notification date: N/A
Application deadline (fall): rolling
Undergraduate student body: 4,232 full time, 1,102 part time; 35% male, 65% female; 0% American Indian, 2% Asian, 29% black, 5% Hispanic, 3% multiracial, 0% Pacific Islander, 56% white, 1% international; 95% from in state; 19% live on campus; 2% of students in fraternities, 2% in sororities
Most popular majors: 13% Business Administration and Management, General, 12% Education, General, 8% Multi/Interdisciplinary Studies, General, 8% Psychology, General, 25% Registered Nursing/Registered Nurse
Expenses: 2014-2015: $10,518 in state, $20,868 out of state; room/board: $7,682
Financial aid: (864) 503-5340; 78% of undergrads determined to have financial need; average aid package $9,704

Voorhees College[1]

Denmark SC
(803) 780-1030
U.S. News ranking: Reg. Coll. (S), second tier
Website: www.voorhees.edu
Admissions email: admissions@voorhees.edu
Private
Application deadline (fall): N/A
Undergraduate student body: N/A full time, N/A part time
Expenses: 2014-2015: $10,780; room/board: $7,346
Financial aid: (803) 780-1150

Winthrop University

Rock Hill SC
(803) 323-2191
U.S. News ranking: Reg. U. (S), No. 26
Website: www.winthrop.edu
Admissions email: admissions@winthrop.edu
Public; founded 1886
Freshman admissions: selective; 2014-2015: 4,546 applied, 3,236 accepted. Either SAT or ACT required. SAT 25/75 percentile: 940-1170. High school rank: 22% in top tenth, 55% in top quarter, 87% in top half
Early decision deadline: N/A, notification date: N/A
Early action deadline: N/A, notification date: N/A
Application deadline (fall): rolling
Undergraduate student body: 4,421 full time, 553 part time; 32% male, 68% female; 0% American Indian, 1% Asian, 30% black, 4% Hispanic, 3% multiracial, 0% Pacific Islander, 58% white, 3% international; 93% from in state; 49% live on campus; 12% of students in fraternities, 11% in sororities
Most popular majors: 23% Business, Management, Marketing, and Related Support Services, 7% Communication, Journalism, and Related Programs, 15% Education, 7% Psychology, 15% Visual and Performing Arts
Expenses: 2015-2016: $14,156 in state, $27,404 out of state; room/board: $8,570
Financial aid: (803) 323-2189; 74% of undergrads determined to have financial need; average aid package $12,387

Wofford College

Spartanburg SC
(864) 597-4130
U.S. News ranking: Nat. Lib. Arts, No. 82
Website: www.wofford.edu
Admissions email: admissions@wofford.edu
Private; founded 1854
Affiliation: United Methodist
Freshman admissions: more selective; 2014-2015: 2,556 applied, 1,978 accepted. Either SAT or ACT required. ACT 25/75 percentile: 24-30. High school rank: 46% in top tenth, 77% in top quarter, 96% in top half
Early decision deadline: 11/1, notification date: 12/1
Early action deadline: 11/15, notification date: 2/1
Application deadline (fall): 2/1
Undergraduate student body: 1,578 full time, 30 part time; 50% male, 50% female; 0% American Indian, 2% Asian, 8% black, 3% Hispanic, 3% multiracial, 0% Pacific Islander, 80% white, 2% international; 56% from in state; 94% live on campus; 44% of students in fraternities, 57% in sororities
Most popular majors: 16% Biology/Biological Sciences, General, 7% Business/Managerial Economics, 10% Finance, General, 6% Psychology, General, 6% Spanish Language and Literature
Expenses: 2015-2016: $38,705; room/board: $11,180
Financial aid: (864) 597-4160; 62% of undergrads determined to have financial need; average aid package $33,209

SOUTH DAKOTA

Augustana College

Sioux Falls SD
(605) 274-5516
U.S. News ranking: Reg. Coll. (Mid.W), No. 2
Website: www.augie.edu
Admissions email: admission@augie.edu
Private; founded 1860
Affiliation: ELCA Lutheran
Freshman admissions: more selective; 2014-2015: 1,545 applied, 947 accepted. Either SAT or ACT required. ACT 25/75 percentile: 23-28. High school rank: 31% in top tenth, 65% in top quarter, 89% in top half
Early decision deadline: N/A, notification date: N/A
Early action deadline: N/A, notification date: N/A
Application deadline (fall): rolling
Undergraduate student body: 1,592 full time, 79 part time; 41% male, 59% female; 0% American Indian, 1% Asian, 2% black, 2% Hispanic, 1% multiracial, 0% Pacific Islander, 87% white, 7% international; 48% from in state; 71% live on campus; 0% of students in fraternities, 0% in sororities
Most popular majors: 11% Biological and Biomedical Sciences, 16% Business, Management, Marketing, and Related Support Services, 16% Education, General, 13% Health Professions and Related Programs, 7% Parks, Recreation, Leisure, and Fitness Studies
Expenses: 2015-2016: $30,090; room/board: $7,402
Financial aid: (605) 274-5216; 62% of undergrads determined to have financial need; average aid package $23,975

Black Hills State University[1]

Spearfish SD
(800) 255-2478
U.S. News ranking: Reg. U. (Mid.W), second tier
Website: www.bhsu.edu
Admissions email: admissions@bhsu.edu
Public
Application deadline (fall): N/A
Undergraduate student body: N/A full time, N/A part time
Expenses: 2014-2015: $7,617 in state, $10,097 out of state; room/board: $6,330
Financial aid: (605) 642-6145

Dakota State University

Madison SD
(888) 378-9988
U.S. News ranking: Reg. U. (Mid.W), No. 92
Website: www.dsu.edu
Admissions email: admissions@dsu.edu
Public; founded 1881
Freshman admissions: selective; 2014-2015: 772 applied, 650 accepted. Either SAT or ACT required. ACT 25/75 percentile: 19-25. High school rank: 7% in top tenth, 20% in top quarter, 49% in top half
Early decision deadline: N/A, notification date: N/A
Early action deadline: N/A, notification date: N/A
Application deadline (fall): rolling
Undergraduate student body: 1,154 full time, 1,582 part time; 54% male, 46% female; 1% American Indian, 1% Asian, 4% black, 4% Hispanic, 2% multiracial, 0% Pacific Islander, 84% white, 1% international; 69% from in state; 32% live on campus; 0% of students in fraternities, 0% in sororities
Most popular majors: Information not available
Expenses: 2015-2016: $8,754 in state, $10,842 out of state; room/board: $6,060
Financial aid: (605) 256-5152; 70% of undergrads determined to have financial need; average aid package $8,144

Dakota Wesleyan University

Mitchell SD
(800) 333-8506
U.S. News ranking: Reg. Coll. (Mid.W), No. 45
Website: www.dwu.edu
Admissions email: admissions@dwu.edu
Private; founded 1885
Affiliation: United Methodist
Freshman admissions: selective; 2014-2015: 651 applied, 478 accepted. Either SAT or ACT required. ACT 25/75 percentile: 18-27. High school rank: 9% in top tenth, 36% in top quarter, 75% in top half
Early decision deadline: N/A, notification date: N/A
Early action deadline: N/A, notification date: N/A
Application deadline (fall): rolling
Undergraduate student body: 675 full time, 138 part time; 42% male, 58% female; 1% American Indian, 0% Asian, 2% black, 3% Hispanic, 2% multiracial, 0% Pacific Islander, 90% white, 2% international
Most popular majors: 7% Business Administration and Management, General, 10% Elementary Education and Teaching, 8% Registered Nursing/Registered Nurse, 8% Sport and Fitness Administration/Management
Expenses: 2015-2016: $24,800; room/board: $6,900
Financial aid: (605) 995-2656; 84% of undergrads determined to have financial need; average aid package $15,500

Mount Marty College

Yankton SD
(800) 658-4552
U.S. News ranking: Reg. Coll. (Mid.W), No. 46
Website: www.mtmc.edu
Admissions email: mmcadmit@mtmc.edu
Private; founded 1936
Affiliation: Roman Catholic
Freshman admissions: selective; 2014-2015: 416 applied, 301 accepted. Either SAT or ACT required. ACT 25/75 percentile: 19-23. High school rank: 13% in top tenth, 36% in top quarter, 70% in top half
Early decision deadline: N/A, notification date: N/A
Early action deadline: N/A, notification date: N/A
Application deadline (fall): 8/30
Undergraduate student body: 530 full time, 578 part time; 42% male, 58% female; 3% American Indian, 1% Asian, 4% black, 9% Hispanic, 0% multiracial, 1% Pacific Islander, 81% white, 0% international; 61% from in state; 66% live on campus; 0% of students in fraternities, 0% in sororities
Most popular majors: 11% Business Administration and Management, General, 12% Criminal Justice/Safety Studies, 17% Education, General, 35% Registered Nursing/Registered Nurse
Expenses: 2015-2016: $24,306; room/board: $7,326
Financial aid: (605) 668-1589; 78% of undergrads determined to have financial need; average aid package $23,212

National American University[1]

Rapid City SD
(855) 448-2318
U.S. News ranking: Reg. U. (Mid.W), unranked
Website: www.national.edu/rc
Admissions email: N/A
For-profit
Application deadline (fall): N/A
Undergraduate student body: N/A full time, N/A part time

Expenses: 2014-2015: $13,287; room/board: $6,975
Financial aid: (605) 394-4880

Northern State University
Aberdeen SD
(800) 678-5330
U.S. News ranking: Reg. Coll. (Mid.W), No. 52
Website: www.northern.edu
Admissions email: admissions@northern.edu
Public; founded 1901
Freshman admissions: selective; 2014-2015: 1,379 applied, 1,143 accepted. Either SAT or ACT required. ACT 25/75 percentile: 19-25. High school rank: 7% in top tenth, 20% in top quarter, 60% in top half
Early decision deadline: N/A, notification date: N/A
Early action deadline: N/A, notification date: N/A
Application deadline (fall): rolling
Undergraduate student body: 1,477 full time, 1,524 part time; 42% male, 58% female; 2% American Indian, 1% Asian, 2% black, 3% Hispanic, 2% multiracial, 0% Pacific Islander, 84% white, 4% international; 82% from in state; 41% live on campus; N/A of students in fraternities, N/A in sororities
Most popular majors: 10% Biological and Biomedical Sciences, 33% Business, Management, Marketing, and Related Support Services, 20% Education, 10% Social Sciences, 8% Visual and Performing Arts
Expenses: 2015-2016: $7,887 in state, $9,975 out of state; room/board: $7,087
Financial aid: (605) 626-2640; 66% of undergrads determined to have financial need; average aid package $10,242

Presentation College[1]
Aberdeen SD
(800) 437-6060
U.S. News ranking: Reg. Coll. (Mid.W), second tier
Website: www.presentation.edu/
Admissions email: N/A
Private
Application deadline (fall): N/A
Undergraduate student body: N/A full time, N/A part time
Expenses: 2014-2015: $17,875; room/board: $8,000
Financial aid: (800) 437-6060

South Dakota School of Mines and Technology
Rapid City SD
(605) 394-2414
U.S. News ranking: Engineering, unranked
Website: www.sdsmt.edu
Admissions email: admissions@sdsmt.edu
Public; founded 1885
Freshman admissions: more selective; 2014-2015: 1,549 applied, 1,360 accepted. Either SAT or ACT required. ACT 25/75 percentile: 24-28. High school rank: 20% in top tenth, 29% in top quarter, 82% in top half
Early decision deadline: N/A, notification date: N/A
Early action deadline: N/A, notification date: N/A
Application deadline (fall): rolling
Undergraduate student body: 2,079 full time, 392 part time; 78% male, 22% female; 2% American Indian, 2% Asian, 2% black, 4% Hispanic, 4% multiracial, 0% Pacific Islander, 84% white, 2% international; 50% from in state; 63% live on campus; 30% of students in fraternities, 45% in sororities
Most popular majors: 11% Chemical Engineering, 12% Civil Engineering, General, 7% Electrical and Electronics Engineering, 8% Industrial Engineering, 28% Mechanical Engineering
Expenses: 2015-2016: $11,170 in state, $14,230 out of state; room/board: $7,300
Financial aid: (605) 394-2274; 56% of undergrads determined to have financial need; average aid package $13,722

South Dakota State University
Brookings SD
(605) 688-4121
U.S. News ranking: Nat. U., No. 187
Website: www.sdstate.edu
Admissions email: SDSU_Admissions@sdstate.edu
Public; founded 1881
Freshman admissions: selective; 2014-2015: 5,133 applied, 4,723 accepted. Either SAT or ACT required. ACT 25/75 percentile: 20-26. High school rank: 13% in top tenth, 35% in top quarter, 69% in top half
Early decision deadline: N/A, notification date: N/A
Early action deadline: N/A, notification date: N/A
Application deadline (fall): rolling
Undergraduate student body: 8,621 full time, 2,330 part time; 47% male, 53% female; 1% American Indian, 1% Asian, 2% black, 2% Hispanic, 2% multiracial, 0% Pacific Islander, 89% white, 3% international; 63% from in state; 42% live on campus; 0% of students in fraternities, 0% in sororities
Most popular majors: 14% Agriculture, Agriculture Operations, and Related Sciences, 6% Engineering, 6% Family and Consumer Sciences/Human Sciences, 23% Health Professions and Related Programs, 8% Social Sciences
Expenses: 2015-2016: $8,349 in state, $10,520 out of state; room/board: $7,562
Financial aid: (605) 688-4695; 61% of undergrads determined to have financial need; average aid package $8,636

University of Sioux Falls
Sioux Falls SD
(605) 331-6600
U.S. News ranking: Reg. Coll. (Mid.W), No. 33
Website: www.usiouxfalls.edu
Admissions email: admissions@usiouxfalls.edu
Private; founded 1883
Affiliation: American Baptist
Freshman admissions: selective; 2014-2015: 1,485 applied, 1,446 accepted. Either SAT or ACT required. ACT 25/75 percentile: 19-25. High school rank: 11% in top tenth, 40% in top quarter, 74% in top half
Early decision deadline: N/A, notification date: N/A
Early action deadline: N/A, notification date: N/A
Application deadline (fall): rolling
Undergraduate student body: 901 full time, 207 part time; 39% male, 61% female; 0% American Indian, 1% Asian, 4% black, 1% Hispanic, 4% multiracial, 0% Pacific Islander, 88% white, 1% international; 60% from in state; 60% live on campus; N/A of students in fraternities, N/A in sororities
Most popular majors: 19% Business Administration and Management, General, 6% Criminal Justice/Safety Studies, 7% Elementary Education and Teaching, 5% Kinesiology and Exercise Science, 22% Registered Nursing/Registered Nurse
Expenses: 2015-2016: $26,240; room/board: $6,900
Financial aid: (605) 331-6623; 78% of undergrads determined to have financial need; average aid package $20,961

University of South Dakota
Vermillion SD
(605) 677-5434
U.S. News ranking: Nat. U., No. 180
Website: www.usd.edu
Admissions email: admiss@usd.edu
Public; founded 1862
Freshman admissions: selective; 2014-2015: 3,542 applied, 3,146 accepted. Either SAT or ACT required. ACT 25/75 percentile: 20-25. High school rank: 15% in top tenth, 37% in top quarter, 72% in top half
Early decision deadline: N/A, notification date: N/A
Early action deadline: N/A, notification date: N/A
Application deadline (fall): rolling
Undergraduate student body: 4,876 full time, 2,665 part time; 37% male, 63% female; 2% American Indian, 1% Asian, 2% black, 3% Hispanic, 3% multiracial, 0% Pacific Islander, 87% white, 2% international; 67% from in state; 33% live on campus; 20% of students in fraternities, 12% in sororities
Most popular majors: 12% Business, Management, Marketing, and Related Support Services, 12% Education, 27% Health Professions and Related Programs, 8% Psychology, 6% Social Sciences
Expenses: 2015-2016: $8,455 in state, $10,426 out of state; room/board: $7,605
Financial aid: (605) 677-5446; 64% of undergrads determined to have financial need; average aid package $6,507

TENNESSEE

Aquinas College
Nashville TN
(800) 649-9956
U.S. News ranking: Reg. Coll. (S), No. 19
Website: www.aquinascollege.edu
Admissions email: admissions@aquinascollege.edu
Private; founded 1961
Affiliation: Roman Catholic
Freshman admissions: more selective; 2014-2015: 154 applied, 94 accepted. Either SAT or ACT required. ACT 25/75 percentile: 20-29. High school rank: 30% in top tenth, 60% in top quarter, 80% in top half
Early decision deadline: N/A, notification date: N/A
Early action deadline: N/A, notification date: N/A
Application deadline (fall): rolling
Undergraduate student body: 191 full time, 224 part time; 21% male, 79% female; 0% American Indian, 4% Asian, 5% black, 3% Hispanic, 2% multiracial, 1% Pacific Islander, 74% white, 2% international; 84% from in state; 13% live on campus; 0% of students in fraternities, 0% in sororities
Most popular majors: 9% Business, Management, Marketing, and Related Support Services, 40% Education, 42% Registered Nursing/Registered Nurse
Expenses: 2015-2016: $20,550; room/board: $8,900
Financial aid: (615) 297-7545

Austin Peay State University
Clarksville TN
(931) 221-7661
U.S. News ranking: Reg. U. (S), No. 68
Website: www.apsu.edu
Admissions email: admissions@apsu.edu
Public; founded 1927
Freshman admissions: selective; 2014-2015: 3,307 applied, 2,952 accepted. Neither SAT nor ACT required. ACT 25/75 percentile: 19-24. High school rank: 13% in top tenth, 36% in top quarter, 73% in top half
Early decision deadline: N/A, notification date: N/A
Early action deadline: N/A, notification date: N/A
Application deadline (fall): 8/5
Undergraduate student body: 6,798 full time, 2,448 part time; 41% male, 59% female; 0% American Indian, 2% Asian, 20% black, 6% Hispanic, 5% multiracial, 0% Pacific Islander, 65% white, 0% international; 89% from in state; 15% live on campus; 8% of students in fraternities, 7% in sororities
Most popular majors: 13% Business, Management, Marketing, and Related Support Services, 8% Education, 11% Health Professions and Related Programs, 8% Homeland Security, Law Enforcement, Firefighting and Related Protective Services, 9% Parks, Recreation, Leisure, and Fitness Studies
Expenses: 2014-2015: $7,462 in state, $23,860 out of state; room/board: $8,106
Financial aid: (931) 221-7907; 81% of undergrads determined to have financial need; average aid package $9,972

Belmont University
Nashville TN
(615) 460-6785
U.S. News ranking: Reg. U. (S), No. 5
Website: www.belmont.edu
Admissions email: buadmission@mail.belmont.edu
Private; founded 1890
Affiliation: Nondenominational Christian
Freshman admissions: more selective; 2014-2015: 5,665 applied, 4,686 accepted. Either SAT or ACT required. ACT 25/75 percentile: 23-29. High school rank: 32% in top tenth, 60% in top quarter, 89% in top half
Early decision deadline: N/A, notification date: N/A
Early action deadline: N/A, notification date: N/A
Application deadline (fall): 8/1
Undergraduate student body: 5,440 full time, 397 part time; 39% male, 61% female; 0% American Indian, 2% Asian, 4% black, 5% Hispanic, 3% multiracial, 0% Pacific Islander, 80% white, 1% international; 34% from in state; 50% live on campus; N/A of students in fraternities, N/A in sororities
Most popular majors: 4% Arts, Entertainment,and Media Management, General, 18% Music Management, 7% Music, Other, 5% Recording Arts Technology/Technician, 12% Registered Nursing/Registered Nurse
Expenses: 2015-2016: $30,000; room/board: $10,970
Financial aid: (615) 460-6403; 53% of undergrads determined to have financial need; average aid package $15,743

Bethel University
McKenzie TN
(731) 352-4030
U.S. News ranking: Reg. U. (S), second tier
Website: www.bethelu.edu
Admissions email: admissions@bethel-college.edu
Private; founded 1842
Affiliation: Cumberland Presbyterian Church
Freshman admissions: selective; 2014-2015: 1,179 applied, 748 accepted. Neither SAT nor ACT required. ACT 25/75 percentile: 17-23. High school rank: N/A
Early decision deadline: N/A, notification date: N/A
Early action deadline: N/A, notification date: N/A
Application deadline (fall): rolling
Undergraduate student body: 3,445 full time, 1,347 part time; 43% male, 57% female; 0% American Indian, 0% Asian, 40% black, 1% Hispanic, 1% multiracial, 0% Pacific Islander, 51% white, 1% international; 85% from in state; 18% live on campus; N/A of students in fraternities, N/A in sororities
Most popular majors: 3% Biological and Biomedical Sciences, 36% Business, Management, Marketing, and Related Support Services, 4% Health Professions and Related Programs, 36% Homeland Security, Law Enforcement, Firefighting and Related Protective Services, 3% Liberal Arts and Sciences, General Studies and Humanities
Expenses: 2015-2016: $15,714; room/board: $8,782
Financial aid: (731) 352-4233; 81% of undergrads determined to have financial need; average aid package $11,665

More at usnews.com/college

Bryan College
Dayton TN
(800) 277-9522
U.S. News ranking: Reg. Coll. (S), No. 30
Website: www.bryan.edu
Admissions email: admissions@bryan.edu
Private; founded 1930
Affiliation: Christian nondenominational
Freshman admissions: selective; 2014-2015: 759 applied, 367 accepted. Either SAT or ACT required. ACT 25/75 percentile: 20-26. High school rank: 16% in top tenth, 48% in top quarter, 76% in top half
Early decision deadline: N/A, notification date: N/A
Early action deadline: N/A, notification date: N/A
Application deadline (fall): rolling
Undergraduate student body: 976 full time, 536 part time; 45% male, 55% female; N/A American Indian, N/A Asian, N/A black, N/A Hispanic, N/A multiracial, N/A Pacific Islander, N/A white, N/A international; 33% from in state; 77% live on campus; N/A of students in fraternities, N/A in sororities
Most popular majors: 50% Business, Management, Marketing, and Related Support Services, 6% Communication, Journalism, and Related Programs, 11% Education, 4% English Language and Literature/Letters, 4% Parks, Recreation, Leisure, and Fitness Studies
Expenses: 2015-2016: $23,300; room/board: $6,690
Financial aid: (423) 775-7339; 77% of undergrads determined to have financial need; average aid package $19,818

Carson-Newman University
Jefferson City TN
(800) 678-9061
U.S. News ranking: Reg. Coll. (S), No. 16
Website: www.cn.edu
Admissions email: admitme@cn.edu
Private; founded 1851
Affiliation: Baptist
Freshman admissions: selective; 2014-2015: 4,880 applied, 3,045 accepted. Either SAT or ACT required. ACT 25/75 percentile: 21-26. High school rank: N/A
Early decision deadline: N/A, notification date: N/A
Early action deadline: N/A, notification date: N/A
Application deadline (fall): rolling
Undergraduate student body: 1,682 full time, 75 part time; 43% male, 57% female; 0% American Indian, 1% Asian, 8% black, 2% Hispanic, 0% multiracial, 0% Pacific Islander, 84% white, 2% international; 76% from in state; 59% live on campus; N/A of students in fraternities, N/A in sororities
Most popular majors: 19% Business, Management, Marketing, and Related Support Services, 13% Education, 16% Health Professions and Related Programs, 9% Psychology, 6% Social Sciences
Expenses: 2015-2016: $25,360; room/board: $8,270
Financial aid: (865) 471-3247; 80% of undergrads determined to have financial need; average aid package $22,244

Christian Brothers University
Memphis TN
(901) 321-3205
U.S. News ranking: Reg. U. (S), No. 27
Website: www.cbu.edu
Admissions email: admissions@cbu.edu
Private; founded 1871
Affiliation: Roman Catholic
Freshman admissions: more selective; 2014-2015: 2,229 applied, 1,108 accepted. Either SAT or ACT required. ACT 25/75 percentile: 21-27. High school rank: 36% in top tenth, 68% in top quarter, 89% in top half
Early decision deadline: N/A, notification date: N/A
Early action deadline: N/A, notification date: N/A
Application deadline (fall): rolling
Undergraduate student body: 1,186 full time, 113 part time; 45% male, 55% female; 0% American Indian, 5% Asian, 32% black, 7% Hispanic, 2% multiracial, 0% Pacific Islander, 45% white, 3% international; 81% from in state; 40% live on campus; 12% of students in fraternities, 12% in sororities
Most popular majors: 10% Biological and Biomedical Sciences, 29% Business, Management, Marketing, and Related Support Services, 12% Engineering, 9% Health Professions and Related Programs, 12% Psychology
Expenses: 2015-2016: $30,106; room/board: $7,000
Financial aid: (901) 321-3305; 78% of undergrads determined to have financial need; average aid package $22,486

Cumberland University
Lebanon TN
(615) 444-2562
U.S. News ranking: Reg. U. (S), second tier
Website: www.cumberland.edu
Admissions email: admissions@cumberland.edu
Private; founded 1842
Freshman admissions: selective; 2014-2015: 713 applied, 331 accepted. ACT required. ACT 25/75 percentile: 20-25. High school rank: 20% in top tenth, 34% in top quarter, 74% in top half
Early decision deadline: N/A, notification date: N/A
Early action deadline: N/A, notification date: N/A
Application deadline (fall): rolling
Undergraduate student body: 984 full time, 270 part time; 42% male, 58% female; 0% American Indian, 1% Asian, 12% black, 3% Hispanic, 0% multiracial, 0% Pacific Islander, 66% white, 2% international
Most popular majors: 4% Business/Commerce, General, 3% Criminal Justice/Law Enforcement Administration, 6% Physical Education Teaching and Coaching, 41% Registered Nursing/Registered Nurse
Expenses: 2015-2016: $21,210; room/board: $8,200
Financial aid: (615) 444-2562; 86% of undergrads determined to have financial need; average aid package $16,664

East Tennessee State University
Johnson City TN
(423) 439-4213
U.S. News ranking: Nat. U., second tier
Website: www.etsu.edu
Admissions email: go2etsu@etsu.edu
Public; founded 1911
Freshman admissions: selective; 2014-2015: 5,252 applied, 4,818 accepted. Either SAT or ACT required. ACT 25/75 percentile: 19-25. High school rank: 19% in top tenth, 44% in top quarter, 76% in top half
Early decision deadline: N/A, notification date: N/A
Early action deadline: N/A, notification date: N/A
Application deadline (fall): rolling
Undergraduate student body: 9,574 full time, 1,976 part time; 43% male, 57% female; 0% American Indian, 1% Asian, 6% black, 2% Hispanic, 3% multiracial, 0% Pacific Islander, 84% white, 3% international; 87% from in state; 20% live on campus; 5% of students in fraternities, 5% in sororities
Most popular majors: 11% Business, Management, Marketing, and Related Support Services, 6% Education, 24% Health Professions and Related Programs, 7% Liberal Arts and Sciences, General Studies and Humanities, 6% Parks, Recreation, Leisure, and Fitness Studies
Expenses: 2014-2015: $7,985 in state, $17,917 out of state; room/board: $7,822
Financial aid: (423) 439-4300

Fisk University
Nashville TN
(888) 702-0022
U.S. News ranking: Nat. Lib. Arts, No. 171
Website: www.fisk.edu
Admissions email: admissions@fisk.edu
Private; founded 1866
Freshman admissions: less selective; 2014-2015: 2,542 applied, 2,121 accepted. Either SAT or ACT required. ACT 25/75 percentile: 17-23. High school rank: 0% in top tenth, 2% in top quarter, 18% in top half
Early decision deadline: N/A, notification date: N/A
Early action deadline: N/A, notification date: N/A
Application deadline (fall): rolling
Undergraduate student body: 705 full time, 25 part time; 37% male, 63% female; 0% American Indian, 1% Asian, 87% black, 1% Hispanic, 1% multiracial, 0% Pacific Islander, 1% white, 0% international; 26% from in state; 78% live on campus; 0% of students in fraternities, 0% in sororities
Most popular majors: Information not available
Expenses: 2014-2015: $20,858; room/board: $10,160
Financial aid: (615) 329-8585

Freed-Hardeman University
Henderson TN
(800) 630-3480
U.S. News ranking: Reg. U. (S), No. 46
Website: www.fhu.edu
Admissions email: admissions@fhu.edu
Private; founded 1869
Affiliation: Church of Christ
Freshman admissions: selective; 2014-2015: 1,044 applied, 975 accepted. Either SAT or ACT required. ACT 25/75 percentile: 22-27. High school rank: 34% in top tenth, 54% in top quarter, 80% in top half
Early decision deadline: N/A, notification date: N/A
Early action deadline: N/A, notification date: N/A
Application deadline (fall): rolling
Undergraduate student body: 1,274 full time, 131 part time; 43% male, 57% female; 0% American Indian, 1% Asian, 5% black, 2% Hispanic, 2% multiracial, 0% Pacific Islander, 86% white, 2% international; 56% from in state; 83% live on campus; 0% of students in fraternities, 0% in sororities
Most popular majors: 13% Business, Management, Marketing, and Related Support Services, 15% Education, 7% Multi/Interdisciplinary Studies, 10% Parks, Recreation, Leisure, and Fitness Studies, 9% Theology and Religious Vocations
Expenses: 2015-2016: $21,500; room/board: $7,464
Financial aid: (731) 989-6662; 78% of undergrads determined to have financial need; average aid package $17,710

King University
Bristol TN
(423) 652-4861
U.S. News ranking: Reg. U. (S), No. 71
Website: www.king.edu
Admissions email: admissions@king.edu
Private; founded 1867
Affiliation: Presbyterian
Freshman admissions: selective; 2014-2015: 928 applied, 526 accepted. Either SAT or ACT required. ACT 25/75 percentile: 20-26. High school rank: 23% in top tenth, 53% in top quarter, 81% in top half
Early decision deadline: N/A, notification date: N/A
Early action deadline: N/A, notification date: N/A
Application deadline (fall): rolling
Undergraduate student body: 2,272 full time, 155 part time; 33% male, 67% female; 0% American Indian, 0% Asian, 6% black, 2% Hispanic, 2% multiracial, 0% Pacific Islander, 81% white, 3% international; 64% from in state; 42% live on campus; 0% of students in fraternities, 0% in sororities
Most popular majors: 44% Adult Health Nurse/Nursing, 32% Business Administration and Management, General, 2% Computer and Information Systems Security/Information Assurance, 2% Multicultural Education, 2% Psychology, General
Expenses: 2015-2016: $26,480; room/board: $8,180
Financial aid: (423) 652-4725; 88% of undergrads determined to have financial need; average aid package $14,128

Lane College
Jackson TN
(731) 426-7533
U.S. News ranking: Nat. Lib. Arts, second tier
Website: www.lanecollege.edu
Admissions email: admissions@lanecollege.edu
Private; founded 1882
Affiliation: Christian Methodist Episcopal
Freshman admissions: least selective; 2014-2015: 5,842 applied, 2,528 accepted. Either SAT or ACT required. ACT 25/75 percentile: 14-17. High school rank: N/A
Early decision deadline: N/A, notification date: N/A
Early action deadline: N/A, notification date: N/A
Application deadline (fall): 8/1
Undergraduate student body: 1,249 full time, 13 part time; 52% male, 48% female; N/A American Indian, N/A Asian, 100% black, N/A Hispanic, N/A multiracial, N/A Pacific Islander, N/A white, N/A international; 55% from in state; 61% live on campus; N/A of students in fraternities, N/A in sororities
Most popular majors: 15% Biological and Biomedical Sciences, 16% Business, Management, Marketing, and Related Support Services, 11% Education, 16% Homeland Security, Law Enforcement, Firefighting and Related Protective Services, 17% Social Sciences
Expenses: 2014-2015: $9,780; room/board: $6,620
Financial aid: (731) 426-7535

Lee University
Cleveland TN
(423) 614-8500
U.S. News ranking: Reg. U. (S), No. 46
Website: www.leeuniversity.edu
Admissions email: admissions@leeuniversity.edu
Private; founded 1918
Affiliation: Pentecostal
Freshman admissions: selective; 2014-2015: 1,745 applied, 1,554 accepted. Either SAT or ACT required. ACT 25/75 percentile: 21-27. High school rank: 20% in top tenth, 49% in top quarter, 75% in top half
Early decision deadline: N/A, notification date: N/A
Early action deadline: N/A, notification date: N/A
Application deadline (fall): rolling
Undergraduate student body: 3,770 full time, 805 part time; 42% male, 58% female; 0% American Indian, 1% Asian, 6% black, 4% Hispanic, 1% multiracial, 0% Pacific Islander, 79% white, 5% international; 43% from in state; 47% live on campus; 10% of students in fraternities, 9% in sororities
Most popular majors: 10% Business, Management,

Marketing, and Related Support Services, 12% Communication, Journalism, and Related Programs, 18% Education, 10% Psychology, 17% Theology and Religious Vocations
Expenses: 2015-2016: $15,000; room/board: $7,045
Financial aid: (423) 614-8300; 72% of undergrads determined to have financial need; average aid package $11,183

LeMoyne-Owen College

Memphis TN
(901) 435-1500
U.S. News ranking: Reg. Coll. (S), second tier
Website: www.loc.edu/
Admissions email: admission@loc.edu
Private; founded 1862
Affiliation: United Church of Christ
Freshman admissions: least selective; 2014-2015: 489 applied, 255 accepted. Either SAT or ACT required. ACT 25/75 percentile: 13-17. High school rank: N/A
Early decision deadline: N/A, notification date: N/A
Early action deadline: N/A, notification date: N/A
Application deadline (fall): 7/1
Undergraduate student body: 968 full time, 38 part time; 44% male, 56% female; 0% American Indian, 0% Asian, 97% black, 0% Hispanic, N/A multiracial, N/A Pacific Islander, 0% white, 1% international; 90% from in state; 5% live on campus; 1% of students in fraternities, 2% in sororities
Most popular majors: 44% Business Administration and Management, General, 5% Computer and Information Sciences, General, 9% Criminal Justice/Law Enforcement Administration, 10% Education, General, 17% Political Science and Government, General
Expenses: 2014-2015: $5,450; room/board: $5,910
Financial aid: (901) 942-7313

Lincoln Memorial University

Harrogate TN
(423) 869-6280
U.S. News ranking: Reg. U. (S), No. 50
Website: www.lmunet.edu
Admissions email: admissions@lmunet.edu
Private; founded 1897
Freshman admissions: selective; 2014-2015: 2,306 applied, 1,715 accepted. Either SAT or ACT required. ACT 25/75 percentile: 19-27. High school rank: N/A
Early decision deadline: N/A, notification date: N/A
Early action deadline: N/A, notification date: N/A
Application deadline (fall): rolling
Undergraduate student body: 1,298 full time, 401 part time; 30% male, 70% female; 0% American Indian, 1% Asian, 5% black, N/A Hispanic, 1% multiracial, N/A Pacific Islander, 86% white, 3% international
Most popular majors: 7% Biological and Biomedical Sciences, 17% Business, Management, Marketing, and Related Support Services, 9% Education, 36% Health Professions and Related Programs, 5% History
Expenses: 2015-2016: $20,546; room/board: $7,300
Financial aid: (423) 869-6336

Lipscomb University

Nashville TN
(615) 966-1776
U.S. News ranking: Reg. U. (S), No. 18
Website: www.lipscomb.edu
Admissions email: admissions@lipscomb.edu
Private; founded 1891
Affiliation: Church of Christ
Freshman admissions: more selective; 2014-2015: 3,699 applied, 2,056 accepted. Either SAT or ACT required. ACT 25/75 percentile: 23-29. High school rank: 25% in top tenth, 51% in top quarter, 78% in top half
Early decision deadline: N/A, notification date: N/A
Early action deadline: N/A, notification date: N/A
Application deadline (fall): rolling
Undergraduate student body: 2,583 full time, 300 part time; 39% male, 61% female; 0% American Indian, 3% Asian, 7% black, 6% Hispanic, 2% multiracial, 0% Pacific Islander, 77% white, 2% international; 66% from in state; 50% live on campus; 23% of students in fraternities, 24% in sororities
Most popular majors: 12% Biological and Biomedical Sciences, 18% Business, Management, Marketing, and Related Support Services, 8% Education, 14% Health Professions and Related Programs, 7% Psychology
Expenses: 2015-2016: $28,624; room/board: $11,032
Financial aid: (615) 269-1791; 65% of undergrads determined to have financial need; average aid package $21,630

Martin Methodist College[1]

Pulaski TN
(931) 363-9804
U.S. News ranking: Reg. Coll. (S), unranked
Website: www.martinmethodist.edu
Admissions email: admit@martinmethodist.edu
Private
Application deadline (fall): N/A
Undergraduate student body: N/A full time, N/A part time
Expenses: 2015-2016: $23,100; room/board: $8,400
Financial aid: (931) 363-9821; 83% of undergrads determined to have financial need; average aid package $10,700

Maryville College

Maryville TN
(865) 981-8092
U.S. News ranking: Nat. Lib. Arts, second tier
Website: www.maryvillecollege.edu
Admissions email: admissions@maryvillecollege.edu
Private; founded 1819
Affiliation: Presbyterian
Freshman admissions: selective; 2014-2015: 2,036 applied, 1,442 accepted. Either SAT or ACT required. ACT 25/75 percentile: 20-26. High school rank: 15% in top tenth, 40% in top quarter, 74% in top half
Early decision deadline: N/A, notification date: N/A
Early action deadline: N/A, notification date: N/A
Application deadline (fall): 5/1
Undergraduate student body: 1,166 full time, 47 part time; 46% male, 54% female; 1% American Indian, 1% Asian, 11% black, 3% Hispanic, 3% multiracial, 0% Pacific Islander, 78% white, 3% international; 72% from in state; 68% live on campus; 0% of students in fraternities, 0% in sororities
Most popular majors: Information not available
Expenses: 2015-2016: $32,866; room/board: $10,442
Financial aid: (865) 981-8100; 86% of undergrads determined to have financial need; average aid package $31,239

Memphis College of Art

Memphis TN
(800) 727-1088
U.S. News ranking: Arts, unranked
Website: www.mca.edu
Admissions email: info@mca.edu
Private; founded 1936
Freshman admissions: N/A; 2014-2015: 958 applied, 360 accepted. Either SAT or ACT required. ACT 25/75 percentile: 19-25. High school rank: N/A
Early decision deadline: N/A, notification date: N/A
Early action deadline: N/A, notification date: N/A
Application deadline (fall): rolling
Undergraduate student body: 332 full time, 34 part time; 35% male, 65% female; 1% American Indian, 2% Asian, 25% black, 8% Hispanic, 5% multiracial, 0% Pacific Islander, 59% white, 0% international; 53% from in state; 44% live on campus; 0% of students in fraternities, 0% in sororities
Most popular majors: 33% Design and Visual Communications, General, 39% Fine/Studio Arts, General, 20% Photography
Expenses: 2015-2016: $30,250; room/board: $8,600
Financial aid: (901) 272-5136; 92% of undergrads determined to have financial need; average aid package $21,964

Middle Tennessee State University

Murfreesboro TN
(615) 898-2111
U.S. News ranking: Nat. U., second tier
Website: www.mtsu.edu
Admissions email: admissions@mtsu.edu
Public; founded 1911
Freshman admissions: selective; 2014-2015: 9,353 applied, 6,740 accepted. Either SAT or ACT required. ACT 25/75 percentile: 19-25. High school rank: 19% in top tenth, 43% in top quarter, 79% in top half
Early decision deadline: N/A, notification date: N/A
Early action deadline: N/A, notification date: N/A
Application deadline (fall): rolling
Undergraduate student body: 16,627 full time, 3,635 part time; 47% male, 53% female; 0% American Indian, 3% Asian, 19% black, 4% Hispanic, 3% multiracial, 0% Pacific Islander, 68% white, 2% international; 96% from in state; 27% live on campus; 6% of students in fraternities, 7% in sororities
Most popular majors: Information not available
Expenses: 2014-2015: $7,370 in state, $24,434 out of state; room/board: $8,302
Financial aid: (615) 898-2830; 77% of undergrads determined to have financial need; average aid package $9,010

Milligan College

Milligan College TN
(423) 461-8730
U.S. News ranking: Reg. Coll. (S), No. 6
Website: www.milligan.edu
Admissions email: admissions@milligan.edu
Private; founded 1866
Affiliation: Christian Churches/Churches of Christ
Freshman admissions: more selective; 2014-2015: 580 applied, 361 accepted. Either SAT or ACT required. ACT 25/75 percentile: 22-26. High school rank: 37% in top tenth, 65% in top quarter, 89% in top half
Early decision deadline: N/A, notification date: N/A
Early action deadline: N/A, notification date: N/A
Application deadline (fall): 8/1
Undergraduate student body: 854 full time, 125 part time; 35% male, 65% female; 0% American Indian, 1% Asian, 5% black, 5% Hispanic, 2% multiracial, 0% Pacific Islander, 83% white, 3% international; 63% from in state; 73% live on campus; 0% of students in fraternities, 0% in sororities
Most popular majors: Information not available
Expenses: 2015-2016: $29,830; room/board: $6,500
Financial aid: (423) 461-8949; 80% of undergrads determined to have financial need; average aid package $21,471

Rhodes College

Memphis TN
(800) 844-5969
U.S. News ranking: Nat. Lib. Arts, No. 51
Website: www.rhodes.edu
Admissions email: adminfo@rhodes.edu
Private; founded 1848
Affiliation: Presbyterian (USA)
Freshman admissions: more selective; 2014-2015: 3,382 applied, 2,029 accepted. Either SAT or ACT required. ACT 25/75 percentile: 27-31. High school rank: 48% in top tenth, 79% in top quarter, 96% in top half
Early decision deadline: 11/1, notification date: 12/1
Early action deadline: 11/15, notification date: 1/15
Application deadline (fall): 1/15
Undergraduate student body: 2,016 full time, 15 part time; 42% male, 58% female; 0% American Indian, 7% Asian, 6% black, 4% Hispanic, 3% multiracial, 0% Pacific Islander, 76% white, 2% international; 26% from in state; 71% live on campus; 35% of students in fraternities, 65% in sororities
Most popular majors: 14% Biological and Biomedical Sciences, 15% Business, Management, Marketing, and Related Support Services, 9% English Language and Literature/Letters, 9% Psychology, 23% Social Sciences
Expenses: 2015-2016: $43,224; room/board: $10,746
Financial aid: (901) 843-3810; 41% of undergrads determined to have financial need; average aid package $34,455

Sewanee–University of the South

Sewanee TN
(800) 522-2234
U.S. News ranking: Nat. Lib. Arts, No. 48
Website: www.sewanee.edu
Admissions email: admiss@sewanee.edu
Private; founded 1857
Affiliation: Episcopal
Freshman admissions: more selective; 2014-2015: 2,977 applied, 1,926 accepted. Neither SAT nor ACT required. ACT 25/75 percentile: 26-30. High school rank: 35% in top tenth, 68% in top quarter, 92% in top half
Early decision deadline: 11/15, notification date: 12/15
Early action deadline: 12/1, notification date: 2/15
Application deadline (fall): 2/1
Undergraduate student body: 1,620 full time, 11 part time; 48% male, 52% female; 0% American Indian, 2% Asian, 5% black, 5% Hispanic, 4% multiracial, 0% Pacific Islander, 82% white, 3% international; 26% from in state; 98% live on campus; 58% of students in fraternities, 56% in sororities
Most popular majors: 11% Biological and Biomedical Sciences, 13% English Language and Literature/Letters, 10% Psychology, 18% Social Sciences, 8% Visual and Performing Arts
Expenses: 2015-2016: $38,700; room/board: $11,050
Financial aid: (931) 598-1312; 48% of undergrads determined to have financial need; average aid package $31,602

South College[1]

Knoxville TN
(865) 251-1800
U.S. News ranking: Reg. Coll. (S), unranked
Website: www.southcollegetn.edu/
Admissions email: N/A
For-profit
Application deadline (fall): N/A
Undergraduate student body: N/A full time, N/A part time
Expenses: 2014-2015: $19,475; room/board: $11,448
Financial aid: (865) 251-1800

Southern Adventist University

Collegedale TN
(423) 236-2844
U.S. News ranking: Reg. Coll. (S), No. 25
Website: www.southern.edu

Admissions email: admissions@southern.edu
Private; founded 1892
Affiliation: Seventh-day Adventist
Freshman admissions: selective; 2014-2015: 2,066 applied, 1,767 accepted. Either SAT or ACT required. ACT 25/75 percentile: 20-26. High school rank: N/A
Early decision deadline: N/A, notification date: N/A
Early action deadline: N/A, notification date: N/A
Application deadline (fall): rolling
Undergraduate student body: 2,252 full time, 476 part time; 44% male, 56% female; 0% American Indian, 7% Asian, 12% black, 19% Hispanic, 3% multiracial, 1% Pacific Islander, 52% white, 5% international
Most popular majors: 6% Biology/Biological Sciences, General, 6% Business Administration and Management, General, 6% Elementary Education and Teaching, 17% Registered Nursing/Registered Nurse, 6% Social Work
Expenses: 2015-2016: $20,650; room/board: $6,000
Financial aid: (423) 236-2835; 70% of undergrads determined to have financial need; average aid package $12,539

Tennessee State University

Nashville TN
(615) 963-5101
U.S. News ranking: Nat. U., second tier
Website: www.tnstate.edu
Admissions email: jcade@tnstate.edu
Public; founded 1912
Freshman admissions: less selective; 2014-2015: 3,934 applied, 2,085 accepted. Either SAT or ACT required. ACT 25/75 percentile: 15-20. High school rank: N/A
Early decision deadline: N/A, notification date: N/A
Early action deadline: N/A, notification date: N/A
Application deadline (fall): 7/1
Undergraduate student body: 5,677 full time, 1,396 part time; 41% male, 59% female; 0% American Indian, 1% Asian, 73% black, 1% Hispanic, N/A multiracial, N/A Pacific Islander, 15% white, 9% international; N/A from in state; 42% live on campus; N/A of students in fraternities, N/A in sororities
Most popular majors: Information not available
Expenses: 2015-2016: $7,128 in state, $21,287 out of state; room/board: $8,143
Financial aid: (615) 963-5701; 85% of undergrads determined to have financial need; average aid package $10,704

Tennessee Technological University

Cookeville TN
(800) 255-8881
U.S. News ranking: Reg. U. (S), No. 35
Website: www.tntech.edu
Admissions email: admissions@tntech.edu
Public; founded 1915
Freshman admissions: selective; 2014-2015: 4,582 applied, 4,326 accepted. Either SAT or ACT required. ACT 25/75 percentile: 21-27. High school rank: 28% in top tenth, 54% in top quarter, 84% in top half
Early decision deadline: N/A, notification date: N/A
Early action deadline: N/A, notification date: N/A
Application deadline (fall): rolling
Undergraduate student body: 9,264 full time, 1,050 part time; 57% male, 43% female; 0% American Indian, 1% Asian, 4% black, 2% Hispanic, 2% multiracial, 0% Pacific Islander, 80% white, 10% international; 98% from in state; 26% live on campus; 9% of students in fraternities, 10% in sororities
Most popular majors: 7% Health and Physical Education/Fitness, General, 6% Liberal Arts and Sciences/Liberal Studies, 6% Mechanical Engineering, 5% Registered Nursing/Registered Nurse, 13% Teacher Education, Multiple Levels
Expenses: 2015-2016: $8,300 in state, $24,500 out of state; room/board: $8,200
Financial aid: (931) 372-3073; 72% of undergrads determined to have financial need; average aid package $9,271

Tennessee Wesleyan College

Athens TN
(423) 746-5286
U.S. News ranking: Reg. Coll. (S), No. 33
Website: www.twcnet.edu
Admissions email: admissions@twcnet.edu
Private; founded 1857
Affiliation: United Methodist
Freshman admissions: selective; 2014-2015: 1,023 applied, 682 accepted. Either SAT or ACT required. ACT 25/75 percentile: 18-25. High school rank: 13% in top tenth, 41% in top quarter, 69% in top half
Early decision deadline: N/A, notification date: N/A
Early action deadline: N/A, notification date: N/A
Application deadline (fall): rolling
Undergraduate student body: 940 full time, 79 part time; 37% male, 63% female; 0% American Indian, 1% Asian, 5% black, 1% Hispanic, 2% multiracial, 0% Pacific Islander, 79% white, 5% international; 91% from in state; 45% live on campus; 13% of students in fraternities, 15% in sororities
Most popular majors: Information not available
Expenses: 2015-2016: $22,900; room/board: $7,310
Financial aid: (423) 746-5209; 49% of undergrads determined to have financial need; average aid package $17,607

Trevecca Nazarene University

Nashville TN
(615) 248-1320
U.S. News ranking: Nat. U., second tier
Website: www.trevecca.edu
Admissions email: admissions_und@trevecca.edu
Private; founded 1901
Affiliation: Nazarene
Freshman admissions: selective; 2014-2015: 1,029 applied, 752 accepted. Either SAT or ACT required. ACT 25/75 percentile: 20-26. High school rank: N/A
Early decision deadline: N/A, notification date: N/A
Early action deadline: N/A, notification date: N/A
Application deadline (fall): 8/1
Undergraduate student body: 1,176 full time, 501 part time; 44% male, 56% female; 1% American Indian, 1% Asian, 9% black, 4% Hispanic, 3% multiracial, 0% Pacific Islander, 71% white, 1% international; 62% from in state; 47% live on campus; 0% of students in fraternities, 0% in sororities
Most popular majors: 41% Business, Management, Marketing, and Related Support Services, 6% Communication, Journalism, and Related Programs, 7% Education, 7% Health Professions and Related Programs, 6% Theology and Religious Vocations
Expenses: 2015-2016: $23,748; room/board: $8,300
Financial aid: (615) 248-1242

Tusculum College

Greeneville TN
(800) 729-0256
U.S. News ranking: Reg. U. (S), second tier
Website: www.tusculum.edu
Admissions email: admissions@tusculum.edu
Private; founded 1794
Affiliation: Presbyterian
Freshman admissions: selective; 2014-2015: 2,537 applied, 1,825 accepted. Either SAT or ACT required. ACT 25/75 percentile: 18-23. High school rank: N/A
Early decision deadline: N/A, notification date: N/A
Early action deadline: N/A, notification date: N/A
Application deadline (fall): rolling
Undergraduate student body: 1,608 full time, 138 part time; 46% male, 54% female; 1% American Indian, 0% Asian, 12% black, 2% Hispanic, 1% multiracial, 0% Pacific Islander, 71% white, 2% international; 78% from in state; 44% live on campus; 0% of students in fraternities, 0% in sororities
Most popular majors: 44% Business Administration and Management, General, 18% Elementary Education and Teaching, 3% Kinesiology and Exercise Science, 16% Psychology, General, 4% Sport and Fitness Administration/Management
Expenses: 2015-2016: $22,670; room/board: $14,110
Financial aid: (423) 636-7377; 87% of undergrads determined to have financial need; average aid package $20,027

Union University

Jackson TN
(800) 338-6466
U.S. News ranking: Reg. U. (S), No. 14
Website: www.uu.edu
Admissions email: admissions@uu.edu
Private; founded 1823
Affiliation: Southern Baptist
Freshman admissions: more selective; 2014-2015: 1,983 applied, 1,360 accepted. Either SAT or ACT required. ACT 25/75 percentile: 22-29. High school rank: 33% in top tenth, 57% in top quarter, 83% in top half
Early decision deadline: N/A, notification date: N/A
Early action deadline: N/A, notification date: N/A
Application deadline (fall): rolling
Undergraduate student body: 1,976 full time, 741 part time; 39% male, 61% female; 0% American Indian, 1% Asian, 19% black, 3% Hispanic, 2% multiracial, 0% Pacific Islander, 70% white, 1% international; 77% from in state; 64% live on campus; 26% of students in fraternities, 28% in sororities
Most popular majors: 17% Multi/Interdisciplinary Studies, Other, 4% Psychology, General, 4% Registered Nursing, Nursing Administration, Nursing Research and Clinical Nursing, Other, 21% Registered Nursing/Registered Nurse, 8% Social Work
Expenses: 2015-2016: $29,190; room/board: $9,440
Financial aid: (731) 661-5015; 79% of undergrads determined to have financial need; average aid package $18,840

University of Memphis

Memphis TN
(901) 678-2111
U.S. News ranking: Nat. U., second tier
Website: www.memphis.edu
Admissions email: recruitment@memphis.edu
Public; founded 1912
Freshman admissions: selective; 2014-2015: 11,408 applied, 5,558 accepted. Either SAT or ACT required. ACT 25/75 percentile: 20-26. High school rank: 16% in top tenth, 43% in top quarter, 77% in top half
Early decision deadline: N/A, notification date: N/A
Early action deadline: N/A, notification date: N/A
Application deadline (fall): 7/1
Undergraduate student body: 12,372 full time, 4,696 part time; 40% male, 60% female; 0% American Indian, 3% Asian, 38% black, 4% Hispanic, 3% multiracial, 0% Pacific Islander, 51% white, 1% international; 35% from in state; 13% live on campus; 8% of students in fraternities, 7% in sororities
Most popular majors: 18% Business, Management, Marketing, and Related Support Services, 10% Education, 7% Health Professions and Related Programs, 6% Liberal Arts and Sciences, General Studies and Humanities, 12% Multi/Interdisciplinary Studies
Expenses: 2015-2016: $8,903 in state, N/A out of state; room/board: $9,061
Financial aid: (901) 678-4825; 79% of undergrads determined to have financial need; average aid package $9,087

University of Tennessee

Knoxville TN
(865) 974-2184
U.S. News ranking: Nat. U., No. 103
Website: admissions.utk.edu/undergraduate
Admissions email: admissions@utk.edu
Public; founded 1794
Freshman admissions: more selective; 2014-2015: 15,442 applied, 11,555 accepted. Either SAT or ACT required. ACT 25/75 percentile: 24-29. High school rank: 50% in top tenth, 90% in top quarter, 100% in top half
Early decision deadline: N/A, notification date: N/A
Early action deadline: N/A, notification date: N/A
Application deadline (fall): 6/1
Undergraduate student body: 20,337 full time, 1,327 part time; 50% male, 50% female; 0% American Indian, 3% Asian, 7% black, 3% Hispanic, 3% multiracial, 0% Pacific Islander, 80% white, 1% international; 90% from in state; 37% live on campus; 16% of students in fraternities, 25% in sororities
Most popular majors: 19% Business, Management, Marketing, and Related Support Services, 7% Communication, Journalism, and Related Programs, 10% Engineering, 9% Psychology, 9% Social Sciences
Expenses: 2015-2016: $11,948 in state, $30,138 out of state; room/board: $9,926
Financial aid: (865) 974-3131; 60% of undergrads determined to have financial need; average aid package $12,313

University of Tennessee–Chattanooga

Chattanooga TN
(423) 425-4662
U.S. News ranking: Reg. U. (S), No. 58
Website: www.utc.edu
Admissions email: utcmocs@utc.edu
Public; founded 1886
Freshman admissions: selective; 2014-2015: 7,399 applied, 5,718 accepted. Either SAT or ACT required. ACT 25/75 percentile: 21-26. High school rank: N/A in top tenth, 47% in top quarter, 85% in top half
Early decision deadline: N/A, notification date: N/A
Early action deadline: N/A, notification date: N/A
Application deadline (fall): 5/1
Undergraduate student body: 8,985 full time, 1,330 part time; 45% male, 55% female; 0% American Indian, 2% Asian, 11% black, 3% Hispanic, 8% multiracial, 0% Pacific Islander, 74% white, 1% international; 94% from in state; 31% live on campus; 8% of students in fraternities, 18% in sororities
Most popular majors: 22% Business Administration and Management, General, 10% Education, General, 6% Engineering, General, 8% Kinesiology and Exercise Science, 7% Psychology, General

Expenses: 2014-2015: $8,138 in state, $24,256 out of state; room/board: $8,110
Financial aid: (423) 425-4677; 63% of undergrads determined to have financial need; average aid package $9,765

University of Tennessee–Martin

Martin TN
(800) 829-8861
U.S. News ranking: Reg. U. (S), No. 50
Website: www.utm.edu
Admissions email: admitme@utm.edu
Public; founded 1900
Freshman admissions: selective; 2014-2015: 3,526 applied, 2,586 accepted. Either SAT or ACT required. ACT 25/75 percentile: 20-25. High school rank: 28% in top tenth, 62% in top quarter, 90% in top half
Early decision deadline: N/A, notification date: N/A
Early action deadline: N/A, notification date: N/A
Application deadline (fall): 8/1
Undergraduate student body: 5,738 full time, 939 part time; 42% male, 58% female; 0% American Indian, 1% Asian, 16% black, 2% Hispanic, 2% multiracial, 0% Pacific Islander, 76% white, 3% international; 95% from in state; 28% live on campus; 14% of students in fraternities, 15% in sororities
Most popular majors: 11% Agriculture, Agriculture Operations, and Related Sciences, 16% Business, Management, Marketing, and Related Support Services, 11% Education, 12% Multi/Interdisciplinary Studies, 8% Parks, Recreation, Leisure, and Fitness Studies
Expenses: 2015-2016: $8,211 in state, $22,593 out of state; room/board: $7,194
Financial aid: (731) 587-7040; 77% of undergrads determined to have financial need; average aid package $13,443

Vanderbilt University

Nashville TN
(800) 288-0432
U.S. News ranking: Nat. U., No. 15
Website: www.vanderbilt.edu
Admissions email: admissions@vanderbilt.edu
Private; founded 1873
Freshman admissions: most selective; 2014-2015: 29,518 applied, 3,865 accepted. Either SAT or ACT required. ACT 25/75 percentile: 32-34. High school rank: 91% in top tenth, 97% in top quarter, 99% in top half
Early decision deadline: 11/1, notification date: 12/15
Early action deadline: N/A, notification date: N/A
Application deadline (fall): 1/1
Undergraduate student body: 6,778 full time, 73 part time; 50% male, 50% female; 0% American Indian, 10% Asian, 8% black, 8% Hispanic, 5% multiracial, 0% Pacific Islander, 58% white, 6% international; 11% from in state; 95% live on campus; 32% of students in fraternities, 54% in sororities
Most popular majors: 11% Economics, General, 5% Mathematics, General, 9% Multi/Interdisciplinary Studies, Other, 5% Political Science and Government, General, 9% Social Sciences, General
Expenses: 2014-2015: $43,838; room/board: $14,382
Financial aid: (615) 322-3591; 49% of undergrads determined to have financial need; average aid package $45,477

Watkins College of Art, Design & Film[1]

Nashville TN
(615) 383-4848
U.S. News ranking: Arts, unranked
Website: www.watkins.edu
Admissions email: admission@watkins.edu
Private
Application deadline (fall): N/A
Undergraduate student body: N/A full time, N/A part time
Expenses: 2014-2015: $20,250; room/board: $9,390
Financial aid: (615) 383-4848

Welch College

Nashville TN
(888) 979-3524
U.S. News ranking: Reg. Coll. (S), No. 63
Website: www.welch.edu
Admissions email: Recruit@welch.edu
Private; founded 1942
Affiliation: Free Will Baptist
Freshman admissions: selective; 2014-2015: 120 applied, 66 accepted. Either SAT or ACT required. ACT 25/75 percentile: 17-25. High school rank: 18% in top tenth, 59% in top quarter, 76% in top half
Early decision deadline: N/A, notification date: N/A
Early action deadline: N/A, notification date: N/A
Application deadline (fall): rolling
Undergraduate student body: 241 full time, 87 part time; 55% male, 45% female; 0% American Indian, 1% Asian, 10% black, 3% Hispanic, 2% multiracial, 0% Pacific Islander, 81% white, 0% international; 40% from in state; 79% live on campus; 75% of students in fraternities, 72% in sororities
Most popular majors: 9% Biological and Biomedical Sciences, 23% Business, Management, Marketing, and Related Support Services, 14% Education, 14% Psychology, 36% Theology and Religious Vocations
Expenses: 2015-2016: $17,398; room/board: $7,048
Financial aid: (615) 844-5250; 92% of undergrads determined to have financial need; average aid package $13,050

TEXAS

Abilene Christian University

Abilene TX
(800) 460-6228
U.S. News ranking: Reg. U. (W), No. 17
Website: www.acu.edu
Admissions email: info@admissions.acu.edu
Private; founded 1906
Affiliation: Church of Christ
Freshman admissions: more selective; 2014-2015: 9,384 applied, 4,736 accepted. Either SAT or ACT required. ACT 25/75 percentile: 21-27. High school rank: 29% in top tenth, 64% in top quarter, 89% in top half
Early decision deadline: N/A, notification date: N/A
Early action deadline: 11/1, notification date: 12/1
Application deadline (fall): 2/15
Undergraduate student body: 3,417 full time, 233 part time; 43% male, 57% female; 0% American Indian, 1% Asian, 8% black, 14% Hispanic, 5% multiracial, 0% Pacific Islander, 67% white, 4% international; 86% from in state; 47% live on campus; 26% of students in fraternities, 30% in sororities
Most popular majors: 6% Accounting, 7% Business Administration and Management, General, 5% Marketing/Marketing Management, General, 6% Psychology, General, 5% Sport and Fitness Administration/Management
Expenses: 2015-2016: $30,830; room/board: $9,310
Financial aid: (325) 674-2643; 65% of undergrads determined to have financial need; average aid package $20,931

Amberton University

Garland TX
(972) 279-6511
U.S. News ranking: Reg. U. (W), unranked
Website: www.amberton.edu
Admissions email: advisor@amberton.edu
Private; founded 1981
Affiliation: Nondenominational Christian
Freshman admissions: N/A; 2014-2015: N/A applied, N/A accepted. Neither SAT nor ACT required. ACT 25/75 percentile: N/A. High school rank: N/A
Early decision deadline: N/A, notification date: N/A
Early action deadline: N/A, notification date: N/A
Application deadline (fall): rolling
Undergraduate student body: 21 full time, 224 part time; 38% male, 62% female; 0% American Indian, 8% Asian, 32% black, 8% Hispanic, N/A multiracial, 0% Pacific Islander, 49% white, 0% international
Most popular majors: Information not available
Expenses: N/A
Financial aid: (972) 279-6511

Angelo State University

San Angelo TX
(325) 942-2041
U.S. News ranking: Reg. U. (W), second tier
Website: www.angelo.edu
Admissions email: admissions@angelo.edu
Public; founded 1928
Freshman admissions: selective; 2014-2015: 3,291 applied, 2,944 accepted. Either SAT or ACT required. ACT 25/75 percentile: 18-24. High school rank: 11% in top tenth, 34% in top quarter, 67% in top half
Early decision deadline: N/A, notification date: N/A
Early action deadline: N/A, notification date: N/A
Application deadline (fall): rolling
Undergraduate student body: 4,645 full time, 779 part time; 46% male, 54% female; 0% American Indian, 1% Asian, 8% black, 32% Hispanic, 3% multiracial, 0% Pacific Islander, 52% white, 3% international; 97% from in state; 38% live on campus; 8% of students in fraternities, 4% in sororities
Most popular majors: 7% Agriculture, Agriculture Operations, and Related Sciences, 14% Business, Management, Marketing, and Related Support Services, 13% Health Professions and Related Programs, 12% Multi/Interdisciplinary Studies, 8% Psychology
Expenses: 2015-2016: $7,864 in state, $18,724 out of state; room/board: $7,702
Financial aid: (325) 942-2246; 67% of undergrads determined to have financial need; average aid package $11,311

Art Institute of Houston[1]

Houston TX
(800) 275-4244
U.S. News ranking: Arts, unranked
Website: www.artinstitute.edu/houston/
Admissions email: N/A
For-profit
Application deadline (fall): N/A
Undergraduate student body: N/A full time, N/A part time
Expenses: 2014-2015: $17,668; room/board: $11,367
Financial aid: (713) 353-4311

Austin College

Sherman TX
(800) 442-5363
U.S. News ranking: Nat. Lib. Arts, No. 79
Website: www.austincollege.edu
Admissions email: admission@austincollege.edu
Private; founded 1849
Affiliation: Presbyterian
Freshman admissions: more selective; 2014-2015: 3,038 applied, 1,652 accepted. Either SAT or ACT required. ACT 25/75 percentile: 22-27. High school rank: 24% in top tenth, 72% in top quarter, 87% in top half
Early decision deadline: N/A, notification date: N/A
Early action deadline: 1/15, notification date: 3/1
Application deadline (fall): rolling
Undergraduate student body: 1,271 full time, 7 part time; 48% male, 52% female; 1% American Indian, 14% Asian, 7% black, 19% Hispanic, 0% multiracial, 0% Pacific Islander, 56% white, 3% international; 90% from in state; 77% live on campus; 27% of students in fraternities, 19% in sororities
Most popular majors: 9% Biological and Biomedical Sciences, 15% Business, Management, Marketing, and Related Support Services, 8% English Language and Literature/Letters, 16% Psychology, 14% Social Sciences
Expenses: 2014-2015: $34,840; room/board: $11,793
Financial aid: (903) 813-2900; 66% of undergrads determined to have financial need; average aid package $30,701

Baylor University

Waco TX
(800) 229-5678
U.S. News ranking: Nat. U., No. 72
Website: www.baylor.edu
Admissions email: Admissions@Baylor.edu
Private; founded 1845
Affiliation: Baptist
Freshman admissions: more selective; 2014-2015: 33,898 applied, 18,766 accepted. Either SAT or ACT required. ACT 25/75 percentile: 24-30. High school rank: 39% in top tenth, 74% in top quarter, 96% in top half
Early decision deadline: N/A, notification date: N/A
Early action deadline: 11/1, notification date: 1/15
Application deadline (fall): 2/1
Undergraduate student body: 13,613 full time, 246 part time; 42% male, 58% female; 0% American Indian, 6% Asian, 7% black, 14% Hispanic, 5% multiracial, 0% Pacific Islander, 64% white, 3% international; 74% from in state; 38% live on campus; 15% of students in fraternities, 28% in sororities
Most popular majors: 5% Accounting, 8% Biology/Biological Sciences, General, 4% Marketing/Marketing Management, General, 5% Psychology, General, 7% Registered Nursing/Registered Nurse
Expenses: 2015-2016: $40,198; room/board: $11,360
Financial aid: (254) 710-2611; 57% of undergrads determined to have financial need; average aid package $26,017

Brazosport College[1]

Lake Jackson TX
(979) 230-3020
U.S. News ranking: Reg. Coll. (W), unranked
Website: www.brazosport.edu
Admissions email: N/A
Public
Application deadline (fall): N/A
Undergraduate student body: N/A full time, N/A part time
Expenses: 2014-2015: $2,295 in state, $4,725 out of state; room/board: $8,700
Financial aid: (979) 230-0337

Concordia University Texas[1]

Austin TX
(800) 865-4282
U.S. News ranking: Reg. U. (W), second tier
Website: www.concordia.edu
Admissions email: admissions@concordia.edu
Private; founded 1926
Affiliation: Lutheran Church-Missouri Synod
Application deadline (fall): 8/1
Undergraduate student body: N/A full time, N/A part time
Expenses: 2015-2016: $28,160; room/board: $9,287
Financial aid: (512) 486-1283; 74% of undergrads determined to have financial need; average aid package $20,814

Dallas Baptist University
Dallas TX
(214) 333-5360
U.S. News ranking: Reg. U. (W), No. 35
Website: www.dbu.edu
Admissions email: admiss@dbu.edu
Private; founded 1898
Affiliation: Baptist
Freshman admissions: selective; 2014-2015: 2,787 applied, 1,288 accepted. Either SAT or ACT required. ACT 25/75 percentile: 18-27. High school rank: 18% in top tenth, 46% in top quarter, 74% in top half
Early decision deadline: N/A, notification date: N/A
Early action deadline: N/A, notification date: N/A
Application deadline (fall): rolling
Undergraduate student body: 2,397 full time, 1,060 part time; 42% male, 58% female; 1% American Indian, 2% Asian, 15% black, 14% Hispanic, 0% multiracial, 0% Pacific Islander, 61% white, 6% international; 92% from in state; 55% live on campus; 10% of students in fraternities, 15% in sororities
Most popular majors: 16% Business Administration and Management, General, 14% Multi/Interdisciplinary Studies, Other, 11% Psychology, General, 7% Religious Education, 9% Speech Communication and Rhetoric
Expenses: 2015-2016: $24,890; room/board: $7,326
Financial aid: (214) 333-5460; 65% of undergrads determined to have financial need; average aid package $15,583

East Texas Baptist University
Marshall TX
(800) 804-3828
U.S. News ranking: Reg. Coll. (W), No. 17
Website: www.etbu.edu
Admissions email: admissions@etbu.edu
Private; founded 1912
Affiliation: Baptist
Freshman admissions: selective; 2014-2015: 941 applied, 545 accepted. Either SAT or ACT required. ACT 25/75 percentile: 18-22. High school rank: 9% in top tenth, 39% in top quarter, 75% in top half
Early decision deadline: N/A, notification date: N/A
Early action deadline: N/A, notification date: N/A
Application deadline (fall): 8/15
Undergraduate student body: 1,113 full time, 118 part time; 48% male, 52% female; 1% American Indian, 0% Asian, 19% black, 10% Hispanic, 3% multiracial, 0% Pacific Islander, 64% white, 2% international; 93% from in state; 84% live on campus; 1% of students in fraternities, 1% in sororities
Most popular majors: 15% Business, Management, Marketing, and Related Support Services, 21% Education, 9% Health Professions and Related Programs, 18% Multi/Interdisciplinary Studies, 5% Psychology
Expenses: 2015-2016: $24,218; room/board: $8,629
Financial aid: (903) 923-2137; 87% of undergrads determined to have financial need; average aid package $18,325

Hardin-Simmons University
Abilene TX
(325) 670-1206
U.S. News ranking: Reg. U. (W), No. 34
Website: www.hsutx.edu/
Admissions email: enroll@hsutx.edu
Private; founded 1891
Affiliation: Baptist
Freshman admissions: selective; 2014-2015: 1,456 applied, 827 accepted. Either SAT or ACT required. ACT 25/75 percentile: 20-25. High school rank: 17% in top tenth, 46% in top quarter, 83% in top half
Early decision deadline: N/A, notification date: N/A
Early action deadline: N/A, notification date: N/A
Application deadline (fall): rolling
Undergraduate student body: 1,469 full time, 171 part time; 48% male, 52% female; 0% American Indian, 1% Asian, 7% black, 15% Hispanic, 3% multiracial, 0% Pacific Islander, 71% white, 2% international; 96% from in state; 48% live on campus; 3% of students in fraternities, 5% in sororities
Most popular majors: 11% Business, Management, Marketing, and Related Support Services, 16% Education, 16% Health Professions and Related Programs, 10% Parks, Recreation, Leisure, and Fitness Studies, 8% Psychology
Expenses: 2015-2016: $24,500; room/board: $7,740
Financial aid: (325) 670-5891; 70% of undergrads determined to have financial need; average aid package $19,036

Houston Baptist University
Houston TX
(281) 649-3211
U.S. News ranking: Reg. U. (W), No. 73
Website: www.hbu.edu
Admissions email: admissions@hbu.edu
Private; founded 1960
Affiliation: Baptist
Freshman admissions: selective; 2014-2015: 12,769 applied, 4,562 accepted. Either SAT or ACT required. SAT 25/75 percentile: 960-1160. High school rank: 24% in top tenth, 57% in top quarter, 80% in top half
Early decision deadline: N/A, notification date: N/A
Early action deadline: N/A, notification date: N/A
Application deadline (fall): rolling
Undergraduate student body: 2,137 full time, 151 part time; 39% male, 61% female; 0% American Indian, 13% Asian, 20% black, 27% Hispanic, 5% multiracial, 0% Pacific Islander, 28% white, 4% international; 96% from in state; 41% live on campus; 10% of students in fraternities, 14% in sororities
Most popular majors: 16% Biology/Biological Sciences, General, 18% Business/Commerce, General, 10% Education, General, 8% Psychology, General, 21% Registered Nursing/Registered Nurse
Expenses: 2015-2016: $29,800; room/board: $7,715
Financial aid: (281) 649-3389; 73% of undergrads determined to have financial need; average aid package $25,617

Howard Payne University
Brownwood TX
(325) 649-8020
U.S. News ranking: Reg. Coll. (W), No. 11
Website: www.hputx.edu
Admissions email: enroll@hputx.edu
Private; founded 1889
Affiliation: Baptist
Freshman admissions: less selective; 2014-2015: 1,057 applied, 868 accepted. Either SAT or ACT required. SAT 25/75 percentile: 860-1070. High school rank: 14% in top tenth, 34% in top quarter, 76% in top half
Early decision deadline: N/A, notification date: N/A
Early action deadline: N/A, notification date: N/A
Application deadline (fall): rolling
Undergraduate student body: 945 full time, 128 part time; 50% male, 50% female; 0% American Indian, 0% Asian, 8% black, 22% Hispanic, 3% multiracial, 0% Pacific Islander, 63% white, 0% international; 97% from in state; 63% live on campus; 15% of students in fraternities, 16% in sororities
Most popular majors: 13% Business, Management, Marketing, and Related Support Services, 14% Education, 7% Psychology, 11% Social Sciences, 14% Theology and Religious Vocations
Expenses: 2015-2016: $25,600; room/board: $7,489
Financial aid: (325) 649-8014; 83% of undergrads determined to have financial need; average aid package $18,654

Huston-Tillotson University
Austin TX
(512) 505-3029
U.S. News ranking: Nat. Lib. Arts, second tier
Website: htu.edu/
Admissions email: admission@htu.edu
Private
Freshman admissions: least selective; 2014-2015: N/A applied, N/A accepted. Either SAT or ACT required. SAT 25/75 percentile: 720-920. High school rank: N/A
Early decision deadline: 12/1, notification date: 1/5
Early action deadline: N/A, notification date: N/A
Application deadline (fall): 5/1
Undergraduate student body: 927 full time, 48 part time; 45% male, 55% female; 0% American Indian, 1% Asian, 70% black, 19% Hispanic, 1% multiracial, 0% Pacific Islander, 4% white, 4% international; 94% from in state; 37% live on campus; N/A of students in fraternities, N/A in sororities
Most popular majors: Information not available
Expenses: 2014-2015: $13,544; room/board: $7,568
Financial aid: (512) 505-3031

Jarvis Christian College
Hawkins TX
(903) 730-4890
U.S. News ranking: Reg. Coll. (W), second tier
Website: www.jarvis.edu
Admissions email: Recruitment@jarvis.edu
Private; founded 1912
Affiliation: Christian Church (Disciples of Christ)
Freshman admissions: least selective; 2014-2015: 739 applied, 591 accepted. Either SAT or ACT required. SAT 25/75 percentile: 660-880. High school rank: 5% in top tenth, 10% in top quarter, 23% in top half
Early decision deadline: N/A, notification date: N/A
Early action deadline: N/A, notification date: N/A
Application deadline (fall): 8/1
Undergraduate student body: 701 full time, 62 part time; 52% male, 48% female; 0% American Indian, N/A Asian, 84% black, 11% Hispanic, N/A multiracial, 0% Pacific Islander, 4% white, N/A international; 83% from in state; 73% live on campus; 12% of students in fraternities, 20% in sororities
Most popular majors: 15% Biological and Biomedical Sciences, 25% Business, Management, Marketing, and Related Support Services, 30% Education, 15% Homeland Security, Law Enforcement, Firefighting and Related Protective Services, 5% Public Administration and Social Service Professions
Expenses: 2015-2016: $11,369; room/board: $8,183
Financial aid: (903) 769-5740; 96% of undergrads determined to have financial need; average aid package $17,996

Lamar University
Beaumont TX
(409) 880-8888
U.S. News ranking: Nat. U., second tier
Website: www.lamar.edu
Admissions email: admissions@lamar.edu
Public; founded 1923
Freshman admissions: less selective; 2014-2015: 4,657 applied, 3,653 accepted. Either SAT or ACT required. SAT 25/75 percentile: 870-1080. High school rank: 15% in top tenth, 38% in top quarter, 71% in top half
Early decision deadline: N/A, notification date: N/A
Early action deadline: N/A, notification date: N/A
Application deadline (fall): 8/10
Undergraduate student body: 6,460 full time, 2,819 part time; 42% male, 58% female; 0% American Indian, 4% Asian, 30% black, 11% Hispanic, 2% multiracial, 0% Pacific Islander, 50% white, 2% international; 98% from in state; 35% live on campus; N/A of students in fraternities, N/A in sororities
Most popular majors: 12% Business, Management, Marketing, and Related Support Services, 8% Engineering, 7% General Studies, 18% Health Professions and Related Programs, 18% Multi/Interdisciplinary Studies, Other
Expenses: 2015-2016: $9,721 in state, $21,421 out of state; room/board: $7,870
Financial aid: (409) 880-8450; 65% of undergrads determined to have financial need; average aid package $6,718

LeTourneau University
Longview TX
(903) 233-4300
U.S. News ranking: Reg. U. (W), No. 32
Website: www.letu.edu
Admissions email: admissions@letu.edu
Private; founded 1946
Affiliation: Christian interdenominational
Freshman admissions: more selective; 2014-2015: 1,761 applied, 870 accepted. Neither SAT nor ACT required. SAT 25/75 percentile: 1030-1310. High school rank: 32% in top tenth, 56% in top quarter, 87% in top half
Early decision deadline: N/A, notification date: N/A
Early action deadline: N/A, notification date: N/A
Application deadline (fall): rolling
Undergraduate student body: 1,341 full time, 909 part time; 53% male, 47% female; 0% American Indian, 1% Asian, 10% black, 9% Hispanic, 4% multiracial, 0% Pacific Islander, 66% white, 4% international; 57% from in state; 75% live on campus; N/A of students in fraternities, N/A in sororities
Most popular majors: 33% Business, Management, Marketing, and Related Support Services, 16% Education, 14% Engineering, 6% Psychology, 7% Transportation and Materials Moving
Expenses: 2015-2016: $27,900; room/board: $9,580
Financial aid: (903) 233-3430; 87% of undergrads determined to have financial need; average aid package $19,491

Lubbock Christian University
Lubbock TX
(806) 720-7151
U.S. News ranking: Reg. U. (W), No. 83
Website: www.lcu.edu
Admissions email: admissions@lcu.edu
Private; founded 1957
Affiliation: Churches of Christ
Freshman admissions: selective; 2014-2015: 828 applied, 781 accepted. Either SAT or ACT required. ACT 25/75 percentile: 19-24. High school rank: 16% in top tenth, 42% in top quarter, 77% in top half
Early decision deadline: N/A, notification date: N/A
Early action deadline: N/A, notification date: N/A

Application deadline (fall): 6/1
Undergraduate student body: 1,222 full time, 217 part time; 39% male, 61% female; 1% American Indian, 1% Asian, 6% black, 23% Hispanic, 0% multiracial, 0% Pacific Islander, 68% white, 2% international; 87% from in state; 36% live on campus; 21% of students in fraternities, 18% in sororities
Most popular majors: 14% Business, Management, Marketing, and Related Support Services, 21% Education, 24% Health Professions and Related Programs, 8% Parks, Recreation, Leisure, and Fitness Studies, 5% Public Administration and Social Service Professions
Expenses: 2015-2016: $20,360; room/board: $6,070
Financial aid: (800) 933-7601; 61% of undergrads determined to have financial need; average aid package $15,364

McMurry University

Abilene TX
(325) 793-4700
U.S. News ranking: Reg. Coll. (W), No. 17
Website: www.mcm.edu
Admissions email: admissions@mcm.edu
Private; founded 1923
Affiliation: Methodist
Freshman admissions: less selective; 2014-2015: 1,031 applied, 633 accepted. Either SAT or ACT required. SAT 25/75 percentile: 810-1010. High school rank: 8% in top tenth, 27% in top quarter, 62% in top half
Early decision deadline: N/A, notification date: N/A
Early action deadline: N/A, notification date: N/A
Application deadline (fall): 8/15
Undergraduate student body: 848 full time, 155 part time; 52% male, 48% female; 1% American Indian, 1% Asian, 18% black, 22% Hispanic, 1% multiracial, 0% Pacific Islander, 56% white, 0% international; 95% from in state; 45% live on campus; 15% of students in fraternities, 18% in sororities
Most popular majors: 28% Business, Management, Marketing, and Related Support Services, 18% Education, 8% Parks, Recreation, Leisure, and Fitness Studies, 8% Psychology, 8% Visual and Performing Arts
Expenses: 2015-2016: $25,588; room/board: $8,162
Financial aid: (325) 793-4709; 91% of undergrads determined to have financial need; average aid package $18,748

Midland College[1]

Midland TX
(432) 685-5502
U.S. News ranking: Reg. Coll. (W), unranked
Website: www.midland.edu/
Admissions email: pebensberger@midland.edu
Public
Application deadline (fall): N/A
Undergraduate student body: N/A full time, N/A part time
Expenses: 2014-2015: $4,380 in state, $5,550 out of state; room/board: $4,510
Financial aid: (432) 685-4757

Midwestern State University

Wichita Falls TX
(800) 842-1922
U.S. News ranking: Reg. U. (W), second tier
Website: www.mwsu.edu
Admissions email: admissions@mwsu.edu
Public; founded 1922
Freshman admissions: selective; 2014-2015: 3,259 applied, 2,009 accepted. Either SAT or ACT required. SAT 25/75 percentile: 900-1100. High school rank: 13% in top tenth, 38% in top quarter, 72% in top half
Early decision deadline: N/A, notification date: N/A
Early action deadline: 8/7, notification date: N/A
Application deadline (fall): 8/7
Undergraduate student body: 3,864 full time, 1,280 part time; 42% male, 58% female; 1% American Indian, 3% Asian, 14% black, 16% Hispanic, 3% multiracial, 0% Pacific Islander, 55% white, 8% international; 92% from in state; 28% live on campus; 8% of students in fraternities, 9% in sororities
Most popular majors: 5% Biology/Biological Sciences, General, 5% Criminal Justice/Safety Studies, 12% Multi/Interdisciplinary Studies, Other, 10% Radiologic Technology/Science - Radiographer, 12% Registered Nursing/Registered Nurse
Expenses: 2014-2015: $7,753 in state, $9,703 out of state; room/board: $6,810
Financial aid: (940) 397-4214; 63% of undergrads determined to have financial need; average aid package $9,339

Our Lady of the Lake University

San Antonio TX
(800) 436-6558
U.S. News ranking: Nat. U., second tier
Website: www.ollusa.edu
Admissions email: admission@lake.ollusa.edu
Private; founded 1895
Affiliation: Roman Catholic
Freshman admissions: less selective; 2014-2015: 5,412 applied, 2,680 accepted. Either SAT or ACT required. SAT 25/75 percentile: 840-1030. High school rank: 13% in top tenth, 34% in top quarter, 71% in top half
Early decision deadline: N/A, notification date: 12/31
Early action deadline: 11/14, notification date: 12/31
Application deadline (fall): 8/1
Undergraduate student body: 1,359 full time, 236 part time; 30% male, 70% female; 1% American Indian, 1% Asian, 10% black, 71% Hispanic, 1% multiracial, 0% Pacific Islander, 13% white, 1% international; 97% from in state; 38% live on campus; 5% of students in fraternities, 7% in sororities
Most popular majors: 14% Business Administration and Management, General, 11% Communication Sciences and Disorders, General, 7% Criminal Justice/Safety Studies, 8% Psychology, General, 9% Social Work
Expenses: 2015-2016: $26,148; room/board: $7,556
Financial aid: (210) 434-6711; 87% of undergrads determined to have financial need; average aid package $20,200

Prairie View A&M University

Prairie View TX
(877) PVA-MU30
U.S. News ranking: Reg. U. (W), second tier
Website: www.pvamu.edu
Admissions email: admission@pvamu.edu
Public; founded 1876
Freshman admissions: least selective; 2014-2015: 4,744 applied, 4,074 accepted. Either SAT or ACT required. SAT 25/75 percentile: 770-940. High school rank: 6% in top tenth, 16% in top quarter, 55% in top half
Early decision deadline: N/A, notification date: N/A
Early action deadline: N/A, notification date: N/A
Application deadline (fall): 6/1
Undergraduate student body: 6,290 full time, 600 part time; 41% male, 59% female; 0% American Indian, 2% Asian, 85% black, 5% Hispanic, 2% multiracial, 0% Pacific Islander, 3% white, 2% international; 92% from in state; 47% live on campus; 1% of students in fraternities, 2% in sororities
Most popular majors: 12% Business, Management, Marketing, and Related Support Services, 12% Engineering Technologies and Engineering-Related Fields, 25% Health Professions and Related Programs, 7% Public Administration and Social Service Professions, 8% Social Sciences
Expenses: 2014-2015: $9,460 in state, $20,928 out of state; room/board: $7,734
Financial aid: (936) 857-2424; 72% of undergrads determined to have financial need; average aid package $14,265

Rice University

Houston TX
(713) 348-7423
U.S. News ranking: Nat. U., No. 18
Website: www.rice.edu
Admissions email: admission@rice.edu
Private; founded 1912
Freshman admissions: most selective; 2014-2015: 17,728 applied, 2,677 accepted. Either SAT or ACT required. SAT 25/75 percentile: 1390-1550. High school rank: 88% in top tenth, 96% in top quarter, 100% in top half
Early decision deadline: 11/1, notification date: 12/15
Early action deadline: N/A, notification date: N/A
Application deadline (fall): 1/1
Undergraduate student body: 3,872 full time, 54 part time; 52% male, 48% female; 0% American Indian, 23% Asian, 7% black, 15% Hispanic, 4% multiracial, 0% Pacific Islander, 38% white, 12% international; 51% from in state; 70% live on campus; 0% of students in fraternities, 0% in sororities
Most popular majors: 9% Biochemistry, 6% Bioengineering and Biomedical Engineering, 5% Chemical Engineering, 6% Mechanical Engineering, 5% Psychology, General
Expenses: 2015-2016: $42,253; room/board: $13,650
Financial aid: (713) 348-4958; 39% of undergrads determined to have financial need; average aid package $39,201

Sam Houston State University

Huntsville TX
(936) 294-1828
U.S. News ranking: Nat. U., second tier
Website: www.shsu.edu
Admissions email: admissions@shsu.edu
Public; founded 1879
Freshman admissions: less selective; 2014-2015: 9,175 applied, 6,759 accepted. Either SAT or ACT required. SAT 25/75 percentile: 880-1070. High school rank: 14% in top tenth, 54% in top quarter, 88% in top half
Early decision deadline: N/A, notification date: N/A
Early action deadline: N/A, notification date: N/A
Application deadline (fall): 8/1
Undergraduate student body: 13,553 full time, 3,266 part time; 40% male, 60% female; 0% American Indian, 1% Asian, 19% black, 19% Hispanic, 3% multiracial, 0% Pacific Islander, 54% white, 1% international; 98% from in state; 20% live on campus; 2% of students in fraternities, 2% in sororities
Most popular majors: 5% Agriculture, Agriculture Operations, and Related Sciences, 22% Business, Management, Marketing, and Related Support Services, 20% Homeland Security, Law Enforcement, Firefighting and Related Protective Services, 12% Multi/Interdisciplinary Studies, 5% Visual and Performing Arts
Expenses: 2015-2016: $9,337 in state, $21,037 out of state; room/board: $8,676
Financial aid: (936) 294-1774; 62% of undergrads determined to have financial need; average aid package $9,698

Schreiner University

Kerrville TX
(800) 343-4919
U.S. News ranking: Reg. Coll. (W), No. 16
Website: www.schreiner.edu
Admissions email: admissions@schreiner.edu
Private; founded 1923
Affiliation: Presbyterian
Freshman admissions: less selective; 2014-2015: 972 applied, 904 accepted. Either SAT or ACT required. SAT 25/75 percentile: 890-1090. High school rank: 13% in top tenth, 40% in top quarter, 74% in top half
Early decision deadline: N/A, notification date: N/A
Early action deadline: N/A, notification date: N/A
Application deadline (fall): 8/1
Undergraduate student body: 1,011 full time, 51 part time; 45% male, 55% female; 0% American Indian, 1% Asian, 4% black, 32% Hispanic, 4% multiracial, 0% Pacific Islander, 59% white, 1% international; 96% from in state; 63% live on campus; 14% of students in fraternities, 15% in sororities
Most popular majors: 8% Education, General, 8% Graphic Design, 9% Health and Physical Education/Fitness, General, 8% Mathematics, General, 8% Psychology, General
Expenses: 2015-2016: $25,086; room/board: $9,170
Financial aid: (830) 792-7217; 88% of undergrads determined to have financial need; average aid package $18,278

Southern Methodist University

Dallas TX
(800) 323-0672
U.S. News ranking: Nat. U., No. 61
Website: www.smu.edu
Admissions email: ugadmission@smu.edu
Private; founded 1911
Affiliation: United Methodist
Freshman admissions: more selective; 2014-2015: 11,817 applied, 6,192 accepted. Either SAT or ACT required. ACT 25/75 percentile: 28-31. High school rank: 46% in top tenth, 79% in top quarter, 95% in top half
Early decision deadline: 11/1, notification date: 12/31
Early action deadline: 11/1, notification date: 12/31
Application deadline (fall): 1/15
Undergraduate student body: 6,193 full time, 198 part time; 50% male, 50% female; 0% American Indian, 7% Asian, 5% black, 12% Hispanic, 3% multiracial, 0% Pacific Islander, 66% white, 7% international; 49% from in state; 53% live on campus; 33% of students in fraternities, 46% in sororities
Most popular majors: 20% Business, Management, Marketing, and Related Support Services, 11% Communication, Journalism, and Related Programs, 9% Engineering, 14% Social Sciences, 7% Visual and Performing Arts
Expenses: 2015-2016: $48,190; room/board: $15,575
Financial aid: (214) 768-3016; 36% of undergrads determined to have financial need; average aid package $37,976

South Texas College[1]

McAllen TX
(956) 872-8323
U.S. News ranking: Reg. Coll. (W), unranked
Website: www.southtexascollege.edu/
Admissions email: N/A
Public
Application deadline (fall): N/A
Undergraduate student body: N/A full time, N/A part time
Expenses: 2014-2015: $3,590 in state, $4,464 out of state; room/board: $4,466
Financial aid: (956) 872-8375

Southwestern Adventist University[1]

Keene TX
(817) 645-3921
U.S. News ranking: Reg. Coll. (W), No. 22
Website: www.swau.edu
Admissions email: admissions@swau.edu
Private; founded 1893
Affiliation: Seventh-day Adventist
Application deadline (fall): rolling
Undergraduate student body: N/A full time, N/A part time
Expenses: 2014-2015: $19,460; room/board: $7,400
Financial aid: (817) 645-3921

Southwestern Assemblies of God University

Waxahachie TX
(888) 937-7248
U.S. News ranking: Reg. U. (W), second tier
Website: www.sagu.edu/
Admissions email: admissions@sagu.edu
Private; founded 1927
Affiliation: Assemblies of God
Freshman admissions: selective; 2014-2015: 1,138 applied, 383 accepted. Either SAT or ACT required. ACT 25/75 percentile: 18-24. High school rank: N/A
Early decision deadline: N/A, notification date: N/A
Early action deadline: N/A, notification date: N/A
Application deadline (fall): rolling
Undergraduate student body: 1,445 full time, 221 part time; 48% male, 52% female; 2% American Indian, 1% Asian, 10% black, 21% Hispanic, 1% multiracial, 0% Pacific Islander, 64% white, 1% international
Most popular majors: 9% Business Administration and Management, General, 16% Education, General, 11% General Studies, 7% Human Services, General, 24% Religious Education
Expenses: 2015-2016: $19,180; room/board: $6,936
Financial aid: N/A; 87% of undergrads determined to have financial need; average aid package $7,477

Southwestern Christian College[1]

Terrell TX
(972) 524-3341
U.S. News ranking: Reg. Coll. (W), unranked
Website: www.swcc.edu
Admissions email: N/A
Private
Application deadline (fall): N/A
Undergraduate student body: N/A full time, N/A part time
Expenses: 2014-2015: $7,764; room/board: $5,355
Financial aid: (972) 524-3341

Southwestern University

Georgetown TX
(800) 252-3166
U.S. News ranking: Nat. Lib. Arts, No. 90
Website: www.southwestern.edu
Admissions email: admission@southwestern.edu
Private; founded 1840
Affiliation: United Methodist
Freshman admissions: more selective; 2014-2015: 3,487 applied, 1,692 accepted. Either SAT or ACT required. SAT 25/75 percentile: 1050-1260. High school rank: 36% in top tenth, 66% in top quarter, 95% in top half
Early decision deadline: N/A, notification date: N/A
Early action deadline: 11/15, notification date: 2/15
Application deadline (fall): rolling
Undergraduate student body: 1,517 full time, 21 part time; 42% male, 58% female; 0% American Indian, 5% Asian, 5% black, 19% Hispanic, 3% multiracial, 0% Pacific Islander, 64% white, 3% international; 88% from in state; 77% live on campus; 22% of students in fraternities, 21% in sororities
Most popular majors: 14% Biological and Biomedical Sciences, 14% Business, Management, Marketing, and Related Support Services, 8% Psychology, 18% Social Sciences, 11% Visual and Performing Arts
Expenses: 2015-2016: $37,560; room/board: $12,108
Financial aid: (512) 863-1259; 63% of undergrads determined to have financial need; average aid package $31,865

St. Edward's University

Austin TX
(512) 448-8500
U.S. News ranking: Reg. U. (W), No. 13
Website: www.stedwards.edu
Admissions email: seu.admit@stedwards.edu
Private; founded 1885
Affiliation: Roman Catholic
Freshman admissions: selective; 2014-2015: 4,423 applied, 3,466 accepted. Either SAT or ACT required. SAT 25/75 percentile: 1010-1210. High school rank: 23% in top tenth, 58% in top quarter, 85% in top half
Early decision deadline: N/A, notification date: N/A
Early action deadline: N/A, notification date: N/A
Application deadline (fall): 5/1
Undergraduate student body: 3,436 full time, 567 part time; 39% male, 61% female; 0% American Indian, 3% Asian, 4% black, 40% Hispanic, 3% multiracial, 0% Pacific Islander, 38% white, 9% international; 88% from in state; 39% live on campus; N/A of students in fraternities, N/A in sororities
Most popular majors: 7% Business Administration and Management, General, 7% Communication, General, 4% International Business/Trade/Commerce, 4% Marketing/Marketing Management, General, 10% Psychology, General
Expenses: 2015-2016: $38,720; room/board: $11,664
Financial aid: (512) 448-8520; 65% of undergrads determined to have financial need; average aid package $28,906

Stephen F. Austin State University

Nacogdoches TX
(936) 468-2504
U.S. News ranking: Reg. U. (W), No. 87
Website: www.sfasu.edu
Admissions email: admissions@sfasu.edu
Public; founded 1923
Freshman admissions: selective; 2014-2015: 10,631 applied, 6,220 accepted. Either SAT or ACT required. SAT 25/75 percentile: 900-1080. High school rank: 13% in top tenth, 40% in top quarter, 77% in top half
Early decision deadline: N/A, notification date: N/A
Early action deadline: N/A, notification date: N/A
Application deadline (fall): rolling
Undergraduate student body: 9,335 full time, 1,689 part time; 37% male, 63% female; 1% American Indian, 1% Asian, 23% black, 14% Hispanic, 3% multiracial, 0% Pacific Islander, 57% white, 1% international; 98% from in state; N/A live on campus; 14% of students in fraternities, 10% in sororities
Most popular majors: 4% Business Administration and Management, General, 5% Human Development and Family Studies, General, 8% Kinesiology and Exercise Science, 13% Multi/Interdisciplinary Studies, Other, 6% Registered Nursing/Registered Nurse
Expenses: 2014-2015: $8,892 in state, $19,752 out of state; room/board: $8,868
Financial aid: (936) 468-2403

St. Mary's University of San Antonio

San Antonio TX
(210) 436-3126
U.S. News ranking: Reg. U. (W), No. 22
Website: www.stmarytx.edu
Admissions email: uadm@stmarytx.edu
Private; founded 1852
Affiliation: Roman Catholic
Freshman admissions: selective; 2014-2015: 4,282 applied, 2,546 accepted. Either SAT or ACT required. SAT 25/75 percentile: 940-1130. High school rank: N/A
Early decision deadline: N/A, notification date: N/A
Early action deadline: N/A, notification date: N/A
Application deadline (fall): rolling
Undergraduate student body: 2,211 full time, 111 part time; 44% male, 56% female; 0% American Indian, 2% Asian, 4% black, 69% Hispanic, 0% multiracial, 0% Pacific Islander, 15% white, 6% international; 92% from in state; 59% live on campus; 1% of students in fraternities, 2% in sororities
Most popular majors: 15% Biological and Biomedical Sciences, 17% Business, Management, Marketing, and Related Support Services, 8% Homeland Security, Law Enforcement, Firefighting and Related Protective Services, 7% Psychology, 16% Social Sciences
Expenses: 2015-2016: $27,160; room/board: $8,908
Financial aid: (210) 436-3141; average aid package $24,476

Sul Ross State University

Alpine TX
(432) 837-8050
U.S. News ranking: Reg. U. (W), second tier
Website: www.sulross.edu
Admissions email: admissions@sulross.edu
Public; founded 1917
Freshman admissions: less selective; 2014-2015: 1,000 applied, 934 accepted. Either SAT or ACT required. ACT 25/75 percentile: 15-21. High school rank: 3% in top tenth, 12% in top quarter, 43% in top half
Early decision deadline: N/A, notification date: N/A
Early action deadline: N/A, notification date: N/A
Application deadline (fall): rolling
Undergraduate student body: 1,238 full time, 793 part time; 43% male, 57% female; 0% American Indian, 0% Asian, 7% black, 65% Hispanic, 1% multiracial, 0% Pacific Islander, 24% white, 0% international; 97% from in state; 45% live on campus; 0% of students in fraternities, 0% in sororities
Most popular majors: 18% Biology/Biological Sciences, General, 12% Business/Commerce, General, 27% Criminal Justice/Safety Studies, 12% History, General, 30% Multi/Interdisciplinary Studies, Other
Expenses: 2015-2016: $7,211 in state, $18,911 out of state; room/board: $7,810
Financial aid: (432) 837-8059

Tarleton State University

Stephenville TX
(800) 687-8236
U.S. News ranking: Reg. U. (W), second tier
Website: www.tarleton.edu
Admissions email: uadm@tarleton.edu
Public; founded 1899
Freshman admissions: less selective; 2014-2015: N/A applied, N/A accepted. Either SAT or ACT required. SAT 25/75 percentile: 860-1050. High school rank: 10% in top tenth, 23% in top quarter, 71% in top half
Early decision deadline: N/A, notification date: N/A
Early action deadline: 3/1, notification date: N/A
Application deadline (fall): 7/21
Undergraduate student body: 8,055 full time, 2,162 part time; 39% male, 61% female; 1% American Indian, 1% Asian, 8% black, 16% Hispanic, 3% multiracial, 0% Pacific Islander, 71% white, 0% international; 98% from in state; 35% live on campus; N/A of students in fraternities, N/A in sororities
Most popular majors: Information not available
Expenses: 2015-2016: $7,933 in state, $18,793 out of state; room/board: $9,324
Financial aid: (254) 968-9070; 65% of undergrads determined to have financial need; average aid package $8,940

Texas A&M International University

Laredo TX
(956) 326-2200
U.S. News ranking: Reg. U. (W), No. 70
Website: www.tamiu.edu
Admissions email: enroll@tamiu.edu
Public; founded 1970
Freshman admissions: less selective; 2014-2015: 6,193 applied, 2,961 accepted. Either SAT or ACT required. SAT 25/75 percentile: 820-1010. High school rank: 20% in top tenth, 51% in top quarter, 85% in top half
Early decision deadline: N/A, notification date: N/A
Early action deadline: N/A, notification date: N/A
Application deadline (fall): 7/1
Undergraduate student body: 4,279 full time, 2,462 part time; 41% male, 59% female; 0% American Indian, 1% Asian, 1% black, 95% Hispanic, 0% multiracial, 0% Pacific Islander, 2% white, 2% international; 99% from in state; 10% live on campus; 2% of students in fraternities, 2% in sororities
Most popular majors: 19% Business, Management, Marketing, and Related Support Services, 13% Health Professions and Related Programs, 12% Homeland Security, Law Enforcement, Firefighting and Related Protective Services, 9% Multi/Interdisciplinary Studies, 11% Psychology
Expenses: 2015-2016: $7,990 in state, $19,684 out of state; room/board: $8,259
Financial aid: (956) 326-2225; 89% of undergrads determined to have financial need; average aid package $11,481

Texas A&M University–College Station

College Station TX
(979) 845-3741
U.S. News ranking: Nat. U., No. 70
Website: www.tamu.edu
Admissions email: admissions@tamu.edu
Public; founded 1876
Freshman admissions: more selective; 2014-2015: 32,190 applied, 22,863 accepted. Either SAT or ACT required. SAT 25/75 percentile: 1060-1310. High school rank: 65% in top tenth, 90% in top quarter, 99% in top half
Early decision deadline: N/A, notification date: N/A
Early action deadline: N/A, notification date: N/A
Application deadline (fall): 12/1
Undergraduate student body: 42,129 full time, 4,964 part time; 51% male, 49% female; 0% American Indian, 5% Asian, 3% black, 21% Hispanic, 3% multiracial, 0% Pacific Islander, 66% white, 1% international; 96% from in state; 24% live on campus; 3% of students in fraternities, 6% in sororities
Most popular majors: 10% Agriculture, Agriculture Operations, and Related Sciences, 8% Biological and Biomedical Sciences, 17% Business,

Management, Marketing, and Related Support Services, 15% Engineering, 9% Multi/Interdisciplinary Studies
Expenses: 2014-2015: $9,180 in state, $26,356 out of state; room/board: $9,522
Financial aid: (979) 845-3236; 44% of undergrads determined to have financial need; average aid package $15,300

Texas A&M University–Commerce

Commerce TX
(903) 886-5000
U.S. News ranking: Nat. U., second tier
Website: www.tamuc.edu/
Admissions email: Admissions@tamuc.edu
Public; founded 1889
Freshman admissions: less selective; 2014-2015: 6,614 applied, 3,164 accepted. Either SAT or ACT required. SAT 25/75 percentile: 870-1080. High school rank: 11% in top tenth, 35% in top quarter, 69% in top half
Early decision deadline: N/A, notification date: N/A
Early action deadline: N/A, notification date: N/A
Application deadline (fall): 8/15
Undergraduate student body: 5,250 full time, 1,898 part time; 40% male, 60% female; 1% American Indian, 2% Asian, 22% black, 16% Hispanic, 4% multiracial, 0% Pacific Islander, 51% white, 3% international; 98% from in state; 31% live on campus; 3% of students in fraternities, 2% in sororities
Most popular majors: 11% Business, Management, Marketing, and Related Support Services, 9% Liberal Arts and Sciences, General Studies and Humanities, 32% Multi/Interdisciplinary Studies, 6% Parks, Recreation, Leisure, and Fitness Studies, 6% Visual and Performing Arts
Expenses: 2015-2016: $7,432 in state, $19,132 out of state; room/board: $8,326
Financial aid: (903) 886-5096; 77% of undergrads determined to have financial need; average aid package $10,814

Texas A&M University–Corpus Christi

Corpus Christi TX
(361) 825-2624
U.S. News ranking: Nat. U., second tier
Website: www.tamucc.edu
Admissions email: admiss@tamucc.edu
Public; founded 1947
Freshman admissions: less selective; 2014-2015: 11,034 applied, 6,687 accepted. Either SAT or ACT required. SAT 25/75 percentile: 870-1070. High school rank: 10% in top tenth, 37% in top quarter, 75% in top half
Early decision deadline: N/A, notification date: N/A
Early action deadline: N/A, notification date: N/A
Application deadline (fall): 7/1
Undergraduate student body: 7,114 full time, 1,944 part time; 41% male, 59% female; 0% American Indian, 2% Asian, 6% black, 48% Hispanic, 2% multiracial, 0% Pacific Islander, 38% white, 3% international; 98% from in state; 16% live on campus; 5% of students in fraternities, 5% in sororities
Most popular majors: 9% Biological and Biomedical Sciences, 16% Business, Management, Marketing, and Related Support Services, 19% Health Professions and Related Programs, 12% Multi/Interdisciplinary Studies, 6% Parks, Recreation, Leisure, and Fitness Studies
Expenses: 2015-2016: $8,620 in state, $20,208 out of state; room/board: N/A
Financial aid: (361) 825-2338; 62% of undergrads determined to have financial need; average aid package $9,093

Texas A&M University–Kingsville

Kingsville TX
(361) 593-2315
U.S. News ranking: Nat. U., second tier
Website: www.tamuk.edu
Admissions email: admissions@tamuk.edu
Public; founded 1925
Freshman admissions: less selective; 2014-2015: 6,503 applied, 5,432 accepted. Either SAT or ACT required. ACT 25/75 percentile: 17-21. High school rank: 11% in top tenth, 38% in top quarter, 74% in top half
Early decision deadline: N/A, notification date: N/A
Early action deadline: N/A, notification date: N/A
Application deadline (fall): 8/1
Undergraduate student body: 4,828 full time, 1,474 part time; 52% male, 48% female; 0% American Indian, 1% Asian, 7% black, 70% Hispanic, 1% multiracial, 0% Pacific Islander, 19% white, 2% international; 99% from in state; 33% live on campus; 2% of students in fraternities, 2% in sororities
Most popular majors: 16% Communication Sciences and Disorders, General, 6% Criminology, 5% Mechanical Engineering, 10% Multi/Interdisciplinary Studies, Other, 6% Psychology, General
Expenses: 2014-2015: $7,434 in state, $18,294 out of state; room/board: $8,131
Financial aid: (361) 593-2173

Texas A&M University–Texarkana[1]

Texarkana TX
(903) 223-3069
U.S. News ranking: Reg. U. (W), second tier
Website: www.tamut.edu
Admissions email: admissions@tamut.edu
Public; founded 1971
Application deadline (fall): rolling
Undergraduate student body: N/A full time, N/A part time
Expenses: 2014-2015: $6,059 in state, $15,235 out of state; room/board: $9,310
Financial aid: (903) 223-3060

Texas Christian University

Fort Worth TX
(817) 257-7490
U.S. News ranking: Nat. U., No. 82
Website: www.tcu.edu
Admissions email: frogmail@tcu.edu
Private; founded 1873
Affiliation: Christian Church (Disciples of Christ)
Freshman admissions: more selective; 2014-2015: 17,029 applied, 8,322 accepted. Either SAT or ACT required. ACT 25/75 percentile: 24-30. High school rank: 42% in top tenth, 73% in top quarter, 96% in top half
Early decision deadline: 11/1, notification date: 1/1
Early action deadline: 11/1, notification date: 1/1
Application deadline (fall): 2/15
Undergraduate student body: 8,338 full time, 309 part time; 40% male, 60% female; 1% American Indian, 3% Asian, 5% black, 11% Hispanic, 0% multiracial, 0% Pacific Islander, 74% white, 5% international; 57% from in state; 48% live on campus; 41% of students in fraternities, 56% in sororities
Most popular majors: 24% Business, Management, Marketing, and Related Support Services, 14% Communication, Journalism, and Related Programs, 7% Education, 14% Health Professions and Related Programs, 7% Social Sciences
Expenses: 2015-2016: $40,720; room/board: $11,800
Financial aid: (817) 257-7858; 39% of undergrads determined to have financial need; average aid package $24,785

Texas College[1]

Tyler TX
(903) 593-8311
U.S. News ranking: Reg. Coll. (W), unranked
Website: www.texascollege.edu
Admissions email: cmarshall-biggins@texascollege.edu
Private
Application deadline (fall): N/A
Undergraduate student body: N/A full time, N/A part time
Expenses: 2014-2015: $10,008; room/board: $7,200
Financial aid: (903) 593-8311

Texas Lutheran University

Seguin TX
(800) 771-8521
U.S. News ranking: Reg. Coll. (W), No. 2
Website: www.tlu.edu
Admissions email: admissions@tlu.edu
Private; founded 1891
Affiliation: Evangelical Lutheran Church in America
Freshman admissions: selective; 2014-2015: 1,516 applied, 847 accepted. Either SAT or ACT required. SAT 25/75 percentile: 920-1130. High school rank: 20% in top tenth, 50% in top quarter, 83% in top half
Early decision deadline: N/A, notification date: N/A
Early action deadline: N/A, notification date: N/A
Application deadline (fall): rolling
Undergraduate student body: 1,229 full time, 77 part time; 48% male, 52% female; 0% American Indian, 1% Asian, 8% black, 31% Hispanic, 1% multiracial, 0% Pacific Islander, 54% white, 0% international; 97% from in state; 59% live on campus; 7% of students in fraternities, 10% in sororities
Most popular majors: 23% Business, Management, Marketing, and Related Support Services, 8% Education, 17% Parks, Recreation, Leisure, and Fitness Studies, 8% Physical Sciences, 8% Psychology
Expenses: 2014-2015: $26,800; room/board: $9,240
Financial aid: (830) 372-8075

Texas Southern University

Houston TX
(713) 313-7071
U.S. News ranking: Nat. U., second tier
Website: www.tsu.edu
Admissions email: admissions@tsu.edu
Public; founded 1947
Freshman admissions: least selective; 2014-2015: 10,239 applied, 5,253 accepted. Either SAT or ACT required. SAT 25/75 percentile: 730-900. High school rank: 6% in top tenth, 19% in top quarter, 54% in top half
Early decision deadline: 12/1, notification date: N/A
Early action deadline: N/A, notification date: N/A
Application deadline (fall): 8/1
Undergraduate student body: 5,842 full time, 1,073 part time; 43% male, 57% female; 1% American Indian, 2% Asian, 82% black, 6% Hispanic, N/A multiracial, 0% Pacific Islander, 2% white, 6% international; 90% from in state; 22% live on campus; 2% of students in fraternities, 3% in sororities
Most popular majors: 7% Accounting, 8% Biology/Biological Sciences, General, 7% Business Administration and Management, General, 6% Criminal Justice/Law Enforcement Administration, 10% General Studies
Expenses: 2014-2015: $8,126 in state, $18,986 out of state; room/board: $15,170
Financial aid: (713) 313-7071; 88% of undergrads determined to have financial need; average aid package $7,833

Texas State University

San Marcos TX
(512) 245-2364
U.S. News ranking: Reg. U. (W), No. 52
Website: www.txstate.edu
Admissions email: admissions@txstate.edu
Public; founded 1899
Freshman admissions: selective; 2014-2015: 18,413 applied, 13,423 accepted. Either SAT or ACT required. SAT 25/75 percentile: 930-1130. High school rank: 11% in top tenth, 43% in top quarter, 88% in top half
Early decision deadline: N/A, notification date: N/A
Early action deadline: N/A, notification date: N/A
Application deadline (fall): 5/1
Undergraduate student body: 26,234 full time, 5,943 part time; 44% male, 56% female; 0% American Indian, 2% Asian, 8% black, 33% Hispanic, 3% multiracial, 0% Pacific Islander, 51% white, 0% international; 98% from in state; 21% live on campus; 5% of students in fraternities, 5% in sororities
Most popular majors: 6% Business Administration and Management, General, 5% Kinesiology and Exercise Science, 4% Marketing/Marketing Management, General, 9% Multi/Interdisciplinary Studies, Other, 6% Psychology, General
Expenses: 2015-2016: $9,944 in state, $21,644 out of state; room/board: $7,840
Financial aid: (512) 245-2315; 58% of undergrads determined to have financial need; average aid package $10,576

Texas Tech University

Lubbock TX
(806) 742-1480
U.S. News ranking: Nat. U., No. 168
Website: www.ttu.edu
Admissions email: admissions@ttu.edu
Public; founded 1923
Freshman admissions: selective; 2014-2015: 21,873 applied, 14,464 accepted. Either SAT or ACT required. SAT 25/75 percentile: 1000-1200. High school rank: 20% in top tenth, 54% in top quarter, 85% in top half
Early decision deadline: N/A, notification date: N/A
Early action deadline: N/A, notification date: N/A
Application deadline (fall): 8/1
Undergraduate student body: 25,589 full time, 3,043 part time; 55% male, 45% female; 0% American Indian, 3% Asian, 6% black, 22% Hispanic, 3% multiracial, 0% Pacific Islander, 61% white, 4% international; 94% from in state; 27% live on campus; 4% of students in fraternities, 8% in sororities
Most popular majors: 20% Business, Management, Marketing, and Related Support Services, 7% Communication, Journalism, and Related Programs, 11% Engineering, 8% Family and Consumer Sciences/Human Sciences, 8% Multi/Interdisciplinary Studies
Expenses: 2015-2016: $9,567 in state, $21,267 out of state; room/board: $8,405
Financial aid: (806) 742-3681; 49% of undergrads determined to have financial need; average aid package $9,733

Texas Wesleyan University

Fort Worth TX
(817) 531-4422
U.S. News ranking: Reg. U. (W), No. 48
Website: www.txwes.edu
Admissions email: admission@txwes.edu
Private; founded 1890
Affiliation: Methodist
Freshman admissions: selective; 2014-2015: 1,855 applied, 706 accepted. Either SAT or ACT

required. SAT 25/75 percentile: 900-1060. High school rank: 12% in top tenth, 39% in top quarter, 77% in top half
Early decision deadline: N/A, notification date: N/A
Early action deadline: N/A, notification date: N/A
Application deadline (fall): rolling
Undergraduate student body: 1,424 full time, 493 part time; 50% male, 50% female; 1% American Indian, 1% Asian, 14% black, 23% Hispanic, 3% multiracial, 0% Pacific Islander, 31% white, 25% international; 96% from in state; 25% live on campus; 2% of students in fraternities, 3% in sororities
Most popular majors: 18% Business, Management, Marketing, and Related Support Services, 15% Education, 8% Homeland Security, Law Enforcement, Firefighting and Related Protective Services, 8% Legal Professions and Studies, 13% Multi/Interdisciplinary Studies
Expenses: 2015-2016: $24,454; room/board: $8,651
Financial aid: (817) 531-4420; 60% of undergrads determined to have financial need; average aid package $21,621

Texas Woman's University

Denton TX
(940) 898-3188
U.S. News ranking: Nat. U., second tier
Website: www.twu.edu
Admissions email: admissions@twu.edu
Public; founded 1901
Freshman admissions: less selective; 2014-2015: 4,582 applied, 3,909 accepted. Neither SAT nor ACT required. SAT 25/75 percentile: 840-1060. High school rank: 14% in top tenth, 29% in top quarter, 79% in top half
Early decision deadline: N/A, notification date: N/A
Early action deadline: N/A, notification date: N/A
Application deadline (fall): 7/15
Undergraduate student body: 6,798 full time, 2,881 part time; 11% male, 89% female; 0% American Indian, 8% Asian, 21% black, 25% Hispanic, 4% multiracial, 0% Pacific Islander, 40% white, 1% international; 100% from in state; 24% live on campus; 0% of students in fraternities, 3% in sororities
Most popular majors: Information not available
Expenses: 2015-2016: $8,522 in state, $20,222 out of state; room/board: $7,443
Financial aid: (940) 898-3050

Trinity University

San Antonio TX
(800) 874-6489
U.S. News ranking: Reg. U. (W), No. 1
Website: www.trinity.edu
Admissions email: admissions@trinity.edu
Private; founded 1869
Affiliation: Presbyterian
Freshman admissions: more selective; 2014-2015: 5,502 applied, 2,664 accepted. Either SAT or ACT required. SAT 25/75 percentile: 1170-1360. High school rank: 38% in top tenth, 70% in top quarter, 93% in top half
Early decision deadline: 11/1, notification date: 12/15
Early action deadline: 11/1, notification date: 12/15
Application deadline (fall): 2/1
Undergraduate student body: 2,259 full time, 38 part time; 48% male, 52% female; 0% American Indian, 6% Asian, 4% black, 18% Hispanic, 5% multiracial, 0% Pacific Islander, 56% white, 7% international; 75% from in state; 75% live on campus; 22% of students in fraternities, 29% in sororities
Most popular majors: 8% Biological and Biomedical Sciences, 21% Business, Management, Marketing, and Related Support Services, 7% Communication, Journalism, and Related Programs, 17% Social Sciences, 8% Visual and Performing Arts
Expenses: 2015-2016: $37,856; room/board: $12,362
Financial aid: (210) 999-8315; 45% of undergrads determined to have financial need; average aid package $34,073

University of Dallas

Irving TX
(800) 628-6999
U.S. News ranking: Reg. U. (W), No. 15
Website: www.udallas.edu
Admissions email: ugadmis@udallas.edu
Private; founded 1956
Affiliation: Roman Catholic
Freshman admissions: selective; 2014-2015: 1,432 applied, 1,219 accepted. Either SAT or ACT required. SAT 25/75 percentile: 1080-1320. High school rank: 25% in top tenth, 58% in top quarter, 87% in top half
Early decision deadline: N/A, notification date: N/A
Early action deadline: 11/1, notification date: 12/1
Application deadline (fall): 7/1
Undergraduate student body: 1,313 full time, 14 part time; 45% male, 55% female; 0% American Indian, 4% Asian, 2% black, 19% Hispanic, 3% multiracial, 0% Pacific Islander, 66% white, 3% international; 45% from in state; 63% live on campus; 0% of students in fraternities, 0% in sororities
Most popular majors: 10% Biological and Biomedical Sciences, 14% English Language and Literature/Letters, 9% Foreign Languages, Literatures, and Linguistics, 11% History, 15% Social Sciences
Expenses: 2015-2016: $35,800; room/board: $11,300
Financial aid: (972) 721-5266; 61% of undergrads determined to have financial need; average aid package $28,690

University of Houston

Houston TX
(713) 743-1010
U.S. News ranking: Nat. U., No. 187
Website: www.uh.edu
Admissions email: admissions@uh.edu
Public; founded 1927
Freshman admissions: selective; 2014-2015: 17,328 applied, 10,915 accepted. Either SAT or ACT required. SAT 25/75 percentile: 1040-1250. High school rank: 32% in top tenth, 63% in top quarter, 89% in top half
Early decision deadline: N/A, notification date: N/A
Early action deadline: N/A, notification date: N/A
Application deadline (fall): 8/1
Undergraduate student body: 23,973 full time, 8,942 part time; 51% male, 49% female; 0% American Indian, 22% Asian, 11% black, 31% Hispanic, 3% multiracial, 0% Pacific Islander, 27% white, 5% international; 98% from in state; 19% live on campus; 3% of students in fraternities, 3% in sororities
Most popular majors: 6% Biological and Biomedical Sciences, 30% Business, Management, Marketing, and Related Support Services, 6% Communication, Journalism, and Related Programs, 8% Psychology, 7% Social Sciences
Expenses: 2014-2015: $10,518 in state, $24,378 out of state; room/board: $9,278
Financial aid: (713) 743-1010; 62% of undergrads determined to have financial need; average aid package $12,119

University of Houston–Clear Lake

Houston TX
(281) 283-2500
U.S. News ranking: Reg. U. (W), No. 81
Website: www.uhcl.edu
Admissions email: admissions@uhcl.edu
Public; founded 1974
Freshman admissions: selective; 2014-2015: 1,761 applied, 601 accepted. Either SAT or ACT required. SAT 25/75 percentile: 960-1150. High school rank: 24% in top tenth, 55% in top quarter, 78% in top half
Early decision deadline: N/A, notification date: N/A
Early action deadline: N/A, notification date: N/A
Application deadline (fall): 6/1
Undergraduate student body: 2,374 full time, 2,703 part time; 33% male, 67% female; 0% American Indian, 6% Asian, 9% black, 35% Hispanic, 3% multiracial, 0% Pacific Islander, 44% white, 2% international; 100% from in state; 3% live on campus; N/A of students in fraternities, N/A in sororities
Most popular majors: 23% Business, Management, Marketing, and Related Support Services, 26% Multi/Interdisciplinary Studies, 6% Parks, Recreation, Leisure, and Fitness Studies, 10% Psychology, 6% Social Sciences
Expenses: 2015-2016: $6,303 in state, $19,263 out of state; room/board: N/A
Financial aid: (281) 283-2480

University of Houston–Downtown

Houston TX
(713) 221-8522
U.S. News ranking: Reg. Coll. (W), No. 31
Website: www.uhd.edu
Admissions email: uhdadmit@uhd.edu
Public; founded 1974
Freshman admissions: less selective; 2014-2015: 3,235 applied, 2,723 accepted. Either SAT or ACT required. SAT 25/75 percentile: 820-980. High school rank: 9% in top tenth, 35% in top quarter, 74% in top half
Early decision deadline: N/A, notification date: N/A
Early action deadline: N/A, notification date: N/A
Application deadline (fall): 7/1
Undergraduate student body: 7,069 full time, 6,761 part time; 40% male, 60% female; 0% American Indian, 9% Asian, 24% black, 41% Hispanic, 1% multiracial, 0% Pacific Islander, 17% white, 5% international; 99% from in state; 0% live on campus; 0% of students in fraternities, 0% in sororities
Most popular majors: 38% Business, Management, Marketing, and Related Support Services, 4% Communication, Journalism, and Related Programs, 10% Homeland Security, Law Enforcement, Firefighting and Related Protective Services, 24% Multi/Interdisciplinary Studies, 7% Psychology
Expenses: 2015-2016: $6,938 in state, $18,638 out of state; room/board: N/A
Financial aid: (713) 221-8041; 74% of undergrads determined to have financial need; average aid package $10,289

University of Houston–Victoria[1]

Victoria TX
(877) 970-4848
U.S. News ranking: Reg. U. (W), second tier
Website: www.uhv.edu/
Admissions email: N/A
Public
Application deadline (fall): 8/15
Undergraduate student body: N/A full time, N/A part time
Expenses: 2014-2015: $6,748 in state, $17,608 out of state; room/board: $7,108
Financial aid: (877) 970-4848

University of Mary Hardin-Baylor

Belton TX
(254) 295-4520
U.S. News ranking: Reg. U. (W), No. 55
Website: www.umhb.edu
Admissions email: admission@umhb.edu
Private; founded 1845
Affiliation: Baptist
Freshman admissions: selective; 2014-2015: 7,037 applied, 5,623 accepted. Either SAT or ACT required. SAT 25/75 percentile: 950-1140. High school rank: 22% in top tenth, 48% in top quarter, 80% in top half
Early decision deadline: N/A, notification date: N/A
Early action deadline: N/A, notification date: N/A
Application deadline (fall): rolling
Undergraduate student body: 2,840 full time, 263 part time; 39% male, 61% female; 1% American Indian, 1% Asian, 15% black, 19% Hispanic, 3% multiracial, 0% Pacific Islander, 58% white, 2% international; 98% from in state; 53% live on campus; N/A of students in fraternities, N/A in sororities
Most popular majors: 11% Business, Management, Marketing, and Related Support Services, 15% Education, 31% Health Professions and Related Programs, 7% Liberal Arts and Sciences, General Studies and Humanities, 5% Psychology
Expenses: 2015-2016: $26,200; room/board: $7,300
Financial aid: (254) 295-4517; 86% of undergrads determined to have financial need; average aid package $16,083

University of North Texas

Denton TX
(940) 565-2681
U.S. News ranking: Nat. U., second tier
Website: www.unt.edu
Admissions email: undergrad@unt.edu
Public; founded 1890
Freshman admissions: selective; 2014-2015: 16,851 applied, 10,472 accepted. Either SAT or ACT required. SAT 25/75 percentile: 990-1210. High school rank: 20% in top tenth, 53% in top quarter, 89% in top half
Early decision deadline: N/A, notification date: N/A
Early action deadline: N/A, notification date: N/A
Application deadline (fall): 8/1
Undergraduate student body: 24,180 full time, 5,543 part time; 48% male, 52% female; 0% American Indian, 6% Asian, 13% black, 21% Hispanic, 4% multiracial, 0% Pacific Islander, 51% white, 3% international; 97% from in state; 19% live on campus; 4% of students in fraternities, 5% in sororities
Most popular majors: 20% Business, Management, Marketing, and Related Support Services, 5% Communication, Journalism, and Related Programs, 14% Multi/Interdisciplinary Studies, 7% Social Sciences, 8% Visual and Performing Arts
Expenses: 2015-2016: $10,091 in state, $21,791 out of state; room/board: $8,200
Financial aid: (940) 565-2302; 62% of undergrads determined to have financial need; average aid package $11,054

University of St. Thomas

Houston TX
(713) 525-3500
U.S. News ranking: Reg. U. (W), No. 30
Website: www.stthom.edu
Admissions email: admissions@stthom.edu
Private; founded 1947
Affiliation: Roman Catholic
Freshman admissions: selective; 2014-2015: 795 applied, 628

accepted. Either SAT or ACT required. SAT 25/75 percentile: 990-1220. High school rank: 28% in top tenth, 49% in top quarter, 80% in top half
Early decision deadline: N/A, notification date: N/A
Early action deadline: 12/1, notification date: 12/15
Application deadline (fall): 5/1
Undergraduate student body: 1,274 full time, 371 part time; 39% male, 61% female; 0% American Indian, 12% Asian, 7% black, 38% Hispanic, 3% multiracial, 0% Pacific Islander, 29% white, 10% international; 96% from in state; 19% live on campus; 0% of students in fraternities, 0% in sororities
Most popular majors: 25% Business, Management, Marketing, and Related Support Services, 9% Health Professions and Related Programs, 8% Liberal Arts and Sciences, General Studies and Humanities, 9% Psychology, 9% Social Sciences
Expenses: 2015-2016: $30,310; room/board: $8,500
Financial aid: (713) 525-2170; 60% of undergrads determined to have financial need; average aid package $21,618

University of Texas–Arlington

Arlington TX
(817) 272-6287
U.S. News ranking: Nat. U., second tier
Website: www.uta.edu
Admissions email: admissions@uta.edu
Public; founded 1895
Freshman admissions: selective; 2014-2015: 10,245 applied, 6,290 accepted. Either SAT or ACT required. SAT 25/75 percentile: 910-1178. High school rank: 27% in top tenth, 72% in top quarter, 96% in top half
Early decision deadline: N/A, notification date: N/A
Early action deadline: N/A, notification date: N/A
Application deadline (fall): rolling
Undergraduate student body: 15,957 full time, 13,926 part time; 40% male, 60% female; 0% American Indian, 11% Asian, 15% black, 24% Hispanic, 3% multiracial, 0% Pacific Islander, 41% white, 5% international; 89% from in state; 13% live on campus; 5% of students in fraternities, 3% in sororities
Most popular majors: 6% Biological and Biomedical Sciences, 12% Business, Management, Marketing, and Related Support Services, 6% Engineering, 36% Health Professions and Related Programs, 6% Liberal Arts and Sciences, General Studies and Humanities
Expenses: 2014-2015: $8,878 in state, $18,102 out of state; room/board: $8,156
Financial aid: (817) 272-3568; 74% of undergrads determined to have financial need; average aid package $12,559

University of Texas–Austin

Austin TX
(512) 475-7440
U.S. News ranking: Nat. U., No. 52
Website: www.utexas.edu
Admissions email: N/A
Public; founded 1883
Freshman admissions: more selective; 2014-2015: 38,785 applied, 15,381 accepted. Either SAT or ACT required. SAT 25/75 percentile: 1170-1390. High school rank: 69% in top tenth, 90% in top quarter, 98% in top half
Early decision deadline: N/A, notification date: N/A
Early action deadline: N/A, notification date: N/A
Application deadline (fall): 12/1
Undergraduate student body: 36,309 full time, 3,214 part time; 48% male, 52% female; 0% American Indian, 19% Asian, 4% black, 22% Hispanic, 3% multiracial, 0% Pacific Islander, 46% white, 5% international; 95% from in state; 19% live on campus; 15% of students in fraternities, 17% in sororities
Most popular majors: 9% Biological and Biomedical Sciences, 12% Business, Management, Marketing, and Related Support Services, 12% Communication, Journalism, and Related Programs, 12% Engineering, 12% Social Sciences
Expenses: 2015-2016: $9,830 in state, $34,836 out of state; room/board: N/A
Financial aid: (512) 475-6203; 43% of undergrads determined to have financial need; average aid package $12,935

University of Texas–Dallas

Richardson TX
(972) 883-2270
U.S. News ranking: Nat. U., No. 140
Website: www.utdallas.edu
Admissions email: interest@utdallas.edu
Public; founded 1969
Freshman admissions: more selective; 2014-2015: 9,587 applied, 5,938 accepted. Either SAT or ACT required. SAT 25/75 percentile: 1140-1370. High school rank: 38% in top tenth, 70% in top quarter, 92% in top half
Early decision deadline: N/A, notification date: N/A
Early action deadline: N/A, notification date: N/A
Application deadline (fall): 7/1
Undergraduate student body: 11,630 full time, 2,670 part time; 57% male, 43% female; 0% American Indian, 28% Asian, 6% black, 18% Hispanic, 4% multiracial, 0% Pacific Islander, 39% white, 4% international; 96% from in state; 29% live on campus; 4% of students in fraternities, 3% in sororities
Most popular majors: 13% Biological and Biomedical Sciences, 32% Business, Management, Marketing, and Related Support Services, 9% Engineering, 9% Psychology, 7% Social Sciences
Expenses: 2014-2015: $11,806 in state, $31,328 out of state; room/board: $9,542
Financial aid: (972) 883-2941; 55% of undergrads determined to have financial need; average aid package $12,812

University of Texas–El Paso

El Paso TX
(915) 747-5890
U.S. News ranking: Nat. U., second tier
Website: www.utep.edu
Admissions email: futureminer@utep.edu
Public; founded 1914
Freshman admissions: less selective; 2014-2015: 7,157 applied, 7,149 accepted. Either SAT or ACT required. ACT 25/75 percentile: 17-23. High school rank: 18% in top tenth, 39% in top quarter, 69% in top half
Early decision deadline: N/A, notification date: N/A
Early action deadline: N/A, notification date: N/A
Application deadline (fall): rolling
Undergraduate student body: 13,106 full time, 6,711 part time; 46% male, 54% female; 0% American Indian, 1% Asian, 3% black, 83% Hispanic, 1% multiracial, 0% Pacific Islander, 7% white, 5% international
Most popular majors: 8% Biological and Biomedical Sciences, 16% Business, Management, Marketing, and Related Support Services, 9% Engineering, 12% Health Professions and Related Programs, 8% Multi/Interdisciplinary Studies
Expenses: 2015-2016: $7,058 in state, $18,759 out of state; room/board: $9,114
Financial aid: (915) 747-5204; 78% of undergrads determined to have financial need; average aid package $12,037

University of Texas of the Permian Basin

Odessa TX
(432) 552-2605
U.S. News ranking: Reg. U. (W), second tier
Website: www.utpb.edu
Admissions email: admissions@utpb.edu
Public; founded 1973
Freshman admissions: selective; 2014-2015: 1,169 applied, 1,017 accepted. Either SAT or ACT required. SAT 25/75 percentile: 880-1068. High school rank: 23% in top tenth, 55% in top quarter, 83% in top half
Early decision deadline: N/A, notification date: N/A
Early action deadline: N/A, notification date: N/A
Application deadline (fall): 8/25
Undergraduate student body: 2,023 full time, 2,638 part time; 42% male, 58% female; 1% American Indian, 2% Asian, 7% black, 47% Hispanic, 1% multiracial, 0% Pacific Islander, 41% white, 1% international; 96% from in state; 22% live on campus; 0% of students in fraternities, 0% in sororities
Most popular majors: 19% Business, Management, Marketing, and Related Support Services, 11% Multi/Interdisciplinary Studies, 7% Parks, Recreation, Leisure, and Fitness Studies, 8% Psychology, 8% Social Sciences
Expenses: 2014-2015: $5,250 in state, $13,938 out of state; room/board: $7,978
Financial aid: (432) 552-2620

University of Texas–San Antonio

San Antonio TX
(210) 458-4599
U.S. News ranking: Nat. U., second tier
Website: www.utsa.edu
Admissions email: prospects@utsa.edu
Public; founded 1969
Freshman admissions: selective; 2014-2015: 14,933 applied, 11,336 accepted. Either SAT or ACT required. SAT 25/75 percentile: 930-1150. High school rank: 19% in top tenth, 64% in top quarter, 92% in top half
Early decision deadline: N/A, notification date: N/A
Early action deadline: N/A, notification date: N/A
Application deadline (fall): 6/1
Undergraduate student body: 20,248 full time, 4,037 part time; 52% male, 48% female; 0% American Indian, 5% Asian, 9% black, 51% Hispanic, 3% multiracial, 0% Pacific Islander, 26% white, 4% international; 97% from in state; 21% live on campus; 5% of students in fraternities, 7% in sororities
Most popular majors: 6% Biological and Biomedical Sciences, 23% Business, Management, Marketing, and Related Support Services, 8% Education, 6% Engineering, 8% Psychology
Expenses: 2015-2016: $8,737 in state, $20,890 out of state; room/board: $7,564
Financial aid: (210) 458-8000; 65% of undergrads determined to have financial need; average aid package $9,553

University of Texas–Tyler

Tyler TX
(903) 566-7203
U.S. News ranking: Reg. U. (W), No. 73
Website: www.uttyler.edu
Admissions email: admrequest@uttyler.edu
Public; founded 1971
Freshman admissions: selective; 2014-2015: 2,156 applied, 1,802 accepted. Either SAT or ACT required. SAT 25/75 percentile: 953-1150. High school rank: 12% in top tenth, 37% in top quarter, 69% in top half
Early decision deadline: N/A, notification date: N/A
Early action deadline: N/A, notification date: N/A
Application deadline (fall): 8/20
Undergraduate student body: 4,282 full time, 1,567 part time; 43% male, 57% female; 0% American Indian, 3% Asian, 9% black, 16% Hispanic, 8% multiracial, 0% Pacific Islander, 59% white, 2% international; 99% from in state; N/A live on campus; 4% of students in fraternities, 3% in sororities
Most popular majors: 19% Business, Management, Marketing, and Related Support Services, 10% Engineering, 23% Health Professions and Related Programs, 7% Multi/Interdisciplinary Studies, 7% Parks, Recreation, Leisure, and Fitness Studies
Expenses: 2014-2015: $7,312 in state, $18,172 out of state; room/board: $11,334
Financial aid: (903) 566-7180

University of the Incarnate Word

San Antonio TX
(210) 829-6005
U.S. News ranking: Reg. U. (W), No. 63
Website: www.uiw.edu
Admissions email: admis@uiwtx.edu
Private; founded 1881
Affiliation: Roman Catholic
Freshman admissions: less selective; 2014-2015: 4,257 applied, 3,968 accepted. Either SAT or ACT required. SAT 25/75 percentile: 850-1070. High school rank: 14% in top tenth, 37% in top quarter, 69% in top half
Early decision deadline: N/A, notification date: N/A
Early action deadline: N/A, notification date: N/A
Application deadline (fall): rolling
Undergraduate student body: 4,324 full time, 2,172 part time; 39% male, 61% female; 0% American Indian, 2% Asian, 8% black, 60% Hispanic, 1% multiracial, 0% Pacific Islander, 19% white, 4% international; 94% from in state; 18% live on campus; 1% of students in fraternities, 1% in sororities
Most popular majors: 11% Biology, General, 37% Business Administration, Management and Operations, 6% Design and Applied Arts, 11% Registered Nursing, Nursing Administration, Nursing Research and Clinical Nursing, 5% Teacher Education and Professional Development, Specific Levels and Methods
Expenses: 2015-2016: $27,798; room/board: $11,364
Financial aid: (210) 829-6008; 81% of undergrads determined to have financial need; average aid package $17,885

Wayland Baptist University

Plainview TX
(806) 291-3500
U.S. News ranking: Reg. U. (W), second tier
Website: www.wbu.edu
Admissions email: admityou@wbu.edu
Private; founded 1908
Affiliation: Southern Baptist Convention
Freshman admissions: less selective; 2014-2015: 548 applied, 533 accepted. Either SAT or ACT required. ACT 25/75 percentile: 17-23. High school rank: 9% in top tenth, 29% in top quarter, 60% in top half
Early decision deadline: N/A, notification date: N/A
Early action deadline: N/A, notification date: N/A
Application deadline (fall): rolling
Undergraduate student body: 1,069 full time, 2,911 part time; 52% male, 48% female; 1% American Indian, 2% Asian, 16% black, 28% Hispanic, 4% multiracial, 1% Pacific Islander, 43% white,

1% international; 69% from in state; 18% live on campus; 1% of students in fraternities, 2% in sororities
Most popular majors: 37% Business Administration and Management, General, 7% Criminal Justice/Law Enforcement Administration, 7% Human Services, General, 28% Liberal Arts and Sciences, General Studies and Humanities, Other, 8% Registered Nursing/Registered Nurse
Expenses: 2015-2016: $16,980; room/board: $6,690
Financial aid: (806) 291-3520; 38% of undergrads determined to have financial need; average aid package $13,512

West Texas A&M University

Canyon TX
(806) 651-2020
U.S. News ranking: Reg. U. (W), second tier
Website: www.wtamu.edu
Admissions email: admissions@mail.wtamu.edu
Public; founded 1910
Freshman admissions: selective; 2014-2015: 5,234 applied, 3,529 accepted. Either SAT or ACT required. ACT 25/75 percentile: 18-23. High school rank: 15% in top tenth, 39% in top quarter, 75% in top half
Early decision deadline: N/A, notification date: N/A
Early action deadline: N/A, notification date: N/A
Application deadline (fall): rolling
Undergraduate student body: 5,654 full time, 1,479 part time; 46% male, 54% female; 1% American Indian, 1% Asian, 6% black, 25% Hispanic, 2% multiracial, 0% Pacific Islander, 62% white, 2% international; 88% from in state; 31% live on campus; 6% of students in fraternities, 5% in sororities
Most popular majors: 9% Agriculture, Agriculture Operations, and Related Sciences, 14% Business, Management, Marketing, and Related Support Services, 11% Health Professions and Related Programs, 11% Liberal Arts and Sciences, General Studies and Humanities, 13% Multi/Interdisciplinary Studies
Expenses: 2015-2016: $6,264 in state, $7,775 out of state; room/board: $7,196
Financial aid: (806) 651-2055; 64% of undergrads determined to have financial need; average aid package $7,790

Wiley College[1]

Marshall TX
(800) 658-6889
U.S. News ranking: Reg. Coll. (W), second tier
Website: www.wileyc.edu
Admissions email: admissions@wileyc.edu
Private; founded 1873
Affiliation: United Methodist
Application deadline (fall): rolling
Undergraduate student body: N/A full time, N/A part time
Expenses: 2014-2015: $11,482; room/board: $6,846
Financial aid: (903) 927-3210

UTAH

Brigham Young University–Provo

Provo UT
(801) 422-2507
U.S. News ranking: Nat. U., No. 66
Website: www.byu.edu
Admissions email: admissions@byu.edu
Private; founded 1875
Affiliation: Church of Jesus Christ of Latter-day Saints
Freshman admissions: more selective; 2014-2015: 11,078 applied, 5,207 accepted. Either SAT or ACT required. ACT 25/75 percentile: 27-31. High school rank: 55% in top tenth, 87% in top quarter, 98% in top half
Early decision deadline: N/A, notification date: N/A
Early action deadline: N/A, notification date: N/A
Application deadline (fall): 2/1
Undergraduate student body: 24,499 full time, 2,664 part time; 55% male, 45% female; 0% American Indian, 2% Asian, 1% black, 6% Hispanic, 3% multiracial, 1% Pacific Islander, 83% white, 3% international; 33% from in state; 17% live on campus; N/A of students in fraternities, N/A in sororities
Most popular majors: 12% Biological and Biomedical Sciences, 12% Business, Management, Marketing, and Related Support Services, 8% Education, 9% Health Professions and Related Programs, 9% Social Sciences
Expenses: 2015-2016: $5,150; room/board: $7,330
Financial aid: (801) 422-4104; 50% of undergrads determined to have financial need; average aid package $7,258

Dixie State University

Saint George UT
(435) 652-7702
U.S. News ranking: Reg. Coll. (W), unranked
Website: www.dixie.edu
Admissions email: admissions@dixie.edu
Public; founded 1911
Freshman admissions: N/A; 2014-2015: 4,038 applied, 4,038 accepted. Neither SAT nor ACT required. ACT 25/75 percentile: 18-23. High school rank: 10% in top tenth, 28% in top quarter, 58% in top half
Early decision deadline: N/A, notification date: N/A
Early action deadline: N/A, notification date: N/A
Application deadline (fall): 8/15
Undergraduate student body: 5,299 full time, 3,271 part time; 47% male, 53% female; 1% American Indian, 1% Asian, 2% black, 10% Hispanic, 3% multiracial, 1% Pacific Islander, 77% white, 3% international; 81% from in state; 4% live on campus; N/A of students in fraternities, N/A in sororities
Most popular majors: 19% Business, Management, Marketing, and Related Support Services, 15% Communication, Journalism, and Related Programs, 13% Education, 11% Multi/Interdisciplinary Studies, 8% Psychology
Expenses: 2014-2015: $4,456 in state, $12,792 out of state; room/board: $5,048
Financial aid: (435) 652-7575; 74% of undergrads determined to have financial need; average aid package $9,835

Southern Utah University

Cedar City UT
(435) 586-7740
U.S. News ranking: Reg. U. (W), No. 70
Website: www.suu.edu
Admissions email: admissionsinfo@suu.edu
Public; founded 1897
Freshman admissions: selective; 2014-2015: 7,968 applied, 5,046 accepted. Either SAT or ACT required. ACT 25/75 percentile: 20-26. High school rank: 18% in top tenth, 43% in top quarter, 72% in top half
Early decision deadline: N/A, notification date: N/A
Early action deadline: N/A, notification date: N/A
Application deadline (fall): 5/1
Undergraduate student body: 5,131 full time, 1,822 part time; 45% male, 55% female; 1% American Indian, 1% Asian, 2% black, 5% Hispanic, 1% multiracial, 1% Pacific Islander, 79% white, 5% international
Most popular majors: 7% Biological and Biomedical Sciences, 12% Business, Management, Marketing, and Related Support Services, 21% Education, 7% Health Professions and Related Programs, 8% Psychology
Expenses: 2015-2016: $6,300 in state, $19,132 out of state; room/board: $6,957
Financial aid: (435) 586-7735; 66% of undergrads determined to have financial need; average aid package $10,519

University of Utah

Salt Lake City UT
(801) 581-8761
U.S. News ranking: Nat. U., No. 115
Website: www.utah.edu
Admissions email: admissions@utah.edu
Public; founded 1850
Freshman admissions: more selective; 2014-2015: 10,991 applied, 8,949 accepted. Either SAT or ACT required. ACT 25/75 percentile: 21-28. High school rank: 22% in top tenth, 49% in top quarter, 82% in top half
Early decision deadline: N/A, notification date: N/A
Early action deadline: N/A, notification date: N/A
Application deadline (fall): 4/1
Undergraduate student body: 17,137 full time, 6,770 part time; 55% male, 45% female; 0% American Indian, 5% Asian, 1% black, 10% Hispanic, 4% multiracial, 1% Pacific Islander, 71% white, 6% international; 80% from in state; 13% live on campus; 5% of students in fraternities, 7% in sororities
Most popular majors: 6% Communication, General, 4% Economics, General, 4% Human Development and Family Studies, General, 4% Kinesiology and Exercise Science, 6% Psychology, General
Expenses: 2015-2016: $8,239 in state, $26,177 out of state; room/board: $8,957
Financial aid: (801) 581-8788; 46% of undergrads determined to have financial need; average aid package $18,259

Utah State University

Logan UT
(435) 797-1079
U.S. News ranking: Nat. U., second tier
Website: www.usu.edu
Admissions email: admit@usu.edu
Public; founded 1888
Freshman admissions: selective; 2014-2015: 12,835 applied, 12,557 accepted. Either SAT or ACT required. ACT 25/75 percentile: 20-26. High school rank: 19% in top tenth, 42% in top quarter, 74% in top half
Early decision deadline: N/A, notification date: N/A
Early action deadline: N/A, notification date: N/A
Application deadline (fall): rolling
Undergraduate student body: 15,823 full time, 8,448 part time; 46% male, 54% female; 2% American Indian, 1% Asian, 1% black, 6% Hispanic, 2% multiracial, 0% Pacific Islander, 81% white, 2% international; 75% from in state; N/A live on campus; 2% of students in fraternities, 2% in sororities
Most popular majors: 9% Communication Sciences and Disorders, General, 8% Economics, General, 4% Elementary Education and Teaching, 4% Multi/Interdisciplinary Studies, Other, 4% Physical Education Teaching and Coaching
Expenses: 2015-2016: $6,663 in state, $19,133 out of state; room/board: $5,790
Financial aid: (435) 797-0173; 75% of undergrads determined to have financial need; average aid package $8,100

Utah Valley University

Orem UT
(801) 863-8466
U.S. News ranking: Reg. Coll. (W), second tier
Website: www.uvu.edu/
Admissions email: InstantInfo@uvu.edu
Public; founded 1941
Freshman admissions: selective; 2014-2015: 7,132 applied, 7,126 accepted. Either SAT or ACT required. ACT 25/75 percentile: 18-24. High school rank: 6% in top tenth, 19% in top quarter, 45% in top half
Early decision deadline: N/A, notification date: N/A
Early action deadline: N/A, notification date: N/A
Application deadline (fall): 8/1
Undergraduate student body: 16,259 full time, 14,904 part time; 55% male, 45% female; 1% American Indian, 1% Asian, 1% black, 10% Hispanic, 2% multiracial, 1% Pacific Islander, 80% white, 2% international; 85% from in state; N/A live on campus; N/A of students in fraternities, N/A in sororities
Most popular majors: 9% Airline/Commercial/Professional Pilot and Flight Crew, 21% Business Administration and Management, General, 11% Elementary Education and Teaching, 10% Psychology, General
Expenses: 2015-2016: $5,386 in state, $15,202 out of state; room/board: N/A
Financial aid: (801) 863-8442; 65% of undergrads determined to have financial need; average aid package $7,777

Weber State University

Ogden UT
(801) 626-6744
U.S. News ranking: Reg. U. (W), No. 77
Website: weber.edu
Admissions email: admissions@weber.edu
Public; founded 1889
Freshman admissions: selective; 2014-2015: 5,188 applied, 5,188 accepted. Neither SAT nor ACT required. ACT 25/75 percentile: 18-24. High school rank: 5% in top tenth, 18% in top quarter, 43% in top half
Early decision deadline: N/A, notification date: N/A
Early action deadline: N/A, notification date: N/A
Application deadline (fall): 8/21
Undergraduate student body: 11,084 full time, 14,251 part time; 46% male, 54% female; 1% American Indian, 2% Asian, 2% black, 10% Hispanic, 2% multiracial, 1% Pacific Islander, 69% white, 2% international; 90% from in state; 4% live on campus; 1% of students in fraternities, 1% in sororities
Most popular majors: 2% Accounting, 2% Criminal Justice/Safety Studies, 2% Psychology, General, 7% Registered Nursing/Registered Nurse, 2% Selling Skills and Sales Operations
Expenses: 2015-2016: $5,339 in state, $14,252 out of state; room/board: $8,400
Financial aid: (801) 626-7569; 62% of undergrads determined to have financial need; average aid package $6,024

Western Governors University[1]

Salt Lake City UT
(866) 225-5948
U.S. News ranking: Reg. U. (W), unranked
Website: www.wgu.edu/
Admissions email: info@wgu.edu
Private; founded 1996
Application deadline (fall): rolling
Undergraduate student body: N/A full time, N/A part time
Expenses: 2014-2015: $6,070; room/board: $6,000
Financial aid: (801) 327-8104

Westminster College

Salt Lake City UT
(801) 832-2200
U.S. News ranking: Reg. U. (W), No. 20
Website: www.westminstercollege.edu
Admissions email: admission@westminstercollege.edu
Private; founded 1875
Freshman admissions: more selective; 2014-2015: 1,784 applied, 1,737 accepted. Either

SAT or ACT required. ACT 25/75 percentile: 22-27. High school rank: 23% in top tenth, 55% in top quarter, 87% in top half
Early decision deadline: N/A, notification date: N/A
Early action deadline: N/A, notification date: N/A
Application deadline (fall): 8/15
Undergraduate student body: 2,075 full time, 158 part time; 46% male, 54% female; 0% American Indian, 2% Asian, 1% black, 10% Hispanic, 3% multiracial, 0% Pacific Islander, 71% white, 5% international; 62% from in state; 32% live on campus; N/A of students in fraternities, N/A in sororities
Most popular majors: 5% Biological and Biomedical Sciences, 23% Business, Management, Marketing, and Related Support Services, 6% Communication, Journalism, and Related Programs, 20% Health Professions and Related Programs, 7% Psychology
Expenses: 2015-2016: $31,228; room/board: $8,712
Financial aid: (801) 832-2500; 60% of undergrads determined to have financial need; average aid package $23,513

VERMONT

Bennington College
Bennington VT
(800) 833-6845
U.S. News ranking: Nat. Lib. Arts, No. 93
Website: www.bennington.edu
Admissions email: admissions@bennington.edu
Private; founded 1932
Freshman admissions: more selective; 2014-2015: 1,101 applied, 740 accepted. Neither SAT nor ACT required. SAT 25/75 percentile: 1170-1400. High school rank: N/A
Early decision deadline: 11/15, notification date: 12/20
Early action deadline: 12/1, notification date: 2/1
Application deadline (fall): 1/15
Undergraduate student body: 629 full time, 31 part time; 34% male, 66% female; 2% American Indian, 3% Asian, 1% black, 5% Hispanic, 3% multiracial, 0% Pacific Islander, 69% white, 13% international; 3% from in state; 94% live on campus; 0% of students in fraternities, 0% in sororities
Most popular majors: 4% Biological and Biomedical Sciences, 12% English Language and Literature/Letters, 5% Foreign Languages, Literatures, and Linguistics, 14% Social Sciences, 42% Visual and Performing Arts
Expenses: 2015-2016: $48,220; room/board: $14,200
Financial aid: (802) 440-4325; 71% of undergrads determined to have financial need; average aid package $42,405

Burlington College[1]
Burlington VT
(802) 862-9616
U.S. News ranking: Nat. Lib. Arts, second tier
Website: www.burlington.edu
Admissions email: admissions@burlington.edu
Private; founded 1972
Application deadline (fall): rolling
Undergraduate student body: N/A full time, N/A part time
Expenses: 2014-2015: $23,546; room/board: $8,600
Financial aid: (802) 862-9616

Castleton State College
Castleton VT
(800) 639-8521
U.S. News ranking: Nat. Lib. Arts, second tier
Website: www.castleton.edu
Admissions email: info@castleton.edu
Public; founded 1787
Freshman admissions: less selective; 2014-2015: 2,397 applied, 1,868 accepted. Either SAT or ACT required. SAT 25/75 percentile: 850-1070. High school rank: 6% in top tenth, 29% in top quarter, 61% in top half
Early decision deadline: N/A, notification date: N/A
Early action deadline: N/A, notification date: N/A
Application deadline (fall): rolling
Undergraduate student body: 1,720 full time, 265 part time; 48% male, 52% female; 0% American Indian, 1% Asian, 2% black, 2% Hispanic, 2% multiracial, 0% Pacific Islander, 85% white, 2% international; 70% from in state; 55% live on campus; N/A of students in fraternities, N/A in sororities
Most popular majors: 12% Business, Management, Marketing, and Related Support Services, 10% Communication, Journalism, and Related Programs, 19% Health Professions and Related Programs, 9% Parks, Recreation, Leisure, and Fitness Studies, 6% Visual and Performing Arts
Expenses: 2014-2015: $10,772 in state, $25,436 out of state; room/board: $9,412
Financial aid: (802) 468-1292

Champlain College
Burlington VT
(800) 570-5858
U.S. News ranking: Reg. Coll. (N), No. 14
Website: www.champlain.edu
Admissions email: admission@champlain.edu
Private; founded 1878
Freshman admissions: selective; 2014-2015: 5,593 applied, 3,589 accepted. Either SAT or ACT required. SAT 25/75 percentile: 1030-1250. High school rank: 19% in top tenth, 44% in top quarter, 84% in top half
Early decision deadline: 11/15, notification date: 12/15
Early action deadline: N/A, notification date: N/A
Application deadline (fall): 2/1
Undergraduate student body: 2,309 full time, 815 part time; 60% male, 40% female; 0% American Indian, 2% Asian, 3% black, 4% Hispanic, 2% multiracial, 0% Pacific Islander, 72% white, 1% international; 31% from in state; 50% live on campus; N/A of students in fraternities, N/A in sororities
Most popular majors: 7% Accounting, 10% Business Administration and Management, General, 10% Cyber/Computer Forensics and Counterterrorism, 10% Game and Interactive Media Design, 7% Speech Communication and Rhetoric
Expenses: 2015-2016: $37,536; room/board: $14,050
Financial aid: (800) 570-5858; 70% of undergrads determined to have financial need; average aid package $21,773

College of St. Joseph[1]
Rutland VT
(802) 773-5286
U.S. News ranking: Reg. U. (N), second tier
Website: www.csj.edu
Admissions email: admissions@csj.edu
Private; founded 1956
Affiliation: Roman Catholic
Application deadline (fall): rolling
Undergraduate student body: N/A full time, N/A part time
Expenses: 2014-2015: $21,200; room/board: $9,400
Financial aid: (802) 773-5900

Goddard College
Plainfield VT
(800) 906-8312
U.S. News ranking: Reg. U. (N), unranked
Website: www.goddard.edu
Admissions email: admissions@goddard.edu
Private; founded 1863
Freshman admissions: N/A; 2014-2015: N/A applied, N/A accepted. Neither SAT nor ACT required. ACT 25/75 percentile: N/A. High school rank: N/A
Early decision deadline: N/A, notification date: N/A
Early action deadline: N/A, notification date: N/A
Application deadline (fall): rolling
Undergraduate student body: 191 full time, 0 part time; 37% male, 63% female; N/A American Indian, N/A Asian, N/A black, N/A Hispanic, N/A multiracial, N/A Pacific Islander, N/A white, N/A international
Most popular majors: Information not available
Expenses: 2014-2015: $14,930; room/board: $1,488
Financial aid: (800) 468-4888

Green Mountain College
Poultney VT
(802) 287-8208
U.S. News ranking: Nat. Lib. Arts, second tier
Website: www.greenmtn.edu
Admissions email: admiss@greenmtn.edu
Private; founded 1834
Affiliation: United Methodist
Freshman admissions: selective; 2014-2015: 973 applied, 665 accepted. Neither SAT nor ACT required. SAT 25/75 percentile: 920-1200. High school rank: N/A
Early decision deadline: N/A, notification date: N/A
Early action deadline: 11/1, notification date: 12/14
Application deadline (fall): rolling
Undergraduate student body: 557 full time, 15 part time; 49% male, 51% female; 1% American Indian, 1% Asian, 5% black, 4% Hispanic, 1% multiracial, N/A Pacific Islander, 60% white, 3% international; 14% from in state; 83% live on campus; N/A of students in fraternities, N/A in sororities
Most popular majors: 8% Agroecology and Sustainable Agriculture, 7% Biology/Biological Sciences, General, 11% Environmental Studies, 13% Parks, Recreation and Leisure Studies, 11% Resort Management
Expenses: 2014-2015: $33,736; room/board: $11,492
Financial aid: (802) 287-8210

Johnson State College
Johnson VT
(800) 635-2356
U.S. News ranking: Reg. U. (N), second tier
Website: www.jsc.edu
Admissions email: JSCAdmissions@jsc.edu
Public
Freshman admissions: less selective; 2014-2015: N/A applied, N/A accepted. Neither SAT nor ACT required. ACT 25/75 percentile: N/A. High school rank: N/A
Early decision deadline: N/A, notification date: N/A
Early action deadline: N/A, notification date: N/A
Application deadline (fall): rolling
Undergraduate student body: 979 full time, 479 part time; 36% male, 64% female; N/A American Indian, N/A Asian, N/A black, N/A Hispanic, N/A multiracial, N/A Pacific Islander, N/A white, N/A international
Most popular majors: Information not available
Expenses: 2014-2015: $10,604 in state, $22,604 out of state; room/board: $9,412
Financial aid: (802) 635-1380

Lyndon State College[1]
Lyndonville VT
(802) 626-6413
U.S. News ranking: Reg. Coll. (N), second tier
Website: www.lyndonstate.edu
Admissions email: admissions@lyndonstate.edu
Public; founded 1911
Application deadline (fall): rolling
Undergraduate student body: N/A full time, N/A part time
Expenses: 2014-2015: $10,700 in state, $21,764 out of state; room/board: $9,412
Financial aid: (802) 626-6218

Marlboro College
Marlboro VT
(800) 343-0049
U.S. News ranking: Nat. Lib. Arts, No. 136
Website: www.marlboro.edu
Admissions email: admissions@marlboro.edu
Private; founded 1946
Freshman admissions: selective; 2014-2015: 212 applied, 173 accepted. Neither SAT nor ACT required. SAT 25/75 percentile: 1080-1370. High school rank: 8% in top tenth, 31% in top quarter, 54% in top half
Early decision deadline: 11/15, notification date: 12/1
Early action deadline: 1/15, notification date: 2/1
Application deadline (fall): rolling
Undergraduate student body: 200 full time, 30 part time; 48% male, 52% female; 1% American Indian, 2% Asian, 0% black, 1% Hispanic, 5% multiracial, 0% Pacific Islander, 73% white, 2% international; 28% from in state; 77% live on campus; 0% of students in fraternities, 0% in sororities
Most popular majors: 13% Area, Ethnic, Cultural, Gender, and Group Studies, 13% English Language and Literature/Letters, 9% Philosophy and Religious Studies, 14% Social Sciences, 27% Visual and Performing Arts
Expenses: 2015-2016: $39,250; room/board: $10,590
Financial aid: (802) 258-9237; 80% of undergrads determined to have financial need; average aid package $30,541

Middlebury College
Middlebury VT
(802) 443-3000
U.S. News ranking: Nat. Lib. Arts, No. 4
Website: www.middlebury.edu
Admissions email: admissions@middlebury.edu
Private; founded 1800
Freshman admissions: most selective; 2014-2015: 8,195 applied, 1,407 accepted. Either SAT or ACT required. SAT 25/75 percentile: 1260-1470. High school rank: 76% in top tenth, 91% in top quarter, 99% in top half
Early decision deadline: 11/1, notification date: 12/15
Early action deadline: N/A, notification date: N/A
Application deadline (fall): 1/1
Undergraduate student body: 2,492 full time, 34 part time; 48% male, 52% female; 0% American Indian, 7% Asian, 3% black, 9% Hispanic, 5% multiracial, 0% Pacific Islander, 65% white, 10% international; 6% from in state; 96% live on campus; 0% of students in fraternities, 0% in sororities
Most popular majors: 15% Economics, General, 6% English Language and Literature/Letters, Other, 7% Environmental Studies, 6% International/Global Studies, 9% Political Science and Government, General
Expenses: 2015-2016: $47,828; room/board: $13,628
Financial aid: (802) 443-5158; 43% of undergrads determined to have financial need; average aid package $41,870

Norwich University
Northfield VT
(800) 468-6679
U.S. News ranking: Reg. U. (N), No. 76
Website: www.norwich.edu
Admissions email: nuadm@norwich.edu
Private; founded 1819
Freshman admissions: selective; 2014-2015: 3,138 applied, 2,063 accepted. Neither SAT nor ACT required. SAT 25/75 percentile: 930-1160. High school rank: 13% in top tenth, 39% in top quarter, 68% in top half
Early decision deadline: N/A, notification date: N/A
Early action deadline: N/A, notification date: N/A
Application deadline (fall): rolling

Undergraduate student body: 2,271 full time, 378 part time; 77% male, 23% female; 0% American Indian, 2% Asian, 4% black, 7% Hispanic, 5% multiracial, 0% Pacific Islander, 78% white, 2% international; 14% from in state; 75% live on campus; N/A of students in fraternities, N/A in sororities
Most popular majors: 5% Architecture, 4% Business Administration and Management, General, 21% Criminal Justice/Law Enforcement Administration, 5% Mechanical Engineering, 8% Registered Nursing/Registered Nurse
Expenses: 2015-2016: $36,092; room/board: $12,484
Financial aid: (802) 485-2015; 85% of undergrads determined to have financial need; average aid package $29,219

Southern Vermont College

Bennington VT
(802) 447-6304
U.S. News ranking: Reg. Coll. (N), second tier
Website: www.svc.edu
Admissions email: admis@svc.edu
Private; founded 1974
Freshman admissions: least selective; 2014-2015: 303 applied, 284 accepted. Either SAT or ACT required. SAT 25/75 percentile: 770-940. High school rank: N/A
Early decision deadline: N/A, notification date: N/A
Early action deadline: N/A, notification date: N/A
Application deadline (fall): N/A
Undergraduate student body: 516 full time, 27 part time; 39% male, 61% female; 1% American Indian, 1% Asian, 13% black, 10% Hispanic, 2% multiracial, 1% Pacific Islander, 59% white, 0% international
Most popular majors: Information not available
Expenses: 2014-2015: $22,370; room/board: $10,500
Financial aid: (877) 563-6076

Sterling College[1]

Craftsbury Common VT
(802) 586-7711
U.S. News ranking: Nat. Lib. Arts, unranked
Website: www.sterlingcollege.edu
Admissions email: admissions@sterlingcollege.edu
Private; founded 1958
Application deadline (fall): rolling
Undergraduate student body: N/A full time, N/A part time
Expenses: 2014-2015: $33,492; room/board: $8,796
Financial aid: (802) 586-7711

St. Michael's College

Colchester VT
(800) 762-8000
U.S. News ranking: Nat. Lib. Arts, No. 105
Website: www.smcvt.edu
Admissions email: admission@smcvt.edu
Private; founded 1904
Affiliation: Roman Catholic
Freshman admissions: selective; 2014-2015: 4,299 applied, 3,459 accepted. Neither SAT nor ACT required. SAT 25/75 percentile: 1050-1250. High school rank: 22% in top tenth, 49% in top quarter, 79% in top half
Early decision deadline: N/A, notification date: N/A
Early action deadline: 11/1, notification date: 12/21
Application deadline (fall): 2/1
Undergraduate student body: 2,064 full time, 59 part time; 46% male, 54% female; 0% American Indian, 2% Asian, 2% black, 5% Hispanic, 2% multiracial, 0% Pacific Islander, 86% white, 3% international; 19% from in state; 95% live on campus; 0% of students in fraternities, 0% in sororities
Most popular majors: 9% Biological and Biomedical Sciences, 17% Business, Management, Marketing, and Related Support Services, 8% English Language and Literature/Letters, 11% Psychology, 14% Social Sciences
Expenses: 2015-2016: $40,750; room/board: $10,975
Financial aid: (802) 654-3243; 62% of undergrads determined to have financial need; average aid package $28,612

University of Vermont

Burlington VT
(802) 656-3370
U.S. News ranking: Nat. U., No. 89
Website: www.uvm.edu
Admissions email: admissions@uvm.edu
Public; founded 1791
Freshman admissions: more selective; 2014-2015: 24,231 applied, 17,796 accepted. Either SAT or ACT required. SAT 25/75 percentile: 1080-1290. High school rank: 29% in top tenth, 68% in top quarter, 94% in top half
Early decision deadline: N/A, notification date: N/A
Early action deadline: 11/1, notification date: 12/15
Application deadline (fall): 1/15
Undergraduate student body: 9,898 full time, 1,094 part time; 45% male, 55% female; 0% American Indian, 2% Asian, 1% black, 4% Hispanic, 3% multiracial, 0% Pacific Islander, 83% white, 3% international; 31% from in state; 51% live on campus; 7% of students in fraternities, 7% in sororities
Most popular majors: 8% Business Administration and Management, General, 4% English Language and Literature, General, 5% Environmental Studies, 6% Psychology, General, 5% Registered Nursing/Registered Nurse
Expenses: 2014-2015: $16,226 in state, $37,874 out of state; room/board: $10,780
Financial aid: (802) 656-5700; 56% of undergrads determined to have financial need; average aid package $22,888

Vermont Technical College

Randolph Center VT
(802) 728-1244
U.S. News ranking: Reg. Coll. (N), No. 24
Website: www.vtc.edu
Admissions email: admissions@vtc.edu
Public; founded 1866
Freshman admissions: less selective; 2014-2015: 567 applied, 393 accepted. Neither SAT nor ACT required. SAT 25/75 percentile: 810-1050. High school rank: 5% in top tenth, 23% in top quarter, 60% in top half
Early decision deadline: N/A, notification date: N/A
Early action deadline: N/A, notification date: N/A
Application deadline (fall): rolling
Undergraduate student body: 996 full time, 548 part time; 54% male, 46% female; 1% American Indian, 2% Asian, 1% black, 2% Hispanic, N/A multiracial, N/A Pacific Islander, 90% white, 2% international; 83% from in state; 38% live on campus; N/A of students in fraternities, N/A in sororities
Most popular majors: Information not available
Expenses: 2015-2016: $13,850 in state, $25,226 out of state; room/board: $9,696
Financial aid: (800) 965-8790; 77% of undergrads determined to have financial need; average aid package $10,716

VIRGINIA

Averett University

Danville VA
(800) 283-7388
U.S. News ranking: Reg. Coll. (S), No. 27
Website: www.averett.edu
Admissions email: admit@averett.edu
Private; founded 1859
Affiliation: Baptist General Association of Virginia
Freshman admissions: less selective; 2014-2015: 1,878 applied, 1,119 accepted. Either SAT or ACT required. SAT 25/75 percentile: 830-1028. High school rank: 11% in top tenth, 30% in top quarter, 58% in top half
Early decision deadline: N/A, notification date: N/A
Early action deadline: N/A, notification date: N/A
Application deadline (fall): rolling
Undergraduate student body: 822 full time, 36 part time; 48% male, 52% female; 1% American Indian, 1% Asian, 28% black, 4% Hispanic, 0% multiracial, 0% Pacific Islander, 61% white, 5% international; 69% from in state; 58% live on campus; 0% of students in fraternities, 1% in sororities
Most popular majors: 6% Accounting, 11% Criminal Justice/Law Enforcement Administration, 5% Liberal Arts and Sciences/Liberal Studies, 7% Management Science, 10% Pre-Medicine/Pre-Medical Studies
Expenses: 2014-2015: $29,150; room/board: $8,600
Financial aid: (434) 791-5646; 87% of undergrads determined to have financial need; average aid package $23,741

Bluefield College

Bluefield VA
(276) 326-4231
U.S. News ranking: Reg. Coll. (S), No. 49
Website: www.bluefield.edu
Admissions email: admissions@bluefield.edu
Private; founded 1922
Affiliation: Baptist
Freshman admissions: least selective; 2014-2015: 648 applied, 635 accepted. Either SAT or ACT required. SAT 25/75 percentile: 800-1010. High school rank: 11% in top tenth, 23% in top quarter, 64% in top half
Early decision deadline: N/A, notification date: N/A
Early action deadline: N/A, notification date: N/A
Application deadline (fall): rolling
Undergraduate student body: 799 full time, 129 part time; 43% male, 57% female; N/A American Indian, 1% Asian, 22% black, 4% Hispanic, 3% multiracial, N/A Pacific Islander, 66% white, 2% international; 63% from in state; 60% live on campus; 6% of students in fraternities, 6% in sororities
Most popular majors: 16% Criminal Justice/Safety Studies, 19% Human Services, General, 8% Kinesiology and Exercise Science, 28% Organizational Leadership, 6% Public Health/Community Nurse/Nursing
Expenses: 2015-2016: $23,296; room/board: $8,760
Financial aid: (276) 326-4215; 89% of undergrads determined to have financial need; average aid package $15,582

Bridgewater College

Bridgewater VA
(800) 759-8328
U.S. News ranking: Nat. Lib. Arts, second tier
Website: www.bridgewater.edu
Admissions email: admissions@bridgewater.edu
Private; founded 1880
Affiliation: Church of the Brethren
Freshman admissions: selective; 2014-2015: 6,169 applied, 2,950 accepted. Either SAT or ACT required. SAT 25/75 percentile: 950-1140. High school rank: 21% in top tenth, 51% in top quarter, 83% in top half
Early decision deadline: N/A, notification date: N/A
Early action deadline: N/A, notification date: N/A
Application deadline (fall): 5/1
Undergraduate student body: 1,766 full time, 19 part time; 46% male, 54% female; 0% American Indian, 1% Asian, 10% black, 4% Hispanic, 5% multiracial, 0% Pacific Islander, 76% white, 1% international; 76% from in state; 80% live on campus; 0% of students in fraternities, 0% in sororities
Most popular majors: 12% Biology/Biological Sciences, General, 17% Business Administration and Management, General, 10% Health and Physical Education/Fitness, General, 6% Liberal Arts and Sciences/Liberal Studies, 6% Mass Communication/Media Studies
Expenses: 2015-2016: $31,480; room/board: $11,520
Financial aid: (540) 828-5376; 81% of undergrads determined to have financial need; average aid package $26,549

Christopher Newport University

Newport News VA
(757) 594-7015
U.S. News ranking: Reg. U. (S), No. 14
Website: www.cnu.edu
Admissions email: admit@cnu.edu
Public; founded 1960
Freshman admissions: selective; 2014-2015: 7,366 applied, 4,116 accepted. Neither SAT nor ACT required. SAT 25/75 percentile: 1060-1250. High school rank: 18% in top tenth, 54% in top quarter, 91% in top half
Early decision deadline: 11/15, notification date: 12/15
Early action deadline: 12/1, notification date: 1/15
Application deadline (fall): 2/1
Undergraduate student body: 4,990 full time, 106 part time; 43% male, 57% female; 0% American Indian, 2% Asian, 8% black, 5% Hispanic, 5% multiracial, 0% Pacific Islander, 75% white, 0% international; 93% from in state; 74% live on campus; 21% of students in fraternities, 26% in sororities
Most popular majors: 13% Biology/Biological Sciences, General, 13% Business Administration and Management, General, 7% Political Science and Government, General, 13% Psychology, General, 12% Speech Communication and Rhetoric
Expenses: 2015-2016: $12,526 in state, $23,428 out of state; room/board: $10,614
Financial aid: (757) 594-7170; 45% of undergrads determined to have financial need; average aid package $8,530

College of William and Mary

Williamsburg VA
(757) 221-4223
U.S. News ranking: Nat. U., No. 34
Website: www.wm.edu
Admissions email: admission@wm.edu
Public; founded 1693
Freshman admissions: most selective; 2014-2015: 14,552 applied, 4,805 accepted. Either SAT or ACT required. SAT 25/75 percentile: 1270-1470. High school rank: 81% in top tenth, 96% in top quarter, 99% in top half
Early decision deadline: 11/1, notification date: 12/1
Early action deadline: N/A, notification date: N/A
Application deadline (fall): 1/1
Undergraduate student body: 6,214 full time, 85 part time; 44% male, 56% female; 0% American Indian, 8% Asian, 7% black, 9% Hispanic, 4% multiracial, 0% Pacific Islander, 59% white, 5% international; 70% from in state; 74% live on campus; 27% of students in fraternities, 32% in sororities
Most popular majors: 10% Biological and Biomedical Sciences, 12% Business, Management, Marketing, and Related Support Services, 7% English Language and Literature/Letters, 8% Psychology, 22% Social Sciences

Expenses: 2015-2016: $16,919 in state, $40,516 out of state; room/board: $10,978
Financial aid: (757) 221-2420; 33% of undergrads determined to have financial need; average aid package $19,711

Eastern Mennonite University

Harrisonburg VA
(800) 368-2665
U.S. News ranking: Nat. Lib. Arts, No. 171
Website: www.emu.edu
Admissions email: admiss@emu.edu
Private; founded 1917
Affiliation: Mennonite Church USA
Freshman admissions: selective; 2014-2015: 1,643 applied, 993 accepted. Either SAT or ACT required. SAT 25/75 percentile: 860-1130. High school rank: N/A
Early decision deadline: N/A, notification date: N/A
Early action deadline: N/A, notification date: N/A
Application deadline (fall): rolling
Undergraduate student body: 1,124 full time, 103 part time; 34% male, 66% female; 0% American Indian, 3% Asian, 9% black, 7% Hispanic, 2% multiracial, 0% Pacific Islander, 74% white, 3% international; 56% from in state; 60% live on campus; N/A of students in fraternities, N/A in sororities
Most popular majors: 10% Biological and Biomedical Sciences, 6% English Language and Literature/Letters, 18% Health Professions and Related Programs, 16% Liberal Arts and Sciences, General Studies and Humanities, 8% Psychology
Expenses: 2014-2015: $30,800; room/board: $9,860
Financial aid: (540) 432-4139

ECPI University[1]

Virginia Beach VA
(866) 499-0336
U.S. News ranking: Reg. Coll. (S), unranked
Website: www.ecpi.edu/
Admissions email: ssaunders@ecpi.edu
For-profit
Application deadline (fall): N/A
Undergraduate student body: N/A full time, N/A part time
Expenses: 2014-2015: $14,245; room/board: $8,250
Financial aid: N/A

Emory and Henry College

Emory VA
(800) 848-5493
U.S. News ranking: Nat. Lib. Arts, No. 174
Website: www.ehc.edu
Admissions email: ehadmiss@ehc.edu
Private; founded 1836
Affiliation: United Methodist
Freshman admissions: selective; 2014-2015: 1,471 applied, 1,055 accepted. Either SAT or ACT required. SAT 25/75 percentile: 860-1115. High school rank: N/A
Early decision deadline: 11/15, notification date: 12/15
Early action deadline: N/A, notification date: N/A
Application deadline (fall): rolling
Undergraduate student body: 994 full time, 18 part time; 51% male, 49% female; 1% American Indian, 0% Asian, 10% black, 2% Hispanic, 3% multiracial, 0% Pacific Islander, 76% white, 1% international; 63% from in state; 80% live on campus; 15% of students in fraternities, 30% in sororities
Most popular majors: 9% Biological and Biomedical Sciences, 10% Business, Management, Marketing, and Related Support Services, 7% Psychology, 26% Social Sciences, 6% Visual and Performing Arts
Expenses: 2014-2015: $30,900; room/board: $10,580
Financial aid: (276) 944-6229; 80% of undergrads determined to have financial need; average aid package $27,315

Ferrum College

Ferrum VA
(800) 868-9797
U.S. News ranking: Reg. Coll. (S), No. 63
Website: www.ferrum.edu
Admissions email: admissions@ferrum.edu
Private; founded 1913
Affiliation: United Methodist
Freshman admissions: least selective; 2014-2015: 3,286 applied, 2,409 accepted. Neither SAT nor ACT required. SAT 25/75 percentile: 740-940. High school rank: 1% in top tenth, 12% in top quarter, 40% in top half
Early decision deadline: N/A, notification date: N/A
Early action deadline: N/A, notification date: N/A
Application deadline (fall): rolling
Undergraduate student body: 1,432 full time, 19 part time; 53% male, 47% female; 0% American Indian, 1% Asian, 30% black, 5% Hispanic, 5% multiracial, 0% Pacific Islander, 55% white, 1% international; 81% from in state; 89% live on campus; 14% of students in fraternities, 26% in sororities
Most popular majors: 9% Business, Management, Marketing, and Related Support Services, 8% Education, 12% Health Professions and Related Programs, 15% Homeland Security, Law Enforcement, Firefighting and Related Protective Services
Expenses: 2015-2016: $30,835; room/board: $10,320
Financial aid: (540) 365-4282

George Mason University

Fairfax VA
(703) 993-2400
U.S. News ranking: Nat. U., No. 135
Website: www.gmu.edu
Admissions email: admissions@gmu.edu
Public; founded 1972
Freshman admissions: more selective; 2014-2015: 22,532 applied, 15,017 accepted. Neither SAT nor ACT required. SAT 25/75 percentile: 1050-1250. High school rank: 26% in top tenth, 65% in top quarter, 95% in top half
Early decision deadline: N/A, notification date: N/A
Early action deadline: 11/1, notification date: 12/15
Application deadline (fall): 1/15
Undergraduate student body: 17,812 full time, 4,531 part time; 49% male, 51% female; 0% American Indian, 18% Asian, 10% black, 12% Hispanic, 4% multiracial, 0% Pacific Islander, 45% white, 4% international; 89% from in state; 28% live on campus; 7% of students in fraternities, 9% in sororities
Most popular majors: 5% Accounting, 5% Biology/Biological Sciences, General, 5% Criminal Justice/Police Science, 5% Information Technology, 7% Psychology, General
Expenses: 2015-2016: $10,952 in state, $31,598 out of state; room/board: $10,510
Financial aid: (703) 993-2353; 55% of undergrads determined to have financial need; average aid package $12,050

Hampden-Sydney College

Hampden-Sydney VA
(800) 755-0733
U.S. News ranking: Nat. Lib. Arts, No. 108
Website: www.hsc.edu
Admissions email: hsapp@hsc.edu
Private; founded 1775
Affiliation: Presbyterian
Freshman admissions: selective; 2014-2015: 3,639 applied, 1,720 accepted. Either SAT or ACT required. SAT 25/75 percentile: 995-1210. High school rank: 8% in top tenth, 30% in top quarter, 70% in top half
Early decision deadline: 11/15, notification date: 12/15
Early action deadline: 1/15, notification date: 2/15
Application deadline (fall): 3/1
Undergraduate student body: 1,105 full time, N/A part time; 100% male, 0% female; 0% American Indian, 2% Asian, 8% black, 2% Hispanic, 5% multiracial, 0% Pacific Islander, 82% white, 0% international; 70% from in state; 95% live on campus; 32% of students in fraternities, N/A in sororities
Most popular majors: 14% Biology/Biological Sciences, General, 19% Business/Managerial Economics, 11% Economics, General, 16% History, General, 7% Psychology, General
Expenses: 2015-2016: $41,730; room/board: $13,060
Financial aid: (434) 223-6119; 64% of undergrads determined to have financial need; average aid package $31,035

Hampton University

Hampton VA
(757) 727-5328
U.S. News ranking: Reg. U. (S), No. 18
Website: www.hamptonu.edu
Admissions email: admissions@hamptonu.edu
Private; founded 1868
Freshman admissions: selective; 2014-2015: 19,473 applied, 5,659 accepted. Neither SAT nor ACT required. SAT 25/75 percentile: 910-1100. High school rank: 17% in top tenth, 52% in top quarter, 91% in top half
Early decision deadline: N/A, notification date: N/A
Early action deadline: 11/1, notification date: 12/31
Application deadline (fall): 3/1
Undergraduate student body: 3,277 full time, 227 part time; 35% male, 65% female; 0% American Indian, 1% Asian, 94% black, 1% Hispanic, 0% multiracial, 0% Pacific Islander, 3% white, 1% international; 23% from in state; 63% live on campus; 5% of students in fraternities, 4% in sororities
Most popular majors: 7% Biology/Biological Sciences, General, 8% Business Administration and Management, General, 5% Political Science and Government, General, 15% Psychology, General, 10% Registered Nursing/Registered Nurse
Expenses: 2015-2016: $23,100; room/board: $10,176
Financial aid: (800) 624-3341; 60% of undergrads determined to have financial need; average aid package $5,789

Hollins University

Roanoke VA
(800) 456-9595
U.S. News ranking: Nat. Lib. Arts, No. 108
Website: www.hollins.edu
Admissions email: huadm@hollins.edu
Private; founded 1842
Freshman admissions: selective; 2014-2015: 1,782 applied, 1,008 accepted. Either SAT or ACT required. SAT 25/75 percentile: 960-1200. High school rank: 15% in top tenth, 53% in top quarter, 83% in top half
Early decision deadline: 11/1, notification date: 11/15
Early action deadline: 12/1, notification date: 12/15
Application deadline (fall): rolling
Undergraduate student body: 580 full time, 16 part time; 0% male, 100% female; 1% American Indian, 3% Asian, 11% black, 5% Hispanic, 2% multiracial, 0% Pacific Islander, 71% white, 6% international; 56% from in state; 77% live on campus; 0% of students in fraternities, 0% in sororities
Most popular majors: 9% Business, Management, Marketing, and Related Support Services, 17% English Language and Literature/Letters, 12% Psychology, 15% Social Sciences, 17% Visual and Performing Arts
Expenses: 2015-2016: $35,635; room/board: $12,300
Financial aid: (540) 362-6332; 80% of undergrads determined to have financial need; average aid package $33,342

James Madison University

Harrisonburg VA
(540) 568-5681
U.S. News ranking: Reg. U. (S), No. 7
Website: www.jmu.edu
Admissions email: admissions@jmu.edu
Public; founded 1908
Freshman admissions: selective; 2014-2015: 22,550 applied, 14,823 accepted. Either SAT or ACT required. SAT 25/75 percentile: 1050-1230. High school rank: 26% in top tenth, 43% in top quarter, 97% in top half
Early decision deadline: N/A, notification date: N/A
Early action deadline: 11/1, notification date: 1/15
Application deadline (fall): 1/15
Undergraduate student body: 18,057 full time, 1,087 part time; 41% male, 59% female; 0% American Indian, 4% Asian, 4% black, 5% Hispanic, 4% multiracial, 0% Pacific Islander, 78% white, 2% international; 75% from in state; 32% live on campus; 3% of students in fraternities, 9% in sororities
Most popular majors: Information not available
Expenses: 2015-2016: $10,018 in state, $25,142 out of state; room/board: $9,396
Financial aid: (540) 568-7820; 41% of undergrads determined to have financial need; average aid package $10,025

Liberty University

Lynchburg VA
(800) 543-5317
U.S. News ranking: Reg. U. (S), No. 80
Website: www.liberty.edu
Admissions email: admissions@liberty.edu
Private; founded 1971
Affiliation: Southern Baptist
Freshman admissions: selective; 2014-2015: 29,501 applied, 5,954 accepted. Either SAT or ACT required. SAT 25/75 percentile: 910-1160. High school rank: 18% in top tenth, 42% in top quarter, 72% in top half
Early decision deadline: N/A, notification date: N/A
Early action deadline: N/A, notification date: N/A
Application deadline (fall): rolling
Undergraduate student body: 27,408 full time, 22,336 part time; 41% male, 59% female; 1% American Indian, 1% Asian, 15% black, 2% Hispanic, 3% multiracial, 0% Pacific Islander, 51% white, 2% international; 26% from in state; 16% live on campus; 0% of students in fraternities, 0% in sororities
Most popular majors: 13% Business, Management, Marketing, and Related Support Services, 11% Health Professions and Related Programs, 7% Parks, Recreation, Leisure, and Fitness Studies, 8% Philosophy and Religious Studies, 8% Psychology
Expenses: 2015-2016: $22,000; room/board: $8,786
Financial aid: (434) 582-2270; 79% of undergrads determined to have financial need; average aid package $9,394

Longwood University

Farmville VA
(434) 395-2060
U.S. News ranking: Reg. U. (S), No. 28
Website: www.whylongwood.com
Admissions email: admissions@longwood.edu
Public; founded 1839
Freshman admissions: selective; 2014-2015: 4,593 applied, 3,349 accepted. Either SAT or ACT required. SAT 25/75 percentile: 930-1090. High school

rank: 10% in top tenth, 36% in top quarter, 78% in top half
Early decision deadline: N/A, notification date: N/A
Early action deadline: 12/1, notification date: 1/15
Application deadline (fall): rolling
Undergraduate student body: 4,183 full time, 391 part time; 34% male, 66% female; 0% American Indian, 1% Asian, 8% black, 5% Hispanic, 4% multiracial, 0% Pacific Islander, 78% white, 1% international; 97% from in state; 71% live on campus; 23% of students in fraternities, 20% in sororities
Most popular majors: 12% Business Administration and Management, General, 8% Health Services/Allied Health/Health Sciences, General, 19% Liberal Arts and Sciences/Liberal Studies, 6% Social Sciences, General, 9% Visual and Performing Arts, General
Expenses: 2015-2016: $11,910 in state, $26,070 out of state; room/board: $10,272
Financial aid: (434) 395-2077; 56% of undergrads determined to have financial need; average aid package $13,742

Lynchburg College

Lynchburg VA
(434) 544-8300
U.S. News ranking: Reg. U. (S), No. 32
Website: www.lynchburg.edu
Admissions email: admissions@lynchburg.edu
Private; founded 1903
Affiliation: Christian Church (Disciples of Christ)
Freshman admissions: selective; 2014-2015: 5,515 applied, 3,681 accepted. Either SAT or ACT required. SAT 25/75 percentile: 900-1090. High school rank: N/A
Early decision deadline: 11/15, notification date: 12/15
Early action deadline: N/A, notification date: N/A
Application deadline (fall): rolling
Undergraduate student body: 1,996 full time, 165 part time; 40% male, 60% female; 1% American Indian, 1% Asian, 11% black, 5% Hispanic, 4% multiracial, 0% Pacific Islander, 73% white, 3% international; 69% from in state; 73% live on campus; 12% of students in fraternities, 14% in sororities
Most popular majors: 13% Business, Management, Marketing, and Related Support Services, 9% Communication, Journalism, and Related Programs, 9% Education, 15% Health Professions and Related Programs, 15% Social Sciences
Expenses: 2015-2016: $35,555; room/board: $9,590
Financial aid: (434) 544-8228; 75% of undergrads determined to have financial need; average aid package $25,845

Mary Baldwin College

Staunton VA
(800) 468-2262
U.S. News ranking: Reg. U. (S), No. 41
Website: www.mbc.edu
Admissions email: admit@mbc.edu
Private; founded 1842
Affiliation: Presbyterian
Freshman admissions: selective; 2014-2015: 5,860 applied, 2,989 accepted. Either SAT or ACT required. SAT 25/75 percentile: 850-1090. High school rank: 14% in top tenth, 42% in top quarter, 82% in top half
Early decision deadline: 11/15, notification date: 12/1
Early action deadline: N/A, notification date: N/A
Application deadline (fall): rolling
Undergraduate student body: 988 full time, 435 part time; 7% male, 93% female; 0% American Indian, 3% Asian, 23% black, 7% Hispanic, 4% multiracial, 0% Pacific Islander, 59% white, 0% international; 69% from in state; 85% live on campus; 0% of students in fraternities, 0% in sororities
Most popular majors: 9% Area, Ethnic, Cultural, Gender, and Group Studies, 8% Business, Management, Marketing, and Related Support Services, 10% History, 16% Psychology, 17% Social Sciences
Expenses: 2015-2016: $30,331; room/board: $9,000
Financial aid: (540) 887-7022; 88% of undergrads determined to have financial need; average aid package $22,492

Marymount University

Arlington VA
(703) 284-1500
U.S. News ranking: Reg. U. (S), No. 53
Website: www.marymount.edu
Admissions email: admissions@marymount.edu
Private; founded 1950
Affiliation: Roman Catholic
Freshman admissions: less selective; 2014-2015: 1,976 applied, 1,659 accepted. Either SAT or ACT required. SAT 25/75 percentile: 910-1100. High school rank: 15% in top tenth, 15% in top quarter, 62% in top half
Early decision deadline: N/A, notification date: N/A
Early action deadline: N/A, notification date: N/A
Application deadline (fall): rolling
Undergraduate student body: 2,127 full time, 236 part time; 35% male, 65% female; 1% American Indian, 9% Asian, 15% black, 16% Hispanic, 4% multiracial, 0% Pacific Islander, 42% white, 10% international; 63% from in state; 34% live on campus; 0% of students in fraternities, 0% in sororities
Most popular majors: 15% Business Administration and Management, General, 7% Information Technology, 5% Interior Design, 7% Psychology, General, 26% Registered Nursing/Registered Nurse
Expenses: 2015-2016: $28,310; room/board: $12,220
Financial aid: (703) 284-1530; 65% of undergrads determined to have financial need; average aid package $17,828

Norfolk State University

Norfolk VA
(757) 823-8396
U.S. News ranking: Reg. U. (S), second tier
Website: www.nsu.edu
Admissions email: admissions@nsu.edu
Public; founded 1935
Freshman admissions: least selective; 2014-2015: N/A applied, N/A accepted. Either SAT or ACT required. SAT 25/75 percentile: 790-950. High school rank: N/A
Early decision deadline: N/A, notification date: N/A
Early action deadline: N/A, notification date: N/A
Undergraduate student body: 4,416 full time, 940 part time; 36% male, 64% female; 0% American Indian, 1% Asian, 83% black, 3% Hispanic, 3% multiracial, 0% Pacific Islander, 5% white, 0% international; 86% from in state; 38% live on campus; N/A of students in fraternities, N/A in sororities
Most popular majors: Information not available
Expenses: 2015-2016: $8,366 in state, $20,124 out of state; room/board: $8,970
Financial aid: (757) 823-8381

Old Dominion University

Norfolk VA
(757) 683-3685
U.S. News ranking: Nat. U., second tier
Website: www.odu.edu
Admissions email: admissions@odu.edu
Public; founded 1930
Freshman admissions: selective; 2014-2015: 9,161 applied, 7,502 accepted. Either SAT or ACT required. SAT 25/75 percentile: 920-1120. High school rank: 10% in top tenth, 33% in top quarter, 76% in top half
Early decision deadline: N/A, notification date: N/A
Early action deadline: 12/1, notification date: 1/15
Application deadline (fall): rolling
Undergraduate student body: 15,261 full time, 4,854 part time; 46% male, 54% female; 0% American Indian, 4% Asian, 27% black, 7% Hispanic, 6% multiracial, 0% Pacific Islander, 50% white, 1% international; 92% from in state; 23% live on campus; 7% of students in fraternities, 6% in sororities
Most popular majors: 14% Business, Management, Marketing, and Related Support Services, 7% English Language and Literature/Letters, 18% Health Professions and Related Programs, 8% Psychology, 14% Social Sciences
Expenses: 2015-2016: N/A in state, $26,538 out of state; room/board: $10,644
Financial aid: (757) 683-3683; 65% of undergrads determined to have financial need; average aid package $9,681

Radford University

Radford VA
(540) 831-5371
U.S. News ranking: Reg. U. (S), No. 37
Website: www.radford.edu
Admissions email: admissions@radford.edu
Public; founded 1910
Freshman admissions: less selective; 2014-2015: 7,704 applied, 6,072 accepted. Neither SAT nor ACT required. SAT 25/75 percentile: 890-1060. High school rank: 5% in top tenth, 20% in top quarter, 60% in top half
Early decision deadline: N/A, notification date: N/A
Early action deadline: 12/1, notification date: 1/15
Application deadline (fall): 2/1
Undergraduate student body: 8,507 full time, 378 part time; 44% male, 56% female; 0% American Indian, 1% Asian, 12% black, 5% Hispanic, 5% multiracial, 0% Pacific Islander, 74% white, 1% international; 95% from in state; 36% live on campus; 13% of students in fraternities, 15% in sororities
Most popular majors: 7% Business Administration and Management, General, 7% Criminal Justice/Safety Studies, 9% Multi/Interdisciplinary Studies, Other, 7% Physical Education Teaching and Coaching, 7% Psychology, General
Expenses: 2015-2016: $9,809 in state, $21,647 out of state; room/board: $8,677
Financial aid: (540) 831-5408; 56% of undergrads determined to have financial need; average aid package $9,421

Randolph College

Lynchburg VA
(800) 745-7692
U.S. News ranking: Nat. Lib. Arts, No. 158
Website: www.randolphcollege.edu/
Admissions email: admissions@randolphcollege.edu
Private; founded 1891
Affiliation: United Methodist
Freshman admissions: selective; 2014-2015: 1,353 applied, 1,096 accepted. Either SAT or ACT required. SAT 25/75 percentile: 950-1200. High school rank: 7% in top tenth, 36% in top quarter, 81% in top half
Early decision deadline: N/A, notification date: N/A
Early action deadline: 11/15, notification date: 1/1
Application deadline (fall): rolling
Undergraduate student body: 657 full time, 18 part time; 36% male, 64% female; 1% American Indian, 3% Asian, 11% black, 5% Hispanic, 3% multiracial, 0% Pacific Islander, 67% white, 10% international; 55% from in state; 85% live on campus; 0% of students in fraternities, 0% in sororities
Most popular majors: 11% Biological and Biomedical Sciences, 9% Business, Management, Marketing, and Related Support Services, 8% English Language and Literature/Letters, 8% History, 8% Psychology
Expenses: 2015-2016: $35,410; room/board: $12,106
Financial aid: (434) 947-8128; 71% of undergrads determined to have financial need; average aid package $28,783

Randolph-Macon College

Ashland VA
(800) 888-1762
U.S. News ranking: Nat. Lib. Arts, No. 125
Website: www.rmc.edu
Admissions email: admissions@rmc.edu
Private; founded 1830
Affiliation: United Methodist
Freshman admissions: selective; 2014-2015: 2,955 applied, 1,783 accepted. Either SAT or ACT required. SAT 25/75 percentile: 980-1190. High school rank: 22% in top tenth, 52% in top quarter, 84% in top half
Early decision deadline: N/A, notification date: N/A
Early action deadline: 11/15, notification date: 1/1
Application deadline (fall): 3/1
Undergraduate student body: 1,365 full time, 29 part time; 46% male, 54% female; 0% American Indian, 2% Asian, 9% black, 4% Hispanic, 4% multiracial, 0% Pacific Islander, 77% white, 2% international; 74% from in state; 84% live on campus; 26% of students in fraternities, 27% in sororities
Most popular majors: 12% Biology/Biological Sciences, General, 10% Business/Managerial Economics, 8% Communication and Media Studies, 9% English Language and Literature, General, 9% Psychology, General
Expenses: 2015-2016: $37,600; room/board: $10,880
Financial aid: (804) 752-7259; 74% of undergrads determined to have financial need; average aid package $26,925

Regent University

Virginia Beach VA
(888) 718-1222
U.S. News ranking: Nat. U., second tier
Website: www.regent.edu
Admissions email: admissions@regent.edu
Private; founded 1978
Affiliation: non-denominational
Freshman admissions: selective; 2014-2015: 1,535 applied, 1,233 accepted. Either SAT or ACT required. SAT 25/75 percentile: 910-1130. High school rank: 8% in top tenth, 51% in top quarter, 81% in top half
Early decision deadline: N/A, notification date: N/A
Early action deadline: N/A, notification date: N/A
Application deadline (fall): 7/28
Undergraduate student body: 1,496 full time, 914 part time; 39% male, 61% female; 1% American Indian, 2% Asian, 21% black, 5% Hispanic, N/A multiracial, N/A Pacific Islander, 59% white, 1% international; 51% from in state; 22% live on campus; N/A of students in fraternities, N/A in sororities
Most popular majors: 18% Business Administration and Management, General, 15% Divinity/Ministry, 10% English Language and Literature, General, 16% Psychology, General, 21% Speech Communication and Rhetoric
Expenses: 2015-2016: $16,638; room/board: $8,250

Financial aid: (757) 226-4125; 76% of undergrads determined to have financial need; average aid package $11,678

Roanoke College

Salem VA
(540) 375-2270
U.S. News ranking: Nat. Lib. Arts, No. 143
Website: www.roanoke.edu
Admissions email: admissions@roanoke.edu
Private; founded 1842
Affiliation: Lutheran
Freshman admissions: selective; 2014-2015: 4,824 applied, 3,344 accepted. Either SAT or ACT required. SAT 25/75 percentile: 980-1210. High school rank: 18% in top tenth, 43% in top quarter, 82% in top half
Early decision deadline: 11/1, notification date: 12/1
Early action deadline: N/A, notification date: N/A
Application deadline (fall): 3/15
Undergraduate student body: 1,978 full time, 76 part time; 40% male, 60% female; 0% American Indian, 2% Asian, 6% black, 4% Hispanic, 4% multiracial, 0% Pacific Islander, 83% white, 2% international; 52% from in state; 75% live on campus; 22% of students in fraternities, 20% in sororities
Most popular majors: 16% Business Administration and Management, General, 8% Communication, General, 6% Criminal Justice/Safety Studies, 7% History, General, 12% Psychology, General
Expenses: 2015-2016: $39,416; room/board: $12,370
Financial aid: (540) 375-2235; 73% of undergrads determined to have financial need; average aid package $30,036

Shenandoah University

Winchester VA
(540) 665-4581
U.S. News ranking: Reg. U. (S), No. 41
Website: www.su.edu
Admissions email: admit@su.edu
Private; founded 1875
Affiliation: United Methodist
Freshman admissions: selective; 2014-2015: 1,907 applied, 1,575 accepted. Either SAT or ACT required. SAT 25/75 percentile: 880-1110. High school rank: N/A
Early decision deadline: N/A, notification date: N/A
Early action deadline: N/A, notification date: N/A
Application deadline (fall): rolling
Undergraduate student body: 1,823 full time, 69 part time; 44% male, 56% female; 2% American Indian, 3% Asian, 14% black, 6% Hispanic, 0% multiracial, 1% Pacific Islander, 65% white, 5% international; 62% from in state; 47% live on campus; 0% of students in fraternities, 0% in sororities
Most popular majors: 6% Biology/Biological Sciences, General, 9% Business Administration and Management, General, 11% Education, 17% Musical Theatre, 35% Registered Nursing/Registered Nurse
Expenses: 2015-2016: $30,760; room/board: $9,920
Financial aid: (540) 665-4538; 74% of undergrads determined to have financial need; average aid package $29,205

University of Mary Washington

Fredericksburg VA
(540) 654-2000
U.S. News ranking: Reg. U. (S), No. 16
Website: www.umw.edu
Admissions email: admit@umw.edu
Public; founded 1908
Freshman admissions: selective; 2014-2015: 5,336 applied, 4,094 accepted. Either SAT or ACT required. SAT 25/75 percentile: 1020-1200. High school rank: 16% in top tenth, 45% in top quarter, 86% in top half
Early decision deadline: N/A, notification date: N/A
Early action deadline: 11/15, notification date: 1/31
Application deadline (fall): rolling
Undergraduate student body: 3,666 full time, 501 part time; 35% male, 65% female; 0% American Indian, 4% Asian, 6% black, 7% Hispanic, 5% multiracial, 0% Pacific Islander, 69% white, 1% international; 89% from in state; 59% live on campus; 0% of students in fraternities, 0% in sororities
Most popular majors: 7% Biological and Biomedical Sciences, 13% Business, Management, Marketing, and Related Support Services, 11% English Language and Literature/Letters, 10% Psychology, 19% Social Sciences
Expenses: 2015-2016: $10,974 in state, $24,814 out of state; room/board: $10,202
Financial aid: (540) 654-2468; 41% of undergrads determined to have financial need; average aid package $8,575

University of Richmond

Univ. of Richmond VA
(804) 289-8640
U.S. News ranking: Nat. Lib. Arts, No. 32
Website: www.richmond.edu
Admissions email: admissions@richmond.edu
Private; founded 1830
Freshman admissions: more selective; 2014-2015: 9,921 applied, 3,155 accepted. Either SAT or ACT required. SAT 25/75 percentile: 1220-1430. High school rank: 59% in top tenth, 87% in top quarter, 98% in top half
Early decision deadline: 11/15, notification date: 12/15
Early action deadline: N/A, notification date: N/A
Application deadline (fall): 1/15
Undergraduate student body: 2,938 full time, 46 part time; 48% male, 52% female; 0% American Indian, 7% Asian, 6% black, 8% Hispanic, 4% multiracial, 0% Pacific Islander, 58% white, 9% international; 20% from in state; 90% live on campus; 19% of students in fraternities, 32% in sororities
Most popular majors: 7% Biological and Biomedical Sciences, 40% Business, Management, Marketing, and Related Support Services, 6% Multi/Interdisciplinary Studies, 6% Psychology, 16% Social Sciences
Expenses: 2015-2016: $48,090; room/board: $11,120
Financial aid: (804) 289-8438; 41% of undergrads determined to have financial need; average aid package $43,016

University of Virginia

Charlottesville VA
(434) 982-3200
U.S. News ranking: Nat. U., No. 26
Website: www.virginia.edu
Admissions email: undergradadmission@virginia.edu
Public; founded 1819
Freshman admissions: most selective; 2014-2015: 31,021 applied, 8,997 accepted. Either SAT or ACT required. SAT 25/75 percentile: 1250-1460. High school rank: 89% in top tenth, 98% in top quarter, 100% in top half
Early decision deadline: N/A, notification date: N/A
Early action deadline: 11/1, notification date: 1/31
Application deadline (fall): 1/1
Undergraduate student body: 15,622 full time, 861 part time; 44% male, 56% female; 0% American Indian, 12% Asian, 6% black, 6% Hispanic, 5% multiracial, 0% Pacific Islander, 61% white, 5% international; 72% from in state; 41% live on campus; 25% of students in fraternities, 28% in sororities
Most popular majors: 8% Biology/Biological Sciences, General, 9% Business/Commerce, General, 10% Economics, General, 8% International Relations and Affairs, 8% Psychology, General
Expenses: 2015-2016: $14,526 in state, $43,822 out of state; room/board: $10,400
Financial aid: (434) 982-6000; 33% of undergrads determined to have financial need; average aid package $24,427

University of Virginia–Wise

Wise VA
(888) 282-9324
U.S. News ranking: Nat. Lib. Arts, second tier
Website: www.uvawise.edu
Admissions email: admissions@uvawise.edu
Public; founded 1954
Freshman admissions: less selective; 2014-2015: 1,113 applied, 766 accepted. Either SAT or ACT required. SAT 25/75 percentile: 840-1050. High school rank: 23% in top tenth, 45% in top quarter, 76% in top half
Early decision deadline: N/A, notification date: N/A
Early action deadline: 12/1, notification date: 12/15
Application deadline (fall): 8/15
Undergraduate student body: 1,407 full time, 775 part time; 40% male, 60% female; 0% American Indian, 1% Asian, 11% black, 2% Hispanic, 0% multiracial, 0% Pacific Islander, 79% white, 0% international; 95% from in state; 35% live on campus; 1% of students in fraternities, 2% in sororities
Most popular majors: 18% Business, Management, Marketing, and Related Support Services, 19% Education, 8% Health Professions and Related Programs, 16% Social Sciences
Expenses: 2015-2016: $9,355 in state, $24,957 out of state; room/board: $10,256
Financial aid: (276) 328-0103; 79% of undergrads determined to have financial need; average aid package $11,602

Virginia Commonwealth University

Richmond VA
(800) 841-3638
U.S. News ranking: Nat. U., No. 156
Website: www.vcu.edu
Admissions email: ugrad@vcu.edu
Public; founded 1838
Freshman admissions: selective; 2014-2015: 15,126 applied, 10,426 accepted. Neither SAT nor ACT required. SAT 25/75 percentile: 1000-1210. High school rank: 19% in top tenth, 47% in top quarter, 85% in top half
Early decision deadline: N/A, notification date: N/A
Early action deadline: N/A, notification date: N/A
Application deadline (fall): 1/15
Undergraduate student body: 20,294 full time, 3,668 part time; 43% male, 57% female; 0% American Indian, 12% Asian, 18% black, 8% Hispanic, 5% multiracial, 0% Pacific Islander, 50% white, 3% international; 93% from in state; 23% live on campus; 7% of students in fraternities, 7% in sororities
Most popular majors: 13% Business, Management, Marketing, and Related Support Services, 7% Health Professions and Related Programs, 8% Homeland Security, Law Enforcement, Firefighting and Related Protective Services, 10% Psychology, 12% Visual and Performing Arts
Expenses: 2015-2016: $12,772 in state, $30,838 out of state; room/board: $11,280
Financial aid: (804) 828-6669; 58% of undergrads determined to have financial need; average aid package $10,318

Virginia Military Institute

Lexington VA
(800) 767-4207
U.S. News ranking: Nat. Lib. Arts, No. 82
Website: www.vmi.edu
Admissions email: admissions@vmi.edu
Public; founded 1839
Freshman admissions: selective; 2014-2015: 2,036 applied, 904 accepted. Either SAT or ACT required. SAT 25/75 percentile: 1070-1250. High school rank: 21% in top tenth, 58% in top quarter, 89% in top half
Early decision deadline: 11/15, notification date: 12/15
Early action deadline: N/A, notification date: N/A
Application deadline (fall): 2/1
Undergraduate student body: 1,700 full time, 0 part time; 89% male, 11% female; 0% American Indian, 4% Asian, 5% black, 5% Hispanic, 2% multiracial, 1% Pacific Islander, 81% white, 1% international; 58% from in state; 100% live on campus; N/A of students in fraternities, N/A in sororities
Most popular majors: 15% Civil Engineering, General, 13% Economics, General, 12% History, General, 19% International Relations and Affairs, 8% Psychology, General
Expenses: 2015-2016: $16,536 in state, $39,550 out of state; room/board: $8,666
Financial aid: (540) 464-7208; 51% of undergrads determined to have financial need; average aid package $18,816

Virginia State University[1]

Petersburg VA
(804) 524-5902
U.S. News ranking: Reg. U. (S), second tier
Website: www.vsu.edu
Admissions email: admiss@vsu.edu
Public
Application deadline (fall): 5/1
Undergraduate student body: N/A full time, N/A part time
Expenses: 2015-2016: $8,226 in state, $17,760 out of state; room/board: $10,252
Financial aid: (804) 524-5992; 90% of undergrads determined to have financial need; average aid package $12,230

Virginia Tech

Blacksburg VA
(540) 231-6267
U.S. News ranking: Nat. U., No. 70
Website: www.vt.edu
Admissions email: vtadmiss@vt.edu
Public; founded 1872
Freshman admissions: more selective; 2014-2015: 20,744 applied, 15,067 accepted. Either SAT or ACT required. SAT 25/75 percentile: 1110-1320. High school rank: 41% in top tenth, 82% in top quarter, 99% in top half
Early decision deadline: 11/1, notification date: 12/15
Early action deadline: N/A, notification date: N/A
Application deadline (fall): 1/15
Undergraduate student body: 23,685 full time, 562 part time; 58% male, 42% female; 0% American Indian, 9% Asian, 4% black, 5% Hispanic, 4% multiracial, 0% Pacific Islander, 70% white, 5% international; N/A from in state; 14% live on campus; 19% of students in fraternities, 14% in sororities
Most popular majors: 8% Biological and Biomedical Sciences, 18% Business, Management, Marketing, and Related Support Services, 23% Engineering, 9% Family and Consumer Sciences/Human Sciences, 8% Social Sciences
Expenses: 2014-2015: $12,017 in state, $27,444 out of state; room/board: $8,270
Financial aid: (540) 231-5179; 45% of undergrads determined to have financial need; average aid package $16,455

Virginia Union University
Richmond VA
(804) 257-5600
U.S. News ranking: Reg. Coll. (S), second tier
Website: www.vuu.edu/
Admissions email: admissions@vuu.edu
Private; founded 1865
Affiliation: Baptist
Freshman admissions: least selective; 2014-2015: N/A applied, N/A accepted. Either SAT or ACT required. SAT 25/75 percentile: 690-860. High school rank: 6% in top tenth, 20% in top quarter, 51% in top half
Early decision deadline: N/A, notification date: N/A
Early action deadline: N/A, notification date: N/A
Application deadline (fall): 6/30
Undergraduate student body: 1,286 full time, 37 part time; 44% male, 56% female; 0% American Indian, 0% Asian, 96% black, 1% Hispanic, 0% multiracial, 0% Pacific Islander, 0% white, 0% international; 51% from in state; 65% live on campus; N/A of students in fraternities, N/A in sororities
Most popular majors: 16% Business, Management, Marketing, and Related Support Services, 9% Computer and Information Sciences and Support Services, 7% Foreign Languages, Literatures, and Linguistics, 13% Psychology, 22% Social Sciences
Expenses: 2015-2016: $15,746; room/board: $8,074
Financial aid: (804) 257-5882; 87% of undergrads determined to have financial need; average aid package $13,322

Virginia Wesleyan College
Norfolk VA
(800) 737-8684
U.S. News ranking: Nat. Lib. Arts, second tier
Website: www.vwc.edu
Admissions email: admissions@vwc.edu
Private; founded 1961
Affiliation: United Methodist
Freshman admissions: less selective; 2014-2015: 2,072 applied, 1,845 accepted. Neither SAT nor ACT required. SAT 25/75 percentile: 870-1100. High school rank: 13% in top tenth, 38% in top quarter, 74% in top half
Early decision deadline: N/A, notification date: N/A
Early action deadline: N/A, notification date: N/A
Application deadline (fall): rolling
Undergraduate student body: 1,420 full time, 81 part time; 38% male, 62% female; 0% American Indian, 1% Asian, 23% black, 8% Hispanic, 6% multiracial, 0% Pacific Islander, 56% white, 1% international; 75% from in state; 61% live on campus; 15% of students in fraternities, 13% in sororities
Most popular majors: 6% Biology/Biological Sciences, General, 19% Business Administration and Management, General, 8% Criminal Justice/Safety Studies, 7% Psychology, General, 11% Social Sciences, General
Expenses: 2015-2016: $34,428; room/board: $8,690
Financial aid: (757) 455-3345; 83% of undergrads determined to have financial need; average aid package $21,185

Washington and Lee University
Lexington VA
(540) 463-8710
U.S. News ranking: Nat. Lib. Arts, No. 14
Website: www.wlu.edu
Admissions email: admissions@wlu.edu
Private; founded 1749
Freshman admissions: most selective; 2014-2015: 5,797 applied, 1,136 accepted. Either SAT or ACT required. SAT 25/75 percentile: 1320-1460. High school rank: 81% in top tenth, 95% in top quarter, 100% in top half
Early decision deadline: 11/1, notification date: 12/22
Early action deadline: N/A, notification date: N/A
Application deadline (fall): 1/1
Undergraduate student body: 1,882 full time, 8 part time; 50% male, 50% female; 0% American Indian, 3% Asian, 2% black, 4% Hispanic, 2% multiracial, 0% Pacific Islander, 83% white, 4% international; 14% from in state; 55% live on campus; 78% of students in fraternities, 81% in sororities
Most popular majors: 6% Accounting and Business/Management, 14% Business Administration and Management, General, 11% Economics, General, 6% History, General, 9% Political Science and Government, General
Expenses: 2015-2016: $46,417; room/board: $10,985
Financial aid: (540) 458-8717; 42% of undergrads determined to have financial need; average aid package $46,604

WASHINGTON

Art Institute of Seattle[1]
Seattle WA
(800) 275-2471
U.S. News ranking: Arts, unranked
Website: www.ais.edu
Admissions email: N/A
For-profit
Application deadline (fall): N/A
Undergraduate student body: N/A full time, N/A part time
Expenses: 2014-2015: $17,560; room/board: $12,132
Financial aid: N/A

Bellevue College[1]
Bellevue WA
(425) 564-1000
U.S. News ranking: Reg. Coll. (W), unranked
Website: bellevuecollege.edu
Admissions email: N/A
Public
Application deadline (fall): N/A
Undergraduate student body: N/A full time, N/A part time
Expenses: 2014-2015: $3,754 in state, $8,944 out of state; room/board: $9,630
Financial aid: (425) 564-2227

Central Washington University
Ellensburg WA
(509) 963-1211
U.S. News ranking: Reg. U. (W), No. 52
Website: www.cwu.edu
Admissions email: cwuadmis@cwu.edu
Public; founded 1891
Freshman admissions: less selective; 2014-2015: 4,041 applied, 3,508 accepted. Either SAT or ACT required. SAT 25/75 percentile: 870-1080. High school rank: N/A
Early decision deadline: N/A, notification date: N/A
Early action deadline: N/A, notification date: N/A
Application deadline (fall): rolling
Undergraduate student body: 8,753 full time, 2,211 part time; 48% male, 52% female; 1% American Indian, 4% Asian, 3% black, 13% Hispanic, 7% multiracial, 1% Pacific Islander, 62% white, 1% international; 94% from in state; 31% live on campus; 0% of students in fraternities, 0% in sororities
Most popular majors: 22% Business, Management, Marketing, and Related Support Services, 14% Education, 7% Homeland Security, Law Enforcement, Firefighting and Related Protective Services, 5% Psychology, 12% Social Sciences
Expenses: 2015-2016: $8,321 in state, $19,958 out of state; room/board: $9,316
Financial aid: (509) 963-1611; 74% of undergrads determined to have financial need; average aid package $11,495

City University of Seattle[1]
Seattle WA
(206) 239-4500
U.S. News ranking: Reg. U. (W), unranked
Website: www.cityu.edu
Admissions email: info@cityu.edu
Private; founded 1973
Application deadline (fall): rolling
Undergraduate student body: N/A full time, N/A part time
Expenses: N/A
Financial aid: (800) 426-5596

Cornish College of the Arts
Seattle WA
(800) 726-ARTS
U.S. News ranking: Arts, unranked
Website: www.cornish.edu
Admissions email: admission@cornish.edu
Private; founded 1914
Freshman admissions: N/A; 2014-2015: 1,134 applied, 970 accepted. Neither SAT nor ACT required. SAT 25/75 percentile: N/A. High school rank: N/A
Early decision deadline: N/A, notification date: N/A
Early action deadline: N/A, notification date: N/A
Application deadline (fall): rolling
Undergraduate student body: 758 full time, 7 part time; 36% male, 64% female; 1% American Indian, 6% Asian, 4% black, 9% Hispanic, 7% multiracial, 0% Pacific Islander, 63% white, 4% international; 48% from in state; 32% live on campus; 0% of students in fraternities, 0% in sororities
Most popular majors: 100% Visual and Performing Arts
Expenses: 2015-2016: $37,240; room/board: $10,680
Financial aid: (206) 726-5014; 80% of undergrads determined to have financial need; average aid package $22,119

Eastern Washington University
Cheney WA
(509) 359-2397
U.S. News ranking: Reg. U. (W), No. 63
Website: www.ewu.edu
Admissions email: admissions@ewu.edu
Public; founded 1882
Freshman admissions: less selective; 2014-2015: 4,987 applied, 3,710 accepted. Either SAT or ACT required. SAT 25/75 percentile: 850-1070. High school rank: N/A
Early decision deadline: N/A, notification date: N/A
Early action deadline: N/A, notification date: N/A
Application deadline (fall): 5/15
Undergraduate student body: 10,061 full time, 2,350 part time; 46% male, 54% female; 1% American Indian, 3% Asian, 3% black, 14% Hispanic, 5% multiracial, 0% Pacific Islander, 64% white, 3% international; 94% from in state; 19% live on campus; 4% of students in fraternities, 5% in sororities
Most popular majors: 17% Business, Management, Marketing, and Related Support Services, 9% Education, 10% Health Professions and Related Programs, 8% Psychology, 9% Social Sciences
Expenses: 2015-2016: $8,204 in state, $22,321 out of state; room/board: $10,265
Financial aid: (509) 359-2314; 66% of undergrads determined to have financial need; average aid package $10,709

Evergreen State College
Olympia WA
(360) 867-6170
U.S. News ranking: Reg. U. (W), No. 35
Website: www.evergreen.edu
Admissions email: admissions@evergreen.edu
Public; founded 1967
Freshman admissions: selective; 2014-2015: 1,544 applied, 1,527 accepted. Either SAT or ACT required. SAT 25/75 percentile: 880-1200. High school rank: 9% in top tenth, 18% in top quarter, 55% in top half
Early decision deadline: N/A, notification date: N/A
Early action deadline: N/A, notification date: N/A
Application deadline (fall): rolling
Undergraduate student body: 3,555 full time, 323 part time; 46% male, 54% female; 2% American Indian, 2% Asian, 6% black, 8% Hispanic, 8% multiracial, 0% Pacific Islander, 65% white, 0% international; 75% from in state; 21% live on campus; N/A of students in fraternities, N/A in sororities
Most popular majors: 17% Biological and Physical Sciences, 83% Liberal Arts and Sciences/Liberal Studies
Expenses: 2015-2016: $8,682 in state, $22,752 out of state; room/board: $9,492
Financial aid: (360) 867-6205; 70% of undergrads determined to have financial need; average aid package $10,111

Gonzaga University
Spokane WA
(800) 322-2584
U.S. News ranking: Reg. U. (W), No. 4
Website: www.gonzaga.edu
Admissions email: admissions@gonzaga.edu
Private; founded 1887
Affiliation: Roman Catholic
Freshman admissions: more selective; 2014-2015: 7,162 applied, 4,835 accepted. Either SAT or ACT required. SAT 25/75 percentile: 1100-1290. High school rank: 38% in top tenth, 71% in top quarter, 95% in top half
Early decision deadline: N/A, notification date: N/A
Early action deadline: 11/15, notification date: 1/15
Application deadline (fall): 2/1
Undergraduate student body: 4,752 full time, 85 part time; 46% male, 54% female; 1% American Indian, 5% Asian, 1% black, 9% Hispanic, 5% multiracial, 0% Pacific Islander, 73% white, 2% international; 50% from in state; 58% live on campus; 0% of students in fraternities, 0% in sororities
Most popular majors: 9% Biological and Biomedical Sciences, 23% Business, Management, Marketing, and Related Support Services, 9% Communication, Journalism, and Related Programs, 10% Engineering, 16% Social Sciences
Expenses: 2015-2016: $37,990; room/board: $10,835
Financial aid: (509) 323-4049; 56% of undergrads determined to have financial need; average aid package $27,809

Heritage University[1]
Toppenish WA
(509) 865-8508
U.S. News ranking: Reg. U. (W), unranked
Website: www.heritage.edu
Admissions email: admissions@heritage.edu
Private
Application deadline (fall): N/A
Undergraduate student body: N/A full time, N/A part time
Expenses: 2014-2015: $18,521; room/board: $9,630
Financial aid: (509) 865-8502

Northwest University
Kirkland WA
(425) 889-5231
U.S. News ranking: Reg. Coll. (W), No. 17
Website: www.northwestu.edu
Admissions email: admissions@northwestu.edu
Private; founded 1934
Affiliation: Assembly of God

Freshman admissions: less selective; 2014-2015: 549 applied, 472 accepted. Either SAT or ACT required. SAT 25/75 percentile: 880-1145. High school rank: N/A
Early decision deadline: N/A, notification date: N/A
Early action deadline: 11/15, notification date: 12/15
Application deadline (fall): rolling
Undergraduate student body: 1,287 full time, 231 part time; 42% male, 58% female; 1% American Indian, 4% Asian, 4% black, 9% Hispanic, 4% multiracial, 1% Pacific Islander, 70% white, 2% international
Most popular majors: Information not available
Expenses: 2015-2016: $28,086; room/board: $7,790
Financial aid: (425) 889-5336; 81% of undergrads determined to have financial need; average aid package $21,680

Olympic College[1]

Bremerton WA
(360) 792-6050
U.S. News ranking: Reg. Coll. (W), unranked
Website: www.olympic.edu
Admissions email: N/A
Public
Application deadline (fall): N/A
Undergraduate student body: N/A full time, N/A part time
Expenses: 2014-2015: $3,720 in state, $4,137 out of state; room/board: $9,630
Financial aid: (800) 259-6718

Pacific Lutheran University

Tacoma WA
(800) 274-6758
U.S. News ranking: Reg. U. (W), No. 14
Website: www.plu.edu
Admissions email: admission@plu.edu
Private; founded 1890
Affiliation: Lutheran
Freshman admissions: selective; 2014-2015: 3,438 applied, 2,579 accepted. Either SAT or ACT required. SAT 25/75 percentile: 980-1210. High school rank: 30% in top tenth, 63% in top quarter, 96% in top half
Early decision deadline: N/A, notification date: N/A
Early action deadline: N/A, notification date: N/A
Application deadline (fall): rolling
Undergraduate student body: 2,855 full time, 104 part time; 37% male, 63% female; 1% American Indian, 7% Asian, 3% black, 8% Hispanic, 8% multiracial, 1% Pacific Islander, 68% white, 4% international; 80% from in state; 43% live on campus; 0% of students in fraternities, 0% in sororities
Most popular majors: 9% Biological and Biomedical Sciences, 12% Business, Management, Marketing, and Related Support Services, 7% Communication, Journalism, and Related Programs, 10% Health Professions and Related Programs, 8% Psychology
Expenses: 2015-2016: $37,950; room/board: $10,330
Financial aid: (253) 535-7134; 76% of undergrads determined to have financial need; average aid package $33,960

Peninsula College[1]

Port Angeles WA
(360) 417-6340
U.S. News ranking: Reg. Coll. (W), unranked
Website: www.pencol.edu
Admissions email: N/A
Public
Application deadline (fall): N/A
Undergraduate student body: N/A full time, N/A part time
Expenses: 2014-2015: $4,191 in state, $4,591 out of state; room/board: $9,630
Financial aid: (360) 417-6390

Seattle Pacific University

Seattle WA
(800) 366-3344
U.S. News ranking: Reg. U. (W), No. 17
Website: www.spu.edu
Admissions email: admissions@spu.edu
Private; founded 1891
Affiliation: Free Methodist
Freshman admissions: selective; 2014-2015: 4,447 applied, 3,709 accepted. Either SAT or ACT required. SAT 25/75 percentile: 1030-1250. High school rank: N/A
Early decision deadline: N/A, notification date: N/A
Early action deadline: 11/15, notification date: 1/5
Application deadline (fall): 2/1
Undergraduate student body: 3,107 full time, 157 part time; 33% male, 67% female; 0% American Indian, 11% Asian, 4% black, 9% Hispanic, 8% multiracial, 0% Pacific Islander, 63% white, 3% international; 61% from in state; 51% live on campus; N/A of students in fraternities, N/A in sororities
Most popular majors: 7% Business/Commerce, General, 5% Physiology, General, 10% Psychology, General, 8% Registered Nursing/Registered Nurse, 6% Speech Communication and Rhetoric
Expenses: 2015-2016: $37,086; room/board: $10,353
Financial aid: (206) 281-2061; 72% of undergrads determined to have financial need; average aid package $31,052

Seattle University

Seattle WA
(206) 296-2000
U.S. News ranking: Reg. U. (W), No. 6
Website: www.seattleu.edu
Admissions email: admissions@seattleu.edu
Private; founded 1891
Affiliation: Roman Catholic (Jesuit)
Freshman admissions: more selective; 2014-2015: 7,392 applied, 5,422 accepted. Either SAT or ACT required. SAT 25/75 percentile: 1060-1280. High school rank: 27% in top tenth, 62% in top quarter, 92% in top half
Early decision deadline: N/A, notification date: N/A
Early action deadline: 11/15, notification date: 12/23
Application deadline (fall): rolling
Undergraduate student body: 4,286 full time, 225 part time; 41% male, 59% female; 1% American Indian, 16% Asian, 3% black, 9% Hispanic, 7% multiracial, 1% Pacific Islander, 45% white, 11% international; 44% from in state; 47% live on campus; 0% of students in fraternities, 0% in sororities
Most popular majors: 24% Business, Management, Marketing, and Related Support Services, 7% Engineering, 13% Health Professions and Related Programs, 6% Social Sciences, 7% Visual and Performing Arts
Expenses: 2015-2016: $39,690; room/board: $11,121
Financial aid: (206) 296-2000; 58% of undergrads determined to have financial need; average aid package $30,502

South Seattle College[1]

Seattle WA
(206) 764-5300
U.S. News ranking: Reg. Coll. (W), unranked
Website: southseattle.edu
Admissions email: N/A
Public
Application deadline (fall): N/A
Undergraduate student body: N/A full time, N/A part time
Expenses: 2014-2015: $3,824 in state, $9,014 out of state; room/board: $9,492
Financial aid: (206) 934-5317

St. Martin's University

Lacey WA
(800) 368-8803
U.S. News ranking: Reg. U. (W), No. 46
Website: www.stmartin.edu
Admissions email: admissions@stmartin.edu
Private; founded 1895
Affiliation: Roman Catholic (Benedictine)
Freshman admissions: selective; 2014-2015: 679 applied, 603 accepted. Either SAT or ACT required. SAT 25/75 percentile: 935-1155. High school rank: 24% in top tenth, 58% in top quarter, 86% in top half
Early decision deadline: N/A, notification date: N/A
Early action deadline: N/A, notification date: N/A
Application deadline (fall): rolling
Undergraduate student body: 1,092 full time, 323 part time; 52% male, 48% female; 1% American Indian, 5% Asian, 5% black, 12% Hispanic, 8% multiracial, 2% Pacific Islander, 58% white, 6% international; 73% from in state; 30% live on campus; 0% of students in fraternities, 0% in sororities
Most popular majors: 9% Biological and Biomedical Sciences, 24% Business, Management, Marketing, and Related Support Services, 12% Engineering, 8% Homeland Security, Law Enforcement, Firefighting and Related Protective Services, 15% Psychology
Expenses: 2015-2016: $33,194; room/board: $10,060
Financial aid: (360) 438-4397; 90% of undergrads determined to have financial need; average aid package $25,247

Trinity Lutheran College[1]

Everett WA
(425) 249-4741
U.S. News ranking: Reg. Coll. (W), No. 25
Website: www.tlc.edu/
Admissions email: admissions@tlc.edu
Private
Application deadline (fall): N/A
Undergraduate student body: N/A full time, N/A part time
Expenses: 2014-2015: $28,240; room/board: $8,400
Financial aid: (425) 249-4777

University of Puget Sound

Tacoma WA
(253) 879-3211
U.S. News ranking: Nat. Lib. Arts, No. 72
Website: www.pugetsound.edu
Admissions email: admission@pugetsound.edu
Private; founded 1888
Freshman admissions: more selective; 2014-2015: 5,583 applied, 4,427 accepted. Either SAT or ACT required. SAT 25/75 percentile: 1110-1330. High school rank: 35% in top tenth, 64% in top quarter, 94% in top half
Early decision deadline: 11/15, notification date: 12/15
Early action deadline: N/A, notification date: N/A
Application deadline (fall): 1/15
Undergraduate student body: 2,525 full time, 28 part time; 43% male, 57% female; 0% American Indian, 7% Asian, 1% black, 7% Hispanic, 9% multiracial, 0% Pacific Islander, 75% white, 0% international; 24% from in state; 65% live on campus; 27% of students in fraternities, 31% in sororities
Most popular majors: 10% Biological and Biomedical Sciences, 11% Business, Management, Marketing, and Related Support Services, 10% Foreign Languages, Literatures, and Linguistics, 10% Psychology, 20% Social Sciences
Expenses: 2015-2016: $44,976; room/board: $11,480
Financial aid: (800) 396-7192; 56% of undergrads determined to have financial need; average aid package $29,668

University of Washington

Seattle WA
(206) 543-9686
U.S. News ranking: Nat. U., No. 52
Website: www.washington.edu
Admissions email: askuwadm@u.washington.edu
Public; founded 1861
Freshman admissions: more selective; 2014-2015: 31,611 applied, 17,451 accepted. Either SAT or ACT required. SAT 25/75 percentile: 1110-1350. High school rank: 92% in top tenth, 98% in top quarter, 100% in top half
Early decision deadline: N/A, notification date: N/A
Early action deadline: N/A, notification date: N/A
Application deadline (fall): 12/1
Undergraduate student body: 27,764 full time, 2,908 part time; 48% male, 52% female; 1% American Indian, 24% Asian, 3% black, 7% Hispanic, 7% multiracial, 0% Pacific Islander, 43% white, 15% international; 84% from in state; 24% live on campus; 16% of students in fraternities, 15% in sororities
Most popular majors: 12% Biological and Biomedical Sciences, 11% Business, Management, Marketing, and Related Support Services, 9% Engineering, 16% Social Sciences, 8% Visual and Performing Arts
Expenses: 2014-2015: $12,394 in state, $33,513 out of state; room/board: $10,833
Financial aid: (206) 543-6101

Walla Walla University

College Place WA
(509) 527-2327
U.S. News ranking: Reg. U. (W), No. 42
Website: www.wallawalla.edu
Admissions email: info@wallawalla.edu
Private; founded 1892
Affiliation: Seventh-day Adventist
Freshman admissions: selective; 2014-2015: 1,689 applied, 976 accepted. Either SAT or ACT required. SAT 25/75 percentile: 930-1230. High school rank: 15% in top tenth, 33% in top quarter, 62% in top half
Early decision deadline: N/A, notification date: N/A
Early action deadline: N/A, notification date: N/A
Application deadline (fall): rolling
Undergraduate student body: 1,589 full time, 100 part time; 49% male, 51% female; 1% American Indian, 7% Asian, 4% black, 13% Hispanic, 1% multiracial, 1% Pacific Islander, 58% white, 12% international; 37% from in state; 56% live on campus; 0% of students in fraternities, 0% in sororities
Most popular majors: 9% Business, Management, Marketing, and Related Support Services, 9% Education, 8% Engineering, 19% Health Professions and Related Programs, 7% Visual and Performing Arts
Expenses: 2015-2016: $26,382; room/board: $6,840
Financial aid: (800) 656-2815; 67% of undergrads determined to have financial need; average aid package $20,874

Washington State University

Pullman WA
(888) 468-6978
U.S. News ranking: Nat. U., No. 140
Website: www.wsu.edu
Admissions email: admissions@wsu.edu
Public; founded 1890
Freshman admissions: selective; 2014-2015: 18,716 applied, 15,029 accepted. Either SAT or ACT required. SAT 25/75

percentile: 910-1130. High school rank: 35% in top tenth, 54% in top quarter, 84% in top half
Early decision deadline: N/A, notification date: N/A
Early action deadline: N/A, notification date: N/A
Application deadline (fall): rolling
Undergraduate student body: 20,843 full time, 3,024 part time; 49% male, 51% female; 1% American Indian, 5% Asian, 3% black, 12% Hispanic, 7% multiracial, 0% Pacific Islander, 65% white, 4% international; 91% from in state; 25% live on campus; 4% of students in fraternities, 7% in sororities
Most popular majors: 18% Business, Management, Marketing, and Related Support Services, 8% Communication, Journalism, and Related Programs, 10% Engineering, 8% Health Professions and Related Programs, 12% Social Sciences
Expenses: 2015-2016: $12,485 in state, $25,567 out of state; room/board: $11,356
Financial aid: (509) 335-9711; 63% of undergrads determined to have financial need; average aid package $13,301

Western Washington University

Bellingham WA
(360) 650-3440
U.S. News ranking: Reg. U. (W), No. 21
Website: www.wwu.edu
Admissions email: admit@cc.wwu.edu
Public; founded 1893
Freshman admissions: selective; 2014-2015: 9,283 applied, 7,850 accepted. Either SAT or ACT required. SAT 25/75 percentile: 1000-1210. High school rank: 21% in top tenth, 51% in top quarter, 90% in top half
Early decision deadline: N/A, notification date: N/A
Early action deadline: N/A, notification date: N/A
Application deadline (fall): 1/31
Undergraduate student body: 13,050 full time, 1,102 part time; 45% male, 55% female; 0% American Indian, 7% Asian, 2% black, 7% Hispanic, 8% multiracial, 0% Pacific Islander, 74% white, 1% international; 91% from in state; 28% live on campus; N/A of students in fraternities, N/A in sororities
Most popular majors: 14% Business, Management, Marketing, and Related Support Services, 6% English Language and Literature/Letters, 6% Health Professions and Related Programs, 13% Social Sciences, 6% Visual and Performing Arts
Expenses: 2014-2015: $8,964 in state, $20,406 out of state; room/board: $10,042
Financial aid: (360) 650-3470; 51% of undergrads determined to have financial need; average aid package $14,092

Whitman College

Walla Walla WA
(509) 527-5176
U.S. News ranking: Nat. Lib. Arts, No. 40
Website: www.whitman.edu
Admissions email: admission@whitman.edu
Private; founded 1883
Freshman admissions: more selective; 2014-2015: 3,653 applied, 1,498 accepted. Either SAT or ACT required. SAT 25/75 percentile: 1200-1430. High school rank: 53% in top tenth, 88% in top quarter, 99% in top half
Early decision deadline: 11/15, notification date: 12/21
Early action deadline: N/A, notification date: N/A
Application deadline (fall): 1/15
Undergraduate student body: 1,467 full time, 31 part time; 44% male, 56% female; 0% American Indian, 5% Asian, 1% black, 8% Hispanic, 6% multiracial, 0% Pacific Islander, 73% white, 4% international; 35% from in state; 67% live on campus; 48% of students in fraternities, 44% in sororities
Most popular majors: 6% Biochemistry and Molecular Biology, 11% Biology/Biological Sciences, General, 6% Economics, General, 7% English Language and Literature, General, 6% Psychology, General
Expenses: 2015-2016: $46,138; room/board: $11,564
Financial aid: (509) 527-5178; 46% of undergrads determined to have financial need; average aid package $34,254

Whitworth University

Spokane WA
(800) 533-4668
U.S. News ranking: Reg. U. (W), No. 10
Website: www.whitworth.edu
Admissions email: admissions@whitworth.edu
Private; founded 1890
Affiliation: Presbyterian Church
Freshman admissions: selective; 2014-2015: 3,277 applied, 2,690 accepted. Neither SAT nor ACT required. SAT 25/75 percentile: 1050-1280. High school rank: N/A
Early decision deadline: N/A, notification date: N/A
Early action deadline: 11/30, notification date: 12/20
Application deadline (fall): 3/1
Undergraduate student body: 2,319 full time, 51 part time; 41% male, 59% female; 1% American Indian, 4% Asian, 2% black, 9% Hispanic, 5% multiracial, 1% Pacific Islander, 76% white, 2% international; 65% from in state; 57% live on campus; 0% of students in fraternities, 0% in sororities
Most popular majors: 11% Business, Management, Marketing, and Related Support Services, 8% Education, 9% Health Professions and Related Programs, 8% Psychology, 10% Social Sciences
Expenses: 2015-2016: $39,096; room/board: $10,714
Financial aid: (800) 533-4668; 70% of undergrads determined to have financial need; average aid package $31,373

WEST VIRGINIA

Alderson Broaddus University

Philippi WV
(800) 263-1549
U.S. News ranking: Reg. Coll. (S), No. 45
Website: www.ab.edu
Admissions email: admissions@ab.edu
Private; founded 1871
Affiliation: American Baptist
Freshman admissions: selective; 2014-2015: 3,880 applied, 1,652 accepted. Either SAT or ACT required. ACT 25/75 percentile: 19-24. High school rank: 11% in top tenth, 32% in top quarter, 68% in top half
Early decision deadline: N/A, notification date: N/A
Early action deadline: N/A, notification date: N/A
Application deadline (fall): 8/25
Undergraduate student body: 993 full time, 45 part time; 51% male, 49% female; 0% American Indian, 1% Asian, 16% black, 4% Hispanic, 1% multiracial, 0% Pacific Islander, 74% white, 3% international; 41% from in state; 82% live on campus; 4% of students in fraternities, 5% in sororities
Most popular majors: 5% Biology/Biological Sciences, General, 4% Elementary Education and Teaching, 6% Psychology, General, 19% Registered Nursing/Registered Nurse, 6% Sport and Fitness Administration/Management
Expenses: 2015-2016: $24,140; room/board: $7,606
Financial aid: (304) 457-6354; 86% of undergrads determined to have financial need; average aid package $25,694

American Public University System

Charles Town WV
(877) 777-9081
U.S. News ranking: Reg. U. (S), unranked
Website: www.apus.edu
Admissions email: N/A
For-profit; founded 1991
Freshman admissions: N/A; 2014-2015: N/A applied, N/A accepted. Neither SAT nor ACT required. ACT 25/75 percentile: N/A. High school rank: N/A
Early decision deadline: N/A, notification date: N/A
Early action deadline: N/A, notification date: N/A
Application deadline (fall): rolling
Undergraduate student body: 3,076 full time, 43,921 part time; 62% male, 38% female; 1% American Indian, 2% Asian, 22% black, 10% Hispanic, 4% multiracial, 1% Pacific Islander, 55% white, 1% international
Most popular majors: 14% Business Administration and Management, General, 10% Criminal Justice/Safety Studies, 7% Homeland Security, 10% International/Global Studies, 5% Kinesiology and Exercise Science
Expenses: 2014-2015: $8,000; room/board: N/A
Financial aid: (877) 372-3535

Bethany College

Bethany WV
(304) 829-7611
U.S. News ranking: Nat. Lib. Arts, second tier
Website: www.bethanywv.edu
Admissions email: enrollment@bethanywv.edu
Private; founded 1840
Affiliation: Christian Church (Disciples of Christ)
Freshman admissions: selective; 2014-2015: 1,394 applied, 865 accepted. Either SAT or ACT required. ACT 25/75 percentile: 17-23. High school rank: 6% in top tenth, 20% in top quarter, 49% in top half
Early decision deadline: N/A, notification date: N/A
Early action deadline: N/A, notification date: N/A
Application deadline (fall): rolling
Undergraduate student body: 719 full time, 186 part time; 53% male, 47% female; 1% American Indian, 0% Asian, 20% black, 4% Hispanic, 3% multiracial, 0% Pacific Islander, 54% white, 2% international; 32% from in state; 97% live on campus; 31% of students in fraternities, 51% in sororities
Most popular majors: 6% Biology/Biological Sciences, General, 6% Physical Education Teaching and Coaching, 21% Psychology, General, 6% Social Work, 17% Speech Communication and Rhetoric
Expenses: 2015-2016: $26,500; room/board: $9,800
Financial aid: (304) 829-7141; 92% of undergrads determined to have financial need; average aid package $31,171

Bluefield State College

Bluefield WV
(304) 327-4065
U.S. News ranking: Reg. Coll. (S), second tier
Website: www.bluefieldstate.edu
Admissions email: bscadmit@bluefieldstate.edu
Public; founded 1895
Freshman admissions: selective; 2014-2015: 1,046 applied, 401 accepted. Either SAT or ACT required. ACT 25/75 percentile: 17-22. High school rank: 20% in top tenth, 49% in top quarter, 78% in top half
Early decision deadline: N/A, notification date: N/A
Early action deadline: N/A, notification date: N/A
Application deadline (fall): rolling
Undergraduate student body: 1,251 full time, 312 part time; 62% male, 38% female; 0% American Indian, 0% Asian, 10% black, 1% Hispanic, 2% multiracial, 0% Pacific Islander, 84% white, 3% international; 97% from in state; 0% live on campus; 4% of students in fraternities, 4% in sororities
Most popular majors: 10% Business, Management, Marketing, and Related Support Services, 13% Education, 14% Engineering Technologies and Engineering-Related Fields, 12% Health Professions and Related Programs, 25% Liberal Arts and Sciences, General Studies and Humanities
Expenses: 2015-2016: $6,120 in state, $11,280 out of state; room/board: N/A
Financial aid: (304) 327-4020; 82% of undergrads determined to have financial need; average aid package $3,557

Concord University

Athens WV
(304) 384-5249
U.S. News ranking: Reg. Coll. (S), No. 47
Website: www.concord.edu
Admissions email: admissions@concord.edu
Public; founded 1872
Freshman admissions: selective; 2014-2015: 2,099 applied, 800 accepted. Either SAT or ACT required. ACT 25/75 percentile: 19-24. High school rank: 18% in top tenth, 48% in top quarter, 78% in top half
Early decision deadline: N/A, notification date: N/A
Early action deadline: N/A, notification date: N/A
Application deadline (fall): rolling
Undergraduate student body: 2,031 full time, 228 part time; 45% male, 55% female; 0% American Indian, 1% Asian, 7% black, 1% Hispanic, 0% multiracial, 0% Pacific Islander, 85% white, 5% international; 86% from in state; 37% live on campus; N/A of students in fraternities, N/A in sororities
Most popular majors: 18% Business, Management, Marketing, and Related Support Services, 18% Education, 21% Liberal Arts and Sciences, General Studies and Humanities, 7% Physical Sciences, 7% Public Administration and Social Service Professions
Expenses: 2014-2015: $6,422 in state, $14,118 out of state; room/board: $7,818
Financial aid: (304) 384-6069; 76% of undergrads determined to have financial need; average aid package $8,896

Davis and Elkins College[1]

Elkins WV
(304) 637-1230
U.S. News ranking: Reg. Coll. (S), No. 63
Website: www.davisandelkins.edu
Admissions email: admiss@davisandelkins.edu
Private
Application deadline (fall): N/A
Undergraduate student body: N/A full time, N/A part time
Expenses: 2014-2015: $27,492; room/board: $8,750
Financial aid: (304) 637-1373

Fairmont State University

Fairmont WV
(304) 367-4892
U.S. News ranking: Reg. U. (S), second tier
Website: www.fairmontstate.edu
Admissions email: admit@fairmontstate.edu
Public; founded 1865
Freshman admissions: selective; 2014-2015: 3,019 applied, 1,783 accepted. Either SAT or ACT required. ACT 25/75 percentile: 18-23. High school

rank: 11% in top tenth, 35% in top quarter, 73% in top half
Early decision deadline: N/A, notification date: N/A
Early action deadline: N/A, notification date: N/A
Application deadline (fall): rolling
Undergraduate student body: 3,270 full time, 515 part time; 45% male, 55% female; 0% American Indian, 0% Asian, 6% black, 2% Hispanic, 2% multiracial, 0% Pacific Islander, 86% white, 2% international; 92% from in state; 21% live on campus; N/A of students in fraternities, N/A in sororities
Most popular majors: 12% Business Administration and Management, General, 11% Criminal Justice/Safety Studies, 9% Education, General, 10% General Studies, 7% Psychology, General
Expenses: 2015-2016: $6,306 in state, $13,306 out of state; room/board: $7,800
Financial aid: (304) 367-4213; 75% of undergrads determined to have financial need; average aid package $8,643

Glenville State College

Glenville WV
(304) 462-4128
U.S. News ranking: Reg. Coll. (S), second tier
Website: www.glenville.edu
Admissions email: admissions@glenville.edu
Public; founded 1872
Freshman admissions: selective; 2014-2015: 1,292 applied, 602 accepted. Either SAT or ACT required. ACT 25/75 percentile: 17-21. High school rank: 10% in top tenth, 35% in top quarter, 66% in top half
Early decision deadline: N/A, notification date: N/A
Early action deadline: N/A, notification date: N/A
Application deadline (fall): rolling
Undergraduate student body: 1,038 full time, 764 part time; 58% male, 42% female; 0% American Indian, 0% Asian, 16% black, 2% Hispanic, 1% multiracial, 0% Pacific Islander, 71% white, 0% international; 87% from in state; 30% live on campus; 3% of students in fraternities, 5% in sororities
Most popular majors: 14% Business Administration and Management, General, 11% Criminalistics and Criminal Science, 14% Elementary Education and Teaching, 12% Secondary Education and Teaching, 17% Social Sciences, Other
Expenses: 2015-2016: $7,032 in state, $15,888 out of state; room/board: $9,702
Financial aid: (304) 462-4103; 82% of undergrads determined to have financial need; average aid package $13,554

Marshall University

Huntington WV
(800) 642-3499
U.S. News ranking: Reg. U. (S), No. 45
Website: www.marshall.edu
Admissions email: admissions@marshall.edu
Public; founded 1837
Freshman admissions: selective; 2014-2015: 5,289 applied, 4,595 accepted. Either SAT or ACT required. ACT 25/75 percentile: 19-24. High school rank: N/A
Early decision deadline: N/A, notification date: N/A
Early action deadline: N/A, notification date: N/A
Application deadline (fall): rolling
Undergraduate student body: 8,142 full time, 1,394 part time; 43% male, 57% female; 0% American Indian, 1% Asian, 7% black, 2% Hispanic, 3% multiracial, 0% Pacific Islander, 85% white, 1% international; 77% from in state; 21% live on campus; N/A of students in fraternities, N/A in sororities
Most popular majors: 19% Business, Management, Marketing, and Related Support Services, 12% Education, 12% Health Professions and Related Programs, 17% Liberal Arts and Sciences, General Studies and Humanities, 6% Psychology
Expenses: 2014-2015: $6,526 in state, $15,026 out of state; room/board: $8,722
Financial aid: (304) 696-3162; 71% of undergrads determined to have financial need; average aid package $10,192

Ohio Valley University

Vienna WV
(877) 446-8668
U.S. News ranking: Reg. Coll. (S), No. 70
Website: www.ovu.edu
Admissions email: admissions@ovu.edu
Private; founded 1958
Affiliation: Church of Christ
Freshman admissions: selective; 2014-2015: 677 applied, 219 accepted. Either SAT or ACT required. ACT 25/75 percentile: 17-23. High school rank: 6% in top tenth, 17% in top quarter, 50% in top half
Early decision deadline: N/A, notification date: N/A
Early action deadline: N/A, notification date: N/A
Application deadline (fall): 8/15
Undergraduate student body: 370 full time, 27 part time; 55% male, 45% female; 0% American Indian, 1% Asian, 11% black, 5% Hispanic, 3% multiracial, 0% Pacific Islander, 66% white, 8% international; 44% from in state; 51% live on campus; 66% of students in fraternities, 66% in sororities
Most popular majors: 15% Business, Management, Marketing, and Related Support Services, 40% Education, 34% Liberal Arts and Sciences, General Studies and Humanities, 10% Psychology, 1% Theology and Religious Vocations
Expenses: 2015-2016: $19,840; room/board: $7,220
Financial aid: (304) 865-6075; 85% of undergrads determined to have financial need; average aid package $14,608

Salem International University[1]

Salem WV
(888) 235-5024
U.S. News ranking: Reg. U. (S), unranked
Website: www.salemu.edu
Admissions email: admissions@salemu.edu
For-profit
Application deadline (fall): N/A
Undergraduate student body: N/A full time, N/A part time
Expenses: 2014-2015: $17,700; room/board: $7,000
Financial aid: (304) 782-5303

Shepherd University

Shepherdstown WV
(304) 876-5212
U.S. News ranking: Reg. U. (S), second tier
Website: www.shepherd.edu
Admissions email: admissions@shepherd.edu
Public; founded 1871
Freshman admissions: less selective; 2014-2015: 1,817 applied, 1,786 accepted. Either SAT or ACT required. SAT 25/75 percentile: 890-1090. High school rank: N/A
Early decision deadline: N/A, notification date: N/A
Early action deadline: 11/15, notification date: 12/1
Application deadline (fall): rolling
Undergraduate student body: 3,093 full time, 683 part time; 41% male, 59% female; 0% American Indian, 2% Asian, 9% black, 3% Hispanic, 1% multiracial, 0% Pacific Islander, 83% white, 0% international; 63% from in state; 34% live on campus; 4% of students in fraternities, 4% in sororities
Most popular majors: 13% Business, Management, Marketing, and Related Support Services, 10% Education, 9% Health Professions and Related Programs, 11% Liberal Arts and Sciences, General Studies and Humanities, 10% Social Sciences
Expenses: 2015-2016: $6,830 in state, $16,628 out of state; room/board: $9,682
Financial aid: (304) 876-5470; 65% of undergrads determined to have financial need; average aid package $11,874

University of Charleston

Charleston WV
(800) 995-4682
U.S. News ranking: Reg. Coll. (S), No. 24
Website: www.ucwv.edu
Admissions email: admissions@ucwv.edu
Private; founded 1888
Freshman admissions: selective; 2014-2015: 1,787 applied, 1,086 accepted. Either SAT or ACT required. ACT 25/75 percentile: 19-23. High school rank: N/A
Early decision deadline: N/A, notification date: N/A
Early action deadline: N/A, notification date: N/A
Application deadline (fall): rolling
Undergraduate student body: 1,355 full time, 194 part time; 43% male, 57% female; N/A American Indian, N/A Asian, N/A black, N/A Hispanic, N/A multiracial, N/A Pacific Islander, N/A white, N/A international
Most popular majors: Information not available
Expenses: 2015-2016: $26,100; room/board: $9,100
Financial aid: (304) 357-4759; 64% of undergrads determined to have financial need; average aid package $19,375

West Liberty University

West Liberty WV
(304) 336-8076
U.S. News ranking: Reg. Coll. (S), No. 60
Website: www.westliberty.edu
Admissions email: admissions@westliberty.edu
Public; founded 1837
Freshman admissions: selective; 2014-2015: 1,896 applied, 1,372 accepted. Either SAT or ACT required. ACT 25/75 percentile: 18-23. High school rank: 12% in top tenth, 35% in top quarter, 69% in top half
Early decision deadline: N/A, notification date: N/A
Early action deadline: N/A, notification date: N/A
Application deadline (fall): rolling
Undergraduate student body: 2,099 full time, 431 part time; 40% male, 60% female; 0% American Indian, 1% Asian, 5% black, 1% Hispanic, 1% multiracial, 0% Pacific Islander, 88% white, 1% international; 70% from in state; 44% live on campus; 3% of students in fraternities, 4% in sororities
Most popular majors: 15% Business, Management, Marketing, and Related Support Services, 18% Education, 6% Health Professions and Related Programs, 18% Liberal Arts and Sciences, General Studies and Humanities, 8% Parks, Recreation, Leisure, and Fitness Studies
Expenses: 2014-2015: $6,415 in state, $13,540 out of state; room/board: $8,550
Financial aid: (304) 336-8016

West Virginia State University

Institute WV
(304) 766-4345
U.S. News ranking: Nat. Lib. Arts, second tier
Website: www.wvstateu.edu
Admissions email: admissions@wvstateu.edu
Public; founded 1891
Freshman admissions: selective; 2014-2015: 2,587 applied, 1,068 accepted. Either SAT or ACT required. ACT 25/75 percentile: 18-22. High school rank: N/A
Early decision deadline: N/A, notification date: N/A
Early action deadline: N/A, notification date: N/A
Application deadline (fall): 8/17
Undergraduate student body: 1,950 full time, 886 part time; 45% male, 55% female; 1% American Indian, 0% Asian, 12% black, 1% Hispanic, N/A multiracial, N/A Pacific Islander, 58% white, 1% international; 89% from in state; 16% live on campus; 1% of students in fraternities, 1% in sororities
Most popular majors: 13% Business Administration and Management, General, 9% Criminal Justice/Safety Studies, 22% General Studies, 6% Psychology, General, 14% Teacher Education and Professional Development, Specific Levels and Methods
Expenses: 2014-2015: $6,228 in state, $14,558 out of state; room/board: $10,476
Financial aid: (304) 766-3131; 79% of undergrads determined to have financial need; average aid package $12,222

West Virginia University

Morgantown WV
(304) 442-3146
U.S. News ranking: Nat. U., No. 175
Website: www.wvu.edu
Admissions email: tech-admissions@mail.wvu.edu
Public; founded 1867
Freshman admissions: selective; 2014-2015: 15,604 applied, 13,386 accepted. Either SAT or ACT required. ACT 25/75 percentile: 21-26. High school rank: 19% in top tenth, 44% in top quarter, 79% in top half
Early decision deadline: N/A, notification date: N/A
Early action deadline: N/A, notification date: N/A
Application deadline (fall): 8/1
Undergraduate student body: 20,863 full time, 1,700 part time; 54% male, 46% female; 0% American Indian, 2% Asian, 5% black, 4% Hispanic, 3% multiracial, 0% Pacific Islander, 81% white, 5% international; 52% from in state; 15% live on campus; 7% of students in fraternities, 6% in sororities
Most popular majors: 12% Business, Management, Marketing, and Related Support Services, 8% Communication, Journalism, and Related Programs, 12% Engineering, 9% Multi/Interdisciplinary Studies, 7% Social Sciences
Expenses: 2014-2015: $6,960 in state, $20,424 out of state; room/board: $9,582
Financial aid: (800) 344-9881; 50% of undergrads determined to have financial need; average aid package $9,060

West Virginia University–Parkersburg

Parkersburg WV
(304) 424-8220
U.S. News ranking: Reg. Coll. (S), unranked
Website: www.wvup.edu
Admissions email: info@mail.wvup.edu
Public
Freshman admissions: N/A; 2014-2015: N/A applied, N/A accepted. Neither SAT nor ACT required. ACT 25/75 percentile: N/A. High school rank: N/A
Early decision deadline: N/A, notification date: N/A
Early action deadline: N/A, notification date: N/A
Application deadline (fall): rolling
Undergraduate student body: 1,674 full time, 1,311 part time; 38% male, 62% female; 0% American

Indian, 0% Asian, 1% black, 0% Hispanic, 3% multiracial, 0% Pacific Islander, 95% white, 0% international
Most popular majors: Information not available
Expenses: 2014-2015: $2,928 in state, $10,416 out of state; room/board: $5,000
Financial aid: (304) 424-8210

West Virginia Wesleyan College
Buckhannon WV
(800) 722-9933
U.S. News ranking: Reg. Coll. (S), No. 14
Website: www.wvwc.edu
Admissions email: admissions@wvwc.edu
Private; founded 1890
Affiliation: United Methodist
Freshman admissions: selective; 2014-2015: 1,789 applied, 1,388 accepted. Either SAT or ACT required. ACT 25/75 percentile: 19-25. High school rank: 27% in top tenth, 56% in top quarter, 85% in top half
Early decision deadline: N/A, notification date: N/A
Early action deadline: N/A, notification date: N/A
Application deadline (fall): rolling
Undergraduate student body: 1,357 full time, 33 part time; 46% male, 54% female; 0% American Indian, 0% Asian, 9% black, 2% Hispanic, 3% multiracial, 0% Pacific Islander, 80% white, 5% international; 62% from in state; 81% live on campus; 25% of students in fraternities, 21% in sororities
Most popular majors: 16% Business, Management, Marketing, and Related Support Services, 8% Education, 11% Health Professions and Related Programs, 10% Parks, Recreation, Leisure, and Fitness Studies, 14% Psychology
Expenses: 2015-2016: $28,992; room/board: $8,066
Financial aid: (304) 473-8080; 73% of undergrads determined to have financial need; average aid package $30,488

Wheeling Jesuit University
Wheeling WV
(800) 624-6992
U.S. News ranking: Reg. Coll. (S), No. 11
Website: www.wju.edu
Admissions email: admiss@wju.edu
Private; founded 1954
Affiliation: Roman Catholic
Freshman admissions: selective; 2014-2015: 1,445 applied, 905 accepted. Either SAT or ACT required. ACT 25/75 percentile: 20-25. High school rank: 16% in top tenth, 38% in top quarter, 71% in top half
Early decision deadline: N/A, notification date: N/A
Early action deadline: N/A, notification date: N/A
Application deadline (fall): rolling
Undergraduate student body: 964 full time, 223 part time; 47% male, 53% female; 0% American Indian, 1% Asian, 4% black, 2% Hispanic, 1% multiracial, 0% Pacific Islander, 78% white, 4% international; 37% from in state; 61% live on campus; 0% of students in fraternities, 0% in sororities
Most popular majors: 21% Business, Management, Marketing, and Related Support Services, 32% Health Professions and Related Programs, 5% Homeland Security, Law Enforcement, Firefighting and Related Protective Services, 5% Physical Sciences, 8% Psychology
Expenses: 2015-2016: $28,030; room/board: $7,070
Financial aid: (304) 243-2304; 73% of undergrads determined to have financial need; average aid package $24,604

WISCONSIN

Alverno College
Milwaukee WI
(414) 382-6100
U.S. News ranking: Reg. U. (Mid.W), No. 64
Website: www.alverno.edu
Admissions email: admissions@alverno.edu
Private; founded 1887
Affiliation: Roman Catholic
Freshman admissions: selective; 2014-2015: 655 applied, 427 accepted. Either SAT or ACT required. ACT 25/75 percentile: 17-22. High school rank: 20% in top tenth, 40% in top quarter, 74% in top half
Early decision deadline: N/A, notification date: N/A
Early action deadline: N/A, notification date: N/A
Application deadline (fall): rolling
Undergraduate student body: 1,283 full time, 440 part time; 0% male, 100% female; 1% American Indian, 5% Asian, 16% black, 21% Hispanic, 3% multiracial, 0% Pacific Islander, 53% white, 1% international; 95% from in state; 12% live on campus; N/A of students in fraternities, 1% in sororities
Most popular majors: 12% Business, Management, Marketing, and Related Support Services, 6% Communication, Journalism, and Related Programs, 9% Education, 44% Health Professions and Related Programs, 5% Liberal Arts and Sciences, General Studies and Humanities
Expenses: 2015-2016: $25,660; room/board: $7,634
Financial aid: (414) 382-6046; 90% of undergrads determined to have financial need; average aid package $18,262

Beloit College
Beloit WI
(608) 363-2500
U.S. News ranking: Nat. Lib. Arts, No. 61
Website: www.beloit.edu
Admissions email: admiss@beloit.edu
Private; founded 1846
Freshman admissions: more selective; 2014-2015: 2,281 applied, 1,581 accepted. Neither SAT nor ACT required. ACT 25/75 percentile: 24-30. High school rank: 42% in top tenth, 75% in top quarter, 95% in top half
Early decision deadline: 11/1, notification date: 11/30
Early action deadline: 12/1, notification date: 1/15
Application deadline (fall): rolling
Undergraduate student body: 1,249 full time, 54 part time; 42% male, 58% female; 0% American Indian, 3% Asian, 5% black, 9% Hispanic, 2% multiracial, 0% Pacific Islander, 70% white, 9% international; 19% from in state; 87% live on campus; 24% of students in fraternities, 28% in sororities
Most popular majors: Information not available
Expenses: 2015-2016: $45,050; room/board: $7,890
Financial aid: (608) 363-2663; 69% of undergrads determined to have financial need; average aid package $33,965

Cardinal Stritch University
Milwaukee WI
(414) 410-4040
U.S. News ranking: Nat. U., second tier
Website: www.stritch.edu
Admissions email: admityou@stritch.edu
Private; founded 1937
Affiliation: Roman Catholic
Freshman admissions: selective; 2014-2015: 711 applied, 590 accepted. Neither SAT nor ACT required. ACT 25/75 percentile: 19-24. High school rank: 10% in top tenth, 37% in top quarter, 73% in top half
Early decision deadline: N/A, notification date: N/A
Early action deadline: N/A, notification date: N/A
Application deadline (fall): rolling
Undergraduate student body: 2,158 full time, 150 part time; 34% male, 66% female; 1% American Indian, 2% Asian, 22% black, 9% Hispanic, 2% multiracial, 0% Pacific Islander, 56% white, 4% international; 87% from in state; 13% live on campus; 1% of students in fraternities, 1% in sororities
Most popular majors: 14% Business Administration and Management, General, 5% Elementary Education and Teaching, 7% Human Resources Management/Personnel Administration, General, 36% Organizational Leadership, 10% Registered Nursing, Nursing Administration, Nursing Research and Clinical Nursing, Other
Expenses: 2015-2016: $27,540; room/board: $7,700
Financial aid: (414) 410-4048; 73% of undergrads determined to have financial need; average aid package $13,949

Carroll University
Waukesha WI
(262) 524-7220
U.S. News ranking: Reg. U. (Mid.W), No. 42
Website: www.carrollu.edu/
Admissions email: ccinfo@carrollu.edu
Private; founded 1846
Affiliation: Presbyterian Church (USA)
Freshman admissions: more selective; 2014-2015: 2,969 applied, 2,400 accepted. Either SAT or ACT required. ACT 25/75 percentile: 21-26. High school rank: N/A
Early decision deadline: N/A, notification date: N/A
Early action deadline: N/A, notification date: N/A
Application deadline (fall): rolling
Undergraduate student body: 2,706 full time, 309 part time; 35% male, 65% female; 0% American Indian, 3% Asian, 1% black, 6% Hispanic, 2% multiracial, 0% Pacific Islander, 86% white, 1% international; 72% from in state; 58% live on campus; N/A of students in fraternities, N/A in sororities
Most popular majors: 11% Business Administration and Management, General, 7% Elementary Education and Teaching, 17% Kinesiology and Exercise Science, 10% Psychology, General, 9% Registered Nursing/Registered Nurse
Expenses: 2015-2016: $29,535; room/board: $8,722
Financial aid: (262) 524-7296; 82% of undergrads determined to have financial need; average aid package $21,258

Carthage College
Kenosha WI
(262) 551-6000
U.S. News ranking: Nat. Lib. Arts, No. 154
Website: www.carthage.edu
Admissions email: admissions@carthage.edu
Private; founded 1847
Affiliation: Evangelical Lutheran Church in America
Freshman admissions: more selective; 2014-2015: 7,164 applied, 5,132 accepted. Either SAT or ACT required. ACT 25/75 percentile: 21-27. High school rank: 29% in top tenth, 50% in top quarter, 80% in top half
Early decision deadline: N/A, notification date: N/A
Early action deadline: N/A, notification date: N/A
Application deadline (fall): rolling
Undergraduate student body: 2,599 full time, 274 part time; 49% male, 51% female; 0% American Indian, 1% Asian, 5% black, 4% Hispanic, 3% multiracial, 0% Pacific Islander, 75% white, 0% international; N/A from in state; 67% live on campus; 8% of students in fraternities, 10% in sororities
Most popular majors: Information not available
Expenses: 2015-2016: $38,375; room/board: $10,460
Financial aid: (262) 551-6001; 79% of undergrads determined to have financial need; average aid package $28,663

Concordia University Wisconsin
Mequon WI
(262) 243-4300
U.S. News ranking: Reg. U. (Mid.W), No. 54
Website: www.cuw.edu
Admissions email: admissions@cuw.edu
Private; founded 1881
Affiliation: Lutheran Church-Missouri Synod
Freshman admissions: selective; 2014-2015: 2,582 applied, 1,947 accepted. ACT required. ACT 25/75 percentile: 21-26. High school rank: 22% in top tenth, 48% in top quarter, 77% in top half
Early decision deadline: N/A, notification date: N/A
Early action deadline: N/A, notification date: N/A
Application deadline (fall): 8/15
Undergraduate student body: 3,112 full time, 1,265 part time; 35% male, 65% female; 1% American Indian, 2% Asian, 16% black, 3% Hispanic, 3% multiracial, 0% Pacific Islander, 71% white, 1% international; 76% from in state; 56% live on campus; 0% of students in fraternities, 0% in sororities
Most popular majors: 13% Business Administration and Management, General, 5% Criminal Justice/Law Enforcement Administration, 4% Criminal Justice/Safety Studies, 7% Occupational Therapy/Therapist, 13% Registered Nursing/Registered Nurse
Expenses: 2015-2016: $27,100; room/board: $9,980
Financial aid: (262) 243-4569; 81% of undergrads determined to have financial need; average aid package $19,601

Edgewood College
Madison WI
(608) 663-2294
U.S. News ranking: Nat. U., No. 175
Website: www.edgewood.edu
Admissions email: admissions@edgewood.edu
Private; founded 1927
Affiliation: Roman Catholic
Freshman admissions: selective; 2014-2015: 1,253 applied, 955 accepted. Either SAT or ACT required. ACT 25/75 percentile: 20-25. High school rank: 17% in top tenth, 44% in top quarter, 84% in top half
Early decision deadline: N/A, notification date: N/A
Early action deadline: N/A, notification date: N/A
Application deadline (fall): 8/15
Undergraduate student body: 1,647 full time, 288 part time; 30% male, 70% female; 0% American Indian, 3% Asian, 2% black, 6% Hispanic, 3% multiracial, 0% Pacific Islander, 80% white, 4% international; 93% from in state; 28% live on campus; N/A of students in fraternities, N/A in sororities
Most popular majors: 5% Biology/Biological Sciences, General, 12% Business/Commerce, General, 5% Communication, General, 9% Psychology, General, 18% Registered Nursing/Registered Nurse
Expenses: 2015-2016: $26,550; room/board: $9,400
Financial aid: (608) 663-2305; 77% of undergrads determined to have financial need; average aid package $20,639

Herzing University[1]
Madison WI
(800) 596-0724
U.S. News ranking: Reg. Coll. (Mid.W), second tier
Website: www.herzing.edu/madison
Admissions email: info@msn.herzing.edu
For-profit
Application deadline (fall): N/A

Undergraduate student body: N/A full time, N/A part time
Expenses: 2014-2015: $12,790; room/board: $9,594
Financial aid: N/A

Lakeland College[1]
Plymouth WI
(920) 565-1226
U.S. News ranking: Reg. U. (Mid.W), second tier
Website: www.lakeland.edu
Admissions email: admissions@lakeland.edu
Private; founded 1862
Affiliation: United Church of Christ
Application deadline (fall): rolling
Undergraduate student body: N/A full time, N/A part time
Expenses: 2014-2015: $24,090; room/board: $8,294
Financial aid: (920) 565-1298

Lawrence University
Appleton WI
(800) 227-0982
U.S. News ranking: Nat. Lib. Arts, No. 57
Website: www.lawrence.edu/
Admissions email: admissions@lawrence.edu
Private; founded 1847
Freshman admissions: more selective; 2014-2015: 2,747 applied, 2,004 accepted. Neither SAT nor ACT required. ACT 25/75 percentile: 25-31. High school rank: 42% in top tenth, 70% in top quarter, 94% in top half
Early decision deadline: 11/1, notification date: 11/15
Early action deadline: 11/15, notification date: 12/20
Application deadline (fall): 1/15
Undergraduate student body: 1,473 full time, 46 part time; 46% male, 54% female; 1% American Indian, 4% Asian, 3% black, 7% Hispanic, 4% multiracial, 0% Pacific Islander, 71% white, 9% international; 35% from in state; 96% live on campus; 21% of students in fraternities, 15% in sororities
Most popular majors: 15% Biological and Biomedical Sciences, 6% English Language and Literature/Letters, 9% Psychology, 18% Social Sciences, 21% Visual and Performing Arts
Expenses: 2015-2016: $43,740; room/board: $9,210
Financial aid: (920) 832-6583; 66% of undergrads determined to have financial need; average aid package $35,069

Maranatha Baptist University
Watertown WI
(920) 206-2327
U.S. News ranking: Reg. Coll. (Mid.W), No. 66
Website: www.mbu.edu
Admissions email: admissions@mbu.edu
Private; founded 1968
Affiliation: Baptist
Freshman admissions: selective; 2014-2015: 345 applied, 262 accepted. Either SAT or ACT required. ACT 25/75 percentile: 20-25. High school rank: N/A
Early decision deadline: N/A, notification date: N/A
Early action deadline: N/A, notification date: N/A
Application deadline (fall): rolling
Undergraduate student body: 670 full time, 272 part time; 44% male, 56% female; 0% American Indian, 1% Asian, 1% black, 3% Hispanic, 5% multiracial, 0% Pacific Islander, 86% white, 1% international; 28% from in state; 71% live on campus; N/A of students in fraternities, N/A in sororities
Most popular majors: 22% Education, 13% Health Professions and Related Programs, 13% Liberal Arts and Sciences, General Studies and Humanities, 15% Multi/Interdisciplinary Studies, 14% Theology and Religious Vocations
Expenses: 2015-2016: $13,940; room/board: $6,550
Financial aid: (920) 206-2319; 86% of undergrads determined to have financial need; average aid package $10,353

Marian University
Fond du Lac WI
(920) 923-7650
U.S. News ranking: Reg. U. (Mid.W), No. 83
Website: www.marianuniversity.edu
Admissions email: admissions@marianuniversity.edu
Private; founded 1936
Affiliation: Roman Catholic
Freshman admissions: selective; 2014-2015: 1,178 applied, 904 accepted. Either SAT or ACT required. ACT 25/75 percentile: 17-23. High school rank: 10% in top tenth, 28% in top quarter, 63% in top half
Early decision deadline: N/A, notification date: N/A
Early action deadline: N/A, notification date: N/A
Application deadline (fall): rolling
Undergraduate student body: 1,293 full time, 335 part time; 29% male, 71% female; 1% American Indian, 1% Asian, 7% black, 7% Hispanic, 0% multiracial, 0% Pacific Islander, 79% white, 3% international; 87% from in state; 34% live on campus; 5% of students in fraternities, 5% in sororities
Most popular majors: 26% Business, Management, Marketing, and Related Support Services, 5% Education, 13% Homeland Security, Law Enforcement, Firefighting and Related Protective Services, 0% Radiologic Technology/Science - Radiographer, 32% Registered Nursing, Nursing Administration, Nursing Research and Clinical Nursing
Expenses: 2015-2016: $27,215; room/board: $6,750
Financial aid: (920) 923-7614; 90% of undergrads determined to have financial need; average aid package $17,414

Marquette University
Milwaukee WI
(800) 222-6544
U.S. News ranking: Nat. U., No. 86
Website: www.marquette.edu
Admissions email: admissions@marquette.edu
Private; founded 1881
Affiliation: Roman Catholic (Jesuit)
Freshman admissions: more selective; 2014-2015: 21,755 applied, 14,513 accepted. Either SAT or ACT required. ACT 25/75 percentile: 25-29. High school rank: 32% in top tenth, 67% in top quarter, 94% in top half
Early decision deadline: N/A, notification date: N/A
Early action deadline: N/A, notification date: N/A
Application deadline (fall): 12/1
Undergraduate student body: 8,078 full time, 332 part time; 48% male, 52% female; 0% American Indian, 5% Asian, 4% black, 10% Hispanic, 3% multiracial, 0% Pacific Islander, 74% white, 4% international; 34% from in state; 54% live on campus; N/A of students in fraternities, N/A in sororities
Most popular majors: 9% Biological and Biomedical Sciences, 24% Business, Management, Marketing, and Related Support Services, 10% Communication, Journalism, and Related Programs, 10% Engineering, 10% Health Professions and Related Programs
Expenses: 2015-2016: $37,170; room/board: $11,220
Financial aid: (414) 288-0200; 57% of undergrads determined to have financial need; average aid package $24,753

Milwaukee Institute of Art and Design[1]
Milwaukee WI
(414) 291-8070
U.S. News ranking: Arts, unranked
Website: www.miad.edu
Admissions email: admissions@miad.edu
Private; founded 1974
Application deadline (fall): 8/1
Undergraduate student body: N/A full time, N/A part time
Expenses: 2015-2016: $33,460; room/board: $9,050
Financial aid: (414) 291-3272; 84% of undergrads determined to have financial need; average aid package $22,913

Milwaukee School of Engineering
Milwaukee WI
(800) 332-6763
U.S. News ranking: Reg. U. (Mid.W), No. 15
Website: www.msoe.edu
Admissions email: explore@msoe.edu
Private; founded 1903
Freshman admissions: more selective; 2014-2015: 2,574 applied, 1,767 accepted. Either SAT or ACT required. ACT 25/75 percentile: 25-30. High school rank: N/A
Early decision deadline: N/A, notification date: N/A
Early action deadline: N/A, notification date: N/A
Application deadline (fall): rolling
Undergraduate student body: 2,434 full time, 162 part time; 76% male, 24% female; 0% American Indian, 3% Asian, 2% black, 4% Hispanic, 2% multiracial, 1% Pacific Islander, 69% white, 12% international; 67% from in state; 35% live on campus; 4% of students in fraternities, 10% in sororities
Most popular majors: 18% Business, Management, Marketing, and Related Support Services, 1% Communication, Journalism, and Related Programs, 68% Engineering, 7% Engineering Technologies and Engineering-Related Fields, 6% Health Professions and Related Programs
Expenses: 2015-2016: $36,540; room/board: $8,613
Financial aid: (414) 277-7511; 76% of undergrads determined to have financial need; average aid package $25,083

Mount Mary University
Milwaukee WI
(800) 321-6265
U.S. News ranking: Reg. U. (Mid.W), No. 75
Website: www.mtmary.edu
Admissions email: mmu-admiss@mtmary.ede
Private; founded 1913
Affiliation: Roman Catholic
Freshman admissions: selective; 2014-2015: 638 applied, 349 accepted. Either SAT or ACT required. ACT 25/75 percentile: 17-22. High school rank: 20% in top tenth, 45% in top quarter, 78% in top half
Early decision deadline: N/A, notification date: N/A
Early action deadline: N/A, notification date: N/A
Application deadline (fall): rolling
Undergraduate student body: 681 full time, 179 part time; 1% male, 99% female; 1% American Indian, 7% Asian, 23% black, 14% Hispanic, 3% multiracial, 0% Pacific Islander, 52% white, 0% international; 95% from in state; 24% live on campus; 0% of students in fraternities, 0% in sororities
Most popular majors: 11% Biology Technician/Biotechnology Laboratory Technician, 6% Fashion Merchandising, 7% Fashion/Apparel Design, 15% Occupational Therapy/Therapist, 6% Speech Communication and Rhetoric
Expenses: 2015-2016: $26,760; room/board: $7,890
Financial aid: (414) 256-1258; 82% of undergrads determined to have financial need; average aid package $22,040

Northland College
Ashland WI
(715) 682-1224
U.S. News ranking: Nat. Lib. Arts, second tier
Website: www.northland.edu
Admissions email: admit@northland.edu
Private; founded 1892
Affiliation: United Church of Christ
Freshman admissions: selective; 2014-2015: 1,020 applied, 647 accepted. Either SAT or ACT required. ACT 25/75 percentile: 21-26. High school rank: 13% in top tenth, 43% in top quarter, 82% in top half
Early decision deadline: N/A, notification date: N/A
Early action deadline: N/A, notification date: N/A
Application deadline (fall): rolling
Undergraduate student body: 567 full time, 17 part time; 51% male, 49% female; 2% American Indian, 0% Asian, 1% black, 4% Hispanic, 2% multiracial, 0% Pacific Islander, 80% white, 1% international; 50% from in state; 74% live on campus; 0% of students in fraternities, 0% in sororities
Most popular majors: 11% Biological and Biomedical Sciences, 12% Business, Management, Marketing, and Related Support Services, 10% Education, 17% Natural Resources and Conservation, 20% Physical Sciences
Expenses: 2015-2016: $32,754; room/board: $8,349
Financial aid: (715) 682-1255; 89% of undergrads determined to have financial need; average aid package $36,066

Ripon College
Ripon WI
(920) 748-8337
U.S. News ranking: Nat. Lib. Arts, No. 116
Website: www.ripon.edu
Admissions email: adminfo@ripon.edu
Private; founded 1851
Freshman admissions: selective; 2014-2015: 1,493 applied, 1,007 accepted. Either SAT or ACT required. ACT 25/75 percentile: 21-27. High school rank: 25% in top tenth, 46% in top quarter, 71% in top half
Early decision deadline: N/A, notification date: N/A
Early action deadline: N/A, notification date: N/A
Application deadline (fall): rolling
Undergraduate student body: 820 full time, 20 part time; 47% male, 53% female; 0% American Indian, 1% Asian, 2% black, 5% Hispanic, 2% multiracial, 0% Pacific Islander, 84% white, 3% international; 73% from in state; 7% live on campus; 30% of students in fraternities, 21% in sororities
Most popular majors: 11% Business/Commerce, General, 11% Health and Physical Education/Fitness, General, 10% History, 11% Political Science and Government, 11% Psychology, General
Expenses: 2015-2016: $36,514; room/board: $8,178
Financial aid: (920) 748-8101; 85% of undergrads determined to have financial need; average aid package $28,608

Silver Lake College
Manitowoc WI
(920) 686-6175
U.S. News ranking: Reg. Coll. (Mid.W), No. 66
Website: www.sl.edu
Admissions email: admslc@silver.sl.edu
Private; founded 1935
Affiliation: Catholic
Freshman admissions: least selective; 2014-2015: 221 applied, 184 accepted. Either SAT or ACT required. ACT 25/75 percentile: 14-20. High school rank: 7% in top tenth, 25% in top quarter, 68% in top half
Early decision deadline: N/A, notification date: N/A
Early action deadline: N/A, notification date: N/A
Application deadline (fall): 9/1
Undergraduate student body: 218 full time, 218 part time; 36% male, 64% female; 0% American Indian, 1% Asian, 20% black, 2% Hispanic, 3% multiracial, 0% Pacific Islander, 58% white,

2% international; 88% from in state; 33% live on campus; 0% of students in fraternities, 0% in sororities
Most popular majors: 13% Accounting, 18% Business Administration and Management, General, 5% Human Resources Management/Personnel Administration, General, 16% Psychology, General, 7% Theology/Theological Studies
Expenses: 2015-2016: $25,060; room/board: $9,715
Financial aid: (920) 686-6122

St. Norbert College

De Pere WI
(800) 236-4878
U.S. News ranking: Nat. Lib. Arts, No. 127
Website: www.snc.edu
Admissions email: admit@snc.edu
Private; founded 1898
Affiliation: Roman Catholic
Freshman admissions: more selective; 2014-2015: 2,149 applied, 1,756 accepted. Either SAT or ACT required. ACT 25/75 percentile: 22-27. High school rank: 31% in top tenth, 61% in top quarter, 88% in top half
Early decision deadline: N/A, notification date: N/A
Early action deadline: N/A, notification date: N/A
Application deadline (fall): rolling
Undergraduate student body: 2,048 full time, 64 part time; 43% male, 57% female; 1% American Indian, 1% Asian, 1% black, 3% Hispanic, 2% multiracial, 0% Pacific Islander, 90% white, 2% international; 78% from in state; 82% live on campus; 12% of students in fraternities, 11% in sororities
Most popular majors: 10% Biology/Biological Sciences, General, 18% Business/Commerce, General, 12% Elementary Education and Teaching, 6% Psychology, General, 9% Speech Communication and Rhetoric
Expenses: 2015-2016: $34,237; room/board: $8,794
Financial aid: (920) 403-3071; 72% of undergrads determined to have financial need; average aid package $24,644

University of Wisconsin–Eau Claire

Eau Claire WI
(715) 836-5415
U.S. News ranking: Reg. U. (Mid.W), No. 33
Website: www.uwec.edu
Admissions email: admissions@uwec.edu
Public; founded 1916
Freshman admissions: selective; 2014-2015: 5,441 applied, 4,552 accepted. Either SAT or ACT required. ACT 25/75 percentile: 22-26. High school rank: 17% in top tenth, 47% in top quarter, 92% in top half
Early decision deadline: N/A, notification date: N/A
Early action deadline: N/A, notification date: N/A
Application deadline (fall): rolling
Undergraduate student body: 9,204 full time, 960 part time; 41% male, 59% female; 0% American Indian, 3% Asian, 1% black, 2% Hispanic, 2% multiracial, 0% Pacific Islander, 89% white, 3% international; 74% from in state; 38% live on campus; N/A of students in fraternities, N/A in sororities
Most popular majors: 23% Business, Management, Marketing, and Related Support Services, 6% Communication, Journalism, and Related Programs, 7% Education, 13% Health Professions and Related Programs, 7% Psychology
Expenses: 2014-2015: $8,744 in state, $16,317 out of state; room/board: $6,986
Financial aid: (715) 836-3373; 55% of undergrads determined to have financial need; average aid package $10,073

University of Wisconsin–Green Bay

Green Bay WI
(920) 465-2111
U.S. News ranking: Reg. U. (Mid.W), No. 75
Website: www.uwgb.edu
Admissions email: uwgb@uwgb.edu
Public; founded 1965
Freshman admissions: selective; 2014-2015: 2,013 applied, 1,700 accepted. Either SAT or ACT required. ACT 25/75 percentile: 20-25. High school rank: N/A
Early decision deadline: N/A, notification date: N/A
Early action deadline: N/A, notification date: N/A
Application deadline (fall): rolling
Undergraduate student body: 4,207 full time, 2,461 part time; 34% male, 66% female; 1% American Indian, 3% Asian, 1% black, 4% Hispanic, 3% multiracial, 0% Pacific Islander, 86% white, 1% international; 93% from in state; 34% live on campus; 1% of students in fraternities, 1% in sororities
Most popular majors: 14% Business Administration and Management, General, 8% Human Biology, 11% Liberal Arts and Sciences/Liberal Studies, 8% Psychology, General, 8% Registered Nursing, Nursing Administration, Nursing Research and Clinical Nursing, Other
Expenses: 2014-2015: $7,676 in state, $15,249 out of state; room/board: $7,224
Financial aid: (920) 465-2075; 69% of undergrads determined to have financial need; average aid package $10,258

University of Wisconsin–La Crosse

La Crosse WI
(608) 785-8939
U.S. News ranking: Reg. U. (Mid.W), No. 29
Website: www.uwlax.edu
Admissions email: admissions@uwlax.edu
Public; founded 1909
Freshman admissions: more selective; 2014-2015: 6,030 applied, 4,564 accepted. Either SAT or ACT required. ACT 25/75 percentile: 23-27. High school rank: 24% in top tenth, 65% in top quarter, 98% in top half
Early decision deadline: N/A, notification date: N/A
Early action deadline: N/A, notification date: N/A
Application deadline (fall): rolling
Undergraduate student body: 9,276 full time, 479 part time; 43% male, 57% female; 0% American Indian, 2% Asian, 1% black, 3% Hispanic, 3% multiracial, 0% Pacific Islander, 90% white, 2% international; 83% from in state; 36% live on campus; N/A of students in fraternities, N/A in sororities
Most popular majors: 14% Biological and Biomedical Sciences, 19% Business, Management, Marketing, and Related Support Services, 9% Education, 10% Health Professions and Related Programs, 10% Psychology
Expenses: 2014-2015: $8,795 in state, $16,368 out of state; room/board: $5,910
Financial aid: (608) 785-8604; 51% of undergrads determined to have financial need; average aid package $7,385

University of Wisconsin–Madison

Madison WI
(608) 262-3961
U.S. News ranking: Nat. U., No. 41
Website: www.wisc.edu
Admissions email: onwisconsin@admissions.wisc.edu
Public; founded 1848
Freshman admissions: more selective; 2014-2015: 30,464 applied, 15,183 accepted. Either SAT or ACT required. ACT 25/75 percentile: 26-31. High school rank: 52% in top tenth, 90% in top quarter, 100% in top half
Early decision deadline: N/A, notification date: N/A
Early action deadline: N/A, notification date: N/A
Application deadline (fall): 2/1
Undergraduate student body: 28,324 full time, 2,965 part time; 49% male, 51% female; 0% American Indian, 5% Asian, 2% black, 5% Hispanic, 3% multiracial, 0% Pacific Islander, 77% white, 7% international; 67% from in state; 25% live on campus; 9% of students in fraternities, 8% in sororities
Most popular majors: 8% Biology/Biological Sciences, General, 8% Economics, General, 6% Political Science and Government, General, 6% Psychology, General, 4% Speech Communication and Rhetoric
Expenses: 2014-2015: $10,410 in state, $26,660 out of state; room/board: $8,600
Financial aid: (608) 262-3060; 39% of undergrads determined to have financial need; average aid package $14,015

University of Wisconsin–Milwaukee

Milwaukee WI
(414) 229-2222
U.S. News ranking: Nat. U., second tier
Website: www.uwm.edu
Admissions email: uwmlook@uwm.edu
Public; founded 1956
Freshman admissions: selective; 2014-2015: 9,635 applied, 7,193 accepted. Either SAT or ACT required. ACT 25/75 percentile: 19-24. High school rank: 9% in top tenth, 27% in top quarter, 64% in top half
Early decision deadline: N/A, notification date: N/A
Early action deadline: N/A, notification date: N/A
Application deadline (fall): rolling
Undergraduate student body: 18,772 full time, 4,307 part time; 49% male, 51% female; 0% American Indian, 6% Asian, 9% black, 9% Hispanic, 3% multiracial, 0% Pacific Islander, 69% white, 3% international; 94% from in state; 18% live on campus; N/A of students in fraternities, N/A in sororities
Most popular majors: 21% Business, Management, Marketing, and Related Support Services, 8% Education, 9% Health Professions and Related Programs, 7% Social Sciences, 7% Visual and Performing Arts
Expenses: 2014-2015: $9,882 in state, $19,610 out of state; room/board: $9,136
Financial aid: (414) 229-6300

University of Wisconsin–Oshkosh

Oshkosh WI
(920) 424-0202
U.S. News ranking: Reg. U. (Mid.W), No. 75
Website: www.uwosh.edu
Admissions email: oshadmuw@uwosh.edu
Public; founded 1871
Freshman admissions: selective; 2014-2015: 5,846 applied, 3,966 accepted. Either SAT or ACT required. ACT 25/75 percentile: 20-24. High school rank: 11% in top tenth, 35% in top quarter, 80% in top half
Early decision deadline: N/A, notification date: N/A
Early action deadline: N/A, notification date: N/A
Application deadline (fall): rolling
Undergraduate student body: 9,020 full time, 4,174 part time; 40% male, 60% female; 1% American Indian, 4% Asian, 2% black, 3% Hispanic, 2% multiracial, 0% Pacific Islander, 87% white, 1% international; 95% from in state; 32% live on campus; 3% of students in fraternities, 3% in sororities
Most popular majors: 19% Business, Management, Marketing, and Related Support Services, 6% Communication, Journalism, and Related Programs, 13% Education, 12% Health Professions and Related Programs, 7% Public Administration and Social Service Professions
Expenses: 2015-2016: $7,490 in state, $15,066 out of state; room/board: $7,516
Financial aid: (920) 424-3377; 63% of undergrads determined to have financial need; average aid package $8,369

University of Wisconsin–Parkside

Kenosha WI
(262) 595-2355
U.S. News ranking: Nat. Lib. Arts, second tier
Website: www.uwp.edu
Admissions email: admissions@uwp.edu
Public; founded 1968
Freshman admissions: selective; 2014-2015: 1,684 applied, 1,202 accepted. Neither SAT nor ACT required. ACT 25/75 percentile: 19-23. High school rank: 8% in top tenth, 30% in top quarter, 70% in top half
Early decision deadline: N/A, notification date: N/A
Early action deadline: N/A, notification date: N/A
Application deadline (fall): 7/15
Undergraduate student body: 3,338 full time, 1,110 part time; 48% male, 52% female; 0% American Indian, 3% Asian, 9% black, 13% Hispanic, 4% multiracial, 0% Pacific Islander, 69% white, 2% international; 85% from in state; 18% live on campus; 1% of students in fraternities, 1% in sororities
Most popular majors: 17% Business Administration and Management, General, 13% Criminal Justice/Safety Studies, 10% Psychology, General, 5% Sociology, 6% Sport and Fitness Administration/Management
Expenses: 2015-2016: $7,341 in state, $15,330 out of state; room/board: $7,712
Financial aid: (262) 595-2004; 67% of undergrads determined to have financial need

University of Wisconsin–Platteville

Platteville WI
(715) 608-1125
U.S. News ranking: Reg. U. (Mid.W), No. 83
Website: www.uwplatt.edu
Admissions email: admit@uwplatt.edu
Public; founded 1866
Freshman admissions: selective; 2014-2015: 4,160 applied, 3,301 accepted. Either SAT or ACT required. ACT 25/75 percentile: 21-25. High school rank: 10% in top tenth, 36% in top quarter, 73% in top half
Early decision deadline: N/A, notification date: N/A
Early action deadline: N/A, notification date: N/A
Application deadline (fall): rolling
Undergraduate student body: 7,147 full time, 900 part time; 65% male, 35% female; 0% American Indian, 1% Asian, 1% black, 3% Hispanic, 2% multiracial, 0% Pacific Islander, 91% white, 1% international; 76% from in state; 47% live on campus; 5% of students in fraternities, 7% in sororities
Most popular majors: 13% Agriculture, Agriculture Operations, and Related Sciences, 10% Business, Management, Marketing, and Related Support Services, 9% Education, 24% Engineering, 11% Homeland Security, Law Enforcement, Firefighting and Related Protective Services
Expenses: 2015-2016: $7,491 in state, $15,064 out of state; room/board: $7,080
Financial aid: (608) 342-1836; 78% of undergrads determined to have financial need; average aid package $7,001

University of Wisconsin–River Falls

River Falls WI
(715) 425-3500
U.S. News ranking: Reg. U. (Mid.W), No. 72
Website: www.uwrf.edu
Admissions email: admit@uwrf.edu
Public; founded 1874
Freshman admissions: selective; 2014-2015: 2,684 applied, 2,082 accepted. Either SAT or ACT required. ACT 25/75 percentile: 20-25. High school rank: 10% in top tenth, 33% in top quarter, 74% in top half
Early decision deadline: N/A, notification date: N/A
Early action deadline: N/A, notification date: N/A
Application deadline (fall): rolling
Undergraduate student body: 5,179 full time, 542 part time; 40% male, 60% female; 0% American Indian, 2% Asian, 2% black, 3% Hispanic, 2% multiracial, 0% Pacific Islander, 89% white, 1% international; 47% from in state; 40% live on campus; 6% of students in fraternities, 4% in sororities
Most popular majors: 18% Agriculture, Agriculture Operations, and Related Sciences, 9% Biological and Biomedical Sciences, 14% Business, Management, Marketing, and Related Support Services, 9% Communication, Journalism, and Related Programs, 15% Education
Expenses: 2014-2015: $7,751 in state, $15,324 out of state; room/board: $6,435
Financial aid: (715) 425-3141; 68% of undergrads determined to have financial need; average aid package $6,846

University of Wisconsin–Stevens Point

Stevens Point WI
(715) 346-2441
U.S. News ranking: Reg. U. (Mid.W), No. 50
Website: www.uwsp.edu
Admissions email: admiss@uwsp.edu
Public; founded 1894
Freshman admissions: selective; 2014-2015: 4,593 applied, 3,729 accepted. Neither SAT nor ACT required. ACT 25/75 percentile: 20-25. High school rank: 14% in top tenth, 40% in top quarter, 80% in top half
Early decision deadline: N/A, notification date: N/A
Early action deadline: N/A, notification date: N/A
Application deadline (fall): rolling
Undergraduate student body: 8,334 full time, 641 part time; 48% male, 52% female; 0% American Indian, 3% Asian, 2% black, 3% Hispanic, 2% multiracial, 0% Pacific Islander, 88% white, 2% international; 90% from in state; 26% live on campus; 2% of students in fraternities, 3% in sororities
Most popular majors: 8% Biology/Biological Sciences, General, 9% Business Administration and Management, General, 5% Communication, General, 4% Psychology, General, 5% Wildlife, Fish and Wildlands Science and Management
Expenses: 2015-2016: $7,682 in state, $18,095 out of state; room/board: $6,993
Financial aid: (715) 346-4771; 61% of undergrads determined to have financial need; average aid package $8,513

University of Wisconsin–Stout

Menomonie WI
(715) 232-1411
U.S. News ranking: Reg. U. (Mid.W), No. 64
Website: www.uwstout.edu
Admissions email: admissions@uwstout.edu
Public; founded 1891
Freshman admissions: selective; 2014-2015: 3,352 applied, 2,744 accepted. Either SAT or ACT required. ACT 25/75 percentile: 20-24. High school rank: 9% in top tenth, 29% in top quarter, 69% in top half
Early decision deadline: N/A, notification date: N/A
Early action deadline: N/A, notification date: N/A
Application deadline (fall): rolling
Undergraduate student body: 6,890 full time, 1,364 part time; 53% male, 47% female; 0% American Indian, 3% Asian, 2% black, 1% Hispanic, 3% multiracial, 0% Pacific Islander, 88% white, 3% international; 68% from in state; 40% live on campus; 2% of students in fraternities, 3% in sororities
Most popular majors: 36% Business, Management, Marketing, and Related Support Services, 10% Education, 8% Engineering Technologies and Engineering-Related Fields, 6% Health Professions and Related Programs, 9% Visual and Performing Arts
Expenses: 2014-2015: $9,025 in state, $16,771 out of state; room/board: $6,434
Financial aid: (715) 232-1363; 60% of undergrads determined to have financial need; average aid package $10,638

University of Wisconsin–Superior

Superior WI
(715) 394-8230
U.S. News ranking: Reg. U. (Mid.W), No. 92
Website: www.uwsuper.edu
Admissions email: admissions@uwsuper.edu
Public; founded 1893
Freshman admissions: selective; 2014-2015: 877 applied, 599 accepted. Either SAT or ACT required. ACT 25/75 percentile: 19-24. High school rank: 7% in top tenth, 17% in top quarter, 62% in top half
Early decision deadline: N/A, notification date: N/A
Early action deadline: N/A, notification date: N/A
Application deadline (fall): 8/1
Undergraduate student body: 1,926 full time, 529 part time; 39% male, 61% female; 3% American Indian, 1% Asian, 2% black, 2% Hispanic, 3% multiracial, 0% Pacific Islander, 83% white, 6% international; 57% from in state; 28% live on campus; 0% of students in fraternities, 0% in sororities
Most popular majors: 17% Business, Management, Marketing, and Related Support Services, 10% Communication, Journalism, and Related Programs, 20% Education, 11% Multi/Interdisciplinary Studies, 7% Public Administration and Social Service Professions
Expenses: 2014-2015: $7,994 in state, $15,567 out of state; room/board: $6,320
Financial aid: (715) 394-8200; 70% of undergrads determined to have financial need; average aid package $11,623

University of Wisconsin–Whitewater

Whitewater WI
(262) 472-1440
U.S. News ranking: Reg. U. (Mid.W), No. 50
Website: www.uww.edu
Admissions email: uwwadmit@mail.uww.edu
Public; founded 1868
Freshman admissions: selective; 2014-2015: 6,833 applied, 4,810 accepted. Neither SAT nor ACT required. ACT 25/75 percentile: 20-25. High school rank: 8% in top tenth, 28% in top quarter, 70% in top half
Early decision deadline: N/A, notification date: N/A
Early action deadline: N/A, notification date: N/A
Application deadline (fall): rolling
Undergraduate student body: 9,979 full time, 992 part time; 50% male, 50% female; 0% American Indian, 2% Asian, 5% black, 5% Hispanic, 4% multiracial, 0% Pacific Islander, 84% white, 1% international; 85% from in state; 40% live on campus; 6% of students in fraternities, 6% in sororities
Most popular majors: 6% Accounting, 7% Finance, General, 5% Physical Education Teaching and Coaching, 6% Social Work, 5% Speech Communication and Rhetoric
Expenses: 2014-2015: $7,600 in state, $15,173 out of state; room/board: $6,194
Financial aid: (262) 472-1130; 62% of undergrads determined to have financial need; average aid package $8,047

Viterbo University[1]

La Crosse WI
(608) 796-3010
U.S. News ranking: Reg. U. (Mid.W), No. 104
Website: www.viterbo.edu
Admissions email: admission@viterbo.edu
Private
Application deadline (fall): N/A
Undergraduate student body: N/A full time, N/A part time
Expenses: 2014-2015: $23,790; room/board: $7,940
Financial aid: (608) 796-3900

Wisconsin Lutheran College

Milwaukee WI
(414) 443-8811
U.S. News ranking: Nat. Lib. Arts, No. 174
Website: www.wlc.edu
Admissions email: admissions@wlc.edu
Private; founded 1973
Affiliation: Wisconsin Evangelical Lutheran Synod
Freshman admissions: selective; 2014-2015: 911 applied, 586 accepted. Either SAT or ACT required. ACT 25/75 percentile: 21-26. High school rank: 13% in top tenth, 41% in top quarter, 79% in top half
Early decision deadline: N/A, notification date: N/A
Early action deadline: N/A, notification date: N/A
Application deadline (fall): rolling
Undergraduate student body: 980 full time, 94 part time; 46% male, 54% female; 1% American Indian, 1% Asian, 5% black, 5% Hispanic, 2% multiracial, 0% Pacific Islander, 83% white, 2% international; 78% from in state; 58% live on campus; N/A of students in fraternities, N/A in sororities
Most popular majors: 6% Biology/Biological Sciences, General, 17% Business Administration and Management, General, 11% Business Administration, Management and Operations, Other, 6% Psychology, General, 8% Registered Nursing/Registered Nurse
Expenses: 2015-2016: $27,040; room/board: $9,250
Financial aid: (414) 443-8856; 80% of undergrads determined to have financial need; average aid package $19,552

WYOMING

University of Wyoming

Laramie WY
(307) 766-5160
U.S. News ranking: Nat. U., No. 168
Website: www.uwyo.edu
Admissions email: Why-wyo@uwyo.edu
Public; founded 1886
Freshman admissions: selective; 2014-2015: 4,187 applied, 4,089 accepted. Either SAT or ACT required. ACT 25/75 percentile: 22-27. High school rank: 19% in top tenth, 48% in top quarter, 79% in top half
Early decision deadline: N/A, notification date: N/A
Early action deadline: N/A, notification date: N/A
Application deadline (fall): 8/10
Undergraduate student body: 8,272 full time, 1,852 part time; 48% male, 52% female; 1% American Indian, 1% Asian, 1% black, 7% Hispanic, 3% multiracial, 0% Pacific Islander, 78% white, 4% international; 69% from in state; 23% live on campus; 5% of students in fraternities, 6% in sororities
Most popular majors: 4% Business Administration and Management, General, 4% Criminal Justice/Safety Studies, 7% Elementary Education and Teaching, 6% Psychology, General, 11% Registered Nursing/Registered Nurse
Expenses: 2015-2016: $4,892 in state, $15,632 out of state; room/board: $10,037
Financial aid: (307) 766-2116; 48% of undergrads determined to have financial need; average aid package $9,422

More at usnews.com/college

A

B

C

D

E

F

M

N

T

U

V

W

X, Y

UNITED STATES MILITARY ACADEMY

WEST POINT®

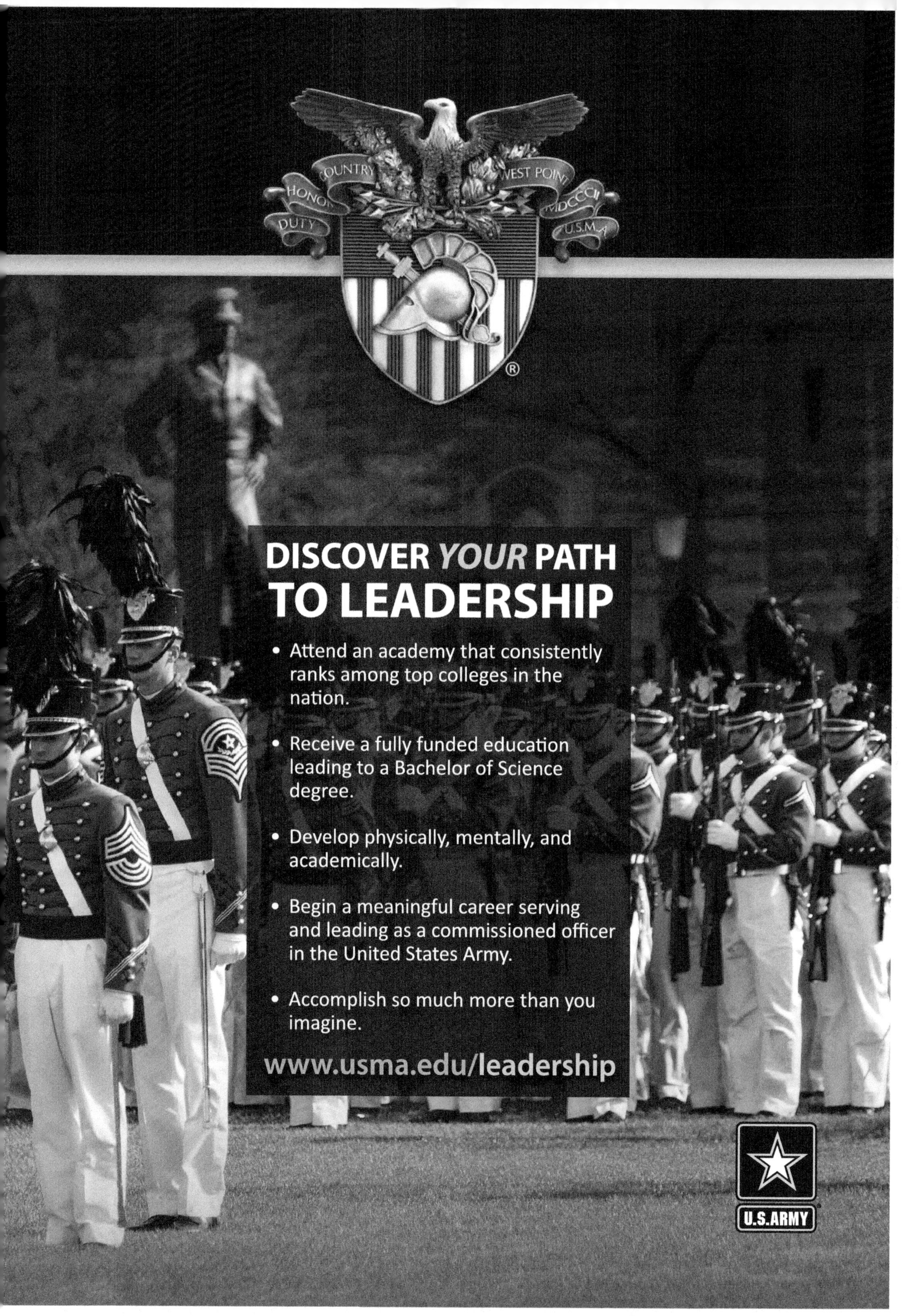
COUNTRY
HONOR
DUTY
WEST POINT
MDCCCII
U.S.M.A.
DISCOVER YOUR PATH
TO LEADERSHIP
• Attend an academy that consistently ranks among top colleges in the nation.
• Receive a fully funded education leading to a Bachelor of Science degree.
• Develop physically, mentally, and academically.
• Begin a meaningful career serving and leading as a commissioned officer in the United States Army.
• Accomplish so much more than you imagine.
www.usma.edu/leadership
U.S.ARMY

CPSIA information can be obtained at www.ICGtesting.com
Printed in the USA
BVOW11s1916071015

421470BV00001B/1/P